W9-BAB-074

FINANCIAL ACCOUNTING

THE IRWIN SERIES IN UNDERGRADUATE ACCOUNTING

Barr and Morris
Short Audit Case
Seventh Edition

Bernstein
Financial Statement Analysis: Theory, Application and Interpretation
Fifth Edition

Bernstein and Maksy
Cases in Financial Statement Reporting and Analysis
Second Edition

Boatsman, Griffin, Vickrey, and Williams
Advanced Accounting
Seventh Edition

Boockholdt
Accounting Information Systems
Third Edition

Brownlee, Ferris, and Haskins
Corporate Financial Reporting: Text and Cases
Second Edition

Dalton
1994 Individual Tax Return
Ninth Edition

Dalton
1994 Corporate Tax Return
Ninth Edition

Danos and Imhoff
Introduction to Financial Accounting
Second Edition

Dyckman, Dukes, and Davis
Intermediate Accounting
Third Edition

Edwards, Hermanson, and Maher
Principles of Financial and Managerial Accounting
Revised Edition

Engler
Managerial Accounting
Third Edition

Engler, Bernstein, and Lambert
Advanced Accounting
Third Edition

Engstrom and Hay
Essentials of Governmental Accounting for Public Administrators

Epstein and Spalding
The Accountant's Guide to Legal Liability and Ethics

FASB 1994–1995 Editions
Current Text: General Standards
Current Text: Industry Standards
Original Pronouncements,
Volume I
Original Pronouncements,
Volume II
Financial Accounting Concepts

Ferris
Financial Accounting and Corporate Reporting: A Casebook
Third Edition

Garrison and Noreen
Managerial Accounting
Seventh Edition

Hay and Engstrom
Essentials of Accounting for Governmental Accounting and Not-for-Profit Organizations
Third Edition

Hay and Wilson
Accounting for Governmental and Nonprofit Entities
Tenth Edition

Hendriksen and Van Breda
Accounting Theory
Fifth Edition

Hermanson and Edwards
Financial Accounting: A Business Perspective
Sixth Edition

Hermanson, Edwards, and Maher
Accounting: A Business Perspective
Sixth Edition

Hermanson, Strawser, and Strawser
Auditing Theory and Practice
Sixth Edition

Hermanson, Walker, Plunkett, and Turner
Computerized Accounting with Peachtree Complete® Accounting
Version 6.0

Hoyle
Advanced Accounting
Fourth Edition

Jesser
Integrated Accounting Computer Applications

Koerber
College Accounting
Revised Edition

Larson and Miller
Financial Accounting
Sixth Edition

Larson and Miller
Fundamental Accounting Principles
Thirteenth Edition

Larson, Spoede, and Miller
Fundamentals of Financial and Managerial Accounting

Maher and Deakin
Cost Accounting
Fourth Edition

Marshall
A Survey of Accounting: What the Numbers Mean
Second Edition

Miller, Redding, and Bahnson
The FASB: The People, the Process and the Politics
Third Edition

Mueller, Gernon, and Meek
Accounting: An International Perspective
Third Edition

Pany and Whittington
Auditing

Pratt and Kulsrud
Corporate, Partnership, Estate, and Gift Taxation
1996 Edition

Pratt and Kulsrud
Federal Taxation
1996 Edition

Pratt and Kulsrud
Individual Taxation
1996 Edition

Rayburn
Cost Accounting: Using a Cost Management Approach
Fifth Edition

Robertson
Auditing
Seventh Edition

Schrader
Accounting for the Small Business
Second Edition

Schroeder and Zlatkovich
A Survey of Accounting

Short
Fundamentals of Financial Accounting
Seventh Edition

Smith and Wiggins
Readings and Problems in Accounting Information Systems

Whittington and Pany
Principles of Auditing
Eleventh Edition

Yacht and Terry
Computer Accounting for Windows

FINANCIAL ACCOUNTING

SIXTH EDITION

Kermit D. Larson
University of Texas–Austin

Paul B.W. Miller
University of Colorado–Colorado Springs

IRWIN

Chicago • Bogota • Boston • Buenos Aires • Caracas
London • Madrid • Mexico City • Sydney • Toronto

Apple Computer, Inc. annual report and logo courtesy of Apple Computer, Inc.

Senior sponsoring editor:	Jeff Shelstad
Developmental editor:	Margaret Haywood
Marketing manager:	Cindy Ledwith
Project editor:	Rita McMullen
Production manager:	Bob Lange
Designer:	Michael Warrell
Cover designer:	Stuart Paterson; Imagehouse, Inc.
Art studio:	Arcata Graphics
Art coordinator:	Eurnice Harris
Compositor:	York Graphic Services, Inc.
Typeface:	10/12 Times Roman
Printer:	Von Hoffmann Press, Inc.

Library of Congress Cataloging-in-Publication Data

Larson, Kermit D.

Financial accounting/Kermit D. Larson, Paul B. W. Miller.—6th ed.

p. cm.

Includes bibliographical references and index.

ISBN 0-256-13338-7.—ISBN 0-256-13378-6 (fully annotated support for teaching) (F.A.S.T. ed.)—0-256-18535-2 (with working papers)

1. Accounting. I. Miller, Paul B. W. II. Title.

HF5635.P974 1995

657—dc20 94–22610

Printed in the United States of America

1 2 3 4 5 6 7 8 9 0 VH 1 0 9 8 7 6 5 4

Dedicated to
Nancy, Julie, Tim, Cindy, Albrecht, and Megan
and to
Diana, David, Greg, and Angela

About the Authors

Kermit D. Larson is the Arthur Andersen & Co. Alumni Centennial Professor Emeritus of Accounting at The University of Texas at Austin, where he has been a member of the faculty since 1966. He served as chairman of the UT Department of Accounting from 1971 to 1975 and was Visiting Associate Professor at Tulane University in 1970. His scholarly articles have been published in a variety of journals such as *The Accounting Review, Journal of Accountancy,* and *Abacus.* He has also co-authored several books, including *Financial and Managerial Accounting* and *Fundamental Accounting Principles,* published by Richard D. Irwin, Inc.

Kermit's professional activities range from service as chairman of the American Accounting Association's Committee on Concepts and Standards, vice president of the American Accounting Association, Southwest regional vice president of the AAA, and director of the AAA Doctoral Consortium, to member of the Constitutional Drafting Committee of the Federation of Schools of Accountancy and member of the Commission on Professional Accounting Education. He has served on the Accounting Accreditation Committee and on the Accounting Standards Committee of the AACSB and has been an expert witness on cases involving mergers, antitrust litigation, and expropriation of assets by foreign governments. Kermit has served on the board of directors and executive committee of Tekcon, Inc., the Strategic Planning Committee of the American Accounting Association, and the National Accountant's Advisory Board of Safeguard Business Systems, Inc. Presently he serves as president of the Richard D. Irwin Foundation.

Paul B. W. Miller is professor of accounting at The University of Colorado at Colorado Springs. He holds a Ph.D. from The University of Texas at Austin and is a CPA. Paul's publications include articles in *The Journal of Accountancy, Accounting Horizons, Advances in Accounting, The Chartered Accountant in Australia, Research in Accounting Regulation,* and *Management Accounting.* He has also co-authored several books, including *Financial and Managerial Accounting, Fundamental Accounting Principles,* and *The FASB: the People, the Process, and the Politics.* Paul has received several teaching excellence awards and was selected by the Colorado Society of CPA's as the first recipient of its Outstanding Accounting Educator Award. His unique experience includes service on the research and technical activities staff of the FASB and as the academic fellow in the office of the chief accountant of the SEC. In addition, he has been a member of the Technical Standards Subcommittee of the Ethics Executive Committee of the AICPA. In the fall of 1994, Paul was a visiting professor at Nihon University in Tokyo.

Preface

This new edition of *Financial Accounting* reflects more extensive changes and improvements than one might expect in a sixth edition. The revision has shifted the focus of the book to include much more attention on the use of accounting information by business owners, lenders, managers, and other parties who are interested in the financial affairs of a business. This is accomplished while maintaining the text's appropriate role of showing students how the information is developed. As a result, *Financial Accounting* (1) develops a general understanding of financial reports and analyses that students will use in their personal and professional affairs, (2) provides a strong foundation for future courses in business and finance, and (3) initiates the course work that would lead to a career in accounting.

Revised to Limit Depth of Coverage and Delete Less Relevant Topics

This revision has been developed in response to the most intensive and far-reaching input from current and potential adopters in the history of all prior editions. Perhaps the most dominant theme of these criticisms and suggestions has been that the authors should take a more proactive role in limiting the depth and range of topical coverage in the financial accounting course. The clear imperative has been that the text should reverse the trend toward being a complete resource for all possible combinations of topical development. As a result, in close contact with reviewers and other instructors, we have taken numerous steps to avoid technical matters better left to intermediate level courses. In addition, we have deleted topics that have become less relevant in the changing climate of business practices. We discuss these revisions in the following paragraphs.

Expanded Prologue and Limited Focus of Chapter 1

The first important change in this direction was to prepare an expanded Prologue that now describes the accounting function in the context of other organizational functions such as finance, human resources, research and development, production, marketing, and executive management. The Prologue also explains the work accountants do—including their certifications and the fields within which accountants work—and the pervasive importance of ethics in accounting. This accomplishes two basic improvements. First, as a separate learning unit, the Prologue emphasizes the overall importance of these topics to an understanding of the role accounting plays in providing information to a variety of decision makers. Instructors who want to give more attention to these topics, as suggested by the Accounting Education Change Commission (AECC), will find the Prologue especially appealing.

Second, as a result of the Prologue revision, Chapter 1 is now a much shorter and more manageable learning unit with a clear focus on financial statements. This includes the information contained in the statements, the basic concepts that guide the development and use of accounting information, and the relationship of the statements to the transactions and events in the life of a business.

Deletions in Chapters 4 and 5

Reviewers and adopters have overwhelmingly encouraged limiting the early examples in the book to proprietorships. As a result, the discussion of corporations has been deleted from Chapter 4 and from the illustrations in Chapter 5. Corporations are considered in the early chapters only as necessary to support student interaction with the financial statements at the back of the book and to recognize the existence of alternative forms of business organization.

Work sheets are now presented as an *optional* step in the accounting cycle. However, we also describe other reasons why an understanding of work sheets is useful. In addition, a more concise recognition of the adjusting entry method of accounting for inventories has eliminated the need for a separate appendix at the end of Chapter 5.

Discounting Notes Receivable

The revision of Chapter 7 recognizes the fact that an increasing number of companies routinely convert their receivables into cash without waiting to receive customer payments. In dealing with this modern business practice, the discussion of discounting notes receivable has been replaced with a more general examination of the various ways receivables may be converted into cash.

Topics Related to Inventories

Because perpetual inventory records are rarely maintained on a LIFO basis, LIFO has been deleted from the discussion of perpetual inventories in Chapter 8. Also, the discussion of lower of cost or market has been simplified to avoid the details of considering ceiling and floor concepts when defining market value. Finally, the treatment of markups and markdowns has been eliminated from the discussion of the retail inventory method. Reviewers agree that all three of these topics are better left to intermediate level courses.

Topics Related to Property, Plant, and Equipment

Sum-of-the-years' digits has been deleted form the discussion of accelerated depreciation, as has the matter of apportioning accelerated depreciation between accounting periods. To help students appreciate the differences between financial accounting and tax accounting, we continue to discuss MACRS. However, the discussion has been condensed to exclude the calculations that underlie MACRS tax rate tables. We also eliminated the discussions of plant asset subsidiary records and tax rules that govern plant asset exchanges.

Consolidated Financial Statements

Adopters indicate that the consolidated statements chapter in prior editions was the one they most frequently omitted. Nevertheless, long-term investments are an extremely important financial consideration in evaluating most large companies. By eliminating the details of consolidated statements, we have been able to develop a more balanced set of asset chapters. This involves a new Chapter 10 that completes the asset coverage by discussing natural resources, intangible assets, and long-term investments. The long-term investments portion naturally concludes with a discussion of investments in international operations.

Leases and Deferred Income Taxes Liabilities

In Chapter 11, the discussion of leases has been significantly shortened. Students learn the differences between capital and operating leases without having to journalize the entries related to capital leases. Also, the appendix on deferred income taxes has been deleted as a technical issue better left to intermediate level courses.

Deletion of Cash Flows Appendix and Direct Method Work Sheet

In explaining cash flows from operating activities in Chapter 14, we first explain the direct method, which is most relevant to managerial evaluations and predictions. However, the direct method work sheet has been deleted. We then explain the indirect method as the dominant method used in financial reporting. This approach avoids the need for a separate appendix dealing with the direct method.

Segmental Reporting

The illustration and discussion of segmental reporting has been eliminated from Chapter 16, based on reviewers suggestions that the topic is better suited for an intermediate level course.

Special Features

Several important features of this text mark its effectiveness. They include the following:

Expanded Focus on the Use of Financial Information

Instructors and reviewers have uniformly called for a new commitment to show students the relevance of accounting information and to teach them how to use the information. We have responded to this in a variety of ways. Most obviously, every chapter now includes a section under the general heading Using the Information. These sections show students how to calculate, interpret, and use information such as:

Return on equity (Chapter 1)
Debt ratio (Chapter 2)
Current ratio (Chapter 3)
Profit margin ratio (Chapter 4)
Acid-test ratio (Chapter 5)
Days' sales uncollected (Chapter 6)
Accounts receivable turnover (Chapter 7)
Merchandise turnover and days' stock on hand (Chapter 8)
Total asset turnover (Chapter 9)
Return on total assets (Chapter 10)
Times fixed interest charges earned (Chapter 11)
Pledged assets to secured liabilities (Chapter 12)
Dividend yield (Chapter 13)
Cash flow analyses (Chapter 14)
Price-earnings ratio (Chapter 15)

In Chapter 16, we review and discuss the relationships between all of these ratios. We also discuss vertical and horizontal analyses and the use of other financial disclosures.

New to this edition are boxed quotations and biographical sketches of persons in business, accounting, and public service. In addition to providing role models for students, these individuals explain how they use accounting information in various decision-making situations.

Numerous sections of the text have been rewritten to explain the accounting issues from the perspective of those who use the information. Also, a large number of the end-of-chapter assignments now require responses that place students in the role of accounting information users. The assignments that require students to compute financial ratios are identified in the text by this symbol:

Broad Exposure to Real World Situations

The text incorporates a variety of features that expose students to real world situations and show the relevance of the material to real world decisions. These features include:

- End-of-chapter questions drawn from the financial statements of Apple Computer, Inc.; Ben & Jerry's Homemade, Inc.; and Federal Expresses Corporation. These financial statements are provided in appendixes to the book.
- Provocative problems at the end of each chapter that call upon students to read and interpret the financial information in Apple Computer's annual report. Also included are many additional provocative problems that are based on real company information.
- A complete rewriting of Chapter 16 that uses the 1993 financial statements of Microsoft Corporation as the basis of the analysis throughout the chapter. The effect is to emphasize the relevance of these issues to real decision situations.
- As a Matter of Opinion inserts that contain brief biographies, pictures, and quotations of persons in business, accounting, and public service. These individuals explain why the material of the chapter is relevant to their business decisions.

Integrated Coverage of Mark-to-Market Accounting (SFAS 115)

The May 1993 issuance of *SFAS 115* represents an accounting milestone in its break from the traditional cost and lower-of-cost-or-market bases of reporting. As a result, we incorporate this new development in several sections of the book. These include short-term investments in Chapter 7, long-term investments in Chapter 10, and alternative valuation methods in Appendix C.

An Emphasis on Analytical Thinking and Communication Skills

The text contains a large number of problems that are identified as analytical essays. Each of them requires students to critically analyze a situation and express their conclusions in writing. Many of the exercises and provocative problems require students to think analytically by working "backward" from outputs to inputs or by analyzing the consequences of errors or omissions. Also, selected chapters include a problem that has as one of its requirements the preparation of a memo, letter, or report to convey information to business colleagues. These promote the development of skills essential for effective business communication. The analytical essays are identified by and the business communication problems by 

Integrated Coverage of Ethics

In addition to the discussion of ethics in the Prologue, several chapters contain As A Matter of Ethics cases that relate closely to the technical issues in the chapter. For each of these cases, a provocative problem requires students to analyze the case and express their conclusions in the form of an essay. These problems are identified by this symbol:

ETHICS

Group Assignments

The instructor's F.A.S.T. Edition of the text contains suggested ways of using selected problem assignments as the basis for group projects. Each chapter includes at least one group project suggestion. The purpose of the group projects is to introduce students to the real life activity of working in teams. We also believe the group projects will help encourage more active student participation in the classroom.

Effective Use of Visual Aids

In response to the visual orientation of most students, we have included a wide range of graphical illustrations that convey the logical relationships between important concepts. The transparency overlay presentation of the work sheet in Chapter 4 is especially noteworthy. Our experience indicates that these overlays are very effective in helping students understand the accounting cycle.

Appendixes That Are Complete Learning Units

The appendixes are intended to give instructors maximum flexibility in selecting and organizing the topical coverage of their courses. The topical appendixes are fully supported with learning objectives, summaries, objective review questions, assignment material, and coverage in the study guides and test bank. Thus, each topical appendix is a complete learning unit.

Extensive and Diverse Assignment Material

The assignment material has been thoroughly revised and carefully developed to include a wide variety of questions, exercises, problems, alternate problems, provocative problems, comprehensive problems, and a serial problem. The serial problem in Chapters 2, 3, 4, and 5 involves a single company's operations and may be started after any of those chapters without going back to rework the problem in earlier chapters.

Responses to the AECC

Many of the features discussed in the previous paragraphs are consistent with or responsive to the recommendations of the Accounting Education Change Commission. These include the emphases on using accounting information, analytical or critical thinking, communication skills, integration of ethics, exposure to real world issues and situations, and group project suggestions. Additional features of the text that address the AECC's concerns include the coverage of international issues in Chapters 1 and 10, the deletion of several procedural discussions, the emphasis placed on decision making, and the overriding educational philosophy of maximizing student involvement in the learning process.

Alternate Problems and Packaging Options

Many instructors have asked that innovative approaches be taken to develop a text that students would want to carry with them to class and to study periods. One way we have responded is to transfer the alternate problems from the text to a separate booklet. The booklet is available in quantity to adopters.

In addition to the hardcover version of the text, a softcover version that includes working papers is available. Various special packaging options are also available depending on the unique needs of each school. Please consult your Irwin representative for details.

Supplements that Support the Text

Financial Accounting is supported by a full range of supplements. They include:

- ***Fully Annotated Support for Teaching Edition.*** Marginal annotations include Fast Hints, Video Notes, and Check Figures. Fast Hints include Important Points to Remember, Critical Thought Questions, Real World parallels, Relevant Exercises, and Alternative Examples.
- ***Solutions Manual.*** The solutions manual contains complete solutions for all assignment material.
- ***Working Papers.*** This volume includes papers for the exercises, the problems or alternate problems, the comprehensive problems, and the serial problem.
- ***Study Guide.*** For each chapter and appendix, this guide reviews the learning objectives and the summaries, outlines the topical coverage, and provides a variety of problems with solutions.
- ***Test Bank.*** The test bank contains a wide variety of test questions, including true/false, multiple-choice, quantitative, matching, and essay questions of varying levels of difficulty.
- ***Computest.*** The extensive features of this test generator program include random question selection based on the user's specification of learning objectives, type of question, and level of difficulty. Users have tremendous flexibility in using the program. They can:
  Preview selected questions before final acceptance.
  Edit questions.
  Add their own questions to the test bank.
  Scramble questions when printing up to 99 versions of an exam.
  Scramble multiple choice answers when printing.
  Insert heading material on the first page.
  Save and recall exams.
  Password protect exam files or the entire test bank.
  Save exams in ASCII format.
- ***Teletest.*** Irwin is happy to serve those without access to administrative support or a computer system. Simply choose your questions from the Test Bank and call Irwin College New Media.
- ***GLAS (General Ledger Applications Software).*** This package contains most of the features of commercial accounting software, yet is easily used by students with little or no computer background. A large number of problem assignments are preloaded on the package. These are identified in the text by this symbol: This software can also be used to solve any other problem that calls for journal entries. Both DOS and Windows versions are available.

- ***SPATS (Spreadsheet Applications Template Software).*** This includes Lotus 1-2-3 (or the equivalent) templates for selected problems and exercises from the text. The templates gradually become more complex, requiring students to build a variety of formulas. "What if" questions are added to show the power of spreadsheets and a simple tutorial is included. Both DOS and Windows versions are available. The problems and exercises for which these templates are available are indicated by this symbol:

- ***Tutorial Software.*** Multiple-choice, true/false, journal entry review, and glossary review questions are randomly accessed by students. Explanations of right and wrong answers are provided and scores are tallied. Both DOS and Windows versions are available.
- ***Practice Sets***
Barns Bluff Camping Equipment Company. This manual practice set utilizes business papers. It also covers special journals. It has been extensively revised for the Sixth Edition.
Republic Lighting Company. This is a manual practice set with a narrative of transactions.
Note: Both Barns Bluff and Republic Lighting have their opening balances preloaded on GLAS. They can each be purchased in a version that includes a GLAS disk.

  In addition, five computerized practice sets are available, all authored by Leland Mansuetti and Keith Weidkamp of Sierra College:
Granite Bay JetSki, Level One
Granite Bay JetSki, Inc., Level Two
Thunder Mountain Snowmobile
Gold Run Snowmobile, Inc.
Wild Goose Marina, Inc.
- ***Solutions Transparencies.*** These transparencies are set in large, boldface type to maximize their effectiveness in large classrooms.
- ***Financial Accounting Teaching Transparencies.*** This set of over 150 color transparencies provides visual support for your complete financial accounting course. A guide for suggested use of each specific transparency with this text is provided.
- ***Financial Accounting Video Library.*** This video series is designed to strengthen your classroom presentations, grab your students' interest, and add variety to your students' learning process. Topics covered include: Plant and Equipment, Partnerships and Corporations, the FASB's Conceptual Framework, and International Accounting. Each of the 10 videos provides approximately 12 minutes of important topical coverage.
- ***Lecture Review Videos.*** These videos are prepared by Kirkwood Community College, Cedar Rapids, IA. Selections from this series of lessons can be used to support and reinforce the concepts and procedures found throughout the text. Each lesson runs approximately 15 minutes.

Acknowledgments

We are grateful for the encouragement, suggestions, reviews, and counsel that have been provided by our students, colleagues, and instructors from across the nation. A tremendous amount of useful information was gained from the participants in the Irwin Accounting Education Seminars. Many others contributed through their responses to the publisher's printed survey and through reviews of various portions of the manuscript. They include:

John B. K. Aheto
Pace University

James Beisel
Longview Community College

John C. Borke
University of Wisconsin-Platteville

Rodger Brannan
University of Minnesota-Duluth

Annhenrie Campbell
California State University-Stanislaus

Kenneth L. Coffey
San Jose Community College

Robert Conway
University of Wisconsin-Platteville

Harvey J. Cooke
Penn Valley Community College

Constance Cooper
University of Cincinnati

David L. Davis
Tallahassee Community College

Diane J. Davis
Indiana University-Purdue/Ft. Wayne

Marvin J. Dittman
Elgin Community College

William J. Engel
Longview Community College

Robert R. Garrett
American River College

Bonnie Givens
Avila College

David Gotlob
Indiana University-Purdue/Ft. Wayne

Maki Ohy Gragg
City College of San Francisco

Duane E. Harper
Johnson County Community College

Charles Hawkins
NW Missouri State University

Linda A. Herrington
Community College of Allegheny County

Sharon J. Huxley
Teikyo Post University

Randy Kidd
Penn Valley Community College

Shirly A. Kleiner
Johnson County Community College

Alvin Koslofsky
San Jose City College

Terrie Kroshus
Inver Hills Community College

Wayne A. Kunert
Inver Hills Community College

Thomas W. Lee
Winona State University

Marie C. Mari
Miami Dade Community College

Linda Spotts Michael
Maple Woods Community College

Barbara Muncaster
Rose State College

Catherine J. Pitts
Highline Community College

Bill Potts
University of Wisconsin-Platteville

Allan M. Rabinowitz
Pace University

Elizabeth Rosa
Allentown College

Richard W. Schneider
Winona State University

Sara Seyedin
Evergreen Valley College

Dennis Stanczak
Indiana University NW

Dick D. Wasson
Southwestern College

Jane G. Wiese
Valencia Community College

Finally, we especially want to recognize Betsey Jones, Sue Ann Meyer, and Barbara Schnathorst for their expertise and their immeasurable contributions to the text and the supplements.

Kermit D. Larson
Paul B. W. Miller

Contents in Brief

Contents

Introduction

Processing Accounting Data

Accounting for Liabilities

Appendixes

Your Introduction to Business, Accounting, and Ethics

What goes on in business and other organizations? How are the activities carried out? Who is responsible for them? And, what part does accounting play? This prologue answers these questions and helps you begin your study of accounting. It provides information on why you should study accounting, even if you are not planning to be an accountant. The presentation includes facts about the kinds of accountants and the work that they do. Finally, the prologue describes the great importance of ethics for accounting and those who use its information.

Learning Objectives

After studying the Prologue, you should be able to:

1. Describe the main purpose of accounting and its internal role for organizations.
2. Describe the external role of accounting for organizations.
3. List the main fields of accounting and the activities carried on in each field.
4. State several reasons for the importance of ethics in accounting.
5. Define or explain the words and phrases listed in the prologue glossary.

Accounting and Its Role in Organizations

The main purpose of **accounting** is to provide useful information to people who make rational investment, credit, and similar decisions.[1] In effect, accountants serve decision makers by providing them with financial information that helps them make better decisions. These decision makers include present and potential investors, lenders, and other users. The other users include managers of organizations, suppliers who sell to them, and customers who buy from them.

LO 1 Describe the main purpose of accounting and its internal role for organizations.

In addition to providing information about profit-oriented businesses, accountants also provide information about nonprofit organizations. Examples of nonprofit organizations include charities, churches, hospitals, museums, schools, and various government agencies. Accounting information

[1] Financial Accounting Standards Board, *Statement of Financial Accounting Concepts No. 1,* "Objectives of Financial Reporting by Business Enterprises" (Norwalk, CT, 1978), par. 34.

about these entities is used by people who manage them. The information is also used by people who donate to or pay taxes to them, who use their services, or who otherwise work with them.

Because it helps so many different kinds of people make decisions, accounting has often been described as a service activity.[2] Later sections describe the role that accounting plays within businesses and other kinds of organizations and how accounting provides information to people external to these organizations. Whether you are planning to be an accountant, an employee, a manager within an organization, or an external user of the information, your knowledge of accounting will help you achieve more success in your career.

What Goes on in Organizations?

Illustration PR–1 is a diagram of some of the major activities of typical businesses that manufacture products and sell them to customers. Similar activities occur in other businesses that sell services to their customers, such as airlines and express delivery companies. The same kinds of activities generally occur in governmental and nonprofit organizations as well.

Note that organizations of all sizes carry out the same functions. In larger companies, many different people are involved in performing them. In smaller companies, one person, or perhaps only a few people, are responsible for doing all of them. The following paragraphs describe these functions in more detail.

Finance. Every organization needs money to operate and grow. Organizations use their money to acquire various kinds of investments, including equipment, buildings, vehicles, and financial holdings. The finance function has the task of planning how to obtain money from such sources as payments from customers, loans from banks, and new investments from owners. Government organizations acquire cash by collecting taxes and fees, while nonprofit organizations acquire most of their cash from contributions by donors. In preparing plans, the finance department identifies and evaluates alternative sources of funds. In addition, finance analyzes alternative investment opportunities to identify which to take and which to reject.

Human Resources. All organizations require efforts from people. As a result, employees must be located, screened, hired, trained, compensated, promoted, and counseled. In some cases, they may be released from employment by being retired or laid off. The human resources function is responsible for handling these tasks. In larger companies, literally hundreds of employees may be engaged in looking after the other employees.

Research and Development. In our dynamic economy, all organizations need to find new ways to meet the needs of their customers and others. Thus, research into new technologies and products or services is essential. This research may involve something as simple as testing a new recipe for pizza or as complex as creating a new technology, such as optical fibers or supercomputers. Once research is completed, the development process uses the new knowledge to design or modify specific products or services. This function is essential to the organization's survival.

[2] Accounting Principles Board, "Basic Concepts and Accounting Principles Underlying Financial Statements of Business Enterprises," *APB Statement No. 4* (New York: AICPA, October 1970), par. 9.

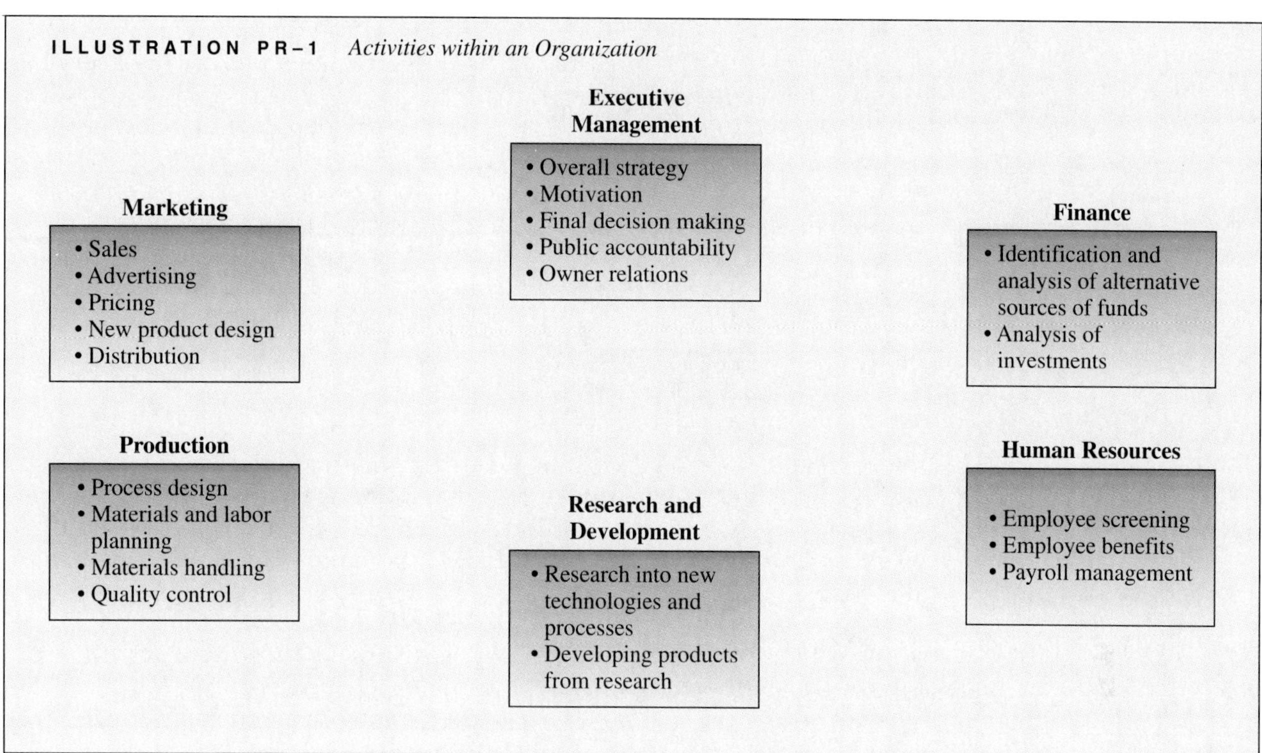

Production. Many companies produce and sell goods to their customers. Producing these goods requires planning, coordinating, and implementing many specific activities. The activities include designing the production process, acquiring materials used in production, and selecting the workers' skills to be applied. In addition, materials handling systems must be implemented to ensure that raw materials and finished goods are delivered on time. Production management also requires a great deal of attention to the quality of the goods. Similar activities in retail and service organizations ensure that quality merchandise and services are delivered to consumers.

Marketing. Companies can sell goods and services only if customers are willing to buy them. Marketing activities help customers know about goods and services and encourage their purchase. These activities include sales efforts by company representatives that present information directly to customers. Marketing also includes advertising that provides information to large numbers of potential customers. Another activity sets prices low enough to encourage sales while being high enough to earn profits. In addition, marketing involves identifying new products that might meet customers' needs. It also includes developing systems that distribute products to customers when and where they need them. These activities are sometimes summed up as the four P's of marketing—product, promotion, price, and place.

Executive Management. All organizations must have leadership, vision, and coordination. Long-term strategies need to be established and employees need to be motivated to do their best. In addition, major decisions have to be made. In many situations, the company must be represented in dealing with the public or with the owners. These tasks are the duty of the company's executive management. In smaller organizations, executive management functions are carried out by the owner or owners. Larger organizations have key

ILLUSTRATION PR–2 *The Internal Role of Accounting*

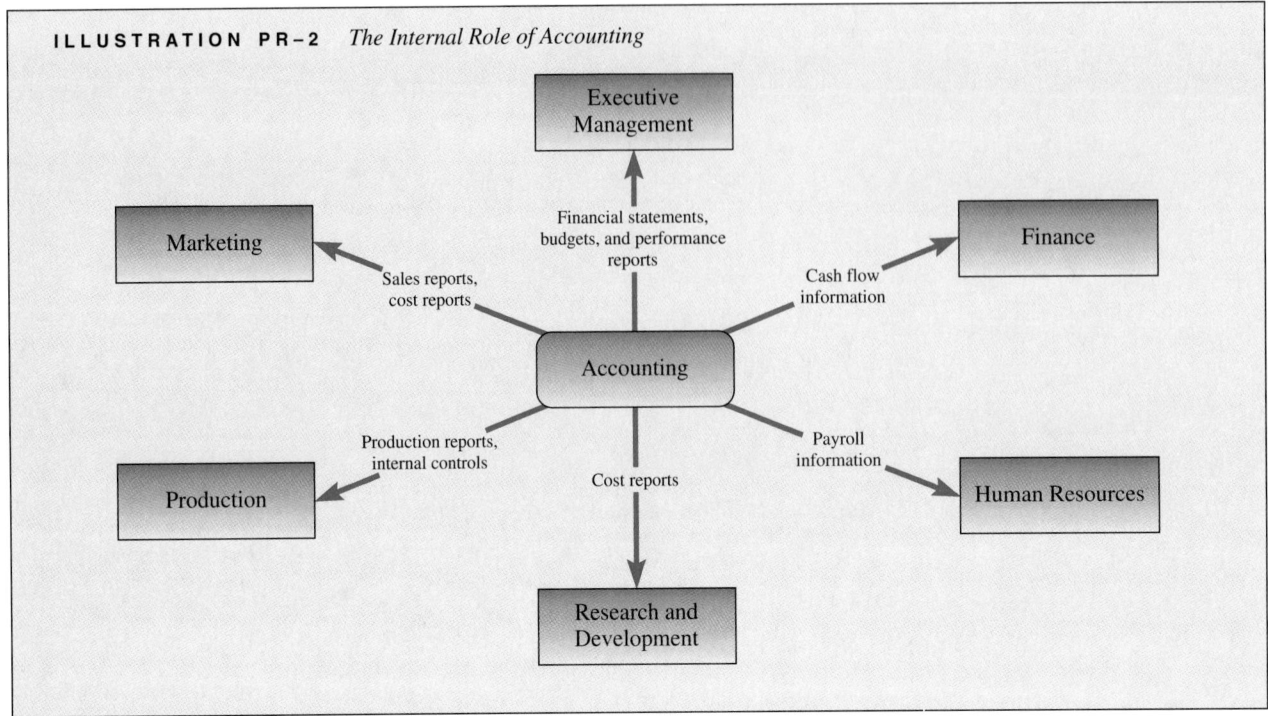

individuals who take on these responsibilities. They may be called the president, the chief executive officer, or the chairman of the board of directors. In nonprofit organizations, the top managers are frequently called executive directors.

Using Accounting to Serve Internal Needs

LO 1 Describe the main purpose of accounting and its internal role for organizations.

The internal role of accounting is to serve all the organization's other functions by providing information that helps them complete their tasks. By providing this information, accounting helps the organization reach its overall goals. Illustration PR–2 shows some of the information provided by accounting within an organization.

The finance function can more usefully project future cash flows and evaluate past decisions if it receives information about actual cash flows. The human resources function can carry out its work more effectively if it has information about the company's employees, including payroll costs. The managers of the research and development function need information about the costs that they have already incurred so that they can decide whether to continue their projects. The managers of the marketing function also use accounting information, especially reports about the company's sales and its marketing costs.

The production division of a company depends heavily on accounting information to determine whether its operating costs are occurring as expected. In carrying out its processes, the production department works within a set of *internal controls* designed and implemented by the accounting department. These controls specify procedures that must be followed before actions can take place. For example, internal controls may require a manager's approval before any materials are moved to the production line. Internal controls ensure the usefulness of the information about the process. They also help prevent unauthorized use of the company's resources. Chapter 6 describes internal control procedures.

Because executive management has overall responsibility for the organization, it depends heavily on accounting information to understand what is happening. One important set of reports includes the *financial statements*. We explain the contents, usefulness, and limits of these statements throughout this book. (Chapter 1 introduces you to the four primary financial statements.) Executive management also receives and uses budget reports that describe future plans. After events have unfolded, the managers use accounting information in performance reports to understand what was done well and to identify where improvements might be made.

Perhaps the most important point to learn at this stage is that accounting activities are not important by themselves. Accounting activities are important only if they provide information that is useful to other parts of the organization.

Using Accounting to Serve External Needs

LO 2 Describe the external role of accounting for organizations.

In addition to using accounting information to meet internal needs, organizations also use it for reporting to various external groups not involved in their daily activities. These external decision makers may include owners who are not managers. For example, these owners can use information about the company's performance and financial strength to help them determine whether to hold their investments.

In making decisions about an organization, internal and external decision makers generally begin by asking questions. The answers are often based on information from the accounting reports. For example, owners (including investors) and managers of businesses use accounting information to help them answer questions like these:

- What resources does the organization own?
- What debts does it owe?
- How much income is it earning?
- Are the expenses appropriate for the amount of sales?
- Are customers' accounts being collected promptly?

Other decision makers include people who have loaned money to the organization. These lenders, also called *creditors,* need information to assess whether the company has enough financial strength and profits to pay its debts. For example, they need answers to questions like these:

- Has the organization promptly paid its debts in the past?
- Does it have the ability to pay its current debts?
- Does it have good prospects for future earnings?
- Should it be granted additional credit now?

People who are considering making new investments in or new loans to the organization also can make better decisions if they have information that helps them predict future events. They need answers to questions similar to the ones just listed.

Accounting information is useful for voters, legislators, and officials concerned about a government agency's receipts and expenditures of funds. Similarly, contributors to a nonprofit organization can use accounting information to understand what happens to their donations.

A company's employees have a special interest in knowing whether an organization represents a stable source of employment. They can rely on accounting information to help them understand their employer's financial health and performance.

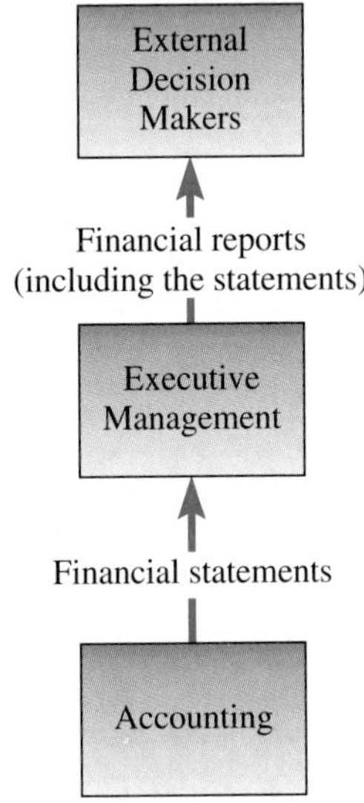

In addition, some government agencies are charged with regulating business activities. They often need useful financial information to carry out that responsibility. Other government agencies are responsible for collecting income taxes. As you know from personal experience, taxpayers use accounting information to determine how much income they have and how much tax they owe.

We explained earlier that executive management is responsible for an organization's relationships with external decision makers. As this diagram shows, accounting provides most of the financial information that executive management presents to external decision makers. The primary focus of this book about financial accounting is to describe the contents and usefulness of the financial statements created for these external reporting activities.

In addition, managers provide other financial information that helps external groups reach decisions. For example, information provided to the government for tax calculations may differ significantly from the information in the financial statements. You need to take one or more special courses in income tax accounting to know what must be reported on tax returns. We describe the work of tax accountants later in this prologue.

Again, remember that financial accounting is important only if it actually provides useful information. This background allows us to look more closely at what accounting is and why you can benefit from learning as much about it as you can.

The Difference between Accounting and Bookkeeping

Because accounting and bookkeeping are both concerned with financial information and records, some people mistakenly think that they are two different names for the same activity. In fact, accounting involves much more than bookkeeping. Although bookkeeping activities are critical to developing useful accounting information, they are only the clerical part of the accounting process. That is, **bookkeeping** is the part of accounting that records transactions and other events, either manually or with computers. In contrast, accounting activities identify how to describe transactions and events in financial statements. Accounting activities also involve designing and implementing systems to produce useful reports and to control the operations of an organization. Accounting involves more professional expertise and judgment than bookkeeping because accountants must analyze complex and unusual events. Also, accountants must be able to interpret and explain the information in the financial reports.

Whether you want to be an accountant, plan to hold some other position in an organization, or expect to be an investor or creditor, you need to understand the source of accounting information. To help you gain this understanding, initially you will study some basic bookkeeping practices. Later in the book, you will use this knowledge to learn how accountants present financial data in useful reports. Eventually, you will be able to use the reports more effectively because you will understand how the information has been processed.

Accounting and Computers

Since computers first became available in the 1950s, they have spread throughout our everyday lives and the business world. From the beginning, computer technology has been applied to accounting and bookkeeping tasks. Computers are widely used in accounting because they efficiently store, process, and summarize large quantities of financial data. Furthermore, computers perform these functions quickly with limited operator involvement. Thus, computers reduce the time, effort, and cost of processing data while improving clerical accuracy. As a result of these advantages, most accounting systems are now computerized. Even so, manual accounting systems are still used by a surprisingly large number of small businesses.

To prepare, analyze, and use accounting information in today's world, you need to understand the important role computers play in most accounting systems. In essence, computers are tools that help accountants provide useful information for decision makers. The huge growth in the number of computers and the explosion of their power have greatly changed how accountants and other people work. However, computers have not eliminated the need for people to learn about accounting. A strong demand exists for people who can design accounting systems, supervise their operation, analyze complex transactions, and interpret reports. A strong demand also exists for people who know how to make better decisions by using computers to analyze accounting reports. While computers have taken over many routine tasks, they are not substitutes for qualified people with abilities to generate and use accounting information.

Why You Should Study Accounting

Because of the wide range of questions answered with accounting information, you will almost certainly use accounting in your future career. (In fact, you probably already use some accounting information every day as you write checks, make deposits, and use charge accounts and credit cards.) To use accounting effectively, you need to understand the words and terms unique to accounting and the concepts that guide the preparation of accounting reports. You should also understand the procedures used to gather accounting information and to summarize it in financial statements. Importantly, your study of accounting will also make you aware of its limitations. For example, much accounting information is based on estimates and predictions instead of precise measurements. By understanding this fact, you can use the information more effectively. Another very good reason for studying accounting is to make it the basis for an interesting and rewarding career. The next section of this prologue describes what accountants do.

The Types of Accountants

LO 3 List the main fields of accounting and the activities carried on in each field.

One way to classify accountants is to identify the kinds of work they perform. In general, accountants work in three broad fields. These fields provide a variety of information to different users. These fields are

- Financial accounting.
- Managerial accounting.
- Tax accounting.

We describe the activities of accountants in these fields later in this prologue.

Another way to classify accountants is to identify the kinds of organizations in which they work. Most accountants are **private accountants.** A private accountant works for a single employer, which is often a business. A large business might employ a hundred or more private accountants, but most companies have fewer.

Many other accountants are **public accountants.** Public accountants provide their services to many different clients. They are called *public accountants* because their services are available to the public. Some public accountants are self-employed. Many others work for public accounting firms that may have thousands of employees or only a few.

Government accountants work for local, state, and federal government agencies. Some government accountants perform accounting services for their own agencies. Other government accountants are involved with business regulation. Still others investigate violations of laws.

Accounting is a profession like law and medicine because accountants have special abilities and responsibilities. The professional status of an accountant is often indicated by one or more special certificates.

The CPA Certificate

Each state in the United States, as well as the District of Columbia, Guam, Puerto Rico, and the Virgin Islands, has an agency (called a *board*) that licenses Certified Public Accountants **(CPAs)**. The licensing process helps ensure that a high standard of professional service is available to the public. Individuals can legally identify themselves as CPAs only if they hold this license.

To become a licensed CPA, an individual must meet education and experience requirements and must pass the CPA examination. In general, most states require an applicant to be a citizen of the United States, to be at least 21 years of age, to have good ethical character, and to hold a college degree with a major in accounting.

The CPA examination covers topics in financial and managerial accounting, as well as income taxes, auditing, and business law. The uniform two-day examination is given in all states and other jurisdictions every May and November. Although the exam is administered by individual state boards, it is prepared and graded by the American Institute of Certified Public Accountants **(AICPA)**, the largest and most influential national professional organization of CPAs.

In addition, many boards issue a certificate only after the applicant has one or more years of experience working under the supervision of a CPA. Nearly all boards reduce the amount of experience if an applicant has completed a specified amount of coursework beyond the undergraduate degree. Some states do not require any work experience. A few states allow applicants to substitute work experience for part of the formal education requirements.

As early as 1969, the AICPA's governing council took the position that CPAs need at least five years of college education (150 semester hours). This position was supported in 1983 by the National Association of State Boards of Accountancy **(NASBA)**. In 1988, the members of the AICPA voted to require all CPAs admitted to the institute after 2000 to have 150 semester hours of college education. As of 1994, more than 30 states had changed their laws to eventually require new CPAs to complete at least 150 semester hours of courses. We expect many more to adopt this requirement before 2000.

Because of the differences among states and the fact that changes are occurring, you should contact your state board to learn the requirements that may apply to you.

Other Professional Certificates

Many private accountants hold CPA certificates because they were public accountants earlier in their careers. Some private accountants hold other certificates in addition to or instead of the CPA license. For example, you may want to obtain a Certificate in Management Accounting **(CMA)** or to become a Certified Internal Auditor **(CIA)**. Holders of these certificates must meet examination, education, and experience requirements similar to those applied to CPAs. Unlike the CPA license, the CMA and CIA certificates are not issued by the government and do not give their holders any legal authority. The CMA is awarded by the Institute of Management Accountants and the CIA is granted by the Institute of Internal Auditors.

The Fields of Accounting

Accountants practice in three fields—financial, managerial, and tax accounting. The actual work done by an accountant depends on both the field and whether the person is employed in private, public, or government accounting. Illustration PR–3 identifies the specific activities of the three types of accountants within these fields.

ILLUSTRATION PR–3 *Activities of Accountants*

Types of Accountants	Fields of Accounting: Financial Accounting	Managerial Accounting	Tax Accounting
Private accountants	Preparing financial statements	General accounting Cost accounting Budgeting Internal auditing	Preparing tax returns Planning
Public accountants	Auditing financial statements	Providing management advisory services	Preparing tax returns Planning
Government accountants	Preparing financial statements Reviewing financial reports Writing regulations Assisting companies Investigating violations	General accounting Cost accounting Budgeting Internal auditing	Reviewing tax returns Assisting taxpayers Writing regulations Investigating violations

Financial Accounting

Financial accounting provides information to decision makers who are not involved in the day-to-day operations of an organization. As described earlier, these external decision makers include investors, creditors, and others. The information is distributed primarily through general purpose financial statements. Financial statements describe the condition of the organization and the events that happened during the year. Chapter 1 explains the form and contents of financial statements.

The Financial Accounting column of Illustration PR–3 shows that financial statements are prepared by a company's private accountants. However, many companies issue their financial statements only after an **audit.** An audit is a thorough check of an organization's accounting systems and records; it is performed to add credibility to the financial statements.[3] For example, banks require audits of the financial statements of companies applying for large loans. Also, federal and state laws require companies to have audits before their securities (stocks and bonds) can be sold to the public. Thereafter, their financial statements must be audited as long as the securities are traded.

When performing an audit, auditors examine the financial statements and the accounting systems and records used to prepare them. Specifically, the auditors must decide whether the statements reflect the company's financial position and operating results in agreement with **generally accepted accounting principles (GAAP).** These principles are rules adopted by the accounting profession as guides for measuring and reporting the financial condition and activities of a business. Chapter 1 discusses the purposes and origins of GAAP, and many later chapters describe specific GAAP requirements.

When an audit is completed, the auditors prepare a report that expresses their professional opinion about the financial statements. The auditors' report must accompany the statements when they are distributed.

[3] To achieve this result, audits are performed by independent CPAs who are public accountants. Little or no credibility would be added to the statements if they were audited by a company's own employees.

As the first column of Illustration PR–3 shows, some government accountants prepare financial statements. These statements describe the financial status of government agencies and results of events occurring during the year. The financial statements of governmental bodies are usually audited by independent CPAs.

Other government accountants are involved with regulating financial accounting practices used by businesses. For example, many accountants work for the Securities and Exchange Commission **(SEC).** Congress created the SEC in 1934 to regulate securities markets, including the flow of information from companies to the public. SEC accountants review companies' financial reports before they are distributed to the public. The purpose of the review is to be sure that the reports comply with the SEC's regulations.

Accountants who work for other regulatory agencies, such as the Federal Trade Commission, may review reports filed by businesses subject to the agencies' authority. Government accountants also help write regulations concerning financial accounting. Because the regulations are complicated, many government accountants help companies understand and comply with them.

As we mentioned briefly, some government accountants investigate possible violations of laws and regulations. For example, accountants who work for the SEC investigate crimes related to securities. Other accountants investigate financial frauds and white-collar crimes in their capacity as agents of the Federal Bureau of Investigation.

Managerial Accounting

The field of managerial accounting involves providing information to organizations' managers. Managerial accounting reports often include much of the same information used in financial accounting. However, managerial accounting reports also include a great deal of information that is not reported outside the company.

Look at the upper and lower sections of the Managerial Accounting column in Illustration PR–3. Notice that private and government accountants have the same four major activities. The middle section of the column shows that public accountants also perform activities related to managerial accounting. These activities are described next.

General Accounting. The task of recording transactions, processing the recorded data, and preparing reports for managers is called **general accounting.** General accounting also includes preparing the financial statements that executive management presents to external users. An organization's own accountants usually design the accounting information system, often with help from public accountants. The general accounting staff is supervised by a chief accounting officer, who is called the organization's **controller.** This title stems from the fact that accounting information is used to control the organization's operations.

Cost Accounting. The managerial accounting activity of **cost accounting** helps managers identify, measure, and control operating costs. Cost accounting may involve accounting for the costs of products, services, or specific activities. Managers need information about these costs to control their amounts. Cost accounting information also is useful for evaluating managers' achievements. Large companies usually employ many cost accountants because cost accounting information is so important.

Budgeting. Budgeting is the process of developing formal plans for an organization's future activities. A primary goal of budgeting is to give managers from different areas in the organization a clear understanding of how their activities affect the entire organization. After the budget has been put into effect, it provides a basis for evaluating actual performance.

Internal Auditing. Just as independent auditing adds credibility to financial statements, **internal auditing** adds credibility to reports produced and used within an organization. Internal auditors not only examine record-keeping processes but also assess whether managers are following established operating procedures. In addition, internal auditors evaluate the efficiency of operating procedures. Almost all large companies and government agencies employ internal auditors.

Management Advisory Services. Public accountants participate in managerial accounting by providing **management advisory services** to their clients. Independent auditors gain an intimate knowledge of a client's accounting and operating procedures when they conduct their examinations. As a result, auditors are in an excellent position to offer suggestions for improving the company's procedures. Most clients expect these suggestions as a useful byproduct of the audit. For example, public accountants often help companies design and install new accounting and internal control systems. This effort includes offering advice on selecting new computer systems. Other advice might relate to budgeting procedures or employee benefit plans.

Tax Accounting

Many taxes raised by federal, state, and city governments are based on the income earned by taxpayers. These taxpayers include both individuals and corporate businesses. The amount of taxes is based on what the laws define to be income. Tax accountants help taxpayers comply with these laws by preparing their tax returns. Another **tax accounting** activity involves planning future transactions to minimize the amount of tax to be paid. The Tax Accounting column of Illustration PR–3 identifies the activities of accountants in this field.

Large companies usually have their own private accountants who are responsible for preparing tax returns and doing tax planning. However, large companies may consult with public accountants when they need special tax expertise. Almost all smaller companies rely on public accountants for their tax work.

Many accountants are employed on the government side of the tax process. For example, the Internal Revenue Service **(IRS)** employs numerous tax accountants. The IRS has the duty of collecting federal taxes and otherwise enforcing tax laws. Most IRS accountants review tax returns filed by taxpayers. Other IRS accountants offer assistance to taxpayers and help write regulations. Still other IRS accountants investigate possible violations of tax laws.

Summary

The preceding description has illustrated how important accounting is for virtually every kind of organization. Regardless of your career goals, you will surely use accounting information and work with accountants. The discussion also shows the variety of opportunities available if you find accounting to be especially enjoyable and challenging. It is likely that you could shape an accounting career to match your personal interests, whatever they might be.

The Importance of Ethics in Accounting

As a student, you realize that ethics and ethical behavior are important features of any society. Disappointing stories in the media often remind us how much ethics affect our society. These stories tell us about attempts to defraud the elderly and other vulnerable people, missed child support payments, harassment, misconduct by public figures, bribery of government officials, and the use of insider information for personal gain in the stock market. Events like these make it difficult for people to trust each other. If trust is lacking, our commercial and personal lives are much more complicated, inefficient, and unpleasant.

LO 4 State several reasons for the importance of ethics in accounting.

This section of the prologue introduces you to the meaning of ethics in general and describes how ethics affect business and accounting in particular. Because the purpose of accounting is to provide useful information that can be trusted, it is essential that accountants be ethical. Can you imagine how difficult it would be for the users of accounting information to rely on it if they could not trust accountants? The need to avoid this difficult situation has prompted the development of special ethics for accountants.

The Meaning of Ethics

According to the dictionary, **ethics** are the "principles that determine the rightness or wrongness of particular acts or activities." Ethics are also "accepted standards of good behavior . . . in a profession or trade."[4] Ethics and laws often coincide, with the result that many unethical actions (such as theft and physical violence) are also illegal. Other actions may not be against the law but are generally recognized as being unethical. For example, the crime of perjury (not telling the truth) occurs only if the liar has been put under an oath. However, not telling the truth is nearly always unethical.[5] Because of differences between laws and ethics, we cannot count on laws to keep us and other people ethical.

In some cases, a person may face difficulty in deciding whether an action is right or wrong. In these situations, the most ethical choice may be to take an unquestionably correct course of action simply to avoid uncertainty and the possible appearance of doing wrong. For example, independent auditors would compromise their independence if they could profit directly from their clients' success. Should this potential conflict of interest prevent auditors from investing in a client if the investment is only a small part of the auditor's personal wealth? To avoid the question of how much would be too much, ethics rules for auditors simply forbid any direct investment in their clients' securities, regardless of the amount.[6] To prevent the appearance of a lack of independence, auditors cannot accept contingent fees that depend on amounts reported in a client's financial statements.[7]

Many controversial issues that we face in school, the workplace, or elsewhere have ethical implications. We should not be surprised when we encounter these ethical issues because they are an unavoidable part of life. However, a commitment to being ethical requires us to think carefully before we act to be certain that we are making ethical choices. Our success in making those choices affects how we feel about ourselves and how others feel about us. In fact, our combined individual choices greatly affect the quality of our entire society and the individual experience that each of us enjoys.

Beyond these relatively abstract ideas, how do ethics relate to business, and more specifically, how do they relate to accounting?

Ethics in Business

We discuss ethics at the beginning of this book because business activity is so central to everyone's life and because useful accounting information is so important for business. Recent history shows that many people have been concerned about what they see as low ethical standards in business. For exam-

---

[4] *The New Lexicon Webster's Dictionary of the English Language* (New York: Lexington Publications, Inc., 1989), p. 324.

[5] The usual exceptions to this rule involve protecting another person against harm.

[6] *AICPA Code of Professional Conduct,* Rule 101.

[7] *AICPA Code of Professional Conduct,* Rule 301.

ple, a survey of more than 1,100 executives, deans of business schools, and members of Congress, showed that 94% of the respondents agreed with the statement that "the business community is troubled by ethical problems."[8] Despite this pessimistic conclusion, we can be encouraged because the survey also showed that the vast majority of the respondents believed high ethical standards are followed by companies that are successful over the long run. This second finding confirms an old saying: "Good ethics is good business." Ethical business practices build trust, which in turn promotes loyalty and productive relationships with customers, suppliers, and employees. As a result, good ethics contribute to a company's reputation and eventually its profitability.

Because of the important public interest in business ethics, many companies have adopted their own codes of ethics that establish standards for their internal activities and their relationships with their customers, suppliers, regulators, the public, and even their competitors. These companies often use their codes as public statements of their commitment to ethical business practices. More importantly, they serve as guides for employees to follow.

Ethics in Accounting

As we mentioned earlier, ethics are important in accounting because accountants are expected to provide useful information for decision makers. These decisions can have a profound effect on many individuals, businesses, and other institutions. As a result, accountants often face ethical issues as they consider what information should be provided to decision makers. For example, accountants' decisions can affect such things as the amount of money a company pays in taxes or distributes to its stockholders. The information also can affect the price that a buyer pays for a business enterprise or the amount of compensation paid to a company's managers and executives. Internal information can affect judgments about the success of a company's specific products or divisions. If inadequate accounting information would cause a successful division to be closed inappropriately, its employees, customers, and suppliers would be significantly harmed. Accountants need to consider all these effects so that they understand what information will be most useful for these important decisions.

In response to the need for guidance for accountants, ethics codes have long been adopted and enforced by professional organizations, including the American Institute of Certified Public Accountants and the Institute of Management Accountants. To keep their codes up to date, these organizations continually monitor their effectiveness and applicability to new ways of operating. The As a Matter of Opinion box presents the views of Herb Finkston, the director of the AICPA's division of professional ethics, on the importance of ethical behavior for accountants and others.

As an example of an ethical accounting issue, assume that the Mayfield Company is managed by an individual paid a yearly bonus based on the company's reported annual income. In the course of the annual audit, the company's independent auditor determines that two alternative accounting principles could be applied to a major transaction that occurred near the end of the year. One interpretation would increase the current year's reported income and the manager's bonus. The other alternative would not affect this year's income but would increase the following year's income. As a result, the manager's bonus would be delayed. Should the auditor's choice between these two alternatives be shaped by the manager's urgent need for the bonus to pay for large personal medical expenses?

---

[8] Touche Ross & Co., *Ethics in American Business* (New York, 1988), pp. 1–2.

AS A MATTER OF
Opinion

Mr. Finkston received his B.A. in accounting from Brooklyn College and his J.D. from Brooklyn Law School. He is a member of the New York State Bar and was a public accountant early in his career. Since 1979, he has been the director of the Division of Professional Ethics of the American Institute of CPAs.

Herbert A. Finkston, CPA

The accounting profession has earned high regard because of its ethical standards. Our standards require ethical behavior in our relationships with our clients and our employers. They also require ethical behavior in our dealings with the public and its interests. And, our standards require us to render high-quality professional services. By adhering to the concepts of objectivity, integrity, and independence, and by continued striving for quality, the profession has won a respected place in the entire business community and among the other professions.

As a student of accounting, be aware of the ethical implications of all that you study. As a member of the accounting profession, or any other profession, practice ethics in all that you do. By doing so, you will bring honor to yourself and your profession.

The starting point for coping with this dilemma is to remember that the goal of financial accounting is to provide useful financial statements for external decision makers. From this point of view, the auditor's choice between the two methods must be based on the quality of the information provided to the outside parties. The users are relying on the auditor to protect their interests by providing them with useful information. On the other hand, the auditor may feel inclined by friendship or compassion to choose the alternative that increases the desperate manager's bonus, even if the information in the financial statements would be less useful for the external users. In summary, the auditor's ethical dilemma is the choice between a professional responsibility to provide useful information and an understandable desire to help the manager.

Suppose that the external users could not trust the accountant to protect their interests. How much usefulness would they assign to the financial statements? Their lack of trust in the accountant would become a lack of trust in the financial statements. These doubts could lead them to decide that investments in or loans to the company are too risky. As a result, they would withhold their funds. In addition, employees, customers, and suppliers might lose their trust in Mayfield Company and go elsewhere. If so, the manager would be worse off, even though the goal of manipulating the financial statements was to make the manager better off by producing a larger bonus.

This example shows why accountants, their clients, and the public need ethical guidance and commitment. This guidance gives accountants a basis for knowing which actions to take, and the commitment provides the courage to do what needs to be done. The guidance also tells clients what they can rightfully expect from their accountants and assures the public that financial statements are trustworthy. This analysis shows how the economic system is harmed when individual accountants fail to act ethically and betray the public's trust.

Another accounting situation involving ethics centers on the information that accountants deal with in their work. For example, auditors have access to confidential salary records and plans for the future. Their clients could be damaged if the auditors released this information to others or chose to enrich themselves with it. To prevent this result, auditors' ethics require them to keep information confidential.[9] In addition, internal accountants are not supposed to use confidential information for personal advantage.[10]

The Ethical Challenge

As you proceed in your study of accounting, you will encounter many other situations in which ethical issues are raised. We encourage you to explore these issues. We also urge you to remember that accounting must be done ethically if it is to be an effective tool in the service of society. Of all the principles of accounting that you learn from this book, the need for ethics is certainly the most fundamental.

In your own approach to life, you are in control of your ethical standards and the ethical decisions that you make. Each of us is individually free to shape our personal morals. To paraphrase former Supreme Court Chief Justice Earl Warren, it can be said that civilized society "floats on a sea of ethics." It is your choice how you elect to navigate this sea. Do not be misled into thinking that your choice does not matter. Eventually, your choice affects everyone, and that is the ethical challenge each of us faces.

Summary of the Prologue in Terms of Learning Objectives

LO 1 The main purpose of accounting is to provide useful information to people who make rational investment, credit, and similar decisions. Accountants serve decision makers by providing them with financial information that helps them reach better decisions. These decision makers include present and potential investors, lenders, and other users. The other users include managers of organizations, suppliers who sell to them, and customers who buy from them. Internally, accounting provides information that assists these and other activities of an organization: finance, human resources, research and development, production, marketing, and executive management.

LO 2 In addition to using accounting information to meet internal needs, organizations also report accounting information to various external parties. These external decision makers include people who invest in the organizations and people who loan money to them. Lenders need information to assess whether the company has enough financial strength and profitability to pay its debts.

LO 3 Accountants work in private, public, and government accounting. All three have members who work in financial, managerial, and tax accounting. Financial accountants prepare or audit financial statements that are distributed to people who are not involved in day-to-day management. Managerial accountants provide information to people who are involved in day-to-day management. Managerial accounting activities include general accounting, cost accounting, budgeting, internal auditing, and management advisory services. Tax accounting includes preparing tax returns and tax planning.

LO 4 Ethics are principles that determine the rightness or wrongness of particular acts or activities. Ethics are also principles of conduct that govern an individual or a profession. The foundation for trust in business activities is the expectation that people are trustworthy. Ethics are especially important for accounting because users of the information have to trust that it has not been manipulated. Without ethics, accounting information could not be trusted, and economic activity would be much more difficult to accomplish.

---

[9] *AICPA Code of Professional Conduct,* Rule 301.

[10] *Institute of Management Accountants Standards of Ethical Conduct.*

Glossary

LO 5 Define or explain the words and phrases listed in the prologue glossary.

Accounting a service activity that provides useful information to people who make rational investment, credit, and similar decisions to help them make better decisions. p. 2

AICPA American Institute of Certified Public Accountants, the largest and most influential national professional organization of certified public accountants in the United States. p. 8

Audit a thorough check of an organization's accounting systems and records that adds credibility to financial statements; the specific goal is to determine whether the statements reflect the company's financial position and operating results in agreement with generally accepted accounting principles. p. 9

Bookkeeping the part of accounting that records transactions and other events, either manually or with computers. p. 6

Budgeting the process of developing formal plans for future activities, which then serve as a basis for evaluating actual performance. p. 10

CIA Certified Internal Auditor; a certification that an individual is professionally competent in internal auditing; granted by the Institute of Internal Auditors. p. 8

CMA Certificate in Management Accounting; a certification that an individual is professionally competent in managerial accounting; awarded by the Institute of Management Accountants. p. 8

Controller the chief accounting officer of an organization. p. 10

Cost accounting a managerial accounting activity designed to help managers identify, measure, and control operating costs. p. 10

CPA Certified Public Accountant; an accountant who has passed an examination and has met education and experience requirements; CPAs are licensed by state boards to practice public accounting. p. 8

Ethics principles that determine the rightness or wrongness of particular acts or activities; also, accepted standards of good behavior in a profession or trade. p. 12

GAAP the abbreviation for *generally accepted accounting principles.* p. 9

General accounting the task of recording transactions, processing the recorded data, and preparing reports for managers; also includes preparing the financial statements that executive management presents to external users. p. 10

Generally accepted accounting principles rules adopted by the accounting profession as guides for measuring and reporting the financial condition and activities of a business. p. 9

Government accountants accountants employed by local, state, and federal government agencies. p. 7

Internal auditing an activity that adds credibility to reports produced and used within an organization; internal auditors not only examine record-keeping processes but also assess whether managers are following established operating procedures; internal auditors also evaluate the efficiency of operating procedures. p. 11

IRS Internal Revenue Service; the federal agency that has the duty of collecting federal taxes and otherwise enforcing tax laws. p. 11

Management advisory services the public accounting activity in which suggestions are offered for improving a company's procedures; the suggestions may concern new accounting and internal control systems, new computer systems, budgeting, and employee benefit plans. p. 11

NASBA National Association of State Boards of Accountancy. p. 8

Private accountant an accountant who works for a single employer, which is often a business. p. 7

Public accountants accountants who provide their services to many different clients. p. 7

SEC Securities and Exchange Commission; the federal agency created by Congress in 1934 to regulate securities markets, including the flow of information from companies to the public. p. 10

Tax accounting the field of accounting that includes preparing tax returns and planning future transactions to minimize the amount of tax; involves private, public, and government accountants. p. 11

Objective Review

Answers to the following questions are listed at the end of this prologue. Be sure that you decide which is the one best answer to each question *before* you check the answers.

LO 1 The primary function of accounting is to:

a. Provide the information that an organization's managers need to control its operations.
b. Provide information that an organization's creditors can use in deciding whether to make additional loans to it.
c. Measure the periodic net income of organizations.
d. Provide financial information that is useful in making rational investment, credit, and similar decisions.
e. Measure the resources owned by organizations and the financial obligations owed by organizations.

LO 2 Accounting serves the external function of providing:

a. Assurance that a company's management has complied with all laws.

b. Information about the company to users who are not involved in its daily activities.
c. Information about the company that is useful only to its managers.
d. Information to potential investors and creditors about a company's plans for the future.
e. Information about the company only to users who are its investors.

LO 3 Public accountants generally perform these services:

a. Income tax services, management advisory services, and independent auditing.
b. Internal auditing, income tax services, and management advisory services.
c. General accounting, independent auditing, and budgeting.
d. Government accounting, private accounting, and independent auditing.
e. Income tax services, cost accounting, and budgeting.

LO 4 Which of the following statements about ethics in accounting is true?

a. Accounting decisions can affect the amount of money a corporation distributes to its stockholders.
b. The AICPA code of ethics has existed for many years.
c. Auditors must protect the confidentiality of information about their clients.
d. The Institute of Management Accountants has a code of ethics for internal accountants.
e. All of the above statements are true.

LO 5 Identify the organization created by Congress to regulate securities markets, including the flow of information from companies to the public.

a. AICPA.
b. NASBA.
c. IRS.
d. SEC.
e. None of the above.

Questions for Class Discussion

1. What is the main purpose of accounting?
2. Why is accounting frequently called a service activity?
3. Identify six different categories of activities carried on within most organizations.
4. Describe the internal role of accounting for organizations.
5. What are three or four questions that business owners and managers might try to answer by looking to accounting information?
6. What is the relationship between accounting and bookkeeping?
7. Why is it necessary for people to study accounting if computers are used to process accounting data?
8. Why do states license Certified Public Accountants?
9. According to the laws in at least 30 states, how many years of college education will a person need to enter the public accounting profession in the future?
10. Identify the three types of services typically offered by public accountants.
11. What are the three broad fields of accounting?
12. What is the purpose of an audit? Describe what Certified Public Accountants do when they perform an audit.
13. What title is frequently used for an organization's chief accounting officer? Why?
14. Identify four managerial accounting activities performed by private and government accountants.
15. Identify two management advisory services typically provided by public accountants.
16. Identify several examples of the types of work performed by government accountants.
17. What do tax accountants do in addition to preparing tax returns?

Apple Computer, Inc.

18. Identify the CPA firm that audited the financial statements of Apple Computer, Inc., reprinted in Appendix F at the end of this book.

Answers to Objective Review Questions

LO 1 (*d*)
LO 2 (*b*)
LO 3 (*a*)
LO 4 (*e*)
LO 5 (*d*)

CHAPTER

1

Financial Statements and Accounting Principles

In this chapter, you start to learn about the useful information that accountants provide to decision makers in financial statements. Next, you study some general principles that guide accountants in developing these statements. This discussion also describes some of the organizations that regulate and influence financial accounting. To continue your introduction to business, this chapter explains several ways that a business can be organized. The chapter also shows you how accountants analyze business transactions to generate useful information. Knowledge of these techniques is important for understanding the usefulness of financial statements. Finally, the chapter teaches you about the return on equity ratio, which is used to indicate a company's success in operating during a reporting period.

Learning Objectives

After studying Chapter 1, you should be able to:

1. Describe the information presented in financial statements, be able to prepare simple financial statements, and analyze a company's performance with the return on equity ratio.
2. Explain the accounting principles introduced in the chapter and describe the process by which generally accepted accounting principles are established.
3. Describe single proprietorships, partnerships, and corporations, including the differences in their owners' responsibilities for the organizations' debts.
4. Analyze business transactions to determine their effects on the accounting equation.
5. Define or explain the words and phrases listed in the chapter glossary.

Financial Statements

Accounting exists for the purpose of providing useful information to people who make rational investment, credit, and similar decisions.[1] These decision makers include an organization's investors, lenders, managers, suppliers, cus-

[1] Financial Accounting Standards Board, *Statement of Financial Accounting Concepts No. 1,* "Objectives of Financial Reporting by Business Enterprises" (Norwalk, CT, 1978), par. 34.

tomers, and other interested people. Be sure to read the As a Matter of Opinion box on page 21 to learn how one decision maker uses accounting information to help him fulfill his responsibilities as a member of a city council.

LO 1 Describe the information presented in financial statements, be able to prepare simple financial statements, and analyze a company's performance with the return on equity ratio.

An organization often provides accounting information to managers and other decision makers in its financial statements. The statements are useful because they describe the organization's financial health and performance in a condensed and highly informative format. Because they provide an overall view of the entire organization, financial statements are a good place to start your study of accounting. We begin by looking at the income statement and the balance sheet. This diagram represents the relationship between these two statements:

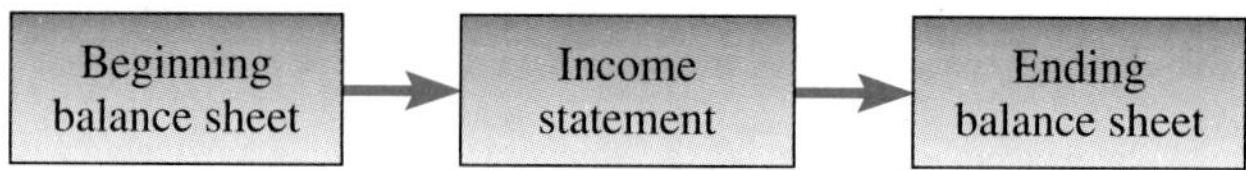

In effect, the income statement for the reporting period links the balance sheets as of the beginning and end of the reporting period.

The Income Statement

Look at the **income statement** in Illustration 1–1. The income statement is useful because it shows whether the business earned a profit (also called *net income*). A company earns a **net income** if its revenues exceed its expenses. A company incurs a **net loss** if its expenses exceed its revenues. The example in Illustration 1–1 shows that the income statement does not simply report the amount of net income or net loss. Instead, it lists the types and amounts of the revenues and expenses. This detailed information is more useful for decision making than just a simple profit or loss number.

Revenues are inflows of assets received in exchange for goods or services provided to customers as part of the major or central operations of the business. Revenues also may occur as decreases in liabilities.[2] (For now, think of assets as economic resources owned by a business and liabilities as the debts owed by a business. These terms are defined more completely on page 21.)

The income statement in Illustration 1–1 shows that the business of Clear Copy Co. earned $3,900 of revenues by providing copy services to customers during the month of December. Examples of revenues for other businesses include sales of products and amounts earned from rent, dividends, and interest.

Expenses are outflows or the using up of assets as a result of the major or central operations of a business. Expenses also may occur as increases in liabilities.[3] The income statement in Illustration 1–1 shows that Clear Copy used up some of its assets by paying for rented office space. The $1,000 cost of the space is reported in Illustration 1–1 as rent expense. The business also paid for an employee's services at a cost of $700. This amount is reported on the income statement as salaries expense.

Notice that the heading of the income statement in Illustration 1–1 begins with the name of the business. The heading also shows the time period covered by the statement. Information about the time period is important for judging whether the company's performance is satisfactory. For example, you

[2] Financial Accounting Standards Board, *Statement of Financial Accounting Concepts No. 6*, "Elements of Financial Statements" (Norwalk, CT, 1985), par. 78.

[3] Ibid., par. 80.

ILLUSTRATION 1–1 *Income Statement for Clear Copy Co.*

CLEAR COPY CO.
Income Statement
For Month Ended December 31, 19X1

Revenues:		
Copy services revenue		$3,900
Operating expenses:		
Rent expense	$1,000	
Salaries expense	700	
Total operating expenses		1,700
Net income		$2,200

ILLUSTRATION 1–2 *Balance Sheet for Clear Copy Co.*

CLEAR COPY CO.
Balance Sheet
December 31, 19X1

Assets		**Liabilities**	
Cash	$ 8,400	Accounts payable . . .	$ 6,200
Store supplies	3,600	**Owner's Equity**	
Copy equipment	26,000	Terry Dow, capital . . .	31,800
		Total liabilities and	
Total assets	$38,000	owner's equity	$38,000

would need to know that Clear Copy earned the $2,200 net income during a one-month period to judge whether that amount is satisfactory.

The Balance Sheet

The purpose of the **balance sheet** is to provide information that helps users understand a company's financial status. As a result, the balance sheet is often called the **statement of financial position.** The balance sheet describes financial position by listing the types and dollar amounts of assets, liabilities, and equity of the business. (Equity is the difference between a company's assets and its liabilities.)

Illustration 1–2 presents the balance sheet for Clear Copy as of December 31, 19X1. Like the income statement, the heading for the balance sheet identifies the company's name. The balance sheet describes conditions that exist at a point in time. Thus, the heading also shows the specific date on which the assets and liabilities are identified and measured. The amounts in the balance sheet are stated as of the close of business on that date.

The balance sheet in Illustration 1–2 reports that the company owned three different assets at the close of business on December 31, 19X1. The assets were cash, store supplies, and copy equipment. The total dollar amount for these assets was $38,000. The balance sheet also shows that there were $6,200 of liabilities. Owner's equity was $31,800. This amount is the difference between the assets and the liabilities.

Notice that the total amounts on the two sides of the balance sheet are equal. This equality is the source of the name *balance sheet.* The name also

AS A MATTER OF

Opinion

Mr. Garcia earned a BBA degree and has done additional graduate work at The University of Texas at Austin. He has been president of the Austin Chapter of CPAs, president of Austin's Hispanic Chamber of Commerce, and president and trustee of the Austin Independent School District and Austin Community College. He has served on the board of directors of the State Bar of Texas and the board of directors of the Greater Austin Chamber of Commerce.

Gustavo L. Garcia, CPA

During my 20-year career in public service, I have served in a variety of both appointed and elected positions. Currently, I am a member of the City Council of Austin, Texas. The council oversees an annual budget of over $1 billion that includes the operation of an airport, an electric utility, a hospital, a general fund, and several other enterprises.

Having a good understanding of accounting has been like having an extra-high-powered flashlight that helps me examine and understand the intricacies of this tremendously complex organization.

My accounting education is like a good friend that helps me decipher the many difficult situations we face daily. My accounting experience allows me to quickly understand the full economic impact and effects of proposed transactions and activities. This valuable insight helps me make decisions that hopefully protect and enhance the economic situation of our city and its citizens.

reflects the fact that the statement reports the balances of the assets, liabilities, and equity on a given date.

Assets, Liabilities, and Equity

In general, the **assets** of a business are the properties or economic resources owned by the business. More precisely, assets are defined as "probable future economic benefits obtained or controlled by a particular entity as a result of past transactions or events."[4] One familiar asset is cash. Another asset consists of amounts owed to the business by its customers for goods and services sold to them on credit. This asset is called **accounts receivable.** In general, individuals who owe amounts to the business are called its **debtors.** Other assets owned by businesses include merchandise held for sale, supplies, equipment, buildings, and land. Assets also can be intangible rights, such as those granted by a patent or copyright.

The **liabilities** of a business are its debts to others. Liabilities are defined more precisely as "probable future sacrifices of economic benefits arising from present obligations of a particular entity to transfer assets or provide services to other entities in the future as a result of past transactions or events."[5] One common liability consists of amounts owed for goods and services bought on credit. This liability is called **accounts payable.** Other liabilities are salaries and wages owed to employees, taxes payable, notes payable, and interest payable.

A liability represents a claim against a business. In general, those who have the right to receive payments from a company are called its **creditors.** From the creditor's viewpoint, a liability is the right to be paid by a business.

[4] Financial Accounting Standards Board, *Statement of Financial Accounting Concepts No. 6,* "Elements of Financial Statements" (Norwalk, CT, 1985), par. 25.

[5] Ibid., par. 35.

(In effect, one company's payable is another company's receivable.) If a business fails to pay its debts, the law gives creditors the right to force the sale of its assets to obtain the money to meet their claims. When the assets are sold under these conditions, the creditors are paid first, up to the full amount of their claims, with the remainder (the residual) going to the owner of the business.

Creditors often use a balance sheet to help them decide whether to loan money to a business. They can use the balance sheet to compare the amounts of existing liabilities and assets. A loan is less risky if the liabilities are small in comparison to the assets. There is less risk because there is a larger cushion if the assets are sold for less than the amounts shown on the balance sheet. On the other hand, a loan is more risky if the liabilities are large compared to the assets. The risk is greater because it is more likely that the assets cannot be sold for enough cash to pay all the debts.

Equity is defined as "the residual interest in the assets of an entity that remains after deducting its liabilities."[6] Equity is also called **net assets.** If a business is organized as a corporation (which we describe later), the owners of the business are called stockholders and the equity is called *stockholders' equity.* Because Clear Copy is owned by one person and is not a corporation, the equity section in Illustration 1–2 is simply called *owner's equity.*

Earlier we defined net income as the difference between revenue and expense for a time period. Net income is also the change in owner's equity that occurred during the period as a result of the company's major or central operations. By describing this change, the income statement links the company's balance sheets from the beginning and end of the reporting period.

We use this background on the balance sheet and income statement to explain more about financial accounting. The next sections of the chapter describe the principles that guide the practice of financial accounting.

Generally Accepted Accounting Principles (GAAP)

LO 2 Explain the accounting principles introduced in the chapter and describe the process by which generally accepted accounting principles are established.

In the Prologue, we explained that financial accounting practice is governed by a set of rules called *generally accepted accounting principles,* or *GAAP.* A good working knowledge of GAAP is essential for all who use or prepare financial statements.

A primary purpose of GAAP is to help ensure that financial reports provide relevant, reliable, and comparable information. In other words, financial accounting practices should produce information that relates to the decisions made by financial statement users. The information should also be reliable so that the decision makers can depend on it. In addition, the information should allow statement users to compare companies. These comparisons are more likely to be useful if all companies use similar practices. GAAP impose limits on the variety of accounting practices that companies can use, thereby making the financial statements more understandable and useful.

The Development of GAAP

From the earliest days of accounting through the first third of the 20th century, GAAP were developed through common usage. In effect, a practice was considered suitable if it was acceptable to most accountants. This history is still reflected in the phrase *generally accepted.* A principle became generally accepted when accountants agreed that it would provide useful and dependable information. However, as the accounting profession grew and the world of business became more complex, many people were not satisfied with the profession's progress in providing additional useful information.

[6] Ibid., par. 49.

The desire for improvement caused many professional accountants, managers, and government regulators to want more uniformity in practice. Thus, in the 1930s, they began to give authority for defining accepted principles to small groups of experienced professional accountants. Since then, several authoritative bodies with different structures and procedures have designated specific practices as generally accepted. Over the years, their authority to prescribe acceptable principles has been greatly increased. We describe the present arrangement for establishing GAAP later in this chapter.

Broad and Specific Accounting Principles

You should understand that GAAP consist of both broad and specific principles. *Broad* principles are rooted in long-used practices. More *specific* principles usually result from the work of authoritative bodies. These specific principles are described in the official pronouncements published by these bodies.

As either a user of financial statements or an accountant, you will be able to perform more effectively if you know about broad and specific principles. To help you gain this knowledge, we describe both kinds in this book. The broad principles are especially helpful for learning about accounting. For this reason, we emphasize them in the beginning chapters. We use the following broad principles in this book:[7]

	First Introduced	
	Chapter	**Page**
Business entity principle	1	27
Objectivity principle	1	27
Cost principle	1	28
Going-concern principle	1	28
Revenue recognition principle	1	33
Time period principle	3	101
Matching principle	3	102
Materiality principle	7	274
Full-disclosure principle	7	280
Consistency principle	8	300
Conservatism principle	8	306

Specific principles are especially important for understanding individual items in the financial statements. They are described throughout the book as we come to them.

Accounting Principles, Auditing Standards, and Financial Accounting

Generally accepted accounting principles are not natural laws like the laws of physics or other sciences. Instead, GAAP are identified in response to the needs of users and others affected by accounting. Thus, GAAP are subject to change as needs change. Current GAAP have developed through the experience and actions of public, private, and government accountants, as well as accounting professors, statement users, and others. In a later section, we describe the rule-making system that allows these groups to form a consensus.

This system reflects the fact that three groups are most affected by financial reporting: *preparers, auditors,* and *users.*

[7] A problem arises in describing accounting principles because different writers have used different words to mean the same thing. For example, broad principles also have been called *concepts, theories, assumptions,* and *postulates.* For simplicity's sake, we have decided to call them *principles* in this book. Don't be confused if you see them called by other names in other books.

Private accountants prepare the financial statements. To make the statements more credible, independent auditors (CPAs) examine the financial statements and the company's accounting system, and develop an audit report. The statements and the audit report are then distributed to the users.

Illustration 1–3 expands this diagram to show how accounting principles and auditing standards relate to the financial reporting process. First, in Illustration 1–3, we show that GAAP are applied in preparing the financial statements. Preparers use GAAP to decide what procedures to follow as they account for business transactions and put the statements together.

Second, in Illustration 1–3, we show that audits are performed in accordance with **generally accepted auditing standards (GAAS).** GAAS are the rules adopted by the accounting profession as guides for conducting audits of financial statements. GAAS tell auditors what they must do in their audits to determine whether the financial statements comply with GAAP.

The application of both GAAP and GAAS assures the users that the financial statements include relevant, reliable, and comparable information. The audit does not, however, ensure them that they can invest in or loan to the company without fear of a loss. The audit reduces the risk created by inadequate information. However, it does not reduce the risk that the company's products and services will not be successfully marketed or that other factors could cause it to fail.

In Illustration 1–3, we also identify the two organizations that are the primary authoritative sources of GAAP and GAAS.

How Accounting Principles Are Established

The primary authoritative source of GAAP is the Financial Accounting Standards Board **(FASB).** The FASB is a nonprofit organization with seven board members who serve full time. (In 1994, a board member's annual salary was $305,000.) The FASB is located in Norwalk, Connecticut, approximately 50 miles from New York City. Board members apply their collected experience as well as the efforts of a 40-member research staff to identify problems in financial accounting and to find ways to solve them. They also seek advice and comments from groups affected by GAAP. The board often holds public hearings for this purpose. In summary, the FASB's job is to improve financial reporting while balancing the interests of the affected groups.[8]

The FASB announces its findings in several different publications. The most important publications are **Statements of Financial Accounting Standards (SFAS).** These statements establish new generally accepted accounting principles in the United States and may affect practice in other countries.

The FASB gains its authority from a variety of sources. The most significant source is the Securities and Exchange Commission (SEC). Congress created this federal agency in 1934 to regulate securities markets, including the

[8] For more detailed information about the board, see Paul B. W. Miller, Rodney J. Redding, and Paul R. Bahnson, *The FASB—the People, the Process, and the Politics,* 3rd ed. (Burr Ridge, IL: Richard D. Irwin, 1994).

ILLUSTRATION 1-3 *Generally Accepted Accounting Principles (GAAP), Generally Accepted Auditing Standards (GAAS), and the Groups that Participate in Financial Accounting*

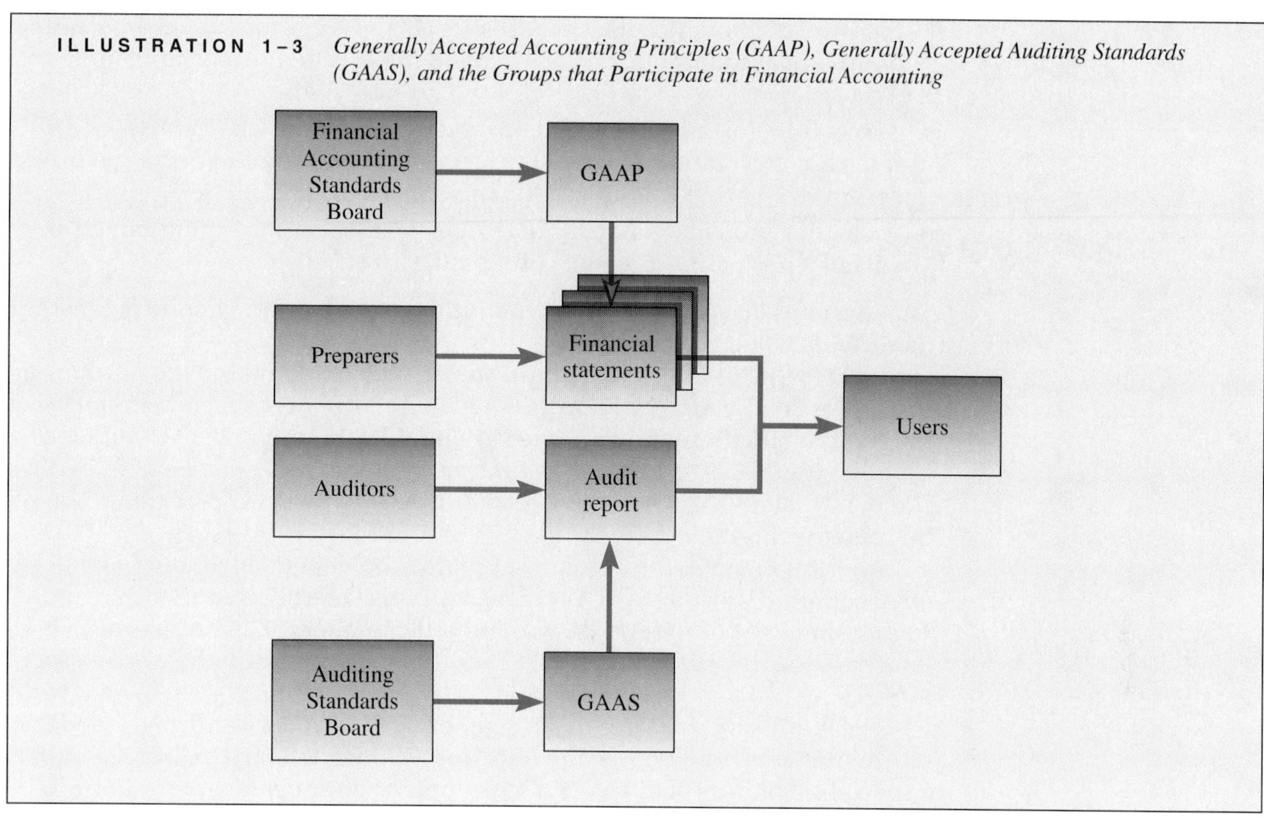

flow of information from companies to the public. When the FASB began operating in 1973, the SEC designated it as the primary authority for establishing GAAP. However, the SEC still retains oversight responsibility over the FASB. This oversight means that the SEC may overrule the FASB if the SEC thinks doing so will protect the public interest. To date, this authority has been exercised only one time.[9]

The FASB also has authority because it has been endorsed by each of the state boards that license certified public accountants. Specifically, state ethics rules are violated if a CPA audits financial statements that do not comply with FASB pronouncements and the CPA fails to identify the problem in the audit report. The CPA's license may be lost as a result of the violation. The AICPA's Code of Professional Conduct includes a similar provision. An auditor who is member of the AICPA may be expelled from the institute for not objecting to financial statements that fail to comply with FASB pronouncements.

Many other professional organizations support the FASB's process by providing input and by giving financial support through the Financial Accounting Foundation.[10] They include:

- American Accounting Association **(AAA)**—a professional association of individuals, primarily college and university accounting faculty.
- Financial Executives Institute **(FEI)**—a professional association of private accountants.

---

[9] The SEC overruled the FASB's Statement of Financial Accounting Standards No. 19 in 1978. This standard concerned accounting for oil and gas producing companies.

[10] Working alongside the FASB is the Governmental Accounting Standards Board (GASB), which identifies special accounting principles to be applied in preparing financial statements for state and local governments. Both the FASB and the GASB operate under the Financial Accounting Foundation.

- Institute of Management Accountants **(IMA)**—a professional association of private accountants, formerly called the National Association of Accountants.
- Association for Investment Management and Research **(AIMR)**—a professional association of people who use financial statements in the process of evaluating companies' financial performance.
- Securities Industry Association **(SIA)**—an association of individuals involved with issuing and marketing securities.

These groups boost the Board's credibility by participating in its process for identifying GAAP.

Prior to the FASB, the accounting profession depended on the Accounting Principles Board **(APB)** to identify GAAP. The APB was a special committee of the AICPA, and its members served as unpaid volunteers. The APB issued 31 *Opinions* from 1959 to 1973. The *Opinions* created GAAP, just like the FASB's standards. Many APB *Opinions* remain in effect, and we describe their requirements throughout this book.

Prior to the APB, the accounting profession depended on the Committee on Accounting Procedure **(CAP)** for identifying GAAP. Like the APB, the CAP was a committee of the AICPA with unpaid members. The CAP issued 51 *Accounting Research Bulletins* from 1936 to 1959. Only a few bulletins remain in effect.

The authority for identifying generally accepted auditing standards (GAAS) presently belongs to the Auditing Standards Board **(ASB).** The ASB is a special committee of the AICPA with unpaid volunteer members. The SEC is an important source of the ASB's authority.

Pronouncements issued by the FASB, APB, CAP, and ASB define specific GAAP and GAAS. They are available for accountants and users of financial statements in publications issued by the FASB and the AICPA. Many of these principles are described in this book and in other books written for advanced students of accounting.

International Accounting Standards

In today's world, people in different countries engage in business with each other more easily than in the past. Some reasons for the increased internationalization of business are improved communication systems, cheaper transportation, and political changes, such as the breakup of the Soviet Union. These developments have opened up many international business opportunities. For example, a company in the United States might sell its products in countries all over the world. Another company in Singapore might raise cash by selling stock to American and Japanese investors. At the same time, it might borrow from creditors in Saudi Arabia and Germany.

Despite this globalization of business, a major problem exists because each country has its own unique set of acceptable accounting practices. Consider, for example, the Singapore company described in the preceding paragraph. Should it prepare financial statements that comply with Singapore accounting standards, or with the standards used in the United States, Japan, Saudi Aradia, or Germany? Should it have to prepare five different sets of reports to gain access to financial markets in all five countries?

Accounting organizations from around the world responded to this problem by creating the International Accounting Standards Committee **(IASC)** in 1973. The IASC is headquartered in London and has the tasks of issuing *International Accounting Standards* that identify preferred accounting practices and then encouraging their worldwide acceptance. By narrowing the range of alternative practices, the IASC hopes to create more harmony among the accounting practices of different countries. If standards could be harmonized, a single set of financial statements could be used by one company in all financial markets.

In many countries, the bodies that set accounting standards have encouraged the IASC to reduce the differences. Both the FASB and the SEC have provided this encouragement and technical assistance. However, the IASC is not as powerful as it could be because it does not have the authority to impose its standards on companies. Although some advances have occurred, progress has been slow. In the United States, interest is growing in moving GAAP toward the IASC's preferred practices. The authority to make such changes continues to rest with the FASB and the SEC.

Understanding Generally Accepted Accounting Principles

LO 2 Explain the accounting principles introduced in the chapter and describe the process by which generally accepted accounting principles are established.

At the beginning of this chapter, we said that the purpose of accounting is to provide useful information to people who make rational investment, credit, and similar decisions. In fact, this description of the purpose of accounting comes from a major FASB project called the *conceptual framework.* This framework also defines several accounting terms that should be understood by financial statement users as well as accountants. For example, we relied on the conceptual framework in preceding discussions when we defined revenues, expenses, assets, liabilities, and equity.

Another purpose of the conceptual framework is to describe the characteristics that make accounting information useful for decisions. Earlier, we referred to the conceptual framework's commonsense ideas that information is useful only if it has both *relevance* and *reliability.*

Now that you have some background on how accounting principles are developed, we can begin to describe some of the broad principles listed on page 23. These broad principles will help you understand financial statements and the procedures used to prepare them.

Business Entity Principle

The **business entity principle** requires every business to be accounted for separately and distinctly from its owner or owners. This principle also requires us to account separately for other entities that might be controlled by the same owners. The reason behind this principle is that separate information for each business is relevant to decisions that its users make.

To illustrate, suppose that the owner of a business wants to see how well it is doing. To be useful, the financial statements for the business should not mix the owner's personal transactions with the business's transactions. For example, the owner's personal expenses should not be subtracted from the company's revenues on its income statement because they do not contribute to the company's success. Thus, the income statement should not report such things as the owner's personal entertainment and transportation expenses. Otherwise, the company's reported net income would be understated and the business would appear less profitable than it really is.

In summary, a company's reports should not include its owner's personal transactions, assets, and liabilities or the transactions, assets, and liabilities of another business. If this principle is not carefully followed, the reported information about the company's financial position and net income is not useful for rational investment and credit decisions.

Objectivity Principle

The **objectivity principle** requires financial statement information to be supported by evidence other than someone's opinion or imagination. This principle should be followed because information is not reliable if it is based only on what the statement preparer thinks might be true. This information would not be reliable because the preparer might have been too optimistic or too pessimistic. In the worst case, an unethical preparer might try to mislead financial statement users by deliberately misrepresenting the truth. The objectivity principle is intended to make financial statements useful by ensuring that they present reliable information.

Cost Principle

The **cost principle** requires financial statement information to be based on costs incurred in business transactions. Sales and purchases are examples of **business transactions.** Business transactions are exchanges of economic consideration between two parties. The consideration may include such things as goods, services, money, or rights to collect money. In applying the cost principle, cost is measured on a cash or cash equivalent basis. If cash is given for an asset or service, the cost of the asset or service is measured as the entire amount of cash paid. If something other than cash is exchanged (such as an old vehicle traded in for a new one), cost is measured as the cash equivalent value of what was given up or of the item received, whichever is more clearly evident.[11]

The *cost principle* is acceptable because it puts relevant information in the financial statements. Cost is the amount initially sacrificed to purchase an asset or service. Cost also approximates the market value of the asset or service when it was acquired. Information about the amount sacrificed and the initial market value of what was received is generally considered to be relevant to decisions. Complying with the cost principle provides this information.

In addition, the cost principle is generally accepted because it is consistent with the *objectivity principle.* Most accountants believe that information based on actual costs is more likely to be objective than information based on estimates of values. For example, reporting purchases of assets and services at cost is more objective than reporting the manager's unsupported estimate of their value. Thus, financial statements based on costs are believed to be more reliable because the information is more objective.

To illustrate, suppose that a business pays $50,000 for land used in its operations. The cost principle tells us to record the purchase at $50,000. It would make no difference if the buyer and several independent appraisers think that the land is worth at least $60,000. The cost principle requires the acquisition to be recorded at the cost of $50,000. However, you learn in later chapters that, to provide more useful information, objective estimates of value are occasionally reported instead of costs.

Going-Concern Principle

The **going-concern principle** (also called the **continuing-concern principle**) requires financial statements to reflect the assumption that the business will continue operating instead of being closed or sold. Thus, a company's balance sheet does not report the liquidation values of operating assets that are expected to be held and used for the long term. Instead, these assets are reported at amounts based on their cost. Many accountants have argued that the going-concern principle leads to reporting relevant information because many decisions about a business are made with the expectation that it will continue to exist in the future.

As a result of applying the cost and going-concern principles, a company's balance sheet seldom describes what the company is worth. Thus, if a com-

[11] FASB, *Accounting Standards—Current Text* (Norwalk, CT, 1994), sec. N35.105. First published as *APB Opinion No. 29,* par. 18.

pany is to be bought or sold, the buyer and seller are well advised to obtain additional information from other sources.[12]

The going-concern principle must be ignored if the company is expected to fail or be liquidated. In these cases, the going-concern principle and the cost principle do not apply. Instead, estimated market values are relevant and costs are not relevant.

Legal Forms of Business Organizations

This section of the chapter describes three legal forms for business organizations. The forms are *single proprietorships, partnerships,* and *corporations.* The particular form chosen for a company creates some differences in its financial statements.

LO 3 Describe single proprietorships, partnerships, and corporations, including the differences in their owners' responsibilities for the organizations' debts.

Single Proprietorships and Partnerships

A **single proprietorship** (or **sole proprietorship**) is owned by one person and is not organized under state or federal laws as a corporation. Small retail stores and service enterprises are often operated as single proprietorships. No special legal requirements must be met to start this kind of business. As a result, single proprietorships are the most numerous of all types of businesses.

A **partnership** is owned by two or more people, called partners, and is not organized as a corporation. Like a single proprietorship, no special legal requirements must be met in starting a partnership. All that is required is an agreement between the partners to operate a business together. The agreement can be either oral or written. However, a written partnership agreement may help the partners avoid or resolve later disputes.

In a strict legal sense, single proprietorships and partnerships are not separate from their owners. Thus, for example, a court can order an owner to sell personal assets to pay the debts of a proprietorship or partnership. In fact, an owner's personal assets may have to be sold to satisfy *all* the debts of a proprietorship or a partnership, even if this amount exceeds the owner's equity in the company. This unlimited liability feature of proprietorships and partnerships is a significant disadvantage.

Despite the lack of separate legal existence from their owners, the *business entity principle* applies to the financial statements of single proprietorships and partnerships. That is, relevant information for ordinary investment and credit decisions is more likely to be reported in the financial statements if each business is treated as being separate from its owner or owners.

Corporations

A **corporation** is a separate legal entity chartered (or *incorporated*) under state or federal laws. Unlike proprietorships or partnerships, corporations are legally separate and distinct from their owners.

A corporation's equity is divided into units called shares of **stock** and its owners are called **shareholders** or **stockholders.** For example, a corporation that has issued 1,000 shares of stock has divided its equity into 1,000 units. A stockholder who owns 500 shares owns 50% of the shares and 50% of the equity. When a corporation issues only one class of stock, it is called **common stock** or *capital stock.* We discuss other classes of stock in Chapter 13.

A very important characteristic of a corporation is its status as a separate legal entity. This characteristic means that the corporation is responsible for its own acts and its own debts. This arrangement relieves the stockholders of

[12] In *SFAS 107,* the FASB established a requirement for supplemental disclosures (in the notes to the financial statements) of the current market values of many assets and liabilities.

personal liability for these acts and debts. This limited liability feature is a major advantage of corporations over proprietorships and partnerships.

The separate legal status of a corporation also means that it can enter into its own contracts. For example, a corporation can buy, own, and sell property in its own name. It also can sue and be sued in its own name. In short, the separate legal status enables a corporation to conduct its business affairs with all the rights, duties, and responsibilities of a person. Of course, a corporation lacks a physical body and must act through its managers, who are its legal agents.

In addition, the separate legal status of a corporation means that its life is not limited by its owners' lives or by a need for them to remain owners. Thus, a stockholder can sell or transfer shares to another person without affecting the operations of the corporation.

There are fewer corporations in the United States than proprietorships and partnerships. However, the corporate form of business offers greater advantages for accumulating and managing capital resources. As a result, corporations control the most economic wealth.

Many nonprofit entities are organized as special corporations that have no shares of stock. This arrangement offers the advantages of separate legal status and limited liability. These corporations are exempt from income taxes if they engage in charitable and educational activities.

Differences in Financial Statements

Despite the major legal differences among the three forms of businesses, there are only a few differences in their financial statements.

One difference is in the equity section of the balance sheet. A proprietorship's balance sheet lists the capital balance beside the single owner's name. Partnership balance sheets use the same approach, unless there are too many owners for their names to fit in the available space. The names of a corporation's stockholders are not listed in the balance sheet. Instead, the total stockholders' equity is divided into **contributed capital** (also called **paid-in capital**) and **retained earnings.** Contributed capital is created by the stockholders' investments. Retained earnings are created by the corporation's profitable activities.

Another difference exists in the term used to describe payments by a company to its owners. When an owner of a proprietorship or a partnership receives cash from the company, the payments are called **withdrawals.** When owners of a corporation receive cash from the company, the payments are called **dividends.** Withdrawals and dividends are not reported on a company's income statement because they are not expenses incurred to generate revenues.

A more significant difference appears in the financial statement description of amounts paid to the company's managers. Because a corporation is a separate legal entity, salaries paid to its managers are reported as expenses on its income statement. In contrast, if the owner of a single proprietorship is also its manager, no salary expense is reported on the income statement for these services. The same is true for a partnership. This different treatment requires special consideration when analyzing the income statement. Our discussion at the end of this chapter describes this analysis in more detail.

To keep things simple while you are beginning to learn accounting, the examples in the first portion of this book are all based on single proprietorships. Chapters 13 and 14 provide additional information about the financial statements of partnerships and corporations.

Using the Balance Sheet Equation to Provide Useful Information

LO 4 Analyze business transactions to determine their effects on the accounting equation.

Up to this stage, you have learned about business and other kinds of organizations and the needs of several different people for useful information about them. You have also learned something about the financial statements providing that information and the broad principles shaping those statements. You are now ready to learn more about financial statements by seeing how they are put together by analyzing each one of a company's transactions. We start in this chapter with a simple example.

The beginning point for accounting systems is the definition of *owner's equity* as the difference between an organization's assets and liabilities. This definition can be stated as the following equation for a single proprietorship:

$$\text{Assets} - \text{Liabilities} = \text{Owner's Equity}$$

Like any equation, this one can be modified by rearranging the terms. The following modified form of the equation is called the **balance sheet equation:**

$$\text{Assets} = \text{Liabilities} + \text{Owner's Equity}$$

Because it serves as the basis for financial accounting information, the balance sheet equation also is called the **accounting equation.** The next section shows you how to use this equation to keep track of changes in a company's assets, liabilities, and owner's equity in a way that provides useful information.

The Effects of Transactions on the Accounting Equation

A transaction is an exchange between two parties of such things as goods, services, money, or rights to collect money. Because the two parties exchange assets and liabilities, transactions affect the components of the accounting equation. Importantly, each and every transaction always leaves the equation in balance. That is, the total assets always equal the sum of the liabilities and the equity regardless of what happens in a transaction. We can show how this equality is preserved by looking at the transactions of a new small business called Clear Copy Co.

Transaction 1. On December 1, 19X1, Terry Dow formed a new photocopying store that was organized as a single proprietorship. Dow planned to be the manager of the store as well as its owner. The marketing plan for the store is to focus primarily on serving business customers who place relatively large orders. Dow invested $30,000 cash in the new company and deposited it in a bank account opened under the name of Clear Copy Co. After this event, the cash (an asset) and the owner's equity each equal $30,000. As you can see, the accounting equation is in balance:

$$\underbrace{\text{Cash, \$30,000}}_{\text{Assets}} = \underbrace{\text{Terry Dow, Capital, \$30,000}}_{\text{Owner's Equity}}$$

The equation shows that the business has one asset, cash, equal to $30,000. It has no liabilities, and the owner's equity is $30,000.

Transactions 2 and 3. Clear Copy's second business transaction used $2,500 of its cash to purchase store supplies. In a third transaction, Clear Copy spent $20,000 to buy photocopying equipment. These events, which we call transactions 2 and 3, were both exchanges of cash for other assets. Neither transaction produced an expense because no value was lost to the company. Instead, the purchases merely changed the form of the assets from cash to supplies and equipment.

The effects of these transactions are shown in color in the equations in Illustration 1–4. Observe that the decreases in cash are exactly equal to the

ILLUSTRATION 1–4 *Changes in the Balance Sheet Equation Caused by Asset Purchases for Cash*

	Assets			=	Owner's Equity	
	Cash +	Store Supplies +	Copy Equipment	=	Terry Dow, Capital	Explanation of Change
(1)	$30,000				$30,000	Investment
(2)	− 2,500	+$2,500				
Bal.	$27,500	$2,500			$30,000	
(3)	−20,000		+$20,000			
Bal.	$ 7,500 +	$2,500 +	$20,000	=	$30,000	

ILLUSTRATION 1–5 *Changes in the Balance Sheet Equation Caused by Asset Purchases on Credit, Revenues Received in Cash, and Expenses Paid in Cash*

	Assets			=	Liabilities +	Owner's Equity	
	Cash +	Store Supplies +	Copy Equipment	=	Accounts Payable +	Terry Dow, Capital	Explanation of Change
Bal.	$7,500	$2,500	$20,000			$30,000	
(4)		+1,100	+ 6,000		+$7,100		
Bal.	$7,500	$3,600	$26,000		$7,100	$30,000	
(5)	+2,200					+ 2,200	Revenue
Bal.	$9,700	$3,600	$26,000		$7,100	$32,200	
(6)	−1,000					− 1,000	Expense
Bal.	$8,700	$3,600	$26,000		$7,100	$31,200	
(7)	− 700					− 700	Expense
Bal.	$8,000 +	$3,600 +	$26,000	=	$7,100 +	$30,500	

increases in the store supplies and the copy equipment. As a result, the equation always remains in balance after each transaction.

Transaction 4. Next, Dow decided that the business needed more store supplies and additional copy equipment. The items to be purchased would have a total cost of $7,100. However, as shown on the last line of the first column in Illustration 1–4, the business had only $7,500 in cash after transaction 3. Because these purchases would almost eliminate Clear Copy's cash, Dow arranged to purchase them on credit from Handy Supply Company. That is, Clear Copy took delivery of the items in exchange for a promise to pay for them later. The supplies cost $1,100, the copy equipment cost $6,000, and the total liability to Handy Supply is $7,100.

The effects of this purchase are shown in Illustration 1–5 as transaction 4. Notice that the purchase increased total assets by $7,100 while the company's liabilities (called *accounts payable*) increased by the same amount. You can see that the transaction did not create an expense because the amount of equity remains unchanged from the original $30,000 balance.

Transaction 5. A primary objective of a business is to increase its owner's wealth. This goal is met when the business produces a profit (also called *net income*). A net income is reflected in the accounting equation as a net increase in owner's equity. Clear Copy's method of generating revenues is to sell photocopying services to its customers. The business will produce a net income only if its revenues are greater than the expenses incurred in earning them. As you should expect, the process of earning copy services revenues and incurring expenses creates changes in the accounting equation.

We can see how the accounting equation is affected by earning revenues in transaction 5. In this transaction, Clear Copy provided copying services to a customer on December 10 and immediately collected $2,200 cash. Illustration 1–5 shows that this event increased cash by $2,200 and increased owner's equity by $2,200. This increase in equity is identified in the last column as a revenue because it was earned by providing services. This information can be used later to prepare the income statement.

Transactions 6 and 7. Also on December 10, Clear Copy paid $1,000 rent to the owner of the building in which its store is located. Paying this amount allowed Clear Copy to occupy the space for the entire month of December. The effects of this event are shown in Illustration 1–5 as transaction 6. On December 12, Clear Copy paid the $700 salary of the company's only employee. This event is reflected in Illustration 1–5 as transaction 7.

Both transactions 6 and 7 produced expenses for the business. That is, they used up cash for the ultimate purpose of providing services to customers. Unlike the asset purchases in transactions 2 and 3, the cash payments in transactions 6 and 7 acquired services. The benefits of these services do not last beyond the end of the month. The equations in Illustration 1–5 show that both transactions reduced cash and Terry Dow's equity. Thus, the accounting equation remains in balance after each event. The last column in Illustration 1–5 includes the notation that these decreases were expenses. This information is useful when the income statement is prepared.

Summary. We said before that a business produces a net income when its revenues exceed its expenses. Net income increases owner's equity. If the expenses exceed the revenues, a net loss occurs and equity is decreased. Remember that the amount of net income or loss is not affected by transactions completed between a business and its owners. Thus, Terry Dow's initial investment of $30,000 is not income to the business, even though it increased the equity.

To keep things simple, and to emphasize the fact that revenues and expenses produce changes in equity, the illustrations in this first chapter add the revenues directly to owner's equity and subtract the expenses directly from owner's equity. In actual practice, however, information about the revenues and expenses is accumulated separately and the amounts are then added to or subtracted from owner's equity. We describe more details about this process in Chapters 2, 3, and 4.

Because of the importance of earning revenues for a company's success, we briefly interrupt the description of Clear Copy's transactions to describe the *revenue recognition principle* that guides us in knowing when to record a company's revenue so that it can be usefully reported in the income statement.

Revenue Recognition Principle

LO 2 Explain the accounting principles introduced in the chapter and describe the process by which generally accepted accounting principles are established.

History shows that managers and auditors have needed guidance to know when to recognize revenue. (*Recognize* means to record an event for the purpose of reporting its effects in the financial statements.) For example, if revenue is recognized too early, the income statement reports net income sooner than it should and the business looks more profitable than it really is. On the other hand, if the revenue is not recognized on time, the income statement shows lower amounts of revenue and net income than it should and the business looks less profitable than it really is. In either case, the income statement does not provide decision makers with useful information about the company's success.

The question of when revenue should be recognized on the income statement is addressed by the **revenue recognition principle** (also called the **realization principle**). This principle includes three important guidelines:

1. *Revenue should be recognized at the time it is earned.* In fact, revenue is partially earned throughout the whole process of providing a service or throughout the whole process of purchasing goods for resale, finding customers who will buy them, and then delivering the goods. However, the amount of revenue earned at any point in the process usually cannot be determined reliably until the entire process is completed and the business acquires the right to collect the selling price. Therefore, in most cases, revenue should not be recognized and reported on the income statement until the earnings process is essentially complete. For most businesses, the earnings process is completed only when services are rendered or when the seller transfers ownership of the goods sold to the buyer. For example, suppose that a customer pays in advance of taking delivery of a good or service. Because the earnings process is not completed, the seller should not recognize any revenue. Instead, the seller must actually complete the earnings process before recognizing the revenue.[13] This practice is known as the *sales basis of revenue recognition.*

2. *The inflow of assets associated with revenue does not have to be in the form of cash.* The most common noncash asset acquired by the seller in a revenue transaction is an account receivable from a customer. These transactions, called *credit sales,* occur because it is convenient for the customer to get the goods or services now and pay for them later. (Remember that Clear Copy took advantage of this convenience in transaction 4 when it bought supplies and equipment on credit.) If objective evidence shows that the seller has the right to collect the account receivable, the seller should recognize the revenue. When the cash is collected later, no additional revenue is recognized. Instead, collecting the cash simply changes the form of the asset from a receivable to cash.

3. *The amount of recognized revenue should be measured as the cash received plus the cash equivalent value (fair market value) of any other asset or assets received.* For example, if the transaction creates an account receivable, the seller should recognize revenue equal to the value of the receivable, which is usually equivalent to the amount of cash to be collected.

The Effects of Additional Transactions on the Accounting Equation

To show how the revenue recognition principle works, we return to the example of Clear Copy Co.

Transactions 8 and 9. Assume that Clear Copy provided copy services for a customer and billed that customer $1,700. This event is identified as transaction 8 in Illustration 1–6. Ten days later, the customer paid Clear Copy the full $1,700 in transaction 9.

Illustration 1–6 shows that transaction 8 created a new asset, the account receivable from the customer. The $1,700 increase in assets produces an equal increase in owner's equity. Notice that this increase in equity is identified as a revenue in the last column of Illustration 1–6.

Transaction 9 occurred when the customer in transaction 8 paid the account receivable. This event merely converted the receivable to cash. Because transaction 9 did not increase total assets and did not affect liabilities, equity did not change. Thus, this transaction did not create any new revenue. The revenue was generated when Clear Copy rendered the services, not when the cash was collected. This emphasis on the earning process instead of cash

[13] FASB, *Accounting Standards—Current Text* (Norwalk, CT, 1994), sec. R75.101. First published as *APB Opinion No. 10,* par. 12.

ILLUSTRATION 1–6 *Changes in the Balance Sheet Equation Caused by Noncash Revenues, the Later Receipt of Cash, the Payment of Payables, and Withdrawals by the Owner*

	Assets				= Liabilities +	Owner's Equity	
	Cash +	Accounts + Receivable	Store + Supplies	Copy Equipment	= Accounts + Payable	Terry Dow, Capital	Explanation of Change
Bal.	$8,000		$3,600	$26,000	$7,100	$30,500	
(8)		+$1,700				+ 1,700	Revenue
Bal.	$8,000	$1,700	$3,600	$26,000	$7,100	$32,200	
(9)	+1,700	−1,700					
Bal.	$9,700	$ -0-	$3,600	$26,000	$7,100	$32,200	
(10)	− 900				− 900		
Bal.	$8,800	$ -0-	$3,600	$26,000	$6,200	$32,200	
(11)	− 400					− 400	Withdrawal
Bal.	$8,400 +	$ -0- +	$3,600 +	$26,000 =	$6,200 +	$31,800	

flows reflects the goal of providing useful information in the income statement by applying the *revenue recognition principle.*

Transaction 10. Another effect on the accounting equation is created by transaction 10. In this transaction, Clear Copy paid $900 to Handy Supply Company on December 24 as partial repayment of the account payable. Illustration 1–6 shows that this transaction decreased Clear Copy's cash by $900 and decreased its liability to Handy Supply by the same amount. As a result, there was no reduction in owner's equity. This event did not create an expense, even though cash flowed out of the company.

Transaction 11. Another type of event, the payment of cash to the company's owner, is identified in Illustration 1–6 as transaction 11. In this case, Clear Copy paid $400 to Terry Dow to use for personal living expenses. Traditionally, a company's payments of cash (or other assets) to its owner are called *withdrawals.* Notice that this decrease in owner's equity is not called an expense in Illustration 1–6. Withdrawals are not expenses because they do not create revenues for the company. And, because withdrawals are not expenses, they are not used to calculate net income.

Summary. Illustration 1–7 presents the effects of the entire series of 11 transactions for Clear Copy. Take time now to see that the equation remained in balance after each transaction. This is because the effects of each transaction are always in balance. In each case, transactions 1, 5, and 8 increased total assets and equity by equal amounts. Also in each case, transactions 2, 3, and 9 increased one asset while decreasing another by an equal amount. Transaction 4 increased total assets and a liability by equal amounts. In each case, transactions 6, 7, and 11 decreased assets and equity by an equal amount. Finally, transaction 10 decreased an asset and a liability by the same amount. The equality of these effects is central to the working of double entry accounting. You learn more about double entry accounting in the next chapter.

Understanding More about the Financial Statements

The purpose of accounting is to provide useful information to people who make rational investment, credit, and similar decisions. This information is often communicated to its users through the financial statements. Accountants prepare these statements from data gathered about transactions and other events. In effect, the statements summarize the economic effects of these transactions and events on the company. Although simpler than actual systems used in practice, the record-keeping system described in this chapter is adequate for preparing the financial statements for Clear Copy.

ILLUSTRATION 1-7 *Changes in the Balance Sheet Equation Created by All Transactions*

	Assets				= Liabilities +	Owner's Equity	
	Cash +	Accounts + Receivable	Store + Supplies	Copy Equipment	= Accounts + Payable	Terry Dow, Capital	Explanation of Change
(1)	$30,000					$30,000	Investment
(2)	− 2,500		+$2,500				
Bal.	$27,500		$2,500			$30,000	
(3)	−20,000			+$20,000			
Bal.	$ 7,500		$2,500	$20,000		$30,000	
(4)			+1,100	+ 6,000	+$7,100		
Bal.	$ 7,500		$3,600	$26,000	$7,100	$30,000	
(5)	+ 2,200					+ 2,200	Revenue
Bal.	$ 9,700		$3,600	$26,000	$7,100	$32,200	
(6)	− 1,000					− 1,000	Expense
Bal.	$ 8,700		$3,600	$26,000	$7,100	$31,200	
(7)	− 700					− 700	Expense
Bal.	$ 8,000		$3,600	$26,000	$7,100	$30,500	
(8)		+$1,700				+ 1,700	Revenue
Bal.	$ 8,000	$1,700	$3,600	$26,000	$7,100	$32,200	
(9)	+ 1,700	−1,700					
Bal.	$ 9,700	$ -0-	$3,600	$26,000	$7,100	$32,200	
(10)	− 900				− 900		
Bal.	$ 8,800	$ -0-	$3,600	$26,000	$6,200	$32,200	
(11)	− 400					− 400	Withdrawal
Bal.	$ 8,400	$ -0-	$3,600	$26,000	$6,200	$31,800	

LO 1 Describe the information presented in financial statements, be able to prepare simple financial statements, and analyze a company's performance with the return on equity ratio.

Up to this point, you have learned about only two financial statements: the income statement and the balance sheet. GAAP also require companies to include two other statements in their reports. They are the statement of changes in owner's equity and the statement of cash flows.

The following chart resembles the one earlier in this chapter that represented the relationship between the income statement and the balance sheet:

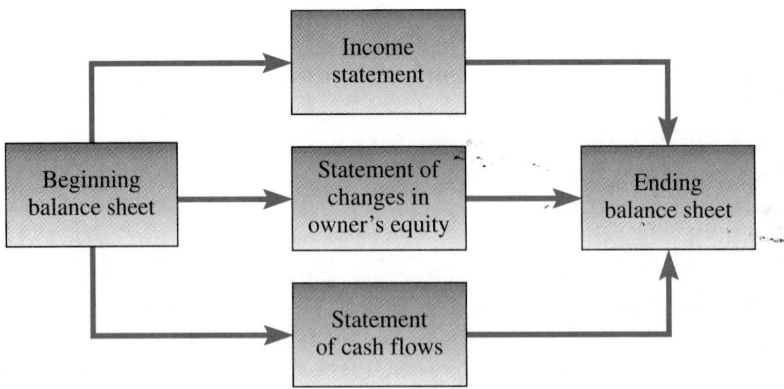

This diagram shows how all four financial statements are linked. The income statement describes how owner's equity changed during the period through the company's income earning activities. The statement of changes in owner's equity describes all changes in equity, including net income, new investments by the owner, and withdrawals by the owner. The statement of cash flows describes how the amount of cash changed between the beginning and ending balance sheets. The statement of cash flows also describes many of the changes in the company's other assets and liabilities. Thus, most of the com-

ILLUSTRATION 1-8 *Financial Statements for Clear Copy Co.*

CLEAR COPY CO.
Income Statement
For Month Ended December 31, 19X1

Revenues:		
Copy services revenue		$3,900
Operating expenses:		
Rent expense	$1,000	
Salaries expense	700	
Total operating expenses		1,700
Net income		$2,200

CLEAR COPY CO.
Statement of Changes in Owner's Equity
For Month Ended December 31, 19X1

Terry Dow, capital, November 30, 19X1		$ -0-
Plus: Investments by owner	$30,000	
Net income	2,200	32,200
Total		$32,200
Less withdrawals by owner		400
Terry Dow, capital, December 31, 19X1		$31,800

CLEAR COPY CO.
Balance Sheet
December 31, 19X1

Assets		**Liabilities**	
Cash	$ 8,400	Accounts payable	$ 6,200
Store supplies	3,600	**Owner's Equity**	
Copy equipment	26,000	Terry Dow, capital . . .	31,800
		Total liabilities and	
Total assets	$38,000	owner's equity	$38,000

pany's activities are described by the three statements in the middle, while the balance sheets describe the company's financial position before and after those activities occurred.

The Income Statement

The top section of Illustration 1–8 shows Clear Copy's income statement as it appeared in Illustration 1–1. Now you can see that it is based on the information about revenues and expenses recorded in the owner's equity column in Illustration 1–7.

Notice that the income statement lists revenues of $3,900. This amount is the result of transactions 5 and 8. For clarity, the revenues are identified as copy services revenue. If the business had earned other kinds of revenues, they would have been listed separately to help users understand more about the company's activities. The income statement then lists the rent and salaries expenses incurred in transactions 6 and 7. The types of expenses are identified to help users form a more complete picture of the events of the time period. Finally, the income statement presents the amount of net income earned during the month.

The Statement of Changes in Owner's Equity

The **statement of changes in owner's equity** presents information about everything that happened to equity during the reporting period. The statement shows the beginning amount of equity, the events that increased it (new investments by the owner and net income), and the events that decreased it (a net loss and withdrawals). This information summarizes the changes in the owner's wealth during the reporting period.

The middle section of Illustration 1–8 shows the statement of changes in owner's equity for Clear Copy Co. The heading refers to December 19X1 because the statement describes events that happened during that time period. The beginning balance of equity is stated as of the close of business on November 30. It is zero because the business did not exist before then. An existing business would report the balance as of the end of the prior reporting period. The Clear Copy statement shows that $30,000 of equity was created by Dow's initial investment. It also shows the $2,200 net income earned during the month. This item links the income statement to the statement of changes in owner's equity. The statement also reports Dow's $400 withdrawal and the $31,800 equity balance at the end of the month.

The Balance Sheet

The lower section of Illustration 1–8 presents Clear Copy's balance sheet (the same statement appeared in Illustration 1–2). The heading shows that the statement describes the company's financial condition at the close of business on December 31, 19X1.

The left side of the balance sheet lists the company's assets. In this case, they are cash, store supplies, and copy equipment. It shows the balance of cash and the costs of the other two assets. The right side of the balance sheet shows that the company owes $6,200 on accounts payable. If any other liabilities had existed (such as bank loans), they would have been listed in this section. The equity section shows an ending balance of $31,800, which equals the amount on the last line of the statement of changes in owner's equity. This item links these two statements.

The Statement of Cash Flows

The fourth financial statement is the **statement of cash flows,** which describes where a company's cash came from and where it went during the period. The statement also shows how much cash was on hand at the beginning of the period, and how much was left at the end. This information is important for both internal and external decision makers because a company must manage its cash well if it is going to survive and prosper.

Illustration 1–9 shows Clear Copy's statement of cash flows for December. The information presented in the statement was recorded in the first column (labeled Cash) of Illustration 1–7. The heading identifies December 19X1 as the time period covered by the statement.

The first section of the statement of cash flows shows the amount of cash used by the company's *operating activities.* This amount includes $3,900 of cash received from customers in transactions 5 and 9. This equals the total revenues only because Clear Copy collected all of its revenues in cash. If some credit sales are not collected, or if credit sales from a prior reporting period are collected, the amount of cash received from customers does not equal the revenues reported on the income statement for the same period.

This first section also lists cash payments for store supplies, rent, and salaries. These cash flows occurred in transactions 2, 6, and 7. Notice that the amounts are shown in parentheses to indicate that they are subtracted. The amounts paid for rent and salaries equal the expenses reported on Clear Copy's income statement because Clear Copy paid cash for the expenses.

The payment for supplies is reported as an operating activity because supplies are expected to be consumed in short-term operations. (We explain this more completely in Chapter 15.) The net outflow from operating activities for

ILLUSTRATION 1–9 *Statement of Cash Flows for Clear Copy Co.*

CLEAR COPY CO.
Statement of Cash Flows
For Month Ended December 31, 19X1

Cash flows from operating activities:		
Cash received from customers	$ 3,900	
Cash paid for store supplies	(2,500)	
Cash paid for rent	(1,000)	
Cash paid to employee	(700)	
Net cash used by operating activities		$ (300)
Cash flows from investing activities:		
Purchase of copy equipment	$(20,000)	
Net cash used by investing activities		(20,000)
Cash flows from financing activities:		
Investments by owner	$ 30,000	
Withdrawals by owner	(400)	
Repayment of debt	(900)	
Net cash provided by financing activities		28,700
Net increase in cash		$ 8,400
Cash balance, November 30, 19X1		-0-
Cash balance, December 31, 19X1		$ 8,400

December was $300. Decision makers are especially interested in this section of the statement of cash flows because companies must generate cash from their operating activities to stay in existence.

The second section of the statement of cash flows describes the cash flows from *investing activities.* In general, investing activities involve buying or selling assets such as land or equipment that are held for long-term use in the business. Clear Copy's only investing activity was the purchase of equipment in transaction 3. Notice that no cash flows are reported for transaction 4, which was a credit purchase. The investing activities section shows that $20,000 of cash was spent. Decision makers are interested in this section of the statement of cash flows because it describes how a company is preparing for the future. If the company is spending cash for productive assets, it should be able to grow. If it is not spending cash, it may not be able to expand its operations. On the other hand, the company might be spending too much on productive assets for its size. The information in the investing section helps decision makers understand what the company has done.

The third section of the statement shows the cash flows related to *financing activities.* Financing activities include borrowing cash from creditors and receiving cash investments from the owner. Financing activities also include loan repayments and cash withdrawals by the owner. The statement of cash flows in Illustration 1–9 shows that Clear Copy obtained $30,000 from Terry Dow's initial investment in transaction 1. If the business had borrowed cash, the amount would appear here as an increase in cash. Decision makers also are interested in the financing section. The sources of cash used by a company can make a difference for the future. For example, excessive borrowing can burden the company with too much debt and reduce its potential for growth.

The financing activities section of Illustration 1–9 shows the $400 withdrawal from transaction 11 and the $900 paid to Handy Supply in transaction 10. The overall effect of the financing activities was a $28,700 net inflow of cash. The information in this section explains why the business did not run out of cash even though it spent $22,500 on assets and used $300 in its operating activities.

The last section of the statement of cash flows shows that the company increased its cash balance by $8,400. Because the company started out with no cash, the ending balance is also $8,400. This final amount links the statement of cash flows to the balance sheet. We present a more detailed explanation of the statement of cash flows in Chapter 15.

Using the Information—The Return on Equity Ratio

LO 1 Describe the information presented in financial statements, be able to prepare simple financial statements, and analyze a company's performance with the return on equity ratio.

An important reason for recording and reporting information about a company's assets, liabilities, equity, and net income is to help the owner judge the business venture's relative success compared to other activities or investments. One way to describe this success is to calculate the **return on equity ratio,** which equals the amount of income achieved in a period divided by the amount of owner's equity. The formula for this ratio is as follows:

$$\text{Return on equity} = \frac{\text{Net income}}{\text{Beginning owner's equity}}$$

For the month of December, the financial statements show that Terry Dow earned a return on equity at the rate of 7.3% for the month. To find this rate, we divide $2,200 of net income by the $30,000 beginning balance of owner's equity.

Interpreting the rate of return achieved by a company requires an understanding of several factors. For example, the rate should be compared with the rates that could be earned on other kinds of investments. Dow's rate for December is high compared to other investments, and may appear very appealing. Recall, however, that the income reported for a single proprietorship does not reflect any expense for the effort exerted by the owner in managing its operations. Thus, it is advisable to reduce the reported income by a fair value for the manager's efforts before calculating the return on equity. Thus, the formula can be restated as follows for a single proprietorship:

$$\text{Modified return on equity} = \frac{\text{Net income} - \text{Value of owner's efforts}}{\text{Beginning owner's equity}}$$

For example, suppose that other employment opportunities show that Dow's efforts are valued at $1,200 per month. If so, the numerator would be only $1,000 ($2,200 minus $1,200). As a result, the modified return would be $1,000/$30,000, which is only 3.3% for the month instead of the 7.3% just shown.

Dow should compare this rate with other investment alternatives to determine whether Clear Copy is producing an adequate return on equity. Because 3.3% per month is close to 40% per year, it is likely that Dow will be encouraged to stay in the business. However, we have not completely measured the income for the month. Chapters 2 and 3 introduce additional revenues and expenses, the net effect of which will be to reduce the net income below the amount shown here.

Summary of the Chapter in Terms of Learning Objectives

LO 1 The income statement shows a company's revenues, expenses, and net income or loss. The balance sheet lists a company's assets, liabilities, and owner's equity. The statement of changes in owner's equity shows the increase in owner's equity from investments by the owner, the decrease from withdrawals, and the increase from net income or the decrease from a net loss. The statement of cash flows shows the events that caused cash to change. It classifies the cash flows as coming from operating, investing, and financing activities. The financial statements are prepared with information about the effects of each transaction on the accounting equation. The company's performance can be analyzed by comparing the company's return on equity with rates on other investments available to the owner.

LO 2 Accounting principles have been developed to help accountants produce relevant and reliable information. Broad accounting principles include the business entity principle, the objectivity principle, the cost principle, the going-concern principle, and the revenue recognition principle. Specific accounting principles for financial accounting are established in the United States primarily by the Financial Accounting Standards Board (FASB), which operates under the oversight of the Securities and Exchange Commission (SEC). Auditing standards are established by the Auditing Standards Board (ASB), a committee of the American Institute of CPAs (AICPA). The International Accounting Standards Committee (IASC) identifies preferred practices and encourages their adoption throughout the world. However, the IASC does not have the authority to impose its standards on companies.

LO 3 A single (or sole) proprietorship is an unincorporated business owned by one individual. A partnership differs from a single proprietorship in that it has more than one owner. Proprietors and partners are personally responsible for the debts of their businesses. A corporation is a separate legal entity. As such, its owners are not personally responsible for its debts.

LO 4 The accounting equation states that Assets = Liabilities + Owners' Equity. Business transactions always have at least two effects on the elements in the accounting equation. The accounting equation is always in balance when business transactions are properly recorded.

Demonstration Problem

After several months of planning, Barbara Schmidt started a haircutting business called The Cutlery. The following events occurred during its first month:

a. On August 1, Schmidt put $3,000 cash into a checking account in the name of The Cutlery. She also invested $15,000 of equipment that she already owned.

b. On August 2, she paid $600 cash for furniture for the shop.

c. On August 3, she paid $500 cash to rent space in a strip mall for August.

d. On August 4, she furnished the shop by installing the old equipment and some new equipment that she bought on credit for $1,200. This amount is to be repaid in three equal payments at the end of August, September, and October.

e. On August 5, The Cutlery opened for business. Receipts from cash sales in the first week and a half of business (ended August 15) were $825.

f. On August 17, Schmidt paid $125 to an assistant for working during the grand opening.

g. Cash receipts from sales during the second half of August were $930.

h. On August 31, Schmidt paid an installment on the accounts payable.

i. On August 31, she withdrew $900 cash for her personal use.

Required

1. Arrange the following asset, liability, and owner's equity titles in a table similar to the one in Illustration 1–7: Cash; Furniture Store; Equipment; Accounts Payable; and Barbara Schmidt, Capital. Show the effects of each transaction on the equation. Explain each of the changes in owner's equity.
2. Prepare an income statement for August.
3. Prepare a statement of changes in owner's equity for August.
4. Prepare a statement of cash flows for August.
5. Prepare a balance sheet as of August 31.

6. Determine the return on equity ratio for August.
7. Determine the modified return on equity ratio for August, assuming that Schmidt's management efforts were worth $1,000.

Planning the Solution

- Set up a table with the appropriate columns, including a final column for describing the events that affect owner's equity.
- Analyze each transaction and show its effects as increases or decreases in the appropriate columns. Be sure that the accounting equation remains in balance after each event.
- To prepare the income statement, find the revenues and expenses in the last column. List those items on the statement, calculate the difference, and label the result as *net income* or *net loss.*
- Use the information in the Explanation of Change column to prepare the statement of changes in owner's equity.
- To prepare the statement of cash flows, include all events listed in the Cash column of the table. Classify each cash flow as operating, investing, or financing. Follow the example in Illustration 1–9.
- Use the information on the last row of the table to prepare the balance sheet.
- Calculate the return on equity by dividing net income by the beginning equity. Calculate the modified return by subtracting the $1,000 value of Schmidt's efforts from the net income, and then dividing the difference by the beginning equity.

Solution to Demonstration Problem

1.

	Assets			= Liabilities +	Owner's Equity	
	Cash +	Furniture +	Shop Equipment	= Accounts Payable +	Barbara Schmidt, Capital	Explanation of Change
a.	$3,000		$15,000		$18,000	Investment
b.	− 600	+$600				
Bal.	$2,400	$600	$15,000		$18,000	
c.	− 500				− 500	Expense
Bal.	$1,900	$600	$15,000		$17,500	
d.			+ 1,200	+$1,200		
Bal.	$1,900	$600	$16,200	$1,200	$17,500	
e.	+ 825				+ 825	Revenue
Bal.	$2,725	$600	$16,200	$1,200	$18,325	
f.	− 125				− 125	Expense
Bal.	$2,600	$600	$16,200	$1,200	$18,200	
g.	+ 930				+ 930	Revenue
Bal.	$3,530	$600	$16,200	$1,200	$19,130	
h.	− 400			− 400		
Bal.	$3,130	$600	$16,200	$ 800	$19,130	
i.	− 900				− 900	Withdrawal
Bal.	$2,230 +	$600 +	$16,200 =	$ 800 +	$18,230	

2.

THE CUTLERY
Income Statement
For Month Ended August 31

Revenues:		
Sales		$1,755
Operating expenses:		
Rent expense	$500	
Salaries expense	125	
Total operating expenses		625
Net income		$1,130

3.

THE CUTLERY
Statement of Changes in Owner's Equity
For Month Ended August 31

Barbara Schmidt, capital, July 31		$ -0-
Plus: Investments by owner	$18,000	
Net income	1,130	19,130
Total		$19,130
Less withdrawals by owner		(900)
Barbara Schmidt, capital, August 31		$18,230

4.

THE CUTLERY
Statement of Cash Flows
For Month Ended August 31

Cash flows from operating activities:		
Cash received from customers	$1,755	
Cash paid for rent	(500)	
Cash paid for wages	(125)	
Net cash provided by operating activities		$1,130
Cash flows from investing activities:		
Cash paid for furniture		(600)
Cash flows from financing activities:		
Cash received from owner	$3,000	
Cash paid to owner	(900)	
Repayment of debt	(400)	
Net cash provided by financing activities		1,700
Net increase in cash		$2,230
Cash balance, July 31		-0-
Cash balance, August 31		$2,230

5.

THE CUTLERY
Balance Sheet
August 31

Assets		**Liabilities**	
Cash	$2,230	Accounts payable	$ 800
Furniture	600	**Owner's Equity**	
Store equipment	16,200	Barbara Schmidt, capital	18,230
Total assets	$19,030	Total liabilities and owner's equity	$19,030

6.

$$\text{Return on equity} = \frac{\text{Net income}}{\text{Beginning owner's equity}} = \frac{\$1,130}{\$18,000} = 6.3\%$$

7.

$$\text{Modified return on equity} = \frac{\text{Net income} - \text{Owner's efforts}}{\text{Beginning owner's equity}} = \frac{\$130}{\$18,000} = 0.7\%$$

Glossary

LO 5 Define or explain the words and phrases listed in the chapter glossary.

AAA the American Accounting Association, a professional association of college and university accounting faculty. p. 25

Accounting equation a description of the relationship between a company's assets, liabilities, and equity; expressed as Assets = Liabilities + Owner's Equity; also called the *balance sheet equation.* p. 31

Accounts payable liabilities created by buying goods and services on credit. p. 21

Accounts receivable assets created by selling goods and services on credit. p. 21

AIMR Association for Investment Management and Research; a professional association of people who use financial statements in the process of evaluating companies' financial performance. p. 26

APB Accounting Principles Board, a former authoritative committee of the AICPA that was responsible for identifying generally accepted accounting principles from 1959 to 1973; predecessor to the FASB. p. 26

ASB the Auditing Standards Board; the authoritative committee of the AICPA that identifies generally accepted auditing standards. p. 26

Assets properties or economic resources owned by the business; more precisely, probable future economic benefits obtained or controlled by a particular entity as a result of past transactions or events. p. 21

Balance sheet a financial statement providing information that helps users understand a company's financial status; lists the types and dollar amounts of assets, liabilities, and equity as of a specific date; also called the *statement of financial position.* p. 20

Balance sheet equation another name for the *accounting equation.* p. 31

Business entity principle the principle that requires every business to be accounted for separately and distinctly from its owner or owners; based on the goal of providing relevant information about the business. p. 27

Business transaction an exchange between two parties of economic consideration, such as goods, services, money, or rights to collect money. p. 28

CAP the Committee on Accounting Procedure; the authoritative body for identifying generally accepted accounting principles from 1936 to 1959. p. 26

Common stock the name given to a corporation's stock when it issues only one kind or class of stock. p. 29

Continuing-concern principle another name for the *going-concern principle.* p. 28

Contributed capital the category of stockholders' equity created by the stockholders' investments. p. 30

Corporation a business chartered, or incorporated, as a separate legal entity under state or federal laws. p. 29

Cost principle the accounting principle that requires financial statement information to be based on costs incurred in business transactions; it requires assets and services to be recorded initially at the cash or cash-equivalent amount given in exchange. p. 28

Creditors individuals or organizations entitled to receive payments from a company. p. 21

Debtors individuals or organizations that owe amounts to a business. p. 21

Dividends payments of cash by a corporation to its stockholders. p. 30

Equity the difference between a company's assets and its liabilities; more precisely, the residual interest in the assets of an entity that remains after deducting its liabilities; also called *net assets.* p. 22

Expenses outflows or the using up of assets as a result of the major or central operations of a business; also, liabilities may be increased. p. 19

FASB Financial Accounting Standards Board, the seven-member nonprofit board that currently has the authority to identify generally accepted accounting principles. p. 24

FEI Financial Executives Institute, a professional association of private accountants. p. 25

GAAS the abbreviation for *generally accepted auditing standards.* p. 24

Generally accepted auditing standards rules adopted by the accounting profession as guides for conducting audits of financial statements. p. 24

Going-concern principle the rule that requires financial statements to reflect the assumption that the business will continue operating instead of being closed or sold, unless evidence shows that it will not continue. p. 28

IASC International Accounting Standards Committee; a committee that attempts to create more harmony among the accounting practices of different countries by identifying preferred practices and encouraging their worldwide acceptance. p. 26

IMA Institute of Management Accountants, a professional association of private accountants, formerly called the National Association of Accountants. p. 26

Income statement the financial statement that shows whether the business earned a profit; it lists the types and amounts of the revenues and expenses. p. 19

Liabilities debts owed by a business or organization; probable future sacrifices of economic benefits arising from present obligations of a particular entity to transfer assets or provide services to other entities in the future as a result of past transactions or events. p. 21

Net assets another name for *equity.* p. 22

Net income the excess of revenues over expenses for a period. p. 19

Net loss the excess of expenses over revenues for a period. p. 19

Objectivity principle the accounting guideline that requires financial statement information to be supported by evidence other than someone's opinion or imagination; objectivity adds to the reliability and usefulness of accounting information. p. 27

Paid-in capital another name for *contributed capital.* p. 30

Partnership a business that is owned by two or more people and that is not organized as a corporation. p. 29

Realization principle another name for the *revenue recognition principle.* p. 34

Retained earnings the category of stockholders' equity created by a corporation's profitable activities. p. 30

Return on equity ratio the ratio of net income to beginning owner's equity; used to judge a business's success compared to other activities or investments; may be modified for proprietorships or partnerships by subtracting the value of the owner's efforts in managing the business from the reported income. p. 40

Revenue recognition principle the rule that (1) requires revenue to be recognized at the time it is earned, (2) allows the inflow of assets associated with revenue to be in a form other than cash, and (3) measures the amount of revenue as the cash plus the cash equivalent value of any noncash assets received from customers in exchange for goods or services. p. 34

Revenues inflows of assets received in exchange for goods or services provided to customers as part of the major or central operations of the business; may occur as inflows of assets or decreases in liabilities. p. 19

Shareholders another name for *stockholders.* p. 29

SIA Securities Industry Association; an association of individuals involved with issuing and marketing securities. p. 26

Single proprietorship a business owned by one individual, not organized as a corporation. p. 29

Sole proprietorship another name for a *single proprietorship.* p. 29

Statement of cash flows a financial statement that describes where a company's cash came from and where it went during the period; the cash flows are classified as being caused by operating, investing, and financing activities. p. 38

Statement of changes in owner's equity a financial statement that shows the beginning balance of owner's equity, the changes in equity that resulted from new investments by the owner, net income (or net loss), and withdrawals, and the ending balance. p. 37

Statement of financial position another name for the *balance sheet.* p. 20

Statements of Financial Accounting Standards (SFAS) the publications of the FASB that establish new generally accepted accounting principles in the United States. p. 24

Stock equity of a corporation divided into units called shares. p. 29

Stockholders the owners of a corporation; also called *shareholders.* p. 29

Withdrawal a payment from a proprietorship or partnership to its owner or owners. p. 30

Objective Review

Answers to the following questions are listed at the end of this chapter. Be sure that you decide which is the one best answer to each question *before* you check the answers.

LO 1 The financial statements usually presented to a company's owner, outside investors, and creditors are the:

a. Revenues, expenses, assets, liabilities, and owner's equity.
b. Income statement, balance sheet, and statement of cash flows.
c. Income statement and balance sheet.
d. Income statement, statement of changes in owner's equity, and balance sheet.
e. Balance sheet, statement of cash flows, income statement, and statement of changes in owner's equity.

LO 2 Generally accepted accounting principles in the United States are currently established by:

a. The SEC, subject to the authority of the U.S. Congress.
b. CPA firms, subject to the auditing standards established by the AICPA.
c. The U.S. Congress, subject to the review of the SEC.
d. The FASB, subject to the oversight of the SEC.
e. The AICPA, subject to the oversight of the FASB.

LO 3 A business organized as a single proprietorship is:

a. Owned by a person who holds all stock issued by the company.
b. Owned by more than one person and is not a separate legal entity.
c. A separate legal entity.
d. Owned by a person who faces limited liability for its debts.
e. Not a separate legal entity and is owned by a person who is personally responsible for all its debts.

LO 4 A new business has the following transactions: (1) the owner invested \$3,600 cash; (2) \$2,600 of supplies were purchased for cash; (3) \$2,300 was received in payment for services rendered by the business; (4) a salary of \$1,000 was paid to an employee; and (5) \$3,000 was borrowed from the bank. After these transactions are completed, the total assets, total liabilities, and total owner's equity of the business are:

a. \$7,900; \$5,300; \$2,600.
b. \$7,900; \$3,000; \$4,900.

c. $10,500; $5,600; $4,900.
d. $7,900; $0; $7,900.
e. $7,900; $3,000; $3,600.

LO 5 An accounting principle that helps accountants prepare reliable financial statements is called the:

a. Objectivity principle.
b. Going-concern principle.
c. Business entity principle.
d. Full-disclosure principle.
e. Consistency principle.

Questions for Class Discussion

1. What information is presented in an income statement?
2. What do accountants mean by the term *revenue*?
3. What do accountants mean by the term *expense*?
4. Why does the user of an income statement need to know the time period that it covers?
5. What information is presented in a balance sheet?
6. Define (*a*) assets, (*b*) liabilities, (*c*) equity, and (*d*) net assets.
7. Identify two categories of generally accepted accounting principles.
8. What FASB pronouncements identify generally accepted accounting principles?
9. Name and describe two qualities of useful information identified by the FASB's conceptual framework.
10. Why do the financial statements of a business present its activities separate from its owner's activities?
11. What does the objectivity principle require for information presented in financial statements? Why?
12. Why are a proprietor's withdrawals not reported on the company's income statement?
13. Is it possible for a transaction to increase a liability without affecting any other asset, liability, or owner's equity? Explain.
14. A business shows office stationery on the balance sheet at its $430 cost, although it cannot be sold for more than $10 as scrap paper. Which accounting principles require this treatment?
15. Why is the revenue recognition principle needed? What does it require?
16. What events or activities change owner's equity?
17. Identify four financial statements that a business presents to its owners and other users.
18. What should a company's return on equity ratio be compared with to determine whether the owner has made a good investment?

19. Find the financial statements of Federal Express Corporation in Appendix G. To what level of significance are the dollar amounts rounded? What time period does the income statement cover?

20. Review the financial statements of Ben & Jerry's Homemade, Inc., in Appendix G. What is the amount of total assets reported at December 26, 1992? How much net cash was provided by operating activities during the 1992 year?

Exercises

Exercise 1–1
The accounting equation
(LO 4)

Determine the missing amount for each of the following equations:

	Assets	= Liabilities	+ Owner's Equity
a.	$ 25,000	$13,500	?
b.	$100,000	?	$28,500
c.	?	$62,500	$31,800

Exercise 1–2
Effects of transactions on the accounting equation
(LO 4)

The following equation shows the effects of five transactions on the assets, liabilities, and owner's equity of Dr. Kirby's dental practice. Write short descriptions of the probable nature of each transaction.

	Assets				=	Liabilities	+	Owner's Equity
	Cash	+ Accounts Receivable	+ Office Supplies	+ Land	=	Accts. Payable	+	M. Kirby, Capital
	$15,000		$5,000	$29,000				$49,000
a.	− 6,000			+ 6,000				
	$ 9,000		$5,000	$35,000				$49,000
b.			+ 800			$800		
	$ 9,000		$5,800	$35,000		$800		$49,000
c.		$2,100						+ 2,100
	$ 9,000	$2,100	$5,800	$35,000		$800		$51,100
d.	− 800					−800		
	$ 8,200	$2,100	$5,800	$35,000		$-0-		$51,100
e.	+ 2,100	−2,100						
	$10,300 +	$ -0- +	$5,800 +	$35,000	=	$-0-	+	$51,100

Exercise 1–3
Using the accounting equation
(LO 4)

Use the accounting equation to determine:

a. The owner's equity in a business having $249,800 of assets and owing $168,300 of liabilities.

b. The liabilities of a business having $100,600 of assets and $84,000 of owner's equity.

c. The assets of a business having $25,100 of liabilities and $75,000 of owner's equity.

Exercise 1–4
Analyzing the accounting equation
(LO 4)

Chris Bevit began operating a new consulting firm on January 15. The accounting equation showed the following balances after each of the company's first five transactions. Analyze the equations and describe each of the five transactions with their amounts.

Balances after Transaction	Cash	+ Accounts Receivable	+ Office Supplies	+ Office Furniture	= Accounts Payable	+ C. Bevit, Capital
1	$60,000	$ -0-	$ -0-	$ -0-	$ -0-	$60,000
2	58,000	-0-	3,500	-0-	1,500	60,000
3	42,000	-0-	3,500	16,000	1,500	60,000
4	42,000	4,000	3,500	16,000	1,500	64,000
5	35,000	4,000	3,500	16,000	1,500	57,000

Exercise 1–5
Determining net income
(LO 1, 4)

A business had the following amounts of assets and liabilities at the beginning and end of a recent year:

	Assets	Liabilities
Beginning of the year	$150,000	$60,000
End of the year	240,000	92,000

Determine the net income earned or net loss incurred by the business during the year under each of the following unrelated assumptions:

a. The owner made no additional investments in the business and withdrew no assets during the year.

b. The owner made no additional investments in the business during the year but withdrew $3,500 per month to pay personal living expenses.

c. The owner withdrew no assets during the year but invested an additional $65,000 cash in the business.

d. The owner withdrew $4,500 per month to pay personal living expenses and invested an additional $20,000 cash in the business at the end of the year.

Exercise 1–6
Analyzing the effects of transactions on the accounting equation
(LO 1, 4)

Cathy Egan began a professional practice on July 1 and plans to prepare financial statements at the end of each month. During July, Egan completed these transactions:

a. Invested $25,000 cash and equipment that had a $5,000 fair market (cash equivalent) value.
b. Paid $800 rent for office space for the month.
c. Purchased $6,000 of additional equipment on credit.
d. Completed work for a client and immediately collected $1,000 cash.
e. Completed work for a client and sent a bill for $3,500 to be paid within 30 days.
f. Purchased $4,000 of additional equipment for cash.
g. Paid an assistant $1,200 as wages for the month.
h. Collected $2,500 of the amount owed by the client described in transaction *e*.
i. Paid for the equipment purchased in transaction *c*.

Required

Create a table like the one in Illustration 1–7, using the following headings for the columns: Cash; Accounts Receivable; Equipment; Accounts Payable; and Cathy Egan, Capital. Then, use additions and subtractions to show the effects of the transactions on the elements of the equation. Show new totals after each transaction. Once you have completed the table, determine Egan's income for July. Determine the modified return on Egan's initial investment, assuming that her management efforts during the month have a value of $1,500.

Exercise 1–7
Analyzing the effects of transactions on the accounting equation
(LO 4)

Following are seven pairs of changes in the elements of the accounting equation. Provide an example of a transaction that creates the described effects:

a. Decreases an asset and decreases equity.
b. Decreases an asset and decreases a liability.
c. Decreases a liability and increases a liability.
d. Increases an asset and decreases an asset.
e. Increases an asset and increases a liability.
f. Increases an asset and increases equity.
g. Increases a liability and decreases equity.

Exercise 1–8
Preparing an income statement
(LO 1)

On July 1, Maia Mears began the practice of tax accounting under the name of Maia Mears, CPA. On July 31, the company's records showed the following items:

Cash	$ 4,000	Owner's withdrawals	$1,500
Accounts receivable	5,000	Tax fees earned	5,000
Office supplies	750	Miscellaneous expenses	180
Tax library	12,000	Rent expense	850
Office equipment	9,000	Salaries expense	2,000
Accounts payable	2,500	Telephone expense	220
Owner's investments	28,000		

Use this information to prepare a July income statement for the business.

Exercise 1–9
Preparing a statement of changes in owner's equity
(LO 1)

Use the facts in Exercise 1–8 to prepare a July statement of changes in owner's equity for the business of Maia Mears, CPA.

Exercise 1–10
Preparing a balance sheet
(LO 1)

Use the facts in Exercise 1–8 to prepare a July 31 balance sheet for the business of Maia Mears, CPA.

Exercise 1–11
Identifying the information in financial statements
(LO 1)

Match each of these numbered items with the financial statement or statements on which it should be presented. Indicate your answer by writing the letter or letters for the correct statement in the blank space next to each item.

A. Income statement
B. Statement of changes in owner's equity
C. Balance sheet
D. Statement of cash flows

___1. Cash received from customers
___2. Office supplies
___3. Rent expense paid in cash
___4. Consulting fees earned and received as cash
___5. Accounts payable
___6. Investments of cash by owner
___7. Accounts receivable
___8. Cash withdrawals by owner

Exercise 1–12
Calculating missing information
(LO 4)

Calculate the amount of the missing item in each of the following independent cases:

	a	b	c	d
Owner's equity, January 1	–0–	$ –0–	$ –0–	$ –0–
Owner's investments during the year	80,000	?	42,000	50,000
Owner's withdrawals during the year	?	(36,000)	(20,000)	(21,000)
Net income (loss) for the year	21,000	54,000	(6,000)	?
Owner's equity, December 31	68,000	66,000	?	57,000

Exercise 1–13
Identifying accounting principles
(LO 2)

Match each of these numbered descriptions with the term that it best describes. Indicate your answer by writing the letter for the correct principle in the blank space next to each description.

A. Broad principle
B. Cost principle
C. Business principle
D. Revenue recognition principle
E. Specific principle
F. Objectivity principle
G. Going-concern principle

___1. Requires every business to be accounted for separately from its owner or owners.
___2. Requires financial statement information to be supported by evidence other than someone's opinion or imagination.
___3. Usually created by a pronouncement from an authoritative body.
___4. Requires financial statement information to be based on costs incurred in transactions.
___5. Derived from long-used accounting practices.
___6. Requires financial statements to reflect the assumption that the business will continue operating instead of being closed or sold.
___7. Requires revenue to be recorded only when the earnings process is complete.

Exercise 1–14
Calculating return on equity
(LO 1)

Use the information for each of the following independent cases to calculate the company's return on equity and its modified return on equity:

	a	b	c	d
Beginning equity	$25,000	$400,000	$150,000	$286,400
Net income	5,400	108,000	45,750	88,965
Value of owner's efforts . .	2,200	50,000	33,000	75,000

Problems

Problem 1–1
Analyzing the effects of transactions on the accounting equation
(LO 4)

Ranca Carr secured her license and opened an architect's office. During a short period, these transactions took place:

a. Carr sold a personal investment in Apple Computer stock for $44,000, and deposited $30,000 of the proceeds in a bank account opened in the name of the business.

b. The business paid $150,000 for a small building to be used as an office. It paid $25,000 in cash and signed a note payable promising to pay the balance over several years.

c. Carr invested $15,000 of her own personal office equipment in the business.
d. Purchased $2,000 of office supplies for cash.
e. Purchased $18,000 of office equipment on credit.
f. Completed a project design on credit and billed the client $2,000 for the work.
g. Paid a local newspaper $500 for an announcement that the office had opened.
h. Designed a house for a client and collected a $9,000 cash commission on completion of the construction.
i. Made a $1,000 payment on the equipment purchased in transaction *e*.
j. Received $1,500 from the client described in transaction *f*.
k. Paid $1,250 cash for the office secretary's wages.
l. Carr withdrew $4,000 from the company bank account to pay personal living expenses.

Required

1. Create a table like the one in Illustration 1–7, using the following headings for the columns: Cash; Accounts Receivable; Office Supplies; Office Equipment; Building; Accounts Payable; Notes Payable; and Ranca Carr, Capital. Leave space for an Explanation column to the right of the Capital column.
2. Use additions and subtractions to show the transactions' effects on the elements of the equation. Show new totals after each transaction. Also, indicate next to each change in the owner's equity whether it was caused by an investment, a revenue, an expense, or a withdrawal.
3. Once you have completed the table, determine the company's net income.
4. Determine the return on the beginning-of-period equity, which consisted of the two amounts invested by Carr in transactions *a* and *c*. Next, assume that Carr could have earned $3,000 for the period from another job and determine the modified return on equity for the period. State whether you think the practice is a good use of Carr's money, if an investment in low-risk bonds would have returned 6% for the same period.

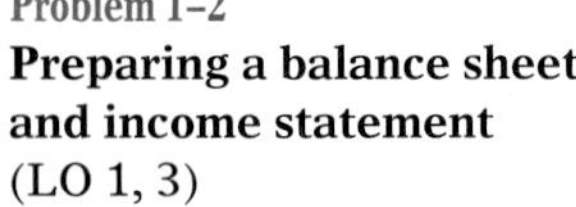

Problem 1–2
Preparing a balance sheet and income statement
(LO 1, 3)

Benny Gates graduated from college in May with a degree in photographic arts. On June 1, Gates invested $30,000 in a new business under the name Benny Gates, Photographer. Gates plans on preparing financial statements for the business at the end of each month. The following transactions occurred during the first month.

June 1 Rented the furnished office and darkroom equipment of a photographer who was retiring. Gates paid $1,600 cash for the rent.
2 Purchased photography supplies for $840 cash.
4 Paid $400 cash for the month's cleaning services.
7 Completed work for a client and immediately collected $300 cash.
13 Completed work for Carl Simone on credit, $1,500.
15 Paid $425 cash for an assistant's salary for the first half of the month.
20 Received payment in full for the work completed for Carl Simone on June 13.
20 Completed work for Wendy Nation on credit, $1,400.
21 Purchased additional photography supplies on credit, $500.
25 Completed work for Billie Carr on credit, $950.
26 Picked up brochures to be used right away to advertise the studio. Gates purchased them from a printer at a cost of $180, which he is to pay within 30 days.
28 Received full payment from Wendy Nation for the work completed on June 20.
29 Paid for the photography supplies purchased on June 21.
30 Paid $100 cash for the month's telephone bill.
30 Paid $240 cash for the month's utilities.
30 Paid $425 cash for an assistant's salary for the second half of the month.
30 Purchased insurance protection for the next 12 months (beginning July 1) by paying a $1,500 premium. Because none of this insurance protection

June had been used up, it was considered to be an asset called Prepaid Insurance.

30 Gates withdrew $560 from the business for personal use.

Required

1. Arrange the following asset, liability, and owner's equity titles in an equation like Illustration 1–7: Cash; Accounts Receivable; Prepaid Insurance; Photography Supplies; Accounts Payable; and Benny Gates, Capital. Include an Explanation column for changes in owner's equity.
2. Show the effects of the transactions on the elements of the equation by recording increases and decreases in the appropriate columns. Indicate an increase with a "+" and a decrease with a "−" before the amount. Do not determine new totals for the items of the equation after each transaction. Next to each change in Benny Gates, Capital, state whether it was caused by an investment, a revenue, an expense, or a withdrawal.
3. After recording the last transaction, determine the final total for each item and insert it on the next line. Verify that the equation is in balance.
4. Use the items in the owner's equity column to prepare a June income statement.
5. Prepare a June statement of changes in owner's equity.
6. Prepare a June 30 balance sheet.

Problem 1–3
Preparing a balance sheet and calculating net income
(LO 1, 3)

The accounting records of Carmen King's dental practice show the following assets and liabilities as of the end of 19X1 and 19X2:

	December 31	
	19X1	**19X2**
Cash	$35,000	$ 12,500
Accounts receivable	19,000	14,900
Dental supplies	3,000	2,200
Dental equipment	92,000	98,000
Office equipment.	36,000	36,000
Land		30,000
Building		120,000
Accounts payable	5,000	25,000
Notes payable		70,000

Late in December 19X2 (just before the amounts in the second column were calculated), King purchased a small office building in the name of the practice, Carmen King, D.D.S., and moved the practice from rented quarters to the new building. The building and the land it occupies cost $150,000. The practice paid $80,000 in cash and a note payable was signed for the balance. King had to invest an additional $35,000 cash in the practice to enable it to pay the $80,000. The practice earned a satisfactory net income during 19X2, which enabled King to withdraw $3,000 per month from the practice for personal living expenses.

Required

1. Prepare balance sheets for the business as of the end of 19X1 and the end of 19X2. (Remember that owner's equity equals the difference between the assets and the liabilities.)
2. By comparing the owner's equity amounts from the balance sheets and using the additional information presented in the problem, prepare a calculation to show how much net income was earned by the business during 19X2.
3. Calculate the return on equity for the dental practice, using the beginning balance of owner's equity for the year. Calculate the modified return on equity, assuming that the owner's efforts were worth $25,000 for the year.

Problem 1–4
Analyzing transactions and preparing financial statements
(LO 1, 3)

Thom Stone began a new financial planning practice and completed these transactions during April:

April 1 Transferred $28,000 from a personal savings account to a checking account opened in the name of the business, Thom Stone, C.F.P.

1 Rented the furnished office of a planner who was retiring, and paid cash for the month's rent of $400.

April 2 Purchased the retiring person's professional library for $7,000 by paying $1,600 in cash and agreeing to pay the balance in six months.
4 Purchased office supplies by paying $450 cash.
6 Completed planning work for Karl Hubbell and immediately collected $500 for doing the work.
9 Purchased $1,900 of office equipment on credit.
15 Completed planning work for Carol Banks on credit in the amount of $2,000.
19 Purchased $250 of office supplies on credit.
21 Paid for the office equipment purchased on April 9.
25 Billed Sy Young $300 for planning work; the balance is due in 30 days.
29 Received $2,000 from Carol Banks for the work completed on April 15.
30 Paid the office assistant's salary of $1,600.
30 Paid the monthly utility bills of $220.
30 Withdrew $500 from the business for personal living expenses.

Required

1. Arrange the following asset, liability, and owner's equity titles in an equation like Illustration 1–7: Cash; Accounts Receivable; Office Supplies; Professional Library; Office Equipment; Accounts Payable; and Thom Stone, Capital. Leave space for an Explanation column to the right of Thom Stone, Capital.
2. Use additions and subtractions to show the effects of each transaction on the items in the equation. Show new totals after each transaction. Next to each change in owner's equity, state whether the change was caused by an investment, a revenue, an expense, or a withdrawal.
3. Use the increases and decreases in the last column of the equation to prepare a monthly income statement.
4. Prepare a monthly statement of changes in owner's equity.
5. Prepare a balance sheet as of the end of the month.
6. Calculate the return on the equity for the month, using the initial investment as the beginning balance of equity.

Problem 1–5
Calculating financial statement amounts
(LO 1)

The following financial statement information is known about five unrelated companies:

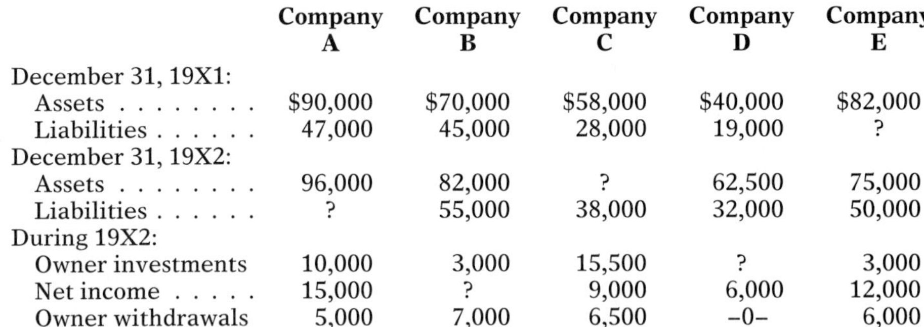

	Company A	Company B	Company C	Company D	Company E
December 31, 19X1:					
Assets	$90,000	$70,000	$58,000	$40,000	$82,000
Liabilities	47,000	45,000	28,000	19,000	?
December 31, 19X2:					
Assets	96,000	82,000	?	62,500	75,000
Liabilities	?	55,000	38,000	32,000	50,000
During 19X2:					
Owner investments	10,000	3,000	15,500	?	3,000
Net income	15,000	?	9,000	6,000	12,000
Owner withdrawals	5,000	7,000	6,500	-0-	6,000

Required

1. Answer the following questions about Company A:
   a. What was the owner's equity on December 31, 19X1?
   b. What was the owner's equity on December 31, 19X2?
   c. What was the amount of liabilities owed on December 31, 19X2?
2. Answer the following questions about Company B:
   a. What was the owner's equity on December 31, 19X1?
   b. What was the owner's equity on December 31, 19X2?
   c. What was the net income for 19X2?
3. Calculate the amount of assets owned by Company C on December 31, 19X2.
4. Calculate the amount of owner investments in Company D made during 19X2.
5. Calculate the amount of liabilities owed by Company E on December 31, 19X1.

Problem 1–6
Identifying effects of transactions on the financial statements
(LO 1, 3)

Identify how each of the following transactions affects the company's financial statements. For the balance sheet, identify how each transaction affects total assets, total liabilities, and owner's equity. For the income statement, identify how each transaction affects net income. For the statement of cash flows, identify how each transaction affects cash flows from operating activities, cash flows from financing activities, and cash flows from investing activities. If there is an increase, place a "+" in the column or columns. If there is a decrease, place a "−" in the column or columns. If there is both an increase and a decrease, place "+/−" in the column or columns. The lines for the first two transactions are completed as examples.

	Balance Sheet			Income Statement	Statement of Cash Flows		
Transaction	**Total Assets**	**Total Liabilities**	**Equity**	**Net Income**	**Operating**	**Financing**	**Investing**
1 Owner invests cash	+		+			+	
2 Purchase supplies on credit	+	+					
3 Sell services for cash							
4 Acquire services on credit							
5 Pay wages with cash							
6 Owner withdraws cash							
7 Borrow cash with note payable							
8 Pay note from (7), including interest							
9 Sell services on credit							
10 Buy office equipment for cash							
11 Pay rent with cash							
12 Collect receivable from (9)							
13 Owner invests equipment							
14 Buy asset with note payable							

Problem 1–7
Analytical essay
(LO 2, 4)

Review the facts presented in Problem 1–1 for transactions *f* and *j*. Identify the transaction that creates a revenue and explain your answer. Then explain why the other transaction did not create a revenue. Next, review the facts for transactions *d* and *k*. Identify the transaction that creates an expense for the current reporting period and explain your answer. Finally, explain why the other transaction did not create an expense.

Problem 1–8
Analytical essay
(LO 4)

Review the facts presented in Problem 1–2. Now assume that all of the company's revenue transactions generated cash (that is, none had been made on credit). Also assume that all of the expense and purchase transactions used cash and none were on credit. Describe the differences, if any, these alternate assumptions would create for the income statement, the statement of changes in owner's equity, and the balance sheet. Construct your answer in general terms without stating the actual dollar amounts of each difference. Be certain to explain why each statement would or would not be affected by the changes in the assumptions.

Provocative Problems

Provocative Problem 1–1
Ann's Bangles and Baubles
(LO 1, 3)

On Friday, September 3, Ann Walker invested $1,000 cash in a small enterprise to participate in a flea market set up in her neighborhood for the Labor Day weekend. In the name of her business, Ann's Bangles and Baubles, she paid $250 rent for space in the market to sell various kinds of costume jewelry. She also paid $50 cash for plastic jewelry boxes, and paid her teenage children $130 to build a booth just for the market. Because she didn't plan to do this again until the next year, she planned to abandon the booth after the market closed. Walker purchased her jewelry from a local wholesaler at a total cost of $900, but, because she had only $570 in cash, could not pay the full price in cash. However, the wholesaler knew that Walker's credit was good, and agreed to accept $500 in cash and the promise that she would pay the $400 balance the day after the market closed. Over the weekend, she sold most of the jewelry for $2,000 cash and paid an assistant $90 cash for helping her. When the market closed, Walker estimated that her unsold goods could be returned to the wholesaler for their original cost of $60. Because of the large number of sales, none of the jewelry boxes was left.

Walker cannot decide whether this venture might be a good thing to repeat in the future. She needs to know whether she earned a satisfactory profit for the time and money that she put into it. Use the methods described in the chapter to develop the information. Prepare (*a*) an income statement for the four-day period ending on Monday, September 6; (*b*) a statement of changes in owner's equity for the same period; and (*c*) a balance sheet as of the close of business on September 6. Then, evaluate whether you think her effort was suitably rewarded by the results, assuming that she could have earned $540 in wages on another job.

Provocative Problem 1–2
Jan's Graphics Co.
(LO 1)

Jan Jericho had an idea near the end of the first semester of his sophomore year that would help him make enough money to pay for the rest of his college education. Because he had really enjoyed his first commercial art course, Jericho decided to provide computerized graphics services to local small businesses for their advertising. His plan was to call on any small business that he could find instead of just advertising his services passively. Besides his enthusiasm, the only asset he owned was a computer system. Jericho had owned the system for two years and estimated that it was worth $2,000 when he started his business. He borrowed about $1,000 cash from a relative, purchased some new software for $800, and began drumming up business.

Now, after the first seven months of operating, he has asked you to help him find out how well he did because he failed to keep adequate accounting records that would allow him to figure it out for himself. You determine that the business now has a checking account, which has a $2,800 balance at December 31. Jericho also has $52 in cash on hand. One of his customers owes him $240 for his last job. In the final week of the year, Jericho sold his computer system and software for $1,800 and used the proceeds as a down payment on a new system and software with a total cost of $6,000. He owes $4,200 to a finance company for the remaining balance of the purchase. The loan from Jericho's relative to the business was still unpaid at the end of the year, but the agreement stated that no interest would be added to the balance. Finally, to cover Jericho's living and education expenses, he has withdrawn $750 cash from the company each month for the seven months since the business started.

To help him determine how well he has done, use the information to prepare a balance sheet as of the end of the year and then calculate the total amount of net income the business earned during the year. Present your calculations in a format that will help other people understand what you have done.

Provocative Problem 1–3
Ben & Jerry's Homemade, Inc.
(LO 2)

Ben & Jerry's Homemade, Inc., is a well-known manufacturer and marketer of superpremium ice cream and frozen yogurt, specializing in unusually flavored products. The company is still managed by its founders, Ben Cohen and Jerry Greenfield, from its headquarters in Waterbury, Vermont. The company's annual filing with the Securities and Exchange Commission for 1992 showed annual sales of nearly $132 million and net income of $6.7 million. The report also included the following information about another company operated by Ben Cohen and Jeffrey Furman, a former officer of the ice cream company:

> **Item 13. Certain relationships and related transactions**
>
> During the year ended December 26, 1992, the Company purchased Rainforest Crunch cashew-brazilnut buttercrunch candy to be included in Ben & Jerry's Rainforest Crunch flavor ice cream for an aggregate purchase price of approximately $1,500,000 from Community Products, Inc., a company of which Messrs. Cohen and Furman are the principal stockholders and of which Mr. Cohen is also president. The candy was purchased from Community Products, Inc., at competitive prices and on standard terms and conditions. Although the Company expects to purchase additional quantities of candy from Community Products, Inc., and had purchase commitments of approximately $1,500,000 as of March 1993, severance of Ben & Jerry's relationship with this supplier would not have a material effect on the Company's business.

Explain why Ben & Jerry's Homemade, Inc., might have included these comments in its report. What accounting principle might be compromised by related-party transactions like the purchases of Rainforest Crunch candy?

Provocative Problem 1–4
Apple Computer, Inc.
(LO 1)

Apple Computer, Inc.

Apple Computer, Inc., is in the business of manufacturing and marketing personal computer systems as well as software and other related products and services. The financial statements and other information from Apple's 1992 annual report are included in Appendix G at the end of the book. Use information from that report to answer the following questions:

1. Examine Apple's consolidated balance sheet. To what level of significance are the dollar amounts rounded?
2. What is the closing date of Apple's most recent annual reporting period?
3. What amount of net income did Apple have during the 1992 year?
4. How much cash (and cash equivalents) did the company hold at the end of the 1992 reporting period?
5. What was the net amount of cash generated by the company's operating activities during the 1992 year?
6. Did the company's investing activities for 1992 create a net cash inflow or outflow? What was the amount of the net flow?
7. Compare 1992's results to 1991's results to determine whether the company's total revenues increased or decreased. If so, what was the amount of the increase or decrease?

8. What was the change in the company's net income between 1991 and 1992?
9. What amount was reported as total assets at the end of the 1992 reporting period?

10. Calculate the return on the beginning shareholders' equity that Apple achieved in 1992.

Answers to Objective Review Questions

LO 1 (*e*)
LO 2 (*d*)
LO 3 (*e*)
LO 4 (*b*)
LO 5 (*a*)

CHAPTER

2

Recording Transactions

In Chapter 1, you were introduced to the accounting equation (Assets = Liabilities + Owner's Equity) and learned how it is affected by business transactions. In this chapter, you learn how the effects of transactions are recorded in accounts. All accounting systems, small or large, manual or computerized, use the procedures described in this chapter to record transactions. No matter how unusual or complicated a business might be, these procedures provide useful information about its transactions.

We begin this chapter by describing how source documents provide useful information about transactions. Then, we describe accounts, explain how they are used, and list several typical accounts. Next, we explain debits and credits and use them to show how transactions affect the accounts. With this background in place, we describe the process of recording events in the journal and ledger. The chapter concludes by describing how to use a company's debt ratio to assess risk.

Learning Objectives

After studying Chapter 2, you should be able to:

1. Describe the events recorded in accounting systems and the importance of source documents and business papers in those systems.
2. Describe how accounts are used to record information about the effects of transactions, how code numbers are used to identify each account, and the meaning of the words *debit* and *credit.*
3. Describe how debits and credits are used to analyze transactions and record their effects in the accounts.
4. Record transactions in a General Journal, describe balance column accounts, and post entries from the journal to the ledger.
5. Prepare a trial balance, explain its usefulness, and calculate a company's debt ratio.
6. Define or explain the words and phrases listed in the chapter glossary.

The Accounting Process

LO 1 Describe the events recorded in accounting systems and the importance of source documents and business papers in those systems.

Chapter 1 explains that accounting provides useful financial information to decision makers. To generate this information, a company uses an accounting process that analyzes economic events, records the results, and classifies and summarizes the information in reports and financial statements. These reports and statements are provided to individuals who find the information to be useful for making investment, credit, and other decisions about the entity. You can see the overall steps in this process in the flowchart in Illustration 2–1.

Business Transactions and Other Events

Notice that the economic events in Illustration 2–1 consist of business transactions and other events. Recall from Chapter 1 that business transactions are completed exchanges between two parties. Also, remember that a company's accounting equation is affected by transactions. The accounting process begins by analyzing transactions to determine how they affect the equation. Then, those effects are captured by recording them in accounting records, informally referred to as *the books.* Additional processing steps summarize and classify the effects of all transactions. The process is not complete until it provides useful information to decision makers in financial statements or other financial reports.

Because business transactions are exchanges between the entity and some other person or organization, they are sometimes called **external transactions.**

In addition, other economic events can affect the accounting equation even though they are not transactions with outside parties. For example, suppose that a company uses a machine in its operations. As a result of using it, the total usefulness of the machine is decreased. That is, the economic benefit of the machine is partially used up. This consumption of the machine's economic benefit is an economic event that decreases assets and decreases owner's equity. Economic events like this one are not transactions between two parties. Nevertheless, they affect the accounting equation and are sometimes called **internal transactions.** The analysis and recording of internal transactions is a main topic of Chapter 3.

In addition, a company can be affected by other events that are not external or internal transactions. For example, natural events, such as storms and floods, can destroy assets and create losses. As another example, market values of the company's assets are likely to change. In some circumstances, those changes are reported in the financial statements, even though transactions have not occurred.

Source Documents and Business Papers

Companies use various documents and other papers when they conduct business. Often called **business papers,** these documents include sales tickets, invoices, checks, purchase orders, bills to customers, bills from suppliers, employee earnings records, and bank statements. Business papers are also called **source documents** because they are the source of the information recorded with accounting entries. Source documents may be printed on paper or they may exist only in computer records.

For example, when you buy a pocket calculator on credit, the store prepares at least two copies of a sales ticket. One copy is given to you. Another is sent to the store's accounting department and triggers an entry in the system to record the sale. (In many systems, this copy is sent electronically without a physical document.) Or, if you pay cash for the calculator, the sale is rung up on a cash register that records and stores the amount of each sale. Some older cash registers print the amount of each sale on a paper tape locked inside the register, while most newer registers store the data electronically. In either

ILLUSTRATION 2-1 *The Accounting Process*

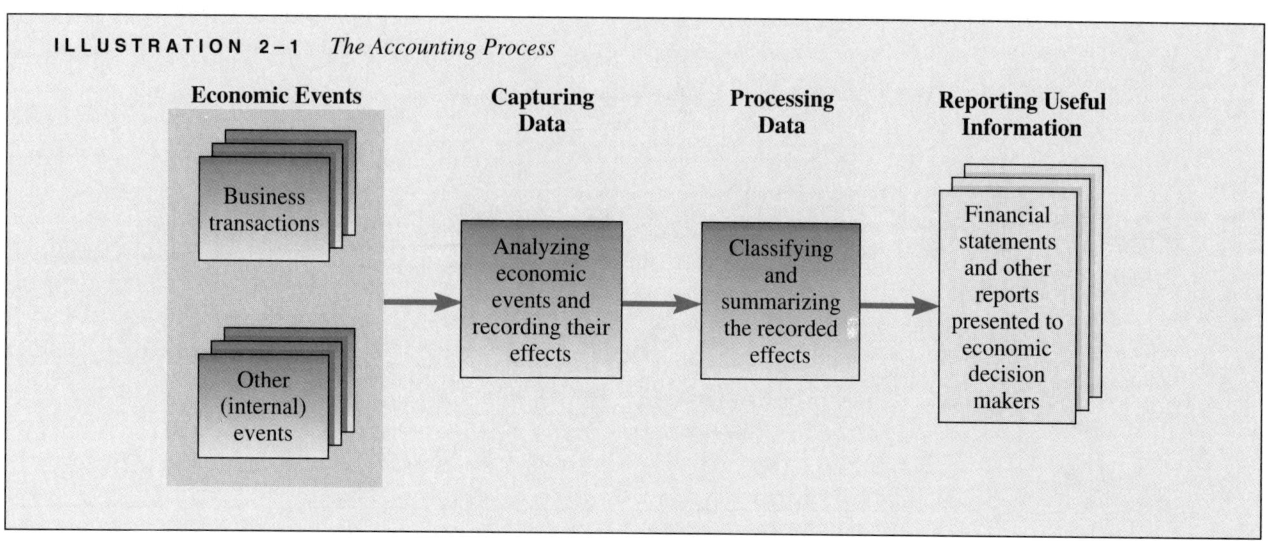

case, the proper keyboard commands at the end of the day cause the cash register to determine the total cash sales for that day. This total is then used to record the day's sales. These systems are designed to ensure that the accounting records include all transactions. They also help prevent mistakes and theft. The As a Matter of Ethics case on page 61 describes a challenge created by an instruction to overlook these accounting procedures. Read the case and think about what you would do if you were Karen Muñoz.

Both buyers and sellers use sales tickets (also called *invoices*) as source documents. For example, if your new calculator is going to be used in your business, your copy of the invoice is a source document that provides information to record the purchase in your accounting records.

To summarize, business papers are the starting point in the accounting process. These source documents, especially if they are created outside the business, provide objective evidence about transactions and the amounts to be recorded for them. As you learned in Chapter 1, this type of evidence is important because it makes the reported information more reliable and useful. The need for credible source documents is created by the *objectivity principle.*

Many years ago, most accounting systems required pen and ink to manually record and process data about transactions. Today, only very small companies use manual systems. Now, large and small companies use computers to record and process the data. However, you will find it easier to understand the steps in the accounting process by learning to prepare accounting data manually. Despite the differences, the general concepts you learn by studying manual methods apply equally well to computerized accounting systems. More importantly, these concepts help you use financial statements because you understand the source of their information.

Recording Information in the Accounts

Accounts are the basic building blocks of accounting systems used to develop a company's financial statements. The diagram in Illustration 2–2 shows how the information about the company's events flows into the accounts. Then, the information flows from the accounts into financial statements that are distributed and used by decision makers.

In one sense, accounts are symbols of the company's assets, liabilities, owner's equity, revenues, and expenses. For example, the amount recorded in an account symbolizing the company's equipment should get larger or smaller as the amount invested in the equipment grows larger or smaller. In another

ILLUSTRATION 2–2 *The Flow of Information through the Accounts into the Financial Statements*

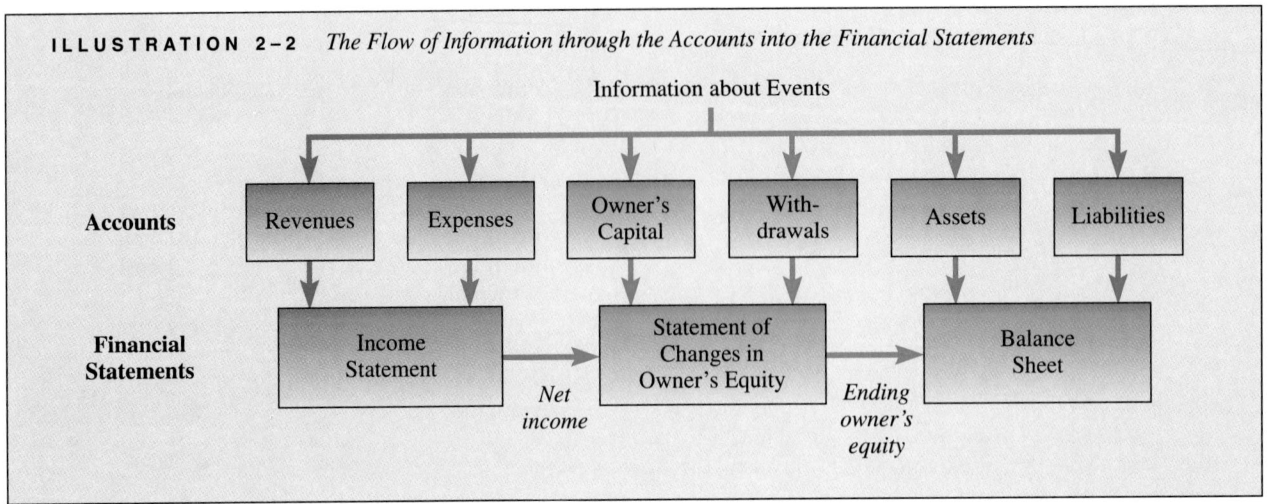

LO 2 Describe how accounts are used to record information about the effects of transactions, how code numbers are used to identify each account, and the meaning of the words *debit* and *credit.*

sense, accounts are special records used to store information about the effects of transactions on assets, liabilities, owner's equity, revenues, and expenses.

When financial statements (or other reports) are needed, the information is taken from the accounts, summarized, and presented in helpful formats. As a result, the usefulness of the statements depends entirely on the completeness of the company's accounts. To provide complete information, a company's accounting system includes a separate account for each revenue and expense on the income statement. The system also includes accounts for changes in owner's equity from new investments and withdrawals. In addition, the system has a separate account for each asset, liability, and owner's equity item on the balance sheet. Because each company is different from all others, each one has its own unique set of accounts according to the information needs of the users of its financial statements. Despite the differences among companies, many accounts are used by all companies. The following paragraphs describe accounts that are widely used in accounting systems.

Asset Accounts

Because most companies own the following kinds of assets, their accounting systems include accounts for them.

Cash. Increases and decreases in the amount of cash are recorded in the *Cash* account. A company's cash consists of money, balances in checking accounts, or any document that a bank accepts for deposit. Thus, cash includes coins, currency, checks, and money orders.

Accounts Receivable. Goods and services are often sold to customers in return for promises to pay in the future. These transactions are called *credit sales* or *sales on account.* The promises from the buyers are called the seller's *accounts receivable.* Accounts receivable are increased by new credit sales and are decreased by customer payments. Because a company sends bills to its credit customers, it needs to know the amount currently due from each of them. Therefore, it creates a separate record of each customer's purchases and payments. We describe the system for maintaining these separate records in Chapter 7. For now, however, we can use the simpler practice of recording all increases and decreases in receivables in a single account called *Accounts Receivable.*

Notes Receivable. A **promissory note** is an unconditional written promise to pay a definite sum of money on demand or on a defined future date (or dates). If a company holds one of these notes signed by another party, it owns a valu-

AS A MATTER OF

Ethics

While taking classes toward her business degree, Karen Muñoz accepted a part-time job at a busy fast-food restaurant in a large downtown mall. As a new employee, she received training from the restaurant's assistant manager, including instructions on operating the cash register. The assistant manager explained that the formal policy is to ring up each sale when an order is placed and the cash is received.

The assistant manager also told Karen that the pressure of the noon-hour rush makes it easier to just accept the customers' cash and make change without ringing up the sales. The assistant manager explained that the formal policy is ignored because it is more important to serve the customers promptly to keep them from going to any of the other restaurants in the mall. Then, after two o'clock, the assistant manager adds up the cash in the drawer and rings up sufficient sales to equal the collected amount. This way, the record in the register always comes out right and there are no problems to explain when the manager arrives at four o'clock to handle the dinner traffic.

Muñoz sees the advantages in this shortcut but wonders whether something is wrong with it. She also wonders what will happen if the manager comes in early some day and finds out that she isn't following the formal policy.

able asset. These assets are called notes receivable and are recorded in a *Notes Receivable* account.

Prepaid Insurance. Insurance contracts provide protection against losses caused by fire, thefts, accidents, or other events. Normally, an insurance policy requires the fee (called a *premium*) to be paid in advance, and the protection usually lasts for a year or even as much as three years. As a result, the unused portion of the coverage may be an asset for a substantial time after the premium is paid.

When an insurance premium is paid in advance, the cost is typically recorded in an asset account called *Prepaid Insurance.* When financial statements are prepared later, the expired portion of the insurance cost is recorded and reported as an expense on the income statement. The total in the Prepaid Insurance account is reduced by the same amount and the remainder of the premium is reported on the balance sheet as an asset.

Office Supplies. All companies use computer diskettes, printer ribbons and cartridges, stationery, paper, pens, and other office supplies. These supplies are assets until they are used. When they are consumed, their cost becomes an expense. Increases and decreases in the cost of the assets are recorded in an *Office Supplies* account.

Store Supplies. Many stores keep plastic and paper bags, gift boxes, cartons, and similar items on hand to use in wrapping purchases for their customers. Increases and decreases in the cost of the assets are recorded in a *Store Supplies* account.

Other Prepaid Expenses. When payments are made for assets that are not used until later, the assets are often called **prepaid expenses.** Then, as the economic benefits of the assets are used up, the cost of the assets becomes an expense. As a practical matter, an asset's cost can be initially recorded as an expense if its benefits will be consumed before the next set of financial statements are prepared. If the asset's benefits will not be used up before the end of the current reporting period, the prepayments are recorded in asset accounts. Prepaid expenses include prepaid insurance and prepaid rent. Other examples include legal fees and accounting fees paid in advance of receiving the services. (In a sense, office and store supplies are also prepaid expenses.) To provide useful information, each prepaid expense is typically accounted for in a separate asset account.

Equipment. Virtually all companies own computers, printers, typewriters, desks, chairs, and other equipment that they use to manage their business. The costs incurred to buy the equipment are recorded in an *Office Equipment* account. The costs of assets used in a store, such as counters, showcases, and cash registers, are recorded in a separate *Store Equipment* account.

Buildings. A building owned by a business provides space for a store, an office, a warehouse, or a factory. Because they produce future benefits, buildings are assets, and their costs are recorded in a *Buildings* account. If several buildings are owned, separate accounts may be used to record the cost incurred in buying each of them.

Land. A *Land* account is used to record increases and decreases in the cost of land owned by a business. The cost of land is separated from the cost of buildings located on the land to provide more useful information in the financial statements. Although the land and the buildings may appear to be inseparable and a single asset, the buildings wear out, or *depreciate,* and their costs become expenses. The land does not depreciate, and its cost does not become an expense. Therefore, the costs of the land and the buildings are recorded in separate accounts to simplify accounting for depreciation.

Liability Accounts

Chapter 1 explained that liabilities are present obligations to transfer assets or provide services to other entities in the future. A business that has liabilities to several different creditors needs information about each debt. Therefore, each category of liabilities is represented by a separate account. The following liability accounts are widely used.

Accounts Payable. When purchases of merchandise, supplies, equipment, or services are made by giving promises to pay, the resulting debts are called *accounts payable.* Because it is useful to know the amount owed to each creditor, accounting systems keep separate records about purchases from and the payments to each of them. We describe these individual records in Chapter 7. For now, however, we can use the simpler practice of recording all increases and decreases in payables in a single account called *Accounts Payable.*

Notes Payable. When an entity signs a promissory note, the resulting liability is appropriately called a note payable. Depending on how soon the liability must be repaid, its amount is recorded in a *Short-Term Notes Payable* account or a *Long-Term Notes Payable* account.

Unearned Revenues. As you learned in Chapter 1, the *revenue recognition principle* allows accountants to report revenues on the income statement only after they are earned. This principle creates the need for a careful approach to recording transactions in which customers pay in advance for products or services. Because the cash from these transactions is received before the revenues are earned, the seller considers them to be **unearned revenues.** (Unearned revenues are prepaid expenses for the buyer.) An unearned revenue is a liability that is satisfied by delivering the product or service in the future. Examples of unearned revenues are subscriptions collected in advance by a magazine publisher, rent collected in advance by a building owner, and professional or other service fees collected in advance.

When the cash is received in advance, the seller records the amount in an appropriately named liability account, such as *Unearned Subscriptions, Unearned Rent,* or *Unearned Professional Fees.* When the products or services are delivered, the earned revenues are transferred to revenue accounts, such as *Subscription Fees Earned, Rent Earned,* or *Professional Fees Earned.*

Other Short-Term Liabilities. Other short-term liabilities include wages payable to employees, taxes payable to government agencies, and interest payable to banks. For complete information, the amount of each of these other debts is recorded in a separate liability account.

Owner's Equity, Withdrawals, Revenue, and Expense Accounts

In Chapter 1, we described four types of transactions that affected the owner's equity in a proprietorship. They are (1) investments by the owner, (2) withdrawals of cash or other assets by the owner, (3) revenues, and (4) expenses. Recall that in Chapter 1 we entered all equity transactions in a single column under the owner's name. We used this simplified procedure to help you understand how transactions affect the accounting equation. However, this simplicity actually created more difficulty later when we needed to prepare an income statement and the statement of changes in owner's equity. Specifically, we had to analyze the items in the single column to see which ones belonged on which statement. In fact, this analysis is not necessary if we use separate accounts for the owner's capital, the owner's withdrawals, each revenue, and each expense. This system allows us to record the effects of each kind of change in owner's equity in its own account. Then, the information in these accounts can be taken directly to the financial statements without further analysis. The following paragraphs describe these equity accounts.

Capital Account. When a person invests in a proprietorship, the invested amount is recorded in an account identified by the owner's name and the word *Capital.* For example, an account called *Terry Dow, Capital* can be used to record Dow's original investment in Clear Copy Co. In addition to the original investment, the owner's capital account is used to record increases in owner's equity from later investments.

Withdrawals Account. When a business earns income, the owner's equity increases. The owner may choose to leave this equity intact or may withdraw assets from the business as needed. Whenever the owner withdraws assets, perhaps to pay personal living expenses, the company's assets and owner's equity are reduced.

In many situations, owners of unincorporated businesses plan to withdraw regular weekly or monthly amounts of cash. The owners may even think of these withdrawals as salaries. However, the owners of unincorporated businesses cannot receive salaries because they are not legally separate from their companies. As a result, they cannot enter into salary (or any other) contracts with themselves. Therefore, withdrawals are neither income to the owners nor expenses of the businesses. They are simply the opposite of investments by the owners.

To record the owner's withdrawals, most accounting systems use an account that has the name of the owner and the word *Withdrawals.* For example, an account called *Terry Dow, Withdrawals* would be used to record Dow's withdrawals from Clear Copy Co. The owner's withdrawals account also may be called the owner's personal account or drawing account.

Revenue and Expense Accounts. To help them understand more about a company, decision makers need information about the amounts of revenue earned and expenses incurred during the reporting period. A business uses a variety of revenue and expense accounts to provide this information on its income statement. As you might expect, various companies have different kinds of revenues and expenses. As a result, we cannot list all the revenue and expense accounts that any particular company might use. Examples of possible revenue accounts are *Sales, Commissions Earned, Professional Fees Earned, Rent Earned,* and *Interest Earned.* Examples of expense accounts are *Advertis-*

ing Expense, Store Supplies Expense, Office Salaries Expense, Office Supplies Expense, Rent Expense, Utilities Expense, and *Insurance Expense.*

You can get an idea of the variety of accounts that a company might use by looking at the list of accounts at the back of this text. This list contains the names of all the accounts you need to solve the exercises and problems in this book.[1]

The Ledger and the Chart of Accounts

Accounts may take on different physical forms, depending on the system. In computerized systems, accounts are stored in files on floppy or hard disks. In manual systems, each account is a separate page in a loose-leaf book or a separate card in a tray of cards. Regardless of their physical form, the collection of all accounts is called the **ledger.** If the accounts are in files on a hard disk, those files are the ledger. If the contents of the files are printed, the hard copy is also called the ledger. If the accounts are pages in a loose-leaf book, the book is the ledger. If the accounts are cards in a file, the file is the ledger. In other words, a ledger is simply a group of accounts.

A company's size affects the number of accounts it uses in its accounting system. A small company may get by with as few as 20 or 30 accounts, while a large company may use several thousand. The **chart of accounts** is a list of all accounts used by a company. The chart also includes the identification number assigned to each account. Companies use systematic methods to assign account identification numbers to help bookkeepers and accountants use the system efficiently. A small business might use this numbering system for its accounts:

101–199 Asset accounts
201–299 Liability accounts
301–399 Owner's equity accounts
401–499 Revenue accounts
501–699 Operating expense accounts

Such a system would not necessarily use all of the accounts between numbers 101 and 699. These numbers create a three-digit code that conveys information to the company's accountants and bookkeepers. For example, the first digit of the code numbers assigned to the asset accounts is a 1, while the first digit of the code numbers assigned to the liability accounts is a 2, and so on. In each case, the first digit of an account's number reveals whether the account appears on the balance sheet or the income statement. The second and third digits may also relate to the accounts' categories. We describe account numbering systems more completely in the next chapter.

Using T-Accounts

In its simplest form, an account looks like the letter **T**:

(Name)	
(Left side)	(Right side)

Because of its shape, this simple form is called a **T-account.** Notice that the **T** format gives the account a left side, a right side, and a convenient place for its name.

[1] Remember that different companies may use different account titles than the titles in the list. For example, a company might use Interest Revenue instead of Interest Earned or Rental Expense instead of Rent Expense. All that is required is that an account title describe the item it represents.

The shape of a T-account provides one side for recording increases in the item while the decreases are recorded on the other side. For example, the following T-account represents Clear Copy's cash account after the transactions in Chapter 1:

Cash

Investment by owner	30,000	Purchase of store supplies	2,500
Copy services revenue earned	2,200	Purchase of copy equipment	20,000
Collection of account receivable	1,700	Payment of rent	1,000
		Payment of salary	700
		Payment of account payable	900
		Withdrawal by owner	1,100

Calculating the Balance of an Account

The **account balance** of any account is the difference between its increases and decreases. Thus, for example, the balance of an asset account is the cost of that asset on the date the balance is calculated. The balance of a liability account is the amount owed on the date of the balance. Putting the increases on one side of the account and the decreases on the other makes it easy to find an account's balance. To determine the balance, simply find the total increases shown on one side (including the beginning balance), find the total decreases shown on the other side, and then subtract the sum of the decreases from the sum of the increases.

For example, the total increases in Clear Copy's Cash account were $33,900, the total decreases were $25,500, and the account balance is $8,400. This T-account shows how the $8,400 balance is calculated:

Cash

Investment by owner	30,000	Purchase of store supplies	2,500
Copy services revenue earned	2,200	Purchase of copy equipment	20,000
Collection of account receivable	1,700	Payment of rent	1,000
		Payment of salary	700
		Payment of account payable	900
		Withdrawal by owner	400
Total increases	33,900	Total decreases	25,500
Less decreases	−25,500		
Balance	8,400		

Debits and Credits

In accounting terms, the left side of a T-account is called the **debit** side, often abbreviated "Dr." The right side is called the **credit** side, abbreviated "Cr."[2] When amounts are entered on the left side of an account, they are called *debits,* and the account is said to be *debited.* When amounts are entered on the right side, they are called *credits,* and the account is said to be *credited.* The difference between the total debits and the total credits in an account is the account balance. The balance may be either a debit balance or a credit balance. It is a debit balance when the sum of the debits exceeds the sum of the credits. It is a credit balance when the sum of the credits exceeds the sum of the debits.

From looking at the Cash account, you might think that the terms *debit* and *credit* mean *increase* and *decrease.* However, a debit can be either an increase or decrease, depending on the type of account. And, a credit is the opposite.

[2] These abbreviations are remnants of 18th-century English bookkeeping practices that used the terms *Debitor* and *Creditor* instead of *debit* and *credit.* These abbreviations use the first and last letters from the words, just as we still do for *Saint* (St.) and *Doctor* (Dr.).

That is, when a debit is an increase in an account, a credit is a decrease in that account. But, if a debit is a decrease in a particular account, then a credit is an increase.

When we work with T-accounts, a debit simply means an entry on the left side and a credit simply means an entry on the right side. For example, notice how Terry Dow's initial investment in Clear Copy Co. is recorded in the Cash and capital accounts:

Cash			Terry Dow, Capital	
Investment 30,000				Investment 30,000

Notice that the increase in the amount of cash is recorded on the left side of the Cash account with a $30,000 debit entry while the increase in owner's equity is recorded on the right side of the capital account with a $30,000 credit entry. This method of recording the transaction is used in *double-entry accounting,* which we explain in the next section.

Using Debits and Credits in Double-Entry Accounting

LO 3 Describe how debits and credits are used to analyze transactions and record their effects in the accounts.

In **double-entry accounting,** every transaction affects and is recorded in at least two accounts. When recording each transaction, *the total amount debited must equal the total amount credited.* Because each transaction is recorded with total debits equal to total credits, the sum of the debits for all entries must equal the sum of the credits for all entries. Furthermore, the sum of the debit account balances in the ledger must equal the sum of the credit account balances. The sum of the debit balances does not equal the sum of the credit balances only if an error has occurred. Thus, an important result of double-entry accounting is that many errors are avoided by being sure that the debits and credits for each transaction are equal.

According to traditional double-entry accounting, increases in assets are recorded on the debit side of asset accounts.[3] Why are asset accounts given debit balances? In fact, there is no specific reason. The choice is simply a convention that makes it easier for accountants by having all accounting systems work the same way. Then, because asset accounts have debit balances, increases in those balances are recorded with debits and decreases are recorded with credits.

Because asset accounts have debit balances, it follows from the logic of the accounting equation (Assets = Liabilities + Owner's Equity) that liability accounts and owner's equity accounts must have credit balances. Therefore, increases in liability and owner's equity accounts are recorded with credit entries. In other words, if asset increases are recorded with debit entries, equal debits and credits for a transaction are possible only if increases in liabilities and owner's equity are recorded on the opposite credit side. Therefore, double-entry accounting systems record increases and decreases in balance sheet accounts as follows:

Assets		=	Liabilities		+	Owner's Equity	
Debited for increases	Credited for decreases		Debited for decreases	Credited for increases		Debited for decreases	Credited for increases

The practices shown in these T-accounts can be expressed as the following rules for recording transactions in a double-entry accounting system:

[3] These double-entry practices originated in 15th-century Italy and have stood the test of more than 500 years of change and progress in business.

1. Increases in assets are debited to asset accounts; therefore, decreases in assets are recorded with credit entries to asset accounts.
2. Increases in liabilities are credited to liability accounts; therefore, decreases in liabilities are recorded with debit entries to liability accounts.
3. Increases in owner's equity are credited to owner's equity accounts; therefore, decreases in owner's equity are recorded with debit entries to owner's equity accounts.

Chapter 1 taught you that owner's equity is increased by owner's investments and by revenues. You also learned that owner's equity is decreased by expenses and by withdrawals. In light of the meaning of debits and credits for owner's equity, these additional rules apply:

4. The owner's investments are credited to the owner's capital account because they increase equity.
5. The owner's withdrawals of assets are debited to the owner's withdrawals account because they decrease equity.
6. Revenues are credited to revenue accounts because they increase equity. The system should include a separate account for each type of revenue.
7. Expenses are debited to expense accounts because they decrease equity. The system should include a separate account for each type of expense.

At this early stage, you may be inclined to memorize these rules. If you do, be sure to rely on the logic that asset increases are debits and asset decreases are credits, and that liabilities and equity are the opposites of assets. Once you have these under your control, they will be second nature to you.

Examples of Debits and Credits

The following series of examples for Clear Copy Co. will help you learn these debit and credit rules. Study each transaction carefully to be sure that you understand it before you go on to the next one.

The numbers in parentheses before each transaction are used throughout the illustration so that you can identify the transaction's effects on the accounts. You should recognize the first 11 transactions because they were used in Chapter 1 to show how transactions affect the accounting equation. The five transactions (numbers 12 through 16) in this chapter show additional kinds of transactions and complete the example.

Before recording a transaction, the bookkeeper first analyzes it to determine what was increased or decreased. Then, the debit and credit rules are applied to decide how to record the increases or decreases. The bookkeeper's analysis for each of the example transactions appears next to the T-accounts. Study the analyses carefully to be sure that you understand the process.

1. On December 1, Terry Dow invested $30,000 in Clear Copy Co.

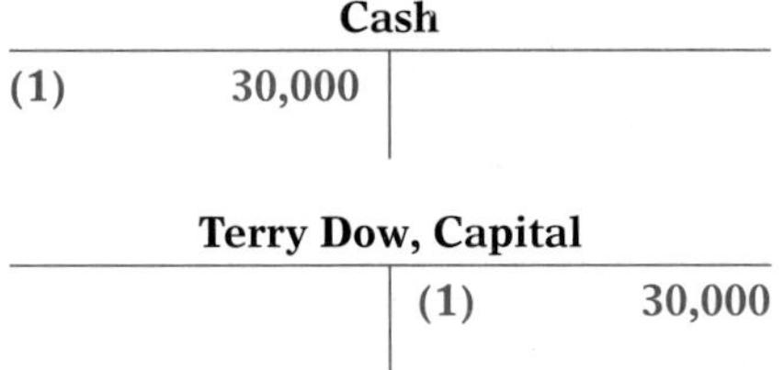

Analysis of the transaction: The transaction increased the company's cash. At the same time, it increased Dow's equity. Increases in assets are debited and increases in owner's equity are credited. Therefore, record the transaction with a debit to Cash and a credit to Terry Dow, Capital, for $30,000.

2. Purchased store supplies by paying $2,500 cash.

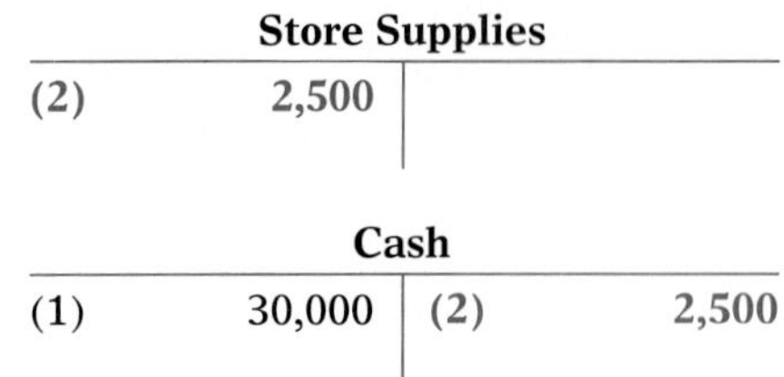

Store Supplies			
(2)	2,500		

Cash			
(1)	30,000	(2)	2,500

Analysis of the transaction: The cost of the store supplies is increased by the purchase and cash is decreased. Increases in assets are debited and decreases are credited. Therefore, record the transaction with a debit to Store Supplies and a credit to Cash for $2,500.

3. Purchased copying equipment by paying $20,000 cash.

Copy Equipment			
(3)	20,000		

Cash			
(1)	30,000	(2)	2,500
		(3)	20,000

Analysis of the transaction: The cost of the copying equipment is increased and cash is decreased. Increases in assets are debited and decreases are credited. Debit Copy Equipment and credit Cash for $20,000.

4. Purchased $1,100 of store supplies and $6,000 of copying equipment on credit from Handy Supply Company.

Store Supplies			
(2)	2,500		
(4)	1,100		

Copy Equipment			
(3)	20,000		
(4)	6,000		

Accounts Payable			
		(4)	7,100

Analysis of the transaction: This transaction increased two assets, store supplies and copy equipment. It also created a new liability. Increases in assets are debits and increases in liabilities are credits. Therefore, debit Store Supplies for $1,100, debit Copy Equipment for $6,000, and credit Accounts Payable for $7,100.

5. Provided copying services to a customer and immediately collected $2,200 cash.

Cash			
(1)	30,000	(2)	2,500
(5)	2,200	(3)	20,000

Copy Services Revenue			
		(5)	2,200

Analysis of the transaction: This revenue transaction increased both assets and owner's equity. Increases in assets are debits and increases in owner's equity are credits. Revenue accounts are increased with credits because revenues increase owner's equity. Therefore, debit Cash $2,200 to record the increase in assets. Credit Copy Services Revenue $2,200 to increase owner's equity and to accumulate information for the income statement.

6. Paid $1,000 cash for rent for December.

Rent Expense			
(6)	1,000		

Cash			
(1)	30,000	(2)	2,500
(5)	2,200	(3)	20,000
		(6)	1,000

Analysis of the transaction: The cost of renting the store during December is an expense, which decreases owner's equity. Because decreases in owner's equity are debits, expenses are recorded as debits. Therefore, debit Rent Expense $1,000 to decrease owner's equity and to accumulate information for the income statement. Also, credit Cash $1,000 to record the decrease in assets.

7. Paid $700 cash for the employee's salary for the pay period ended on December 12.

Salaries Expense

	Debit		Credit
(7)	700		

Cash

	Debit		Credit
(1)	30,000	(2)	2,500
(5)	2,200	(3)	20,000
		(6)	1,000
		(7)	700

Analysis of the transaction: The employee's salary is an expense that decreased owner's equity. Debit Salaries Expense $700 to decrease owner's equity and to accumulate information for the income statement. Also, credit Cash $700 to record the decrease in assets.

8. Completed copying work on credit and billed the customer $1,700 for the services.

Accounts Receivable

	Debit		Credit
(8)	1,700		

Copy Services Revenue

	Debit		Credit
		(5)	2,200
		(8)	1,700

Analysis of the transaction: This revenue transaction gave Clear Copy the right to collect $1,700 from the customer. Thus, it increased both assets and owner's equity. Therefore, debit Accounts Receivable $1,700 for the increase in assets and credit Copy Services Revenue $1,700 to increase owner's equity and to accumulate information for the income statement.

9. The customer paid the $1,700 account receivable created in transaction 8.

Cash

	Debit		Credit
(1)	30,000	(2)	2,500
(5)	2,200	(3)	20,000
(9)	1,700	(6)	1,000
		(7)	700

Accounts Receivable

	Debit		Credit
(8)	1,700	(9)	1,700

Analysis of the transaction: One asset was increased and another decreased. Debit Cash $1,700 to record the increase in cash, and credit Accounts Receivable $1,700 to record the decrease in the account receivable.

10. Paid Handy Supply Company $900 cash on the $7,100 owed for the supplies and equipment purchased on credit in transaction 4.

Accounts Payable

	Debit		Credit
(10)	900	(4)	7,100

Cash

	Debit		Credit
(1)	30,000	(2)	2,500
(5)	2,200	(3)	20,000
(9)	1,700	(6)	1,000
		(7)	700
		(10)	900

Analysis of the transaction: A payment to a creditor decreases an asset and a liability by the same amount. Decreases in liabilities are debited, and decreases in assets are credited. Debit Accounts Payable $900 and credit Cash $900.

11. Terry Dow withdrew $400 from Clear Copy Co. for personal living expenses.

Terry Dow, Withdrawals

	Debit		Credit
(11)	400		

Cash

	Debit		Credit
(1)	30,000	(2)	2,500
(5)	2,200	(3)	20,000
(9)	1,700	(6)	1,000
		(7)	700
		(10)	900
		(11)	400

Analysis of the transaction: This event reduced owner's equity and assets by the same amount. The Terry Dow, Withdrawals account is debited $400 to decrease owner's equity and to accumulate information for the statement of changes in owner's equity. Cash is credited $400 to record the asset reduction.

12. Signed a contract with a customer and accepted $3,000 cash in advance of providing any services.

Cash

	Debit		Credit
(1)	30,000	(2)	2,500
(5)	2,200	(3)	20,000
(9)	1,700	(6)	1,000
(12)	3,000	(7)	700
		(10)	900
		(11)	400

Unearned Copy Services Revenue

	Debit		Credit
		(12)	3,000

Analysis of the transaction: The $3,000 inflow of cash increased assets but a revenue was not earned. Instead, the transaction creates a liability that will be satisfied by doing the client's copying work in the future. Record the asset increase by debiting Cash for $3,000 and record the liability increase by crediting Unearned Copy Services Revenue for $3,000.

13. Paid $2,400 cash for the premium on a two-year insurance policy.

Prepaid Insurance

	Debit		Credit
(13)	2,400		

Cash

	Debit		Credit
(1)	30,000	(2)	2,500
(5)	2,200	(3)	20,000
(9)	1,700	(6)	1,000
(12)	3,000	(7)	700
		(10)	900
		(11)	400
		(13)	2,400

Analysis of the transaction: The advance payment of the insurance premium creates an asset (a prepaid expense) by decreasing another asset. The new asset is recorded with a $2,400 debit to Prepaid Insurance and the payment is recorded with a $2,400 credit to Cash.

14. Paid $120 cash for additional store supplies.
15. Paid $230 cash for the December utilities bill.
16. Paid $700 cash for the employee's salary for two weeks ended December 26.

Store Supplies

	Debit		Credit
(2)	2,500		
(4)	1,100		
(14)	120		

Utilities Expense

	Debit		Credit
(15)	230		

Salaries Expense

	Debit		Credit
(7)	700		
(16)	700		

Cash

	Debit		Credit
(1)	30,000	(2)	2,500
(5)	2,200	(3)	20,000
(9)	1,700	(6)	1,000
(12)	3,000	(7)	700
		(10)	900
		(11)	400
		(13)	2,400
		(14)	120
		(15)	230
		(16)	700

Analysis of the transactions: These transactions are similar because each of them decreased cash. They are different from each other because the store supplies are assets while the utilities and employee's salary are expenses. The $120 cost of the supplies should be debited to the Store Supplies asset account, while the $230 for utilities and the $700 salary should be debited to separate expense accounts. Each transaction requires its own credit to Cash.

Accounts and the Accounting Equation

Illustration 2–3 shows the accounts of Clear Copy Co. after the 16 transactions have been recorded and the balances computed. The three columns in the illustration relate the accounts to the assets, liabilities, and owner's equity elements of the accounting equation. When we take the totals of the balance in each of the three columns, we find that total assets are $40,070 ($7,950 + $0 + $2,400 + $3,720 + $26,000). The total liabilities are $9,200 ($6,200 + $3,000), and the total of the equity accounts is $30,870 ($30,000 − $400 + $3,900 − $1,000 − $1,400 − $230). Thus, the total assets of $40,070 equals the $40,070 sum of the liabilities and the owner's equity ($9,200 + $30,870). The withdrawals, revenue, and expense accounts in the box record the events that change equity; their balances are reported as events on the income statement and statement of changes in owner's equity. Their balances are eventually combined with the balance of the capital account to produce the amount of equity reported on the balance sheet. Chapter 4 describes the bookkeeping (closing) process for combining these balances.

Transactions Are First Recorded in the Journal

In the preceding pages, we used debits and credits to show how transactions affect accounts. This process of analyzing transactions and recording their effects directly in the accounts is helpful as a learning exercise. However, real accounting systems do not record transactions directly in the accounts. If the bookkeeper recorded the effects directly in the accounts, errors would be easily made and difficult to track down and correct.

LO 4 Record transactions in a General Journal, describe balance column accounts, and post entries from the journal to the ledger.

To help avoid errors, accounting systems record transactions in a **journal** before recording them in the accounts. This practice provides a complete record of each transaction in one place and links the debits and credits for each transaction. After the debits and credits for each transaction are entered in the journal, they are transferred to the ledger accounts. This two-step process

ILLUSTRATION 2–3 *The Ledger for Clear Copy Co.*

Assets = **Liabilities** + **Owner's Equity**

Assets

Cash

(1)	30,000	(2)	2,500
(5)	2,200	(3)	20,000
(9)	1,700	(6)	1,000
(12)	3,000	(7)	700
		(10)	900
		(11)	400
		(13)	2,400
		(14)	120
		(15)	230
		(16)	700
Total	36,900	Total	28,950
	−28,950		
Balance	7,950		

Accounts Receivable

(8)	1,700	(9)	1,700
	−1,700		
Balance	0		

Prepaid Insurance

(13)	2,400		
Balance	2,400		

Store Supplies

(2)	2,500		
(4)	1,100		
(14)	120		
Balance	3,720		

Copy Equipment

(3)	20,000		
(4)	6,000		
Balance	26,000		

Liabilities

Accounts Payable

(10)	900	(4)	7,100
Total	900	Total	7,100
			−900
		Balance	6,200

Unearned Copy Services Revenue

		(12)	3,000
		Balance	3,000

Owner's Equity

Terry Dow, Capital

		(1)	30,000
		Balance	30,000

Terry Dow, Withdrawals

(11)	400		
Balance	400		

Copy Services Revenue

		(5)	2,200
		(8)	1,700
		Balance	3,900

Rent Expense

(6)	1,000		
Balance	1,000		

Salaries Expense

(7)	700		
(16)	700		
Balance	1,400		

Utilities Expense

(15)	230		
Balance	230		

The accounts in this box record increases and decreases in owner's equity. Their balances are reported on the income statement or the statement of changes in owner's equity.

$40,070 = **$9,200** + **$30,870**

produces useful records for the auditor about a company's transactions. At the same time, the process helps the bookkeeper avoid errors. And, if errors are made, the process makes it easier to find and correct them.

The process of recording transactions in a journal is called *journalizing.* The process of transferring journal entry information to the ledger is called **posting.** This sequence of steps is represented in Illustration 2–4. Various source documents provide the evidence that transactions have occurred. Next, these transactions are recorded in the journal. Finally, the journal entries are posted to the ledger. This sequence causes the journal to be called the **book of original entry** while the ledger is sometimes called the **book of final entry.**

ILLUSTRATION 2–4 *The Sequence of Steps in Recording Transactions*

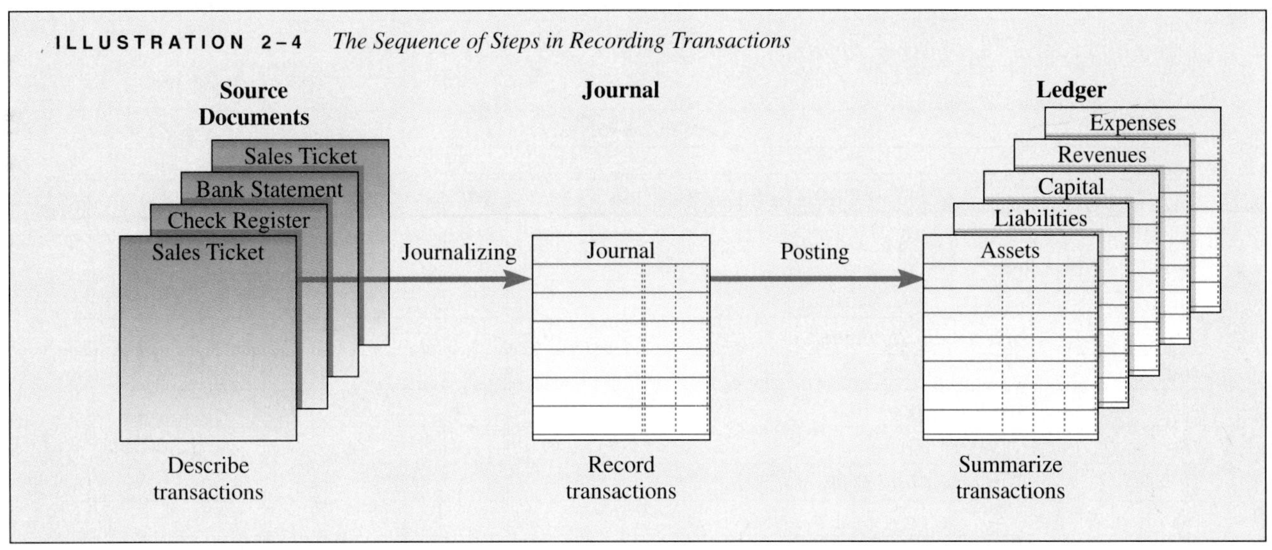

The General Journal

The most flexible type of journal is the **General Journal.** The General Journal can be used to record any kind of transaction. A journal entry records this information about each transaction:

1. The transaction's date.
2. The names of the affected accounts.
3. The amount of each debit and credit.
4. An explanation of the transaction.
5. The identifying numbers of the accounts.

Illustration 2–5 shows how the first four transactions for Clear Copy would be recorded in a typical General Journal in a manual system. The General Journals used in computerized systems may look like the manual journal page, or they may differ. Regardless of their form or appearance, journals serve the same purpose in every system.

Notice that the fourth entry in Illustration 2–5 uses three accounts to record the credit purchase of store supplies and additional copying equipment. A transaction that affects at least three accounts is recorded in the General Journal with a **compound journal entry.**

Recording Transactions in a General Journal

A bookkeeper follows routine procedures when recording entries in the General Journal. The following steps were used to record the entries in Illustration 2–5. As you read these steps, compare them to the illustration to see how they produced the journal entries:

1. Enter the year at the top of the first column of the first line on the page.
2. Enter the month on the first line of the journal entry in the first column. (Successive entries in the same month on the same page of the journal would not show the month again.)
3. Enter the day's date for the transaction in the second column on the first line of each entry.
4. Enter the names of the accounts to be debited. The account titles are taken from the chart of accounts and are aligned with the left margin of the Account Titles and Explanation column.

ILLUSTRATION 2-5 *A General Journal Showing Transactions for Clear Copy Co.*

General Journal — Page 1

Date		Account Titles and Explanation	PR	Debit	Credit
19X1 Dec.	1	Cash		30,000 00	
		Terry Dow, Capital			30,000 00
		Investment by owner.			
	2	Store Supplies		2,500 00	
		Cash			2,500 00
		Purchased law books for cash.			
	3	Copy Equipment		20,000 00	
		Cash			20,000 00
		Purchased copy equipment for cash.			
	6	Store Supplies		1,100 00	
		Copy Equipment		6,000 00	
		Accounts Payable			7,100 00
		Purchased supplies and equipment on credit.			

5. Enter the amount debited to each account in the Debit column of the journal on the same line as the account title.
6. Enter the names of the accounts to be credited. The account titles are taken from the chart of accounts and are indented far enough from the left margin of the column to distinguish them from the debited accounts (perhaps as much as an inch).
7. Enter the amount credited to each account in the Credit column of the journal on the same line as the account title.
8. Provide a brief explanation of the transaction to help an auditor or other person understand what happened. The explanation is indented about half as far as the credited account titles to avoid confusing the explanation with either a debit or credit entry. (For clarity, this book italicizes the explanations.)
9. Skip a single line between each journal entry to keep them separate.

Once the journalizing process is completed, the journal entry provides a complete and useful description of the event's effects on the organization.

In a manual system, nothing is entered in the **Posting Reference (PR) column** when a transaction is initially recorded in the journal. As a control over the posting process, the account numbers are not entered until the entries are posted to the ledger. (Because the old word for page was *folio,* and because each account used to be a separate page in a book, the Posting Reference column in the journal is occasionally called the *folio column.*)

ILLUSTRATION 2-6 *The Cash Account for Clear Copy Co. in the Balance Column Format*

		Cash			Account No. 101
Date	**Explanation**	**PR**	**Debit**	**Credit**	**Balance**
19X1 Dec. 1		G1	30,000 00		30,000 00
2		G1		2,500 00	27,500 00
3		G1		20,000 00	7,500 00
10		G1	2,200 00		9,700 00

Computerized Journals. Journals in computerized accounting systems serve the same purpose of providing a complete record of each transaction. In some systems, they even look like the manual journal page in Illustration 2–5. In addition, they may include error-checking routines that ensure that the debits in the entry equal the credits. They often provide shortcuts that allow the computer operator to enter account numbers instead of names, or to enter the account names and numbers with pull-down menus or other easy-to-use techniques.

Balance Column Accounts

T-accounts are used only in textbook illustrations and in accounting classes to show how accounts work. T-accounts are helpful because they allow you to disregard some details and concentrate on the main ideas. Actual accounting systems use **balance column accounts** like the one in Illustration 2–6.

The balance column account format is similar to a T-account because it has columns for entering each debit and credit. It differs by providing space for each entry's date. It also provides a space for explaining any highly unusual entries and identifying beginning balances. Its main difference is its third column for showing the balance of the account after each entry is posted. As a result, the amount on the last line in this column is the account's current balance. Notice that Clear Copy's Cash account in Illustration 2–6 was debited on December 1 for the $30,000 investment by Terry Dow, which gave the account a $30,000 debit balance. The account was then credited on December 2 for $2,500, and its new $27,500 balance was entered in the third column. On December 3, it was credited again, this time for $20,000, and its balance was reduced to $7,500. Finally, the Cash account was debited for $2,200 on December 10, and its balance was increased to $9,700.

When the balance column format is used, the heading of the Balance column does not indicate whether the account has a debit or credit balance. However, this omission should not create any problems because every account has a *normal balance.* The normal balance of each type of account (asset, liability, owner's equity, revenue, or expense) is the same as the debit or credit entry used to record an increase in the account. This table shows the normal balances for accounts:

Type of Account	Increases are Recorded as	Normal Balance
Asset	Debits	Debit
Liability	Credits	Credit
Owner's equity:		
Capital	Credits	Credit
Withdrawals . .	Debits	Debit
Revenue	Credits	Credit
Expense	Debits	Debit

Abnormal Balances. Some unusual events may cause an account to have an abnormal balance. For example, a credit customer might accidentally pay its balance twice, which would give the account receivable a credit balance instead of a zero balance. If an abnormal balance is created, the bookkeeper can identify it by circling the amount or by entering the balance in red or some other nonstandard color. Many computerized systems automatically provide a code beside the balance, such as *dr* or *cr* to identify the kind of balance.

Zero Balances. If an account has a zero balance, it is customary to indicate that fact by writing 0.00 or -0- in the Balance column. This practice avoids confusion between a zero balance and an accidentally omitted balance.

Posting Journal Entries

Illustration 2–4 on page 73 shows that journal entries are posted to the accounts in the ledger. To ensure that the ledger is up to date, journal entries are posted as promptly as possible, which may be daily, weekly, or as time permits. All entries need to be posted before the end of the reporting period to provide the accounts with updated balances when the financial statements are prepared.

When posting the entries to the ledger, the bookkeeper copies the debits in the journal entries into the accounts as debits, and the credits in the journal entries are copied into the accounts as credits. The diagrams in Illustration 2–7 identify and label the six steps used in a manual system to post each debit and credit from the journal entry. Use the diagram in the upper section of the illustration to see how each of these six steps for the debit is completed:

1. Find the account that was debited in the journal entry.
2. Enter the date of the journal entry in the account on the next available line for the debit.
3. Write the amount debited in the journal entry in the Debit column of the account.
4. To show where the debit came from, enter the letter *G* and the journal page number in the Posting Reference (PR) column for the account. (The letter *G* shows that the posted entry came from the General Journal. Other journals are identified by their own letters. We discuss other journals in Appendix E at the end of the book.)
5. Calculate and enter the account's new balance in the third column.
6. To show that the posting process is complete, enter the account number in the Posting Reference column on the entry's line in the journal. (If posting is interrupted, the bookkeeper can use the journal's Posting Reference column to take up the process where it was stopped.)

The six steps for posting credit entries are similar. Use the diagram in the lower section of the illustration to see how each of these six steps for the credit is completed:

1. Find the account that was credited in the journal entry.
2. Enter the date of the journal entry in the account on the next available line for the credit.

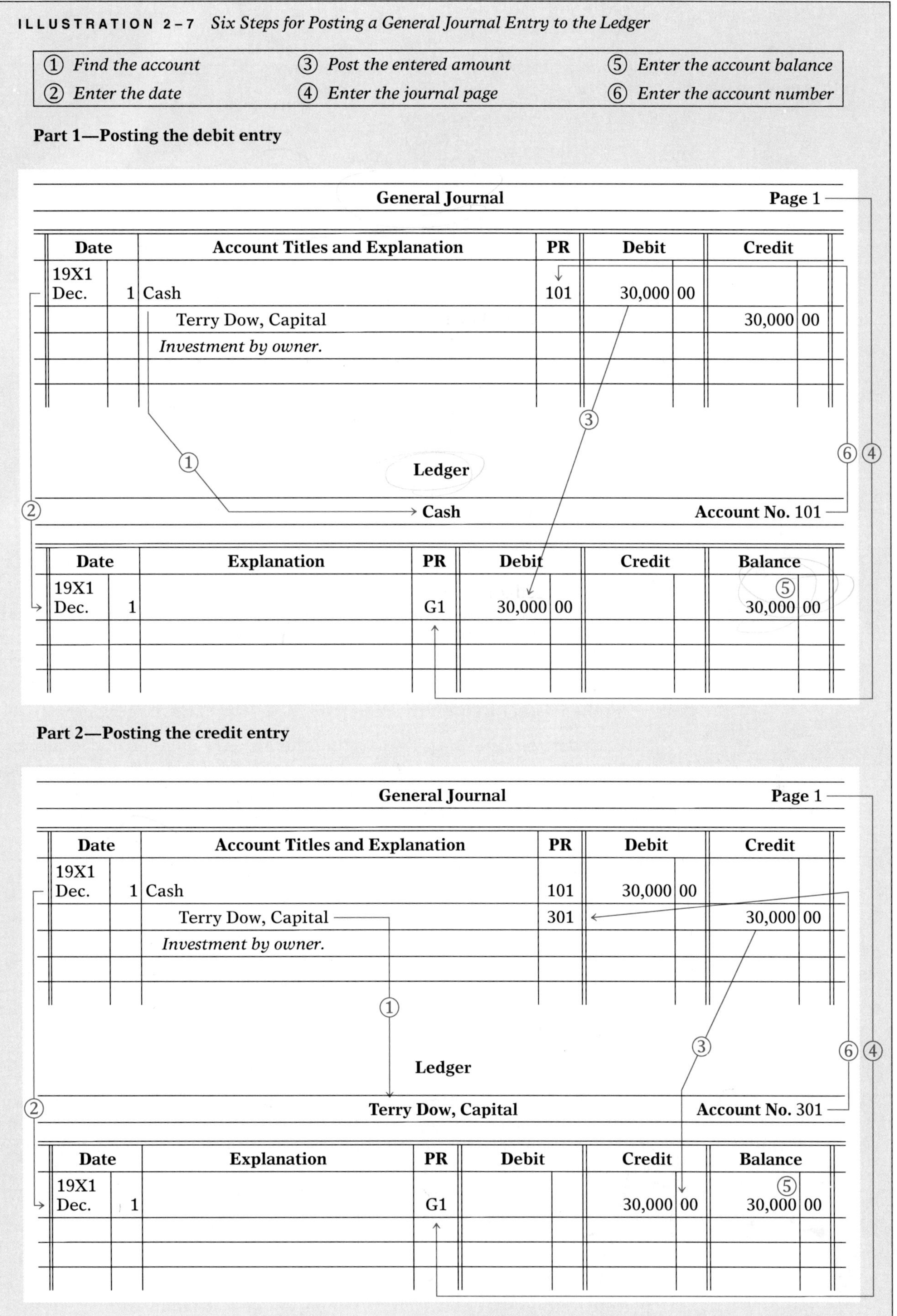

ILLUSTRATION 2–7 *Six Steps for Posting a General Journal Entry to the Ledger*

① *Find the account*	③ *Post the entered amount*	⑤ *Enter the account balance*
② *Enter the date*	④ *Enter the journal page*	⑥ *Enter the account number*

Part 1—Posting the debit entry

General Journal — **Page 1**

Date		Account Titles and Explanation	PR	Debit	Credit
19X1 Dec.	1	Cash	101	30,000 00	
		Terry Dow, Capital			30,000 00
		Investment by owner.			

Ledger

Cash — **Account No. 101**

Date		Explanation	PR	Debit	Credit	Balance
19X1 Dec.	1		G1	30,000 00		30,000 00

Part 2—Posting the credit entry

General Journal — **Page 1**

Date		Account Titles and Explanation	PR	Debit	Credit
19X1 Dec.	1	Cash	101	30,000 00	
		Terry Dow, Capital	301		30,000 00
		Investment by owner.			

Ledger

Terry Dow, Capital — **Account No. 301**

Date		Explanation	PR	Debit	Credit	Balance
19X1 Dec.	1		G1		30,000 00	30,000 00

ILLUSTRATION 2–8

CLEAR COPY CO.
Trial Balance
December 31, 19X1

	Debit	Credit
Cash	$ 7,950	
Accounts receivable	-0-	
Prepaid insurance	2,400	
Store supplies	3,720	
Copy equipment	26,000	
Accounts payable		$ 6,200
Unearned copy services revenue		3,000
Terry Dow, capital		30,000
Terry Dow, withdrawals	400	
Copy services revenue		3,900
Rent expense	1,000	
Salaries expense	1,400	
Utilities expense	230	
Totals	$43,100	$43,100

3. Write the amount credited in the journal entry in the Credit column of the account.
4. To show where the credit came from, enter the letter *G* and the journal page number in the Posting Reference (PR) column for the account.
5. Calculate and enter the account's new balance in the third column.
6. To show that the posting process is complete, enter the account number in the Posting Reference column on the entry's line in the journal.

Notice that the final step of inserting the account number in the journal's Posting Reference column creates a link between the ledger and the journal entry. This link provides a cross-reference that helps the bookkeeper and the auditor trace an amount from one record to the other.

Posting in Computerized Systems. Computerized accounting systems do not require any additional effort by the operator to post the journal entries to the ledger. The programs in the systems are designed to automatically transfer the debit and credit entries from the journal into the database. In effect, the journal entries are posted directly into the accounts in the ledger without any additional steps. Many systems include error-detection routines that test the reasonableness of the journal entry and the account balance when the new entry is recorded.

Preparing and Using the Trial Balance

LO 5 Prepare a trial balance, explain its usefulness, and calculate a company's debt ratio.

Recall that a double-entry accounting system records every transaction with equal debits and credits. As a result, the bookkeeper can tell that an error has occurred if the sum of the debit entries in the ledger does not equal the sum of the credit entries. The bookkeeper also knows that an error has occurred if the sum of the debit account balances does not equal the sum of the credit balances.

One purpose for preparing a **trial balance** is to find out if the debit and credit account balances are equal. A trial balance is a summary of the ledger that is a list of the accounts and their balances. The account balances are placed in either the debit or credit column of the trial balance. Illustration 2–8 presents the trial balance for Clear Copy Co. after the 16 entries described earlier in the chapter have been posted to the ledger.

The trial balance also serves as a helpful internal document for preparing the financial statements. The task of preparing the statements is simplified if the accountant can take the account balances from the trial balance instead of looking them up in the ledger. (The statement preparation process is described in more detail in Chapter 3.)

The bookkeeper uses these five steps to prepare a trial balance:

1. Find the balance of each account in the ledger.
2. List each account and place its balance beside it. Debit balances are entered in the Debit column and credit balances are entered in the Credit column. (If an account has a zero balance, it may be included in the trial balance with a zero in the column for its normal balance.)
3. Compute the total of the debit balances.
4. Compute the total of the credit balances.
5. Verify that the sum of the debit balances equals the sum of the credit balances.

The trial balance for Clear Copy Co. in Illustration 2–8 is presented in a typical format. Notice that the total of the debit balances does equal the total of the credit balances. If the two totals are not equal, we would know that at least one error occurred. However, the fact that the two totals are equal does not prove that all errors were avoided.

The Information Provided by a Trial Balance

When a trial balance does not balance (that is, the columns are not equal), we know that at least one error has occurred. The error (or errors) may have occurred during these steps in the accounting process: (1) preparing journal entries, (2) posting journal entries to the ledger, (3) calculating account balances, (4) copying account balances to the trial balance, or (5) totaling the trial balance columns.

If the trial balance does balance, the accounts are likely to be free from errors that create unequal debits and credits. However, bookkeeping accuracy is not assured if the column totals are equal because some errors do not create unequal debits and credits. For example, the bookkeeper may debit a correct amount to the wrong account in preparing the journal entry or in posting a journal entry to the ledger. This error would cause two accounts to have incorrect balances but the trial balance would not be out of balance. Another error would debit and credit the same incorrect amount for a transaction to the correct accounts. This error would give those two accounts incorrect balances but would not create unequal debits and credits. As a result, the fact that the trial balance column totals are equal does not prove that all journal entries have been recorded and posted correctly. However, equal totals do suggest that several types of errors probably have not occurred.

Searching for and Correcting Errors

If the trial balance does not balance, at least one error has occurred. The error (or errors) need to be found and corrected before going on to prepare the financial statements. The search for the error is more efficient if the bookkeeper checks the journalizing, posting, and trial balance preparation steps in reverse order.

First, the bookkeeper should verify that the trial balance columns were correctly added, in the hope that the error was simple. Second, if that step does not find the error, the bookkeeper should verify that account balances were accurately copied from the ledger. Third, the bookkeeper should check to see if a debit or credit balance was mistakenly listed in the trial balance as a credit or debit. (A clue that this kind of error occurred is provided by the fact that the difference between the total debits and total credits in the trial balance would equal twice the amount of the incorrectly listed account balance.)

If the error remains undiscovered, the bookkeeper's fourth step is to recalculate each account balance. Then, if the error is not found, it is necessary to verify that each journal entry was properly posted to the accounts. Finally, the only remaining (and least likely) source of the error would be an original journal entry that did not have equal debits and credits.

One frequent error is called a *transposition.* This error occurs when two digits are switched or transposed within a number. For example, a $691 debit in a journal entry may be posted to the ledger as $619. We can get an idea that a transposition has occurred if the difference between the two trial balance columns is evenly divisible by nine. For example, suppose that a posting error places a $619 debit in an account instead of the journal's correct amount of $691. As a result, the total credits in the trial balance would be larger than the total debits by $72 ($691 − $619). This number is evenly divisible by 9 ($72/9 = 8). Furthermore, the quotient (8) equals the difference between the two transposed numbers. The number of digits in the quotient also signals the location of the transposition. In this example, the fact that the quotient (8) has only one digit tells us that the transposition occurred in the first digit of the transposed numbers, starting from the right.[4]

Correcting Errors

If errors are discovered in either the journal or the ledger, they need to be corrected to ensure that the financial statements provide useful information. The approach to correcting the records depends on the nature of the errors and when they are discovered.

If an error in a journal entry is discovered before the error is posted, it can be corrected in a manual system by drawing a single line through the incorrect information. Then, the correct information can be written above it to create a record of the change for the auditor. (Most computerized systems allow the operator to simply replace the incorrect information.) If a correct amount in the journal was posted incorrectly in the ledger, the bookkeeper can correct it the same way.

If an error in a journal entry is not discovered before it is posted, the correction may have to be done differently. For example, suppose that a journal entry incorrectly debited (or credited) the wrong account. If the journal entry has already been posted to that incorrect account, the bookkeeper generally does not strike through both erroneous entries in the journal and ledger. Instead, the usual practice is to correct the error in the original journal entry by creating another journal entry. This *correcting entry* removes the amount from the wrong account and moves it to the right account. For example, suppose that the bookkeeper recorded a purchase of office supplies with this incorrect debit in the journal entry to the Office Equipment account and then posted it to the accounts in the ledger:

Oct.	14	Office Equipment	1,600.00	
		Cash		1,600.00
		To record the purchase of office supplies.		

[4] If the transposition error had posted $961 instead of the correct $691, the difference would have been $270, and the quotient would have been $30 ($270/9). The fact that the quotient has two digits would tell us to carefully examine the second digits from the right for a transposition of two numbers with a difference of 3.

As a result of posting this incorrect entry, the Office Supplies account balance is too small (understated) by $1,600 and the Office Equipment account balance is too large (overstated) by the same amount. Three days later, the error is discovered and the following entry is made to correct both account balances:

Oct.	17	Office Supplies	1,600.00	
		Office Equipment		1,600.00
		To correct the entry of October 14 that incorrectly debited Office Equipment instead of Office Supplies.		

The credit in the correcting entry cancels the error from the first entry, and the debit correctly records the supplies. The explanation in the correcting entry allows the auditor to know exactly what happened.

Similar correcting entries may be needed in computerized accounting systems. The exact procedure depends on the particular program being used.

Other Formatting Conventions

When amounts are entered manually on ruled accounting paper in a journal, ledger, or trial balance, commas are not needed to indicate thousands and decimal points are not needed to separate dollars and cents. However, commas and decimal points do appear in financial statements and other reports.

As a matter of convenience, dollar signs are not used in journals and ledgers. However, they do appear in financial statements and other reports, including trial balances. This book follows the practice of putting a dollar sign beside the first amount in each column of numbers and the first amount appearing after a ruled line indicating that an addition or subtraction has been performed. The financial statements in Illustrations 1–8 and 1–9 on pages 37 and 39 demonstrate how dollar signs are used in this book. Different companies use various conventions for dollar signs. For example, dollar signs are used beside only the first and last numbers in the columns in the financial statements for Apple Computer, Inc., in Appendix F.

If an amount entered manually in a ledger or a journal consists of even dollars without cents, a convenient shortcut uses a dash in the cents column instead of two zeros. To simplify the illustrations, this book usually shows exact dollar amounts.

Using the Information—The Debt Ratio

With so much emphasis in this chapter on bookkeeping activities, it might be easy to temporarily overlook the fact that accounting records are created for the purpose of providing useful information in financial statements. This chapter closes by describing a ratio that users apply to assess a company's risk of failing to pay its debts when they are due.

In particular, it is useful to distinguish debt from owner's equity because they create different risks for the owner and the creditors. Therefore, both internal and external users of accounting information are assisted if the balance sheet provides facts about the nature and amounts of debts and equity.

The **debt ratio** describes the relationship between the amounts of the company's liabilities and assets. The debt ratio is calculated with this formula:

$$\text{Debt ratio} = \frac{\text{Total liabilities}}{\text{Total assets}}$$

The debt ratio provides information about the risk created for the owner and company's lenders when the company goes into debt. In particular, relatively large amounts of liabilities may make it difficult for the company to pay the interest on its debts or to repay the debts themselves. In an extreme case, the company might not be able to repay a large amount of debt, even after liquidating its assets. If so, the creditors would not be paid their full claims, and the owners would not receive any payment. (In fact, proprietors or partners might have to contribute additional assets to pay the creditors.) This higher level of risk is indicated by a higher value for the debt ratio.

On the other hand, a lower value for the debt ratio suggests that the company has potential for growth if it can borrow more money to acquire more assets and increase the company's profits.

The dividing line between low and high debt ratio values varies among industries. It also varies according to a company's age, stability, profitability, and cash flows. In addition, changing economic conditions can affect asset values or interest rates and thus cause the dividing line to change. Therefore, it is not possible to state precisely whether a specific value is too high or too low.

As an example, the data in the trial balance in Illustration 2–8 produce the following debt ratio for Clear Copy Co. at the end of 19X1:

$$\text{Debt ratio} = \frac{\$9{,}200}{\$40{,}070} = 0.230$$

This value would appear to be low compared to many companies. A more careful analysis may suggest that the company could be in a position to borrow more without creating additional risk. Other variations of the debt ratio are described in Chapter 16.

Summary of the Chapter in Terms of Learning Objectives

LO 1 Accounting systems record transactions and other events that affect a company's assets, liabilities, and equity. The other events include internal transactions that use up assets or external events that cause the company's assets or liabilities to change. Source documents describe information that is recorded with accounting entries.

LO 2 Accounts are the basic building blocks of accounting systems. In one sense, accounts are symbols of the company's assets, liabilities, owner's equity, revenues, and expenses. In another sense, accounts are special records used to store information about transactions. The ledger is the collection of accounts used by an organization. Each account is assigned an identification number based on a code that indicates what kind of account it is. Debits record increases in assets, withdrawals, and expenses. Credits record decreases in these same accounts. Credits also record increases in liabilities, the owner's capital account, and revenues, while debits record decreases in these accounts.

LO 3 To understand how a transaction affects a business, first determine what accounts were increased or decreased. Every transaction affects at least two accounts, and the sum of the debits for each transaction equals the sum of the credits. As a result, the effects of business transactions never create an imbalance in the accounting equation (Assets = Liabilities + Owner's Equity).

LO 4 Transactions are first recorded in a journal that provides a record of all their effects in one location. Then, each entry in the journal is posted to the accounts in the ledger. This process places information in the accounts that is used to produce the company's financial statements. Balance column accounts are widely used in accounting systems. These accounts include columns for debit entries, credit entries, and the balance after each entry.

LO 5 A trial balance is a list of the accounts in the ledger that shows their debit and credit balances in separate columns. The trial balance is a convenient summary of the ledger's contents. It also reveals the existence of some kinds of errors if the sum of the debit account balances does not equal the sum of the credit account balances. A company's debt ratio is the ratio between its total liabilities and total assets. Its size provides information about the risk faced by the company's owners and creditors and may indicate whether the company might be capable of increasing its income by going further into debt.

Demonstration Problem

This demonstration problem is based on the same facts as the demonstration problem at the end of Chapter 1. The following events occurred during the first month of Barbara Schmidt's new haircutting business called The Cutlery:

a. On August 1, Schmidt put $3,000 cash into a checking account in the name of The Cutlery. She also invested $15,000 of equipment that she already owned.

b. On August 2, she paid $600 cash for furniture for the shop.

c. On August 3, she paid $500 cash to rent space in a strip mall for August.

d. On August 4, she furnished the shop by installing the old equipment and some new equipment that she bought on credit for $1,200. This amount is to be repaid in three equal payments at the end of August, September, and October.

e. On August 5, The Cutlery opened for business. Receipts from cash sales in the first week and a half of business (ended August 15) were $825.

f. On August 17, Schmidt paid $125 to an assistant for working during the grand opening.

g. Cash receipts from sales during the second half of August were $930.

h. On August 31, Schmidt paid an installment on the accounts payable.

i. On August 31, she withdrew $900 cash for her personal use.

Required

1. Prepare general journal entries for the preceding transactions.
2. Open the following accounts: Cash, 101; Furniture, 161; Store Equipment, 165; Accounts Payable, 201; Barbara Schmidt, Capital, 301; Barbara Schmidt, Withdrawals, 302; Haircutting Services Revenue, 403; Wages Expense, 623; and Rent Expense, 640.
3. Post the journal entries to the ledger accounts.
4. Prepare a trial balance as of August 31.

Planning the Solution

- Analyze each transaction to identify the accounts affected by the transaction and the amount of each effect.
- Use the debit and credit rules to prepare a journal entry for each transaction.
- Post each debit and each credit in the journal entries to the appropriate ledger accounts and cross-reference each amount in the Posting Reference columns in the journal and account.
- Calculate each account balance and list the accounts with their balances on a trial balance.
- Verify that the total debits in the trial balance equal total credits.

Solution to Demonstration Problem

1. General journal entries:

Page 1

Date		Account Titles and Explanations	PR	Debit	Credit
Aug.	1	Cash	101	3,000.00	
		Store Equipment	165	15,000.00	
		Barbara Schmidt, Capital	301		18,000.00
		Owner's initial investment.			

Date		Account Titles and Explanations	PR	Debit	Credit
Aug.	2	Furniture	161	600.00	
		Cash	101		600.00
		Purchased furniture for cash.			
	3	Rent Expense	640	500.00	
		Cash	101		500.00
		Paid rent for August.			
	4	Store Equipment	165	1,200.00	
		Accounts Payable	201		1,200.00
		Purchased additional equipment on credit.			
	15	Cash	101	825.00	
		Haircutting Services Revenue	403		825.00
		Cash receipts from 10 days of operations.			
	17	Wages Expense	623	125.00	
		Cash	101		125.00
		Paid wages to assistant.			
	31	Cash	101	930.00	
		Haircutting Services Revenue	403		930.00
		Cash receipts from second half of August.			
	31	Accounts Payable	201	400.00	
		Cash	101		400.00
		Paid an installment on accounts payable.			
	31	Barbara Schmidt, Withdrawals	302	900.00	
		Cash	101		900.00
		Owner withdrew cash from the business.			

2., 3. Accounts in the ledger:

Cash — **Account No. 101**

Date		Explanation	PR	Debit	Credit	Balance
Aug.	1		G1	3,000.00		3,000.00
	2		G1		600.00	2,400.00
	3		G1		500.00	1,900.00
	15		G1	825.00		2,725.00
	17		G1		125.00	2,600.00
	31		G1	930.00		3,530.00
	31		G1		400.00	3,130.00
	31		G1		900.00	2,230.00

Furniture — **Account No. 161**

Date		Explanation	PR	Debit	Credit	Balance
Aug.	2		G1	600.00		600.00

Store Equipment — **Account No. 165**

Date		Explanation	PR	Debit	Credit	Balance
Aug.	1		G1	15,000.00		15,000.00
	4		G1	1,200.00		16,200.00

Accounts Payable — Account No. 201

Date		Explanation	PR	Debit	Credit	Balance
Aug.	4		G1		1,200.00	1,200.00
	31		G1	400.00		800.00

Barbara Schmidt, Capital — Account No. 301

Date		Explanation	PR	Debit	Credit	Balance
Aug.	1		G1		18,000.00	18,000.00

Barbara Schmidt, Withdrawals — Account No. 302

Date		Explanation	PR	Debit	Credit	Balance
Aug.	31		G1	900.00		900.00

Haircutting Services Revenue — Account No. 403

Date		Explanation	PR	Debit	Credit	Balance
Aug.	15		G1		825.00	825.00
	31		G1		930.00	1,755.00

Wages Expense — Account No. 623

Date		Explanation	PR	Debit	Credit	Balance
Aug.	17		G1	125.00		125.00

Rent Expense — Account No. 640

Date		Explanation	PR	Debit	Credit	Balance
Aug.	3		G1	500.00		500.00

4.

THE CUTLERY
Trial Balance
August 31, 19X1

	Debit	Credit
Cash	$ 2,230	
Furniture	600	
Store equipment	16,200	
Accounts payable		$ 800
Barbara Schmidt, capital		18,000
Barbara Schmidt, withdrawals	900	
Haircutting services revenue		1,755
Wages expense	125	
Rent expense	500	
Totals	$20,555	$20,555

Glossary

LO 6 Define or explain the words and phrases listed in the chapter glossary.

Accounts the basic building blocks of accounting systems used to develop a company's financial statements; symbols of the company's assets, liabilities, owner's equity, revenues, and expenses; special records used to store information about the effects of transactions. p. 59

Account balance the difference between the increases (including the beginning balance) and decreases recorded in an account. p. 65

Balance column account an account with debit and credit columns for recording entries and a third column for showing the balance of the account after each entry is posted. p. 75

Book of final entry another name for a ledger. p. 72

Book of original entry another name for a journal. p. 72

Business papers various kinds of documents and other papers that companies use when they conduct their business; sometimes called *source documents.* p. 58

Chart of accounts a list of all the accounts used by a company; includes the identification number assigned to each account. p. 64

Compound journal entry a journal entry that affects at least three accounts. p. 73

Credit an entry that decreases asset and expense accounts, or increases liability, owner's equity, and revenue accounts; recorded on the right side of a T-account. p. 65

Debit an entry that increases asset and expense accounts, or decreases liability, owner's equity, and revenue accounts; recorded on the left side of a T-account. p. 65

Debt ratio the ratio between a company's liabilities and assets; used to describe the risk associated with the company's debts. p. 81.

Double-entry accounting an accounting system that records the effects of transactions and other events in at least two accounts with equal debits and credits. p. 66

External transactions exchanges between the entity and some other person or organization. p. 58

General Journal the most flexible type of journal; can be used to record any kind of transaction. p. 73

Internal transactions a term occasionally used to describe economic events that affect an entity's accounting equation but that are not transactions between two parties. p. 58

Journal a record in which the effects of transactions are first recorded; amounts are posted from the journal to the ledger; also called the *book of original entry.* p. 71

Ledger the collection of all accounts used by a business. p. 64

Posting the process of copying journal entry information to the ledger. p. 71

Posting Reference (PR) column a column in journals and accounts used to cross-reference journal and ledger entries. p. 74

Prepaid expenses assets created by payments for economic benefits that are not used until later; as the benefits are used up, the cost of the assets becomes an expense. p. 61

Promissory note an unconditional written promise to pay a definite sum of money on demand or on a defined future date (or dates). p. 60

Source documents another name for *business papers;* these documents are the source of information recorded with accounting entries. p. 58

T-account a simple account form widely used in accounting education to illustrate how debits and credits work. p. 64

Trial balance a summary of the ledger that lists the accounts and their balances; the total debit balances should equal the total credit balances. p. 78

Unearned revenues liabilities created by advance cash payments from customers for products or services; satisfied by delivering the products or services in the future. p. 62

Objective Review

Answers to the following questions are listed at the end of this chapter. Be sure that you decide which is the one best answer to each question *before* you check the answers.

LO 1 Examples of accounting source documents include:

a. Journals and ledgers.
b. Income statements and balance sheets.
c. External transactions and internal transactions.
d. Bank statements and sales tickets.
e. All of the above.

LO 2 Which of the following answers properly classifies these commonly used accounts: (1) Prepaid Rent, (2) Unearned Fees, (3) Buildings, (4) Owner's Capital, (5) Wages Payable, (6) Owner's Withdrawals, (7) Office Supplies?

	Assets	Liabilities	Owner's Equity
a.	1, 3, 7	2, 5	4, 6
b.	1, 3, 7	2, 5, 6	4
c.	1, 3, 7	5, 6	2, 4
d.	1, 7	5, 6	2, 3, 4
e.	1, 7	2, 5	3, 4, 6

LO 3 Double-entry accounting requires that:

a. All transactions that create debits to asset accounts must create credits to liability or owner's equity accounts.
b. All transactions be recorded with equal debits and credits.
c. The total debits must equal the total credits for all recorded transactions and other events.
d. Only the effects of external transactions can be recorded.
e. Both (*b*) and (*c*) are correct.

LO 4 When The Davis Company was created, the owner invested $15,000 cash and land with a fair market value of $23,000. The company also assumed responsibility for an $18,000 note payable originally issued to finance the purchase of the land. The journal entry used to record this initial investment should consist of:

a. One debit and one credit.
b. Two debits and one credit.
c. Two debits and two credits.

d. Debits that total $38,000 and credits that total $33,000.

e. None of the above is correct.

LO 5 A trial balance has total debits of $14,000 and total credits of $17,000. Which of the following errors would create this imbalance?

a. A $1,500 debit to Wages Expense in a journal entry was incorrectly posted to the ledger as a $1,500 credit.

b. A $3,000 debit to Wages Expense in a journal entry was incorrectly posted to the ledger as a $3,000 credit.

c. A $1,500 credit to Fees Earned in a journal entry was incorrectly posted to the ledger as a $1,500 debit.

d. A $3,000 credit to Fees Earned in a journal entry was incorrectly posted to the ledger account as a $3,000 debit.

e. None of the above is correct.

LO 6 Which of the following terms describes a list of all of a company's accounts and their identifying numbers?

a. A journal.

b. A ledger.

c. A trial balance.

d. A source document.

e. A chart of accounts.

Questions for Class Discussion

1. What kinds of economic events affect a company's accounting equation?
2. What are the three fundamental steps in the accounting process?
3. Why are business papers called *source documents?*
4. What are accounts? What is a ledger?
5. What determines the quantity and types of accounts used by a company?
6. What is the difference between a note receivable and an account receivable?
7. What kinds of transactions increase owner's equity? What kinds decrease owner's equity?
8. Does debit always mean increase and credit always mean decrease?
9. Why are most accounting systems called *double-entry?*
10. If assets are valuable resources and asset accounts have debit balances, why do expense accounts have debit balances?
11. Why does the bookkeeper prepare a trial balance?
12. Should a transaction be recorded first in a journal or the ledger? Why?
13. Are debits or credits listed first in general journal entries? Are the debits or the credits indented?
14. What is a compound journal entry?
15. What kinds of transactions can be recorded in a General Journal?
16. Why are posting reference numbers entered in the journal when entries are posted to the accounts?
17. If a wrong amount was journalized and posted to the accounts, how should the error be corrected?
18. When are dollar signs used in accounting reports?

19. Review the 1992 consolidated statement of cash flows for Ben & Jerry's Homemade, Inc., in Appendix G. What was the total effect on the company's Cash account of the sales of property, plant, and equipment? Were these transactions recorded with debits or credits to the Cash account?

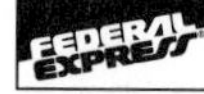

20. Review the 1993 consolidated statement of cash flows for Federal Express Corporation in Appendix G. What was the total effect on the company's Cash account of the purchases of property and equipment? Were these transactions recorded with debits or credits to the Cash account?

Exercises

Exercise 2–1
Increases, decreases, and normal balances of accounts
(LO 2, 3)

Complete the following table by (1) identifying the type of account listed on each line, (2) entering *debit* or *credit* in the blank spaces to identify the kind of entry that would increase or decrease the account balance, and (3) identifying the type of normal balance that the account would have.

Account	Type of Account	Increase	Decrease	Normal Balance
a. Accounts payable				
b. Accounts receivable				
c. B. Baxter, capital				
d. B. Baxter, withdrawals				
e. Cash				
f. Equipment				
g. Fees earned				
h. Land				
i. Postage expense				
j. Prepaid insurance				
k. Rent expense				
l. Unearned revenue				

Exercise 2–2
Entries to increase or decrease accounts
(LO 2, 3)

Identify whether a debit or credit entry would be made to record the indicated change in each of the following accounts:

a. To increase Rent Earned.
b. To increase Owner, Withdrawals.
c. To decrease Owner, Capital.
d. To decrease Cash.
e. To decrease Prepaid Insurance.
f. To decrease Unearned Fees.
g. To increase Rent Expense.
h. To increase Accounts Payable.
i. To increase Office Equipment.

Exercise 2–3
Analyzing the effects of a transaction on the accounts
(LO 3)

Franklin Consulting Company recently notified a client that it would have to pay a $32,000 fee for consulting services. Unfortunately, the client did not have enough cash to pay the entire bill. Fran Franklin, the owner of the company, agreed to accept the following items in full payment: $5,000 cash and computer equipment worth $50,000. Franklin also had to assume responsibility for a $23,000 note payable related to the equipment. Which of the following effects would be recorded by Franklin for this transaction? (Your answer may include more than one of the listed effects. Some of the effects of the transaction may not be listed.)

a. $23,000 increase in a liability account.
b. $5,000 increase in the Cash account.
c. $5,000 increase in a revenue account.
d. $32,000 increase in the F. Franklin, Capital account.
e. $32,000 increase in a revenue account.

Exercise 2–4
Recording the effects of transactions directly in T-accounts
(LO 3)

Open the following T-accounts: Cash; Accounts Receivable; Office Supplies; Office Equipment; Accounts Payable; R. J. Wainwright, Capital; Services Revenue; and Utilities Expense. Next, record these transactions of the Wainwright Company by recording the debit and credit entries directly in the T-accounts. Use the letters beside each transaction to identify the entries. Finally, determine the balance of each account.

a. R. J. Wainwright invested $8,500 cash in the business.
b. Purchased $250 of office supplies for cash.
c. Purchased $4,700 of office equipment on credit.
d. Received $1,000 cash as fees for services provided to a customer.
e. Paid for the office equipment purchased in transaction *c.*
f. Billed a customer $1,800 as fees for services.
g. Paid the monthly utility bills with $350 cash.
h. Collected $750 of the account receivable created in transaction *f.*

Exercise 2–5
Preparing a trial balance
(LO 5)

After recording the transactions of Exercise 2–4 in T-accounts and calculating the balance of each account, prepare the trial balance for the ledger. Use November 30, 19X1, as the date.

Exercise 2–6
Effects of posting errors on the trial balance
(LO 5)

Complete the following table by filling in the blanks. For each of the listed posting errors, enter in column (1) the amount of the difference that the error would create between the two trial balance columns (show a zero if the columns would balance). If there would be a difference between the two columns, identify in column (2) the trial balance column that would be larger. The answer for the first error is provided as an example.

Description	(1) Difference between debit and credit columns	(2) Column with the larger total
a. A $1,600 debit to Utilities Expense was posted as a $1,060 debit.	$540	credit
b. A $28,000 debit to Automobiles was posted as a debit to Accounts Payable.		
c. A $3,300 credit to Fees Earned was posted as a $330 credit.		
d. A $960 debit to Office Supplies was not posted at all.		
e. A $1,500 debit to Prepaid Rent was posted as a debit to Rent Expense.		
f. A $2,700 credit to Cash was posted twice as two credits to the Cash account.		
g. A $6,600 debit to the owner's withdrawals account was debited to the owner's capital account.		

Exercise 2–7
Analyzing a trial balance error
(LO 5)

As the bookkeeper for a company, you are disappointed to learn that the column totals in your new trial balance are not equal. After going through a careful analysis, you have discovered only one error. Specifically, the balance of the Office Equipment account has a debit balance of $15,600 on the trial balance. However, you have figured out that a correctly recorded credit purchase of a computer for $3,500 was posted from the journal to the ledger with a $3,500 debit to Office Equipment and another $3,500 debit to Accounts Payable. Answer each of the following questions and present the dollar amount of any misstatement.

a. Is the balance of the Office Equipment account overstated, understated, or correctly stated in the trial balance?
b. Is the balance of the Accounts Payable account overstated, understated, or correctly stated in the trial balance?
c. Is the debit column total of the trial balance overstated, understated, or correctly stated?
d. Is the credit column total of the trial balance overstated, understated, or correctly stated?
e. If the debit column total of the trial balance was $240,000 before correcting the error, what is the total of the credit column?

Exercise 2–8
Preparing a corrected trial balance
(LO 5)

On January 1, Rob Gregory created a new business called RG Public Relations Consulting. Near the end of the year, he hired a new bookkeeper without making a careful reference check. As a result, a number of mistakes have been made in preparing the following trial balance:

RG PUBLIC RELATIONS CONSULTING
Trial Balance
December 31

	Debit	Credit
Cash	$ 11,000	
Accounts receivable		$15,800
Office supplies	5,300	
Office equipment	41,000	
Accounts payable		18,930
R. Gregory, capital	51,490	
R. Gregory, withdrawals	18,000	
Services revenue		45,600
Wages expense		12,000
Rent expense		9,600
Advertising expense		2,500
Totals	$126,790	$104,680

Gregory's analysis of the situation has uncovered these errors:

a. The sum of the debits in the Cash account is $74,350 and the sum of the credits is $61,080.

b. A $550 payment from a credit customer was posted to cash but was not posted to Accounts Receivable.

c. A credit purchase of office supplies for $800 was completely unrecorded.

d. A transposition error occurred in copying the balance of the Services Revenue account to the trial balance. The correct amount was $46,500.

Other errors were made in placing account balances in the trial balance columns and in taking the totals of the columns. Use all this information to prepare a correct trial balance.

Exercise 2–9
Analyzing account entries and balances
(LO 2, 3)

Use the information in each of the following situations to calculate the unknown amount:

1. During June, Sunnyside Company had $65,000 of cash receipts and $67,500 of cash disbursements. The June 30 Cash balance was $11,200. Determine how much cash the company had on hand at the close of business on May 31.
2. On May 31, Sunnyside Company had a $65,000 balance in Accounts Receivable. During June, the company collected $59,300 from its credit customers. The June 30 balance in Accounts Receivable was $67,000. Determine the amount of sales on account that occurred in June.
3. Sunnyside Company had $98,000 of accounts payable on May 31 and $91,000 on June 30. Total purchases on account during June were $180,000. Determine how much cash was paid on accounts payable during June.

Exercise 2–10
Analyzing transactions
(LO 2, 3)

Seven transactions were posted to these T-accounts. Provide a short description of each transaction. Include the amounts in your descriptions.

Cash

	Debit		Credit
(*a*)	3,500	(*b*)	1,800
(*e*)	1,250	(*c*)	300
		(*f*)	1,200
		(*g*)	350

Truck

	Debit		Credit
(*a*)	5,500		

Accounts Payable

	Debit		Credit
(*f*)	1,200	(*d*)	4,800

Plumbing Supplies

	Debit		Credit
(*c*)	300		

Plumbing Equipment

	Debit		Credit
(*a*)	2,800		
(*d*)	4,700		

Plumbing Fees Earned

	Debit		Credit
		(*e*)	1,800

Prepaid Insurance

	Debit		Credit
(*b*)	1,800		

Vinnie Doran, Capital

	Debit		Credit
		(*a*)	11,800

Gas and Oil Expense

	Debit		Credit
(*g*)	350		

Exercise 2–11
General journal entries
(LO 4)

Use the information in the T-accounts in Exercise 2–10 to prepare general journal entries for the seven transactions. (Omit the account numbers.)

Exercise 2–12
General journal entries
(LO 4)

Prepare general journal entries to record the following transactions of Wayne's Water-Taxi Service.

May	1	Wayne Oldham invested $15,000 cash and a boat with a $65,000 fair value in a new company that will operate a water-taxi service in the harbor.
	1	Rented space in a marina by paying $6,000 for the next three months in advance.
	2	Purchased a two-way radio for the boat for $2,800 cash.
	15	Collected $5,300 in fares over the preceding two weeks.
	31	Paid $1,750 cash for gas and oil used by the boat during May.

Exercise 2–13
T-accounts and the trial balance
(LO 3, 5)

Use the information provided in Exercise 2–12 to prepare a May 31 trial balance for Wayne's Water-Taxi Service. First, open these T-accounts: Cash; Prepaid Rent; Boat; Equipment; Wayne Oldham, Capital; Fares Earned; and Gas and Oil Expense. Then post the general journal entries to the T-accounts. Finally, prepare the trial balance.

Exercise 2–14
Analyzing and journalizing revenue transactions
(LO 4)

Examine the following transactions and identify those that created revenues for the business. Prepare general journal entries to record those transactions and explain why the other transactions did not create revenues.

a. Received $25,500 cash from Dr. J. Runner, the owner of the medical practice.
b. Provided $900 of medical services to a patient on credit.
c. Received $1,050 cash for medical services provided to patient.
d. Received $6,100 from a patient in payment for medical services to be provided next year.
e. Received $3,000 from a patient in partial payment of an account receivable.
f. Borrowed $100,000 from the bank by signing a promissory note.

Exercise 2–15
Analyzing and journalizing expense transactions
(LO 4)

Examine the following transactions and identify those that created expenses for the business. Prepare general journal entries to record those transactions and explain why the other transactions did not create expenses.

a. Paid $9,400 cash for medical supplies purchased 30 days previously.
b. Paid the $750 salary of the doctor's assistant.
c. Paid $30,000 cash for medical equipment.
d. Paid utility bill with $620 cash.
e. Paid $700 to the owner of the medical practice as a withdrawal.

Exercise 2–16
Calculating the debt ratio
(LO 5)

Calculate the debt ratio for each of the following cases:

Case	Assets	Liabilities	Owner's Equity
1	$290,000	$110,000	$180,000
2	61,000	51,000	10,000
3	205,000	101,000	104,000
4	177,000	22,000	155,000
5	124,000	92,000	32,000
6	180,000	60,000	120,000

Problems

Problem 2–1
Recording transactions in T-accounts; preparing a trial balance
(LO 2, 3, 5)

Bobbie Benson opened a consulting firm and completed these transactions during June:

a. Invested $40,000 cash and office equipment with a $15,000 fair value in a business called Benson Consulting.
b. Purchased land and a small office building. The land was worth $15,000 and the building was worth $85,000. The purchase price was paid with $20,000 cash and a long-term note payable for $80,000.
c. Purchased $1,200 of office supplies on credit.
d. Bobbie Benson transferred title of an automobile to the business. The car was worth $9,000.
e. Purchased $3,000 of additional office equipment on credit.
f. Paid $750 salary to an assistant.
g. Provided services to a client and collected $3,000 cash.
h. Paid $400 for the month's utilities.
i. Paid account payable created in transaction *c.*
j. Purchased $10,000 of new office equipment by paying $9,300 cash and trading in old equipment with a recorded cost of $700.
k. Completed $2,600 of services for a client. This amount is to be paid within 30 days.
l. Paid $750 salary to an assistant.
m. Received $1,900 payment on the receivable created in transaction *k.*
n. The owner withdrew $2,000 cash from the business.

Required

1. Open the following T-accounts: Cash; Accounts Receivable; Office Supplies; Automobiles; Office Equipment; Building; Land; Accounts Payable; Long-Term Notes Payable; Bobbie Benson, Capital; Bobbie Benson, Withdrawals; Fees Earned; Salaries Expense; and Utilities Expense.
2. Record the effects of the listed transactions by entering debits and credits directly in the T-accounts. Use the transaction letters to identify each debit and credit entry.
3. Determine the balance of each account and prepare a trial balance as of June 30.

Problem 2–2
Recording transactions in T-accounts; preparing a trial balance
(LO 2, 3, 5)

At the beginning of March, Avery Wilson created a custom computer programming company called Softouch. The following transactions occurred during the month:

a. Created the business by investing $35,000 cash, office equipment with a value of $2,000, and $15,000 of computer equipment.
b. Purchased land for an office. The land was worth $18,000, which was paid with $1,800 cash and a long-term note payable for $16,200.
c. Purchased a portable building with $25,000 cash and moved it onto the land.
d. Paid $2,000 cash for the premiums on two one-year insurance policies.
e. Provided services to a client and collected $1,900 cash.
f. Purchased additional computer equipment for $7,500. Paid $3,500 cash and signed a long-term note payable for the $4,000 balance.
g. Completed $4,000 of services for a client. This amount is to be paid within 30 days.
h. Purchased $750 of additional office equipment on credit.
i. Completed another software job for $6,000 on credit.
j. Received a bill for rent on a computer that was used on the completed job. The $400 rent must be paid within 30 days.

k. Collected $2,400 from the client described in transaction *g*.
l. Paid $500 wages to an assistant.
m. Paid the account payable created in transaction *h*.
n. Paid $225 cash for some repairs to an item of computer equipment.
o. The owner wrote a $3,200 check on the company's bank account to pay some personal expenses.
p. Paid $500 wages to an assistant.
q. Paid $1,000 cash to advertise in the local newspaper.

Required

1. Open the following T-accounts: Cash; Accounts Receivable; Prepaid Insurance; Office Equipment; Computer Equipment; Building; Land; Accounts Payable; Long-Term Notes Payable; Avery Wilson, Capital; Avery Wilson, Withdrawals; Fees Earned; Wages Expense; Computer Rental Expense; Advertising Expense; and Repairs Expense.
2. Record the transactions by entering debits and credits directly in the accounts. Use the transaction letters to identify each debit and credit. Prepare a trial balance as of March 31.
3. Calculate the company's debt ratio. Use $78,675 as the ending total assets.

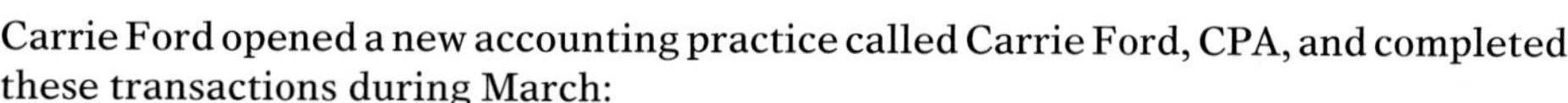

Problem 2–3
Preparing and posting general journal entries; preparing a trial balance
(LO 4, 5)

Carrie Ford opened a new accounting practice called Carrie Ford, CPA, and completed these transactions during March:

Mar.	1	Invested $25,000 in cash and office equipment that had a fair value of $6,000.
	1	Prepaid $1,800 cash for three months' rent for an office.
	3	Made credit purchases of office equipment for $3,000 and office supplies for $600.
	5	Completed work for a client and immediately received $500 cash.
	9	Completed a $2,000 project for a client, who will pay within 30 days.
	11	Paid the account payable created on March 3.
	15	Paid $1,500 cash as the annual premium on an insurance policy.
	20	Received $1,600 as partial payment for the work completed on March 9.
	23	Completed work for another client for $660 on credit.
	27	Carrie Ford withdrew $1,800 cash from the business to pay some personal expenses.
	30	Purchased $200 of additional office supplies on credit.
	31	Paid $175 for the month's utility bill.

Required

1. Prepare general journal entries to record the transactions.
2. Open the following accounts (use the balance column format): Cash (101); Accounts Receivable (106); Office Supplies (124); Prepaid Insurance (128); Prepaid Rent (131); Office Equipment (163); Accounts Payable (201); Carrie Ford, Capital (301); Carrie Ford, Withdrawals (302); Accounting Fees Earned (401); and Utilities Expense (690).
3. Post the entries to the accounts and enter the balance after each posting.
4. Prepare a trial balance as of the end of the month.

Problem 2–4
Interpreting journals, posting, and correcting a trial balance
(LO 4, 5)

Ada Evans started a business called The Pine Bough on August 1 and completed several transactions during the month. Her accounting and bookkeeping skills are not well polished, and she needs some help gathering information at the end of the month.

Part 1. She recorded the following journal entries during the month. Although the entries are correct, Evans forgot to provide explanations of the events. Analyze each entry and present a reasonable explanation of what happened.

Date		Account	Debit	Credit
Aug.	1	Cash	15,000.00	
		Automobiles	11,000.00	
		Ada Evans, Capital		26,000.00
	3	Store Supplies	323.00	
		Cash		323.00
	7	Cash	500.00	
		Accounts Receivable	2,500.00	
		Fees Earned		3,000.00
	8	Store Equipment	3,200.00	
		Accounts Payable		3,200.00
	15	Cash	400.00	
		Fees Earned		400.00
	17	Prepaid Insurance	625.00	
		Cash		625.00
	23	Cash	2,500.00	
		Accounts Receivable		2,500.00
	25	Accounts Payable	3,200.00	
		Cash		3,200.00
	27	Office Equipment	4,700.00	
		Ada Evans, Capital		4,700.00
	28	Ada Evans, Withdrawals	1,230.00	
		Cash		1,230.00
	29	Store Supplies	727.00	
		Accounts Payable		727.00
	31	Salaries Expense	1,570.00	
		Cash		1,570.00

Part 2. Evans remembers something about trial balances, so she knows that the following one has at least one error. To help her find the mistakes, you need to repeat the posting process for the journal entries from Part 1. Use these balance column accounts in your ledger: Cash (101); Accounts Receivable (106); Store Supplies (125); Prepaid Insurance (128); Automobiles (151); Office Equipment (163); Store Equipment (165); Accounts Payable (201); Ada Evans, Capital (301); Ada Evans, Withdrawals (302); Fees Earned (401); and Salaries Expense (622). Once you have posted the entries, prepare a correct trial balance, and then describe the errors that Evans made.

THE PINE BOUGH
Trial Balance
August 31

Cash	$11,452	
Accounts receivable	-0-	
Store supplies	1,500	
Prepaid insurance	625	
Automobiles	11,000	
Office equipment	7,400	
Store equipment		$ 3,200
Accounts payable		7,270
Ada Evans, capital		30,700
Ada Evans, withdrawals	123	
Fees earned		3,400
Salaries expense	1,750	
Totals	$33,850	$44,570

Problem 2–5
Journalizing, posting, and preparing financial statements
(LO 4, 5)

Jan Dell started a new business, Dimple Dell Day Care, and completed these transactions during October of the current year:

Oct.	1	Invested $35,000 in cash, $2,500 in teaching supplies, and school equipment worth $9,000.
	2	Paid $750 cash for one month's rent for suitable space in a shopping center.
	3	Paid a liability insurance policy premium of $1,400 for the first month.
	4	Purchased a van for picking up the kids by paying $14,000 cash.
	10	Purchased $800 of additional teaching supplies on credit.
	21	Paid $4,000 cash for helpers' salaries.
	23	Paid one-half of the account payable created on October 10.
	28	Collected $9,000 cash from customers.
	29	Paid $1,150 for the month's utility bills.
	31	Withdrew $1,200 cash from the business to pay some personal expenses.

Required

1. Open the following accounts: Cash (101); Teaching Supplies (126); Trucks (153); School Equipment (167); Accounts Payable (201); Jan Dell, Capital (301); Jan Dell, Withdrawals (302); Day Care Fees Earned (401); Salaries Expense (622); Insurance Expense (637); Rent Expense (640); and Utilities Expense (690).
2. Prepare general journal entries to record the transactions, post them to the accounts, and prepare a trial balance as of October 31.
3. Prepare an income statement for the month ended October 31.
4. Prepare a statement of changes in owner's equity for the month ended October 31.
5. Prepare a balance sheet dated October 31.

Problem 2–6
Analytical essay
(LO 3)

Consider the facts in Problem 2–2 and focus on transactions *h* and *o*. Explain how transaction *h* affects the balance sheet, income statement, and statement of changes in owner's equity differently from transaction *o*. Describe how the effects of transaction *o* would differ if the company's owner had written the check to pay the company's property taxes instead of the described purpose.

Problem 2–7
Analytical essay
(LO 3, 5)

Consider the facts in Problem 2–3 and assume that the following mistakes were made in journalizing and posting the transactions. Explain how each mistake would affect the account balances and the column totals in the trial balance.

a. The March 1 investment by Ford was recorded correctly in the journal but the debit to Cash was incorrectly posted to the Cash account as $52,000.

b. The March 5 transaction was incorrectly recorded in the journal as a collection of an account receivable.

c. In recording the March 15 transaction in the journal, the account that should have been debited was credited and the account that should have been credited was debited.

d. The March 30 transaction was recorded correctly in the journal, and the debit was correctly posted, but the credit was not posted at all.

e. The $175 payment on March 31 was recorded incorrectly in both accounts in the journal as a $715 payment.

Serial Problem

Emerald Computer Services

(This comprehensive problem starts in this chapter and continues in Chapters 3, 4, and 5. Because of its length, this problem is most easily solved if you use the Working Papers that accompany this text.)

On October 1, 19X1, Tracy Green created a single proprietorship called Emerald Computer Services. Emerald will provide consulting services, including computer system installations and custom program development. Green has adopted the calendar year for reporting, and expects to prepare the company's first set of financial statements as of December 31, 19X1. The initial chart of accounts for the accounting system includes these items:

No.	Account
101	Cash
106	Accounts Receivable
126	Computer Supplies
128	Prepaid Insurance
131	Prepaid Rent
163	Office Equipment
167	Computer Equipment
201	Accounts Payable
301	Tracy Green, Capital
302	Tracy Green, Withdrawals
403	Computer Services Revenue
623	Wages Expense
655	Advertising Expense
676	Mileage Expense
677	Miscellaneous Expenses
684	Repairs Expense, Computer

Required

1. Prepare journal entries to record each of the following transactions for Emerald Computer Services.
2. Open balance column accounts for the company and post the journal entries to them.
3. Prepare a trial balance as of November 30.

Transactions:

Oct. 1 Tracy Green invested $30,000 cash in the business, along with a $12,000 computer system and $6,000 of office equipment.

2 Rented office space for $750 per month and paid the first four months' rent in advance.

3 Purchased computer supplies on credit for $880 from AAA Supply Co.

4 Paid $1,440 cash for one year's premium on a property and liability insurance policy.

5 Billed Bravo Productions $2,200 for installing a new computer.

7 Paid for the computer supplies purchased from AAA Supply Co.

9 Hired Fran Sims as a part-time assistant for $125 per day, as needed. These wages will be paid once each month.

11 Billed Bravo Productions another $800 for services.

14 Received $2,200 from Bravo Productions on their account.

16 Paid $470 to repair computer equipment damaged when moving into the new office.

18 Paid $1,240 for an advertisement in the local newspaper.

21 Received $800 from Bravo Productions on their account.

24 Paid Fran Sims for seven days' work.

27 Billed Charles Company $2,150 for services.

31 Paid $2,000 to Tracy Green for personal use.

Nov. 1 Reimbursed Tracy Green's business automobile mileage for 700 miles at $0.25 per mile.

4 Received $3,100 cash from Delta Fixtures, Inc., for computer services.

6 Purchased $640 of computer supplies from AAA Supply Co.

7 Billed Fox Run Estates $2,900 for services.

Nov. 10 Notified by Alpha Printing Co. that Emerald's bid of $2,500 for an upcoming project was accepted.
17 Paid $150 for Tracy Green's home utilities bill.
19 Received $1,250 from Charles Company against the bill dated October 27.
21 Donated $500 to the United Way in the company's name.
24 Completed work for Alpha Printing Co. and sent them a bill for $2,500.
26 Sent another bill to Charles Company for the past due amount of $900.
27 Paid $2,000 to Tracy Green as a withdrawal.
28 Reimbursed Tracy Green's business automobile mileage for 800 miles at $0.25 per mile.
30 Paid Fran Sims for 14 days' work.

Provocative Problems

Provocative Problem 2–1
Ella Fant Interiors
(LO 2)

Following are preliminary financial statements for Ella Fant Interiors:

ELLA FANT INTERIORS
Income Statement
June 30

Revenue:		
Investments by owner		$ 725
Unearned professional fees		10,575
Total		$11,300
Operating expenses:		
Prepaid insurance	$ 750	
Rent expense	450	
Telephone expense	300	
Professional library	8,000	
Travel and entertainment expense	3,100	
Utilities expense	400	
Withdrawals by owner	325	
Total operating expenses		13,325
Net income (loss)		$ (2,025)

ELLA FANT INTERIORS
Balance Sheet
For Month Ended June 30

Assets	
Cash	$13,000
Accounts receivable	2,900
Insurance expense	250
Prepaid rent	900
Office supplies	250
Buildings	30,000
Land	12,000
Salaries expense	3,300
Short-term notes payable	13,500
Total assets	$76,100
Liabilities	
Accounts payable	$ 2,725
Professional fees earned	8,400
Total liabilities	$11,125
Owner's Equity	
Ella Fant, capital	64,975
Total liabilities and owner's equity	$76,100

Ella Fant operates an interior decorating business. For the first few months of the company's life (through May), the accounting records were maintained by an outside bookkeeping service. According to those records, Fant's capital balance was $40,000 as of May 31. To save on expenses, Fant decided to keep the records herself. She managed to record June's transactions properly, but was a bit rusty when the time came to prepare the financial statements. The preceding income statement and balance sheet are her first versions. Fant is bothered that the company operated at a loss during the month, even though she had been very busy. Use the account balances included in the original financial statements to prepare revised statements (except for the capital account), including a statement of changes in owner's equity for the month.

Provocative Problem 2–2
Accounting related communications
(LO 2)

To increase sales and income, the Jackson Company decided to market its professional services more aggressively than it had in the past. The new efforts will include committing to providing services several months in the future. Previously, the company had simply recorded the names of customers who wanted future services and then promised that they would be called when their work could be scheduled. In quite a few cases, the customers had grown tired of waiting and found someone else to do the work.

Under the new policy, customers are promised a firm date for the services. In addition, they are asked to provide a 25% cash deposit against the estimated charge for the future services. This deposit not only brings cash into the Jackson Company earlier but also promises to greatly reduce the number of customers who turn to other companies for the work.

As a result of this policy, Jan Hughes, the controller, has tried to explain to the manager that the company's balance sheet will now show a liability account called Unearned Professional Fees equal to the amount of cash deposited on undelivered jobs. The manager, Tom Jackson, does not quite understand the meaning of this account and why it is used instead of the Professional Fees Earned account on the income statement. In particular, Jackson argues that the biggest effort in the business is getting people to sign up for the services, so it seems reasonable to just go ahead and credit the revenue account instead of the liability account.

Prepare a memorandum to the manager dated September 15 that explains why using the Unearned Professional Fees account provides more useful information in the financial statements. The memo will be signed by the controller.

Provocative Problem 2–3
Paradise Pedals
(LO 4, 5)

At the end of the summer, Pat Hand closed down a small business that operated in Paradise Park. The business rented out two-passenger bicycles and sold shirts, sunglasses, and hats. Hand started the summer with $9,000 in cash and an agreement to rent a small building in the park for up to five years. The $2,400 annual rent must be paid every year, even though the business is open from only June 1 through August 31. At the beginning of the summer, Hand paid cash for the first year's rent and nine bicycles at the price of $250 each.

Over the summer, Hand also purchased shirts, sunglasses, and hats on credit for the total cost of $6,000. By August 31, all but $125 of the payables were paid. Over the summer, cash had been paid for $650 of utility bills and $3,000 of wages to several part-time workers. The owner had also withdrawn $250 of cash from the business each week for 13 weeks.

The summer's revenues included $7,500 in bicycle rentals and $13,500 for shirts, sunglasses, and hats. All revenue was collected in cash, except for $80 owed by a local day-care center for some shirts.

Upon closing on August 31, Hand returned the unsold inventory of sunglasses to the distributor for a full cash refund of their $50 original cost. The owner took home the unsold inventory of shirts and hats as gifts for friends and family. Their original cost was $135. Finally, each of the nine used bicycles was sold for $110 cash.

Use the information to prepare an income statement describing the summer's business activities for the three months ended August 31. Also prepare a statement of changes in owner's equity for the same three months and a balance sheet as of August 31. The company's name is Paradise Pedals. As a first step in gathering the data, develop a list of brief explanations of the transactions. Next, post the amounts directly to T-accounts without using a general journal. Then use the T-account balances to prepare the statements. (Record the shirts, hats, and sunglasses in an account called Cost of Goods Sold and then reduce the balance for the unsold merchandise. Also record the difference between the original cost and the selling price of the bicycles in an account called Depreciation Expense.)

Provocative Problem 2–4
Fenwick Real Estate Agency
(LO 2, 5)

Lester Fenwick started a real estate agency and completed seven transactions, including Fenwick's initial investment of $8,500 cash. After these transactions, the following trial balance was prepared. Analyze the accounts and balances appearing in the trial balance and prepare a list that describes each of the seven transactions and its amount.

LESTER FENWICK, REALTOR
Trial Balance

Cash	$11,300	
Office supplies	330	
Prepaid insurance	1,600	
Office equipment	8,250	
Accounts payable		$ 8,250
Lester Fenwick, capital		8,500
Lester Fenwick, withdrawals	3,900	
Commissions earned		12,000
Advertising expense	3,370	
Totals	$28,750	$28,750

Provocative Problem 2–5
Apple Computer, Inc.
(LO 2)

Refer to the financial statements and related information for Apple Computer, Inc., in Appendix F. Find the answers to the following questions by analyzing the information in the report:

1. What four broad categories of expenses are reported on Apple's income statement?
2. What six current assets are reported on Apple's balance sheet?
3. What seven current liabilities are reported on Apple's balance sheet?
4. How large are the provisions for income taxes reported by Apple on its income statements for 1992 and 1991?
5. How much cash did Apple spend on new short-term investments during 1992? How much cash did Apple receive upon selling short-term investments during 1992? Use information in the cash flow statement to explain the change between the beginning and ending balances of short-term investments for 1992.
6. Using the sum of the company's current liabilities and deferred income taxes as the total liabilities, what is Apple's debt ratio at the end of 1992?

Provocative Problem 2–6
As a Matter of Ethics: Essay

Review the As a Matter of Ethics case on page 61. Discuss the nature of the dilemma faced by Karen Muñoz and evaluate the alternative courses of action that she should consider.

Answers to Objective Review Questions

LO 1 (*d*)
LO 2 (*a*)
LO 3 (*e*)
LO 4 (*c*)
LO 5 (*a*)
LO 6 (*e*)

CHAPTER

3

Adjusting the Accounts and Preparing the Statements

You learned in Chapter 2 that companies use accounting systems to collect information about transactions and other economic events. That chapter showed you how journals and ledgers are used to capture information about external transactions. This chapter explains how the accounting system gathers information about the effects of events that are not external transactions. The process adjusts the account balances at the end of the reporting period to reflect all relevant events. As a result, the adjusted accounts contain the amounts to be reported on the financial statements according to generally accepted accounting principles. The chapter ends with a description of the current ratio, which is used by decision makers to assess the company's ability to pay its liabilities in the near future.

Learning Objectives

After studying Chapter 3, you should be able to:

1. Explain why an organization prepares financial statements at the end of regular accounting periods and why unrecorded economic events lead to adjusting the accounts at the end of each period.
2. Explain why the revenue recognition and matching principles lead to adjusting entries and why the accrual basis of accounting produces more useful information than the cash basis.
3. Prepare adjusting entries for prepaid expenses, depreciation, unearned revenues, accrued expenses, and accrued revenues.
4. Prepare a schedule that includes the unadjusted trial balance, the adjustments, and the adjusted trial balance, and use the adjusted trial balance to prepare financial statements.
5. Prepare journal entries to record cash receipts and cash disbursements related to assets and liabilities originally recorded as accrued revenues and accrued expenses.
6. Define each asset and liability category for the balance sheet, classify balance sheet items, prepare a classified balance sheet, and calculate the current ratio.
7. Define or explain the words and phrases listed in the chapter glossary.

After studying Appendix A at the end of Chapter 3, you should be able to:

8. Explain the advantages of initially recording prepaid and unearned items in income statement accounts and prepare adjusting entries under this bookkeeping approach.

Accounting Periods and Fiscal Years

LO 1 Explain why an organization prepares financial statements at the end of regular accounting periods and why unrecorded economic events lead to adjusting the accounts at the end of each period.

To be useful, information must reach decision makers frequently and promptly. Otherwise, problems can arise and opportunities can be missed while they wait for the information. To provide frequent and prompt information, accounting systems are designed to produce periodic reports at regular intervals. As a result, the accounting process is based on the **time period principle.** According to this principle, an organization's activities are identified with specific time periods, such as a month, a quarter, or a year. Then, the financial statements or other reports are prepared for each reporting period. The time periods covered by the reports are called **accounting periods.** Most organizations use one year as their primary accounting period. As a result, they prepare annual financial statements. However, nearly all organizations also prepare **interim financial reports** that cover one or three months of activity.

The annual reporting period is not always the same as the calendar year ending December 31. In fact, an organization can adopt a **fiscal year** consisting of any 12 consecutive months.[1] Companies that do not experience much seasonal variation in sales volume within the year often choose the calendar year as their fiscal year. On the other hand, companies that experience major seasonal variations in sales often choose a fiscal year that corresponds to their **natural business year.** The natural business year ends when sales activities are at their lowest point during the year. For example, the natural business year for retail stores ends around January 31, after the Christmas and January selling seasons. As a result, they often start their annual accounting periods on February 1. The financial statements of the Federal Express Corporation in Appendix G at the end of the book reflect a fiscal year that ends on May 31.

Why Are the Accounts Adjusted at the End of an Accounting Period?

After all external transactions are recorded, several accounts in the ledger need to be updated before their balances appear in the financial statements at the end of an accounting period. This need arises from the fact that some economic events remain unrecorded because they did not occur as external transactions.

For example, the costs of some assets expire as time passes. Notice that the third item in the trial balance of Clear Copy Co. in Illustration 3–1 is Prepaid Insurance and that it has a balance of $2,400. This amount is the original cost of the premium for two years of insurance protection beginning on December 1, 19X1. By December 31, one month's coverage has been used up, and $2,400 is no longer the cost of the remaining prepaid insurance. Because the coverage costs an average of $100 per month ($2,400/24 months), the Prepaid Insurance account balance should be reduced by that amount. In addition, the income statement should report $100 as insurance expense.

Similarly, the $3,720 balance in the Store Supplies account includes the cost of some supplies used up during December. The cost of the consumed supplies should be reported as an expense for the month.

[1] Some companies actually choose a 52-week fiscal year, with the result that their annual reports end on a different date each year. For example, this practice is reflected in the annual report for Apple Computer, Inc., in Appendix F and Ben & Jerry's Homemade, Inc., in Appendix G.

ILLUSTRATION 3-1

CLEAR COPY CO.
Trial Balance
December 31, 19X1

	Debit	Credit
Cash	$ 7,950	
Accounts receivable	-0-	
Prepaid insurance	2,400	
Store supplies	3,720	
Copy equipment	26,000	
Accounts payable		$ 6,200
Unearned copy services revenue		3,000
Terry Dow, capital		30,000
Terry Dow, withdrawals	400	
Copy services revenue		3,900
Rent expense	1,000	
Salaries expense	1,400	
Utilities expense	230	
Totals	$43,100	$43,100

Because of these unrecorded events, the balances of the Prepaid Insurance, Store Supplies, and Copy Equipment accounts should be *adjusted* before they are presented on the December 31 balance sheet. In addition, the balances of the Unearned Copy Services Revenue, Copy Services Revenue, and Salaries Expense accounts should be adjusted before they appear on the December income statement. The financial statements simply would not be as useful without these *adjustments.*

The next section of the chapter explains how the adjusting process is accomplished. As you study the material, remember that our goal is to provide useful information in the financial statements.

The Adjusting Process

LO 2 Explain why the revenue recognition and matching principles lead to adjusting entries and why the accrual basis of accounting produces more useful information than the cash basis.

The adjusting process is consistent with two accounting principles, the *revenue recognition principle* and the *matching principle.*

Chapter 1 explained that the *revenue recognition principle* requires revenue to be reported on the income statement only when it is earned, not before and not after. For most firms, revenue is earned when a service or a product is delivered to the customer. For example, if Clear Copy Co. provides services to a customer during December, the revenue is earned during December. As a result, it should be reported on the December income statement, even if the customer paid for the services in November or will pay for them in January. One major goal for the adjusting process is to ensure that revenue is reported, or recognized, in the time period when it is earned.

The goal of the **matching principle** is to report expenses on the income statement in the same accounting period as the revenues that were earned as a result of the expenses. For example, assume that a business earns revenues during December while it operates out of rented store space. According to the *revenue recognition principle,* the business should report its revenues on the December income statement. In earning those revenues, the business incurs rent expense. The *matching principle* tells us that the rent should be reported on the income statement for December, even if the rent was paid in November or will be paid in January. As a result, the rent expense for December is matched with December's revenues. This matching of expenses with revenues is a major goal of the adjusting process.

ILLUSTRATION 3–2 *Allocating the $2,400 Cost for Insurance Protection over 24 Months in 19X1, 19X2, and 19X3*

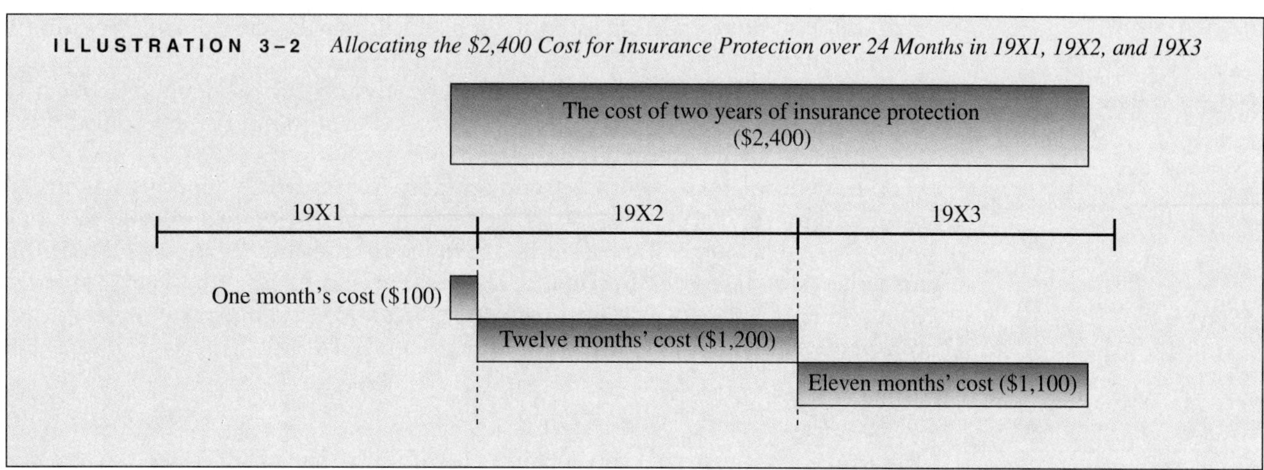

Accrual Basis Compared with Cash Basis Accounting

When the adjusting process assigns revenues to the periods in which they are earned and matches expenses with the revenues, the company is using **accrual basis accounting.** The objective of the accrual basis is to provide useful information that reports the economic effects of revenues and expenses when they are earned or incurred, not when cash is received or paid.

The alternative to accrual accounting is **cash basis accounting.** Under the cash basis, revenues are recognized when cash is received and expenses are reported when cash is paid. For example, if revenue is earned in December but cash is not received from the customer until January, the cash basis reports the revenue in January. Because revenues are reported when cash is received and expenses are deducted when cash is paid, cash basis net income for a period is the difference between revenues received in cash (called *receipts*) and expenses paid with cash (called *expenditures* or *disbursements*).

In describing the objectives of financial reporting in the conceptual framework, the Financial Accounting Standards Board concluded that "information about enterprise earnings and its components measured by accrual accounting generally provides a better indication of enterprise performance than information about current cash receipts and payments."[2] Although some small companies use a cash basis for preparing their internal statements and reports, cash-basis financial statements are not consistent with generally accepted accounting principles.

Accrual accounting provides more useful information because it increases the *comparability* between financial statements for two or more periods. For example, Clear Copy paid $2,400 for two years of insurance coverage beginning on December 1. Under accrual accounting, $100 of insurance expense is reported on the December 19X1 income statement. During 19X2, $1,200 of expense will be reported (the average monthly cost is $100). During 19X3, $1,100 expense will be reported for the first 11 months of the year. This allocation of the insurance cost among the three fiscal years is represented graphically in Illustration 3–2.

In contrast, a cash basis income statement for December 19X1 would report insurance expense of $2,400. The income statements for 19X2 and 19X3 would not report any insurance expense from this policy. To provide useful information about the company's activities and assets, the accrual basis shows that each of the 24 months had $100 of insurance expense. The balance sheet

[2] *Statement of Financial Accounting Concepts No. 1,* "Objectives of Financial Reporting by Business Enterprises" (Norwalk, CT, 1978), par. 44.

also reports the remaining unexpired premium as the cost of the prepaid insurance asset. However, the cash basis would never report an asset. In summary, the cash basis information would be less useful for decisions because the reported income for 19X1, 19X2, and 19X3 would not reflect comparable measures of the cost of having insurance in those years.

The accrual basis is generally acceptable for external reporting because it produces more useful information. The cash basis is not acceptable for a balance sheet or income statement because it provides highly incomplete information about assets, liabilities, revenues, and expenses. However, information about cash flows is useful for other decisions, as shown by the fact that companies must provide a statement of cash flows.

Adjusting Specific Accounts

LO 3 Prepare adjusting entries for prepaid expenses, depreciation, unearned revenues, accrued expenses, and accrued revenues.

The process of adjusting the accounts is similar to the process used to analyze and record transactions. Each account balance and the economic events that affect it are analyzed to determine whether an adjustment is needed. If an adjustment is needed, an **adjusting entry** is recorded to bring the asset or liability account balance up to date. The adjustment also updates the related expense or revenue account. Like other journal entries, adjusting entries are posted to the accounts. The following paragraphs explain why adjusting entries are needed to provide useful information.

Adjusting entries for prepaid expenses, depreciation, and unearned revenues involve previously recorded assets and liabilities. These entries are made to record the effects of economic events (including the passing of time) that have changed these assets and liabilities. On the other hand, adjusting entries for accrued expenses and accrued revenues involve liabilities and assets that have not yet been recorded. Adjusting entries record the effects of economic events that created these liabilities and assets as well as the related expenses and revenues.

Prepaid Expenses

A prepaid expense is an economic benefit paid for in advance of its use. When it is paid for, the company acquires an asset that will expire or be used up. As the asset is used, its cost becomes an expense.

Prepaid Insurance. For example, recall that Clear Copy paid $2,400 for two years of insurance protection that went into effect on December 1, 19X1. (The allocation of this cost to 19X1, 19X2, and 19X3 is described in Illustration 3–2.) As each day of December went by, some of the benefit of the insurance protection expired, and a portion of the asset's cost became an expense. By December 31, one month's insurance coverage had expired. This expense is measured as $100, which is 1/24 of $2,400. The following adjusting entry causes the accounts to reflect more useful amounts for the asset and expense as of December 31:

		Adjustment a		
Dec.	31	Insurance Expense	100.00	
		Prepaid Insurance		100.00
		To record the expense created by expired insurance.		

This entry records the expense with a debit, and reduces the cost of the asset with a credit to the asset account. Posting the adjusting entry has the following effect on the accounts:

Insurance Expense

Date		Explanation	Debit	Credit	Balance
Dec.	31	(a)	100		100

Prepaid Insurance

Date		Explanation	Debit	Credit	Balance
Dec.	26		2,400		2,400
	31	(a)		100	2,300

After the entry is posted, the $100 balance in Insurance Expense and the $2,300 balance in Prepaid Insurance are ready to be presented on the financial statements.

The allocation process in Illustration 3–2 shows that another adjusting entry in 19X2 transfers $1,200 from Prepaid Insurance to Insurance Expense. A third adjusting entry in 19X3 transfers the remaining $1,100 to the expense account.

Store Supplies. Store supplies are another prepaid expense that is adjusted. For example, Clear Copy purchased $3,720 of store supplies in December and used some of them up during the month. Consuming these supplies created an expense equal to their cost. However, the daily consumption of the supplies was not recorded in the accounts because the information was not needed. Due to the fact that the account balances are not presented in financial statements until the end of the month, bookkeeping effort can be reduced by making only one adjusting entry to record the total cost of all supplies consumed in the month.

Because an income statement is to be prepared for December, the cost of the store supplies used during the month needs to be determined and then recognized as an expense. To learn the amount used, Terry Dow counts (or, takes an inventory of) the remaining unused supplies. Then, the cost of the remaining supplies is deducted from the cost of the purchased supplies. For example, suppose that Dow finds that $2,670 of supplies remain out of the $3,720 purchased in December. The $1,050 difference between these two amounts is the cost of the consumed supplies. This amount is the month's store supplies expense. This adjusting entry records the expense with a debit and reduces the asset account balance with an equal credit:

		Adjustment b		
Dec.	31	Store Supplies Expense	1,050.00	
		Store Supplies		1,050.00
		To record the expense created by using store supplies.		

Posting the adjusting entry has the following effect on the accounts:

Store Supplies Expense

Date		Explanation	Debit	Credit	Balance
Dec.	31	(b)	1,050		1,050

Store Supplies

Date		Explanation	Debit	Credit	Balance
Dec.	2		2,500		2,500
	6		1,100		3,600
	26		120		3,720
	31	(b)		1,050	2,670

As a result, the balance of the store supplies account now equals the $2,670 cost revealed by the manager's inventory.

Other Prepaid Expenses. Unlike the two previous examples, some prepaid expenses are both acquired and fully used up within a single accounting period. For example, a company usually pays monthly rent on the first day of each month. Every month, the payment creates a prepaid expense that fully expires by the end of the month. In these cases, the bookkeeper can conveniently ignore the fact that the payment creates an asset and initially record the transaction with a debit to the expense account instead of the asset account. (These practices are described more completely in Appendix A at the end of this chapter.)

Depreciation

In accounting, the term **plant and equipment** describes tangible long-lived assets used to produce or sell goods and services. Examples of plant and equipment are land, buildings, machines, vehicles, and professional libraries. Except for land, plant and equipment assets eventually wear out or otherwise lose their usefulness and value. Therefore, the goal of providing complete information requires income statements to report the cost of using these assets as expenses during their useful lives. The expense created by allocating the original cost of assets is called **depreciation.** Depreciation expense is recorded with an adjusting entry similar to the entries used to record the consumption of prepaid expenses. That is, the cost of the asset is transferred from the asset account to the expense account. The entry is slightly more complicated because a special account is used to record the reduced balance in the asset account.

For example, Clear Copy uses copy equipment to earn revenue. This equipment's cost should be depreciated to provide a complete income statement. Early in December, Clear Copy made two purchases of equipment for $20,000 and $6,000. Using information received from the manufacturer and other sources, Terry Dow predicts that the equipment will have a four-year useful life. Dow also predicts that the company will be able to sell the equipment for $8,000 at the end of the four years. Therefore, the net cost expected to expire over the useful life is $18,000 ($26,000 − $8,000). When this net cost is divided by the 48 months in the asset's predicted life, the result is an average monthly cost of $375 ($18,000/48). This average cost is recorded as depreciation expense for each month with this adjusting entry:

		Adjustment c		
Dec.	31	Depreciation Expense	375.00	
		Accumulated Depreciation, Copy Equipment		375.00
		To record the expense created by using the copying equipment.		

Posting the adjusting entry has the following effect on the accounts:

Depreciation Expense, Copy Equipment

Date		Explanation	Debit	Credit	Balance
Dec.	31	(c)	375		375

Copy Equipment

Date		Explanation	Debit	Credit	Balance
Dec.	3		20,000		20,000
	6		6,000		26,000

Accumulated Depreciation, Copy Equipment

Date		Explanation	Debit	Credit	Balance
Dec.	31	(c)		375	375

The account called Depreciation Expense, Copy Equipment shows the amount of expense that will appear on the December income statement. The December 31 balance sheet will show the balances of both the Copy Equipment account and its related account for Accumulated Depreciation.

Using a Contra Account. In most cases, a decrease in an asset account is recorded by entering a credit directly in the account. However, this practice is not used when depreciation is recorded. Instead, the effects of depreciation on the asset's cost are recorded in what is called a **contra account.** A contra account's balance is subtracted from a related account's balance to provide more information in the financial statements. In this example, the account called Accumulated Depreciation, Copy Equipment is a contra account.

A contra account is used to record accumulated depreciation to provide more information about the asset on the balance sheet. Specifically, this approach lets the users observe both the original cost of the assets and the amount of depreciation charged to expense in the past. By knowing both the original cost and the accumulated depreciation, decision makers can more completely assess the company's productive capacity and the potential need to replace the assets. In this example, Clear Copy's balance sheet shows both the $26,000 original cost of the equipment and the $375 balance in the accumulated depreciation contra account. This information lets statement users see that the equipment is almost new. In contrast, if Clear Copy simply reported the net remaining cost of $25,625, the users would not know whether the equipment is new or so old that it needs immediate replacement.

The word *accumulated* in the contra account's title reflects the fact that this account reports the cumulative amount of depreciation expense recognized in all prior periods since the assets were put into service. For example, the Copy Equipment and the Accumulated Depreciation accounts would look like this on February 28, 19X2, after three monthly adjusting entries:

Copy Equipment

Date		Explanation	Debit	Credit	Balance
Dec.	3		20,000		20,000
	6		6,000		26,000

Accumulated Depreciation, Copy Equipment

Date		Explanation	Debit	Credit	Balance
Dec.	31	(*c*)		375	375
Jan.	31			375	750
Feb.	28			375	1,125

These account balances would be presented on the February 28 balance sheet as follows:

Copy equipment	$26,000
Less accumulated depreciation	1,125
Net	$24,875

Later chapters describe how other contra accounts are used in other situations.

Unearned Revenues

An unearned revenue is created when a customer's payment is received in advance of delivering the goods or services. For example, Clear Copy agreed on December 26 to provide copying services for a customer for the fixed fee of $1,500 per month. On that day, the customer paid the first two months' fees in advance to cover the period from December 27 to February 26. This entry would be made to record the cash receipt:

Dec.	26	Cash	3,000.00	
		Unearned Copy Services Revenue		3,000.00
		Received advanced payment for copying services to be provided over 2 months.		

This advance payment increased cash and created an obligation to do copying work over the next two months. By December 31, the business has provided five days' service and earned one-sixth of the $1,500 revenue for the first month. This amount is $250 ($1,500/6). The company has also discharged one-twelfth of the total $3,000 liability because five days is one-twelfth of two months. According to the *revenue recognition principle,* the $250 of revenue should appear on the December income statement. Notice that these events have occurred without any external transactions. The following adjusting entry updates the accounts by reducing the liability and recognizing the earned revenue:

		Adjustment d		
Dec.	31	Unearned Copy Services Revenue	250.00	
		Copy Services Revenue ($1,500/6)		250.00
		Earned revenue that was received in advance.		

The accounts look like this after the entry is posted:

Unearned Copy Services Revenue

Date		Explanation	Debit	Credit	Balance
Dec.	26			3,000	3,000
	31	(d)	250		2,750

Copy Services Revenue

Date		Explanation	Debit	Credit	Balance
Dec.	10			2,200	2,200
	12			1,700	3,900
	31	(d)		250	4,150

In effect, the adjusting entry transfers $250 of earned revenue from the liability account to the revenue account.

Accrued Expenses

Most expenses are recorded when they are paid with cash. In making the journal entry to record the transaction, the credit to the Cash account is accompanied by a debit to the expense account. However, some expenses incurred during the period may remain unrecorded at the end of an accounting period because they have not been paid for. These incurred but unpaid expenses are called **accrued expenses.** One typical example of an accrued expense is the unpaid wages earned by employees for work they have already completed.

Accrued Salaries. For example, Clear Copy's only employee earns $70 per day or $350 for a five-day workweek that begins on Monday and ends on Friday. The employee's salary is paid every two weeks on Friday. During December, these wages were paid on the 12th and the 26th, recorded in the journal and posted to the ledger. The Salaries Expense and Cash accounts show these entries:

Salaries Expense

Date		Explanation	Debit	Credit	Balance
Dec.	12		700		700
	26		700		1,400

Cash

Date		Explanation	Debit	Credit	Balance
Dec.	12	Salaries		700	xxx
	26	Salaries		700	xxx

The calendar for December 31, 19X1, in the margin shows us that three working days (December 29, 30, and 31) come after the December 26 payday. Thus, the employee has earned three days' salary at the close of business on Wednesday, December 31. Because this salary has not been paid, this expense has not yet been recorded. But, the financial statements would be incomplete if they neglected to report this additional expense and the liability to the employee for the unpaid salary. Therefore, this adjusting entry should be recorded on December 31 to produce a complete record of the company's expenses and liabilities:

December 19X1

S	M	T	W	T	F	S
	1	2	3	4	5	6
7	8	9	10	11	12	13
14	15	16	17	18	19	20
21	22	23	24	25	26	27
28	29	30	31			

		Adjustment e		
Dec.	31	Salaries Expense	210.00	
		Salaries Payable		210.00
		To record three days' accrued salary.		

After this entry is posted, the Salaries Expense and liability accounts appear as follows:

Salaries Expense

Date		Explanation	Debit	Credit	Balance
Dec.	12		700		700
	26		700		1,400
	31	(e)	210		1,610

Salaries Payable

Date		Explanation	Debit	Credit	Balance
Dec.	31	(e)		210	210

As a result of this entry, $1,610 of salaries expense is reported on the income statement. In addition, the balance sheet reports a $210 liability to the employee.

Accrued Interest Expense. Another typical accrued expense recorded with an adjusting entry at the end of the period is interest incurred on accounts and notes payable. Interest expense is incurred simply with the passage of time. Therefore, unless interest is paid on the last day of the accounting period, some additional amount will have accrued since the previous payment. A company's financial statements will be incomplete unless this expense and additional liability are recorded. The adjusting entry for interest is similar to the one used to accrue the unpaid salary.

Accrued Revenues

Many revenues are recorded when cash is received from the customer. Other revenues are recorded when goods and services are sold on credit. However, some earned revenues may remain unrecorded at the end of the accounting period. Although these **accrued revenues** are earned, they are unrecorded because the customer has not yet paid for them or the seller has not yet billed the customer. For example, suppose that Clear Copy agreed to provide copying services for a bank at a fixed fee of $2,700 per month. The terms of the agreement call for Clear Copy to provide services from the 12th of one month through the 11th of the following month. On this second date, the bank will pay $2,700 cash to Clear Copy. Thus, the company will be entitled to receive $2,700 on January 11, 19X2, for services it provides from December 12 through January 11. As of December 31, 20 days of services have been provided to the bank, but no payment has been received. No journal entry has recorded the revenues because no obvious transaction has occurred. Because 20 days equal two-thirds of a month, Clear Copy has earned two-thirds of one month's fee, or $1,800 ($2,700 × 2/3). According to the *revenue recognition principle,* this revenue should be reported on the December income statement because it was earned in that month. In addition, the balance sheet should report that the bank owes the company $1,800. Clear Copy makes this adjusting entry to record the effects of the agreement:

		Adjustment f		
Dec.	31	Accounts Receivable	1,800.00	
		Copy Services Revenue		1,800.00
		To record 20 days' accrued revenue.		

The debit to the receivable reflects the fact that the bank owes Clear Copy for the provided services. After this entry is posted, the affected accounts look like this:

Accounts Receivable

Date		Explanation	Debit	Credit	Balance
Dec.	12		1,700		1,700
	22			1,700	-0-
	31	(f)	1,800		1,800

Copy Services Revenue

Date		Explanation	Debit	Credit	Balance
Dec.	10			2,200	2,200
	12			1,700	3,900
	31	(d)		250	4,150
	31	(f)		1,800	5,950

Accounts receivable are reported on the balance sheet at $1,800, and $5,950 of revenues are reported on the income statement.

Accrued Interest Income. We mentioned earlier that interest is an accrued expense recorded with an adjusting entry. Interest is also an accrued revenue when a company is entitled to receive it from a debtor. If a company has notes or accounts receivable that produce interest income, the bookkeeper records an adjusting entry to recognize any accrued but uncollected interest revenue. The entry also records the interest receivable from the debtor as an asset.

Take time to read the As a Matter of Ethics case on p. 114. It tells about pressure being applied to an accountant to omit some adjusting entries that are needed to present complete financial statements. Consider the situation and determine what you would do if you were in this accountant's place.

The Adjusted Trial Balance

An **unadjusted trial balance** is prepared before adjustments have been recorded. As you might expect, an **adjusted trial balance** uses the account balances after the adjusting entries have been posted to the ledger. In Illustration 3–3, parallel columns show the unadjusted trial balance, the adjustments, and the adjusted trial balance for Clear Copy as of December 31, 19X1. Notice that several new accounts have been added because of the ad-

ILLUSTRATION 3–3 *The Unadjusted Trial Balance, Adjustments, and Adjusted Trial Balance for Clear Copy Co. as of December 31, 19X1*

	Unadjusted Trial Balance		Adjustments		Adjusted Trial Balance	
Cash	$ 7,950				$ 7,950	
Accounts receivable			(*f*)1,800		1,800	
Store supplies	3,720			(*b*)1,050	2,670	
Prepaid insurance	2,400			(*a*) 100	2,300	
Copy equipment	26,000				26,000	
Accumulated depreciation, copy equipment				(*c*) 375		$ 375
Accounts payable		$ 6,200				6,200
Salaries payable				(*e*) 210		210
Unearned copy services revenue		3,000	(*d*) 250			2,750
Terry Dow, capital		30,000				30,000
Terry Dow, withdrawals	400				400	
Copy services revenue		3,900		(*d*) 250 (*f*)1,800		5,950
Depreciation expense, copy equipment			(*c*) 375		375	
Salaries expense	1,400		(*e*) 210		1,610	
Insurance expense			(*a*) 100		100	
Rent expense	1,000				1,000	
Store supplies expense			(*b*)1,050		1,050	
Utilities expense	230				230	
Totals	$43,100	$43,100	$3,785	$3,785	$45,485	$45,485

LO 4 Prepare a schedule that includes the unadjusted trial balance, the adjustments, and the adjusted trial balance, and use the adjusted trial balance to prepare financial statements.

justing entries. (The order of the accounts has also been changed to list them in the order of the account numbers listed at the back of this book.) Also notice that the letters in the adjustments columns identify the debits and credits that were recorded with adjusting entries presented earlier in the chapter.

Preparing Financial Statements from the Adjusted Trial Balance

Chapter 2 explained that the trial balance summarizes the information in the ledger by showing the account balances. This summary is easier to work with than the entire ledger when preparing financial statements. By now, you should understand that the accountant would use the adjusted trial balance for this purpose because it includes the adjusted balances that should appear in the statements.

Illustrations 3–4 and 3–5 show how the account balances are transferred from the adjusted trial balance to the statements. For completeness, the trial balance includes the identification numbers for the accounts.

Because the amount of net income is used on the statement of changes in owner's equity, the first phase of the preparation process produces the company's income statement. The arrows in the lower section of Illustration 3–4 show how the balances of the revenue and expense accounts are transferred into the income statement. (These accounts are presented in color.) The revenue is listed on the statement first, and then the expenses. The total expenses are subtracted from the revenues to find the net income of $1,585.

The second phase prepares the statement of changes in owner's equity. In developing this statement, the accountant combines the net income from the income statement with the balances of Terry Dow's capital and withdrawals accounts. The $30,000 capital account balance came entirely from the initial

ILLUSTRATION 3–4 *Preparing the Income Statement and the Statement of Changes in Owner's Equity from the Adjusted Trial Balance*

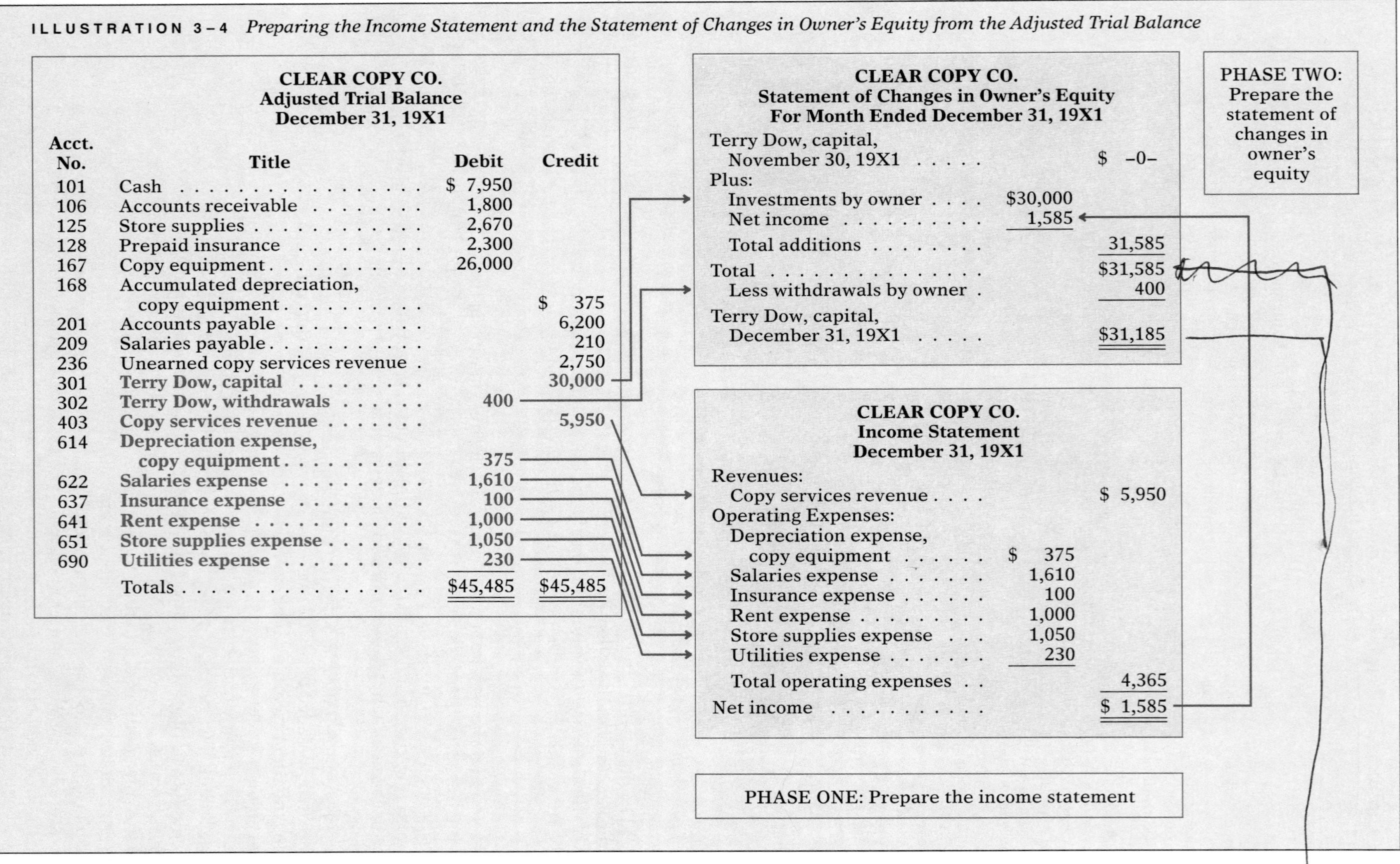

CLEAR COPY CO.
Adjusted Trial Balance
December 31, 19X1

Acct. No.	Title	Debit	Credit
101	Cash	$ 7,950	
106	Accounts receivable	1,800	
125	Store supplies	2,670	
128	Prepaid insurance	2,300	
167	Copy equipment	26,000	
168	Accumulated depreciation, copy equipment		$ 375
201	Accounts payable		6,200
209	Salaries payable		210
236	Unearned copy services revenue		2,750
301	**Terry Dow, capital**		30,000
302	**Terry Dow, withdrawals**	400	
403	**Copy services revenue**		5,950
614	**Depreciation expense, copy equipment**	375	
622	**Salaries expense**	1,610	
637	**Insurance expense**	100	
641	**Rent expense**	1,000	
651	**Store supplies expense**	1,050	
690	**Utilities expense**	230	
	Totals	$45,485	$45,485

CLEAR COPY CO.
Statement of Changes in Owner's Equity
For Month Ended December 31, 19X1

Terry Dow, capital, November 30, 19X1		$ -0-
Plus:		
Investments by owner	$30,000	
Net income	1,585	
Total additions		31,585
Total		$31,585
Less withdrawals by owner		400
Terry Dow, capital, December 31, 19X1		$31,185

PHASE TWO: Prepare the statement of changes in owner's equity

CLEAR COPY CO.
Income Statement
December 31, 19X1

Revenues:		
Copy services revenue		$ 5,950
Operating Expenses:		
Depreciation expense, copy equipment	$ 375	
Salaries expense	1,610	
Insurance expense	100	
Rent expense	1,000	
Store supplies expense	1,050	
Utilities expense	230	
Total operating expenses		4,365
Net income		$ 1,585

PHASE ONE: Prepare the income statement

ILLUSTRATION 3–5 *Preparing the Balance Sheet from the Adjusted Trial Balance and the Statement of Changes in Owner's Equity*

CLEAR COPY CO.
Adjusted Trial Balance
December 31, 19X1

Acct. No.	Title	Debit	Credit
101	Cash	$ 7,950	
106	Accounts receivable	1,800	
125	Store supplies	2,670	
128	Prepaid insurance	2,300	
167	Copy equipment	26,000	
168	Accumulated depreciation, copy equipment		$ 375
201	Accounts payable		6,200
209	Salaries payable		210
236	Unearned copy services revenue		2,750
301	Terry Dow, capital		30,000
302	Terry Dow, withdrawals	400	
403	Copy services revenue		5,950
614	Depreciation expense, copy equipment	375	
622	Salaries expense	1,610	
637	Insurance expense	100	
641	Rent expense	1,000	
651	Store supplies expense	1,050	
690	Utilities expense	230	
	Totals	$45,485	$45,485

PHASE THREE: Prepare the balance sheet

CLEAR COPY CO.
Balance Sheet
December 31, 19X1

Assets		
Cash		$ 7,950
Accounts receivable		1,800
Store supplies		2,670
Prepaid insurance		2,300
Copy equipment	$26,000	
Less accumulated depreciation	(375)	25,625
Total assets		$40,345
Liabilities		
Accounts payable	$ 6,200	
Salaries payable	210	
Unearned copy services revenue	2,750	
Total liabilities		$ 9,160
Owner's Equity		
Terry Dow, capital, December 31, 19X1		31,185
Total liabilities and owner's equity		$40,345

Statement of Changes in Owner's Equity (from Illustration 3–4)

AS A MATTER OF

Ethics

Bill Palmer is the accountant for the Crown Company. Just as Palmer was about to prepare adjusting entries to record some accrued expenses at the end of the company's first year, he was called into the company president's office. The president asked about the accrued expenses and then instructed Palmer not to make the adjustments. Although Palmer expressed concern about these instructions, the president said that the expenses should not be reported until next year because they would be paid in January or later.

As Palmer was turning to leave, the president asked how much the current year's revenues would be increased by the purchase order that was recently received from the Fisher Company. Palmer explained that there will be no effect on sales until the next year because Fisher will not take delivery until the middle of January. The exasperated president pointed out that the order had already been received and Crown was ready to make the delivery. Even though Fisher's order indicated the merchandise should not be delivered until January 15, the president told Palmer to record the sale in December.

Palmer knows that the combination of recording the sales to Fisher Company and not accruing the expenses will have a large effect on the income statement. In fact, it would report a net income instead of a net loss. Palmer is unsure about following the president's instructions. He also wonders how the company's independent auditors would react if they reviewed the statements and records and found that the adjusting entries were not made. What do you think Palmer should do?

investment in December. (In other situations, the accountant would have to analyze the capital account to identify the beginning balance and any new investments made during the period.) The bottom line of the statement shows the December 31 balance of owner's equity.

The third phase of the preparation process is represented in Illustration 3–5. In this phase, the balances of the asset and liability accounts (presented in color) are transferred to the asset and liability sections of the balance sheet. Notice in particular how the balance of the accumulated depreciation account is shown as a deduction from the cost of the copy equipment. And, notice that the December 31 balance of Terry Dow's capital is taken from the statement of changes in owner's equity. The $30,000 balance of the capital account cannot be used on the balance sheet because it does not include the changes in equity created by the month's revenues, expenses, and withdrawals. (The next chapter explains how the capital account is updated through the closing process.) The completed balance sheet shows the total cost of the company's assets, its total liabilities, and the owner's equity.

Removing Accrued Assets and Liabilities from the Accounts

After a new reporting period begins, cash is received from customers for revenues that were accrued at the end of the prior period. In addition, a company pays out cash to settle the unpaid expenses that were accrued with adjusting entries. This section explains the journal entries to remove the accrued assets and liabilities from the accounts.

Accrued Expenses

LO 5 Prepare journal entries to record cash receipts and cash disbursements related to assets and liabilities originally recorded as accrued revenues and accrued expenses.

Earlier, Clear Copy Co. recorded three days of accrued wages for its employee with this adjusting entry:

Dec.	31	Salaries Expense	210.00	
		Salaries Payable		210.00
		To record three days' accrued salary.		

When the next payday comes on Friday, January 9, the following entry removes the accrued liability and records additional salaries expense for January:

Jan.	9	Salaries Payable (3 days at $70)	210.00	
		Salaries Expense (7 days at $70)	490.00	
		Cash		700.00
		Paid two weeks salary, including three days accrued in December.		

The first debit in the January 9 entry records the payment of the liability for the three days' salary accrued on December 31. The second debit records the salary for January's first seven working days (including the New Year's Day holiday) as an expense of the new accounting period. The credit records the total amount of cash paid to the employee.

Accrued Revenue

On December 31, the following adjusting entry was made to record 20 days' accrued revenue earned under Clear Copy's contract with the bank:

Dec.	31	Accounts Receivable	1,800.00	
		Copy Services Revenue		1,800.00
		To record 20 days' accrued revenue.		

When the first month's fee is received on January 11, the company makes the following entry to eliminate the receivable and recognize the revenue earned in January:

Jan.	11	Cash	2,700.00	
		Accounts Receivable		1,800.00
		Copy Services Revenue		900.00
		Received cash for accrued and earned copy services revenue.		

The first credit in the entry records the collection of the receivable. The second credit records the earned revenue.

Classifying Balance Sheet Items

LO 6 Define each asset and liability category for the balance sheet, classify balance sheet items, prepare a classified balance sheet, and calculate the current ratio.

Up to this point, we have presented only **unclassified balance sheets.** (For example, see Illustration 3–5.) To keep the statements simple, we did not separate the assets and liabilities into categories. However, the information on a balance sheet is more useful if assets and liabilities are classified into relevant groups. Readers of these **classified balance sheets** have more information to use in making their decisions. For example, they can use the data to assess the likelihood that funds will be available to meet the liabilities when they become due.

All companies do not use the same categories of assets and liabilities on their balance sheets. However, most companies classify them into the categories shown for National Electric Supply in Illustration 3–6. Assets are classified as (1) current assets, (2) investments, (3) plant and equipment, and (4) intangible assets. Liabilities are either current or long-term.

ILLUSTRATION 3-6 *A Classified Balance Sheet*

NATIONAL ELECTRICAL SUPPLY CO.
Balance Sheet
December 31, 19X1

Assets			
Current assets:			
Cash		$ 6,500	
Short-term investments		2,100	
Accounts receivable		4,400	
Notes receivable		1,500	
Merchandise inventory		27,500	
Prepaid expenses		2,400	
Total current assets			$ 44,400
Investments:			
Chrysler Corporation common stock		$ 18,000	
Land held for future expansion		48,000	
Total investments			66,000
Plant and equipment:			
Store equipment	$ 33,200		
Less accumulated depreciation	8,000	$ 25,200	
Buildings	$170,000		
Less accumulated depreciation	45,000	125,000	
Land		73,200	
Total plant and equipment			223,400
Intangible assets:			
Trademark			10,000
Total assets			$343,800
Liabilities			
Current liabilities:			
Accounts payable	$ 15,300		
Wages payable	3,200		
Notes payable	3,000		
Current portion of long-term liabilities	7,500		
Total current liabilities		$ 29,000	
Long-term liabilities:			
Notes payable (net of current portion)		150,000	
Total liabilities			$179,000
Owner's Equity			
B. Brown, capital			164,800
Total liabilities and owner's equity			$343,800

Current Assets

Current assets are cash and other assets that are reasonably expected to be sold, collected, or consumed within one year or within the normal **operating cycle of the business,** whichever is longer.[3] In addition to cash, current assets typically include short-term investments in marketable securities, accounts receivable, notes receivable, goods expected to be sold to customers (called *merchandise* or *inventory*), and prepaid expenses.

[3] FASB, *Accounting Standards—Current Text* (Norwalk, CT, 1994), Sec. B05.105. First published as *Accounting Research Bulletin No. 43,* Chapter 3A, par. 4.

ILLUSTRATION 3–7 *The Phases of Operating Cycles for Companies that Sell Services and Merchandise*

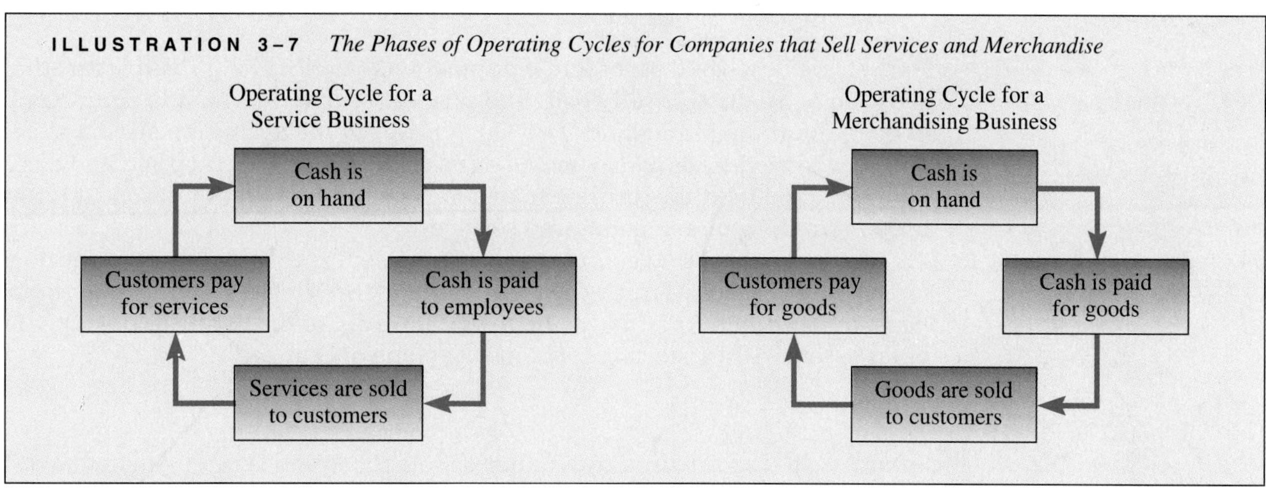

The Operating Cycle. The length of a company's operating cycle depends on its activities. The diagrams in Illustration 3–7 represent the phases of operating cycles for service and merchandising companies. For a company that sells services, the operating cycle is the average time between paying the employees who perform the services and receiving the cash from customers. For a company that sells goods, the operating cycle is the average time between paying for the merchandise and receiving cash from customers.

Most operating cycles are shorter than one year. As a result, most companies use a one-year period in deciding which assets are current. However, a few companies have an operating cycle longer than one year. For example, a company may routinely allow customers to take several years to pay for their purchases. Some producers of beverages and other products may allow their products to age for several years. In both cases, these companies would use the longer operating cycle in deciding which assets are current.[4]

Other Details. The balance sheet in Illustration 3–6 lists current assets first. This practice gives a prominent position to assets that are most easily converted into cash. Items within the current asset category are traditionally listed in the order of how quickly they will be converted to cash. Prepaid expenses are usually listed last because they will not be converted to cash.

A company's individual prepaid expenses are usually small compared to other assets on the balance sheet. As a result, they are often combined and shown as a single item. Thus, it is likely that the Prepaid expenses item in Illustration 3–6 includes such things as prepaid insurance, prepaid rent, office supplies, and store supplies.

Investments

The second balance sheet classification is long-term investments. In many cases, notes receivable and investments in stocks and bonds are not current assets because they will be held for more than one year (or one operating cycle). Investments also include land that is not being used in operations because it is held for future expansion. Notice that the short-term investments on the second line in Illustration 3–6 are current assets and are not presented in the Investments section. We explain the differences between short- and long-term investments in a later chapter.

[4] In these unusual situations, the companies provide supplemental information about their current assets and liabilities that allows users to compare them with other companies.

Plant and Equipment

Earlier, we described plant and equipment as tangible long-lived assets that are used to produce or sell goods and services. Examples include equipment, vehicles, buildings, and land. Two key phrases in the definition are *long-lived* and *used to produce or sell goods and services.* Although it is tangible and has a long life, land held for future expansion is not a plant asset because it is not used to produce or sell goods and services.

The term *plant and equipment* is often used as a balance sheet caption. Other widely used titles for the same category are *Property, plant, and equipment,* or *Land, buildings, and equipment.* The order of the listing or the types of plant assets within the category varies among organizations.

Intangible Assets

Some assets that are used to produce or sell goods and services do not have a physical form. These assets are called **intangible assets.** Examples of intangible assets are goodwill, patents, trademarks, copyrights, and franchises. Their value comes from the privileges or rights granted to or held by the owner.

Current Liabilities

Obligations due to be paid or liquidated within one year (or the operating cycle) are classified as **current liabilities.** Current liabilities are usually satisfied by paying out current assets. Typical current liabilities are accounts payable, notes payable, wages payable, taxes payable, interest payable, and unearned revenues. Also, any portion of a long-term liability due to be paid within one year (or a longer operating cycle) is a current liability. Illustration 3–6 shows how the current portion of long-term liabilities is usually described on a balance sheet. Unearned revenues are classified as current liabilities because they will be settled by delivering goods or services within the year (or the operating cycle). Different companies present current liabilities in different orders. Generally, the first position goes to the liabilities that will be paid first.

Long-Term Liabilities

The second liability classification consists of **long-term liabilities.** These liabilities are not due to be paid within one year, or the operating cycle. Notes payable and bonds payable are usually long-term liabilities. If a company has both short- and long-term notes payable, it probably uses separate accounts for them in its ledger.

Equity on the Balance Sheet

The format of the balance sheet's equity section depends on whether the company is a single proprietorship, a partnership, or a corporation.

Single Proprietorships and Partnerships

If a business is a single proprietorship, the equity section consists of a single line showing the owner's equity as of the balance sheet date. For example, the balance sheet in Illustration 3–5 shows "Terry Dow, capital, December 31, 19X1" and the amount of $31,185. When total liabilities exceed total assets, the negative equity amount (often called a *deficit*) is subtracted from total liabilities.

If a business is organized as a partnership, separate equity accounts are used for each partner. Changes in each partner's equity are reported in a statement of changes in partners' equity that is similar to the statement of changes in owner's equity. The balance sheet shows the equity of each partner in a format like this:

Partners' Equity	
Shirley Tucker, capital	$17,300
Mark Jackson, capital	24,800
Total partners' equity	$42,100

Corporations

Corporations are established under state or federal laws. These laws may require the company's financial statements to distinguish between the equity created by investments from stockholders and the equity created by the corporation's net incomes less any reductions for **dividends.** A dividend is a distribution, generally a cash payment, made by a corporation to its stockholders. A cash dividend reduces the assets and the equity of a corporation in the same way that a withdrawal reduces the assets and equity of a proprietorship.

As described in Chapter 1, the total stockholders' equity is divided into *contributed capital* (also called *paid-in capital*) and *retained earnings.* Contributed capital is created by the stockholders' investments and retained earnings are created by the corporation's profitable activities. The components of stockholders' equity are usually shown on a corporate balance sheet like this:

Stockholders' Equity	
Contributed capital: Common stock	$400,000
Retained earnings	124,400
Total stockholders' equity	$524,400

If a corporation issues only one kind of stock, it is called **common stock** or *capital stock.* (Other types of stock are described in Chapter 13.) The $400,000 amount assigned to common stock in the example is the amount invested in the corporation by its original stockholders when they bought the stock from the corporation. (The company's financial statements do not reflect any subsequent sales of stock by investors to other investors.) The retained earnings of $124,400 represents the stockholders' equity arising from prior years' net incomes in excess of any net losses and dividends paid to the stockholders.

Alternative Balance Sheet Formats

Different companies choose different formats for their balance sheets. For example, the balance sheet in Illustration 1–8 (on p. 37) places the liabilities and owner's equity to the right of the assets. This format creates an **account form balance sheet.** If the items are arranged vertically, as shown in Illustration 3–6, the format creates a **report form balance sheet.** Both forms are widely used, and neither is considered more useful than the other.

Using Code Numbers for Accounts

We briefly described a possible three-digit account numbering system in Chapter 2. In these systems, the code number assigned to an account not only identifies the account but also provides information about the account's financial statement category.

In the following simple system, the first digit in an account's number identifies its primary balance sheet or income statement category. For example, account numbers beginning with a 1 are assigned to asset accounts and account numbers beginning with a 2 are assigned to liability accounts. Under this system, the following numbers could be assigned to the accounts of a company that buys and sells merchandise:

101 to 199 Assets
201 to 299 Liabilities
301 to 399 Owner's Equity (including withdrawals)
401 to 499 Revenues
501 to 599 Cost of Goods Sold (these accounts are described in Chapter 5)
601 to 699 Operating Expenses
701 to 799 Gains
801 to 899 Losses

In this system, the second digit of each account number identifies its subclassification within the primary category, such as the following codes:

101 to 199 Assets
- 101 to 139 Current assets (second digit is 0, 1, 2, or 3)
- 141 to 149 Long-term investments (second digit is 4)
- 151 to 179 Plant assets (second digit is 5, 6, or 7)
- 181 to 189 Natural resources (second digit is 8)
- 191 to 199 Intangible assets (second digit is 9)

201 to 299 Liabilities
- 201 to 249 Current liabilities (second digit is 0, 1, 2, 3, or 4)
- 251 to 299 Long-term liabilities (second digit is 5, 6, 7, 8, or 9)

Finally, the third digit completes the unique code for each account. For example, specific current asset accounts might be assigned the following numbers:

101 to 199 Assets
- 101 to 139 Current assets
  - 101 Cash
  - 106 Accounts Receivable
  - 110 Rent Receivable
  - 128 Prepaid Insurance

This code is used for the accounts listed inside the front and back covers of the book.

A three-digit account numbering system may be adequate for many smaller businesses. However, a numbering system for a more complex business might use four, five, or even more digits.

Using the Information—The Current Ratio

Most financial statement users find it helpful to evaluate a company's ability to pay its debts in the near future. This ability obviously affects decisions by suppliers about allowing the company to buy on credit. It would affect decisions by a bank about lending money to the company and the terms of the loan, including the interest rate, due date, and any assets to be pledged as security against the loan. The ability to pay debts also affects a business owner's decisions about obtaining cash to pay existing debts when they come due.

The **current ratio** is widely used to describe the company's ability to pay its short-term obligations. It is calculated by dividing the current assets by the current liabilities:

$$\text{Current ratio} = \frac{\text{Current assets}}{\text{Current liabilities}}$$

Using the balance sheet in Illustration 3–6, National Electrical Supply Co.'s current ratio at the end of 19X1 would be calculated as follows:

$$\text{Current ratio} = \frac{\$44{,}400}{\$29{,}000} = 1.5$$

This value suggests that the company's short-term obligations can be satisfied with the short-term resources on hand. If the ratio were to be closer to one, the company might expect to face more difficulty in paying the liabilities. However, the company's sales may generate sufficient new cash to pay the liabilities. If the ratio drops below 1, the company is more likely to have difficulty because its current liabilities are greater than its current assets.

Summary of the Chapter in Terms of Learning Objectives

LO 1 Decision makers need to have information frequently and promptly to be able to act before problems arise or opportunities are missed. As a result, companies prepare reports at least once each year, but generally more often, such as once each month or once every three months. Adjusting entries are needed at the end of each reporting period to capture information about unrecorded events that are not external transactions.

LO 2 Adjusting entries are needed under the revenue recognition principle because revenues can be earned in a reporting period different from the period in which cash is received. The matching principle requires adjusting to ensure that expenses are reported in the same period as the revenue earned from them. Thus, expenses are reported when incurred even though they may be paid for in another period. Expenses can also create liabilities that are paid in a later period. The revenue recognition and matching principles shape the practices of accrual accounting. Accrual accounting information is more useful than cash basis accounting information for many decisions because it reports the economic effects of events when they occur, not when the cash flows happen. In contrast, cash basis accounting reports revenues when cash is received and reports expenses when cash is paid. The cash basis is not consistent with generally accepted accounting principles for reporting income and financial position. However, companies are required by GAAP to provide a statement of cash flows.

LO 3 Adjusting entries are used (*a*) to record expenses when prepaid expenses expire, (*b*) to record depreciation expense as the cost of using plant and equipment assets, (*c*) to record revenues when the company converts unearned revenues to earned revenues, (*d*) to accrue expenses and related liabilities, and (*e*) to accrue revenues and related assets.

LO 4 The effects of adjustments can be shown in a six-column schedule that presents the unadjusted trial balance in the first two columns, the adjusting entries in the next two columns, and the adjusted trial balance in the final two columns. The adjusted trial balance shows all ledger accounts, including assets, liabilities, revenues, expenses, and owner's equity. As a result, it can be used to prepare the income statement, the statement of changes in owner's equity, and the balance sheet.

LO 5 Payments of accrued expenses in the next accounting period are recorded with a debit to the accrued liability and may include another debit for any additional expense incurred since the beginning of the new period. When accrued revenues are collected, the entry credits the previously recorded asset (a receivable) and may include another credit for any additional revenue earned during the new period.

LO 6 Classified balance sheets usually report four categories of assets: current assets, investments, plant and equipment, and intangible assets. The two categories of liabilities are current and long-term. Owner's equity for proprietorships and partners' equity for partnerships are reported by putting the capital account balances on the balance sheet. A corporation reports stockholders' equity as contributed capital and retained earnings. A company's current ratio describes its ability to pay its current liabilities out of its current assets. The value of the ratio equals the amount of the current assets divided by the current liabilities.

Demonstration Problem

The following information relates to Best Plumbing Company on December 31, 19X2. The company uses the calendar year as its annual reporting period.

a. The company's weekly payroll is $2,800, paid every Friday for a five-day workweek. December 31, 19X2, falls on a Wednesday, but the employees will not be paid until Friday, January 2, 19X3.

b. Eighteen months earlier, on July 1, 19X1, the company purchased equipment that cost $10,000 and had no salvage value. Its useful life is predicted to be five years.

c. On October 1, 19X2, the company agreed to work on a new housing project. For installing plumbing in 24 new homes, the company was paid $144,000 in advance. When the $144,000 cash was received on October 1, 19X2, that amount was credited to the Unearned Plumbing Revenue account. Between October 1 and December 31, 19X2, work on 18 homes was completed.

d. On September 1, 19X2, the company purchased a one-year insurance policy for $1,200. The transaction was recorded with a $1,200 debit to Prepaid Insurance.

Required

1. Prepare the adjusting entries needed on December 31, 19X2, to record the previously unrecorded effects of the events.
2. Complete the following table describing your adjusting entries. Your answer should indicate the amount entered in the listed accounts by each entry; the amount of the asset or liability that will appear on the December 31, 19X2, balance sheet; and whether the item on the balance sheet will be a current asset, an item related to plant and equipment, a current liability, or a long-term liability:

Entry	Account	Amount in the Entry	Amount on the Balance Sheet	Balance Sheet Category
a	Wages Payable	$	$	
b	Accumulated Depreciation, Equipment	$	$	
c	Unearned Plumbing Revenue	$	$	
d	Prepaid Insurance	$	$	

3. Complete the following table describing your adjusting entries. Your answer should indicate how much the entry changed (if at all) the company's reported income, its reported total assets, and its reported total liabilities. If the change is a decrease, enter the amount in parentheses:

Entry	Reported Net Income	Reported Total Assets	Reported Total Liabilities
a	$	$	$
b	$	$	$
c	$	$	$
d	$	$	$

Planning the Solution

- Analyze the information for each situation to determine which accounts need to be updated with an adjustment.
- Calculate the size of each adjustment and prepare the necessary journal entries.

- Show the amount entered by each adjustment in the designated accounts, determine the adjusted balance, and then determine the balance sheet classification that the account falls within.
- Determine each entry's effect on reported net income, reported total assets, and reported total liabilities.

Solution to Demonstration Problem

1. Adjusting journal entries:

a.	Dec.	31	Wages Expense	1,680.00	
			Wages Payable		1,680.00
			To accrue wages for the last three days of the year ($2,800 × 3/5).		
b.	Dec.	31	Depreciation Expense, Equipment	2,000.00	
			Accumulated Depreciation, Equipment		2,000.00
			To record depreciation expense for the full year ($10,000/5 = $2,000).		
c.	Dec.	31	Unearned Plumbing Revenue	108,000.00	
			Plumbing Services Revenue		108,000.00
			To recognize plumbing revenues earned ($144,000 × 18/24).		
d.	Dec.	31	Insurance Expense	400.00	
			Prepaid Insurance		400.00
			To adjust for the expired portion of insurance ($1,200 × 4/12).		

2.

Entry	Account	Amount in the Entry	Amount on the Balance Sheet	Balance Sheet Category
a	Wages Payable	$1,680 cr	$1,680	Current liability
b	Accumulated Depreciation, Equipment	$2,000 cr	$3,000	Plant and equipment
c	Unearned Plumbing Revenue	$108,000 dr	$36,000	Current liability
d	Prepaid Insurance	$400 cr	$800	Current asset

3.

Entry	Reported Net Income	Reported Total Assets	Reported Total Liabilities
a	$(1,680)	no effect	$1,680
b	$(2,000)	$(2,000)	no effect
c	$108,000	no effect	$(108,000)
d	$(400)	$(400)	no effect

APPENDIX

A

Recording Prepaid and Unearned Items in Income Statement Accounts

LO 8 Explain the advantages of initially recording prepaid and unearned items in income statement accounts and prepare adjusting entries under this bookkeeping approach.

This appendix explains alternative bookkeeping procedures that bring about the same results for the financial statements. Because the same information is presented in the statements, there is no conceptual basis for preferring either procedure over the other. The choice between them is simply a matter of convenience. In overview, the accountant first selects the procedure for initially recording prepaid expenses and unearned revenues. That choice shapes adjusting entries made at the end of the period. The alternative sequences of entries are described in Illustrations A–1 and A–2.

Prepaid Expenses

According to the approach presented in Chapter 3, the initial entry for a prepaid expense records a debit to an asset with a credit to cash. Then, as the prepaid expense is used up, the cost is transferred to the expense account. This sequence of entries is shown on the left side of the diagram in Illustration A–1 for Clear Copy Co.'s purchase of insurance coverage. The company paid $2,400 on December 26 for coverage that began on December 1, 19X1, and that will continue for 24 months. Initially, the $2,400 cost is debited to the Prepaid Insurance account and no entry is recorded in the Insurance Expense account. Then, at the end of the reporting period, an adjusting entry transfers one month's cost ($100) from the asset account to the expense account. Thus, the balance sheet shows a $2,300 asset and the income statement reports $100 of insurance expense.

An alternative sequence of entries appears in the right side of Illustration A–1. Under this sequence, the initial entry debits Insurance Expense for $2,400. The adjusting entry credits the Insurance Expense account for $2,300 to reduce it to the $100 balance that it should have. The adjustment also creates a $2,300 debit balance in the Prepaid Insurance account. Notice that the company's balance sheet shows the $2,300 asset and the income statement shows $100 of insurance expense.

The diagram shows that the same result is reached by both routes. It does not matter which method a company uses, as long as the financial statements report the same amounts.

A company prefers one sequence of entries over the other based on the typical life of the prepaid expense. If a company's prepaid expenses typically last a year or more, it makes sense to record them initially with debits to asset accounts and let the adjusting process record the expenses later. If the company's prepaid expenses last only briefly, such as one to three months, it is more convenient to record them initially as expense. As a result, adjusting entries are not needed to record the expense and eliminate the asset account's bal-

ILLUSTRATION A–1 *Alternative Bookkeeping Entries for Prepaid Expenses*

Acquire prepaid expense:

Initial entry records prepaid insurance

Prepaid Insurance 2,400
Cash 2,400

Prepaid Insurance

Date		Expl.	Debit	Credit	Balance
Dec.	26		2,400		2,400

Insurance Expense

Date		Expl.	Debit	Credit	Balance

Initial entry records insurance expense

Insurance Expense 2,400
Cash 2,400

Prepaid Insurance

Date		Expl.	Debit	Credit	Balance

Insurance Expense

Date		Expl.	Debit	Credit	Balance
Dec.	26		2,400		2,400

Make the following adjustments at the end of the reporting period:

Insurance Expense 100
Prepaid Insurance 100

Prepaid Insurance

Date		Expl.	Debit	Credit	Balance
Dec.	26		2,400		2,400
	31			100	2,300

Insurance Expense

Date		Expl.	Debit	Credit	Balance
Dec.	31		100		100

Prepaid Insurance 2,300
Insurance Expense 2,300

Prepaid Insurance

Date		Expl.	Debit	Credit	Balance
Dec.	31		2,300		2,300

Insurance Expense

Date		Expl.	Debit	Credit	Balance
Dec.	26		2,400		2,400
	31			2,300	100

Prepare the financial statements:

Balance Sheet
December 31, 19X1
Prepaid insurance $2,300

Income Statement
For Month Ended December 31, 19X1
Insurance expense . . . . $ 100

ance in most situations. However, an adjustment would be needed at the end of the reporting period to recognize any unexpired prepaid expense as an asset.

In fact, a company might combine the two methods. For example, the first approach might be used for some prepaid expenses that last longer (such as insurance). Other prepaid expenses that are quickly consumed (such as rent or supplies) would be recorded with the second method. Remember that the actual bookkeeping sequence does not matter as long as the financial statements report useful amounts in accordance with generally accepted accounting principles.

ILLUSTRATION A–2 *Alternative Bookkeeping Entries for Unearned Revenues*

Receive unearned revenue:

Initial entry records unearned revenue

Cash	3,000	
Unearned Copy Services Revenue		3,000

Unearned Copy Services Revenue

Date		Expl.	Debit	Credit	Balance
Dec.	26			3,000	3,000

Copy Services Revenue

Date		Expl.	Debit	Credit	Balance

Initial entry records copy services revenue

Cash	3,000	
Copy Services Revenue .		3,000

Unearned Copy Services Revenue

Date		Expl.	Debit	Credit	Balance

Copy Services Revenue

Date		Expl.	Debit	Credit	Balance
Dec.	26			3,000	3,000

Make the following adjustments at the end of the reporting period:

Unearned Copy Services Revenue	250	
Copy Services Revenue . . .		250

Unearned Copy Services Revenue

Date		Expl.	Debit	Credit	Balance
Dec.	26			3,000	3,000
	31		250		2,750

Copy Services Revenue

Date		Expl.	Debit	Credit	Balance
Dec.	31			250	250

Copy Services Revenue	2,750	
Unearned Copy Services Revenue		2,750

Unearned Copy Services Revenue

Date		Expl.	Debit	Credit	Balance
Dec.	31			2,750	2,750

Copy Services Revenue

Date		Expl.	Debit	Credit	Balance
Dec.	26			3,000	3,000
	31		2,750		250

Prepare the financial statements:

Balance Sheet
December 31, 19X1

Unearned copy services revenue .	$2,750

Income Statement
For Month Ended December 31, 19X1

Copy services revenue	$ 250

Unearned Revenues

Unearned revenues also can be recorded with two different approaches. Under the sequence on the left side of Illustration A–2, the initial entry to record the unearned revenue debits cash and credits the liability to the customer. For example, Clear Copy received $3,000 in advance and promised to provide services over the period from December 26, 19X1, through February 26, 19X2. Thus, by December 31, the company had earned $250 (one-sixth of one month's revenue), and owes only $2,750 to the customer. The adjusting entry updates the account balances to record the revenue and reduce the liability. The bottom of the diagram shows that the balance sheet reports $2,750 as the unearned revenue and the income statement reports $250 of revenue.

Alternatively, the company could initially record the advance payment as revenue. This sequence of entries appears in the right side of Illustration A–2. At the end of the reporting period, an adjusting entry reduces the revenue account to the $250 balance that it ought to have. At the same time, the company needs to recognize the $2,750 liability for future services.

As before, it does not matter which sequence a company uses, as long as the financial statements report the same amounts.

The choice between the two methods is purely practical. If most unearned revenues are earned quickly, it makes sense to initially record them as if they have been earned because it is likely that no additional entry will be needed. On the other hand, if it takes many months to earn the revenues, it makes sense to initially record the liability and reduce it as revenue is earned.

Summary of Appendix A in Terms of the Learning Objective

LO 8 The same financial statement measures can be developed by different bookkeeping procedures. Under one approach to recording a prepaid expense or unearned revenue, the system initially records the asset or liability. These accounts are later reduced and the expense or revenue increased with an adjusting entry. Alternatively, the system can initially record the expense or revenue, and then, if necessary, adjust the account to reflect the asset or liability. The choice between the alternatives is purely practical.

Glossary

LO 7 Define or explain the words and phrases listed in the chapter glossary.

Account form balance sheet a balance sheet that places the liabilities and owner's equity to the right of the assets. p. 119

Accounting period the length of time covered by periodic financial statements and other reports. p. 101

Accrual basis accounting the approach to preparing financial statements based on recognizing revenues when they are earned and matching expenses to those revenues; the basis for generally accepted accounting principles. p. 103

Accrued expenses incurred but unpaid expenses that are recorded during the adjusting process; recorded with a debit to an expense and a credit to a liability. p. 108

Accrued revenues earned but uncollected revenues that are recorded during the adjusting process; recorded with a credit to a revenue and a debit to an expense. p. 109

Adjusted trial balance a trial balance prepared after adjustments have been recorded. p. 110

Adjusting entry a journal entry at the end of an accounting period that recognizes revenues earned or expenses incurred in that period while updating the related liability and asset accounts. p. 104

Cash basis accounting the approach to preparing financial statements based on recognizing revenues when the cash is received and reporting expenses when the cash is paid; not generally accepted. p. 103

Classified balance sheet a balance sheet that presents the assets and liabilities in relevant groups. p. 115

Common stock the most basic category of a corporation's stock; if the corporation issues only one class of stock, all of it is common. p. 119

Contra account an account used to provide more complete information; its balance is subtracted from the balance of an associated account on a financial statement or report. p. 107

Current assets cash or other assets that are reasonably expected to be sold, collected, or consumed within one year or within the normal operating cycle of the business, whichever is longer. p. 116

Current liabilities obligations due to be paid or liquidated within one year or the operating cycle, whichever is longer. p. 118

Current ratio a description of a company's ability to pay its short-term obligations; calculated by dividing the current assets by the current liabilities. p. 120

Depreciation the expense created by allocating the cost of plant and equipment to the periods in which they are used; represents the expense of using the assets. p. 106

Dividends a distribution, generally a cash payment, made by a corporation to its stockholders; similar to a withdrawal for a proprietorship. p. 119

Fiscal year the 12 consecutive months (or 52 weeks) selected as an organization's annual accounting period. p. 101

Intangible assets assets without a physical form that are used to produce or sell goods and services; their value comes from the privileges or right granted to or held by the owner. p. 118

Interim financial reports financial reports covering less than one year; usually based on one- or three-month periods. p. 101

Long-term liabilities obligations that are not due to be paid within one year or the operating cycle, whichever is longer. p. 118

Matching principle the broad principle that requires expenses to be reported in the same period as the revenues that were earned as a result of the expenses. p. 102

Natural business year a 12-month period that ends when a company's sales activities are at their lowest point. p. 101

Operating cycle of a business the average time between paying cash for employee salaries or merchandise and receiving cash from customers. p. 116

Plant and equipment tangible long-lived assets used to produce goods or services. p. 106

Report form balance sheet a balance sheet that places the assets above the liabilities and owner's equity. p. 119

Time period principle a broad principle that requires identifying the activities of a business with specific time periods such as months, quarters, or years. p. 101

Unadjusted trial balance a trial balance prepared before adjustments have been recorded. p. 110

Unclassified balance sheet a balance sheet that does not separate the assets and liabilities into categories. p. 115

Objective Review

Answers to the following questions are listed at the end of the chapter. Be sure that you decide which is the one best answer to each question *before* you check the answers.

LO 1 A company selects an annual reporting period that:

a. Is called the fiscal year.
b. Always ends at the close of the natural business year.
c. Always ends at the close of the calendar business year.
d. Is never divided into shorter interim periods.
e. None of the above are correct.

LO 2 On April 1, 19X1, Collins Company paid a $4,800 premium for two years of insurance coverage.

a. Under the cash basis, no insurance expense will be reported for 19X2.
b. Under the accrual basis, $4,800 of insurance expense will be reported for 19X1.
c. Under the cash basis, $600 of insurance expense will be reported for 19X3.
d. Under the accrual basis, no adjusting entry for insurance will be needed at the end of 19X2.
e. Under the cash basis, $2,400 of insurance expense will be reported for 19X2.

LO 3 At the end of its fiscal year, Corona Company omitted an adjustment to record $200 of accrued service revenues. The company also neglected to record $700 of insurance premiums that had expired; this cost had been initially debited to the Prepaid Insurance account. As a result of these oversights, the income statement for the reporting period will:

a. Understate net income by $500.
b. Overstate revenues by $200 and understate expenses by $700.
c. Overstate revenues by $200 and overstate expenses by $700.
d. Understate revenues by $200 and overstate expenses by $700.
e. Understate revenues by $200 and understate expenses by $700.

LO 4 The following information has been taken from Jones Company's unadjusted and adjusted trial balances:

	Unadjusted		Adjusted	
	Debit	Credit	Debit	Credit
Prepaid insurance	$6,200		$5,900	
Salaries payable .				$1,400
Office supplies . .	900		800	

The adjusting entries must have included these items:

a. A $300 debit to Prepaid Insurance, a $1,400 credit to Salaries Payable, and a $100 credit to Office Supplies.
b. A $300 credit to Prepaid Insurance, a $1,400 debit to Salaries Payable, and a $100 credit to Office Supplies.
c. A $300 credit to Insurance Expense, a $1,400 debit to Salaries Expense, and a $100 debit to Office Supplies Expense.
d. A $300 debit to Insurance Expense, a $1,400 credit to Salaries Payable, and a $100 debit to Office Supplies.
e. A $300 debit to Insurance Expense, a $1,400 debit to Salaries Expense, and a $100 debit to Office Supplies Expense.

LO 5 On December 31, 19X1, Holland Photo Company recorded $1,600 of accrued salaries with an adjusting entry. On January 5, 19X2, a total of $8,000 was paid to the employees for their salaries earned since the prior payday. This information allows you to know that:

a. The company uses cash basis accounting.
b. The January 5 entry includes a $6,400 credit to Cash.

c. The salaries expense assigned to 19X2 is $8,000.
d. The salaries expense assigned to 19X2 is $6,400.
e. The salaries expense assigned to 19X1 is $6,400.

LO 6 A company owns these assets:

1. Land used in operating the business.
2. Office supplies.
3. Receivables from customers due in 10 months.
4. Common stock issued by another company that the company expects to hold for the long term.
5. Insurance protection for the next nine months.
6. Land held for the possibility of use in future operations.
7. Trucks used to provide services to customers.
8. Trademarks used in advertising the company's services.

These assets should appear on the balance sheet as follows:

	Current Assets	Investments	Plant and Equipment	Intangible Assets
a.	2	4, 6	1, 7	3, 5, 8
b.	2, 3, 4	6	1, 7	5, 8
c.	2, 3	4, 6	1, 7	5, 8
d.	2, 3, 5	4	1, 6, 7	8
e.	2, 3, 5	4, 6	1, 7	8

LO 7 Identify the term that describes a cash distribution to a corporation's stockholders:

a. Paid-out capital.
b. Retained earnings.
c. A dividend.
d. An intangible asset.
e. A withdrawal.

LO 8 Blalock Company initially records prepaid and unearned items in income statement accounts. In preparing adjusting entries at the end of the company's first accounting period:

a. Unpaid salaries will be recorded with a debit to Prepaid Salaries and a credit to Salaries Expense.
b. The cost of unused office supplies will be recorded with a debit to Supplies Expense and a credit to Office Supplies.
c. Unearned fees will be recorded with a debit to Consulting Fees Earned and a credit to Unearned Consulting Fees.
d. Earned but unbilled consulting fees will be recorded with a debit to Unearned Consulting Fees and a credit to Consulting Fees Earned.
e. None of the above is correct.

The letter [A] identifies the questions, exercises, and problems based on Appendix A at the end of the chapter.

Questions for Class Discussion

1. Why do companies provide periodic reports to decision makers?
2. What type of business is most likely to select a fiscal year that corresponds to the natural business year instead of the calendar year?
3. What is the primary purpose for making adjustments at the end of the accounting period?
4. What kind of assets require adjusting entries to record depreciation?
5. What contra account is used when recording and reporting the effects of depreciation? Why is it used?
6. What is an accrued expense? Give an example.
7. How does an unearned revenue arise? Give an example of an unearned revenue.
8. How is an unearned revenue classified on the balance sheet?
9. What is an accrued revenue? Give an example.
10. Which accounting principles lead most directly to the adjustment process?
11. What does the matching principle require?
12. Is the cash basis of accounting consistent with the matching principle?
13. What is the difference between the cash and accrual bases of accounting?
14. What classes of assets and liabilities are shown on a typical classified balance sheet?
15. What are the characteristics of a current asset?
16. What is a company's operating cycle?
17. Identify two examples of assets classified as investments on the balance sheet.
18. What are the characteristics of plant and equipment?

19. Review the consolidated balance sheets of Federal Express Corporation in Appendix G. Assume that all accrued expenses existing at the end of each year are paid within a few months. What was the total amount of accrued expenses in the company's adjusting entries at the end of the 1993 fiscal year?

20. Review the consolidated balance sheet of Ben & Jerry's Homemade, Inc., in Appendix G. As a simplification, assume that the company did not sell any property, plant, and equipment during 1992. How much depreciation was recorded in the adjusting entries at the end of 1992?

[A]21. If a company initially records prepaid expenses

with debits to expense accounts, what type of account is debited in the adjusting entries for prepaid expenses?

A22. Suppose that one company initially records unearned revenues with credits to a liability account while another records them with credits to revenue accounts. Will their financial statements differ as a result of this variation in their procedures? Why or why not?

Exercises

Exercise 3–1
Adjusting entries for expenses
(LO 3)

Prepare adjusting journal entries for the financial statements for the year ended December 31, 19X1, for each of these independent situations:

a. The Supplies account had a $150 debit balance on January 1, 19X1; $1,340 of supplies were purchased during the year; and the December 31, 19X1, count showed that $177 of supplies are on hand.

b. The Prepaid Insurance account had a $2,800 debit balance at December 31, 19X1, before adjusting for the costs of any expired coverage. An analysis of the company's insurance policies showed that $2,300 of coverage had expired.

c. The Prepaid Insurance account had a $3,500 debit balance at December 31, 19X1, before adjusting for the costs of any expired coverage. An analysis of the company's insurance policies showed that $520 of unexpired insurance remained in effect.

d. Depreciation on the company's equipment for 19X1 was estimated to be $8,000.

e. Six months' property taxes are estimated to be $5,400. They have accrued since June 30, 19X1, but are unrecorded and unpaid at December 31, 19X1.

Exercise 3–2
Adjusting entries for accrued expenses
(LO 3)

The Haywood Company has five part-time employees, and each earns $120 per day. They are normally paid on Fridays for work completed on Monday through Friday of the same week. They were all paid in full on Friday, December 28, 19X1. The next week, all five of the employees worked only four days because New Year's Day was an unpaid holiday. Show the adjusting entry that would be recorded on Monday, December 31, 19X1, and the journal entry that would be made to record paying the employees' wages on Friday, January 4, 19X2.

Exercise 3–3
Identifying adjusting entries
(LO 3)

For each of these adjusting entries, enter the letter of the explanation that most closely describes the transaction in the blank space beside the entry.

A. To record the year's consumption of a prepaid expense.
B. To record accrued interest expense.
C. To record accrued income.
D. To record the year's depreciation expense.
E. To record the earning of previously unearned income.
F. To record accrued salaries expense.

	Account	Debit	Credit
___1.	Depreciation Expense	99,000.00	
	Accumulated Depreciation		99,000.00
___2.	Insurance Expense	6,000.00	
	Prepaid Insurance		6,000.00
___3.	Interest Receivable	22,000.00	
	Interest Earned		22,000.00
___4.	Salaries Expense	37,500.00	
	Salaries Payable		37,500.00
___5.	Interest Expense	63,000.00	
	Interest Payable		63,000.00
___6.	Unearned Professional Fees	86,000.00	
	Professional Fees Earned		86,000.00

Exercise 3–4
Missing data in supplies expense calculations
(LO 3)

Determine the missing amounts in each of these four independent situations.

	(a)	(b)	(c)	(d)
Supplies on hand—January 1	$100	$ 800	$ 680	$?
Supplies purchased during the year	700	2,700	?	12,000
Supplies on hand—December 31	250	?	920	1,600
Supplies expense for the year	?	650	4,800	13,150

Exercise 3–5
Adjustments and payments of accrued items
(LO 3, 5)

The following three situations require adjusting journal entries to prepare financial statements as of June 30. For each situation, present the adjusting entry and the entry that would record the payment of the accrued liability during July.

a. The total weekly salaries expense for all employees is $6,000. This amount is paid at the end of the day on Friday of each week with five working days. June 30 falls on Tuesday of this year, which means that the employees had worked two days since the last payday. The next payday is July 3.

b. The company has a $390,000 note payable that requires 0.8% interest to be paid each month on the 20th of the month. The interest was last paid on June 20 and the next payment is due on July 20.

c. On June 1, the company retained an attorney at a flat monthly fee of $1,000. This amount is payable on the 12th of the following month.

Exercise 3–6
Amounts of cash and accrual basis expenses
(LO 2, 4)

On March 1, 19X1, a company paid a $32,400 premium on a three-year insurance policy for protection beginning on that date. Fill in the blanks in the following table:

Balance Sheet Asset under the		
	Accrual Basis	Cash Basis
12/31/X1	$______	$______
12/31/X2	______	______
12/31/X3	______	______
12/31/X4	______	______

Insurance Expense under the		
	Accrual Basis	Cash Basis
19X1	$______	$______
19X2	______	______
19X3	______	______
19X4	______	______
Total	$______	$______

Exercise 3–7
Unearned and accrued revenues
(LO 2, 4)

The owner of a duplex apartment building prepares annual financial statements based on a March 31 fiscal year.

a. The tenants of one of the apartments paid five months' rent in advance on November 1, 19X1. The monthly rental is $1,000 per month. Because more than one month's rent was paid in advance, the journal entry credited the Unearned Rent account when the payment was received. No other entry had been recorded prior to March 31, 19X2. Give the adjusting journal entry that should be recorded on March 31, 19X2.

b. On January 1, 19X2, the tenants of the other apartment moved in and paid the first month's rent. The $900 payment was recorded with a credit to the Rent Earned account. However, the tenants have not paid the rent for February or March. They have agreed to pay it as soon as possible. Give the adjusting journal entry that should be recorded on March 31, 19X2.

c. On April 3, 19X2, the tenants described in part *b* paid $2,700 rent for February, March, and April. Give the journal entry to record the cash collection.

Exercise 3–8
Preparing financial statements
(LO 4)

Use the following adjusted trial balance of the Hamburg Trucking Company to prepare (*a*) an income statement for the year ended December 31, 19X1; (*b*) a statement of changes in owner's equity for the year ended December 31, 19X1; and (*c*) an unclassified balance sheet as of December 31, 19X1. The owner did not make any new investments during 19X1.

	Debit	Credit
Cash	$ 5,500	
Accounts receivable	18,000	
Office supplies	2,000	
Trucks	180,000	
Accumulated depreciation, trucks		$ 45,000
Land	75,000	
Accounts payable		11,000
Interest payable		3,000
Long-term notes payable		52,000
B. Hamburg, capital		161,000
B. Hamburg, withdrawals	19,000	
Trucking fees earned		128,000
Depreciation expense, trucks	22,500	
Salaries expense	60,000	
Office supplies expense	7,000	
Repairs expense, trucks	11,000	
Total	$400,000	$400,000

Exercise 3–9
Classified balance sheet and current ratio
(LO 6)

Use the information provided in Exercise 3–8 to prepare a classified balance sheet for the Hamburg Trucking Company as of December 31, 19X1. Determine the value of the current ratio as of the balance sheet date.

Exercise 3–10
Identifying the effects of adjusting entries
(LO 3, 4)

Following are two income statements for the Carlton Financial Consulting Co. for the year ended on December 31. The left column was prepared before any adjusting entries were recorded and the right column includes the effects of adjusting entries. Analyze the statements and prepare the adjusting entries that must have been recorded. Thirty percent of the additional consulting fees were earned but not billed and the other 70% were earned by performing services that the customers had paid for in advance.

CARLTON FINANCIAL CONSULTING CO.
Income Statements
For Year Ended December 31

	Before Adjustments	After Adjustments
Revenues:		
Consulting fees earned	$ 48,000	$ 60,000
Commissions earned	85,000	85,000
Total revenues	$133,000	$145,000
Operating expenses:		
Depreciation expense, computers		$ 3,000
Depreciation expense, office furniture		3,500
Salaries expense	$ 25,000	29,900
Insurance expense		2,600
Rent expense	9,000	9,000
Office supplies expense		960
Advertising expense	6,000	6,000
Utilities expense	2,500	2,640
Total operating expenses	$ 42,500	$ 57,600
Net income	$ 90,500	$ 87,400

Exercise 3–11
Calculating the current ratio
(LO 6)

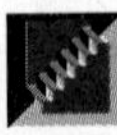

Calculate the current ratio in each of the following cases:

	Current Assets	Current Liabilities
Case 1	$84,000	$31,000
Case 2	96,000	75,000
Case 3	45,000	48,000
Case 4	84,500	82,600
Case 5	65,000	97,000

[A]Exercise 3–12
Adjustments for prepaid items recorded in expense and revenue accounts
(LO 8)

The Elder Painting Co. was organized on December 1 by Terry Elder. In setting up the bookkeeping procedures, Elder decided to debit expense accounts when the company prepays its expenses and to credit revenue accounts when customers pay for services in advance. Prepare general journal entries for items *a* through *d* and adjusting journal entries as of December 31 for items *e* through *g*:

a. Shop supplies were purchased on December 1 for $1,000.
b. The company prepaid insurance premiums of $480 on December 2.
c. On December 15, the company received an advance payment of $4,000 from one customer for two painting projects.
d. On December 28, the company received $1,200 from a second customer for painting services to be performed in January.
e. By counting them on December 31, Elder determined that $640 of shop supplies were on hand.
f. An analysis of the insurance policies in effect on December 31 showed that $80 of insurance coverage had expired.
g. As of December 31, only one project had been completed. The fee for this particular project was $2,100.

[A]Exercise 3–13
Alternative procedures for revenues received in advance
(LO 8)

The Falcon Company experienced the following events and transactions during March:

Mar. 1 Received $1,000 in advance of performing work for T. Carson.
5 Received $4,200 in advance of performing work for B. Gamble.
10 Completed the job for T. Carson.
16 Received $3,750 in advance of performing work for S. Curtin.
25 Completed the job for B. Gamble.
31 The job for S. Curtin is still unfinished.

a. Give journal entries (including any adjusting entry as of the end of the month) to record these events using the procedure of initially crediting the Unearned Fees account when a payment is received from a customer in advance of performing services.
b. Show journal entries (including any adjusting entry as of the end of the month) to record these events using the procedure of initially crediting the Fees Earned account when a payment is received from a customer in advance of performing services.
c. Under each method, determine the amount of earned fees that should be reported on the income statement for March and the amount of unearned fees that should appear on the balance sheet as of March 31.

Problems

Problem 3–1
Adjusting journal entries
(LO 3, 5)

The Montgomery Company's annual accounting period ends on December 31, 19X2. The following information concerns the adjusting entries to be recorded as of that date:

a. The Office Supplies account started the year with a $1,000 balance. During 19X2, the company purchased supplies at a cost of $4,200, which was added to the Office Supplies account. The inventory of supplies on hand at December 31 had a cost of $880.
b. An analysis of the company's insurance policies provided these facts:

Policy	Date of Purchase	Years of Coverage	Total Cost
1	April 1, 19X1	2	$5,280
2	April 1, 19X2	3	4,356
3	August 1, 19X2	1	900

The total premium for each policy was paid in full at the purchase date, and the Prepaid Insurance account was debited for the full cost.

c. The company has five employees who earn a total of $700 in salaries for every working day. They are paid each Monday for their work in the five-day workweek ending on the preceding Friday. December 31, 19X2, falls on Tuesday, and all five employees worked the first two days of the week. Because New Year's Day is a paid holiday, they will be paid salaries for five full days on Monday, January 6, 19X3.

d. The company purchased a building on August 1, 19X2. The building cost $570,000 and is expected to have a $30,000 salvage value at the end of its predicted 30-year life.

e. Because the company is not large enough to occupy the entire building, it arranged to rent some space to a tenant at $800 per month, starting on November 1, 19X2. The rent was paid on time on November 1, and the amount received was credited to the Rent Earned account. However, the tenant has not paid the December rent. The company has worked out an agreement with the tenant, who has promised to pay both December's and January's rent in full on January 15. The tenant has agreed not to fall behind again.

f. On November 1, the company also rented space to another tenant for $725 per month. The tenant paid five months' rent in advance on that date. The payment was recorded with a credit to the Unearned Rent account.

Required

1. Use the information to prepare adjusting entries as of December 31, 19X2.
2. Prepare journal entries to record the subsequent cash transactions described in parts *c* and *e*.

Problem 3–2
Adjusting entries and financial statements
(LO 3, 4, 6)

The following six-column table includes the unadjusted trial balance for Carter's Carpentry School as of December 31, 19X1. The school is owned and operated by Carl Carter. Carter provides one-on-one training to individuals who pay tuition directly to the business, and also offers extension training to groups in off-site locations. Presented after the table are facts leading to eight adjusting entries as of December 31, 19X1.

	Unadjusted Trial Balance		Adjustments		Adjusted Trial Balance	
Cash	$ 13,000					
Accounts receivable						
Teaching supplies	5,000					
Prepaid insurance	7,500					
Prepaid rent	1,000					
Professional library	15,000					
Accumulated depreciation, professional library		$ 4,500				
Equipment	35,000					
Accumulated depreciation, equipment		8,000				
Accounts payable		18,000				
Salaries payable						
Unearned extension fees		5,500				
Carl Carter, capital		31,800				
Carl Carter, withdrawals	20,000					
Tuition fees earned		51,000				
Extension fees earned		19,000				
Depreciation expense, equipment						
Depreciation expense, professional library						
Salaries expense	24,000					
Insurance expense						
Rent expense	11,000					
Teaching supplies expense						
Advertising expense	3,500					
Utilities expense	2,800					
Totals	$137,800	$137,800				

Additional facts:

a. An analysis of the company's policies shows that $1,500 of insurance coverage has expired.

b. An inventory shows that teaching supplies costing $1,300 are on hand at the end of the year.

c. The estimated annual depreciation on the equipment is $6,000.

d. The estimated annual depreciation on the professional library is $3,000.

e. The school offers off-campus services for specific employers. On November 1, the company agreed to do a special six-month course for a client. The contract calls for a monthly fee of $1,100, and the client paid the first five months' fees in advance. When the cash was received, the Unearned Extension Fees account was credited.

f. On October 15, the school agreed to teach a four-month class for an individual for $1,500 tuition per month payable at the end of the class. The services have been provided as agreed, and no payment has been received.

g. The school's only employee is paid weekly. As of the end of the year, two days' wages have accrued at the rate of $100 per day.

h. The balance in the Prepaid Rent account represents the rent for December.

Required

1. Enter the adjusting entries in the two adjustments columns in the table. Identify the debits and credits of each entry with the letters in the list of additional facts.
2. Complete the adjusted trial balance.
3. Prepare the company's income statement and the statement of changes in owner's equity for 19X1, and prepare the classified balance sheet as of December 31, 19X1. Carter did not make additional investments in the business during the year.
4. Calculate the current ratio and the debt ratio as of December 31, 19X1, and calculate the modified return on equity for the company, under the assumption that Carter's time in the business is worth $15,000 per year.

Problem 3–3
Comparing the unadjusted and adjusted trial balances
(LO 4, 6)

In the following six-column table for the Decker Company, the first two columns contain the unadjusted trial balance for the company as of March 31, 19X1. The last two columns contain the adjusted trial balance as of the same date.

	Unadjusted Trial Balance		Adjustments		Adjusted Trial Balance	
Cash	$ 13,500				$ 13,500	
Accounts receivable	6,000				11,230	
Office supplies	9,000				1,500	
Prepaid insurance	3,660				2,440	
Office equipment	36,000				36,000	
Accumulated depreciation, office equipment		$ 6,000				$ 9,000
Accounts payable		4,650				5,100
Interest payable						400
Salaries payable						3,300
Unearned consulting fees		8,000				7,150
Long-term notes payable		22,000				22,000
Webster Decker, capital		14,210				14,210
Webster Decker, withdrawals	15,000				15,000	
Consulting fees earned		78,000				84,080
Depreciation expense, office equipment					3,000	
Salaries expense	35,500				38,800	
Interest expense	700				1,100	
Insurance expense					1,220	
Rent expense	6,600				6,600	
Office supplies expense					7,500	
Advertising expense	6,900				7,350	
Totals	$132,860	$132,860			$145,240	$145,240

Required

1. Insert the adjusting journal entries that must have been recorded by the company in the two middle columns. Label each entry with a letter, and provide a short description of the purpose for recording it. (Use the working papers that accompany the text or recreate the table.)
2. Prepare the company's income statement for the year ended March 31, 19X1.
3. Prepare the company's statement of changes in owner's equity for the year ended March 31, 19X1. The owner did not make any new investments during the year.
4. Prepare the company's classified balance sheet as of March 31, 19X1.
5. Calculate the company's current ratio and debt ratio as of March 31, 19X1.

Problem 3–4
Accrual basis income
(LO 2, 3, 5)

The records for Jan Kauffman's home nursing business were kept on the cash basis instead of the accrual basis. However, the company is now applying for a loan and the bank wants to know what its net income for 19X2 was under generally accepted accounting principles. Here is the income statement for 19X2 under the cash basis:

KAUFFMAN'S HOME NURSING
Income Statement (Cash Basis)
For Year Ended December 31, 19X2

Revenues	$175,000
Expenses	110,000
Net income	$ 65,000

This additional information was gathered to help the accountant convert the income statement to the accrual basis:

	As of 12/31/X1	As of 12/31/X2
Accrued revenues	$ 4,000	$5,500
Unearned revenues	22,000	7,000
Accrued expenses	4,900	3,000
Prepaid expenses	9,000	6,900

All prepaid expenses from the beginning of the year were consumed or expired, all unearned revenues from the beginning of the year were earned, and all accrued expenses and revenues from the beginning of the year were paid or collected.

Required

Prepare an accrual basis income statement for this business for 19X2. Provide schedules that explain how you converted from cash revenues and expenses to accrual revenues and expenses.

Problem 3–5
Identifying adjusting and subsequent entries
(LO 3)

For these adjusting and transaction entries, enter the letter of the explanation that most closely describes the adjustment or transaction in the blank space beside each entry. (You can use some letters more than once.)

A. To record collection of an accrued revenue.
B. To record the year's depreciation expense.
C. To record collection of an unearned revenue.
D. To record the earning of previously unearned income.
E. To record payment of an accrued expense.
F. To record an accrued expense.
G. To record accrued income.
H. To record payment of a prepaid expense.
I. To record the year's consumption of a prepaid expense.

	Account	Debit	Credit
___ 1.	Rent Expense	1,000.00	
	Prepaid Rent		1,000.00
___ 2.	Cash	6,500.00	
	Unearned Professional Fees		6,500.00
___ 3.	Depreciation Expense	3,000.00	
	Accumulated Depreciation		3,000.00
___ 4.	Interest Expense	4,000.00	
	Interest Payable		4,000.00
___ 5.	Prepaid Rent	3,500.00	
	Cash		3,500.00
___ 6.	Salaries Expense	5,000.00	
	Salaries Payable		5,000.00
___ 7.	Unearned Professional Fees	2,000.00	
	Professional Fees Earned		2,000.00
___ 8.	Cash	8,000.00	
	Accounts Receivable		8,000.00
___ 9.	Insurance Expense	6,000.00	
	Prepaid Insurance		6,000.00
___10.	Salaries Payable	1,500.00	
	Cash		1,500.00
___11.	Cash	9,000.00	
	Interest Receivable		9,000.00
___12.	Interest Receivable	7,000.00	
	Interest Earned		7,000.00

Problem 3–6
Balance sheet classifications
(LO 6)

In the blank space beside each numbered balance sheet item, enter the letter of its balance sheet classification. If the item should not appear on the balance sheet, enter a Z in the blank.

A. Current assets
B. Investments
C. Plant and equipment
D. Intangible assets
E. Current liabilities
F. Long-term liabilities
G. Owner's equity
H. Stockholders' equity

___ 1. S. Sherman, capital
___ 2. Accounts payable
___ 3. Depreciation expense, trucks
___ 4. S. Sherman, withdrawals
___ 5. Investment in Ben & Jerry's Homemade, Inc. (long-term holding)
___ 6. Notes payable—due in three years
___ 7. Unearned fees revenue
___ 8. Prepaid insurance
___ 9. Common stock (issued)
___10. Interest receivable
___11. Accumulated depreciation, trucks
___12. Building
___13. Cash
___14. Retained earnings
___15. Office equipment
___16. Automobiles
___17. Repairs expense
___18. Prepaid property taxes
___19. Current portion of long-term note payable
___20. Land (in use)

Problem 3–7
Preparing financial statements from the adjusted trial balance and computing ratios
(LO 4, 6)

This adjusted trial balance is for the Krumbell Wrecking Co. as of December 31, 19X1:

	Debit	Credit
Cash	$ 11,000	
Accounts receivable	22,000	
Interest receivable	5,000	
Notes receivable (due in 90 days)	80,000	
Office supplies	4,000	
Trucks	90,000	
Accumulated depreciation, trucks		$ 36,000
Equipment	70,000	
Accumulated depreciation, equipment		5,000
Land	35,000	
Accounts payable		44,000
Interest payable		6,000
Salaries payable		5,500
Unearned wrecking fees		11,000
Long-term notes payable		65,000
W. Krumbell, capital		123,900
W. Krumbell, withdrawals	19,000	
Wrecking fees earned		210,000
Interest earned		8,000
Depreciation expense, trucks	9,000	
Depreciation expense, equipment	5,000	
Salaries expense	90,000	
Wages expense	16,000	
Interest expense	12,000	
Office supplies expense	13,000	
Advertising expense	25,000	
Repairs expense, trucks	8,400	
Total	$514,400	$514,400

Required

1. Use the information in the trial balance to prepare (*a*) the income statement for the year ended December 31, 19X1 (under the assumption that the owner made no new investments during the year); (*b*) the statement of changes in owner's equity for the year ended December 31, 19X1; and (*c*) the classified balance sheet as of December 31, 19X1.

2. Calculate the following ratios for the company:
   a. Current ratio as of December 31, 19X1.
   b. Debt ratio as of December 31, 19X1.
   c. Modified return on equity for the year ended December 31, 19X1, under the assumption that the proprietor's efforts are valued at $30,000.

[A]Problem 3–8
Recording prepaid expenses and unearned revenues
(LO 2, 8)

The following events occurred for a company during the last two months of its fiscal year ended December 31:

Nov.	1	Paid $1,000 for November's rent.
	1	Paid $1,440 for insurance through October 31 of the following year.
	15	Received $2,200 for services to be provided within 30 days.
Dec.	1	Paid $1,000 for December's rent.
	12	Performed the services as agreed on November 15.
	15	Received $5,100 for services to be provided within 30 days.
	31	The company had not performed the services as agreed on December 15. The company also prepared financial statements as of this date.

Required

1. Prepare journal entries under the approach that initially recognizes assets for prepaid expenses and liabilities for unearned revenues received in advance. Include entries to recognize that an asset or liability has been completely consumed or settled, as well as any adjusting entries that should be made at the end of the year.

2. Prepare journal entries under the approach that initially recognizes expenses for prepaid expenses and revenues for unearned revenues received in advance. Include any adjusting entries that should be made at the end of the year.
3. Use the information in the entries to provide numbers for the following table:

	Part 1	Part 2	Difference
Rent expense for two months	$______	$______	$______
Insurance expense for two months . . .	______	______	______
Fees earned for two months	______	______	______
Prepaid insurance as of December 31 .	______	______	______
Prepaid rent as of December 31	______	______	______
Unearned fees as of December 31 . . .	______	______	______

Explain the contents of the Difference column.

Problem 3–9
Analytical essay
(LO 3, 4, 5)

Review the information presented in paragraphs *c*, *d*, and *e* of Problem 3–1. Describe how each of the following errors from 19X2 would affect the company's income statements for 19X2 and 19X3 and its balance sheets as of December 31, 19X2, and 19X3 (treat each case as independent from the others). None of the errors were repeated in 19X3, but they remained undiscovered until well into 19X4.

1. The company mistakenly recorded the $1,400 of accrued salary expense described in part *c* as if the amount was only $1,000. However, the employees were paid the correct amount of $1,400 on January 6, 19X3. At that time, the Salaries Payable account was debited for $1,000 and the remainder of the $3,500 payment to the employees was debited to the Salaries Expense account for 19X3.
2. The company failed to record the $7,500 depreciation expense on the building described in part *d*.
3. The company failed to record the $800 of accrued rent income described in part *e*. Instead, the revenue was recorded on January 15 as income earned in 19X3.

[A]Problem 3–10
Analytical essay
(LO 3, 4, 8)

On November 1, 19X1, Carson Company and Winslow Company each paid $6,000 for six months' rent on their offices. Carson recorded its payment with a debit to the Prepaid Rent account. On the other hand, Winslow debited the Rent Expense account for $6,000. Both companies use calendar years as their accounting periods. Describe the differences between the adjusting entries the two companies should make on December 31, 19X1. Be sure to explain how the two companies' different bookkeeping procedures affect the financial statements.

Serial Problem

Emerald Computer Services

(This comprehensive problem was introduced in Chapter 2, and continues in Chapters 4 and 5. If the Chapter 2 segment has not been completed, the assignment can begin at this point. However, you will need to use the facts presented on pages 95–97 in Chapter 2. Because of its length, this problem is most easily solved if you use the Working Papers that accompany this text.).

After the success of its first two months, Tracy Green has decided to continue operating Emerald Computer Services. (The transactions that occurred in these months are described in Chapter 2.) Before proceeding into December, Green adds these new accounts to the chart of accounts for the ledger:

No.	Account
164	Accumulated Depreciation, Office Equipment
168	Accumulated Depreciation, Computer Equipment
210	Wages Payable
233	Unearned Computer Fees
612	Depreciation Expense, Office Equipment
613	Depreciation Expense, Computer Equipment
637	Insurance Expense
640	Rent Expense
652	Computer Supplies Expense

Required

1. Prepare journal entries to record each of the transactions for Emerald Computer Services for December 3 through 29. Post the entries to the accounts in the ledger.
2. Prepare adjusting entries to record the events described on December 31. Post the entries to the accounts in the ledger.
3. Prepare an adjusted trial balance as of December 31, 19X1.
4. Prepare an income statement for the three months ended December 31, 19X1.
5. Prepare a statement of changes in owner's equity for the three months ended December 31, 19X1.
6. Prepare a balance sheet as of December 31, 19X1.

Transactions and other data:

Dec. 3 Paid $700 to the Town Center Mall for the company's share of mall advertising costs.
4 Paid $400 to repair the company's computer.
6 Received $2,500 from Alpha Printing Co. for the receivable from the prior month.
10 Paid Fran Sims for six days' work at the rate of $125 per day.
12 Notified by Alpha Printing Co. that Emerald's bid of $4,000 on a proposed project was accepted. Alpha Company paid a $1,000 advance to Emerald.
13 Purchased $770 of computer supplies on credit from AAA Supply Co.
15 Sent a reminder to Fox Run Estates to pay the fee for services originally recorded on November 7.
19 Completed project for Delta Fixtures, Inc., and received $3,750 cash.
21 Paid $2,000 to Tracy Green as a cash withdrawal.
22–26 Took the week off for the holidays.
28 Received $1,900 from Fox Run Estates on their receivable.
29 Reimbursed Tracy Green's business automobile mileage of 400 miles at $0.25 per mile.
31 The following information was collected to be used in adjusting entries prior to preparing financial statements for the company's first three months:

a. The December 31 inventory of computer supplies was $480.
b. Three months have passed since the annual insurance premium was paid.
c. As of the end of the year, Fran Sims has not been paid for four days of work at the rate of $125 per day.
d. The computer is expected to have a four-year life with no salvage value.
e. The office equipment is expected to have a three-year life with no salvage value.
f. Prepaid rent for three of the four months has expired.

Provocative Problems

Provocative Problem 3–1
Phillips Law Practice
(LO 3, 4)

The 19X1 and 19X2 balance sheets for Phillips Law Practice reported the following assets and liabilities:

	19X1	19X2
Accounts receivable	$45,000	$62,000
Prepaid insurance	4,800	3,600
Interest payable	5,750	9,250
Unearned legal fees	17,000	25,000

The company's records show that the following amounts of cash were spent and received during 19X2:

Cash spent to pay insurance premiums . .	$ 12,500
Cash spent to pay interest	14,000
Cash received on accounts receivable . . .	120,000
Cash received in advance for legal fees . .	108,000

Calculate the amounts to be reported on Phillips Law Practice's 19X2 income statement for (*a*) insurance expense, (*b*) interest expense, and (*c*) total legal fees earned.

Provocative Problem 3–2
We-Fix-Anything
(LO 2, 3, 4, 6)

Early in January, Chris Williams created a new business called We-Fix-Anything. Unfortunately, Williams has not maintained any double-entry accounting records, although all cash receipts and disbursements have been carefully recorded. In addition, all unpaid invoices for the company's expenses and purchases are kept in a file until they are paid. The cash records have been summarized in this schedule:

Cash receipts:		
Investment by owner	$43,000	
Customer repairs	66,000	
Total		$109,000
Cash payments:		
Shop equipment	$21,200	
Repair supplies	25,000	
Rent	8,400	
Insurance premiums	900	
Newspaper advertising	2,000	
Utility bills	1,600	
Employee's wages	8,000	
Chris Williams	20,000	
Total cash payments		87,100
Cash balance as of December 31		$ 21,900

Williams wants to know the net income for the first year and the company's financial position at the end of the year. Provide this information by preparing an accrual basis income statement, a statement of changes in owner's equity, and a classified balance sheet. Also compute the current ratio, the debt ratio, and the modified return on equity, assuming that Williams's efforts are worth $22,500 per year.

The following information will help you: The shop equipment was bought in January and is predicted to have a useful life of 10 years, with a $1,200 salvage value. There is a $4,000 unpaid invoice in the file; it is for supplies that have been purchased and received. An inventory shows that $8,200 of supplies are on hand at the end of the year. The shop space is rented for $600 per month under a five-year lease. The lease contract required Williams to pay the first and the final two months' rents in advance. The insurance premiums acquired two policies on January 2. The first is a one-year policy that cost $500, and the second is a two-year policy that cost $400. There are $190 of earned but unpaid wages and customers owe the shop $3,750 for services they have received.

Provocative Problem 3–3
Apple Computer, Inc.
(LO 6)

Apple Computer, Inc.

Refer to the financial statements and related information for Apple Computer, Inc., in Appendix F. Find the answers to the following questions by analyzing the information in the report:

1. Does the company present a classified balance sheet? What title is given to the financial statement?
2. Identify the classifications of assets presented on the balance sheet.
3. What is the total amount of accumulated depreciation (and amortization) as of September 25, 1992? (*Amortization* is the term used for the depreciation of intangible assets.)
4. What is the company's current ratio at the end of its 1992 and 1991 fiscal years?
5. What is the company's debt ratio at the end of its 1992 and 1991 fiscal years? (Include deferred income taxes in the liabilities.)

Provocative Problem 3–4
As a Matter of Ethics: Essay

ETHICS

Review the As a Matter of Ethics case on page 114. Discuss the ethical dilemma faced by Bill Palmer and describe the alternative courses of action that he might take. Explain how your answer would differ given the following assumptions: (*a*) Palmer knows that the company's financial statements are not going to be audited; (*b*) Palmer knows that the president's bonus depends on the amount of income reported in the first year; and (*c*) Palmer's job depends on complying with the president's wishes.

Answers to Objective Review Questions

LO 1 (*a*)
LO 2 (*a*)
LO 3 (*e*)
LO 4 (*e*)
LO 5 (*d*)
LO 6 (*e*)
LO 7 (*c*)
LO 8 (*c*)

CHAPTER

4

The Work Sheet and Closing Process

This chapter continues your study of the accounting process by describing procedures that the accountant performs at the end of each reporting period. You learn about an optional work sheet that accountants use to draft adjusting entries and the financial statements. Studying the work sheet allows you to get an overall perspective on the steps in the accounting cycle. The chapter also describes the closing process that prepares the revenue, expense, and withdrawals accounts for the next reporting period and updates the owner's capital account. In addition, the chapter describes the profit margin ratio that decision makers use to assess a company's performance.

Learning Objectives

After studying Chapter 4, you should be able to:

1. Explain why work sheets are prepared and prepare a work sheet for a service business.
2. Prepare financial statements from the information in a work sheet.
3. Explain why accounts are closed at the end of each accounting period and prepare closing entries for a service business.
4. Describe each step in the accounting cycle.
5. Calculate the profit margin ratio and describe what it reveals about a company's performance.
6. Define or explain the words and phrases listed in the chapter glossary.

After studying Appendix B at the end of Chapter 4, you should be able to:

7. Explain when and why reversing entries are used and prepare reversing entries.

Using Work Sheets at the End of Accounting Periods

When organizing the information presented in formal reports to internal and external decision makers, accountants prepare numerous analyses and informal reports. These informal reports are important tools for accountants. Traditionally, they are called **working papers,** especially when they are prepared by public accountants. One widely used working paper is simply called the **work sheet.** The work sheet is not formally distributed to decision makers. It is prepared by accountants for internal use.

LO 1 Explain why work sheets are prepared and prepare a work sheet for a service business.

Why Study the Work Sheet?

If the work sheet is used only by accountants, it is reasonable to ask why it is presented in this introductory text that is studied by many people who are not planning to become accountants. In fact, there are several reasons:

1. Studying the work sheet is an effective way for you to see the entire accounting process from beginning to end. In a sense, it gives a bird's-eye view of the process between the occurrence of economic events and the presentation of their effects in financial statements. This view of the process shows how events, accounts, and financial statements are interrelated. The knowledge gained from this overview is valuable for managers and other decision makers because it helps them understand and use the information in the statements.
2. Work sheets are also used when managers are planning major transactions, such as asset purchases or new borrowings before launching a new product. The work sheet can be used to project how these kinds of events will affect the company. By understanding the work sheet, decision makers can make more effective analyses.
3. Work sheets are useful in many situations faced by accountants. For example, auditors use work sheets to organize audits, to gain an overall perspective on their client's financial statements, and to develop modifications of the statements before issuing them. Private accountants also use work sheets to prepare interim (monthly or quarterly) statements.

In light of these reasons, all business students should know about work sheets. Keep these reasons in mind as you move ahead into the details.

Where Does the Work Sheet Fit into the Accounting Process?

In practice, the work sheet is an optional step in the accounting process; it simplifies the accountant's efforts in preparing financial statements. Even though it is optional, it is widely used because it is so helpful. Specifically, the accountant completes the work sheet before preparing the adjusting entries at the end of the reporting period. It helps the accountant gather information about the accounts, the needed adjustments, and the financial statements. When the work sheet is finished, it contains information that is recorded in the journal and then presented in the statements.

Preparing the Work Sheet

Illustration 4–1 shows a blank work sheet. Notice that it has five sets of double columns for the

1. Unadjusted trial balance.
2. Adjustments.
3. Adjusted trial balance.
4. Income statement.
5. Statement of changes in owner's equity and the balance sheet.

The work sheet does not provide a separate set of double columns for the statement of changes in owner's equity because the statement usually includes only a few items. Notice that the work sheet can be completed manually or with a computer. In fact, this format is especially well-suited for using a spreadsheet program.

Step 1—Enter the Unadjusted Trial Balance

To see how this step works, move the first transparent overlay into position to create Illustration 4–2.

The accountant starts preparing the work sheet by listing the number and title of every account expected to appear on the company's financial statements. Then, the unadjusted debit or credit balance of each account is found in the ledger and recorded in the first two columns. Because these columns serve as the unadjusted trial balance, the totals of the columns should be equal.

The illustration shows this first step for Clear Copy Co. with information from Chapter 2. The account balances include the effects of December's external transactions. They do not reflect any of the adjustments described in Chapter 3.

In some situations, the accountant determines later that additional accounts need to be inserted on the work sheet. If the sheet is completed manually, the additional accounts are inserted below the initial list. If a computer spreadsheet program is used, the new lines are easily inserted between existing lines.

Because a later step in the example requires two lines for the Copy Services Revenue account, Illustration 4–2 includes an extra blank line below that account. If this need is not anticipated when the work sheet is being prepared manually, the accountant can adapt by squeezing two entries on one line. This problem is avoided with computer spreadsheets because new lines can be readily inserted.

Step 2—Enter the Adjustments and Prepare the Adjusted Trial Balance

Turn the next overlay into position to create Illustration 4–3. The work sheet now appears as it would after the second step is completed.

Step 2 begins by entering adjustments for economic events that were not external transactions. These events include consumption of prepaid expenses, depreciation, and accruals of revenues, assets, expenses, and liabilities. The illustration shows the six adjustments for Clear Copy Co. that were explained in Chapter 3:

(*a*) Expiration of $100 of prepaid insurance.
(*b*) Consumption of $1,050 of store supplies.
(*c*) Depreciation of copy equipment by $375.
(*d*) Earning of $250 of previously unearned revenue.
(*e*) Accrual of $210 of salaries owed to the employee.
(*f*) Accrual of $1,800 of revenue owed by a customer.

As a control to ensure equal debits and credits, the components of each adjustment are identified on the work sheet with a letter. Some accountants explain the adjustments with a list at the bottom of the work sheet or on a separate page.[1] As a test for clerical accuracy, they add the totals of the two columns to be sure they are equal.

After the adjustments are entered on the work sheet, the adjusted trial balance is prepared by combining the adjustments with the unadjusted balances. Debits and credits are combined just as they would be in determining an account's balance. For example, the Prepaid Insurance account in Illustration 4–3 has a $2,400 debit balance in the unadjusted trial balance. This amount is combined with the $100 credit entry (*a*) in the Adjustments columns to give the account a $2,300 debit balance in the adjusted trial balance. Salaries Expense has a $1,400 balance in the unadjusted trial balance and is combined with the $210 debit entry (*e*) in the Adjustments columns. When the

[1] Auditors' work sheets cross-reference each adjustment to a detailed analysis and other supporting evidence.

ILLUSTRATION 4-1 *Preparing the Work Sheet at the End of the Accounting Period*

CLEAR COPY CO.
Work Sheet
For Month Ended December 31, 19X1

The heading should identify the entity, the document, and the time period.

Account		Unadjusted Trial Balance		Adjustments		Adjusted Trial Balance		Income Statement		Statement of Changes in Owner's Equity and Balance Sheet	
No.	Title	Dr.	Cr.	Dr.	Cr.	Dr.	Cr.	Dr.	Cr.	Dr.	Cr.

The work sheet can be prepared manually or with a computer spreadsheet program.

The worksheet collects and summarizes the information used to prepare financial statements, adjusting entries, and closing entries.

debit balance is combined with the debit from the adjustment, the account has a $1,610 debit balance in the adjusted trial balance.

The accountant next calculates the totals of the Adjusted Trial Balance columns to ensure that the debits and credits are equal. If the work sheet is used, there is no need to actually prepare an adjusted trial balance after the adjusting journal entries have been posted to the ledger.

The main advantage of step 2 is that it accumulates information about the needed adjustments and shows how they affect the accounts.

Step 3—Extend the Adjusted Trial Balance Amounts to the Financial Statement Columns

Turn the third transparent overlay into position to create Illustration 4–4 and to see the effects of step 3.

In this step, the accountant assigns each adjusted account balance to its financial statement. The assignment is accomplished by extending each amount into one of the appropriate columns across the page. The revenue and expense accounts are extended into the Income Statement columns. The asset, liability, and owner's capital and withdrawals account balances are extended into the columns for the statement of changes in owner's equity and balance sheet. Notice that accounts with debit balances in the adjusted trial balance are extended to the Debit columns (such as Cash and Salaries Expense) and accounts with Credit balances are extended to the credit columns (such as Accounts Payable and Copy Services Revenue).

Next, the column totals are taken. In this situation, the paired column totals are not equal. The inequality exists because the total debit balance for the expenses does not equal the credit balance for the revenue. This imbalance also creates an equal and opposite imbalance in the Statement of Changes in Owner's Equity and Balance Sheet columns. This imbalance is dealt with in step 4.

The objective of step 3 is to help the accountant prepare the financial statements as they will appear after the adjustments are journalized and posted. The advantages of the work sheet are that the accountant has an organized set of data and an overview of what the statements will look like.

Step 4—Enter the Net Income (or Loss) and Balance the Financial Statement Columns

Now turn the final transparent overlay into place to create Illustration 4–5, which shows the completed work sheet. The accountant begins this last step by entering Net income and Totals on the next two lines in the account title column. Next, the accountant computes the net income by finding the excess of the Income Statement Credit column total over the Debit column total. The amount of the net income is then inserted on the net income line in the Debit column, and a new total is computed for each column. (If the initial total of the debits is greater than the initial total credits, the expenses exceed the revenues, and the company has incurred a net loss. If so, the difference is entered in the Credit column instead of the Debit column.) The total debits and total credits in the Income Statement columns are now equal.

The accountant next enters the net income in the Credit column of the Balance Sheet columns. (If there were a net loss, it would be entered in the Debit column.) Notice that this entry causes the total debits in the last two columns to equal the total credits.

Even if all five pairs of columns do balance, there is no guarantee that the work sheet is free from errors. For example, if the accountant incorrectly extends an asset account's balance into the Income Statement Debit column, the

ILLUSTRATION 4–6 *Step Five: Prepare the Financial Statements from the Work Sheet Information*

CLEAR COPY CO.
Income Statement
For Month Ended December 31, 19X1

Revenues:		
Copy services revenue		$5,950
Operating expenses:		
Depreciation expense, copy equipment	$ 375	
Salaries expense	1,610	
Insurance expense	100	
Rent expense	1,000	
Store supplies expense	1,050	
Utilities expense	230	
Total operating expenses		4,365
Net income		$1,585

CLEAR COPY CO.
Statement of Changes in Owner's Equity
For Month Ended December 31, 19X1

Terry Dow, Capital, November 30, 19X1		$ 0
Plus:		
Investments by owner	$30,000	
Net income	1,585	31,585
Total		$31,585
Less withdrawals by owner		400
Terry Dow, capital, December 31, 19X1		$31,185

CLEAR COPY CO.
Balance Sheet
December 31, 19X1

Assets		
Cash		$ 7,950
Accounts receivable		1,800
Store supplies		2,670
Prepaid insurance		2,300
Copy equipment	$26,000	
Accumulated depreciation, copy equipment	(375)	25,625
Total assets		$40,345
Liabilities		
Accounts payable		$ 6,200
Salaries payable		210
Unearned copy services revenue		2,750
Total liabilities		$ 9,160
Owner's Equity		
Terry Dow, capital		31,185
Total liabilities and owner's equity		$40,345

columns balance but net income is understated. Or, if the accountant extends an expense amount into the Balance Sheet Debit column, the columns balance but the net income is overstated. Although these errors may not be immediately obvious, they are discovered when the accountant begins to actually prepare the financial statements. For example, it would be readily apparent that an asset does not belong on the income statement or that an expense does not belong on the balance sheet.

At this point, the work sheet is complete. If the accountant discovers new information or an error, the change can be easily included in the work sheet, especially if it is being prepared with a computer spreadsheet.

Step 5—Prepare the Financial Statements from the Work Sheet Information

LO 2 Prepare financial statements from the information in a work sheet.

The final step uses the information in the last four columns to prepare the financial statements in Illustration 4–6. (These statements are identical to the ones in Illustration 3–4 and 3–5 on pages 112 and 113.)

The sequence is the same as we have seen before. The income statement is completed first. The net income is then added to the information about the owner's investments and withdrawals to calculate the ending balance of the capital account. In addition, the accountant analyzes the capital account to determine whether the owner made any new investments during the reporting period. Finally, the balance sheet is completed by using the ending balance of owner's equity from the statement of changes in owner's equity.

Once the accountant is satisfied that the work sheet has captured information about all relevant events, the adjusting entries are recorded in the journal and posted to the ledger.

Summary of the Advantages of Using a Work Sheet

At this point, it should be clear that we ended up with exactly the same financial statements and adjusting entries that we developed in Chapter 3 without using a work sheet. Therefore, it is fair to ask why accountants go to the trouble of preparing work sheets.

First, the example in this chapter is greatly simplified. Real companies have many more adjusting entries and accounts than Clear Copy. A work sheet makes it easier to organize all the additional information.

Second, the work sheet can be used to prepare *interim* financial statements without recording the adjusting entries in the journal and ledger. Thus, a company can prepare statements for 11 monthly periods and one annual period while actually going through the formal adjustment process only once at the end of the year. This advantage is not apparent from the Clear Copy example because the company's statements are prepared for only one month.

Third, the work sheet can be used ahead of time to anticipate the effects of transactions and other planned economic events that have not yet happened.

In addition to explaining these accounting advantages, a main goal for describing the work sheet is to provide you with an overview of the accounting process. If you are able to complete the work sheet on your own, you demonstrate that you have learned the following basic concepts:

- Debits equal credits for transaction entries, adjusting entries, the ledger, and trial balances.
- Asset, withdrawals, and expense accounts have debit balances.
- Contra asset, liability, capital, and revenue accounts have credit balances.
- Net income is the difference between revenues and expenses.
- Owner's equity is increased by investments and net income, and is decreased by withdrawals and losses.
- Assets equal liabilities plus owner's equity.
- The accounting process is designed to provide useful information to be reported in the financial statements. (In other words, the accounting process is a means to an end, not an end in itself.)

By knowing how to complete a work sheet, you can prove to yourself that you understand these important principles. Even if you never complete another work sheet after this course, you have learned a great deal. But, if you do go on to study more accounting, mastering these techniques not only confirms your understanding of these concepts, but also gives you skills that help you perform more efficiently.

Regardless of the career path that you end up taking, it is likely that you will encounter one kind of accountant's work sheet or another. Another goal of this discussion is to make those future encounters less mysterious than they would be otherwise.

Alternate Formats of the Work Sheet

Because the work sheet is an informal working paper, its format is not dictated by generally accepted accounting principles. Different accountants use different formats according to their needs and personal preferences. For example, some accountants omit the adjusted trial balance. Others use different work sheet columns to draft the *closing entries* described later in the chapter.

Some work sheets have separate columns for the statement of changes in owner's equity and the balance sheet. The decision about which format is preferred rests with the accountant who creates the work sheet. We have chosen a familiar format that will help you understand the accounting process.

Closing Entries

LO 3 Explain why accounts are closed at the end of each accounting period and prepare closing entries for a service business.

After preparing the work sheet, journalizing and posting adjusting entries, and presenting the financial statements, the accountant carries out another step at the end of each year. Specifically, the accountant creates **closing entries** to:

- Prepare the revenue, expense, and withdrawals accounts for the upcoming year.
- Update the owner's capital account for the events of the year just ended.

Understanding the closing process will help you understand more about how the accounting system accumulates the information presented in the financial statements. It will also help you see how the financial statements are interrelated.

Closing the accounts involves the four steps diagrammed in Illustration 4–7 for Clear Copy Co. The company has the following adjusted balances in its ledger for its revenue, expense, capital, and withdrawals accounts on December 31:

	Debit	Credit
Copy services revenue		$ 5,950
Depreciation expense, copy equipment	$ 375	
Salaries expense	1,610	
Insurance expense	100	
Rent expense	1,000	
Store supplies expense	1,050	
Utilities expense	230	
Terry Dow, capital		30,000
Terry Dow, withdrawals	400	

These balances were used to prepare the company's income statement in Illustration 4–6. The statement shows that revenue was $5,950, total expenses were $4,765, and net income was $1,585. The statement of changes in owner's equity reports that the equity was increased by Dow's $30,000 investment and the net income of $1,585. The equity was decreased by $400 of withdrawals. As a result, the ending capital balance should be $31,185 ($30,000 + $1,585 − $400). The capital account is updated through the following four steps in the closing process:

Step 1. Transfer the credit balances in the revenue accounts to the **Income Summary** account. The Income Summary account is created especially for the closing process and is used only for this purpose. This step concentrates all the revenue account credit balances in the single summary account. This step also closes the revenue accounts by giving them zero balances. This clearing of the accounts allows them to be used to record new revenues in the upcoming year. The first closing entry for Clear Copy is

Dec.	31	Copy Services Revenue	5,950.00	
		Income Summary		5,950.00
		To close the revenue account and create the Income Summary account.		

The $5,950 credit balance in Income Summary equals the total revenues for the year. If the company has more than one revenue account, all of their balances are closed and the total is credited to the Income Summary account.

Step 2. Transfer the debit balances in the expense accounts to the Income Summary account. This step concentrates all the expense account debit balances in the Income Summary account. It also closes each expense account by giving it a zero balance that allows it to be used to record new expenses in the upcoming year. The second closing entry for Clear Copy is

Dec.	31	Income Summary	4,365.00	
		Depreciation Expense, Copy Equipment		375.00
		Salaries Expense		1,610.00
		Insurance Expense		100.00
		Rent Expense		1,000.00
		Store Supplies Expense		1,050.00
		Utilities Expense		230.00
		To close the expense accounts.		

Illustration 4–7 shows that posting this entry gives each expense account a zero balance and prepares it to accept entries for expenses in 19X2. The entry also makes the balance of the Income Summary account equal to December's net income of $1,585. In effect, all the debit and credit balances of the expense and revenue accounts have now been concentrated in the Income Summary account.

Step 3. Transfer the balance of the Income Summary account to the owner's capital account. This third closing entry closes the Income Summary account and adds the company's net income to the owner's capital account:

Dec.	31	Income Summary	1,585.00	
		Terry Dow, Capital		1,585.00
		To close the Income Summary account and add the net income to the capital account.		

After this entry is posted, the Income Summary account has a zero balance. It will continue to have a zero balance until the closing process occurs at the end of the next year. The owner's capital account has been increased by the amount of the net income, but still does not include the effects of the withdrawal that occurred in December.

Step 4. Transfer the debit balance of the withdrawals account to the capital account. The fourth closing entry gives the withdrawals account a zero balance, which allows it to accumulate the next year's payments to the owner. It also reduces the capital account balance to the amount reported on the statement of changes in owner's equity. This entry would be made for Clear Copy:

Dec.	31	Terry Dow, Capital	400.00	
		Terry Dow, Withdrawals		400.00
		To close the withdrawals account and reduce the balance of the capital account.		

The capital account has now been fully updated to equal the $31,185 ending balance reported on the statement of changes in owner's equity and balance sheet in Illustration 4–6.

ILLUSTRATION 4-7 *Closing Entries for Clear Copy Co.*

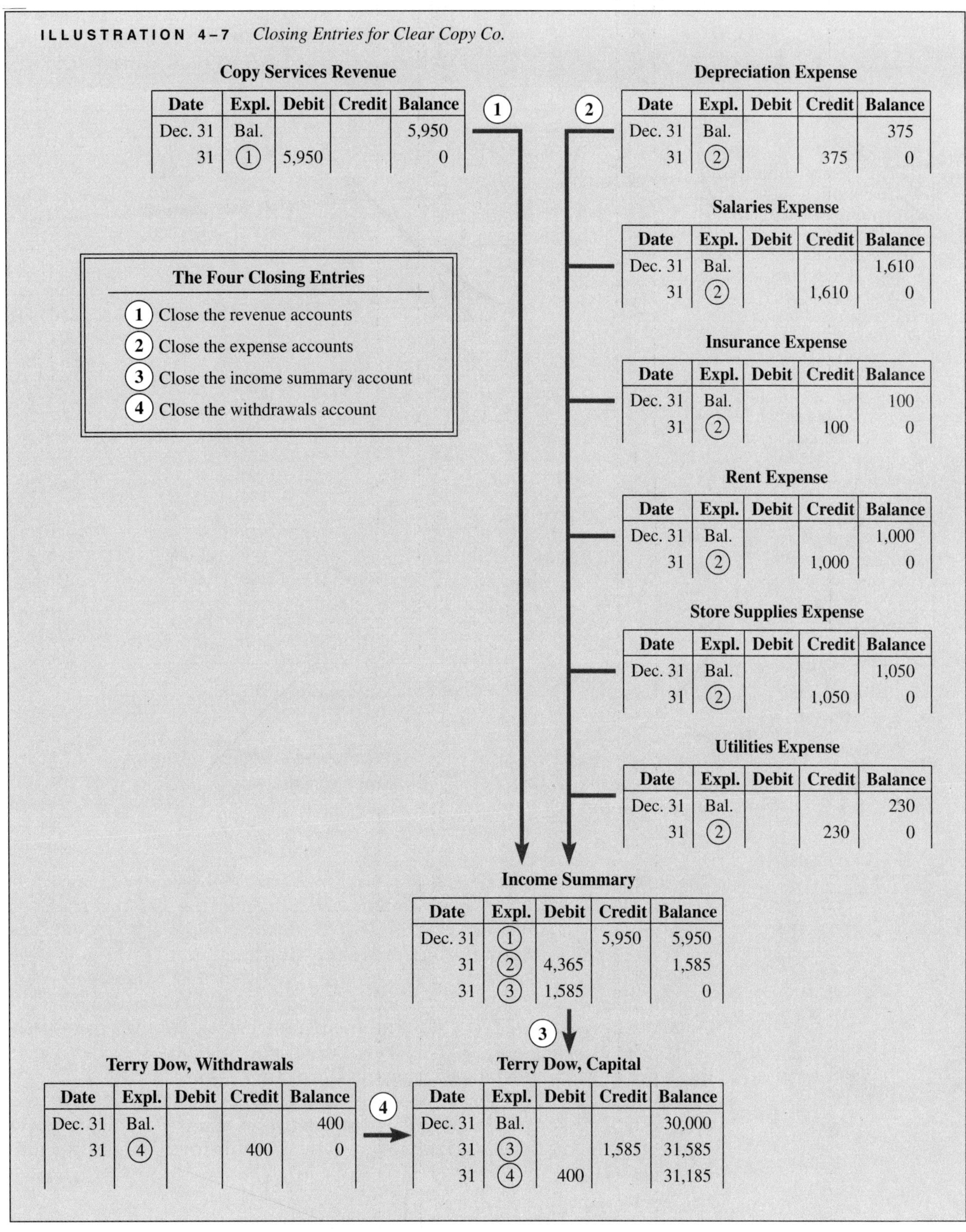

The Four Closing Entries

1. Close the revenue accounts
2. Close the expense accounts
3. Close the income summary account
4. Close the withdrawals account

Copy Services Revenue

Date	Expl.	Debit	Credit	Balance
Dec. 31	Bal.			5,950
31	(1)	5,950		0

Depreciation Expense

Date	Expl.	Debit	Credit	Balance
Dec. 31	Bal.			375
31	(2)		375	0

Salaries Expense

Date	Expl.	Debit	Credit	Balance
Dec. 31	Bal.			1,610
31	(2)		1,610	0

Insurance Expense

Date	Expl.	Debit	Credit	Balance
Dec. 31	Bal.			100
31	(2)		100	0

Rent Expense

Date	Expl.	Debit	Credit	Balance
Dec. 31	Bal.			1,000
31	(2)		1,000	0

Store Supplies Expense

Date	Expl.	Debit	Credit	Balance
Dec. 31	Bal.			1,050
31	(2)		1,050	0

Utilities Expense

Date	Expl.	Debit	Credit	Balance
Dec. 31	Bal.			230
31	(2)		230	0

Income Summary

Date	Expl.	Debit	Credit	Balance
Dec. 31	(1)		5,950	5,950
31	(2)	4,365		1,585
31	(3)	1,585		0

Terry Dow, Withdrawals

Date	Expl.	Debit	Credit	Balance
Dec. 31	Bal.			400
31	(4)		400	0

Terry Dow, Capital

Date	Expl.	Debit	Credit	Balance
Dec. 31	Bal.			30,000
31	(3)		1,585	31,585
31	(4)	400		31,185

Sources of Closing Entry Information

The accountant can identify the accounts to be closed and the amounts to be used in the closing entries by referring to the individual revenue and expense accounts in the ledger. However, the work sheet provides this information in a more convenient format. To locate the information on the work sheet, look again at the income statement columns in Illustration 4–5. All accounts with

ILLUSTRATION 4–8 *The Adjusted Trial Balance, Closing Entries, and Post-Closing Trial Balance for Clear Copy Co.*

	Adjusted Trial Balance		Closing Entries		Post-Closing Trial Balance	
Cash	$ 7,950				$ 7,950	
Accounts receivable	1,800				1,800	
Store supplies	2,670				2,670	
Prepaid insurance	2,300				2,300	
Copy equipment	26,000				26,000	
Accumulated depreciation, copy equipment		$ 375				$ 375
Accounts payable		6,200				6,200
Salaries payable		210				210
Unearned copy services revenue		2,750				2,750
Terry Dow, capital		30,000	(4)$ 400	(3)$ 1,585		31,185
Terry Dow, withdrawals	400			(4) 400		
Copy services revenue		5,950	(1) 5,950			
Depreciation expense, copy equipment	375			(2) 375		
Salaries expense	1,610			(2) 1,610		
Insurance expense	100			(2) 100		
Rent expense	1,000			(2) 1,000		
Store supplies expense	1,050			(2) 1,050		
Utilities expense	230			(2) 230		
Income Summary			(2) 4,365 (3) 1,585	(1) 5,950		
Totals	$45,485	$45,485	$12,300	$12,300	$40,720	$40,720

balances in these columns are closed and the amounts in the work sheet are used in the closing entries. The balance of the owner's withdrawals account appears in the last debit column in the work sheet.

The Post-Closing Trial Balance

The six-column table in Illustration 4–8 summarizes the effects of the closing process. The first two columns contain the adjusted trial balance from the work sheet, with two additional lines for the Income Summary account. The next two columns present the four closing entries, numbered (1) through (4) to correspond to the four steps in the closing process. The last two columns contain the **post-closing trial balance,** which lists the balances of the accounts not closed.[2] These accounts represent the company's assets, liabilities, and owner's equity as of the end of 19X1. These items and amounts are the same as those presented in the balance sheet in Illustration 4–6.

Illustration 4–9 presents the post-closing trial balance as a separate two-column table that can be used instead of the six-column table. Regardless of the format, the post-closing trial balance is the last step in the annual accounting process.

Permanent (Real) Accounts and Temporary (Nominal) Accounts

The terms **permanent accounts** and **real accounts** both describe the asset, liability, and owner's capital accounts because they are not closed as long as the

[2] Some accountants use work sheets that include these four columns instead of the financial statement columns. Although there are advantages for both formats, the financial statements are not changed by choosing one or the other.

ILLUSTRATION 4–9 *Separate Post-Closing Trial Balance for Clear Copy Co.*

Cash	$ 7,950	
Accounts receivable	1,800	
Store supplies	2,670	
Prepaid insurance	2,300	
Copy equipment	26,000	
Accumulated depreciation, copy equipment		$ 375
Accounts payable		6,200
Salaries payable		210
Unearned copy services revenue		2,750
Terry Dow, capital		31,185
Totals	$40,720	$40,720

company continues to own the assets, owe the liabilities, and have owner's equity. These accounts exist permanently because they describe real items.

In contrast, the terms **temporary accounts** and **nominal accounts** both describe the revenue, expense, income summary, and withdrawals accounts. These terms are used because the accounts are opened at the beginning of the year, used to record events, and then closed at the end of the year. These accounts exist only temporarily because they describe nominal events instead of real items.

The Ledger for Clear Copy Co.

To complete the Clear Copy example, look at Illustration 4–10, the company's entire ledger as of December 31, 19X1. Review the accounts and observe that the temporary accounts (the withdrawals account and all accounts with numbers greater than 400) have been closed.

ILLUSTRATION 4–10 *The Ledger for Clear Copy Co. as of December 31, 19X1 (After adjustments and closing entries have been posted)*

Asset Accounts

Cash — **Acct. No. 101**

Date		Explanation	Debit	Credit	Balance
19X1 Dec.	1		30,000 00		30,000 00
	2			2,500 00	27,500 00
	3			20,000 00	7,500 00
	10		2,200 00		9,700 00
	12			1,000 00	8,700 00
	12			700 00	8,000 00
	22		1,700 00		9,700 00
	24			900 00	8,800 00
	24			400 00	8,400 00
	26		3,000 00		11,400 00
	26			2,400 00	9,000 00
	26			120 00	8,880 00
	26			230 00	8,650 00
	26			700 00	7,950 00

ILLUSTRATION 4-10 *(continued)*

Accounts Receivable — **Acct. No. 106**

Date		Explanation	Debit	Credit	Balance
19X1 Dec.	12		1,700 00		1,700 00
	22			1,700 00	0 00
	31		1,800 00		1,800 00

Store Supplies — **Acct. No. 125**

Date		Explanation	Debit	Credit	Balance
19X1 Dec.	2		2,500 00		2,500 00
	6		1,100 00		3,600 00
	26		120 00		3,720 00
	31			1,050 00	2,670 00

Prepaid Insurance — **Acct. No. 128**

Date		Explanation	Debit	Credit	Balance
19X1 Dec.	26		2,400 00		2,400 00
	31			100 00	2,300 00

Copy Equipment — **Acct. No. 167**

Date		Explanation	Debit	Credit	Balance
19X1 Dec.	3		20,000 00		20,000 00
	6		6,000 00		26,000 00

Accumulated Depreciation, Copy Equipment — **Acct. No. 168**

Date		Explanation	Debit	Credit	Balance
19X1 Dec.	31			375 00	375 00

ILLUSTRATION 4–10 *(continued)*
Liability and Equity Accounts

Accounts Payable — **Acct. No.** 201

Date		Explanation	Debit		Credit		Balance	
19X1 Dec.	6				7,100	00	7,100	00
	24		900	00			6,200	00

Salaries Payable — **Acct. No.** 209

Date		Explanation	Debit		Credit		Balance	
19X1 Dec.	31				210	00	210	00

Unearned Copy Services Revenue — **Acct. No.** 236

Date		Explanation	Debit		Credit		Balance	
19X1 Dec.	26				3,000	00	3,000	00
	31		250	00			2,750	00

Terry Dow, Capital — **Acct. No.** 301

Date		Explanation	Debit		Credit		Balance	
19X1 Dec.	1				30,000	00	30,000	00
	31				1,585	00	31,585	00
	31		400	00			31,185	00

Terry Dow, Withdrawals — **Acct. No.** 302

Date		Explanation	Debit		Credit		Balance	
19X1 Dec.	24		400	00			400	00
	31				400	00	0	00

ILLUSTRATION 4–10 *(continued)*
Revenue and Expense Accounts (including Income Summary)

Copy Services Revenue — **Acct. No. 403**

Date		Explanation	Debit		Credit		Balance	
19X1 Dec.	10				2,200	00	2,200	00
	12				1,700	00	3,900	00
	31				250	00	4,150	00
	31				1,800	00	5,950	00
	31		5,950	00			0	00

Depreciation Expense, Copy Equipment — **Acct. No. 614**

Date		Explanation	Debit		Credit		Balance	
19X1 Dec.	31		375	00			375	00
	31				375	00	0	00

Salaries Expense — **Acct. No. 622**

Date		Explanation	Debit		Credit		Balance	
19X1 Dec.	12		700	00			700	00
	26		700	00			1,400	00
	31		210	00			1,610	00
	31				1,610	00	0	00

Insurance Expense — **Acct. No. 637**

Date		Explanation	Debit		Credit		Balance	
19X1 Dec.	31		100	00			100	00
	31				100	00	0	00

Rent Expense — **Acct. No. 641**

Date		Explanation	Debit		Credit		Balance	
19X1 Dec.	12		1,000	00			1,000	00
	31				1,000	00	0	00

ILLUSTRATION 4-10 *(continued)*

Store Supplies Expense **Acct. No. 651**

Date		Explanation	Debit		Credit		Balance	
19X1 Dec.	31		1,050	00			1,050	00
	31				1,050	00	0	00

Utilities Expense **Acct. No. 690**

Date		Explanation	Debit		Credit		Balance	
19X1 Dec.	26		230	00			230	00
	31				230	00	0	00

Income Summary **Acct. No. 901**

Date		Explanation	Debit		Credit		Balance	
19X1 Dec.	31				5,950	00	5,950	00
	31		4,365	00			1,585	00
	31		1,585	00			0	00

Closing Entries for Corporations

Up to this point, all examples of journal entries have concerned the activities and accounts of single proprietorships. At this stage, it is helpful to briefly describe how the accounting process records closing entries for corporations.

Chapter 3 explained that a corporation's balance sheet presents the stockholders' equity as contributed capital and retained earnings. Despite this difference, the first two steps of the closing process are exactly the same. Specifically, a corporation's revenue and expense accounts are closed to the Income Summary account.

The third step differs only by closing the Income Summary account to the corporation's Retained Earnings account. For example, suppose that the first two closing entries for a corporation have created a $98,500 credit balance in the Income Summary account. This third closing entry would close that account and update the Retained Earnings account:

Dec.	31	Income Summary	98,500.00	
		Retained Earnings		98,500.00
		To close the Income Summary account and update Retained Earnings.		

The fourth closing entry is also different because corporations do not use withdrawals accounts. The accounting practices for dividends paid to stockholders are described in Chapter 13.

A Review of the Accounting Cycle

LO 4 Describe each step in the accounting cycle.

Chapters 2, 3, and 4 have described the accounting procedures that are completed during each reporting period, beginning with recording external transactions in the journal and ending with preparing the post-closing trial balance. Because these steps are repeated each period, they are often called the **accounting cycle.** In Illustration 4–11, a flow chart shows the steps in order. Steps 1 and 2 take place every day as the company engages in business transactions. When the end of the accounting period arrives and financial statements are needed, the other steps are completed. Review this illustration and the following list of the steps to be sure that you understand how each one helps accountants provide useful information in the financial statements:

Step	Description
1. **Journalizing**	Analyzing transactions and recording debits and credits in a journal.
2. **Posting**	Copying the debits and credits from the journal entries to the accounts in the ledger.
3. **Preparing an unadjusted trial balance**	Summarizing the ledger accounts and partially testing clerical accuracy. (This step is omitted if the work sheet is used.)
4. **Completing the work sheet**	Identifying the effects of adjustments on the financial statements before entering them in the ledger and posting them to the accounts; also drafting the adjusted trial balance, the income statement, the statement of changes in owner's equity, and the balance sheet. Involves extending account balances into the appropriate financial statement columns and determining the size of the net income or net loss. (The work sheet is optional.)
5. **Adjusting the accounts**	Identifying adjustments in account balances to record nontransaction events and then recording them with journal entries. (If the work sheet is prepared, the information in the adjustments columns is used for the entries.) The journal entries are posted to the ledger to bring the account balances up to date.
6. **Preparing the financial statements**	Using the information on the adjusted trial balance (or the work sheet) to prepare an income statement, a statement of changes in owner's equity, a balance sheet, and a statement of cash flows. (Techniques for preparing the cash flow statement are described in Chapter 15.)
7. **Closing the temporary accounts**	Preparing journal entries to close the revenue, expense, and withdrawals accounts and to update the owner's capital (or retained earnings) account. These entries are posted to the ledger.
8. **Preparing a post-closing trial balance**	Partially testing the clerical accuracy of the adjusting and closing procedures.

Illustration 4–11 also identifies an optional ninth step of making reversing entries at the beginning of the following period. These entries are described in Appendix B, which begins on page 165.

A Practical Point

As a matter of practicality, accountants do not physically make all adjusting and closing entries on the last day of the fiscal year. In nearly all situations, many facts about accruals and other nontransaction events are not known until after several days, a few weeks, or even a month after the end of the year.

ILLUSTRATION 4–11 *The Accounting Cycle*

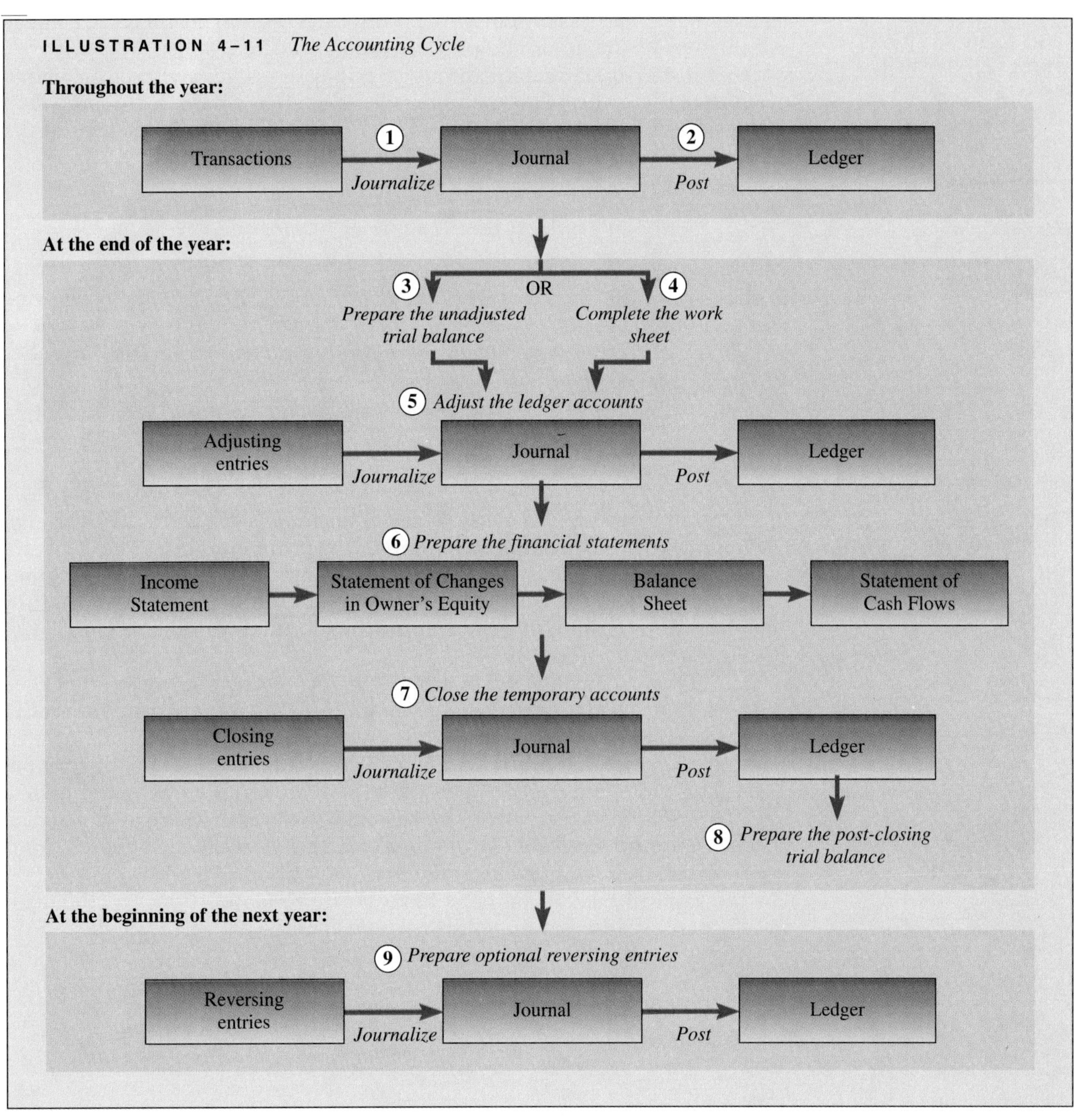

As a result, the adjusting and closing entries are recorded later but dated as of the last day of the year. As a result, the financial statements reflect what is known on the date that they prepared instead of what was known on the financial statement date. For example, a company might receive a utility bill on January 14 for costs incurred from December 1 through December 31. Upon receiving the bill, the company's accountant would record the expense and the payable as of December 31. The income statement for December reflects the full expense and the December 31 balance sheet includes the payable, even though the exact amounts were not actually known on December 31.

Using the Information—the Profit Margin

By now, it should be clear that accountants go to great lengths to ensure that a company's accounts include the effects of all of its assets, liabilities, revenues, and expenses. One of the primary goals of this attention to completeness is to provide information that helps internal and external decision makers evaluate the results achieved in the reporting period. This information describes

LO 5 Calculate the profit margin ratio and describe what it reveals about a company's performance.

management's success in generating profits and may suggest ways to achieve even better results. It also helps users predict future results.

One widely used analytical tool describes the company's net income in proportion to its sales. This measure is developed by dividing the company's net income by its revenues. The ratio is called either the **profit margin** or the **return on sales.** It is calculated with this formula:

$$\text{Profit margin} = \frac{\text{Net income}}{\text{Revenues}}$$

In effect, this ratio measures the average proportion of each dollar of revenue that ends up as profit.

The Clear Copy Co. achieved the following profit margin for December 19X1:

$$\text{Profit margin} = \frac{\$1{,}585}{\$5{,}950} = 26.9\%$$

In effect, 26.9 cents out of every dollar of revenue is profit for the company.

It is not possible to determine whether the profit margin for the company is suitable without additional information about normal margins for other companies of similar size in the same industry. In addition, it is appropriate to modify a sole proprietorship's net income by subtracting the value of the owner's management efforts.

The size of a company's ratio usually reflects its marketing strategy. For example, some companies (like large retail stores) attempt to increase profits by selling a large volume of goods and accept a low profit on each sale to have attractive prices. Their profit margin may even be less than 1%. Other companies (like smaller specialty or boutique retail stores) plan to obtain higher profits by selling a lower volume to customers who are willing to pay higher prices. Their profit margin may be 10% or higher. A company's chosen strategy is also shaped by its industry and its competition.

The following profit margins have been calculated from the financial statements presented in Appendixes F and G at the end of the book:

Apple Computer, Inc.	**1992**	**1991**	**1990**
Net income	$530,373	$309,841	$474,895
Revenues	$7,086,542	$6,308,849	$5,558,435
Profit margin	7.5%	4.9%	8.5%
Ben & Jerry's Homemade, Inc.	**1992**	**1991**	**1990**
Net income	$6,675,340	$3,739,383	$2,609,245
Revenues	$131,968,814	$96,997,339	$77,024,037
Profit margin	5.1%	3.9%	3.4%
Federal Express Corporation	**1993**	**1992**	**1991**
Net income (loss)	$53,866	$(113,782)	$5,898
Revenues	$7,808,043	$7,550,060	$7,688,296
Profit margin	0.7%	−1.5%	0.1%

Apple achieved the highest profit margins, which would be expected in light of its general strategy to produce unique personal computers and market them with higher prices. The drop in the profit margin for Apple in 1991 reflects a change in strategy that was implemented to build a larger share of the market. Ben & Jerry's is a relatively small competitor in the super-premium ice cream industry. As a result of selling in this segment of the market, their profit margins are higher than other producers with more standard products. However, the competition from larger super-premium companies keeps Ben & Jerry's from enjoying a higher margin. Federal Express has had some difficulties re-establishing its earlier success in generating profits. Its low margin in 1993 is closer to normal, and shows that the competition and the nature of the express delivery business emphasizes volume at a competitive price.

Ratio values for several years for a single company are also helpful in detecting trends. For example, a declining profit margin percentage would indicate that steps might need to be taken to control expenses or increase selling prices. The decline for Apple from 1990 to 1991 was reversed in 1992. On the other hand, the trend for Ben & Jerry's is positive and may indicate that it has gained a stronger position in its industry. Because of the low profit in 1991 and the loss in 1992, there is no clear trend for Federal Express.

Summary of the Chapter in Terms of Learning Objectives

LO 1 Accountants often use work sheets at the end of an accounting period in the process of preparing adjusting entries, the adjusted trial balance, and the financial statements. The work sheet is only a tool for accountants and is not distributed to investors or creditors. The work sheet described in this chapter has five pairs of columns for the unadjusted trial balance, the adjustments, the adjusted trial balance, the income statement, and the statement of changes in owner's equity and the balance sheet. Other formats are used in practice.

LO 2 The income statement is prepared from the Income Statement columns of the work sheet by taking the revenues from the Credit column and the expenses from the Debit column. The net income is the difference between the debits and credits. The statement of changes in owner's equity combines the pre-closing balance of the capital account (including the beginning balance plus any new investments), the net income from the Income Statement columns, and the owner's withdrawals. The balance sheet combines all assets, contra assets, and liabilities from the last two columns of the work sheet with the ending balance of owner's equity presented in the statement of changes in owner's equity.

LO 3 The temporary accounts are closed at the end of each accounting period for two reasons. First, this process prepares the revenue, expense, and withdrawals accounts for the next reporting period by giving them zero balances. Second, it updates the owner's equity account to include the effects of all economic events recorded for the year. The revenue and expense account balances are initially transferred to the Income Summary account, which is then closed to the owner's capital account. Finally, the withdrawals account is closed to the capital account.

LO 4 The accounting cycle consists of eight phases: (1) journalizing external transactions and (2) posting the entries during the year, and, at the end of the year: (3) preparing either an unadjusted trial balance or (4) a work sheet, (5) preparing and posting adjusting entries, (6) preparing the financial statements, (7) preparing and posting closing entries, and (8) preparing the post-closing trial balance.

LO 5 The profit margin ratio describes a company's income earning activities by showing the period's net income as a percentage of total revenue. It is found by dividing the reporting period's net income by the revenue for the same period. The ratio can be usefully interpreted only in light of additional facts about the company and its industry.

Demonstration Problem

This six-column table shows the December 31, 19X1, adjusted trial balance of Westside Appliance Repair Company:

	Adjusted Trial Balance		Closing Entries		Post-Closing Trial Balance	
Cash	$ 83,300					
Notes receivable	60,000					
Prepaid insurance	19,000					
Prepaid rent	5,000					
Equipment	165,000					
Accumulated depreciation, equipment		$ 52,000				
Accounts payable		37,000				
Long-term notes payable		58,000				
B. Westside, capital		173,500				
B. Westside, withdrawals	25,000					
Repair services revenue		294,000				
Interest earned		6,500				
Depreciation expense, equipment	26,000					
Wages expense	179,000					
Rent expense	47,000					
Insurance expense	7,000					
Interest expense	4,700					
Income summary						
Totals	$621,000	$621,000				

The beginning balance of the capital account was $140,500, and the owner invested $33,000 cash in the company on June 15, 19X1.

Required

1. Prepare closing entries for Westside Appliance Repair Co.
2. Complete the six-column schedule.
3. Post the closing entries to this capital account:

B. Westside, Capital **Acct. No. 301**

Date		Explanation	Debit	Credit	Balance
19X1					
Jan.	1	Beginning balance			140,500.00
June	15	New investment		33,000.00	173,500.00

Planning the Solution

- Prepare entries to close the revenue accounts to Income Summary, to close the expense accounts to Income Summary, to close Income Summary to the capital account, and to close the withdrawals account to the capital account.
- Enter the four closing entries in the second pair of columns in the six-column schedule, and then extend the balances of the asset and liability accounts to the third pair of columns.
- Enter the post-closing balance of the capital account in the last column. Examine the totals of the columns to verify that they are equal.
- Post the third and fourth closing entries to the capital account.

1.

Solution to Demonstration Problem

Closing entries:

19X1				
Dec.	31	Repair Services Revenue	294,000.00	
		Interest Earned	6,500.00	
		Income Summary		300,500.00
		To close the revenue accounts and create the Income Summary account.		
	31	Income Summary	263,700.00	
		Depreciation Expense, Equipment		26,000.00
		Wages Expense		179,000.00
		Rent Expense		47,000.00
		Insurance Expense		7,000.00
		Interest Expense		4,700.00
		To close the expense accounts.		
	31	Income Summary	36,800.00	
		B. Westside, Capital		36,800.00
		To close the Income Summary account and add the net income to the capital account.		
	31	B. Westside, Capital	25,000.00	
		B. Westside, Withdrawals		25,000.00
		To close the withdrawals account and reduce the balance of the capital account.		

2.

	Adjusted Trial Balance		Closing Entries		Post-Closing Trial Balance	
Cash	$ 83,300				$ 83,300	
Notes receivable	60,000				60,000	
Prepaid insurance	19,000				19,000	
Prepaid rent	5,000				5,000	
Equipment	165,000				165,000	
Accumulated depreciation, equipment		$ 52,000				$ 52,000
Accounts payable		37,000				37,000
Long-term notes payable		58,000				58,000
B. Westside, capital		173,500	(4) 25,000	(3) 36,800		185,300
B. Westside, withdrawals	25,000			(4) 25,000		
Repair services revenue		294,000	(1) 294,000			
Interest earned		6,500	(1) 6,500			
Depreciation expense, equipment	26,000			(2) 26,000		
Wages expense	179,000			(2) 179,000		
Rent expense	47,000			(2) 47,000		
Insurance expense	7,000			(2) 7,000		
Interest expense	4,700			(2) 4,700		
Income summary			(2) 263,700	(1) 300,500		
			(3) 36,800			
Totals	$621,000	$621,000	$ 626,000	$ 626,000	$332,300	$332,300

3.

B. Westside, Capital **Acct. No. 301**

Date		Explanation	Debit	Credit	Balance
19X1					
Jan.	1	Beginning balance			140,500.00
June	15	New investment		33,000.00	173,500.00
Dec.	31	Net income		36,800.00	210,300.00
	31	Withdrawals	25,000.00		185,300.00

APPENDIX

B

Reversing Entries

LO 7 Explain when and why reversing entries are used and prepare reversing entries.

This appendix explains the option of using **reversing entries** for accrued assets and liabilities created by adjusting entries at the end of a reporting period. Reversing entries are used for the practical purpose of simplifying a company's bookkeeping process.

Illustration B–1 shows how reversing works. The top of the diagram shows the adjusting entry that Clear Copy Co. recorded on December 31, 19X1, for the employee's earned but unpaid salary. The entry recorded three days' salary to increase the total expense to $1,610. The entry also recognized a liability for $210. Then, this expense is reported on the income statement and the expense account is closed. As a result, the ledger for 19X2 starts off with a $210 liability and a zero balance in the Salaries Expense account. At this point, the choice is made between using or not using reversing entries.

Bookkeeping without Reversing Entries

The path down the left side of Illustration B–1 was described in Chapter 3. When the next payday occurs on January 9, the bookkeeper records the payment with a compound entry that debits both the expense and liability accounts. Posting the entry creates a $490 balance in the expense account and reduces the liability account balance to zero because the debt has been settled.

The disadvantage of this approach is the complex entry on January 9. Paying the accrued liability causes the entry to differ from the routine entries made on all other paydays. To construct the proper entry on January 9, the bookkeeper must be informed of the effect of the adjusting entry. Reversing entries overcome this disadvantage.

Bookkeeping with Reversing Entries

The right side of Illustration B–1 shows how a reversing entry on January 1 overcomes the disadvantage of the complex January 9 entry.[3] The reversing entry is the exact opposite of the adjusting entry recorded on December 31. Specifically, the Salaries Payable liability is debited for $210, with the result that the account has a zero balance after the entry is posted. Technically, the Salaries Payable account now understates the liability, but no problem exists because financial statements will not be prepared before the liability is actually settled on January 9.

[3] Although the reversing entry would probably not be made on New Year's Day, it would be recorded in the journal as if it had been.

ILLUSTRATION B-1 *Reversing Entries for Accrued Expenses*

Accrue salaries expense on December 31, 19X1

Salaries Expense	210	
Salaries Payable		210

Salaries Expense

Date	Expl.	Debit	Credit	Balance
19X1				
Dec.	(7)	700		700
	(16)	700		1,400
	(*e*)	210		1,610

Salaries Payable

Date	Expl.	Debit	Credit	Balance
19X1				
Dec. 31	(*e*)		210	210

No reversing entry recorded on January 1, 19X2

NO ENTRY

Salaries Expense

Date	Expl.	Debit	Credit	Balance
19X2				

Salaries Payable

Date	Expl.	Debit	Credit	Balance
19X1				
Dec. 31	(*e*)		210	210
19X2				

Reversing entry recorded on January 1, 19X2

Salaries Payable	210	
Salaries Expense		210

Salaries Expense

Date	Expl.	Debit	Credit	Balance
19X2				
Jan. 1			210	(210)

Salaries Payable

Date	Expl.	Debit	Credit	Balance
19X1				
Dec. 31	(*e*)		210	210
19X2				
Jan. 1		210		0

Pay the accrued and current salaries on January 9, the first payday in 19X2

Salaries Expense	490	
Salaries Payable	210	
Cash		700

Salaries Expense

Date	Expl.	Debit	Credit	Balance
19X2				
Jan. 9		490		490

Salaries Payable

Date	Expl.	Debit	Credit	Balance
19X1				
Dec. 31	(*e*)		210	210
19X2				
Jan. 9		210		0

Salaries Expense	700	
Cash		700

Salaries Expense

Date	Expl.	Debit	Credit	Balance
19X2				
Jan. 1			210	(210)
Jan. 9		700		490

Salaries Payable

Date	Expl.	Debit	Credit	Balance
19X1				
Dec. 31	(*e*)		210	210
19X2				
Jan. 1		210		0

Under both approaches, the expense and liability accounts have the same balances after the subsequent payment on January 9:

Salaries Expense	$ 490
Salaries Payable	$ 0

The credit to the Salaries Expense account is unusual because it gives the account an *abnormal credit balance,* as indicated by the circle. This account's balance is also temporarily incorrect, but no problem exists because financial statements will not be prepared before January 9.

The reason for reversing is the simple entry for the payment on January 9. Notice that it merely debits the Salaries Expense account for the full $700 paid. This entry is the same as all other entries made to record 10 days' salary for the employee.

Look next at the accounts on the lower right side. After the payment entry is posted, the Salaries Expense account has the $490 balance that it should have to reflect seven days' salary of $70 per day. The zero balance in the Salaries Payable account is now appropriate. Then, the lower section of the illustration shows that the expense and liability accounts have exactly the same balances whether reversing occurs or not.

As a general rule, adjusting entries that create new asset or new liability accounts are the best candidates for reversing.

Summary of Appendix B in Terms of the Learning Objective

LO 7 Optional reversing entries can be applied to accrued assets and liabilities, including accrued interest earned, accrued interest expense, accrued taxes, and accrued salaries or wages. The goal of reversing entries is to simplify subsequent journal entries. The financial statements are not affected by the choice. Reversing entries are used simply as a matter of convenience in bookkeeping.

Glossary

LO 6 Define or explain the words and phrases listed in the chapter glossary.

Accounting cycle eight recurring steps performed each accounting period, starting with recording transactions in the journal and continuing through the post-closing trial balance. p. 158

Closing entries journal entries recorded at the end of each accounting period to prepare the revenue, expense, and withdrawals accounts for the upcoming year and update the owner's capital account for the events of the year that was just finished. p. 149

Income Summary the special account used only in the closing process to temporarily hold the amounts of revenues and expenses before the net difference is added to (or subtracted from) the owner's Capital account or the Retained Earnings account for a corporation. p. 149

Nominal accounts another name for *temporary accounts.* p. 153

Permanent accounts accounts that are used to describe assets, liabilities, and owner's equity; they are not closed as long as the company continues to own the assets, owe the liabilities, or have owner's equity; the balances of these accounts appear on the balance sheet. p. 152

Post-closing trial balance a trial balance prepared after the closing entries have been posted; the final step in the accounting cycle. p. 152

Profit margin the ratio of a company's net income to its revenues; measures the average proportion of each dollar of revenue that ends up as profit. p. 160

Real accounts another name for *permanent accounts.* p. 152

Return on sales another name for *profit margin.* p. 160

Reversing entries optional entries recorded at the beginning of a new year that prepare the accounts for simplified journal entries subsequent to accrual adjusting entries. p. 165

Temporary accounts accounts that are used to describe revenues, expenses, and owner's withdrawals; they are closed at the end of the reporting period. p. 153

Work sheet a 10-column spreadsheet used to draft a company's unadjusted trial balance, adjusting entries, adjusted trial balance, and financial statements; an optional step in the accounting process. p. 143

Working papers analyses and other informal reports prepared by accountants when organizing the useful information presented in formal reports to internal and external decision makers. p. 143

Objective Review

Answers to the following questions are listed at the end of this chapter. Be sure that you decide which is the one best answer to each question *before* you check the answers.

LO 1 In preparing a work sheet at the end of the fiscal year, an accountant incorrectly extended the $99,400 salaries expense balance from the Adjusted Trial Balance column to the Statement of Changes in Owner's Equity and Balance Sheet Debit column. As a result of this error:

a. The Adjusted Trial Balance columns will not balance.
b. The net income calculated on the work sheet will be understated.
c. The net income calculated on the work sheet will be overstated.
d. When the work sheet is completed, the totals of the last pair of columns will not be equal.
e. Both *b* and *d* are correct.

LO 2 After using the 10-column work sheet, the accountant prepares the financial statements in the following order:

a. Balance sheet, income statement, statement of changes in owner's equity.
b. Income statement, statement of changes in owner's equity, balance sheet.
c. Income statement, balance sheet, statement of changes in owner's equity.
d. Statement of changes in owner's equity, balance sheet, income statement.
e. The order does not matter.

LO 3 When closing entries are prepared:

a. The accounts for expenses, revenues, and the owner's withdrawals are closed to the Income Summary account.
b. The expense accounts are first closed to the revenue accounts, and the revenue accounts are then closed to the Income Summary account.
c. The final balance of the Income Summary account equals net income or net loss for the period.
d. All temporary accounts have zero balances when the process is completed.
e. None of the above is correct.

LO 4 The steps in the accounting cycle:

a. Are the procedures used to prepare a 10-column work sheet.
b. Begin with preparing the unadjusted trial balance.
c. Are completed only once in the life of a business.
d. Are concluded by preparing a balance sheet.
e. None of the above is correct.

LO 5 The profit margin is the ratio between a company's net income and:

a. Total expenses.
b. Total assets.
c. Total liabilities.
d. Total revenues.
e. Total withdrawals (or dividends).

LO 6 Temporary accounts include the following:

a. Assets, expenses, and the owner's withdrawals account.
b. Revenues, liabilities, and the owner's capital account.
c. Assets, liabilities, and the owner's capital account.
d. Revenues, expenses, and the owner's withdrawals account.
e. All the accounts that are not closed at the end of the accounting period.

LO 7 Reversing entries:

a. Are used by all companies that apply accrual accounting.
b. Are journalized and posted at the end of the accounting period after adjusting entries are posted but before the closing entries are posted.
c. Delay reporting accrued expenses to the next period.
d. Have no effect on the financial statements.
e. None of the above is correct.

The letter [B] identifies the questions, exercises, and problems based on Appendix B at the end of the chapter.

Questions for Class Discussion

1. What tasks are performed with the work sheet?
2. Is it possible to prepare adjusting entries and the financial statements without using the work sheet? What is gained by using a work sheet?
3. At what point in the accounting cycle is the work sheet prepared?
4. Where does the accountant obtain the amounts entered in the Unadjusted Trial Balance columns of the work sheet?
5. Why are the debit and credit entries in the Adjustments columns of the work sheet identified with letters?
6. What internal document is produced by combining the amounts in the Unadjusted Trial Balance col-

umns with the amounts in the Adjustments columns of the work sheet?

7. Why does the accountant extend the items in the Adjusted Trial Balance columns to the appropriate financial statement columns?
8. Why are revenue and expense accounts called temporary? Are there any other temporary accounts?
9. What two purposes are accomplished by recording closing entries?
10. What are the four steps in preparing closing entries?
11. What accounts are affected by closing entries? What accounts are not affected?
12. Describe the similarities and differences between adjusting and closing entries.
13. What is the purpose of the Income Summary account?
14. What accounts are listed on the post-closing trial balance?
15. Explain whether an error has occurred if a post-closing trial balance includes the item, Depreciation expense, building.
16. What is the name of the account used by a corporation to close the Income Summary account?
17. List all eight steps in the accounting cycle. What is the optional ninth step, and when is it accomplished?
18. If a company has a profit margin of 22.5% and net income of $1,012,500, what was the total amount of its revenues for the reporting period?

19. Refer to the current liability section of the balance sheet for Federal Express Corporation in Appendix G at the end of the book. Use the footnote to list the specific items included in the accrued expense liability.

20. Refer to the financial statements of Ben & Jerry's Homemade, Inc., in Appendix G. What journal entry was recorded as of December 26, 1992, to close the company's Income Summary account?

B21. How are the financial statements of a company affected by the accountant's choice to use or not use reversing entries?

B22. How do reversing entries simplify a company's bookkeeping efforts?

B23. If a company accrued unpaid salaries expense of $500 at the end of a fiscal year, what reversing entry could be made? When would it be made?

Exercises

Exercise 4–1
Extending adjusted account balances on a work sheet
(LO 1)

These accounts are from the Adjusted Trial Balance columns in a company's 10-column work sheet. In the blank space beside each account, write the letter of the appropriate financial statement column to which the account balance should be extended.

A. Debit column for the income statement.
B. Credit column for the income statement.
C. Debit column for the statement of changes in owner's equity and balance sheet.
D. Credit column for the statement of changes in owner's equity and balance sheet.

__1. R. Jefferson, Withdrawals
__2. Interest Earned
__3. Accumulated Depreciation, Machinery
__4. Service Fees Revenue
__5. Accounts Receivable
__6. Rent Expense
__7. Depreciation Expense, Machinery
__8. Accounts Payable
__9. Cash
__10. Office Supplies
__11. R. Jefferson, Capital
__12. Wages Payable
__13. Machinery
__14. Insurance Expense
__15. Interest Expense
__16. Interest Receivable

Exercise 4–2
Preparing adjusting entries from work sheet information
(LO 1)

Use the following information from the Adjustments columns of a 10-column work sheet to prepare adjusting journal entries:

No.		Adjustments Debit		Adjustments Credit	
109	Interest receivable	(*d*)	380		
124	Office supplies			(*b*)	1,350
128	Prepaid insurance			(*a*)	1,000
164	Accumulated depreciation, office equipment			(*c*)	3,500
209	Salaries payable			(*e*)	660
409	Interest earned			(*d*)	380
612	Depreciation expense, office equipment	(*c*)	3,500		
620	Office salaries expense	(*e*)	660		
636	Insurance expense, office equipment	(*a*)	432		
637	Insurance expense, store equipment	(*a*)	568		
650	Office supplies expense	(*b*)	1,350		
	Totals		6,890		6,890

Exercise 4–3
Preparing and posting closing entries
(LO 2, 4)

Open the following T-accounts with the provided balances. Prepare closing journal entries and post them to the accounts.

B. Holley, Capital

		Dec. 31	44,000

Rent Expense

Dec. 31	9,600		

B. Holley, Withdrawals

Dec. 31	21,000		

Salaries Expense

Dec. 31	24,000		

Income Summary

Insurance Expense

Dec. 31	3,500		

Services Revenue

		Dec. 31	77,000

Depreciation Expense

Dec. 31	15,000		

Exercise 4–4
Completing the income statement columns
(LO 2)

These partially completed Income Statement columns from a 10-column work sheet are for the Winston Sail'em Boat Rental Company. Use the information to determine the amount that should be entered on the Net income line of the work sheet.

	Debit	Credit
Rent earned		99,000
Salaries expense	35,300	
Insurance expense	4,400	
Dock rental expense	12,000	
Boat supplies expense	6,220	
Depreciation expense, boats	21,500	
Totals		
Net income		
Totals		

Exercise 4–5
Using the work sheet to draft closing entries
(LO 3)

Use the information in Exercise 4–4 to draft closing entries for the Winston Sail'em Boat Rental Company. The owner's name is C. Winston, and the pre-closing balance of the withdrawals account is $18,000.

Exercise 4–6
Extending accounts in the work sheet
(LO 1)

The last 6 columns of a 10-column work sheet for the Plummer Plumbing Co. follow. Complete the work sheet by extending the account balances into the appropriate financial statement columns and by entering the amount of net income for the reporting period.

No.	Title	Adjusted Trial Balance		Income Statement		Statement of Changes in Owner's Equity and Balance Sheet	
101	Cash	$ 8,200					
106	Accounts receivable	24,000					
153	Trucks	41,000					
154	Accumulated depreciation, trucks		$ 16,500				
193	Franchise	30,000					
201	Accounts payable		14,000				
209	Salaries payable		3,200				
233	Unearned fees		2,600				
301	F. Plummer, capital		64,500				
302	F. Plummer, withdrawals	14,400					
401	Plumbing fees earned		79,000				
611	Depreciation expense, trucks	11,000					
622	Salaries expense	31,500					
640	Rent expense	12,000					
677	Miscellaneous expenses	7,700					
	Totals	$179,800	$179,800				
	Net income						
	Totals						

Exercise 4–7
Preparing closing entries and the post-closing trial balance
(LO 3)

Complete the following six-column table for Plummer Plumbing Co. by providing four closing entries and the post-closing trial balance:

No.	Title	Adjusted Trial Balance		Closing Entries		Post-closing Trial Balance	
101	Cash	$ 8,200					
106	Accounts receivable	24,000					
153	Trucks	41,000					
154	Accumulated depreciation, trucks		$ 16,500				
193	Franchise	30,000					
201	Accounts payable		14,000				
209	Salaries payable		3,200				
233	Unearned fees		2,600				
301	F. Plummer, capital		64,500				
302	F. Plummer, withdrawals	14,400					
401	Plumbing fees earned		79,000				
611	Depreciation expense, trucks	11,000					
622	Salaries expense	31,500					
640	Rent expense	12,000					
677	Miscellaneous expenses	7,700					
901	Income summary						
	Totals	$179,800	$179,800				

Exercise 4–8
Preparing a work sheet
(LO 1)

The following unadjusted trial balance contains the accounts and balances of the Fine Painting Co. as of December 31, 19X1, the end of its fiscal year:

No.	Title	Debit	Credit
101	Cash	$18,000	
126	Supplies	12,000	
128	Prepaid insurance	2,000	
167	Equipment	23,000	
168	Accumulated depreciation, equipment		$ 6,500
209	Salaries payable		
301	B. Fine, capital		31,900
302	B. Fine, withdrawals	6,000	
404	Services revenue		36,000
612	Depreciation expense, equipment		
622	Salaries expense	11,000	
637	Insurance expense		
640	Rent expense	2,400	
652	Supplies expense		
	Totals	$74,400	$74,400

Required

Use the following information about the company's adjustments to complete a 10-column work sheet for the company:

a. The cost of expired insurance coverage was $300.
b. The cost of unused supplies on hand at the end of the year was $1,600.
c. Depreciation of the equipment for the year was $3,250.
d. Earned but unpaid salaries at the end of the year were $250.

Exercise 4–9
Adjusting and closing entries
(LO 3)

Use the information in Exercise 4–8 to prepare adjusting and closing journal entries for Fine Painting Co. (It is helpful but not mandatory to prepare the 10-column work sheet.)

Exercise 4–10
Closing entries for a corporation
(LO 3)

The following balances of the retained earnings and temporary accounts are for High Ridge, Inc., from its adjusted trial balance:

	Debit	Credit
Retained earnings		$43,200
Services revenue		62,000
Interest earned		5,800
Salaries expense	$23,500	
Insurance expense	4,050	
Rental expense	6,400	
Supplies expense	3,100	
Depreciation expense, trucks	10,600	

Required

a. Prepare the first three closing entries for this corporation.
b. Determine the amount of retained earnings to be reported on the company's balance sheet.

Exercise 4–11
The steps in the accounting cycle
(LO 4)

List the following steps of the accounting cycle in the proper order:

a. Preparing the post-closing trial balance.
b. Journalizing and posting adjusting entries.
c. Preparing the unadjusted trial balance.
d. Journalizing and posting closing entries.
e. Journalizing transactions.
f. Posting the transaction entries.
g. Preparing the financial statements.

Exercise 4–12
Calculating the profit margin
(LO 5)

Use the following information to calculate the profit margin for each case:

	Net Income	Revenue
a.	$ 1,745	$ 10,540
b.	48,372	131,651
c.	55,102	84,262
d.	27,513	450,266
e.	39,632	144,638

[B]Exercise 4–13
Reversing entries
(LO 7)

The following information was used to prepare adjusting entries for the Monterey Company as of August 31, the end of the company's fiscal year:

a. The company has earned $3,000 of unrecorded service fees.
b. The expired portion of prepaid insurance is $2,400.
c. The earned portion of the Unearned Fees account balance is $1,700.
d. Depreciation expense for the office equipment is $3,300.
e. Employees have earned but have not been paid salaries of $2,250.

Required

Prepare the reversing entries that would simplify the bookkeeping effort for recording subsequent events related to these adjustments.

[B]Exercise 4–14
Reversing entries
(LO 7)

The following two conditions existed for Lomax Company on September 30, 19X1, the end of its fiscal year:

a. Lomax rents a building from its owner for $2,400 per month. By a prearrangement, the company delayed paying September's rent until October 5. On this date, the company paid the rent for both September and October.
b. Lomax rents space in a building it owns to a tenant for $655 per month. By prearrangement, the tenant delayed paying the September rent until October 8. On this date, the tenant paid the rent for both September and October.

Required

1. Prepare the adjusting entries that Lomax should record for these situations as of September 30.
2. Assuming that Lomax does not use reversing entries, prepare journal entries to record Lomax's payment of rent on October 5 and the collection of rent on October 8 from Lomax's tenant.
3. Assuming that Lomax does use reversing entries, prepare those entries and the journal entries to record Lomax's payment of rent on October 5 and the collection of rent on October 8 from Lomax's tenant.

Problems

Problem 4–1
The work sheet; adjusting and closing entries; financial statements; and profit margin
(LO 1, 2, 3, 5)

Dunagin's Repairs opened for business on January 1, 19X1. By the end of the year, the company's unadjusted trial balance appeared as follows:

DUNAGIN'S REPAIRS
Unadjusted Trial Balance
December 31, 19X1

No.	Title	Debit	Credit
101	Cash	$ 3,000	
124	Office supplies	3,800	
128	Prepaid insurance	2,650	
167	Equipment	48,000	
168	Accumulated depreciation, equipment		
201	Accounts payable		$ 12,000
210	Wages payable		
301	R. Dunagin, capital		30,000
302	R. Dunagin, withdrawals	15,000	
401	Repair fees earned		77,750
612	Depreciation expense, equipment		
623	Wages expense	36,000	
637	Insurance expense		
640	Rent expense	9,600	
650	Office supplies expense		
690	Utilities expense	1,700	
	Totals	$119,750	$119,750

Required

1. Enter the unadjusted trial balance on a blank 10-column work sheet form and complete the work sheet using this information:
   a. An inventory of the office supplies at the end of the year showed that $700 of supplies were on hand.
   b. The cost of expired insurance coverage was $660.
   c. The year's depreciation on the equipment was $4,000.
   d. The earned but unpaid wages at the end of the year were $500.
2. Present the adjusting entries and closing entries as they would appear in the journal.

3. Use the information in the work sheet to prepare an income statement, a statement of changes in owner's equity, and a classified balance sheet.
4. Determine the company's profit margin.

Problem 4–2
Work sheet, journal entries, financial statements, and profit margin
(LO 1, 2, 3, 5)

This unadjusted trial balance is for Blue Mesa Construction as of the end of its fiscal year. The beginning balance of the owner's capital account was $12,660 and the owner invested another $15,000 cash in the company during the year:

BLUE MESA CONSTRUCTION
Unadjusted Trial Balance
September 30, 19X2

No.	Title	Debit	Credit
101	Cash	$ 18,000	
126	Supplies	9,400	
128	Prepaid insurance	6,200	
167	Equipment	81,000	
168	Accumulated depreciation, equipment		$ 20,250
201	Accounts payable		4,800
203	Interest payable		
208	Rent payable		
210	Wages payable		
213	Estimated property taxes payable		
251	Long-term notes payable		25,000
301	T. Morrison, capital		27,660
302	T. Morrison, withdrawals	36,000	
401	Construction fees earned		140,000
612	Depreciation expense, equipment		
623	Wages expense	41,000	
633	Interest expense	1,500	
637	Insurance expense		
640	Rent expense	13,200	
652	Supplies expense		
683	Property taxes expense	5,000	
684	Repairs expense	2,510	
690	Utilities expense	3,900	
	Totals	$217,710	$217,710

Required

1. Prepare a 10-column work sheet for 19X2, starting with the unadjusted trial balance and including these additional facts:
   a. The inventory of supplies at the end of the year had a cost of $2,500.
   b. The cost of expired insurance for the year is $4,000.
   c. Annual depreciation on the equipment is $9,000.
   d. The September utilities expense was not included in the trial balance because the bill arrived after it was prepared. Its $400 amount needs to be recorded.
   e. The company's employees have earned $1,500 of accrued wages.
   f. The lease for the office requires the company to pay total rent for the year equal to 10% of the company's annual revenues. The rent is paid to the building owner with monthly payments of $1,100. If the annual rent exceeds the total monthly payments, the company must pay the excess before October 31. If the total is less than the amount previously paid, the building owner will refund the difference by October 31.
   g. Additional property taxes of $800 have been assessed on the equipment but have not been paid or recorded in the accounts.
   h. The long-term note payable bears interest at 1% per month, which the company is required to pay by the tenth of the following month. The balance of the Interest Expense account equals the amount paid during the year. The interest for September has not yet been paid or recorded. In addition, the company is required to make a $5,000 payment on the note on November 30, 19X2.
2. Use the work sheet to prepare the adjusting and closing entries.
3. Prepare an income statement, a statement of changes in owner's equity, and a classified balance sheet. Calculate the company's profit margin for the year.

Problem 4–3
Closing entries, financial statements, ratios
(LO 2, 3, 5)

The adjusted trial balance for the Kessler Company as of December 31, 19X1, follows:

KESSLER COMPANY
Adjusted Trial Balance
December 31, 19X1

No.	Title	Debit	Credit
101	Cash	$ 14,000	
104	Short-term investments	16,000	
126	Supplies	6,100	
128	Prepaid insurance	3,000	
167	Equipment	40,000	
168	Accumulated depreciation, equipment		$ 15,000
173	Building	115,000	
174	Accumulated depreciation, building		35,000
183	Land	45,000	
201	Accounts payable		15,500
203	Interest payable		1,500
208	Rent payable		2,500
210	Wages payable		500
213	Estimated property taxes payable		800
233	Unearned professional fees		6,500
251	Long-term notes payable		66,000
301	H. Kessler, capital		86,700
302	H. Kessler, withdrawals	30,000	
401	Professional fees earned		112,000
406	Rent earned		12,000
407	Dividends earned		2,900
409	Interest earned		1,000
606	Depreciation expense, building	10,000	
612	Depreciation expense, equipment	5,000	
623	Wages expense	28,000	
633	Interest expense	4,100	
637	Insurance expense	9,000	
640	Rent expense	2,400	
652	Supplies expense	6,400	
682	Postage expense	3,200	
683	Property taxes expense	8,000	
684	Repairs expense	7,900	
688	Telephone expense	1,200	
690	Utilities expense	3,600	
	Totals	$357,900	$357,900

An analysis of other information reveals that the company is required to make a $3,900 payment on the long-term note payable during 19X2. Also, the owner invested $20,000 cash early in the year.

Required

1. Present the income statement, statement of changes in owner's equity, and balance sheet.

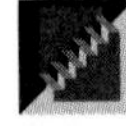

2. Present the four closing entries made at the end of the year.
3. Use the information in the financial statements to calculate the values of these ratios:
   a. Return on equity (use the capital account from the adjusted trial balance in the denominator).
   b. Modified return on equity when the proprietor's efforts are valued at $25,000 for the year.
   c. Debt ratio.
   d. Current ratio.
   e. Profit margin (use total revenues as the denominator).
   f. Modified profit margin when the proprietor's efforts are valued at $25,000 for the year.

[B]Problem 4–4
Adjusting, reversing, and subsequent entries
(LO 7)

This six-column table for Milton's Pool Parlor includes the unadjusted trial balance as of December 31, 19X1:

MILTON'S POOL PARLOR
December 31, 19X1

	Unadjusted Trial Balance		Adjustments		Adjusted Trial Balance	
Cash	$ 11,000					
Accounts receivable						
Supplies	4,500					
Equipment	150,000					
Accumulated depreciation, equipment		$ 15,000				
Interest payable						
Salaries payable						
Unearned membership fees		24,000				
Notes payable		50,000				
U. Milton, capital		58,250				
U. Milton, withdrawals	30,000					
Membership fees earned		90,000				
Depreciation expense, equipment						
Salaries expense	38,000					
Interest expense	3,750					
Supplies expense						
Totals	$237,250	$237,250				

Required

1. Complete the six-column table by entering adjustments that reflect the following information:
   a. As of December 31, employees have earned $800 of unpaid and unrecorded wages. The next payday is January 4, and the total wages to be paid will be $1,200.
   b. The cost of supplies on hand at December 31 is $1,800.
   c. The note payable requires an interest payment to be made every three months. The amount of unrecorded accrued interest at December 31 is $1,250, and the next payment is due on January 15. This payment will be $1,500.
   d. An analysis of the unearned membership fees shows that $16,000 remains unearned at December 31.
   e. In addition to the membership fees included in the revenue account balance, the company has earned another $12,000 in fees that will be collected on January 21. The company is also expected to collect $7,000 on the same day for new fees earned during January.
   f. Depreciation expense for the year is $15,000.
2. Prepare journal entries for the adjustments drafted in the six-column table.
3. Prepare journal entries to reverse the effects of the adjusting entries that involve accruals.
4. Prepare journal entries to record the cash payments and collections described for January.

Problem 4–5
Performing the steps in the accounting cycle
(LO 1, 2, 3, 4)

On June 1, Jo Farr created a new travel agency called International Tours. These events occurred during the company's first month:

June 1 Farr created the new company by investing $20,000 cash and computer equipment worth $30,000.

2 The company rented furnished office space by paying $1,600 rent for the first month.

3 The company purchased $1,200 of office supplies for cash.

June 10 The company paid $3,600 for the premium on a one-year insurance policy.
14 The owner's assistant was paid $800 for two weeks' salary.
24 The company collected $6,800 of commissions from airlines on tickets obtained for customers.
28 The assistant was paid another $800 for two weeks' salary.
29 The company paid the month's $750 telephone bill.
30 The company paid $350 cash to repair the company's computer.
30 The owner withdrew $1,425 cash from the business.

The company's chart of accounts included these accounts:

101	Cash	405	Commissions Earned
106	Accounts Receivable	612	Depreciation Expense, Computer Equipment
124	Office Supplies	622	Salaries Expense
128	Prepaid Insurance	637	Insurance Expense
167	Computer Equipment	640	Rent Expense
168	Accumulated Depreciation, Computer Equipment	650	Office Supplies Expense
209	Salaries Payable	684	Repairs Expense
301	J. Farr, Capital	688	Telephone Expense
302	J. Farr, Withdrawals	901	Income Summary

Required

1. Use the balance-column format to create each of the listed accounts.
2. Prepare journal entries to record the transactions for June and post them to the accounts.
3. Prepare a 10-column work sheet that starts with the unadjusted trial balance as of June 30. Use the following information to draft the adjustments for the month:
   a. Two-thirds of one month's insurance coverage was consumed.
   b. There were $800 of office supplies on hand at the end of the month.
   c. Depreciation on the computer equipment was estimated to be $825.
   d. The assistant had earned $160 of unpaid and unrecorded salary.
   e. The company had earned $1,750 of commissions that had not yet been billed.

   Complete the remaining columns of the worksheet.
4. Prepare journal entries to record the adjustments drafted on the work sheet and post them to the accounts.
5. Prepare an income statement, a statement of changes in owner's equity, and a balance sheet.
6. Prepare journal entries to close the temporary accounts and post them to the accounts.
7. Prepare a separate post-closing trial balance.

Problem 4–6
Analytical essay
(LO 1, 2)

This problem relies on the information provided in Problem 4–2. Analyze each of the following errors and describe how it would affect the 10-column work sheet and the company's financial statements.

1. The adjustment for supplies consumption credited the Supplies account for $2,500 and debited the same amount to the Supplies Expense account.
2. The adjustment for property taxes debited the Equipment account for $800 and credited the same amount to the Estimated Property Taxes Payable account.
3. When completing the adjusted trial balance in the work sheet, the $18,000 cash balance was incorrectly entered in the Credit column.
4. When transferring the adjusted trial balance amounts to the financial statement columns, the Prepaid Insurance account balance was extended to the Debit column for the income statement.

[B]Problem 4–7
Analytical essay
(LO 7)

On December 31, 19X1, the Castle Rock Company recorded a $10,000 liability to its employees for wages earned in 19X1 that will be paid on January 5, the first payday in 19X2. In addition, they will receive another $5,000 for wages earned in 19X2. The accountant did not prepare a reversing entry as of January 1, 19X2, but did not inform the bookkeeper about the liability accrued for the wages. As a result, the bookkeeper recorded a $15,000 debit to Wages Expense on January 5, and a $15,000 credit to Cash.

Describe the effects of this error on the financial statements for 19X1. Describe any erroneous account balances that will exist during 19X2. Suggest a reasonable point in time at which the error would be discovered.

Serial Problem

Emerald Computer Services

(The first two segments of this comprehensive problem were in Chapters 2 and 3, and the final segment is presented in Chapter 5. If the Chapter 2 and 3 segments have not been completed, the assignment can begin at this point. However, you should use the facts on pages 96–97 in Chapter 2 and pages 139–140 in Chapter 3. Because of its length, this problem is most easily solved if you use the Working Papers that accompany this text.)

The transactions of Emerald Computer Services for October through December 19X1 have been recorded in the problem segments in Chapters 2 and 3, as well as the year-end adjusting entries. Prior to closing the revenue and expense accounts for 19X1, the accounting system is modified to include the Income Summary account, which is given the number 901.

Required

1. Record and post the appropriate closing entries.
2. Prepare a post-closing trial balance.

Provocative Problems

Provocative Problem 4–1
Tender Tunes
(LO 1)

The following balance sheet was prepared at the end of the company's fiscal year:

TENDER TUNES
Balance Sheet
December 31, 19X1

Assets

Current assets:		
Cash		$ 6,500
Office supplies		1,500
Prepaid insurance		600
Total current assets		$ 8,600
Plant and equipment:		
Automobiles	$42,000	
Accumulated depreciation, automobiles	(17,000)	$25,000
Office equipment	$40,000	
Accumulated depreciation, office equipment	(13,500)	26,500
Total plant and equipment		$51,500
Total assets		$60,100

Liabilities

Current liabilities:	
Accounts payable	$ 4,200
Interest payable	400
Salaries payable	1,100
Unearned fees	1,800
Total current liabilities	$ 7,500
Noncurrent liabilities:	
Long-term notes payable	40,000
Total liabilities	$47,500

Owner's Equity

Charlie Griffin, capital	12,600
Total liabilities and owner's equity	$60,100

The company's accountant also prepared and posted the following adjusting and closing entries:

Dec.	31	Insurance Expense	800.00	
		Prepaid Insurance		800.00
		To record consumed insurance coverage.		
	31	Office Supplies Expense	4,100.00	
		Office Supplies		4,100.00
		To record consumed office supplies.		
	31	Depreciation Expense, Automobiles	8,500.00	
		Accumulated Depreciation, Automobiles		8,500.00
		To record depreciation on automobiles.		
	31	Depreciation Expense, Office Equipment	3,500.00	
		Accumulated Depreciation, Office Equipment		3,500.00
		To record depreciation on equipment.		

Dec.	31	Unearned Fees	730.00	
		Fees Earned		730.00
		To record earning of fees paid in advance.		
	31	Salaries Expense	1,100.00	
		Salaries Payable		1,100.00
		To record accrued salaries.		
	31	Interest Expense	400.00	
		Interest Payable		400.00
		To record accrued interest expense.		
	31	Fees Earned	61,000.00	
		Income Summary		61,000.00
		To close the revenue account and open the Income Summary account.		
	31	Income Summary	45,960.00	
		Depreciation Expense, Automobiles		8,500.00
		Depreciation Expense, Office Equipment		3,500.00
		Salaries Expense		15,000.00
		Interest Expense		3,200.00
		Insurance Expense		800.00
		Rent Expense		7,200.00
		Office Supplies Expense		4,100.00
		Gas, Oil, and Repairs Expense		2,350.00
		Telephone Expense		1,310.00
		To close the expense accounts.		
	31	Income Summary	15,040.00	
		Charlie Griffin, Capital		15,040.00
		To close income summary.		
	31	Charlie Griffin, Capital	16,000.00	
		Charlie Griffin, Withdrawals		16,000.00
		To close withdrawals account.		

Use the information in the balance sheet and the journal entries to complete a 10-column work sheet. (The five steps should be completed in reverse order.)

Provocative Problem 4–2
California Car Wash
(LO 1, 2, 3)

Use the following Unadjusted Trial Balance information to complete a 10-column work sheet. Instead of the usual column headings, use the following headings on the work sheet:

Unadjusted Trial Balance: Debit and Credit
Adjustments: Debit and Credit
Adjusted Trial Balance: Debit and Credit
Closing Entries: Debit and Credit
Post-Closing Trial Balance: Debit and Credit

Notice that these headings combine the six-column table we used in Chapter 3 to develop the adjusted trial balance with the six-column table we used in Chapter 4 to develop the post-closing trial balance. The information for the adjustments is

a. Three customers owe the company $550 for services provided but not billed.
b. A count of the supplies shows that $3,700 has been consumed.
c. The insurance coverage expired at the rate of $35 per month for 12 months.
d. The annual depreciation expense for the equipment is $2,000.
e. December's utility costs of $135 were not included in the unadjusted trial balance.
f. The employees had earned $623 of accrued wages as of December 31.

Unadjusted Trial Balance

No.	Title	Dr.	Cr.
101	Cash	$ 3,200	
106	Accounts receivable	500	
126	Soap supplies	6,000	
128	Prepaid insurance	2,100	
167	Equipment	15,000	
168	Accumulated depreciation, equipment		$ 4,000
201	Accounts payable		1,350
210	Salaries payable		
301	K. McGowan, capital		25,900
302	K. McGowan, withdrawals	13,500	
401	Fees earned		44,450
612	Depreciation expense, equipment		
623	Wages expense	18,000	
637	Insurance expense		
640	Rent expense	6,000	
652	Soap supplies expense		
690	Utilities expense	11,400	
901	Income summary		
	. . . .		
	Totals	$75,700	$75,700

Provocative Problem 4–3
Accounting related communications
(LO 3)

As the end of the calendar year is approaching, Controller Jerry James is getting the Woodward Company's accounting department ready to prepare the annual financial statements. One concern is the expense of the services provided by an external consultant under a three-month contract that runs from November 30, 19X1, through February 28, 19X2. The total fee for the contract is based on the hours of the consultant's time, with the result that the total fee is not known.

The controller is concerned that the company's financial statements could not be prepared until March because the amount of consulting expense will not be known until then. To avoid this problem, the controller has asked you to prepare a letter to Pat Patterson, the consultant, that would ask for a progress report by the end of the first week of January. This report would specifically identify the hours and charges that will be billed for the consultant's time in December.

Draft the letter that will be sent to Patterson requesting this information. It will be signed by the controller on December 15, 19X1.

Provocative Problem 4–4
Apple Computer, Inc.
(LO 4)

Apple Computer, Inc.

Refer to the consolidated balance sheet for Apple Computer, Inc., in Appendix F at the end of this book. Assume that a ledger account exists for each item in the balance sheet and prepare a post-closing trial balance for the company as of September 25, 1992. Also assume that the company uses an account with a credit balance called Allowance for Doubtful Accounts that is contra to the Accounts Receivable account. For simplicity, the amounts in the trial balance can be stated in thousands of dollars as they are presented in the balance sheet. (Note: The account for the Accumulated Translation Adjustment is an owners' equity account. You may omit an account for Notes Receivable from Shareholders.)

Comprehensive Problem

Piper's Plumbing and Heating
(Review of Chapters 1–4)

Following is the unadjusted trial balance of Piper's Plumbing and Heating as of November 30, 19X1. The account balances include the effects of transactions during the first 11 months of the year.

PIPER'S PLUMBING AND HEATING
Unadjusted Trial Balance
November 30, 19X1

No.	Title	Debit	Credit
101	Cash	$ 17,000	
124	Office supplies	9,400	
126	Repair supplies	86,500	
128	Prepaid insurance	2,400	
153	Trucks	82,000	
154	Accumulated depreciation, trucks		$ 40,000
173	Building	185,000	
174	Accumulated depreciation, building		32,000
201	Accounts payable		13,500
210	Wages payable		
233	Unearned heating fees		3,700
301	Bill Piper, capital		174,600
302	Bill Piper, withdrawals	30,000	
401	Plumbing fees earned		180,000
402	Heating fees earned		95,000
606	Depreciation expense, building		
611	Depreciation expense, trucks		
623	Wages expense	65,000	
637	Insurance expense		
650	Office supplies expense		
652	Repair supplies expense		
669	Gas, oil, and repairs expense	13,500	
672	General and administrative expenses	48,000	
	Totals	$538,800	$538,800

The following transactions occurred during December 19X1:

Dec.	2	Received $1,000 for completed heating work.
	5	Paid $11,325 on accounts payable.
	6	Paid $4,100 insurance premium in advance.
	7	Received $3,300 cash for plumbing work completed.
	10	Purchased $1,500 of repair supplies on credit.
	14	Paid $3,000 for wages earned December 1 to 14.
	17	Purchased $325 of office supplies on credit.
	21	Received $2,200 cash for plumbing work completed and $14,000 cash for heating work.
	24	Paid $1,430 for truck repairs related to an accident.
	28	Paid $3,300 for wages earned December 15 to 28.
	30	Received $600 cash for plumbing work completed and $4,500 cash for heating work.

Required

1. Use the balance column format to create the accounts listed in the November 30 trial balance. Enter the unadjusted November 30 balances in the accounts.
2. Prepare and post journal entries to record the transactions for December; omit entering the account numbers in the posting reference column.
3. Prepare a 10-column work sheet as of December 31. Start by entering the unadjusted balances from the accounts as of that date. Continue by entering adjustments for the following items, and then complete the rest of the work sheet.
   a. At the end of the year, the office supplies inventory was $730.

b. At the end of the year, the repair supplies inventory was $7,600.
c. At the end of the year, the unexpired portion of the prepaid insurance was $3,800.
d. Annual depreciation on the trucks was $20,000.
e. Annual depreciation on the building was $5,000.
f. At the end of the year, the employees had earned $990 in accrued wages.
g. At the end of the year, the balance of unearned heating fees was $600.

4. Prepare adjusting journal entries and post them to the accounts.
5. Prepare an income statement and a statement of changes in owner's equity for 19X1 and a balance sheet as of December 31, 19X1. The owner did not make any new investments during the year.
6. Prepare closing journal entries and post them to the accounts.
7. Prepare a post-closing trial balance.
8. Calculate the following ratios for 19X1:
   a. Return on equity.
   b. Modified return on equity, assuming that the proprietor's management efforts are valued at $32,000 for the year.
   c. The profit margin.

Answers to Objective Review Questions

LO 1 (*c*)
LO 2 (*b*)
LO 3 (*d*)
LO 4 (*e*)
LO 5 (*d*)
LO 6 (*d*)
LO 7 (*d*)

CHAPTER

5

Accounting for Merchandising Activities

The first four chapters in this book used only service companies as examples of businesses that prepare financial statements. This chapter introduces you to some of the business and accounting practices used by companies that engage in merchandising activities. These companies buy goods and then resell them to customers. This chapter shows how the financial statements describe the special transactions and assets related to these activities. In particular, you will learn about the additional financial statement elements created by merchandising activities. To help you understand where the information comes from, we describe how accountants close the accounts of merchandising companies and design income statements.

Learning Objectives

After studying Chapter 5, you should be able to:

1. Describe merchandising activities and their effects on financial statements.
2. Analyze and record sales of merchandise.
3. Describe how the ending inventory and the cost of goods sold are determined with perpetual and periodic inventory accounting systems.
4. Describe various formats for income statements and prepare closing entries for a merchandising business.
5. Complete a work sheet that includes the inventory-related accounts and explain an adjusting entry approach to recording the change in the Merchandise Inventory account.
6. Calculate the acid-test ratio and describe what it reveals about a company's liquidity.
7. Define or explain the words and phrases in the chapter glossary.

The Nature of Merchandising Activities

The first four chapters have described the financial statements and accounting records of Clear Copy Co. Because it provides services to its customers, Clear Copy is a service company. Other examples of service companies include hotels, hospitals, car rental agencies, airlines, theaters, ski resorts, and golf courses. In return for services provided to its customers, a service company receives commissions, fares, or fees as revenue. Its net income for a reporting period is the difference between its revenues and the operating expenses incurred in providing the services.

LO 1 Describe merchandising activities and their effects on financial statements.

In contrast, a merchandising company earns net income by buying and selling **merchandise,** which consists of goods that the company acquires specifically to be sold.[1] To achieve a net income, the revenue from selling the merchandise needs to exceed not only the cost of the merchandise sold to customers but also the company's other operating expenses for the reporting period.

The accounting term for the revenues from selling merchandise is *sales* and the term used to describe the expense of buying and preparing the merchandise is *cost of goods sold.*[2] The company's other expenses are often called *operating expenses.* This condensed income statement for Meg's Mart shows you how these three elements of net income are related to each other:

MEG'S MART
Condensed Income Statement
For Year Ended December 31, 19X2

Net sales	$314,700
Cost of goods sold	(230,400)
Gross profit from sales	$ 84,300
Total operating expenses	(62,800)
Net income	$ 21,500

This income statements tells us that Meg's Mart sold goods to its customers for $314,700. The company acquired those goods at a total cost of $230,400. As a result, it earned $84,300 of **gross profit,** which is the difference between the net sales and the cost of goods sold. In addition, the company incurred $62,800 of operating expenses and achieved $21,500 of net income for the year.

A merchandising company's balance sheet includes an additional element that is not on the balance sheet of a service company. In Illustration 5–1, we present the classified balance sheet for Meg's Mart. Notice that the current asset section includes an item called **merchandise inventory.** Even though they also have inventories of supplies, most companies simply refer to merchandise inventory as **inventory.** This asset consists of goods the company owns on the balance sheet date and expects to sell to its customers. The $21,000 amount listed for the inventory is the cost incurred in buying the goods, shipping them to the store, and otherwise making them ready for sale.

The next sections of the chapter provide more information about these unique elements of the financial statements for merchandising companies.

Total Revenue from Sales

LO 2 Analyze and record sales of merchandise.

This schedule shows how Meg's Mart calculates its *net sales* for 19X2:

MEG'S MART
Calculation of Net Sales
For Year Ended December 31, 19X2

Sales		$321,000
Less: Sales returns and allowances . .	$2,000	
Sales discounts	4,300	6,300
Net sales		$314,700

The components of this calculation are described in the following paragraphs.

[1] A merchandising company can be either a wholesaler or a retailer. Wholesalers buy goods from manufacturers and sell them to retailers or other wholesalers. Retailers buy goods from wholesalers and sell them to individual customers.

[2] Many service companies also use the word *sales* to describe their revenues.

ILLUSTRATION 5–1 *Classified Balance Sheet for a Merchandising Company*

MEG'S MART
Balance Sheet
December 31, 19X2

Assets			
Current assets:			
Cash		$ 8,200	
Accounts receivable		11,200	
Merchandise inventory		21,000	
Prepaid expenses		1,100	
Total current assets			$41,500
Plant and equipment:			
Office equipment	$ 4,200		
Less accumulated depreciation	1,400	$ 2,800	
Store equipment	$30,000		
Less accumulated depreciation	6,000	24,000	
Total plant and equipment			26,800
Total assets			$68,300
Liabilities			
Current liabilities:			
Accounts payable		$16,000	
Salaries payable		800	
Total liabilities			$16,800
Owner's Equity			
Meg Harlowe, capital			51,500
Total liabilities and owner's equity			$68,300

Sales

The sales item in this calculation is the total cash and credit sales made by the company during the year. Each cash sale was rung up on one of the company's cash registers when it was completed. At the end of each day, the registers were read and the total cash sales for the day were recorded with a journal entry like this one for November 3:

Nov.	3	Cash	1,205.00	
		Sales		1,205.00
		Sold merchandise for cash.		

This journal entry records an increase in the company's cash for the amount received from the customers. It also records the revenue in the Sales account.

In addition, a journal entry would be prepared each day to record the credit sales made on that day. For example, this entry records $450 of credit sales on November 3:

Nov.	3	Accounts Receivable	450.00	
		Sales		450.00
		Sold merchandise on credit.		

This entry records the increase in the company's assets in the form of the accounts receivable from the customers. It also records the revenue from the credit sales.[3]

Sales Returns and Allowances

To meet their customers' needs, most companies allow customers to *return* any unsuitable merchandise for a full refund. If a customer keeps the unsatisfactory goods and is given a partial refund of the selling price, the company is said to have provided a sales *allowance.* Either way, returns and allowances involve dissatisfied customers and the possibility of lost future sales. Careful managers try to reduce customer dissatisfaction by minimizing returns and allowances. A company's accountants can help by providing information to the manager about actual returns and allowances. Thus, many accounting systems record returns and allowances in a separate *contra-revenue* account like the one used in this entry to record a $200 cash refund:

Nov.	3	Sales Returns and Allowances	200.00	
		Cash		200.00
		Customer returned defective merchandise.		

The company could record the refund with a debit to the Sales account. Although this practice would provide the same measure of net sales, it would not provide information that the manager can use to monitor the refunds and allowances. By using the Sales Returns and Allowances contra account, the information is readily available. To simplify the reports provided to external decision makers, published income statements usually omit this detail and present only the amount of net sales.

Sales Discounts

When goods are sold on credit, the expected amounts and dates of future payments need to be clearly stated to avoid misunderstandings. The **credit terms** for a sale describe the amounts and timing of payments that the buyer agrees to make in the future. The specific terms usually reflect the ordinary practices of most companies in the industry. For example, companies in an industry might customarily expect to be paid 10 days after the end of the month in which a sale occurred. These credit terms would be stated on sales invoices or tickets as "n/10 EOM," with the abbreviation **EOM** standing for "end of the month." In other industries, invoices become due and payable 30 calendar days after the invoice date. These terms are abbreviated as "n/30," and the 30-day period is called the **credit period.**

When the credit period is long, the seller often grants a **cash discount** if the customer pays promptly. These early payments are desirable because the seller receives the cash more quickly and can use it to carry on its activities. In addition, prompt payments reduce future efforts and costs of billing customers. These advantages are usually worth the cost of offering the discounts.

If cash discounts for early payment are granted, they are described in the credit terms on the invoice. For example, the terms of "2/10, n/60" mean that a 60-day credit period passes before full payment is due. However, to encourage early payment, the seller allows the buyer to deduct 2% of the invoice amount from the payment if it is made within 10 days of the invoice date. The **discount period** is the period in which the reduced payment can be made.

[3] Chapter 7 describes how stores account for sales to customers who use third-party credit cards, such as those issued by banks.

At the time of a credit sale, the seller does not know that the customer will pay within the discount period and take advantage of a cash discount. As a result, the discount is usually not recorded until the customer pays within the discount period. For example, suppose that Meg's Mart completed a credit sale on November 12 at a gross selling price of $100, subject to terms of 2/10, n/60. The sale is recorded with this entry:

Nov.	12	Accounts Receivable	100.00	
		Sales		100.00
		Sold merchandise under terms of 2/10, n/60.		

Even though the customer may pay less than the purchase price, the entry records the receivable and the revenue as if the full amount will be collected.

In fact, the customer has two alternatives. One option is to wait 60 days until January 11 and pay the full $100. If this option is chosen, Meg's Mart records the collection with this entry:

Jan.	11	Cash	100.00	
		Accounts Receivable		100.00
		Collected account receivable.		

The customer's other option is to pay $98 within a 10-day period that runs through November 22. If the customer pays on November 22, Meg's Mart records the collection with this entry:

Nov.	22	Cash	98.00	
		Sales Discounts	2.00	
		Accounts Receivable		100.00
		Received payment for the November 12 sale less the discount.		

Cash discounts granted to customers are called **sales discounts.** Because management needs to monitor the amount of cash discounts to assess their effectiveness and their cost, their amounts are recorded in a contra-revenue account called Sales Discounts. The balance of this account is deducted from the balance of the Sales account when calculating the company's net sales. Although information about the amount of discounts is useful internally, it is seldom reported on income statements distributed to external decision makers.

Measuring Inventory and Cost of Goods Sold

A merchandising company's balance sheet includes a current asset called *inventory* and its income statement includes the item called *cost of goods sold.* Both of these items are affected by the company's merchandise transactions. The amount of the asset on the balance sheet equals the cost of the inventory on hand at the end of the fiscal year. The amount of the cost of goods sold is the cost of the merchandise that was sold to customers during the year.

Two different inventory accounting systems may be used to collect information about the cost of the inventory on hand and the cost of goods sold. They are described in the following paragraphs.

Periodic and Perpetual Inventory Systems

LO 3 Describe how the ending inventory and the cost of goods sold are determined with perpetual and periodic inventory accounting systems.

The two basic types of inventory accounting systems are called *perpetual* and *periodic*. As suggested by their name, **perpetual inventory systems** maintain a continuous record of the amount of inventory on hand. This perpetual record is maintained by adding the cost of each newly purchased item to the inventory account and subtracting the cost of each sold item from the account. When an item is sold, its cost is recorded in the Cost of Goods Sold account. Users of perpetual systems can refer to the balance of the inventory account to determine the cost of the items that remain on hand. They can also refer to the balance of the Cost of Goods Sold account to determine the cost of the merchandise sold to customers.

Before the development of inexpensive and easy-to-use computer programs, perpetual systems were generally applied only by businesses that made a limited number of sales each day, such as automobile dealers or major appliance stores. Because there were relatively few transactions, the perpetual accounting system could be operated efficiently. However, the availability of improved technology has greatly increased the number of companies that use perpetual systems.

Under **periodic inventory systems,** a company does not continuously update its records of the quantity and cost of goods on hand or sold. Instead, the company simply records the cost of new merchandise in a temporary *Purchases* account. When merchandise is sold, only the revenue is recorded. When financial statements are prepared, the company takes a *physical inventory* by counting the quantities of merchandise on hand and determines the inventory's total cost from records that show each item's original cost. This total cost is then used to determine the cost of goods sold.

Traditionally, periodic systems were always used by companies such as drug and department stores that sold large quantities of low-valued items. Without computers and scanners, it was not feasible for accounting systems to track such small items as toothpaste, pain killers, clothing, and housewares through the inventory and into the customers' hands.

Although perpetual systems are now more affordable, they are still not used by all merchandising companies. As a result, it will be helpful for you to understand how periodic systems work. In addition, studying periodic systems will help you visualize the flow of goods through inventory without having to learn the more complicated sequence of journal entries used in perpetual systems. (More information on perpetual systems is provided in Chapter 8.)

Calculating the Cost of Goods Sold with a Periodic Inventory System

As mentioned earlier, a store that uses a periodic inventory system does not record the cost of merchandise items when they are sold. Rather, the accountant waits until the end of the reporting period and determines the cost of all the goods sold during the period. To make this calculation, the accountant must have information about:

1. The cost of the merchandise on hand at the beginning of the period.
2. The cost of merchandise purchased during the period.
3. The cost of unsold goods on hand at the end of the period.

Look at Illustration 5–2 to see how this information can be used to measure the cost of goods sold for Meg's Mart.

In Illustration 5–2, note that Meg's Mart had $251,400 of goods available for sale during the period. They were available because the company had $19,000 of goods on hand when the period started and purchased an additional $232,400 of goods during the year. The available goods were then either sold during the period or on hand at the end of the period. Because the count

ILLUSTRATION 5-2 *The Flow of Goods and Costs through Inventory*

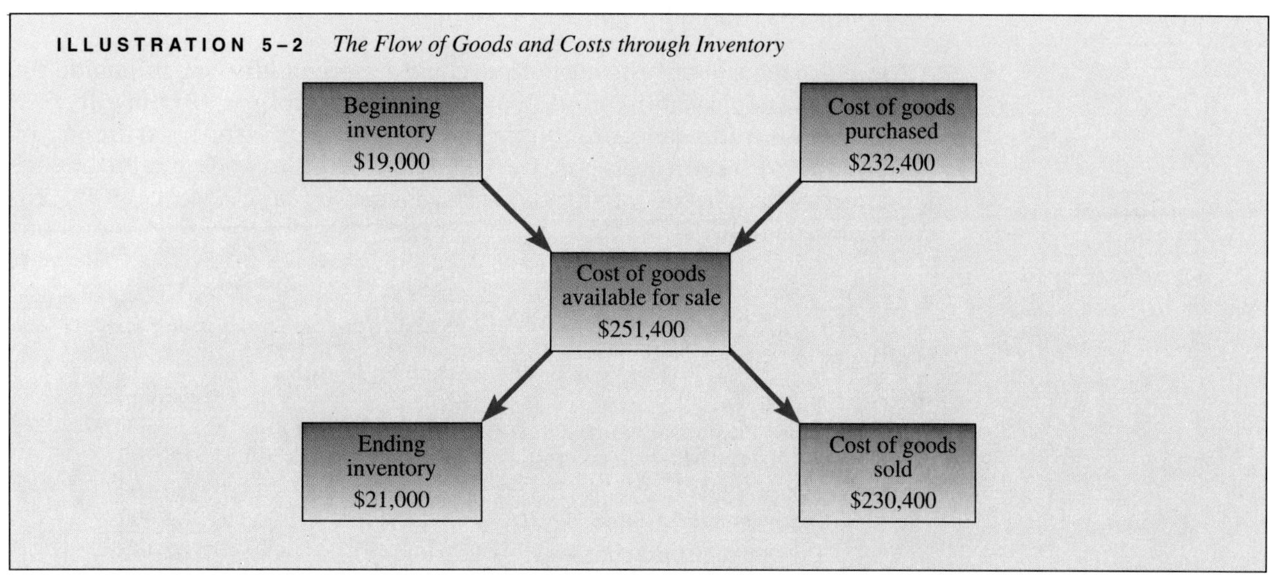

showed that $21,000 were on hand at the end of the year, we can conclude that $230,400 must have been sold. This schedule presents the calculation:

MEG'S MART
Calculation of Cost of Goods Sold
For Year Ended December 31, 19X2

Beginning inventory	$ 19,000
Cost of goods purchased	232,400
Cost of goods available for sale	$251,400
Less ending inventory	(21,000)
Cost of goods sold	$230,400

The following paragraphs explain how the accounting system accumulates the information that the accountant needs to make this calculation.

Measuring and Recording Merchandise Inventory

The merchandise on hand at the beginning of an accounting period is called the *beginning inventory* and the merchandise on hand at the end is called the *ending inventory.* (Because a new reporting period starts as soon as the old period ends, the ending inventory of one period is always the beginning inventory of the next.) When a periodic inventory system is used, the dollar amount of the ending inventory is determined by (1) counting the unsold items in the store and the stockroom, (2) multiplying the counted quantity of each type of good by its cost, and (3) adding all the costs of the different types of goods. The cost of goods sold is found by subtracting the cost of the ending inventory from the cost of the goods available for sale.

Through the closing process described later in the chapter, the periodic system records the cost of the ending inventory in the *Merchandise Inventory* account. The balance in this account is not changed during the next accounting period. In fact, entries are made to the Merchandise Inventory account *only* at the end of the period. Thus, neither the purchases of new merchandise nor the cost of goods sold is entered in the Merchandise Inventory account. As a result, the account no longer shows the cost of the merchandise on hand as soon as any goods are purchased or sold in the current period. Because the account's balance describes the beginning inventory of the period, it cannot be used on a new balance sheet without being updated by the closing entries described later in this chapter.

Recording the Cost of Purchased Merchandise

A complete measure of the cost of purchased merchandise must include the effects of (1) any cash discounts provided by the suppliers, (2) the effects of any returns and allowances for unsatisfactory items received from the suppliers, and (3) any freight costs paid by the buyer to get the goods into the buyer's inventory. The net cost of the goods purchased by Meg's Mart for 19X2 is calculated as follows:

MEG'S MART
Calculation of Cost of Goods Purchased
For Year Ended December 31, 19X2

Purchases		$235,800
Less: Purchases returns and allowances . .	$1,500	
Purchases discounts	4,200	5,700
Net purchases		$230,100
Add transportation-in		2,300
Cost of goods purchased		$232,400

The following paragraphs explain how these amounts are found and then accumulated in the accounts.

The Purchases Account. Under a periodic inventory system, the cost of merchandise bought for resale is debited to a temporary account called *Purchases.* For example, Meg's Mart would record a $1,000 credit purchase of merchandise on November 2 with this entry:

Nov.	2	Purchases	1,000.00	
		Accounts Payable		1,000.00
		Purchased merchandise on credit, invoice dated November 2, terms 2/10, n/30.		

The accountant uses the Purchases account to accumulate the cost of all merchandise bought during a period. This temporary account is a holding place for information used at the end of the year to calculate the cost of goods sold.

Purchases Discounts. When stores buy merchandise on credit, they may be offered cash discounts for paying within the discount period. These cash discounts are called **purchases discounts** by the buyer. When the buyer pays within the discount period, the accounting system records a credit to a contra-purchases account called *Purchases Discounts.* The following entry uses this account to record the payment for the merchandise purchased on November 2:

Nov.	12	Accounts Payable	1,000.00	
		Purchases Discounts		20.00
		Cash		980.00
		Paid for the purchase of November 2 less the discount.		

By recording the amount of discounts taken, the accountant can help the manager determine whether any discounts are missed. For example, if all purchases are made on credit and all suppliers offer a 2% discount, the balance of the Purchases Discounts contra account should equal 2% of the balance of the

Purchases account. If the accountant did not use the contra account, the $20 credit entry would be recorded as a reduction of the Purchases account balance. As a result, it would be more difficult to determine whether all discounts were taken.

The accountant uses the balance of the Purchases Discounts account to compute the net cost of the purchases for the period. However, published financial statements usually do not include this calculation because it is useful only for managers.

A Cash Management Technique. To ensure that discounts are not missed, most companies set up a system to pay all invoices within the discount period. Furthermore, careful cash management ensures that no invoice is paid until the last day of the discount period. A helpful technique for reaching both of these goals files every invoice in such a way that it automatically comes up for payment on the last day of its discount period. For example, a simple manual system uses 31 folders, one for each day in the month. After an invoice is recorded in the journal, it is placed in the file folder for the last day of its discount period. Thus, if the last day of an invoice's discount period is November 12, it is filed in folder number 12. Then, the invoice and any other invoices in the same folder are removed and paid on November 12. Computerized systems can accomplish the same result by using a code that identifies the last date in the discount period. When that date is reached, the computer automatically provides a reminder that the account should be paid.

Read the short As a Matter of Ethics case and consider what you would do if you were faced with the situation it describes.

Trade Discounts. Cash discounts represent real reductions below the original negotiated prices for merchandise. Thus, they differ from **trade discounts** offered by sellers in the process of negotiating the selling price. Trade discounts are offered as a percentage reduction in the **list price** of the goods. Because the list price is only the starting point in setting the final price for the goods, it is not recorded in the buyer's accounting records as their cost. (Similarly, the seller records the net price as the amount of the sale.) For example, if Meg's Mart purchased items with a $1,200 list price, net of a 25% *trade discount,* the purchase would be recorded as its negotiated price of $900 [$1,200 − (25% × $1,200)]. Any cash discounts on this purchase would be based on the $900 price and would be recorded in the Purchases Discounts account.

Purchases Returns and Allowances. Some merchandise received from suppliers is not acceptable and must be returned. In other cases, the purchaser may keep imperfect but marketable merchandise because the supplier grants an allowance against the purchase price.

Even though the seller does not charge the buyer for the returned goods or gives an allowance for imperfect goods, the buyer incurs costs in receiving, inspecting, identifying, and possibly returning defective merchandise. The occurrence of these costs can be signaled to the manager by recording the cost of the returned merchandise or the seller's allowance in a separate contra-purchases account called *Purchases Returns and Allowances.* For example, this journal entry is recorded on November 14 when Meg's Mart returns defective merchandise for a $265 refund of the original purchase price:

Nov.	14	Accounts Payable	265.00	
		Purchases Returns and Allowances		265.00
		Returned defective merchandise.		

AS A MATTER OF

Ethics

Renee Fleck was recently hired by Mid-Mart, a medium-sized retailing company that purchases most of its merchandise on credit. She overlapped on the new job for several days with the outgoing employee in her position, Martin Hull, so that he could help her learn the ropes.

One of Fleck's responsibilities is to see that the payables are paid promptly to maintain the company's credit standing with its suppliers and to take advantage of all cash discounts. Hull told Fleck that the current system has accomplished both goals easily and has also made another contribution to the company's profits. He explained that the computer system has been programmed to prepare checks for amounts net of the cash discounts. Even though the checks are dated as of the last day of the discount period, they are not mailed until five days later. Because the accounts are always paid, the company has had virtually no trouble with its suppliers. "It's simple," Hull explained to Fleck. "We get the free use of the cash for an extra five days, and who's going to complain? Even when somebody does, we just blame the computer system and the people in the mail room."

A few days later, Hull had departed and Fleck assumed her new duties. The first invoice that she examined had a 10-day discount period on a $10,000 purchase. The transaction occurred on April 9 subject to terms of 2/10, n/30. Fleck had to decide whether she should mail the $9,800 check on April 19th or wait until the 24th.

As we described for Purchases Discounts, the accountant uses the balance of the Purchases Returns and Allowances account to compute the net cost of goods purchased during the period. However, published financial statements generally do not include this information because it is useful only for managers.

Discounts and Returned Merchandise. If part of a shipment of goods is returned within the discount period, the buyer can take the discount only on the remaining balance of the invoice. For example, suppose that Meg's Mart is offered a 2% cash discount on $5,000 of merchandise. Two days later, the company returns $800 of the goods before the invoice is paid. When the $4,200 balance is paid within the discount period, Meg's Mart can take the 2% discount only on that amount. Specifically, the company can deduct only an $84 discount (2% × $4,200).

Transportation Costs. Depending on the terms negotiated with its suppliers, a company may be responsible for paying the shipping costs for transporting the acquired goods to its own place of business. Because these costs are part of the sacrifice of making the goods ready for sale, generally accepted accounting principles require them to be added to the cost of the purchased goods.

The freight charges could be recorded with a debit to the Purchases account. However, more complete information about these costs is provided to management if they are debited to a special supplemental account called *Transportation-In.* The accountant adds this account's balance to the net purchase price of the acquired goods to find the total cost of goods purchased. (See the schedule on page 192.)

The use of this account is demonstrated by the following entry, which records a $75 freight charge for incoming merchandise:

Nov.	24	Transportation-In	75.00	
		Cash		75.00
		Paid freight charges on purchased merchandise.		

ILLUSTRATION 5–3 *Identifying Ownership Responsibilities and Risks*

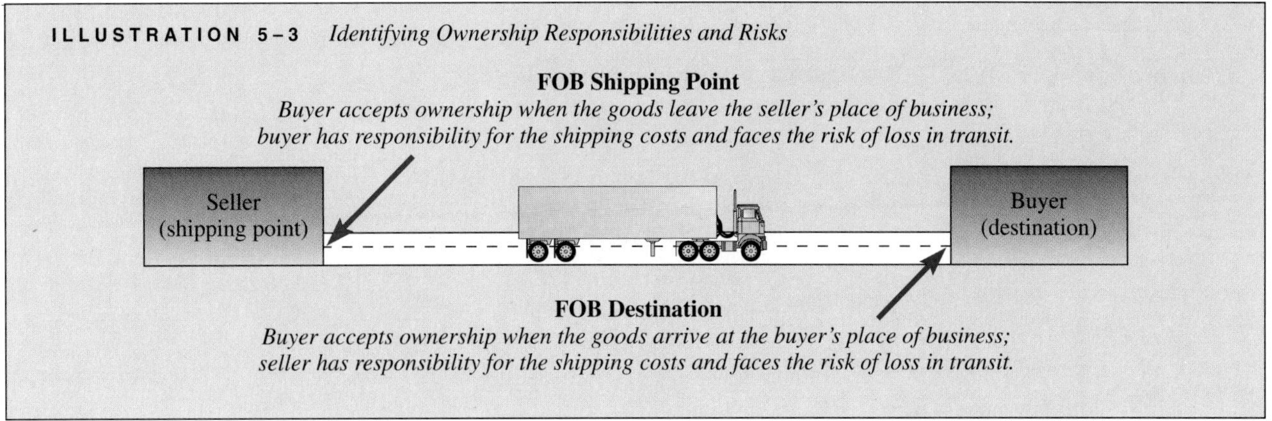

FOB Shipping Point
Buyer accepts ownership when the goods leave the seller's place of business;
buyer has responsibility for the shipping costs and faces the risk of loss in transit.
Seller
(shipping point)
Buyer
(destination)
FOB Destination
Buyer accepts ownership when the goods arrive at the buyer's place of business;
seller has responsibility for the shipping costs and faces the risk of loss in transit.

Because detailed information about freight charges is relevant only for managers, it is seldom found in external financial statements.

Freight paid to bring purchased goods into the inventory is accounted for separately from freight paid on goods sent to customers. The shipping cost of incoming goods is included in the cost of goods sold, while the shipping cost for outgoing goods is a selling expense.

Identifying Ownership Responsibilities and Risks. When a merchandise transaction is planned, the buyer and seller need to establish which party will be responsible for paying any freight costs and which will bear the risk of loss during transit.

The basic issue to be negotiated is the point at which ownership is transferred from the buyer to the seller. The place of the transfer is called the **FOB** point, which is the abbreviation for the phrase, *free on board.* The meaning of different FOB points is explained by the diagram in Illustration 5–3.

Under an *FOB shipping point* agreement (also called *FOB factory*), the buyer accepts ownership at the seller's place of business. As a result, the buyer is responsible for paying the shipping costs and bears the risk of damage or loss while the goods are in shipment. In addition, the goods are part of the buyer's inventory while they are in transit because the buyer already owns them.

Alternatively, an *FOB destination* agreement causes ownership of the goods to pass at the buyer's place of business. If so, the seller is responsible for paying the shipping charges and bears the risk of damage or loss in transit. Furthermore, the seller does not record the sales revenue until the goods arrive at the destination because the transaction is not complete before that point in time.

Debit and Credit Memoranda

Buyers and sellers often find that they need to adjust the amount that is owed between them. For example, purchased merchandise may not meet specifications, unordered goods may be received, different quantities may be received than were ordered and billed, and billing errors may occur.

In some cases, the original balance can be adjusted by the buyer without a negotiation. For example, a seller may make an error on an invoice. If the buying company discovers the error, it can make its own adjustment and notify the seller by sending a **debit memorandum** or a **credit memorandum.** A debit memorandum is a business document that informs the recipient that the sender has *debited* the account receivable or payable. It provides the notification with words like these: "We debit your account," followed by the amount

ILLUSTRATION 5–4 *The Use of Debit and Credit Memoranda*

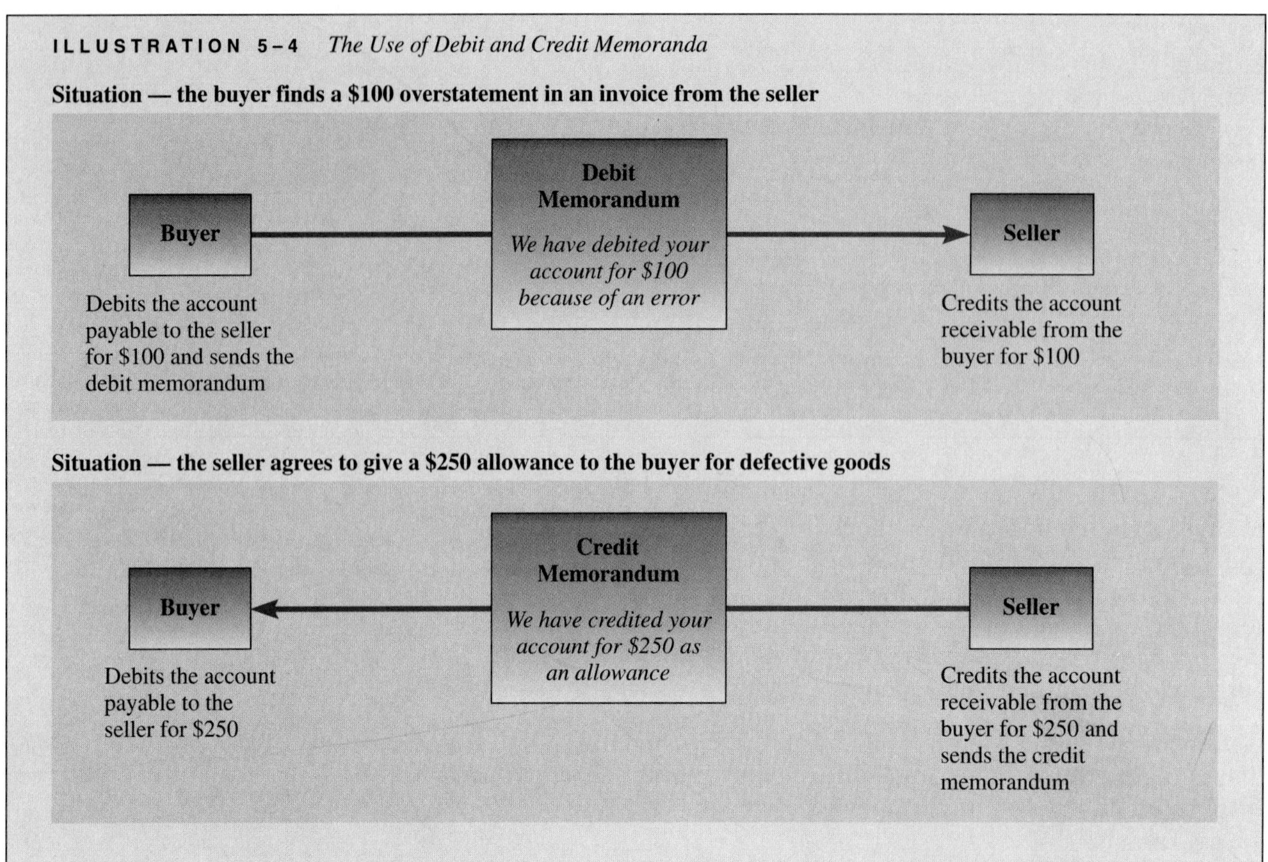
Situation — the buyer finds a $100 overstatement in an invoice from the seller
Buyer
Debit Memorandum
We have debited your account for $100 because of an error
Seller
Debits the account payable to the seller for $100 and sends the debit memorandum
Credits the account receivable from the buyer for $100
Situation — the seller agrees to give a $250 allowance to the buyer for defective goods
Buyer
Credit Memorandum
We have credited your account for $250 as an allowance
Seller
Debits the account payable to the seller for $250
Credits the account receivable from the buyer for $250 and sends the credit memorandum

and an explanation. On the other hand, a credit memorandum informs the recipient that the sender has credited the receivable or payable. See Illustration 5–4 for two situations that involve these documents.

The debit memorandum in Illustration 5–4 is based on a case in which a buyer initially records an invoice as an account payable and later discovers an error by the seller that overstated the total bill by $100. The buyer corrects the balance of its liability and formally notifies the seller of the mistake with a debit memorandum reading: "We have debited your account for $100 because of an error." Additional information is also provided about the invoice, its date, and the nature of the error. The buyer sends a *debit* memorandum because the correction debits the account payable to reduce its balance. The buyer's debit to the payable is offset by a credit to the Purchases account.

When the seller receives its copy of the debit memorandum, it records a *credit* to the buyer's account receivable to reduce its balance. An equal debit is recorded in the Sales account. Neither company uses a contra account because the adjustment was created by an error.

In other situations, an adjustment can be made only after negotiations between the buyer and the seller. For example, suppose that a buyer claims that some merchandise does not meet specifications. The amount of the allowance to be given by the seller can be determined only after discussion. Assume that a buyer accepts delivery of merchandise and records the transaction with a $750 debit to the Purchases account and an equal credit to Accounts Payable. Later, the buyer discovers that some of the merchandise is flawed, and can be sold only if it is marked down substantially. After a phone call and brief negotiations, the seller agrees to grant a $250 allowance against the original purchase price.

The seller records the allowance with a debit to the Sales Returns and Allowances contra account and a credit to Accounts Receivable. Then, the seller formally notifies the buyer of the allowance with a credit memorandum. A *credit* memorandum is used because the adjustment credited the receivable to reduce its balance. When the buyer receives the credit memorandum, it debits Accounts Payable and credits Purchases Returns and Allowances. Contra accounts provide both companies' managers with useful information about the allowance.

Inventory Shrinkage

Merchandising companies lose merchandise in a variety of ways, including shoplifting and deterioration while an item is on the shelf or in the warehouse. These losses are called **shrinkage.**

Even though perpetual inventory systems track all goods as they move into and out of the company, they are not able to directly measure shrinkage caused by shoplifting or thefts by employees. However, these systems allow the accountant to measure shrinkage by comparing a physical count with recorded quantities.

Because periodic inventory systems do not identify quantities on hand, they cannot provide direct measures of shrinkage. In fact, all that they can determine is the cost of the goods on hand and the goods that passed out of the inventory. The amount that passed out includes the cost of goods sold, stolen, or destroyed. For example, suppose that shoplifters took merchandise that cost $500. Because the goods were not on hand for a physical count, the ending inventory's cost is $500 smaller than it would have been. Ultimately, the $500 is included in the cost of the goods sold.

Chapter 8 describes perpetual systems and how they provide more complete information about shrinkage. Chapter 8 also describes how an accountant can estimate shrinkage when a periodic system is used.

Alternative Income Statement Formats

LO 4 Describe various formats for income statements and prepare closing entries for a merchandising business.

Within the framework of generally accepted accounting principles, companies have flexibility in selecting a format for their financial statements. In fact, practice shows that many different formats are used. This section of the chapter describes several possible formats that Meg's Mart could use for its income statement.

In Illustration 5–5, we present a *classified* income statement that would probably be distributed only to the company's managers because of the details that it includes. The sales and cost of goods sold sections are the same as the calculations presented earlier in the chapter. The difference between the net sales and cost of goods sold is the gross profit for the year.

Also notice that the operating expenses section classifies the expenses into two categories. **Selling expenses** include the expenses of promoting sales through displaying and advertising the merchandise, making sales, and delivering goods to customers. **General and administrative expenses** support the overall operations of a business and include the expenses of such activities as accounting, human resource management, and financial management.

Some expenses may be divided between categories because they contribute to both activities. For example, Illustration 5–5 reflects the fact that Meg's Mart divided the total rent expense of $9,000 for its store building between the two categories. Ninety percent ($8,100) was selling expense and the remaining 10% ($900) was general and administrative expense.[4] The cost allo-

[4] These expenses can be recorded in a single account or in two separate accounts. If they are recorded in one account, the accountant allocates its balance between the two expenses when preparing the statements.

ILLUSTRATION 5–5 *Classified Income Statement for Internal Use*

MEG'S MART
Income Statement
For Year Ended December 31, 19X2

Sales				$321,000
Less: Sales returns and allowances			$ 2,000	
Sales discounts			4,300	6,300
Net sales				$314,700
Cost of goods sold:				
Merchandise inventory, December 31, 19X1			$ 19,000	
Purchases		$235,800		
Less: Purchases returns and allowances	$1,500			
Purchases discounts	4,200	5,700		
Net purchases		$230,100		
Add transportation-in		2,300		
Cost of goods purchased			232,400	
Goods available for sale			$251,400	
Merchandise inventory, December 31, 19X2			21,000	
Cost of goods sold				230,400
Gross profit from sales				$ 84,300
Operating expenses:				
Selling expenses:				
Depreciation expense, store equipment		$ 3,000		
Sales salaries expense		18,500		
Rent expense, selling space		8,100		
Store supplies expense		1,200		
Advertising expense		2,700		
Total selling expenses			$ 33,500	
General and administrative expenses:				
Depreciation expense, office equipment		$ 700		
Office salaries expense		25,300		
Insurance expense		600		
Rent expense, office space		900		
Office supplies expense		1,800		
Total general and administrative expenses			29,300	
Total operating expenses				62,800
Net income				$ 21,500

cation should reflect an economic relationship between the prorated amounts and the activities. For example, the allocation in this case could be based on relative rental values.

In Illustration 5–6, we use the **multiple-step income statement** format that would probably be used in external reports. The only difference between this format and the one in Illustration 5–5 is that it leaves out the detailed calculations of net sales and cost of goods sold. The format is called multiple-step because it shows several intermediate totals between sales and net income.

In contrast, we present a **single-step income statement** for Meg's Mart in Illustration 5–7. This simpler format presents only one intermediate total for total operating expenses.

In practice, many companies use combination formats that have some of the features of both the single- and multiple-step statements. Combination formats are used in the income statements in Appendixes F and G at the end of the book for Apple Computer, Ben & Jerry's, and Federal Express. As long as

ILLUSTRATION 5–6 *Multiple-Step Income Statement*

MEG'S MART
Income Statement
For Year Ended December 31, 19X2

Net sales			$314,700
Cost of goods sold			230,400
Gross profit from sales			$ 84,300
Operating expenses:			
Selling expenses:			
Depreciation expense, store equipment	$ 3,000		
Sales salaries expense	18,500		
Rent expense, selling space	8,100		
Store supplies expense	1,200		
Advertising expense	2,700		
Total selling expenses		$33,500	
General and administrative expenses:			
Depreciation expense, office equipment	$ 700		
Office salaries expense	25,300		
Insurance expense	600		
Rent expense, office space	900		
Office supplies expense	1,800		
Total general and administrative expenses		29,300	
Total operating expenses			62,800
Net income			$ 21,500

ILLUSTRATION 5–7 *Single-Step Income Statement*

MEG'S MART
Income Statement
For Year Ended December 31, 19X2

Net sales		$314,700
Cost of goods sold	$230,400	
Selling expenses	33,500	
General and administrative expenses	29,300	
Total operating expenses		293,200
Net income		$ 21,500

the income statement elements are presented logically, management can choose the format that it wants to use.[5]

Closing Entries for Merchandising Companies

To help understand how information flows through the accounting system into the financial statements, we now discuss the process for closing the temporary accounts of merchandising companies. The process is demonstrated with data from the adjusted trial balance for Meg's Mart in Illustration 5–8. In addition, the accountant knows from a physical count that the cost of the ending inventory is $21,000.

[5] Later chapters describe other possible elements, such as extraordinary gains and losses, that have designated locations in the income statement.

ILLUSTRATION 5-8 *Adjusted Trial Balance for Meg's Mart at December 31, 19X2*

Cash	$ 8,200	
Accounts receivable	11,200	
Merchandise inventory	19,000	
Office supplies	550	
Store supplies	250	
Prepaid insurance	300	
Office equipment	4,200	
Accumulated depreciation, office equipment		$ 1,400
Store equipment	30,000	
Accumulated depreciation, store equipment		6,000
Accounts payable		16,000
Salaries payable		800
Meg Harlowe, capital		34,000
Meg Harlowe, withdrawals	4,000	
Sales		321,000
Sales returns and allowances	2,000	
Sales discounts	4,300	
Purchases	235,800	
Purchases returns and allowances		1,500
Purchases discounts		4,200
Transportation-in	2,300	
Depreciation expense, store equipment	3,000	
Depreciation expense, office equipment	700	
Office salaries expense	25,300	
Sales salaries expense	18,500	
Insurance expense	600	
Rent expense, office space	900	
Rent expense, selling space	8,100	
Office supplies expense	1,800	
Store supplies expense	1,200	
Advertising expense	2,700	
Totals	$384,900	$384,900

LO 4 Describe various formats for income statements and prepare closing entries for a merchandising business.

The trial balance includes these unique accounts for merchandising activities: Merchandise Inventory, Sales, Sales Returns and Allowances, Sales Discounts, Purchases, Purchases Returns and Allowances, Purchases Discounts, and Transportation-In. Their presence in the ledger causes the closing entries to be slightly different from the ones described in Chapter 4. However, the process still consists of four steps.

Step 1—Record the Ending Inventory and Close the Temporary Accounts That Have Credit Balances

The first step accomplishes two goals: First, it adds the $21,000 cost of the ending inventory to the balance of the Merchandise Inventory account. Second, it closes the temporary accounts that have credit balances, including the Sales account and the two contra-purchases accounts. The first closing entry for Meg's Mart is

Dec.	31	Merchandise Inventory	21,000.00	
		Sales	321,000.00	
		Purchases Returns and Allowances	1,500.00	
		Purchases Discounts	4,200.00	
		Income Summary		347,700.00
		To close temporary accounts with credit balances and record the ending inventory.		

Posting this entry gives zero balances to the three temporary accounts that had credit balances in the adjusted trial balance. It also momentarily increases the balance of the Merchandise Inventory account to $40,000. However the next entry reduces the balance of this account.

Step 2—Remove the Beginning Inventory and Close the Temporary Accounts That Have Debit Balances

The second step also accomplishes two results: First, it subtracts the cost of the beginning inventory from the Merchandise Inventory account. Second, it closes the temporary accounts that have debit balances, including the expense accounts, the two contra-sales accounts, the Purchases account, and the Transportation-In account. The second closing entry for Meg's Mart is

Dec.	31	Income Summary	326,200.00	
		Merchandise Inventory		19,000.00
		Sales Returns and Allowances		2,000.00
		Sales Discounts		4,300.00
		Purchases		235,800.00
		Transportation-In		2,300.00
		Depreciation Expense, Store Equipment		3,000.00
		Depreciation Expense, Office Equipment		700.00
		Office Salaries Expense		25,300.00
		Sales Salaries Expense		18,500.00
		Insurance Expense		600.00
		Rent Expense, Office Space		900.00
		Rent Expense, Selling Space		8,100.00
		Office Supplies Expense		1,800.00
		Store Supplies Expense		1,200.00
		Advertising Expense		2,700.00
		To close temporary accounts with debit balances and to remove the beginning inventory balance.		

Posting this entry reduces the balance of the Merchandise Inventory account down to $21,000, which is the amount produced by the physical count at December 31, 19X2. It also gives zero balances to the 14 temporary accounts that had debit balances.

The following Merchandise Inventory account shows you how the first two closing entries create an ending balance equal to the $21,000 cost provided by the physical count:

Merchandise Inventory **Acct. No. 119**

Date		Explanation	Debit	Credit	Balance
19X1					
Dec.	31	Ending balance for 19X1			19,000.00
19X2					
Dec.	31	First closing entry	21,000.00		40,000.00
	31	Second closing entry (Ending balance for 19X2)		19,000.00	21,000.00

As mentioned earlier in the chapter, this account has the $21,000 balance throughout 19X3 until the accounts are closed at the end of that year.

Step 3—Close the Income Summary Account to the Owner's Capital Account

The third closing entry for a merchandising company is the same as the third closing entry for a service company. Specifically, it closes the Income Summary account and updates the balance of the owner's capital account. The third closing entry for Meg's Mart is

Dec.	31	Income Summary	21,500.00	
		Meg Harlowe, Capital		21,500.00
		To close the Income Summary account.		

The amount in the entry equals the net income reported on the income statement.

Step 4—Close the Owner's Withdrawals Account to the Owner's Capital Account

The fourth closing entry for a merchandising company is the same as the fourth closing entry for a service company. Specifically, it closes the owner's withdrawals account and reduces the balance of the owner's capital account to the amount shown on the balance sheet. The fourth closing entry for Meg's Mart is

Dec.	31	Meg Harlowe, Capital	4,000.00	
		Meg Harlowe, Withdrawals		4,000.00
		To close the withdrawals account.		

When this entry is posted, all the temporary accounts are cleared and ready to record events in 19X3. In addition, the owner's capital account has been fully updated to reflect the events of 19X2.

A Work Sheet for a Merchandising Company

LO 5 Complete a work sheet that includes the inventory-related accounts and explain an adjusting entry approach to recording the change in the Merchandise Inventory account.

Illustration 5–9 presents a version of the work sheet that the accountant for Meg's Mart could prepare in the process of developing its 19X2 financial statements. It differs in two ways from the 10-column work sheet described in Chapter 4.

The first difference is the deletion of the adjusted trial balance columns. This simplification has nothing to do with the fact that Meg's Mart is a retail business. This commonly used format is designed to simplify the work sheet by reducing its size. The omission of the columns causes the accountant to first compute the adjusted balances and then extend them directly into the financial statement columns.

The second difference appears on the line for the Merchandise Inventory account (shown in color). The unadjusted trial balance includes the beginning inventory balance of $19,000. This amount is extended into the debit column for the income statement. Then, the ending balance is entered in the credit column for the income statement and the debit column for the balance sheet. This step allows the cost of goods sold to be included in net income while the correct ending balance is included for the balance sheet.

The adjustments in the work sheet reflect the following economic events:

(*a*) Expiration of $600 of prepaid insurance.
(*b*) Consumption of $1,200 of store supplies.

ILLUSTRATION 5-9 *Work Sheet for Meg's Mart for the Year Ended December 31, 19X2*

		Unadjusted Trial Balance		Adjustments		Income Statement		Statement of Changes in Owner's Equity and Balance Sheet	
No.	**Account**	**Dr.**	**Cr.**	**Dr.**	**Cr.**	**Dr.**	**Cr.**	**Dr.**	**Cr.**
101	Cash	8,200						8,200	
106	Accounts receivable	11,200						11,200	
119	**Merchandise inventory**	**19,000**				19,000	21,000	21,000	
124	Office supplies	2,350			*(c)* 1,800			550	
125	Store supplies	1,450			*(b)* 1,200			250	
128	Prepaid insurance	900			*(a)* 600			300	
163	Office equipment	4,200						4,200	
164	Accum. depr., office equip.		700		*(e)* 700				1,400
165	Store equipment	30,000						30,000	
166	Accum. depr., store equip.		3,000		*(d)* 3,000				6,000
201	Accounts payable		16,000						16,000
209	Salaries payable				*(f)* 800				800
301	Meg Harlowe, capital		34,000						34,000
302	Meg Harlowe, withdrawals	4,000						4,000	
413	Sales		321,000				321,000		
414	Sales returns and allow.	2,000				2,000			
415	Sales discounts	4,300				4,300			
505	Purchases	235,800				235,800			
506	Purchases ret. and allow.		1,500				1,500		
507	Purchases discounts		4,200				4,200		
508	Transportation-in	2,300				2,300			
612	Depr. expense, store equip.			*(d)* 3,000		3,000			
613	Depr. expense, office equip.			*(e)* 700		700			
620	Office salaries expense	25,000		*(f)* 300		25,300			
621	Sales salaries expense	18,000		*(f)* 500		18,500			
637	Insurance expense			*(a)* 600		600			
641	Rent expense, office space	900				900			
642	Rent expense, selling space	8,100				8,100			
650	Office supplies expense			*(c)* 1,800		1,800			
651	Store supplies expense			*(b)* 1,200		1,200			
655	Advertising expense	2,700				2,700			
	Totals	380,400	380,400	8,100	8,100	326,200	347,700	79,700	58,200
	Net income					21,500			21,500
	Totals					347,700	347,700	79,700	79,700

(c) Consumption of $1,800 of office supplies.

(d) Depreciation of the store equipment for $3,000.

(e) Depreciation of the office equipment for $700.

(f) Accrual of $300 of unpaid office salaries and $500 of unpaid store salaries.

Once the adjusted amounts are extended into the financial statement columns, the accountant can use this information to develop the company's financial statements.

The Adjusting Entry Approach to Recording the Change in the Merchandise Inventory Account

LO 5 Complete a work sheet that includes the inventory-related accounts and explain an adjusting entry approach to recording the change in the Merchandise Inventory account.

The previously described closing entry approach to recording the change in the inventory account is widely used in practice. However, it is not the only bookkeeping method that can be applied at the end of the year. One other possible approach records two adjusting journal entries right before the closing entries are prepared. Because these entries are recorded, the first two closing entries do not include changes in the Merchandise Inventory account. This adjusting entry approach is preferred by some accountants. It is also used by computerized accounting systems that allow only temporary accounts to be affected by closing entries.

The Adjusting Entries

Under this adjusting approach, Meg's Mart removes the beginning balance from the Merchandise Inventory account by recording this adjusting entry at the end of 19X2:

Dec.	31	Income Summary	19,000.00	
		Merchandise Inventory		19,000.00
		To remove the beginning balance from the Merchandise Inventory account.		

This second adjusting entry produces the correct ending balance in the Merchandise Inventory account:

Dec.	31	Merchandise Inventory	21,000.00	
		Income Summary		21,000.00
		To insert the correct ending balance into the Merchandise Inventory account.		

After this entry is posted, the Merchandise Inventory account has a $21,000 debit balance. In addition, the Income Summary account has a $2,000 credit balance.

The Closing Entries

If the two adjusting entries for inventory are used, the closing entries differ only by not including the Merchandise Inventory account. Thus, Meg's Mart records the following two closing entries for 19X2 under the adjusting entry approach:

Dec.	31	Sales	321,000.00	
		Purchases Returns and Allowances	1,500.00	
		Purchases Discounts	4,200.00	
		Income Summary		326,700.00
		To close temporary accounts with credit balances.		

Dec.	31	Income Summary	307,200.00	
		Sales Returns and Allowances		2,000.00
		Sales Discounts		4,300.00
		Purchases		235,800.00
		Transportation-In		2,300.00
		Depreciation Expense, Store Equipment		3,000.00
		Depreciation Expense, Office Equipment		700.00
		Office Salaries Expense		25,300.00
		Sales Salaries Expense		18,500.00
		Insurance Expense		600.00
		Rent Expense, Office Space		900.00
		Rent Expense, Selling Space		8,100.00
		Office Supplies Expense		1,800.00
		Store Supplies Expense		1,200.00
		Advertising Expense		2,700.00
		To close temporary accounts with debit balances.		

The third and fourth entries are the same as before, although the amount debited to the Income Summary account is now based on four previous entries instead of two:

Dec.	31	Income Summary	21,500.00	
		Meg Harlowe, Capital		21,500.00
		To close the Income Summary account.		
Dec.	31	Meg Harlowe, Capital	4,000.00	
		Meg Harlowe, Withdrawals		4,000.00
		To close the withdrawals account.		

The Adjusting Entry Approach and the Work Sheet. If the accountant uses the adjusting entry approach to update the inventory account, the two adjustments are included in the adjustments columns in the work sheet, and a line for the Income Summary account is inserted at the bottom of the work sheet. This procedure is not demonstrated here.

Using the Information—The Acid-Test Ratio

LO 6 Calculate the acid-test ratio and describe what it reveals about a company's liquidity.

You have learned in this chapter that a company's current assets may include a merchandise inventory. Thus, you can now understand that a major part of a company's current assets may not be immediately available for paying its existing liabilities. In effect, the inventory must be sold and the accounts receivable must be collected before cash is available. As a result, the current ratio (which we described in Chapter 3) may not provide a complete description of a company's ability to pay its current liabilities.

To deal with this limitation, financial statement users often calculate the **acid-test ratio** to assess the company's ability to settle its current debts with its existing assets. The acid-test ratio is similar to the current ratio, but differs because it focuses on the company's immediate future.

The acid-test ratio is calculated just like the current ratio except that its numerator omits inventory and prepaid expenses. The prepaid expenses are omitted because they are not usually converted into cash quickly. The remaining current assets (cash, short-term investments, and receivables) are called the company's *quick assets.* The formula for the ratio is

$$\text{Acid-test ratio} = \frac{\text{Quick assets}}{\text{Current liabilities}}$$

The acid-test ratio for Meg's Mart is computed as follows:

$$\text{Acid-test ratio} = \frac{\$8,200 + \$11,200}{\$16,000 + \$800} = 1.2$$

In contrast, the current ratio (current assets/current liabilities) for Meg's Mart has this value:

$$\text{Current ratio} = \frac{\$41,500}{\$16,800} = 2.5$$

The difference between these two ratio values describes how the company's inventory and prepaid expenses affect its ability to pay short-term obligations with existing resources.

As an approximate rule of thumb, an acid-test ratio value of at least 1.0 suggests that the company is not likely to face a liquidity crisis in the near future. However, a value lower than 1.0 is not necessarily threatening if the company can generate adequate cash from sales or the accounts payable are not due until later in the year. On the other hand, a value higher than 1.0 may hide a liquidity crisis if the payables are due at once but the receivables are scheduled to be collected late in the year. These possibilities reinforce the point that a single ratio is seldom enough to indicate strength or weakness. However, it can identify areas that the analyst should look into more deeply.

Summary of the Chapter in Terms of Learning Objectives

LO 1 Merchandising companies purchase and sell merchandise. Their financial statements include the cost of the merchandise inventory in the current assets on the balance sheet and sales and cost of goods sold on the income statement. The difference between these last two numbers is called the gross profit.

LO 2 The seller first records the sale at the negotiated price. Any returns or allowances are recorded in a contra account to provide information to the manager. Cash collections are less than the sales revenues if credit customers take advantage of cash discounts. Discounts are recorded in a contra-sales account to provide the manager with additional information. Trade discounts are used to negotiate the selling price recorded as the sales revenue.

LO 3 A perpetual inventory system continuously tracks the cost of goods on hand and the cost of goods sold. A periodic system merely accumulates the cost of goods purchased during the year and does not provide continuous information about the cost of the inventory or the sold goods. At year-end, the cost of the inventory is determined and used on the balance sheet and to calculate the cost of goods sold. The cost of goods available for sale equals the beginning inventory plus the cost of goods purchased. The cost of goods sold equals the cost of goods available for sale minus the cost of the ending inventory. The cost of goods purchased is affected by purchases discounts, purchases returns and allowances, and transportation-in. These amounts are recorded in contra and supplemental accounts to provide information to management and are seldom reported in external statements.

LO 4 Companies have flexibility in choosing formats for their income statements. Internal statements have more details, including the calculations of net sales and the cost of goods sold. Classified income statements describe expenses incurred in different activities. Multiple-step statements include several intermediate totals and single-step statements do not. Merchandising companies' closing entries differ because they include accounts for inventory, sales, and purchases. The widely used closing-entry approach records the ending inventory and closes all temporary accounts that have credit balances. It then removes the cost of the beginning inventory and closes the temporary accounts with debit balances.

LO 5 The work sheet for a merchandising company uses special entries to update the inventory. The beginning inventory balance is extended into the income statement debit column and the cost of the ending inventory is entered in the income statement credit column and balance sheet debit column. Many accountants omit the adjusted trial balance columns to reduce the size of the work sheet. The adjusting entry approach to recording the ending inventory in the accounts uses two adjusting entries that remove the beginning cost from and add the ending cost to the inventory account. This approach is often used in computer systems.

LO 6 The acid-test ratio is used to assess a company's ability to pay its current liabilities with its existing quick assets (cash, short-term investments, and receivables). The costs of the merchandise inventory and prepaid expenses are not included in the numerator. A ratio value equal to or greater than one is usually considered to be adequate.

Demonstration Problem

Use the following adjusted trial balance and additional information to complete the requirements:

YE OLDE JUNQUE AND STUFF
Adjusted Trial Balance
December 31, 19X2

Cash	$ 19,000	
Merchandise inventory	52,000	
Store supplies	1,000	
Equipment	40,000	
Accumulated depreciation, equipment		$ 16,500
Accounts payable		8,000
Salaries payable		1,000
Ann Teak, capital		69,000
Ann Teak, withdrawals	8,000	
Sales		320,000
Sales discounts	20,000	
Purchases	147,000	
Purchases discounts		12,000
Transportation-in	11,000	
Depreciation expense	5,500	
Salaries expense	60,000	
Insurance expense	12,000	
Rent expense	24,000	
Store supplies expense	6,000	
Advertising expense	21,000	
Totals	$426,500	$426,500

A physical count shows that the cost of the year's ending inventory is $50,000.

Required

1. Prepare schedules that calculate the company's net sales and cost of goods sold for the year.
2. Present a single-step income statement for 19X2.
3. Prepare closing entries.

Planning the Solution

- The calculation of net sales deducts discounts from sales. The calculation of cost of goods sold adds the cost of goods purchased for the year to the beginning inventory and then subtracts the cost of the ending inventory.
- To prepare the single-step income statement, find the net sales and then list the operating expenses. Use the cost of goods sold number calculated in the first requirement.
- The first closing entry debits the inventory account for the cost of the ending inventory and debits all temporary accounts with credit balances. The second closing entry credits the inventory account with the cost of the beginning inventory and credits all temporary accounts with debit balances. The third entry closes the Income Summary account to the owner's capital account and the fourth closing entry closes the owner's withdrawals account to the owner's capital account.

Solution to Demonstration Problem

1.

Sales		$320,000
Less sales discounts		(20,000)
Net sales		$300,000
Beginning inventory		$ 52,000
Purchases	$147,000	
Less purchases discounts	(12,000)	
Plus transportation-in	11,000	
Cost of goods purchased		146,000
Cost of goods available for sale		$198,000
Less ending inventory		(50,000)
Cost of goods sold		$148,000

2.

YE OLDE JUNQUE AND STUFF
Income Statement
For Year Ended December 31, 19X2

Net sales		$300,000
Operating expenses:		
Cost of goods sold	$148,000	
Depreciation expense	5,500	
Salaries expense	60,000	
Insurance expense	12,000	
Rent expense	24,000	
Store supplies expense	6,000	
Advertising expense	21,000	
Total expenses		276,500
Net income		$ 23,500

3.

Dec.	31	Merchandise Inventory	50,000.00	
		Sales	320,000.00	
		Purchases Discounts	12,000.00	
		Income Summary		382,000.00
		To close temporary accounts with credit balances and record the ending inventory.		

Dec.	31	Income Summary	358,500.00	
		Merchandise Inventory		52,000.00
		Sales Discounts		20,000.00
		Purchases		147,000.00
		Transportation-In		11,000.00
		Depreciation Expense		5,500.00
		Salaries Expense		60,000.00
		Insurance Expense		12,000.00
		Rent Expense		24,000.00
		Store Supplies Expense		6,000.00
		Advertising Expense		21,000.00
		To close temporary accounts with debit balances and to remove the beginning inventory balance.		
	31	Income Summary	23,500.00	
		Ann Teak, Capital		23,500.00
		To close the Income Summary account.		
	31	Ann Teak, Capital	8,000.00	
		Ann Teak, Withdrawals		8,000.00
		To close the withdrawals account.		

Glossary

LO 7 Define or explain the words and phrases in the chapter glossary.

Acid-test ratio a ratio used to assess the company's ability to settle its current debts with its existing assets; it is the ratio between a company's quick assets (cash, short-term investments, and receivables) and its current liabilities. p. 206

Cash discount a reduction in a payable that is granted if it is paid within the discount period. p. 188

Credit memorandum a notification that the sender has entered a credit in the recipient's account maintained by the sender. p. 195

Credit period the time period that can pass before a customer's payment is due. p. 188

Credit terms the description of the amounts and timing of payments that a buyer agrees to make in the future. p. 188

Debit memorandum a notification that the sender has entered a debit in the recipient's account maintained by the sender. p. 195

Discount period the time period in which a cash discount is available. p. 188

EOM the abbreviation for *end-of-month*; used to describe credit terms for some transactions. p. 188

FOB the abbreviation for *free on board*; the designated point at which ownership of goods passes to the buyer; FOB shipping point (or factory) means that the buyer pays the shipping costs and FOB destination means that the seller pays the shipping costs. p. 195

General and administrative expenses expenses that support the overall operations of a business and include the expenses of such activities as providing accounting services, human resource management, and financial management. p. 197

Gross profit the difference between net sales and the cost of goods sold. p. 186

Inventory the goods that a company owns and expects to sell to its customers. p. 186

List price the nominal price of an item before any trade discount is deducted. p. 193

Merchandise goods acquired specifically to be sold to earn net income. p. 186

Merchandise inventory another term for *inventory*. p. 186

Multiple-step income statement an income statement format that shows several intermediate totals between sales and net income. p. 198

Periodic inventory system a method of accounting that records the cost of inventory purchased but does not track the quantity on hand or sold to customers; the records are updated periodically to reflect the results of physical counts of the items on hand. p. 190

Perpetual inventory system a method of accounting that maintains continuous records of the amount of inventory on hand and sold. p. 190

Purchases discount a cash discount taken against an amount owed to a supplier of goods. p. 192

Sales discount a cash discount taken by customers against an amount owed to the seller. p. 189

Selling expenses the expenses of promoting sales by displaying and advertising the merchandise, making sales, and delivering goods to customers. p. 197

Shrinkage inventory losses that occur through shoplifting and deterioration. p. 197

Single-step income statement an income statement format that does not present intermediate totals other than total expenses. p. 198

Trade discount a reduction below a list or catalog price that is negotiated in setting the selling price of goods. p. 193

Objective Review

Answers to the following questions are listed at the end of this chapter. Be sure that you decide which is the one best answer to each question *before* you check the answers.

LO 1 Which of the following items is not unique to the financial statements of merchandising companies?

a. Cost of goods sold.
b. Accounts receivable.
c. Gross profit.
d. Merchandise inventory.
e. Net sales.

LO 2 A cash discount is offered to:

a. Reduce the price of goods to only certain customers.
b. Reduce the seller's cost of billing and collecting its accounts.
c. Deceive customers into thinking that they are saving money.
d. Provide cash to the seller more quickly.
e. Both (*b*) and (*d*) are correct.

LO 3 Under a periodic inventory system, the cost of goods sold is:

a. Subtracted from the cost of goods available for sale to determine the gross profit from sales.
b. Added to cost of goods purchased to determine the cost of goods available for sale.
c. Equal to the cost of the beginning inventory plus the cost of goods purchased minus the cost of the ending inventory.
d. Equal to the cost of the ending inventory plus the cost of goods purchased minus the cost of the beginning inventory.
e. Subtracted from sales to determine net sales.

LO 4 Which one of the following procedures is applied when closing entries are used to update the merchandise inventory account under a periodic system?

a. The closing entries include a credit to Merchandise Inventory for the cost of the beginning inventory.
b. The closing entries include a debit to Merchandise Inventory for the cost of the ending inventory.
c. The closing entries include a debit to Merchandise Inventory for the cost of the beginning inventory.
d. The closing entries include a credit to Merchandise Inventory for the cost of the ending inventory.
e. Both (*a*) and (*b*) are correct.

LO 5 Which one of the following procedures is applied when adjusting entries are used to update the merchandise inventory account under a periodic system?

a. The adjusting entries include a debit to Merchandise Inventory for the cost of the beginning inventory.
b. The adjusting entries include a debit to Merchandise Inventory for the cost of the ending inventory.
c. The adjusting entries close the purchases-related accounts to the Income Summary account.
d. The adjusting entries include a credit to Merchandise Inventory for the cost of the ending inventory.
e. Both (*a*) and (*b*) are correct.

LO 6 The Lyons Company has the following current assets and liabilities: Cash, $100; Accounts receivable, $250; Inventory, $600; Prepaid expenses, $50; Accounts payable, $375; Unearned sales, $125. The correct values of the acid-test and current ratios are:

	Acid-test	Current ratio
a.	0.93	2.00
b.	2.53	1.90
c.	0.20	2.53
d.	0.70	2.00
e.	1.07	2.67

LO 7 General and administrative expenses would include all but which of the following expenses?

a. Salaries for the selling employees.
b. Salaries for the accounting employees.
c. Interest expense on long-term borrowing.
d. Depreciation on equipment used in human resources management.
e. All of the above are general and administrative expenses.

Questions for Class Discussion

1. What item on the balance sheet is unique to merchandising companies? What items on the income statement are unique to merchandising companies?
2. What is a merchandising company's gross profit?
3. Explain how a business can earn a gross profit on its sales and still have a net loss.
4. Why should the manager of a merchandising business be interested in knowing the amount of its sales returns and allowances? Is this information likely to be reported outside the company?
5. Why would a company offer a cash discount?
6. How long are the credit and discount periods under credit terms of 2/10, n/60?
7. Why are sales discounts recorded in a contra-revenue account instead of being debited directly to the Sales account?
8. How is the cost of goods sold determined with a periodic inventory accounting system?
9. What is the difference between a sales discount and a purchases discount?

10. A company purchased merchandise that cost $165,000 during the year that just ended. Determine the company's cost of goods sold in each of the following four situations: (*a*) there were no beginning or ending inventories; (*b*) there was a beginning inventory of $35,000 and no ending inventory; (*c*) there was a $30,000 beginning inventory and a $42,000 ending inventory; and (*d*) there was no beginning inventory but there was a $21,000 ending inventory.
11. In counting the ending inventory, an employee omitted the contents of one shelf that contained merchandise with a cost of $2,300. How would this omission affect the company's balance sheet and income statement?
12. Distinguish between cash discounts and trade discounts. Is the amount of a trade discount on purchased merchandise recorded in the Purchases Discounts account?
13. Why would a company's manager be concerned about the quantity of its purchases returns if its suppliers allow unlimited returns?
14. What is the meaning of the abbreviation *FOB*? What is the meaning of the term *FOB destination*?
15. What do the sender and the recipient of a debit memorandum record in their accounts?
16. What is the difference between single-step and multiple-step income statement formats?
17. Does the cost of the beginning or ending inventory appear on the unadjusted trial balance of a company that uses a periodic inventory system?
18. How does the choice between the adjusting and closing entry approaches to bookkeeping for inventories affect the reported amount of the ending inventory and net income?

19. Refer to the income statement for Ben & Jerry's Homemade, Inc., in Appendix G at the end of the book. What term is used instead of cost of goods sold? Does the company present the calculation of the cost of goods sold?

Apple Computer, Inc.

20. Use the income statement for Apple Computer, Inc., in Appendix F to calculate the gross profit for each of the three years to the nearest million dollars.

Exercises

Exercise 5–1
Calculating net sales
(LO 2)

Calculate the company's net sales in each of the following situations:

	a.	b.	c.	d.
Sales	$125,000	$505,000	$33,700	$256,700
Sales discounts	3,200	13,500	300	4,000
Sales returns and allowances	19,000	3,000	6,000	600

Exercise 5–2
Calculating cost of goods sold
(LO 3)

Determine each of the missing numbers in the following situations:

	a.	b.	c.
Purchases	$45,000	$80,000	$61,000
Purchases discounts	2,000	?	1,300
Purchases returns and allowances	1,500	3,000	2,200
Transportation-in	?	7,000	8,000
Beginning inventory	3,500	?	18,000
Cost of goods purchased	44,700	79,000	?
Ending inventory	2,200	15,000	?
Cost of goods sold	?	83,200	68,260

Exercise 5–3
Merchandising terms
(LO 2, 3)

Insert the letter for each term in the blank space beside the definition that it most closely matches:

A. Cash discount
B. Credit period
C. Discount period
D. FOB destination
E. FOB shipping point
F. Gross profit
G. Inventory
H. Purchases discount
I. Sales discount
J. Trade discount

___ 1. An agreement that ownership of goods passes at the buyer's place of business.

___ 2. The time period in which a cash discount is available.

___ 3. The difference between net sales and the cost of goods sold.

___ 4. A reduction in a receivable or payable that is granted if it is paid within the discount period.

___ 5. A cash discount taken against an amount owed to a supplier of goods.

___ 6. An agreement that ownership of goods passes at the seller's place of business.

___ 7. A reduction below a list or catalog price that is negotiated in setting the selling price of goods.

___ 8. A cash discount taken by customers against an amount owed to the seller.

___ 9. The time period that can pass before a customer's payment is due.

___10. The goods that a company owns and expects to sell to its customers.

Exercise 5–4
Recording journal entries for merchandise transactions
(LO 3)

Prepare journal entries to record the following transactions for a retail store:

March 2 Purchased merchandise from Alfa Company under the following terms: $1,800 invoice price; 2/15, n/60; FOB factory.

3 Paid $125 for shipping charges on the purchase of March 2.

4 Returned unacceptable merchandise to Alfa Company that had an invoice price of $300.

17 Sent a check to Alfa Company for the March 2 purchase, net of the discount and the returned merchandise.

18 Purchased merchandise from Bravo Company under the following terms: $2,500 invoice price; 2/10, n/30; FOB destination.

21 After brief negotiations, received a credit memorandum from Bravo Company granting a $700 allowance on the purchase of March 18.

28 Sent a check to Bravo Company paying for the March 18 purchase, net of the discount and the allowance.

Exercise 5–5
Analyzing and recording merchandise transactions and returns
(LO 2, 3)

On May 12, Wilcox Company accepted delivery of $20,000 of merchandise and received an invoice dated May 11, with terms of 3/10, n/30, FOB Garner Company's factory. When the goods were delivered, Wilcox Company paid $185 to Express Shipping Service for the delivery charges on the merchandise. The next day, Wilcox Company returned $800 of defective goods to the seller, which received them one day later. On May 21, Wilcox Company mailed a check to Garner Company for the amount owed on that date. It was received the following day.

Required

a. Present the journal entries that Wilcox Company should record for these transactions.

b. Present the journal entries that Garner Company should record for these transactions.

Exercise 5–6
Analyzing and recording merchandise transactions and discounts
(LO 2, 3)

Sandra's Store purchased merchandise from a manufacturer with an invoice price of $11,000 and credit terms of 3/10, n/60, and paid within the discount period.

Required

a. Prepare the journal entries that the purchaser should record for the purchase and payment.

b. Prepare the journal entries that the seller should record for the sale and collection.

c. Assume that the buyer borrowed enough cash to pay the balance on the last day of the discount period at an annual interest rate of 8% and paid it back on the last day of the credit period. Calculate how much the buyer saved by following this strategy. (Use a 365-day year.)

Exercise 5–7
Calculating expenses and cost of goods sold
(LO 2, 3)

The following information appeared in a company's income statement:

Sales	$300,000
Sales returns	15,000
Sales discounts	4,500
Beginning inventory	25,000
Purchases	180,000
Purchases returns and allowances	6,000
Purchases discounts	3,600
Transportation-in	11,000
Gross profit from sales	105,000
Net income	55,000

Required

Calculate the (*a*) total operating expenses, (*b*) cost of goods sold, and (*c*) ending inventory.

Exercise 5–8
Calculating expenses and income
(LO 2, 3)

Fill in the blanks in the following income statements. Identify any losses by putting the amount in parentheses.

	a.	b.	c.	d.	e.
Sales	$40,000	$85,000	$24,000	$?	$59,000
Cost of goods sold:					
Beginning inventory	$ 4,000	$ 6,200	$ 5,000	$ 3,500	$ 6,400
Purchases	24,000	?	?	16,000	14,000
Ending inventory	?	(5,400)	(6,000)	(3,300)	?
Cost of goods sold	$22,700	$31,800	$?	$?	$14,000
Gross profit	$?	$?	$ 2,500	$22,800	$?
Expenses	6,000	21,300	8,100	1,300	15,000
Net income (loss)	$?	$31,900	$(5,600)	$21,500	$?

Exercise 5–9
Multiple-step income statement and other calculations
(LO 4)

The following accounts and balances are taken from the year-end adjusted trial balance of The Vintage Shop, a single proprietorship. Use the information in these columns to complete the requirements.

	Debit	Credit
Merchandise inventory	$ 28,000	
Sales		$425,000
Sales returns and allowances	16,500	
Sales discounts	4,000	
Purchases	240,000	
Purchases returns and allowances		18,000
Purchases discounts		2,000
Transportation-in	6,000	
Selling expenses	35,000	
General and administrative expenses	95,000	

The count of the ending inventory shows that its cost is $37,000.

Required

a. Calculate the company's net sales for the year.

b. Calculate the company's cost of goods purchased for the year.

c. Calculate the company's cost of goods sold for the year.

d. Prepare a multiple-step income statement for the year that lists net sales, cost of goods sold, gross profit, the operating expenses, and net income.

Exercise 5–10
Detailed income statement
(LO 4)

Use the information provided in Exercise 5–9 to prepare a detailed income statement that shows the calculation of net sales and cost of goods sold.

Exercise 5–11
Closing entries
(LO 4)

The Vintage Shop described in Exercise 5–9 is owned and operated by Otto Vintage. The ending balance of Vintage's withdrawals account is $25,000. Prepare four closing entries for this company. Post the entries to a balance column account for Merchandise Inventory that includes the beginning balance.

Exercise 5–12
Adjusting entry approach
(LO 5)

The Vintage Shop described in Exercise 5–9 is owned and operated by Otto Vintage. The ending balance of Vintage's withdrawals account is $25,000. Assume that the company uses the adjusting entry approach to update its inventory account. Prepare adjusting and closing journal entries for this company, and post them to a balance column account for Merchandise Inventory that includes the beginning balance.

Exercise 5–13
Preparing reports from closing entries
(LO 4)

The following closing entries for Fox Fixtures Co. were made on March 31, the end of its annual accounting period:

1. Merchandise Inventory	11,000.00	
Sales	445,000.00	
Purchases Returns and Allowances	22,000.00	
Purchases Discounts	11,400.00	
Income Summary		489,400.00
To close temporary accounts with credit balances and record the ending inventory.		
2. Income Summary	453,300.00	
Merchandise Inventory		15,000.00
Sales Returns and Allowances		25,000.00
Sales Discounts		16,000.00
Purchases		286,000.00
Transportation-In		8,800.00
Selling Expenses		69,000.00
General and Administrative Expenses		33,500.00
To close temporary accounts with debit balances and to remove the beginning inventory balance.		

Required

Use the information in the closing entries to prepare:

a. A calculation of net sales.

b. A calculation of cost of goods purchased.

c. A calculation of cost of goods sold.

d. A multiple-step income statement for the year that lists net sales, cost of goods sold, gross profit, the operating expenses, and net income.

Exercise 5–14
Preparing a work sheet for a merchandising proprietorship
(LO 5)

The following unadjusted trial balance was taken from the ledger of Johnson's Newsstand at the end of its fiscal year. (To reduce your effort, the account balances are relatively small.)

JOHNSON'S NEWSSTAND
Unadjusted Trial Balance
December 31

No.	Account		
101	Cash	$ 3,700	
106	Accounts receivable	1,800	
119	Merchandise inventory	1,200	
125	Store supplies	600	
201	Accounts payable		$ 140
209	Salaries payable		
301	Tod Johnson, capital		5,785
302	Tod Johnson, withdrawals	375	
413	Sales		6,000
414	Sales returns and allowances	145	
505	Purchases	3,200	
506	Purchases discounts		125
507	Transportation-in	80	
622	Salaries expense	700	
640	Rent expense	250	
651	Store supplies expense		
	Totals	$12,050	$12,050

Required

Use the preceding information and the following additional facts to complete an eight-column work sheet for the company (do not include columns for the adjusted trial balance).

a. The ending inventory of store supplies was $450.
b. Accrued salaries at the end of the year were $60.
c. The ending merchandise inventory was $1,360.

Exercise 5–15
Acid-test ratio
(LO 6)

Calculate the current and acid-test ratios in each of the following cases:

	Case X	Case Y	Case Z
Cash	$ 800	$ 910	$1,100
Short-term investments			500
Receivables		990	800
Inventory	2,000	1,000	4,000
Prepaid expenses	1,200	600	900
Total current assets	$4,000	$3,500	$7,300
Current liabilities	$2,200	$1,100	$3,650

Problems

Problem 5–1
Journal entries for merchandising activities
(LO 2, 3)

Prepare general journal entries to record the following transactions of the Belton Company and determine the cost of goods purchased and net sales for the month. (Use a separate account for each receivable and payable; for example, record the purchase on July 1 in Accounts Payable—Jones Co.)

July 1 Purchased merchandise from the Jones Company for $3,000 under credit terms of 1/15, n/30, FOB factory.
2 Sold merchandise to Terra Co. for $800 under credit terms of 2/10, n/60, FOB shipping point.
3 Paid $100 for freight charges on the purchase of July 1.
8 Sold $1,600 of merchandise for cash.
9 Purchased merchandise from the Keene Co. for $2,300 under credit terms of 2/15, n/30, FOB destination.
12 Received a $200 credit memorandum acknowledging the return of merchandise purchased on July 9.
13 Received the balance due from the Terra Co. for the credit sale dated July 2, net of the discount.
16 Paid the balance due to the Jones Company within the discount period.
19 Sold merchandise to Urban Co. for $1,250 under credit terms of 2/10, n/60, FOB shipping point.
21 Issued a $150 credit memorandum to Urban Co. for an allowance on goods sold on July 19.
22 Received a debit memorandum from Urban Co. for an error that overstated the total invoice by $50.
24 Paid the Keene Co. the balance due after deducting the discount.
30 Received the balance due from the Urban Co. for the credit sale dated July 19, net of the discount.
31 Sold merchandise to Terra Co. for $5,000 under credit terms of 2/10, n/60, FOB shipping point.

Problem 5–2
Income statement calculations and formats
(LO 2, 3, 4)

The following amounts appeared on the Gershwin Company's adjusted trial balance as of October 31, the end of its fiscal year:

	Debit	Credit
Merchandise inventory	$ 25,000	
Other assets	140,000	
Liabilities		$ 37,000
G. Gershwin, capital		117,650
G. Gershwin, withdrawals	17,000	
Sales		210,000
Sales returns and allowances	15,000	
Sales discounts	2,250	
Purchases	90,000	
Purchases returns and allowances		4,300
Purchases discounts		1,800
Transportation-in	3,100	
Sales salaries expense	28,000	
Rent expense, selling space	10,000	
Store supplies expense	3,000	
Advertising expense	18,000	
Office salaries expense	16,000	
Rent expense, office space	2,500	
Office supplies expense	900	
Totals	$370,750	$370,750

A physical count shows that the cost of the ending inventory is $27,000.

Required

1. Calculate the company's net sales for the year.
2. Calculate the company's cost of goods purchased for the year.
3. Calculate the company's cost of goods sold for the year.
4. Present a multiple-step income statement that lists the company's net sales, cost of goods sold, and gross profit, as well the components and amounts of selling expenses and general and administrative expenses.
5. Present a condensed single-step income statement that lists these expenses: cost of goods sold, selling expenses, and general and administrative expenses.

Problem 5–3
Closing entries and interpreting information about discounts and returns
(LO 1, 2, 4)

Use the data for the Gershwin Company in Problem 5–2 to meet the following requirements:

Required

1. Prepare closing entries for the company as of October 31.
2. All of the company's purchases were made on credit and the suppliers uniformly offer a 3% discount. Does it appear that the company's cash management system is accomplishing the goal of taking all available discounts?
3. In prior years, the company has experienced a 4% return rate on its sales, which means that approximately 4% of its gross sales were for items that were eventually returned outright or that caused the company to grant allowances to customers. How does this year's record compare to prior years' results?

Problem 5–4
Adjusting entries, closing entries, and interpreting information about discounts and returns
(LO 1, 2, 4, 5)

Use the data for the Gershwin Company in Problem 5–2 to meet the following requirements:

Required

1. Prepare adjusting entries to update the Merchandise Inventory account at October 31 and then prepare closing entries for the company as of October 31.
2. All of the company's purchases were made on credit and the suppliers uniformly offer a 2.1% discount. Does it appear that the company's cash management system is accomplishing the goal of taking all available discounts?
3. In prior years, the company has experienced a 9% return rate on its sales, which means that approximately 9% of its gross sales were for items that were eventually returned outright or that caused the company to grant allowances to customers. How does this year's record compare to prior years' results?

Problem 5–5
Work sheet, income statements, and acid-test ratio
(LO 4, 5, 6)

The following unadjusted trial balance was prepared at the end of the fiscal year for Ruth's Place:

RUTH'S PLACE
Unadjusted Trial Balance
December 31

No.	Account		
101	Cash	$ 4,000	
119	Merchandise inventory	9,900	
125	Store supplies	5,000	
128	Prepaid insurance	2,000	
165	Store equipment	45,000	
166	Accumulated depreciation, store equipment		$ 6,000
201	Accounts payable		8,000
301	Ruth Helm, capital		35,200
302	Ruth Helm, withdrawals	3,500	
413	Sales		90,000
415	Sales discounts	1,000	
505	Purchases	38,000	
506	Purchases returns and allowances		800
508	Transportation-in	1,800	
612	Depreciation expense, store equipment		
622	Salaries expense	16,000	
637	Insurance expense		
640	Rent expense	5,000	
651	Store supplies expense		
655	Advertising expense	8,800	
	Totals	$140,000	$140,000

Required

1. Use the unadjusted trial balance and the following information to prepare an eight-column work sheet for the company:
   a. The ending inventory of store supplies is $650.
   b. Expired insurance for the year is $1,200.
   c. Depreciation expense for the year is $9,000.
   d. The ending merchandise inventory is $11,500.
2. Prepare a detailed multiple-step income statement for use by the store's owner.
3. Prepare a single-step income statement that would be provided to decision makers outside the company.
4. Compute the company's current and acid-test ratios as of December 31.

Problem 5–6
Analytical essay
(LO 2)

Briefly explain why a company's manager would want to obtain useful information by having the accounting system record a customer's return of unsatisfactory goods in the Sales Returns and Allowances account instead of the Sales account. In addition, explain whether the information would be useful for external decision makers.

Problem 5–7
Analytical essay
(LO 3)

A retail company's accountant recently compiled the cost of the ending merchandise inventory to use in preparing the financial statements. In developing the measure, the accountant did not know that $10,000 of incoming goods had been shipped by a supplier on December 31 under an FOB factory agreement. These goods had been recorded as a purchase, but they were not included in the physical count because they were not on hand. Explain how this overlooked fact would affect the company's financial statements and these ratios: return on equity, debt ratio, current ratio, profit margin, and acid-test ratio.

Serial Problem

Emerald Computer Services

(The first three segments of this comprehensive problem were presented in Chapters 2, 3, and 4. If those segments have not been completed, you can begin the assignment at this point. However, you need to use the facts presented on pages 96–97 in Chapter 2, pages 139–140 in Chapter 3, and page 179 in Chapter 4. Because of its length, this problem is most easily solved if you use the Working Papers that accompany this text.)

Earlier segments of this problem have described how Tracy Green created Emerald Computer Services on October 1, 19X1. The company has been successful, and its list of customers has started to grow. To accommodate the growth, the accounting system is ready to be modified to set up separate accounts for each customer. The following list of customers includes the account number used for each account and any balance as of the end of 19X1. Green decided to add a fourth digit with a decimal point to the 106 account number that had been used for the single Accounts Receivable account. This modification allows the existing chart of accounts to continue being used. The list also shows the balances that two customers owed as of December 31, 19X1:

Account	No.	Dec. 31 Balance
Alpha Printing Co.	106.1	
Bravo Productions	106.2	
Charles Company	106.3	$ 900
Delta Fixtures, Inc.	106.4	
Echo Canyon Ranch	106.5	
Fox Run Estates	106.6	$1,000
Golf Course Designs, Inc.	106.7	
Hotel Pollo del Mar	106.8	
Indiana Manuf. Co.	106.9	

In response to frequent requests from customers, Green has decided to begin selling computer software. The company will extend credit terms of 1/10, n/30 to customers who purchase merchandise. No cash discount will be available on consulting fees. The following additional accounts were added to the general ledger to allow the system to account for the company's new merchandising activities:

Account	No.
Merchandise Inventory	119
Sales	413
Sales Returns and Allowances	414
Sales Discounts	415
Purchases	505
Purchases Returns and Allowances	506
Purchases Discounts	507
Transportation-In	508

Because the accounting system does not use reversing entries, all revenue and expense accounts have zero balances as of January 1, 19X2.

Required

1. Prepare journal entries to record each of the following transactions for Emerald Computer Services.
2. Post the journal entries to the accounts in the company's general ledger. (Use asset, liability, and capital accounts that start with the balance as of December 31, 19X1.)
3. Prepare a six-column table similar to Illustration 3–3 that presents the unadjusted trial balance, the March 31 adjustments, and the adjusted trial balance.

   Do not prepare closing entries and do not journalize the adjusting entries or post them to the ledger.
4. Prepare an interim income statement for the three months ended March 31, 19X2. Use a detailed multiple-step format that shows calculations of net sales, total revenues, cost of goods sold, total expenses, and net income.
5. Prepare an interim statement of changes in owner's equity for the three months ended March 31, 19X2.
6. Prepare an interim balance sheet as of March 31, 19X2.

Transactions:

Jan. 4 Paid Fran Sims for five days, including one day in addition to the four unpaid days from the prior year.

6 Tracy Green invested an additional $12,000 cash in the business.

7 Purchased $2,800 of merchandise from SoftHead Co. on terms of 1/10, n/30, FOB shipping point.

Jan.	8	Received $1,000 from Fox Run Estates as final payment on its account.
	10	Completed 5-day project for Alpha Printing Co. and billed them $3,000, which is the total price of $4,000 less the advance payment of $1,000.
	13	Sold merchandise with a retail value of $2,100 to Delta Fixtures, Inc., with terms of 1/10, n/30, FOB shipping point.
	14	Paid $350 for freight charges on the merchandise purchased on Jan. 7.
	16	Received $1,500 cash from Golf Course Designs, Inc., for computer services.
	17	Paid SoftHead Co. for the purchase on Jan. 7, net of the discount.
	21	Delta Fixtures, Inc., returned $200 of defective merchandise from its purchase on Jan. 13.
	22	Received the balance due from Delta Fixtures, Inc., net of the discount and the credit for the returned merchandise.
	23	Returned defective merchandise to SoftHead Co. and accepted credit against future purchases. Its cost, net of the discount, was $198.
	26	Sold $2,900 of merchandise on credit to Hotel Pollo del Mar.
	28	Purchased $4,000 of merchandise from SoftHead Co. on terms of 1/10, n/30, FOB destination.
	29	Received a $198 credit memo from SoftHead Co. concerning the merchandise returned on Jan. 23.
	31	Paid Fran Sims for 10 days' work.
Feb.	1	Paid $2,250 to the Town Hall Mall for another three months' rent.
	3	Paid SoftHead Co. for the balance due, net of the cash discount, less the $198 amount in the credit memo.
	4	Paid $400 to the local newspaper for advertising.
	11	Received the balance due from Alpha Printing Co. for fees billed on Jan. 10.
	16	Paid $2,000 to Tracy Green as a withdrawal.
	23	Sold $1,600 of merchandise on credit to Golf Course Designs, Inc.
	26	Paid Fran Sims for eight days' work.
	27	Reimbursed Tracy Green's business automobile mileage for 600 miles at $0.25 per mile.
Mar.	8	Purchased $1,200 of computer supplies from AAA Supply Co. on credit.
	9	Received the balance due from Golf Course Designs, Inc., for merchandise sold on Feb. 23.
	15	Repaired the company's computer at the cost of $430.
	16	Received $2,130 cash from Indiana Manuf. Co. for computing services.
	19	Paid the full amount due to AAA Supply Co. Includes amounts created on Dec. 13 and Mar. 8.
	24	Billed Bravo Productions for $2,950 of computing services.
	25	Sold $900 of merchandise on credit to Echo Canyon Ranch.
	30	Sold $1,110 of merchandise on credit to Charles Company.
	31	Reimbursed Tracy Green's business automobile mileage for 400 miles at $0.25 per mile.

Information for the March 31 adjustments and financial statements:

a. The March 31 inventory of computing supplies is $670.

b. Three more months have passed since the company purchased the annual insurance policy at the cost of $1,440.

c. Fran Sims has not been paid for seven days of work.

d. Three months have passed since any prepaid rent cost has been transferred to expense.

e. Depreciation on the computer for January through March is $750.

f. Depreciation on the office equipment for January through March is $500.

g. The March 31 inventory of merchandise is $2,182.

Provocative Problems

Provocative Problem 5–1
WonderFull Store
(LO 2, 3, 4)

Wanda Wonder, the owner of the WonderFull Store, has operated the company for several years, but has never used an accrual accounting system. To have more useful information, Wonder has engaged you to help prepare an income statement for 19X2. Based on data that you have gathered from the cash-basis accounting system and other documents, you have been able to prepare the following balance sheets as of the beginning and end of 19X2:

	December 31	
	19X1	19X2
Cash	$ 5,400	$ 42,250
Accounts receivable	18,500	22,600
Merchandise inventory	39,700	34,000
Equipment (net of depreciation)	87,000	56,000
Total assets	$150,600	$154,850
Accounts payable	$ 28,300	$ 36,250
Wages payable	2,200	1,700
Wanda Wonder, capital	120,100	116,900
Total liabilities and owner's equity	$150,600	$154,850

The store's cash records also provided the following facts for 19X2:

Amount collected on accounts receivable	$339,900
Payments for:	
Accounts payable	198,050
Employees' wages	52,000
All other operating expenses	29,000
Withdrawals by the owner	24,000

You have determined that all merchandise purchases and sales were made on credit, and that no equipment was either purchased or sold during the year.

Use the preceding information to calculate the amounts of the company's sales, cost of goods purchased, cost of goods sold, depreciation expense, and wages expense for 19X2. Then, prepare a multiple-step income statement that shows the company's gross profit.

Provocative Problem 5–2
Using the information
(LO 6)

Calculate the current and acid-test ratios for each of these three cases, and comment on your findings.

	Case A	Case B	Case C
Current assets:			
Cash	$ 500	$3,100	$ 600
Short-term investments	1,500	2,600	400
Accounts receivable	3,000	2,800	1,100
Interest receivable	200	900	–0–
Merchandise inventory	4,000	1,000	7,000
Office supplies	300	500	1,000
Prepaid insurance	1,100	600	900
Prepaid rent	900	–0–	500
Current liabilities:			
Accounts payable	$1,300	$2,400	$4,000
Interest payable	300	700	100
Salaries payable	600	800	200
Notes payable	2,800	1,100	700

Provocative Problem 5–3
Apple Computer, Inc.
(LO 2, 6)

Apple Computer, Inc.

Use the financial statements for Apple Computer, Inc., in Appendix F at the end of the book to find the answers to these questions:

1. Although Apple manufactures most of the goods that it sells, assume that the amounts reported for inventories and cost of sales were all purchased ready for resale and then calculate the total cost of goods purchased during fiscal year 1992.

2. Calculate the current and acid-test ratios as of the end of the 1992 and 1991 fiscal years. (Assume that the Other current assets are not quick assets.) Comment on what you find.

Provocative Problem 5–4
As a Matter of Ethics: Essay

Describe the problem faced by Renee Fleck in the As a Matter of Ethics case on page 194 and evaluate her alternative courses of action.

Answers to Objective Review Questions

LO 1 (*b*)
LO 2 (*e*)
LO 3 (*c*)
LO 4 (*e*)
LO 5 (*b*)
LO 6 (*d*)
LO 7 (*a*)

CHAPTER

6

Accounting for Cash

Cash is an asset that every business owns and uses. Cash includes such specific items as currency, coins, checking accounts (also called *demand deposits*), and perhaps savings accounts (also called *time deposits*). Most organizations own at least some assets known as *cash equivalents,* which are very similar to cash. In studying this chapter, you will learn the principles of internal control that guide businesses in managing and accounting for cash. The chapter shows how to establish and use a petty cash fund and how to reconcile a checking account. Also, you will learn a method of accounting for purchases that helps management determine whether cash discounts on purchases are being lost and, if so, how much has been lost.

Learning Objectives

After studying Chapter 6, you should be able to:

1. Explain the concept of liquidity and the difference between cash and cash equivalents, and calculate days' sales uncollected.
2. Explain why internal control procedures are needed in a large organization and state the broad principles of internal control.
3. Describe internal control procedures used to protect cash received from cash sales, cash received through the mail, and cash disbursements.
4. Explain the operation of a petty cash fund and be able to prepare journal entries to record petty cash fund transactions.
5. Explain why the bank balance and the book balance of cash should be reconciled and be able to prepare a reconciliation.
6. Tell how recording invoices at net amounts helps gain control over cash discounts taken and be able to account for invoices recorded at net amounts.
7. Define or explain the words and phrases listed in the chapter glossary.

Cash, Cash Equivalents, and the Concept of Liquidity

In previous chapters, you learned that a company can own many different kinds of assets, such as accounts receivable, merchandise inventory, equipment, buildings, and land. These assets all have value, but most of them are not easily used as a means of payment when buying other assets, acquiring services, or paying off liabilities. Usually cash must be used as the method of payment. Another way to state this is to say that cash is more *liquid* than these other assets.

In more general terms, the **liquidity** of an asset refers to how easily the asset can be converted into other types of assets or be used to buy services or satisfy obligations. All assets can be evaluated in terms of their relative liquidity. Assets such as cash are said to be **liquid assets** because they can be easily converted into other types of assets or used to buy services or pay liabilities.

LO 1 Explain the concept of liquidity and the difference between cash and cash equivalents, and calculate days' sales uncollected.

As you know, a company needs more than valuable assets to stay in business. That is, the company must own some liquid assets so that bills are paid on time and purchases can be made for cash when necessary.

For financial accounting, the asset *cash* includes not only currency and coins but also amounts on deposit in bank accounts, including checking accounts (sometimes called demand deposits) and some savings accounts (also called time deposits). Cash also includes items that are acceptable for deposit in those accounts, especially customers' checks made payable to the company.

To increase their return, many companies invest their idle cash balances in assets called **cash equivalents.** These assets are short-term, highly liquid investments that satisfy two criteria:

1. The investment must be readily convertible to a known amount of cash.
2. The investment must be sufficiently close to its maturity date so that its market value is relatively insensitive to interest rate changes.

In general, only investments purchased within three months of their maturity dates satisfy these criteria.[1] Examples of cash equivalents include short-term investments in U.S. Treasury bills, commercial paper (short-term corporate notes payable), and money market funds.

Because cash equivalents are so similar to cash, most companies combine them with cash on the balance sheet. Others show them separately. For example, IBM Corporation shows these items on its published balance sheet:

(in millions)	December 31	
	1992	**1991**
Cash	$1,090	$1,171
Cash equivalents	3,356	2,774

Note that IBM had more than twice as much invested in cash equivalents as it did in cash.

As you would expect, cash is an important asset for every business. Because cash is so important, companies need to be careful about keeping track of it. They also need to carefully control access to cash by employees and others who might want to take it for their own use. A good accounting system supports both goals. It can keep track of how much cash is on hand, and it helps control who has access to the cash. Because of the special importance of cash, this chapter describes the practices companies follow to account for and protect cash.

Internal Control

LO 2 Explain why internal control procedures are needed in a large organization and state the broad principles of internal control.

In a small business, the manager often controls the entire operation through personal supervision and direct participation in all its activities. For example, he or she commonly buys all the assets and services used in the business. The manager also hires and supervises all employees, negotiates all contracts, and signs all checks. As a result, the manager knows from personal contact and observation whether the business actually received the assets and services for

[1] FASB, *Accounting Standards—Current Text* (Norwalk, CT, 1993), sec. C25.106. First published in *Statement of Financial Accounting Standards No. 95,* par. 8.

which the checks were written. However, as a business grows, it becomes increasingly difficult to maintain this close personal contact. At some point the manager must delegate responsibilities and rely on formal procedures rather than personal contact in controlling the operations of the business.

The procedures a company uses to control its operations make up its **internal control system.** A properly designed internal control system encourages adherence to prescribed managerial policies. In doing so, it promotes efficient operations and protects the assets from waste, fraud, and theft. The system also helps ensure that accurate and reliable accounting data are produced.

Specific internal control procedures vary from company to company and depend on such factors as the nature of the business and its size. However, the same broad principles of internal control apply to all companies. These broad principles are

1. Clearly establish responsibilities.
2. Maintain adequate records.
3. Insure assets and bond employees.
4. Separate record-keeping and custody over assets.
5. Divide responsibility for related transactions.
6. Use mechanical devices whenever feasible.
7. Perform regular and independent reviews.

We discuss these seven principles in the following paragraphs. Throughout, we describe how various internal control procedures prevent fraud and theft. Remember, however, that these procedures are needed to ensure that the accounting records are complete and accurate.

Clearly Establish Responsibilities

To have good internal control, responsibility for each task must be clearly established and assigned to one person. When responsibility is not clearly spelled out, it is difficult to determine who is at fault when something goes wrong. For example, if two sales clerks share access to the same cash register and there is a shortage, it may not be possible to tell which clerk is at fault. Neither can prove that he or she did not cause the shortage. To prevent this problem, one clerk should be given responsibility for making all change. Alternatively, the business can use a register with separate cash drawers for each operator.

Maintain Adequate Records

A good record-keeping system helps protect assets and ensures that employees follow prescribed procedures. Reliable records are also a source of information that management uses to monitor the operations of the business. For example, if detailed records of manufacturing equipment and tools are maintained, items are unlikely to be lost or otherwise disappear without any discrepancy being noticed. As another example, expenses and other expenditures are less likely to be debited to the wrong accounts if a comprehensive chart of accounts is established and followed carefully. If the chart is not in place or is not used correctly, management may never discover that some expenses are excessive.

Numerous preprinted forms and internal business papers should be designed and properly used to maintain good internal control. For example, if sales slips are properly designed, sales personnel can record the needed information efficiently without errors or delays to customers. And, if all sales slips are prenumbered and controlled, each salesperson can be held responsible for the sales slips issued to him or her. As a result, a salesperson is not able to pocket cash by making a sale and destroying the sales slip. Computerized point-of-sale systems can achieve the same control results.

Insure Assets and Bond Key Employees

Assets should be covered by adequate casualty insurance, and employees who handle cash and negotiable assets should be bonded. An employee is said to be *bonded* when the company purchases an insurance policy, or bond, against losses from theft by that employee. Bonding clearly reduces the loss suffered by a theft. It also tends to discourage theft because bonded employees know that an impersonal bonding company must be dealt with when a theft is discovered.

Separate Record-Keeping and Custody over Assets

A fundamental principle of internal control is that the person who has access to or is otherwise responsible for an asset should not maintain the accounting record for that asset. When this principle is followed, the custodian of an asset, knowing that a record of the asset is being kept by another person, is not as likely to misplace, steal, or waste the asset. And, the record-keeper, who does not have access to the asset, has no reason to falsify the record. As a result, two people would have to agree to commit a fraud (called *collusion*) if the asset were to be stolen and the theft concealed in the records. Because collusion is necessary to commit the fraud, it is less likely to happen.

Divide Responsibility for Related Transactions

Responsibility for a transaction or a series of related transactions should be divided between individuals or departments so that the work of one acts as a check on the other. However, this principle does not call for duplication of work. Each employee or department should perform an unduplicated portion.

For example, responsibility for placing orders, receiving the merchandise, and paying the vendors should not be given to one individual or department. Doing so creates a situation in which mistakes and perhaps fraud are more likely to occur. Having a different person check incoming goods for quality and quantity may encourage more care and attention to detail than having it done by the person who placed the order. And, designating a third person to approve the payment of the invoice offers additional protection against error and fraud. Finally, giving a fourth person the authority to actually write checks adds another measure of protection.

Use Mechanical Devices Whenever Feasible

Cash registers, check protectors, time clocks, and mechanical counters are examples of control devices that should be used whenever feasible. A cash register with a locked-in tape makes a record of each cash sale. A check protector perforates the amount of a check into its face, and makes it difficult to change the amount. A time clock registers the exact time an employee arrives on the job and the exact time the employee departs. Using mechanical change and currency counters is faster and more accurate than counting by hand and reduces the possibility of loss.

Perform Regular and Independent Reviews

Even a well-designed internal control system has a tendency to deteriorate as time passes. Changes in personnel and computer equipment present opportunities for shortcuts and other omissions. The stress of time pressures tends to bring about the same results. Thus, regular reviews of internal control systems are needed to be sure that the standard procedures are being followed.

Where possible, these reviews should be performed by internal auditors who are not directly involved in operations. From their independent perspective, internal auditors can evaluate the overall efficiency of operations as well as the effectiveness of the internal control system.

Many companies also have audits by independent auditors who are CPAs. After testing the company's financial records, the CPAs give an opinion as to whether the company's financial statements are presented fairly in accordance with generally accepted accounting principles. However, before CPAs decide on how much testing they must do, they evaluate the effectiveness of the internal control system. When making their evaluation, they can find areas for improvement and offer suggestions.

Computers and Internal Control

LO 2 Explain why internal control procedures are needed in a large organization and state the broad principles of internal control.

The broad principles of internal control should be followed for both manual and computerized accounting systems. However, computers have several important effects on internal control. Perhaps the most obvious is that computers provide rapid access to large quantities of information. As a result, management's ability to monitor and control business operations can be greatly improved.

Computers Reduce Processing Errors

Computers reduce the number of errors in processing information. Once the data are entered correctly, the possibility of mechanical and mathematical errors is largely eliminated. On the other hand, data entry errors may occur because the process of entering data may be more complex in a computerized system. Also, the lack of human involvement in later processing may cause data entry errors to go undiscovered.

Computers Allow More Extensive Testing of Records

The regular review and audit of computerized records can include more extensive testing because information can be accessed so rapidly. To reduce costs when manual methods are used, managers may select only small samples of data to test. But, when computers are used, large samples or even complete data files can be reviewed and analyzed.

Computerized Systems May Limit Hard Evidence of Processing Steps

Because many data processing steps are performed by the computer, fewer items of documentary evidence may be available for review. However, computer systems can actually create additional evidence by recording more information about who made entries and even when they were made. And, the computer can be programmed to require the use of passwords before making entries so that access to the system is limited. Therefore, internal control may depend more on reviews of the design and operation of the computerized processing system and less on reviews of the documents left behind by the system.

Separation of Duties Must Be Maintained

Because computerized systems are so efficient, companies often need fewer employees. This savings carries the risk that the separation of critical responsibilities may not be maintained. In addition, companies that use computers need employees with special skills to program and operate them. The duties of such employees must be controlled to minimize undetected errors and the risk of fraud. For example, better control is maintained if the person who designs and programs the system does not serve as the operator. Also, control over programs and files related to cash receipts and disbursements should be separated. To prevent fraud, check-writing activities should not be controlled by the computer operator. However, achieving a suitable separation of duties can be especially difficult in small companies that have only a few employees.

Internal Control for Cash

LO 3 Describe internal control procedures used to protect cash received from cash sales, cash received through the mail, and cash disbursements.

Now that we have covered the principles of good internal control in general, it is helpful to see how they are applied to cash, the most liquid of all assets. A good system of internal control for cash should provide adequate procedures for protecting both cash receipts and cash disbursements. In designing the procedures, three basic guidelines should always be observed:

1. Duties should be separated so that people responsible for actually handling cash are not responsible for keeping the cash records.
2. All cash receipts should be deposited in the bank, intact, each day.
3. All cash payments should be made by check.

The reason for the first principle is that a division of duties helps avoid errors. It also requires two or more people to collude if cash is to be embezzled (stolen) and the theft concealed in the accounting records. One reason for the second guideline is that the daily deposit of all receipts produces a timely independent test of the accuracy of the count of the cash received and the deposit. It also helps prevent loss or theft and keeps an employee from personally using the money for a few days before depositing it.

Finally, if all payments are made by check, the bank records provide an independent description of cash disbursements. This arrangement also tends to prevent thefts of cash. (One exception to this principle allows small disbursements of currency and coins to be made from a petty cash fund. Petty cash funds are discussed later in this chapter.) Note especially that the daily intact depositing of receipts and making disbursements by check allow you to use the bank records as a separate and external record of essentially all cash transactions. Later in the chapter, you learn how the bank records are used to confirm the accuracy of your own records.

The exact procedures used to achieve control over cash vary from company to company. They depend on such factors as company size, number of employees, the volume of cash transactions, and the sources of cash. Therefore, the procedures described in the following paragraphs illustrate many but not all situations.

Cash from Cash Sales

Cash sales should be recorded on a cash register at the time of each sale. To help ensure that correct amounts are entered, each register should be placed so that customers can read the amounts displayed. Also, clerks should be required to ring up each sale before wrapping the merchandise and should give the customer a receipt. Finally, each cash register should be designed to provide a permanent, locked-in record of each transaction. In some systems, the register is directly connected to a computer. The computer is programmed to accept cash register transactions and enter them in the accounting records. In other cases, the register simply prints a record of each transaction on a paper tape locked inside the register.

We stated earlier that custody over cash should be separated from recordkeeping for cash. For cash sales, this separation begins with the cash register. The salesclerk who has access to the cash in the register should not have access to its locked-in record. At the end of each day, the salesclerk should count the cash in the register, record the result, and turn over the cash and this record of the count to an employee in the cashier's office. The employee in the cashier's office, like the salesclerk, has access to the cash and should not have access to the computerized accounting records (or the register tape). A third employee, preferably from the accounting department, examines the computerized record of register transactions (or the register tape) and compares its total with the cash receipts reported by the cashier's office. The computer record (or register tape) becomes the basis for the journal entry to record cash sales. Note that the accounting department employee has access to the records for cash but does not have access to the actual cash. The salesclerk and the employee from the cashier's office have access to the cash but not to the accounting records. Thus, their accuracy is automatically checked, and none of them can make a mistake or divert any cash without the difference being revealed.

Cash Received through the Mail

Control of cash that comes in through the mail begins with the person who opens the mail. Preferably, two people should be present when the mail is opened. One should make a list (in triplicate) of the money received. The list should record each sender's name, the amount, and the purpose for which the money was sent. One copy is sent to the cashier with the money. A second copy goes to the accounting department. A third copy is kept by the clerk who opened the mail. The cashier deposits the money in the bank, and the bookkeeper records the amounts received in the accounting records. Then, when the bank balance is reconciled by a fourth person (this process is discussed later in the chapter), errors or fraud by the clerk, the cashier, or the bookkeeper are detected. They are detected because the bank's record of the amount of cash deposited and the records of three people must agree. Note how this arrangement makes errors and fraud nearly impossible, unless the employees enter into collusion. If the clerk does not report all receipts accurately, the customers will question their account balances. If the cashier does not deposit all receipts intact, the bank balance does not agree with the bookkeeper's cash balance. The bookkeeper and the fourth person who reconciles the bank balance do not have access to cash and, therefore, have no opportunity to divert any to themselves. Thus, undetected errors and fraud are made highly unlikely.

Cash Disbursements

The previous discussions clearly show the importance of gaining control over cash from sales and cash received through the mail. Most large embezzlements, however, are actually accomplished through payments of fictitious invoices. Therefore, controlling cash disbursements is perhaps even more critical than controlling cash receipts.

As described earlier, the key to controlling cash disbursements is to require all expenditures to be made by check, except very small payments from petty cash. And, if authority to sign checks is assigned to some person other than the business owner, that person should not have access to the accounting records. This separation of duties helps prevent an employee from concealing fraudulent disbursements in the accounting records.

In a small business, the manager usually signs checks and normally knows from personal contact that the items being paid for were actually received. However, this arrangement is impossible in a larger business. Instead, internal control procedures must be substituted for personal contact. The procedures are designed to assure the check signer that the obligations to be paid were properly incurred and should be paid. Often these controls are achieved through a voucher system.

The Voucher System and Control

LO 3 Describe internal control procedures used to protect cash received from cash sales, cash received through the mail, and cash disbursements.

A **voucher system** is a set of procedures designed to control the incurrence of obligations and disbursements of cash. This kind of system:

1. Establishes procedures for incurring obligations that result in cash disbursements, such as permitting only authorized individuals to make purchase commitments.
2. Provides established procedures for verifying, approving, and recording these obligations.
3. Permits checks to be issued only in payment of properly verified, approved, and recorded obligations.
4. Requires that every obligation be recorded at the time it is incurred and that every purchase be treated as an independent transaction, complete in itself.

A good voucher system produces these results for every transaction, even if several purchases are made from the same company during a month or other billing period.

When a voucher system is used, control over cash disbursements begins as soon as the company incurs an obligation that will result in cash being paid out. A key factor in making the system work is that only specified departments and individuals are authorized to incur such obligations. Managers should also limit the kind of obligations that each department or individual can incur. For example, in a large retail store, only a specially created purchasing department should be authorized to incur obligations through merchandise purchases. In addition, the procedures for purchasing, receiving, and paying for merchandise should be divided among several departments. These departments include the one that originally requested the purchase, the purchasing department, the receiving department, and the accounting department. To coordinate and control the responsibilities of these departments, several different business papers are used. Illustration 6–1 shows how these papers are accumulated in a **voucher.** A voucher is an internal business paper used to accumulate other papers and information needed to control the disbursement of cash and to ensure that the transaction is properly recorded. The following explanation of each paper going into the voucher shows how companies use this system to gain control over cash disbursements for merchandise purchases.

Purchase Requisition

In a large retail store, department managers generally are not allowed to place orders directly with suppliers. If each manager could deal directly with suppliers, the amount of merchandise purchased and the resulting liabilities would not be well controlled. Therefore, to gain control over purchases and the resulting liabilities, department managers are usually required to place all orders through the purchasing department. When merchandise is needed, the department managers inform the purchasing department of their needs by preparing and signing a **purchase requisition.** On the requisition, the manager lists the merchandise needed by the department and requests that it be purchased. Two copies of the purchase requisition are sent to the purchasing department. The manager of the requisitioning department (identified in Illustration 6–1 as Department A) keeps a third copy as a back up. The purchasing department sends one copy to the accounting department. When it is received, the accounting department creates a new voucher.

ILLUSTRATION 6–1 *The Accumulation of Documents in the Voucher*

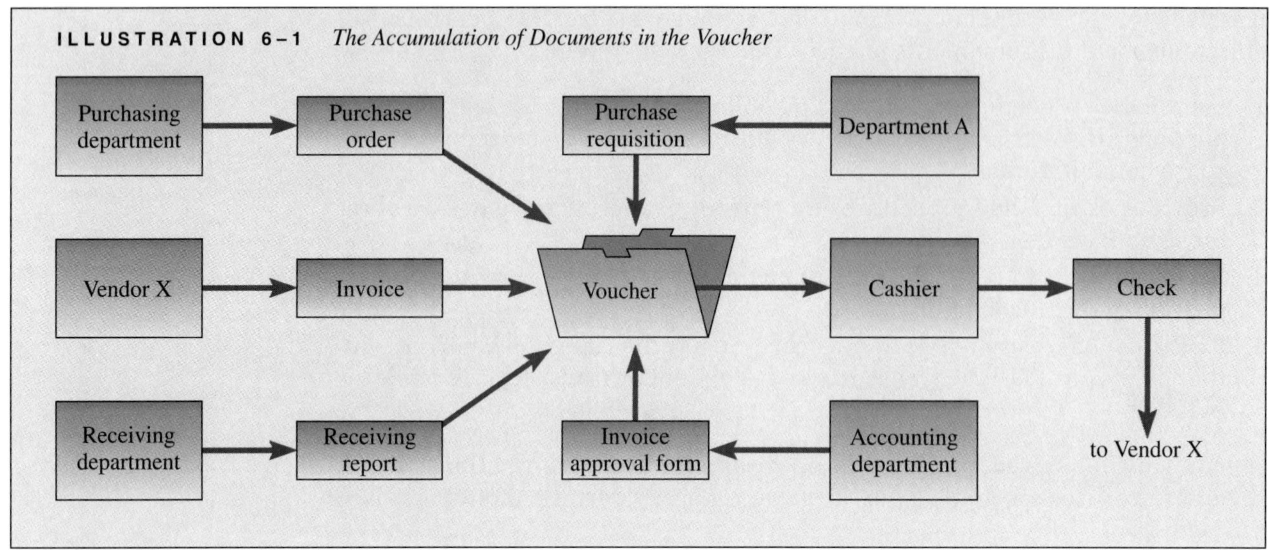

Purchase Order

A **purchase order** is a business paper used by the purchasing department to place an order with the seller or **vendor,** which usually is a manufacturer or wholesaler. The purchase order authorizes the vendor to ship the ordered merchandise at the stated price and terms.

When a purchase requisition is received by the purchasing department, it prepares at least four copies of a purchase order. The copies are distributed as follows:

Copy 1 is sent to the vendor as a request to purchase and as authority to ship the merchandise.

Copy 2, with a copy of the purchase requisition attached, is sent to the accounting department, where it is used in approving the payment of the invoice for the purchase; this copy is shown in Illustration 6–1.

Copy 3 is sent to the department originally issuing the requisition to inform its manager that the action has been taken.

Copy 4 is retained on file by the purchasing department.

Invoice

An **invoice** is an itemized statement prepared by the vendor that lists the customer's name, the items sold, the sales prices, and the terms of sale. In effect, the invoice is the bill sent to the buyer by the seller. (From the vendor's point of view, it is a *sales invoice.*) The vendor sends the invoice to the buyer or **vendee,** who treats it as a *purchase invoice.* On receiving a purchase order, the vendor ships the ordered merchandise to the buyer and mails a copy of the invoice that covers the shipment. The goods are delivered to the buyer's receiving department and the invoice is sent directly to the buyer's accounting department, where it is placed in the voucher. Illustration 6–1 also presents this document flow.

Receiving Report

Most large companies maintain a special department that receives all merchandise or other purchased assets. When each shipment arrives, this receiving department counts the goods and checks them for damage and agreement with the purchase order. Then, it prepares four or more copies of a **receiving report.** This report is a form used within the business to notify the appropriate persons that ordered goods were received and to describe the quantities and condition of the goods. As shown in Illustration 6–1, one copy is sent to the accounting department and placed in the voucher. Copies are also sent to the original requisitioning department and the purchasing department to notify them that the goods have arrived. The receiving department retains a copy in its files.

Invoice Approval Form

After the receiving report arrives, the accounting department should have copies of these papers on file in the voucher:

1. The *purchase requisition* listing the items to be ordered.
2. The *purchase order* listing the merchandise that was actually ordered.
3. The *invoice* showing the quantity, description, price, and total cost of the goods shipped by the seller.
4. The *receiving report* listing the quantity and condition of the items actually received by the buyer.

With the information on these papers, the accounting department is in a position to make an entry recording the purchase and to approve its eventual payment before the end of the discount period. In approving the invoice for payment, the accounting department checks and compares the information on all the papers. To facilitate the checking procedure and to ensure that no step is omitted, the department commonly uses an **invoice approval form.** (See Illustration 6–2.) This form is a document on which the accounting department notes that it has performed each step in the process of checking an invoice and approving it for recording and payment. An invoice approval form may be a separate business paper that is filed in the voucher or it may be preprinted on the voucher. It may also be stamped on the invoice. For clarity, the flowchart in Illustration 6–1 shows the form as a separate document.

As each of the steps in the checking procedure is finished, the clerk initials the invoice approval form and records the current date. Initials in each space on the form indicate that the following administrative actions have been taken:

1. **Requisition check** . . . . The items on the invoice were actually requisitioned, as shown on the copy of the purchase requisition.
2. **Purchase order check** . . . . . The items on the invoice were actually ordered, as shown on the copy of the purchase order.
3. **Receiving report check** . . . . The items on the invoice were actually received, as shown on the copy of the receiving report.
4. **Invoice check:**
   Price approval . . . . The invoice prices are stated as agreed with the vendor.
   Calculations . . . . The invoice has no mathematical errors.
   Terms . . . . The terms are stated as agreed with the vendor.

The Voucher

After an invoice is checked and approved, the voucher is complete. At this point, the voucher is a record that summarizes the transaction. The voucher shows that the transaction has been certified as correct and authorizes its recording as an obligation of the buyer. The voucher also contains approval for paying the obligation on the appropriate date. Of course, the actual physi-

ILLUSTRATION 6-2 *An Invoice Approval Form*

	By	Date
Purchase order number	______	______
Requisition check	______	______
Purchase order check	______	______
Receiving report check	______	______
Invoice check:		
Price approval	______	______
Calculations	______	______
Terms	______	______
Approved for payment	______	______

cal form used for vouchers varies substantially from company to company. In general, they are designed so that the invoice and other documents from which they are prepared are placed inside the voucher, which is often a folder. The information printed on the inside of a typical voucher is shown in Illustration 6–3, and the information on the outside is shown in Illustration 6–4.

The preparation of a voucher requires a clerk to enter the specified information in the proper blanks. The information is taken from the invoice and all the supporting documents filed inside the voucher. Once the steps are completed, the voucher is sent to the appropriate authorized individual (sometimes called the *auditor*), who completes one final review of the information, approves the accounts and amounts to be debited (called the *accounting distribution*), and approves the voucher for recording.

After a voucher is approved and recorded, it is filed until its due date, when it is sent to the cashier's office for payment. Here, the person responsible for issuing checks relies on the approved voucher and its signed supporting documents as proof that the obligation was properly incurred and should be paid. As described earlier, the purchase requisition and purchase order attached to the voucher confirm that the purchase was authorized. The receiving report shows that the items were received, and the invoice approval form verifies that the invoice was checked for errors. As a result, there is little chance for error. There is even less chance for fraud without collusion, unless all the documents and signatures are forged.

The Voucher System and Expenses

LO 3 Describe internal control procedures used to protect cash received from cash sales, cash received through the mail, and cash disbursements.

Under a voucher system, obligations should be approved for payment and recorded as liabilities as soon as possible after they are incurred. As shown in the example, this practice should be followed for all purchases. It should also be followed for all expenses. For example, when a company receives a monthly telephone bill, the charges (especially long-distance calls) should be examined for accuracy. A voucher should be prepared, and the telephone bill should be filed inside the voucher. The voucher is then recorded with a journal entry. If the amount is due at once, a check should be issued. Otherwise, the voucher should be filed for payment on the due date.

The requirement that vouchers be prepared for expenses as they are incurred helps ensure that every expense payment is approved only when adequate information is available. However, invoices or bills for such things as equipment repairs are sometimes not received until weeks after the work is done. If no records of the repairs exist, it may be difficult to determine whether the invoice or bill correctly states the amount owed. Also, if no records exist, it may be possible for a dishonest employee to arrange with an outsider for more than one payment of an obligation, or for payment of exces-

ILLUSTRATION 6–3 *Inside of a Voucher*

VALLEY SUPPLY COMPANY Voucher No. 93–767
Eugene, Oregon

Date Oct. 1, 19X1
Pay to A. B. Seay Wholesale Company
City Salem State Oregon

For the following: (attach all invoices and supporting papers)

Date of Invoice	Terms	Invoice Number and Other Details	Amount
Sept. 30, 19X1	2/10, n/60	Invoice No. C-11756	800.00
		Less discount	16.00
		Net amount payable	784.00

Payment approved
N. O. Neal
Auditor

ILLUSTRATION 6–4 *Outside of a Voucher*

Voucher No. 93–767

ACCOUNTING DISTRIBUTION

Account Debited	Amount
Purchases	800.00
Transportation-In	
Store Supplies	
Office Supplies	
Sales Salaries	
Other	
Total Vouch. Pay. Cr.	800.00

Due date October 10, 19X1

Pay to A. B. Seay Wholesale Company
City Salem
State Oregon

Summary of charges:
Total charges 800.00
Discount 16.00
Net payment 784.00

Record of payment:
Paid
Check No.

sive amounts, or for payment for goods and services not received. A properly functioning voucher system helps prevent all of these undesirable results.

The Petty Cash Fund

A basic principle for controlling cash disbursements requires that all disbursements be made by check. However, an exception to this rule is made for *petty cash disbursements*. Every business must make many small payments for items such as postage, express charges, repairs, and small items of supplies. If firms made such payments by check, they would end up writing many checks

ILLUSTRATION 6–5 *A Petty Cash Receipt*

No. - 1 - $ 10.00

RECEIVED OF PETTY CASH

Date Nov. 2 19 X1

For Washing windows

Charge to Miscellaneous Expenses

Approved by CAB

Received by Bob Tone

TOPS-Form 3008

LO 4 Explain the operation of a petty cash fund and be able to prepare journal entries to record petty cash fund transactions.

for small amounts. This arrangement would be both time consuming and expensive. Therefore, to avoid writing checks for small amounts, a business establishes a petty cash fund and uses the money in this fund to make payments such as those listed earlier.

Establishing a petty cash fund requires estimating the total amount of small payments likely to be made during a short period, such as a month. Then, a check is drawn by the company cashier's office for an amount slightly in excess of this estimate. This check is recorded with a debit to the Petty Cash account (an asset) and a credit to Cash. The check is cashed, and the currency is turned over to a member of the office staff designated as the *petty cashier.* This person is responsible for the safekeeping of the cash, for making payments from this fund, and for keeping accurate records.

The petty cashier should keep the petty cash in a locked box in a safe place. As each disbursement is made, the person receiving payment signs a *petty cash receipt* (see Illustration 6–5). The receipt is then placed in the petty cashbox with the remaining money. Under this system, the cashbox should always contain petty cash receipts and cash equal to the amount of the fund. The total should remain constant. For example, a $100 petty cash fund could have (*a*) $100 in cash, (*b*) $80 in cash and $20 in receipts, or (*c*) $10 in cash and $90 in receipts. Notice that each disbursement reduces the cash and increases the sum of the receipts in the petty cashbox. When the cash is nearly gone, the fund should be reimbursed.

To reimburse the fund, the petty cashier presents the receipts to the company cashier. The company cashier stamps all receipts *paid* so that they cannot be reused, retains them, and gives the petty cashier a check for their sum. When this check is cashed and the proceeds returned to the cashbox, the money in the box is restored to its original amount, and the fund is ready to begin a new cycle of operations.

At the time a check is written to reimburse the petty cash fund, the petty cashier should sort the paid receipts according to the type of expense or other accounts to be debited in recording payments from the fund. Each group is then totaled and used in making the entry to record the reimbursement.

ILLUSTRATION 6–6 *Summary of Petty Cash Payments*

Miscellaneous expenses:		
Nov. 2, washing windows	$10.00	
Nov. 17, washing windows	10.00	
Nov. 27, computer repairs	26.50	$46.50
Transportation-in:		
Nov. 5, delivery of merchandise purchased	$ 6.75	
Nov. 20, delivery of merchandise purchased	8.30	15.05
Delivery expense:		
Nov. 18, customer's package delivered		5.00
Office supplies:		
Nov. 15, purchased office supplies		4.75
Total		$71.30

Illustration of a Petty Cash Fund

To avoid writing numerous checks for small amounts, a company established a petty cash fund on November 1, designating one of its office clerks, Carl Burns, as petty cashier. A $75 check was drawn, cashed, and the proceeds turned over to Burns. The following entry recorded the check:

Nov.	1	Petty Cash	75.00	
		Cash		75.00
		Established a petty cash fund.		

Notice that this entry transfers $75 from the regular Cash account to the Petty Cash account. After the petty cash fund is established, the Petty Cash account is not debited or credited again unless the size of the total fund is changed. For example, the fund should be increased if it is being exhausted and reimbursed too frequently. Another entry like the preceding one would be made to record an increase in the size of the fund. That is, there would be a debit to Petty Cash and credit to Cash for the amount of the increase. If the fund is too large, some of the money in the fund should be redeposited in the checking account. Such a reduction in the fund is recorded with a debit to Cash and a credit to Petty Cash.

During November, Carl Burns, the petty cashier, made several payments from the cash fund. Each time, he asked the person who received payment to sign a receipt. On November 27, after making a $26.50 payment for repairs to an office computer, Burns decided there might not be enough cash in the fund for another payment. Therefore, he summarized and totaled the petty cash receipts as shown in Illustration 6–6. Then, the summary and the petty cash receipts were given to the company cashier in exchange for a $71.30 check to reimburse the fund. Burns cashed the check, put the $71.30 proceeds in the petty cashbox, and then was ready to make additional payments from the fund. The reimbursing check is recorded with the following journal entry:

Nov.	27	Miscellaneous Expenses	46.50	
		Transportation-In	15.05	
		Delivery Expense	5.00	
		Office Supplies	4.75	
		Cash		71.30
		Reimbursed petty cash.		

Information for this entry came from the petty cashier's summary of payments. Note that the debits in the entry record the petty cash payments. Even if the petty cash fund is not low on funds at the end of an accounting period, it may be reimbursed at that time to record the expenses in the proper period. Otherwise, the financial statements show an overstated petty cash asset and understated expenses or assets that were paid for out of petty cash. (Of course, the amounts involved are seldom if ever significant to users of the financial statements.)

Cash Over and Short

Sometimes, a petty cashier fails to get a receipt for a payment. Then, when the fund is reimbursed, he or she may forget the purpose of the expenditure. This mistake causes the fund to be short. If, for whatever reason, the petty cash fund is short at reimbursement time, the shortage is recorded as an expense in the reimbursing entry with a debit to the **Cash Over and Short account.** This account is an income statement account that records the income effects of cash overages and cash shortages arising from omitted petty cash receipts and from errors in making change.

Errors in making change are discovered when there are differences between the cash in a cash register and the record of the amount of cash sales. Even though a cashier is careful, some customers may be given too much or too little change. As a result, at the end of a day, the actual cash from a cash register may not equal the cash sales rung up. For example, assume that a cash register shows cash sales of $550 but the actual count of cash in the register is $555. The entry to record the cash sales and the overage would be:

Nov.	23	Cash	555.00	
		Cash Over and Short		5.00
		Sales		550.00
		Day's cash sales and overage.		

On the other hand, if there were a shortage of cash in the register on the next day, the entry to record cash sales and the shortage would look like the following:

Nov.	24	Cash	621.00	
		Cash Over and Short	4.00	
		Sales		625.00
		Day's cash sales and shortage.		

Because customers are more likely to dispute being shortchanged, the Cash Over and Short account usually has a debit balance by the end of the accounting period. Because it is a debit, this balance represents an expense. This expense can be shown on the income statement as a separate item in the general and administrative expense section. Or, because the amount is usually small, you can combine it with other small expenses and report them as a single item called *miscellaneous expenses.* If Cash Over and Short has a credit balance at the end of the period, it usually is shown on the income statement as part of *miscellaneous revenues.*

Reconciling the Bank Balance

At least once every month, banks send depositors a bank statement that shows the activity in their accounts during the month. Different banks use a variety of formats for their bank statements. However, all of them include the following items of information in one place or another:

1. The balance of the depositor's account at the beginning of the month.

ILLUSTRATION 6–7 *A Typical Bank Statement*

First National Bank P.O. BOX 1727 AUSTIN, TEXAS 78767 512/473-4343

VALLEY COMPANY
1300 FALCON LEDGE
AUSTIN, TEXAS 78746

ACCOUNT NUMBER	DATE OF THIS STATEMENT	DATE OF LAST STATEMENT	PAGE NO.
494 504 2	10/31/95	9/30/95	1

A

BALANCE OF PREVIOUS STATEMENT ON 9/30/95	1,609.58
5 DEPOSITS AND OTHER CREDITS TOTALING	1,155.00
10 CHECKS AND OTHER DEBITS TOTALING	723.00
SERVICE CHARGE AMOUNT	.00
INTEREST AMOUNT AT 5.2500%	8.42
CURRENT BALANCE AS OF THIS STATEMENT	2,050.00
AVERAGE BALANCE AS OF THIS STATEMENT	1,924.95
TOTAL INTEREST PAID TO DATE	124.00

B

CHECKING ACCOUNT TRANSACTIONS

DATE	AMOUNT	TRANSACTION DESCRIPTION
10/02	240.00+	DEPOSIT
10/09	180.00+	DEPOSIT
10/12	23.00−	CHARGE FOR PRINTING NEW CHECKS
10/15	100.00+	DEPOSIT
10/16	150.00+	DEPOSIT
10/23	485.00+	NOTE COLLECTION LESS FEE
10/25	30.00−	NSF CHECK AND NSF CHARGE
10/31	8.42+	INTEREST PAID

C

DATE	CHECK NO	AMOUNT	DATE	CHECK NO	AMOUNT
10/03	119	55.00	10/16	123	25.00
10/19	120	200.00	10/23	125*	10.00
10/10	121	120.00	10/26	127*	50.00
10/14	122	75.00	10/29	128	135.00

*INDICATES A SKIP IN CHECK NUMBER SEQUENCE

D

DAILY BALANCE SUMMARY

DATE	BALANCE	DATE	BALANCE	DATE	BALANCE
10/01	1,609.58	10/12	1,831.58	10/23	2,256.58
10/02	1,849.58	10/14	1,756.58	10/25	2,226.58
10/03	1,794.58	10/15	1,856.58	10/26	2,176.58
10/09	1,974.58	10/16	1,981.58	10/29	2,041.58
10/10	1,854.58	10/19	1,781.58	10/31	2,050.00

FOR QUESTIONS ON DIRECT DEPOSITS, PLEASE CALL 473-4522, BETWEEN 9:00–4:00 MONDAY-FRIDAY OR WRITE P. O. BOX 1727, AUSTIN, TEXAS 78767.

2. Deposits and any other amounts added to the account during the month.
3. Checks and any other amounts deducted from the account during the month.
4. The account balance at the end of the month.

LO 5 Explain why the bank balance and the book balance of cash should be reconciled and be able to prepare a reconciliation.

Of course, all this information is presented as it appears in the bank's records. Examine Illustration 6–7, a typical bank statement, to find the four items just listed.

Note that section A of Illustration 6–7 summarizes the changes in the account. Section B lists specific debits and credits to the account (other than canceled checks). Section C lists all paid checks in numerical order and section D shows the daily account balances.

Enclosed with the monthly statement are the depositor's **canceled checks** and any debit or credit memoranda that have affected the account. Canceled checks are checks that the bank has paid and deducted from the customer's

AS A MATTER OF

Ethics

Nancy Tucker is an internal auditor for a large corporation and is in the process of making surprise counts of three $200 petty cash funds in various offices in the headquarters building. She arrived at the office of one of the fund custodians shortly before lunch while he was on the telephone. Tucker explained the purpose of her visit, and the custodian asked politely that she come back after lunch so that he could finish the business he was conducting by long distance. She agreed and returned around 1:30. The custodian opened the petty cashbox and showed her nine new $20 bills with consecutive serial numbers plus receipts that totaled $20. Would you suggest that the auditor take any further action or comment on these events in her report to management?

account during the month. Additional deductions that may appear on the bank statement for an individual include withdrawals through automatic teller machines (ATM withdrawals) and periodic payments arranged in advance by the depositor.[2] Other deductions from the depositor's account may include service charges and fees assessed by the bank, customer checks deposited that prove to be uncollectible, and corrections of previous errors. Except for the service charges, the bank notifies the depositor of the deduction in each case with a debit memorandum at the time that the bank reduces the balance. For completeness, a copy of each debit memorandum is usually sent with the monthly statement.[3]

In addition to deposits made by the depositor, the bank may add amounts to the depositor's account. Examples of additions would be amounts the bank has collected on behalf of the depositor and corrections of previous errors. Credit memoranda notify the depositor of all additions when they are first recorded. For completeness, a copy of each credit memorandum may be sent with the monthly statement.

Another item commonly added to the bank balance on the statement is interest earned by the depositor. Many checking accounts pay the depositor interest based on the average cash balance maintained in the account. The bank calculates the amount of interest earned and credits it to the depositor's account each month. In Illustration 6–7, note that the bank credited $8.42 of interest to the account of Valley Company. (The methods used to calculate interest are discussed in the next chapter.)

When the business deposits all receipts intact and when all payments (other than petty cash payments) are drawn from the checking account, the bank statement is a device for proving the accuracy of the depositor's cash records. The test of the accuracy begins by preparing a **bank reconciliation,** which is an analysis that explains the difference between the balance of a checking account in the depositor's records and the balance on the bank statement.

---

[2] Because of the need to make all disbursements by check, most business checking accounts do not allow ATM withdrawals.

[3] To clarify, the depositor's account is a liability on the bank's records. Thus, a deposit increases the account balance, and the bank records it with a *credit* to the account. On the other hand, the deposit is an increase in the depositor's asset, so the depositor records it with a *debit* to the Cash account. Checks reduce the account balance, and the bank records them as a *debit* while the depositor records them with a *credit.* Debit memos from the bank produce *credits* on the depositor's books, and credit memos lead to *debits.*

Need for Reconciling the Bank Balance

For virtually all checking accounts, the balance on the bank statement does not agree with the balance in the depositor's accounting records. Therefore, to prove the accuracy of both the depositor's records and those of the bank, you must *reconcile* the two balances. In other words, you must explain or account for the differences between them.

Numerous factors cause the bank statement balance to differ from the depositor's book balance. Some are:

1. **Outstanding checks.** These checks were written (or drawn) by the depositor, deducted on the depositor's records, and sent to the payees. However, they are called **outstanding checks** because they did not reach the bank for payment and deduction before the statement date.
2. **Unrecorded deposits.** Companies often make deposits at the end of each business day, after the bank is closed. These deposits made in the bank's night depository are not recorded by the bank until the next business day. Therefore, a deposit placed in the night depository on the last day of the month cannot appear on the bank statement for that month. In addition, deposits mailed to the bank toward the end of the month may be in transit and unrecorded when the statement is prepared.
3. **Charges for uncollectible items and for service.** Occasionally, a company deposits a customer's check that bounces, or turns out to be uncollectible. Usually, the balance in the customer's account is not large enough to cover the check. In these cases, the check is called a nonsufficient funds (NSF) check. In other situations, the customer's account has been closed. In processing deposited checks, the bank credits the depositor's account for the full amount. Later, when the bank learns that the check is uncollectible, it debits (reduces) the depositor's account for the amount of the check. Also, the bank may charge the depositor a fee for processing the uncollectible check. At the same time, the bank notifies the depositor of each deduction by mailing a debit memorandum. Although each deduction should be recorded by the depositor on the day the debit memorandum is received, sometimes an entry is not made until the bank reconciliation is prepared.

   Other charges to a depositor's account that a bank might report on the bank statement include the printing of new checks. Also, the bank may assess a monthly service charge for maintaining the account. Notification of these charges is not provided until the statement is mailed.
4. **Credits for collections and for interest.** Banks sometimes act as collection agents for their depositors by collecting promissory notes and other items. When the bank collects an item, it deducts a fee and adds the net proceeds to the depositor's account. At the same time, it sends a credit memorandum to notify the depositor of the transaction. As soon as the memorandum is received, it should be recorded by the depositor. However, these items may remain unrecorded until the time of the bank reconciliation.

   Many bank accounts earn interest on the average cash balance in the account during the month. If an account earns interest, the bank statement includes a credit for the amount earned during the past month. Notification of earned interest is provided only by the bank statement.
5. **Errors.** Regardless of care and systems of internal control for automatic error detection, both banks and depositors make errors. Errors by the

bank may not be discovered until the depositor completes the bank reconciliation. Also, the depositor's errors often are not discovered until the balance is reconciled.

Steps in Reconciling the Bank Balance

To obtain the benefits of separated duties, an employee who does not handle cash receipts, process checks, or maintain cash records should prepare the bank reconciliation. In preparing to reconcile the balance, this employee must gather information from the bank statement and from other sources in the records. The person who performs the reconciliation must do the following:

- Compare the deposits listed on the bank statement with the deposits shown in the accounting records. Identify any discrepancies and determine which is correct. Make a list of any errors or unrecorded deposits.
- Examine all other credits on the bank statement and determine whether each was recorded in the books. These items include collections by the bank, correction of previous bank statement errors, and interest earned by the depositor. List any unrecorded items.
- Compare the canceled checks listed on the bank statement with the actual checks returned with the statement. For each check, make sure that the correct amount was deducted by the bank and that the returned check was properly charged to the company's account. List any discrepancies or errors.
- Compare the canceled checks listed on the bank statement with the checks recorded in the books. (To make this process easier, the bank statement normally lists canceled checks in numerical order.) Prepare a list of any outstanding checks.

  Although an individual may occasionally write a check and fail to record it in the books, companies with reasonable internal controls rarely, if ever, write a check without recording it. Nevertheless, prepare a list of any canceled checks unrecorded in the books.
- Determine whether any outstanding checks listed on the previous month's bank reconciliation are not included in the canceled checks listed on the bank statement. Prepare a list of any of these checks that remain outstanding at the end of the current month. Send this list to the cashier's office for follow-up with the payees to see if the checks were actually received.
- Examine all other debits to the account shown on the bank statement and determine whether each one was recorded in the books. These include bank charges for newly printed checks, NSF checks, and monthly service charges. List those not yet recorded.

When this information has been gathered, the employee can complete the reconciliation like the one in Illustration 6–8 by using these steps:

1. Start with the bank balance of the cash account.
2. Identify and list any unrecorded deposits and any bank errors that understated the bank balance. Add them to the bank balance.
3. Identify and list any outstanding checks and any bank errors that overstated the bank balance. Subtract them from the bank balance.
4. Compute the adjusted balance. This amount is also called the *correct* or *reconciled* balance.
5. Start with the book balance of the cash account.

ILLUSTRATION 6-8 *A Typical Bank Reconciliation*

VALLEY COMPANY
Bank Reconciliation
October 31, 1995

① Bank statement balance	$2,050.00	⑤ Book balance	$1,404.58
② Add:		⑥ Add:	
Deposit of 10/31	145.00	Proceeds of note less collection fee	$ 485.00
		Interest earned	8.42
		Total	$ 493.42
Total	$2,195.00	Total	$1,898.00
③ Deduct:		⑦ Deduct:	
Outstanding checks:		NSF check plus service charge	$ 30.00
No. 124	$ 150.00		
No. 126	200.00	Check printing charge	23.00
Total	$ 350.00	Total	$ 53.00
④ Reconciled balance	$1,845.00	⑧ Reconciled balance	$1,845.00

⑨ The two balances both equal $1,845.00

6. Identify and list any unrecorded credit memoranda from the bank (perhaps for the proceeds of a collected note), interest earned, and any errors that understated the book balance. Add them to the book balance.
7. Identify and list any unrecorded debit memoranda from the bank (perhaps for an NSF check from a customer), service charges, and any errors that overstated the book balance. Subtract them from the book balance.
8. Compute the reconciled balance. This is also the correct balance.
9. Verify that the two adjusted balances from steps 4 and 8 are equal. If so, they are reconciled. If not, check for mathematical accuracy and for any missing data.

When the reconciliation is complete, the employee should send a copy to the accounting department so that any needed journal entries can be recorded. For example, entries are needed to record any unrecorded debit and credit memoranda and any of the company's mistakes. Another copy should go to the cashier's office, especially if the bank has made an error that needs to be corrected.

Illustration of a Bank Reconciliation

We can illustrate a bank reconciliation by preparing one for Valley Company as of October 31. In preparing to reconcile the bank account, the Valley Company employee gathered the following facts:

- The bank balance shown on the bank statement was $2,050.
- The cash balance according to the accounting records was $1,404.58.
- A $145 deposit was placed in the bank's night depository on October 31 and was unrecorded by the bank when the bank statement was mailed.
- Enclosed with the bank statement was a copy of a credit memorandum showing that the bank had collected a note receivable for the company on October 23. The note's proceeds of $500 (less a $15 collection fee) were credited to the company's account. This credit memorandum had not been recorded by the company.

- The bank statement also showed a credit of $8.42 for interest earned on the average cash balance in the account. Because there had been no prior notification of this item, it had not been recorded on the company's books.
- A comparison of canceled checks with the company's books showed that two checks were outstanding—No. 124 for $150 and No. 126 for $200.
- Other debits on the bank statement that had not been previously recorded on the books included (*a*) a $23 charge for checks printed by the bank; and (*b*) an NSF (nonsufficient funds) check for $20 plus the related processing fee of $10. The NSF check had been received from a customer, Frank Green, on October 16 and had been included in that day's deposit.

Illustration 6–8 shows the bank reconciliation that reflects these items. The numbers in the circles beside the various parts of the reconciliation correspond to the numbers of the steps listed earlier.

Preparing a bank reconciliation helps locate any errors made by either the bank or the depositor. It also identifies unrecorded items that should be recorded on the company's books. For example, in Valley Company's reconciliation, the adjusted balance of $1,845.00 is the correct balance as of October 31, 1995. However, at that date, Valley Company's accounting records show a $1,404.58 balance. Therefore, journal entries must be made to increase the book balance to the correct balance. This process requires four entries. The first is

Nov.	2	Cash	485.00	
		Collection Expense	15.00	
		Notes Receivable		500.00
		To record the collection fee and proceeds of a note collected by the bank.		

This entry records the net proceeds of Valley Company's note receivable that had been collected by the bank, the expense of having the bank perform that service, and the reduction in the Notes Receivable account.

The second entry records the interest credited to Valley Company's account by the bank:

Nov.	2	Cash	8.42	
		Interest Earned		8.42
		To record interest earned on the average cash balance maintained in the checking account.		

Interest earned is a revenue, and the entry recognizes both the revenue and the related increase in Cash.

The third entry records the NSF check that was returned as uncollectible. The $20 check was received from Green in payment of his account and deposited. The bank charged $10 for handling the NSF check and deducted $30 from Valley Company's account. Therefore, the company must reverse the entry made when the check was received and also record the $10 processing fee:

Nov.	2	Accounts Receivable—Frank Green	30.00	
		Cash		30.00
		To charge Frank Green's account for his NSF check and for the bank's fee.		

This entry reflects the fact that Valley Company followed customary business practice and added the NSF $10 fee to Green's account. Thus, it will try to collect the entire $30 from Green.

The fourth entry debits Miscellaneous Expenses for the check printing charge. The entry is

Nov.	2	Miscellaneous Expenses	23.00	
		Cash		23.00
		Check printing charge.		

After these entries are recorded, the balance of cash is increased to the correct amount of $1,845.00 ($1,404.58 + $485.00 + 8.42 − $30.00 − $23.00).

Other Internal Control Procedures

Internal control principles apply to every phase of a company's operations including merchandise purchases, sales, cash receipts, cash disbursements, and owning and operating plant assets. Many of these procedures are discussed in later chapters. At this point, we consider a way that a company can gain more control over *purchases discounts.*

LO 6 Tell how recording invoices at net amounts helps gain control over cash discounts taken and be able to account for invoices recorded at net amounts.

Recall that entries such as the following have recorded the receipt and payment of an invoice for a purchase of merchandise:

Oct.	2	Purchases	1,000.00	
		Accounts Payable		1,000.00
		Purchased merchandise, terms 2/10, n/60.		
	12	Accounts Payable	1,000.00	
		Purchases Discounts		20.00
		Cash		980.00
		Paid the invoice of October 2.		

These entries reflect the **gross method of recording purchases.** That is, the invoice was recorded at its gross amount of $1,000 before considering the cash discount. Many companies record invoices in this way. However, the **net method of recording purchases** records invoices at their *net* amounts (after cash discounts). This method is widely thought to provide more useful information to management.

To illustrate the net method, assume that a company purchases merchandise with a $1,000 invoice price and terms of 2/10, n/60. On receiving the goods, the purchasing company deducted the offered $20 discount from the gross amount and recorded the purchase at the $980 net amount:

Oct.	2	Purchases	980.00	
		Accounts Payable		980.00
		Purchased merchandise on credit.		

If the invoice for this purchase is paid within the discount period, the entry to record the payment debits Accounts Payable and credits Cash for $980. However, if payment is not made within the discount period and the discount is *lost,* an entry such as the following must be made either before or when the invoice is paid:

Dec.	1	Discounts Lost	20.00	
		Accounts Payable		20.00
		To record the discount lost.		

A check for the full $1,000 invoice amount is then written, recorded, and mailed to the creditor.[4]

Advantage of the Net Method

When invoices are recorded at *gross* amounts, the amount of discounts taken is deducted from the balance of the Purchases account on the income statement to arrive at the cost of merchandise purchased. However, the amount of any lost discounts does not appear in any account or on the income statement. Therefore, lost discounts may not come to the attention of management.

On the other hand, when purchases are recorded at *net* amounts, the amount of discounts taken does not appear on the income statement. Instead, an expense for **discounts lost** is brought to management's attention through its appearance on the income statement as an operating expense.

Recording invoices at their net amounts supplies management with useful information about the amount of discounts missed through oversight, carelessness, or some other reason. Thus, this practice gives management better control over the people responsible for paying bills on time so that cash discounts can be taken. When the accounts record the fact that discounts are missed, someone has to explain why. As a result, it is likely that fewer discounts are lost through carelessness.

Using the Information—Days' Sales Uncollected

LO 1 Explain the concept of liquidity and the difference between cash and cash equivalents, and calculate days' sales uncollected.

Many companies attract customers by selling to them on credit. As a result, cash flows from customers are postponed until the accounts receivable are collected. To evaluate the liquidity of a company's assets, investors want to know how quickly the company converts its accounts receivable into cash. One way financial statement users evaluate the liquidity of the receivables is to look at the **days' sales uncollected.** This is calculated by taking the ratio between the present balance of receivables and the credit sales over the preceding year, and then multiplying by the number of days in the year. Since the amount of credit sales usually is not reported, net sales is typically used in the calculation. Thus, the formula for the calculation is

$$\text{Days' sales uncollected} = \frac{\text{Accounts receivable}}{\text{Net sales}} \times 365$$

For example, Meg's Mart (see p. 187) had accounts receivable of $11,200 at the end of 19X2 and net sales of $314,700 (see page 198) for the year. By dividing $11,200 by $314,700, we find that the receivables balance represents 3.56% of the year's sales. Because there are 365 days in a year, the $11,200 balance is 3.56% of 365 days of sales, or 13 days of sales.

The number of days' sales uncollected is used as an estimate of how much time is likely to pass before cash receipts from credit sales equal the amount of the existing accounts receivable. In evaluating this number, financial statement users should compare it to days' sales uncollected calculations for other companies in the same industry. In addition, they may make comparisons between the current and prior periods.

[4] Alternatively, the lost discount can be recorded with the late payment in a single entry.

Summary of the Chapter in Terms of Learning Objectives

LO 1 The liquidity of an asset refers to how easily the asset can be converted into other types of assets or used to buy services or satisfy obligations. Cash is the most liquid asset. To increase their return, companies may invest their idle cash balances in cash equivalents. These investments are readily convertible to a known amount of cash and are purchased so close to their maturity date that their market values are relatively insensitive to interest rate changes. In evaluating the liquidity of a company, financial statement users may calculate days' sales uncollected.

LO 2 Internal control systems are designed to encourage adherence to prescribed managerial policies. In doing so, they promote efficient operations and protect assets against theft or misuse. They also help ensure that accurate and reliable accounting data are produced. Principles of good internal control include establishing clear responsibilities, maintaining adequate records, insuring assets and bonding employees, separating record-keeping and custody of assets, dividing responsibilities for related transactions, using mechanical devices whenever feasible, and performing regular independent reviews of internal control practices.

LO 3 To maintain control over cash, custody must be separated from record-keeping for cash. All cash receipts should be deposited intact in the bank on a daily basis, and all payments (except for minor petty cash payments) should be made by check. A voucher system helps maintain control over cash disbursements by ensuring that payments are made only after full documentation and approval.

LO 4 The petty cashier, who should be a responsible employee, makes small payments from the petty cash fund and obtains signed receipts for the payments. The Petty Cash account is debited when the fund is established or increased in size. Petty cash disbursements are recorded with a credit to cash whenever the fund is replenished.

LO 5 A bank reconciliation is produced to prove the accuracy of the depositor's and the bank's records. In completing the reconciliation, the bank statement balance is adjusted for such items as outstanding checks and unrecorded deposits made on or before the bank statement date but received by the bank after. The depositor's cash account balance is adjusted to the correct balance. The difference arises from such items as service charges, collections the bank has made for the depositor, and interest earned on the average checking account balance.

LO 6 When the net method of recording invoices is used, missed cash discounts are reported as an expense. In contrast, when the gross method is used, discounts taken are reported as reductions in the cost of the purchased goods. Therefore, the net method directs management's attention to instances where the company failed to take advantage of discounts.

Demonstration Problem

Set up a table for a bank reconciliation as of September 30 with the following headings:

Bank Balance		Book Balance			Not Shown on the Reconciliation
Add	Deduct	Add	Deduct	Must Adjust	

For each item that follows, place an x in the appropriate columns to indicate whether the item should be added to or deducted from the book or bank balance, or whether it should not appear on the reconciliation. If the book balance is to be adjusted, place a *Dr.* or *Cr.* in the Must Adjust column to indicate whether the Cash balance should be debited or credited.

1. Interest earned on the account.
2. Deposit made on September 30 after the bank was closed.
3. Checks outstanding on August 31 that cleared the bank in September.
4. NSF check from customer returned on September 15 but not recorded by the company.
5. Checks written and mailed to payees on September 30.
6. Deposit made on September 5 that was processed on September 8.
7. Bank service charge.
8. Checks written and mailed to payees on October 5.
9. Check written by another depositor but charged against the company's account.
10. Principal and interest collected by the bank but not recorded by the company.
11. Special charge for collection of note in No. 10 on company's behalf.
12. Check written against the account and cleared by the bank; erroneously omitted by the bookkeeper.

Planning the Solution

- Examine each item to determine whether it affects the book balance or the bank balance.
- If it acts to increase the balance, place an *x* in the Add column. If it acts to decrease the balance, place an *x* in the Deduct column.
- If the item increases or decreases the book balance, enter a *Dr.* or *Cr.* in the adjustment column.
- If the item does not affect either balance, place an *x* in the Not Shown on the Reconciliation column.

Solution to Demonstration Problem

	Bank Balance		Book Balance			Not Shown on the Reconciliation
	Add	Deduct	Add	Deduct	Must Adjust	
1. Interest earned on the account.			x		Dr.	
2. Deposit made on September 30 after the bank was closed.	x					
3. Checks outstanding on August 31 that cleared the bank in September.						x
4. NSF check from customer returned on September 15 but not recorded by the company.				x	Cr.	
5. Checks written and mailed to payees on September 30.		x				
6. Deposit made on September 5 that was processed on September 8.						x
7. Bank service charge.				x	Cr.	
8. Checks written and mailed to payees on October 5.						x
9. Check written by another depositor but charged against the company's account.	x					
10. Principal and interest collected by the bank but not recorded by the company.			x		Dr.	
11. Special charge for collection of note in No. 11 on company's behalf.				x	Cr.	
12. Check written against the account and cleared by the bank; erroneously omitted by the bookkeeper.				x	Cr.	

Glossary

LO 7 Define or explain the words and phrases listed in the chapter glossary.

Bank reconciliation an analysis that explains the difference between the balance of a checking account shown in the depositor's records and the balance shown on the bank statement. p. 238

Canceled checks checks that the bank has paid and deducted from the customer's account during the month. p. 237

Cash equivalents temporary liquid investments that can be easily and quickly converted to cash. p. 223

Cash Over and Short account an income statement account used to record cash overages and cash shortages arising from omitted petty cash receipts and from errors in making change. p. 236

Days' sales uncollected the number of days of average credit sales volume accumulated in the accounts receivable balance, calculated as the product of 365 times the ratio of the accounts receivable balance divided by credit (or net) sales. p. 244

Discounts lost an expense resulting from failing to take advantage of cash discounts on purchases. p. 244

Gross method of recording purchases a method of recording purchases at the full invoice price without deducting any cash discounts. p. 243

Internal control system procedures adopted by a business to encourage adherence to prescribed managerial policies; in doing so, the system also promotes operational efficiencies and protects the business assets from waste, fraud, and theft, and helps ensure that accurate and reliable accounting data are produced. p. 224

Invoice an itemized statement prepared by the vendor that lists the customer's name, the items sold, the sales prices, and the terms of sale. p. 230

Invoice approval form a document on which the accounting department notes that it has performed each step in the process of checking an invoice and approving it for recording and payment. p. 231

Liquid asset an asset, such as cash, that is easily converted into other types of assets or used to buy services or pay liabilities. p. 223

Liquidity a characteristic of an asset that refers to how easily the asset can be converted into another type of asset or used to buy services or to satisfy obligations. p. 223

Net method of recording purchases a method of recording purchases at the full invoice price less any cash discounts. p. 243

Outstanding checks checks that were written (or drawn) by the depositor, deducted on the depositor's records, and sent to the payees; however, they had not reached the bank for payment and deduction before the statement date. p. 239

Purchase order a business paper used by the purchasing department to place an order with the vendor; authorizes the vendor to ship the ordered merchandise at the stated price and terms. p. 230

Purchase requisition a business paper used to request that the purchasing department buy the needed merchandise or other items. p. 229

Receiving report a form used within the business to notify the appropriate persons that ordered goods were received and to describe the quantities and condition of the goods. p. 230

Vendee the buyer or purchaser of goods or services. p. 230

Vendor the seller of goods or services, usually a manufacturer or wholesaler. p. 230

Voucher an internal business paper used to accumulate other papers and information needed to control the disbursement of cash and to ensure that the transaction is properly recorded. p. 229

Voucher system a set of procedures designed to control the incurrence of obligations and disbursements of cash. p. 229

Objective Review

Answers to the following questions are listed at the end of this chapter. Be sure that you decide which is the one best answer to each question *before* you check the answers.

LO 1 Which of the following assets should be classified as a cash equivalent?

a. Land purchased as an investment.
b. Accounts receivable.
c. Common stock purchased as a short-term investment.
d. A 90-day Treasury bill issued by the U.S. government.
e. None of the above.

LO 2 The broad principles of internal control require that:

a. Responsibility for a series of related transactions (such as placing orders for, receiving, and paying for merchandise) should be lodged in one person so that responsibility is clearly assigned.
b. An employee who has custody over an asset should also keep the accounting records for that asset to ensure that the records are kept current.
c. Responsibility for specific tasks should be shared by more than one employee so that one serves as a check on the other.
d. Employees who handle cash and negotiable assets should be bonded.
e. All of the above are correct.

LO 3 Regarding internal control procedures for cash receipts:

a. All cash disbursements, other than from petty cash, should be made by check.
b. At the end of each day, each salesclerk who receives cash should analyze and correct any errors in the cash register's record of receipts before the records are submitted to the accounting department.
c. An accounting department employee should count the cash received from sales and promptly deposit the cash receipts in the bank.
d. Mail containing cash receipts should be opened by an accounting department employee who is responsible for recording the amount of the receipts and for depositing the receipts in the bank.
e. All of the above are correct.

LO 4 When a petty cash fund is used:

a. The balance in the Petty Cash account should be reported in the balance sheet as a long-term investment since this amount is kept in the fund on a long-term basis.
b. The petty cashier's summary of petty cash payments serves as a journal entry that is posted to the appropriate General Ledger accounts.
c. At the time that they are made, payments from the petty cash fund should be recorded with entries that include a credit to the Cash account.

d. At the time that they are made, payments from the petty cash fund should be recorded with entries that include a credit to the Petty Cash account.

e. Reimbursements of the petty cash fund should be credited to the Cash account.

LO 5 In the process of preparing a bank reconciliation:

a. Outstanding checks should be added to the bank balance of cash.

b. Outstanding checks should be subtracted from the book balance of cash.

c. All of the reconciling items shown on a bank reconciliation must be entered in the accounting records after the reconciliation is completed.

d. Items that appear on the reconciliation as corrections to the book balance of cash should be entered in the accounting records.

e. Items that appear on the reconciliation as corrections to the bank statement balance should be entered in the accounting records.

LO 6 When invoices are recorded at net amounts:

a. The Purchases account is debited for the amount of any purchases discounts offered plus the amount to be paid if a purchase discount is taken.

b. The amount of purchases discounts lost is not recorded in a separate account.

c. The amount of purchases discounts taken is not recorded in a separate account.

d. Purchases discounts taken are recorded in a Purchases Discounts account.

e. The cash expenditures for purchases will always be less than if the invoices are recorded at gross amounts.

LO 7 A form used within a business to notify the appropriate persons that ordered goods were received and to describe the quantities and condition of the goods is called a (an):

a. Invoice.

b. Invoice approval form.

c. Purchase order.

d. Receiving report.

e. Voucher.

Questions for Class Discussion

1. Why does a company need to own liquid assets?
2. Why does a company own cash equivalent assets in addition to cash?
3. List the seven broad principles of internal control.
4. Why should the person who keeps the record of an asset not be the person responsible for custody of the asset?
5. Internal control procedures are important in every business, but at what stage in the development of a business do they become critical?
6. Why should responsibility for a sequence of related transactions be divided among different departments or individuals?
7. What are some of the effects of computers on internal control?
8. Why should all receipts be deposited intact on the day of receipt?
9. When merchandise is purchased for a large store, why are department managers not permitted to deal directly with suppliers?
10. Do all companies need a voucher system? At what approximate point in a company's growth would you recommend installing a voucher system?
11. Why are some cash payments made from a petty cash fund?
12. Explain how a petty cash fund operates.
13. Why would it be helpful to reimburse a petty cash fund at the end of an accounting period?
14. What are two results of reimbursing the petty cash fund?
15. What is a bank statement? What kind of information appears on a bank statement?
16. What is the meaning of the phrase *to reconcile a bank balance?*
17. Why should you reconcile the bank statement balance of cash and the depositor's book balance of cash?
18. What valuable information becomes readily available to management when invoices are recorded at net amounts? Is this information as readily available when invoices are recorded at gross amounts?

19. Refer to the Federal Express financial statements in Appendix G. What was the difference in the number of days' sales uncollected on May 31, 1993, and 1992? (In making the calculations, use the amounts that are reported as receivables, less allowance for doubtful accounts.)

Apple Computer, Inc.

20. Apple Computer's consolidated statement of cash flows (see Appendix F) describes the changes in cash and cash equivalents that occurred during the year ended September 25, 1992. What amount was provided (or used) by investing activities and what amount was provided (or used) by financing activities?

Exercises

Exercise 6–1
Analyzing internal control
(LO 2, 3)

Seinfeld Company is a young business that has grown rapidly. The company's bookkeeper, who was hired two years ago, left town suddenly after the company's manager discovered that a great deal of money had disappeared over the past 18 months. An audit disclosed that the bookkeeper had written and signed several checks made payable to the bookkeeper's sister, and then recorded the checks as salaries expense. The sister, who cashed the checks but had never worked for the company, left town with the bookkeeper. As a result, the company incurred an uninsured loss of $123,000.

Evaluate Seinfeld Company's internal control system and indicate which principles of internal control appear to have been ignored in this situation.

Exercise 6–2
Recommending internal control procedures
(LO 2, 3)

What internal control procedures would you recommend in each of the following situations?

a. An antique store has one employee who is given cash and sent to garage sales each weekend. The employee pays cash for merchandise to be resold at the antique store.

b. Fun in the Sun has one employee who sells sun visors and beach chairs at the beach. Each day, the employee is given enough visors and chairs to last through the day and enough cash to make change. The money is kept in a box at the stand.

Exercise 6–3
Internal control over cash receipts
(LO 2, 3)

Some of Carver Company's cash receipts from customers are sent to the company in the mail. Carver's bookkeeper opens the letters and deposits the cash received each day. What internal control problem is inherent in this arrangement? What changes would you recommend?

Exercise 6–4
Petty cash fund
(LO 4)

A company established a $400 petty cash fund on March 1. One week later, on March 8, the fund contained $74.50 in cash and receipts for these expenditures: postage, $73.00; transportation-in, $38.00; miscellaneous expenses, $122.00; and store supplies, $92.50.

Prepare the journal entries to (*a*) establish the fund and (*b*) reimburse it on March 8. (*c*) Now assume that the fund was not only reimbursed on March 8 but also increased to $600 because it was exhausted so quickly. Give the entry to reimburse the fund and increase it to $600.

Exercise 6–5
Petty cash fund
(LO 4)

A company established a $300 petty cash fund on May 9. On May 31, the fund had $123.20 in cash and receipts for these expenditures: transportation-in, $24.20; miscellaneous expenses, $66.10; and store supplies, $84.90. The petty cashier could not account for the $1.60 shortage in the fund. Prepare (*a*) the May 9 entry to establish the fund and (*b*) the May 31 entry to reimburse the fund and reduce it to $225.

Exercise 6–6
Bank reconciliation
(LO 5)

Cisco Company deposits all receipts intact on the day received and makes all payments by check. On April 30, 19X1, after all posting was completed, its Cash account showed a $9,540 debit balance. However, Cisco's April 30 bank statement showed only $7,881 on deposit in the bank on that day. Prepare a bank reconciliation for Cisco, using the following information:

a. Outstanding checks, $1,440.

b. Included with the April canceled checks returned by the bank was a $15 debit memorandum for bank services.

c. Check No. 658, returned with the canceled checks, was correctly drawn for $327 in payment of the utility bill and was paid by the bank on April 22. However, it had been recorded with a debit to Utilities Expense and a credit to Cash as though it were for $372.

d. The April 30 cash receipts, $3,129, were placed in the bank's night depository after banking hours on that date and were unrecorded by the bank at the time the April bank statement was prepared.

Exercise 6–7
Adjusting entries resulting from bank reconciliation
(LO 5)

Give the journal entries that Cisco Company should make as a result of having prepared the bank reconciliation in the previous exercise.

Exercise 6–8
Completion of bank reconciliation
(LO 5)

Complete the following bank reconciliation by filling in the missing amounts:

SAZAR COMPANY
Bank Reconciliation
September 30, 19X1

Bank statement balance . . .	$19,260	Book balance of cash	$?
Add:		Add:	
Deposit of Sept. 30	$ 8,575	Collection of note	$15,000
Bank error	?	Interest earned	450
Total	$?	Total	$?
Total	$27,915	Total	$23,640
Deduct:		Deduct:	
Outstanding checks	?	NSF check	$ 550
		Recording error	?
		Service charge	20
		Total	$?
Reconciled balance	$23,010	Reconciled balance	$?

Exercise 6–9
Recording invoices at gross or net amounts
(LO 6)

The September 30, 19X1, credit balance in the Sales account of Tiny's Toys showed it had sold merchandise for $73,500 during the month. The company began September with a $140,350 merchandise inventory and ended the month with a $118,500 inventory. It had incurred $17,150 of operating expenses during the month and recorded the following transactions:

Sept. 3 Received merchandise purchased at a $3,150 invoice price, invoice dated August 31, terms 2/10, n/30.

8 Received a $650 credit memorandum (invoice price) for merchandise received on September 3 and returned for credit.

15 Received merchandise purchased at a $7,000 invoice price, invoice dated September 13, terms 2/10, n/30.

22 Paid for the merchandise received on September 15, less the discount.

29 Paid for the merchandise received on September 3. Payment was delayed because the invoice was mistakenly filed for payment today. This error caused the discount to be lost. The filing error occurred after the credit memorandum received on September 8 was attached to the invoice dated August 31.

Prepare journal entries to record the transactions assuming Tiny's Toys records invoices (*a*) at gross amounts and (*b*) at net amounts.

Exercise 6–10
Liquidity of accounts receivable
(LO 1)

Electric Services Company reported net sales for 19X1 and 19X2 of $345,000 and $520,000. The end-of-year balances of accounts receivable were December 31, 19X1, $30,000; and December 31, 19X2, $76,000. Calculate the days' sales uncollected at the end of each year and describe any changes in the apparent liquidity of the company's receivables.

Problems

Problem 6–1
Establishing, reimbursing, and increasing petty cash fund
(LO 4)

A company completed the following petty cash transactions during July of the current year:

July 1 Drew a $250 check, cashed it, and gave the proceeds and the petty cash box to Tom Albertson, the petty cashier.

3 Purchased stationery, $37.00.

11 Paid $12.50 postage to express mail a contract to a customer.

14 Paid $11.25 COD charges on merchandise purchased for resale.

17 Paid $29.00 for stamps.

19 Purchased paper for the copy machine, $16.25.

July 22 Reimbursed Sarah Oliver, the manager of the business, $24.00 for business car mileage.
24 Paid $37.50 COD charges on merchandise purchased for resale.
26 Paid City Delivery $12.00 to deliver merchandise sold to a customer.
31 Albertson sorted the petty cash receipts by accounts affected and exchanged them for a check to reimburse the fund for expenditures. However, there was only $65.35 in cash in the fund, and he could not account for the shortage. In addition, the size of the petty cash fund was increased to $300.

Required

1. Prepare a general journal entry to record establishing the petty cash fund.
2. Prepare a summary of petty cash payments that has these categories: Office supplies, Postage expense, Transportation-in, Mileage expense, and Delivery expense. Sort the payments into the appropriate categories and total the expenses in each category.
3. Prepare the general journal entry to record the reimbursement and the increase of the fund.

Problem 6–2
Petty cash fund; reimbursement and analysis of errors
(LO 4)

The Thayer Company has only a General Journal in its accounting system and uses it to record all transactions. However, the company recently set up a petty cash fund to facilitate payments of small items. The following petty cash transactions were noted by the petty cashier as occurring during October (the last month of the company's fiscal year):

Oct. 2 Received a company check for $275 to establish the petty cash fund.
16 Received a company check to replenish the fund for the following expenditures made since October 2 and to increase the fund to $375:
a. Payment of $63.50 to *Travis Times* for an advertisement in the newspaper.
b. Purchased postage stamps for $58.
c. Purchased office supplies for $70.75.
d. Payment of $75 for janitorial service.
e. Discovered that $12.35 remained in the petty cash box.
31 The petty cashier noted that $182.20 remained in the fund. Having decided that the October 16 increase in the fund was too large, received a company check to replenish the fund for the following expenditures made since October 16 but causing the fund to be reduced to $325:
f. Reimbursement to office manager for business mileage, $36.
g. Purchased office supplies for $57.80.
h. Paid $52 to Austin Trucking Co. to deliver merchandise sold to a customer.
i. Payment of $47 COD delivery charges on merchandise purchased for resale.

Required

1. Prepare general journal entries to record the establishment of the fund on October 2 and its replenishments on October 16 and on October 31.
2. Explain how the company's financial statements would be affected if the petty cash fund is not replenished and no entry is made on October 31. (Hint: The amount of office supplies that appears on a balance sheet is determined by a physical count of the supplies on hand.)

Problem 6–3
Preparation of bank reconciliation and recording adjustments
(LO 5)

The following information was available to reconcile Kramer Company's book cash balance with its bank statement balance as of March 31, 19X1:

a. The March 31 cash balance according to the accounting records was $24,789, and the bank statement balance for that date was $34,686.
b. Check No. 573 for $834 and Check No. 582 for $300, both written and entered in the accounting records in March, were not among the canceled checks returned.

Two checks, No. 531 for $1,761 and No. 542 for $285, were outstanding on February 28 when the bank and book statement balances were last reconciled. Check No. 531 was returned with the March canceled checks but Check No. 542 was not.

c. When the March checks were compared with entries in the accounting records, it was found that Check No. 567 had been correctly drawn for $1,925 to pay for office supplies but was erroneously entered in the accounting records as though it were drawn for $1,952.

d. Two debit memoranda were included with the returned checks and were unrecorded at the time of the reconciliation. One of the debit memoranda was for $570 and dealt with an NSF check for $555 that had been received from a customer, Barbara White, in payment of her account. It also assessed a $15 fee for processing. The second debit memorandum covered check printing and was for $67. These transactions were not recorded by Kramer before receiving the statement.

e. A credit memorandum indicated that the bank had collected a $15,000 note receivable for the company, deducted a $15 collection fee, and credited the balance to the company's account. This transaction was not recorded by Kramer before receiving the statement.

f. The March 31 cash receipts, $5,897, had been placed in the bank's night depository after banking hours on that date and did not appear on the bank statement.

Required

1. Prepare a bank reconciliation for the company as of March 31.
2. Prepare the general journal entries necessary to bring the company's book balance of cash into conformity with the reconciled balance.

Problem 6–4
Preparation of bank reconciliation and recording adjustments
(LO 5)

Mountainview Co. reconciled its bank and book statement balances of cash on October 31 and showed two checks outstanding at that time, No. 1388 for $1,597 and No. 1393 for $745. The following information was available for the November 30, 19X1, reconciliation:

From the November 30 bank statement:

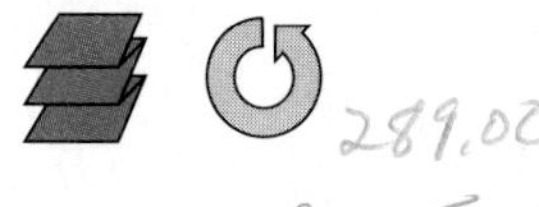

Balance of previous statement on 10/31/X1	27,418.00
5 Deposits and other credits totaling	17,176.00
9 Checks and other debits totaling	16,342.00
Current balance as of 11/30/X1	28,252.00

Checking Account Transactions

Date	Amount	Transaction Description
11/5	1,698.00+	Deposit
11/12	3,426.00+	Deposit
11/17	905.00−	NSF check
11/21	6,297.00+	Deposit
11/25	3,618.00+	Deposit
11/30	17.00+	Interest
11/30	2,120.00+	Credit memorandum

Date	Check No.	Amount	Date	Check No.	Amount
11/3	1388	1,597.00	11/22	1404	3,185.00
11/7	1401*	4,363.00	11/20	1405	1,442.00
11/4	1402	1,126.00	11/28	1407*	329.00
11/22	1403	614.00	11/29	1409*	2,781.00

* Indicates a skip in check sequence.

From Mountainview Co.'s accounting records:

Cash Receipts Deposited

Date			Cash Debit
Nov.	5		1,698.00
	12		3,426.00
	21		6,297.00
	25		3,618.00
	30		2,435.00
			17,474.00

Cash Disbursements

Check No.		Cash Credit
1401		4,363.00
1402		1,126.00
1403		614.00
1404		3,135.00
1405		1,442.00
1406		1,322.00
1407		329.00
1408		425.00
1409		2,781.00
		15,537.00

Cash — Acct. No. 101

Date		Explanation	PR	Debit	Credit	Balance
Oct.	31	Balance				25,076.00
Nov.	30	Total receipts	R12	17,474.00		42,550.00
	30	Total disbursements	D23		15,537.00	27,013.00

Check No. 1404 was correctly drawn for $3,185 to pay for computer equipment; however, the bookkeeper misread the amount and entered it in the accounting records with a debit to Computer Equipment and a credit to Cash as though it were for $3,135.

The NSF check was originally received from a customer, Jerry Skyles, in payment of his account. Its return was not recorded when the bank first notified the company. The credit memorandum resulted from the collection of a $2,150 note for Mountainview by the bank. The bank had deducted a $30 collection fee. The collection has not been recorded.

Required

1. Prepare a November 30 bank reconciliation for the company.
2. Prepare the general journal entries needed to adjust the book balance of cash to the reconciled balance.

Problem 6–5
Analytical essay
(LO 4)

In Problem 6–1, several transactions involved payments of cash from a petty cash fund. Then, the transaction on July 31 reimbursed the fund and increased its size to $300. Now assume that the July 31 transaction reimbursed but did not increase the size of the fund. Also assume that when the payments from petty cash were recorded, the company's bookkeeper made an entry in the following general form:

July	31	xxxxxxxxxxxx (Expense)	xxx	
		xxxxxxxxxxxx (Expense)	xxx	
		xxxxxxxxxxxx (Asset)	xxx	
		Petty Cash		xxx

Explain why this entry is not correct. Also explain the effects of the error on the General Ledger and on the balance sheet.

Problem 6–6
Analytical essay
(LO 5)

The bank statement in Problem 6–4 discloses three places where the canceled checks returned with the bank statement are not numbered sequentially. In other words, some of the prenumbered checks in the sequence are missing. Several possible situations would explain why the canceled checks returned with a bank statement might not be numbered sequentially. Describe three situations, each of which is a possible explanation of why the canceled checks returned with a bank statement are not numbered sequentially.

Provocative Problems

Provocative Problem 6–1
Accounting related communications
(LO 5)

On March 26, Summerfield Office Supply received Miles Brokaw's check number 629, dated March 24, in the amount of $1,420. The check was to pay for merchandise Brokaw had purchased on February 25. The merchandise was shipped from Summerfield's office at 1715 Westgate Boulevard, Austin, Texas, 78704 to Brokaw's home at 823 Congress, Austin, Texas, 78701. On March 27, Summerfield's cashier deposited the check in the company's bank account. The bank returned the check to Summerfield with the March 31 bank statement. Also included was a debit memorandum indicating that Brokaw's check was returned for nonsufficient funds and the bank was charging Summerfield a $25 NSF processing fee. Immediately after reconciling the bank statement on April 2, Marla Decker, Summerfield's accountant, asks you to write a letter for her signature using the company's letterhead stationery. Your letter to Brokaw should explain the amount owed and request prompt payment.

Provocative Problem 6–2
Commerce Company
(LO 2, 3)

The Commerce Company has enjoyed rapid growth since it was created several years ago. Last year, for example, its sales exceeded $4 million. However, its purchasing procedures have not kept pace with its growth. A plant supervisor or department head who needs raw materials, plant assets, or supplies, telephones a request to the purchasing department manager. The purchasing department manager then prepares a purchase order in duplicate, sends one copy to the company selling the goods, and keeps the other copy in the files. When the seller's invoice is received, it is sent directly to the purchasing department. When the goods arrive, receiving department personnel count and inspect the items and prepare only one copy of a receiving report, which is then sent to the purchasing department. The purchasing department manager attaches the receiving report and the file copy of the purchase order to the invoice. If all is in order, the invoice is stamped *approved for payment* and signed by the purchasing department manager. The invoice and its supporting documents are then sent to the accounting department to be recorded and filed until due. On its due date, the invoice and its supporting documents are sent to the office of the company treasurer, and a check is prepared and mailed. The number of the check is entered on the invoice and the invoice is sent to the accounting department for an entry to record its payment.

Do the procedures of Commerce make it fairly easy for someone in the company to initiate the payment of fictitious invoices by the company? If so, who is most likely to commit the fraud and what would that person have to do to receive payment of a fictitious invoice? What changes should be made in the company's purchasing procedures, and why should each change be made?

Provocative Problem 6–3
Apple Computer, Inc.
(LO 1)

Apple Computer, Inc.

For this problem, turn to the financial statements of Apple Computer, Inc., in Appendix F. Use the information presented in the financial statements to answer these questions:

1. For both 1992 and 1991, determine the total amount of cash and cash equivalents that Apple held at the end of the fiscal year. Determine the percentage that this amount represents of total current assets, total current liabilities, total shareholders' equity, and total assets.
2. For both 1992 and 1991, determine the total amount of cash, cash equivalents, and short-term investments that Apple held at the end of the year. Determine the percentage that this amount represents of total current assets, total current liabilities, total shareholders' equity, and total assets.
3. For 1992, use the information in the statement of cash flows to determine the percentage change between the beginning of the year and end of the year holding of cash and cash equivalents.
4. What was the number of days' sales uncollected at the end of the 1992 fiscal year and at the end of the 1991 fiscal year? (In making the calculations, use the amounts that are reported as accounts receivable, net of allowance for doubtful accounts.)

Provocative Problem 6–4
As a Matter of Ethics: essay

Review the As a Matter of Ethics case on page 238. Discuss the nature of the problem faced by Nancy Tucker and evaluate the alternative courses of action she should consider.

Answers to Objective Review Questions

LO 1 (*d*)
LO 2 (*d*)
LO 3 (*a*)
LO 4 (*e*)
LO 5 (*d*)
LO 6 (*c*)
LO 7 (*d*)

CHAPTER

7

Short-Term Investments and Receivables

The focus of the prior chapter was on accounting for cash, which is the most liquid of all assets. This chapter continues the discussion of liquid assets by focusing on short-term investments, accounts receivable, and short-term notes receivable.

Learning Objectives

After studying Chapter 7, you should be able to:

1. Prepare journal entries to account for short-term investments and explain how fair (market) value gains and losses on such investments are reported.
2. Prepare entries to account for credit card sales.
3. Prepare entries to account for transactions with credit customers, including accounting for bad debts under the allowance method and the direct write-off method.
4. Calculate the interest on promissory notes and prepare entries to record the receipt of promissory notes and their payment or dishonor.
5. Explain how receivables can be converted into cash before they are due, and calculate accounts receivable turnover.
6. Define or explain the words and phrases listed in the chapter glossary.

Because companies use cash to acquire assets and to pay expenses and obligations, good managers plan to maintain a cash balance large enough to meet expected payments plus some surplus for unexpected needs. Also, idle cash balances may exist during some months of each year because of seasonal fluctuations in sales volume. Rather than leave this unneeded cash in checking accounts that pay low rates of interest at best, most companies invest them in securities that earn higher returns.

Short-Term Investments

Recall from Chapter 6 that cash equivalents are investments readily convertible into a known amount of cash; generally, they mature not more than three months after purchase. Some investments of idle cash balances do not meet these criteria of cash equivalents but, nevertheless, are classified as current assets. Although these **short-term investments** or **temporary investments** do not qualify as cash equivalents, they serve a similar purpose. Like cash equiv-

LO 1 Prepare journal entries to account for short-term investments and explain how fair (market) value gains and losses on such investments are reported.

alents, short-term investments can be converted into cash easily and are held as a source of cash to satisfy the needs of current operations. Management usually expects to convert them into cash within one year or the current operating cycle of the business, whichever is longer.[1]

Short-term investments may be made in the form of government or corporate debt obligations (called *debt securities*) or in the form of stock (called *equity securities*). Some investments in debt securities are classified as current assets because they mature within one year or the current operating cycle of the business. Other securities that do not mature in a short time can be classified as current assets only if they are marketable. In other words, the reporting company must be able to sell them without excessive delays. For example, stocks that are actively traded on a stock exchange qualify as marketable.

When short-term investments are purchased, the purchaser should record them at cost. For example, assume that on January 10, Alpha Company purchased Ford Motor Company's short-term notes payable for $40,000. Alpha's entry to record the transaction is

Jan.	10	Short-Term Investments	40,000.00	
		Cash		40,000.00
		Bought $40,000 of Ford Motor Company notes due May 10.		

Assume that when these notes mature on May 10, the cash proceeds are $40,000 plus $1,200 interest. When the receipt is recorded, this entry credits the interest to a revenue account:

May	10	Cash	41,200.00	
		Short-Term Investments		40,000.00
		Interest Earned		1,200.00
		Received cash proceeds from matured notes.		

To determine the cost of an investment, the investor must include any commissions paid. For example, assume that on June 2, 19X1, Bailey Company purchased 1,000 shares of Xerox Corporation common stock as a short-term investment. The purchase price was 70⅛ ($70.125 per share) plus a $625 broker's commission. The entry to record the transaction is:[2]

June	2	Short-Term Investments	70,750.00	
		Cash		70,750.00
		Bought 1,000 shares of Xerox stock at 70⅛ plus $625 broker's commission.		

Notice that the commission is not recorded in a separate account.

[1] FASB, *Accounting Standards—Current Text* (Norwalk, CT, 1993), sec. B05.105. First published as *Accounting Research Bulletin No. 43,* chap. 3A, par. 4.

[2] Stock prices are quoted on stock exchanges on the basis of dollars and ⅛ dollars per share. For example, a stock quoted at 23⅛ sold for $23.125 per share and one quoted at 36½ sold for $36.50 per share.

When cash dividends are received on stock held as a short-term investment, they are credited to a revenue account as follows:

Dec.	12	Cash	1,000.00	
		Dividends Earned		1,000.00
		Received dividend of $1 per share on 1,000 shares of Xerox stock.		

Reporting Short-Term Investments in the Financial Statements

In past years, companies reported their short-term investments at the lower of cost or market value. The losses on reducing cost to market value were subtracted in the calculation of net income on the income statement. Recently, however, these reporting requirements have changed.

In May 1993, the FASB issued a new standard that requires companies to report most short-term investments at their fair (market) values.[3] The exact requirements of the new standard vary, depending on whether the investments are classified as (1) investments in securities held to maturity, (2) investments in trading securities, or (3) investments in securities available for sale.

Short-Term Investments in Securities Held to Maturity

If a company has the positive intent and ability to hold investments in debt securities until they mature, the investments are classified as **investments in securities held to maturity.**[4] As we mentioned earlier, these investments cannot qualify as current assets unless their maturity dates fall within one year or the current operating cycle of the business. Short-term investments in debt securities that will be held until maturity are reported at cost.

Short-Term Investments in Trading Securities

Some short-term investments in securities are actively managed. In other words, frequent purchases and sales generally are made with the objective of generating profits on short-term differences in price. Most often, such investments are made by financial institutions such as banks or insurance companies. The FASB notes that these **investments in trading securities** are bought principally for the purpose of selling them in the near term.

According to SFAS 115, companies must report investments in trading securities at their fair (market) values. The related gains and losses of fair (market) value are reported on the income statement and closed to Retained Earnings as part of net income or loss.

Short-Term Investments in Securities Available for Sale

Investments in securities available for sale include all securities investments that do not qualify as investments in trading securities or as investments in securities held to maturity. Securities available for sale are purchased to earn

---

[3] FASB, "Accounting for Certain Investments in Debt and Equity Securities," *Statement of Financial Accounting Standards No. 115* (Norwalk, CT, 1993). The requirements of SFAS 115 also apply to long-term investments in debt and marketable equity securities. You learn more about this in Chapter 10.

[4] Ibid., par. 7.

interest, dividends, and perhaps increases in market value. They are not actively managed like trading securities. Many industrial and commercial companies have short-term investments in securities available for sale.

As in the case of trading securities, SFAS 115 requires companies to adjust the reported amount of securities available for sale to reflect all changes in fair value. Unlike trading securities, however, the fair value gains and losses on securities available for sale are not reported on the income statement. Instead, they are reported in the stockholders' equity section of the balance sheet.

For example, assume that Bailey Company did not have any short-term investments prior to its purchase of the Xerox stock on June 2, 19X1. Later during 19X1, Bailey purchased two other short-term investments. Assume that all three are classified as securities available for sale. On December 31, 19X1, the cost and fair values of these securities are

Short-Term Investments in Securities Available for Sale on December 31, 19X1	**Costs**	**Fair (Market) Values**
Sears, Roebuck Co. common stock	$ 42,600	$ 43,500
Chrysler Corporation notes payable . . .	30,500	30,200
Xerox Corporation common stock	70,750	78,250
Total	$143,850	$151,950

The difference between the $143,850 cost and the $151,950 fair (market) value amounts to an $8,100 gain in fair value. Because the amount of the gain has not yet been confirmed by the sale of the security, accountants describe this gain as an **unrealized holding gain.** The following entry records the gain:

Dec.	31	Short-Term Investments, Fair Value Adjustment	8,100.00	
		Unrealized Holding Gain (Loss)		8,100.00
		To reflect fair values of short-term investments in securities available for sale.		

After posting this entry, the cost and fair value adjustment of the short-term investments appear in the accounts as follows:

Short-term investments	$143,850
Short-term investments, fair value adjustment . .	8,100
Total	$151,950

Note that the cost of the investments is maintained in one account and the adjustment to fair values is recorded in a separate account. Keeping the Short-Term Investments account at cost facilitates calculating realized gains or losses that must be recorded when securities are sold.

Depending on whether the fair value adjustment account has a debit or credit balance, it is added or subtracted from the cost to determine the fair value amount reported on the balance sheet. Bailey's December 31, 19X1, balance sheet includes the following:

Assets		
Current assets:		
Cash and cash equivalents	$ xx,xxx	
Short-term investments	151,950	
Accounts receivable	xxx,xxx	
Stockholders' Equity		
Contributed capital:		
Common stock	$xxx,xxx	
Retained earnings	xx,xxx	
Unrealized holding gain on securities held for sale	8,100	
Total stockholders' equity		$xxx,xxx

Notice that the unrealized holding gain is reported as a separate item in stockholders' equity. It is not reported on the income statement and is not closed to Retained Earnings. If the fair value of the securities available for sale had been less than cost, the **unrealized holding loss** would have appeared in stockholders' equity as a deduction.

When a short-term investment in securities available for sale is sold, the cash proceeds from the sale are compared with the cost of the investment to determine the *realized* gain or loss. This realized gain or loss is reported on the income statement and closed to Retained Earnings as part of the net income or loss.

For example, assume that on May 14, 19X2, Bailey sold its investment in Xerox common stock for $81,000. The entry to record the sale is

May	14	Cash	81,000.00	
		Short-Term Investments		70,750.00
		Gain on Sale of Short-Term Investments		10,250.00
		To record sale of Xerox common stock.		

Note that the realized gain is calculated by comparing the proceeds with cost, not with the previously reported fair value of the stock. Then, at the next balance sheet date, the unrealized gain or loss account is adjusted so the securities available for sale are reported at their new fair values.

For example, assume that Bailey did not buy or sell any other securities during 19X2. As a result, the securities available for sale on December 31, 19X2, include the Sears common stock and the Chrysler notes payable. The costs and December 31, 19X2, fair values of these securities are as follows:

Short-Term Investments in Securities Available for Sale on December 31, 19X2	Costs	Fair (Market) Values
Sears common stock	$42,600	$41,200
Chrysler notes payable	30,500	29,900
Total	$73,100	$71,100

Recall the December 31, 19X1, entry that recorded the $8,100 excess of fair values over costs. That entry gave the Short-Term Investments, Fair Value Adjustment account a debit balance of $8,100, and gave the Unrealized Holding Gain (Loss) account a credit balance of $8,100. On December 31, 19X2, these account balances must be revised to show that the $73,100 costs exceed the $71,100 fair values by $2,000. The required adjustments are calculated as follows:

	Short-Term Investments, Fair Value Adjustment	Unrealized Holding Gain (Loss)
Existing balances	$ 8,100 Debit	$ 8,100 Credit
Required balances, December 31, 19X2 . .	2,000 Credit	2,000 Debit
Necessary adjustment	$10,100 Credit	$10,100 Debit

The following adjusting entry updates the account balances:

Dec.	31	Unrealized Holding Gain (Loss)	10,100.00	
		Short-Term Investments, Fair Value Adjustment		10,100.00
		To reflect fair values of short-term investments in securities held for sale.		

Credit Sales and Receivables

In addition to cash, cash equivalents, and short-term investments, the liquid assets of a business include receivables that result from credit sales to customers. In the following sections, we discuss the procedures to account for sales when customers use credit cards issued by banks or credit card companies. Then, we focus on accounting for credit sales when a business grants credit directly to its customers. This situation requires the company (1) to maintain a separate account receivable for each customer and (2) to account for bad debts that result from credit sales. In addition, we discuss how to account for notes receivable, many of which arise from extending credit to customers.

Credit Card Sales

LO 2 Prepare entries to account for credit card sales.

Many customers use credit cards such as VISA, MasterCard, or American Express to charge purchases from various businesses. This practice gives the customers the ability to make purchases without carrying cash or writing checks. It also allows them to defer their payments to the credit card company. Further, once credit is established with the credit card company, the customer does not have to open an account with each store. Finally, customers who use credit cards can make single monthly payments instead of several to different creditors.

There are good reasons why businesses allow customers to use credit cards instead of maintaining their own accounts receivable. First, the business does not have to evaluate the credit standing of each customer or make decisions about who should get credit and how much. Second, the business avoids the risk of extending credit to customers who cannot or do not pay. Instead, this risk is faced by the credit card company. Third, the business typically receives cash from the credit card company sooner than it would if it granted credit directly to its customers.

In dealing with some credit cards, usually those issued by banks, the business deposits a copy of each credit card sales receipt in its bank account just like it deposits a customer's check. Thus, the business receives a credit to its checking account without delay. Other credit cards require the business to send a copy of each receipt to the credit card company. Until payment is received, the business has an account receivable from the credit card company. In return for the services provided by the credit card company, a business

AS A MATTER OF

Fact

A Return to the Past?

Before 1938, banks reported market (also known as fair or current) values for financial instruments. A return to market value reporting is now occurring, driven by the S&L and banking crisis. Ironically, it was another financial disaster, the Great Depression, that fueled the 1938 conversion from market value to historical cost financial reporting.

In the late 1920s and early 1930s, bank examiners were concerned primarily with protecting bank depositors (Federal Deposit Insurance Corp. protection did not exist). During this time, examiners determined market values for bank assets and liabilities to arrive at bank equity. If a bank's liabilities exceeded or even approximated its assets, its capital was determined to be impaired.

To satisfy regulatory capital requirements, problem bank owners had to provide additional capital, merge with another bank or close. At the onset of the Depression, bank examiners generally were blamed for excessive bank closings and the troubled economy. This set the stage for a series of bank conferences with regulators in 1938 at which bank asset appraisal procedures were relaxed.

Source: Dan W. Swenson and Thomas E. Buttross, "A Return to the Past: Disclosing Market Values of Financial Instruments." Reprinted with permission from the *Journal of Accountancy,* January 1993, pp. 71–77. Opinions of the authors are their own and do not necessarily reflect policies of the AICPA.

pays a fee ranging from 2 to 5% of credit card sales. This charge is deducted from the credit to the checking account or the cash payment to the business.

The procedures used in accounting for credit card sales depend on whether cash is received immediately on deposit or is delayed until paid by the credit card company. If cash is received immediately, the entry to record \$100 of credit card sales with a 4% fee is

Jan.	25	Cash	96.00	
		Credit Card Expense	4.00	
		Sales		100.00
		To record credit card sales less a 4% credit card expense.		

If the business must send the receipts to the credit card company and wait for payment, this entry on the date of the sale records them:

Jan.	25	Accounts Receivable, Credit Card Company	100.00	
		Sales		100.00
		To record credit card sales.		

When cash is received from the credit card company, the entry to record the receipt and the deduction of the fee is

Feb.	10	Cash	96.00	
		Credit Card Expense	4.00	
		Accounts Receivable, Credit Card Company		100.00
		To record cash receipt less 4% credit card expense.		

In the last two entries, notice that the credit card expense was not recorded until cash was received from the credit card company. This practice is merely a matter of convenience. By following this procedure, the business avoids having to calculate and record the credit card expense each time sales are recorded. Instead, the expense related to many sales can be calculated once and recorded when cash is received. However, the *matching principle* requires reporting credit card expense in the same period as the sale. Therefore, if the sale and the cash receipt occur in different periods, the seller accrues and reports the credit card expense in the period of the sale by using an adjusting entry at the end of the year. For example, this year-end adjustment accrues $24 of credit card expense on a $600 receivable that the Credit Card Company has not yet paid.

Dec.	31	Credit Card Expense	24.00	
		Accounts Receivable, Credit Card Company .		24.00
		To accrue credit card expense that is unrecorded at the end of the year.		

Then, the following entry records the cash collection in January:

Jan.	5	Cash	576.00	
		Accounts Receivable, Credit Card Company .		576.00
		To record collection of the amount due from Credit Card Company.		

Some firms report credit card expense in the income statement as a type of discount that is deducted from sales to get net sales. Other companies classify it as a selling expense or even as an administrative expense. Arguments can be made for all three alternatives but there is little practical difference in the result.

Maintaining a Separate Account for Each Credit Customer

LO 3 Prepare entries to account for transactions with credit customers, including accounting for bad debts under the allowance method and the direct write-off method.

In previous chapters, we recorded credit sales by debiting a single Accounts Receivable account. However, a business with more than one credit customer must design its accounting system to show how much each customer has purchased, how much each customer has paid, and how much remains to be collected from each customer. This information provides the basis for sending bills to the customers. To have this information on hand, businesses that extend credit directly to their customers must maintain a separate account receivable for each of them.

One possible way of keeping a separate account for each customer would be to include all of these accounts in the same ledger that contains the financial statement accounts. However, this approach is usually not used because there are too many customers. Instead, the **General Ledger,** which is the ledger that contains the financial statement accounts, has only a single Accounts Receivable account. In addition, a supplementary record is established in which a separate account is maintained for each customer. This supplementary record is the **Accounts Receivable Ledger.**

Illustration 7–1 shows the relationship between the Accounts Receivable account in the General Ledger and the individual customer accounts in the Accounts Receivable Ledger. In Part A of Illustration 7–1, notice that the $3,000 sum of the two balances in the Accounts Receivable Ledger is equal to the balance of the Accounts Receivable account in the General Ledger as of February 1. To maintain this relationship, each time that credit sales are

ILLUSTRATION 7-1 *The Accounts Receivable Account and the Accounts Receivable Ledger*

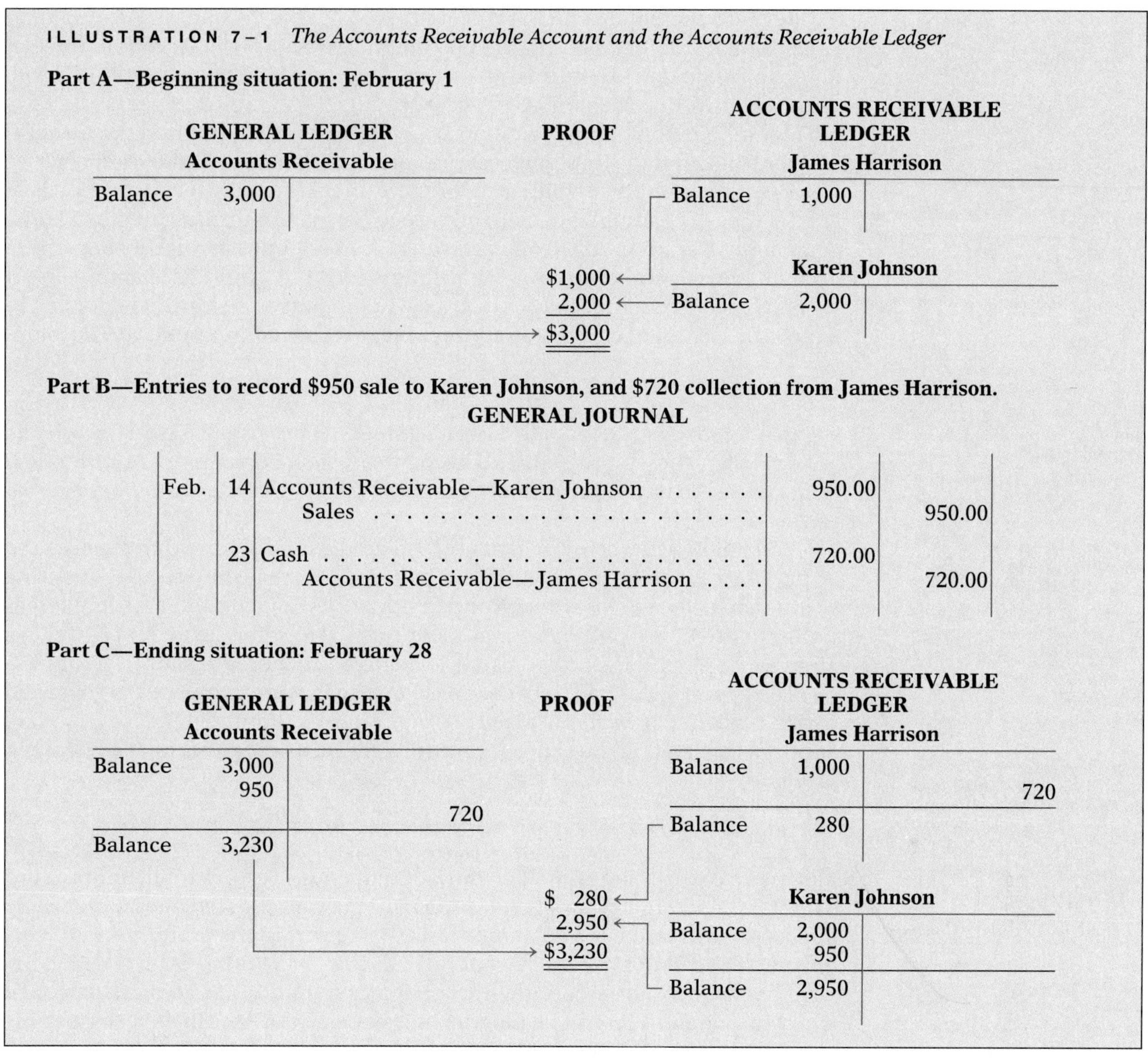

Part B—Entries to record $950 sale to Karen Johnson, and $720 collection from James Harrison.

GENERAL JOURNAL

Feb.	14	Accounts Receivable—Karen Johnson	950.00	
		Sales		950.00
	23	Cash	720.00	
		Accounts Receivable—James Harrison		720.00

posted with a debit to the Accounts Receivable account in the General Ledger, they are also posted with debits to the appropriate customer accounts in the Accounts Receivable Ledger. Also, cash receipts from credit customers must be posted with credits to both the Accounts Receivable account in the General Ledger and to the appropriate customer accounts.

Part C—Ending situation: February 28
GENERAL LEDGER
Accounts Receivable
Balance 3,000
950
720
Balance 3,230
PROOF
$ 280
2,950
$3,230
ACCOUNTS RECEIVABLE LEDGER
James Harrison
Balance 1,000
720
Balance 280
Karen Johnson
Balance 2,000
950
Balance 2,950

Part B shows the general journal entry to record a credit sale on February 14 to customer Karen Johnson. It also shows the entry to record the collection of $720 from James Harrison.

Part C presents the general ledger account and the Accounts Receivable Ledger as of February 28. Notice how the General Ledger account shows the effects of the sales and the collection, and that it has a $3,230 balance. The same events are reflected in the accounts for the two customers: Harrison now has a balance of only $280, and Johnson owes $2,950. The $3,230 sum of their accounts equals the debit balance of the General Ledger account.

Note that posting debits or credits to Accounts Receivable twice does not violate the requirement that debits equal credits. The equality of debits and credits is maintained *in the General Ledger.* The Accounts Receivable Ledger is simply a supplementary record that provides detailed information concerning each customer.

Because the balance in the Accounts Receivable account is always equal to the sum of the balances in the customers' accounts, the Accounts Receivable account is said to control the Accounts Receivable Ledger and is an example of a **controlling account.** Also, the Accounts Receivable Ledger is an example of a supplementary record that is controlled by an account in the General Ledger; this kind of supplementary record is called a **subsidiary ledger.**

The Accounts Receivable account and the Accounts Receivable Ledger are not the only examples of controlling accounts and subsidiary ledgers. Most companies buy on credit from several suppliers and must use a controlling account and subsidiary ledger for accounts payable. Another example might be an Office Equipment account that would control a subsidiary ledger in which the cost of each item of equipment is recorded in a separate account.

Bad Debts

When a company grants credit to its customers, there usually are a few who do not pay what they promised. The accounts of such customers are called **bad debts.** These bad debt amounts that cannot be collected are an expense of selling on credit.

You might ask why merchants sell on credit if it is likely that some of the accounts prove to be uncollectible. The answer is that they believe granting credit increases revenues and profits. They are willing to incur bad debt losses if the net effect is to increase sales and profits. Therefore, bad debt losses are an expense of selling on credit that is incurred to increase sales.

The reporting of bad debts expense on the income statement is governed by the *matching principle.* This principle requires that the expense from bad debts be reported in the same accounting period as the revenues they helped produce.

Matching Bad Debt Expenses with Sales

Managers realize that some portion of credit sales result in bad debts. However, the fact that a specific credit sale will not be collected does not become apparent until later. If a customer fails to pay within the credit period, most businesses send out several repeat billings and make other efforts to collect. Usually, they do not accept the fact that a customer is not going to pay until every reasonable means of collection has been exhausted. In many cases, this point may not be reached until one or more accounting periods after the period in which the sale was made. Thus, matching this expense with the revenue it produced requires the company to estimate its unknown amount at the end of the year. The **allowance method of accounting for bad debts** accomplishes this matching of bad debts expense with revenues.

Allowance Method of Accounting for Bad Debts

At the end of each accounting period, the allowance method of accounting for bad debts requires estimating the total bad debts expected to result from the period's sales. An allowance is then provided for the loss. This method has two advantages: (1) the expense is charged to the period in which the revenue is recognized; and (2) the accounts receivable are reported on the balance sheet at the estimated amount of cash to be collected.

Recording the Estimated Bad Debts Expense

Under the allowance method of accounting for bad debts, the seller calculates bad debts expense at the end of each accounting period. Then, it is recorded with an adjusting entry. For example, assume that Fritz Company had credit sales of $300,000 during the first year of its operations. At the end of the year, $20,000 remains uncollected. Based on the experience of similar businesses,

Fritz Company estimates that $1,500 of accounts receivable will be uncollectible. This estimated expense is recorded with the following adjusting entry:

Dec.	31	Bad Debts Expense	1,500.00	
		Allowance for Doubtful Accounts		1,500.00
		To record the estimated bad debts.		

The debit in this entry causes the expense to appear on the income statement of the year in which the sales were made. As a result, the estimated $1,500 expense of selling on credit is matched with the $300,000 of revenue it helped produce.

Note that the credit of the entry is to a contra account called **Allowance for Doubtful Accounts.** A contra account must be used because at the time of the adjusting entry, you do not know which customers will not pay. Therefore, because specific bad accounts are not identifiable at the time of the adjusting entry, they cannot be removed from the subsidiary Accounts Receivable Ledger. Because the customer accounts are left in the subsidiary ledger, the controlling account for Accounts Receivable cannot be reduced. Instead, the Allowance for Doubtful Accounts account *must* be credited.

Bad Debts in the Accounts and in the Financial Statements

The process of evaluating customers and approving them for credit usually is not assigned to the selling department of a business. Otherwise, given the primary objective of increasing sales, the selling department might not use good judgment in approving customers for credit. Because the sales department is not responsible for granting credit, it should not be held responsible for bad debts expense. Therefore, bad debts expense normally appears on the income statement as an administrative expense rather than a selling expense.

Recall from the previous example that Fritz Company has $20,000 of outstanding accounts receivable at the end of its first year of operations. Thus, after the bad debts adjusting entry is posted, the company's Accounts Receivable and Allowance for Doubtful Accounts accounts show these balances:

Accounts Receivable

Dec. 31	20,000		

Allowance for Doubtful Accounts

		Dec. 31	1,500

The Allowance for Doubtful Accounts credit balance of $1,500 has the effect of reducing accounts receivable (net of the allowance) to their estimated **realizable value.** The term *realizable value* means the expected proceeds from converting the assets into cash. Although $20,000 is legally owed to Fritz Company by all of its customers, only $18,500 is likely to be realized in cash collections from customers.

When the balance sheet is prepared, the allowance for doubtful accounts is subtracted from the accounts receivable to show the amount that is expected to be realized from the accounts. For example, this information could be reported as follows:

Current assets:		
Cash and cash equivalents		$11,300
Short-term investments, at fair market value (cost is $16,200)		14,500
Accounts receivable	$20,000	
Less allowance for doubtful accounts	(1,500)	18,500
Merchandise inventory		52,700
Prepaid expenses		1,100
Total current assets		$98,100

In this example, compare the presentations of short-term investments and accounts receivable, and note that contra accounts are subtracted in both cases. Even though the contra account to the Short-Term Investments account is not shown on the statement, you can easily determine that its balance is $1,700 by comparing the $16,200 cost with the $14,500 net amount. Sometimes, the contra account to Accounts Receivable is presented in a similar fashion, as follows:

Accounts receivable (net of $1,500 estimated uncollectible accounts)	$18,500

Writing Off a Bad Debt

When specific accounts are identified as uncollectible, they are written off against the Allowance for Doubtful Accounts. For example, after spending a year trying to collect from Jack Vale, the Fritz Company finally decided that his $100 account was uncollectible and made the following entry to write it off:

Jan.	23	Allowance for Doubtful Accounts	100.00	
		Accounts Receivable—Jack Vale		100.00
		To write off an uncollectible account.		

Posting the credit of the entry to the Accounts Receivable account removes the amount of the bad debt from the controlling account. Posting it to the Jack Vale account removes the amount of the bad debt from the subsidiary ledger. By removing it from the subsidiary ledger, Fritz Company avoids the cost of sending additional bills to Vale. After the entry is posted, the general ledger accounts appear as follows:

Accounts Receivable

Dec. 31	20,000		
		Jan. 23	100

Allowance for Doubtful Accounts

		Dec. 31	1,500
Jan. 23	100		

Notice two aspects of the entry and the accounts. First, although bad debts are an expense of selling on credit, the allowance account is debited in the write-off. The expense account is *not* debited. The expense account is not debited because the estimated expense was previously recorded at the end of the period in which the sale occurred. At that time, the expense was estimated and recorded with an adjusting entry.

Second, although the write-off removed the amount of the account receivable from the ledgers, it did not affect the estimated realizable value of Fritz Company's net accounts receivable, as the following tabulation shows:

	Before	**After**
Accounts receivable	$20,000	$19,900
Less allowance for doubtful accounts . . .	1,500	1,400
Estimated realizable accounts receivable . .	$18,500	$18,500

Thus, neither total assets nor net income are affected by the decision to write off a specific account. However, both total assets and net income are affected by the recognition of the year's bad debts expense in the adjusting entry. Again, a primary purpose of writing off a specific account is to avoid the cost of additional collection efforts.

Bad Debt Recoveries

When a customer fails to pay and the account is written off, his or her credit standing is jeopardized. Therefore, the customer may choose to voluntarily pay all or part of the amount owed after the account is written off as uncollectible. This payment helps restore the credit standing. Thus, when this event happens, it should be recorded in the customer's subsidiary account where the information will be retained for use in future credit evaluations.

When a company collects an account that was previously written off, it makes two journal entries. The first reverses the original write-off and reinstates the customer's account. The second entry records the collection of the reinstated account. For example, assume that on August 15 Jack Vale pays in full the account that Fritz Company had previously written off. The entries to record the bad debt recovery are

Aug.	15	Accounts Receivable—Jack Vale	100.00	
		Allowance for Doubtful Accounts		100.00
		To reinstate the account of Jack Vale written off on January 23.		
	15	Cash	100.00	
		Accounts Receivable—Jack Vale		100.00
		Received full payment of account.		

In this case, Jack Vale paid the entire amount previously written off. In other situations, the customer may pay only a portion of the amount owed. The question then arises of whether the entire balance of the account should be returned to accounts receivable or just the amount paid. The answer is a matter of judgment. If you believe the customer will later pay in full, the entire amount owed should be recorded. However, only the amount paid should be recorded if you believe that no more will be collected.

Estimating the Amount of Bad Debts Expense

As you already learned, the allowance method of accounting for bad debts requires an adjusting entry at the end of each accounting period to record management's estimate of the bad debts expense for the period. That entry takes the following form:

Dec.	31	Bad Debts Expense	????	
		Allowance for Doubtful Accounts		????
		To record the estimated bad debts.		

How does a business determine the amount to record in this entry? There are two alternative approaches. One focuses on the income statement relationship between bad debts expense and sales. The other focuses on the balance sheet relationship between accounts receivable and the allowance for doubtful accounts. Both alternatives require a careful analysis of past experience.

Estimating Bad Debts by Focusing on the Income Statement

The income statement approach to estimating bad debts is based on the idea that some particular percentage of a company's credit sales for the period will become uncollectible.[5] Hence, in the income statement, the amount of bad debts expense should equal that amount.

[5] Note that the factor to be considered is *credit* sales. Naturally, cash sales do not produce bad debts, and they generally should not be used in the calculation. However, if cash sales are relatively small compared to credit sales, there is no practical difference in the result.

For example, suppose that Baker Company had credit sales of $400,000 in 19X2. Based on past experience and the experience of similar companies, Baker Company estimates that 0.6% of credit sales will be uncollectible. Using this prediction, Baker Company can expect $2,400 of bad debts expense to result from the year's sales ($400,000 × 0.006 = $2,400). The adjusting entry to record this estimated expense is

Dec.	31	Bad Debts Expense	2,400.00	
		Allowance for Doubtful Accounts		2,400.00
		To record the estimated bad debts.		

This entry does not mean the December 31, 19X2, balance in Allowance for Doubtful Accounts will be $2,400. A $2,400 balance would occur only if the account had a zero balance immediately prior to posting the adjusting entry. For several reasons, however, the unadjusted balance of Allowance for Doubtful Accounts is not likely to be zero.

First, unless Baker Company was created during the current year, the Allowance for Doubtful Accounts would have had a credit balance at the beginning of the year. The beginning-of-year credit balance would have resulted from entries made in past years to record estimated bad debts expense and to write off uncollectible accounts. The cumulative effect of these entries would show up as a credit balance at the beginning of the current year.

Second, because bad debts expense must be estimated each year, the total amount of expense recorded in past years is not likely to equal the amounts that were written off as uncollectible. Although annual expense estimates are based on past experience, some residual difference between recorded expenses and amounts written off should be expected to show up in the unadjusted Allowance for Doubtful Accounts balance.

Third, some of the amounts written off as uncollectible during the current year probably relate to credit sales made during the current year. These debits affect the unadjusted Allowance for Doubtful Accounts balance. In fact, they may cause the account to have a debit balance prior to posting the adjusting entry for bad debts expense.

For these reasons, you should not expect the Allowance for Doubtful Accounts to have an unadjusted balance of zero at the end of the year. As we stated earlier, this means that the adjusted balance reported on the balance sheet normally does not equal the amount of expense reported on the income statement.

Remember that expressing bad debts expense as a percentage of sales is an estimate based on past experience. As new experience is gained over time, the percentage used may appear to have been too large or too small. When this happens, a different rate should be used in future periods.

Estimating Bad Debts by Focusing on the Balance Sheet

The balance sheet approach to estimating bad debts is based on the idea that some portion of the end-of-period accounts receivable balance will not be collected. From this point of view, the goal of the bad debts adjusting entry is to make the Allowance for Doubtful Accounts balance equal to the portion of outstanding accounts receivable estimated to be uncollectible. To obtain this required balance in the Allowance for Doubtful Accounts account, simply compare its balance before the adjustment with the required balance. The difference between the two is debited to Bad Debts Expense and credited to Allowance for Doubtful Accounts. Estimating the required balance of the Allowance account can be done in two ways: (1) by the simplified approach and (2) by aging the accounts receivable.

The Simplified Balance Sheet Approach. Using the simplified balance sheet approach, a company estimates that a certain percentage of its outstanding receivables will prove to be uncollectible. This estimated percentage is based on past experience and the experience of similar companies. It also may be affected by current conditions such as recent prosperity or economic difficulties faced by the firm's customers. Then, the total dollar amount of all outstanding receivables is multiplied by the estimated percentage to determine the estimated dollar amount of uncollectible accounts. This amount must appear in the balance sheet as the balance of the Allowance for Doubtful Accounts. To put this balance in the account, you must prepare an adjusting entry that debits Bad Debts Expense and credits Allowance for Doubtful Accounts. The amount of the adjustment is the amount necessary to provide the required balance in Allowance for Doubtful Accounts.

For example, assume that Baker Company (of the previous illustration) has $50,000 of outstanding accounts receivable on December 31, 19X2. Past experience suggests that 5% of the outstanding receivables are uncollectible. Thus, after the adjusting entry is posted, the Allowance for Doubtful Accounts should have a $2,500 credit balance (5% of $50,000). Assume that before the adjustment the account appears as follows:

Allowance for Doubtful Accounts

		Dec. 31, 19X1, balance	2,000
Feb. 6	800		
July 10	600		
Nov. 20	400		
		Unadjusted balance	200

The $2,000 beginning balance appeared on the December 31, 19X1, balance sheet. During 19X2, accounts of specific customers were written off on February 6, July 10, and November 20. As a result, the account has a $200 credit balance prior to the December 31, 19X2, adjustment. The adjusting entry to give the Allowance the required $2,500 balance is

Dec.	31	Bad Debts Expense	2,300.00	
		Allowance for Doubtful Accounts		2,300.00
		To record the estimated bad debts.		

After this entry is posted, the Allowance has a $2,500 credit balance, as shown here:

Allowance for Doubtful Accounts

		Dec. 31, 19X1, balance	2,000
Feb. 6	800		
July 10	600		
Nov. 20	400		
		Unadjusted balance	200
		Dec. 31	2,300
		Dec. 31, 19X2, balance	2,500

Aging Accounts Receivable. Both the income statement approach and the simplified balance sheet approach use knowledge gained from past experience to estimate the amount of bad debts expense. Another balance sheet approach produces a more refined estimate based on past experience and on information about current conditions.

ILLUSTRATION 7–2 *Estimating Bad Debts by Aging the Accounts*

BAKER COMPANY
Schedule of Accounts Receivable by Age
December 31, 19X2

Customer's Name	Total	Not Due	1 to 30 Days Past Due	31 to 60 Days Past Due	61 to 90 Days Past Due	Over 90 Days Past Due
Charles Abbot	$ 450.00	$ 450.00				
Frank Allen	710.00			$ 710.00		
George Arden	500.00	300.00	$ 200.00			
Paul Baum	740.00				$ 100.00	$ 640.00
ZZ Services	1,000.00	810.00	190.00			
Totals	$49,900.00	$37,000.00	$6,500.00	$3,500.00	$1,900.00	$1,000.00
Rate		×2%	×5%	×10%	×25%	×40%
Estimated uncollectible accounts . . .	$ 2,290.00	$ 740.00	$ 325.00	$ 350.00	$ 475.00	$ 400.00

This method involves **aging of accounts receivable.** Under this method, each account receivable is examined in the process of estimating the amount that is uncollectible. Specifically, the receivables are classified by how long they have been outstanding. Then, estimates of uncollectible amounts are made under the assumption that the longer an amount is outstanding, the more likely it will be uncollectible.

To age the accounts receivable outstanding at the end of the period, you must examine each account and classify the outstanding amounts in terms of how much time has passed since they were created. The selection of the classes to be used depends on the judgment of each company's management. However, the classes are often based on 30-day (or one month) periods. After the outstanding amounts have been classified (or aged), past experience is used to estimate a percentage of each class that will become uncollectible. These percentages are applied to the amounts in the classes to determine the required balance of the Allowance for Doubtful Accounts. The calculation is completed by setting up a schedule like the one in Illustration 7–2 for Baker Company.

In Illustration 7–2, notice that each customer's account is listed with its total balance. Then, each balance is allocated to five categories based on the age of the unpaid charges that make up the balance. (In computerized systems, this allocation is done automatically.) When all accounts have been aged, the amounts in each category are totaled and multiplied by the estimated percentage of uncollectible accounts for each category.

For example, in Illustration 7–2, Baker Company is owed $3,500 that is 31 to 60 days past due. Baker's management estimates that 10% of the amounts in this age category will not be collected. Thus, the dollar amount of uncollectible accounts in this category is $350 ($3,500 × 10%). The total in the first column tells us that the adjusted balance in Baker Company's Allowance for Doubtful Accounts should be $2,290 ($740 + $325 + $350 + $475 + $400). Because the Allowance has an unadjusted credit balance of $200, the aging of accounts receivable approach requires the following change in its balance:

Unadjusted balance	$ 200 credit
Required balance	2,290 credit
Required adjustment	$2,090 credit

As a result, Baker should record the following adjusting entry:

Dec.	31	Bad Debts Expense	2,090.00	
		Allowance for Doubtful Accounts		2,090.00
		To record the estimated bad debts.		

For instructional purposes, suppose that Baker's Allowance had an unadjusted *debit* balance of $500. In this case, the calculation of the adjustment amount and the entry would be:

Unadjusted balance	$ 500 debit
Required balance	2,290 credit
Required adjustment	$2,790 credit

Dec.	31	Bad Debts Expense	2,790.00	
		Allowance for Doubtful Accounts		2,790.00
		To record the estimated bad debts.		

Recall from page 270 that when the income statement approach was used, Baker's bad debts expense for 19X2 was estimated to be $2,400. When the simplified balance sheet approach was used (see page 271), the estimate was $2,300. And when aging of accounts receivable was used the first time, the estimate was $2,090. Do not be surprised that the amounts are different; after all, each approach is only an estimate of what will prove to be true. However, the aging of accounts receivable is based on a more detailed examination of specific outstanding accounts and is usually the most reliable.[6]

Direct Write-Off Method of Accounting for Bad Debts

The allowance method of accounting for bad debts satisfies the requirements of the *matching principle.* Therefore, it is the method that should be used in most cases. However, another method may be suitable under certain limited circumstances. Under this **direct write-off method of accounting for bad debts,** no attempt is made to estimate uncollectible accounts or bad debts expense at the end of each period. In fact, no adjusting entry is made. Instead, bad debts expense is recorded when specific accounts are written off as uncollectible. For example, note the following entry to write off a $52 uncollectible account:

Nov.	23	Bad Debts Expense	52.00	
		Accounts Receivable—Dale Hall		52.00
		To write off the uncollectible account under the direct write-off method.		

[6] In many cases, the aging analysis is supplemented with information about specific customers that allows management to decide whether those accounts should be classified as uncollectible. This information often is supplied by the sales and credit department managers.

The debit of the entry charges the uncollectible amount directly to the current year's Bad Debts Expense account. The credit removes the balance of the account from the subsidiary ledger and from the controlling account.

If an account previously written off directly to Bad Debts Expense is later collected in full, the following entries record the recovery:

Mar.	11	Accounts Receivable—Dale Hall	52.00	
		Bad Debts Expense		52.00
		To reinstate the account of Dale Hall previously written off.		
	11	Cash	52.00	
		Accounts Receivable—Dale Hall		52.00
		In full payment of account.		

Sometimes an amount previously written off directly to Bad Debts Expense is recovered in the year following the write-off. If there is no balance in the Bad Debts Expense account from previous write-offs and no other write-offs are expected, the credit portion of the entry recording the recovery can be made to a Bad Debt Recoveries revenue account.

The direct write-off method usually mismatches revenues and expenses. The mismatch occurs because bad debts expense is not recorded until an account becomes uncollectible, which often does not occur during the same period as the credit sale. Despite this weakness, the direct write-off method may be used when a company's bad debts expenses are very small in relation to other financial statement items such as total sales and net income. In such cases, the direct write-off method is justified by the materiality principle, which we explain next.

The Materiality Principle

The basic idea of the **materiality principle** is that the requirements of accounting principles may be ignored if the effect on the financial statements is unimportant to their users. In other words, failure to follow the requirements of an accounting principle is acceptable when the failure does not produce an error or misstatement large enough to influence a financial statement reader's judgment of a given situation.

Installment Accounts and Notes Receivable

Many companies allow their credit customers to make periodic payments over several months. When this is done, the selling company's assets may be in the form of **installment accounts receivable** or notes receivable. As is true for other accounts receivable, the evidence behind installment accounts receivable includes sales slips or invoices that describe the sales transactions. A note receivable, on the other hand, is a written document that promises payment and is signed by the customer. In either case, when payments are made over several months or if the credit period is long, the customer is usually charged interest. Although the credit period of installment accounts and notes receivable may be more than one year, they should be classified as current assets if the company regularly offers customers such terms.

Generally, creditors prefer notes receivable over accounts receivable when the credit period is long and the receivable relates to a single sale for a fairly large amount. Notes are also used to replace accounts receivable when customers ask for additional time to pay their past-due accounts. In these situations, creditors prefer notes to accounts receivable for legal reasons. If a

ILLUSTRATION 7–3 *A Promissory Note*

$1,000.00 Eugene, Oregon March 9, 19X1

Thirty days after date I promise to pay to

the order of Frank Tomlinson

One thousand and no / 100 -- dollars

for value received with interest at 12%

payable at First National Bank of Eugene, Oregon

Hugo Brown

lawsuit is needed to collect from a customer, a note represents a clear written acknowledgment by the debtor of the debt, its amount, and its terms.

Promissory Notes

LO 4 Calculate the interest on promissory notes and prepare entries to record the receipt of promissory notes and their payment or dishonor.

A **promissory note** is an unconditional written promise to pay a definite sum of money on demand or at a fixed or determinable future date. In the promissory note in Illustration 7–3, Hugo Brown promises to pay Frank Tomlinson or to his order (that is, according to Tomlinson's instructions) a definite sum of money ($1,000), called the **principal of the note,** at a fixed future date (April 8, 19X1). As the one who signed the note and promised to pay it at maturity, Hugo Brown is the **maker of the note.** As the person to whom the note is payable, Frank Tomlinson is the **payee of the note.** To Hugo Brown, the illustrated note is a liability called a *note payable.* To Frank Tomlinson, the same note is an asset called a *note receivable.*

The Hugo Brown note bears **interest** at 12%. Interest is the charge assessed for the use of money. To a borrower, interest is an expense. To a lender, it is a revenue. The rate of interest that a note bears is stated on the note.

Calculating Interest

Unless otherwise stated, the rate of interest on a note is the rate charged for the use of the principal for one year. The formula for calculating interest is

$$\begin{matrix}\text{Principal} & & \text{Annual} & & \text{Time of the} & & \\ \text{of the} & \times & \text{rate of} & \times & \text{note expressed} & = & \text{Interest} \\ \text{note} & & \text{interest} & & \text{in years} & & \end{matrix}$$

For example, interest on a $1,000, 12%, six-month note is calculated as:

$$\$1{,}000 \times 12\% \times \frac{6}{12} = \$60$$

The **maturity date of a note** is the day on which the note (principal and interest) must be repaid. Many notes mature in less than a full year, and the period covered by them is often expressed in days. When the time of a note is expressed in days, the maturity date is the specified number of days after the note's date. As a simple example, a one-day note dated June 15 matures and is due on June 16. Also, a 90-day note dated July 10 matures on October 8. This October 8 due date is calculated as follows:

Number of days in July	31
Minus the date of the note	10
Gives the number of days the note runs in July	21
Add the number of days in August	31
Add the number of days in September	30
Total through September 30	82
Days in October needed to equal the 90-day time of the note, also the maturity date of the note (October 8)	8
Total time the note runs in days	90

In other situations, the period of a note is expressed in months. In these cases, the note matures and is payable in the month of its maturity on the same day of the month as its original date. For example, a three-month note dated July 10 is payable on October 10.

To simplify interest calculations for notes that have periods expressed in days, a common practice has been to treat a year as having just 360 days. Although this practice is not applied as frequently as it used to be, we use it in this book to make it easier for you to work the exercises and problems assigned by your instructor. We also assume a 360-day year in the following discussion. Suppose, for example, that there is a 90-day, 12%, $1,000 note. The amount of interest is calculated as follows:

$$\text{Interest} = \text{Principal} \times \text{Rate} \times \frac{\text{Exact days}}{360}$$

or

$$\text{Interest} = \$1{,}000 \times 12\% \times \frac{90}{360} = \$30$$

Recording the Receipt of a Note

To simplify record-keeping, notes receivable are usually recorded in a single Notes Receivable account. Only one account is needed because the individual original notes are on hand. Therefore, the maker, rate of interest, due date, and other information may be learned by examining each note.[7]

When a company receives a note at the time of a sale, an entry such as this one is recorded:

Dec.	5	Notes Receivable	650.00	
		Sales		650.00
		Sold merchandise, terms six-month, 9% note.		

A business also may accept a note from an overdue customer as a way of granting a time extension on the past-due account receivable. When this happens, the business may collect part of the past-due balance in cash. This partial payment forces a concession from the customer, reduces the customer's debt (and the seller's risk), and produces a note for a smaller amount. For example, Symplex Company agrees to accept $232 in cash and a $600, 60-day, 15% note from Joseph Cook to settle his $832 past-due account. Symplex makes the following entry to record the receipt of the cash and note:

[7] If the company holds a large number of notes, it may be more efficient to set up a controlling account and a subsidiary ledger.

Oct.	5	Cash	232.00	
		Notes Receivable	600.00	
		Accounts Receivable—Joseph Cook		832.00
		Received cash and a note in settlement of an account.		

When Cook pays the note on the due date, Symplex records the receipt as follows:

Dec.	4	Cash	615.00	
		Notes Receivable		600.00
		Interest Earned		15.00
		Collected the Joseph Cook note, including interest of $600 × 15% × 60/360.		

Dishonored Notes Receivable

Sometimes, the maker of a note is not able to pay the note at maturity. When a note's maker is unable or refuses to pay at maturity, the note is said to be dishonored. This act of **dishonoring a note** does not relieve the maker of the obligation to pay. Furthermore, the payee should use every legitimate means to collect. However, collection may require lengthy legal proceedings.

The usual practice is to have the balance of the Notes Receivable account show only the amount of notes that have not matured. Therefore, when a note is dishonored, the lender removes the amount of the note from the Notes Receivable account and charges it back to an account receivable from its maker. To illustrate, Symplex Company holds an $800, 12%, 60-day note of George Hart. At maturity, Hart dishonors the note. To remove the dishonored note from the Notes Receivable account, the company makes the following entry:

Oct.	14	Accounts Receivable—George Hart	816.00	
		Interest Earned		16.00
		Notes Receivable		800.00
		To charge the account of George Hart for his dishonored note, including interest of $800 × 12% × 60/360.		

Charging a dishonored note back to the account of its maker serves two purposes. First, it removes the amount of the note from the Notes Receivable account, leaving in the account only notes that have not matured. It also records the dishonored note in the maker's account. The second purpose is important. If the maker of the dishonored note again applies for credit in the future, his or her account will show all past dealings, including the dishonored note. Restoring the account also reminds the business to continue collection efforts.

Note that Hart owes both the principal and the interest. Therefore, the entry records the full amount owed in Hart's account and credits the interest to Interest Earned. This procedure assures that the interest will be included in future efforts to collect from Hart.

End-of-Period Adjustments

When notes receivable are outstanding at the end of an accounting period, the accrued interest should be calculated and recorded. This procedure recognizes the interest revenue when it is earned and recognizes the additional asset owned by the note's holder. For example, on December 16, Perry Company accepted a $3,000, 60-day, 12% note from a customer in granting an extension on a past-due account. When the company's accounting period ends on December 31, $15 of interest will have accrued on this note ($\$3,000 \times 12\% \times 15/360$). The following adjusting entry records this revenue:

Dec.	31	Interest Receivable	15.00	
		Interest Earned		15.00
		To record accrued interest.		

The adjusting entry causes the interest earned to appear on the income statement of the period in which it was earned. It also causes the interest receivable to appear on the balance sheet as a current asset.

Collecting Previously Accrued Interest

When the note is collected, Perry Company's entry to record the cash receipt is

Feb.	14	Cash	3,060.00	
		Interest Earned		45.00
		Interest Receivable		15.00
		Notes Receivable		3,000.00
		Received payment of a note and its interest.		

Observe that the entry's credit to Interest Receivable records collection of the interest accrued at the end of the previous period. Only the $45 of interest earned between January 1 and February 14 is recorded as revenue.

Converting Receivables into Cash before They Are Due

LO 5 Explain how receivables can be converted into cash before they are due, and calculate accounts receivable turnover.

Many companies grant credit to customers and then hold the receivables until they are paid by the customers. However, some companies convert receivables into cash without waiting until they are due. This is done either by selling the receivables or by using them as security for a loan. In certain industries such as textiles and furniture, this has been a common practice for years. More recently, the practice has spread to other industries.

Selling Accounts Receivable

A business may sell its accounts receivable to a finance company or bank. The buyer, which is called a *factor*, charges the seller a *factoring fee* and then collects the receivables as they come due. By incurring the factoring fee cost, the seller receives the cash earlier and passes the risk of bad debts to the factor. The seller also avoids the cost of billing and accounting for the receivables.

For example, assume that a business sells $20,000 of its accounts receivable and is charged a 2% factoring fee. The seller records the sale with the following entry:

Aug.	15	Cash	19,600.00	
		Factoring Fee Expense	400.00	
		Accounts Receivable		20,000.00
		Sold accounts receivable for cash, less a 2% factoring fee.		

Pledging Accounts Receivable as Security for a Loan

When a business borrows money and pledges its accounts receivable as security for the loan, the business records the loan with an entry such as the following:

Aug.	20	Cash	35,000.00	
		Notes Payable		35,000.00
		Borrowed money on a note secured by the pledge of accounts receivable.		

Under the pledging arrangement, the risk of bad debts is not transferred to the lender. The borrower retains ownership of the receivables. However, if the borrower defaults on the loan, the creditor has the right to be paid from the cash receipts as the accounts receivable are collected.

Because pledged receivables are committed as security for a loan from a particular creditor, the borrower's financial statements should disclose the fact that accounts receivable have been pledged. For example, the following footnote to the financial statements provides the necessary information: "Accounts receivable in the amount of $40,000 are pledged as security for a $35,000 note payable to Western National Bank."

Discounting Notes Receivable

Notes receivable also can be converted into cash before they mature, usually by discounting the notes receivable at a bank. For example, if a company discounts a $50,000 note receivable at a cost of $700, it records the discounting with the following entry:

Aug.	25	Cash	49,300.00	
		Interest Expense	700.00	
		Notes Receivable		50,000.00
		Discounted a note receivable.		

Notes receivable may be discounted with recourse or without recourse. If a note is discounted with recourse and the original maker of the note fails to pay the bank when the note matures, the original payee of the note must pay. Thus, a company that discounts a note with recourse has a contingent liability until the bank is paid. A **contingent liability** is an obligation to make a future payment if and only if an uncertain future event actually occurs. The company should disclose the contingent liability in its financial statements with a footnote such as: "The company is contingently liable for a $50,000 note receivable discounted with recourse."

In the previous entry, notice the debit to Interest Expense. This indicates that the discounting transaction is understood to be a loan. In some cases, discounting a note with recourse is considered to be a sale.[8] When the transaction is a sale, the debit should be to Loss on Sale of Notes instead of to Interest Expense.

When a note is discounted *without recourse,* the bank assumes the risk of a bad debt loss and the original payee does not have a contingent liability. A note discounted without recourse is clearly understood to be sold.

---

[8] The criteria for deciding whether discounting with recourse is a loan or a sale are explained in more advanced accounting courses.

Full-Disclosure Principle

The disclosure of contingent liabilities in footnotes is consistent with the **full-disclosure principle.** This principle requires financial statements (including the footnotes) to present all relevant information about the operations and financial position of the entity. A company should report any facts important enough to affect a statement reader's evaluation of the company's operations, financial position, or cash flows. This principle does not require companies to report excessive detail. It simply means that significant information should not be withheld and that enough information should be provided to make the reports understandable. Examples of items that are reported to satisfy the full-disclosure principle include the following:

Contingent Liabilities. In addition to discounted notes, a company should disclose any items for which the company is contingently liable. Examples are possible additional tax assessments, debts of other parties that the company has guaranteed, and unresolved lawsuits against the company. Information about these facts helps users predict future events that might affect the company.

Long-Term Commitments under Contracts. A company should disclose that it has signed a long-term lease requiring material annual payments, even though the obligation does not appear in the accounts. Also, a company should reveal that it has pledged certain of its assets as security for loans. These facts show statement readers that the company has restricted its flexibility.

Accounting Methods Used. When more than one accounting method can be applied, a company must describe the one it uses, especially when the choice can materially affect reported net income.[9] For example, a company must describe the methods it uses to account for inventory and depreciation. (These methods are explained in future chapters.) This information helps users understand how the company determines its net income.

Using the Information—Accounts Receivable Turnover

In Chapter 6, you learned how to calculate *days' sales uncollected,* which provides information about the short-term liquidity of a company. In evaluating short-term liquidity, you also may want to calculate **accounts receivable turnover.** The formula for this ratio is

$$\text{Accounts receivable turnover} = \frac{\text{Net sales}}{\text{Average accounts receivable}}$$

Recall that days' sales uncollected relates to the accounts receivable balance at the end of the year. In contrast, notice that the denominator in the turnover formula is the average accounts receivable balance during the year. The average is often calculated as:

$$\frac{\text{The beginning balance} + \text{The ending balance}}{2}$$

This method of estimating the average balance provides a useful result if the seasonal changes in the accounts receivable balances during the year are not too large.

[9] FASB, *Accounting Standards—Current Text* (Norwalk, CT, 1993), sec. A10.105. First published as *APB Opinion No. 22,* pars. 12, 13.

Accounts receivable turnover indicates how often the company converted its average accounts receivable balance into cash during the year. Thus, a turnover of 12 suggests that the average accounts receivable balance was converted into cash 12 times during the year.

Accounts receivable turnover also provides useful information for evaluating how efficient management has been in granting credit to produce revenues. A ratio that is high in comparison with competing companies suggests that management should consider using more liberal credit terms to increase sales. A low ratio suggests that management should consider less liberal credit terms and more aggressive collection efforts to avoid an excessive investment in accounts receivable.

Summary of the Chapter in Terms of Learning Objectives

LO 1 Short-term investments are recorded at cost; dividends and interest on the investments are recorded in appropriate income statement accounts. On the balance sheet, investments in securities held to maturity are reported at cost; investments in trading securities and securities available for sale are reported at their fair values. Unrealized gains and losses on trading securities are included in income, but unrealized gains and losses on securities available for sale are reported as a separate stockholders' equity item.

LO 2 When credit card receipts are deposited in a bank account, the credit card expense is recorded at the time of the deposit. When credit card receipts must be submitted to the credit card company for payment, Accounts Receivable is debited for the sales amount. Then, credit card expense is recorded when cash is received from the credit card company. However, any unrecorded credit card expense should be accrued at the end of each accounting period.

LO 3 Under the allowance method, bad debts expense is recorded with an adjustment at the end of each accounting period that debits the expense and credits the Allowance for Doubtful Accounts. The amount of the adjustment is determined by either (*a*) focusing on the income statement relationship between bad debts expense and credit sales or (*b*) focusing on the balance sheet relationship between accounts receivable and the Allowance for Doubtful Accounts. The latter approach may involve using a simple percentage relationship or aging the accounts. Uncollectible accounts are written off with a debit to the Allowance for Doubtful Accounts. The direct write-off method charges Bad Debts Expense when accounts are written off as uncollectible. This method is suitable only when the amount of bad debts expense is immaterial.

LO 4 Interest rates are typically stated in annual terms. When a note's time to maturity is more or less than one year, the amount of interest on the note must be determined by expressing the time as a fraction of one year and multiplying the note's principal by that fraction and the annual interest rate. Dishonored notes are credited to Notes Receivable and debited to Accounts Receivable and to the account of the maker.

LO 5 To obtain cash from receivables before they are due, a company may sell accounts receivable to a factor, who charges a factoring fee. Also, a company may borrow money by signing a note payable that is secured by pledging the accounts receivable. Notes receivable may be discounted at a bank, with or without recourse. The full-disclosure principle requires companies to disclose the amount of accounts receivable that have been pledged and the contingent liability for notes discounted with recourse.

Demonstration Problem

Garden Company had the following transactions during 19X2:

May 8 Purchased 300 shares of Federal Express common stock as a short-term investment in a security available for sale. The cost of $40 per share plus $975 in broker's commissions was paid in cash.

July 14 Wrote off a $750 account receivable arising from a sale several months ago. (Garden Company uses the allowance method.)

Aug. 15 Accepted a $2,000 down payment and a $10,000 note receivable from a customer in exchange for an inventory item that normally sells for $12,000. The note was dated August 15, bears 12% interest, and matures in six months.

Sept. 2 Sold 100 shares of Federal Express stock at $47 per share, and continued to hold the other 200 shares. The broker's commission on the sale was $225.

15 Received $9,850 in return for discounting without recourse the $10,000 note (dated August 15) at the local bank.

Dec. 2 Purchased 400 shares of McDonald's stock for $60 per share plus $1,600 in commissions. The stock is to be held as a short-term investment in a security available for sale.

Required

1. Prepare journal entries to record these transactions on the books of Garden Company.
2. Prepare adjusting journal entries as of December 31, 19X2, for the following items (assume 19X2 is the first year of operation):
   a. The market prices of the equity securities held by Garden Company are $48 per share for the Federal Express stock, and $55 per share for the McDonald's stock.
   b. Bad debts expense is estimated by an aging of accounts receivable. The unadjusted balance of the Allowance for Doubtful Accounts account is a $1,000 debit, while the required balance is estimated to be a $20,400 credit.

Planning the Solution

- Examine each item to determine which accounts are affected and produce the needed journal entries.
- With respect to the year-end adjustments, adjust the stock investments to fair value and record the bad debts expense.

Solution to Demonstration Problem

			Debit	Credit
May	8	Short-Term Investments	12,975.00	
		Cash		12,975.00
		Purchased 300 shares of Federal Express. Cost is (300 × $40) + $975.		
July	14	Allowance for Doubtful Accounts	750.00	
		Accounts Receivable		750.00
		Wrote off an uncollectible account.		
Aug.	15	Cash	2,000.00	
		Notes Receivable	10,000.00	
		Sales		12,000.00
		Sold merchandise to customer for $2,000 cash and $10,000 note receivable.		
Sept.	2	Cash	4,475.00	
		Gain on Sale of Investment		150.00
		Short-Term Investments		4,325.00
		Sold 100 shares of Federal Express for $47 per share less a $225 commission. The original cost is ($12,975 × 100/300).		
	15	Cash	9,850.00	
		Loss on Sales of Notes	150.00	
		Notes Receivable		10,000.00
		Discounted note receivable dated August 15.		
Dec.	2	Short-Term Investments	25,600.00	
		Cash		25,600.00
		Purchased 400 shares of McDonald's for $60 per share plus $1,600 in commissions.		
	31	Short-Term Investments, Fair Value Adjustment	2,650.00	
		Unrealized Holding Gain (Loss)		2,650.00
		To reflect fair values of short-term investments in securities available for sale.		

Short-Term Investments in Securities Available for Sale	Shares	Cost per Share	Total Cost	Market Value per Share	Total Market Value	Difference
Federal Express	200	$43.25	$ 8,650	$48.00	$ 9,600	
McDonald's	400	64.00	25,600	55.00	22,000	
Total			$34,250		$31,600	$2,650

			Debit	Credit
	31	Bad Debts Expense	21,400.00	
		Allowance for Doubtful Accounts		21,400.00
		To adjust the allowance account from $1,000 debit balance to $20,400 credit balance.		

Glossary

LO 6 Define or explain the words and phrases listed in the chapter glossary.

Accounts Receivable Ledger a supplementary record (also called a subsidiary ledger) having an account for each customer. p. 264

Accounts receivable turnover a measure of how long it takes a company to collect its accounts, calculated by dividing credit sales (or net sales) by the average accounts receivable balance. p. 280

Aging accounts receivable a process of classifying accounts receivable in terms of how long they have been outstanding for the purpose of estimating the amount of uncollectible accounts. p. 272

Allowance for Doubtful Accounts a contra asset account with a balance equal to the estimated amount of accounts receivable that will be uncollectible. p. 267

Allowance method of accounting for bad debts an accounting procedure that (1) estimates and reports bad debts expense from credit sales during the period of the sales, and (2) reports accounts receivable at the amount of cash proceeds that is expected from their collection (their estimated realizable value). p. 266

Bad debts accounts receivable from customers that are not collected; the amount is an expense of selling on credit. p. 266

Contingent liability an obligation to make a future payment if, and only if, an uncertain future event actually occurs. p. 279

Controlling account a general ledger account with a balance that is always equal to the sum of the balances in a related subsidiary ledger. p. 266

Direct write-off method of accounting for bad debts a method that makes no attempt to estimate uncollectible accounts or bad debts expense at the end of each period; instead, when an account is found to be uncollectible, it is written off directly to Bad Debts Expense; this method is generally considered to be inferior to the allowance method. p. 273

Dishonoring a note failure by a promissory note's maker to pay the amount due at maturity. p. 277

Full-disclosure principle the accounting principle that requires financial statements (including the footnotes) to contain all relevant information about the operations and financial position of the entity; it also requires that the information be presented in an understandable manner. p. 280

General Ledger the ledger that contains all the financial statement accounts of an organization. p. 264

Installment accounts receivable accounts receivable that allow the customer to make periodic payments over several months and that typically earn interest for the seller. p. 274

Interest the charge assessed for the use of money. p. 275

Investments in securities available for sale investments in debt and equity securities that do not qualify as investments in trading securities or as investments in securities held to maturity p. 259

Investments in securities held to maturity investments in debt securities that the owner positively intends and has the ability to hold until maturity. p. 259

Investments in trading securities investments in debt and equity securities that the owner actively manages, so that frequent purchases and sales generally are made with the objective of generating profits on short-term differences in price. p. 259

Maker of a note one who signs a note and promises to pay it at maturity. p. 275

Materiality principle the idea that the requirements of an accounting principle may be ignored if the effect on the financial statements is unimportant to their users. p. 274

Maturity date of a note the date on which a note and any interest are due and payable. p. 275

Payee of a note the one to whom a promissory note is made payable. p. 275

Principal of a note the amount that the signer of a promissory note agrees to pay back when it matures, not including the interest. p. 275

Promissory note an unconditional written promise to pay a definite sum of money on demand or at a fixed or determinable future date. p. 275

Realizable value the expected proceeds from converting assets into cash. p. 267

Short-term investments investments that can be converted into cash quickly (but less quickly than cash equivalents), and that management intends to sell as a source of cash to satisfy the needs of current operations; short-term investments include such things as government or corporate debt obligations and marketable equity securities. p. 257

Subsidiary ledger a collection of accounts (other than general ledger accounts) that contains the details underlying the balance of a controlling account in the General Ledger. p. 266

Temporary investments another name for *short-term investments.* p. 257

Unrealized holding gain an increase in the fair (market) value of a security that has not yet been confirmed by the sale of the security. p. 260

Unrealized holding loss a decrease in the fair (market) value of a security that has not yet been confirmed by the sale of the security. p. 261

Objective Review

Answers to the following questions are listed at the end of this chapter. Be sure that you decide which is the one best answer to each question *before* you check the answers.

LO 1 In accounting for short-term investments:

a. Securities held to maturity are reported on the balance sheet at their fair (market) values.
b. Unrealized holding gains and losses on investments in securities available for sale are reported on the income statement and closed to Retained Earnings.
c. Unrealized holding gains and losses on investments in trading securities are included in earnings and reported on the income statement.
d. Investments in trading securities are reported on the balance sheet at cost.
e. The same accounting procedures are used for trading securities and securities available for sale.

LO 2 In accounting for credit card sales:

a. The seller does not incur any credit card expense when the seller must submit accumulated sales receipts to the credit card company and then time passes before cash is received from the company.
b. The entry to record credit card sales always includes a debit to Accounts Receivable.
c. The seller does not incur any credit card expense when the bank credits the seller's checking account immediately on the seller's deposit of sales receipts.
d. The seller records credit card sales with a debit to Cash when the bank credits the seller's checking account immediately on the seller's deposit of sales receipts.
e. Credit card expense that results from credit sales made in Period One should be reported as expense in Period Two if the cash from the sale is received in Period Two.

LO 3 Just before adjusting entries are made at year-end, Clayton Company's Accounts Receivable balance is $440,000 and the Allowance for Doubtful Accounts has a debit balance of $1,400. Credit sales for the year were $1,050,000, and the experience of past years suggests that 2% of credit sales prove to be uncollectible. However, an aging of accounts receivable results in a $31,500 estimate of uncollectible accounts at the end of the year. Using the aging of accounts receivable method, the Bad Debts Expense for the year is

a. $32,900.
b. $31,500.
c. $30,100.
d. $21,000.
e. None of the above is correct.

LO 4 White Corporation purchased $7,000 of merchandise from Stamford Company on December 16, 19X1. Stamford accepted White's $7,000, 90-day, 12% note as payment. Assuming Stamford's annual accounting period ends on December 31, and Stamford does not make reversing entries, which entry should Stamford make on March 16, 19X2, when the note is paid?

a.	Cash	7,210.00	
	Interest Earned		210.00
	Notes Receivable		7,000.00
b.	Cash	7,210.00	
	Interest Earned		175.00
	Interest Receivable		35.00
	Notes Receivable		7,000.00
c.	Cash	7,175.00	
	Interest Earned		175.00
	Notes Receivable		7,000.00
d.	Cash	7,210.00	
	Notes Receivable		7,210.00

e. None of the above.

LO 5 Vesco Company discounts without recourse a $25,000 note receivable at a cost of $1,000. Vesco's entry to record the transaction should include a:

a. Debit to Factoring Fee Expense for $1,000.
b. Credit to Notes Receivable for $24,000.
c. Debit to Loss on Sale of Notes for $1,000.
d. Debit to Interest Expense for $1,000.
e. None of the above.

LO 6 A temporary investment is

a. An uncollectible receivable.
b. A potential liability that will become an actual liability if and only if certain events occur.
c. An account receivable that allows the customer to make periodic payments over several months and which typically earns interest.
d. A short-term investment called by another name.
e. A promissory note.

Questions for Class Discussion

1. Under what conditions should investments be classified as current assets?
2. If a short-term investment in securities held for sale cost $6,780 and was sold for $7,500, how should the difference between the two amounts be recorded?
3. On a balance sheet, what valuation must be reported for short-term investments in trading securities?
4. If a company purchases short-term investments in securities available for sale for the first time, and their fair (market) values fall below cost, what ac-

count is credited for the amount of the unrealized loss?

5. For which category of short-term investments are unrealized holding gains included in earnings and reported on the income statement?
6. How do businesses benefit from allowing their customers to use credit cards?
7. What is the relationship between the Accounts Receivable controlling account and the Accounts Receivable Subsidiary Ledger?
8. How is the equality of a controlling account and its subsidiary ledger maintained?
9. In meeting the requirements of the matching principle, why must bad debts expenses be matched with sales on an estimated basis?
10. What term describes the balance sheet valuation of accounts receivable less the allowance for doubtful accounts?
11. What is a contra account? Why is estimated bad debts expense credited to a contra account rather than to the Accounts Receivable controlling account?
12. Classify the following accounts: (*a*) Accounts Receivable, (*b*) Allowance for Doubtful Accounts, and (*c*) Bad Debts Expense.
13. Explain why writing off a bad debt against the allowance account does not reduce the estimated realizable value of a company's accounts receivable.
14. Why does the Bad Debts Expense account usually not have the same adjusted balance as the Allowance for Doubtful Accounts?
15. Why does the direct write-off method of accounting for bad debts commonly fail to match revenues and expenses?
16. What is the essence of the accounting principle of materiality?
17. Why might a business prefer a note receivable to an account receivable?
18. What does the full-disclosure principle require in a company's financial statements?

19. Review the consolidated balance sheets of Federal Express Corporation presented in Appendix G. Assuming the company records all of its receivables in one controlling account, what was the balance of that account on May 31, 1993?

20. Review the consolidated balance sheets of Federal Express Corporation presented in Appendix G. Assuming that during the year ended May 31, 1993, $5 million of Federal Express Corporation's receivables were written off as uncollectible and no amounts written off were subsequently collected during the year, what amount of bad debts expense did the company record during that year?

Exercises

Exercise 7–1
Transactions involving short-term investments
(LO 1)

Prepare general journal entries to record the following transactions involving Best Plumbing's short-term investments, all of which occurred during 19X1:

a. On April 15, paid $90,000 to purchase $90,000 of Westside Company's short-term (60-day) notes payable, which are dated April 15, and pay interest at an 8% rate.
b. On May 10, bought 600 shares of American Steel common stock at 10½ plus a $126 brokerage fee.
c. On June 15, received a check from Westside Company in payment of the principal and 60 days' interest on the notes purchased in transaction *a*.
d. On June 25, paid $75,000 to purchase Stockard Corporation's 7% notes payable, $75,000 principal value, due June 25, 19X2.
e. On August 16, received a $1.25 per share cash dividend on the American Steel common stock purchased in transaction *b*.
f. On September 3, sold 300 shares of American Steel common stock for $15 per share, less a $90 brokerage fee.
g. On December 26, received a check from Stockard Corporation for six months' interest on the notes purchased in *d*.

Exercise 7–2
Recording fair values of short-term investments
(LO 1)

On December 31, 19X1, Compustat Company held the following short-term investments in securities available for sale:

	Cost	Fair Value
J.C. Penney Co. common stock	$37,200	$41,100
Exxon Corporation bonds payable	50,400	48,500
Transamerica notes payable	69,600	63,900
Times Mirror Company common stock	85,500	84,100

Compustat had no short-term investments prior to 19X1. Prepare the December 31 adjusting entry to record the change in fair value of the investments.

Exercise 7–3
Adjusting the short-term investment accounts to reflect changes in fair value
(LO 1)

Rexlon Company's annual period ends on December 31. The total cost and fair (market) value of the company's short-term investments in securities available for sale were as follows:

	Total Cost	Total Fair Value
Short-term investments in securities available for sale:		
On December 31, 19X1	$56,250	$52,500
On December 31, 19X2	63,750	68,125

Prepare the December 31, 19X2, adjusting entry to update the fair values of the short-term investments.

Exercise 7–4
Credit card transactions
(LO 2)

Nickels Company allows customers to use two credit cards in charging purchases. With the Southwest Bank Card, Nickels receives an immediate credit on depositing sales receipts in its checking account. Southwest Bank assesses a 3% service charge for credit card sales. The second credit card that Nickels accepts is Americard. Nickels sends the accumulated Americard receipts to Americard on a weekly basis and is paid by Americard approximately 15 days later. Americard charges 2.5% of sales for using its card. Prepare entries in journal form to record the following credit card transactions of Nickels Company:

May 4 Sold merchandise for $2,500, accepting the customer's Southwest Bank Card. At the end of the day, the Southwest Bank Card receipts were deposited in the company's account at the bank.

5 Sold merchandise for $550, accepting the customer's Americard.

12 Mailed $9,520 of credit card receipts to Americard, requesting payment.

28 Received Americard's check for the May 12 billing, less the normal service charge.

Exercise 7–5
Subsidiary ledger accounts
(LO 3)

Littlefield Corporation recorded the following transactions during April 19X1:

Apr.	2	Accounts Receivable—Barbara Fowler	2,500.00	
		Sales		2,500.00
	10	Accounts Receivable—Robert Guerrero	260.00	
		Sales		260.00
	18	Accounts Receivable—Chris Layton	1,800.00	
		Sales		1,800.00
	23	Sales Returns and Allowances	562.00	
		Accounts Receivable—Chris Layton		562.00
	30	Accounts Receivable—Barbara Fowler	1,125.00	
		Sales		1,125.00

Required

1. Open a General Ledger having T-accounts for Accounts Receivable, Sales, and Sales Returns and Allowances. Also, open a subsidiary Accounts Receivable Ledger having a T-account for each customer. Post the preceding entries to the general ledger accounts and the customer accounts.
2. List the balances of the accounts in the subsidiary ledger, total the balances, and compare the total with the balance of the Accounts Receivable controlling account.

Exercise 7–6
Allowance for doubtful accounts
(LO 3)

On December 31, at the end of its annual accounting period, a company estimated its bad debts as one-fourth of 1% of its $1,240,000 of credit sales made during the year, and made an addition to its Allowance for Doubtful Accounts equal to that amount. On the following February 3, management decided the $1,390 account of Colin Smith was uncollectible and wrote it off as a bad debt. Two months later, on April 2, Smith unexexpectedly paid the amount previously written off. Give the journal entries required to record these events.

Exercise 7–7
Bad debts expense
(LO 3)

At the end of each year, a company uses the simplified balance sheet approach to estimate bad debts. On December 31, 19X1, it has outstanding accounts receivable of $176,600 and estimates that 3.5% will be uncollectible. (*a*) Give the entry to record bad debts expense for 19X1 under the assumption that the Allowance for Doubtful Accounts had a $1,470 credit balance before the adjustment. (*b*) Give the entry under the assumption that the Allowance for Doubtful Accounts has a $1,235 debit balance before the adjustment.

Exercise 7–8
Dishonor of a note
(LO 4)

Prepare journal entries to record these transactions:

Aug. 12 Accepted a $4,500, three-month, 10% note dated today from Clive Nelson in granting a time extension on his past-due account.
Nov. 12 Nelson dishonored his note when presented for payment.
Dec. 31 After exhausting all legal means of collecting, wrote off the account of Nelson against the Allowance for Doubtful Accounts.

Exercise 7–9
Selling and pledging accounts receivable
(LO 5)

On March 31, Jester Company had accounts receivable in the amount of $82,500. Prepare journal entries to record the following transactions for April. Also prepare any footnotes to the April 30 financial statements that should be reported a result of these transactions.

Apr. 5 Sold merchandise to customers on credit, $23,600.
8 Sold $6,800 of accounts receivable to Union Bank. Union Bank charges a 1.5% fee.
17 Received payments from customers, $5,200.
24 Borrowed $15,000 from Union Bank, pledging $22,000 of accounts receivable as security for the loan.

Exercise 7–10
Accounts receivable turnover
(LO 5)

The following is from the financial statements of Fine Furniture Company:

	19X3	19X2	19X1
Net sales	$1,080,000	$860,000	$750,000
Accounts receivable (December 31)	81,900	80,100	76,800

Calculate Fine Furniture's accounts receivable turnover for 19X2 and 19X3. Compare the two results and give a possible explanation for any significant change.

Problems

Problem 7–1
Accounting for short-term investments
(LO 1)

Ridgeway Company had no short-term investments prior to 19X1, but had the following transactions involving short-term investments in securities available for sale during 19X1:

Jan. 3 Purchased 1,200 shares of General Mills common stock at 62¼ plus a $1,494 brokerage fee.
26 Paid $250,000 to buy six-month U.S. Treasury bills, $250,000 principal amount, 6%, dated January 26.
Mar. 11 Purchased 3,000 shares of Texaco common stock at 59½ plus a $3,570 brokerage fee.
May 4 Purchased 700 shares of Unisys common stock at 11½ plus a $161 brokerage fee.
July 28 Received a check for the principal and accrued interest on the U.S. Treasury bills that matured on July 26.
29 Received a $1.60 per share cash dividend on the General Mills common shares.
Aug. 4 Sold 600 shares of General Mills common stock at 76 less a $912 brokerage fee.
19 Received a $3.10 per share cash dividend on the Texaco common shares.

Oct. 28 Received a $1.75 per share cash dividend on the remaining General Mills common shares owned.

Nov. 19 Received a $2.95 per share cash dividend on the Texaco common shares.

On December 31, 19X1, the market prices of the securities held by Ridgeway were General Mills, 79¼; Texaco, 61⅞; and Unisys, 14¾.

Required

1. Prepare journal entries to record the preceding transactions.
2. Prepare a schedule to compare the cost and fair (market) values of Ridgeway's short-term investments in securities available for sale.
3. Prepare an adjusting entry, if necessary, to record the fair value adjustment of the short-term investments.

Problem 7–2
Credit sales and credit card sales
(LO 2)

Werner Company allows a few customers to make purchases on credit. Other customers may use either of two credit cards. West Bank deducts a 2% service charge for sales on its credit card but immediately credits the checking account of its commercial customers when credit card receipts are deposited. Werner deposits the West Bank credit card receipts at the close of each business day.

When customers use SilverCard, Werner accumulates the receipts for several days before submitting them to SilverCard for payment. SilverCard deducts a 3% service charge and usually pays within one week of being billed. Werner completed the following transactions. (Terms of all credit sales are 2/15, n/30; all sales are recorded at the gross price.)

June 3 Sold merchandise on credit to Sandra Kish for $985.

9 Sold merchandise for $3,980 to customers who used their West Bank credit cards. Sold merchandise for $4,300 to customers who used their SilverCard.

11 Sold merchandise for $2,460 to customers who used their SilverCard.

13 Wrote off the account of John Farlow against Allowance for Doubtful Accounts. The $278 balance in Farlow's account stemmed from a credit sale in October of last year.

14 The SilverCard receipts accumulated since June 9 were submitted to the credit card company for payment.

18 Received Kish's check paying for the purchase of June 3.

23 Received the amount due from SilverCard.

Required

Prepare journal entries to record the preceding transactions and events.

Problem 7–3
Estimating bad debts expense
(LO 3)

On December 31, 19X1, Hallmart Company's records showed the following results for the year:

Cash sales	$ 601,250
Credit sales	1,178,000

In addition, the unadjusted trial balance included the following items:

Accounts receivable	$ 356,700 debit
Allowance for doubtful accounts	5,250 debit

Required

1. Prepare the adjusting entry needed on the books of Hallmart to recognize bad debts under each of the following independent assumptions:
   a. Bad debts are estimated to be 1% of total sales.
   b. Bad debts are estimated to be 2% of credit sales.
   c. An analysis suggests that 5% of outstanding accounts receivable on December 31, 19X1, will become uncollectible.
2. Show how Accounts Receivable and the Allowance for Doubtful Accounts would appear on the December 31, 19X1, balance sheet given the facts in requirement 1(*b*).

3. Show how Accounts Receivable and the Allowance for Doubtful Accounts would appear on the December 31, 19X1, balance sheet given the facts in requirement 1(*c*).

Problem 7–4
Aging accounts receivable
(LO 3)

Artex Company had credit sales of $1.3 million in 19X1. On December 31, 19X1, the company's Allowance for Doubtful Accounts had a credit balance of $6,700. The accountant for Artex has prepared a schedule of the December 31, 19X1, accounts receivable by age, and on the basis of past experience has estimated the percentage of the receivables in each age category that will become uncollectible. This information is summarized as follows:

December 31, 19X1 Accounts Receivable	Age of Accounts Receivable	Expected Percentage Uncollectible
$365,000	Not due (under 30 days)	1.00%
177,000	1 to 30 days past due	2.50
38,000	31 to 60 days past due	7.75
20,000	61 to 90 days past due	45.00
6,000	over 90 days past due	70.00

Required

1. Calculate the amount that should appear in the December 31, 19X1, balance sheet as the Allowance for Doubtful Accounts.
2. Prepare the journal entry to record bad debts expense for 19X1.
3. On June 30, 19X2, Artex concluded that a customer's $1,875 receivable (created in 19X1) was uncollectible and that the account should be written off. What effect will this action have on Artex's 19X2 net income? Explain your answer.

Problem 7–5
Recording accounts receivable transactions and bad debts adjustments
(LO 3)

Gilcrest Company began operations on January 1, 19X1. During the next two years, the company completed a number of transactions involving credit sales, accounts receivable collections, and bad debts. These transactions are summarized as follows:

19X1

a. Sold merchandise on credit for $817,500, terms n/30.
b. Wrote off uncollectible accounts receivable in the amount of $12,500.
c. Received cash of $476,500 in payment of outstanding accounts receivable.
d. In adjusting the accounts on December 31, concluded that 1.5% of the outstanding accounts receivable would become uncollectible.

19X2

e. Sold merchandise on credit for $1,017,000, terms n/30.
f. Wrote off uncollectible accounts receivable in the amount of $19,200.
g. Received cash of $788,500 in payment of outstanding accounts receivable.
h. In adjusting the accounts on December 31, concluded that 1.5% of the outstanding accounts receivable would become uncollectible.

Required

Prepare journal entries to record the 19X1 and 19X2 summarized transactions of Gilcrest and the adjusting entries to record bad debts expense at the end of each year.

Problem 7–6
Analysis and journalizing of notes receivable transactions
(LO 4, 5)

Prepare journal entries to record the following transactions of Brackenridge Company:

19X1
Dec. 1 Accepted a $6,000, 90-day, 10% note dated this day in granting Tish McCoy a time extension on her past-due account.
31 Made an adjusting entry to record the accrued interest on the McCoy note.
31 Closed the Interest Earned account.

19X2
Mar. 1 Received McCoy's payment for the principal and interest on the note dated December 1.

Mar. 5 Accepted a $3,200, 9%, 60-day note dated this day in granting a time extension on the past-due account of Gary Roster.

17 Accepted a $1,000, 90-day, 10% note dated this day in granting T. Z. Hanks a time extension on his past-due account.

31 Discounted, with recourse, the Roster note at First Bank at a cost of $20. The transaction was considered to be a loan.

May 5 Received notice from First Bank that Roster defaulted on the note. Paid the bank the principal plus interest due on the note. (Hint: Create an account receivable for the maturity value of the note.)

June 16 Hanks dishonored his note when presented for payment.

July 5 Received payment from Roster of the maturity value of his dishonored note plus interest for 60 days beyond maturity at 9%.

16 Accepted a $3,400, 90-day, 12% note dated this day in granting a time extension on the past-due account of Stanley Frasier.

Aug. 6 Accepted a $1,300, 60-day, 10% note dated this day in granting Susan Faltinski a time extension on her past-due account.

31 Discounted, without recourse, the Faltinski note at First Bank at a cost of $10.

Oct. 14 Received payment of principal plus interest from Frasier for the note of July 16.

Dec. 1 Wrote off the T. Z. Hanks account against Allowance for Doubtful Accounts.

Problem 7–7
Entries and fair value adjustments for short-term investments
(LO 1)

Reitz Company has relatively large idle cash balances and invests them in common stocks that it holds available for sale. Following is a series of events and other facts relevant to the short-term investment activity of the company:

19X1

Mar. 2 Purchased 1,600 shares of Borden at $18.75 plus $900 commission.

Apr. 6 Purchased 700 shares of Chrysler at $56.00 plus $1,176 commission.

Aug. 15 Purchased 1,800 shares of Pennzoil at $55.50 plus $2,997 commission.

Dec. 31 These per share market values were known for the stocks in the portfolio: Borden, $20.15; Chrysler, $49.00; Pennzoil, $57.25.

19X2

Jan. 10 Sold 1,600 shares of Borden at $21.75 less $1,044 commission.

May 3 Sold 1,800 shares of Pennzoil at $49.50 less $2,673 commission.

Oct. 22 Purchased 2,000 shares of Heinz at $36.25 plus $2,175 commission.

Nov. 5 Purchased 800 shares of Reebok at $28.00 plus $672 commission.

Dec. 31 These per share market values were known for the stocks in the portfolio: Chrysler, $36.75; Heinz, $32.50; Reebok, $30.00.

19X3

Feb. 19 Purchased 3,800 shares of Continental Airlines at $23.00 plus $2,622 commission.

April 11 Sold 2,000 shares of Heinz at $31.25 less $1,875 commission.

Aug. 9 Sold 700 shares of Chrysler at $40.00 less $840 commission.

Sept. 6 Purchased 2,000 shares of Goodyear at $47.50 plus $2,850 commission.

Dec. 12 Sold 800 shares of Reebok at $45.50 less $1,092 commission.

31 These per share market values were known for the stocks in the portfolio: Continental Airlines, $25.75; Goodyear, $56.50.

Required

1. Prepare journal entries to record the events and any year-end adjustments needed to record the fair values of the short-term investments.
2. Prepare a schedule that shows the total cost, total fair value adjustment, and total fair value of the investments at the end of each year.
3. For each year, prepare a schedule that shows the realized gains and losses included in earnings and the total unrealized gain or loss at the end of each year.

Problem 7–8
Analytical essay
(LO 1)

Cloron Company did not own any short-term investments prior to 19X2. After purchasing some short-term investments in 19X2, the company's accountant made the following December 31, 19X2, adjusting entry:

Dec.	31	Short-Term Investments, Fair Value Adjustment	5,670.00	
		Holding Gain (Loss)		5,670.00
		To record fair value of short-term investments in securities available for sale.		

When Cloron's accountant reviewed the year-end adjustments with an office manager of the company, the accountant commented that the previous adjustment might have been different if the company had owned short-term investments on December 31, 19X1. The office manager thought the accountant must be confused. The manager said that the December 31, 19X2, adjustment was supposed to record a gain that occurred during 19X2, and therefore should not be affected by any events that occurred during 19X1.

Required

Explain why the accountant's comment is correct.

Problem 7–9
Analytical essay
(LO 3)

Review the facts about Hallmart Company in Problem 7–3.

Required

1. Recall that Allowance for Doubtful Accounts is a contra asset account. Nevertheless, Hallmart's unadjusted trial balance shows that this account has a $5,250 debit balance. Explain how this contra asset account could have a debit balance.
2. In Problem 7–3, requirement 1(*c*) indicates that 5% of the outstanding accounts receivable ($356,700 × 5% = $17,835) will become uncollectible. Given this conclusion, explain why the adjusting entry should not include a $17,835 credit to Accounts Receivable.

Provocative Problems

Provocative Problem 7–1
Accounting related communications
(LO 3)

As the accountant for JWest Company, you recently attended a sales managers' meeting devoted to a discussion of the company's credit policies. At the meeting, you reported that bad debts expense for the past year was estimated to be $35,000 and accounts receivable at the end of the year amounted to $645,000 less a $21,000 allowance for doubtful accounts. Chris Albertson, one of the sales managers, expressed confusion over the fact that bad debts expense and the allowance for doubtful accounts were different amounts. To save time at the meeting, you agreed to discuss the matter with Albertson after the meeting.

Required

Because the meeting lasted longer than expected, Albertson had to leave early to catch a plane back to his sales district. As a result, you need to write a memorandum to him explaining why a difference in bad debts expense and the allowances for doubtful accounts is not unusual. (Assume that the company estimates bad debts expense to be 2% of sales.)

Provocative Problem 7–2
Builders Depot
(LO 3)

Builders Depot has been in business for six years and has used the direct write-off method of accounting for bad debts. The following information is available from the accounting records for the first five years:

	19X5	19X4	19X3	19X2	19X1
Sales	$2,243,000	$1,170,000	$2,600,000	$3,400,000	$950,000
Net income	336,200	175,000	390,200	509,500	142,200
Bad debts written off during year	13,940	18,410	47,960	11,720	2,100
Bad debts by year of sale*	21,300	11,990	29,790	32,910	10,640

*Results from classifying bad debt losses so that the losses appear in the same years as the sales that produced them. For example, the $21,300 for 19X5 includes $12,500 of bad debts that became uncollectible during 19X6.

You are the manager of Builders Depot and want to change the method of accounting for bad debts from the direct write-off method to the allowance method. Kelly Skyles, the president of the company, feels this is not necessary.

Required

1. Prepare a five-year schedule for Skyles showing:
   a. Net income if bad debts expense is defined to be bad debts by year of sale.
   b. The dollar amount of difference between net income using the direct write-off method and the answer to *a*.
   c. The answer to requirement *b* as a percentage of the answer to requirement *a*.
   d. Bad debts by year of sale as a percentage of sales.
   e. Bad debts written off during the year as a percentage of sales.
2. Use the schedule to support your argument for using the allowance method to account for bad debts.

Provocative Problem 7–3
Apple Computer, Inc.
(LO 1, 5)

Apple Computer, Inc.

Refer to the financial statements and related disclosures from Apple Computer, Inc.'s 1992 annual report in Appendix F. Based on your examination of this information, answer the following:

1. Apple's most liquid assets include cash and cash equivalents, short-term investments, and accounts receivable. What total amount of those assets did Apple have on September 25, 1992?
2. Express Apple's total liquid assets as of September 25, 1992, (as previously defined) as a percentage of current liabilities. Do the same for 1991. Comment on Apple's ability to satisfy current liabilities at the end of fiscal year 1992, as compared to the end of fiscal year 1991.
3. What criteria did Apple use to classify items as cash equivalents? Short-term investments?
4. Calculate Apple's accounts receivable turnover for 1992. (In making the calculations, use accounts receivable net of allowance for doubtful accounts.)

Answers to Objective Review Questions

LO 1 (*c*) LO 2 (*d*) LO 3 (*a*) LO 4 (*b*) LO 5 (*c*) LO 6 (*d*)

CHAPTER

8

Inventories and Cost of Goods Sold

The operations of merchandising businesses involve the purchase and resale of tangible goods. In Chapter 5, when we first introduced the topic of accounting for merchandisers, we left several important matters for later consideration. In this chapter, we return to the topic and examine the methods businesses use at the end of each period to assign dollar amounts to merchandise inventory and to cost of goods sold. The principles and procedures that we explain in this chapter are used in department stores, grocery stores, automobile dealerships, and any other businesses that purchase goods for resale.

Learning Objectives

After studying Chapter 8, you should be able to:

1. Describe (*a*) how the matching principle relates to accounting for merchandise; (*b*) the types of items that should be included in merchandise inventory; and (*c*) the elements that make up the cost of merchandise.
2. Calculate the cost of an inventory based on (*a*) specific invoice prices, (*b*) weighted-average cost, (*c*) FIFO, and (*d*) LIFO, and explain the financial statement effects of choosing one method over the others.
3. Explain the effect of an inventory error on the income statements of the current and succeeding years.
4. Describe perpetual inventory systems and prepare entries to record merchandise transactions and maintain subsidiary inventory records under a perpetual inventory system.
5. Calculate the lower-of-cost-or-market amount of an inventory.
6. Use the retail method and the gross profit method to estimate an inventory and calculate merchandise turnover and days' stock on hand.
7. Define or explain the words and phrases listed in the chapter glossary.

The assets that a business buys and holds for resale are called *merchandise inventory*. As a rule, the items held as merchandise inventory are sold within one year or one operating cycle. Therefore, merchandise inventory is a current asset, usually the largest current asset on the balance sheet of a merchandiser.

Matching Merchandise Costs with Revenues

LO 1 Describe (*a*) how the matching principle relates to accounting for merchandise; (*b*) the types of items that should be included in merchandise inventory; and (*c*) the elements that make up the cost of merchandise.

Accounting for inventories affects both the balance sheet and the income statement. However, "the major objective [in accounting for the goods in the inventory] is the matching of appropriate **costs** against revenues in order that there may be a proper determination of the realized income."[1] The matching process is already a familiar topic. For inventories, it consists of deciding how much of the cost of the goods available for sale during a period should be deducted from the period's revenue and how much should be carried forward as inventory to be matched against a future period's revenue.

In a periodic inventory system, when the cost of goods available for sale is allocated between cost of goods sold and ending inventory, the key problem is assigning a cost to the ending inventory. Remember, however, that by assigning a cost to the ending inventory, you are also determining cost of goods sold. This is true because the ending inventory is subtracted from the cost of goods available for sale to determine cost of goods sold.

Items to Include in Merchandise Inventory

The merchandise inventory of a business includes all goods owned by the business and held for sale, regardless of where the goods may be located at the time inventory is counted. In applying this rule, most items present no problem. All that is required is to see that all items are counted, that nothing is omitted, and that nothing is counted more than once. However, goods in transit, goods sold but not delivered, goods on consignment, and obsolete and damaged goods require special attention.

Should merchandise be included in the inventory of a business if the goods are in transit from a supplier to a business on the date the business takes an inventory? The answer to this question depends on whether the rights and risks of ownership have passed from the supplier to the purchaser. If ownership has passed to the purchaser, they should be included in the purchaser's inventory. If the buyer is responsible for paying the freight charges, ownership usually passes as soon as the goods are loaded on the means of transportation. (As mentioned in Chapter 5, the terms would be FOB the seller's factory or warehouse.) On the other hand, if the seller is to pay the freight charges, ownership passes when the goods arrive at their destination (FOB destination).

Goods on consignment are goods shipped by their owner (known as the **consignor**) to another person or firm (called the **consignee**) who is to sell the goods for the owner. Consigned goods belong to the consignor and should appear on the consignor's inventory.

Damaged goods and deteriorated or obsolete goods should not be counted in the inventory if they are not salable. If such goods can be sold at a reduced price, they should be included in the inventory at a conservative estimate of their **net realizable value** (sales price less the cost of making the sale). Thus, the accounting period in which the goods deteriorated, were damaged, or became obsolete suffers the resultant loss.

Elements of Merchandise Cost

As applied to merchandise, cost means the sum of the expenditures and charges directly or indirectly incurred in bringing an article to its existing condition and location.[2] Therefore, the cost of an inventory item includes the invoice price, less any discount, plus any additional or incidental costs necessary to put the item into place and condition for sale. The additional costs may

[1] FASB, *Accounting Standards—Current Text* (Norwalk, CT, 1993), sec. I78.104. First published as *Accounting Research Bulletin No. 43,* Ch. 4, par. 4.

[2] Ibid., sec. I78.402. First published as *Accounting Research Bulletin No. 43,* ch. 4, par. 5.

ILLUSTRATION 8–1 *Inventory Tickets Used to Tag Inventory Items as They Are Counted*

Inventory Ticket No. 786	Quantity counted ________
Item ________	Sales price $________
Counted by ________	Cost price $________
Checked by ________	Purchase date ________

include import duties, transportation-in, storage, insurance, and any other related costs such as those incurred during an aging process (for example, the aging of wine).

All of these costs should be included in the cost of merchandise. When calculating the cost of a merchandise inventory, however, some concerns do not include the incidental costs of acquiring merchandise. They price the inventory on the basis of invoice prices only. As a result, the incidental costs are allocated to cost of goods sold during the period in which they are incurred.

In theory, a share of each incidental cost should be assigned to every unit purchased. This causes a portion of each to be carried forward in the inventory to be matched against the revenue of the period in which the inventory is sold. However, the effort of computing costs on such a precise basis may outweigh the benefit from the extra accuracy. Therefore, many businesses take advantage of the *materiality principle* and charge such costs to cost of goods sold.

Taking an Ending Inventory

As you learned in Chapter 5, when a *periodic inventory system* is used, the dollar amount of the ending inventory is determined as follows: count the units of each product on hand, multiply the count for each product by its cost per unit, and add the costs for all products. In making the count, items are less likely to be counted twice or omitted from the count if you use prenumbered **inventory tickets** like the one in Illustration 8–1.

Before beginning the inventory count, a sufficient number of the tickets, at least one for each product on hand, is issued to the employees who make the count. Next, the employees count the quantity of each product. From the count and the price tag attached to the merchandise, the required inventory tickets are filled in and attached to the counted items. When the count is completed, inventory tickets are attached to all counted items. After checking for uncounted items, the employees remove the tickets and send them to the accounting department. To ensure that no ticket is lost or left attached to merchandise, the accounting department verifies that all the prenumbered tickets issued have been returned.

In the accounting department, the unit and cost data on the tickets are aggregated by multiplying the number of units of each product by its unit cost. This gives the dollar amount of each product in the inventory, and the total for all the products is the dollar total of the inventory.

Assigning Costs to Inventory Items

One of the major issues in accounting for merchandise involves determining the unit cost amounts assigned to items in the inventory. When all units are purchased at the same unit cost, this process is easy. However, when identical items were purchased at different costs, a problem arises as to which costs apply to the ending inventory and which apply to the goods sold. There are four commonly used methods of assigning costs to goods in the ending inventory and to goods sold. They are (1) specific invoice prices; (2) weighted-average cost; (3) first-in, first-out; and (4) last-in, first-out. All four methods are generally accepted.

LO 2 Calculate the cost of an inventory based on (*a*) specific invoice prices, (*b*) weighted-average cost, (*c*) FIFO, and (*d*) LIFO, and explain the financial statement effects of choosing one method over the others.

To illustrate the four methods, assume that a company has 12 units of Product X on hand at the end of its annual accounting period. Also, assume that the inventory at the beginning of the year and the purchases during the year were as follows:

Jan. 1	Beginning inventory	10 units @ $100 =	$1,000
Mar. 13	Purchased	15 units @ $108 =	1,620
Aug. 17	Purchased	20 units @ $120 =	2,400
Nov. 10	Purchased	10 units @ $125 =	1,250
Total	. . . .	55 units	$6,270

Specific Invoice Prices

When each item in an inventory can be clearly related to a specific purchase and its invoice, **specific invoice inventory pricing** may be used to assign costs. For example, assume that 6 of the 12 unsold units of Product X were from the November purchase and 6 were from the August purchase. With this information, specific invoice prices can be used to assign cost to the ending inventory and to the goods sold as follows:

Total cost of 55 units available for sale		$6,270
Less ending inventory priced by means of specific invoices:		
6 units from the November purchase at $125 each	$750	
6 units from the August purchase at $120 each	720	
12 units in the ending inventory		1,470
Cost of goods sold		$4,800

Weighted Average

When using **weighted-average inventory pricing,** multiply the per unit costs of the beginning inventory and of each purchase by the number of units in the beginning inventory and in each purchase. Then, divide the total of these amounts by the total number of units available for sale to find the weighted-average cost per unit as follows:

10 units @ $100 =	$1,000
15 units @ $108 =	1,620
20 units @ $120 =	2,400
10 units @ $125 =	1,250
55	$6,270

$6,270/55 = $114 weighted-average cost per unit

After determining the weighted-average cost per unit, use this average to assign costs to the inventory and to the units sold as follows:

Total cost of 55 units available for sale	$6,270
Less ending inventory priced on a weighted-average cost basis: 12 units at $114 each	1,368
Cost of goods sold	$4,902

First-In, First-Out

First-in, first-out inventory pricing (FIFO) assumes the items in the beginning inventory are sold first. Additional sales are assumed to come in the order in which they were purchased. Thus, the costs of the last items received are assigned to the ending inventory, and the remaining costs are assigned to goods sold. For example, when first-in, first-out is used, the costs of Product X are assigned to the inventory and goods sold as follows:

Total cost of 55 units available for sale		$6,270
Less ending inventory priced on a basis of FIFO:		
10 units from the November purchase at $125 each	$1,250	
2 units from the August purchase at $120 each	240	
12 units in the ending inventory		1,490
Cost of goods sold		$4,780

Understand that FIFO is acceptable whether or not the physical flow of goods actually follows a first-in, first-out pattern. The physical flow of products depends on the nature of the product and the way the products are stored. If a product is perishable (for example, fresh tomatoes), the business attempts to sell it in a first-in, first-out pattern. Other products, for example, bolts or screws kept in a large bin, may tend to be sold on a last-in, first-out basis. In either case, the FIFO method of allocating cost may be used.

Last-In, First-Out

Under the **last-in, first-out inventory pricing (LIFO)** method, the cost of the last goods received are charged to cost of goods sold and matched with revenue from sales. Again, this method is acceptable even though the physical flow of goods may not be on a last-in, first-out basis.

One argument for the use of LIFO is based on the fact that a going concern must replace the inventory items it sells. When goods are sold, replacements are purchased. Thus, a sale causes the replacement of goods. From this point of view, a correct matching of costs with revenues would require you to match replacement costs with the sales that made replacements necessary. Although the costs of the most recent purchases are not quite the same as replacement costs, they usually are close approximations of replacement costs. Because LIFO assigns the most recent purchase costs to the income statement, LIFO (compared to FIFO or weighted average) comes closest to matching replacement costs with revenues.

Under LIFO, costs are assigned to the 12 remaining units of Product X and to the goods sold as follows:

Total cost of 55 units available for sale		$6,270
Less ending inventory priced on a basis of LIFO:		
10 units in the beginning inventory at $100 each	$1,000	
2 units from the March purchase at $108 each	216	
12 units in the ending inventory		1,216
Cost of goods sold		$5,054

Notice that when LIFO is used to match costs and revenues, the ending inventory cost is the cost of the oldest 12 units.

Comparison of Methods

In a stable market where prices remain unchanged, the choice of an inventory pricing method is not important. When prices are unchanged over a period of time, all methods give the same cost figures. However, in a changing market

ILLUSTRATION 8–2 *The Income Statement Effects of Alternative Inventory Pricing Methods*

	Specific Invoice Prices	Weighted Average	FIFO	LIFO
Sales	$6,000	$6,000	$6,000	$6,000
Cost of goods sold:				
Merchandise inventory, January 1	$1,000	$1,000	$1,000	$1,000
Purchases	5,270	5,270	5,270	5,270
Cost of goods available for sale	$6,270	$6,270	$6,270	$6,270
Merchandise inventory, December 31	1,470	1,368	1,490	1,216
Cost of goods sold	$4,800	$4,902	$4,780	$5,054
Gross profit	$1,200	$1,098	$1,220	$ 946
Operating expenses	500	500	500	500
Income before taxes	$ 700	$ 598	$ 720	$ 446
Income taxes expense (30%)	210	179	216	134
Net income	$ 490	$ 419	$ 504	$ 312

where prices are rising or falling, each method may give a different result. These differences are shown in Illustration 8–2, where we assume that Product X sales were $6,000 and operating expenses were $500. In Illustration 8–2, note the differences that resulted from the choice of an inventory pricing method.

Because purchase prices were rising throughout the period, FIFO resulted in the lowest cost of goods sold, the highest gross profit, and the highest net income. On the other hand, LIFO resulted in the highest cost of goods sold, the lowest gross profit, and the lowest net income. As you would expect, the results of using the weighted-average method fall between FIFO and LIFO. The results of using specific invoice prices depend entirely on which units were actually sold.

Each of the four pricing methods is generally accepted, and arguments can be made for using each. In one sense, one might argue that specific invoice prices exactly match costs and revenues. However, this method is practical only for relatively high-priced items when just a few units are kept in stock and sold. Weighted-average costs tend to smooth out price fluctuations. FIFO provides an inventory valuation on the balance sheet that most closely approximates current replacement cost. LIFO causes the last costs incurred to be assigned to cost of goods sold. Therefore, it results in a better matching of current costs with revenues on the income statement.

Because the choice of an inventory pricing method often has material effects on the financial statements, the choice of a method should be disclosed in the footnotes to the statements. This information is important to an understanding of the statements and is required by the *full-disclosure principle.*[3]

Tax Effect of LIFO

The income statements in Illustration 8–2 are assumed to be those of a corporation. Therefore, the income statements include income taxes expense (at an assumed rate of 30%). Note that because purchase prices were rising, a tax advantage was gained by using LIFO. This advantage arises because LIFO assigns the largest dollar amounts to cost of goods sold when purchase prices are increasing. As a result, the smallest income is reported when LIFO is used. This in turn results in the smallest income tax expense.

---

[3] Ibid., sec. A10.105, 106. First published as *APB Opinion No. 22,* pars. 12, 13.

AS A MATTER OF
Fact

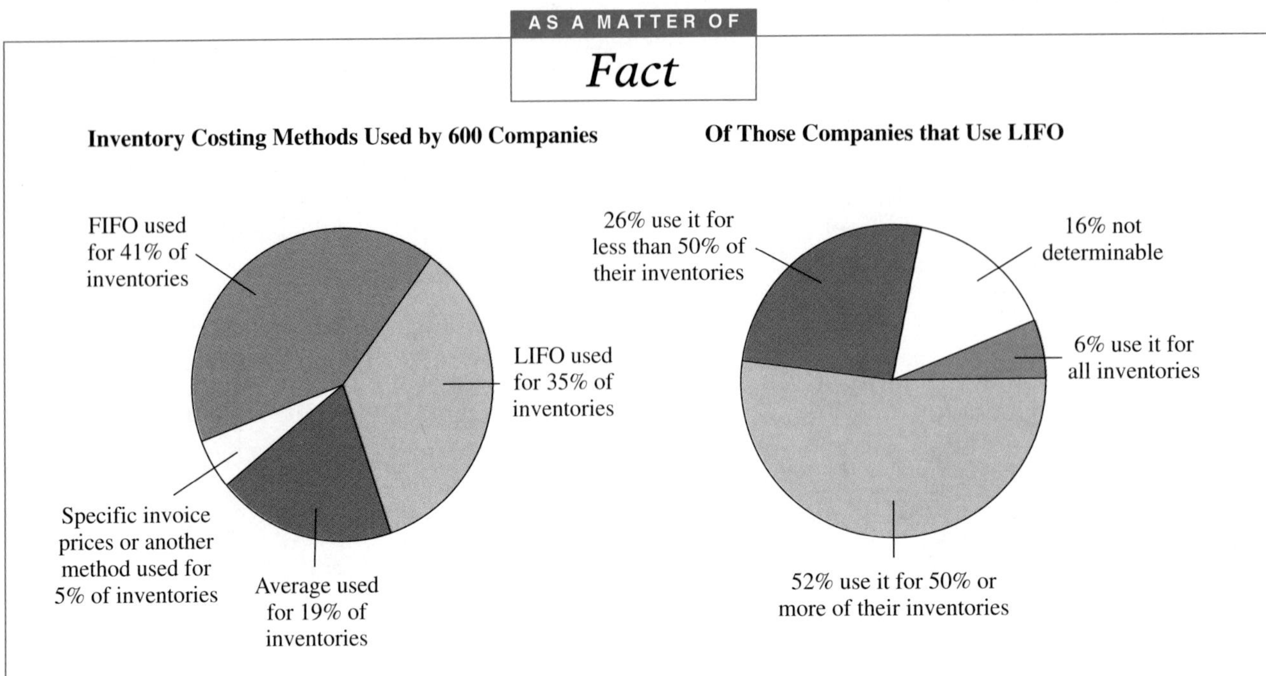

Source of data: American Institute of Certified Public Accountants, *Accounting Trends and Techniques,* New York, 1992, p. 142. Copyright © 1993 (1992) by American Institute of Certified Public Accounts, Inc.

The Consistency Principle

Because the choice of an inventory pricing method can have a material effect on the financial statements, some companies might be inclined to make a new choice each year. Their objective would be to select whichever method would result in the most favorable financial statements. If this were allowed, however, readers of financial statements would find it extremely difficult to compare the company's financial statements from one year to the next. If income increased, the reader would have difficulty deciding whether the increase resulted from more successful operations or from the change in the accounting method. The **consistency principle** is used to avoid this problem.

The *consistency principle* requires that a company use the same accounting methods period after period, so that the financial statements of succeeding periods will be comparable.[4] The *consistency principle* is not limited just to inventory pricing methods. Whenever a company must choose between alternative accounting methods, consistency requires that the company continue to use the selected method period after period. As a result, a reader of a company's financial statements may assume that in keeping its records and in preparing its statements, the company used the same procedures employed in previous years. Only on the basis of this assumption can meaningful comparisons be made of the data in a company's statements year after year.

In achieving comparability, the *consistency principle* does not mean that a company can never change from one accounting method to another. Rather, if a company justifies a different acceptable method or procedure as an improvement in financial reporting, a change may be made. However, when such a change is made, the *full-disclosure principle* requires that the nature of

[4] FASB, *Statement of Financial Accounting Concepts No. 2,* "Qualitative Characteristics of Accounting Information" (Norwalk, CT, 1980), par. 120.

ILLUSTRATION 8–3 *Effects of Inventory Errors—Periodic Inventory System*

	19X1		19X2		19X3	
Sales		$100,000		$100,000		$100,000
Cost of goods sold:						
Beginning inventory	$20,000		$16,000*		$20,000	
Purchases	60,000		60,000		60,000	
Goods for sale	$80,000		$76,000		$80,000	
Ending inventory	16,000*		20,000		20,000	
Cost of goods sold		64,000		56,000		60,000
Gross profit		$36,000		$ 44,000		$ 40,000

* Should have been $20,000.

the change, justification for the change, and the effect of the change on net income be disclosed in footnotes to the statements.[5]

Inventory Errors—Periodic System

LO 3 Explain the effect of an inventory error on the income statements of the current and succeeding years.

Companies that use the *periodic inventory system* must be especially careful in taking the end-of-period inventory. If an error is made, it will cause misstatements in cost of goods sold, gross profit, net income, current assets, and owners' equity. Also, the ending inventory of one period is the beginning inventory of the next. Therefore, the error will carry forward and cause misstatements in the succeeding period's cost of goods sold, gross profit, and net income. Furthermore, since the amount involved in an inventory often is large, the misstatements can materially reduce the usefulness of the financial statements.

To illustrate the effects of an inventory error, assume that in each of the years 19X1, 19X2, and 19X3, a company had $100,000 in sales. If the company maintained a $20,000 inventory throughout the period and made $60,000 in purchases in each of the years, its cost of goods sold each year was $60,000 and its annual gross profit was $40,000. However, assume the company incorrectly calculated its December 31, 19X1, inventory at $16,000 rather than $20,000. Note the effects of the error in Illustration 8–3.

Observe in Illustration 8–3 that the $4,000 understatement of the December 31, 19X1, inventory caused a $4,000 overstatement in 19X1 cost of goods sold and a $4,000 understatement in gross profit and net income. Also, because the ending inventory of 19X1 became the beginning inventory of 19X2, the error caused an understatement in the 19X2 cost of goods sold and a $4,000 overstatement in gross profit and net income. However, by 19X3 the error had no effect.

In Illustration 8–3, the December 31, 19X1, inventory is understated. Had it been overstated, it would have caused opposite results—the 19X1 net income would have been overstated and the 19X2 income understated.

Because inventory errors correct themselves by causing offsetting errors in the next period, you might be inclined to think that they are not serious. Do not make this mistake. Management, creditors, and owners base many important decisions on fluctuations in reported net income. Therefore, inventory errors must be avoided.

[5] FASB, *Accounting Standards—Current Text* (Norwalk, CT, 1993), sec. A06.113. First published as *APB Opinion No. 20,* par. 17.

Perpetual Inventory Systems

LO 4 Describe perpetual inventory systems and prepare entries to record merchandise transactions and maintain subsidiary inventory records under a perpetual inventory system.

The previous discussion of inventories focused on the periodic inventory system. Under the periodic system, the Merchandise Inventory account is updated only once each accounting period, at the end of the period. Then, the Merchandise Inventory account reflects the current balance of inventory only until the first purchase or sale in the following period. Thereafter, the Merchandise Inventory account no longer reflects the current balance.

By contrast, a *perpetual inventory system* updates the Merchandise Inventory account after each purchase and after each sale. As long as all entries have been posted, the account shows the current amount of inventory on hand. The system takes its name from the fact that the Merchandise Inventory account is perpetually up to date. When a perpetual system is used, management is able to monitor the inventory on hand on a regular basis. This aids in planning future purchases.

Before the widespread use of computers in accounting, only companies that sold a limited number of products of relatively high value used perpetual inventory systems. The cost and effort of maintaining perpetual inventory records were simply too great for other types of companies. However, since computers have made the record-keeping chore much easier, an increasing number of firms are switching from periodic to perpetual systems.

Comparing Journal Entries under Periodic and Perpetual Inventory Systems

By using parallel columns in Illustration 8–4, we show the typical journal entries made under periodic and perpetual inventory systems. Observe the entries for the purchase of transaction 1. The perpetual system does not use a Purchases account. Instead, the cost of the items purchased is debited directly to Merchandise Inventory. Also, in transaction 2, the perpetual system credits the cost of purchase returns directly to the Merchandise Inventory account instead of using a Purchases Returns and Allowances account.

Transaction 3 involves the sale of merchandise. Note that the perpetual system requires two entries to record the sale, one to record the revenue and another to record cost of goods sold. Thus, the perpetual system uses a Cost of Goods Sold account. In the periodic system, the elements of cost of goods sold are not transferred to such an account. Instead, they are transferred to Income Summary in the process of recording the closing entries.

The closing entries under the two systems are shown as item 4 in Illustration 8–4. Under the periodic system, all of the cost elements related to inventories are transferred to Income Summary. By comparison, under the perpetual system, those cost elements were already recorded in a Cost of Goods Sold account. Thus, the closing entries simply transfer the balance in the Cost of Goods Sold account to Income Summary. Of course, Sales must be closed under both inventory systems. In Illustration 8–4, both inventory systems result in the same amounts of sales, cost of goods sold, and end-of-period merchandise inventory.

Subsidiary Inventory Records—Perpetual System

When a company sells more than one product and uses the perpetual inventory system, the Merchandise Inventory account serves as a controlling account to a subsidiary Merchandise Inventory Ledger. This ledger contains a separate record for each product in stock. This ledger may be computerized or kept on a manual basis. In either case, the record for each product shows the number of units and cost of each purchase, the number of units and cost of each sale, and the resulting balance of product on hand.

Illustration 8–5 shows an example of a subsidiary merchandise inventory record. This particular record is for Product Z, which is stored in Bin 8 of the stockroom. In this case, the record also shows the company's policy of maintaining no more than 25 or no less than 5 units of Product Z on hand.

ILLUSTRATION 8-4 *A Comparison of Entries under Periodic and Perpetual Inventory Systems*

X Company purchases merchandise for $15 per unit and sells it for $25. The company begins the current period with five units of product on hand, which cost a total of $75.

Periodic			Perpetual		
1. *Purchased on credit 10 units of merchandise for $15 per unit.*					
Purchases	150		Merchandise Inventory	150	
Accounts Payable		150	Accounts Payable		150
2. *Returned three units of merchandise purchased in (1).*					
Accounts Payable	45		Accounts Payable	45	
Purchases Ret. and Allow.		45	Merchandise Inventory		45
3. *Sold eight units for $200 cash.*					
Cash	200		Cash	200	
Sales		200	Sales		200
			Cost of Goods Sold	120	
			Merchandise Inventory		120
4. *Closing entries:*					
Merchandise Inventory (Ending)	60		Income Summary	120	
Sales	200		Cost of Goods Sold		120
Purchases Ret. and Allow.	45		Sales	200	
Income Summary		305	Income Summary		200
Income Summary	225				
Merchandise Inv. (Beginning)		75			
Purchases		150			

	Units	Cost
Beginning inventory	5	$ 75
Purchases	10	150
Purchase returns	(3)	(45)
Goods available	12	$180
Goods sold	(8)	(120)
Ending inventory	4	$ 60

ILLUSTRATION 8-5 *A Subsidiary Inventory Record Using FIFO*

Item *Product Z* Location in stockroom *Bin 8*

Maximum *25* Minimum *5*

	Purchased			Sold			Balance		
Date	Units	Cost	Total	Units	Cost	Total	Units	Cost	Total
1/1							10	10.00	100.00
1/5				5	10.00	50.00	5	10.00	50.00
1/8	20	10.50	210.00				5	10.00	
							20	10.50	260.00
1/10				3	10.00	30.00	2	10.00	
							20	10.50	230.00

AS A MATTER OF *Opinion*

Mr. Brown is vice president and director of auditing for JCPenney Company, a $16 billion national retail and catalog chain that includes 1,300 JCPenney stores, 450 Thrift Drug stores, the JCPenney Life Insurance Company, and 180,000 employees.

Mr. Brown began his career with Peat, Marwick, Mitchell & Co., and was director of auditing for Mohasco Industries before joining JCPenney. He is a Certified Internal Auditor, a Certified Public Accountant, and a graduate of the University of Kansas with a B.S. in Business Administration and Accounting.

Mr. Brown has been chairman of the Institute of Internal Auditors, an international professional organization recognized worldwide as the leading authority on internal auditing. He has also served as chairman of the Internal Audit Group of the National Retail Foundation, the international association of retailers.

Charles L. Brown

To maximize customer satisfaction and return to stockholders, the goal of any retailer is to consistently have the right merchandise at the right time and at a price customers are willing to pay. In addition to knowing our customers, a fully integrated and automated perpetual inventory system is the *heart* of a successful department store operation. It provides information on how fast customers are buying, by store and by item (including sizes and colors). As a result, we can anticipate future buying patterns.

Our perpetual inventory system also provides the basis for Electronic Data Interchange (EDI). This automates replenishment to stores from suppliers and reduces the cycle time from ordering to selling. In addition to providing financial information, the perpetual system automates invoice matching with payments to suppliers and allows us to determine shrinkage (inventory losses) by store and by time.

Accounting truly becomes the language of business when the accounting system is integrated into an active, day-to-day, management decision-making process. Perpetual inventory systems are an important example of this integration.

In Illustration 8–5, note that the beginning inventory consisted of 10 units that cost $10 each. The first transaction occurred on January 5 and was a sale of 5 units at $17 per unit. Next, 20 units were purchased on January 8 at a cost of $10.50 per unit. Then, 3 units were sold on January 10 for $17 per unit. The entries to record the January 10 sale are

Jan.	10	Cash (or Accounts Receivable)	51.00	
		Sales		51.00
		3 × $17.00 = $51		
	10	Cost of Goods Sold	30.00	
		Merchandise Inventory		30.00
		3 × $10.00 = $30.00		

In the second entry, notice that the cost per unit assigned to these three units was $10. This indicates that a first-in, first-out basis is being assumed for this product. In addition to FIFO, perpetual inventory systems can be designed to accommodate an average cost flow assumption. Perpetual inventory systems rarely use LIFO in the subsidiary records. If a company wants its financial statements to reflect LIFO, special adjustments are made at the end of each accounting period to convert the balances from FIFO or average to LIFO. The details of using weighted average and LIFO with perpetual systems are explained in a more advanced accounting course.

All companies should take a physical inventory at least annually, even if a perpetual inventory system is used. By taking a physical inventory, management confirms the accuracy of the perpetual inventory records. When the physical inventory shows that the perpetual records are incorrect, a special adjusting entry should be prepared to update the accounts.

Lower of Cost or Market

LO 5 Calculate the lower-of-cost-or-market amount of an inventory.

As we have discussed, the cost of the ending inventory is determined by using one of the four pricing methods (FIFO, LIFO, weighted average, or specific invoice prices). However, the cost of the inventory is not necessarily the amount reported on the balance sheet. Generally accepted accounting principles require that the inventory be reported at market value whenever market is lower than cost. Thus, merchandise inventory is shown on the balance sheet at the **lower of cost or market (LCM)**.

Market Normally Means Replacement Cost

In applying lower of cost or market (LCM) to merchandise inventories, what do accountants mean by the term *market*? In this situation, market does not mean the expected sales price. Instead, market normally means *replacement cost.*[6] That is the price a company would pay if it bought new items to replace those in its inventory.

The theory of LCM is that when the sales price of merchandise falls, the replacement cost also is likely to fall. The decline from the previously incurred cost to replacement cost represents a loss of value that should be recognized when the loss occurs. This is accomplished at the end of the period by writing the ending merchandise down from cost to replacement cost.

		Per Unit				
Product	**Units on Hand**	**Cost**	**Replacement Cost**	**Total Cost**	**Total Replacement Cost**	**Lower of Cost or Replacement Cost**
X	20	$8	$7	$160	$140	$140
Y	10	5	6	50	60	50
Z	5	9	7	45	35	35
Total cost originally incurred				$255		
LCM (applied to whole inventory)					$235	
LCM (applied to each product)						$225

Note that when LCM is applied to the whole inventory, the total is $235, which is $20 lower than the $255 cost. And when the method is applied separately to each product, the sum is only $225. In general, a company may apply LCM three different ways:

1. LCM may be applied separately to each product.
2. LCM may be applied to major categories of products.
3. If the products are not too different, LCM may be applied to the inventory as a whole.

The Conservatism Principle

Generally accepted accounting principles require writing inventory down to market when market is less than cost. On the other hand, inventory generally cannot be written up to market when market exceeds cost. If writing inventory down to market is justified, why not also write inventory up to market? What is the reason for this apparent inconsistency?

[6] Exceptions to the normal definition of market as replacement cost are explained in more advanced accounting courses.

The reason is that the gain from a market value increase is not realized until a sales transaction provides verifiable evidence of the amount of the gain. But why, then, are inventories written down when market is below cost?

Accountants often justify the lower of cost or market rule by citing the **conservatism principle.** This principle attempts to guide the accountant in uncertain situations where amounts must be estimated. In general terms, it implies that when "two estimates of amounts to be received or paid in the future are about equally likely, . . . the less optimistic" should be used.[7] Because the value of inventory is uncertain, writing the inventory down when its market value falls is clearly the less optimistic estimate of the inventory's value to the company.

The Retail Method of Estimating Inventories

LO 6 Use the retail method and the gross profit method to estimate an inventory and calculate merchandise turnover and days' stock on hand.

Most companies prepare financial statements on a quarterly or monthly basis. These monthly or quarterly statements are called **interim statements,** because they are prepared between the regular year-end statements. The cost of goods sold information that is necessary to prepare interim statements is readily available if a perpetual inventory system is used. However, a periodic system requires a physical inventory to determine cost of goods sold. To avoid the time-consuming and expensive process of taking a physical inventory each month or quarter, some companies use the **retail inventory method** to estimate cost of goods sold and ending inventory. Then, they take a physical inventory at the end of each year. Other companies also use the retail inventory method to prepare the year-end statements. However, all companies should take a physical inventory at least once each year to correct any errors or shortages.

Estimating an Ending Inventory by the Retail Method

When the retail method is used to estimate an inventory, the company's records must show the amount of inventory it had at the beginning of the period both at *cost* and at *retail.* You already understand the cost of an inventory. The retail amount of an inventory simply means the dollar amount of the inventory at the marked selling prices of the inventory items.

In addition to the beginning inventory, the accounting records must also show the net amount of goods purchased during the period both at cost and at retail. This is the balance of the Purchases account less returns and discounts. Also, the records must show the amount of net sales at retail. With this information, you can estimate the ending inventory as follows:

Step 1: Compute the amount of goods available for sale during the period both at cost and at retail.

Step 2: Divide the goods available at cost by the goods available at retail to obtain a **retail method cost ratio.**

Step 3: Deduct sales (at retail) from goods available for sale (at retail) to determine the ending inventory at retail.

Step 4: Multiply the ending inventory at retail by the cost ratio to reduce the inventory to a cost basis.

Look at Illustration 8–6 to see these calculations.

This is the essence of Illustration 8–6: (1) The company had $100,000 of goods (at marked selling prices) for sale during the period. (2) The cost of these goods was 60% of their $100,000 marked retail sales value. (3) The company's records (its Sales account) showed that $70,000 of these goods were sold, leaving $30,000 (retail value) of unsold merchandise in the ending inven-

[7] FASB, *Statement of Financial Accounting Concepts No. 2* (Norwalk, CT, 1980) par. 95.

ILLUSTRATION 8-6 *Calculating the Ending Inventory Cost by the Retail Method*

		At Cost	At Retail
(Step 1)	Goods available for sale:		
	Beginning inventory	$20,500	$ 34,500
	Net purchases	39,500	65,500
	Goods available for sale	$60,000	$100,000
(Step 2)	Cost ratio: ($60,000/$100,000) × 100 = 60%		
(Step 3)	Deduct net sales at retail		70,000
	Ending inventory at retail		$ 30,000
(Step 4)	Ending inventory at cost ($30,000 × 60%) . .	$18,000	

tory. (4) Since cost in this store is 60% of retail, the estimated cost of this ending inventory is $18,000.

An ending inventory calculated as in Illustration 8–6 is an estimate arrived at by deducting sales (goods sold) from goods available for sale. As we said before, this method may be used for interim statements or even for year-end statements. Nonetheless, a store must take a physical count of the inventory at least once each year to correct any errors or shortages.

Using the Retail Method to Reduce a Physical Inventory to Cost

In retail stores, items for sale normally have price tags that show selling prices. So, when a store takes a physical inventory, it commonly takes the inventory at the marked selling prices of the items on hand. It then reduces the dollar total of this inventory to a cost basis by applying its cost ratio. It does this because the selling prices are readily available and the application of the cost ratio eliminates the need to look up the invoice price of each item on hand.

For example, assume that the company in Illustration 8–6 estimates its inventory by the retail method and takes a physical inventory at the marked selling prices of the goods. Also, assume that the total retail amount of this physical inventory is $29,600. The company may calculate the cost for this inventory simply by applying its cost ratio to the inventory total as follows:

$$\$29{,}600 \times 60\% = \$17{,}760$$

The $17,760 cost figure for this company's ending physical inventory is a satisfactory figure for year-end statement purposes. It is also acceptable to the Internal Revenue Service for tax purposes.

Inventory Shortage

An inventory determined as in Illustration 8–6 is an estimate of the amount of goods on hand. Since it is arrived at by deducting sales from goods for sale, it does not reveal any shortages due to breakage, loss, or theft. However, you can estimate the amount of such shortages by comparing the inventory as calculated in Illustration 8–6 with the amount that results from taking a physical inventory.

For example, in Illustration 8–6, we estimated that the ending inventory at retail was $30,000. Then, we assumed that this same company took a physical inventory and counted only $29,600 of merchandise on hand (at retail). Therefore, the company must have had an inventory shortage at retail of $30,000 − $29,600 = $400. Stated in terms of cost, the shortage is $400 × 60% = $240.

ILLUSTRATION 8-7 *The Gross Profit Method of Estimating Inventory*

Goods available for sale:		
Inventory, January 1, 19X1		$ 12,000
Net purchases	$20,000	
Add transportation-in	500	20,500
Goods available for sale		$ 32,500
Less estimated cost of goods sold:		
Sales	$31,500	
Less sales returns	(1,500)	
Net sales	$30,000	
Estimated cost of goods sold (70% × $30,000)		(21,000)
Estimated March 27 inventory and inventory loss		$ 11,500

Gross Profit Method of Estimating Inventories

Sometimes, a business that does not use a perpetual inventory system or the retail method may need to estimate the cost of its inventory. For example, if a fire destroys the inventory or it is stolen, the business must estimate the inventory so that it can file a claim with its insurance company. In cases such as this, the cost of the inventory can be estimated by the **gross profit method.** With this method, the historical relationship between cost of goods sold and sales is applied to sales of the current period as a way of estimating cost of goods sold during the current period. Then, cost of goods sold is subtracted from the cost of goods available for sale to get the estimated cost of the ending inventory.

To use the gross profit method, several items of accounting information must be available. This includes information about the normal gross profit margin or rate, the cost of the beginning inventory, the cost of net purchases, transportation-in, and the amount of sales and sales returns.

For example, assume that the inventory of a company was totally destroyed by a fire on March 27, 19X1. The company's average gross profit rate during the past five years has been 30% of net sales. On the date of the fire, the company's accounts showed the following balances:

Sales	$31,500
Sales returns	1,500
Inventory, January 1, 19X1	12,000
Net purchases	20,000
Transportation-in	500

With this information, the gross profit method may be used to estimate the company's inventory loss. To apply the gross profit method, the first step is to recognize that whatever portion of each dollar of net sales was gross profit, the remaining portion was cost of goods sold. Thus, if the company's gross profit rate averages 30%, then 30% of each net sales dollar was gross profit, and 70% was cost of goods sold. In Illustration 8–7, we show how the 70% is used to estimate the inventory that was lost.

To understand Illustration 8–7, recall that an ending inventory is normally subtracted from goods available for sale to determine the cost of goods sold. Then observe in Illustration 8–7 that the opposite subtraction is made. Estimated cost of goods sold is subtracted from goods available for sale to determine the estimated ending inventory.

As we mentioned, the gross profit method is often used to estimate the amount of an insurance claim. The method is also used by accountants to see if an inventory amount determined by management's physical count of the items on hand is reasonable.

Using the Information—Merchandise Turnover and Days' Stock on Hand

In prior chapters, we explained some ratios that you can use to evaluate a company's short-term liquidity. These ratios include the current ratio, the acid-test ratio, days' sales uncollected, and accounts receivable turnover. A company's ability to pay its short-term obligations also depends on how rapidly it sells its merchandise inventory. To evaluate this, you may calculate **merchandise turnover,** which is the number of times the average inventory was sold during the accounting period. The formula for this ratio is

$$\text{Merchandise turnover} = \frac{\text{Cost of goods sold}}{\text{Average merchandise inventory}}$$

In this ratio, the average merchandise inventory is usually calculated by adding the beginning and ending inventory amounts and dividing the total by two. However, if the company's sales vary by season of the year, you may want to take an average of the inventory amounts at the end of each quarter.

Analysts use merchandise turnover in evaluating short-term liquidity. In addition, they may use it to assess whether management is doing a good job of controlling the amount of inventory kept on hand. A ratio that is high compared to the ratios of competing companies may indicate that the amount of merchandise held in inventory is too low. As a result, sales may be lost because customers are unable to find what they want. A ratio that is low compared to other companies may indicate an inefficient use of assets. In other words, the company may be holding more merchandise than is needed to support its sales volume.

Earlier in the chapter, we explained how the choice of an inventory costing method (such as FIFO, weighted average, or LIFO) affects the reported amounts of inventory and cost of goods sold. The choice of an inventory costing method also affects the calculated amount of merchandise turnover. Therefore, comparing the merchandise turnover ratios of different companies may be misleading unless they use the same costing method.

Another inventory statistic that is used to evaluate the liquidity of the merchandise inventory is **days' stock on hand.** This is similar to the days' sales uncollected measure described in Chapter 6. The formula for days' stock on hand is

$$\text{Days' stock on hand} = \frac{\text{Ending inventory}}{\text{Cost of goods sold}} \times 365$$

Notice the difference in the focus of merchandise turnover and days' stock on hand. Merchandise turnover is an average that occurred during an accounting period. By comparison, the focus of days' stock on hand is on the end-of-period inventory. Days' stock on hand is an estimate of how many days it will take to convert the inventory on hand at the end of the period into accounts receivable or cash.

Summary of the Chapter in Terms of Learning Objectives

LO 1 The allocation of the cost of goods available for sale between cost of goods sold and ending inventory is an accounting application of the *matching principle.* Merchandise inventory should include all goods owned by the business and held for resale. This includes items the business has placed on consignment with other parties but excludes items that the business has taken on consignment from other parties. The cost of merchandise includes not only the invoice price less any discounts but also any additional or incidental costs incurred to put the merchandise into place and condition for sale.

LO 2 When specific invoice prices are used to price an inventory, each item in the inventory is identified and the cost of the item is determined by referring to the item's purchase invoice. With weighted-average cost, the total cost of the beginning inventory and of purchases is divided by the total number of units available to determine the weighted-average cost per unit. Multiplying this cost by the number of units in the ending inventory yields the cost of the inventory. FIFO prices the ending inventory based on the assumption that the first units purchased are the first units sold. LIFO is based on the assumption that the last units purchased are the first units sold. All of these methods are acceptable.

LO 3 When the periodic inventory system is used, an error in counting the ending inventory affects assets (inventory), net income (cost of goods sold), and owners' equity. Since the ending inventory is the beginning inventory of the next period, an error at the end of one period affects the cost of goods sold and the net income of the next period. These next period effects offset the financial statement effects in the previous period.

LO 4 Under a perpetual inventory system, purchases and purchases returns are recorded in the Merchandise Inventory account. At the time sales are recorded, the cost of goods sold is credited to Merchandise Inventory. As a result, the Merchandise Inventory is kept up to date throughout the accounting period.

LO 5 When lower of cost or market is applied to merchandise inventory, market usually means replacement cost. Lower of cost or market may be applied separately to each product, to major categories of products, or to the merchandise inventory as a whole.

LO 6 When the retail method is used, sales are subtracted from the retail amount of goods available for sale to determine the ending inventory at retail. This is multiplied by the cost ratio to reduce the inventory amount to cost. To calculate the cost ratio, divide the cost of goods available by the retail value of goods available (including markups but excluding markdowns).

With the gross profit method, multiply sales by (1 − the gross profit rate) to estimate cost of goods sold. Then, subtract the answer from the cost of goods available for sale to estimate the cost of the ending inventory.

Analysts use merchandise turnover and days' stock on hand in evaluating a company's short-term liquidity. They also use merchandise turnover to evaluate whether the amount of merchandise kept in inventory is too high or too low.

Demonstration Problem

Tale Company uses a periodic inventory system and had the following beginning inventory and purchases during 19X1:

Date		Item X Units	Item X Unit Cost
1/1	Inventory	400	$14
3/10	Purchase	200	15
5/9	Purchase	300	16
9/22	Purchase	250	20
11/28	Purchase	100	21

At December 31, 19X1, there were 550 units of X on hand.

Required

1. Using the preceding information, apply FIFO inventory pricing and calculate the cost of goods available for sale in 19X1, the ending inventory, and the cost of goods sold.

2. In preparing the financial statements for 19X1, the bookkeeper was instructed to use FIFO but failed to do so and computed the cost of goods sold according to LIFO. Determine the size of the misstatement of 19X1's income from this error. Also determine the effect of the error on the 19X2 income. Assume no income taxes.

Planning the Solution

- Multiply the units of each purchase and the beginning inventory by the appropriate unit costs to determine the total costs. Then, calculate the cost of goods available for sale.
- For FIFO, calculate the ending inventory by multiplying the units on hand by the unit costs of the latest purchases. Then, subtract the ending inventory from the cost of goods available for sale.
- For LIFO, calculate the ending inventory by multiplying the units on hand by the unit costs of the beginning inventory and the earliest purchases. Then, subtract the total ending inventory from the cost of goods available for sale.
- Compare the ending 19X1 inventory amounts under FIFO and LIFO to determine the misstatement of 19X1 income that resulted from using LIFO. The 19X2 and 19X1 errors are equal in amount but have opposite effects.

Solution to Demonstration Problem

1. FIFO basis:

1/1 inventory (400 @ $14)		$ 5,600
Purchases:		
3/10 purchase (200 @ $15).	$3,000	
5/9 purchase (300 @ $16)	4,800	
9/22 purchase (250 @ $20).	5,000	
11/28 purchase (100 @ $21)	2,100	14,900
Cost of goods available for sale		$20,500
Ending inventory at FIFO cost:		
11/28 purchase (100 @ $21)	$2,100	
9/22 purchase (250 @ $20).	5,000	
5/9 purchase (200 @ $16)	3,200	
Ending inventory		10,300
Cost of goods sold		$10,200

2. LIFO basis:

Cost of goods available for sale		$20,500
Ending inventory at LIFO cost:		
1/1 inventory (400 @ $14)	$5,600	
3/10 purchase (150 @ $15).	2,250	
LIFO cost of ending inventory.		7,850
Cost of goods sold		$12,650

If LIFO is mistakenly used when FIFO should have been used, cost of goods sold in 19X1 would be overstated by $2,450, which is the difference between the FIFO and LIFO amounts of ending inventory. Income would be understated in 19X1 by $2,450. In 19X2, income would be overstated by $2,450 because of the understatement of the beginning inventory.

Glossary

LO 7 Define or explain the words and phrases listed in the chapter glossary.

Conservatism principle the accounting principle that guides accountants to select the less optimistic estimate when two estimates of amounts to be received or paid are about equally likely. p. 306

Consignee one who receives and holds goods owned by another party for the purpose of selling the goods for the owner. p. 295

Consignor an owner of goods who ships them to another party who will then sell the goods for the owner. p. 295

Consistency principle the accounting requirement that a company use the same accounting methods period after period so that the financial statements of succeeding periods will be comparable. p. 300

Days' stock on hand an estimate of how many days it will take to convert the inventory on hand at the end of the period into accounts receivable or cash; calculated by dividing the ending inventory by cost of goods sold and multiplying the result by 365. p. 309

First-in, first-out inventory pricing (FIFO) the pricing of an inventory under the assumption that the first items received were the first items sold. p. 298

Gross profit inventory method a procedure for estimating an ending inventory in which the past gross profit rate is used to estimate cost of goods sold, which is then subtracted from the cost of goods available for sale to determine the estimated ending inventory. p. 308

Interim statements monthly or quarterly financial statements prepared in between the regular year-end statements. p. 306

Inventory ticket a form attached to the counted items in the process of taking a physical inventory. p. 296

Last-in, first-out inventory pricing (LIFO) the pricing of an inventory under the assumption that the last items received were the first items sold. p. 298

Lower of cost or market (LCM) the required method of reporting merchandise inventory on the balance sheet, in which market is normally defined as replacement cost on the date of the balance sheet. p. 305

Merchandise turnover the number of times a company's average inventory was sold during an accounting period, calculated by dividing cost of goods sold by the average merchandise inventory balance. p. 309

Net realizable value the expected sales price of an item less any additional costs to sell. p. 295

Retail inventory method a method for estimating an ending inventory based on the ratio of the amount of goods for sale at cost to the amount of goods for sale at marked selling prices. p. 306

Retail method cost ratio the ratio of goods available for sale at cost to goods available for sale at retail prices. p. 306

Specific invoice inventory pricing the pricing of an inventory where the purchase invoice of each item in the ending inventory is identified and used to determine the cost assigned to the inventory. p. 297

Weighted-average inventory pricing an inventory pricing system in which the unit prices of the beginning inventory and of each purchase are weighted by the number of units in the beginning inventory and each purchase. The total of these amounts is then divided by the total number of units available for sale to find the unit cost of the ending inventory and of the units that were sold. p. 297

Objective Review

Answers to the following questions are listed at the end of this chapter. Be sure that you decide which is the one best answer to each question *before* you check the answers.

LO 1 Kramer Gallery purchased an original painting for $11,400. Additional costs incurred in obtaining and selling the artwork included $130 for transportation-in, $150 for import duties, $100 for insurance during shipment, $180 for advertising costs, $400 for framing, and $800 for sales commissions. In calculating the cost of inventory, what total cost should be assigned to the painting?

a. $11,400.

b. $11,530.

c. $11,780.

d. $12,180.

e. $13,160.

LO 2 The following data relate to a single inventory item for Montgomery Co.:

Date	Units	Unit Cost
May 1 Beginning inventory	110	$5
2 Purchase	30	6
17 Sale	40	
19 Purchase	25	4
26 Sale	20	

Using a perpetual inventory system and costing inventory by LIFO, the ending inventory is

a. $260.

b. $520.

c. $525.

d. $530.

e. $830.

LO 3 Falk Company maintains its inventory records on a periodic basis. In making the physical count of inventory at 19X1 year-end, an error was made that overstated the 19X1 ending inventory by $10,000. What impact, if any, will this error have on cost of goods sold in 19X1 and 19X2?

a. 19X1 overstated by $10,000; 19X2 understated by $10,000.

b. 19X1 understated by $10,000; 19X2 overstated by $10,000.

c. 19X1 overstated by $10,000; no impact on 19X2.

d. 19X1 understated by $10,000; no impact on 19X2.

e. 19X1 understated by $10,000; no impact on 19X2 cost of goods sold, but 19X2 ending inventory will be overstated by $10,000.

LO 4 With a perpetual inventory system:

a. The Merchandise Inventory account balance shows the amount of merchandise on hand.

b. Subsidiary inventory records are maintained for each type of product.

c. A sale of merchandise requires two entries, one to record the revenue and one to record the cost of goods sold.

d. A separate Cost of Goods Sold account is used.

e. All of the above are correct.

LO 5 A company's ending inventory includes the following items:

Product	Units on Hand	Unit Cost	Market Value per Unit
A	20	$ 6	$ 5
B	40	9	8
C	10	12	15

Applied separately to each product, the inventory's lower of cost or market amount is

a. $520.
b. $540.
c. $570.
d. $600.
e. None of the above.

LO 6 The following data relates to Taylor Company's inventory during the year:

	Cost	Retail
Beginning inventory	$324,000	$530,000
Purchases	204,000	343,000
Purchases returns	3,600	8,000
Markups		9,000
Markdowns		75,000
Sales		320,000

Using the retail method, the estimated cost of the ending inventory is:

a. $129,400.
b. $287,400.
c. $290,370.
d. $314,368.
e. $479,000.

LO 7 The accounting principle that guides accountants to select the less optimistic estimate when two estimates of amounts to be received or paid are about equally likely is the:

a. Retail principle.
b. Lower of cost or market principle.
c. Consistency principle.
d. Conservatism principle.
e. None of the above.

Questions for Class Discussion

1. Where is merchandise inventory disclosed in the financial statements?
2. If Campbell sells goods to Thompson, FOB Campbell's factory, and the goods are still in transit from Campbell to Thompson, which company should include the goods in its inventory?
3. Of what does the cost of an inventory item consist?
4. Why are incidental costs often ignored in pricing an inventory? Under what accounting principle is this permitted?
5. Give the meanings of the following when applied to inventory: (*a*) FIFO; (*b*) LIFO; (*c*) cost; and (*d*) perpetual inventory.
6. If prices are rising, will the LIFO or the FIFO method of inventory valuation result in the higher gross profit?
7. If prices are falling, will the LIFO or the FIFO method of inventory valuation result in the higher ending inventory?
8. If prices are falling, will the LIFO or the FIFO method of inventory valuation result in the lower cost of goods sold?
9. May a company change its inventory pricing method each accounting period?
10. Does the accounting principle of consistency preclude any changes from one accounting method to another?
11. What effect does the full-disclosure principle have if a company changes from one acceptable accounting method to another?
12. What is meant when it is said that under a periodic inventory system, inventory errors correct themselves?
13. If inventory errors under a periodic inventory system correct themselves, why be concerned when such errors are made?
14. What guidance for accountants is provided by the principle of conservatism?
15. What accounts are used in a periodic inventory system but not in a perpetual inventory system?
16. What account is used in a perpetual inventory system but not in a periodic system?
17. What is the usual meaning of the word *market* as it is used in determining the lower of cost or market for merchandise inventory?
18. In deciding whether to reduce an item of merchandise to the lower of cost or market, what is the importance of the item's net realizable value?
19. Refer to the financial statements of Ben & Jerry's Homemade, Inc., in Appendix G. Calculate the merchandise turnover for 1992.

Apple Computer, Inc.

20. Refer to Apple Computer, Inc.'s financial statements in Appendix F and Ben & Jerry's Homemade, Inc.'s financial statements in Appendix G. On September 25, 1992, what percentage of Apple's current assets was represented by inventories? On December 26, 1992, what percentage of Ben & Jerry's current assets was represented by inventory?

Exercises

Exercise 8–1
Alternative cost flow assumptions, periodic inventory system
(LO 2)

Serges Company began a year and purchased merchandise as follows:

Jan.	1	Beginning inventory	80 units	@ $60.00 =	$ 4,800
Feb.	16	Purchased	400 units	@ $56.00 =	22,400
Sept.	2	Purchased	160 units	@ $50.00 =	8,000
Nov.	26	Purchased	320 units	@ $46.00 =	14,720
Dec.	4	Purchased	240 units	@ $40.00 =	9,600
		Total	1,200 units		$59,520

Required

The company uses a periodic inventory system, and the ending inventory consists of 300 units, 100 from each of the last three purchases. Determine the share of the $59,520 cost of the units for sale that should be assigned to the ending inventory and to goods sold under each of the following: (*a*) costs are assigned on the basis of specific invoice prices, (*b*) costs are assigned on a weighted-average cost basis, (*c*) costs are assigned on the basis of FIFO, and (*d*) costs are assigned on the basis of LIFO. Assuming the company has enough income to require that it pay income taxes, which method provides a current tax advantage?

Exercise 8–2
Alternative cost flow assumptions, periodic inventory system
(LO 2)

Finest Company began a year and purchased merchandise as follows:

Jan.	1	Beginning inventory	80 units	@ $40.00 =	$ 3,200
Feb.	16	Purchased	400 units	@ $46.00 =	18,400
Sept.	2	Purchased	160 units	@ $50.00 =	8,000
Nov.	26	Purchased	320 units	@ $56.00 =	17,920
Dec.	4	Purchased	240 units	@ $60.00 =	14,400
		Total	1,200 units		$61,920

Required

The company uses a periodic inventory system, and the ending inventory consists of 300 units, 100 from each of the last three purchases. Determine the share of the $61,920 cost of the units for sale that should be assigned to the ending inventory and to goods sold under each of the following: (*a*) costs are assigned on the basis of specific invoice prices, (*b*) costs are assigned on a weighted-average cost basis, (*c*) costs are assigned on the basis of FIFO, and (*d*) costs are assigned on the basis of LIFO. Assuming the company has enough income to require that it pay income taxes, which method provides a current tax advantage?

Exercise 8–3
Analysis of inventory errors
(LO 3)

Coe Company had $435,000 of sales during each of three consecutive years, and it purchased merchandise costing $300,000 during each of the years. It also maintained a $105,000 inventory from the beginning to the end of the three-year period. However, in accounting under a periodic inventory system, it made an error at the end of year 1 that caused its ending year 1 inventory to appear on its statements at $90,000, rather than the correct $105,000.

Required

1. State the actual amount of the company's gross profit in each of the years.
2. Prepare a comparative income statement like Illustration 8–2 to show the effect of this error on the company's cost of goods sold and gross profit in year 1, year 2, and year 3.

Exercise 8–4
Perpetual inventory system—FIFO cost flow
(LO 4)

In its beginning inventory on January 1, 19X1, Stable Company had 120 units of merchandise that cost $8 per unit. Prepare general journal entries for Stable to record the following transactions during 19X1, assuming a perpetual inventory system and a first-in, first-out cost flow:

April	3	Purchased on credit 300 units of merchandise at $10.00 per unit.
	9	Returned 60 defective units from the April 3 purchase to the supplier.
July	16	Purchased for cash 180 units of merchandise at $8.50 per unit.

Aug. 5 Sold 200 units of merchandise for cash at a price of $12.50 per unit.
Dec. 31 Prepare entries to close the revenue and expense accounts to Income Summary.

Exercise 8–5
Lower of cost or market
(LO 5)

Crystal Corporation's ending inventory includes the following items:

Product	Units on Hand	Unit Cost	Replacement Cost per Unit
W	40	$30	$34
X	50	48	40
Y	60	26	24
Z	44	20	20

Replacement cost is determined to be the best measure of market. Calculate lower of cost or market for the inventory (*a*) as a whole and (*b*) applied separately to each product.

Exercise 8–6
Estimating ending inventory—retail method
(LO 6)

During an accounting period, Felder Company sold $220,000 of merchandise at marked retail prices. At the period end, the following information was available from its records:

	At Cost	At Retail
Beginning inventory	$ 62,180	$102,000
Net purchases	115,820	176,125

Use the retail method to estimate Felder's ending inventory at cost.

Exercise 8–7
Reducing physical inventory to cost—retail method
(LO 6)

Assume that, in addition to estimating its ending inventory by the retail method, Felder Company of Exercise 8–6 also took a physical inventory at the marked selling prices of the inventory items. Assume further that the total of this physical inventory at marked selling prices was $50,500. Then, (*a*) determine the amount of this inventory at cost and (*b*) determine the store's inventory shrinkage from breakage, theft, or other causes, at retail and at cost.

Exercise 8–8
Estimating ending inventory—gross profit method
(LO 6)

On January 1, a store had a $216,000 inventory at cost. During the first quarter of the year, it purchased $735,000 of merchandise, returned $10,500, and paid freight charges on purchased merchandise totaling $22,300. During the past several years, the store's gross profit on sales has averaged 25%. Under the assumption the company had $890,000 of sales during the first quarter of the year, use the gross profit method to estimate its inventory at the end of the first quarter.

Exercise 8–9
Merchandise turnover and days' stock on hand
(LO 6)

From the following information for Jester Company, calculate merchandise turnover for 19X3 and 19X2 and days' stock on hand at December 31, 19X3, and 19X2.

	19X3	19X2	19X1
Cost of goods sold	$367,900	$243,800	$223,600
Inventory (December 31)	77,120	69,400	73,200

Comment on Jester's efficiency in using its assets to support increasing sales from 19X2 to 19X3.

Problems

Problem 8–1
Alternative cost flows—periodic system
(LO 2)

Hart Company began a year with 3,000 units of Product A in its inventory that cost $25 each, and it made successive purchases of the product as follows:

Jan. 29	4,500 units @ $30 each
Apr. 4	5,000 units @ $35 each
Sept. 8	4,800 units @ $40 each
Dec. 9	4,500 units @ $45 each

The company uses a periodic inventory system. On December 31, a physical count disclosed that 6,000 units of Product A remained in inventory.

Required

1. Prepare a calculation showing the number and total cost of the units available for sale during the year.
2. Prepare calculations showing the amounts that should be assigned to the ending inventory and to cost of goods sold assuming (*a*) a FIFO basis, (*b*) a LIFO basis, and (*c*) a weighted-average cost basis. Round your calculation of the weighted-average cost per unit to three decimal places.

Problem 8–2
Income statement comparisons and cost flow assumptions
(LO 2)

MDI Company sold 7,800 units of its product at $55 per unit during 19X1. Incurring operating expenses of $8 per unit in selling the units, it began the year and made successive purchases of the product as follows:

January 1 beginning inventory	800 units costing $30.00 per unit
Purchases:	
March 3	1,000 units costing $31.00 per unit
June 9	2,000 units costing $32.00 per unit
October 17	4,500 units costing $33.00 per unit
December 6	600 units costing $34.00 per unit

Required

Prepare a comparative income statement for the company, showing in adjacent columns the net incomes earned from the sale of the product assuming the company uses a periodic inventory system and prices its ending inventory on the basis of: (*a*) FIFO, (*b*) LIFO, and (*c*) weighted-average cost. Assume an income tax rate of 30%. Round your calculation of the weighted-average cost per unit to three decimal places.

Problem 8–3
Analysis of inventory errors
(LO 3)

Ying Company keeps its inventory records on a periodic basis. The following amounts were reported in the company's financial statements:

	Financial Statements for Year Ended December 31,		
	19X1	**19X2**	**19X3**
(*a*) Cost of goods sold	$130,000	$154,000	$140,000
(*b*) Net income	40,000	50,000	42,000
(*c*) Total current assets	210,000	230,000	200,000
(*d*) Owner's equity	234,000	260,000	224,000

In making the physical counts of inventory, the following errors were made:

Inventory on December 31, 19X1	Understated	$12,000
Inventory on December 31, 19X2	Overstated	6,000

Required

1. For each of the preceding financial statement items—(*a*), (*b*), (*c*), and (*d*)—prepare a schedule similar to the following and show the adjustments that would have been necessary to correct the reported amounts.

	19X1	**19X2**	**19X3**
Cost of goods sold:			
Reported	____	____	____
Adjustments: 12/31/X1 error	____	____	____
12/31/X2 error	____	____	____
Corrected	====	====	====

2. What is the error in the aggregate net income for the three-year period that resulted from the inventory errors?

Problem 8–4
Lower of cost or market
(LO 5)

The following information pertains to the physical inventory of Home Appliance Center taken at December 31:

Product	Units on Hand	Per Unit Cost	Per Unit Replacement Cost
Kitchen:			
Refrigerators	165	$380	$405
Stoves	120	203	181
Dishwashers	158	140	165
Microwaves	200	50	40
Entertainment:			
Stereos	140	250	312
Televisions	360	304	320
Cleaning/Maintenance:			
Washers	245	190	146
Dryers	280	188	162
Vacuum Cleaners . .	104	67	79

Required

In each of the these independent cases, calculate the lower of cost or market (*a*) for the inventory as a whole, (*b*) for the inventory by major category, and (*c*) for the inventory, applied separately to each product.

Problem 8–5
Retail inventory method
(LO 6)

The records of The Unlimited provided the following information for the year ended December 31:

	At Cost	At Retail
January 1 beginning inventory	$ 160,450	$ 264,900
Purchases	1,113,140	1,828,200
Purchases returns	17,600	34,100
Sales		1,570,200
Sales returns		15,600

Required

1. Prepare an estimate of the company's year-end inventory by the retail method.
2. Under the assumption the company took a year-end physical inventory at marked selling prices that totaled $478,800, prepare a schedule showing the store's loss from theft or other cause at cost and at retail.

Problem 8–6
Gross profit method
(LO 6)

Cafferty Company wants to prepare interim financial statements for the first quarter of 19X1. The company uses a periodic inventory system but would like to avoid making a physical count of inventory. During the last five years, the company's gross profit rate has averaged 35%. The following information for the year's first quarter is available from its records:

January 1 beginning inventory	$ 600,520
Purchases	1,890,400
Purchases returns	26,100
Transportation-in	13,800
Sales	2,382,300
Sales returns	18,900

Required

Use the gross profit method to prepare an estimate of the company's March 31 inventory.

Problem 8–7
Analytical essay
(LO 3)

Starlite Furniture uses a periodic inventory system to account for its merchandise. Describe what effect, if any, the following independent errors would have on Starlite's financial statements for 19X2 and 19X3:

a. Goods held on consignment by Starlite were included in its December 31, 19X2, inventory.

b. Merchandise stored in one of Starlite's warehouses was double counted in the inventory taken on December 31, 19X1.

c. Starlite purchased and received merchandise in December 19X2, but did not record the purchase until 19X3. (Assume payment for the merchandise was not due until January 19X3.)

Provocative Problems

Provocative Problem 8–1
Dow Chemical Company
(LO 2)

The Dow Chemical Company manufactures and supplies more than 2,000 products and services, including chemicals and performance products, plastics, hydrocarbons and energy, and consumer specialities. In the company's 1992 annual report, the footnotes to the financial statements included the following:

Inventories

A reduction of certain inventories resulted in the liquidation of some quantities of LIFO inventory, which decreased pretax income by $6 [million] in 1992 and which increased pretax income by $11 [million] in 1991 and $44 [million] in 1990.

The amount of reserve required to reduce inventories from the first-in, first-out basis to the last-in, first-out basis on December 31, 1992 and 1991, was $162 [million] and $216 [million], respectively. The inventories that were valued on a LIFO basis represented 42 percent and 40 percent of the total inventories on December 31, 1992 and 1991, respectively.
(Courtesy of Dow Chemical Company and Subsidiaries.)

Discuss the financial statement effects of experiencing a reduction in inventory when LIFO is used and explain how this applies to Dow Chemical.

Provocative Problem 8–2
Times Mirror Company
(LO 2)

The Times Mirror Company is a media and information company that does business in three principal areas: print media, professional information and book publishing, and electronic media. Times Mirror uses the FIFO method for books and certain finished products and LIFO for newsprint, paper, and certain other inventories. The 1991 annual report of Times Mirror included the following footnote to its financial statements:

Note G—Inventories

Inventories consist of the following (in thousands):

	1991	1990	1989
Newsprint, paper, and other raw materials	$ 59,557	$ 54,951	$ 41,165
Books and other finished products	71,788	72,692	68,282
Work-in-process	20,596	24,654	21,782
	$151,941	$152,297	$131,229

Inventories determined on the last-in, first-out method were $51,133,000, $46,323,000 and $33,194,000 at December 31, 1991, 1990, and 1989, respectively, and would have been higher by $7,427,000 in 1991, $16,986,000 in 1990 and $15,756,000 in 1989 had the first-in, first-out method (which approximates current cost) been used exclusively.
(Courtesy of Times Mirror Company.)

Times Mirror reported a net income of $81,954,000 in 1991. Retained earnings on December 31, 1991, was $1,722,734,000. If Times Mirror had used FIFO for all of its inventories, what would the total inventories reported on December 31, 1991, and January 1, 1991, have been? Assuming the average income tax rate applicable to the company was 30% in all past years, what would have been reported as 1991 net income if FIFO had been used for all inventories? What would have been the balance of retained earnings on December 31, 1991? Comment on Times Mirror's policy of using FIFO for some inventories and LIFO for other inventories in light of the consistency principle.

Provocative Problem 8–3
Apple Computer, Inc.
(Analysis and review problem)

Apple Computer, Inc.

Refer to the financial statements and related disclosures from Apple Computer, Inc.'s 1992 annual report in Appendix F. Based on your examination of this information, answer the following:

1. What was the total amount of inventories held as current assets by Apple at September 25, 1992? At September 27, 1991?
2. Inventories represented what percentage of total assets at September 25, 1992? At September 27, 1991?
3. Comment on the relative size of inventories Apple holds compared to other types of assets.
4. What method did Apple use to determine the inventory amounts reported on its balance sheet?
5. Calculate merchandise turnover for fiscal year 1992 and days' stock on hand at September 25, 1992, and September 27, 1991. (Use cost of sales for cost of goods sold.)

Answers to Objective Review Questions

LO 1 (*d*)
LO 2 (*b*)
LO 3 (*b*)
LO 4 (*e*)
LO 5 (*b*)
LO 6 (*b*)
LO 7 (*d*)

CHAPTER

9

Plant and Equipment

The focus of this chapter is long-term, tangible assets used in the operations of a business. In studying the chapter, you will learn what distinguishes them from other types of assets, how to determine their cost, and how companies allocate their cost to the periods that benefit from their use.

Learning Objectives

After studying Chapter 9, you should be able to:

1. Describe the differences between plant assets and other kinds of assets, calculate the cost and record the purchase of plant assets, and explain the use of total asset turnover in evaluating a company's efficiency in using its assets.
2. Explain depreciation accounting (including the reasons for depreciation), calculate depreciation by the straight-line and units-of-production methods, and calculate depreciation after revising the estimated useful life of an asset.
3. Describe the use of accelerated depreciation for financial accounting and tax accounting purposes and calculate accelerated depreciation under (*a*) the declining-balance method, and (*b*) the Modified Accelerated Cost Recovery System.
4. Describe the difference between revenue and capital expenditures and account properly for costs such as repairs and betterments incurred after the original purchase of plant assets.
5. Prepare entries to account for the disposal of plant assets and to record the exchange of plant assets.
6. Define or explain the words and phrases listed in the chapter glossary.

Plant Assets Compared to Other Types of Assets

Tangible assets that are used in the production or sale of other assets or services and that have a useful life longer than one accounting period are called *plant assets.* In the past, such assets were often described as *fixed assets.* However, now more descriptive terms such as *plant and equipment* or perhaps *property, plant, and equipment* are used more often.

The main difference between plant assets and merchandise is that plant assets are held for use while merchandise is held for sale. For example, a business that buys a computer for the purpose of reselling it should report the computer on the balance sheet as merchandise inventory. If the same retailer owns another computer that is used to account for business operations and to prepare reports, it is classified as plant and equipment.

LO 1 Describe the differences between plant assets and other kinds of assets, calculate the cost and record the purchase of plant assets, and explain the use of total asset turnover in evaluating a company's efficiency in using its assets.

The characteristic that distinguishes plant assets from tangible current assets is the length of their useful lives. For example, supplies are usually consumed within a short time after they are placed in use. Thus, their cost is assigned to the single period in which they are used. By comparison, plant assets have longer useful lives that extend over more than one accounting period. As the usefulness of plant assets expires over these periods, their cost must be allocated among them. This allocation should be accomplished in a systematic and rational manner.[1]

Plant assets are not the same as long-term investments. Although both are held for more than one accounting period, investments are not used in the primary operations of the business. For example, land that is held for future expansion is classified as a long-term investment. On the other hand, land on which the company's factory is located is a plant asset. In addition, standby equipment held for use in case of a breakdown or during peak periods of production is a plant asset. However, equipment that is removed from service and held for sale is no longer considered a plant asset.

Cost of a Plant Asset

When a plant asset is purchased, it should be recorded at cost. This cost includes all normal and reasonable expenditures necessary to get the asset in place and ready to use. For example, the cost of a factory machine includes its invoice price, less any cash discount for early payment, plus freight, unpacking, and assembling costs. The cost of an asset also includes the costs of installing a machine before placing it in service. Examples are the costs to build a concrete base or foundation for a machine, to provide electrical connections, and to adjust the machine before using it in operations.

An expenditure cannot be charged to and reported as part of the cost of a plant asset unless the expenditure is reasonable and necessary. For example, if a machine is damaged by being dropped during unpacking, the repairs should not be added to its cost. Instead, they should be charged to an expense account. Also, a fine paid for moving a heavy machine on city streets without proper permits is not part of the cost of the machine. However, if proper permits are obtained, their cost is included in the cost of the asset. Sometimes, costs in addition to the purchase price are incurred to modify or customize a new plant asset. These items should be charged to the asset's cost.

When a plant asset is constructed by a business for its own use, cost includes material and labor costs plus a reasonable amount of indirect overhead costs such as the costs of heat, lights, power, and depreciation on the machinery used to construct the asset. Cost also includes design fees, building permits, and insurance during construction. However, insurance costs for coverage after the asset has been placed in service are an operating expense.

When land is purchased for a building site, its cost includes the total amount paid for the land, including any real estate commissions. It also includes fees for insuring the title, legal fees, and any accrued property taxes paid by the purchaser. Payments for surveying, clearing, grading, draining, and landscaping also are included in the cost of land. Other costs of land include assessments by the local government, whether incurred at the time of purchase or later, for such things as installing streets, sewers, and sidewalks. These assessments are included because they add a more or less permanent value to the land.

[1] See FASB, *Statement of Financial Accounting Concepts No. 6*, "Elements of Financial Statements of Business Enterprises" (Norwalk, CT, 1985), par. 149.

Land purchased as a building site may have an old building that must be removed. In such cases, the total purchase price should be charged to the Land account. Also, the cost of removing the old building, less any amounts recovered through the sale of salvaged materials, should be charged to the Land account.

Because land has an unlimited life and is not consumed when it is used, it is not subject to depreciation. However, **land improvements,** such as parking lot surfaces, fences, and lighting systems have limited useful lives. Although these costs increase the usefulness of the land, they must be charged to separate Land Improvement accounts so that they can be depreciated. Of course, a separate Building account must be charged for the costs of purchasing or constructing a building that will be used as a plant asset.

Land, land improvements, and buildings often are purchased in a single transaction for a lump-sum price. When this occurs, you must allocate the cost of the purchase among the different types of assets, based on their relative market values. These market values may be estimated by appraisal or by using the tax-assessed valuations of the assets.

For example, assume that a company pays $90,000 cash to acquire land appraised at $30,000, land improvements appraised at $10,000, and a building appraised at $60,000. The $90,000 cost is allocated on the basis of appraised values as follows:

	Appraised Value	Percentage of Total	Apportioned Cost
Land	$ 30,000	30%	$27,000
Land improvements	10,000	10	9,000
Building	60,000	60	54,000
Totals	$100,000	100%	$90,000

Nature of Depreciation

LO 2 Explain depreciation accounting (including the reasons for depreciation), calculate depreciation by the straight-line and units-of-production methods, and calculate depreciation after revising the estimated useful life of an asset.

Because plant assets are purchased for use, you can think of a plant asset as a quantity of usefulness that contributes to the operations of the business throughout the service life of the asset. And, because the life of any plant asset (other than land) is limited, this quantity of usefulness expires as the asset is used. This expiration of a plant asset's quantity of usefulness is generally described as *depreciation.* In accounting, this term describes the process of allocating and charging the cost of the usefulness to the accounting periods that benefit from the asset's use.

For example, when a company buys an automobile for use as a plant asset, it acquires a quantity of usefulness in the sense that it obtains a quantity of transportation. The total cost of the transportation is the cost of the car less the expected proceeds to be received when the car is sold or traded in at the end of its service life. This net cost must be allocated to the accounting periods that benefit from the car's use. In other words, the asset's cost must be depreciated. Note that the depreciation process does not measure the decline in the car's market value each period. Nor does it measure the physical deterioration of the car each period. Under generally accepted accounting principles, depreciation is a process of allocating a plant asset's cost to income statements of the years in which it is used.

Because depreciation represents the cost of using a plant asset, you should not begin recording depreciation charges until the asset is actually put to use providing services or producing products.

Service (Useful) Life of a Plant Asset

The **service life** of a plant asset is the length of time it will be used in the operations of the business. This service life (or useful life) may not be as long as the asset's potential life. For example, although computers have a potential life of six to eight years, a company may plan to trade in its old computers for new ones every three years. In this case, the computers have a three-year service life. Therefore, this company should charge the cost of the computers (less their expected trade-in value) to depreciation expense over this three-year period.

Several factors often make the service life of a plant asset hard to predict. Wear and tear from use determine the service life of many assets. However, two additional factors, **inadequacy** and **obsolescence,** often need to be considered.

When a business grows more rapidly than anticipated, the capacity of the assets may become too small for the productive demands of the business. As this happens, the assets become inadequate. Obsolescence, like inadequacy, is hard to anticipate because the timing of new inventions and improvements normally cannot be predicted. Yet, new inventions and improvements may cause a company to discard an obsolete asset long before it wears out.

Many times, a company is able to predict the service life of a new asset based on the company's past experience with similar assets. In other cases, when it has no experience with a particular type of asset, a company must depend on the experience of others or on engineering studies and judgment.

Salvage Value

The total amount of depreciation that should be taken over an asset's service life is the asset's cost minus its estimated **salvage value.** The salvage value of a plant asset is the amount that you expect to receive from selling the asset at the end of its life. If you expect an asset to be traded in on a new asset, the salvage value is the expected trade-in value.

Sometimes, a company must incur additional costs to dispose of plant assets. For example, a company may plan to clean and paint an old machine before offering it for sale. In this case, the estimated salvage value is the expected proceeds from the sale of the asset less the cleaning and painting costs.

Allocating Depreciation

Many depreciation methods for allocating a plant asset's total cost among the several accounting periods in its service life have been suggested and used in the past. However, at present, most companies use the *straight-line method* of depreciation in their financial accounting records for presentation in their financial statements. Some types of assets are depreciated according to the *units-of-production method.* We explain these two methods next, and then consider some *accelerated depreciation* methods.

Straight-Line Method

Straight-line depreciation charges each year in the asset's life with the same amount of expense. To determine the annual expense, the total cost to be depreciated over the asset's life is calculated by first subtracting the asset's estimated salvage value from its cost. This total amount to be depreciated is then divided by the estimated number of accounting periods in the asset's service life.

For example, if an asset costs $7,000, has an estimated service life of five years, and has an estimated $2,000 salvage value, its depreciation per year by the straight-line method is $1,000. This amount is calculated as follows:

$$\frac{\text{Cost} - \text{Salvage}}{\text{Service life in years}} = \frac{\$7{,}000 - \$2{,}000}{5 \text{ years}} = \$1{,}000 \text{ per year}$$

ILLUSTRATION 9–1 *The Financial Statement Effects of Straight-Line Depreciation*

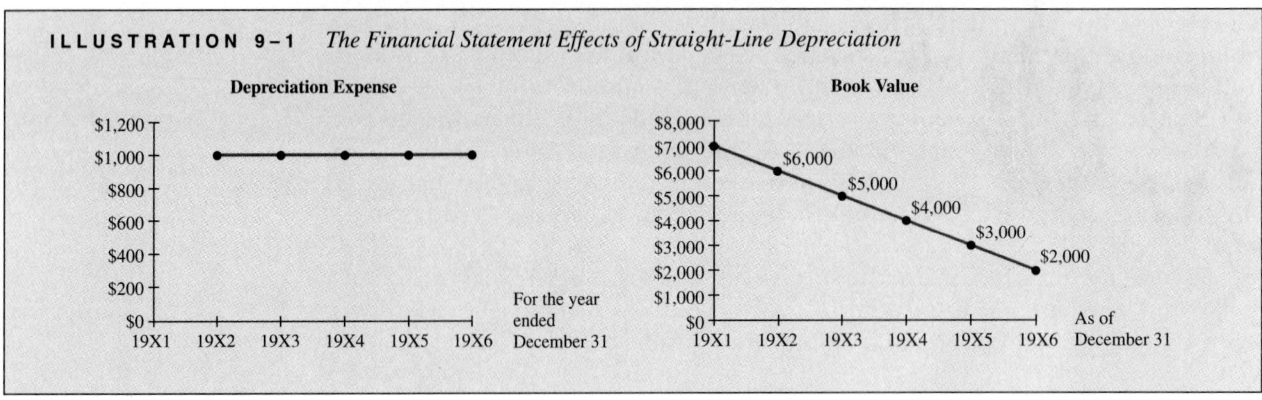

If this asset is purchased on December 31, 19X1, and used throughout its predicted service life of five years, the straight-line method will allocate an equal amount of depreciation to each of those years (19X2 through 19X6). The left graph in Illustration 9–1 shows that this $1,000 per year amount will be reported each year as an expense. The right graph shows the amount that will be reported on each of the six balance sheets that will be produced while the company actually owns the asset. This **book value** of the asset is its original cost less accumulated depreciation. The book value goes down by $1,000 each year. Both graphs show why this method is called *straight line.*

Units-of-Production Method

The purpose of recording depreciation is to provide relevant information about the cost of consuming an asset's usefulness. In general, this means that each accounting period an asset is used should be charged with a fair share of its cost. The straight-line method charges an equal share to each period. If plant assets are used about the same amount in each accounting period, this method produces a reasonable result. However, the use of some plant assets varies greatly from one accounting period to another. For example, a contractor may use a particular piece of construction equipment for a month and then not use it again for a few months.

Because the use of such equipment varies from period to period, **units-of-production depreciation** may provide a better matching of expenses with revenues than straight-line depreciation. Under the units-of-production method, the cost of an asset minus its estimated salvage value is divided by the total number of units that management predicts it will produce during its service life. Units of production may be expressed as units of product or in any other unit of measure such as hours of use or miles driven. In effect, this method computes the amount of depreciation per unit of service provided by the asset. Then, the amount of depreciation taken in an accounting period is determined by multiplying the units produced in that period by the depreciation per unit.

For example, a truck that cost $24,000 has a predicted salvage value of $4,000 and an estimated service life of 125,000 miles. The depreciation per mile, or the depreciation per unit of service, is $0.16, which is calculated as follows:

$$\text{Depreciation per unit of production} = \frac{\text{Cost} - \text{Salvage value}}{\text{Predicted units of production}}$$

$$= \frac{\$24{,}000 - \$4{,}000}{125{,}000 \text{ miles}}$$

$$= \$0.16 \text{ per mile}$$

If the truck is driven 20,000 miles during its first year, depreciation for the first year is \$3,200 (20,000 miles at \$0.16 per mile). If the truck is driven 15,000 miles in the second year, depreciation for the second year is 15,000 miles times \$0.16 per mile, or \$2,400.

Depreciation for Partial Years

Of course, plant assets may be purchased or disposed of at any time during the year. When an asset is purchased (or disposed of) at some time other than the beginning or end of an accounting period, depreciation must be recorded for part of a year. Otherwise, the year of purchase or the year of disposal is not charged with its share of the asset's depreciation.

For example, assume that a machine was purchased and placed in service on October 8, 19X1, and that the annual accounting period ends on December 31. The machine cost \$4,600; it has an estimated service life of five years and an estimated salvage value of \$600. Because the machine was purchased and used nearly three months during 19X1, the annual income statement should reflect depreciation expense on the machine for that part of the year. The amount of depreciation to be reported is often based on the assumption that the machine was purchased on the first of the month nearest the actual date of purchase. Therefore, since the purchase occurred on October 8, three months' depreciation is recorded on December 31. If the purchase had been on October 16 or later during October, depreciation would be calculated as if the purchase had been on November 1. Using straight-line depreciation, the three months' depreciation of \$200 is calculated as follows:

$$\frac{\$4,600 - \$600}{5} \times \frac{3}{12} = \$200$$

A similar calculation is necessary when the disposal of an asset occurs during a year. For example, suppose that the preceding asset is sold on June 24, 19X6. On the date of the disposal, depreciation should be recognized. The partial year's depreciation, calculated to the nearest whole month, is

$$\frac{\$4,600 - \$600}{5} \times \frac{6}{12} = \$400$$

Depreciation on the Balance Sheet

In presenting information about the plant assets of a business, both the cost and accumulated depreciation of plant assets should be reported. For example, Apple Computer, Inc.'s balance sheet at the close of its 1992 fiscal year included the following:

(Dollars in thousands)	1992	1991
Property, plant, and equipment:		
Land and buildings	\$ 255,808	\$ 198,107
Machinery and equipment	516,335	485,872
Office furniture and equipment	155,317	146,433
Leasehold improvements	208,180	205,602
	\$1,135,640	\$1,036,014
Accumulated depreciation and amortization	(673,419)	(588,036)
Net property, plant, and equipment	\$ 462,221	\$ 447,978

Notice that Apple reported only the total amount of accumulated depreciation and amortization for all plant and equipment. This is the usual practice in published financial statements. In fact, many companies show plant and equipment on one line with the net amount of cost less accumulated depreciation. When this is done, however, the amount of accumulated depreciation is disclosed in a footnote. To satisfy the *full-disclosure principle,* companies also describe the depreciation method or methods used.[2] Usually, they do this in a footnote.

Reporting both the cost and the accumulated depreciation of plant assets may help balance sheet readers compare the status of different companies. For example, a company that holds assets having an original cost of $50,000 and accumulated depreciation of $40,000 may be in a quite different situation than another company with new assets that cost $10,000. Although the net undepreciated cost is the same in both cases, the first company may have more productive capacity available but probably is facing the need to replace its older assets. These differences are not conveyed if the balance sheets report only the $10,000 book values.

From the discussion so far, you should recognize that depreciation is a process of cost allocation rather than valuation. Plant assets are reported on balance sheets at their remaining undepreciated costs (book value), not at market values.

Some people argue that financial statements should report the market value of plant assets. However, this practice has not gained general acceptance. Instead, most accountants believe that financial statements should be based on the *going-concern principle* described in Chapter 1. This principle states that, unless there is adequate evidence to the contrary, the accountant should assume the company will continue in business. This leads to a related assumption that plant assets will be held and used long enough to recover their original costs through the sale of products and services. Therefore, since the plant assets will not be sold, their market values are not reported in the financial statements. Instead, the assets are carried on the balance sheet at cost less accumulated depreciation. This is the remaining portion of the original cost that is expected to be recovered in future periods.

Inexperienced financial statement readers may make the mistake of thinking that the accumulated depreciation shown on a balance sheet represents funds accumulated to buy new assets when the presently owned assets must be replaced. However, you know that accumulated depreciation is a contra account with a credit balance that cannot be used to buy anything. If a business has funds available to buy assets, the funds are shown on the balance sheet as liquid assets such as *Cash,* not as accumulated depreciation.

Revising Depreciation Rates

Because the calculation of depreciation must be based on an asset's *predicted* useful life, depreciation expense is an estimate. Therefore, during the life of an asset, new information may indicate that the original prediction of useful life was inaccurate. If your estimate of an asset's useful life changes, what should be done? The answer is to use the new estimate of the remaining useful life to calculate depreciation in the future. In other words, revise the estimate of annual depreciation expense in the future by spreading the remaining cost to be depreciated over the revised remaining useful life. This approach should be followed whether the depreciation method is straight-line, units-of-production, or some other method.

For example, assume that a machine was purchased seven years ago at a cost of $10,500. At that time, the machine was predicted to have a 10-year life with a $500 salvage value. Therefore, it was depreciated by the straight-line method at the rate of $1,000 per year [($10,500 − $500)/10 = $1,000]. At the beginning of the asset's eighth year, its book value is $3,500, calculated as follows:

[2] FASB, *Accounting Standards—Current Text* (Norwalk, CT, 1993), sec. D40.101. First published as *APB Opinion No. 12,* par. 5.

Cost	$10,500
Less seven years' accumulated depreciation	7,000
Book value	$ 3,500

At the beginning of its eighth year, the predicted number of years remaining in the useful life is changed from three to five years. The estimated salvage value is also changed to $300. Depreciation for each of the machine's five remaining years should be calculated as follows:

$$\frac{\text{Book value} - \text{Revised salvage value}}{\text{Revised remaining useful life}} = \frac{\$3{,}500 - \$300}{5 \text{ years}} = \$640 \text{ per year}$$

Thus, $640 of depreciation should be recorded for the machine at the end of the eighth and each remaining year in its useful life.

Because this asset was depreciated at the rate of $1,000 per year for the first seven years, you might contend that depreciation expense was overstated during the first seven years. While that view may have merit, accountants have concluded that past years' financial statements generally should not be restated to reflect facts that were not known when the statements were originally prepared.

A revision of the predicted useful life of a plant asset is an example of a **change in an accounting estimate.** Such changes result "from new information or subsequent developments and accordingly from better insight or improved judgment." Generally accepted accounting principles require that changes in accounting estimates, such as a change in estimated useful life or salvage value, be reflected only in future financial statements, not by modifying past statements.[3]

Accelerated Depreciation

LO 3 Describe the use of accelerated depreciation for financial accounting and tax accounting purposes and calculate accelerated depreciation under (*a*) the declining-balance method, and (*b*) the Modified Accelerated Cost Recovery System.

An annual survey of 600 industrial companies indicates that straight-line is the most widely used method of depreciation. However, note in the following table that **accelerated depreciation** methods were used 14% of the time in 1992.

	Depreciation Methods Used	
	1992	**1991**
Straight-line	78%	77%
An accelerated method	14	15
Units-of-production	7	7
Other	1	1
Total	100%	100%

Source: *Accounting Trends & Techniques,* Copyright © 1993 (1992) by American Institute of Certified Public Accountants, Inc., Table 3–12, p. 341.

Accelerated depreciation methods produce larger depreciation charges during the early years of an asset's life and smaller charges in the later years. Although more than one accelerated method is used in financial reporting, the most commonly used is the declining-balance method.

[3] FASB, *Accounting Standards—Current Text* (Norwalk, CT, 1994), sec. A35.104 and sec. A06.130. First published as *APB Opinion No. 20,* par. 13 and par. 31.

AS A MATTER OF

Ethics

Fascar Company has struggled financially for more than two years. The economic situation surrounding the company has been depressed and there are no signs of improvement for at least two more years. As a result, net income has been almost zero, and the future seems bleak.

The operations of Fascar require major investments in equipment. As a result, depreciation is a large factor in the calculation of income. Because competition in Fascar's industry normally has required frequent replacements of equipment, the equipment has been depreciated over only three years. However, Fascar's president has recently instructed Sue Ann Meyer, the company's accountant, to revise the estimated useful lives of existing equipment to six years and to use a six-year life on new equipment.

Meyer suspects that the president's instruction is motivated by a desire to improve the reported income of the company. In trying to determine whether to follow the president's instructions, Meyer is torn between her loyalty to her employer and her responsibility to the public, the stockholders, and others who use the company's financial statements. She also wonders what the independent CPA who audits the financial statements will think about the change.

Declining-Balance Method

Under **declining-balance depreciation,** a depreciation rate of up to twice the straight-line rate is applied each year to the book value of the asset at the beginning of the year. Because the book value *declines* each year, the amount of depreciation gets smaller each year.

When the depreciation rate used is twice the straight-line rate, the method is called the *double-declining-balance method.* To use the double-declining-balance method: (1) calculate the straight-line depreciation rate for the asset; (2) double it; and (3) calculate depreciation expense for the year by applying this rate to the asset's book value at the beginning of that year. Note that the salvage value is not used in the calculation.

For example, assume that the double-declining-balance method is used to calculate depreciation on a new $10,000 asset; it has an estimated life of five years and an estimated salvage value of $1,000. The steps to follow are

1. Divide 100% by five years to determine the straight-line annual depreciation rate of 20% per year.
2. Double this 20% rate to get a declining-balance rate of 40% per year.
3. Calculate the annual depreciation charges as shown in the following table:

Year	Beginning Book Value	Annual Depreciation (40% of Book Value)*	Accumulated Depreciation at the Year-End	Ending Book Value ($10,000 Cost Less Accumulated Depreciation)
First	$10,000	$4,000	$4,000	$6,000
Second	6,000	2,400	6,400	3,600
Third	3,600	1,440	7,840	2,160
Fourth	2,160	864	8,704	1,296
Fifth	1,296	296*	9,000	1,000
Total		$9,000		

*Fifth year depreciation is $1,296 − $1,000 = $296.

In the fifth year of the table, notice that the annual depreciation of $296 for the fifth year does not equal 40% × $1,296, or $518.40. Instead, the $296 was calculated by subtracting the $1,000 salvage value from the $1,296 book value at the beginning of the fifth year. This was done because, according to generally accepted accounting principles, an asset should not be depreciated below its salvage value. If the declining-balance procedure had been applied in the fifth year, the $518.40 of annual depreciation would have reduced the ending book value to $777.60, which is less than the $1,000 estimated salvage value.

Earlier in the chapter we discussed the calculation of a partial year's depreciation when the straight-line method is used. Recall that when an asset is purchased (or disposed of) at some time other than the end of an accounting period, depreciation must be recorded for part of a year. Declining balance depreciation does not complicate this calculation. For example, if depreciation must be calculated for three months, the annual amount of depreciation is simply multiplied by 3/12. So, if an asset that cost $10,000 is purchased three months before the end of the year and the annual declining-balance depreciation rate is 20%, depreciation for the last three months is $10,000 × 20% × 3/12 = $500.

Accelerated Depreciation for Tax Purposes

Some people fail to understand why the records a company keeps for financial accounting purposes may be different from the records it keeps for tax accounting purposes. Some may even suspect fraud when they hear there are differences between the two sets of records. In fact, differences between the two are normal and to be expected. Accelerated depreciation provides an example of this.

Many companies prefer to use accelerated depreciation for the purpose of calculating their taxable income. Accelerated methods reduce taxable income in the early years of an asset's life and increase taxable income in the later years. The effect of this is to defer income tax payments. Taxes are decreased in the early years and increased in the later years.

Beginning in 1981, a United States federal income tax law installed new rules for depreciating assets. Those rules were revised beginning in 1987 and are now called the **Modified Accelerated Cost Recovery System (MACRS).** MACRS allows straight-line depreciation and for most kinds of property also provides an accelerated method. MACRS separates depreciable assets purchased after December 31, 1986, into eight different types or classes. These include 3 year, 5 year, 7 year, 10 year, 15 year, 20 year, 27½ year, and 31½ year classes. For example, computer equipment and general-purpose, heavy trucks are in the five-year class while office furniture is in the seven-year class.

When calculating depreciation for tax purposes, salvage values are ignored. Also, depreciation methods for personal property are based on the assumption that the asset is purchased half-way through the year and sold or retired half-way through the year. This *half-year convention* is required regardless of when the asset was actually purchased or sold.[4]

To simplify accelerated calculations under MACRS, the Internal Revenue Service provides a table for each class of assets. The table shows the percentage of original cost to be deducted as depreciation on each year's tax return. For example, Illustration 9–2 shows the accelerated depreciation rates for the three-year, five-year, and seven-year classes. In the table, note that it takes four years to fully depreciate the assets in the three-year class. Also, it takes six years to depreciate the assets in the five-year class, and eight years to depreciate the assets in the seven-year class. This happens because the half-

[4] Under certain conditions, a half-quarter convention must be used. Depreciation methods for real property are based on a half-month convention.

ILLUSTRATION 9-2 *Accelerated Depreciation Rates under MACRS Using the Half-Year Convention*

	For Assets in the		
Year	Three-Year Class	Five-Year Class	Seven-Year Class
1 . . .	33.33%	20.00%	14.29%
2 . . .	44.45	32.00	24.49
3 . . .	14.81	19.20	17.49
4 . . .	7.41	11.52	12.49
5 . . .		11.52	8.93
6 . . .		5.76	8.92
7 . . .			8.93
8 . . .			4.46
Total	100.00%	100.00%	100.00%

year convention provides one-half of one year's depreciation during the first year and one-half of one year's depreciation during the last year.

Remember that the half-year convention also applies to straight-line depreciation under MACRS. Thus, under straight-line, it also takes four years to fully depreciate an asset in the three-year class.

As an example of how MACRS is applied, assume an asset in the five-year class (for example, a general-purpose, heavy truck) is purchased in 19X1 at a cost of $10,000. In the following table, the second column shows the MACRS accelerated rates for assets in the five-year class, which includes the truck. The remaining columns in the table show the effects of applying accelerated depreciation under MACRS to the $10,000 truck:

Year	MACRS Accelerated Depreciation Rate	Beginning Tax Basis	(Depreciation Rate × $10,000)	Ending Tax Basis
19X1	20.00%	$10,000	$2,000	$8,000
19X2	32.00	8,000	3,200	4,800
19X3	19.20	4,800	1,920	2,880
19X4	11.52	2,880	1,152	1,728
19X5	11.52	1,728	1,152	576
19X6	5.76	576	576	-0-
Total	100.00%			

While MACRS is now required for tax purposes, MACRS is not consistent with *generally accepted accounting principles.* It is not consistent because it allocates depreciation over an arbitrary period that usually is much shorter than the estimated service life of the asset. For example, general-purpose, heavy trucks in the 5-year class normally have useful lives of up to 10 years. Even when straight-line depreciation is used under MACRS, acceleration occurs because the length of life assumed for tax purposes is shorter than the expected service life of the asset. As a result, companies typically have to keep one set of depreciation records for tax purposes and another set for financial accounting purposes.

Revenue and Capital Expenditures

By this time, you have learned that some expenditures are recorded as expenses right away while others are recorded as assets with expenses coming later. After a plant asset is acquired and put into service, additional expenditures may be incurred to operate, maintain, repair, and improve it. In recording these additional expenditures, the accountant must decide whether they should be debited to expense accounts or asset accounts. The issue is whether more useful information is provided by reporting these expenditures as current expenses or by adding them to the plant asset's cost and depreciating them over its remaining useful life.

LO 4 Describe the difference between revenue and capital expenditures and account properly for costs such as repairs and betterments incurred after the original purchase of plant assets.

Expenditures that are recorded as expenses and deducted from revenues on the current period's income statement are called **revenue expenditures.** They are reported on the income statement because they do not provide material benefits in future periods. Examples of revenue expenditures that relate to plant assets are supplies, fuel, lubricants, and electrical power.

In contrast to revenue expenditures, **capital expenditures** produce economic benefits that do not fully expire before the end of the current period. Because they are debited to asset accounts and reported on the balance sheet, they are also called **balance sheet expenditures.** Capital expenditures increase or improve the kind or amount of service that an asset provides.

Because the information in the financial statements is affected for several years by the choice you make in recording costs as revenue or capital expenditures, be careful in deciding how to classify them. In making these decisions, it may be helpful to identify the costs as ordinary repairs, extraordinary repairs, betterments, or purchases of assets with low costs.

Ordinary Repairs

Ordinary repairs are made to keep an asset in normal, good operating condition. These expenditures are necessary if an asset is to provide its expected level of service over its estimated useful life. However, ordinary repairs do not extend the useful life beyond the original estimate and do not increase the productivity of the asset beyond the levels originally estimated. For example, machines must be cleaned, lubricated, and adjusted, and small parts must be replaced when they wear out. These ordinary repairs typically are made every year, and accountants treat them as *revenue expenditures.* Thus, their costs should be reported on the current income statement as expenses.

Extraordinary Repairs

In contrast to ordinary repairs that keep a plant asset in its normal, good operating condition, **extraordinary repairs** extend the asset's service life beyond the original estimate. Because they benefit future periods, the costs of extraordinary repairs are *capital expenditures.* They may be debited to the asset account. However, by tradition, they are debited to the repaired asset's accumulated depreciation account to show that they restore the effects of past years' depreciation.

For example, a machine was purchased for $8,000 and depreciated under the assumption it would last eight years and have no salvage value. At the beginning of the machine's seventh year, when the machine's book value is $2,000, it is given a major overhaul at a cost of $2,100. The overhaul extends the machine's estimated useful life three years. Thus, the company now predicts that the machine will be used for five more years. The $2,100 cost of the extraordinary repair should be recorded as follows:

Jan.	12	Accumulated Depreciation, Machinery	2,100.00	
		Cash		2,100.00
		To record extraordinary repairs.		

This entry increases the book value of the asset from $2,000 to $4,100. For the remaining five years of the asset's life, depreciation should be based on this new book value. The effects of the extraordinary repairs are as follows:

	Before	Extraordinary Repair	After
Original cost	$ 8,000		$ 8,000
Accumulated depreciation	(6,000)	$2,100	(3,900)
Book value	$ 2,000		$ 4,100
Annual depreciation expense for remaining years ($4,100/5 years)			$ 820

Notice that because the $2,100 cost of the extraordinary repairs is included in the $4,100 book value, it is depreciated over the asset's remaining life of five years.

Betterments

A **betterment** (or an improvement) occurs when a plant asset is modified to make it more efficient or productive. A betterment often involves adding a component to an asset or replacing one of its old components with an improved or superior component. While a betterment makes an asset more productive, it may not increase the asset's useful life. For example, replacing the manual controls on a machine with automatic controls reduces future labor costs. But, the machine still wears out just as fast as it would have with the manual controls.

A betterment benefits future periods and should be debited to the asset account as a capital expenditure. Then, the new book value (less salvage) should be depreciated over the remaining service life of the asset. For example, suppose that a company paid $80,000 for a machine with an eight-year service life and no salvage value. On January 2, after three years and $30,000 of depreciation, it adds an automatic control system to the machine at a cost of $18,000. As a result, the company's labor cost to operate the machine in future periods will be reduced. The cost of the betterment is added to the Machinery account with this entry:

			Debit	Credit
Jan.	2	Machinery	18,000.00	
		Cash		18,000.00
		To record the installation of the automatic control system.		

At this point, the remaining cost to be depreciated is $80,000 + $18,000 − $30,000 = $68,000. Because five years remain in the useful life, the annual depreciation expense hereafter will be $13,600 per year ($68,000/5 years).

Plant Assets with Low Costs

Even with the help of computers, keeping individual plant asset records can be expensive. Therefore, many companies do not keep detailed records for assets that cost less than some minimum amount such as $50 or $100. Instead, they treat the acquisition as a revenue expenditure, and charge the cost directly to an expense account at the time of purchase. As long as the amounts are small, this practice is acceptable under the *materiality principle.* That is, treating these capital expenditures as revenue expenditures is unlikely to mislead a user of the financial statements.

Plant Asset Disposals

A variety of events might lead to the disposal of plant assets. Some assets wear out or become obsolete. Other assets may be sold because of changing business plans. Sometimes, an asset is discarded or sold because it is damaged by a fire or other accident. Regardless of what leads to a disposal, the journal entry or entries related to the disposal should:

LO 5 Prepare entries to record the disposal of plant assets and the exchange of plant assets.

1. Record depreciation expense up to the date of the disposal and bring the accumulated depreciation account up to date.
2. Remove the asset and accumulated depreciation account balances that relate to the disposal.
3. Record any cash received or paid as a result of the disposal.
4. Record any gain or loss that results from comparing the book value of the asset with the cash received or paid as a result of the disposal.

For example, assume a machine that cost $9,000 was totally destroyed in a fire on June 25. Accumulated depreciation at the end of the previous year was $3,000 and unrecorded depreciation for the first six months of the current year is $500. The following entry brings the accumulated depreciation account up to date:

June	25	Depreciation Expense	500.00	
		Accumulated Depreciation, Machinery		500.00
		To record depreciation up to the date of the fire.		

Assume the owner of the machine carried insurance against fire losses and received a $4,400 cash settlement for the loss. The following entry records the loss of the machine and the cash settlement:

June	25	Cash	4,400.00	
		Loss on Fire[5]	1,100.00	
		Accumulated Depreciation, Machinery	3,500.00	
		Machinery		9,000.00
		To record the destruction of machinery, the receipt of insurance settlement, and the net loss resulting from the fire.		

Notice that the two entries accomplish all four of the necessary changes that occurred as a result of the asset disposal. Of course, an asset disposal might involve a gain instead of a loss. Also, a disposal might involve a cash payment instead of a receipt. Regardless of the specific facts, entries similar to these must be made so the income statement shows any gain or loss resulting from the disposal and the balance sheet reflects the necessary changes in the asset and accumulated depreciation accounts.

Exchanging Plant Assets

Many plant assets are sold for cash when they are retired from use. Others, such as machinery, automobiles, and office equipment, are commonly exchanged for new assets. In a typical exchange of assets, a trade-in allowance is received on the old asset, and any balance is paid in cash.

Accounting for the exchange of nonmonetary assets depends on whether the old and the new assets are similar in the functions they perform. For example, trading an old truck for a new truck is an exchange of similar assets. An example of exchanging dissimilar assets would be trading a parcel of land for a truck.

[5] Note that the recorded loss of $1,100 probably does not equal the economic loss from the fire. The economic loss depends on the difference between the cost of replacing the asset and any insurance settlement. A difference between this economic loss and the reported loss arises from the fact that the accounting records do not attempt to reflect the replacement value of plant assets.

Exchanges of Dissimilar Assets

If a company exchanges a plant asset for another asset that is *dissimilar* in use or purpose, any gain or loss on the exchange must be recorded. The gain or loss can be determined by comparing the book value of the assets given up with the fair market value of the assets received. For example, assume that a company exchanges an old machine plus $16,500 cash for some merchandise inventory. The old machine originally cost $18,000 and had accumulated depreciation of $15,000 at the time of the exchange. Also assume that the fair market value of the merchandise received in the exchange was $21,000. This entry would record the exchange:

Jan.	5	Merchandise Inventory (or Purchases)	21,000.00	
		Accumulated Depreciation, Machinery	15,000.00	
		Machinery		18,000.00
		Cash		16,500.00
		Gain on Exchange of Machinery		1,500.00
		Exchanged old machine and cash for merchandise inventory.		

Note that the book value of the assets given up totaled $19,500, which included $16,500 cash plus $3,000 ($18,000 − $15,000) for the machine. Because the merchandise had a fair market value of $21,000, the entry recorded a gain of $1,500 ($21,000 − $19,500).

Another way to calculate the gain or loss is to compare the machine's book value with the trade-in allowance granted for the machine. Since the fair market value of the machine was $21,000 and the cash paid was $16,500, the trade-in allowance granted for the merchandise was $4,500. The difference between the machine's $3,000 book value and the $4,500 trade-in allowance equals the $1,500 gain on the exchange.

Exchanges of Similar Assets

In general, accounting for exchanges of similar assets depends on whether the book value of the asset given up is less or more than the trade-in allowance received for the asset.[6] When the trade-in allowance is less than the book value, the difference is recognized as a loss. However, when the trade-in allowance is more than the book value, no gain is recognized.

Recognition of a Loss. To illustrate the recognition of a loss on an exchange of similar assets, assume the machine that cost $18,000 and has accumulated depreciation of $15,000 is traded in on a similar but new machine. The new machine has a $21,000 cash price, and a $1,000 trade-in allowance is received. The $20,000 balance of the cost is paid in cash. The book value of the old machine and the loss on the exchange are calculated as follows:

Cost of old machine	$18,000
Less accumulated depreciation	15,000
Book value	$ 3,000
Less trade-in allowance	1,000
Loss on exchange	$ 2,000

[6] These general rules apply to exchanges of similar assets when the exchange includes a cash payment or when no cash is received or paid. The accounting is more complex when the exchange involves a cash receipt. Such cases are explained in more advanced accounting texts. See FASB, *Accounting Standards—Current Text* (Norwalk, CT, 1994), sec. N35.109. First published as *APB Opinion No. 29,* par. 22.

The entry to record this exchange transaction is:

Jan.	5	Machinery	21,000.00	
		Loss on Exchange of Machinery	2,000.00	
		Accumulated Depreciation, Machinery	15,000.00	
		Machinery		18,000.00
		Cash		20,000.00
		Exchanged old machine and cash for a similar machine.		

The $21,000 debit to Machinery puts the new machine in the accounts at its cash price. The debit to Loss on Exchange of Machinery records the loss. The old machine is removed from the accounts with the $15,000 debit to Accumulated Depreciation and the $18,000 credit to Machinery.

Nonrecognition of a Gain. When similar assets are exchanged and the trade-in allowance of the asset given up is more than its book value, the difference between the trade-in allowance and the book value may be perceived as a gain. However, generally accepted accounting principles do not allow the recognition of this gain. Instead, the new asset is recorded at the sum of the old asset's book value plus any cash paid.

For example, assume that the exchange for the $21,000 machine in the previous section involved a trade-in allowance of $4,500 instead of $1,000. As a result, the balance to be paid in cash is only $16,500. Since the $4,500 trade-in allowance exceeds the $3,000 book value of the old asset, the difference is a gain. However, you cannot recognize the gain in the accounts. Rather, it is absorbed into the cost of the new machine, which is calculated as follows:

Cost of old machine	$18,000
Less accumulated depreciation	15,000
Book value of old machine	$ 3,000
Cash given in the exchange	16,500
Cost recorded for the new machine	$19,500

The following entry records the exchange:

Jan.	5	Machinery	19,500.00	
		Accumulated Depreciation, Machinery	15,000.00	
		Machinery		18,000.00
		Cash		16,500.00
		Exchanged old machine and cash for a similar but new machine.		

Observe that the $19,500 recorded for the new machine equals its cash price less the unrecognized $1,500 gain on the exchange ($21,000 – $1,500 = $19,500). In other words, the $1,500 gain was absorbed into the amount at which the new machine was recorded. The $19,500 is the *cost basis* of the new machine and is the amount used to calculate its depreciation and/or any gain or loss on its sale.

In summary, when similar plant assets are exchanged and there is a cash payment, losses are recognized but gains are not recognized. This rule is based on the opinion that "revenue [or a gain] should not be recognized merely because one productive asset is substituted for a similar productive asset but rather should be considered to flow from the production and sale of the goods or services to which the substituted productive asset is committed."[7] As a result, the effect of a gain is delayed. In future income statements, the gain appears in the form of smaller depreciation charges or perhaps as a gain on the sale of the asset. In the previous example, depreciation calculated on the recorded $19,500 cost basis of the new machine is smaller than it would be if it was based on the machine's $21,000 cash price.

Using the Information— Total Asset Turnover

LO 1 Describe the differences between plant assets and other kinds of assets, calculate the cost and record the purchase of plant assets, and explain the use of total asset turnover in evaluating a company's efficiency in using its assets.

We have not yet discussed all of the different assets a business might own. Nevertheless, you can see from this and previous chapters that a company's assets are usually very important factors in determining the company's ability to earn profits. Managers spend a great deal of time and energy deciding which assets a company should acquire, how much should be acquired, and how the assets can be used more efficiently. Outside investors and other financial statement readers also are interested in evaluating whether a company uses its assets efficiently.

One way to describe the efficiency of a company's use of its assets is to calculate **total asset turnover.** The formula for this calculation is

$$\text{Total asset turnover} = \frac{\text{Net sales}}{\text{Average total assets}}$$

In this calculation, average total assets is often approximated by averaging the total assets at the beginning of the year with total assets at the end of the year.

For example, suppose that a company with total assets of $9,650,000 at the beginning of the year and $10,850,000 at the end of the year generated sales of $44,000,000 during the year. The company's total asset turnover for the year is calculated as follows:

$$\text{Total asset turnover} = \frac{\$44{,}000{,}000}{(\$9{,}650{,}000 + \$10{,}850{,}000)/2} = 4.3$$

Thus, in describing the efficiency of the company in using its assets to generate sales, we can say that it turned its assets over 4.3 times during the year. Or, we might say that each $1.00 of assets produced $4.30 of sales during the year.

As is true for other financial ratios, a company's total asset turnover is meaningful only when compared to the results in other years and of similar companies. Interpreting the total asset turnover also requires that users understand the company's operations. Some operations are capital intensive, meaning that a relatively large amount must be invested in assets to generate sales. This suggests a relatively low total asset turnover. On the other hand, if operations are labor intensive, sales are generated more by the efforts of people than the use of assets. Thus, we would expect a higher total asset turnover.

Summary of the Chapter in Terms of Learning Objectives

LO 1 Plant assets are tangible items that have a useful life longer than one accounting period. Plant assets are not held for sale but are used in the production or sale of other assets or services. The cost of plant assets includes all normal and reasonable expenditures necessary to get the assets in place and ready to use. The cost of a lump-sum purchase should be allocated among the individual assets based on their relative market values. Total asset turnover measures the efficiency of a company's use of its assets to generate sales.

[7] APB, "Accounting for Nonmonetary Transactions," *APB Opinion No. 29* (New York: AICPA, May 1973), par. 16.

LO 2 The cost of plant assets that have limited service lives must be allocated to the accounting periods that benefit from their use. The straight-line method of depreciation divides the cost minus salvage value by the number of periods in the service life of the asset to determine the depreciation expense of each period. The units-of-production method divides the cost minus salvage value by the estimated number of units the asset will produce to determine the depreciation per unit. If the estimated useful life of a plant asset is changed, the remaining cost to be depreciated is spread over the remaining (revised) useful life of the asset.

LO 3 Accelerated depreciation methods such as the declining-balance method are acceptable for financial accounting purposes if they are based on realistic estimates of useful life. However, they are not widely used at the present time. The Modified Accelerated Cost Recovery System (MACRS), which is used for tax purposes, is not based on realistic estimates of useful life. Thus, MACRS is not acceptable for financial accounting purposes.

LO 4 The benefit of revenue expenditures expires during the current period. Thus, revenue expenditures are debited to expense accounts and matched with current revenues. Capital expenditures are debited to asset accounts because they benefit future periods. Ordinary repairs are revenue expenditures. Examples of capital expenditures include extraordinary repairs and betterments. Amounts paid for assets with low costs are technically capital expenditures but can be treated as revenue expenditures if they are not material.

LO 5 When a plant asset is discarded or sold, the cost and accumulated depreciation are removed from the accounts. Any cash proceeds are recorded and compared to the asset's book value to determine gain or loss. When nonmonetary assets are exchanged and they are dissimilar, the new asset is recorded at its fair value, and either a gain or a loss on disposal is recognized. When similar assets are exchanged, losses are recognized but gains are not. Instead, the new asset account is debited for the book value of the old asset plus any cash paid.

Demonstration Problem

On July 14, 19X1, Tulsa Company paid $600,000 to acquire a fully equipped factory. The purchase included the following:

Asset	Appraised Value	Estimated Salvage Value	Estimated Service Life	Depreciation Method
Land	$160,000			Not depreciated
Land improvements . .	80,000	$ -0-	10 years	Straight line
Building	320,000	100,000	10 years	Double declining balance
Machinery.	240,000	20,000	10,000 units	Units of production*
Total	$800,000			

* The machinery was used to produce 700 units in 19X1 and 1,800 units in 19X2.

Required

1. Allocate the total $600,000 cost among the separate assets.
2. Calculate the 19X1 (six months) and 19X2 depreciation expense for each type of asset and calculate the total each year for all assets.

Planning the Solution

- Complete a three-column worksheet showing these amounts for each asset: appraised value, percent of total value, and allocated cost.
- Using the allocated costs, compute the amount of depreciation for 19X1 (only one-half year) and 19X2 for each asset. Then, summarize those calculations in a table showing the total depreciation for each year.

Solution to Demonstration Problem

1. Allocation of total cost among the assets:

Asset	Appraised Value	Percent of Total Value	Allocated Cost
Land	$160,000	20%	$120,000
Land improvements	80,000	10	60,000
Building	320,000	40	240,000
Machinery	240,000	30	180,000
Total	$800,000	100%	$600,000

2. Depreciation for each asset:

Land Improvements:

Cost	$60,000
Salvage value	-0-
Net cost	$60,000
Service life	10 years
Annual expense ($60,000/10)	$6,000
19X1 depreciation ($6,000 × 6/12)	$3,000
19X2 depreciation	$6,000

Building:

Straight-line rate = 100%/10 = 10%

Double-declining-balance rate = 10% × 2 = 20%

19X1 depreciation ($240,000 × 20% × 6/12)	$24,000
19X2 depreciation[($240,000 − $24,000) × 20%]	$43,200

Machinery:

Cost	$180,000
Salvage value	20,000
Net cost	$160,000
Total expected units	10,000
Expected cost per unit ($160,000/10,000)	$ 16

Year	Units × Unit Cost	Depreciation
19X1	700 × $16	$11,200
19X2	1,800 × $16	28,800

Total depreciation expense:

	19X1	19X2
Land improvements	$ 3,000	$ 6,000
Building	24,000	43,200
Machinery	11,200	28,800
Total	$38,200	$78,000

Glossary

LO 6 Define or explain the words and phrases listed in the chapter glossary.

Accelerated depreciation depreciation methods that produce larger depreciation charges during the early years of an asset's life and smaller charges in the later years. p. 327

Balance sheet expenditure another name for *capital expenditure.* p. 331

Betterment a modification to an asset to make it more efficient, usually by replacing one of its components with an improved or superior component. p. 332

Book value the amount assigned to an item in the accounting records and in the financial statements; for a plant asset, book value is its original cost less accumulated depreciation. p. 324

Capital expenditure an expenditure that produces economic benefits that do not fully expire before the end of the current period; because it creates or adds to existing assets, it should appear on the balance sheet as the cost of an asset. Also called a *balance sheet expenditure.* p. 331

Change in an accounting estimate a change in a calculated amount used in the financial statements that results from new information or subsequent developments and from better insight or improved judgment. p. 327

Declining-balance depreciation a depreciation method in which a plant asset's depreciation charge for the period is determined by applying a constant depreciation rate (up to twice the straight-line rate) each year to the asset's beginning book value. p. 328

Extraordinary repairs major repairs that extend the service life of a plant asset beyond original expectations; treated as a capital expenditure. p. 331

Inadequacy a condition in which the capacity of plant assets becomes too small for the productive demands of the business. p. 323

Land improvements assets that increase the usefulness of land but that have a limited useful life and are subject to depreciation. p. 322

Modified Accelerated Cost Recovery System (MACRS) the system of depreciation required by federal income tax law for assets placed in service after 1986. p. 329

Obsolescence a condition in which, because of new inventions and improvements, a plant asset can no longer be used to produce goods or services with a competitive advantage. p. 323

Ordinary repairs repairs made to keep a plant asset in normal, good operating condition; treated as a revenue expenditure. p. 331

Revenue expenditure an expenditure that should appear on the current income statement as an expense and be deducted from the period's revenues because it does not provide a material benefit in future periods. p. 331

Salvage value the amount that management predicts will be recovered at the end of a plant asset's service life through a sale or as a trade-in allowance on the purchase of a new asset. p. 323

Service life the length of time in which a plant asset will be used in the operations of the business. p. 323

Straight-line depreciation a method that allocates an equal portion of the total depreciation for a plant asset (cost minus salvage) to each accounting period in its service life. p. 323

Total asset turnover a measure of how efficiently a company uses its assets to generate sales; calculated by dividing net sales by average total assets. p. 336

Units-of-production depreciation a method that allocates an equal portion of the total depreciation for a plant asset (cost minus salvage) to each unit of product or service that it produces, or on a similar basis, such as hours of use or miles driven. p. 324

Objective Review

Answers to the following questions are listed at the end of this chapter. Be sure that you decide which is the one best answer to each question *before* you check the answers.

LO 1 The recent purchase of a new production machine by the Wallace Company involved the following dollar amounts:

Gross purchase price	$700,000
Sales tax	49,000
Freight to move machine to plant	3,500
Assembly costs	3,000
Cost of foundation for machine	2,500
Cost of spare parts to be used in maintaining the machine	4,200
Purchase discount taken	21,000

The amount to be recorded as the cost of the machine is:

a. $737,000.

b. $733,500.

c. $728,000.

d. $679,000.

e. $741,200.

LO 2 Clandestine Gift Shop purchased a new machine for $96,000 on January 1, 19X1. Its predicted useful life is five years or 100,000 units of product, and salvage value is $8,000. During 19X1, 10,000 units of product were produced. Assuming (1) straight-line depreciation and (2) units-of-production depreciation, respectively, the book value of the machine on December 31, 19X1, is:

	Straight Line	Units of Production
a.	$76,800	$86,400.
b.	$78,400	$79,200.
c.	$76,800	$86,400.
d.	$70,400	$78,400.
e.	$78,400	$87,200.

LO 3 On January 1, 19X1, Temperware Industries paid $77,000 to purchase office furniture having an estimated salvage value of $14,000. The furniture has an estimated service life of 10 years, but it is in the 7-year class for tax purposes. What is the 19X1 depreciation on the furniture using (1) double-declining-balance method for financial accounting purposes and (2) straight-line under MACRS with the half-year convention?

	Double Declining Balance	MACRS Straight-Line
a.	$15,400	$11,000.
b.	$12,600	$ 7,700.
c.	$12,600	$ 6,300.
d.	$15,400	$ 5,500.
e.	$ 7,700	$ 3,850.

LO 4 At the beginning of the fifth year of a machine's estimated six-year useful life, the machine was completely overhauled and its estimated useful life was extended to nine years in total. The machine originally cost $108,000, and the overhaul cost was $12,000. The cost of the overhaul should be recorded as follows:

a.	Depreciation Expense	12,000.00	
	Cash		12,000.00
b.	Machinery	12,000.00	
	Accumulated Depreciation, Machinery		12,000.00
c.	Repairs Expense	12,000.00	
	Cash		12,000.00
d.	Accumulated Depreciation, Machinery	12,000.00	
	Cash		12,000.00
e.	Machinery	12,000.00	
	Cash		12,000.00

LO 5 Standard Company traded an old truck for a new one. The original cost of the old truck was $30,000, and its accumulated depreciation at the time of the trade was $23,400. The new truck had a cash price of $45,000. However, Standard received a $3,000 trade-in allowance. Standard should record the new truck at the cost of:

a. $48,600.
b. $45,000.
c. $42,000.
d. $41,400.
e. $ 6,600.

LO 6 Repairs made to keep a plant asset in normal, good operating condition are called:

a. Betterment.
b. Extraordinary repair.
c. Ordinary repairs.
d. Capital expenditure.
e. Balance sheet expenditure.

Questions for Class Discussion

1. What characteristics of a plant asset make it different from other assets?
2. What is the balance sheet classification of land held for future expansion? Why is the land not classified as a plant asset?
3. In general, what is included in the cost of a plant asset?
4. After discovering that the cost of buying a special machine would be $37,500, Mack Company decided to build the machine itself for a total cash outlay of $30,000. It recorded the machine's construction with a debit to Machinery for $37,500, a credit to Cash for $30,000, and a credit to Gain on Construction of Machinery for $7,500. Why was this not a proper entry?
5. What is the difference between land and land improvements?
6. For accounting purposes, what is the meaning of the term *depreciation?* What is accomplished by recording depreciation?
7. Does the recording of depreciation cause a plant asset to appear on the balance sheet at market value?
8. Does the balance of the account, Accumulated Depreciation, Machinery, represent funds accumulated to replace the machinery when it wears out? What does the balance of Accumulated Depreciation represent?
9. Early in the sixth year of a machine's life, it was decided that the machine's total useful life would be eight years instead of the six years originally estimated. How should this new information be reflected in the accounts?
10. Why is the Modified Accelerated Cost Recovery System not generally accepted for financial accounting purposes?
11. What is the difference between revenue expenditures and capital expenditures and how should they be recorded?
12. What is the difference between ordinary repairs and extraordinary repairs and how should they be recorded?
13. What is a betterment? How should a betterment to a machine be recorded?
14. What accounting principle justifies charging the $75 cost of a plant asset immediately to an expense account?
15. What are some of the events that might lead to the disposal of a plant asset?
16. What causes a loss to be recorded on the sale of a plant asset? An exchange of a plant asset?
17. Should a gain on an exchange of plant assets be recorded?
18. How is total asset turnover calculated? Why would a financial statement user be interested in calculating total asset turnover?

19. Refer to the consolidated balance sheets for Federal Express Corporation in Appendix G. What phrase does Federal Express use to describe its plant assets? What is the book value of plant assets as of May 31, 1993, and May 31, 1992?

20. Using the consolidated balance sheet and consolidated statement of income for Ben & Jerry's Homemade, Inc., in Appendix G, calculate total asset turnover for the year ended December 26, 1992.

Exercises

Exercise 9–1
Cost of a plant asset
(LO 1)

Hot Sox purchased a machine for $23,000, terms 2/10, n/60, FOB shipping point. The seller prepaid the freight charges, $520, adding the amount to the invoice and bringing its total to $23,520. The machine required a special steel mounting and power connections costing $1,590, and another $750 was paid to assemble the machine and get it into operation. In moving the machine onto its steel mounting, it was dropped and damaged. The repairs cost $380. Later, $60 of raw materials were consumed in adjusting the machine so that it would produce a satisfactory product. The adjustments were normal for this type of machine and were not the result of the damage. However, the items produced while the adjustments were being made were not sellable. Prepare a calculation to show the cost of this machine for accounting purposes. (Assume Hot Sox pays for the purchase within the discount period.)

Exercise 9–2
Lump-sum purchase of plant assets
(LO 1)

Piper Plumbing Company paid $184,125 for real estate plus $9,800 in closing costs. The real estate included land appraised at $83,160; land improvements appraised at $27,720; and a building appraised at $87,120. Prepare a calculation showing the allocation of the total cost among the three purchased assets and present the journal entry to record the purchase.

Exercise 9–3
Recording costs of real estate
(LO 1)

After planning to build a new manufacturing plant, Jammers Casual Wear purchased a large lot on which a small building was located. The negotiated purchase price for this real estate was $150,000 for the lot plus $80,000 for the building. The company paid $23,000 to have the old building torn down and $34,000 for landscaping the lot. Finally, it paid $960,000 in construction costs, which included the cost of a new building plus $57,000 for lighting and paving a parking lot next to the building. Present a single journal entry to record the costs incurred by Jammers, all of which were paid in cash.

Exercise 9–4
Alternative depreciation methods
(LO 2, 3)

Moon Paper Company installed a computerized machine in its factory at a cost of $84,600. The machine's useful life was estimated at 10 years, or 363,000 units of product, with a $12,000 trade-in value. During its second year, the machine produced 35,000 units of product. Determine the machine's second-year depreciation under the (*a*) straight-line, (*b*) units-of-production, and (*c*) double-declining-balance methods.

Exercise 9–5
Alternative depreciation methods; partial year's depreciation
(LO 2, 3)

On April 1, 19X1, Lake Excavating Services purchased a trencher for $500,000. The machine was expected to last five years and have a salvage value of $50,000. Calculate depreciation expense for 19X2, using (*a*) the straight-line method and (*b*) the double-declining-balance method.

Exercise 9–6
Revising depreciation rates
(LO 2)

Gemini Fitness Club used straight-line depreciation for a machine that cost $43,500, under the assumption it would have a four-year life and a $4,500 trade-in value. After two years, Gemini determined that the machine still had three more years of remaining useful life, after which it would have an estimated $3,600 trade-in value. (*a*) Calculate the machine's book value at the end of its second year. (*b*) Calculate the amount of depreciation to be charged during each of the remaining years in the machine's revised useful life.

Exercise 9–7
Income statement effects of alternative depreciation methods
(LO 2, 3)

Starnes Enterprises recently paid $156,800 for equipment that will last five years and have a salvage value of $35,000. By using the machine in its operations for five years, the company expects to earn $57,000 annually, after deducting all expenses except depreciation. Present a schedule showing income before depreciation, depreciation expense, and net income for each year and the total amounts for the five-year period, assuming (*a*) straight-line depreciation and (*b*) double-declining-balance depreciation.

Exercise 9–8
MACRS depreciation
(LO 2, 3)

In January 19X1, Labenski Labs purchased computer equipment for $98,000. The equipment will be used in research and development activities for four years and then sold at an estimated salvage value of $20,000. The equipment is in the five-year class for tax purposes, and the half-year convention is required. Prepare schedules showing the depreciation under MACRS for each year's tax returns, assuming (*a*) straight-line depreciation and (*b*) accelerated depreciation. (To calculate accelerated depreciation, use the MACRS rates in Illustration 9–2.)

Exercise 9–9
Ordinary repairs, extraordinary repairs, and betterments
(LO 4)

Eden Extract Company paid $175,000 for equipment that was expected to last four years and have a salvage value of $20,000. Prepare journal entries to record the following costs related to the equipment:

a. During the second year of the equipment's life, $14,000 cash was paid for a new component that was expected to increase the equipment's productivity by 10% each year.
b. During the third year, $3,500 cash was paid for repairs necessary to keep the equipment in good working order.
c. During the fourth year, $9,300 was paid for repairs that were expected to increase the service life of the equipment from four to six years.

Exercise 9–10
Extraordinary repairs
(LO 4)

Hot Dog Heaven owns a building that appeared on its balance sheet at the end of last year at its original $374,000 cost less $280,500 accumulated depreciation. The building has been depreciated on a straight-line basis under the assumption that it would have a 20-year life and no salvage value. During the first week in January of the current year, major structural repairs were completed on the building at a cost of $44,800. The repairs did not increase the building's capacity, but they did extend its expected life for 7 years beyond the 20 years originally estimated.

a. Determine the building's age as of the end of last year.
b. Give the entry to record the repairs, which were paid with cash.
c. Determine the book value of the building after the repairs were recorded.
d. Give the entry to record the current year's depreciation.

Exercise 9–11
Partial year's depreciation; disposal of plant asset
(LO 2, 5)

Plum Hill Industries purchased and installed a machine on January 1, 19X1, at a total cost of $185,500. Straight-line depreciation was taken each year for four years, based on the assumption of a seven-year life and no salvage value. The machine was disposed of on July 1, 19X5, during its fifth year of service. Present the entries to record the partial year's depreciation on July 1, 19X5, and to record the disposal under each of the following unrelated assumptions: (*a*) The machine was sold for $70,000 cash; (*b*) Plum Hill received an insurance settlement of $60,000 resulting from the total destruction of the machine in a fire.

Exercise 9–12
Exchanging plant assets
(LO 5)

The Rourke Group traded in an old tractor for a new tractor, receiving a $56,000 trade-in allowance and paying the remaining $164,000 in cash. The old tractor cost $190,000, and straight-line depreciation of $105,000 had been recorded under the assumption that it would last eight years and have a $22,000 salvage value. Answer the following questions:

a. What was the book value of the old tractor?
b. What is the loss on the exchange?
c. What amount should be debited to the new Tractor account?

Exercise 9–13
Recording plant asset disposal or exchange
(LO 5)

On January 2, 19X1, Kelly Camera Shop disposed of a machine that cost $84,000 and had been depreciated $45,250. Present the journal entries to record the disposal under each of the following unrelated assumptions:

a. The machine was sold for $32,500 cash.
b. The machine was traded in on a new machine of like purpose having a $117,000 cash price. A $40,000 trade-in allowance was received, and the balance was paid in cash.
c. A $30,000 trade-in allowance was received for the machine on a new machine of like purpose having a $117,000 cash price. The balance was paid in cash.
d. The machine was traded for vacant land adjacent to the shop to be used as a parking lot. The land had a fair value of $75,000, and Kelly paid $25,000 cash in addition to giving the seller the machine.

Lamb's Antiques reported net sales of $2,431,000 for 19X2 and $3,771,000 for 19X3. End of year balances for total assets were 19X1, $793,000; 19X2, $850,000; and 19X3, $941,000. Calculate Lamb's total asset turnover for 19X2 and 19X3, and comment on the store's efficiency in the use of its assets.

Exercise 9–14
Evaluating efficient use of assets
(LO 1)

Problems

Problem 9–1
Real estate costs; partial year's depreciation
(LO 1, 2)

In 19X1, ProSports paid $1,400,000 for a tract of land and two buildings on it. The plan was to demolish Building One and build a new store in its place. Building Two was to be used as a company office and was appraised at a value of $291,500, with a useful life of 20 years and an $80,000 salvage value. A lighted parking lot near Building One had improvements (Land Improvements One) valued at $185,500 that were expected to last another 14 years and have no salvage value. Without considering the buildings or improvements, the tract of land was estimated to have a value of $848,000.

ProSports incurred the following additional costs:

Cost to demolish Building One	$ 211,300
Cost of additional landscaping	83,600
Cost to construct new building (Building Three), having a useful life of 25 years and a $195,050 salvage value	1,009,500
Cost of new land improvements near Building Two (Land, Improvements Two) which have a 20-year useful life and no salvage value	79,000

Required

1. Prepare a schedule having the following column headings: Land, Building Two, Building Three, Land Improvements One, and Land Improvements Two. Allocate the costs incurred by ProSports to the appropriate columns and total each column.
2. Prepare a single journal entry dated March 31 to record all the incurred costs, assuming they were paid in cash on that date.
3. Using the straight-line method, prepare December 31 adjusting entries to record depreciation for the nine months of 19X1 during which the assets were in use.

Problem 9–2
Plant asset costs; partial year's depreciation; alternative methods, including MACRS
(LO 1, 2, 3)

Valley Wide Industries recently negotiated a lump-sum purchase of several assets from a vending machine service company that was going out of business. The purchase was completed on March 1, 19X1, at a total cash price of $1,575,000, and included a building, land, certain land improvements, and 12 vehicles. The estimated market value of each asset was building, $816,000; land, $578,000; land improvements, $85,000; and vehicles, $221,000.

Required

1. Prepare a schedule to allocate the lump-sum purchase price to the separate assets that were purchased. Also present the journal entry to record the purchase.
2. Calculate the 19X1 depreciation expense on the building using the straight-line method, assuming a 15-year life and a $51,300 salvage value.
3. Calculate the 19X1 depreciation expense on the land improvements assuming an eight-year life and double-declining-balance depreciation.
4. The vehicles are in the five-year class for tax purposes, but are expected to last seven years and have a salvage value of $29,400. Prepare a schedule showing each year's depreciation for the vehicles under MACRS, assuming (*a*) straight-line and (*b*) accelerated depreciation. (To calculate accelerated depreciation, use the MACRS rates in Illustration 9–2.)

Problem 9–3
Alternative depreciation methods; partial year's depreciation; disposal of plant asset
(LO 2, 3, 5)

Part 1. A machine that cost $105,000 with a four-year life and an estimated $10,000 salvage value, was installed in Patterson Company's factory on January 1. The factory manager estimated that the machine would produce 237,500 units of product during its life. It actually produced the following units: year 1, 60,700; year 2, 61,200; year 3, 59,800; and year 4, 59,100. Note the total number of units produced by the end of year 4 exceeded the original estimate. Nevertheless, the machine should not be depreciated below the estimated salvage value.

Required

1. Prepare a calculation showing the amount that should be charged to depreciation over the machine's four-year life.
2. Prepare a form with the following column headings:

Year	Straight Line	Units of Production	Double Declining Balance

Then show the depreciation for each year and the total depreciation for the machine under each depreciation method.

Part 2. Patterson purchased a used machine for $83,500 on January 2. It was repaired the next day at a cost of $1,710 and installed on a new platform that cost $540. The company predicted that the machine would be used for six years and would then have a $7,300 salvage value. Depreciation was to be charged on a straight-line basis. A full year's depreciation was charged on December 31, the end of the first year of the machine's use. On September 30 of its sixth year in service, it was retired from service.

Required

1. Prepare journal entries to record the purchase of the machine, the cost of repairing it, and the installation. Assume that cash was paid.
2. Prepare entries to record depreciation on the machine on December 31 of its first year and on September 30 in the year of its disposal.
3. Prepare entries to record the retirement of the machine under each of the following unrelated assumptions: (*a*) it was sold for $6,750; (*b*) it was sold for $18,000; and (*c*) it was destroyed in a fire and the insurance company paid $12,000 in full settlement of the loss claim.

Problem 9–4
Partial year's depreciation; revising depreciation rates; revenue and capital expenditures
(LO 2, 3, 4)

Finlay General Contractors completed these transactions involving the purchase and operation of heavy equipment:

19X1

Jun. 30 Paid $127,720 cash for a new front-end loader, plus $7,600 in state sales tax and $1,250 for transportation charges. The loader was estimated to have a four-year life and a $17,370 salvage value.

Oct. 4 Paid $1,830 to enclose the cab and install air conditioning in the loader. This increased the estimated salvage value of the loader by $555.

Dec. 31 Recorded straight-line depreciation on the loader.

19X2

Feb. 16 Paid $460 to repair the loader after the operator backed it into a tree.

July 1 Paid $2,250 to overhaul the loader's engine. As a result, the estimated useful life of the loader was increased by two years.

Dec. 31 Recorded straight-line depreciation on the loader.

Required

Prepare journal entries to record the transactions.

Problem 9–5
Partial year's depreciation; revising depreciating rates; exchanging plant assets
(LO 2, 3, 5)

Syracuse Systems completed the following transactions involving delivery trucks:

19X1

Mar. 29 Paid cash for a new delivery truck, $38,830 plus $2,330 state sales tax. The truck was estimated to have a five-year life and a $6,000 trade-in value.

Dec. 31 Recorded straight-line depreciation on the truck.

19X2

Dec. 31 Recorded straight-line depreciation on the truck. However, due to new information obtained earlier in the year, the original estimated service life of the truck was changed from five years to four years, and the original estimated trade-in value was increased to $7,000.

19X3

July 5 Traded in the old truck and paid $27,130 in cash for a new truck. The new truck was estimated to have a six-year life and a $6,250 trade-in value. The invoice for the exchange showed these items:

Price of the new truck	$45,100
Trade-in allowance granted on the old truck . .	(19,500)
Balance of purchase price	$25,600
State sales taxes	1,530
Total paid in cash	$27,130

Dec. 31 Recorded straight-line depreciation on the new truck.

Required

Prepare journal entries to record the transactions.

Problem 9–6
Partial year's depreciation; alternative methods; disposal of plant assets
(LO 2, 3, 5)

Menck Interiors completed the following transactions involving machinery:

Machine No. 15–50 was purchased for cash on May 1, 19X1, at an installed cost of $52,900. Its useful life was estimated to be six years with a $4,300 trade-in value. Straight-line depreciation was recorded for the machine at the end of 19X1, 19X2, and 19X3; on April 29, 19X4, it was traded for Machine No. 17–95, a similar asset with an installed cash price of $61,900. A trade-in allowance of $30,110 was received for Machine No. 15–50, and the balance was paid in cash.

Machine No. 17–95's life was predicted to be four years with an $8,200 trade-in value. Double-declining-balance depreciation was recorded on each December 31 of its life. On November 2, 19X5, it was traded for Machine No. BT–311, which was a dissimilar asset with an installed cash price of $179,000. A trade-in allowance of $27,000 was received for Machine No. 17–95, and the balance was paid in cash.

It was estimated that Machine No. BT–311 would produce 200,000 units of product during its five-year useful life, after which it would have a $35,000 trade-in value. Units-of-production depreciation was recorded for the machine for 19X5, when it produced 31,000 units of product. Between January 1, 19X6, and August 21, 19X8, the machine produced 108,000 more units. On the latter date, it was sold for $81,200.

Required

Prepare journal entries to record: (*a*) the purchase of each machine, (*b*) the depreciation expense recorded on the first Decamber 31 of each machine's life, and (*c*) the disposal of each machine. (Only one entry is needed to record the exchange of one machine for another.)

Problem 9–7
Analytical essay
(LO 4)

It is January 9, 19X2, and you have just been hired as an accountant for Brinks Supply Company. The previous accountant brought the accounting records up to date through December 31, 19X1, the end of the fiscal year, including the year-end adjusting entries. In reviewing the entries made last year, you discover the following three items:

1. An expenditure to have a factory machine reconditioned by the manufacturer so it would last three years longer than originally estimated was recorded as a debit to Repairs Expense, Machinery.
2. The lubrication of factory machinery was recorded as a debit to Machinery.
3. The installation of a security system for the building was recorded as a debit to Building Improvements. The new system allowed the company to reduce the number of security guards.

Required

For each of the three items, explain why you think a correction is or is not necessary. Also, describe any correcting entry that should be made.

Provocative Problems

Provocative Problem 9–1
Accounting related communications
(LO 1, 5)

While examining the accounting records of Fortunato Company on December 15, 19X5, you discover two 19X5 entries that appear questionable. The first entry recorded the cash proceeds from an insurance settlement as follows:

Apr.	30	Cash	29,000.00	
		Loss on Fire	8,800.00	
		Accumulated Depreciation, Machinery	25,200.00	
		Machinery		63,000.00
		Received payment of fire loss claim.		

Your investigation shows that this entry was made to record the receipt of an insurance company's $29,000 check to settle a claim resulting from the destruction of a machine in a small fire on April 2, 19X5. The machine originally cost $58,800 and was put in operation on January 3, 19X2. It was depreciated on a straight-line basis for three years, under the assumptions that it would have a seven-year life and no salvage value. During the first week of January 19X5, the machine was overhauled at a cost of $4,200. The overhaul did not increase the machine's capacity or its salvage value. However, it was expected that the overhaul would lengthen the machine's service life two years beyond the seven originally expected.

The second entry that appears questionable was made to record the receipt of a check from selling a portion of a tract of land. The land was adjacent to the company's plant and had been purchased the year before. It cost $105,000, and another $18,000 was paid for clearing and grading it. Both amounts had been debited to the Land account. The land was to be used for storing finished products but, sometime after the grading was completed, it became obvious the company did not need the entire tract. Fortunato received an offer from a purchaser to buy the north section for $94,550 or the south section for $60,450. The company decided to sell the north section and recorded the receipt of the purchaser's check with the following entry:

Nov.	16	Cash	94,550.00	
		Land		94,550.00
		Sold unneeded land.		

Required

Write a memo to the company's Corrections File describing any errors made in recording these transactions. Since the Corrections File is used in making the year-end adjusting journal entries, show the entry or entries needed to correct each error described in your memo.

Provocative Problem 9–2
Manufax Company
(LO 1, 2)

Manufax Company temporarily recorded the costs of a new plant in a single account called Land and Buildings. Now, management has asked you to examine this account and prepare any necessary entries to correct the account balances. In doing so, you find the following debits and credits to the account:

		Debits	
Jan.	4	Cost of land and building acquired for new plant site	$ 564,000
	9	Attorney's fee for title search	1,500
	18	Cost of demolishing old building on plant site	37,500
	30	Nine months' liability and fire insurance during construction	6,075
Sept.	28	Payment to building contractor on completion	819,000
Oct.	1	Architect's fee for new building	25,200
	10	City assessment for street improvements	42,000
	21	Cost of landscaping new plant site	10,500
			$1,505,775

Credits

Jan. 21	Proceeds from sale of salvaged materials from building . . .	$ 7,900
Oct. 5	Refund of one month's liability and fire insurance premium . . .	675
Dec. 31	Depreciation at 2½% per year . . .	28,069
		$ 36,644
	Debit balance . . .	$1,469,131

An account called Depreciation Expense, Land and Buildings was debited in recording the $28,069 of depreciation. Your investigation suggests that 40 years is a reasonable life expectancy for a building of the type involved and that an assumption of zero salvage value is reasonable.

To summarize your analysis, set up a schedule with columns headed Date, Description, Total Amount, Land, Buildings, and Other Accounts. Next, enter the items found in the Land and Buildings account on the schedule, distributing the amounts to the proper columns. Show credits on the schedule by enclosing the amounts in parentheses. Also, draft any required correcting entry or entries, under the assumption that the accounts have not been closed.

Provocative Problem 9–3
Apple Computer, Inc.
(LO 1, 2)

Apple Computer, Inc.

Refer to the annual report for Apple Computer, Inc., in Appendix F. Give particular attention to the balance sheet, statement of income, and notes to financial statements before answering the following questions:

1. What percentage of the original cost of Apple's property, plant, and equipment remains to be depreciated as of September 25, 1992, and September 27, 1991? (Assume the assets have no salvage value.)
2. What method of depreciation does Apple use in depreciating its plant assets?
3. What was the net change in total property, plant, and equipment (before depreciation) during the year ended September 25, 1992? What was the amount of cash generated by (or used for) investment in property, plant, and equipment during the year ended September 25, 1992? What is one possible explanation for the difference between these two amounts?
4. Calculate Apple's total asset turnover for the year ended September 25, 1992.

Provocative Problem 9–4
As a Matter of Ethics: Essay

Review the As a Matter of Ethics case on page 328 and write a short essay discussing the situation faced by Sue Ann Meyer. Include a discussion of the alternative courses of action available to Meyer and indicate how you think she should deal with the situation.

Answers to Objective Review Questions

LO 1 (*a*)	LO 3 (*d*)	LO 5 (*b*)
LO 2 (*e*)	LO 4 (*d*)	LO 6 (*c*)

CHAPTER

10

Natural Resources, Intangible Assets, and Long-Term Investments

In Chapters 6 through 9, you learned about current assets and plant assets. This chapter concludes the focus on assets with a discussion of natural resources, intangible assets, and long-term investments. Natural resources and intangible assets are particularly important in evaluating the future prospects of certain companies.

Many companies make long-term investments in assets such as real estate, and debt and equity securities issued by other companies. Also, an increasing number of companies invest in foreign countries or have international operations. The financial statement effects of these investments are often very important. As a result, your study of these topics in this chapter will enrich your ability to understand and interpret financial reports.

Learning Objectives

After studying Chapter 10, you should be able to:

1. Identify assets that should be classified as natural resources or as intangible assets and prepare entries to account for them, including entries to record depletion and amortization.
2. State the criteria for classifying assets as long-term investments and describe the categories of securities that are classified as long-term investments.
3. Describe the methods used to report long-term securities investments in the financial statements.
4. Describe the primary accounting problems of having investments in international operations and prepare entries to account for sales to foreign customers.
5. Explain the use of return on total assets in evaluating a company's efficiency in using its assets.
6. Define or explain the words and phrases listed in the chapter glossary.

Natural Resources

Natural resources include such things as standing timber, mineral deposits, and oil reserves. Because they are physically consumed when they are used, they are known as *wasting assets.* In their natural state, they represent inventories of raw materials that will be converted into a product by cutting, mining, or pumping. However, until the conversion takes place, they are noncurrent assets and appear on a balance sheet under captions such as Timberlands, Mineral deposits, or Oil reserves. Sometimes, this caption ap-

LO 1 Identify assets that should be classified as natural resources or as intangible assets and prepare entries to account for them, including entries to record depletion and amortization.

pears under the property, plant, and equipment category of assets and sometimes it is a separate category.

Natural resources are initially recorded at cost. Like the cost of plant assets, the cost of natural resources is allocated to the periods in which they are consumed. The cost created by consuming the usefulness of natural resources is called **depletion.** On the balance sheet, natural resources are shown at cost less *accumulated depletion.* The amount by which such assets are depleted each year by cutting, mining, or pumping is usually calculated on a units-of-production basis.

For example, if a mineral deposit has an estimated 500,000 tons of available ore and is purchased for $500,000, the depletion charge per ton of ore mined is $1. Thus, if 85,000 tons are mined and sold during the first year, the depletion charge for the year is $85,000 and is recorded as follows:

Dec.	31	Depletion Expense, Mineral Deposit	85,000.00	
		Accumulated Depletion, Mineral Deposit . . .		85,000.00
		To record depletion of the mineral deposit.		

On the balance sheet prepared at the end of the first year, the mineral deposit should appear at its $500,000 cost less accumulated depletion of $85,000. Because the 85,000 tons of ore were sold during the year, the entire $85,000 depletion charge is reported on the income statement. However, if a portion of the ore had remained unsold at year-end, the depletion cost related to the unsold ore should be carried forward on the balance sheet as part of the cost of the unsold ore inventory, which is a current asset.

The conversion of natural resources through mining, cutting, or pumping often requires the use of machinery and buildings. Because the usefulness of these assets is related to the depletion of the natural resource, their costs should be depreciated over the life of the natural resource in proportion to the annual depletion charges. In other words, depreciation should be calculated using the units-of-production method. For example, if a machine is installed in a mine and one-eighth of the mine's ore is mined and sold during a year, one-eighth of the machine's cost (less salvage value) should be charged to depreciation expense.

Intangible Assets

Some assets represent certain legal rights and economic relationships beneficial to the owner. Because they have no physical existence, they are called **intangible assets.** Patents, copyrights, leaseholds, leasehold improvements, goodwill, and trademarks are intangible assets. We discuss each of these items in more detail in the following sections. Although notes and accounts receivable are also intangible in nature, they are not used to produce products or provide services. Therefore, they are not listed on the balance sheet as intangible assets; instead, they are classified as current assets or investments.

When an intangible asset is purchased, it is recorded at cost. Thereafter, its cost must be systematically written off to expense over its estimated useful life through the process of **amortization.** Generally accepted accounting principles require that the amortization period for an intangible asset be 40 years or less.[1]

Amortization of intangible assets is similar to depreciation of plant assets and depletion of natural resources in that all three are processes of cost allocation. However, only the straight-line method can be used for amortizing intangibles unless the reporting company can demonstrate that another method is

[1] FASB, *Accounting Standards—Current Text* (Norwalk, CT, 1994), sec. I60.110. First published as *APB Opinion No. 17,* par. 29.

more appropriate. Also, while the effects of depreciation and depletion on the assets are recorded in a contra account (Accumulated Depreciation or Accumulated Depletion), amortization is usually credited directly to the intangible asset account. As a result, the full original cost of intangible assets generally is not reported on the balance sheet. Instead, only the remaining amount of unamortized cost is reported.

Normally, intangible assets are shown in a separate section of the balance sheet that follows immediately after plant and equipment. However, not all companies follow this tradition. For example, IBM's December 31, 1992, balance sheet included an item called *Investments and Other Assets.* A footnote related to this item indicated that it included $274 million of goodwill, which is an intangible asset.

The following paragraphs describe several specific intangible assets.

Patents

The federal government grants **patents** to encourage the invention of new machines, mechanical devices, and production processes. A patent gives its owner the exclusive right to manufacture and sell a patented machine or device, or to use a process, for 17 years. When patent rights are purchased, the cost of acquiring the rights is debited to an account called Patents. Also, if the owner engages in lawsuits to defend a patent, the cost of the lawsuits should be debited to the Patents account. However, the costs of research and development leading to a new patent are not debited to an asset account.[2]

Although a patent gives its owner exclusive rights to the patented device or process for 17 years, the cost of the patent should be amortized over its predicted useful life, which might be less than the full 17 years. For example, if a patent that cost $25,000 has an estimated useful life of 10 years, the following adjusting entry is made at the end of each of those years to write off one-tenth of its cost:

Dec.	31	Amortization Expense, Patents	2,500.00	
		Patents		2,500.00
		To write off patent costs over the expected 10-year life.		

The entry's debit causes $2,500 of patent costs to appear on the income statement as one of the costs of the product manufactured and sold under the protection of the patent. Note that we have followed the convention of crediting the Patents account rather than a contra account.

Copyrights

A **copyright** is granted by the federal government or by international agreement. In most cases, a copyright gives its owner the exclusive right to publish and sell a musical, literary, or artistic work during the life of the composer, author, or artist and for 50 years thereafter. Most copyrights have value for a much shorter time, and their costs should be amortized over the shorter period. Often, the only identifiable cost of a copyright is the fee paid to the Copyright Office. If this fee is not material, it may be charged directly to an expense account. Otherwise, the copyright costs should be capitalized (recorded as a capital expenditure), and the periodic amortization of a copyright should be debited to an account called *Amortization Expense, Copyrights.*

[2] FASB, *Accounting Standards—Current Text* (Norwalk, CT, 1994), sec. R50.108. First published as *Statement of Financial Accounting Standards No. 2,* par. 12.

Leaseholds

Property is rented under a contract called a **lease.** The person or company that owns the property and grants the lease is called the **lessor.** The person or company that secures the right to possess and use the property is called the **lessee.** The rights granted to the lessee by the lessor under the lease are called a **leasehold.** A leasehold is an intangible asset for the lessee.

Some leases require no advance payment from the lessee but do require monthly rent payments. In such cases, a Leasehold account is not needed and the monthly payments are debited to a Rent Expense account. Sometimes, a long-term lease requires the lessee to pay the final year's rent in advance when the lease is signed. If so, the lessee records the advance payment with a debit to its Leasehold asset account. Because the usefulness of the advance payment is not consumed until the final year is reached, the Leasehold account balance remains intact until that year. At that time, the balance is transferred to Rent Expense.

Often, a long-term lease gains value because the current rental rates for similar property increase while the required payments under the lease remain constant. In such cases, the increase in value of the lease is not reported on the lessee's balance sheet since no extra cost was incurred to acquire it. However, if the property is subleased and the new tenant makes a cash payment to the original lessee for the rights under the old lease, the new tenant should debit the payment to a Leasehold account. Then, the balance of the Leasehold account should be amortized to Rent Expense over the remaining life of the lease.

Leasehold Improvements

Long-term leases often require the lessee to pay for any alterations or improvements to the leased property, such as new partitions and store fronts. Normally, the costs of these **leasehold improvements** are debited to an account called *Leasehold Improvements.* Also, since the improvements become part of the property and revert to the lessor at the end of the lease, the lessee must amortize the cost of the improvements over the life of the lease or the life of the improvements, whichever is shorter. The amortization entry commonly debits Rent Expense and credits Leasehold Improvements.

Goodwill

The term **goodwill** has a special meaning in accounting. In theory, a business has an intangible asset called goodwill when its rate of expected future earnings is greater than the rate of earnings normally realized in its industry. Above-average earnings and the existence of theoretical goodwill may be demonstrated with the following information about Companies A and B, both of which are in the same industry:

	Company A	Company B
Net assets (other than goodwill)	$100,000	$100,000
Normal rate of return in this industry	10%	10%
Normal return on net assets	$ 10,000	$ 10,000
Expected net income	10,000	15,000
Expected earnings above average	$ -0-	$ 5,000

Company B is expected to have an above-average earnings rate compared to its industry and, therefore, is said to have goodwill. This goodwill may be the result of excellent customer relations, the location of the business, the quality and uniqueness of its products, monopolistic market advantages, a superior

AS A MATTER OF

Fact

Intangible Assets	Number of Companies 1992	1991	1990	1989
Goodwill recognized in a business combination	383	383	379	367
Patents, patent rights	62	59	62	62
Trademarks, brand names, copyrights	50	48	46	38
Noncompete covenants	21	18	20	11
Licenses, franchises, memberships	17	17	16	19
Other—described	45	42	37	41

Excerpted with permission from *Accounting Trends & Techniques*, Annual Survey of Accounting Practices Followed in 600 Stockholders' Reports, Forty-Seventh Edition, Copyright © 1993 by American Institute of Certified Public Accountants, Inc., Table 2–18, p. 177.

management and workforce, or a combination of these and other factors.[3] Consequently, a potential investor would be willing to pay more for Company B than for Company A. Thus, goodwill is theoretically an asset that has value.

Normally, goodwill is purchased only when a business is acquired in its entirety. In determining the purchase price of a business, the buyer and seller may estimate the amount of goodwill in several different ways. If the business is expected to have $5,000 each year in above-average earnings, its goodwill may be valued at, say, four times its above-average earnings, or $20,000. Or, if the $5,000 is expected to continue indefinitely, they may think of it as a return on an investment at a given rate of return, say, 10%. In this case, the estimated amount of goodwill is $5,000/10% = $50,000. However, in the final analysis, the value of goodwill is confirmed only by the price the seller is willing to accept and the buyer is willing to pay.

To keep financial statement information from being too subjective, accountants have agreed that goodwill should not be recorded unless it is purchased. The amount of goodwill is measured by subtracting the fair market value of the purchased business's net assets (excluding goodwill) from the purchase price.

Like other intangible assets, goodwill must be amortized on a straight-line basis over its estimated useful life. However, estimating the useful life of goodwill is very difficult and highly arbitrary in most situations. As a result, you can expect to find companies reporting amortization expense for goodwill based on an estimated useful life of 5 years upward, but not more than 40 years.

Trademarks and Trade Names

Companies often adopt unique symbols or select unique names that they use in marketing their products. Sometimes, the ownership and exclusive right to use such a **trademark** or **trade name** can be established simply by demonstrating that one company has used the trademark or trade name before other businesses. However, ownership generally can be established more definitely by registering the trademark or trade name at the U.S. Patent Office.

[3] Of course, the value of the location may be reflected in a higher cost for the land owned and used by the company.

The cost of developing, maintaining, or enhancing the value of a trademark or trade name, perhaps through advertising, should be charged to expense in the period or periods incurred. However, if a trademark or trade name is purchased, the purchase cost should be debited to an asset account and amortized over time.

Amortization of Intangibles

Some intangibles, such as patents, copyrights, and leaseholds, have limited useful lives that are determined by law, contract, or the nature of the asset. Other intangibles, such as goodwill, trademarks, and trade names, have indeterminable lives. In general, the cost of intangible assets should be amortized over the periods expected to be benefited by their use, which in no case is longer than their legal existence. However, as we stated earlier, generally accepted accounting principles require that the amortization period of intangible assets never be longer than 40 years. This limitation applies even if the life of the asset (for example, goodwill) may continue indefinitely into the future.

Classifying Investments

LO 2 State the criteria for classifying assets as long-term investments and describe the categories of securities that are classified as long-term investments.

In Chapter 7, you learned how to account for short-term investments in debt and equity securities. (We encourage you to review pages 257–262 before you study this section.) Recall that short-term investments are current assets; they are expected to be converted into cash within one year or the current operating cycle of the business, whichever is longer. In general, short-term investments are held as "an investment of cash available for current operations."[4] They either mature within one year or the current operating cycle or are easily sold and therefore qualify as being *marketable.*

Securities investments that do not qualify as current assets are called **long-term investments.** Long-term investments include investments in bonds and stocks that are not marketable or that, although marketable, are not intended to serve as a ready source of cash. Long-term investments also include funds earmarked for a special purpose, such as bond sinking funds, and land or other assets owned but not used in the regular operations of the business. In general, these assets are reported on the balance sheet in a separate *Long-term investments* section.

Recall from Chapter 7 that accounting for short-term investments depends on whether the investments are in (1) trading securities, (2) debt securities held to maturity, or (3) debt and equity securities available for sale. Investments in trading securities always are short-term investments; they are reported as current assets. The other two types of investments may be long-term or short-term.

In Illustration 10–1, the boxes on the left side show the different long-term investments in securities. Note that they include (1) debt securities held to maturity, (2) debt and equity securities available for sale, (3) equity securities which give the investor a significant influence over the investee, and (4) equity securities which give the investor control over the investee. We discuss each of these types of investments in the following sections.

Long-Term Investments in Securities

Much of what you learned about short-term investments in Chapter 7 also applies to long-term investments. For example, at the time of purchase, investments are recorded at cost, which includes any commissions or brokerage fees paid to make the purchase. After the purchase, the accounting treatment depends on the type of investment.

[4] FASB, *Accounting Standards—Current Text* (Norwalk, CT, 1994), sec. B05.105. Previously published in *Accounting Research Bulletin No. 43,* ch. 3, sec. A, par. 4.

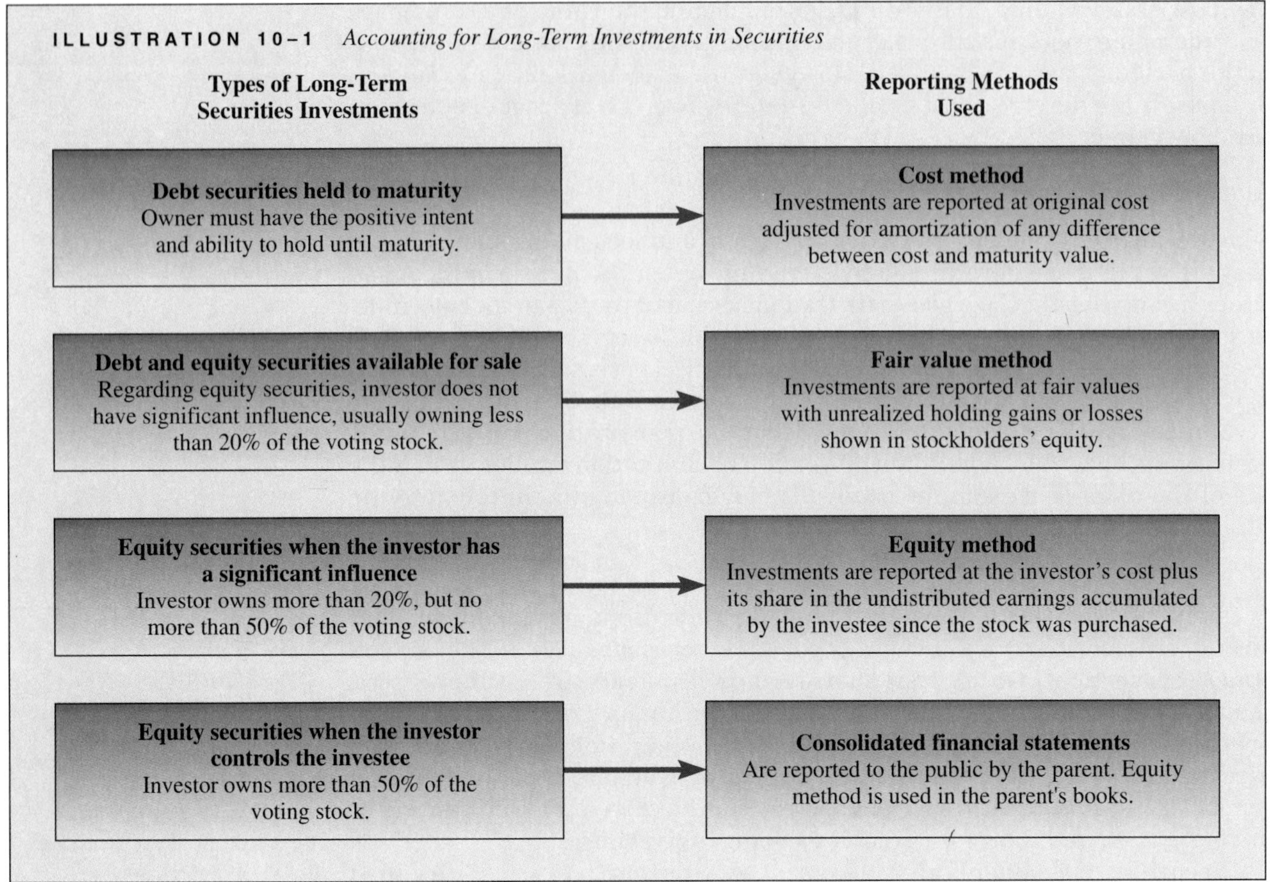

ILLUSTRATION 10-1 Accounting for Long-Term Investments in Securities
Types of Long-Term Securities Investments
Reporting Methods Used
Debt securities held to maturity
Owner must have the positive intent and ability to hold until maturity.
Cost method
Investments are reported at original cost adjusted for amortization of any difference between cost and maturity value.
Debt and equity securities available for sale
Regarding equity securities, investor does not have significant influence, usually owning less than 20% of the voting stock.
Fair value method
Investments are reported at fair values with unrealized holding gains or losses shown in stockholders' equity.
Equity securities when the investor has a significant influence
Investor owns more than 20%, but no more than 50% of the voting stock.
Equity method
Investments are reported at the investor's cost plus its share in the undistributed earnings accumulated by the investee since the stock was purchased.
Equity securities when the investor controls the investee
Investor owns more than 50% of the voting stock.
Consolidated financial statements
Are reported to the public by the parent. Equity method is used in the parent's books.

LO 3 Describe the methods used to report long-term securities investments in the financial statements.

Investments in Debt Securities Held to Maturity

Debt securities held to maturity may be short-term or long-term investments. In either case, the owner must have the positive intent and the ability to hold the securities until they mature.[5] At the time of purchase, these investments are recorded at cost. Then, interest revenue is recorded as it accrues.

The cost of an investment in debt securities may be more or less than the maturity value of the securities. When the investment is long-term, any difference between cost and maturity value must be amortized over the remaining life of the security. Chapter 12 explains the process of amortizing this difference. In this chapter, however, we assume that the costs of debt investments equal their maturity values.

For example, on August 31, 19X1, Francis, Inc., paid $29,500 plus a brokerage fee of $500 to buy $30,000 par value of Candice Corp.'s 7% bonds payable. The bonds pay interest semiannually on August 31 and February 28. The amount of each payment is $300,000 × 7% × 6⁄12 = $1,050. Francis has the positive intent to hold the bonds until they mature on August 31, 19X3. The following entry records the purchase:

19X1				
Aug.	31	Investment in Candice Corp. Bonds	30,000.00	
		Cash		30,000.00
		Purchased bonds to be held to maturity.		

[5] FASB, "Accounting for Certain Investments in Debt and Equity Securities," *Statement of Accounting Standards No. 115* (Norwalk, CT, 1994), par. 6.

On December 31, 19X1, at the end of its accounting period, Francis accrues interest receivable with the following entry:

Dec.	31	Interest Receivable	700.00	
		Interest Earned		700.00
		$1,050 × 4/6 = $700.		

In this entry, the $700 represents 4/6 of the semiannual cash receipt for interest. As a result of these entries, Francis's financial statements for 19X1 show the following items:

On the income statement for 19X1:	
Interest earned	$ 700
On the December 31, 19X1, balance sheet:	
Assets:	
Long-term investments:	
Investment in Candice Corp. bonds	$30,000

On February 28, 19X2, Francis records the receipt of interest with the following entry:

19X2				
Feb.	28	Cash	1,050.00	
		Interest Receivable		700.00
		Interest Earned		350.00
		Received 6 months' interest on Candice Corp. bonds.		

When the bonds mature, this entry records the proceeds from the matured bonds:

19X3				
Aug.	31	Cash	30,000.00	
		Investment in Candice Corp. Bonds		30,000.00
		Received cash from matured bonds.		

Investments in Securities Available for Sale

On the left side of Illustration 10–1, notice that only the top two boxes include debt securities. In other words, debt securities that do not qualify as securities held to maturity are classified as securities available for sale. In the second box on the left side of Illustration 10–1, you can see that securities available for sale also include certain equity securities. To be included in this group of long-term investments, the investor in equity securities must not have a significant influence over the investee. Normally, this means that the investor owns less than 20% of the investee corporation's voting stock.[6]

Debt Securities Available for Sale. Accounting for debt securities available for sale is similar to debt securities held to maturity. At the time of purchase, the debt securities are recorded at cost. Then, interest is recorded as it accrues.

[6] The 20% limit is not an absolute rule. Other factors may overrule. FASB, *Accounting Standards—Current Text* (Norwalk, CT, 1994), sec. I82.107–108. First published in *FASB Interpretation No. 35*, pars. 3–4.

For example, assume that in the previous discussion, the bonds purchased by Francis, Inc., were not classified as debt securities held to maturity. Instead, assume they were securities available for sale. In other words, assume that Francis did not necessarily intend to hold the bonds to maturity. The previous entries to record the purchase of the bonds on August 31, the accrual of interest on December 31, 19X1, and the receipt of interest on February 28, 19X2, would be exactly the same. If Francis were to sell the bonds before they mature, any gain or loss realized on the sale would be reported in the income statement.

The only difference between debt securities held to maturity and debt securities available for sale involves the amount reported on the balance sheet. Debt securities held to maturity are reported at cost (adjusted for the amortized amount of any difference between cost and maturity value.) Debt securities available for sale are reported at their fair value. We explain this more completely after discussing equity securities available for sale.

Equity Securities Available for Sale. Chapter 7 (pages 259–262) explained the procedures of accounting for short-term investments in equity securities available for sale. These same procedures are used for long-term investments. At the time of purchase, the investments are recorded at cost. As dividends are received, they are credited to Dividends Earned and reported in the income statement. When the shares are sold, the proceeds from the sale are compared with the cost of the investment and any gain or loss realized on the sale is reported in the income statement.

Continuing with Francis, Inc., assume that on October 10, 19X1, Francis purchased 1,000 shares of Intex Corp.'s common stock at their par value of $86,000. The following entry records the purchase:

Oct.	10	Investment in Intex Corp. Common Stock	86,000.00	
		Cash		86,000.00
		Purchased 1,000 shares.		

On November 2, Francis received a $1,720 quarterly dividend on the Intex shares. The following entry records the receipt:

Nov.	2	Cash	1,720.00	
		Dividends Earned		1,720.00
		Received dividend of $1.72 per share.		

On December 20, Francis sold 500 of the Intex shares for $45,000, and records the sale with the following entry:

Dec.	20	Cash	45,000.00	
		Investment in Intex Corp. Common Stock . . .		43,000.00
		Gain on Sale of Long-Term Investment		2,000.00
		$86,000/2 = $43,000		

Reporting the Fair Values of Securities Available for Sale. On the balance sheet, long-term investments in securities available for sale are reported at their fair values. This includes both debt and equity securities. Unrealized holding gains (losses) are reported as a separate item in the equity section.

For example, assume that Francis had no prior investments in securities available for sale, other than the bonds purchased on August 31 and the stock purchased on October 10. The following table shows the book values and fair values of these investments on December 31, 19X1:

	Book Value	Fair (Market) Value
Candice Corp. bonds payable	$30,000	$29,050
Intex Corp. common stock, 500 shares	43,000	45,500
Total	$73,000	$74,550

The entry to record the fair value of the investments is

Dec.	31	Long-Term Investments, Fair Value Adjustment	1,550.00	
		Unrealized Holding Gain (Loss)		1,550.00
		To record change in fair value of securities available for sale.		

In preparing Francis's December 31, 19X1, balance sheet, the cost of the investments normally would be combined with the balance in the Long-Term Investments, Fair Value Adjustment account and reported as a single amount. Thus, Francis's balance sheet would include the following items:

Assets:	
Long-term investments:	
Securities available for sale (at fair value) . .	$74,550
Stockholders' equity:	
Common stock	xxx
Retained Earnings	xxx
Unrealized Holding Gain	1,550

Investment in Equity Securities; Investor Has a Significant Influence or Has Control

Sometimes, an investor buys a large block of a corporation's voting stock and is able to exercise a significant influence over the investee corporation. An investor who owns 20% or more of a corporation's voting stock is normally presumed to have a significant influence over the investee. There may be cases, however, where the accountant concludes that the 20% test of significant influence should be overruled by other, more persuasive, evidence.

If an investor owns more than 50% of a corporation's voting stock, the investor can dominate all of the other stockholders in electing the corporation's board of directors. Thus, the investor usually has control over the investee corporation's management.[7]

As we stated earlier, the method of accounting for a stock investment depends on the relationship between the investor and the investee. In studying Illustration 10–1, note that if the investor has a significant influence, the *equity method* of accounting and reporting is used. Finally, if the investor controls the investee, the investor uses the equity method in its records, but reports *consolidated financial statements* to the public. We discuss the equity method and consolidated statements in the following sections.

The Equity Method of Accounting for Common Stock Investments

If a common stock investor has significant influence over the investee, the **equity method** of accounting for the investment must be used. When the stock

[7] Ibid., sec. C51.102. First published in *Statement of Financial Accounting Standards No. 94,* par. 13.

is acquired, the investor records the purchase at cost. For example, on January 1, 19X1, Gordon Company purchased 3,000 shares (30%) of JWM, Inc., common stock for a total cost of $70,650. This entry records the purchase on Gordon's books:

Jan.	1	Investment in JWM Common Stock	70,650.00	
		Cash		70,650.00
		Purchased 3,000 shares.		

Under the equity method, the earnings of the investee corporation not only increase the investee's net assets but also increase the investor's equity claims against the investee's assets. Therefore, when the investee closes its books and reports the amount of its earnings, the investor takes up its share of those earnings in its investment account. For example, assume that JWM reported net income of $20,000 for 19X1. Gordon's entry to record its 30% share of these earnings is

Dec.	31	Investment in JWM Common Stock	6,000.00	
		Earnings from Investment in JWM, Inc.		6,000.00
		To record 30% equity in investee's earnings of $20,000.		

The debit records the increase in Gordon Company's equity in JWM. The credit causes 30% of JWM's net income to appear on Gordon Company's income statement as earnings from the investment. As with any other revenue, Gordon closes the earnings to Income Summary.

If the investee corporation incurs a net loss instead of a net income, the investor records its share of the loss and reduces (credits) its investment account. Then, the investor closes the loss to Income Summary.

Under the equity method, the receipt of cash dividends is not recorded as revenue because the investor has already recorded its share of the earnings reported by the investee. Instead, dividends received from the investee simply convert the form of the investor's asset from a stock investment to cash. Thus, the equity method records dividends as a reduction in the balance of the investment account.

For example, assume that JWM declared and paid $10,000 in cash dividends on its common stock. Gordon's entry to record its 30% share of these dividends, which it received on January 9, 19X2, is

Jan.	9	Cash	3,000.00	
		Investment in JWM Common Stock		3,000.00
		To record receipt of 30% of the $10,000 dividend paid by JWM, Inc.		

Thus, when the equity method is used, the carrying value of a common stock investment equals the cost of the investment plus the investor's equity in the *undistributed* earnings of the investee. For example, after the preceding transactions are recorded on the books of Gordon Company, the investment account appears as follows:

Investment in JWM Common Stock

Date		Explanation	Debit	Credit	Balance
19X1					
Jan.	1	Investment	70,650		70,650
Dec.	31	Share of earnings	6,000		76,650
19X2					
Jan.	9	Share of dividend		3,000	73,650

If Gordon prepared a balance sheet on January 9, the investment in JWM would be reported as $73,650. This is the original cost of the investment, plus Gordon's equity in JWM's earnings since the date of purchase, less Gordon's equity in JWM's dividends since the date of purchase.

When an equity method stock investment is sold, the gain or loss on the sale is determined by comparing the proceeds from the sale with the carrying value (book value) of the investment on the date of sale. For example, suppose that Gordon Company sold its JWM stock for $80,000 on January 10, 19X2. The entry to record the sale is

Jan.	10	Cash	80,000.00	
		Investment in JWM Common Stock		73,650.00
		Gain on Sale of Investments		6,350.00
		Sold 3,000 shares of stock for $80,000.		

Investments That Require Consolidated Financial Statements

Corporations often own stock in and may even control other corporations. For example, if Par Company owns more than 50% of the voting stock of Sub Company, Par Company can elect Sub Company's board of directors and thus control its activities and resources. The controlling corporation, Par Company, is known as the **parent company** and Sub Company is called a **subsidiary.**

When a corporation owns all the outstanding stock of a subsidiary, it can take over the subsidiary's assets, cancel the subsidiary's stock, and merge the subsidiary into the parent company. However, there often are financial, legal, and tax advantages if a large business is operated as a parent corporation that controls one or more subsidiary corporations. In fact, many large companies are parent corporations that own one or more subsidiaries.

When a business operates as a parent company with subsidiaries, separate accounting records are maintained by each corporation. From a legal viewpoint, the parent and each subsidiary are still separate entities with all the rights, duties, and responsibilities of individual corporations. However, investors in the parent company indirectly are investors in the subsidiaries. To evaluate their investments, parent company investors must consider the financial status and operations of the subsidiaries as well as the parent. This information is provided in **consolidated financial statements.**

Consolidated statements show the financial position, the results of operations, and the cash flows of all corporations under the parent's control, including the subsidiaries. These statements are prepared as if the business is organized as a single company. Although the parent uses the equity method in its accounts, the investment account is not reported on the parent's financial statements. Instead, the individual assets and liabilities of the affiliated companies are combined on a single balance sheet. Also, their revenues and expenses are combined on a single income statement and their cash flows are combined on a single statement of cash flows. More detailed explanations of consolidated statements are included in more advanced accounting courses.

Investments in International Operations

LO 4 Describe the primary accounting problems of having investments in international operations and prepare entries to account for sales to foreign customers.

In today's complex world, many companies conduct business activities in more than one country. In fact, the operations of some large corporations involve so many different countries that they are called **multinational businesses.** The problems of managing and accounting for companies that have international operations can be very complex. Because of this complexity, the following pages present only a brief discussion. A more detailed study of these issues is reserved for advanced business courses.

Two primary problems in accounting for international operations occur because businesses with transactions in more than one country have to deal with more than one currency. These two problems are (1) accounting for sales or purchases denominated in a foreign currency and (2) preparing consolidated financial statements with foreign subsidiaries. To simplify the discussion of these problems, we assume that the companies have a base of operations in the United States and prepare their financial statements in the U.S. dollar. Hence, the **reporting currency** of such firms is the U.S. dollar.

Exchange Rates between Currencies

Active markets for the purchase and sale of foreign currencies exist all over the world. In these markets, U.S. dollars can be exchanged for Canadian dollars, British pounds, French francs, Japanese yen, or other currencies. The price of one currency stated in terms of another currency is called a **foreign exchange rate.** For example, assume that the current exchange rate for British pounds and U.S. dollars was $1.7515 on January 31, 19X1. This rate means that one pound could have been acquired for $1.7515. On the same day, assume that the exchange rate between German marks and U.S. dollars was $0.5321. This number means that one mark could be purchased for $0.5321. Foreign exchange rates fluctuate daily (or even hourly) in accordance with the changing supply and demand for each currency and expectations about future events.

Sales or Purchases Denominated in a Foreign Currency

When a U.S. company makes a credit sale to a foreign customer, a special problem can arise in accounting for the sale and the account receivable. If the sales terms require the foreign customer's payment to be in U.S. dollars, no special accounting problem arises. But, if the terms of the sale state that payment is to be made in a foreign currency, the U.S. company must go through special steps to account for the sale and the account receivable.

For example, suppose that a U.S. company, the Boston Company, makes a credit sale to London Outfitters, a British company. The sale occurs on December 12, 19X1, and the price is £10,000, which is due on February 10, 19X2. Naturally, Boston Company keeps its accounting records in U.S. dollars. Therefore, to record the sale, Boston Company must translate the sales price from pounds to dollars. This is done using the current exchange rate on the date of the sale. Assuming that the current exchange rate on December 12 is $1.80, Boston records the sale as follows:

Dec.	12	Accounts Receivable—London Outfitters	18,000.00	
		Sales (10,000 × $1.80)		18,000.00
		To record a sale at £10,000, when the exchange rate equals $1.80.		

Now, assume that Boston Company prepares annual financial statements on December 31, 19X1. On that date, the current exchange rate has increased to $1.84. Therefore, the current dollar value of Boston Company's receivable is $18,400 (10,000 × $1.84). This amount is now $400 greater than the amount originally recorded on December 12. According to generally accepted accounting principles, the receivable must be reported in the balance sheet at its current dollar value. Hence, Boston Company must make the following entry to record the increase in the dollar value of the receivable:

Dec.	31	Accounts Receivable—London Outfitters	400.00	
		Foreign Exchange Gain or Loss		400.00
		To record the effects of the increased value of the British pound on our receivable.		

The Foreign Exchange Gain or Loss is closed to the Income Summary account and reported on the income statement.[8]

Assume that Boston Company receives London Outfitters' payment of £10,000 on February 10, and immediately exchanges the pounds for U.S. dollars. On this date, the exchange rate for pounds has declined to $1.78. Therefore, Boston Company receives only $17,800 (10,000 × $1.78). The firm records the receipt and the loss associated with the decline in the exchange rate as follows:

Feb.	10	Cash	17,800.00	
		Foreign Exchange Gain or Loss	600.00	
		Accounts Receivable—London Outfitters . . .		18,400.00
		Received foreign currency payment of account and converted it into dollars.		

Accounting for credit purchases from a foreign supplier is similar to the previous example of a credit sale to a foreign customer. If the U.S. company is required to make a payment in a foreign currency, the account payable must be translated into dollars before it can be recorded by the U.S. company. Then, if the exchange rate changes, an exchange gain or loss must be recognized by the U.S. company at any intervening balance sheet date and at the payment date.

Consolidated Statements with Foreign Subsidiaries

A second problem of accounting for international operations involves the preparation of consolidated financial statements when the parent company has one or more foreign subsidiaries. For example, suppose that a U.S. company owns a controlling interest in a French subsidiary. The reporting currency of the U.S. parent is the dollar. However, the French subsidiary maintains its financial records in francs. Before preparing consolidated statements, the parent must translate financial statements of the French company into U.S. dollars. After the translation is completed, the preparation of consolidated statements is not any different than for any other subsidiary.[9]

[8] Ibid., sec. F60.122. First published as FASB, *Statement of Financial Accounting Standards No. 52,* par. 15.

[9] The problem grows much more complicated when the accounts of the French subsidiary are maintained in accordance with French version of GAAP. The French statements must be converted to U.S. GAAP before the consolidation can be completed.

The procedures for translating a foreign subsidiary's account balances depend on the nature of the subsidiary's operations. In simple terms, the general process requires the parent company to select appropriate foreign exchanges rates and then to apply those rates to the account balances of the foreign subsidiary.

Using the Information—Return on Total Assets

LO 5 Explain the use of return on total assets in evaluating a company's efficiency in using its assets.

After studying this and the previous chapters, you have learned about all of the important classes of assets that businesses own. Recall from Chapter 9 that in evaluating the efficiency of a company in using its assets, a ratio that is often calculated and reviewed is total asset turnover. Another ratio that provides information about a company's efficiency in using its assets is **return on total assets.** You can calculate the *return on total assets* with this formula:

$$\text{Return on total assets} = \frac{\text{Net income}}{\text{Average total assets}}$$

For example, Reebok International, a worldwide distributor of sports and fitness products, earned a net income of \$114.8 million during 1992. At the beginning of 1992, Reebok had total assets of \$1,422.3 million, and at the end of the year total assets were \$1,345.3 million. If the average total assets owned during the year is approximated by averaging the beginning and ending asset balances, Reebok's return on total assets for 1992 was:

$$\text{Return on total assets} = \frac{\$114.8}{(\$1,422.3 + \$1,345.3)/2} = 8.3\%$$

As we have seen for other ratios, a company's return on total assets should be compared with past performance and with the ratios of similar companies. In addition, you must be careful not to place too much importance on the evaluation of any single ratio. For example, Reebok's return on total assets and total asset turnover over a four-year period were as follows:

Year	Return on Total Assets	Total Asset Turnover
1992	8.3%	2.2
1991	16.7	1.9
1990	13.9	1.7
1989	15.8	1.6

Notice that the change in return on total assets suggests that the company's efficiency in using its assets declined. However, the total asset turnover improved each year. A possible explanation for this might be that Reebok decided to increase expenses at a faster rate than sales in an effort to gain an increasing share of the market for its products. Such a strategy would explain a reduced return on total assets and an increased total asset turnover.

Summary of Chapter in Terms of Learning Objectives

LO 1 The cost of a natural resource is recorded in an asset account. Then, depletion of the natural resource is recorded by allocating the cost to expense according to a units-of-production basis. The depletion is credited to an accumulated depletion account. Intangible assets are recorded at the cost incurred to purchase the assets. The allocation of intangible asset cost to expense is done on a straight-line basis and is called amortization. Normally, amortization is recorded with credits made directly to the asset account instead of a contra account.

LO 2 Securities investments are classified as current assets if they are held as a source of cash to be used in current operations and if they mature within one year or the current operating cycle of the business or are marketable. All other investments in securities are long-term investments, which also include assets held for a special purpose and not used in operations.

Long-term investments in securities are classified in four groups: (*a*) debt securities held to maturity, (*b*) debt and equity securities available for sale, (*c*) equity securities when the investor has a significant influence over the investee, and (*d*) equity securities when the investor controls the investee.

LO 3 Debt held to maturity is reported at its original cost adjusted for amortization of any difference between cost and maturity value. Debt and equity securities available for sale are reported at their fair values with unrealized gains or losses shown in the stockholders' equity section of the balance sheet. Gains and losses realized on the sale of the investments are reported in the income statement.

The equity method is used if the investor has a significant influence over the investee. This situation usually exists when the investor owns 20% or more of the investee's voting stock. If an investor owns more than 50% of another corporation's voting stock and controls the investee, the investor's financial reports are prepared on a consolidated basis.

Under the equity method, the investor records its share of the investee's earnings with a debit to the investment account and a credit to a revenue account. Dividends received satisfy the investor's equity claims, and reduce the investment account balance.

LO 4 If a U.S. company makes a credit sale to a foreign customer and the sales terms call for payment with a foreign currency, the company must translate the foreign currency into dollars to record the receivable. If the exchange rate changes before payment is received, foreign exchange gains or losses are recognized in the year in which they occur. The same treatment is used if a U.S. company makes a credit purchase from a foreign supplier and is required to make payment in a foreign currency. Also, if a U.S. company has a foreign subsidiary that maintains its accounts in a foreign currency, the account balances must be translated into dollars before they can be consolidated with the parent's accounts.

LO 5 Return on total assets is used along with other ratios such as total asset turnover to evaluate the efficiency of a company in using its assets. Return on total assets is usually calculated as the annual net income divided by the average amount of total assets.

Demonstration Problem

The following transactions relate to Brown Company's long-term investment activities during 19X1 and 19X2. Brown did not own any long-term investments prior to 19X1. Show the appropriate journal entries and the portions of each year's balance sheet and income statement that describe these transactions.

19X1

Sept. 9 Purchased 1,000 shares of Packard, Inc., common stock for $80,000 cash. These shares represent 30% of Packard's outstanding shares.

Oct. 2 Purchased 2,000 shares of AT&T common stock for $60,000 cash. These shares represent less than a 1% ownership in AT&T.

	17	Purchased as a long-term investment 1,000 shares of Apple Computers common stock for $40,000 cash. These shares are less than 1% of Apple's outstanding shares.
Nov.	1	Received $5,000 cash dividend from Packard.
	30	Received $3,000 cash dividend from AT&T.
Dec.	15	Received $1,400 cash dividend from Apple.
	31	Packard's 19X1 net income was $70,000.
	31	Market values for the investments in marketable equity securities are Packard, $84,000; AT&T, $48,000; and Apple Computers, $45,000.
	31	After closing the accounts, selected account balances on Brown Company's books are

Common stock	$500,000
Retained earnings	350,000

19X2		
Jan.	1	Packard, Inc., was taken over by other investors, and Brown sold its shares for $108,000 cash.
May	30	Received $3,100 cash dividend from AT&T.
June	15	Received $1,600 cash dividend from Apple.
Aug.	17	Sold the AT&T stock for $52,000 cash.
	19	Purchased 2,000 shares of Coca-Cola common stock for $50,000 as a long-term investment. The stock represents less than a 5% ownership in Coca-Cola.
Dec.	15	Received $1,800 cash dividend from Apple.
	31	Market values of the investments in marketable equity securities are Apple, $39,000 and Coca-Cola, $48,000.
	31	After closing the accounts, selected account balances on Brown Company's books are

Common stock	$500,000
Retained earnings	410,000

Planning the Solution

- Account for the investment in Packard under the equity method.
- Account for the investments in AT&T, Apple, and Coca-Cola as long-term investments in securities available for sale.
- Prepare the information for the two balance sheets by including the appropriate assets and stockholders' equity accounts.

Solution to Demonstration Problem

Journal entries during 19X1:

Sept.	9	Investment in Packard Common Stock	80,000.00	
		Cash		80,000.00
		Acquired 1,000 shares representing a 30% equity in Packard, Inc.		
Oct.	2	Investment in AT&T Common Stock	60,000.00	
		Cash		60,000.00
		Acquired 2,000 shares as a long-term investment in securities available for sale.		
	17	Investment in Apple Common Stock	40,000.00	
		Cash		40,000.00
		Acquired 1,000 shares as a long-term investment in securities available for sale.		

Nov.	1	Cash	5,000.00	
		Investment in Packard Common Stock		5,000.00
		Received dividend from Packard, Inc.		
	30	Cash	3,000.00	
		Dividends Earned		3,000.00
		Received dividend from AT&T.		
Dec.	15	Cash	1,400.00	
		Dividends Earned		1,400.00
		Received dividend from Apple.		
	31	Investment in Packard Common Stock	21,000.00	
		Earnings from Investment in Packard		21,000.00
		To record our 30% share of Packard's annual earnings of $70,000.		
	31	Unrealized Holding Gain (Loss)	7,000.00	
		Long-Term Investments, Fair Value Adjustment		7,000.00
		To record change in fair value of securities available for sale.		

	Cost	Fair (Market) Value
AT&T	$ 60,000	$48,000
Apple	40,000	45,000
Total	$100,000	$93,000

Required credit balance of Long-Term Investments Fair Value Adjustment account ($100,000 − $93,000)	$ 7,000
Existing balance	–0–
Necessary credit	$ 7,000

December 31, 19X1, balance sheet items:

Assets

Long-term investments:		
Securities available for sale (at fair value)	$93,000	
Investment in Packard, Inc.	96,000	
Total		$189,000

Stockholders' Equity

Common stock	$500,000
Retained earnings	350,000
Unrealized holding gain (loss)	(7,000)

Income statement items for the year ended December 31, 19X1:

Dividends earned	$ 4,400
Earnings from equity method investment	21,000

Journal entries during 19X2:

Jan.	1	Cash	108,000.00	
		Investment in Packard Common Stock		96,000.00
		Gain on Sale of Investments		12,000.00
		Sold 1,000 shares for cash.		
May	30	Cash	3,100.00	
		Dividends Earned		3,100.00
		Received dividend from AT&T.		
June	15	Cash	1,600.00	
		Dividends Earned		1,600.00
		Received dividend from Apple.		
Aug.	17	Cash	52,000.00	
		Loss on Sale of Investments	8,000.00	
		Investment in AT&T Common Stock		60,000.00
		Sold 2,000 shares for cash.		
	19	Investment in Coca-Cola Common Stock	50,000.00	
		Cash		50,000.00
		Acquired 2,000 shares as a long-term investment in securities available for sale.		
Dec.	15	Cash	1,800.00	
		Dividends Earned		1,800.00
		Received dividend from Apple.		
	31	Long-Term Investments, Fair Value Adjustment	4,000.00	
		Unrealized Holding Gain (Loss)		4,000.00
		To record change in fair value of securities available for sale.		

	Cost	Fair (Market) Value
Apple	$40,000	$39,000
Coca-Cola	50,000	48,000
Total	$90,000	$87,000

Required credit balance of Long-Term Investments Fair Value Adjustment account ($90,000 − $87,000)	$ 3,000
Existing credit balance	7,000
Necessary debit	$ 4,000

December 31, 19X2, balance sheet items:

Assets

Long-term investments:	
Securities available for sale (fair value)	$ 87,000

Stockholders' Equity

Common stock	$500,000
Retained earnings	410,000
Unrealized holding gain (loss)	(3,000)

Income statement items for the year ended December 31, 19X2:

Dividends earned	$ 6,500
Gain on sale of investments	12,000
Loss on sale of investments	(8,000)

Glossary

LO 6 Define or explain the words and phrases listed in the chapter glossary.

Amortization the process of systematically writing off the cost of an intangible asset to expense over its estimated useful life. p. 349

Consolidated financial statements financial statements that show the results of all operations under the parent's control, including those of any subsidiaries; assets and liabilities of all affiliated companies are combined on a single balance sheet, revenues and expenses are combined on a single income statement, and cash flows are combined on a single statement of cash flows as though the business were in fact a single company. p. 359

Copyright an exclusive right granted by the federal government or by international agreement to publish and sell a musical, literary, or artistic work for a period of years. p. 350

Depletion the cost created by consuming the usefulness of natural resources. p. 349

Equity method an accounting method used when the investor has influence over the investee; the investment account is initially debited for cost and then increased to reflect the investor's share of the investee's earnings and decreased to reflect the investor's receipt of dividends paid by the investee. p. 357

Foreign exchange rate the price of one currency stated in terms of another currency. p. 360

Goodwill an intangible asset of a business that represents future earnings greater than the average in its industry; recognized in the financial statements only when a business is acquired at a price in excess of the fair market value of its net assets (excluding goodwill). p. 351

Intangible asset an asset representing certain legal rights and economic relationships; it has no physical existence but is beneficial to the owner. p. 349

Lease a contract under which the owner of property (the lessor) grants to the lessee the right to use the property. p. 351

Leasehold the rights granted to a lessee by the lessor under the terms of a lease contract. p. 351

Leasehold improvements improvements to leased property made and paid for by the lessee. p. 351

Lessee the individual or company that acquires the right to use property under the terms of a lease. p. 351

Lessor the individual or company that owns property to be used by a lessee under the terms of a lease. p. 351

Long-term investments investments in stocks and bonds that are not marketable or, if marketable, are not intended to be a ready source of cash in case of need; also funds earmarked for a special purpose, such as bond sinking funds, and land or other assets not used in regular operations. p. 353

Multinational business a company that operates in a large number of different countries. p. 360

Parent company a corporation that owns a controlling interest in another corporation (more than 50% of the voting stock is required). p. 359

Patent exclusive right granted by the federal government to manufacture and sell a patented machine or device, or to use a process, for 17 years. p. 350

Reporting currency the currency in which a company presents its financial statements. p. 360

Return on total assets a measure of a company's operating efficiency, calculated by expressing net income as a percentage of average total assets. p. 362

Subsidiary a corporation that is controlled by another corporation (the parent) because the parent owns more than 50% of the subsidiary's voting stock. p. 359

Trademark a unique symbol used by a company in marketing its products or services. p. 352

Trade name a unique name used by a company in marketing its products or services. p. 352

Objective Review

Answers to the following questions are listed at the end of this chapter. Be sure that you decide which is the one best answer to each question *before* you check the answers.

LO 1 Prospect Mining Company paid $650,000 for an ore deposit. The deposit had an estimated 325,000 tons of ore that would be fully mined during the next 10 years. During the current year, 91,000 tons were mined, processed, and sold. The amount of depletion for the year is:

a. $65,000.
b. $91,000.
c. $182,000.
d. $156,000.
e. $-0-.

LO 2 Which of the following criteria must be satisfied for a stock investment to be classified as long term?

a. The stock must not be held longer than one year.
b. The stock must not be a marketable security.
c. The stock must be common shares.
d. The stock must not be a marketable security that is held as a ready source of cash.
e. The stock must be a marketable security.

LO 3 On January 1, 19X1, Brenner Wholesale Corporation purchased 7,000 shares (35%) of Outback Cargo Company's common stock at a total cost of $140,000. Outback Cargo's net income over the next three years totaled $450,000, and the company declared and paid $200,000 in dividends on its outstanding common shares. Brenner Wholesale sold its Outback Cargo Company shares on January 3, 19X4, for $34.50 per share. The entry to record the sale is as follows:

		Debit	Credit
a.	Cash	241,500	
	Investment in Outback Cargo Company, Common Stock		70,000
	Gain on Sale of Investments		171,500
b.	Cash	241,500	
	Investment in Outback Cargo Company, Common Stock		140,000
	Gain on Sale of Investments		101,500
c.	Cash	241,500	
	Loss on Sale of Investments	56,000	
	Investment in Outback Cargo Company, Common Stock		297,500
d.	Cash	241,500	
	Investment in Outback Cargo Company, Common Stock		227,500
	Gain on Sale of Investments		14,000
e.	Cash	241,500	
	Investment in Outback Cargo Company, Common Stock		241,500

LO 4 If a U.S. company makes a credit sale of merchandise to a French customer and the sales terms require the customer's payment to be in francs:

a. The United States company will incur an exchange loss if the foreign exchange rate between francs and dollars increases from $0.189 at the date of sale to $0.199 at the date the account is settled.

b. The French company will incur an exchange loss if the foreign exchange rate between francs and dollars decreases from $0.189 at the date of sale to $0.179 at the date the account is settled.

c. The French company may eventually have to record an exchange gain or loss.

d. The U.S. company may be required to record an exchange gain or loss on the date of the sale.

e. None of the above is correct.

LO 5 A company had net income of $140,000 for 19X1 and $100,000 for 19X2. At December 31, 19X1, and 19X2, total assets reported were $800,000 and $900,000, respectively. The return on total assets for 19X2 was:

a. 11.1%.

b. 11.8%.

c. 12.5%.

d. 13.3%.

e. Cannot be determined from the information provided.

LO 6 A company that owns more than 50% of another corporation and controls that corporation is called a:

a. Subsidiary.

b. Consolidated company.

c. Multinational business.

d. Parent company.

e. None of the above is correct.

Questions for Class Discussion

1. What is the name for the process of allocating the cost of natural resources to expense as the natural resources are used?
2. What are the characteristics of an intangible asset?
3. Is the declining-balance method an acceptable means of calculating depletion of natural resources?
4. What general procedures are followed in accounting for intangible assets?
5. Define (*a*) lease, (*b*) lessor, (*c*) lessee, (*d*) leasehold, and (*e*) leasehold improvement.
6. When does a business have goodwill? Under what conditions can goodwill appear in a company's balance sheet?
7. X Company bought an established business and paid for goodwill. If X Company plans to incur substantial advertising and promotional costs each year to maintain the value of the goodwill, must the company also amortize the goodwill?
8. Under what conditions should a stock investment be classified on the balance sheet as a long-term investment?
9. What types of assets are classified as long-term investments?
10. In accounting for common stock investments, when should the equity method be used?
11. Under what circumstances would a company prepare consolidated financial statements?
12. When a long-term stock investment is classified as a security available for sale, what events related to the investment are reported on the investor's income statement?
13. Under what circumstances are long-term investments in debt securities reported at their original cost adjusted for amortization of any difference between cost and maturity value?
14. What are two basic problems of accounting for international operations?
15. If a U.S. company makes a credit sale to a foreign customer and the customer is required to make payment in U.S. dollars, can the U.S. company have an exchange gain or loss as a result of the sale?

16. A U.S. company makes a credit sale to a foreign customer, and the customer is required to make payment in a foreign currency. The foreign exchange rate was $1.40 on the date of the sale and is $1.30 on the date the customer pays the receivable. Will the U.S. company record an exchange gain or an exchange loss?
17. On December 31, 19X1, a U.S. company has an account receivable from a British customer that requires the customer to pay £6,000 to the U.S. company. How do you determine the amount to be reported on the U.S. company's December 31 balance sheet?
18. In preparing its December 31, 19X1, financial statements, a U.S. company had to report an account receivable that was denominated in a foreign currency. The receivable stemmed from a sale made on November 14, 19X1. In translating the receivable into dollars, should the accountant use the foreign exchange rate on November 14 or on December 31?

19. Refer to Federal Express Corporation's consolidated balance sheets in Appendix G. What percentage of total assets is represented by goodwill at May 31, 1993?

20. Refer to Ben & Jerry's Homemade, Inc., financial statements in Appendix G. Calculate the return on total assets for 1992.

Exercises

Exercise 10–1
Depletion of natural resources
(LO 1)

On March 30, 19X1, Clementine Investments paid $7,275,000 for an ore deposit containing 4,850,000 tons. The company also installed machinery in the mine that cost $339,500, had an estimated 10-year life with no salvage value, and was capable of removing all the ore in 8 years. The machine will be abandoned when the ore is completely mined. Clementine began operations on July 1, 19X1, and mined and sold 582,000 tons of ore during the remaining six months of the year. Give the December 31, 19X1, entries to record the depletion of the ore deposit and the depreciation of the mining machinery.

Exercise 10–2
Amortization of intangible assets
(LO 1)

Majestic Productions purchased the copyright to a painting for $369,000 on January 1, 19X1. The copyright legally protects its owner for 24 more years. However, the company plans to market and sell prints of the original for only 15 more years. Prepare journal entries to record (*a*) the purchase of the copyright and (*b*) the annual amortization of the copyright on December 31, 19X1.

Exercise 10–3
Estimating goodwill
(LO 1)

Rocky Lane has devoted years to developing a profitable business that earns an attractive return. Lane is now considering the possibility of selling the business and is attempting to estimate the value of the goodwill in the business. The fair value of the net assets of the business (excluding goodwill) is $625,000, and in a typical year net income is about $90,000. Most businesses of this type are expected to earn a return of about 12% on net assets. Estimate the value of the goodwill assuming (*a*) the value is equal to eight times the excess earnings above average, and (*b*) the value can be found by capitalizing the excess earnings above average at a rate of 10%.

Exercise 10–4
Classifying stock investments, recording fair values
(LO 2, 3)

During 19X1, Stockton Company's investments in securities included five items. These securities, with their December 31, 19X1, market values, are as follows:

a. Antel Corporation bonds payable: $167,400 cost; $182,000 market value. Stockton positively intends and is able to hold these bonds until they mature in 19X4.
b. Foxfire, Inc., common stock: 30,800 shares; $132,980 cost; $143,500 market value. Stockton owns 22% of Foxfire's voting stock and has a significant influence on Foxfire.
c. Techcon Corp. common stock: 10,300 shares; $67,900 cost; $73,240 market value. The goal of this investment is to earn dividends over the next few years.
d. Bali common stock: 4,500 shares; $46,120 cost; $45,770 market value. The goal of this investment is expected increase in market value of the stock over the next three to five years. Bali has 30,000 common shares outstanding.
e. Joskey common stock: 18,400 shares; $57,100 cost; $59,900 market value. This stock is marketable and is held as an investment of cash available for operations.

State whether each of these investments should be classified as a current asset or as a long-term investment. Also, for each of the long-term items, indicate in which of the four types of long-term investments the item should be classified. Then, prepare a journal entry dated December 31, 19X1, to record the fair value of the long-term investments in securities available for sale. Assume that Stockton had no long-term investments prior to 19X1.

Exercise 10–5
Investments in securities available for sale
(LO 3)

Pratt Company began operations in 19X1 and regularly makes long-term investments in securities available for sale. The total cost and fair value of these investments at the end of several years were

	Cost	Market Value
On December 31, 19X1	$170,000	$164,800
On December 31, 19X2	194,000	206,000
On December 31, 19X3	264,000	312,000
On December 31, 19X4	398,000	354,000

Required

Prepare journal entries to record the fair value of Pratt's investments at the end of each year.

Exercise 10–6
Stock investment transactions; equity method
(LO 3)

Prepare general journal entries to record the following events on the books of MCM Company:

19X1

Jan. 14 Purchased 18,000 shares of Putnam, Inc., common stock for $156,900 plus broker's fee of $1,000. Putnam has 90,000 shares of common stock outstanding and has acknowledged the fact that its policies will be significantly influenced by MCM.

Oct. 1 Putnam declared and paid a cash dividend of $2.60 per share.

Dec. 31 Putnam announced that net income for the year amounted to $650,000.

19X2

Apr. 1 Putnam declared and paid a cash dividend of $2.70 per share.

Dec. 31 Putnam announced that net income for the year amounted to $733,100.

31 MCM sold 6,000 shares of Putnam for $119,370.

Exercise 10–7
Receivables denominated in a foreign currency
(LO 4)

On June 2, 19X1, Comco Company made a credit sale to a French company. The terms of the sale required the French company to pay 980,000 francs on January 3, 19X2. Comco prepares quarterly financial statements on March 31, June 30, September 30, and December 31. The foreign exchange rates for francs during the time the receivable was outstanding were

June 2, 19X1	$0.16720
June 30, 19X1	0.17100
September 30, 19X1	0.17225
December 31, 19X1	0.16885
January 3, 19X2	0.17310

Calculate the foreign exchange gain or loss that Comco should report on each of its quarterly income statements during the last three quarters of 19X1 and the first quarter of 19X2. Also calculate the amount that should be reported on Comco's balance sheets at the end of the last three quarters of 19X1.

Exercise 10–8
Foreign currency transactions
(LO 4)

Donham Company of Montvale, New Jersey, sells its products to customers in the United States and in England. On December 3, 19X1, Donham sold merchandise on credit to Swensons, Ltd., of London, England, at a price of £6,500. The exchange rate on that day was £1 equals $1.4685. On December 31, 19X1, when Donham prepared its financial statements, the exchange rate was £1 for $1.4230. Swensons, Ltd., paid its bill in full on January 3, 19X2, at which time the exchange rate was £1 for $1.4460. Donham immediately exchanged the £6,500 for U.S. dollars. Prepare journal entries on December 3, December 31, and January 3, to account for the sale and account receivable on the books of Donham.

Exercise 10–9
Return on total assets
(LO 5)

The following information is available from the financial statements of NRE Company:

	19X1	19X2	19X3
Total assets, December 31 . .	$320,000	$580,000	$1,200,000
Net income	46,000	75,000	106,000

Calculate NRE's return on total assets for 19X2 and 19X3. Comment on the company's efficiency in using its assets in 19X2 and 19X3.

Problems

Problem 10–1
Intangible assets and natural resources
(LO 1)

Part 1. Five years ago, Zeno Insurance Company leased space in a building for 15 years. The lease contract calls for annual rental payments of $28,000 to be made on each July 1 throughout the life of the lease and also provides that the lessee must pay for all additions and improvements to the leased property. Because recent nearby construction has made the location more valuable, Zeno decided to sublease the space to Bogart & Company for the remaining 10 years of the lease. On June 25, Bogart paid $75,000 to Zeno for the right to sublease the property and agreed to assume the obligation to pay the $28,000 annual rental charges to the building owner, beginning the next July 1. After taking possession of the leased space, Bogart paid for improving the office portion of the leased space at a cost of $90,950. The improvement was paid for on July 8 and is estimated to have a life equal to the 17 years remaining in the life of the building.

Required

Prepare entries for Bogart & Company to record (*a*) its payment to Zeno for the right to sublease the building space, (*b*) its payment of the next annual rental charge to the building owner, and (*c*) payment for the improvements. Also, prepare the adjusting entries required on December 31 of the first year of the sublease to amortize (*d*) a proper share of the $75,000 cost of the sublease and (*e*) a proper share of the office improvement.

Part 2. On February 20 of the current year, Amazon Industries paid $8,700,000 for land estimated to contain 11.6 million tons of recoverable ore of a valuable mineral. It installed machinery costing $348,000, which had a 12-year life and no salvage value, and was capable of exhausting the ore deposit in 9 years. The machinery was paid for on May 24, six days before mining operations began. The company removed 744,000 tons of ore during the first seven months' operations.

Required

Prepare entries to record (*a*) the purchase of land, (*b*) the installation of the machinery, (*c*) the first seven months' depletion under the assumption that the land will be valueless after the ore is mined, and (*d*) the first seven months' depreciation on the machinery, which will be abandoned after the ore is fully mined.

Problem 10–2
Goodwill
(LO 1)

Flowers Unlimited has the following balance sheet on December 31, 19X1:

Cash	$ 57,800
Merchandise inventory	43,650
Buildings	320,000
Accumulated depreciation	(112,000)
Land	101,750
Total assets	$411,200
Accounts payable	$ 9,400
Long-term note payable	124,925
D. E. Flowers, capital	276,875
Total liabilities and owner's equity	$411,200

In this industry, earnings average 32% of owner's equity. Flowers Unlimited, however, is expected to earn $100,000 annually. The owner believes that the balance sheet amounts are reasonable estimates of fair market values for all assets except goodwill, which does not appear on the financial statement. In discussing a plan to sell the company, D. E. Flowers has suggested to the potential buyer that goodwill can be measured by capitalizing the amount of above-average earnings at a rate of 12%. On the other hand, the potential buyer thinks that goodwill should be valued at six times the amount of excess earnings above the average for the industry.

Required

1. Calculate the amount of goodwill claimed by Flowers.
2. Calculate the amount of goodwill according to the potential buyer.
3. Suppose that the buyer finally agrees to pay the full price requested by Flowers. If the amount of expected earnings (before amortization of goodwill) is obtained and the goodwill is amortized over the longest permissible time period, what amount of net income will be reported for the first year after the company is purchased?
4. If the buyer pays the full price requested by Flowers, what rate of return on the purchaser's investment will be earned as net income the first year?

Problem 10–3
Accounting for stock investments
(LO 3)

Austex Company was organized on January 2, 19X1. The following transactions and events subsequently occurred:

19X1

Jan. 7	Austex purchased 50,000 shares (20%) of Staat, Inc.'s outstanding common stock for $565,500.
Apr. 30	Staat declared and paid a cash dividend of $1.10 per share.
Dec. 31	Staat announced that its net income for 19X1 was $480,000. Market value of the stock was $11.80 per share.

19X2

Nov. 30	Staat declared and paid a cash dividend of $0.70 per share.
Dec. 31	Staat announced that its net income for 19X2 was $630,000. Market value of the stock was $12.18 per share.

19X3

Jan. 5	Austex sold all of its investment in Staat for $682,000 cash.

Part 1. Assume that Austex has a significant influence over Staat because it owns 20% of the stock.

Required

1. Give the entries on the books of Austex to record the preceding events.
2. Calculate the carrying value per share of Austex's investment as reflected in the investment account on January 4, 19X3.
3. Calculate the change in Austex's equity from January 7, 19X1, through January 5, 19X3, that resulted from its investment in Staat.

Part 2. Assume that even though Austex owns 20% of Staat's outstanding stock, a thorough investigation of the surrounding circumstances indicates that it does not have a significant influence over the investee.

Required

1. Give the entries on the books of Austex to record the preceding events. Also prepare an entry dated January 5, 19X3, to remove any balances related to the fair value adjustment.
2. Calculate the cost per share of Austex's investment as reflected in the investment account on January 4, 19X3.
3. Calculate the change in Austex's equity from January 7, 19X1, through January 5, 19X3, that resulted from its investment in Staat.

Problem 10–4
Accounting for long-term investments
(LO 2, 3)

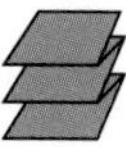

Leling Company's long-term investments portfolio at December 31, 19X1, consisted of the following:

Securities Available for Sale	Cost	Fair (Market) Value
10,000 shares of Company X common stock	$163,500	$145,000
1,500 shares of Company Y common stock	65,000	62,000
120,000 shares of Company Z common stock	40,000	35,600

Leling made the following long-term investments transactions during 19X2:

Jan. 17 Sold 750 shares of Company Y common stock for $36,000 less a brokerage fee of $180.

Mar. 3 Purchased 5,000 shares of Company A common stock for $300,000 plus a brokerage fee of $1,500. The shares represent a 30% ownership in Company A.

May 12 Purchased 3,000 shares of Company B common stock for $96,000 plus a brokerage fee of $400. The shares represent a 10% ownership in Company B.

Sept. 2 Purchased 250,000 shares of Company C common stock for $480,000 plus a brokerage fee of $2,400. The shares represent a 51% ownership in Company C.

Dec. 11 Purchased 10,000 shares of Company D common stock for $89,000 plus a brokerage fee of $445. The shares represent a 5% ownership in Company D.

20 Sold 10,000 shares of Company X common stock for $160,000 less a brokerage fee of $800.

The fair (market) values of Leling's investments at December 31, 19X2, follow: A, $18,000; B, $92,000; C, $506,500; D, $90,800; Y, $38,200; Z, $31,000.

Required

1. Determine what amount should be reported on Leling's December 31, 19X2, balance sheet for its investments in equity securities available for sale.
2. Prepare a December 31, 19X2, adjusting entry, if necessary, to record the fair value adjustment of the long-term investments in securities available for sale.
3. What amount of gain or loss on those transactions relating to securities available for sale should be reported on Leling's December 31, 19X2, income statement?

Problem 10–5
Foreign currency transactions
(LO 4)

Lupold Company is a U.S. company that has customers in several foreign countries. The company had the following transactions in 19X1 and 19X2:

19X1

May 22 Sold merchandise for 15,000 marks to Weishaar Imports of Germany, payment in full to be received in 90 days. On this day, the foreign exchange rate for marks was $0.5654.

Sept. 9 Sold merchandise to Campos Company of Mexico for $24,780 cash. The exchange rate for pesos was $0.322154.

Aug. 25 Received Weishaar Imports' payment for its purchase of May 22, and exchanged the marks for dollars. The current foreign exchange rate for marks was $0.5995.

Nov. 29 Sold merchandise on credit to ONI Company, located in Japan. The price of 1.1 million yen was to be paid 60 days from the date of sale. The exchange rate for yen was $0.009195 on November 29.

Dec. 23 Sold merchandise for 158,000 francs to Martinique Company of France, payment in full to be received in 30 days. The exchange rate for francs was $0.16722.

Dec. 31 Prepared adjusting entries to recognize exchange gains or losses on the annual financial statements. Rates for exchanging foreign currencies on this day included the following:

Marks (Germany)	$0.5690
Pesos (Mexico)	0.331256
Yen (Japan)	0.010110
Francs (France)	0.16530

19X2

Jan. 24 Received full payment from Martinique for the sale of December 23 and immediately exchanged the francs for dollars. The exchange rate for francs was $0.16342.

30 Received ONI's full payment for the sale of November 29 and immediately exchanged the yen for dollars. The exchange rate for yen was $0.010290.

Required

1. Prepare general journal entries to account for these transactions of Lupold.
2. Calculate the foreign exchange gain or loss to be reported on Lupold's 19X1 income statement.

Problem 10–6
Analytical essay
(LO 3)

On January 3, Tragor Company purchased 20,000 shares of Entech Company common stock for $10 per share, or $200,000. Tragor's purchase represents a 30% ownership in Entech. Tragor did not own any investments prior to the Entech stock purchase. Entech did not declare any dividends on its common stock during the year, and on December 31 reported a net loss of $80,000. The market value of the Entech stock on December 31 was $11.00 per share. The accountant for Tragor made the following adjusting entry to update the account balances for the investment in Entech:

Dec.	31	Long-Term Investments, Fair Value Adjustment .	20,000.00	
		Unrealized Holding Gain (Loss)		20,000.00
		(20,000 × 11) − $200,000 = $20,000		

Describe the method that Tragor's accountant used to account for the investment in Entech. Explain why this method is incorrect. Without providing specific amounts, determine what impact the accountant's error had on the financial statements.

Provocative Problems

Provocative Problem 10–1
Accounting related communications
(LO 2, 3)

You are the accountant for PCI Company. The owner of PCI, Lester Murphy, has finished reviewing the financial statements you prepared for 19X3 and questions the $40,000 loss reported on PCI's sale of its investment in the stock of Runyan Company.

PCI acquired 100,000 shares of Runyan's outstanding common stock on December 31, 19X1, at a cost of $500,000. This stock purchase represented a 30% interest in Runyan. The 19X2 income statement showed that the investments made by PCI proved to be very profitable and that the earnings from all investments were $340,000. On January 5, 19X3, PCI sold the Runyan stock for $580,000. Runyan did not pay any dividends during 19X2 and reported $400,000 net income for the year.

Murphy believes that because the purchase price of the Runyan stock was $500,000 and it was sold for $580,000, the 19X3 income statement should report an $80,000 gain on the sale.

Draft a memo to Murphy explaining why the $40,000 loss on the sale of the Runyan stock is correctly reported.

Provocative Problem 10–2
Riteway and Best Companies
(A review problem)

UNI Company is considering buying either Riteway Company or Best Company, similar businesses that acquired their equipment and began operating four years ago. In evaluating the two companies, UNI has determined that they have not used the same accounting procedures, so their financial statements are not comparable. Over the past four years, Riteway has reported an average annual net income of $197,840 and Best has reported $254,190. The current balance sheets of the two companies show the following:

	Riteway	Best
Cash	$ 131,500	$ 144,400
Accounts receivable	972,400	1,077,000
Allowance for doubtful accounts	(57,000)	-0-
Merchandise inventory	1,268,200	1,666,000
Store equipment	496,800	420,800
Accumulated depreciation, store equipment	(293,310)	(168,320)
Total assets	$2,518,590	$3,139,880
Total liabilities	$1,176,800	$1,408,600

Riteway has used the allowance method of accounting for bad debts and Best has used the direct write-off method. An examination of each company's accounts revealed that only $30,000 of Riteway's accounts are probably uncollectible and that Best's estimated uncollectible accounts total $54,000.

Because Best uses FIFO, its ending inventory amounts approximate replacement cost. However, Riteway uses LIFO. As a result, Riteway's current inventory is reported $176,000 below replacement cost.

In taking depreciation for the past four years, both companies have assumed 10-year lives and no salvage value for their equipment. However, Riteway has used double-declining balance depreciation, while Best has used straight-line. UNI believes that straight-line depreciation results in reporting equipment on the balance sheet at its approximate fair market value.

UNI is willing to pay fair market value for the net assets (including goodwill) of either business. UNI estimates goodwill to be four times the average annual earnings in excess of 14% of the fair market value of the net tangible assets (assets, other than goodwill, minus liabilities).

Required

Prepare the following schedules: (*a*) the net tangible assets of each company at fair market values assessed by UNI, (*b*) the revised net incomes of the companies based on adjusted amounts of bad debts expense, FIFO inventories, and straight-line depreciation, (*c*) the calculation of each company's goodwill, and (*d*) the maximum purchase price UNI would pay for each business, if it assumed the liabilities of the purchased business. (Note: Round all calculations to the nearest dollar.)

Provocative Problem 10–3
Apple Computer, Inc.
(LO 1, 4, 5)

Apple Computer, Inc.

Examine Apple Computer, Inc.'s financial statements and supplemental information in Appendix F and answer the following questions:

1. Are Apple's financial statements consolidated? How can you tell?
2. Does Apple have more than one subsidiary? How can you tell?
3. Does Apple have any foreign operations? How can you tell?
4. Is there a foreign exchange gain or loss on the income statement? Provide an explanation for what you find or do not find.
5. What intangible assets does Apple own? Assuming it will not take advantage of any renewal options, what is the maximum time period that Apple can use to amortize these intangibles?
6. Calculate Apple's return on total assets for 1992.

Answers to Objective Review Questions

LO 1 (*c*)	LO 3 (*d*)	LO 5 (*b*)
LO 2 (*d*)	LO 4 (*e*)	LO 6 (*d*)

CHAPTER

11

Current and Long-Term Liabilities

As you already know, liabilities are one of the three elements of the balance sheet. Previous chapters have described liabilities for accounts payable, notes payable, wages payable, and unearned revenues. In this chapter, you will learn about liabilities arising from warranties, income taxes, borrowing, asset purchases, leases, and payrolls. We also describe contingent liabilities and the important concepts of present value. As you study this chapter, you will learn how accountants define, classify, and measure liabilities for the purpose of reporting useful information about them.

Learning Objectives

After studying Chapter 11, you should be able to:

1. Define liabilities and explain the difference between current and long-term liabilities.
2. Explain the uncertainties that may exist about liabilities.
3. Describe how accountants record and report transactions and liabilities for warranties, income taxes, and short-term notes payable.
4. Explain the nature of contingencies.
5. Describe present value concepts and calculate the present value of an amount to be paid at a future date and of a series of equal amounts paid at future dates.
6. Describe how accountants allocate interest expense among the years in the life of long-term interest-bearing and noninterest-bearing notes payable.
7. Describe payroll expenses and liabilities and prepare journal entries to account for them.
8. Calculate the times fixed interest charges earned ratio and describe what it reveals about a company's situation.
9. Define or explain the words and phrases listed in the chapter glossary.

Defining and Classifiying Liabilities

In its conceptual framework, the FASB defined liabilities as "probable *future* sacrifices of economic benefits arising from *present* obligations of a particular entity to transfer assets or provide services to other entities in the future as a result of *past* transactions or events."[1] As shown in the diagram, this definition involves three dimensions in time:

---

[1] Financial Accounting Standards Board, *Statement of Financial Accounting Concepts No. 6,* "Elements of Financial Statements" (Norwalk, CT, 1985), par. 35. (Emphasis added.)

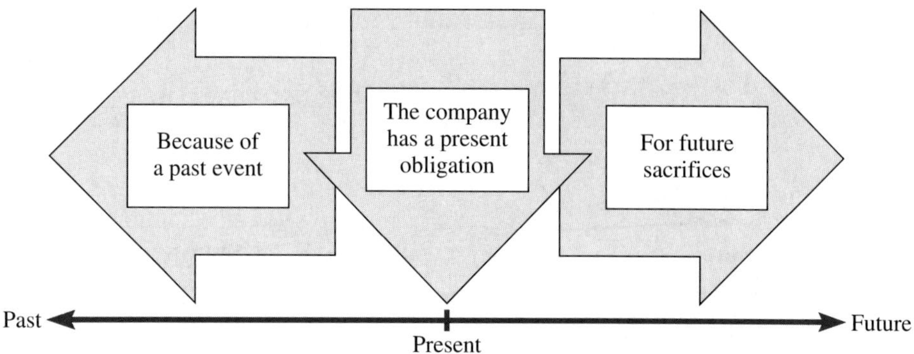

- The company is obligated in the present
- To pay out assets or deliver services in the future
- Because of an event in the past

LO 1 Define liabilities and explain the difference between current and long-term liabilities.

This definition also tells us that all expected future payments are not liabilities. For example, suppose that a company expects to pay wages to its employees in the coming months. These future payments are not liabilities because the company is not presently obligated to pay them. The company is not presently obligated because there has been no past transaction. The liabilities will be created in the future only when the employees actually work for the company.

Because liabilities are created by past transactions, they are normally enforceable as legal claims. However, a liability may be reported on a company's balance sheet in some circumstances even though the obligation is not legally enforceable at that time. For example, a company's obligation to repair defective products is reported as a liability even though the customers' claims are not enforceable until the products prove to be defective.

Current and Long-Term Liabilities

Information about liabilities is presented in a company's balance sheet. The information is more useful when the balance sheet classifies the liabilities as current and long-term.

Current liabilities are expected to be paid by using existing current assets or creating other current liabilities.[2] Current liabilities are due within one year or the company's operating cycle, whichever is longer.[3] Current liabilities include accounts payable, short-term notes payable, wages payable, warranty liabilities, lease liabilities, payroll and other taxes payable, and unearned revenues.

Obligations that are not expected to be paid within one year (or a longer operating cycle) are reported on the balance sheet as *long-term liabilities.* Long-term liabilities include long-term notes payable, warranty liabilities, lease liabilities, and bonds payable. As you can tell from the two lists, some kinds of liabilities may be both current and long term. A specific debt is assigned to a category on the basis of how soon it will be paid. In fact, a single liability can be divided between the two categories if the company expects to make payments in both the near and more distant future.

---

[2] FASB, *Accounting Standards—Current Text* (Norwalk, CT, 1994), sec. B05.402. First published as *Accounting Research Bulletin No. 43,* Ch. 3A, par. 7.

[3] The operating cycle is described in Chapter 3. It is the typical length of time between acquiring goods or providing services and receiving the cash from the customers who buy the goods or services.

A few liabilities do not have a fixed due date because they are payable on the creditor's demand. They are reported as current liabilities because they may have to be paid within the year or a longer operating cycle.

Liabilities and Uncertainty

LO 2 Explain the uncertainties that may exist about liabilities.

Because liabilities involve future sacrifices, and because information about the future is imperfect, liabilities often involve one kind of uncertainty or another. The uncertainty may exist for the amount to be paid, the date on which payments will occur, and the person or other entity who will be paid. In some cases, there may be uncertainty about the existence of the obligation.

The FASB's definition of liability includes the phrase "*probable* future sacrifices" to guide accountants when they face these uncertainties. In effect, companies may be required to report liabilities even if they don't know who or how much will be paid or when the payment will occur.

In many situations, everything is known when the liability is created. For example, assume that a company purchases goods on credit from AAA Office Supply Company and creates a $100 account payable on August 15, 19X1. There is no uncertainty on any of the points. The company knows that it is required to make the payment, and it knows who and how much will be paid and when. Other liabilities are not as certain.

When the Identity of the Creditor Is Uncertain. Some liabilities have uncertainty about who will be paid. For example, a corporation's board of directors creates a liability with a known amount when it declares a dividend payable to the stockholders. Because the dividend will be paid to the investors who actually own stock on a specified future date, the recipients are not known with certainty until that date. Despite this uncertainty, the corporation has a liability that is reported on the balance sheet.

When the Due Date Is Uncertain. In other situations, a company may have an obligation of a known amount to a known creditor, but not know exactly when the debt will be settled. For example, a copy services company may accept fees in advance from a customer who expects to need copies later. Thus, the copy service company has a liability that will be settled by providing services at an unknown future date. Even though this uncertainty exists, the company's balance sheet is complete only if it includes this liability to its customer. (These obligations are usually reported as current liabilities because they are settled in the short term.)

When the Amount Is Uncertain. In addition, a company may know that an obligation exists but may not know exactly how much will be required to settle it. For example, a company uses electrical power every day but is billed only after the meter has been read. The cost has been incurred and the liability has been created, even though the bill has not been received. As a result, a liability to the power company is reported with an estimated amount if the balance sheet is prepared before the bill arrives. These obligations that are believed to exist but have uncertain amounts are called **estimated liabilities.** A common example of an estimated liability involves warranties offered by a seller. Other estimated liabilities, such as income tax obligations, are recorded and reported in interim financial statements.

Warranty Liabilities

An estimated liability is created when a company sells products covered by a warranty. In effect, a **warranty** obligates the seller or manufacturer to pay for replacing or repairing the product when it breaks or otherwise fails to perform within a specified period. For example, a used car might be sold with a warranty that covers parts and labor.

LO 3 Describe how accountants record and report transactions and liabilities for warranties, income taxes, and short-term notes payable.

To provide useful information about the seller's activities, accountants comply with the *full disclosure* and the *matching principles* by reporting all expenses that help produce a sale in the same period as the revenue. The company also reports an obligation under the warranty as a liability, even though it is uncertain about the existence, amount, payee, and date of its future sacrifices. Furthermore, the obligation is legally unenforceable until the product breaks and is returned for repairs. Nonetheless, future payments are probable, and the amount of the liability can be estimated using the company's past experience with warranties.

For example, suppose that a dealer sells a used car for $8,000 on December 1, 19X1, with a one-year or 12,000-mile warranty that covers repair parts and labor charges. Experience shows that the warranty expense averages about 4% of a car's selling price. In this case, the expense is expected to be $320 ($8,000 × 4%). The dealer's accounting system would record the expense and liability with this entry:

19X1				
Dec.	1	Warranty Expense	320.00	
		Estimated Warranty Liability		320.00
		To record the warranty expense and liability at 4% of the selling price.		

This entry causes the expense to be reported on the income statement for 19X1. It also causes the warranty liability to appear on the balance sheet for December 31, 19X1.

Now, suppose that the customer returns the car for warranty repairs on January 9, 19X2. The dealer performs the work by replacing parts that cost $90 and using labor at a cash cost of $110. The accounting system would record the partial settlement of the estimated warranty liability with this entry:

19X2				
Jan.	9	Estimated Warranty Liability	200.00	
		Auto Parts Inventory		90.00
		Cash		110.00
		To record the cost of warranty repairs.		

Notice that this entry does not record any additional expense in 19X2 for the repairs. Instead, the entry shows that the balance of the estimated warranty liability has been reduced. The warranty expense was already included in the net income for 19X1, the year the car was sold under the warranty. The entry also reflects the fact that the company expects to provide additional repairs in the future to satisfy the obligation to the buyer.

What happens if the total warranty costs actually turn out to be different from the predicted $320? In fact, some difference is highly likely for any particular car. Over the longer term, management should monitor the actual warranty costs to see whether the 4% rate provides useful information. If actual experience reveals a large difference, the rate should be modified for future sales.

Other estimated liabilities are created for contracts to provide future services, income taxes, property taxes, and employee benefits such as pensions and health care.

Estimated Liabilities in Interim Financial Statements

Most companies prepare interim financial statements throughout the year, primarily for internal users but occasionally for external users. This practice may require the accountant to include additional estimated liabilities on the balance sheet.

Income Tax Liabilities for Corporations

This section describes how corporations account for income taxes in their financial statements. A proprietorship's financial statements do not include income taxes because they are assessed directly against the owner.

Income tax expense for a corporation creates a liability that exists until payments are made to the government. Because the taxes are created by the process of earning income, a liability is created as soon as the income is earned. However, the taxes must be paid quarterly under federal regulations. Thus, the estimated liability is created every day but is paid only once every three months.

For example, suppose that Foster Corporation prepares monthly financial statements. Based on the income earned in the month, an entry such as the following is recorded at the end of each month:

Jan.	31	Income Taxes Expense	12,100.00	
		Estimated Income Taxes Payable		12,100.00
		Accrued income tax expense and liability based on the estimated income for the month of January.		

The liability will increase until the first quarterly payment is made. An entry such as this one records the payment:

Apr.	10	Estimated Income Taxes Payable	50,000.00	
		Cash		50,000.00
		Paid the quarterly income taxes based on the estimated income for the first quarter of the year.		

The process of accruing and then paying the taxes continues throughout the year.

However, by the time that the annual financial statements are prepared at the end of the year, the company's accountant knows the amount of income that has been earned and the actual amount of income taxes that must be paid. This information allows the accountant to change the *estimated* liability into an *actual* liability. Suppose, for example, that Foster Corporation's accounts include a $22,000 credit balance in the Estimated Income Taxes Liability account at December 31, 19X1. Information about the company's income for the year shows that the actual liability should be $33,500. This entry records the additional expense and changes the estimated liability to a known liability:

Dec.	31	Income Tax Expense	11,500.00	
		Estimated Income Taxes Payable	22,000.00	
		Income Taxes Payable		33,500.00
		To record additional tax expense and change the estimated liability to an actual liability.		

The actual liability will be settled when the company makes its final quarterly payment early in 19X2.

Deferred Income Tax Liabilities

Another special type of income tax liability is often created for a corporation when the amount of income reported on its annual income statement is not the same as the amount of income reported on its annual income tax return. The difference arises because income tax laws define income differently from GAAP. In turn, the differences between the laws and GAAP arise because Congress uses the tax law to stimulate the economy and otherwise influence behavior.

The differences between the law and GAAP create what accountants call *temporary differences* that cause revenues and expenses to be reported in different years for the tax return and the income statement. For example, the tax law usually causes a company to report larger amounts of depreciation expense on its tax returns than it shows on its income statements in the early years of an asset's life. Because it is believed that information about the income tax expense on the income statements is more useful if it is based on the amount of GAAP income for the year, the reported tax expense is greater than the amount of tax actually paid. In effect, these temporary differences cause some of the company's income tax payments to be postponed into later years.

When tax payments are postponed, the corporation reports a **deferred income tax liability** equal to the estimated additional taxes expected to be paid in the future. For example, the balance sheet for Apple Computer, Inc., in Appendix F shows that the company had a deferred income tax liability of $610,803,000 at the end of its 1992 fiscal year. The financial statements in Appendix G for Federal Express and Ben & Jerry's Homemade also reported deferred tax liabilities. In some circumstances, temporary differences may cause a company to pay income taxes before they are reported on the income statement as expense. If so, the company reports a *deferred income tax asset* on its balance sheet that is similar to a prepaid expense. The procedures used to account for deferred tax assets and liabilities are described in intermediate accounting courses and textbooks.

Accounting for Contingencies

LO 4 Explain the nature of contingencies.

We have showed you that accountants often have to deal with uncertainty when they describe liabilities in the financial statements. Because of the need to provide useful information to investors and creditors who would otherwise be unaware of the risks created by those uncertainties, a great deal of effort goes into accounting for **contingencies.** In effect, a contingency (1) arises from a past event, (2) has an uncertain effect, and (3) will be cleared up when another later event occurs and confirms that the effect did or did not take place. The challenge to accountants is to provide financial statements that adequately describe these uncertainties and their effects. The practices used to account for contingencies involve several considerations.[4]

First, the past event may have created a gain or a loss. Because of the *conservatism principle,* a company can describe a contingent gain only in the footnotes to its statements. In other words, the gain cannot be reported until the future confirming event actually occurs. Conservatism also causes accountants to report some losses that might have occurred to avoid unpleasant surprises for investors and creditors. Second, the accountant must try to assess the likelihood that the future confirming event will actually occur. Third, the accountant must estimate the amount of the loss that will be confirmed if the later event does occur.

If the future event that will confirm the loss is to be probable and if the amount of the loss can be reasonably estimated, the company is required to

[4] FASB, *Accounting Standards—Current Text* (Norwalk, CT, 1994), sec. C59.105. First published as *FASB Statement No. 5,* par. 8.

report the loss and credit an estimated liability.[5] In effect, these principles produce the same results as accounting for known liabilities. For example, a warranty liability is a contingency for which payments are probable and can be estimated. Unlike liabilities with known amounts, these estimated liabilities must be carefully monitored by the accountant to ensure that the estimates result in useful information.

On the other hand, if the likelihood that the loss will be confirmed is so low as to be remote, the company is not required to report the loss in either the financial statements or the footnotes.

Other situations do require a footnote description. First, a loss that will probably be confirmed but that has a highly uncertain amount must be described in a footnote to avoid surprising users later. Second, the footnotes must describe any loss that has only a reasonably possible chance of being confirmed. In these circumstances, the company must report what accountants often describe as a **contingent liability.** Because of uncertainty about the liability's existence, amount, or both, the contingent liability is not recognized on the balance sheet. However, enough information is provided in the footnotes to allow the statement users to understand the possible effects of the contingency.

The following paragraphs describe potential legal claims and debt guarantees, two contingent liabilities usually described in footnotes.

Potential Legal Claims

Companies are subject to lawsuits for damages from a variety of accidents and other events. To provide useful information, the accountant must determine whether the company should recognize a liability on its balance sheet and a loss on its income statement for damages claimed by a plaintiff. If the liability is not recognized, the accountant also decides whether useful information would be provided by a footnote. The problem is complicated by the fact that reporting the liability or describing the potential loss might be interpreted by the court as an acknowledgment of responsibility for the damages. According to the FASB, the potential claim is reported as a liability only if a payment is probable and the amount can be reasonably estimated. Otherwise, the nature of the claim is described in a footnote. The defendant does not have to provide a footnote description if there is only a remote chance that the lawsuit will be lost.

Debt Guarantees

A company may cosign a note payable for a debt owed by a supplier, customer, or a related company. By cosigning, the company becomes a *guarantor* that is contingently liable for the debt. The guarantor does not report a liability on its own balance sheet unless it is probable that the original debtor will default. However, the guarantor must provide a footnote describing the guarantee.

Chapter 7 described how a company can become a guarantor and be contingently liable when it discounts a note receivable *with recourse.* The contingent liability will become an actual liability if the original maker of the note fails to pay it at maturity.

Other Uncertainties

All companies and other organizations face major uncertainties from future economic events, including natural disasters and the development of new competing products. If these events do occur, they may destroy the company's

[5] In some circumstances, a contingency may cause the accountant to reduce the recorded value of an asset instead of recording a liability. For example, you learned in Chapter 7 that bad debt losses are recorded with a credit to a contra-asset account to reduce the net amount reported on the balance sheet for receivables.

AS A MATTER OF

Opinion

Diana Scott is a graduate of Wittenberg University. She worked for Price Waterhouse in its national office in New York before joining the FASB staff as a project manager in 1985. After leaving that position in 1991, she joined the management consulting firm of Towers Perrin in Chicago, where she is a consultant on post-retirement benefit accounting and plan design.

Diana Scott

Over the past several years, accountants have begun to pay much more attention to the potential future payments businesses may be obligated to make as a result of current operations. A good example involves the promises of employers to pay health care benefits for their retired employees. Prior to the FASB's standard on this topic (*SFAS 106*), companies generally did not report this obligation except by reporting an expense for actual payments they had already made. The standard requires them to provide information about their obligations and to recognize the expenses for probable future payments.

Are there other obligations that we presently ignore but someday may have to recognize as liabilities? I would not be surprised. One that comes to mind is potential claims from injuries to product users. Some juries have given large awards many years after a product was sold. Another possible liability is the cost of cleaning up toxic wastes discarded before anyone was aware of the danger.

Nobody can say whether these particular examples will eventually result in new liabilities or disclosures. But, I have no doubt that accounting will continue to evolve in response to an increasing emphasis on the obligations of doing business responsibly.

assets or drive it out of business. However, these uncertainties are not liabilities because they are future events. Financial statements are not useful if they include the possible effects of events that have not yet occurred.

In contrast, a company may have to report a liability for a lawsuit because the plaintiff's claim is based on an event that has already occurred. A debt guarantee may create a liability because the note was cosigned. The uncertainty in these two cases surrounds the effect of the past event, not whether the event actually occurred.

Be sure to read the comment by Diana Scott in "As a Matter of Opinion." She discusses additional liabilities that companies may need to describe in the future if accounting principles are changed.

Accounting for Known Liabilities

Most liabilities arise in situations with little uncertainty. The procedures used to account for these debts are described in the rest of the chapter. The topics include:

- Short-term notes payable.
- Long-term notes payable.
- Lease liabilities.
- Payroll liabilities.

In addition, the chapter introduces you to the useful present value calculations that accountants use when accounting for long-term liabilities and interest expense.

Short-Term Notes Payable

A short-term note payable may be created when a company purchases merchandise on credit and then extends the credit period by signing a note that replaces the account. Short-term notes payable also arise when money is borrowed from a bank.

LO 3 Describe how accountants record and report transactions and liabilities for warranties, income taxes, and short-term notes payable.

Note Given to Extend a Credit Period

In some cases, a company may create a note payable to replace an account payable. For example, a creditor may ask that an interest-bearing note be substituted for an account that does not bear interest. In other situations, the borrower's weak financial condition may encourage the creditor to obtain a note and close the account to ensure that additional credit sales are not made to this customer.

For example, assume that Broke Company wishes to extend its past-due $600 account payable to Smart Company. After some negotiations, Smart agrees to accept $100 cash and a 60-day, 12%, $500 note payable to replace the account. The accountant for Broke would record the substitution with this entry:

Aug.	23	Accounts Payable—Smart Company	600.00	
		Cash		100.00
		Notes Payable		500.00
		Paid $100 cash and gave a 60-day, 12% note to extend the due date on the account.		

Notice that signing the note does not pay off the entire debt. Instead, the debt's form is merely changed from an account to a note payable. Smart Company may prefer to have the note because it earns interest and because it provides reliable documentation of the debt's existence, term, and amount.

When the note becomes due, Broke will pay the note and interest by giving Smart a check for $510 and then record the payment with this entry:

Oct.	22	Notes Payable	500.00	
		Interest Expense	10.00	
		Cash		510.00
		Paid note with interest ($500 × 12% × 60/360).		

This entry shows that the payment does eliminate the liability. It also records interest expense that will be deducted from revenues on the income statement. (The amount of the interest expense is found by multiplying the principal of the note by the original rate for the fraction of the year the note was outstanding.)

Borrowing from a Bank

When making a loan, a bank typically requires the borrower to sign a promissory note. When the note matures, the borrower pays back a larger amount. The difference between the two amounts is *interest.* In many situations, the note states that the signer of the note promises to pay the *principal* (the amount borrowed) plus the interest. If so, the *face value* of the note equals the principal.

In other situations, the bank may have the borrower sign a note with a face value that includes both the principal and the interest. In these cases, the signer of the note borrows less than the note's face value. The difference between the borrowed amount and the note's face value is interest. Because the borrowed amount is less than the face value, the difference is sometimes called the **discount on note payable.** To illustrate these two kinds of loans, assume that Robin Goode borrows $2,000 from a bank on behalf of the Goode Company. The loan is made on September 30 and will be repaid in 60 days. It has a 12% annual interest rate.

Face Value Equals the Amount Borrowed. Suppose that the bank requires Goode to sign a loan with a face value equal to the borrowed $2,000. If so, the note will include the following phrase: "I promise to pay $2,000 plus interest at 12% sixty days after September 30." The Goode Company would record the increase in cash and the new liability with this entry:

Sept.	30	Cash	2,000.00	
		Notes Payable		2,000.00
		Borrowed cash with a 60-day, 12% note.		

When the note and interest are paid 60 days later, Goode records the event with this entry:

Nov.	29	Notes Payable	2,000.00	
		Interest Expense	40.00	
		Cash		2,040.00
		Paid note with interest ($2,000 × 12% × 60/360).		

This entry eliminates the $2,000 liability account balance so that it will not be reported on the balance sheet. It also records the $40 interest expense that will be reported on the income statement. Notice that the interest was paid in addition to the note's face value.

Face Value Equals the Amount Borrowed and the Interest. If Goode's bank wishes to do so, it may draw up a note that includes the 12% interest in its face value. If so, the note contains the following promise: "I promise to pay $2,040 sixty days after September 30." Notice that the note does not refer to the rate that was used to compute the $40 of interest included in the $2,040 face value. In all other respects, the note is exactly the same. However, the lack of a stated rate of interest sometimes causes an agreement like this one to be called a **noninterest-bearing note.** In fact, the title is imprecise because the note does bear interest that is included in the face value.

Although the economic substance of the transaction is the same, bookkeeping practices may differ because the note's face value exceeds the amount borrowed. If Goode prefers, the transaction can be recorded with this entry:

Sept.	30	Cash	2,000.00	
		Discount on Notes Payable	40.00	
		Notes Payable		2,040.00
		Borrowed cash with a 60-day, 12% note (discount = $2,000 × 12% × 60/360).		

As shown by its debit balance, the Discount on Notes Payable account is contra to the Notes Payable account. For example, if a balance sheet is prepared on September 30, the $40 balance of the discount is subtracted from the $2,040 balance in the Notes Payable account to reflect the $2,000 net amount borrowed.

When the note matures 60 days later on November 29, the entry to record Goode's $2,040 payment to the bank is slightly more complicated:

Nov.	29	Notes Payable	2,040.00	
		Interest Expense	40.00	
		Cash		2,040.00
		Discount on Notes Payable		40.00
		Paid note with interest.		

The first debit reflects the fact that the liability has been settled. The second debit records the interest expense that has been incurred during the 60 days that the note was in effect. The first credit records the $2,040 cash disbursement to the bank. The second credit eliminates the balance in the discount contra account that was created when the loan was recorded.

Adjustments at the End of the Reporting Period

If the end of a fiscal year (or an interim reporting period) falls between the signing of a note payable and its maturity date, the need for complete information leads the accountant to record the accrued but unpaid interest on the note. For example, suppose that Robin Goode borrowed $2,000 on December 16, 19X1, instead of September 30. The 60-day note will mature on February 14, 19X2. Because the company's fiscal year ends on December 31, the accountant records interest expense for the 15 days in December. The actual entries depend on the form of the note and how the borrowing transaction was initially recorded.

Face Value Equals the Amount Borrowed. If the note's face value equals the amount borrowed, the interest accrual is recorded by recognizing the expense for the elapsed portion of the note's life. The borrower also records the previously unrecorded additional liability for the unpaid interest. To illustrate, assume that the $2,000 note signed by Goode on December 16 bears 12% interest. Because 15 out of the 60 days covered by the note have elapsed by December 31, one-fourth (15 days/60 days) of the $40 total interest is an expense of 19X1. The borrower records this expense with the following adjusting entry at the end of 19X1:

19X1				
Dec.	31	Interest Expense	10.00	
		Interest Payable		10.00
		To record accrued interest on note payable ($2,000 × 12% × 15/360).		

This entry accomplishes the dual purpose of recognizing the interest expense and the increase in the borrower's debts.

When the note matures on February 14, Goode records this entry:

19X2				
Feb.	14	Interest Expense	30.00	
		Interest Payable	10.00	
		Notes Payable	2,000.00	
		Cash		2,040.00
		Paid note with interest ($2,000 × 12% × 45/360).		

The entry recognizes the 45 days of interest expense for 19X2 and removes the balances of the two liability accounts.

Face Value Equals the Amount Borrowed and the Interest. If the face value of the note signed by the borrower includes the interest, there is no difference in the underlying economic substance. That is, the borrower has incurred interest expense with the passing of time and has an additional liability for the unpaid interest.

For example, assume that Goode signed a $2,040 noninterest-bearing note on December 15. If the accountant recorded the original borrowing transaction with the contra account for the note's discount, this adjusting entry is needed to record the accrual of 15 days of interest at the end of 19X1:

Dec.	31	Interest Expense	10.00	
		Discount on Notes Payable		10.00
		To record accrued interest on note payable ($2,000 × 12% × 15/360).		

This entry reduces the balance of the contra account for the discount from $40 to $30, and thereby increases the net liability to $2,010 ($2,040 − $30). Although the interest liability is not recorded separately, there is no significant difference for the users of the company's financial statements.

When the note matures, this entry (1) recognizes the $30 of interest expense incurred in the 45 days since the beginning of the year, (2) removes the account for the note payable, and (3) removes the remaining balance of the contra account:

19X2				
Feb.	14	Interest Expense	30.00	
		Notes Payable	2,040.00	
		Discount on Notes Payable		30.00
		Cash		2,040.00
		Paid note with interest ($2,000 × 12% × 45/360).		

After this entry is recorded, the liability and contra-liability accounts have zero balances, and $30 of interest expense has been recorded for the 19X2 income statement.

Long-Term Liabilities

In addition to current liabilities, companies often have liabilities that are repaid after one year (or a longer operating cycle). These *long-term liabilities* can arise when money is borrowed from a bank or when a note is issued to buy an asset. A long-term liability also may be created when a company enters into a multiyear lease agreement that is economically the same as buying the asset. Each of these liability arrangements is described in this chapter. In addition, large companies often borrow money by issuing *bonds* to a number of creditors. These securities are usually long-term liabilities that exist as long as 30 years or more. Accounting for bonds is described in Chapter 12.

Because of the size and extended lives of long-term liabilities, accounting for them is often more complicated than accounting for short-term liabilities. In particular, the accountant may need to apply present value techniques to measure a long-term liability when it is created and to assign interest expense to each of the years in the liability's life.

Present Value Concepts

LO 5 Describe present value concepts and calculate the present value of an amount to be paid at a future date and of a series of equal amounts paid at future dates.

Information based on present value concepts is useful for internal and external decisions about a company's financing and investing activities. Thus, accountants often provide present value information when they describe long-term liabilities in the financial statements and the footnotes to the statements. As a result of this widespread use, all business students need to understand how present value concepts and calculations are used in accounting.

The most fundamental present value concept is based on the economic fact that an amount of cash to be paid or received in the future has less value than the same amount of cash to be paid or received today. For example, the value of $1 to be paid out in a year is less than the value of $1 to be paid out today.[6]

According to these concepts, $1 to be paid (or received) one year from now has a **present value** that is less than $1. The difference between the present value and the future cash payment (receipt) depends on the interest rate. In effect, the present value is the amount of money that can be borrowed (invested) currently at a given interest rate such that it will grow to equal the future payment (receipt). This amount to be borrowed (invested) is the value in the present of the amount to be paid (received) in the future.

For example, if 8% annual interest must be paid, an obligation to pay $1 one year from now has a present value of $0.9259. This amount can be verified by determining that $0.9259 borrowed today at 8% annual interest will create $0.0741 of interest expense in one year (8% × $0.9259 = $0.0741). When the $0.0741 interest is added to the $0.9259 borrowed, the original liability plus the interest equals $1, as shown here:

Amount borrowed	$0.9259
Interest for one year at 8%	0.0741
Total debt after one year	$1.0000

Similarly, the present value of $1 to be paid back after two years is $0.8573 if the 8% annual interest rate is *compounded.* This amount can be verified by determining that $0.8573 borrowed at 8% will create $0.0686 of interest during the first year of the debt (8% × $0.8573 = $0.0686). When the $0.0686 interest is added to the $0.8573 original liability, the resulting combined liability after one year is

Amount borrowed	$0.8573
First year's interest at 8%	0.0686
Total debt after one year	$0.9259

Because this $0.9259 debt remains outstanding for another year at 8%, it creates $0.0741 of interest expense (8% × $0.9259 = $0.0741). As we saw, the accumulated total debt after two years equals $1.0000:

Total debt after one year	$0.9259
Second year's interest at 8%	0.0741
Total debt after two years	$1.0000

[6] Because this chapter focuses on liabilities, it relates present value concepts to future cash outflows, payables, and interest expense. The same concepts also apply to future cash inflows, receivables, and interest income.

ILLUSTRATION 11–1 *Compounding Increases the Amount of Interest Paid and the Balance Due*

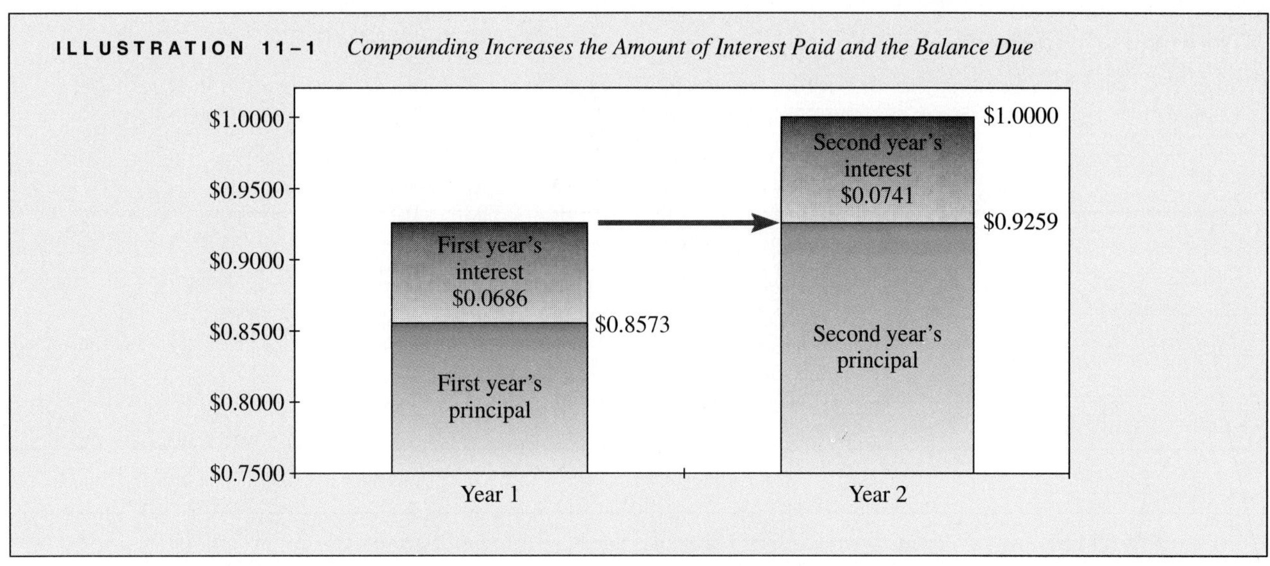

This example shows you how the $0.8573 present value of the original debt accumulates interest to become a future amount of $1.0000 after two years. These results are caused by the fact that the annual 8% interest rate is compounded, which means that the interest produces additional interest at the same 8% rate.[7]

The compounding process for this simple situation is shown graphically in Illustration 11–1. Notice that the first year's interest is added to the first year's principal to become the second year's principal. As a result, the amount of interest in the second year is greater than the amount in the first year.

Present Value Tables

The present value of $1 to be paid after a number of periods in the future can be calculated by using this formula: $1/(1 + i)^n$. The symbol i in the equation is the interest rate per period and n is the number of periods until the future payment must be made. For example, the present value of $1 to be paid after two periods at 8% is $\$1/(1.08)^2$, which equals $1/1.1664, which in turn equals $0.8573.

Although you can use this formula to find present values, other techniques are available. For example, many electronic calculators are preprogrammed to find present values. Alternatively, you can use a **present value table** that shows present values computed with the formula at various interest rates for different time periods. In fact, many students find it helpful to learn how to make the calculations with the tables, and then move on to use a calculator when they become comfortable with present value concepts.

Table 11–1 shows present values of a future payment of $1 for up to 10 periods at five different interest rates. For simplicity, the present values have been rounded to four decimal places.[8] (This table is taken from a larger and more complete table in Appendix E at the end of the book.)

To see how the table can help you, notice that the first value in the 8% column in Table 11–1 is 0.9259. We used this value in the previous section as the present value of $1 at 8%. Go down one row in the same 8% column to find the present value of $1 discounted at 8% for two years. You should find the value of 0.8573 that we just used in the second example. This value means that

---

[7] Benjamin Franklin is said to have described compounding with this expression: "The money money makes makes more money."

[8] Four decimal places are sufficient for the applications described in this book. Other situations may require more precision.

TABLE 11–1 *Present Value of $1*

Periods	Rate 2%	4%	6%	8%	10%
1	0.9804	0.9615	0.9434	0.9259	0.9091
2	0.9612	0.9246	0.8900	0.8573	0.8264
3	0.9423	0.8890	0.8396	0.7938	0.7513
4	0.9238	0.8548	0.7921	0.7350	0.6830
5	0.9057	0.8219	0.7473	0.6806	0.6209
6	0.8880	0.7903	0.7050	0.6302	0.5645
7	0.8706	0.7599	0.6651	0.5835	0.5132
8	0.8535	0.7307	0.6274	0.5403	0.4665
9	0.8368	0.7026	0.5919	0.5002	0.4241
10	0.8203	0.6756	0.5584	0.4632	0.3855

ILLUSTRATION 11–2 *Finding the Present Value of a Series of Unequal Payments*

Years from Now	Expected Payments	Present Value of $1 at 10%	Present Value of Expected Payments
1	$2,000	0.9091	$1,818
2	3,000	0.8264	2,479
3	5,000	0.7513	3,757
Total present value of the payments . .			$8,054

$0.8573 is the present value of the obligation to pay $1 after two periods discounted with an interest rate of 8%. (The word *discounted* is used because the present value is smaller than the future value.)

Using a Present Value Table

To demonstrate how an accountant can measure a liability by using a present value table like Table 11–1, assume that a company plans to borrow cash and then repay it as follows:

To be paid back after one year	$ 2,000
To be paid back after two years	3,000
To be paid back after three years	5,000
Total to be paid back	$10,000

If the company will have to pay 10% interest on this loan, how much will it be able to borrow? The answer is that it can borrow the present value of the three future payments, discounted at 10%. This value is calculated in Illustration 11–2 with values from Table 11–1.

The calculation in Illustration 11–2 finds the present value of each payment by multiplying its amount by the present value of $1 for the number of years until it is expected to be paid. By adding the present values of the three payments, we find that the company can borrow $8,054 at 10% in exchange for its promise to make the three payments at the scheduled dates. The $1,946 difference between the $8,054 borrowed and the $10,000 to be repaid is the future interest expense to be incurred over the three years. By applying the 10% rate to each year's beginning balance, each year's interest expense can be calculated as follows:

ILLUSTRATION 11–3 *The Accumulation of Interest and the Effect of Payments on the Loan Balance*

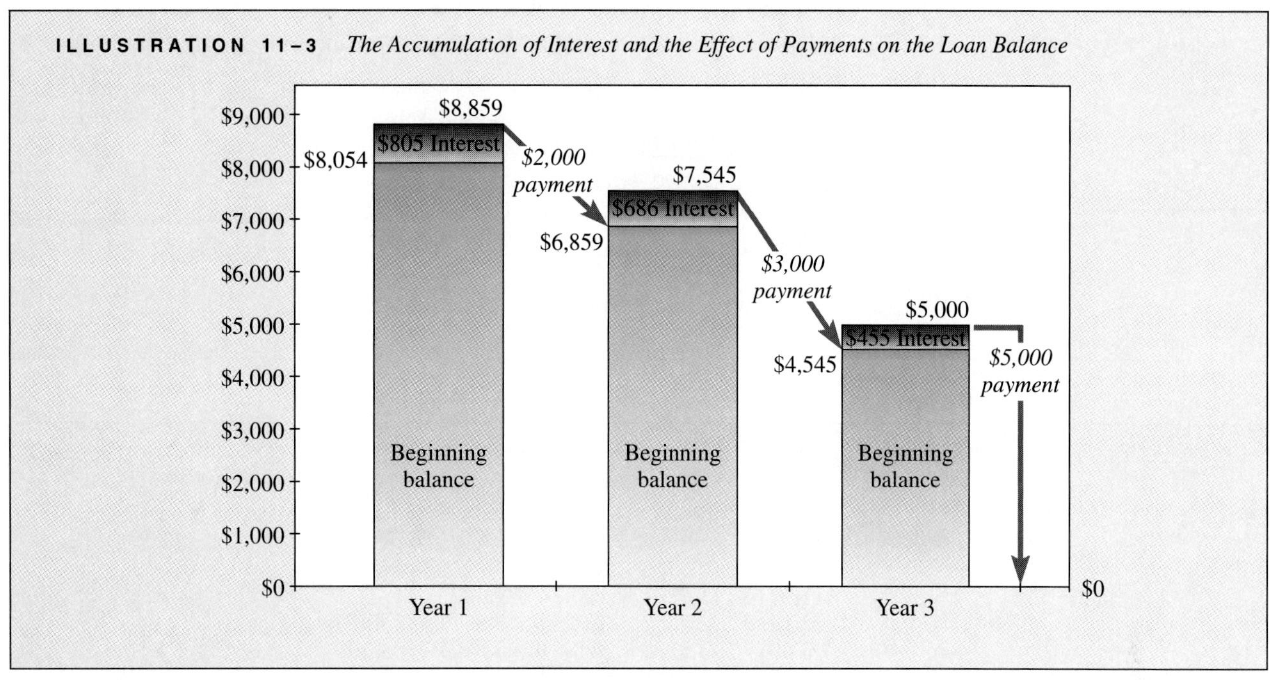

Amount borrowed	$8,054
First year's interest at 10%	805
Total	$8,859
Less first payment	(2,000)
Balance owed after one year	$6,859
Second year's interest at 10%	686
Total	$7,545
Less second payment	(3,000)
Balance owed after two years	$4,545
Third year's interest at 10%	455
Total	$5,000
Less third payment	(5,000)
Balance owed after three years	$ -0-

Over its three-year life, the loan generates $1,946 of interest, which is assigned to (or allocated among) the three years as $805, $686, and $455. The amount of interest reported in each year declines because the balance of the loan is reduced by the payments. We show the accumulation of interest and the reduction of the balance for the payments in Illustration 11–3. After the $5,000 payment is made at the end of the third year, the balance drops to $0.

Present Values of Annuities

The $8,054 present value of the loan in Illustration 11–2 is the sum of the present values of the three different payments. If the expected cash flows for a liability are not equal, their combined present value can be found only by separately calculating each of their present values. In other cases, a loan may create an **annuity,** which is a series of equal payments occurring at equal time intervals. When an annuity exists, the present value of the payments can be found with fewer calculations.

For example, suppose that a company can repay a 6% loan by making four $5,000 payments at the end of each of the next four years. The amount to be borrowed under this loan equals the present value of the four payments dis-

ILLUSTRATION 11–4 *Finding the Present Value of a Series of Equal Payments (an Annuity) by Discounting Each Payment*

Years from Now	Expected Payments	Present Value of $1 at 6%	Present Value of Expected Payments
1	$5,000	0.9434	$ 4,717
2	5,000	0.8900	4,450
3	5,000	0.8396	4,198
4	5,000	0.7921	3,961
Total		3.4651	$17,326

TABLE 11–2 *Present Value of an Annuity of $1*

	Rate				
Payments	2%	4%	6%	8%	10%
1	0.9804	0.9615	0.9434	0.9259	0.9091
2	1.9416	1.8861	1.8334	1.7833	1.7355
3	2.8839	2.7751	2.6730	2.5771	2.4869
4	3.8077	3.6299	3.4651	3.3121	3.1699
5	4.7135	4.4518	4.2124	3.9927	3.7908
6	5.6014	5.2421	4.9173	4.6229	4.3553
7	6.4720	6.0021	5.5824	5.2064	4.8684
8	7.3255	6.7327	6.2098	5.7466	5.3349
9	8.1622	7.4353	6.8017	6.2469	5.7590
10	8.9826	8.1109	7.3601	6.7101	6.1446

counted at 6%. The present value calculation is shown in Illustration 11–4. The present value of each expected payment is calculated by multiplying it by the appropriate value from Table 11–1. The illustration shows that the company can borrow $17,326 under these terms.

Because the series of $5,000 payments is an annuity, the accountant can determine the present value with one of two shortcuts: As shown in the third column of Illustration 11–4, the first shortcut adds the present values of $1 at 6% for 1 through 4 periods from Table 11–1. Then, this total of 3.4651 can be multiplied by the $5,000 annual payment to get the combined present value of $17,326. This shortcut requires only one multiplication instead of four.

The second shortcut uses an *annuity table* that shows the present values of annuities of various numbers of payments at different discount rates. The next section describes how to use an annuity table. In addition, calculators include functions that allow you to find the present value of an annuity with only a few steps.

Present Value of an Annuity with $1 Periodic Payments

Table 11–2 helps you work with annuity situations. Instead of having to take the sum of the individual present values from Table 11–1, you can go directly to the annuity table to find the present (table) value that relates to a specific number of $1 payments and a specific interest rate. Then, you multiply this table value by the size of the payment to find the combined present value of all the payments in the annuity.

For example, the annuity in Illustration 11–4 has four payments and the interest rate is 6%. By entering Table 11–2 on the row for four payments and going across until reaching the column for 6%, we find the value of 3.4651. This amount equals the present value of an annuity with four payments of $1, discounted at 6%. To find the present value of the annuity with four payments of $5,000, multiply this table value by $5,000 to find the same $17,326 present value of the annuity.

The present values in Table 11–2 can be found by adding the values in Table 11–1 for single payments with the same interest rate, starting with the value for one period and continuing through the row for the number of payments. For example, the 1.8861 annuity table value for a two payment annuity discounted at 4% is equal to the sum of the present values in Table 11–1 at 4% for the first two rows (0.9615 + 0.9246). In fact, the values shown in Table 11–2 were computed with a formula.[9] (Because the table shows only four decimal places, there are some insignificant rounding differences of ±0.0001). Table 11–2 is taken from a more complete table in Appendix E at the end of the book.

Now let's apply Table 11–2 to a different example to test your understanding. Suppose that you need to find the present value of an annuity of seven $20,000 payments discounted at 10%. Enter the table on the seventh row and go across to the column for 10%, where you should find the value of 4.8684. Multiply this number by $20,000 to find that the present value of the annuity is $97,368 (4.8684 × $20,000).

Compounding Periods Shorter than a Year

In the previous examples, all interest rates were applied to one-year periods and compounded annually. That is, the interest was added to the principal at the end of the year and the total was used to determine the interest for the following year. In many real situations, interest is compounded over shorter periods. For example, the interest rate on bonds is usually described as an annual rate but the interest is actually paid every six months. To find the present value of future payments to be made on bonds, accountants use the number of semiannual periods instead of the number of years and a discount rate equal to half of the annual rate.

To illustrate a calculation based on a six-month interest period, suppose that a borrower wants to know the present value of a series of 10 $4,000 semiannual payments to be made over five years. These payments are to be discounted with an *annual* interest rate of 8%. This rate is divided in half to become 4% per six-month compounding period. To find the present value of the series of $4,000 payments, enter Table 11–2 on the tenth row and go across to the 4% column. The table value is 8.1109, and the present value of the annuity is $32,444 (8.1109 × $4,000).

Study Appendix E at the end of the book to learn more about present value concepts. The appendix includes more complete present value tables and provides future value tables. It also includes exercises that will help you understand discounting.

Allocating Interest over the Life of a Liability

Earlier in the chapter, we stated that accountants use present value concepts to measure liabilities and to assign or allocate interest expense to each reporting period in a liability's life. Under this approach, the liability is initially measured as the present value of the future payments. Over the life of the note, the amount of interest allocated to each period equals the product of multiplying the original interest rate by the balance of the liability at the beginning of the period. The balance at any point in time equals the original balance plus any allocated interest less any payments.[10]

---

[9] The formula for these values is: $\dfrac{1 - \dfrac{1}{(1+i)^n}}{i}$

[10] The liability's balance at any date also equals the present value of all remaining future payments, discounted at the original interest rate.

LO 6 Describe how accountants allocate interest expense among the years in the life of long-term interest-bearing and noninterest-bearing notes payable.

Measuring the Balance and Interest for an Annuity. Present value concepts also can be applied to an annuity to find its balance at future dates and the amount of interest assigned to each period. To illustrate, return to the note that promises to make a series of $5,000 payments at the end of each of the next four years. We can use these concepts to determine how much interest expense to report in each of the four years and the balance at the end of each year.

Suppose that the loan is taken out on January 1, 19X1, at a 6% annual interest rate. Because the note creates an annuity, we can use Table 11–2 to find the present value, which equals the amount borrowed and is the liability's original balance. The table value of 3.4651 is found on the fourth row of Table 11–2 in the 6% column. Therefore, the original balance is $17,326 (3.4651 × $5,000).

Illustration 11–5 shows the calculations for each year's interest and ending balance. Each year's 6% interest is added to the beginning balance and each year's $5,000 payment is then subtracted to find the ending balance. This ending balance is the beginning balance for the next year. Notice that the balance of the liability is reduced to zero at the end of 19X4. (The interest for 19X4 is rounded down by one dollar to cause the ending balance to equal $0.)

Issuing a Note to Buy an Asset

When buying a high-cost asset, a company may decide to issue a long-term note payable to the seller instead of first borrowing cash from a bank and then paying the seller. If so, the purchased asset is recorded in the accounts at its fair value. For example, suppose that a company buys equipment on January 2 with a fair market value of $60,000 by issuing a note. In addition, assume that the note bears 8% interest and matures in three years. If 8% is the current market rate for this kind of note, the buyer records the purchase with this entry:

Jan.	2	Store Equipment	60,000.00	
		Notes Payable		60,000.00
		Issued a $60,000, three-year, 8% note payable for store equipment.		

In most credit purchases of major assets, the seller requires the buyer to make a cash **down payment** on the date of purchase. For this example, suppose that the buyer pays a 25% down payment to the seller. The buyer would record the purchase with this entry:

Jan.	2	Store Equipment	60,000.00	
		Cash		15,000.00
		Notes Payable		45,000.00
		Made a $15,000 down payment and issued a $45,000, three-year, 8% note payable for store equipment.		

The credit to the Notes Payable account equals the note's own fair value. The amount also equals the difference between the asset's fair value and the cash down payment.

Allocating Interest on a Note Issued to Buy an Asset

Over the life of the note, the issuer reports annual interest expense equal to the original interest rate times each year's beginning balance for the liability. Let's return to the example of the note with the initial principal balance of $45,000 and an 8% market interest rate with all interest to be paid at the end of the third year. Note the interest allocation in Illustration 11–6.

ILLUSTRATION 11-5 *Allocating Interest and Finding the Balance of an Annuity with $5,000 Payments*

	19X1	19X2	19X3	19X4
Beginning balance	$17,326	$13,366	$9,168	$4,718
Plus interest at 6%	1,040	802	550	282*
Total	$18,366	$14,168	$9,718	$5,000
Less payment	(5,000)	(5,000)	(5,000)	(5,000)
Ending balance	$13,366	$ 9,168	$4,718	$ -0-

*Adjusted for rounding.

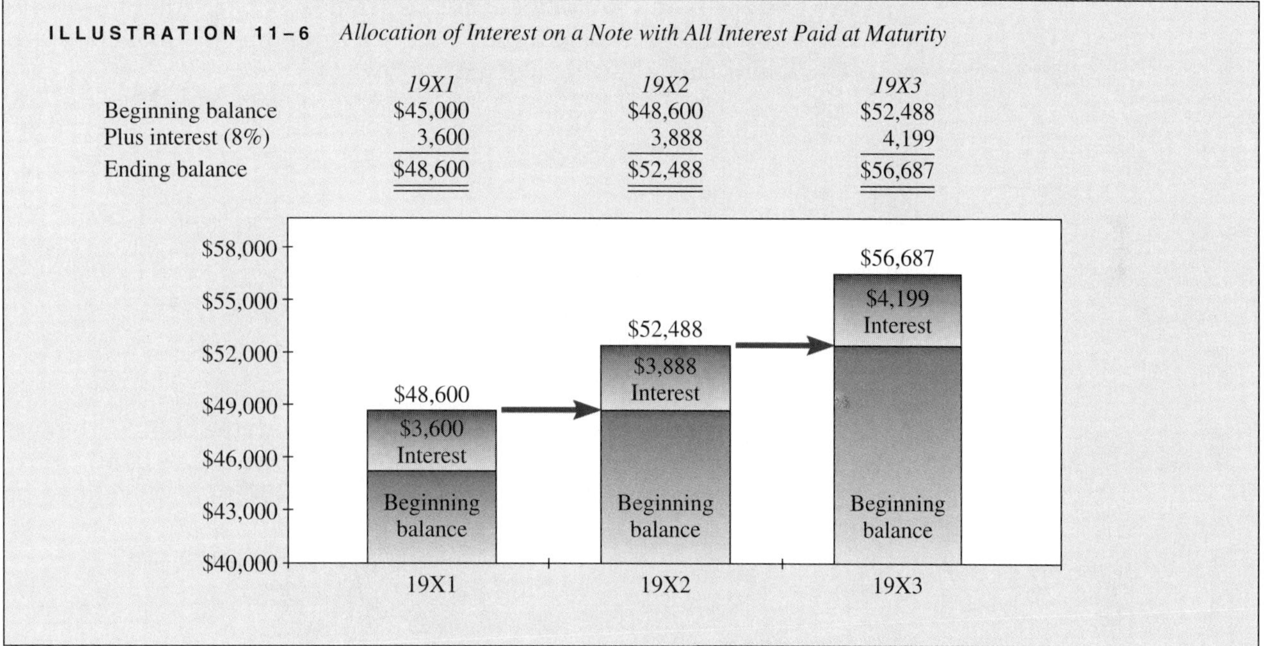

ILLUSTRATION 11-6 *Allocation of Interest on a Note with All Interest Paid at Maturity*

	19X1	*19X2*	*19X3*
Beginning balance	$45,000	$48,600	$52,488
Plus interest (8%)	3,600	3,888	4,199
Ending balance	$48,600	$52,488	$56,687

In the illustration, we show that the interest is allocated by multiplying each year's beginning balance by the original 8% interest rate. The interest is added to the beginning balance to find the ending balance, which then becomes the next year's beginning balance. Because the balance grows through compounding, the amount of interest allocated to each year increases over the life of the note. The final ending balance of $56,687 equals the original $45,000 borrowed plus the total interest of $11,687. The graph in Illustration 11-6 shows that the interest is compounded by being added to each year's balance.

Noninterest-Bearing Notes

LO 6 Describe how accountants allocate interest expense among the years in the life of long-term interest-bearing and noninterest-bearing notes payable.

Earlier in the chapter, we described notes that include all interest in their initial face values. These notes can be used to purchase assets directly from a seller. Because the interest is included in the note's face value, the face value is greater than the asset's fair value. As a result, the financial statements would not provide useful information if the asset and the note were both recorded at the note's face amount. Instead, the asset is recorded at its fair value or at the note's fair value, whichever is more clearly determinable.[11] The note's fair value can be estimated by finding the present value of its payments discounted at the market interest rate when it was issued.

[11] FASB, *Accounting Standards—Current Text* (Norwalk, CT, 1994), sec. I69.105. First published as *APB Opinion No. 21,* par. 12.

For example, suppose that the Harley Company buys machinery on January 2, 19X1, by issuing a noninterest-bearing, five-year, $10,000 note payable. Although the company's managers have a rough idea about the asset's market value, they do not consider the information to be reliable. However, they do know that the current market interest rate is 10% per year because they recently borrowed $15,000 cash at that rate. Because of their confidence in the rate's reliability, they decide to use it to estimate the note's fair value, and then use that amount to record the asset.

When the note is issued, its fair value equals the present value of the $10,000 payment due after five years discounted at 10%. Table 11–1 shows us that the present value of $1 discounted at 10% for five years is 0.6209. By multiplying the $10,000 future cash flow by 0.6209, the company's accountant estimates that the note's fair value is $6,209. Thus, it is likely that the asset's fair value is also $6,209. This information is captured for the financial statements by making the following journal entry:

19X1				
Jan.	2	Machinery	6,209.00	
		Discount on Notes Payable	3,791.00	
		Long-Term Notes Payable		10,000.00
		Exchanged a five-year noninterest-bearing note for a machine.		

The credit to Long-Term Notes Payable is combined with the debit to the contra account for the discount to provide a useful measure of the liability created by this transaction. The net amount of the liability is calculated as follows:

Long-term note payable	$10,000
Less discount	(3,791)
Net liability	$ 6,209

Allocating the Interest Created by a Noninterest-Bearing Note Payable

Earlier, we described how accountants allocate interest to each period in a liability's life by multiplying the period's beginning balance by the original interest rate. The same procedure is used with noninterest-bearing notes. In the example that we just used, the accountant's goal is to allocate the $3,791 total interst expense among the five years in the note's life. At the same time, the balance of the discount account is made smaller, and the net liability is increased. Because the discount is reduced to zero, this process is often referred to as *amortizing the discount.* However, you should realize that the process is nothing more than allocating the interest and determining the liability's balance.

Look at the table in Illustration 11–7. Note that we allocate the interest among the five years by multiplying the beginning net liability balance by the original 10% interest rate. Just as you have seen before, the interest expense is added to the beginning liability balance to find the ending liability balance. The column for 19X1 shows that interest expense for that year is $621, which is 10% of the initial net liability balance of $6,209. Because no payment is made, the interest is added to the balance, and the ending net liability is $6,830. This

ILLUSTRATION 11–7 *Allocating Interest Expense over the Life of a Noninterest-Bearing Note Payable*

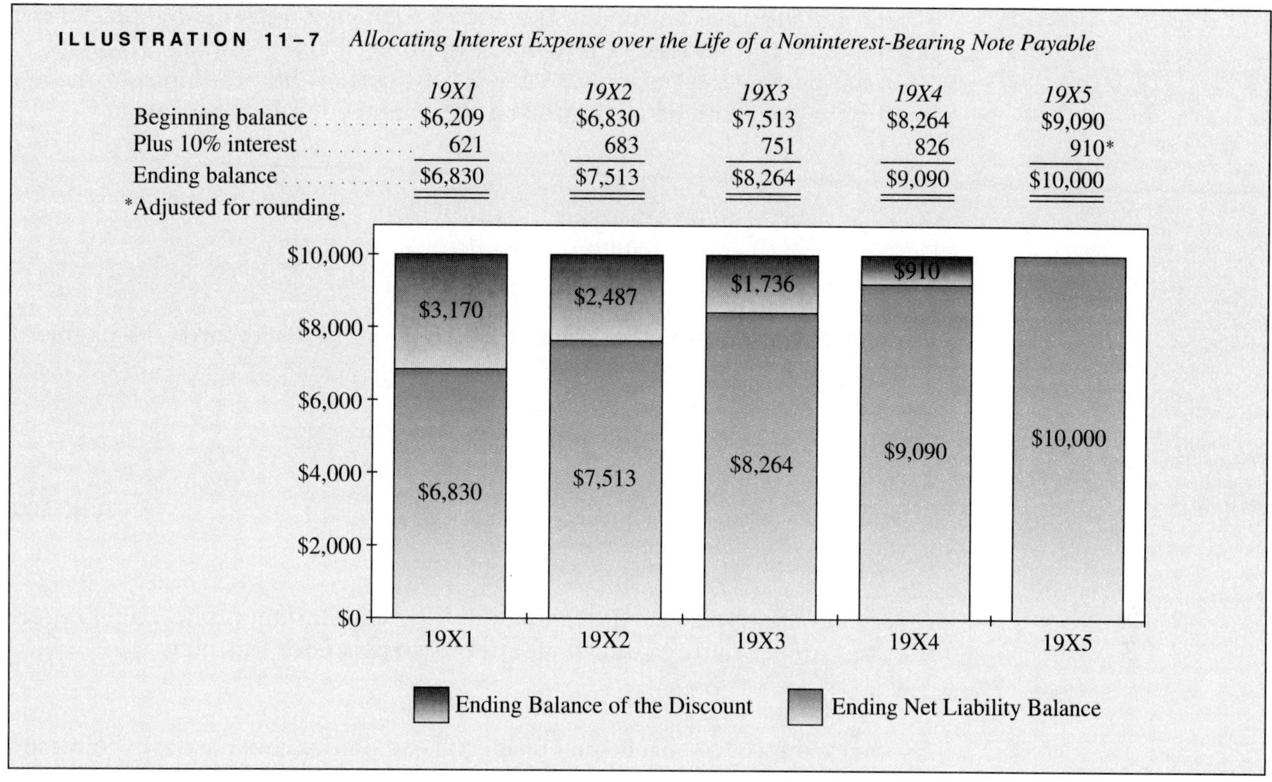

	19X1	*19X2*	*19X3*	*19X4*	*19X5*
Beginning balance	$6,209	$6,830	$7,513	$8,264	$9,090
Plus 10% interest	621	683	751	826	910*
Ending balance	$6,830	$7,513	$8,264	$9,090	$10,000

*Adjusted for rounding.

process continues throughout the five years until the note is paid.[12] (Notice that the interest expense for 19X5 is modified for rounding.)

In Illustration 11–7, we show that the net liability balance grows over the five years until it reaches the maturity amount of $10,000. Note also that the discount balance decreases to $0 after five years. In the following table, you can see how the balance of the discount is reduced:

	19X1	**19X2**	**19X3**	**19X4**	**19X5**
Beginning discount	$3,791	$3,170	$2,487	$1,736	$ 910
Less interest	(621)	(683)	(751)	(826)	(910)
Ending discount	$3,170	$2,487	$1,736	$ 910	$ -0-

The first year's interest and reduction of the discount are recorded when the accountant makes this year-end adjusting entry:

19X1				
Dec.	31	Interest Expense	621.00	
		Discount on Notes Payable		621.00
		To record interest expense accrued on a noninterest-bearing note.		

[12] Notice that the ending balance for any of the five years equals the present value of the future $10,000 payment discounted at the original interest rate for the number of years until the note matures. For example, the present value of the maturity amount at the end of 19X3 equals $10,000 discounted for two years at 10%, which is $8,264 ($10,000 × 0.8264). This amount appears in Illustration 11–7 as the ending balance for 19X3.

Similar entries are recorded at the end of each year until the balance of the discount account equals $0, and the net liability balance equals $10,000.

After posting the December 31, 19X1, adjusting entry for interest, the net liability balance can be presented on the balance sheet as follows:

Long-term note payable	$10,000
Less discount	(3,170)
Net liability	$ 6,830

When the note matures on January 2, 19X6, the issuer records the payment with this entry:

19X6				
Jan.	2	Long-Term Notes Payable	10,000.00	
		Cash		10,000.00
		Paid noninterest-bearing note.		

After this entry is posted, the company's financial statements no longer report the net liability or any additional interest expense for this note.

Liabilities from Leasing

As an alternative to purchasing property, companies can lease it by agreeing to make a series of rental payments to the property owner, who is called the **lessor.** Because a lease gives the property's user (called the **lessee**) exclusive control over the property's usefulness, the lessee can use it to earn revenues. In addition, some leases create liabilities if they obligate the lessees to make future payments to the lessors.

According to the generally accepted accounting principles described in *Statement of Financial Accounting Standards No. 13* issued by the FASB, the lessee's financial statements must report a leased asset and a lease liability under specified conditions. The asset and liability are reported only if the lessor essentially transfers ownership or unique control of the property to the lessee. In general, these **capital leases** cover a number of years and create long-term liabilities that are paid off with a series of equal payments.

When a capital lease is created, the lessee recognizes a leased asset and depreciates it over its useful life. The lessee also recognizes a lease liability and allocates interest expense to the years in the lease. The interest allocation process is the same as we have seen for notes payable.

Leases that are not capital leases are called **operating leases.** With an operating lease, the lessee does not report the lease as an asset. The only asset that would be reported is prepaid rent. The balance sheet shows a liability only if there is accrued and unpaid rent expense. The lessee's income statement reports rent expense and does not report either interest or depreciation expense.

Intermediate accounting textbooks describe more details about the characteristics of leases that cause them to be accounted for as capital or operating. These books also describe the financial accounting practices used by the lessor and lessee for capital leases.

Payroll Liabilities

An employer's income statement and current liabilities on the balance sheet typically include payroll-related items. Expenses and liabilities also arise from employee benefits and payroll taxes levied on the employer. Other liabilities (but no additional expenses) are created by withholding income and payroll taxes from employees' salaries and wages. These items are discussed in the next sections.

LO 7 Describe payroll expenses and liabilities and prepare journal entries to account for them.

FICA Taxes on Employees

The federal Social Security system provides qualified workers who retire at age 62 with monthly cash payments for the rest of their lives. The retirees also receive *Medicare benefits* beginning at age 65. In addition, the system provides monthly payments to surviving families of deceased workers who qualify for the assistance. These benefits are paid with **FICA taxes** collected under the Federal Insurance Contributions Act. The taxes for retirees and survivors are often called *Social Security taxes* to distinguish them from Medicare taxes.

Among other things, the law requires employers to withhold FICA taxes from each employee's salary or wages paid on each payday. The two components of these taxes for Social Security and Medicare are calculated separately. In 1994, the amount withheld from each employee's pay for Social Security was 6.2% of the first $60,600 earned by the employee in the calendar year. The Medicare tax was 1.45% of all wages earned by the employee.

The employer is required to promptly pay the withheld taxes to the Internal Revenue Service. Substantial penalties can be levied against individual managers and employees of a company that fails to turn the withheld taxes over to the IRS on time. These penalties apply to anyone who has check-signing authority for the company and reflect the fact that the liability to the government is on behalf of the company's employees. Until all these taxes are paid, they are included in the employer's current liabilities.

Employee's Federal Income Tax Withholdings

With very few exceptions, employers must withhold an amount of federal income tax from each employee's paycheck. The amount withheld is determined from tables published by the IRS. The amount depends on the employee's annual earnings rate and the number of *withholding allowances* claimed by the employee. In 1994, each allowance exempted $2,400 of the employee's annual earnings from withholding. (The size of the allowance increases each year because it is indexed for the effects of inflation.) Employees can claim allowances for themselves and their dependents. They also can claim additional allowances if they anticipate major reductions in their taxable income for medical expenses or other deductible items. The income taxes withheld from employees also must be paid promptly to the IRS. Until they are paid, withholdings are reported as a current liability on the employer's balance sheet.

Other Withholdings from Wages

In addition to Social Security, Medicare, and income taxes, an employer may withhold other amounts from employees' earnings according to their instructions. These withholdings may include amounts for charitable contributions, medical insurance premiums, investment purchases, and union dues. These withholdings are the employer's current liabilities until they are paid.

Recording Payroll Expenses and Other Withholdings

A general journal entry records the payroll expenses and liabilities at the end of each pay period. As an example, this entry shows some of the various types of liabilities and expenses that may be created:

Jan.	31	Salaries Expense	2,000.00	
		FICA Taxes Payable		153.00
		Employees' Federal Income Taxes Payable		213.00
		Employees' Medical Insurance Payable		85.00
		Employees' Union Dues Payable		25.00
		Accrued Payroll Payable		1,524.00
		To record the payroll for the pay period ended January 31.		

The debit to Salaries Expense records the fact that the company's employees earned gross salaries of $2,000. The first four credits record liabilities that the employer owes on behalf of its employees for their FICA taxes, income taxes, medical insurance, and union dues. The fifth credit to the Accrued Payroll Payable account records the fact that the employees will receive only $1,524 of the $2,000 that they earned.

When employees are actually paid, another entry (or a series of entries) records the checks written and distributed to them. The following journal entry records the payment of the employees' take-home pay on January 31:

Jan.	31	Accrued Payroll Payable	1,524.00	
		Cash		1,524.00
		To record paying the take-home pay for January 31.		

Many companies find it convenient to maintain separate payroll checking accounts; these allow them to keep paychecks separate from the regular checks that they write for other payments.

Employer's Payroll Taxes

In addition to the taxes assessed on the employees, other taxes must be paid by the employer. They include FICA and unemployment taxes.

Employer's FICA Tax

Employers also pay FICA taxes equal to the FICA taxes withheld from their employees. Unlike the employee's portion, this tax creates an additional expense and liability for the employer. In effect, the employer's total payroll expense is greater than the gross compensation earned by the employees.

Federal and State Unemployment Taxes

The federal government participates with states in a joint program for providing unemployment benefits. The federal government protects workers by approving the state programs. The state's costs are reduced when the federal program pays some of the administrative expenses. The joint program is funded by federal and state taxes on employers.

The Federal Unemployment Tax (FUTA). Employers are subject to a federal unemployment tax on wages paid to their employees. In 1994, the Federal Unemployment Tax Act (called *FUTA*) required employers to pay a tax of as much as 6.2% of the first $7,000 in salary or wages paid to each employee. However, the federal tax can be reduced by a credit of up to 5.4% for taxes paid to a state program. As a result, the net federal unemployment tax is normally only 0.8% of the first $7,000. (Because the tax is not withheld from their paychecks, employees may be unaware that this tax is paid.)

State Unemployment Insurance Taxes (SUTA). State unemployment programs are funded by a payroll tax on employers. In most states, the maximum rate is 5.4% of the first $7,000 paid to each employee. However, the state may assign a **merit rating** according to the employer's past record for creating or not creating unemployment. A good rating is based on stable employment and allows the employer to actually pay less than the maximum 5.4% rate while getting full credit against the federal taxes. A history of high turnover or seasonal hirings and layoffs may create an unfavorable rating that causes the employer to pay the full 5.4% rate.

A favorable merit rating may offer important cash savings. For example, suppose that an employer receives a merit rating that reduces the applied state rate from 5.4% to 0.5%. If it has 100 employees who each earn at least $7,000 per year, the company will save $34,300 annually. At the 5.4% rate, it will pay $37,800 (5.4% × $700,000) but will pay only $3,500 at the 0.5% rate (0.5% × $700,000).

Recording the Employer's Payroll Taxes

The employer's payroll taxes are an additional expense above the amount earned by the employees. As a result, these taxes are usually recorded in a journal entry separate from the one recording the basic payroll expense and withholding liabilities.

For example, assume that the previously recorded $2,000 salaries expense was earned by employees who have earned less than $7,000 so far in the year. Also, assume that the federal unemployment tax rate was 0.8% and that the state unemployment tax rate was 5.4%. The FICA portion of the employer's tax expense equals 7.65% of the $2,000 gross pay. The state unemployment (SUTA) taxes are $108, which is 5.4% of the $2,000 gross pay. The federal unemployment (FUTA) taxes are $16, which is 0.8% of $2,000. This entry records the employer's payroll tax expense and the related liabilities:

Jan.	31	Payroll Taxes Expense	277.00	
		FICA Taxes Payable		153.00
		State Unemployment Taxes Payable		108.00
		Federal Unemployment Taxes Payable		16.00
		To record payroll taxes.		

In this situation, the liabilities owed by the employer are for its own expenses instead of expenses incurred by its employees.

Employee Benefits

In addition to salaries and wages earned by employees and payroll taxes paid by employers, many companies provide a variety of other **employee benefits.** For example, an employer may pay all or part of the premiums for medical, dental, life, and disability insurance. Many employers also contribute to pension plans or offer special stock purchase plans for their employees.

By the time that payroll taxes and employee benefits costs are added to the employees' basic earnings, employers often find that their total payroll cost exceeds the employees' gross earnings by 25% or more. The following paragraphs describe two specific employee benefits.

Employer Contributions to Insurance and Pension Plans

The entries that record employee benefit costs are similar to the entries recording payroll taxes. To return to the same example, suppose that the employer agreed to pay an amount for medical insurance equal to the $85 withheld from the employees' paychecks and to contribute an additional 10% of the employees' $2,000 gross salary to a retirement program. This entry would record these benefits:

			Debit	Credit
Jan.	7	Employee Benefits Expense	285.00	
		Employees' Medical Insurance Payable		85.00
		Employees' Retirement Program Payable . . .		200.00
		To record employee benefits.		

The additional expense is reported on the employer's income statement. The liabilities remain on the books until they are paid. Additional accounting requirements for these benefits were created by the FASB and are covered in more advanced accounting courses.

Vacation Pay

Another widely offered benefit is paid vacations. For example, many employees earn 2 weeks' vacation by working 50 weeks. This benefit increases the employer's payroll expenses above their apparent amount because the employees are paid for 50 weeks of work over the 52 weeks in the year. Although the total annual salary is the same, the cost per week worked is greater than the amount paid per week. For example, suppose than an employee is paid $20,800 for 52 weeks of employment, but works only 50 weeks. The weekly salary expense to the employer is $416 ($20,800/50 weeks) instead of the $400 paid weekly to the employee ($20,800/52 weeks). The $16 difference between these two amounts is recorded as salary expense and a liability for vacation pay. When the employee actually takes vacation, the employer reduces the vacation pay liability and does not record additional expense.

Using the Information—Times Fixed Interest Charges Earned

LO 8 Calculate the times fixed interest charges earned ratio and describe what it reveals about a company's situation.

A company incurs interest expense that is reported on its income statement when it issues notes or bonds and when it enters into capital leases. Because they are related to the amount of the company's debt, interest expense may continue on into the future at essentially the same amount, even if the company's sales increase or decrease. As a result, the amount of interest is often considered to be a fixed cost. That is, the interest can be fixed in amount. Although fixed costs can be advantageous when a company is growing, they create the risk that the company might not be able to pay them if sales decline. The following example shows a company's results for the current year and two possible outcomes for the next year:

	Current Year	Next Year: If Sales Increase	Next Year: If Sales Decrease
Sales	$600,000	$900,000	$300,000
Expenses (75% of sales)	450,000	675,000	225,000
Income before interest	$150,000	$225,000	$ 75,000
Interest expense (fixed)	60,000	60,000	60,000
Net income	$ 90,000	$165,000	$ 15,000

As we show in the table, expenses other than interest are projected to stay at 75% of sales. In contrast, the interest is expected to remain at $60,000 per year. Note in the second column that the company's income would nearly double if its sales increased by 50%. However, the company's profits would fall drastically if the sales decreased by 50%. These numbers show that a company's risk is affected by the amount of fixed interest charges that it incurs each year.

The risk created by these fixed expenses can be described numerically with the **times fixed interest charges earned.** You can use the following formula to find the ratio:

$$\text{Times fixed interest charges earned} = \frac{\text{Income before interest}}{\text{Interest expense}}$$

For this company's current year, the income before interest is $150,000. Therefore, this ratio is $150,000/$60,000, which equals 2.5 times. This result suggests that the company faces a relatively low degree of risk. Its sales would have to go down by a large amount before the company would not be able to cover its interest expenses. This condition should provide comfort to the company's creditors and its owners.

The ratio is best interpreted in light of information about the variability of the company's net income before interest. If this amount is stable from year to year, or is growing, the company can afford to take on some of the risk created by borrowing. However, if the company's income before interest varies greatly from year to year, fixed interest charges can increase the risk that the owner will not earn a return or that the company will be unable to pay the interest.

Summary of Chapter in Terms of Learning Objectives

LO 1 Liabilities are probable future sacrifices of economic benefits arising from present obligations of a particular entry to transfer assets or provide services to other entities in the future as a result of past transactions or events. Current liabilities are due within one year or one operating cycle, whichever is longer. Long-term liabilities are not expected to be paid within one year or a longer operating cycle.

LO 2 A liability may have uncertainties about its existence, the identity of the creditor, the due date, or its amount. Because information about liabilities is useful for investment and credit decisions, accountants recognize liabilities and their effects in the financial statements even when all the facts about them are not known.

LO 3 Liabilities for warranties and income taxes are recorded with amounts that are expected to be paid. This practice recognizes the expense in the time period that it occurs, even if the exact amount is not known. Subsequent entries reduce the liability when actual costs are incurred, but no additional expense is recorded. Short-term notes payable arise when a company replaces an existing account receivable or borrows cash from a lender. The notes may be interest-bearing, in which case the face value of the note equals the amount borrowed and the note specifies a rate of interest to be paid until maturity. Noninterest-bearing notes include interest in their face value, which exceeds the amount borrowed.

LO 4 Contingencies arise from past events, have an uncertain effect on a company, and will be cleared up when another later event occurs and confirms whether the effect did take place. Because of the conservatism principle, contingent gains are not recognized in the financial statements. Contingent losses are recognized only when confirmation is probable and their amount can be estimated. Contingent losses also can be disclosed in the footnotes to the financial statements, possibly as contingent liabilities. Examples of contingent liabilities are potential legal claims and debt guarantees.

LO 5 Present value concepts are used to measure liabilities that involve future cash flows. The primary present value concept is that today's value of an amount of cash to be paid or received in the future is less than today's value of the same amount of cash to be paid or received today. Another present value concept is that interest is compounded, which means that the interest is added to the balance and used to determine interest for succeeding periods. The present value of a single future cash flow can be determined with a formula, a present value table, or a calculator. An annuity is a series of equal payments occurring at equal time intervals. The present value of an annuity can be determined with a formula, a present value table, or a calculator.

LO 6 Accountants use present value concepts to allocate interest expense among the years in a note's life by multiplying the note's beginning balance for the year by the original interest rate. The ending balance is found by adding the allocated interest and deducting any payments. Noninterest-bearing notes are frequently recorded with a discount account that is contra to the liability account. The balance of the discount account is made smaller (amortized) in the process of recognizing interest expense over the note's life.

LO 7 Payroll expenses are created for gross earnings of the employees and payroll taxes levied against the employer. Payroll liabilities arise for take-home pay, amounts withheld from the employees, employee benefits, and the employer's payroll taxes. Payroll taxes are assessed for Social Security, Medicare, and unemployment programs.

LO 8 The times-fixed-interest-charges-earned ratio is calculated by dividing a company's net income before interest by the amount of fixed interest charges incurred. This ratio describes the cushion that exists to protect the company's ability to pay interest and earn a profit for its owners against declines in its sales.

Demonstration Problem

The following series of transactions and other events took place at the Kern Company during its calendar reporting year. Describe their effects on the financial statements by presenting the journal entries described in each situation.

a. Throughout September 19X1, Kern sold $140,000 of merchandise that was covered by a 180-day warranty. Prior experience shows that the costs of fulfilling the warranty will equal 5% of the sales revenue. Calculate September's warranty expense and the increase in the warranty liability and show how it would be recorded with a September 30 adjusting entry. Also show the journal entry that would be made on October 8 to record an expenditure of $300 cash to provide warranty service on an item sold in September.

b. On October 12, Kern arranged with a supplier to replace an overdue $10,000 account payable by paying $2,500 cash and signing a note for the remainder. The note matured in 90 days and had a 12% interest rate. Show the entries that would be recorded on October 12, December 31, and Janaury 10, 19X2 (when the note matures).

c. Kern acquired a machine on December 1 by giving a $60,000, noninterest-bearing note due in one year. The market rate of interest for this type of debt was 10%. Show the entries that would be made when the note is created, as of December 31, 19X1, and at maturity on December 1, 19X2.

On January 1, 19X2, Kern Company borrowed cash by agreeing to make three $40,000 payments at the end of each of 19X2, 19X3, and 19X4. The interest rate for the loan was 8%.

d. Calculate the present value of the three payments to determine how much cash the company was able to borrow under these terms.

e. Present a table that shows how much interest expense will be assigned to 19X2, 19X3, and 19X4 and the ending balance for each of the three years.

Planning the Solution

- For (*a*), compute the warranty expense for September and record it with an estimated liability. Record the October expenditure as a decrease in the liability.
- For (*b*), eliminate the liability for the account payable and create the liability for the note payable. Calculate the interest expense for the 80 days that the note is outstanding in 19X1 and record it as an additional liability. Record the payment of the note, being sure to include the interest for the 10 days in 19X2.

- For (*c*), measure the cost of the machinery by finding the present value of the $60,000 cash expected to be paid when the note matures. Record the note at its face value, and use a contra-liability account to record the discount. Accrue 30 days' interest at December 31 by reducing the discount account. At maturity, the journal entry should record additional interest expense for 19X2, eliminate the note payable account balance, and eliminate the discount account balance.
- For (*d*), find the present value of the annuity of three annual payments discounted at the 8% interest rate.
- For (*e*), prepare a table with three columns for 19X2, 19X3, and 19X4. For each year, show the amount of interest as 8% of the beginning balance and subtract the payment to find the ending balance, which becomes the beginning balance for the next year. The ending balance for the third year should be zero.

Solution to Demonstration Problem

a. Warranty expense = 5% × $140,000 = $7,000

Sept.	30	Warranty Expense	7,000.00	
		Estimated Warranty Liability		7,000.00
		To record warranty expense and liability at 5% of sales for the month.		
Oct.	8	Estimated Warranty Liability	300.00	
		Cash		300.00
		To record the cost of the warranty service.		

b. Interest expense for 19X1 = 12% × $7,500 × 80/360 = $200
Interest expense for 19X2 = 12% × $7,500 × 10/360 = $25

Oct.	12	Accounts Payable	10,000.00	
		Notes Payable		7,500.00
		Cash		2,500.00
		Paid $2,500 cash and gave a 90-day, 12% note to extend the due date on the account.		
Dec.	31	Interest Expense	200.00	
		Interest Payable		200.00
		To accrue interest on note payable.		
Jan.	10	Interest Expense	25.00	
		Interest Payable	200.00	
		Notes Payable	7,500.00	
		Cash		7,725.00
		Paid note with interest, including accrued interest payable.		

c. Cost of the asset = present value of the note
Present value of the note = $60,000 × Table 11–1 value for n = 1 and i = 10%
Present value of the note = $60,000 × 0.9091 = $54,546
Discount on the note = $60,000 − $54,546 = $5,454

Dec.	1	Machinery	54,546.00	
		Discounts on Notes Payable		5,454.00
		Notes Payable		60,000.00
		Exchanged a one-year, noninterest-bearing note for a machine.		

Interest expense for 19X1 = 10% × $54,546 × 30/360 = $455
Interest expense for 19X2 = $5,454 − $455 = $4,999

Dec.	31	Interest Expense	455.00	
		Discount on Notes Payable		455.00
		To accrue interest on noninterest-bearing note payable.		
19X2				
Dec.	1	Interest Expense	4,999.00	
		Notes Payable	60,000.00	
		Cash		60,000.00
		Discount on Notes Payable		4,999.00
		Paid noninterest-bearing note payable.		

d. Amount borrowed = present value of the annuity
= $40,000 × Table 11–2 value for $n = 3$ and $i = 8\%$
= $40,000 × 2.5771 = $103,084

e. Table for finding interest and the ending balance:

	19X2	19X3	19X4
Beginning balance	$103,084	$71,331	$37,037
Plus interest (8%)	8,247	5,706	2,963
Total	$111,331	$77,037	$40,000
Less payment	(40,000)	(40,000)	(40,000)
Ending balance	$ 71,331	$37,037	$ -0-

Glossary

LO 9 Define or explain the words and phrases listed in the chapter glossary.

Annuity a series of equal payments occurring at equal time intervals. p. 391

Capital lease a lease that causes the lessor to essentially transfer ownership or unique control of the asset to the lessee. p. 398

Contingency an event with an uncertain effect arising from a past event that will be cleared up when another later confirming event occurs. p. 381

Contingent liability a possible obligation that is reported in the footnotes because of uncertainty about its existence, amount, or both. p. 382

Deferred income tax liability the estimated liability for income taxes to be paid in the future for temporary differences created by past transactions. p. 381

Discount on note payable the difference between the face value of a noninterest-bearing note payable and the amount borrowed; the discount equals the amount of interest that will be paid on the note over its life. p. 384

Down payment a cash payment to the seller from a buyer who is acquiring an asset on credit. p. 394

Employee benefits additional compensation paid to or on behalf of employees, such as premiums for medical, dental, life, and disability insurance, contributions to pension plans, and vacations. p. 401

Estimated liability an obligation that is believed to exist but has an uncertain amount that can be estimated. p. 378

FICA taxes taxes assessed on both employers and employees under the Federal Insurance Contributions Act; these taxes fund Social Security and Medicare programs. p. 399

Lessee the user of leased property. p. 398

Lessor the owner of leased property. p. 398

Merit rating a rating assigned to an employer by a state according to the employer's past record for creating or not creating unemployment; a higher rating produces a lower unemployment tax rate. p. 401

Noninterest-bearing note a note that does not have a stated rate of interest; the interest is included in the face value of the note. p. 385

Operating lease a lease that is not a capital lease. p. 398

Present value the amount of money that currently can be borrowed (invested) at a given interest rate such that it will grow to equal a specified future payment (receipt). p. 388

Present value table a numeric table that shows present values computed with a formula at various interest rates for various time periods; tables exist for single future payments and annuities. p. 389

Times fixed interest charges earned the ratio of a company's net income before interest divided by the amount of fixed interest charges; used to describe the risk created by variable amounts of income. p. 402

Warranty an agreement that obligates the seller or manufacturer to repair or replace a product within a specified period. p. 378

Objective Review

Answers to the following questions are listed at the end of this chapter. Be sure that you decide which is the one best answer to each question *before* you check the answers.

LO 1 Which of the following items would normally be classified as a current liability for a company that has a 14-month operating cycle?

a. A note payable due in 14 months.
b. Salaries payable.
c. A note payable due in 10 months.
d. The portion of a long-term note that is due to be paid in 14 months.
e. All of the above.

LO 2 Estimated liabilities would include an obligation to pay:

a. A known amount to a known person if an uncertain future event actually occurs.
b. An uncertain but reasonably estimated amount to a specific person on a specific date.
c. A known amount to a specific person on an uncertain due date.
d. A known amount to an uncertain person on a known due date.
e. All of the above.

LO 3 An automobile was sold for $15,000 on June 1, 19X1, with a one-year or 10,000-mile warranty. The warranty covers parts and labor. Based on past experience, warranty expense is estimated at 1.5% of the selling price. On March 1, 19X2, the customer returned the car for warranty repairs that used replacement parts with a cost of $75 and labor with a cost of $60. The amount that should be recorded as warranty expense at the time of the March 1 repairs is:

a. $ 0.
b. $ 60.
c. $ 75.
d. $135.
e. $225.

LO 4 A future payment should be reported as a liability on a company's balance sheet if the payment is contingent on a future event that:

a. Is probable and the amount of the payment cannot be reasonably estimated.
b. Is probable and the amount of the payment can be reasonably estimated.
c. Is probable and the amount of the payment is known.
d. Is not probable and the amount of the payment is known.
e. Both (*b*) and (*c*) are correct.

LO 5 A company enters into an agreement to make four annual payments of $1,000 each, starting one year from now. The annual interest rate is 8%. The present value of these four payments is:

a. $2,923.
b. $2,940.
c. $3,312.
d. $4,000.
e. $6,733.

LO 6 On January 1, 19X1, Fairview Co. signed a $6,000 three-year note payable bearing 6% annual interest. The original principal and all interest is to be paid on December 31, 19X3. The interest will compound every year. How much interest should be allocated to each of the three years?

	19X1	19X2	19X3
a.	$360	$360	$360
b.	$0	$0	$1,080
c.	$382	$382	$382
d.	$360	$382	$404
e.	$0	$0	$1,146

LO 7 Midtown Repairs pays its one employee $3,000 per month. The company's net FUTA rate is 0.8% on the first $7,000 earned by the employee, the SUTA rate is 4.0% on the first $7,000, the Social Security tax rate is 6.2% of the first $60,600, and the Medicare tax rate is 1.45% of all amounts earned by the employee. The journal entry to record the company's payroll taxes for March (the third month of the year) would include a total expense of:

a. $277.50
b. $293.50
c. $373.50
d. $1,120.50
e. $4,093.20

LO 8 The times fixed interest charges earned ratio:

a. Describes the risk faced by a company that goes into debt with fixed interest charges.

b. Equals the company's income before interest divided by the annual interest expense.
c. Takes on a smaller value as the amount of fixed interest charges gets larger.
d. Is best interpreted in light of information about the variability of the company's net income before interest.
e. All of the above are correct.

LO 9 Which one of the following terms is not associated with leases?

a. Operating lease.
b. Lessor.
c. Contingent liability.
d. Lessee.
e. Capital lease.

Questions for Class Discussion

1. What is a liability?
2. Is every expected future payment a liability?
3. What is the difference between a current and a long-term liability?
4. If a liability is payable in 15 months, should it be classified as current or long-term?
5. What is an estimated liability?
6. Why would a corporation accrue an income tax liability for interim reports?
7. What is a contingency? Under what circumstances is a contingency reported as a liability on the balance sheet?
8. Suppose that a company has a facility located in an area where disastrous weather conditions often occur. Under what conditions should it report a probable loss from a future disaster as a liability on its balance sheet?
9. Why are warranty liabilities usually recognized on the balance sheet as actual liabilities even when they are uncertain and unenforceable?
10. Why would a creditor want a past-due account to be replaced by a note?
11. What factors affect the present value of a future $2,000 payment?
12. Suppose that a company has an option to pay either $10,000 after one year or $5,000 after six months and another $5,000 after one year. Which choice always has the smaller present value?
13. Suppose that a company promises to pay a lender $4,000 at the end of four years. If the annual interest rate is 8% and the interest is included in the $4,000, what is (*a*) the amount that the company originally borrowed, (*b*) the amount of interest allocated to the first year, and (*c*) the balance owed after one year has passed?
14. How would a lease create an asset and a liability for the lessee?
15. Under what circumstances would an operating lease cause the lessee to report an asset or a liability on its balance sheet? Could it ever report both an asset and a liability?
16. Indicate whether the employer or the employee pays each of these taxes: (*a*) FICA taxes, (*b*) FUTA taxes, (*c*) SUTA taxes, and (*d*) withheld income taxes.
17. What is an employer's unemployment merit rating? Why are these ratings assigned to employers?
18. Suppose that two companies have net income after interest of $100,000. The first company has fixed interest charges of $200,000 and the second one has fixed interest charges of $40,000. Which one is in a more risky situation in terms of being affected by a drop in sales?

19. Examine the 1993 balance sheet for Federal Express Corporation in Appendix G. How much of the company's long-term debt is due to be paid during the 1994 fiscal year?

20. Examine the balance sheet for Ben & Jerry's in Appendix G. Has the company entered into any capital leases for its equipment? How do you know?

Class Exercises

Exercise 11–1
Classifying liabilities
(LO 1)

The following list of items might appear as liabilities on the balance sheet of a company that has a two-month operating cycle. Identify the proper classification of each item. In the space beside each item write *C* if it is a current liability, an *L* if it is a long-term liability, or an *N* if it is not a liability.

___*a.* Wages payable
___*b.* Notes payable in 60 days
___*c.* Mortgage payable (payments due after next 12 months)

__*d.* Notes receivable in 90 days
__*e.* Bonds payable (mature in 10 years)
__*f.* Mortgage payable (payments due in next 12 months)
__*g.* Notes payable in 6–12 months
__*h.* Income taxes payable
__*i.* Accounts receivable
__*j.* Notes payable in 13–24 months

Exercise 11–2
Warranty expense and liability
(LO 3)

Sassower Co. sold a computer to a customer on December 4, 19X1, for $8,000 cash. Based on prior experience, the company expects to eventually incur warranty costs equal to 5% of this selling price. On January 18, 19X2, the customer returned the computer for repairs that were completed on the same day. The cost of the repairs consisted of $198 for the materials taken from the parts inventory and $40 of labor that was fully paid with cash.

a. How much warranty expense should the company report for December for this computer?
b. How large is the warranty liability for this computer as of December 31, 19X1?
c. How much warranty expense should the company report for January for this computer?
d. How large is the warranty liability for this computer as of January 31, 19X2?
e. Show the journal entries that would be made to record (1) the sale; (2) the adjustment as of December 31, 19X1, to record the warranty expense; and (3) the repairs that occurred in January.

Exercise 11–3
Short-term note payable calculations and entries
(LO 3)

On December 11, 19X1, the Snyder Company borrowed $42,000 and signed a 60-day, 9% note payable with a face value of $42,000.

a. What is the maturity date of this note?
b. How much interest will accrue on the note as of December 31, 19X1? (For simplicity, use a 360-day year to calculate the interest.)
c. How much cash will the company have to pay at maturity?
d. Present the journal entries that would be made to record: (1) issuing the note; (2) accruing interest at December 31, 19X1; and (3) paying the note at maturity.

Exercise 11–4
Interest-bearing and noninterest-bearing notes payable
(LO 3)

The Knightwood Co. borrowed $50,000 on September 1, 19X1, for 90 days at 8% interest by signing a note.

a. On what date will this note mature?
b. How much interest expense is created by this note? (Assume a 360-day year.)
c. Suppose that the face value of the note equals the principal of the loan. Show the general journal entries to record issuing the note and paying it at maturity.
d. Suppose that the face value of the note includes the principal of the loan and the interest to be paid at maturity. Show the general journal entries to record issuing the note and paying it at maturity.

Exercise 11–5
Interest-bearing and noninterest-bearing short-term notes payable with year-end adjustments
(LO 3)

The Shelby Co. borrowed $30,000 on December 1, 19X1, for 90 days at 10% interest by signing a note.

a. On what date will this note mature?
b. How much interest expense is created by this note in 19X1? (Assume a 360-day year.)
c. How much interest expense is created by this note in 19X2? (Assume a 360-day year.)
d. Suppose that the face value of the note equals the principal of the loan. Show the general journal entries to record issuing the note, to accrue interest at the end of 19X1, and to record paying the note at maturity.
e. Suppose that the face value of the note includes the principal of the loan and the interest to be paid at maturity. Show the general journal entries to record issuing the note, to accrue interest at the end of 19X1, and to record paying the note at maturity.

Exercise 11–6
Present value of a future payment and accumulating interest
(LO 5)

On January 1, 19X1, a company has agreed to pay $15,000 after three years. If the annual interest rate is 6%, determine how much cash the company can borrow with this promise. Present a three-column table that shows the beginning balance, interest, and ending balance for 19X1, 19X2, and 19X3.

Exercise 11–7
Present value of liabilities
(LO 5)

Find the amount of money that can be borrowed with each of the following promises:

	Future Payment	Number of Years	Interest Rate
a.	$80,000	1	6%
b.	80,000	5	6
c.	80,000	5	8
d.	60,000	7	10
e.	10,000	1	2
f.	25,000	9	4

Exercise 11–8
Present value of two cash flows and interest accumulation
(LO 5)

A company borrowed cash by promising to pay $5,000 after one year and $8,000 after two years. The interest rate on the loan is 6%. Determine the amount of:

a. Cash that was borrowed.
b. Interest that will be accumulated in the first year.
c. The balance of the loan after the first payment is made.
d. Interest that will be accumulated in the second year.
e. The balance of the loan after the second payment is made.

Exercise 11–9
Present value of annuities
(LO 5)

A company recently borrowed money and agreed to pay it back with a series of three annual payments of $10,000 each. It also borrowed cash and agreed to pay it back with a series of seven annual payments of $4,000 each. The annual interest rate for the loans was 10%.

a. Use Table 11–1 to find the present value of these two annuities.
b. Use Table 11–2 to find the present value of these two annuities.

Exercise 11–10
Semiannual compounding
(LO 5)

A company borrowed cash on January 2, 19X1, by promising to make four payments of $3,000 each at June 30, 19X1; December 31, 19X1; June 30, 19X2; and December 31, 19X2.

a. How much cash was the company able to borrow if the interest rate was 12%, compounded semiannually?
b. How much cash was the company able to borrow if the interest rate was 16%, compounded semiannually?
c. How much cash was the company able to borrow if the interest rate was 20%, compounded semiannually?

Exercise 11–11
Finding the initial balance of an annuity
(LO 6)

The Detter Company borrowed some cash on January 2, 19X1, by agreeing to make four payments of $4,200 on December 31 of 19X1 through 19X4. The annual interest rate was 8%. How much was the company able to borrow?

Exercise 11–12
Allocating interest among the years covered by an annuity
(LO 6)

Use the facts described about the annuity in Exercise 11–11 to prepare a table that shows the amount of interest assigned to each of the four years and the ending balance for each of the four years.

Exercise 11–13
Recording an asset purchase in exchange for a note
(LO 6)

The Carson Company purchased some machinery on March 10 that had a cost of $56,000. Show the journal entry that would be made to record this purchase under these four separate situations:

a. The company paid cash for the full purchase price.
b. The company gave an interest-bearing note for the full purchase price.

c. The company gave an interest-bearing note for 80% of the purchase price and paid the remainder with a cash down payment.

d. The company gave a noninterest-bearing one-year note for $61,600.

Exercise 11–14
Calculations concerning a noninterest-bearing note
(LO 6)

On January 2, 19X1, the Brewster Co. acquired land by issuing a noninterest-bearing note for $20,000. The fair market value of the land was not reliably known, but the company knew that the market interest rate for the note was 6%. The note matures in three years on January 1, 19X4.

a. What is the present value of the note at the time of the purchase?

b. What is the initial balance of the discount on the note payable?

c. Prepare a table that shows the amount of interest that will be allocated to each of the three years in the note's life and the ending balance of the net liability for each year.

d. Prepare a table that determines the ending balance of the discount on the note for each of the three years.

Exercise 11–15
Journal entries for a noninterest-bearing note
(LO 6)

Use the data in Exercise 11–14 to prepare journal entries for these dates:

a. January 2, 19X1 (land purchase).

b. December 31, 19X1 (accrual entry).

c. December 31, 19X2 (accrual entry).

d. December 31, 19X3 (accrual entry).

e. January 1, 19X4 (the payment of the note).

Exercise 11–16
Payroll taxes
(LO 7)

The Juneau Co. has a single employee on its payroll. The employee and the company are subject to the following taxes:

Tax	Rate	Applied to
FICA—Social Security	6.20%	First $60,600
FICA—Medicare	1.45%	Gross pay
FUTA	0.80%	First $7,000
SUTA	3.20%	First $7,000

Compute the amounts of the four taxes on the employee's gross earnings for July under each of these three separate situations:

	Gross Salary through June	Gross Salary for July
a.	$ 5,000	$ 900
b.	20,000	3,500
c.	60,000	10,000

Exercise 11–17
Payroll tax journal entries
(LO 7)

Use the data in requirement *a* of Exercise 11–16 to prepare journal entries to record the gross salary and withholdings for the employee and the company's payroll taxes. The employee's withheld income taxes are $125.

Exercise 11–18
Times fixed interest charges earned ratio
(LO 8)

Use the following information for a proprietorship to compute the ratio for times fixed interest charges earned:

	Net Income or (loss)	Fixed Interest Charges
a.	$ 85,000	$ 16,000
b.	85,000	40,000
c.	85,000	90,000
d.	240,000	120,000
e.	(25,000)	60,000
f.	96,000	6,000

Problems

Problem 11–1
Estimated product warranty liabilities
(LO 3)

On November 10, 19X1, Bright Beam Co. began to buy and then resell high-powered flashlights for $40 each. The flashlights are covered under a warranty that requires the company to replace any nonworking flashlight within 90 days. When a flashlight is returned, the company simply throws it away and mails a new one from inventory to the customer. The company's cost for a new flashlight is only $7. The manufacturer has advised the company to expect warranty costs to equal 8% of the total sales. These events occurred in 19X1 and 19X2:

19X1	
Nov. 15	Sold flashlights for $8,000 cash.
30	Recognized warranty expense for November with an adjusting entry.
Dec. 8	Replaced 15 flashlights that were returned under the warranty.
15	Sold flashlights for $22,000 cash.
29	Replaced 40 flashlights that were returned under the warranty.
31	Recognized warranty expense for December with an adjusting entry.
19X2	
Jan. 14	Sold flashlights for $11,000 cash.
20	Replaced 63 flashlights that were returned under the warranty.
31	Recognized warranty expense for January with an adjusting entry.

Required

1. How much warranty expense should be reported for November and December of 19X1?
2. How much warranty expense should be reported for January 19X2?
3. What is the balance of the estimated warranty liability as of December 31, 19X1?
4. What is the balance of the estimated warranty liability as of January 31, 19X2?
5. Prepare journal entries to record the transactions and adjustments.

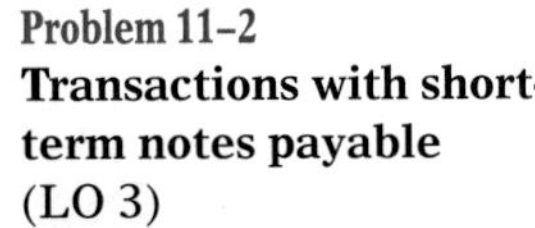

Problem 11–2
Transactions with short-term notes payable
(LO 3)

The Northside Co. entered into the following transactions involving short-term liabilities during 19X1 and 19X2:

19X1	
Mar. 14	Purchased merchandise on credit from Pete Winston Co. for $12,500. The terms were 1/10, n/30.
Apr. 14	Replaced the account payable to Pete Winston Co. with a 60-day note bearing 10% annual interest. Northside paid $3,500 cash, with the result that the balance of the note was $9,000.
May 21	Borrowed $20,000 from the Central Bank by signing an interest-bearing note for $20,000. The annual interest rate was 12%, and the note has a 90-day term.
?	Paid the note to Pete Winston Co. at maturity.
?	Paid the note to Central Bank at maturity.
Dec. 15	Borrowed $35,000 from the Eastern Bank by signing a noninterest-bearing note for $36,050 that matures in 120 days. (This amount is based on a 9% interest rate.)
31	Recorded an accrual adjusting entry for the interest on the note to the Eastern Bank.
19X2	
?	Paid the note to Eastern Bank at maturity.

Required

1. Determine the maturity dates of the three notes just described.
2. Determine the interest due at maturity for the three notes. (Assume a 360-day year.)

3. Determine the interest to be recorded in the adjusting entry at the end of 19X1.
4. Determine the interest to be recorded in 19X2.
5. Prepare journal entries for all the preceding events and adjustments.

Problem 11–3
Accounting for estimated and actual income taxes
(LO 3)

McKeag Corp. prepares interim financial statements each month. As part of the process, estimated income taxes are accrued each month as 30% of the company's income for that month. The estimated income taxes are paid in the first month of each quarter for the amount accrued in the prior quarter.

These facts are known about the last quarter of 19X1:

a. The September 30 adjusted balance of the Estimated Income Taxes Payable account is $8,000.

b. The company determines that the following amounts of net income occurred for these months:

October 19X1	$ 8,500
November 19X1	6,000
December 19X1	10,000

c. A quarterly payment of $8,000 is made on October 6.

d. After the tax return is completed, it is determined that the December 31 adjusted balance of the actual Income Taxes Payable account should be $7,480.

Required

1. Determine the balance of the estimated liability account after the accrual for December but before the adjustment to record the actual liability.
2. Determine the total income tax expense recorded in the last quarter by including the adjustment needed to produce the proper ending balance in the actual income tax liability account.
3. Present journal entries to record the entries related to income taxes for the fourth quarter of 19X1.

Problem 11–4
Present values of possible liabilities
(LO 5, 6)

Sherlock Enterprises is negotiating the purchase of a new building. The seller has offered Sherlock the following three payment plans:

Plan A: $100,000 cash would be paid at once.

Plan B: $114,000 cash would be paid after two years.

Plan C: $58,000 cash would be paid at the end of each of the next two years.

The company's owner knows that the market interest rate is 8%.

Required

1. Use the market interest rate to determine the present value of each of the three possible payment plans.
2. Show the journal entry that would be made to record the acquisition under each of the three plans. (Assume that the note's face value would include all interest to be paid.)
3. Identify the plan that creates the lowest cost for the company.
4. Assume that Plan B is adopted and the present value of the cash flows is used as the building's cost. Determine the amount of interest expense that will be reported in each of the two years in the note's life.

Problem 11–5
Exchanging a noninterest-bearing note for a plant asset
(LO 6)

On January 2, 19X1, Watts Company acquired an item of equipment by issuing a $55,000 noninterest-bearing five-year note payable on December 31, 19X5. A reliable cash price for the equipment was not readily available. The market annual rate of interest for similar notes was 4% on the day of the exchange.

Required

(Round all amounts in your answers to the nearest whole dollar.)

1. Determine the initial net liability created by issuing this note.
2. Present a table showing the calculation of the amount of interest expense allocated to each year the note is outstanding and the carrying amount of the net liability at the end of each of those years.

3. Present a table that shows the balance of the discount at the end of each year the note is outstanding.
4. Prepare general journal entries to record the purchase of the equipment, the accrual of interest expense at the end of 19X1 and 19X2, and the accrual of interest expense and the payment of the note on December 31, 19X5.
5. Show how the note should be presented on the balance sheet as of December 31, 19X3.

Problem 11–6
Payroll costs, withholdings, and taxes
(LO 7)

The Boston Company pays its employees every week. The employees' gross earnings are subject to these taxes:

	Rate	Applied To
FICA—Social Security	6.20%	First $60,600
FICA—Medicare	1.45%	Gross pay
FUTA	0.80%	First $7,000
SUTA	3.20%	First $7,000

The company is preparing its payroll calculations for the week ended October 20. The payroll records show the following information for the company's four employees:

		This Week	
Name	Gross pay through 10/13	Gross Pay	Withholding Tax
Fran	$21,000	$1,500	$165
Lynn	85,000	2,500	325
Shane	60,000	2,000	285
Terry	5,500	1,000	122

In addition to the gross pay, the company and each employee pays one-half of the weekly health insurance premium of $66. The company also contributes 10% of each employee's gross earnings to a pension fund.

Required

Use this information to determine:

1. Each employee's FICA withholdings for Social Security.
2. Each employee's FICA withholdings for Medicare.
3. The employer's FICA taxes for Social Security.
4. The employer's FICA taxes for Medicare.
5. The employer's FUTA taxes.
6. The employer's SUTA taxes.
7. Each employee's take-home pay.
8. The employer's total payroll-related expense for each employee.

Problem 11–7
Understanding the times fixed interest charges earned ratio
(LO 9)

These condensed income statements are for two companies:

Adams Co.		Beene Co.	
Sales	$100,000	Sales	$100,000
Variable expenses (65%) . . .	65,000	Variable expenses (85%) . . .	85,000
Net income before interest . .	$ 35,000	Net income before interest . .	$ 15,000
Interest (fixed)	25,000	Interest (fixed)	5,000
Net income	$ 10,000	Net income	$ 10,000

Required

1. What is the times fixed interest charges earned ratio for Adams Co.?
2. What is the times fixed interest charges earned ratio for Beene Co.?
3. What happens to each company's net income if sales increase by 20%?
4. What happens to each company's net income if sales increase by 40%?
5. What happens to each company's net income if sales increase by 80%?

6. What happens to each company's net income if sales decrease by 10%?
7. What happens to each company's net income if sales decrease by 20%?
8. What happens to each company's net income if sales decrease by 50%?
9. Comment on what you observe and relate it to the ratio values that you found in questions 1 and 2.

Problem 11–8
Analytical essay
(LO 6)

This problem requires you to demonstrate your understanding of noninterest-bearing notes, interest allocation, and present values by explaining how it would be possible to use incomplete information to discover other facts about a loan. Suppose that a company borrowed some cash on January 1, 19X1, with a four-year noninterest-bearing note payable. A year later, on December 31, 19X1, you know only these two items of information:

a. The net liability (net of the remaining discount) as of December 31, 19X1.
b. The interest expense reported for the year ended December 31, 19X1.

Write brief explanations of the calculations you would make to identify the following additional facts about the loan:

1. The amount borrowed on January 1, 19X1.
2. The market interest rate on January 1, 19X1.
3. The amount of interest that will be reported for 19X2.

Problem 11–9
Analytical essay
(LO 6)

After a long analysis, the manager of the Greenfield Company has decided to acquire a truck through a long-term noncancellable lease instead of buying it outright. Under the terms of the lease, Greenfield must make regular monthly payments throughout the four-year term of the lease and provide for all the operating costs, including gas, insurance, and repairs. At the end of the lease, the lessor will simply give Greenfield the legal title to the truck. Describe why Greenfield should account for the lease as if it is essentially a purchase.

Provocative Problems

Provocative Problem 11–1
Scoggins Company
(LO 6)

The Scoggins Company is analyzing the following four options for acquiring a fleet of vehicles.

Option A	Purchase the fleet by paying $600,000 cash.
Option B	Purchase the fleet by giving a three-year noninterest-bearing note with a face value of $700,000.
Option C	Purchase the fleet by promising to make three payments of $220,000 at the end of the each of the next three years.
Option D	Lease the fleet for two years with four semiannual payments of $180,000, with the first one to occur immediately. At the end of the lease, Scoggins will obtain legal title to all the vehicles.

Required

1. Use an annual interest rate of 8% to find the present value of each of the four alternative payment options.
2. Use an annual interest rate of 8% to calculate the annual amounts of interest that would be reported over the life of the last three options.
3. Present journal entries that would be made to record the acquisition under each of the four options. Use the present value of the future payments from question 1 as the cost of the asset for the last three options.
4. Explain which option ought to be selected on the basis of having the lowest cost.

Provocative Problem 11–2
Excellent Shirt Company
(LO 7)

All 60 regular employees of the Excellent Shirt Company earn at least $7,000 per year. The company operates in a state with a maximum SUTA tax rate of 5.4% on the first $7,000 gross wages of each employee. The company's excellent record has earned a merit rating that reduces its SUTA rate to 3.5%.

The company has recently received an order for a line of leather vests from a chain of clothing stores. The order should be very profitable and probably will be repeated each year for at least three or four years. The company can produce the vests with its present production facility, but it will have to add 10 more workers for six weeks at 40 hours per week to make the vests and pack them for shipment.

The company is considering two different approaches to getting the workers. That is, it can either go through a local temporary employment service (called Templuyees) or actually hire them as employees and then lay them off after six weeks. Excellent Shirt would pay Temployees $12 per hour for each worker, and Temployees would pay their wages and all payroll taxes and benefits. Alternatively, Excellent Shirt would pay its new employees a wage rate of $8.50 per hour, plus these additional payroll taxes: FICA tax, 7.65%; FUTA tax, 0.8%; and SUTA tax, 5.0%. The SUTA rate would jump to 5.0% because the company would receive a less favorable merit rating from the state because of the unemployment claims it would create by laying off the workers every year. This higher rate would apply to all of the company's employees. In addition, Excellent Shirt would provide health care insurance to these employees at the rate of $24 per employee per week.

Compare the total costs under the two alternatives to determine whether Excellent Shirt should use the services of Temployees or hire the additional workers that it needs. Provide a complete analysis and explanation.

Provocative Problem 11–3
Accounting-related communications
(LO 4)

Sam Ishikawa is the new manager of accounting and finance for a medium-sized manufacturing company. Now that the end of the year is approaching, his problem is determining whether and how to describe some of the company's contingencies in the financial statements. The general manager, Sue Peebles, raised objections to two specific contingencies in his preliminary proposal.

First, Peebles objected to the proposal to report nothing about a patent infringement suit that the company has filed against a competitor. The manager's written comment on his proposal was, "We KNOW that we have them cold on this one! There is no way that we're not going to win a very large settlement!"

Second, she objected to his proposal to recognize an expense and a liability for warranty service on units of a new product that was just introduced in the company's fourth quarter. Her scribbled comment on this point was, "There is no way that we can estimate this warranty cost. Besides, we don't owe anybody anything until the products break down and are returned for service. Let's just report an expense if and when we do the repairs."

Develop a short written response for Ishikawa to the objections raised by the general manager in a one-page memorandum dated December 15.

Provocative Problem 11–4
Apple Computer, Inc.
(LO 1, 3, 4, 6, 8)

Apple Computer, Inc.

Answer the following questions by using the information in the financial statements and footnotes for Apple Computer, Inc., that appear in Appendix F at the end of the book:

1. Examine the company's balance sheet to find the amount of long-term debt that it had on September 25, 1992. Also, what is the amount of the company's current notes payable?
2. Examine the statement of cash flows to find the amount of interest paid during fiscal year 1992. Does the company appear to be at risk from having large fixed interest payments compared to its operating income?
3. Does the footnote on "Commitments and Contingencies" provide information that allows the reader to determine whether the company has entered into any operating or capital leases?
4. What evidence would you look for as an indication that the company has any temporary differences between the income reported on the income statement and the income reported on its tax return? Can you find any evidence of these differences for Apple?

Comprehensive Problem

Schwartz Exterminator Company
(Review of Chapters 1–10)

The Schwartz Exterminator Company provides pest control services and sells extermination products manufactured by other companies. The following six-column table contains the company's unadjusted trial balance as of December 31, 19X4.

SCHWARTZ EXTERMINATOR COMPANY
Six-Column Table
December 31, 19X4

	Unadjusted Trial Balance		Adjustments		Adjusted Trial Balance	
Cash	$ 15,000					
Accounts receivable	24,000					
Allowance for doubtful accounts		$ 3,064				
Merchandise inventory	18,000					
Trucks	22,000					
Accum. depreciation, trucks		-0-				
Equipment	75,000					
Accum. depreciation, equipment		21,500				
Accounts payable		6,000				
Estimated warranty liability		1,200				
Unearned extermination services revenue		-0-				
Long-term notes payable		60,000				
Discount on notes payable	15,898					
Arnold Schwartz, capital		58,800				
Arnold Schwartz, withdrawals	21,000					
Extermination services revenue		70,000				
Interest earned		436				
Sales		135,000				
Purchases	81,000					
Depreciation expense, trucks	-0-					
Depreciation expense, equip.	-0-					
Wages expense	45,000					
Interest expense	-0-					
Rent expense	16,000					
Bad debts expense	-0-					
Miscellaneous expenses	6,202					
Repairs expense	11,000					
Utilities expense	5,900					
Warranty expense	-0-					
Totals	$356,000	$356,000				

The following information applies to the company and its situation at the end of the year:

a. The bank reconciliation as of December 31, 19X4, includes these facts:

Balance per bank	$13,200
Balance per books	15,000
Outstanding checks	2,600
Deposit in transit	3,500
Interest earned	44
Service charges (miscellaneous expense)	17

Included with the bank statement was a canceled check that the company had failed to record. (This information allows you to determine the amount of the check, which was a payment of an account payable.)

b. An examination of customers' accounts shows that accounts totaling $2,500 should be written off as uncollectible. In addition, the owner has determined that the ending balance of the Allowance for Doubtful Accounts account should be $4,300.

c. A truck was purchased and placed in service on July 1, 19X4. Its cost is being depreciated with the straight-line method using these facts and predictions:

Original cost	$22,000
Expected salvage value	6,000
Useful life (years)	4

d. Two items of equipment (a sprayer and an injector) were purchased and put into service early in January 19X2. Their costs are being depreciated with the straight-line method using these facts and predictions:

	Sprayer	**Injector**
Original cost	$45,000	$30,000
Expected salvage value	3,000	2,500
Useful life (years)	8	5

e. On October 1, 19X4, the company was paid $2,640 in advance to provide monthly service on an apartment complex for one year. The company began providing the services in October. When the cash was received, the full amount was credited to the Extermination Services Revenue account.

f. The company offers a warranty for all of the products it sells. The expected cost of providing warranty service is 2% of sales. No warranty expense has been recorded for 19X4. All costs of servicing products under the warranties in 19X4 were properly debited to the liability account.

g. The $60,000 long-term note is a five-year, noninterest-bearing note that was given to Second National Bank on December 31, 19X2. The market interest rate on the date of the loan was 8%.

h. The ending inventory of merchandise was counted and determined to have a cost of $16,300.

Required

1. Use the provided information to determine the amounts of the following items:
   a. The correct ending balance of Cash and the amount of the omitted check.
   b. The correct ending balance of the Allowance for Doubtful Accounts.
   c. The annual depreciation expense for the truck that was acquired during the year (calculated to the nearest month).
   d. The annual depreciation expense for the two items of equipment that were used during the year.
   e. The correct ending balances of the accounts for Extermination Services Revenue and Unearned Extermination Services Revenue.
   f. The correct ending balances of the accounts for Warranty Expense and the Estimated Warranty Liability.
   g. The correct ending balances of the accounts for Interest Expense and the Discount on Note Payable.
   h. The cost of goods sold for the year.
2. Use the results of question 1 to complete the six-column table by first entering the appropriate adjustments for items *a* through *g* and then completing the adjusted trial balance columns. (Hint: item *b* requires two entries.)
3. Present general journal entries to record the adjustments entered on the six-column table.
4. Present a single-step income statement, a statement of changes in owner's equity, and a classified balance sheet.

Answers to Objective Review Questions

LO 1 (*e*)	**LO 4** (*e*)	**LO 7** (*a*)
LO 2 (*b*)	**LO 5** (*c*)	**LO 8** (*e*)
LO 3 (*a*)	**LO 6** (*d*)	**LO 9** (*c*)

CHAPTER

12

Installment Notes Payable and Bonds

In Chapter 11, you learned that some notes payable require a single payment on the date the note matures. In those cases, the single payment includes the borrowed amount plus interest. You also learned about other notes requiring a series of payments that include interest plus a part of the principal. We begin this chapter with a more complete discussion of these installment notes. Then, we turn to bonds, which are securities in the form of liabilities created by companies, government bodies, and nonprofit entities. We also describe how investors account for bonds that they own.

Learning Objectives

After studying Chapter 12, you should be able to:

1. Calculate the payments on an installment note payable and describe their effects on the financial statements.
2. Describe the various characteristics of different types of bonds and prepare entries to record bond issuances and retirements.
3. Estimate the price of bonds issued at a discount and describe their effects on the issuer's financial statements.
4. Estimate the price of bonds issued at a premium and describe their effects on the issuer's financial statements.
5. Describe how investments in bonds are presented in the investor's financial statements.
6. Calculate and describe how to use the ratio of pledged assets to secured liabilities.
7. Define or explain the words and phrases listed in the chapter glossary.

Although some long-term notes may call for a single payment when they mature, many of them require the borrower to make a series of payments to the lender. The first section of this chapter describes these **installment notes.** Later sections of the chapter describe bond liabilities and investments.

Installment Notes Payable

When an installment note is used to borrow money, the borrower must capture information about the debt in the accounting records so that it can be usefully described in the financial statements. The borrower captures this information by initially recording the note with an entry similar to the one used for a single-payment note. That is, the increase in cash is recorded with a debit and

ILLUSTRATION 12–1 *Installment Note with Payments of Accrued Interest and Equal Amounts of Principal*

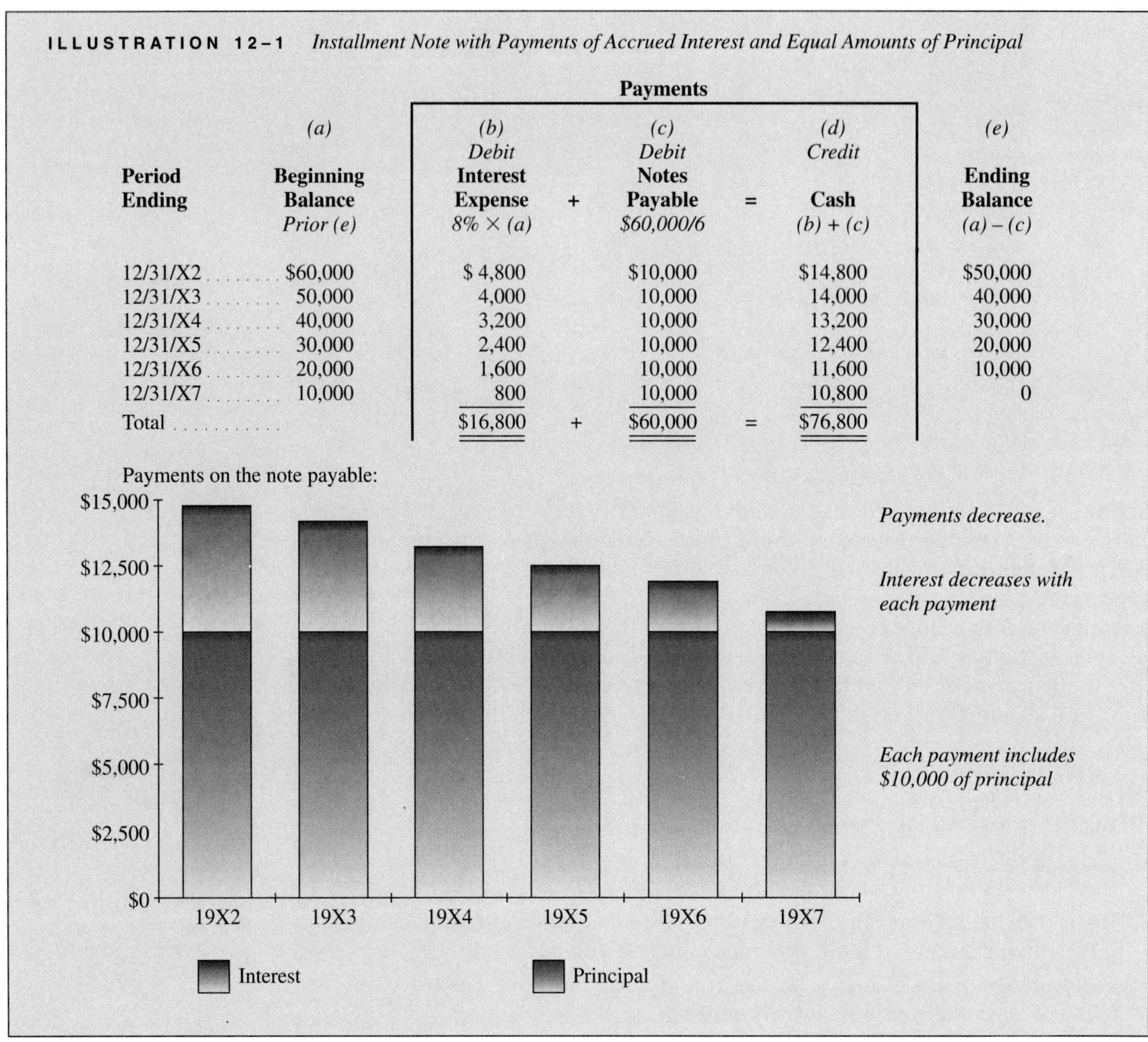

		Payments			
	(a)	*(b)* Debit	*(c)* Debit	*(d)* Credit	*(e)*
Period Ending	**Beginning Balance** *Prior (e)*	**Interest Expense** *8% × (a)* +	**Notes Payable** *$60,000/6* =	**Cash** *(b) + (c)*	**Ending Balance** *(a) – (c)*
12/31/X2	$60,000	$ 4,800	$10,000	$14,800	$50,000
12/31/X3	50,000	4,000	10,000	14,000	40,000
12/31/X4	40,000	3,200	10,000	13,200	30,000
12/31/X5	30,000	2,400	10,000	12,400	20,000
12/31/X6	20,000	1,600	10,000	11,600	10,000
12/31/X7	10,000	800	10,000	10,800	0
Total		$16,800 +	$60,000 =	$76,800	

LO 1 Calculate the payments on an installment note payable and describe their effects on the financial statements.

the increase in the liability is recorded with a credit to the Notes Payable account. For example, suppose that a company borrows $60,000 by signing an 8% installment note that requires six annual payments. The borrower records the note as follows:

19X1				
Dec.	31	Cash	60,000.00	
		Notes Payable		60,000.00
		Borrowed $60,000 by signing an 8% installment note.		

Installment notes payable like this one require the borrower to pay back the debt with a series of periodic payments. Usually, each payment includes all interest expense that has accrued up to the date of the payment plus some portion of the original amount borrowed (the *principal*). The terms of installment notes generally specify one of two alternative payment patterns. Some notes require installment payments that include interest and equal amounts of principal while other notes simply call for equal payments.

Installment Notes with Payments of Accrued Interest and Equal Amounts of Principal

Installment note agreements requiring payments of accrued interest plus equal amounts of principal create cash flows that decrease in size over the life of the note. This pattern occurs because each payment reduces the liability's principal balance, with the result that the following period's interest expense is reduced. The next payment is smaller because the amount of interest is reduced. For example, suppose that the $60,000, 8% note that we just recorded requires the borrower to make six payments equal to the accrued interest plus $10,000 of principal at the end of each year.

We describe the payments, interest, and changes in the balance of this note in the table in Illustration 12–1. Column *a* of the table shows the beginning balance of the note. Columns *b*, *c*, and *d* describe each cash payment and how it is divided between interest and principal. Column *b* calculates the interest expense that accrues during each year at 8% of the beginning balance. Column *c* shows the portion of the payment applied to principal. It shows that each payment reduces the liability with a $10,000 debit to the Notes Payable account. Column *d* calculates each annual payment, which consists of the interest in column *b* plus $10,000. (Notice that the credit to the Cash account equals the debits to the expense and the liability account.) Finally, column *e* shows the ending balance of the liability, which equals the beginning balance in column *a* minus the principal portion of the payment in column *c*. Over the life of the note, the table shows that the total interest expense is $16,800 and the total reduction in principal is $60,000. Thus, the total cash payments are $76,800.

The graph in the lower section of Illustration 12–1 shows these three points: (1) the total payment gets smaller as the loan balance is reduced, (2) the amount of interest included in each payment gets steadily smaller, and (3) the amount of principal in each payment remains constant at $10,000.

The borrower's bookkeeper records the effects of the first two payments with these journal entries:

19X2				
Dec.	31	Interest Expense	4,800.00	
		Notes Payable	10,000.00	
		Cash		14,800.00
		To record first installment payment.		
19X3				
Dec.	31	Interest Expense	4,000.00	
		Notes Payable	10,000.00	
		Cash		14,000.00
		To record second installment payment.		

These entries accomplish these three results: The balance of the liability on the balance sheet is reduced by $10,000, each year's interest expense is reported on the income statement, and the cash balance on the balance sheet is reduced. After all six payments are recorded, the balance of the Notes Payable account for the note will be eliminated.

Installment Notes with Equal Payments

In contrast to the previous pattern, many installment note agreements require the borrower to make a series of equal payments. Notice that these payments actually consist of changing amounts of interest and principal. We demonstrate this result in Illustration 12–2 for our example. The $60,000 note requires the borrower to make a series of six equal payments of $12,979 at the

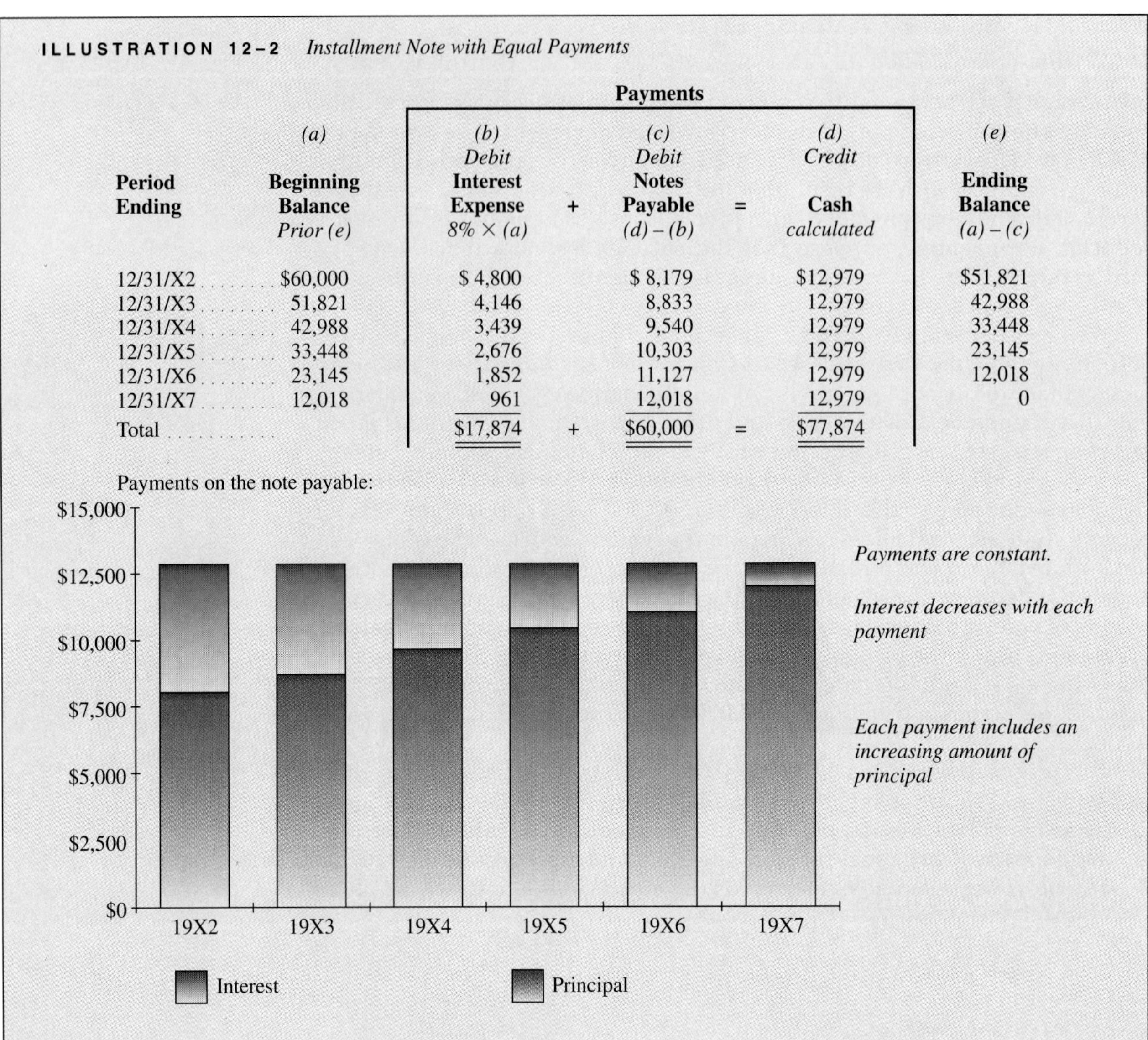

ILLUSTRATION 12–2 *Installment Note with Equal Payments*

Period Ending	(a) Beginning Balance *Prior (e)*	(b) Debit Interest Expense *8% × (a)*	+	(c) Debit Notes Payable *(d) – (b)*	=	(d) Credit Cash *calculated*	(e) Ending Balance *(a) – (c)*
		Payments					
12/31/X2	$60,000	$ 4,800		$ 8,179		$12,979	$51,821
12/31/X3	51,821	4,146		8,833		12,979	42,988
12/31/X4	42,988	3,439		9,540		12,979	33,448
12/31/X5	33,448	2,676		10,303		12,979	23,145
12/31/X6	23,145	1,852		11,127		12,979	12,018
12/31/X7	12,018	961		12,018		12,979	0
Total		$17,874	+	$60,000	=	$77,874	

end of each year. (The payments are this amount because $60,000 is the present value of an annuity of six annual payments of $12,979, discounted at 8%. We show you how to make this calculation later in this section.)

Allocating Each Payment between Interest and Principal. Each payment of $12,979 includes both interest and principal. Look at the table in Illustration 12–2 to see how an accountant allocates the total amount of each payment between interest and principal. The lower section of the illustration shows the same information in a graph.

The table is essentially the same as the table in Illustration 12–1. Again, column *a* shows the liability's beginning balance for each year. Column *b* presents the interest that will accrue each year at 8% of the beginning balance. Column *c* calculates the change in the principal of the liability caused by each payment. The debit to the liability account in this column is the difference between the total payment in column *d* and the interest expense in column *b*. Finally, column *e* presents the ending balance after each payment is made.

Even though all six payments are equal, the amount of interest decreases each year because the balance of the liability gets smaller. Then, because the amount of interest gets smaller, the amount of the payment applied to the principal gets larger. This effect is presented graphically in Illustration 12–2.

Because the tables in Illustration 12–1 and 12–2 show how the principal balance is reduced (or amortized) by the periodic payments, they are often referred to as *installment note amortization schedules.*[1]

The bookkeeper records the effects of the first two payments with these journal entries:

19X2				
Dec.	31	Interest Expense	4,800.00	
		Notes Payable	8,179.00	
		Cash		12,979.00
		To record first installment payment.		
19X3				
Dec.	31	Interest Expense	4,146.00	
		Notes Payable	8,833.00	
		Cash		12,979.00
		To record second installment payment.		

The amounts in these entries come from the table in Illustration 12–2. The borrower would record similar entries for each of the remaining payments. Over the six years, the Notes Payable account balance will be eliminated.

To be sure that you understand the differences between the two payment patterns, compare the numbers and graphs in Illustration 12–1 and Illustration 12–2. Notice that the series of equal payments leads to a greater amount of interest expense over the life of the note. This result occurs because the first three payments in Illustration 12–2 are smaller and thus do not reduce the principal as quickly as the first three payments in Illustration 12–1.

Calculating the Equal Periodic Payments on an Installment Note. In the previous example, we simply gave you the size of the equal annual payments on the installment note. Now, we show you how to calculate the size of the payment on your own.

Because this kind of note has a series of equal payments, you can calculate the size of each payment with a present value table for an annuity such as Table 12–2 on page 445.[2] To make the calculation with the table, start with this equation:

$$\text{Payment} \times \text{Annuity table value} = \text{Present value of the annuity}$$

Then, modify the equation to get this version:

$$\text{Payment} = \frac{\text{Present value of the annuity}}{\text{Annuity table value}}$$

Because the balance of an installment note equals the present value of the series of payments, the equation can again be modified to become this formula:

$$\text{Payment} = \frac{\text{Note balance}}{\text{Annuity table value}}$$

For this example, the initial note balance is $60,000. The annuity table value in the formula is based on the note's interest rate and the number of payments. The interest rate is 8% and there are six payments. Therefore, enter

---

[1] Many business calculators are preprogrammed to make these amortization calculations for annuities.

[2] This chapter provides present value tables that include additional interest rates and additional periods (or payments). You should use them to solve the exercises and problems at the end of the chapter.

Table 12–2 on the sixth row and go across to the 8% column, where you will find the value of 4.6229. These numbers can now be substituted into the formula to find the payment:

$$\text{Payment} = \frac{\$60{,}000}{4.6229} = \$12{,}979$$

This formula can be used for all installment notes that require equal periodic payments.[3]

Borrowing by Issuing Bonds

LO 2 Describe the various characteristics of different types of bonds and prepare entries to record bond issuances and retirements.

Companies often borrow money by issuing **bonds.**[4] Like notes payable, bonds involve written promises to pay interest at a stated annual rate and to pay the principal, which is also referred to as the **par value of the bonds.** Most bonds require that the borrower make semiannual interest payments and pay the par value of the bonds (also known as the *face amount*) at a specified future date called the *maturity date of the bonds.* The amount of interest that must be paid each year is determined by multiplying the par value of the bonds by the stated rate of interest established when the bonds were issued.

Differences between Notes Payable and Bonds

When a business borrows money by signing a note payable, the money is generally obtained from a single lender, such as a bank. In contrast, a group of bonds (often called a *bond issue*) typically consists of a large number of bonds, usually in denominations of $1,000, that are sold to many different lenders. After bonds are originally issued, they are often bought and sold by these investors. Thus, any particular bond may actually be owned by a number of people before it matures.

Although practice varies, the interest on most bonds is paid every six months. In contrast, interest on notes is usually paid monthly, quarterly, or annually.

Differences between Stocks and Bonds

The phrase *stocks and bonds* often appears on the financial pages of newspapers or comes up as a topic of conversation. Stocks and bonds are not the same things and you should understand the differences between them. A share of stock represents an ownership right in the corporation. For example, a person who owns 1,000 of a corporation's 10,000 outstanding shares controls one-tenth of the total stockholders' equity. On the other hand, if a person owns a $1,000, 11%, 20-year bond, the bondholder has a receivable from the issuer. The bond owner has the right to receive (1) 11% interest ($110) each year that the bond is outstanding and (2) $1,000 when the bond matures 20 years after its issue date. The issuing company is obligated to make these payments and thus has a liability to the bondholder.

Advantages of Issuing Bonds

Companies that issue bonds are usually trying to increase their rate of return on equity. For example, assume a company that has $1 million of equity is considering spending $500,000 to expand its capacity. Management predicts that the $500,000 will allow the company to earn an additional $125,000 of income before paying any interest. The managers are considering three possi-

[3] Business calculators also can be used to find the size of the payments.

[4] In addition, bonds are issued by nonprofit organizations, as well as the federal government and other governmental units, such as cities, states, and school districts. Although the examples in this chapter deal with business situations, all issuers use the same practices to account for their bonds.

ILLUSTRATION 12–3 *Financing with Bonds or Stock*

	Plan A Don't expand	Plan B Increase Equity	Plan C Issue Bonds
Income before interest	$ 100,000	$ 225,000	$ 225,000
Interest			(50,000)
Net income	$ 100,000	$ 225,000	$ 175,000
Equity.	$1,000,000	$1,500,000	$1,000,000
Return on equity	10.0%	15.0%	17.5%

ble plans: Under Plan A, the expansion will not occur. Under Plan B, the expansion will occur, and the needed funds will be obtained from the owners. Under Plan C, the company will sell $500,000 of bonds that pay 10% annual interest ($50,000). Illustration 12–3 shows how the plans would affect the company's net income, equity, and return on equity.

Analysis of the alternatives in the illustration shows that the owners will enjoy a greater rate of return and be better off if the expansion is made and if the funds are obtained by issuing the bonds. Even though the projected total income under Plan C would be smaller than Plan B's income, the rate of return on the equity would be larger because there would be less equity. This result occurs whenever the expected rate of return from the new assets is greater than the rate of interest on the bonds.

In addition, issuing bonds allows the current owner or owners of a business to remain in control of the company.

Characteristics of Bonds

Over the years, financial experts have created many different kinds of bonds with various characteristics. We describe some of the more common features of bonds in the following paragraphs.

Serial Bonds

Some companies issue several groups of bonds that mature at different dates. As a result, the bonds are repaid gradually over a number of years. Because these bonds mature in series, they are called **serial bonds.** For example, $1 million of serial bonds might mature at the rate of $100,000 each year from 6 to 15 years after the bonds were issued. There would be 10 groups (or series) of bonds of $100,000 each. One series would mature after six years, another after seven years, and another each successive year until the final series is repaid.

Sinking Fund Bonds

In contrast to serial bonds, **sinking fund bonds** all mature on the same date. To reduce some of the risk for owners, these bonds require the issuer to create a *sinking fund,* which is a separate pool of assets used only to retire the bonds at maturity. In effect, the issuer must start to set aside the cash to pay off the bonds long before they mature.

Convertible Bonds

Some companies issue **convertible bonds** that can be exchanged by the bondholders for a fixed number of shares of the issuing company's common stock. These bonds offer issuers the advantage that they might be settled without paying back the cash initially borrowed. Convertible bonds also offer the bondholders the potential to participate in future increases in the market value of the stock. However, if the stock does not appreciate, the bondholders continue to receive periodic interest and will receive the par value when the bond matures. In most cases, the bondholders can decide whether and when to convert the bonds to stock. However, the issuer can force conversion by exercising an option to buy the bonds back at a price less than the market value of the stock.

Registered Bonds and Bearer Bonds

A company that issues **registered bonds** keeps a record of the names and addresses of the bonds' owners. Then, over the life of the bonds, the company makes interest payments by sending checks to these registered owners. When one investor sells a bond to another investor, the issuer must be notified of the change. Registered bonds offer the issuer the practical advantage of not having to actually issue bond certificates to the investors. This arrangement also protects investors against loss or theft of the bonds.

Unregistered bonds are called **bearer bonds,** because they are payable to whoever holds them (called the *bearer*). Since there may be no record of sales or exchanges, the holder of a bearer bond is presumed to be its rightful owner. As a result, lost or stolen bonds are difficult to replace.

Many bearer bonds are also **coupon bonds.** This term reflects the fact that interest coupons are attached to each bond. Each coupon matures on a specific interest payment date. The owner detaches each coupon when it matures and presents it to a bank or broker for collection. At maturity, the owner follows the same process and presents the bond certificates to a bank or broker. Because there is no readily available record of who actually receives the interest, the income tax law was changed in 1982 to discourage companies from issuing any new coupon bonds.

Secured Bonds and Debentures

When bonds are secured, specific assets of the issuing company are pledged (or *mortgaged*) as collateral. This arrangement gives the bondholders additional protection against default by the issuer. If the issuing company fails to pay the interest or maturity value, the secured bondholders can demand that the collateral be sold and the proceeds used to repay the debt.

In contrast to secured bonds, unsecured bonds are potentially more risky because they are supported by only the issuer's general credit standing. Unsecured bonds also are called **debentures.** Because of the greater risk of default, a company generally must be financially strong to successfully issue debentures at a favorable rate of interest.

Bond Market Values

Bonds are securities and can be easily traded between investors. Because they are bought and sold in the market, they have a market value. As a matter of convenience, bond market values are expressed as a percentage of their face value. For example, a company's bonds might be trading at 103½, which means that they can be bought or sold for 103.5% of their face value. If other bonds are trading at 95, they can be bought or sold at 95% of their face value.

The Process of Issuing Bonds

When a company issues bonds, it normally sells them to an investment firm called an *underwriter.* In turn, the underwriter resells the bonds to the public. In some situations, the issuer may sell the bonds directly to investors as the cash is needed.

The legal document that identifies the rights and obligations of the bondholders and the issuer is called the **bond indenture.** In effect, the bond indenture is the legal contract between the issuer and the bondholders. Although the practice is less common today, each bondholder may receive an actual bond certificate as evidence of the company's debt. However, most companies reduce their costs by not issuing certificates to registered bondholders.

If the underwriter sells the bonds to a large number of investors, the bondholders' interests are represented and protected by a *trustee*. The trustee monitors the issuer's actions to ensure that it complies with the obligations in the bond indenture. Most trustees are large banks or trust companies.

Accounting for the Issuance of Bonds

Before bonds are issued, the terms of the indenture are drawn up and accepted by the trustee. If the bonds are to be offered to the general public by the underwriter, they must be registered with the Securities and Exchange Commission (SEC), which means that the issuer must provide extensive financial information in special reports. Then, if certificates are to be issued, they are printed and distributed to the bondholders.

For example, suppose that the Barnes Company receives authorization from the SEC to issue $800,000 of 9%, 20-year bonds dated January 1, 1995, that are due on December 31, 2014. They will pay interest semiannually on each June 30 and December 31. After the bond indenture is accepted by the trustee on behalf of the bondholders, all or a portion of the bonds may be sold to the underwriter. If all the bonds are sold at their par value, Barnes Company makes this entry to record the sale:

1995				
Jan.	1	Cash	800,000.00	
		Bonds Payable		800,000.00
		Sold bonds at par.		

This entry reflects the fact that the company's cash and long-term liabilities are increased.

Six months later, the first semiannual interest payment is made, and Barnes records the cash flow with this entry:

1995				
June	30	Interest Expense	36,000.00	
		Cash		36,000.00
		Paid semiannual interest on bonds (9% × $800,000 × ½).		

The entry records the decrease in cash and captures information about the expense to be reported on the company's income statement.

The bonds will mature 20 years later, and the Barnes Company will pay the maturity value to the bondholders at that time. This entry will be recorded for the payment:

2014				
Dec.	31	Bonds Payable	800,000.00	
		Cash		800,000.00
		Paid bonds at maturity.		

This entry will remove the liability from the accounts, and the debt will no longer appear on the company's balance sheet.

Selling Bonds between Interest Dates

Like the previous example, many bonds are sold on their original issue date. However, circumstances may cause a company to actually sell some of the bonds later. If so, it is likely that the selling date will fall between interest payment dates. When this happens, the purchasers normally make a payment to the issuer equal to any interest accrued since the issue date or the preceding interest payment date. This accrued interest is then refunded to the purchasers on the next interest date. For example, assume that the Fields Company sold $100,000 of its 9% bonds at par on March 1, 19X1, which was two months after the original issue date. The interest on the bonds is payable semiannually on each June 30 and December 31. Because two months have passed, the issuer collects two months' interest from the buyer at the time of the sale. This amount is $1,500 ($100,000 × 9% × 2/12). This situation is represented by the following diagram:

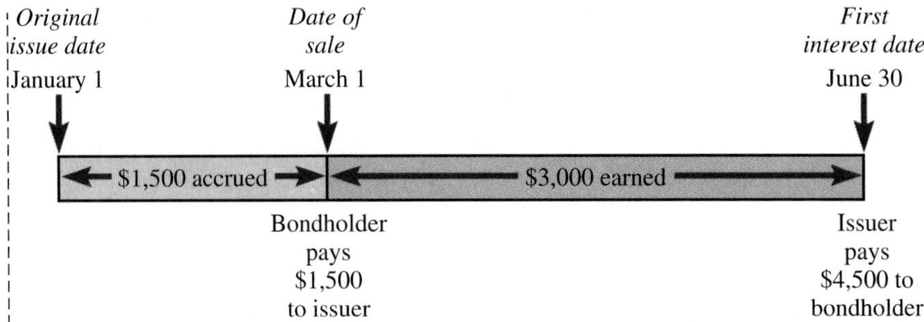

The issuer's entry to record the sale is

Mar.	1	Cash	101,500.00	
		Interest Payable		1,500.00
		Bonds Payable		100,000.00
		Sold $100,000 of bonds with two months' accrued interest.		

This entry records the fact that the transaction creates separate liabilities for $100,000 when the bond matures and $1,500 on the next interest payment date. Altogether, the company receives $101,500 in cash.

When the June 30 semiannual interest date arrives, the issuer pays a full six months' interest of $4,500 ($100,000 × 9% × ½) to the bondholder. This payment includes the four months' interest of $3,000 earned by the bondholder from March 1 to June 30 plus the refund of the two months' accrued interest collected by the issuer when the bonds were sold. The issuer's entry to record this first payment is

June	30	Interest Payable	1,500.00	
		Interest Expense	3,000.00	
		Cash		4,500.00
		Paid semiannual interest on the bonds.		

This entry records the expense and eliminates the payable to the bondholders for their earlier payment.

The practice of collecting and then refunding the accrued interest with the next interest payment may seem like a roundabout way to do business. However, this practice greatly simplifies the bond issuer's administrative efforts. To understand this point, suppose that company sells bonds to individual bondholders on 15 or 20 different dates between the original issue date and the first interest payment date. If the issuer did not collect the accrued interest from the buyers, it would have to pay different amounts of cash to each of them in accordance with how much time had passed since they purchased their bonds. To make the correct payments, the issuer would have to keep detailed records of the purchasers and the dates on which they bought their bonds. Issuers avoid this extra record-keeping by having each buyer pay in the accrued interest at the time of purchase. Then, the company simply pays a full six months' interest to all purchasers, regardless of when they bought the bonds.

Bond Interest Rates

The interest rate to be paid out by the issuer of bonds is specified in the indenture and on the bond certificates. Because it is stated in the indenture, this rate is called the **contract rate** of the bonds. (This rate also is known as the *coupon rate,* the *stated rate,* or the *nominal rate.*) The amount of interest to be paid each year is determined by multiplying the par value of the bonds by the contract rate. The contract rate is usually stated on an annual basis, even if the interest is to be paid semiannually. For example, suppose that a company issues a $1,000, 8% bond that pays interest semiannually. As a result, the annual interest of $80 (8% × $1,000) will be paid in two semiannual payments of $40 each.

Although the contract rate sets the amount of interest that the issuer pays in *cash,* the contract rate is not necessarily the rate of interest *expense* actually incurred by the issuer. In fact, the interest expense depends on the market value of the issuer's bonds, which, in turn, depends on the purchasers' opinions about the riskiness of lending to the issuer. This perceived risk (as well as the supply of and demand for bonds) is reflected in the **market rate** for bond interest. The market rate is the consensus rate that borrowers are willing to pay and that lenders are willing to earn at the level of risk inherent in the bonds. This rate changes often (even daily) in response to changes in the supply of and demand for bonds. The market rate tends to go up when the demand for bonds decreases or the supply increases. The rate tends to go down when the supply of bonds decreases or the demand increases.

Because many factors affect the bond market, various companies face different interest rates for their bonds. The market rate for a specific set of bonds depends on the level of risk investors assign to them. As the level of risk increases, the rate increases. Market rates also are affected by the length of the bonds' life. Specifically, longer-term bonds have higher rates because they are more risky.

Many bond issuers offer a contract rate of interest equal to the rate they expect the market to demand as of the bonds' issuance date. If the contract and market rates are equal, the bonds sell at their par value because this amount also equals their fair market value. However, if the contract and market rates are not equal, the bonds are not sold at their par value. Instead, they are sold at a *premium* above their par value or at a *discount* below their par value. They sell at a premium when the contract rate is greater than the market rate, and they sell at a discount when the contract rate is less than the market rate. We can depict the relationship between the interest rates and the bonds' value in this table:

When the contract rate is		The bond sells
Above the market rate	→	At a premium
At the market rate	→	At par value
Below the market rate	→	At a discount

Over the last two decades, some companies have issued *zero-coupon bonds* that do not provide any periodic interest payments. Because this contract rate of 0% is always below the market rate, these bonds are always issued at prices less than their face values.

Bonds Sold at a Discount

LO 3 Estimate the price of bonds issued at a discount and describe their effects on the issuer's financial statements.

As we described in the prior section, a **discount on bonds payable** arises when a company issues bonds with a contract rate below the market rate. Because the market adjusts the price downward below the par value, the bondholders receive the market rate of interest consistent with the level of risk. The expected market price of the bonds can be found by calculating the *present value* of the expected cash flows. This process involves using the current market interest rate to find the present value of the cash flows from the bond.

To illustrate how expected bond prices can be calculated, assume that a company offers to issue bonds with a $100,000 par value, an 8% annual contract rate, and a five-year life. Also assume that the market rate of interest for this company's bonds is 10%.[5] In exchange for the purchase price received from the buyers, these bonds obligate the issuer to pay out two different future cash flows:

1. $100,000 at the end of the bonds' five-year life.
2. $4,000 (4% × $100,000) at the end of each six-month interest period throughout the five-year life of the bonds.

In turn, the buyers have the right to receive these amounts.

To estimate the bonds' issue price, use the market rate of interest to calculate the present value of the future cash flows to be paid (or received). To use the annuity table of present values, you must work with *semiannual* compounding periods. Thus, the annual market rate of 10% is changed to the semiannual rate of 5%. Likewise, the five-year life of the bonds is changed to 10 semiannual periods.

The actual calculation requires two steps: First, you find the present value of the $100,000 maturity payment. Second, you find the present value of the annuity of 10 payments of $4,000 each.

The present values can be found by using Table 12–1 (on page 445) for the single maturity payment and Table 12–2 for the annuity. To complete the first step, enter Table 12–1 on row 10 and go across until you reach the 5% column. The table value is 0.6139. Second, enter Table 12–2 on row 10 and go across until you reach the 5% column, where the table value is 7.7217. Finally, use these table values to reduce the future cash flows to their present value. This schedule shows the results when you multiply the cash flow amounts by the table values and add them together:

Cash Flow	Table	Table Value	Amount	Present Value
Par value	12–1	0.6139	$100,000	$61,390
Interest (annuity)	12–2	7.7217	4,000	30,887
Total.				$92,277

If 5% is the appropriate interest rate for the bonds in the current market, the maximum price that informed buyers would offer for the bonds is $92,277. This amount is also the minimum price that the issuer would accept.

If the issuer does accept $92,277 cash for its bonds on the original issue date of December 31, 19X1, the accountant records the event with this entry:

[5] The spread between the contract rate and the market rate of interest on a new bond issue is seldom more than a fraction of a percent. However, we use a difference of 2% here to emphasize the effects.

19X1				
Dec.	31	Cash	92,277.00	
		Discount on Bonds Payable	7,723.00	
		Bonds Payable		100,000.00
		Sold bonds at a discount on the original issue date.		

The account for the Discount on Bonds Payable is *contra* to the liability account for Bonds Payable. This entry will cause the bonds to appear in the long-term liability section of the issuer's balance sheet as follows:

Long-term liabilities:		
Bonds payable, 8%, due December 31, 19X6	$100,000	
Less discount	7,723	$92,277

This presentation shows that the discount is deducted from the par value of the bonds to produce the **carrying amount** of the bonds payable. As we saw in the last chapter for notes payable, the carrying amount is the net amount at which the bonds are reflected on the balance sheet.

Allocating Interest and Amortizing the Discount

In the previous example, the issuer received $92,277 for its bonds and will pay the bondholders $100,000 after five years have passed. Because the $7,723 discount is eventually paid to the bondholders at maturity, it is part of the cost of using the $92,277 for five years. This table shows that the total interest cost of $47,723 is the difference between the amount repaid and the amount borrowed:

Amount repaid:	
Ten payments of $4,000	$ 40,000
Maturity amount	100,000
Total repaid	$140,000
Less amount borrowed	(92,277)
Total interest expense	$ 47,723

This calculation verifies that the total expense also equals the sum of the 10 cash payments and the discount:

Ten payments of $4,000	$40,000
Plus discount	7,723
Total interest expense	$47,723

In describing these bonds and the interest expense, the issuer's accountant must accomplish two things: First, the total interest expense of $47,723 must be allocated among the 10 six-month periods in the bonds' life. Second, the carrying value of the bonds must be updated for each balance sheet. Two alternative methods accomplish these objectives. They are the straight-line and the interest method of allocating interest.

Straight-Line Method. The **straight-line method** of allocating the interest is the simpler of the two methods. This method allocates an equal portion of the total interest expense to each of the six-month interest periods. Because the process involves reducing the original discount on the bonds over the life of the bonds, it is also called *amortizing the bond discount.*

In applying the straight-line method to the present example, the accountant would divide the five years' total expense of $47,723 by 10 (the number of semiannual periods in the bonds' life). The result is $4,772 per period.[6] The same number can be found by dividing the $7,723 original discount by 10. That result is $772, which is the amount of discount to be amortized in each interest period. When the $772 of amortized discount is added to the $4,000 cash payment, the total interest expense for each six-month period is $4,772.

When the semiannual cash payment is made, the issuer uses the following entry to record the interest expense and update the balance of the bond liability:

19X2				
June	30	Interest Expense	4,772.00	
		Discount on Bonds Payable		772.00
		Cash		4,000.00
		To record six months' interest and discount amortization.		

The debit in this entry records the $4,772 interest expense for the six-month period. The credit to cash records the amount actually paid out to the bondholders. The $772 credit to the Discount account actually *increases* the bonds' carrying value. The increase comes about by *decreasing* the balance of the contra account that is subtracted from the Bonds Payable account.

Illustration 12–4 presents a table similar to the amortization tables that you have studied for notes payable. It shows how the interest expense is allocated among the 10 six-month periods in the bonds' life. It also shows how amortizing the bond discount causes the balance of the net liability to increase until it reaches $100,000 at the end of the bonds' life. Notice the following points as you analyze Illustration 12–4:

1. The $92,277 beginning balance in column *a* equals the cash received from selling the bonds. It also equals the $100,000 face amount of the bonds less the initial $7,723 discount from selling the bonds below par.
2. The semiannual interest expense of $4,772 in column *b* for each row equals the amount obtained by dividing the total expense of $47,723 by 10.
3. The credit to the Discount on Bonds Payable account in column *c* equals one-tenth of the total discount of $7,723.
4. The $4,000 interest payment in column *d* is the result of multiplying the $100,000 par value of the bonds by the 4% semiannual contract rate of interest.
5. The ending balance in column *e* equals the beginning balance in column *a* plus the $772 discount amortization in column *c*. This ending balance then becomes the beginning balance on the next row in the table.
6. The balance in column *e* continues to grow each period by the $772 of discount amortization until it finally equals the par value of the bonds when they mature.

The three payment columns show that the company incurs a $4,772 interest expense each period, but pays only $4,000. The $772 unpaid portion of the expense is appropriately added to the balance of the liability. It is added to the liability by being taken from the contra account balance. This table shows you

[6] For simplicity, all calculations have been rounded to the nearest whole dollar. Use the same practice when solving the exercises and problems at the end of the chapter.

ILLUSTRATION 12-4 *Allocating Interest Expense and Amortizing the Bond Discount with the Straight-Line Method*

		Payments					
	(a)	*(b)* *Debit*		*(c)* *Credit*		*(d)* *Credit*	*(e)*
Period Ending	**Beginning Balance**	**Interest Expense**	=	**Discount on Bonds**	+	**Cash**	**Ending Balance**
	Prior (e)	*$47,723/10*		*$7,723/10*		*4% × $100,000*	*(a) + (c)*
6/30/X2	$92,277	$ 4,772		$ 772		$ 4,000	$ 93,049
12/31/X2	93,049	4,772		772		4,000	93,821
6/30/X3	93,821	4,772		772		4,000	94,593
12/31/X3	94,593	4,772		772		4,000	95,365
6/30/X4	95,365	4,772		772		4,000	96,137
12/31/X4	96,137	4,772		772		4,000	96,909
6/30/X5	96,909	4,772		772		4,000	97,681
12/31/X5	97,681	4,772		772		4,000	98,453
6/30/X6	98,453	4,772		772		4,000	99,225
12/31/X6	99,225	4,775*		775*		4,000	100,000
Total		$47,723	=	$7,723	+	$40,000	

* Adjusted for rounding.

how the balance of the discount is partially amortized every six months until it is eliminated:

Period Ending	**Beginning Discount Balance**	**Amount Amortized**	**Ending Discount Balance**
6/30/X2	$7,723	$ (772)	$6,951
12/31/X2	6,951	(772)	6,179
6/30/X3	6,179	(772)	5,407
12/31/X3	5,407	(772)	4,635
6/30/X4	4,635	(772)	3,863
12/31/X4	3,863	(772)	3,091
6/30/X5	3,091	(772)	2,319
12/31/X5	2,319	(772)	1,547
6/30/X6	1,547	(772)	775
12/31/X6	775	(775)	-0-
Total		$(7,723)	

Interest Method. Straight-line allocations of interest used to be widely applied in practice. However, generally accepted accounting principles now allow the straight-line method to be used only if the results do not differ materially from those obtained by using the **interest method** to allocate the interest over the life of the bonds.[7] This process is often called the *interest method of amortizing the bond discount* because it gradually reduces the discount down to zero over the life of the bonds.

The interest method is exactly the same process for allocating interest that you learned in Chapter 11 for notes payable. It is also the same approach that you have seen for installment notes. Specifically, the period's interest expense is found by multiplying the beginning balance of the liability by the original market interest rate.

[7] FASB, *Accounting Standards—Current Text* (Norwalk, CT, 1994), sec. I69.108. First published in *APB Opinion No. 21,* par. 15.

ILLUSTRATION 12–5 *Allocating Interest Expense and Amortizing the Bond Discount with the Interest Method*

		Payments			
	(a)	(b) Debit	(c) Credit	(d) Credit	(e)
Period Ending	**Beginning Balance**	**Interest Expense** =	**Discount on Bonds** +	**Cash**	**Ending Balance**
	Prior (e)	*5% × (a)*	*(b) − (d)*	*4% × $100,000*	*(a) + (c)*
6/30/X2	$92,277	$ 4,614	$ 614	$ 4,000	$ 92,891
12/31/X2	92,891	4,645	645	4,000	93,536
6/30/X3	93,536	4,677	677	4,000	94,213
12/31/X3	94,213	4,711	711	4,000	94,924
6/30/X4	94,924	4,746	746	4,000	95,670
12/31/X4	95,670	4,784	784	4,000	96,454
6/30/X5	96,454	4,823	823	4,000	97,277
12/31/X5	97,277	4,864	864	4,000	98,141
6/30/X6	98,141	4,907	907	4,000	99,048
12/31/X6	99,048	4,952	952	4,000	100,000
Total		$47,723 =	$7,723 +	$40,000	

In Illustration 12–5, we present an amortization table for our example. The key difference between Illustrations 12–4 and 12–5 lies in the calculation of the interest expense in column *b*. Instead of assigning an equal amount of interest to each interest period, the interest method assigns an increasing amount of interest over the bonds' life because the balance of the liability is getting bigger over the five years. The interest expense in column *b* equals the original 5% market interest rate times the beginning balance of the liability. Notice that both methods allocate the same $47,723 of total expense among the five years, but with different patterns.

The amount of discount amortized in any period is the difference between the interest expense in column *b* and the cash payment in column *d*. In effect, the accrued but unpaid portion of the interest expense in column *c* is added to the net liability in column *a* to get the ending balance in column *e*.

In the following table, you can see how the balance of the discount is amortized by the interest method until it reaches zero:

Period Ending	Beginning Discount Balance	Amount Amortized	Ending Discount Balance
6/30/X2	$7,723	$ (614)	$7,109
12/31/X2	7,109	(645)	6,464
6/30/X3	6,464	(677)	5,787
12/31/X3	5,787	(711)	5,076
6/30/X4	5,076	(746)	4,330
12/31/X4	4,330	(784)	3,546
6/30/X5	3,546	(823)	2,723
12/31/X5	2,723	(864)	1,859
6/30/X6	1,859	(907)	952
12/31/X6	952	(952)	–0–
Total		$(7,723)	

When the interest method is used to allocate interest, the journal entries that record the expense and update the liability balance are the same as the entries made under the straight-line method, except for the differences in the amounts. For example, the entry to record the interest payment at the end of the first interest period is

ILLUSTRATION 12–6 *Comparing the Straight-Line and Interest Methods of Allocating Interest on a Bond Sold at a Discount*

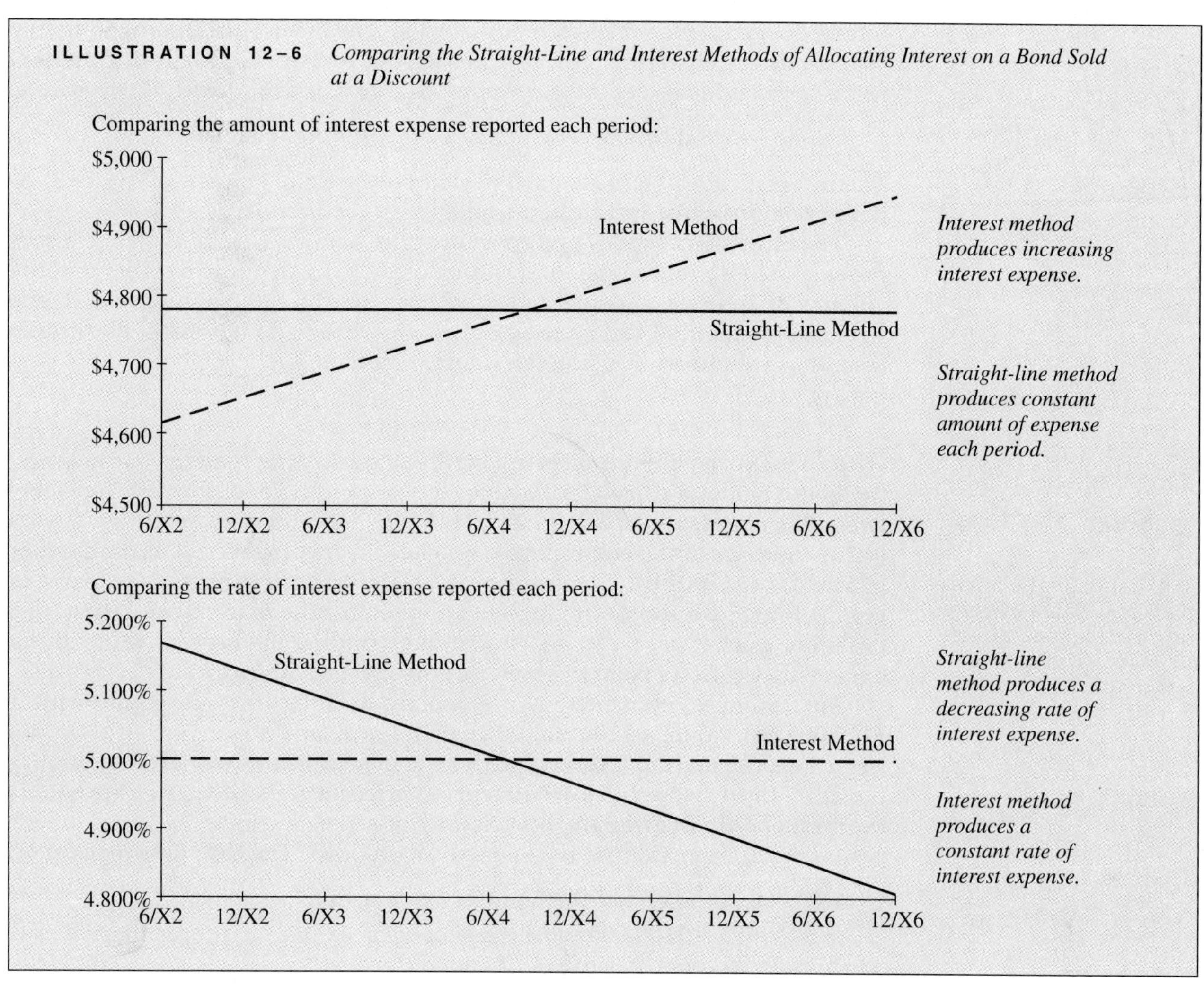

19X2				
June	30	Interest Expense	4,614.00	
		Discount on Bonds Payable		614.00
		Cash		4,000.00
		To record six months' interest and discount amortization.		

The accountant uses the numbers in Illustration 12–5 to make similar entries throughout the five-year life of the bonds.

Comparing the Straight-Line and Interest Methods. With this background in place, we can now look more closely at the differences between the straight-line and interest methods of allocating interest among the periods in the bonds' life. In Illustration 12–6, the two graphs illustrate the differences for bonds issued at a discount.

The horizontal solid line in the first graph in Illustration 12–6 represents the amounts of interest expense reported each period under straight-line. The upward sloping dashed line represents the increasing amounts of interest reported under the interest method. The amounts increase because the constant 5% rate is applied to the growing balance of the liability.

The horizontal dashed line in the second graph in Illustration 12–6 represents the constant rate of 5% that the interest method uses to determine the interest expense for every six-month period. The downward sloping solid line represents the changing interest rates produced by the straight-line method when the bond is issued at a discount. The rate is found with this formula:

Rate = Interest expense/Beginning balance

The interest rates decrease each period because the amount of interest expense remains constant while the balance of the liability is growing.

The interest method is preferred over the straight-line method because it provides a more reasonable description of the growth of the liability and the amount of interest expense incurred each period. As we mentioned, the straight-line method can be used only if the results do not differ materially from those obtained by using the interest method.

Bonds Sold at a Premium

LO 4 Estimate the price of bonds issued at a premium and describe their effects on the issuer's financial statements.

When bonds carry a contract interest rate that is *greater* than the market rate, the bonds sell at a price greater than the par value. If so, the difference between the par and the market values is called the **premium.** In effect, buyers bid up the price of the bonds until it reaches the level that creates the current market rate of interest. In other words, the buyers are willing to pay extra to get the higher contract rate. As we explained for the discount situation, this premium market price can be estimated by finding the present value of the expected cash flows from the bonds at the market interest rate.

For example, assume that a company decides to issue bonds with a $100,000 par value, a 12% annual contract rate, and a five-year life. On the issue date, the market interest rate for the bonds is only 10%. Thus, potential buyers of these bonds bid up their market price until the effective rate equals the market rate. To estimate this price, we use the 5% semiannual market rate to find the present value of the expected cash flows. The cash flows consist of:

1. $100,000 at the end of the bonds' five-year life.
2. $6,000 (6% × $100,000) at the end of each six-month interest period through the five-year life of the bonds.

As we saw before, the actual calculation requires two steps: First, we need to find the present value of the $100,000 maturity payment. Second, we need to find the present value of the annuity of 10 payments of $6,000 each.

The present values can be found by using Table 12–1 (page 445) for the single maturity payment and Table 12–2 for the annuity. To complete the first step, enter Table 12–1 on row 10 and go across until you reach the 5% column. The table value is 0.6139. Second, enter Table 12–2 on row 10 and go across until you reach the 5% column, where the table value is 7.7217. Finally, use these table values to reduce the future cash flows to their present value. This schedule shows the results when you multiply the cash flow amounts by the table values and add them together:

Cash Flow	Table	Table Value	Amount	Present Value
Par value	12–1	0.6139	$100,000	$ 61,390
Interest (annuity)	12–2	7.7217	6,000	46,330
Total.				$107,720

If 5% is the appropriate interest rate for the bonds in the current market, the maximum price that informed buyers would offer for the bonds is $107,720. This amount is also the minimum price that the issuer would accept.

If the issuer does accept $107,720 cash for its bonds on the original issue date of December 31, 19X1, the accountant records the event with this entry:

19X1				
Dec.	31	Cash	107,720.00	
		Premium on Bonds Payable		7,720.00
		Bonds Payable		100,000.00
		Sold bonds at a premium on the original issue date.		

The account for the Premium on Bonds Payable is supplemental to the liability account for Bonds Payable. This entry causes the bonds to appear in the long-term liability section of the issuer's balance sheet as follows:

Long-term liabilities:		
Bonds payable, 8%, due December 31, 19X6	$100,000	
Plus premium	7,720	$107,720

This presentation shows that the premium is added to the par value of the bonds to produce their carrying amount.

Allocating Interest Expense and Amortizing the Premium

Over the life of these premium bonds, the issuer pays back $160,000, which consists of the 10 periodic interest payments of $6,000 plus the $100,000 par value. Because it borrowed $107,720, the total interest expense will be $52,280. This table shows the calculation:

Amount repaid:	
Ten payments of $6,000	$ 60,000
Maturity amount	100,000
Total repaid	$160,000
Less amount borrowed	(107,720)
Total interest expense	$ 52,280

The following calculation confirms that the total expense also equals the difference between the 10 cash payments and the premium:

Ten payments of $6,000	$60,000
Less premium	(7,720)
Total interest expense	$52,280

The premium is subtracted because it will not be paid to the bondholders when the bonds mature.

This total interest expense can be allocated over the 10 semiannual periods with either the straight-line or the interest method. Because the interest method is preferred, it is the only one illustrated for these bonds. Illustration 12–7 shows an amortization schedule for the bonds using this method.

Again, column *a* of the illustration shows the beginning balance, and column *b* shows the amount of expense at 5% of the beginning balance. But, the amount of cash paid out in column *d* is larger than the expense because the payment is based on the higher 6% contract rate. As a result, the excess payment over the expense reduces the principal. These amounts are shown in column *c*. Thus, the two debits in the payment columns equal the one credit. Finally, column *e* shows the new ending balance after the amortized premium in column *c* is deducted from the beginning balance in column *a*.

ILLUSTRATION 12-7 *Allocating Interest Expense and Amortizing the Bond Premium with the Interest Method*

Period Ending	(a) Beginning Balance	(b) Debit Interest Expense	+	(c) Debit Premium on Bonds	=	(d) Credit Cash	(e) Ending Balance
		Payments					
	Prior (e)	*5% × (a)*		*(d) − (b)*		*6% × $100,000*	*(a) − (c)*
6/30/X2	$107,720	$ 5,386		$ 614		$ 6,000	$107,106
12/31/X2	107,106	5,355		645		6,000	106,461
6/30/X3	106,461	5,323		677		6,000	105,784
12/31/X3	105,784	5,289		711		6,000	105,073
6/30/X4	105,073	5,254		746		6,000	104,327
12/31/X4	104,327	5,216		784		6,000	103,543
6/30/X5	103,543	5,177		823		6,000	102,720
12/31/X5	102,720	5,136		864		6,000	101,856
6/30/X6	101,856	5,093		907		6,000	100,949
12/31/X6	100,949	5,051*		949		6,000	100,000
Total		$52,280	+	$7,720	=	$60,000	

* Adjusted for rounding.

The following table shows how the premium is reduced by the amortization process over the life of the bonds:

Period Ending	Beginning Premium Balance	Amount Amortized	Ending Premium Balance
6/30/X2	$7,720	$ (614)	$7,106
12/31/X2	7,106	(645)	6,461
6/30/X3	6,461	(677)	5,784
12/31/X3	5,784	(711)	5,073
6/30/X4	5,073	(746)	4,327
12/31/X4	4,327	(784)	3,543
6/30/X5	3,543	(823)	2,720
12/31/X5	2,720	(864)	1,856
6/30/X6	1,856	(907)	949
12/31/X6	949	(949)	–0–
Total		$(7,720)	

The effect of premium amortization on interest expanse and the balance of the liability can be seen in this journal entry that would be recorded on June 30, 19X2, when the issuer makes the first semiannual interest payment:

19X2				
June	30	Interest Expense	5,386.00	
		Premium on Bonds Payable	614.00	
		Cash		6,000.00
		To record six months' interest and premium amortization.		

The *debit* to the Premium on Bonds Payable account shows that the company has reduced its total liability. The amount of the reduction is the $614 excess of the $6,000 credit to cash over the $5,386 debit to the Interest Expense account.

Similar entries are recorded at each payment date until the bonds mature at the end of 19X6. However, the interest method causes the company to report decreasing amounts of interest expense and increasing amounts of premium amortization.

Accounting for Accrued Interest Expense

If a bond's interest period does not coincide with the issuing company's accounting period, the financial statements would be incomplete if the accountant did not record an adjusting entry to recognize the interest expense that has accrued since the most recent interest payment. For example, assume that the bonds described in Illustration 12–7 were issued on September 1, 19X1, instead of December 31, 19X1. As a result, four months' of interest (and premium amortization) will have accrued at the end of the 19X1 calendar year. Because the reporting period ends on that date, an adjusting entry is needed to capture this information about the bonds for the financial statements. Specifically, the four months' interest equals $3,591, which is 4/6 of the first six months' interest of $5,386. The premium amortization is $409, which is 4/6 of the first six months' amortization of $614. The sum of the interest expense and the amortization is $4,000 ($3,591 + $409), which also equals 4/6 of the $6,000 cash payment that is due on March 1, 19X2. The accountant would record these effects with this adjusting entry:

19X1				
Dec.	31	Interest Expense	3,591.00	
		Premium on Bonds Payable	409.00	
		Interest Payable		4,000.00
		To record four months' accrued interest and premium amortization.		

Similar entries will be made on each December 31 throughout the five-year life of the bonds.

When the $6,000 cash payment occurs on the next interest date, the journal entry recognizes the interest expense and amortization for the intervening two months (January and February of 19X2) and eliminates the Interest Payable liability created by the adjusting entry. For this example, the accountant would make the following entry to record the payment on March 1, 19X2:

19X2				
Mar.	1	Interest Payable	4,000.00	
		Interest Expense ($5,386 × 2/6)	1,795.00	
		Premium on Bonds Payable ($614 × 2/6)	205.00	
		Cash		6,000.00
		To record two months' interest and amortization and eliminate the accrued interest liability.		

The interest payments made each September are recorded normally because the entire six-month interest period is included within a single fiscal year.

Retiring Bonds Payable

Many bond indentures give the issuing company an option to retire the bonds prior to maturity. Most options allow the issuer to *call* the bonds before they mature by paying the par value plus a *call premium* to the bondholders. If this option exists, the company is said to have issued **callable bonds.** Companies include call provisions in their bond agreements to allow them to eliminate

LO 2 Describe the various characteristics of different types of bonds and prepare entries to record bond issuances and retirements.

the debt if market interest rates decline significantly. The call provision makes it easier for a company to replace the older high-interest bonds with new bonds that have a lower rate. Even if a specific set of bonds is not callable, the issuer may be able to achieve a similar savings by issuing low interest bonds and using the proceeds to buy the older bonds on the open market.

Whenever bonds are called or repurchased, the issuer is unlikely to pay a price that equals the bonds' carrying value. This condition arises because a bond's market value changes when the market interest rate changes. Therefore, a decision to retire bonds may result in reporting a gain or loss equal to the difference between the bonds' carrying value and the amount paid for them.[8]

For example, assume that a company previously issued bonds with a par value of $100,000. Their carrying value is $104,000 immediately after the June 30 interest payment date. The market interest rate has increased since the bonds were issued, and they are currently trading in the market at the quoted price of 98½ (98.5% of par value). If the issuer buys and retires all of the outstanding bonds at this price, it recognizes a $5,500 gain for the difference between the bonds' carrying value of $104,000 and the retirement price of $98,500. The information is recorded in the accounting system with this entry:

July	1	Bonds Payable	100,000.00	
		Premium on Bonds Payable	4,000.00	
		Gain on Retirement of Bonds		5,500.00
		Cash		98,500.00
		To record the retirement of bonds.		

Although a company generally must call all of its bonds when it exercises a call option, it may retire as many or as few bonds as it desires through open market transactions. If it retires less than the entire set of bonds, it recognizes a gain or loss for the difference between the carrying value of those bonds and the amount paid to acquire them.

Be sure to read "As a Matter of Fact" on the next page; it describes how call options can affect bondholders. It also includes a brief description of zero-coupon bonds.

Mortgages as Security for Notes Payable and Bonds

Earlier in this chapter, we said that some bonds are secured by collateral agreements, while others, called *debentures,* are not secured. These risk-reducing arrangements are also widely used for notes payable, including car and home loans. Unsecured bonds and notes are more risky because the issuer's obligation to pay interest and principal has the same low priority as all other unsecured liabilities in the event of bankruptcy. If the company's financial troubles leave it unable to pay its debts in full, the unsecured creditors (including the holders of debentures) lose a proportion or all of their balances.

Thus, a company's ability to borrow money with or without collateral agreements depends on its credit rating. In many cases, debt financing is simply unavailable if the borrower cannot provide security to the creditors with a collateral agreement. Even if unsecured loans are available, the creditors are

[8] Any material gain or loss from retiring bonds or other debt is considered to be *extraordinary* and is reported separately on the debtor's income statement. FASB, *Accounting Standards—Current Text* (Norwalk, CT, 1994), sec. D14.104. First published in *FASB Statement of Financial Accounting Standards No. 4,* par. 8.

AS A MATTER OF

Fact

Wall Street Awaits Refinancing Boom as Interest Rates Show Sharp Decline

When does a 30-year bond turn into a 10-year bond or even a 5-year bond? When the bond is "called," or redeemed before its maturity. That's happening more and more, as states, municipalities, and corporations take advantage of low interest rates to refinance huge amounts of long-term debt. And it's bad news for bond investors.

At best, a call means that people who bought bonds for their retirement or their kids' college education will get their money back and be forced to reinvest the funds at a lower rate. "Nobody wants to see a bond yielding 10% called and receive principal back when bonds are yielding 6.5%," says Jeffrey Kratz, head of investor relations at John Nuveen & Co. in Chicago.

But people who bought high-yielding bonds at a premium—paying more than face value to get a higher yield investment—fare even worse. In addition to the lost investment opportunity, they actually lose money. That's because the bonds are typically called at par, costing investors the premium. "The easiest way to get killed is if you paid a premium," says Herbert Davidson, vice president of fixed income at Financial Management Group Inc. in McLean, Va.

Holders of zero-coupon bonds are another group getting badly hurt by calls. These bonds sell at a deep discount, with the price rising as the bond gets closer to maturity. But when a zero is called, its value is still discounted and "the yields you hoped to earn turn out to be illusory," says Mr. Davidson.

A bond issuer usually retains the right to call the bond, albeit at a premium, after 10 years. The bond can usually be called at par a few years later. There are other sorts of calls, as well. Housing bonds, for example, are usually written with "extraordinary redemption features," meaning they can be redeemed at any time for a very wide range of reasons.

When shopping for new bonds, investors should be aware that call protection isn't what it used to be. With lower interest rates and heavy demand for bonds, "issuers can get away with shorter call features," says James F. Lynch, editor of the Lynch Municipal Bond Advisory in Santa Fe, NM. That means that the first call date on a bond may be only 7 or 8 years from issue, rather than the traditional 10 years. Some bonds can be called even sooner—with housing bonds, it can be as early as 12 to 36 months from issue.

And remember, while brokers may quote you an attractive yield to maturity, the only meaningful figure in today's market is yield to first call. Use that figure when making your investments, and you're less likely to be surprised.

Source: Lynn Asinof, "Bond Calls Leave Investors Hung Up," *The Wall Street Journal,* October 3, 1991, pp. C1, C18. Reprinted by permission of *The Wall Street Journal,* © Dow Jones & Company, Inc. 1991.

likely to charge a much higher rate of interest to compensate for the additional risk. To borrow the funds at a more economical rate, many notes payable and bonds are secured by collateral agreements called *mortgages.*

A **mortgage** is a legal agreement that helps protect a lender if a borrower fails to make the required payments on a note payable or on bonds payable. A mortgage gives the lender the right to be paid out of the cash proceeds from the sale of the borrower's specific assets identified in the mortgage.

A separate legal document, call the *mortgage contract,* describes the terms of a mortgage. The mortgage contract is given to the lender who accepts a note payable or to the trustee for the bondholders. Mortgage contracts usually require a borrower to pay all property taxes on the mortgaged assets, to maintain it properly, and to carry adequate insurance against fire and other types of losses. These requirements are designed to keep the property from losing value and thus avoid diminishing the lender's security. Importantly, mortgage contracts grant the lender the right to *foreclose* on the property if the borrower fails to pay in accordance with the terms of the debt agreement. If a foreclosure occurs, a court either orders the property to be sold or simply grants legal title of the mortgaged property to the lender. If the property is sold, the proceeds are first applied to court costs and then to the claims of the mortgage holder. If there are any additional proceeds, the borrower is entitled to receive them. However, this cash is subject to any claims from the company's unsecured creditors.

Given the relevance of information about a company's collateral agreements, the footnotes to the financial statements may describe the amounts of assets pledged as security against liabilities. A later section in the chapter describes two ratios that can be used to assess a borrower's situation with respect to its security agreements.

Investments in Bonds

LO 5 Describe how investments in bonds are presented in the investor's financial statements.

So far in this chapter, the discussion of bonds has focused on their effects on the issuer and its financial statements. At this point, we shift our attention to the purchasers of bonds.

Bonds purchased as an investment are recorded in the accounts at their cost, including any broker's fees. If necessary, the purchaser also pays the seller (either the original issuer or another investor) any interest that has accrued since the previous interest payment date. This portion of the payment is recorded with a debit to the Interest Receivable asset account.

For example, suppose that a company purchases bonds from another investor with a par value of $50,000. They were issued by the Fox Company, pay 9% interest, and mature after 10 years. The purchase occurs on May 1, 19X1, which is four months after their most recent interest payment date. The accrued interest on May 1 is $1,500 ($50,000 × 9% × 4/12). The purchase price is 92 and the investor pays an additional $400 for broker's fees. The transaction is recorded with this journal entry:

19X1				
May	1	Investment in Fox Company Bonds	46,400.00	
		Interest Receivable	1,500.00	
		Cash		47,900.00
		Purchased bonds, including broker's fee and accrued interest.		

The $46,400 recorded cost of the bonds equals the sum of their market value of $46,000 (92% × $50,000 par value) plus the $400 broker's fee. When the next interest payment is received, the investor recognizes interest income of only $750, which is the amount earned in May and June ($50,000 × 9% × 2/12).

Bond investors generally do not record a discount or a premium in a separate contra or supplemental account. Instead, the investment account is initially debited for the net cost. Subsequent to the purchase, the accounting practices used by the investor depend on whether the bond investment is classified as short-term or long-term.

Short-Term Investments in Bonds

If the investment in bonds is purchased with the intent of selling it within the next year (or longer operating cycle), it is classified as short-term. If so, the only income received from the investment is the cash interest paid by the bond issuer plus any change in market value between the purchase and the sale of the investment. Thus, interest income is recorded without including any amortization of a discount or premium. To continue the example of the investment in the Fox Company bonds, the investor would receive a cash payment of $2,250 on June 30, 19X1 (9% × $50,000 × 1/2). Remember that the investor paid the previous owner $1,500 for the interest accrued as of the purchase date. Therefore, only the $750 difference is considered to be income. These facts are captured for the financial statements with this journal entry on June 30, 19X1:

19X1				
June	30	Cash	2,250.00	
		Interest Receivable		1,500.00
		Interest Earned		750.00
		To record the first semiannual receipt of interest.		

Recall from Chapter 7, if a balance sheet is prepared while the investor still owns these bonds, the FASB's *Statement of Financial Accounting Standards Number 115* requires the financial statements to reflect any change in their market value. This departure from the *cost principle* is justified by the need to provide more complete information about the investor's assets.

The market value as of the reporting date is presented on the balance sheet. For example, if the Fox Company bonds increased in value to $49,000 at the end of the fiscal year, they would be reported on the investor's balance sheet at that amount. The method used to report the gain on the market value change depends on whether the investment is classified as a trading security or as a security available for sale.

Long-Term Investments in Bonds

If an investment in bonds is to be held for the long term (more than one year or a longer operating cycle), it is a different kind of asset than a short-term investment. In these circumstances, it is likely that the investor has purchased the bonds primarily for the interest income with little regard for possible changes in their market value.

This presumption leads to two accounting practices: First, periodic interest income from the investment includes the effects of amortizing the premium or discount. This practice causes the carrying value of the bonds to move toward maturity value over their life. The procedures for amortizing a discount or premium on bond investments are the same as those used for the issuer, but with opposite effects. For example, amortizing the discount increases interest revenue instead of increasing interest expense.

Second, as discussed in Chapter 10, *FASB Statement No. 115* allows changes in the market value of bond investments to be ignored if the investor has the intent and ability to hold them to maturity. When bonds are held for eventual sale before maturity, however, changes in their market value must be reflected on the investor's balance sheet.

Sales of Bonds by Investors

Under many normal circumstances, an investor may decide to sell bonds after holding them for several months or even years. In other situations, as described earlier in "As a Matter of Fact," the issuer may call the bonds and force the investor to sell. In any of these circumstances, it is highly unlikely that the selling price of the bonds will equal their carrying value in the investor's accounts. Thus, the sale of a bond investment is likely to produce a gain or loss for the difference between their carrying value and the selling price.

Using the Information—Pledged Assets to Secured Liabilities

LO 6 Calculate and describe how to use the ratio of pledged assets to secured liabilities.

As you have learned in this chapter, creditors can reduce their risk with agreements that can force borrowers to sell specific assets to settle overdue debts. Investors who consider buying a company's secured debt obligations need to determine whether the pledged assets of the debtor provide adequate security. One method of evaluating this is to calculate the ratio of **pledged assets to secured liabilities.** This is calculated by dividing the book value of the company's assets pledged as collateral by the book value of the liabilities secured by these collateral agreements:

$$\text{Pledged assets to secured liabilities} = \frac{\text{Book value of pledged assets}}{\text{Book value of secured liabilities}}$$

For example, suppose that a company has assets with a book value of \$2,300,000 pledged against loans with a balance of \$1,000,000. The ratio is \$2,300,000/\$1,000,000 = 2.3 to 1. Although there are no hard and fast guidelines for interpreting the values of this ratio, 2.3 to 1 may be sufficiently high to provide the existing secured creditors with some comfort that the debts are safely covered by the assets.

The pledging of assets for the benefit of secured creditors also affects unsecured creditors. As an increasing portion of the assets are pledged, the unsecured creditors are less likely to receive a full repayment. In evaluating their position, unsecured creditors may gain some information from the ratio of pledged assets to secured creditors. For two reasons, an unusually large ratio may suggest that the unsecured creditors are at risk. First, secured creditors may have demanded an unusually large ratio because the value of the assets in liquidation is low. Second, the secured creditors may perceive that the ability of the company to meet its obligations from operating cash flows is weak.

In using this ratio, a creditor must be aware of the fact that the reported book value of the company's assets is unlikely to reflect their fair value. Thus, creditors would have better information if they could determine the assets' current market value and then use it in the ratio instead of book value. Major creditors may be able to get this information directly by asking the borrower to provide recent appraisals or other evidence of the assets' fair value. Other creditors may not have this option. In addition, using the ratio requires knowledge about the amounts of secured liabilities and pledged assets. This information may or may not be clearly identified in the financial statements. Again, it may be necessary to go directly to the borrower to obtain the information or to estimate it from other sources.

Present Value Tables

TABLE 12-1 *Present Value of $1*

	Rate							
Periods	3%	4%	5%	6%	7%	8%	10%	12%
1	0.9709	0.9615	0.9524	0.9434	0.9346	0.9259	0.9091	0.8929
2	0.9426	0.9246	0.9070	0.8900	0.8734	0.8573	0.8264	0.7972
3	0.9151	0.8890	0.8638	0.8396	0.8163	0.7938	0.7513	0.7118
4	0.8885	0.8548	0.8227	0.7921	0.7629	0.7350	0.6830	0.6355
5	0.8626	0.8219	0.7835	0.7473	0.7130	0.6806	0.6209	0.5674
6	0.8375	0.7903	0.7462	0.7050	0.6663	0.6302	0.5645	0.5066
7	0.8131	0.7599	0.7107	0.6651	0.6227	0.5835	0.5132	0.4523
8	0.7894	0.7307	0.6768	0.6274	0.5820	0.5403	0.4665	0.4039
9	0.7664	0.7026	0.6446	0.5919	0.5439	0.5002	0.4241	0.3606
10	0.7441	0.6756	0.6139	0.5584	0.5083	0.4632	0.3855	0.3220
20	0.5537	0.4564	0.3769	0.3118	0.2584	0.2145	0.1486	0.1037
30	0.4120	0.3083	0.2314	0.1741	0.1314	0.0994	0.0573	0.0334

TABLE 12-2 *Present Value of an Annuity of $1*

	Rate							
Payments	3%	4%	5%	6%	7%	8%	10%	12%
1	0.9709	0.9615	0.9524	0.9434	0.9346	0.9259	0.9091	0.8929
2	1.9135	1.8861	1.8594	1.8334	1.8080	1.7833	1.7355	1.6901
3	2.8286	2.7751	2.7232	2.6730	2.6243	2.5771	2.4869	2.4018
4	3.7171	3.6299	3.5460	3.4651	3.3872	3.3121	3.1699	3.0373
5	4.5797	4.4518	4.3295	4.2124	4.1002	3.9927	3.7908	3.6048
6	5.4172	5.2421	5.0757	4.9173	4.7665	4.6229	4.3553	4.1114
7	6.2303	6.0021	5.7864	5.5824	5.3893	5.2064	4.8684	4.5638
8	7.0197	6.7327	6.4632	6.2098	5.9713	5.7466	5.3349	4.9676
9	7.7861	7.4353	7.1078	6.8017	6.5152	6.2469	5.7590	5.3282
10	8.5302	8.1109	7.7217	7.3601	7.0236	6.7101	6.1446	5.6502
20	14.8775	13.5903	12.4622	11.4699	10.5940	9.8181	8.5136	7.4694
30	19.6004	17.2920	15.3725	13.7648	12.4090	11.2578	9.4269	8.0552

Summary of the Chapter in Terms of Learning Objectives

LO 1 Typical installment notes require one of two alternative payment patterns: (*a*) payments that include interest plus equal amounts of principal or (*b*) equal payments. In either case, interest is allocated to each period in a note's life by multiplying the carrying value by the original interest rate. If a note is repaid with equal payments, the payment's size is found by dividing the borrowed amount by the annuity table value for the interest rate and the number of payments.

LO 2 An installment note is usually created when a company borrows money from a single creditor. In contrast, bonds are issued to many investors. Serial bonds mature at different points in time. Companies that issue sinking fund bonds must accumulate a fund of assets to use to pay out the par value of the bonds at the maturity date. Convertible bonds can be exchanged by the bondholders for shares of the issuing company's stock. If bonds are registered, each bondholder's name and address are recorded by the issuing company. In contrast, bearer bonds are payable to whoever holds the bonds. Some bonds are secured by mortgages on the issuer's assets while other bonds, called debentures, are unsecured. When bonds are sold between interest dates, the accrued interest is collected from the purchasers, who are then refunded that amount on the next interest payment date. Bonds can be retired early by the issuer by exercising a call option or by purchases on the open market. The issuer must recognize a gain or loss for the difference between the amount paid out and the bonds' carrying value.

LO 3 The cash paid to bondholders on semiannual interest payment dates is calculated as one-half of the result of multiplying the par value of the bonds by their contract interest rate. The market value of a bond can be estimated by using the market interest rate to find the present values of the interest payments and the par value. Bonds are issued at a discount when the contract rate is less than the market rate. Then, the issuer records the issuance with a credit to the Bonds Payable account for the par value and a debit to Discount on Bonds Payable. The amount of interest assigned to each interest period can be allocated with the straight-line method if the result is not materially different from the results of applying the interest method. The interest method assigns interest to a period by multiplying the beginning carrying value by the original market interest rate.

LO 4 Bonds are issued at a premium when the contract rate is higher than the market interest rate. The issuer records the premium in a supplemental account. The balance of this account is reduced over the life of the bonds through the interest allocation process.

LO 5 Investments in bonds can be either short-term or long-term, depending on the investor's intent. Interest income on short-term investments consists only of the cash received from the issuer, while interest income from long-term bonds must include the effects of amortizing any discount or premium. Investments in bonds are also written up or down to their market value at the balance sheet date, except for those that the investor intends and is capable of holding to maturity.

LO 6 Secured and unsecured creditors are both concerned about the relationship between the amounts of assets owned by the debtor and the amounts of secured liabilities. The secured creditors are safer when the ratio of pledged assets to secured liabilities is larger, while the risks of unsecured creditors are increased in this circumstance.

Demonstration Problem

The Staley Tile Company patented and successfully test-marketed a new product. However, to expand its ability to produce and market the product, the company needed to raise $1.2 million of additional financing. On January 1, 19X1, the company borrowed the money under these three arrangements:

1. Staley signed a $400,000, 10% installment note that will be repaid in five annual payments. Each payment will include principal of $80,000 plus interest. The payments will be made on December 31 of 19X1 through 19X5.
2. Staley also signed a $400,000, 10% installment note that will be repaid with five equal annual installments. The payments will be made on December 31 of 19X1 through 19X5.
3. Staley issued five-year bonds with a par value of $400,000. The bonds have a 12% annual contract rate and pay interest on June 30 and December 31. The annual market interest rate for the bonds was 10% on January 1, 19X1.

Required

1. For the first installment note, (*a*) prepare an amortization table and (*b*) present the entry for the first payment.
2. For the second installment note, (*a*) calculate the size of each payment, (*b*) prepare an amortization table, and (*c*) present the entry for the first payment.
3. For the bonds, (*a*) estimate the issue price of the bonds; (*b*) present the January 1, 19X1, entry to record issuing the bonds; (*c*) prepare an amortization table using the interest method; (*d*) present the June 30, 19X1, entry to record the first payment of interest; and (*e*) present a entry to record retiring the bonds at the call price of $416,000 on January 1, 19X3.

Planning the Solution

- For the first installment note, prepare a table similar to Illustration 12–1 and use the numbers in the first line for the entry.
- For the second installment note, divide the borrowed amount by the annuity table factor (from Table 12–2 on page 445) for 10% and five payments. Prepare a table similar to Illustration 12–2 and use the numbers in the first line for the entry.
- For the bonds, estimate the issue price by using the market rate to find the present value of the bonds' cash flows. Then, use this result to record issuing the bonds. Next, develop an amortization table like Illustration 12–7, and use it to get the numbers that you need for the journal entry. Finally, use the table to find the carrying value as of the date of the retirement of the bonds that you need for the journal entry.

Solution to Demonstration Problem

Part 1:
Table:

		Payments						
	(*a*)	(*b*) *Debit*		(*c*) *Debit*		(*d*) *Credit*	(*e*)
Period Ending	**Beginning Balance**	**Interest Expense**	**+**	**Notes Payables**	**=**	**Cash**	**Ending Balance**
	Prior (e)	*10% × (a)*		*$400,000/5*		*(b) + (c)*	*(a) − (c)*
19X1	$400,000	$ 40,000		$ 80,000		$120,000	$320,000
19X2	320,000	32,000		80,000		112,000	240,000
19X3	240,000	24,000		80,000		104,000	160,000
19X4	160,000	16,000		80,000		96,000	80,000
19X5	80,000	8,000		80,000		88,000	-0-
Total		$120,000		$400,000		$520,000	

Journal entry:

19X1				
Dec.	31	Interest Expense	40,000.00	
		Notes Payable	80,000.00	
		Cash		120,000.00
		To record first installment payment.		

Part 2:
Payment = Note Balance/Table Value = $400,000/3.7908 = $105,519.
Table value is for five payments and an interest rate of 10%.

Table:

Period Ending	(a) Beginning Balance	(b) Debit Interest Expense	+	(c) Debit Notes Payables	=	(d) Credit Cash	(e) Ending Balance
		Payments					
19X1	$400,000	$ 40,000		$ 65,519		$105,519	$334,481
19X2	334,481	33,448		72,071		105,519	262,410
19X3	262,410	26,241		79,278		105,519	183,132
19X4	183,132	18,313		87,206		105,519	95,926
19X5	95,926	9,593		95,926		105,519	–0–
Total		$127,595		$400,000		$527,595	

Journal entry:

19X1				
Dec.	31	Interest Expense	40,000.00	
		Notes Payable.	65,519.00	
		Cash		105,519.00
		To record first installment payment.		

Part 3:
Estimated issue price of the bonds:

Cash Flow	Table	Table Value	Amount	Present Value
Par value	12–1	0.6139	$400,000	$245,560
Interest (annuity)	12–2	7.7217	24,000	185,321
Total.				$430,881

Table value is for 10 payments and an interest rate of 5%.
Journal entry:

19X1				
Jan.	1	Cash	430,881.00	
		Premium on Bonds Payable		30,881.00
		Bonds Payable		400,000.00
		Sold bonds at a premium.		

Table:

Period Ending	(a) Beginning Balance	(b) Debit Interest Expense	+	(c) Debit Premium on Bonds	=	(d) Credit Cash	(e) Ending Balance
		Payments					
	Prior (e)	*5% × (a)*		*(d) − (b)*		*6% × $400,000*	*(a) − (c)*
6/30/X1	$430,881	$ 21,544		$ 2,456		$ 24,000	$428,425
12/31/X1	428,425	21,421		2,579		24,000	425,846
6/30/X2	425,846	21,292		2,708		24,000	423,138
12/31/X2	423,138	21,157		2,843		24,000	420,295
6/30/X3	420,295	21,015		2,985		24,000	417,310
12/31/X3	417,310	20,866		3,134		24,000	414,176
6/30/X4	414,176	20,709		3,291		24,000	410,885
12/31/X4	410,885	20,544		3,456		24,000	407,429
6/30/X5	407,429	20,371		3,629		24,000	403,800
12/31/X5	403,800	20,200*		3,800		24,000	400,000
Total		$209,119		$30,881		$240,000	

* Adjusted for rounding.

Journal entries:

19X1				
June	30	Interest Expense	21,544.00	
		Premium on Bonds Payable	2,456.00	
		Cash		24,000.00
		Paid semiannual interest on the bonds.		
19X3				
Jan.	1	Bonds Payable	400,000.00	
		Premium on Bonds Payable	20,295.00	
		Cash		416,000.00
		Gain on Retirement of Bonds		4,295.00
		To record the retirement of bonds (carrying value determined as of Dec. 31, 19X2).		

Glossary

LO 7 Define or explain the words or phrases listed in the chapter glossary.

Bearer bonds bonds that are made payable to whoever holds them (called the bearer); these bonds are not registered. p. 426

Bond a company's long-term liability that requires periodic payments of interest and final payment of its par value when it matures; usually issued in denominations of $1,000. p. 424

Bond indenture the contract between the bond issuer and the bondholders; it identifies the rights and obligations of the parties. p. 426

Callable bonds bonds that give the issuer an option of retiring them before they mature. p. 439

Carrying amount the net amount at which bonds are reflected on the balance sheet; equals the par value of the bonds less any unamortized discount or plus any unamortized premium. p. 431

Contract rate the interest rate specified in the bond indenture; it is multiplied by the par value of the bonds to determine the amount of interest to be paid each year. p. 429

Convertible bonds bonds that can be exchanged by the bondholders for a fixed number of shares of the issuing company's common stock. p. 425

Coupon bonds bonds that have interest coupons attached to their certificates; the bondholders detach the coupons when they mature and present them to a bank for collection. p. 426

Debentures unsecured bonds that are supported by only the general credit standing of the issuer. p. 426

Discount on bonds payable the difference between the par value of a bond and its lower issue price or paying amount; arises when the contract rate is lower than the market rate. p. 430

Installment notes promissory notes that require the borrower to make a series of payments consisting of interest and principal. p. 419

Interest method (interest allocation) a method that allocates interest expense to a reporting period by multiplying the beginning paying value by the original market interest rate. p. 433

Market rate the consensus interest rate that borrowers are willing to pay and that lenders are willing to earn at the level of risk inherent in the bonds. p. 429

Mortgage a legal agreement that protects a lender by giving the lender the right to be paid out of the cash proceeds from the sale of the borrower's specific assets identified in the mortgage. p. 441

Par value of a bond the amount that the bond issuer agrees to pay at maturity and the amount on which interest payments are based; also called the *face amount.* p. 424

Pledged assets to secured liabilities the ratio of the book value of a company's pledged assets to the book value of its secured liabilities. p. 444

Premium on bonds payable the difference between the par value of a bond and its higher issue price or paying amount; arises when the contract rate is higher than the market rate. p. 436

Registered bonds bonds owned by investors whose names and addresses are recorded by the issuing company; the interest payments are made with checks to the bondholders. p. 426

Serial bonds bonds that mature at different dates with the result that the entire debt is repaid gradually over a number of years. p. 425

Sinking fund bonds bonds that require the issuing company to make deposits to a separate pool of assets; the bondholders are repaid at maturity from the assets in this pool. p. 425

Straight-line method (interest allocation) a method that allocates an equal amount of interest to each accounting period in the life of the bonds. p. 431

Objective Review

Answers to the following questions are listed at the end of this chapter. Be sure that you decide which is the one best answer to each question *before* you check the answers.

LO 1 Which one of the following situations always occurs when an installment note requires a series of equal payments?

a. The interest expense for a given period is calculated by multiplying the original face amount of the note by the interest rate.
b. The payments consist of an increasing amount of interest and a decreasing amount of principal.
c. The payments consist of changing amounts of principal, but the interest portion of the payment remains constant.
d. The payments consist of changing amounts of interest, but the principal portion of the payment remains constant.
e. The payments consist of a decreasing amount of interest and an increasing amount of principal.

LO 2 On May 1, a company sold $500,000 of 9% bonds that pay semiannual interest on each January 1 and July 1. The bonds were sold at par value plus accrued interest as of May 1. The bond issuer's entry to record the first semiannual interest payment on July 1 should include:

a. A debit to Interest Payable for $15,000.
b. A credit to Cash for $45,000.
c. A debit to Bonds Payable for $22,500.
d. A debit to Interest Payable for $7,500.
e. A credit to Interest Payable for $15,000 and a debit to Interest Expense for $22,500.

LO 3 A company recently sold a group of five-year 6% bonds with a $100,000 par value. The interest is to be paid semiannually and the market interest rate was 8%. What was the bonds' selling price?

a. $ 87,367.
b. $ 91,893.
c. $ 92,016.
d. $100,000.
e. $116,225.

LO 4 On December 31, 19X1, Cello Corporation received $109,444 from the sale of 16% bonds payable that mature in eight years, have a $100,000 par value, and pay interest on June 30 and December 31. The bonds were sold to yield a 14% market rate of interest. Using the interest method, the company would record the second interest payment (on December 31, 19X2), with a debit to Premium on Bonds Payable of:

a. $7,661.
b. $ 339.
c. $ 678.
d. $7,637.
e. $ 363.

LO 5 Which of the following statements about a bond investment is true?

a. The investor should report interest accrued as of the date of purchase as interest earned when it is collected.
b. If the bond was purchased at a premium, the amount of interest earned and recorded in each period exceeds the amount of cash received.
c. If the bond is held as a long-term investment, any premium or discount on the investment must be amortized in the process of measuring the interest income.
d. The investment should be initially recorded at cost, excluding any brokerage fees.
e. If the bond is held as a short-term investment, any premium or discount on the investment must be amortized in the process of measuring the interest income.

LO 6 Which of the following ratios is useful to creditors for assessing the risk of not being paid when a secured debt becomes due:

a. Inventory turnover.
b. Accounts receivable turnover.
c. Pledged assets to secured liabilities.
d. Total assets to secured liabilities.
e. Both *c* and *d* are useful in these circumstances.

LO 7 Bearer bonds:

a. Are owned by investors whose names and addresses are recorded by the issuing company.
b. Mature at different dates with the result that the entire bond issue is repaid gradually over a period of years.
c. Are paid at maturity out of a special designated pool of assets.
d. Are payable to whoever holds them.
e. None of the above.

Questions for Class Discussion

1. Describe two alternative payment patterns for installment notes.
2. How is the interest portion of an installment note payment calculated?
3. What is the difference between notes payable and bonds payable?
4. What is the primary difference between a share of stock and a bond?

5. What is the main advantage of issuing bonds instead of obtaining funds from the company's owners?
6. What is a bond indenture? What provisions are usually included in an indenture?
7. What role is played by the underwriter when bonds are issued?
8. What are the duties of a trustee for bondholders?
9. Why does a company that issues bonds between interest dates collect accrued interest from the bonds' purchasers?
10. What are the *contract* and *market interest rates* for bonds?
11. What factors affect the market interest rates for bonds?
12. If you know the par value of bonds, the contract rate and the market interest rate, how can you estimate the market value of the bonds?
13. When the straight-line method is used to allocate interest on a bond issued at a discount, how does the issuer determine the amount of interest expense for each period?
14. When the interest method is used to allocate interest for any bond, how does the issuer determine the interest expense for each period?
15. Does the straight-line or interest method produce an allocation of interest that creates a constant rate of interest over a bond's life? Explain your answer.
16. What is the cash price of a $2,000 bond that is sold at 98¼? What is the cash price of a $6,000 bond that is sold at 101½?
17. In what sense do the accounting practices applied to bond investments depart from the cost principle?
18. Explain whether secured or unsecured creditors should be alarmed to observe that the pledged assets to secured liabilities ratio for a borrower has grown substantially.

19. Refer to the financial statements for Federal Express Corporation presented in Appendix G. What amount of the company's long-term debt was classified as a current liability on May 31, 1993?

20. Refer to the financial statements for Ben & Jerry's Homemade, Inc., presented in Appendix G. Is there any indication in the balance sheet that the company has issued bonds?

Exercises

When solving the following exercises, round all dollar amounts to the nearest whole dollar. Also assume that none of the companies use reversing entries.

Exercise 12–1
Installment note with payments of accrued interest and equal amounts of principal
(LO 1)

On December 31, 19X1, Akron Co. borrowed $16,000 by signing a four-year, 5% installment note. The note requires annual payments of accrued interest and equal amounts of principal on December 31 of each year from 19X2 through 19X5.

a. How much principal will be included in each of the four payments?
b. Prepare an amortization table for this installment note like the one presented in Illustration 12–1 on page 420.

Exercise 12–2
Journal entries for an installment note with payments of accrued interest and equal amount of principal
(LO 1)

Use the data in Exercise 12–1 to prepare journal entries that Akron Co. would make to record the loan on December 31, 19X1, and the four payments starting on December 31, 19X2, through the final payment on December 31, 19X5.

Exercise 12–3
Installment note with equal payments
(LO 1)

On December 31, 19X1, Gates Co. borrowed $10,000 by signing a four-year, 5% installment note. The note requires four equal payments of accrued interest and principal on December 31 of each year from 19X2 through 19X5.

a. Calculate the size of each of the four equal payments.
b. Prepare an amortization table for this installment note like the one presented in Illustration 12–2 on page 422.

Exercise 12–4
Journal entries for an installment note with equal payments
(LO 1)

Use the data in Exercise 12–3 to prepare journal entries that Gates Co. would make to record the loan on December 31, 19X1, and the four payments starting on December 31, 19X2, through the final payment on December 31, 19X5.

Exercise 12–5
Calculating installment note payments
(LO 1)

The owner of Ripley's Restaurant borrowed $80,000 from a bank and signed an installment note that calls for eight annual payments of equal size, with the first payment due one year after the note was signed. Use Table 12–2 on page 445 to calculate the size of the annual payment for each of the following annual interest rates:

a. 5%
b. 7%
c. 10%
d. 12%

Exercise 12–6
Journal entries for bond issuance and interest payments
(LO 2)

On January 1, 19X1, the Tennyson Co. issued $300,000 of 20-year bonds that pay 8% interest semiannually on June 30 and December 31. The bonds were sold to investors at their par value.

a. How much interest will the issuer pay to the holders of these bonds every six months?
b. Show the journal entries that the issuer would make to record (1) the issuance of the bonds on January 1, 19X1, (2) the first interest payment on June 30, 19X1, and (3) the second interest payment on December 31, 19X1.

Exercise 12–7
Journal entries for bond issuance with accrued interest
(LO 2)

On March 1, 19X1, the Tennyson Co. issued $300,000 of 20-year bonds dated January 1, 19X1. The bonds pay 8% interest semiannually on June 30 and December 31. The bonds were sold to investors at their par value plus the two months' interest that had accrued since the original issue date.

a. How much accrued interest was paid to the issuer by the purchasers of these bonds on March 1, 19X1?
b. Show the journal entries that the issuer would make to record (1) the issuance of the bonds on March 1, 19X1; (2) the first interest payment on June 30, 19X1; and (3) the second interest payment on December 31, 19X1.

Exercise 12–8
Calculating the present value of a bond
(LO 3)

The Carraway Co. issued bonds with a par value of $200,000 on their initial issue date. The bonds mature in 10 years and pay 10% annual interest in two semiannual payments. On the issue date, the annual market rate of interest for the bonds turned out to be 12%.

a. What is the size of the semiannual interest payment for these bonds?
b. How many semiannual interest payments will be made on these bonds over their life?
c. Use the information about the interest rates to decide whether the bonds were issued at par, a discount, or a premium.
d. Estimate the market value of the bonds as of the date they were issued.

Exercise 12–9
Calculating the present value of a bond and recording the issuance
(LO 3)

The Sesame Co. issued bonds with a par value of $150,000 on their initial issue date. The bonds mature in 15 years and pay 8% annual interest in two semiannual payments. On the issue date, the annual market rate of interest for the bonds turned out to be 10%.

a. What is the size of the semiannual interest payment for these bonds?
b. How many semiannual interest payments will be made on these bonds over their life?
c. Use the information about the interest rates to decide whether the bonds were issued at par, a discount, or a premium.
d. Estimate the market value of the bonds as of the date they were issued.
e. Present the journal entry that would be made to record the bonds' issuance.

Exercise 12–10
Straight-line allocation of interest for bonds sold at a discount
(LO 3)

The Columbia Co. issued bonds with a par value of $50,000 on January 1, 19X2. The annual contract rate on the bonds is 8%, and the interest is paid semiannually. The bonds mature after three years. The annual market interest rate at the date of issuance was 12%, and the bonds were sold for $45,085.

a. What is the amount of the original discount on these bonds?
b. How much total interest expense will be recognized over the life of these bonds?

c. Present an amortization table like Illustration 12–4 on page 433 for these bonds; use the straight-line method of allocating the interest and amortizing the discount.

Exercise 12–11
Interest method allocation of interest for bonds sold at a discount
(LO 3)

The Cheyenne Company issued bonds with a par value of $30,000 on January 1, 19X2. The annual contract rate on the bonds is 8%, and the interest is paid semiannually. The bonds mature after three years. The annual market interest rate at the date of issuance was 10%, and the bonds were sold for $28,477.

a. What is the amount of the original discount on these bonds?

b. How much total interest expense will be recognized over the life of these bonds?

c. Present an amortization table like Illustration 12–5 on page 434 for these bonds; use the interest method of allocating the interest and amortizing the discount.

Exercise 12–12
Calculating the present value of a bond
(LO 3)

The Downhome Co. issued bonds with a par value of $60,000. The bonds mature in 10 years and pay 12% annual interest in two semiannual payments. On the issue date, the annual market rate of interest for the bonds turned out to be 10%.

a. What is the size of the semiannual interest payment for these bonds?

b. How many semiannual interest payments will be made on these bonds over their life?

c. Use the information about the interest rates to decide whether the bonds were issued at par, a discount, or a premium.

d. Estimate the market value of the bonds as of the date they were issued.

Exercise 12–13
Calculating the present value of a bond and recording the issuance
(LO 3)

The Allan Co.issued bonds with a par value of $25,000 on their initial issue date. The bonds mature in 15 years and pay 8% annual interest in two semiannual payments. On the issue date, the annual market rate of interest for the bonds turned out to be 6%.

a. What is the size of the semiannual interest payment for these bonds?

b. How many semiannual interest payments will be made on these bonds over their life?

c. Use the information about the interest rates to decide whether the bonds were issued at par, a discount, or a premium.

d. Estimate the market value of the bonds as of the date they were issued.

e. Present the journal entry that would be made to record the bonds' issuance.

Exercise 12–14
Interest method allocation of interest for bonds sold at a premium
(LO 3)

The Cypress Company issued bonds with a par value of $40,000 on January 1, 19X2. The annual contract rate on the bonds was 12%, and the interest is paid semiannually. The bonds mature after three years. The annual market interest rate at the date of issuance was 10%, and the bonds were sold for $42,030.

a. What is the amount of the original premium on these bonds?

b. How much total interest expense will be recognized over the life of these bonds?

c. Present an amortization table like Illustration 12–7 on page 438 for these bonds; use the interest method of allocating the interest and amortizing the premium.

Exercise 12–15
Retiring bonds payable
(LO 2)

On January 1, 19X1, the Amsterdam Co. issued $700,000 of its 10%, 15-year bonds at the price of 95½. Three years later, on January 1, 19X4, the company retired 30% of these bonds by buying them on the open market at 105¾. All interest had been properly accounted for and paid through December 31, 19X3, the day before the purchase. The company used the straight-line method to allocate the interest and amortize the original discount.

a. How much money did the company receive when it first issued the entire group of bonds?

b. How large was the original discount on the entire group of bonds?

c. How much amortization did the company record on the entire group of bonds between January 1, 19X1, and December 31, 19X3?

d. What was the carrying value of the entire group of bonds as of the close of business on December 31, 19X3? What was the carrying value of the retired bonds on this date?

e. How much money did the company pay on January 1, 19X4, to purchase the bonds that it retired?

f. What is the amount of the gain or loss from retiring the bonds?

g. Provide the general journal entry that the company would make to record the retirement of the bonds.

Exercise 12–16
Bonds as temporary investments
(LO 5)

On May 16, 19X2, the Camden Company purchased bonds issued by the Baltimore Corp. The bonds are dated December 31, 19X1, and have a total par value of $30,000. The contract interest rate is 12%, and the bonds mature six years after the issue date. Interest is paid semiannually on June 30 and December 31. Camden Company bought the bonds at 105 plus accrued interest and also paid a $400 broker's fee. Camden intends to hold the bonds as a temporary investment.

a. What was the total purchase price of this investment?

b. How much interest had accrued on the bonds as of the date of purchase?

c. Present the journal entry that the investor made to record the purchase.

d. How much interest income will be earned between the purchase date and the first interest payment date?

e. Present the journal entry that the investor will make to record the first interest payment that it will receive on June 30.

Exercise 12–17
Computing asset-to-liability ratios
(LO 6)

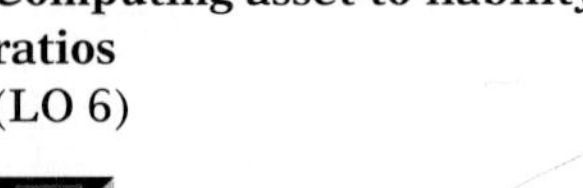

Use the following information to compute the ratio of pledged assets to secured liabilities:

	Alcon Co.	Berry Co.
Pledged assets	$155,000	$ 84,000
Total assets.	180,000	300,000
Secured liabilities	90,000	66,000
Unsecured liabilities	140,000	160,000

Problems

When solving the following problems, round all dollar amounts to the nearest whole dollar. Also assume that none of the companies use reversing entries.

Problem 12–1
Installment notes
(LO 1)

On November 30, 19X1, the Stanley Company borrowed $50,000 from a bank by signing a four-year installment note bearing interest at 12%. The terms of the note require equal payments each year on November 30.

Required

1. Calculate the size of each installment payment. (Use Table 12–2 on page 445.)
2. Complete an installment note amortization schedule for this note similar to Illustration 12–2 on page 422.
3. Present the journal entries that the borrower would make to record accrued interest as of December 31, 19X1 (the end of the annual reporting period) and the first payment on the note.
4. Now assume that the note does not require equal payments but does require four payments that include accrued interest and an equal amount of principal in each payment. Complete an installment notes amortization schedule for this note similar to Illustration 12–1 on page 420. Prepare the journal entries that the borrower would make to record accrued interest as of December 31, 19X1 (the end of the annual reporting period) and the first payment on the note.

Problem 12–2
Calculating bond prices and recording issuances with journal entries
(LO 2, 3, 4)

Helmer Co. issued a group of bonds on January 1, 19X1, that pay interest semiannually on June 30 and December 31. The par value of the bonds is $40,000, the annual contract rate is 8%, and the bonds mature in 10 years.

Required

For each of these three situations, (*a*) determine the issue price of the bonds and (*b*) show the journal entry that would record the issuance.

1. The market interest rate at the date of issuance was 6%.
2. The market interest rate at the date of issuance was 8%.
3. The market interest rate at the date of issuance was 10%.

Problem 12–3
Straight-line method of allocating interest and amortizing a bond discount
(LO 3)

Abbot Company issued $125,000 of bonds that pay 6% annual interest with two semiannual payments. The date of issuance was January 1, 19X1, and the interest is paid on June 30 and December 31. The bonds mature after 10 years and were issued at the price of $108,014.

Required

1. Prepare a general journal entry to record the issuance of the bonds.
2. Determine the total interest expense that will be recognized over the life of these bonds.
3. Prepare the first four lines of an amortization table like Illustration 12–4 based on the straight-line method of allocating the interest.
4. Prepare the first four lines of a separate table that shows the beginning balance of the discount, the amount of straight-line amortization of the discount, and the ending balance.
5. Present the journal entries that the bond issuer would make to record the first two interest payments.

Problem 12–4
Interest method of allocating bond interest and amortizing a discount
(LO 2, 3)

The Martin Company issued $50,000 of bonds that pay 4% annual interest with two semiannual payments. The date of issuance was January 1, 19X1, and the interest is paid on June 30 and December 31. The bonds mature after three years and were issued at the price of $47,292. The market interest rate was 6%.

Required

1. Prepare a general journal entry to record the issuance of the bonds.
2. Determine the total interest expense that will be recognized over the life of these bonds.
3. Prepare the first four lines of an amortization table like Illustration 12–5 based on the interest method.
4. Prepare the first four lines of a separate table that shows the beginning balance of the discount, the amount of interest method amortization of the discount, and the ending balance.
5. Present the journal entries that the bond issuer would make to record the first two interest payments.

Problem 12–5
Interest method of amortizing bond premium and retiring bonds
(LO 2, 4)

The Jones Company issued $100,000 of bonds that pay 9% annual interest with two semiannual payments. The date of issuance was January 1, 19X1, and the interest is paid on June 30 and December 31. The bonds mature after three years and were issued at the price of $102,619. The market interest rate was 8%.

Required

1. Prepare a general journal entry to record the issuance of the bonds.
2. Determine the total interest expense that will be recognized over the life of these bonds.
3. Prepare the first four lines of an amortization table like Illustration 12–7 based on the interest method.
4. Prepare the first four lines of a separate table that shows the beginning balance of the premium, the amount of interest method amortization of the premium, and the ending balance.

5. Present the journal entries that the bond issuer would make to record the first two interest payments.
6. Present the journal entry that would be made to record the retirement of these bonds on December 31, 19X2, at the price of 98.

Problem 12–6
Straight-line amortization table, accrued interest, and bond investment
(LO 3, 4, 5)

The Schaffner Co. issued bonds with a par value of $100,000 and a five-year life on May 1, 19X1. The contract interest rate is 7%. The bonds pay interest on October 31 and April 30. They were issued on the original issue date at a price of $95,948.

Required

1. Prepare an amortization table for these bonds that covers their entire life. Use the straight-line method of allocating interest.
2. Show the journal entries that the issuer would make to record the first two interest payments and to accrue interest as of December 31, 19X1.
3. The Gilchrist Company purchased 10% of the bonds on the issue date to hold as a long-term investment until maturity. Show the journal entries that would be made by this company to record the first interest payment that it collects, assuming that it uses the interest method of allocating the interest revenue earned over the bonds' life. The original annual market rate on the bonds was 8%.

Problem 12–7
Bond premium amortization and finding the present value of remaining cash flows
(LO 5)

The Briggs Company issued bonds with a par value of $80,000 and a five-year life on January 1, 19X1. The bonds pay interest on June 30 and December 31. The contract interest rate is 8.5%. The bonds were issued at a price of $81,625. The market interest rate was 8% on the original issue date.

Required

1. Prepare an amortization table for these bonds that covers their entire life. Use the interest method.
2. Show the journal entries that the issuer would make to record the first two interest payments.
3. Use the original market interest rate to calculate the present value of the remaining cash flows for these bonds as of December 31, 19X3. Compare your answer with the amount shown on the amortization table as the balance for that date, and explain your findings.

Problem 12–8
Analytical essay
(LO 3, 4)

Review the transactions presented in Problem 12–4 for the Martin Company. Instead of the facts described in the problem, assume that the market interest rate on January 1, 19X1, was 3% instead of 6%. Without presenting any specific numbers, describe how this change would affect the amounts presented on the company's financial statements.

Problem 12–9
Analytical essay
(LO 3, 4)

An unsecured major creditor of the Hawkins Company has been monitoring the company's financing activities. Two years before, the ratio of its pledged assets to secured liabilities had been 1.4. One year ago, the ratio had climbed to 2.0, and the most recent financial report shows that the ratio value is now 3.1. Briefly describe what this trend may indicate about the company's activities, specifically from the point of view of this creditor.

Provocative Problems

When solving the following provocative problems, round all dollar amounts to the nearest whole dollar.

Provocative Problem 12–1
Star Manufacturing Company
(LO 2)

Star Manufacturing Company is planning major additions to its operating capacity and needs approximately $400,000 to finance the expansion. The company has been considering three alternative proposals for issuing bonds that pay annual interest over the eight years in their lives. The alternatives are

Plan A: Issue $400,000 of 8% bonds.
Plan B: Issue $450,000 of 6% bonds.
Plan C: Issue $360,000 of 10% bonds.

The market rate of interest for all of these bonds is expected to be 8%.

Required

1. For each plan, calculate:
   a. The expected cash proceeds from issuing the bonds.
   b. The expected annual cash outflow for interest.
   c. The expected interest expense for the first year. (Use the interest method to amortize bond premium or discount.)
   d. The amount that must be paid at maturity.
2. Which plans have the smallest and largest cash demands on the company prior to the final payment at maturity? Which plans required the smallest and largest payment at maturity?

Provocative Problem 12–2
Angela Company
(LO 3)

The Angela Company issued $500,000 of zero-coupon bonds on January 1, 19X1. These bonds are scheduled to mature seven years later on December 31, 19X7. Under the terms of the bond agreement, the company will pay out $500,000 to the bondholders on the maturity date without making any periodic interest payments. The market rate of interest for these bonds was 10% when they were issued.

Required

1. Estimate the amount of cash that Angela received when it issued these bonds (assume annual compounding).
2. Present the journal entry that Angela's accountant would use to record the issuance of these bonds.
3. Calculate the total amount of interest expense that will be incurred over the life of the bonds.
4. Prepare an amortization table that shows the amount of interest expense that will be allocated to each year in the bonds' life with the interest method.
5. Present the journal entry that Angela's accountant would use to record the interest expense from these bonds for the year ended December 31, 19X1.

Provocative Problem 12–3
Hankamer Company
(LO 2, 3, 4)

Following are the first two lines of an amortization table for a group of bonds issued by the Hankamer Company. They were issued on January 1, 19X1; pay interest semiannually; and have a par value of $100,000.

		Payments					
	(a)	*(b)* Debit		*(c)* Credit		*(d)* Credit	*(e)*
Period Ending	?	?	=	?	+	?	?
6/30/X1	$93,789	$5,627		$627		$5,000	$94,416
12/31/X1	94,416	5,665		665		5,000	95,081

Required

1. What are the five missing column headings?
2. Which method is being used to allocate the interest?
3. What is the contract rate of interest?
4. What is the original market interest rate?
5. Complete the table.

Provocative Problem 12–4
Apple Computer, Inc.
(LO 1, 5, 6)
Apple Computer, Inc.

Use the financial statements and the footnotes in Appendix F to answer these questions about Apple Computer, Inc.

a. Has Apple issued any bonds or long-term notes payable?
b. What is the carrying value of Apple's short-term notes payable at the end of the

1992 fiscal year? Are they secured or unsecured? What is their typical life? What was the average interest rate on the notes outstanding at the end of the 1992 fiscal year?

c. Does Apple own any short-term investments? If so, what is their carrying value and how does the company determine this amount?

d. Does Apple own any long-term investments? If so, what is their carrying value?

Answers to Objective Review Questions

LO 1 (*e*)
LO 2 (*a*)
LO 3 (*b*)
LO 4 (*e*)
LO 5 (*c*)
LO 6 (*e*)
LO 7 (*d*)

CHAPTER

13

Corporations, Proprietorships, and Partnerships

Of the three common types of business organizations, corporations are fewest in number. However, the sales volume of corporations is approximately nine times the combined sales of unincorporated businesses. Thus, from an overall economic point of view, corporations are clearly the most important. As you study this chapter you will learn how corporations are organized and operated, and some of the procedures used to account for corporations. You will also learn more about proprietorships and partnerships.

Learning Objectives

After studying Chapter 13, you should be able to:

1. Explain the unique characteristics of the corporate form of business.
2. Record the issuance of par value stock and no-par stock with or without a stated value, and explain the concept of minimum legal capital.
3. Record transactions that involve dividends and stock subscriptions and explain the effects of stock subscriptions on the balance sheet.
4. State the differences between common and preferred stock, and allocate dividends between the common and preferred stock of a corporation.
5. Describe convertible preferred stock and explain the meaning of the par value, call price, market value, and book value of corporate stock.
6. Explain the legal status of a proprietorship, prepare entries to account for the owner's equity of a proprietorship, and prepare a statement of changes in owner's equity.
7. Explain the concepts of mutual agency and unlimited liability for a partnership, record the investments and withdrawals of partners, and allocate the net incomes or losses of a partnership among the partners.
8. Calculate the dividend yield and describe its meaning.
9. Define or explain the words and phrases listed in the chapter glossary.

CORPORATIONS

Characteristics of Corporations

LO 1 Explain the unique characteristics of the corporate form of business.

Corporations have become the dominant type of business because of the advantages created by their unique characteristics. We describe these characteristics in the following sections.

Corporations Are Separate Legal Entities

A corporation is a separate legal entity. As a separate entity, a corporation conducts its affairs with the same rights, duties, and responsibilities as a person. However, because it is not a real person, a corporation can act only through its agents, who are its officers and managers.

Stockholders Are Not Liable for the Corporation's Debts

Because a corporation is a separate legal entity, it is responsible for its own acts and its own debts. Its shareholders are not liable for either. From the viewpoint of an investor, this lack of stockholders' liability is perhaps the most important advantage of the corporate form of business.

Ownership Rights of Corporations Are Easily Transferred

The ownership of a corporation is represented by shares of stock that generally can be transferred and disposed of any time the owners wish to do so. Also, the transfer of shares from one stockholder to another usually has no effect on the corporation or its operations.[1]

Corporations Have Continuity of Life

A corporation's life may continue indefinitely because it is not tied to the physical lives of its owners. In some cases, a corporation's life may be initially limited by the laws of the state of its incorporation. However, the corporation's charter can be renewed and its life extended when the stated time expires. Thus, a corporation may have a perpetual life as long as it continues to be successful.

Stockholders Are Not Agents of the Corporation

As we previously stated, a corporation acts through its agents, who are the officers or managers of the corporation. Stockholders who are not officers or managers of the corporation do not have the power to bind the corporation to contracts. Instead, a stockholder's participation in the affairs of the corporation is limited to the right to vote in the stockholders' meetings.

Ease of Capital Accumulation

Buying stock in a corporation is often more attractive to investors than investing in other forms of business. Stock investments are attractive because (1) stockholders are not liable for the corporation's actions and debts, (2) stock usually can be transferred easily, (3) the life of the corporation is not limited, and (4) stockholders are not agents of the corporation. These advantages make it possible for some corporations to accumulate large amounts of capital from the combined investments of many stockholders. In a sense, a

[1] However, a transfer of ownership can create significant effects if it brings about a change in who controls the company's activities.

corporation's capacity for raising capital is limited only by its ability to convince investors that it can use (and has used) their funds profitably.

Governmental Regulation of Corporations

Corporations are created by fulfilling the requirements of a state's incorporation laws. These laws subject a corporation to state regulation and control. Single proprietorships and partnerships may escape some of these regulations. In addition, they may avoid having to file some governmental reports required of corporations.

Taxation of Corporations

Corporations are subject to the same property and payroll taxes as single proprietorships and partnerships. In addition, corporations are subject to taxes that are not levied on either of the other two. The most burdensome of these are federal and state income taxes that together may take 40% or more of a corporation's pretax income. However, the tax burden does not end there. The income of a corporation is taxed *twice,* first as income of the corporation and again as personal income to the stockholders when cash is distributed to them as dividends. This differs from single proprietorships and partnerships, which are not subject to income taxes as business units. Their income is taxed only as the personal income of their owners.[2]

The tax situation of a corporation is generally viewed as a disadvantage. However, in some cases, it can work to the advantage of stockholders because corporation and individual tax rates are progressive. That is, higher levels of income are taxed at higher rates and lower levels of income are taxed at lower rates. Therefore, taxes may be saved or at least delayed if a large amount of income is divided among two or more tax-paying entities. Thus, an individual who has a large personal income and pays taxes at a high rate may benefit if some of the income is earned by a corporation that person owns, as long as the corporation avoids paying dividends. By not paying dividends, the corporation's income is taxed only once at the lower corporate rate, at least temporarily until dividends are paid.

Organizing a Corporation

A corporation is created by securing a charter from a state government. The requirements that must be met to be chartered vary among the states. Usually, a charter application must be signed by three or more subscribers to the prospective corporation's stock (such persons are called the *incorporators* or *promoters*). Then, the application must be filed with the appropriate state official. When it is properly completed and all fees are paid, the charter is issued and the corporation is formed. The subscribers then purchase the corporation's stock, meet as stockholders, and elect a board of directors. The directors are responsible for guiding the company's business affairs.

Organization Costs

The costs of organizing a corporation, such as legal fees, promoters' fees, and amounts paid to secure a charter, are called **organization costs.** On the corporation's books, these costs are debited to an asset account called Organization Costs. In a sense, this intangible asset benefits the corporation throughout its life. Thus, you could argue that the cost should be amortized over the life of

[2] Some corporations that have a limited number of shareholders can elect to be treated like a partnership for tax purposes. These companies are called *Subchapter S Corporations.*

the corporation, which may be unlimited. However, generally accepted accounting principles require any intangible asset to be amortized over a period that is no longer than 40 years.[3]

Income tax rules permit a corporation to write off organization costs as a tax deduction over a minimum of five years. Thus, to make record-keeping simple, many corporations use a five-year amortization period for financial statement purposes. Although the five-year period is arbitrary, it is widely used in practice. Because organization costs are usually not material in amount, the *materiality principle* also supports the arbitrarily short amortization period.

Management of a Corporation

Although the organizational structures of all corporations are not always the same, the ultimate control of a corporation rests with its stockholders. However, this control is exercised only indirectly through the election of the board of directors. Individual stockholders' rights to participate in management begin and end with a vote in the stockholders' meetings, where each of them has one vote for each share of stock owned.

Normally, a corporation holds a stockholders' meeting once each year to elect directors and transact other business as required by the corporation's bylaws. A group of stockholders that owns or controls the votes of 50% plus one share of a corporation's stock can easily elect the board and thereby control the corporation. However, in most companies, only a very few stockholders attend the annual meeting or even care about getting involved in the voting process. As a result, a much smaller percentage may be able to dominate the election of board members.

Stockholders who do not attend stockholders' meetings must be given an opportunity to delegate their voting rights to an agent. A stockholder does this by signing a document called a **proxy** that gives a designated agent the right to vote the stock. Prior to a stockholders' meeting, a corporation's board of directors typically mails to each stockholder an announcement of the meeting and a proxy that names the existing board chairperson as the voting agent of the stockholder. The announcement asks the stockholder to sign and return the proxy.

A corporation's board of directors is responsible for and has final authority for managing the corporation's activities. However, it can act only as a collective body. An individual director has no power to transact corporate business. Although the board has final authority, it usually limits its actions to establishing broad policy. Day-to-day direction of corporate business is delegated to executive officers appointed by the board.

Traditionally, the chief executive officer (CEO) of the corporation is the president. Under the president, several vice presidents may be assigned specific areas of management responsibility, such as finance, production, and marketing. In addition, the corporate secretary keeps the minutes of the meetings of the stockholders and directors and ensures that all legal responsibilities are fulfilled. In a small corporation, the secretary is also responsible for keeping a record of the stockholders and the changing amounts of their stock interest.

Many corporations have a different structure in which the chairperson of the board of directors is also the chief executive officer. With this arrangement, the president is usually designated the chief operating officer (COO), and the rest of the structure is essentially the same.

[3] FASB, *Accounting Standards—Current Text* (Norwalk, CT, 1994), sec. I60.110. First published in *APB Opinion No. 17,* par. 29.

Stock Certificates and the Transfer of Stock

When investors buy a corporation's stock, they may receive a stock certificate as proof that they purchased the shares.[4] In many corporations, only one certificate is issued for each block of stock purchased. This certificate may be for any number of shares. Other corporations may use preprinted certificates, each of which represents 100 shares, plus blank certificates that may be made out for any number of shares.

When selling shares of a corporation, a stockholder completes and signs a transfer endorsement on the back of the certificate and sends it to the corporation's secretary or the transfer agent. The secretary or agent cancels and files the old certificate and issues a new certificate to the new stockholder. If the old certificate represents more shares than were sold, the corporation issues two new certificates. One certificate goes to the new stockholder for the sold shares and the other to the original stockholder for the remaining unsold shares.

Registrar and Transfer Agent

If a corporation's stock is traded on a major stock exchange, the corporation must have a *registrar* and a *transfer agent.* The registrar keeps the stockholder records and prepares official lists of stockholders for stockholders' meetings and for dividend payments. Registrars and transfer agents usually are large banks or trust companies that have the computer facilities and staff to carry out this kind of work.

When a corporation has a transfer agent and a stockholder wants to transfer ownership of some shares to another party, the owner completes the transfer endorsement on the back of the stock certificate and sends the certificate to the transfer agent, usually with the assistance of a stockbroker. The transfer agent cancels the old certificate and issues one or more new certificates and sends them to the registrar. The registrar enters the transfer in the stockholder records and sends the new certificate or certificates to the proper owners.

Authorization and Issuance of Stock

LO 2 Record the issuance of par value stock and no-par stock with or without a stated value, and explain the concept of minimum legal capital.

When a corporation is organized, its charter authorizes it to issue a specified number of shares of stock. If all of the authorized shares have the same rights and characteristics, the stock is called *common stock.* However, a corporation may be authorized to issue more than one class of stock, including preferred stock. (We discuss preferred stock later in this chapter.)

Because a corporation cannot issue more than the number of shares authorized in its charter, its founders usually obtain authorization to issue more shares than they plan to sell when the company is first organized. By doing so, the corporation avoids having to get the state's approval to sell more shares when additional capital is needed to finance an expansion of the business. A corporation's balance sheet must disclose the numbers of shares authorized and issued. These facts are reported in the stockholders' equity section of the statement. For example, Federal Express Corporation's balance sheet shows this information:

	1993	1992
Common stock, $.10 par value; 100,000,000 shares authorized, 54,743,000 and 54,100,000 shares issued	$5,474,300	$5,410,000

[4] The issuance of certificates is less common than it used to be. Instead, many stockholders maintain accounts with the corporation or their stockbrokers and never receive certificates.

Sale of Stock for Cash

When stock is sold for cash and immediately issued, an entry like the following is made to record the sale and issuance:

June	5	Cash	300,000.00	
		Common Stock, $10 Par Value		300,000.00
		Sold at par and issued 30,000 shares of $10 par value common stock.		

Exchanging Stock for Noncash Assets

A corporation may accept assets other than cash in exchange for its stock. In the process, the corporation also may assume some liabilities, such as a mortgage on some of the property. These transactions are recorded with an entry like this one:

June	10	Machinery	10,000.00	
		Buildings	65,000.00	
		Land	15,000.00	
		Long-Term Notes Payable		50,000.00
		Common Stock, $10 Par Value		40,000.00
		Exchanged 4,000 shares of $10 par value common stock for machinery, buildings, and land.		

This entry records the acquired assets and the new liability at their fair market values as of the date of the transaction. It also records the difference between the combined fair values of the assets and the liability as an increase in stockholders' equity. If reliable fair values for the assets and liabilities cannot be determined, the fair market value of the stock may be used to estimate their values.

A corporation also may give shares of its stock to its promoters in exchange for their services in organizing the company. In this case, the corporation receives the intangible asset of being organized in exchange for its stock. The company's bookkeeper records this transaction as follows:

June	5	Organization Costs	5,000.00	
		Common Stock, $10 Par Value		5,000.00
		Gave the promotors 500 shares of $10 par value common stock in exchange for their services in organizing the corporation.		

Par Value and Minimum Legal Capital

Many stocks have a **par value**, which is an arbitrary value assigned to the stock when it is authorized. A corporation may choose to issue stock with a par value of any amount, but par values of $100, $25, $10, $5, $1, and even $0.01 are widely used. When a corporation issues par value stock, the par value is printed on each certificate and is used in accounting for the stock.

In many states, the par value of a corporation's stock also establishes the **minimum legal capital** for the corporation. Laws that establish minimum legal capital normally require stockholders to invest assets equal in value to at least that amount. Otherwise, the stockholders are liable to the corporation's creditors for the deficiency. Usually, the minimum legal capital is defined as the par value of the issued stock. In other words, persons who buy stock from a corporation must give the corporation assets equal in value to at least the par value of the stock or be subject to making up the difference later. For example, if a corporation issues 1,000 shares of $100 par value stock, the minimum legal capital of the corporation is $100,000. Minimum legal capital requirements also make it illegal to pay any dividends if they reduce the stockholders' equity below the minimum amount.

The requirements for minimum legal capital are intended to protect the creditors of a corporation. Because a corporation's creditors cannot demand payment from the personal assets of the stockholders, the assets of the corporation are all that is available to satisfy the creditors' claims. To protect a corporation's creditors under these conditions, the minimum legal capital requirement limits a corporation's ability to distribute its assets to its stockholders. The idea is that assets equal to the amount of minimum legal capital cannot be paid to the stockholders unless all creditor claims are paid first.

Because par value determines the amount of minimum legal capital in many states, it is traditionally used in accounting for the part of stockholders' equity derived from the issuance of stock. However, par value does *not* establish a stock's market value or the price at which a corporation must issue the stock. If purchasers are willing to pay more, a corporation may sell and issue its stock at a price above par.

Stock Premiums and Discounts

Premiums on Stock

When a corporation sells its stock at a price above the par value, the stock is said to be issued at a premium. For example, if a corporation sells and issues its $10 par value common stock at $12 per share, the stock is sold at a $2 per share premium. A **premium on stock** is the amount in excess of par paid by the purchasers of newly issued stock. It is not a revenue and does not ever appear on the income statement. Rather, a premium is part of the investment of stockholders and is simply a part of stockholders' equity.

In accounting for stock sold at a price greater than its par value, the premium is recorded separately from the par value and is called *contributed capital in excess of par value.* For example, assume that a corporation sells and issues 10,000 shares of its $10 par value common stock for cash at $12 per share. The sale is recorded as follows:

Dec.	1	Cash	120,000.00	
		Common Stock, $10 Par Value		100,000.00
		Contributed Capital in Excess of Par Value, Common Stock		20,000.00
		Sold and issued 10,000 shares of $10 par value common stock at $12 per share.		

When a balance sheet is prepared, any contributed capital in excess of par value is added to the par value of the stock in the equity section, as shown in the following example:

Stockholders' Equity	
Common stock, $10 par value, 25,000 shares authorized, 20,000 shares issued and outstanding	$200,000
Contributed capital in excess of par value, common stock	30,000
Total contributed capital	$230,000
Retained earnings	82,400
Total stockholders' equity	$312,400

Discounts on Stock

If stock is issued at a price below par value, the difference between par and the issue price is called a **discount on stock.** Most states prohibit the issuance of stock at a discount because the stockholders would be investing less than minimum legal capital. In states that allow stock to be issued at a discount, its purchasers usually become contingently liable to the corporation's creditors for the amount of the discount. Therefore, stock is seldom issued at a discount. However, if stock is issued at less than par, the discount is not an expense and does not appear on the income statement. Rather, the amount of the discount is debited to a discount account that is contra to the common stock account. The balance of the discount account is then subtracted from the par value of the stock on the balance sheet.

No-Par Stock

At one time, all stocks were required to have a par value. Today, nearly all states permit the issuance of stocks that do not have a par value. The primary advantage of **no-par stock** is that it may be issued at any price without having a discount liability attached. Also, printing a par value of, say, $100 on a stock certificate may cause an inexperienced person to think that the share must be worth $100, when it actually may be worthless. Therefore, eliminating par value may encourage a closer analysis of the factors that give a stock value. These factors include such things as expectations about future earnings and dividends, and prospects for the economy as a whole.

In some states, the entire proceeds from the sale of no-par stock becomes minimum legal capital. In this case, the entire proceeds are credited to a no-par stock account. For example, if a corporation issues 1,000 shares of no-par stock at $42 per share, the transaction is recorded like this:

Oct.	20	Cash	42,000.00	
		Common Stock, No-Par		42,000.00
		Sold and issued 1,000 shares of no-par common stock at $42 per share.		

In other states, the board of directors of a corporation can place a **stated value** on its no-par stock. The stated value becomes the minimum legal capital and is credited to the no-par stock account. If the stock is issued at an amount in excess of stated value, the excess is credited to Contributed Capital in Excess of Stated Value, No-Par Common Stock. For example, suppose that a corporation issues 1,000 shares of no-par common stock with a stated value of $25 per share for cash of $42 per share. The transaction is recorded as follows:

Oct.	20	Cash	42,000.00	
		Common Stock, No-Par		25,000.00
		Contributed Capital in Excess of Stated Value, No-Par Common Stock		17,000.00
		Sold 1,000 shares of no-par stock having a $25 per share stated value at $42 per share.		

Sale of Stock through Subscriptions

Usually, stock is sold for cash and immediately issued. However, corporations sometimes sell stock through **stock subscriptions.** For example, when a new corporation is formed, the organizers may realize that the new business has limited immediate needs for cash but will need additional capital in the future. To get the corporation started on a sound footing, the organizers may sell

LO 3 Record transactions that involve dividends and stock subscriptions and explain the effects of stock subscriptions on the balance sheet.

the stock to investors who agree to contribute some cash now and to make additional contributions in the future. When stock is sold through subscriptions, the investor agrees to buy a certain number of the shares at a specified price. The agreement also states when payments are to be made.

To illustrate the sale of stock through subscriptions, assume that Northgate Corporation accepted subscriptions on May 6 to 5,000 shares of its $10 par value common stock at $12 per share. The subscription contracts called for a 10% down payment with the balance to be paid in two equal installments due after three and six months. Northgate records the subscriptions with the following entry:

May	6	Subscriptions Receivable, Common Stock	60,000.00	
		Common Stock Subscribed		50,000.00
		Contributed Capital in Excess of Par Value, Common Stock		10,000.00
		Accepted subscriptions to 5,000 shares of $10 par value common stock at $12 per share.		

At the time that subscriptions are accepted, the firm debits the Subscriptions Receivable account (an asset) for the sum of the stock's par value and premium. This is the total amount the subscribers agreed to pay. Notice that the *Common Stock Subscribed* account (an equity) is credited for par value and that the premium is credited to Contributed Capital in Excess of Par Value, Common Stock.

The receivables are converted into cash when the subscribers pay for their stock. And, when all the payments are received, the subscribed stock is issued. Northgate records the receipt of the down payment and the two installment payments with these entries:

May	6	Cash	6,000.00	
		Subscriptions Receivable, Common Stock . . .		6,000.00
		Collected 10% down payments on the common stock subscriptions.		
Aug.	6	Cash	27,000.00	
		Subscriptions Receivable, Common Stock . . .		27,000.00
		Collected the first installment payments on the common stock subscriptions.		
Nov.	6	Cash	27,000.00	
		Subscriptions Receivable, Common Stock . . .		27,000.00
		Collected the second installment payments on the common stock subscriptions.		

In this case, the down payments accompanied the subscriptions. Therefore, the accountant could have combined the May 6 entries to record the subscriptions and the down payments as follows:

May	6	Cash	6,000.00	
		Subscriptions Receivable, Common Stock	54,000.00	
		Common Stock Subscribed		50,000.00
		Contributed Capital in Excess of Par Value, Common Stock		10,000.00
		Accepted subscriptions to 5,000 shares of $10 par value common stock at $12 per share and received down payments of 10% of the subscription price.		

When stock is sold through subscriptions, the stock usually is not issued until the subscriptions are paid in full. Also, if dividends are declared before subscribed stock has been issued, the dividends go only to the holders of outstanding shares, not to the subscribers. However, as soon as the subscriptions are paid, the stock is issued. The entry to record the issuance of the Northgate common stock is as follows:

Nov.	6	Common Stock Subscribed	50,000.00	
		Common Stock, $10 Par Value		50,000.00
		Issued 5,000 shares of common stock sold through subscriptions.		

Subscriptions are usually collected in full, but not always. Sometimes, a subscriber fails to pay the agreed amount. When this default happens, the subscription contract is canceled. If the subscriber has made a partial payment on the contract, the amount may be refunded. Or, the company may issue a smaller amount of stock with a fair value equal to the partial payment. Or, the state law may allow the subscriber's partial payment to be kept by the corporation to compensate it for any damages.

Subscriptions Receivable and Subscribed Stock on the Balance Sheet

Subscriptions receivable are reported on the balance sheet as current or long-term assets, depending on when collection is expected.[5] If a corporation prepares a balance sheet after accepting subscriptions to its stock but before the stock is issued, both the issued stock and the subscribed stock should be reported on the balance sheet as follows:

Common stock, $10 par value, 25,000 shares authorized, 20,000 shares issued and outstanding	$200,000
Common stock subscribed, 5,000 shares	50,000
Total common stock issued and subscribed	$250,000
Contributed capital in excess of par value, common stock	40,000
Total contributed capital	$290,000

Corporate Dividends

Many corporations pay cash dividends to their stockholders in regular amounts at regular dates. These cash flows provide a return to the investors and usually affect the stock's market value. Three dates are involved in the process of declaring dividends.

The day the directors vote to pay a dividend is called the **date of declaration.** Stockholders receive a dividend only if the directors formally vote to declare one. By declaring a dividend, the directors create a legal liability of the corporation to its stockholders.

In its declaration, the directors specify a future date on which the persons listed in the corporation's records are identified as those who will receive the dividend. In most cases, this **date of record** follows the date of declaration by at least two weeks. Persons who buy stock in time to be recorded as stockholders on the date of record will receive the dividend.

[5] If collection of stock subscriptions is uncertain, they are subtracted from contributed capital on the balance sheet.

The declaration by the board of directors also specifies a **date of payment**, which follows the date of record by enough time to allow the corporation to prepare checks payable to the stockholders. If a balance sheet is prepared between the date of declaration and the date of payment, the liability for the dividend is reported as a current liability.

Accounting for Dividends

Because the act of declaring a dividend creates a liability for the corporation, the accountant needs to prepare a journal entry to record the new obligation. This entry would be recorded if the directors of a company with 5,000 outstanding shares declare a $1 per share dividend on January 9, payable on February 1:

Jan.	9	Cash Dividends Declared	5,000.00	
		Common Dividend Payable		5,000.00
		Declared a $1 per share cash dividend on the common stock.		

Cash Dividend Declared is a temporary account that accumulates information about the total dividends declared during the reporting period. It serves the same purpose as the Withdrawals account for a proprietorship. Note that it is not an expense account. The credited account describes the corporation's liability to its stockholders.

No entry is needed at the date of record, unless the tabulation of the stockholder list shows that a larger or smaller dividend will actually be paid than the directors anticipated on the declaration date.

On the payment date, the following entry records the settlement of the liability and the reduction of the cash balance:

Feb.	1	Common Dividend Payable	5,000.00	
		Cash		5,000.00
		Paid the $1 per share cash dividend to the common stockholders.		

At the end of the annual reporting period, an additional entry closes the balance of the Cash Dividends Declared account against Retained Earnings. If the company declared four quarterly dividends of $5,000, the account has a $20,000 balance at the end of the year, and the accountant makes this closing entry:

Dec.	31	Retained Earnings	20,000.00	
		Cash Dividends Declared		20,000.00
		To close the Cash Dividends Declared account.		

If one of the declared dividends remains unpaid on December 31, this closing entry is still recorded because the act of declaration reduces retained earnings. The liability account continues to have a balance until the dividends are paid, and its amount is presented on the December 31 balance sheet.

Deficits and Dividends

A corporation with a debit balance of retained earnings is said to have a **deficit**. A deficit arises when a company incurs cumulative losses and pays dividends greater than the cumulative profits earned in other years. A deficit is deducted on a corporation's balance sheet, as in this example:

Stockholders' Equity	
Common stock, $10 par value, 5,000 shares authorized and outstanding	$50,000
Deduct retained earnings deficit	(6,000)
Total stockholders' equity	$44,000

In most states, a corporation with a deficit is not allowed to pay a cash dividend to its stockholders. This legal restriction is designed to protect the creditors of the corporation by preventing the distribution of assets to stockholders at a time when the company is in financial difficulty.

Rights of Common Stockholders

LO 4 State the differences between common and preferred stock, and allocate dividends between the common and preferred stock of a corporation.

When investors buy a corporation's common stock, they acquire all the *specific* rights granted by the corporation's charter to its common stockholders. They also acquire the *general* rights granted stockholders by the laws of the state in which the company is incorporated. State laws vary, but common stockholders usually have the following general rights:

1. The right to vote at stockholders' meetings.
2. The right to sell or otherwise dispose of their stock.
3. The right of first opportunity to purchase any additional shares of common stock issued by the corporation. This right is called the common stockholders' **preemptive right.** It gives stockholders the opportunity to protect their proportionate interest in the corporation. For example, a stockholder who owns 25% of a corporation's common stock has the first opportunity to buy 25% of any new common stock issued. This arrangement enables the stockholder to maintain a 25% interest.
4. The right to share equally with other common stockholders in any dividends, with the result that each common share receives the same amount.
5. The right to share equally in any assets that remain after creditors are paid when the corporation is liquidated, with the result that each common share receives the same amount.

In addition, stockholders have the right to receive timely reports that describe the corporation's financial position and the results of its activities.

Preferred Stock

As mentioned earlier in this chapter, a corporation may be authorized to issue more than one kind or class of stock. If two classes are issued, one is generally called **preferred stock** and the other is called *common stock.* Preferred stock often has a par value, but like common stock, may be sold at a price greater than par (or perhaps less). Separate contributed capital accounts are used to record the issuance of preferred stock. For example, if 50 shares of preferred stock with a $100 par value are issued for $6,000 cash, the entry is

June	1	Cash	6,000.00	
		Preferred Stock		5,000.00
		Contributed Capital in Excess of Par Value, Preferred Stock		1,000.00
		Issued preferred stock for cash.		

The term *preferred* is used because the preferred shares have a higher priority (or senior status) relative to common shares in one or more ways. These typically include a preference for receiving dividends and a preference in the distribution of assets if the corporation is liquidated.

In addition to the preferences it receives, preferred stock carries all the rights of common stock, unless they are nullified in the corporation's charter. For example, most preferred stock does not have the right to vote.

Preferred Dividends

A preference for dividends gives preferred stockholders the right to receive their dividends before the common stockholders receive a dividend. In other words, a dividend cannot be paid to common stockholders unless preferred stockholders also receive one. The amount of dividends that the preferred stockholders must receive is usually expressed as a dollar amount per share or as a percentage applied to the par value. For example, holders of a 9%, $100 par value, preferred stock must be paid dividends at the rate of $9 per share per year before the common shareholders can receive any dividend. A preference for dividends does not, however, grant an absolute right to dividends. If the board of directors does not declare a dividend, neither the preferred nor the common stockholders receive one.

Cumulative and Noncumulative Preferred Stock

Preferred stock can be either **cumulative** or **noncumulative.** For noncumulative, the right to receive dividends is forfeited in any year that the dividends are not declared. When preferred stock is cumulative and the board of directors fails to declare a dividend to the preferred stockholders, the unpaid dividend is called a **dividend in arrears.** The accumulation of dividends in arrears on cumulative preferred stock does not guarantee that they will be paid. However, the cumulative preferred stockholders must be paid both the current dividend and all dividends in arrears before any dividend can be paid to the common stockholders.

To show the difference between cumulative and noncumulative preferred stock, assume that a corporation's outstanding stock includes 1,000 shares of $100 par, 9% preferred stock and 4,000 shares of $50 par common stock. During the first two years of the corporation's operations, the board of directors declared cash dividends of $5,000 in 19X1 and $42,000 in 19X2. The allocations of the total dividends are as follows:

	Preferred	Common
Assuming noncumulative preferred:		
19X1	$ 5,000	$ -0-
19X2:		
First: current preferred dividend	$ 9,000	
Remainder to common		$33,000
* * * * *		
Assuming cumulative preferred:		
19X1	$ 5,000	$ -0-
19X2:		
First: dividends in arrears	$ 4,000	
Next: current preferred dividend	9,000	
Remainder to common		$29,000
Totals	$13,000	$29,000

Notice that the allocation of the 19X2 dividends depends on whether the preferred stock is noncumulative or cumulative. With noncumulative preferred stock, the preferred stockholders never receive the $4,000 that was skipped in 19X1. However, when the preferred stock is cumulative, the $4,000 in arrears is paid in 19X2 before the common stockholders receive a dividend.

Disclosure of Dividends in Arrears in the Financial Statements

Dividends are not like interest expense, which is incurred as time passes and therefore must be accrued. A liability for a dividend does not come into existence until the dividend is declared by the board of directors. Thus, if a preferred dividend date passes and the corporation's board fails to declare the dividend on its cumulative preferred stock, the dividend in arrears is not a liability. Accordingly, it does not appear as a liability on the balance sheet. However, when preparing financial statements, the *full-disclosure principle* requires the corporation to report the amount of preferred dividends in arrears as of the balance sheet date. Normally, this information is given in a footnote. If there is no such disclosure, readers of the financial statements should assume that preferred dividends are not in arrears.

Participating Preferred Stock—A Defense Against Hostile Takeovers

The dividends on most preferred stocks are limited to a maximum amount each year. The maximum is defined as a stated percentage of the stock's par value or as a specific dollar amount per share. Once the preferred stockholders receive this amount, the common stockholders receive any and all additional dividends. Preferred stocks that have this limitation are called *nonparticipating.* However, the owners of **participating preferred stock** have the right to share with the common stockholders in any additional dividends paid in excess of the stated percentage dividend on the preferred.

Although many corporations are authorized to issue participating preferred stock, the shares are issued only rarely. That is, companies obtain authorization to issue the shares even though management does not expect to ever sell them. They do this to defend against a *takeover* of the corporation by an unfriendly investor (or a group of investors) who would buy enough voting common stock to gain control over operations. Using terminology from spy novels, the financial world refers to this kind of a plan as a *poison pill* that the company will "swallow" if it is threatened with capture by an enemy.

A typical poison pill works as follows: The common stockholders on a given date are granted the right to purchase a large amount of participating preferred stock at a very low price. This right cannot be transferred. Thus, if the stock is sold, the buyer does not gain the right. In addition, this right cannot be exercised unless the directors identify a buyer of a large block of common shares as an unfriendly buyer.

If an unfriendly investor were identified and the preferred stock were issued, future dividends would be divided between the preferred shares and the common shares. This would transfer some of the value of the common shares to the preferred shares. As a result, the stock owned by the unfriendly buyer would lose much of its value and be worth much less than the buyer's cost. The ultimate effect is to eliminate the potential benefit of attempting a hostile takeover.

Why Preferred Stock Is Issued

A corporation might issue preferred stock for several reasons. One reason is to raise capital without sacrificing control of the corporation. For example, suppose that the organizers of a business have $100,000 cash to invest but wish to organize a corporation that needs $200,000 of capital to get off to a good start. If they sold $200,000 of common stock, they would have only 50% control and would have to negotiate extensively with the other stockholders in making policy. However, if they issue $100,000 of common stock to themselves and can sell outsiders $100,000 of 8%, cumulative preferred stock that has no voting rights, they can retain control of the corporation.

A second reason for issuing preferred stock is to boost the return earned by the common stockholders. Using the previous example to illustrate, suppose that the corporation's organizers expect the new company to earn an annual after-tax income of $24,000. If they sell and issue $200,000 of common stock, this income produces a 12% return on the $200,000 of common stockholders' equity. However, if they issue $100,000 of 8% preferred stock to the outsiders and $100,000 of common stock to themselves, their own return increases to 16% per year, as shown here:

Net after-tax income	$24,000
Less preferred dividends at 8%	(8,000)
Balance to common stockholders (equal to 16% on their $100,000 investment)	$16,000

In this case, the common stockholders earn 16% because the assets contributed by the preferred stockholders are invested to earn $12,000 while the preferred dividend payments amount to only $8,000.

The use of preferred stock to increase the return to common stockholders is an example of **financial leverage.** Whenever the dividend rate on preferred stock is less than the rate that the corporation earns on its assets, the effect of issuing preferred stock is to increase (or *lever*) the rate earned by common stockholders. Financial leverage also occurs when debt is issued and paid an interest rate less than the rate earned from using the assets the creditors loaned to the corporation.

There are other reasons for issuing preferred stock. For example, a corporation's preferred stock may appeal to some investors who believe that its common stock is too risky or that the dividend rate on the common stock will be too low. Also, if a corporation's management wants to issue common stock but believes the current market price for the common stock is too low, the corporation may issue preferred stock that is convertible into common stock. If and when the price of the common stock increases, the preferred stockholders can convert their shares into common shares.

Convertible Preferred Stock

LO 5 Describe convertible preferred stock and explain the meaning of the par value, call price, market value, and book value of corporate stock.

As we just mentioned, an issue of preferred stock can be made more attractive to some investors by giving them the right to exchange the preferred shares for a fixed number of common shares. **Convertible preferred stock** offers investors a higher potential return than does nonconvertible preferred stock. If the company prospers and its common stock increases in value, the convertible preferred stockholders can share in the prosperity by converting their preferred stock into the more valuable common stock. Conversion is at the option of the investors and therefore does not occur unless it is to their advantage. (The investors can enjoy the results of the increased value of the common stock without converting the preferred stock because the preferred stock's market value reflects the change in the common stock's value.)

Stock Values

In addition to a par value, stocks may have a *call price,* a *market value,* and a book value.

Call Price of Callable Preferred Stock

Some issues of preferred stock are callable. This means that the issuing corporation has the right to retire the **callable preferred stock** by paying a specified amount to the preferred stockholders. The amount that must be paid to call and retire a preferred share is its **call price** or *redemption value.* This amount is set at the time the stock is issued. Normally, the call price includes the par value of the stock plus a premium that provides the stockholders with some

ILLUSTRATION 13–1 *Stockholders' Equity with Preferred and Common Stock*

Stockholders' Equity		
Preferred stock, $100 par value, 7%, cumulative, 2,000 shares authorized, 1,000 shares issued and outstanding	$100,000	
Contributed capital in excess of par value, preferred stock	5,000	
Total capital contributed by preferred stockholders		$105,000
Common stock, $25 par value, 12,000 shares authorized, 10,000 shares issued and outstanding	$250,000	
Contributed capital in excess of par value, common stock	10,000	
Total capital contributed by common stockholders		260,000
Total contributed capital		$365,000
Retained earnings		82,000
Total stockholders' equity		$447,000

additional return on their investment. When the issuing corporation calls and retires a preferred stock, it must pay not only the call price but also any dividends in arrears.

Market Value

The market value of a share of stock is the price at which it can be bought or sold. Market values are influenced by a wide variety of factors including expected future earnings, dividends, and events in the economy at large. Market values of frequently traded stocks are reported daily in newspapers such as *The Wall Street Journal.* The market values of stocks that are not actively traded can be more difficult to determine. Analysts use a variety of techniques to estimate the value of such stocks, and most of these techniques use accounting information as an important input to the valuation process.

Book Value

The **book value of a share of stock** equals the share's portion of the stockholders' equity as it is recorded in the company's accounts. If a corporation has only common stock, the book value per share equals the total stockholders' equity divided by the number of outstanding shares. For example, if a company has 10,000 outstanding shares and total stockholders' equity of $285,000, the stock's book value is $28.50 per share ($285,000/10,000 shares).

Computing the book values of stock is more complex when both common and preferred shares are outstanding. To calculate the book values of each class of stock, first allocate the total stockholders' equity between the two classes. The preferred stockholders' portion equals the preferred stock's call price (or par value if the preferred is not callable) plus any cumulative dividends in arrears. The remaining stockholders' equity is then allocated to the common shares. To determine the book value per share of preferred, divide the portion of stockholders' equity assigned to preferred by the number of preferred shares outstanding. Similarly, the book value per share of common is the stockholders' equity assigned to common divided by the number of outstanding common shares. For example, assume a corporation has the stockholders' equity as shown in Illustration 13–1.

If the preferred stock is callable at $108 per share and two years of cumulative preferred dividends are in arrears, the book values of the corporation's shares are calculated as follows:

Total stockholders' equity		$447,000
Less equity applicable to preferred shares:		
Call price (1,000 × $108)	$108,000	
Cumulative dividends in arrears		
($100,000 × 7% × 2)	14,000	(122,000)
Equity applicable to common shares		$325,000
Book value of preferred shares ($122,000/1,000) . .		$ 122.00
Book value of common shares ($325,000/10,000) . .		$ 32.50

In their annual reports to shareholders, corporations sometimes report the increase in the book value of the corporation's shares that has occurred during a year. Also, book value may have significance in contracts. For example, a stockholder may enter into a contract to sell shares at their book value at some future date. However, this agreement may not be wise because the stock is likely to have a market value that differs from its book value.

Similarly, book value should not be confused with the liquidation value of a stock. If a corporation is liquidated, its assets probably will sell at prices that are quite different from the amounts at which they are carried on the books.

PROPRIETORSHIPS

LO 6 Explain the legal status of a proprietorship, prepare entries to account for the owner's equity of a proprietorship, and prepare a statement of changes in owner's equity.

Chapter 1 explained that a proprietorship (sometimes called a *single proprietorship* or *sole proprietorship*) is a business owned by one person that is not organized as a corporation. Legally, a proprietorship is not a separate entity; it does not exist apart from the owner. In other words, a proprietorship is no more than a business carried on by an individual.

Because a proprietorship is not a separate legal entity, it is not subject to income taxes. Instead, the income is taxed as personal income of the owner. The taxes are assessed whether the owner withdraws cash from the business or not.

Unlimited Liability of the Proprietor

Because a proprietorship is not legally separate from its owner, the owner is personally responsible for the liabilities of the proprietorship. Thus, the personal assets of the owner are available to satisfy the claims of the business creditors. This situation is called *unlimited liability.*

Accounting for Proprietorships

Although a proprietorship is not a separate legal entity, managing a proprietorship requires using information about the activities, assets, and related liabilities of the business as if it were separate from its owner. Thus, the accounting records and financial statements for a proprietorship are based on the assumption that the business is a separate entity. (See the discussion of the *business entity principle* in Chapter 1, page 27.)

Accounting for a proprietorship and for a corporation are the same except in regard to owners' equity. In a proprietorship, contributed capital and retained earnings are not recorded in separate accounts. Instead, all of the owner's equity is recorded in a single *capital* account. For example, assume that Terry Dow started a consulting business and invested $10,000 cash. The entry to record this event on the books of the proprietorship is

Jan.	1	Cash	10,000.00	
		Terry Dow, Capital		10,000.00
		To record owner's investment.		

When the owner of a proprietorship withdraws cash from the business, the withdrawal is recorded in a special *withdrawals* account. For example, assume that Dow withdrew $7,000 from the business for personal use. The entry to record the withdrawal is

Nov.	1	Terry Dow, Withdrawals	7,000.00	
		Cash		7,000.00
		To record owner's cash withdrawal.		

Now assume that Dow's first year of operations resulted in a net income of $12,000, which appears as a credit balance in the Income Summary account. The following entry closes the Income Summary account:

Dec.	31	Income Summary	12,000.00	
		Terry Dow, Capital		12,000.00
		To close Income Summary.		

Then, the withdrawals account is closed with the following entry:

Dec.	31	Terry Dow, Capital	7,000.00	
		Terry Dow, Withdrawals		7,000.00
		To close the withdrawals account.		

The changes in the owner's capital account during an accounting period are reported on the statement of changes in owner's equity. This statement for Dow's consulting business appears as follows:

TERRY DOW, CONSULTANT
Statement of Changes in Owner's Equity
For Year Ended December 31, 19X1

Terry Dow, capital, January 1, 19X1		$ -0-
Plus: Investments by owner	$10,000	
Net income	12,000	22,000
Total		$22,000
Less withdrawals by owner		7,000
Terry Dow, capital, December 31, 19X1		$15,000

On the balance sheet for a proprietorship, the owner's equity section includes a single item—the capital account balance of the owner. For example, the December 31 balance sheet for Dow's consulting business would include the following item:

Owner's Equity

Terry Dow, capital	$15,000

PARTNERSHIPS

A **partnership** can be defined as *an unincorporated association of two or more persons to carry on a business for profit as co-owners.* Many businesses, such as small retail and service businesses, are organized as partnerships. Also, many professional practitioners—including physicians, lawyers, and certified public accountants—have traditionally organized their practices as partnerships.

Characteristics of Partnerships

LO 7 Explain the concepts of mutual agency and unlimited liability for a partnership, record the investments and withdrawals of partners, and allocate the net incomes or losses of a partnership among the partners.

A partnership is a voluntary association between the partners. All that is required to form a partnership is that two or more legally competent people (that is, people who are of age and of sound mental capacity) must agree to be partners. Their agreement becomes a **partnership contract.** Although it should be in writing, the contract is binding even if it is only expressed orally.[6]

The life of a partnership is always limited. Death, bankruptcy, or anything that takes away the ability of one of the partners to enter into or fulfill a contract automatically ends a partnership. In addition, a partnership may be terminated at will by any one of the partners. Before agreeing to join a partnership, you should understand clearly two important characteristics of a partnership: **mutual agency** and **unlimited liability.**

Mutual Agency

Generally, the relationship between the partners in a partnership involves **mutual agency.** Under normal circumstances, every partner is a fully authorized agent of the partnership. As its agent, a partner can commit or bind the partnership to any contract that is within the apparent scope of the partnership's business. For example, a partner in a merchandising business can sign contracts that bind the partnership to buy merchandise, lease a store building, borrow money, or hire employees. These activities are all within the scope of the business of a merchandising firm. On the other hand, a partner in a law firm, acting alone, cannot bind his or her partners to a contract to buy merchandise for resale or rent a retail store building. These actions are not within the normal scope of a law firm's business.

Partners may agree to limit the power of any one or more of the partners to negotiate certain contracts for the partnership. Such an agreement is binding on the partners and on outsiders who know that it exists. However, it is not binding on outsiders who do not know that it exists. Outsiders who are not aware of the agreement have the right to assume that each partner has normal agency powers for the partnership.

Because mutual agency exposes all partners to the risk of unwise actions by any one partner, people should carefully evaluate potential partners before agreeing to join a partnership. The importance of this advice is underscored by the fact that most partnerships are also characterized by unlimited liability.

Unlimited Liability of Partners

When a partnership cannot pay its debts, the creditors normally can satisfy their claims from the *personal* assets of the partners. Also, if some partners do not have enough assets to meet their share of the partnership's debts, the creditors can turn to the assets of the remaining partners who are able to pay. Because partners may be called on to pay all the debts of the partnership, each partner is said to have *unlimited liability* for the partnership's debts. Mutual

[6] In some cases, courts have ruled that partnerships have been created by the actions of the partners, even when there was no expressed agreement to form a partnership.

agency and unlimited liability are the main reasons why most partnerships have only a few members.

Limited Partnerships

Partnerships in which all of the partners have unlimited liability are called **general partnerships.** Sometimes, however, individuals who want to invest in a partnership are not willing to accept the risk of unlimited liability. Their needs can be met by using a **limited partnership.** A limited partnership has two classes of partners, general and limited. At least one partner has to be a **general partner** who must assume unlimited liability for the debts of the partnership. The remaining **limited partners** have no personal liability beyond the amounts that they invest in the business. Usually, a limited partnership is managed by the general partner or partners. The limited partners have no active role except for major decisions specified in the partnership agreement.

Partnership Accounting

Accounting for a partnership does not differ from accounting for a proprietorship except for transactions that directly affect the partners' equity. Because ownership rights in a partnership are divided among two or more partners, partnership accounting uses:

- A capital account for each partner.
- A withdrawals account for each partner.
- An accurate measurement and division of earnings.

When partners invest in a partnership, their capital accounts are credited for the invested amounts. Partners' withdrawals of assets are debited to their withdrawals accounts. In closing the accounts at the end of the year, the partners' capital accounts are credited or debited for their shares of the net income or loss. Finally, the withdrawals account of each partner is closed to that partner's capital account. These closing procedures are like those used for a single proprietorship. The only difference is that separate capital and withdrawals accounts are maintained for each partner.

Nature of Partnership Earnings

Because they are its owners, partners are not employees of the partnership. If partners devote their time and services to the affairs of their partnership, they are understood to do so for profit, not for salary. Therefore, when the partners calculate the net income of a partnership, salaries to the partners are not deducted as expenses on the income statement. However, when a net income or loss of the partnership is allocated among the partners, the partners may agree to base part of the allocation on salary allowances that reflect the relative amounts of service provided by the partners. Likewise, if the services of one partner are much more valuable than those of another, salary allowances provide for the unequal service contributions.

Partners are also understood to have invested in a partnership for profit, not for interest. Nevertheless, partners may agree that the division of partnership earnings should include a return based on their invested capital. For example, if one partner contributes five times as much capital as another, it is only fair that this fact be taken into consideration when earnings are allocated among the partners. Thus, a partnership agreement may provide for interest allowances based on the partners' capital balances. Like salary allowances, interest allowances are not expenses to be reported on the income statement.

Division of Earnings

In the absence of a contrary agreement, the law states that the income or loss of a partnership is to be shared equally by the partners. However, partners may agree to any method of sharing. If they agree on how they will share income but say nothing about losses, then losses are shared in the same way as income.

Several methods of sharing partnership earnings can be used. Three frequently used methods divide earnings (1) on a stated fractional basis, (2) in the ratio of capital investments, or (3) using salary and interest allowances and any remainder in a fixed ratio.

Earnings Allocated on a Stated Fractional Basis

The easiest way to divide partnership earnings is to give each partner a fraction of the total. All that is necessary is for the partners to agree on the fractional share that each will receive. For example, assume that the partnership agreement of B. A. Jones and S. A. Meyers states that Jones will receive two-thirds and Meyers will receive one-third of the partnership earnings. In accounting for the partnership, this agreement shapes the entry to close the Income Summary account. If the partnership's net income is $30,000, the earnings are allocated to the partners and the Income Summary account is closed with the following entry:

Dec.	31	Income Summary	30,000.00	
		B. A. Jones, Capital		20,000.00
		S. A. Meyers, Capital		10,000.00
		To close the Income Summary account and allocate the earnings.		

When earnings are shared on a fractional basis, the fractions may reflect the relative capital investments of the partners. For example, suppose that B. Donner and H. Flack formed a partnership and agreed to share earnings in the ratio of their investments. Because Donner invested $50,000 and Flack invested $30,000, Donner will receive five-eighths of the earnings ($50,000/$80,000) while Flack will receive three-eighths of the earnings ($30,000/$80,000).

Salaries and Interest as Aids in Sharing

As we have mentioned, partners' service contributions are not always equal. Also, the capital contributions of the partners often are not equal. If the service contributions are not equal, the partners may use salary allowances to compensate for the differences. Or, when capital contributions are not equal, they may allocate part of the earnings with interest allowances that compensate for the unequal investments. When investment and service contributions are both unequal, the allocation of net incomes and losses may include both interest and salary allowances.

For example, in Kathy Stanley and Gary Wilson's new partnership, Stanley is to provide services that they agree are worth an annual salary of $36,000. Wilson is less experienced in the business, so his service contribution is worth only $24,000. Also, Stanley will invest $30,000 in the business and Wilson will invest $10,000. To compensate Stanley and Wilson fairly in light of the differences in their service and capital contributions, they agree to share incomes or losses as follows:

1. The partners are to be granted annual salary allowances of $36,000 to Stanley and $24,000 to Wilson.

ILLUSTRATION 13-2 *Sharing Income When Income Exceeds Salary and Interest Allowances*

	Share to Stanley	Share to Wilson	Income to Be Allocated
Total net income			$70,000
Allocated as salary allowances:			
Stanley	$36,000		
Wilson		$24,000	
Total allocated as salary allowances			60,000
Balance of income after salary allowances			$10,000
Allocated as interest:			
Stanley (10% on $30,000)	3,000		
Wilson (10% on $10,000)		1,000	
Total allocated as interest			4,000
Balance of income after salary and interest allowances			$ 6,000
Balance allocated equally:			
Stanley	3,000		
Wilson		3,000	
Total allocated equally			6,000
Balance of income			$ -0-
Shares of the partners	$42,000	$28,000	
Percentages of total net income	60%	40%	

ILLUSTRATION 13-3 *Sharing Income When Salary and Interest Allowances Exceed Income*

	Share to Stanley	Share to Wilson	Income to Be Allocated
Total net income			$ 50,000
Allocated as salary allowances:			
Stanley	$36,000		
Wilson		$24,000	
Total allocated as salary allowances			60,000
Balance of income after salary allowances			$(10,000)
Allocated as interest:			
Stanley (10% on $30,000)	3,000		
Wilson (10% on $10,000)		1,000	
Total allocated as interest			4,000
Balance of income after salary and interest allowances			$(14,000)
Balance allocated equally:			
Stanley	(7,000)		
Wilson		(7,000)	
Total allocated equally			(14,000)
Balance of income			$ -0-
Shares of the partners	$32,000	$18,000	
Percentages of total net income	64%	36%	

2. The partners are to be granted an interest allowance equal to 10% of each partner's beginning-of-year capital balance.
3. The remaining balance of income or loss is to be shared equally.

Note that the provisions for salaries and interest in this partnership agreement are called *allowances.* Also remember that, in the legal sense, partners do not work for salaries and do not invest in a partnership to earn interest. Rather, they work and invest for profits. Therefore, when a partnership agreement provides for salary and interest allowances to the partners, these allowances are not reported on the income statement as salaries and interest expense. They are only a means of splitting up the net income or net loss of the partnership.

Under the Stanley and Wilson partnership agreement, a first year's net income of $70,000 is shared as shown in Illustration 13–2. Notice that Stanley gets $42,000, or 60% of the income, while Wilson gets $28,000, or 40%.

In Illustration 13–2, notice that the $70,000 net income exceeds the salary and interest allowances of the partners. However, the method of sharing agreed to by Stanley and Wilson must be followed even if the net income is smaller than the salary and interest allowances. For example, if the first year's net income was $50,000, it would be allocated to the partners as shown in Illustration 13–3. Notice that this circumstance provides Stanley with 64% of the total income, while Wilson gets only 36%.

A net loss would be shared by Stanley and Wilson in the same manner as the $50,000 net income. The only difference is that the income-and-loss-sharing procedure would begin with a negative amount of income because of the net loss. After the salary and interest allowances, the remaining balance to be allocated equally would then be a larger negative amount.

Using the Information—Dividend Yield

LO 8 Calculate the dividend yield and describe its meaning.

Investors buy shares of a company's stock in anticipation of receiving a return from cash dividends and from increases in the stock's value. Stocks that pay large dividends on a regular basis are sometimes called *income stocks.* They are attractive to investors who want dependable cash flows from their investments. In contrast, other stocks pay little or no dividends, but are still attractive to investors because they expect the market value of the stocks to increase rapidly. The stocks of companies that do not distribute cash but use it to finance rapid expansion are often called *growth stocks.*

One way to determine whether a company stock should be viewed as an income stock or growth stock is to examine the **dividend yield.** The following formula shows that this ratio is a rate of return based on the annual cash dividends and the stock's market value:

$$\text{Dividend yield} = \frac{\text{Annual cash dividends per share}}{\text{Market value per share}}$$

Dividend yield may be calculated on a historical basis using the prior year's actual dividends or on an expected basis. For example, suppose that a stock with a current market value of $40 is expected to pay a dividend of $2.40 per share over the coming year. By computing the ratio of the expected dividends to the market value, we can discover that the stock's expected dividend yield is 6% per year ($2.40/$40).

An investor can determine whether this rate is similar to rates provided by other investments that are clearly based on regular cash flows (such as bonds). This comparison allows the investor to decide whether the stock is valued for its regular dividends or its growth potential. For example, if bonds are yielding around 5% per year, the 6% yield on the stock suggests that the company's dividends are the main source of its value. On the other hand, if bond yields are substantially higher (such as 12 to1 5%), the stock's current value is apparently being shaped by the potential for its higher expected future value. As an extreme, many growth stocks do not pay any dividends at all.

Although income stocks tend to have relatively stable market values, their values can vary substantially in anticipation of changes in the company's ability to pay future dividends or changes in rates of returns on other available investments. Thus, investors need to examine much more information in addition to the dividend yield before deciding to buy, sell, or keep a stock.

Summary of the Chapter in Terms of Learning Objectives

LO 1 Corporations are separate legal entities. As such, their stockholders are not liable for the corporate debts. Stocks issued by corporations are easily transferred between stockholders, and the life of corporations does not end with the incapacity or death of a stockholder. A corporation acts through its agents, who are its officers and managers, not its stockholders. Corporations tend to be closely regulated by government and are subject to income taxes.

LO 2 When stock is issued, the par or stated value is credited to the stock account and any excess is credited to a separate contributed capital account. If the stock has no par or stated value, the entire proceeds are credited to the stock account. Stockholders must contribute assets equal to the minimum legal capital of a corporation or be potentially liable for the deficiency. And, as long as any liabilities remain unpaid, the minimum legal capital cannot be paid to stockholders.

LO 3 If a corporation sells stock through subscriptions, the unpaid portion is recorded as a receivable, and the subscribers' equity is recorded in contributed capital accounts. The balance of the Common Stock Subscribed account is transferred to the Common Stock account when the shares are issued, which normally occurs after all payments are received. Three dates are involved when cash dividends are distributed to stockholders. The board of directors binds the company to pay the dividend on the date of declaration. The recipients of the dividend are identified on the date of record. The cash is paid to the stockholders on the date of payment.

LO 4 Preferred stock has a priority (or senior status) relative to common stock in one or more ways. Usually, common stockholders cannot be paid dividends unless a specified amount of dividends also is paid to preferred shareholders. Preferred stock also may have a priority status if the corporation is liquidated. The dividend preference for many preferred stocks is cumulative. Many companies are authorized to issue participating preferred stocks as a poison pill against hostile takeovers.

LO 5 Convertible preferred stock can be exchanged by its holders for common stock. If preferred stock is callable, the amount that must be paid to retire the stock is its call price plus any dividends in arrears. Market value is the price that a stock commands when it is bought or sold. The book value of preferred stock is any dividends in arrears plus its par value or, if it is callable, its call price. The remaining stockholders' equity is divided by the number of outstanding common shares to determine the book value per share of the common stock.

LO 6 Proprietorships are not separate legal entities but are treated as separate entities for accounting purposes. The owner's equity of a proprietorship is recorded in a single capital account and withdrawals are recorded in a withdrawals account that is closed to the capital account at the end of each period. A statement of changes in owner's equity shows the change in the owner's capital account balance during a period that resulted from investments and withdrawals by the owner and from the net income or loss.

LO 7 Mutual agency means that every partner can bind a partnership to contracts that are within the normal scope of the business. In a general partnership, each partner has unlimited liability for the debts of the partnership. A partnership agreement should specify the method of allocating the partnership's net income or loss among the partners. This allocation may be done on a fractional basis, or salary and interest allowances may be used to compensate partners for differences in their service and capital contributions.

LO 8 The dividend yield is the ratio between a stock's annual dividends and its market value. It describes the rate of return to the stockholders from the company's dividends. The yield can be compared with the rates of return offered by other kinds of investments to determine whether the stock should be viewed as an income or growth stock.

Demonstration Problem

Barton Corporation was created on January 1, 19X1. The following transactions relating to stockholders' equity occurred during the first two years of the company's operations. Prepare the journal entries to record these transactions. Also prepare the balance sheet presentation of the organization costs, liabilities, and stockholders' equity as of December 31, 19X1, and December 31, 19X2. Include appropriate footnotes.

19X1

Jan. 1 Authorized the issuance of 2 million shares of $5 par value common stock and 100,000 shares of $100 par value preferred stock. The preferred stock pays a 10% annual dividend and is cumulative.

1 Issued 200,000 shares of common stock for cash at $12 per share.

1 Issued 100,000 shares of common stock in exchange for a building valued at $820,000 and merchandise inventory valued at $380,000.

1 Accepted subscriptions for 150,000 shares of common stock at $12 per share. The subscribers made no down payments, and the full purchase price was due on April 1, 19X1.

1 Paid a cash reimbursement to the company's founders for $100,000 of organization costs; these costs are to be amortized over 10 years.

1 Issued 12,000 shares of preferred stock for cash at $110 per share.

Apr. 1 Collected the full subscription price for the January 1 common stock and issued the stock.

Dec. 31 The Income Summary account for 19X1 had a $125,000 credit balance before being closed to Retained Earnings; no dividends were declared on either the common or preferred stocks.

19X2

June 4 Issued 100,000 shares of common stock for cash at $15 per share.

Dec. 10 Declared dividends payable on January 10, 19X3, as follows:

To preferred stockholders for 19X1	$120,000
To preferred stockholders for 19X2	120,000
To common stockholders for 19X2	300,000

31 The Income Summary account for 19X2 had a $1 million credit balance before being closed to Retained Earnings.

Planning the Solution

- Record journal entries for the events in 19X1.
- Close the accounts related to retained earnings.
- Determine the balances for the 19X1 balance sheet.
- Determine the following amounts to use in the balance sheet and the accompanying note:
  a. The number of shares issued.
  b. The amount of dividends in arrears.
  c. The unamortized balance of organization costs.

- Prepare the specified portions of the 19X1 balance sheet.
- Record journal entries for the events in 19X2.
- Close the accounts related to retained earnings.
- Determine the balances for the 19X2 balance sheet.
- Determine the following amounts to use in the balance sheet and the accompanying note:
  a. The number of shares issued.
  b. The unamortized balance of organization costs.
- Prepare the specified portions of the 19X2 balance sheet.

Solution to Demonstration Problem

Date		Account	Debit	Credit
19X1 Jan.	1	Cash	2,400,000.00	
		Common Stock		1,000,000.00
		Contributed Capital in Excess of Par Value, Common Stock		1,400,000.00
		Issued 200,000 shares of common stock.		
	1	Building	820,000.00	
		Merchandise Inventory	380,000.00	
		Common Stock		500,000.00
		Contributed Capital in Excess of Par Value, Common Stock		700,000.00
		Issued 100,000 shares of common stock.		
	1	Subscriptions Receivable	1,800,000.00	
		Common Stock Subscribed		750,000.00
		Contributed Capital in Excess of Par Value, Common Stock		1,050,000.00
		Accepted subscriptions for 150,000 shares of common stock.		
	1	Organization Costs	100,000.00	
		Cash		100,000.00
		Reimbursed the founders for organization costs.		
	1	Cash	1,320,000.00	
		Preferred Stock		1,200,000.00
		Contributed Capital in Excess of Par Value, Preferred Stock		120,000.00
		Issued 12,000 shares of preferred stock.		
Apr.	1	Cash	1,800,000.00	
		Subscriptions Receivable		1,800,000.00
		Collected balance due on common stock subscription.		
	1	Common Stock Subscribed	750,000.00	
		Common Stock		750,000.00
		Issued 150,000 shares of subscribed common stock.		
Dec.	31	Income Summary	125,000.00	
		Retained Earnings		125,000.00
		To close the Income Summary account and update Retained Earnings.		
19X2 June	4	Cash	1,500,000.00	
		Common Stock		500,000.00
		Contributed Capital in Excess of Par Value, Common Stock		1,000,000.00
		Issued 100,000 shares of common stock.		

Dec.	10	Cash Dividends Declared	540,000.00	
		Common Dividend Payable		300,000.00
		Preferred Dividend Payable		240,000.00
		Declared current dividends and dividends in arrears to common and preferred stockholders, payable on January 10, 19X3.		
Dec.	31	Income Summary	1,000,000.00	
		Retained Earnings		1,000,000.00
		To close the Income Summary account and update Retained Earnings.		
	31	Retained Earnings	540,000.00	
		Cash Dividends Declared		540,000.00
		To close the Cash Dividends Declared account.		

Balance sheet presentations:

	As of December 31, 19X1	As of December 31, 19X2
Assets		
Organization costs	$ 90,000	$ 80,000
Liabilities		
Common dividend payable		$ 300,000
Preferred dividend payable		240,000
Total liabilities		$ 540,000
Stockholders' Equity		
Contributed capital:		
Preferred stock, $100 par value, 10% cumulative dividends, 100,000 shares authorized, 12,000 shares issued and outstanding	$1,200,000	$1,200,000
Contributed capital in excess of par, preferred stock	120,000	120,000
Total capital contributed by preferred stockholders	$1,320,000	$1,320,000
Common stock, $5 par value, 2,000,000 shares authorized, 450,000 shares issued and outstanding in 19X1, and 550,000 shares in 19X2	$2,250,000	$2,750,000
Contributed capital in excess of par, common stock	3,150,000	4,150,000
Total capital contributed by common stockholders	$5,400,000	$6,900,000
Total contributed capital	$6,720,000	$8,220,000
Retained earnings (see Note 1)	125,000	585,000
Total stockholders' equity	$6,845,000	$8,805,000

Note 1: As of December 31, 19X1, there were $120,000 of dividends in arrears on the preferred stock.

Glossary

LO 9 Define or explain the words and phrases listed in the chapter glossary.

Book value of a share of stock one share's portion of the stockholders' equity recorded in the accounts. p. 474

Call price of preferred stock the amount that must be paid to call and retire a preferred share. p. 473

Callable preferred stock preferred stock that the issuing corporation, at its option, may retire by paying a specified amount (the call price) to the preferred stockholders plus any dividends in arrears. p. 473

Convertible preferred stock a preferred stock that can be exchanged for shares of the issuing corporation's common stock at the option of the preferred stockholder. p. 473

Cumulative preferred stock preferred stock on which undeclared dividends accumulate until they are paid; common stockholders cannot receive a dividend until all cumulative dividends have been paid. p. 471

Date of declaration the date on which a corporation's board of directors votes to pay a dividend; the dividend becomes a liability on this date. p. 468

Date of payment the date on which a corporation actually disburses a cash dividend directly to the stockholders. p. 469

Date of record the date on which a corporation's records are examined to identify the stockholders who will receive a dividend. p. 468

Deficit a debit balance in the Retained Earnings account; this situation arises when a company's cumulative losses and dividends are greater than the cumulative profits earned in other years. p. 469

Discount on stock the difference between the par value of stock and its issue price when it is issued at a price below par value. p. 466

Dividend in arrears an unpaid dividend on cumulative preferred stock; it must be paid before any regular dividends on the preferred stock and before any dividends on the common stock. p. 471

Dividend yield a company's annual cash dividends per share divided by the market value per share. p. 481

Financial leverage the achievement of an increased return on common stock by paying dividends on preferred stock or interest at a rate that is less than the rate of return earned with the assets invested in the corporation by the preferred stockholders or creditors. p. 473

General partner a partner who assumes unlimited liability for the debts of the partnership; the general partner in a limited partnership is usually responsible for its management. p. 478

General partnership a partnership in which all partners have unlimited liability for partnership debts. p. 478

Limited partners partners who have no personal liability for debts of the partnership beyond the amounts they have invested in the partnership. p. 478

Limited partnership a partnership that has two classes of partners, limited partners and one or more general partners. p. 478

Minimum legal capital an amount of assets defined by state law that stockholders must invest and leave invested in a corporation; this provision is intended to protect the creditors of the corporation. p. 464

Mutual agency the legal relationship among the partners whereby each partner is an agent of the partnership and is able to bind the partnership to contracts within the apparent scope of the partnership's business. p. 477

Noncumulative preferred stock a preferred stock on which the right to receive dividends is forfeited for any year that the dividends are not declared. p. 471

No-par stock a class of stock that does not have a par value; no-par stock can be issued at any price without creating a discount liability. p. 466

Organization costs the costs of bringing a corporation into existence, including legal fees, promoters' fees, and amounts paid to the state to secure the charter. p. 461

Par value an arbitrary value assigned to a share of stock when the stock is authorized. p. 464

Participating preferred stock preferred stock that gives its owners the right to share in dividends in excess of the stated percentage or amount. p. 472

Partnership an unincorporated association of two or more persons to carry on a business for profit as co-owners. p. 477

Partnership contract the agreement between partners that sets forth the terms under which the affairs of the partnership will be conducted. p. 477

Preemptive right the right of common stockholders to protect their proportionate interest in a corporation by having the first opportunity to buy additional shares of common stock issued by the corporation. p. 470

Preferred stock stock that gives its owners a priority status over common stockholders in one or more ways, such as the payment of dividends or the distribution of assets on liquidation. p. 470

Premium on stock the difference between the par value of stock and its issue price when it is issued at a price above par value. p. 465

Proxy a legal document that gives an agent of a stockholder the power to exercise the voting rights of that stockholder's shares. p. 462

Stated value of no-par stock an arbitrary amount assigned to no-par stock by the corporation's board of directors; this amount is credited to the no-par stock account when the stock is issued. p. 466

Stock subscription a contractual commitment by an investor to purchase unissued shares of stock and become a stockholder. p. 466

Unlimited liability of partners the legal relationship among general partners that makes each of them responsible for paying all the debts of the partnership if the other partners are unable to pay their shares. p. 477

Objective Review

Answers to the following questions are listed at the end of this chapter. Be sure that you decide which is the one best answer to each question *before* you check the answers.

LO 1 A characteristic of the corporate form of organization is:

a. That ownership rights are easily transferred.
b. That stockholders have a mutual agency relationship with the corporation.
c. The ease of capital accumulation.
d. The lack of governmental regulation compared to single proprietorships and partnerships.
e. Both (*a*) and (*c*) are correct.

LO 2 Verde Corporation has no-par common stock with a stated value of $10 per share. The company issued 7,000 shares of its stock in exchange for some equipment valued at $105,000. The entry to record the transaction would include:

a. A credit to Retained Earnings for $35,000.

b. A credit to Contributed Capital in Excess of Stated Value, No-Par Common Stock for $35,000.

c. A debit to Equipment for $70,000.

d. A credit to Common Stock, No-Par for $105,000.

e. A credit to Contributed Capital in Excess of Stated Value, No-Par Common Stock for $70,000.

LO 3 Sweeps Corporation accepted subscriptions for 9,000 shares of $10 par value common stock at $48 per share. A 10% down payment was made on the date of the subscription contract, and the balance was to be paid in full six months later. The entries to record receipt of the final balance and the issuance of the stock would include:

a. A debit to Common Stock Subscribed for $432,000.

b. A credit to Contributed Capital in Excess of Par Value, Common Stock for $307,800.

c. A credit to Common Stock, $10 Par Value for $90,000.

d. A credit to Subscriptions Receivable, Common Stock for $432,000.

e. A debit to Subscriptions Receivable, Common Stock for $388,800.

LO 4 Bearcat Corporation has stockholders' equity as follows:

Preferred stock, $50 par value, 10%, cumulative and nonparticipating, 10,000 shares authorized, 9,000 shares issued and outstanding	$ 450,000
Contributed capital in excess of par value, preferred stock	50,000
Total capital contributed by preferred stockholders	$ 500,000
Common stock, $10 par value, 100,000 shares authorized, 27,000 shares issued and outstanding	$ 270,000
Contributed capital in excess of par value, common stock	540,000
Total capital contributed by common stockholders	$ 810,000
Total contributed capital	$1,310,000
Retained earnings	1,260,000
Total stockholders' equity	$2,570,000

Dividends have not been declared for the past two years, but in the third year, Bearcat Corporation declared $288,000 of dividends distributable to both preferred and common stockholders. Determine the amount of dividends to be paid to the common stockholders.

a. $ 90,000.

b. $135,000.

c. $153,000.

d. $243,000.

e. $288,000.

LO 5 World Cinema, Inc.'s callable preferred stock has a call price of $108 plus any dividends in arrears. The stockholders' equity of the company is as follows:

Preferred stock, $90 par value, 10%, cumulative and nonparticipating, 5,000 shares authorized, 1,000 shares issued and outstanding (dividends are in arrears for two years)	$ 90,000
Contributed capital in excess of par value, preferred stock	6,000
Total capital contributed by preferred stockholders	$ 96,000
Common stock, $20 par value, 50,000 shares authorized, 12,000 shares issued and outstanding	$240,000
Contributed capital in excess of par value, common stock	120,000
Total capital contributed by common stockholders	$360,000
Total contributed capital	$456,000
Retained earnings	174,000
Total stockholders' equity	$630,000

The book values per share of the preferred and common shares are:

a. Preferred, $126.00; common, $42.00.

b. Preferred, $96.00; common, $32.50.

c. Preferred, $90.00; common, $45.00.

d. Preferred, $108.00; common, $43.50.

e. Preferred, $114.00; common, $31.00.

LO 6 Which one of the following practices is not used in accounting for a proprietorship?

a. Cash taken from the business for the personal use of the owner should be debited to the owner's withdrawals account.

b. The owner's investments in the business should be credited to the owner's capital account.

c. In making closing entries, an Income Summary balance that represents a net loss should be credited to the owner's capital account.

d. The owner's equity section of the balance sheet should show the owner's capital account balance on the date of the balance sheet.

e. The statement of changes in owner's equity shows the changes in the owner's capital account that occurred during the period.

LO 7 Mixon and Reed form a partnership with initial investments of $70,000 and $35,000, respectively. The partners agree to annual salary allowances of $42,000 to Mixon and $28,000 to Reed. Also, they agree to an interest allowance equal to 10% of each partner's beginning-of-the-year capital balance. The remaining income or loss is to be shared equally. How would a first-year net income of $21,000 be shared between Mixon and Reed?

a. Mixon, $13,300; Reed, $ 7,700.

b. Mixon, $19,250; Reed, $ 1,750.

c. Mixon, $12,600; Reed, $ 8,400.

d. Mixon, $12,250; Reed, $ 8,750.

e. Mixon, $10,500; Reed, $10,500.

LO 8 Which one of the following situations produces an expected dividend yield of 10% for the common stock?

a. The dividends paid during the last calendar year were $100,000 and the net income for the same period was $1,000,000.

b. The dividends expected to be paid in the next year are $100,000 and the expected net income for the same period is $1,000,000.

c. The dividends expected to be paid in the next year are $120,000 and the net income for the prior year was $1,200,000.

d. The dividends expected to be paid in the next year are $2 per share and the current market value of the stock is $20 per share.

e. None of the above.

LO 9 A preferred stock that can be exchanged for shares of its issuing corporation's common stock at the option of the stockholder is:

a. Participating preferred stock.

b. Noncumulative preferred stock.

c. Callable preferred stock.

d. Convertible preferred stock.

e. Cumulative preferred stock.

Questions for Class Discussion

1. Why is the income of a corporation said to be taxed twice?
2. Who is responsible for directing the affairs of a corporation?
3. What is a proxy?
4. What are organization costs? List several examples of these costs.
5. How are organization costs classified on the balance sheet?
6. What are the duties and responsibilities of a corporation's registrar and transfer agent?
7. What happens on the date of declaration, the date of record, and the date of payment?
8. List the general rights of common stockholders.
9. What is the preemptive right of common stockholders?
10. What is a stock premium? What is a stock discount?
11. What is the main advantage of no-par stock?
12. What is the difference between cumulative and noncumulative preferred stock?
13. What are the balance sheet classifications of these accounts: (*a*) Subscriptions Receivable, Common Stock, and (*b*) Common Stock Subscribed?
14. What is the difference between the par value and the call price of a share of stock?
15. Why would an investor find convertible preferred stock attractive?
16. Kurt and Ellen are partners in operating a store. Without consulting Kurt, Ellen contracts to purchase merchandise for the store. Kurt contends that he did not authorize the order and refuses to take delivery. Is the partnership obligated to pay? Why or why not?
17. Would your answer to Question 16 differ if Kurt and Ellen were partners in a public accounting firm?
18. What does the term *unlimited liability* mean when it is applied to a partnership?

19. Examine the balance sheet for Ben & Jerry's Homemade, Inc., in Appendix G at the end of the book and determine the classes of stock that the company has issued.

20. Examine the statement of changes in stockholders' equity (called the *consolidated statement of changes in common stockholders' investment*) for Federal Express Corporation in Appendix G at the end of the book and determine how many shares of common stock the company issued during the year ended May 31, 1993. Examine the company's balance sheet and determine the par value per share.

Exercises

Exercise 13–1
Recording stock issuances
(LO 2)

Present the general journal entries that an accountant would prepare to record the following issuances of stock in three different situations:

a. Two thousand shares of $10 par value common stock are issued for $35,000 cash.

b. One thousand shares of no-par common stock are issued to the corporation's promoters in exchange for their efforts in creating it. Their efforts are estimated to be worth $15,000, and the stock has no stated value.

c. One thousand shares of no-par common stock are issued to the corporation's promoters in exchange for their efforts in creating it. Their efforts are estimated to be worth $15,000, and the stock has a $1 per share stated value.

Exercise 13–2
Accounting for par and no-par stock issuances
(LO 2)

Printers, Inc., issued 4,000 shares of its common stock for $96,000 cash on March 16. Present the journal entries that the company's accountant would use to record this event under each of the following situations:

a. The stock has no par or stated value.
b. The stock has a stated value of $8 per share.
c. The stock has a $20 par value.

Exercise 13–3
Interpreting journal entries for stock issuances and subscriptions
(LO 2, 3)

Each of these journal entries was recently recorded by four different corporations. Provide an explanation for the event or transaction described by each entry.

a.	Cash	40,000.00	
	Common Stock, No-Par		40,000.00
b.	Merchandise Inventory	45,000.00	
	Machinery	65,000.00	
	Notes Payable		72,000.00
	Common Stock, $25 Par Value		20,000.00
	Contributed Capital in Excess of Par Value, Common Stock		18,000.00
c.	Organization Costs	45,000.00	
	Common Stock, No-Par		33,000.00
	Contributed Capital in Excess of Stated Value, No-Par Common Stock		12,000.00
d.	Cash	25,000.00	
	Subscriptions Receivable, Common Stock	75,000.00	
	Common Stock Subscribed		60,000.00
	Contributed Capital in Excess of Par Value, Common Stock		40,000.00

Exercise 13–4
Stock subscriptions
(LO 3)

On February 15, Quality Care Corp. accepted subscriptions at $19 per share for 8,000 shares of its $10 par value common stock. The subscriptions called for 40% of the subscription price to be paid as a down payment with the balance due on April 15. Show the journal entries that the company's accountant would make to record these three events:

a. Accepting the subscriptions and the down payments.
b. Receiving the balance of the subscriptions on the due date.
c. Issuing the stock on the same date.

Exercise 13–5
Dividends on common and noncumulative preferred stock
(LO 4)

The outstanding stock of D. B. Copper Corp. includes 20,000 shares of noncumulative preferred stock with a $10 par value and a 7.5% dividend rate, as well as 50,000 shares of common stock with a $1 par value. During its first four years of operation, the corporation declared and paid the following total amounts of dividends:

19X1	$ 5,000
19X2	12,000
19X3	50,000
19X4	98,000

Determine the amount of dividends paid in each year to each class of stockholders. Also determine the total dividends paid to each class in the four years combined.

Exercise 13–6
Dividends on common and cumulative preferred stock
(LO 4)

Use the data in Exercise 13–5 to determine the amount of dividends paid in each year to each class of stockholders, assuming that the preferred stock is cumulative. Also determine the total dividends paid to each class in the four years combined.

Exercise 13–7
Using preferred stock to create leverage
(LO 4)

An individual entrepreneur is planning to start a new business and needs $625,000 of start-up capital. This person has $500,000 in personal assets that can be invested and thus needs to raise another $125,000 in cash. The founder will buy 10,000 shares of common stock for $500,000 and has two alternative plans for raising the additional cash. One plan is to sell 2,500 shares of common stock to one or more investors for $125,000 cash. The second is to sell 1,250 shares of cumulative preferred stock to one or more investors for $125,000 cash (this stock has a $100 par value, an annual 7% dividend rate, and would be issued at par).

1. If the business is expected to earn $90,000 of after-tax net income in the first year, what rate of return on beginning equity will the founder earn under each alternative? Which of the two plans will provide the higher return to the founder?
2. If the business is expected to earn $21,000 of after-tax net income in the first year, what rate of return on beginning equity will the founder earn under each alternative? Which of the two plans will provide the higher return to the founder?

Exercise 13–8
Identifying characteristics of preferred stock
(LO 5)

Match each of the numbered descriptions with the characteristic of preferred stock that it best describes. Indicate your answer by writing the letter for the correct characteristic in the blank space next to each description.

A. Callable
B. Convertible
C. Cumulative
D. Noncumulative
E. Nonparticipating
F. Participating

___1. The holders of the stock can exchange it for shares of common stock.
___2. The issuing corporation can retire the stock by paying a prearranged price.
___3. The holders of the stock are entitled to receive dividends in excess of the stated rate under some conditions.
___4. The holders of the stock are not entitled to receive dividends in excess of the stated rate.
___5. The holders of the stock lose any dividends that are not declared.
___6. The holders of the stock are entitled to receive current and all past dividends before common stockholders receive any dividends.

Exercise 13–9
Characteristics of corporations and partnerships
(LO 1, 7)

By entering a check mark in the appropriate column, indicate whether each of the following characteristics applies to corporations or partnerships:

Corporations	Partnerships		
		1.	Limited liability for owners.
		2.	Owners are agents of the business.
		3.	Income is taxed twice in normal circumstances.
		4.	Separate legal entity.
		5.	Creation requires only an agreement among the owners.
		6.	Unlimited life.
		7.	Ownership rights cannot be transferred easily.
		8.	Income is taxed only once under normal circumstances.
		9.	Creation requires government approval.
		10.	Limited life.
		11.	Owners are not agents of the business.
		12.	Ownership rights are easily transferred.
		13.	Unlimited liability for owners.
		14.	Not a separate legal entity.
		15.	Capital is easily accumulated.

Exercise 13–10
Characteristics of corporations and partnerships
(LO 1, 7)

On the following list of eight general characteristics of business organizations, write a brief description of how each characteristic applies to corporations and partnerships:

		Corporations	Partnerships
1.	Life		
2.	Owners' liability		
3.	Legal status		
4.	Tax status of income		
5.	Owner's authority		
6.	Ease of formation		
7.	Transferability of ownership		
8.	Ability to raise large amounts of capital		

Exercise 13–11
Comparative entries for partnership and corporation
(LO 1, 7)

Andy Anderson and Bobbie Buelow created a new business on April 11 when they each invested $60,000 cash in the company. On December 15, they decided that they would each receive $15,000 of the company's cash as a distribution. The checks were prepared and given to Anderson and Buelow on December 20. On December 31, the company's accountant determined that the company's net income was $44,000.

1. Assume that this company is a partnership and present the journal entries that the accountant would make to record these events: (*a*) investments by the owners, (*b*) the cash distribution to the owners, and (*c*) the closing of the Income Summary and the owners' withdrawals accounts.
2. Assume that this company is a corporation and present the journal entries that the accountant would make to record these events: (*a*) investments by the owners, (*b*) the cash distribution to the owners, and (*c*) the closing of the Income Summary and dividends accounts. When the company was created, each owner acquired 2,000 shares of $25 par value common stock.

Exercise 13–12
Book value per share of stock
(LO 5)

The balance sheet for High Beams, Inc., includes the following information:

Stockholders' Equity	
Preferred stock, 6% cumulative, $50 par value, $60 call price, 5,000 shares issued and outstanding	$ 250,000
Common stock, $20 par value, 40,000 shares issued and outstanding	800,000
Retained earnings	535,000
Total stockholders' equity	$1,585,000

Determine the book value per share of the preferred and common stock under these two situations:

a. No preferred dividends are in arrears.
b. Three years of preferred dividends are in arrears.

Exercise 13–13
Proprietorship transactions
(LO 6)

On May 1, K. Malone opened a checking account for a new proprietorship business and invested $40,000 cash, land worth $50,000, and a building worth $175,000. The owner also arranged for the business to assume responsibility for the $85,000 long-term note payable mortgaged by the land and building. On October 3, the owner withdrew $16,000 cash. After closing the revenue and expense accounts on December 31, the Income Summary account had a credit balance of $48,000. Show the general journal entries that would be made to record the owner's initial investment, the cash withdrawal, and the closing of the Income Summary and withdrawal accounts. Also determine the ending balance of the owner's capital account.

Exercise 13–14
Income allocation for a partnership
(LO 7)

Sells and Haskins began a partnership by investing $120,000 and $80,000, respectively. During its first year, the partnership earned $40,000. Show how the partnership's income would be allocated to the partners under each of the following situations:

a. The partners did not establish a method of sharing income.

b. The partners agreed to share incomes and losses in proportion to their initial investments.

c. The partners agreed to share incomes and losses with an $18,000 per year salary allowance to Sells, a $10,000 per year salary allowance to Haskins, 8% interest on their initial investments, and the balance equally.

Exercise 13–15
Calculating dividend yield
(LO 8)

Calculate the dividend yield for each of these situations:

	Expected Annual Dividend per Share	Stock's Market Price per Share
a.	$6.00	$ 64.00
b.	3.00	30.50
c.	5.50	65.00
d.	0.60	43.00
e.	1.00	25.00
f.	7.50	108.00

Problems

Problem 13–1
Stock subscriptions
(LO 2, 3, 4)

On March 1, Mercer Corporation received authorization to issue up to 20,000 shares of $10 par value preferred stock that pays a 9% cumulative dividend. The company also is authorized to issue up to 100,000 shares of common stock that has no par value; however, the board of directors established a $2 stated value for this stock. The company then completed these transactions over the next three months:

Mar. 6 Accepted subscriptions to 15,000 shares of common stock at $5 per share. The subscribers each made down payments of 30% of the subscription price. The balance is due on May 6.

20 Issued 1,000 shares of common stock to the corporation's promoters for their services in organizing the corporation. The board valued the services at $5,000.

30 Accepted subscriptions to 4,000 shares of preferred stock at $12 per share. The subscribers each made down payments of 40% of the subscription price. The balance is due on May 30.

May 6 Collected the balance due on the March 6 common stock subscriptions and issued the shares.

12 Accepted subscriptions to 2,500 shares of preferred stock at $14 per share. The subscribers each made down payments of 40% of the subscription price. The balance is due on July 12.

30 Collected the balance due on the March 30 preferred stock subscriptions and issued the shares.

At the end of May, the balance of retained earnings is $16,000.

Required

Use the information about the transactions to prepare the stockholders' equity section of the company as of May 31. (Note: you will find it useful to prepare journal entries for the transactions to help you process the data.)

Problem 13–2
Stockholders' equity transactions
(LO 2, 3, 5, 8)

Alabama Energy, Inc., was chartered at the beginning of the year and engaged in a number of transactions. The following journal entries affected its stockholders' equity during its first year of operations:

a.	Cash	300,000.00	
	Common Stock, $25 Par Value		250,000.00
	Contributed Capital in Excess of Par Value, Common Stock		50,000.00

		Debit	Credit
b.	Organization Costs	150,000.00	
	Common Stock, $25 Par Value		125,000.00
	Contributed Capital in Excess of Par Value, Common Stock		25,000.00
c.	Cash	43,000.00	
	Accounts Receivable	15,000.00	
	Office Equipment	21,500.00	
	Building	60,000.00	
	Accounts Payable		22,000.00
	Notes Payable		37,500.00
	Common Stock, $25 Par Value		50,000.00
	Contributed Capital in Excess of Par Value, Common Stock		30,000.00
d.	Cash	120,000.00	
	Common Stock, $25 Par Value		75,000.00
	Contributed Capital in Excess of Par Value, Common Stock		45,000.00
e.	Cash Dividends Declared	15,000.00	
	Common Dividend Payable		15,000.00
f.	Common Dividend Payable	15,000.00	
	Cash		15,000.00
g.	Income Summary	60,000.00	
	Retained Earnings		60,000.00
h.	Retained Earnings	15,000.00	
	Cash Dividends Declared		15,000.00

Required

1. Provide explanations for the journal entries.
2. Prepare answers for the following questions:
   a. What is the net income for the year?
   b. How many shares of common stock are outstanding?
   c. What is the minimum legal capital?
   d. What is the total contributed capital?
   e. What is the total retained earnings?
   f. What is the total stockholders' equity?
   g. What is the book value per share of the common stock at the end of the year?
   h. The dividend yield on this stock is 2%. Expected dividends for the upcoming year are $1 per year. What is the stock's current market value?
   i. The market interest rate on bonds ranged from 8 to 10%. Does the value of this company's stock appear to be based on income or growth?

Problem 13–3
Allocating dividends between preferred and common stock
(LO 4)

Moving Along, Inc., has 5,000 outstanding shares of $100 par value, 5% preferred stock and 40,000 shares of $1 par value common stock. During the last seven-year period, the company paid out the following total amounts in dividends to its preferred and common stockholders:

19X1	$ 5,000
19X2	11,000
19X3	22,500
19X4	65,000
19X5	18,000
19X6	35,000
19X7	45,000

No dividends were in arrears for the years prior to 19X1.

Required

1. Determine the amounts of dividends paid to the two classes of stock in each year and for all seven years combined under these two assumptions:

a. The preferred stock is noncumulative.
b. The preferred stock is cumulative.

2. Comment on the difference between the answers in Part 1.

Problem 13–4
Calculating book values
(LO 5)

Duplex Communications, Inc.'s common stock is currently selling on a stock exchange today at $85 per share, and a recent balance sheet shows the following information:

Stockholders' Equity

Preferred stock, 5%, $? par value, 1,000 shares authorized, issued, and outstanding	$ 50,000
Common stock, $? par value, 4,000 shares authorized, issued, and outstanding	80,000
Retained earnings	150,000
Total stockholders' equity	$280,000

Required

1. What is the market value of the corporation's common stock?
2. What are the par values of the preferred stock and the common stock?
3. If no dividends are in arrears, what are the book values of the preferred stock and the common stock?
4. If two years' preferred dividends are in arrears, what are the book values of the preferred stock and the common stock?
5. If two years' preferred dividends are in arrears and the preferred stock is callable at $55 per share, what are the book values of the preferred stock and the common stock?

Problem 13–5
Allocating partnership income
(LO 7)

Tinker, Evers, and Chance created a partnership and invested $42,000, $83,000, and $75,000, respectively, at the beginning of the year. During its first year, the partnership achieved a net income of $78,000. Tinker, Evers, and Chance each withdrew $15,000 cash from the partnership on December 31.

Required

1. Prepare schedules that show how the partners would allocate the partnership's net income among themselves under each of the following agreements:
   a. The partners divide the income equally.
   b. The partners share the income in proportion to their initial investments.
   c. The partners agreed to provide annual salary allowances of $30,000 to Tinker, $13,000 to Evers, and $13,000 to Chance and 8% interest allowances on the partners' initial investments. Any remaining income (or deficit) is to be shared equally.
2. Prepare a schedule that shows the equity balances of each of the three partners as of the end of the year under agreement *c* above.

Problem 13–6
Analytical essay
(LO 1, 7)

Jan Carston and Carey Glenwood want to create a new software development business. Each of them can contribute fairly large amounts of capital. However, they know that the business will need additional equity capital from other investors after its first year. With respect to their individual activities, they are both planning to devote full-time effort to getting the first products out the door within the year. They plan to hire three employees initially and expect to distribute a substantial amount of cash every year for their personal expenses. Carston has proposed organizing the business as a general partnership, but Glenwood thinks that a corporation offers more advantages. They have asked you to prepare a brief analysis that supports choosing the corporate form. What main points would you include in your analysis?

Problem 13–7
Analytical essay
(LO 5)

In your role as an assistant to a company manager, you are frequently called on to explain certain financial points that the manager does not completely understand. Just recently, the manager encountered the phrase *book value* being applied to stock and didn't exactly understand what the term means and how it relates to the stock's market value. Write a short explanation of the significance of the book value of a company's preferred stock.

Provocative Problems

Provocative Problem 13–1
We've Got It, Inc.
(LO 2, 7)

For a number of years, Berry Benson and Connie Karle have operated a retailing company called We've Got It. They organized the company as a partnership and have shared income and losses in a 2:3 ratio. Benson gets 40% while Karle gets 60%. Because the business is growing beyond their ability to keep up with it, they have agreed to accept a third person, Mickey Rogers, into the business. Part of the new arrangement involves creating a new corporation, called We've Got It, Inc. The corporate charter authorizes 50,000 shares of $10 par value common stock. The deal requires three steps: First, the partners must settle up the old business by revaluing the assets to their fair market values and dividing the previously unrecognized gains and losses. Second, the partnership must transfer its assets and liabilities to the corporation, which will issue shares to the partners in exchange for their equity in the partnership. The shares will be considered to be worth $10 each when the exchange is made. Third, Rogers will pay $10 cash for all authorized shares not issued to the former partners. You have been engaged to help the three phases of the deal go smoothly.

The following spreadsheet has been developed to help you accomplish the first phase of modifying the partnership's accounts to reflect the fair market values for the assets and to modify the partners' equity balances:

WE'VE GOT IT
Account Modification Spreadsheet
July 31

Accounts	Unmodified Trial Balance	Modifications (a)	(b)	(c)	(d)	(e)	Modified Trial Balance
Debits							
Cash	21,000						
Accts. receivable	31,000						
Merch. inventory	150,000	(25,000)					
Store equipment	128,000						
Buildings	280,000						
Land	87,000						
Total	697,000						
Credits							
Allowance for doubtful accounts	(3,000)						
Acc. depr., equip.	(48,000)						
Acc. depr., bldgs.	(82,000)						
Accounts payable	(32,000)						
Notes payable	(172,000)						
Benson, capital	(160,000)	10,000					
Karle, capital	(200,000)	15,000					
Total	(697,000)						

Numbers in parentheses are credits.

The partners have agreed that the following modifications need to be included in the first phase (they will divide any gains and losses from the changes in recorded value according to their regular income and loss ratio):

a. The merchandise inventory is to be written down to its fair value of $125,000.

b. An account receivable from a customer for $1,000 is known to be uncollectible and will be written off against the allowance for doubtful accounts.

c. After writing off that account, the allowance for doubtful accounts will be adjusted to 5% of the gross accounts receivable.

d. The net recorded value of the store equipment will be decreased to $65,000 by increasing the balance of the accumulated depreciation account.

e. The gross recorded value of the building is to be increased to its replacement cost of $360,000. At the same time, the balance of the accumulated depreciation account is to be adjusted to equal 25% of the replacement cost to represent the fact the building's fair market value is 75% of its replacement cost.

Your first task is to complete the spreadsheet by entering the effects of each of the five modifications as debits and credits to the affected accounts. The first items have been entered in the spreadsheet as an example. You should provide supporting calculations as needed. Second, determine how many shares each partner is entitled to receive in exchange for the partner's equity. Third, determine how many shares Rogers will purchase for cash. Fourth, present the journal entries that the corporation will use to record the issuance of the shares to all three stockholders. Finally, present a balance sheet for the corporation immediately after the transactions are completed (the notes payable are due within 90 days).

Provocative Problem 13–2
Endor Corporation and Kenobe Company
(LO 4)

Having received a large lump sum of severance pay, Lou Franklin is thinking about investing the money in one of two securities: Endor Corporation common stock or the preferred stock issued by Kenobe Company. The companies manufacture similar products and compete in the same market, and both have been operating about the same length of time—four years for Endor and three years for Kenobe. The two companies also have similar amounts of stockholders' equity, as shown here:

Endor Corporation

Common stock, $1 par value, 800,000 shares authorized, 500,000 shares issued and outstanding	$ 500,000
Retained earnings	820,000
Total stockholders' equity	$1,320,000

Kenobe Company

Preferred stock, $50 par value, 6% cumulative, 6,000 shares authorized, issued, and outstanding	$ 300,000*
Common stock, $20 par value, 50,000 shares authorized, issued, and outstanding	1,000,000
Retained earnings	60,000
Total stockholders' equity	$1,360,000

* The current and two prior years' dividends are in arrears on the preferred stock.

Endor did not pay a dividend on its common stock during its first year's operations; however, it has paid a cash dividend of $0.09 per share in each of the past three years. The stock is currently selling for $3.00 per share. In contrast, the preferred stock of Kenobe Company is selling for $45 per share. Franklin has expressed a leaning for the preferred stock as an investment because it appears to be a bargain at $5 below par value and $14 below book value. Besides, Franklin has told you, "The dividends are guaranteed because it is a preferred stock." Franklin also believes that the common stock of Endor is overpriced at 14% above book value and 200% above par value, while it is paying only a $0.09 per share dividend. In conclusion, your friend asks how anyone could prefer a common stock yielding only 3% to a preferred stock that is supposed to pay 6%.

1. Is the preferred stock of Kenobe Company actually selling at $14 below its book value, and is the common stock of Endor Corporation actually selling at 14% above book value and 200% above par?
2. Analyze the stockholders' equity sections and express your opinion of the two stocks as investments by describing some of the factors Franklin should consider in choosing between them.

Provocative Problem 13–3
Apple Computer, Inc.
(LO 3, 4, 5, 8)

Apple Computer, Inc.

Use the information provided in the financial statements of Apple Computer, Inc., and the footnotes in Appendix F to answer the following questions:

1. Does it appear that Apple has been authorized to issue any preferred stock? If so, has any been issued as of September 25, 1992?
2. How many shares of common stock have been authorized? How many have been issued as of September 25, 1992?
3. What is the par value of the common stock? What is its book value at September 25, 1992?

4. Are any shares of common stock subscribed? Are there any shares that cannot be issued to the public because they have been promised to others?
5. What was the highest market value of the stock during 1992? What was the lowest?
6. Did Apple declare any dividends on its capital stock during 1992? If so, how large were the dividends (in total, and per share)? If the price of the stock was $48 per share at the end of fiscal year 1992, and dividends were expected to continue at the same rate, what was the dividend yield of the stock? Does it appear that Apple is a growth or income stock?

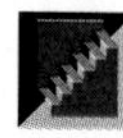

Answers to Objective Review Questions

LO 1 (*e*)
LO 2 (*b*)
LO 3 (*c*)
LO 4 (*c*)
LO 5 (*a*)
LO 6 (*c*)
LO 7 (*b*)
LO 8 (*d*)
LO 9 (*d*)

CHAPTER

14

Additional Corporate Transactions; Reporting Income and Retained Earnings; Earnings per Share

Because of their size and complexity, corporations often enter into special financing activities and other transactions that involve changes in stockholders' equity. They also experience unique gains and losses that are reported in special ways on the income statement. In addition, firms often describe corporate activities in terms of their earnings per share. The first section of this chapter deals with all three of these topics, including stock dividends, stock splits, and transactions involving the company's own stock. The second section of the chapter explains how information about income and retained earnings is classified and reported. The third section explains how accountants report earnings per share. Understanding these topics will help you interpret and use corporate financial statements.

Learning Objectives

After studying Chapter 14, you should be able to:

1. Describe stock dividends and stock splits and explain their effects on a corporation's assets and stockholders' equity.
2. Record purchases and sales of treasury stock and retirements of stock and describe their effects on stockholders' equity.
3. Describe restrictions and appropriations of retained earnings and explain how they are described in financial reports.
4. Explain how to report the income effects of discontinued segments, extraordinary items, changes in accounting principles and estimates, and prior period adjustments.
5. Calculate earnings per share for companies with simple capital structures and explain the difference between primary and fully diluted earnings per share.
6. Calculate the price-earnings ratio and describe its meaning.
7. Define or explain the words and phrases listed in the chapter glossary.

CORPORATE DIVIDENDS AND OTHER STOCK TRANSACTIONS

In Chapter 1, we briefly described a corporation's retained earnings as the stockholders' equity that is created by the company's profitable activities. It is equal to the total cumulative amount of the reported net income less any net losses and dividends declared since the company started operating. In effect, retained earnings are the stockholders' residual interest in the corporation that was not created by their investments. Information about retained earnings is helpful to investors and other users of financial statements for predicting future cash flows for dividends and other events.

LO 1 Describe stock dividends and stock splits and explain their effects on a corporation's assets and stockholders' equity.

Retained Earnings and Dividends

Most state laws allow a corporation to pay cash dividends if retained earnings exist. However, in addition to retained earnings, a corporation must have enough cash available to pay the dividend. And, even if there is sufficient cash and retained earnings, the directors may decide against declaring a dividend because the cash is needed in the business.

Although cash may be paid out in dividends, companies also keep some cash in reserve to meet emergencies, to take advantage of unexpected opportunities, or to avoid having to borrow for future expansion.

Chapter 13 described how cash dividends are recorded in the accounts. The declaration of a dividend reduces the retained earnings and creates a current liability to the stockholders. On the date of record, the recipients of the dividend are identified, but no entry is recorded in the accounts. On the date of payment, cash is sent to the qualifying stockholders, and the liability is removed from the books.

Dividends Based on Contributed Capital

Generally, the Dividends Declared account is closed to the Retained Earnings account. However, in limited circumstances, some state laws allow cash dividends to be paid as a return of capital contributed by the stockholders. If so, the Dividends Declared account is closed with a debit entry to one of the contributed capital accounts instead of Retained Earnings. Because these dividends return part of the original investment to the stockholders, they are often called **liquidating dividends.** They usually occur when the company is completing a major downsizing, perhaps in preparation for a merger or even dissolution. In most cases, the equity that originated from the par or stated value of the outstanding stock cannot be used as a basis for liquidating dividends until all creditors have been paid. This situation normally occurs only when the corporation is actually going out of business.

Stock Dividends

Sometimes, a corporation's directors may declare a **stock dividend.** This means the company distributes additional shares of its own stock to its stockholders without receiving any payment in return. Stock dividends and cash dividends are very different. A cash dividend reduces the corporation's assets and stockholders' equity, and a stock dividend does neither. A stock dividend simply transfers some equity from retained earnings into contributed capital.

Why Stock Dividends Are Distributed

If stock dividends do not affect assets or total stockholders' equity, why are they declared and distributed? Directors can use stock dividends to keep the market value of the stock affordable. For example, if a profitable corporation grows but does not pay cash dividends, the price of its common stock increases in anticipation of continued growth and future dividends. Eventually, the price of a share may become so high that it discourages some investors from buying the stock. Thus, the corporation may declare stock dividends to increase the number of outstanding shares and thereby keep the per share price low enough to be attractive to smaller investors.

Another reason for declaring a stock dividend is to provide tangible evidence of management's confidence that the company is doing well. The stock dividend may substitute for a cash dividend, thereby saving cash that can then be used to expand the business.

The Effect of Stock Dividends on Stockholders' Equity Accounts

Although a stock dividend does not affect the corporation's assets or total stockholders' equity, it does affect the components of stockholders' equity. This effect is recorded by transferring part of the retained earnings to the contributed capital accounts. Because this treatment increases the company's contributed capital, it is often described as *capitalizing* retained earnings.

If a corporation declares a **small stock dividend,** accounting principles require it to capitalize retained earnings equal to the market value of the shares to be distributed. This practice is based on the concept that a small stock dividend is likely to be perceived as similar to a cash dividend because it has a small impact on the price of the stock. A dividend is considered small if it is less than or equal to 25% of the previously outstanding shares.

A **large stock dividend,** one that distributes more than 25% of the outstanding shares before the dividend, is likely to have a noticeable effect on the stock's market price per share. It is not likely to be perceived as a substitute for a cash dividend. Therefore, a large stock dividend is recorded by capitalizing an amount of retained earnings only to the minimum required by the state law governing the corporation. In most cases, the law requires capitalizing retained earnings equal to the par or stated value of the shares.

For example, assume that Northwest Corporation's stockholders' equity consists of the following amounts just before the declaration of a stock dividend:

NORTHWEST CORPORATION
Stockholders' Equity
December 31, 19X1

Common stock, $10 par value, 15,000 shares authorized, 10,000 shares issued and outstanding	$100,000	
Contributed capital in excess of par value, common stock	8,000	
Total contributed capital	$108,000	
Retained earnings	35,000	
Total stockholders' equity		$143,000

Recording a Small Stock Dividend

To illustrate how a small stock dividend is recorded, let's assume that the directors of Northwest Corporation declared a 10% stock dividend on December 31. The 1,000 dividend shares (10% of the 10,000 outstanding shares) are to be distributed on January 20 to the January 15 stockholders of record.

If the market value of Northwest Corporation's stock on December 31 is $15 per share, the dividend declaration is recorded with this entry:

Dec.	31	Stock Dividends Declared	15,000.00	
		Common Stock Dividend Distributable		10,000.00
		Contributed Capital in Excess of Par Value, Common Stock		5,000.00
		To record the declaration of a 1,000-share common stock dividend.		

The debit is recorded in the temporary account called Stock Dividends Declared. This account serves the same purpose as the Cash Dividends Declared account described in the preceding chapter. A complete chart of accounts includes separate accounts for cash and stock dividends because the financial statements must report stock and cash dividends as separate events. If stock dividends are not frequently declared, a company can get by without a separate account for Stock Dividends Declared. Instead, it can record the debit directly to the Retained Earnings account. This expedient approach is satisfactory as long as the information is suitably reported in the financial statements.

The two credits in the previous entry also need to be explained. The first credit puts the par value of the dividend shares in a contributed capital account called Common Stock Dividend Distributable. This account balance exists only until the shares are actually issued. The second credit records the premium on the dividend shares at this time, even though the shares have not yet been issued. This account is the same one that is used for all other issuances at an amount more than par value.

As part of the year-end closing process, the accountant for the Northwest Corporation closes the Stock Dividends Declared account to Retained Earnings with this entry:

Dec.	31	Retained Earnings	15,000.00	
		Stock Dividends Declared		15,000.00
		To close the Stock Dividends Declared account.		

On January 20, the company distributes the new shares to the stockholders and records the event with this entry:

Jan.	20	Common Stock Dividend Distributable	10,000.00	
		Common Stock		10,000.00
		To record the distribution of a 1,000-share common stock dividend.		

The combined effect of these three entries is the transfer (or capitalization) of $15,000 of retained earnings to contributed capital. The amount of capitalized retained earnings equals the market value of the 1,000 issued shares ($15 × 1,000 shares).

This example demonstrates that a stock dividend has no effect on the corporation's assets or total stockholders' equity. Nor does the dividend affect the percentage of the company owned by individual stockholders. For example, assume that Pat Johnson owned 200 shares of Northwest Corporation's stock prior to the 10% stock dividend. When the corporation sent each stockholder one new share for each 10 shares held, Johnson received 20 new shares (10% × 200 shares).

Looking at Illustration 14–1, you can see what the 10% stock dividend does to Northwest Corporation's total contributed capital and retained earnings. Note that nothing happens to the total book value of Johnson's shares. Before the stock dividend, Johnson owned 2% of the corporation's stock, which is 200 out of the 10,000 outstanding shares. The book value of this holding was $2,860 (2% × $143,000, or 200 × $14.30 per share). After the dividend, the 200 shares have become 220 shares, but the holding still equals 2% of the 11,000 shares now outstanding. The book value is still $2,860 (2% × $143,000, or 220 × $13.00 per share). In other words, the only change in Johnson's investment is that it now consists of 220 new shares instead of 200 old shares. Also, the only effect on the stockholders' equity is a transfer of $15,000 from retained earnings to contributed capital. There is no change in the corporation's total assets, in its total equity, or in the percentage of equity owned by Johnson. Of course, Johnson's main concern is whether the 220 shares are now worth more than the 200 shares used to be.

ILLUSTRATION 14–1 *The Effect of Northwest Corporation's 10% Stock Dividend*

Before the 10% stock dividend

Stockholders' equity:	
Common stock (10,000 shares)	$100,000
Contributed capital in excess of par value, common stock	8,000
Retained earnings	35,000
Total stockholders' equity	$143,000

Book value per share = $143,000/10,000 shares = $14.30
Book value of Johnson's 200 shares = $14.30 × 200 = $2,860

After the 10% stock dividend

Stockholders' equity:	
Common stock (11,000 shares)	$110,000
Contributed capital in excess of par value, common stock	13,000
Retained earnings	20,000
Total stockholders' equity	$143,000

Book value per share = $143,000/11,000 shares = $13.00
Book value of Johnson's 220 shares = $13 × 220 = $2,860

Stock Dividends on the Balance Sheet

Because a stock dividend does not reduce the corporation's assets, it is never a liability on a balance sheet prepared between the declaration and distribution dates. Instead, the amount of any declared but undistributed stock dividend appears on the balance sheet as a component of the contributed capital in the stockholders' equity section. For example, the stockholders' equity of Northwest Corporation looks like this just after the 10% stock dividend is declared on December 31:

NORTHWEST CORPORATION
Stockholders' Equity
December 31, 19X1

Common stock, $10 par value, 15,000 shares authorized, 10,000 shares issued and outstanding	$100,000
Common stock dividend distributable, 1,000 shares	10,000
Total common stock issued and to be issued	$110,000
Contributed capital in excess of par value, common stock	13,000
Total contributed capital	$123,000
Retained earnings	20,000
Total stockholders' equity	$143,000

This updated section of the balance sheet shows three differences: First, the amount of equity attributed to the common stock increased from $100,000 to $110,000 because 1,000 additional shares are ready to be issued. Second, the contributed capital in excess of par increased by $5,000, which equals the excess of the stock's $15 per share market value over its $10 per share par value for the 1,000 shares. Finally, the balance of retained earnings decreased by $15,000 from the pre-dividend amount of $35,000 to $20,000.

Recording a Large Stock Dividend

When a stock dividend is declared that exceeds 25% of the outstanding shares, the corporation capitalizes retained earnings equal to the minimum amount required by the law. Usually, that is the par or stated value of the newly issued shares. For example, suppose Northwest Corporation's board declared a 30% stock dividend on December 31 instead of 10%. Because the dividend is greater than the arbitrary limit of 25%, it is considered to be large. As a result, only the par value of the new 3,000 shares is capitalized. Thus, the company would record the declaration with this entry:

Dec.	31	Stock Dividends Declared	30,000.00	
		Common Stock Dividend Distributable		30,000.00
		To record the declaration of a 3,000-share common stock dividend at par value.		

This entry causes the company's retained earnings to be decreased by the $30,000 par value of the dividend shares. It also causes the company's contributed capital to increase by the same amount.

Stock Splits

Recall that one goal for stock dividends is to manage the stock's market value. Stock dividends divide the company into a larger number of smaller pieces. The total value of the company is unchanged, but the value of each new share is smaller. The same result can be accomplished through a **stock split.** When a stock split occurs, the corporation calls in its outstanding shares and issues two or more new shares in exchange for each of the old ones.[1] Suppose that a company has 100,000 outstanding shares of $20 par value common stock that have a current market value of $88 per share. The market value can be cut in half by carrying out a two-for-one split, in which the 100,000 old shares are replaced by 200,000 new shares with a $10 par value and a market value in the neighborhood of $44 per share. Splits can be accomplished at any ratio, including two-for-one, three-for-one, or even higher. In fact, it is possible for the ratio to be less than one, causing the stockholders to end up with fewer shares. These **reverse stock splits** increase the stock's market value instead of reducing it.

A stock split does not affect the total stockholders' equity reported on the balance sheet. It also does not affect a stockholder's percentage interest in the corporation. The contributed capital and retained earnings accounts are unchanged by a split, and no journal entry is made. The only effect on the accounts is a change in the account title used for the common stock. The earlier example described a two-for-one split for a $10 par value stock. After the split, the account name would be changed to Common Stock, $5 Par Value. Although nothing else changes in the accounts, the disclosures about the stock on the balance sheet are changed to reflect the additional outstanding shares and the revised par value per share.

Treasury Stock

LO 2 Record purchases and sales of treasury stock and retirements of stock and describe their effects on stockholders' equity.

For a variety of reasons, corporations often acquire shares of their own stock. They may give some shares to employees as compensation. Others they may use to acquire control of other corporations. Sometimes, they repurchase shares to avoid a hostile takeover by an investor seeking to control the company. Less frequently, a corporation may buy a large number of shares to maintain a suitable market for the stock. This practice was widespread in 1987 after many stocks lost a great deal of market value very quickly. By buying the shares, corporations helped their stockholders get a better price and brought more stability to the market. The same practice may be needed in other specific circumstances. For example, a recent annual report for W. R. Grace & Co. gave this reason for large-scale purchases of its own stock:

[1] To reduce the administrative cost and effort, most splits are accomplished by simply issuing new certificates to the stockholders for the additional shares they are entitled to receive. The stockholders do not have to turn the old certificates in, but simply continue to hold them.

AS A MATTER OF

Ethics

Falcon Corporation's board of directors and officers have been discussing and planning the agenda for the corporation's 19X1 annual stockholders' meeting. The first item considered by the directors and officers was whether to report a large government contract that Falcon has just signed. Although this contract will significantly increase income and cash flows in 19X1 and beyond, management saw no need to reveal the news at the stockholders' meeting. "After all," one officer said, "the meeting is intended to be the forum for describing the past year's activities, not the plans for the next year."

After agreeing not to mention the contract, the group moved on to the next topic for the stockholders' meeting. This topic was a motion for the stockholders to approve a compensation plan awarding managers options to acquire large quantities of shares over the next several years. According to the plan, the managers will have a three-year option to buy shares at a fixed price that equals the market value of the stock as measured 30 days after the upcoming stockholders' meeting. In other words, the managers will be able to buy stock in 19X2, 19X3, or 19X4 by paying the 19X1 market value. Obviously, if the stock increases in value over the next several years, the managers will realize large profits without having to invest any cash. The financial vice president asks the group whether they should reconsider their decision about the government contract in light of its possible relevance to the vote on the stock option plan.

> The year began with the unexpected need to repurchase 13.6 million Grace common shares plus some preferred shares for nearly $600 million. This unplanned action [was] made necessary when Grace's largest shareholder divested its entire holdings . . . [and] was done to avoid a potentially dangerous downturn in the market value of your Grace shares.

Regardless of the reason for their acquisition, a corporation's reacquired shares are called **treasury stock.**

In many respects, treasury stock is similar to unissued stock. Neither unissued nor treasury stock is an asset of the corporation. Neither receive cash or stock dividends, and no one can exercise the vote attached to the shares. However, treasury stock does have one potentially significant difference from unissued stock. Specifically, the company can reissue treasury stock at a price less than par without a discount liability, as long as it was initially issued at a price equal to or greater than par.

In addition, treasury stock purchases require management to exercise ethical sensitivity. Corporate funds are being paid to specific stockholders instead of all stockholders. As a result, managers must be careful to ensure that the purchase is in the best interest of all the stockholders. These concerns cause most companies to be very open with their stockholders about their treasury stock and other activities related to stock. Read "As a Matter of Ethics" and consider whether Falcon Corporation's management is showing proper consideration for its stockholders.

Purchasing Treasury Stock

The act of purchasing treasury stock reduces the corporation's assets and stockholders' equity by equal amounts.[2] This effect is illustrated by the two balance sheets of the Curry Corporation in Illustrations 14–2 and 14–3. The first balance sheet shows the account balances on April 30, 19X1, before a

[2] This text discusses the *cost method* of accounting for treasury stock; it is the most widely used. The *par value* method is discussed in more advanced accounting courses.

ILLUSTRATION 14–2 *Curry Corporation's Balance Sheet Prior to the Purchase of Treasury Stock*

CURRY CORPORATION
Balance Sheet
April 30, 19X1

Assets		**Stockholders' Equity**	
Cash	$ 30,000	Contributed capital:	
Other assets	95,000	Common stock, $10 par value, authorized and issued 10,000 shares	$100,000
		Retained earnings	25,000
Total assets	$125,000	Total stockholders' equity	$125,000

ILLUSTRATION 14–3 *Curry Corporation's Balance Sheet Immediately After Purchasing Treasury Stock*

CURRY CORPORATION
Balance Sheet
April 30, 19X1

Assets		**Stockholders' Equity**	
Cash	$ 18,500	Contributed capital:	
Other assets	95,000	Common stock, $10 par value, authorized and issued 10,000 shares, of which 1,000 are in the treasury	$100,000
		Retained earnings, of which $11,500 is restricted by the purchase of treasury stock	25,000
		Total	$125,000
		Less cost of treasury stock	(11,500)
Total assets	$113,500	Total stockholders' equity	$113,500

treasury stock purchase. The second balance sheet shows the account balances after the company purchased 1,000 of its own shares for $11,500 cash.

This entry records the purchase of the 1,000 shares:

May	1	Treasury Stock, Common	11,500.00	
		Cash		11,500.00
		Purchased 1,000 shares of treasury stock at $11.50 per share.		

The entry reduces the stockholders' equity by debiting the Treasury Stock account, which is contra to equity. To see the effects of the transaction, look at the balance sheet in Illustration 14–3.

Notice that the company's cash balance in the asset section is reduced from $30,000 to $18,500 by the purchase. Thus, the total assets are reduced by $11,500. The equity also is reduced by the same amount, which is reflected on the balance sheet by deducting the cost of the treasury stock in the equity section. The purchase does not reduce the balance of either the Common

Stock account or the Retained Earnings account. However, two disclosures in this section describe the effects of the transaction. First, the statement tells the reader that 1,000 of the issued shares are in the treasury of the corporation. Thus, only 9,000 shares are outstanding. Second, the purchase has placed a restriction on the company's retained earnings. This restriction is described in the next section.

Restricting Retained Earnings by the Purchase of Treasury Stock

LO 3 Describe restrictions and appropriations of retained earnings and explain how they are described in financial reports.

Cash dividends and purchases of treasury stock have a similar effect on a corporation's assets and stockholders' equity. That is, they both transfer corporate cash to stockholders and reduce assets and equity. Therefore, most states restrict the amount of cash dividends and treasury stock purchases to the amount of retained earnings.

Unlike a cash dividend, a treasury stock purchase does not directly reduce the balance of the Retained Earnings account. If it did reduce the balance, the balance sheet would continue to report the amount of retained earnings available for dividends. However, the use of the contra-equity account makes it necessary for the corporation to disclose any statutory restrictions on retained earnings. Thus, the balance sheet in Illustration 14–3 identifies the amount of the **restricted retained earnings** created by the treasury stock purchase. In many cases, the restriction is described in a footnote to the financial statements. In addition to this restriction, other limits on dividends are established by statute and by contract.

Reissuing Treasury Stock

Treasury stock may be reissued by selling it at cost, above cost, or below cost. If it is reissued by being sold at its cost, the journal entry is the opposite of the entry that was made to record the purchase.

If treasury stock is sold for more than cost, the amount received in excess of cost is credited to a special account called Contributed Capital, Treasury Stock Transactions. For example, if Curry Corporation receives $12 cash per share for 500 treasury shares originally purchased at $11.50 per share, the accountant records the transaction with the following entry:

June	3	Cash	6,000.00	
		Treasury Stock, Common		5,750.00
		Contributed Capital, Treasury Stock Transactions		250.00
		Received $12 per share for 500 treasury shares that cost $11.50 per share.		

Notice that the company does not report a gain from this transaction.

When treasury stock is sold for less than its cost, the entry to record the sale depends on whether there is a credit balance in the Contributed Capital, Treasury Stock Transactions account. If there is no balance, the excess of cost over the sales price is debited to Retained Earnings. However, if the contributed capital account has a credit balance, the excess of the cost over the sales price is debited for an amount up to the balance in that account. When the credit balance in the contributed capital account is eliminated, any remaining difference between the cost and the selling price is debited to Retained Earnings.

For example, if Curry Corporation sells its remaining 500 shares of treasury stock at $10 per share, the company's equity is reduced by $750 (500 shares × \$1.50 per share excess of cost over selling price). The reissuance is recorded with this entry:

July	10	Cash	5,000.00	
		Contributed Capital, Treasury Stock Transactions	250.00	
		Retained Earnings	500.00	
		Treasury Stock, Common		5,750.00
		Received \$10 per share for 500 treasury shares that cost \$11.50 per share.		

This entry eliminates the \$250 credit balance in the contributed capital account created on June 3 and then reduces the retained earnings balance by the remaining \$500 of the excess of the cost over the selling price. Thus, the purchase and reissuance of the treasury shares caused the Curry Corporation to incur a \$500 decrease in retained earnings and total stockholders' equity. Notice that the company does not report a loss from this transaction.

Retiring Stock

Instead of acquiring treasury stock with the intent of reissuing it in the future, a corporation may simply purchase its own stock to retire it. It cancels the shares, which become the same as unissued stock. Like purchases of treasury stock, purchases and retirements of stock are permissible under state laws only if they do not jeopardize the best interests of creditors and other stockholders.

When stock is purchased for retirement, the accountant must remove all the contributed capital amounts related to the retired shares. If the purchase price for the shares exceeds the net amount removed from contributed capital, the excess is debited to Retained Earnings. On the other hand, if the purchase price is less than the net amount removed from contributed capital, the difference is credited to a special contributed capital account.

For example, assume that the Carolina Corporation originally issued its \$10 par value common stock at \$12 per share. As a result, the \$2 per share premium was credited to the Contributed Capital in Excess of Par Value, Common Stock account. When the corporation purchased and retired 1,000 shares of this stock at \$12 per share on April 12, it recorded the effects of this event with this entry:

Apr.	12	Common Stock	10,000.00	
		Contributed Capital in Excess of Par Value, Common Stock	2,000.00	
		Cash		12,000.00
		Purchased and retired 1,000 shares of common stock at \$12 per share.		

This entry restores the accounts to the balances that they would have had if the stock had never been issued.

On the other hand, if the corporation paid only \$11 per share instead of \$12, the retirement causes equity to increase by \$1 per share, the difference between cost and the original issuance price. This increase in equity is recorded as follows:

Apr.	12	Common Stock	10,000.00	
		Contributed Capital in Excess of Par Value,		
		Common Stock	2,000.00	
		Cash		11,000.00
		Contributed Capital from the Retirement of		
		Common Stock		1,000.00
		Purchased and retired 1,000 shares of common stock at $11 per share.		

Even though this transaction increased equity, the amount is not a gain. The concept underlying this treatment is that transactions in a corporation's own stock cannot affect income or increase retained earnings.

The same idea governs the accounting for a retirement accomplished with a purchase price that is greater than the stock's original issuance price. For example, suppose that the Carolina Corporation retired 1,000 shares of its stock at $15 per share, which is $3 per share greater than the $12 original issue price. This entry would be used to account for the event:

Apr.	12	Common Stock	10,000.00	
		Contributed Capital in Excess of Par Value,		
		Common Stock	2,000.00	
		Retained Earnings	3,000.00	
		Cash		15,000.00
		Purchased and retired 1,000 shares of common stock at $15 per share.		

Even though this transaction decreased equity, the amount is not a loss. The $3,000 is debited to Retained Earnings. If there had been a credit balance in a contributed capital account related to retirements, it would have been debited up to the amount of its balance.

All three retirement examples reduced the company's assets and equity by the amount paid for the stock. However, no income effects are recognized. The only effects on equity are recorded in the contributed capital and retained earnings accounts.

Appropriating Retained Earnings

As explained earlier, treasury stock purchases often result in statutory restrictions on paying dividends from the corporation's retained earnings. Also, a corporation's directors may voluntarily limit dividends because of a special need for cash, such as to purchase new facilities. When they do this, the directors may notify the stockholders and other financial statement users of this change in policy by setting up an amount of **appropriated retained earnings.** In contrast to statutory or contractual retained earnings restrictions, these appropriations are strictly voluntary and nonbinding. They serve only to notify the statement readers of the directors' decision to not pay out cash.

In fact, appropriated retained earnings are seldom seen on today's balance sheets. Instead, management usually explains in a letter attached to the financial statements why dividends have not been declared.

REPORTING INCOME AND RETAINED EARNINGS INFORMATION

When a company's only revenue and expense transactions are created by routine, continuing operations, a single-step income statement is adequate for describing the results of its activities. This format shows the revenues followed by a list of operating expenses and the net income. In today's complex business world, however, a period's activities often include many income-related events that are not part of a company's continuing and otherwise normal activities.

LO 4 Explain how to report the income effects of discontinued segments, extraordinary items, changes in accounting principles and estimates, and prior period adjustments.

The accountant's goal is to provide useful information in a format that helps the statement users understand past period events and predict the future period results. To see how this goal is accomplished, look at the income statement in Illustration 14–4. Notice that the statement is separated into five sections.

Continuing Operations

The top section of the income statement (labeled ①) shows the revenues, expenses, and income generated by the company's continuing operations. This portion looks like the single-step income statement that we first discussed in Chapter 5. Income statement users rely on the information in this section to predict what will happen. As such, this section usually contains the most important information in the income statement. Previous chapters have explained the nature of the items and measures included in income from continuing operations.

Discontinued Segments

Most large companies have several lines of business and deal with different groups of customers. For example, International Business Machines not only produces and sells computer hardware and software but also delivers system design and repair services. Information about these **segments of the business** is of particular interest to users of the company's financial statements. According to GAAP, a segment is a component of a company's operations that serves a particular line of business or class of customers. A segment has assets, activities, and financial results of operations that can be distinguished from other parts of the business.

Reporting Income Statement Information about Discontinued Segments

When a company incurs a gain or loss from selling or closing down a segment, the gain or loss must be reported in a separate section of the income statement.[3] Section ② of the income statement in Illustration 14–4 includes this information. Note that the income from operating the discontinued segment prior to its disposal also is reported in section 2. When the income statement presents the results of several years side-by-side, it is necessary to go back and restate the prior years' results to separate out the revenues and expenses of the discontinued segment.

Separate information about a discontinued segment can be useful on its own. However, the primary purpose of reporting the gains or losses from discontinued operations separately is to more clearly present the results of continuing operations. The effect is to provide useful information for predicting the income that will be earned by the segments that will continue to operate in the future.

Distinguishing the Results of Operating a Discontinued Segment from the Gain or Loss on Disposal

Section ② of Illustration 14–4 reports both the income from *operating* the discontinued Division A during the year and the loss that occurred from disposing of the division's assets. The income tax effects of operating and disposing of the segment are also disclosed in section ②. As a result, the tax effects

[3] FASB, *Accounting Standards—Current Text* (Norwalk, CT, 1994), sec. I13.105. Originally published as *APB Opinion No. 30,* par. 8.

ILLUSTRATION 14-4 *Income Statement for a Corporation*

CONNELLY CORPORATION
Income Statement
For Year Ended December 31, 19X4

①	Net sales		$8,440,000
	Gain on sale of equipment		38,000
	Total		$8,478,000
	Expenses:		
	Cost of goods sold	$5,950,000	
	Depreciation expense	35,000	
	Other selling, general, and administrative expenses	515,000	
	Interest expense	20,000	
	Income taxes expense	595,500	
	Total expenses		(7,115,500)
	Unusual loss on relocating a plant		(45,000)
	Infrequent gain on sale of surplus land		72,000
	Income from continuing operations		$1,389,500
②	**Discontinued segment:**		
	Income from operating Division A (net of $180,000 income taxes)	$ 420,000	
	Loss on disposal of Division A (net of $66,000 tax benefit)	(154,000)	266,000
	Income before extraordinary items and cumulative effect of a change in accounting principle		$1,655,500
③	**Extraordinary items:**		
	Gain on sale of unused land condemned by the state for a highway interchange (net of $61,200 income taxes)	$ 142,800	
	Loss from earthquake damage (net of $270,000 income tax benefit)	(630,000)	(487,200)
④	**Cumulative effect of a change in accounting principle:**		
	Effect on prior years' income (through December 31, 19X3) of changing to a different depreciation method (net of $24,000 income taxes)		56,000
	Net income		$1,224,300
⑤	**Earnings per common share** (200,000 shares outstanding):		
	Income from continuing operations		$6.95
	Discontinued operations		1.33
	Income before extraordinary items and cumulative effect of a change in accounting principle		$8.28
	Extraordinary items		(2.44)
	Cumulative effect of a change in accounting principle		0.28
	Net income		$6.12

related to the discontinued segment are separated from the presentation of continuing operations in section ①. If the tax effects of the discontinued segment were not separated from the continuing operations, the result would not be as useful.

This discussion presents only a highly summarized description of the requirements for reporting the results of discontinued segments. The details are covered in more advanced accounting courses.

Extraordinary Items

Section ③ of the income statement in Illustration 14–4 reports **extraordinary gains and losses** that occurred during the year. Extraordinary gains and losses are both unusual and infrequent. An **unusual gain or loss** is abnormal or otherwise unrelated to the ordinary activities and environment of the business. An **infrequent gain or loss** is not expected to occur again in the company's operating environment.[4] Reporting extraordinary items in a separate category makes it easier for users to predict what will happen in the future, apart from these extraordinary events.

In light of these definitions of *unusual* and *infrequent,* very few items qualify as extraordinary gains or losses by meeting both criteria. For example, none of the following events are considered extraordinary.

1. Write-downs or write-offs of assets, unless the change in value is caused by a major unusual and infrequent calamity, a condemning or expropriating of property by a domestic or foreign government, or a prohibition against using the assets under a newly enacted law.
2. Gains or losses from exchanging foreign currencies or translating account balances expressed in one currency into another currency.
3. Gains and losses from disposing of a business segment.
4. Effects of a labor action, including one against the company, its competitors, or its major suppliers.
5. Adjustment of accruals on long-term contracts.[5]

Gains or losses that are neither unusual nor infrequent are reported as part of the results of continuing operations. Gains or losses that are either unusual or infrequent but not both are not extraordinary. These items are listed on the income statement in the continuing operations section below the regular revenues, expenses, gains, and losses. For example, section ① of Illustration 14–4 includes a "Gain on sale of equipment" that is neither unusual nor infrequent with the revenues. However, an unusual loss and an infrequent gain are reported at the end of the section. The proper classification of these items is not always clear without carefully examining the circumstances.

In addition, some items are treated as extraordinary gains or losses, even if they do not otherwise meet the criteria. In particular, any gains and losses from retiring debt are reported as extraordinary.

Changes in Accounting Principles

In general, the *consistency principle* requires a company to continue applying a specific accounting method or principle once it is chosen. (In this context, the term *accounting principles* describes accounting methods, such as FIFO and straight-line depreciation.) However, a company may change from one acceptable accounting principle to another as long as it justifies the change as an improvement in the information provided in its financial statements. In addition, companies often change accounting principles when they adopt new standards issued by the FASB.

When a company changes accounting principles, it usually affects the amount of reported income in more than one way. For example, let's consider Connelly Corporation's income statement in Illustration 14–4. The company purchased its only depreciable asset early in 19X1 for $320,000. The asset has a $40,000 salvage value and has been depreciated with the double-declining-balance method for three of the eight years in its predicted useful life. (This

[4] Ibid., sec. I17.107. Originally published as *APB Opinion No. 30,* par. 20.
[5] Ibid., sec. I17.110. Originally published as *APB Opinion No. 30,* par. 23.

ILLUSTRATION 14–5 *Calculating the Cumulative Effect of a Change in Accounting Principle*

Year	Double-Declining Depreciation Amount	Straight-Line Depreciation Amount	Pre-Tax Difference	Tax Rate	After-Tax Cumulative Effect
Prior to change:					
19X1	$ 80,000	$ 35,000	$45,000		
19X2	60,000	35,000	25,000		
19X3	45,000	35,000	10,000		
Subtotal	$185,000	$105,000	$80,000	30%	$56,000†
Year of change:					
19X4	$ 33,750	35,000*			
Years after change:					
19X5		35,000			
19X6		35,000			
19X7		35,000			
19X8		35,000			
Total		$210,000			

* Reported on the 19X4 income statement as depreciation expense.
† Reported on the 19X4 income statement as the cumulative adjustment for difference in the three years prior to the change in 19X4, net of $24,000 additional taxes to be paid (30% × $80,000).

company is subject to a 30% income tax rate.) During 19X4, the company decided that its income statement would be more useful if the annual depreciation were calculated with the straight-line method instead of double-declining-balance.

In Illustration 14–5, we compare the results of applying the two depreciation methods to the first three years in the asset's service life and show how the company would determine what to report on its 19X4 income statement. The table shows that the accelerated method caused $185,000 of depreciation to be allocated to 19X1 through 19X3. If the straight-line method had been used from the beginning, only $105,000 of depreciation would have been allocated to those years. To give the accounts the balances that they would have had under the straight-line method, the company needs to decrease accumulated depreciation for this asset by the $80,000 gross difference. Offsetting this debit is a credit of $24,000 (30% × $80,000) to a deferred income tax liability for additional taxes to be paid in the future. The remaining $56,000 is the resulting credit to equity created by this change. Because the change increases equity, the company adds it to the income for the year in which the change is made effective.

Reporting Requirements for Changes in Accounting Principles

The income statement in Illustration 14–4 on page 510 shows the acceptable method of reporting the effects of a change in accounting principles by the Connelly Corporation. Section ① of the income statement includes $35,000 of depreciation expense for the current year. This amount is shown in the straight-line method column for 19X4 in Illustration 14–5. Thus, the income for the year of the change is based on the new accounting principle. The annual depreciation of $35,000 also will be used in 19X5 through 19X8. In Illustration 14–5, we calculate the $56,000 catch-up adjustment reported in section ④ of the income statement in Illustration 14–4. This item is the cumulative effect of the change in accounting principle.

In addition to the information in the financial statements, two points about the change should be explained: First, a footnote should describe the change and why it is an improvement over the old principle. Second, the footnote should describe what 19X4's income would have been under the old method if the change had not occurred. For this example, the footnote would reveal that leaving the method unchanged would have caused the depreciation for 19X4 to be $33,750 under double-declining instead of $35,000 under straight-line. This footnoted amount appears in Illustration 14–5 as the declining-balance depreciation for 19X4.

Earnings per Share Section of the Income Statement

Section ⑤ of Illustration 14–4 provides detailed information about earnings per share results for the year. This information is included on the face of the income statement in accordance with GAAP. This section is more complete than the minimum reporting requirements to show the possible categories companies can and often do report. A later section of the chapter explains the basic procedures to compute earnings per share.

Prior Period Adjustments for Correcting Material Errors

Companies do not report the effect of a **prior period adjustment** on their current income statements. Instead, prior period adjustments appear in the statement of retained earnings (or the statement of changes in stockholders' equity), net of any income tax effects. Prior period adjustments modify the beginning balance of retained earnings for events occurring prior to the earliest year described in the financial statements. Under GAAP, prior period adjustments only record the effects of correcting material errors in earlier years. These errors include arithmetic mistakes, using unacceptable accounting principles, or failing to consider relevant facts.[6] An error would occur if an accountant mistakenly omits depreciation, applies an unacceptable depreciation method, or overlooks important facts in predicting an asset's useful life. For example, assume that the accountant for the Connelly Corporation failed to detect an error in a 19X2 journal entry for the purchase of land incorrectly debited to an expense account. This statement of retained earnings includes a prior period adjustment to correct the error discovered in 19X4:

CONNELLY CORPORATION
Statement of Retained Earnings
For Year Ended December 31, 19X4

Retained earnings, December 31, 19X3, as previously stated	$4,745,000
Prior period adjustment:	
Cost of land incorrectly charged to expense	
(net of $63,000 income taxes)	147,000
Retained earnings, December 31, 19X3, as adjusted	$4,892,000
Plus net income	1,162,500
Less cash dividends declared	(240,000)
Retained earnings, December 31, 19X4	$5,814,500

Changes in Accounting Estimates

Many of the items disclosed in financial statements are based on estimates and predictions. Future events are certain to reveal some of these estimates and predictions were inaccurate, even though they were based on the best data available at the time. Because these inaccuracies are not the result of

[6] Ibid, sec. A35.104. Originally published as *APB Opinion No. 20,* par. 13.

ILLUSTRATION 14–6

ALBERTSON'S INC.
Consolidated Stockholders' Equity
(in thousands, except per share data)

	Common Stock $1.00 Par Value	Capital in Excess of Par	Retained Earnings	Treasury Stock	Total
Balance at January 30, 1992	$132,131	$ 718	$1,066,603		$1,199,452
Exercise of stock options	199	4,191			4,390
Cash dividends $0.32 per share . .			(84,631)		(84,631)
Net earnings			269,217		269,217
Balance at January 28, 1993	132,330	4,909	1,251,189		1,388,428
Exercise of stock options	245	4,238			4,483
Purchase treasury shares				$(517,526)	(517,526)
Issue treasury shares		19,615		244,912	264,527
Retire treasury shares	(5,788)	(25,010)	(241,816)	272,614	
Two-for-one stock split	126,620	(1,635)	(124,985)		
Other			953		953
Cash dividends, $0.36 per share . .			(91,167)		(91,167)
Net earnings			339,681		339,681
Balance at February 3, 1994	$253,407	$ 2,117	$1,133,855		$1,389,379

Courtesy of Albertson's Inc.

mistakes, they are not accounting errors. Thus, any corrections of these estimates are not reported as prior period adjustments. Instead, they are **changes in accounting estimates.** For example, depreciation is based on predicted useful lives and salvage values. As new information becomes available, it may be used to change predictions and modify the amounts reported as depreciation expense. Unlike changes in accounting principles, changes in accounting estimates are not accounted for with cumulative catch-up adjustments. Instead, the revised estimates are applied in determining revenues and expenses for the current and future periods. In Chapter 9, we explained one common change in an accounting estimate when we discussed revising depreciation rates.

Statement of Changes in Stockholders' Equity

Most corporations actually do not present a separate statement of retained earnings. Instead, they provide a **statement of changes in stockholders' equity** that lists the beginning and ending balances of each equity account and describes all the changes that occurred during the year. For example, Albertson's Inc., which operates a large chain of retail stores, presents this information in a format that provides a column for each component of equity and uses the rows to describe the events of the year. (See Illustration 14–6.) Notice that the company acquired treasury stock in fiscal year 1994 and then either sold or retired all the shares. The statement also indicates a stock split, but the credit to the common stock account reveals it was actually a 100% stock dividend. (For reasons not explained in the report, the dividend was recorded with a partial transfer of contributed capital in excess of par to the common stock account.)

EARNINGS PER SHARE

LO 5 Calculate earnings per share for companies with simple capital structures and explain the difference between primary and fully diluted earnings per share.

Among the most widely quoted items of accounting information is the **earnings per share** results achieved by a corporation. This number represents the amount of income earned by each share of a company's common stock. For example, this excerpt from *The Wall Street Journal* reported the earnings per share J. C. Penney Co. achieved and expects to achieve:

> J. C. Penney Co. expects to post another record year for earnings and revenue, William R. Howell, chairman and chief executive, said at the company's annual meeting. Mr. Howell said he is comfortable with analysts' estimates of earnings between $4.15 and $4.22 a share for the fiscal year ending Jan. 29, 1995, a gain of 10% to 12% from fiscal 1994 earnings of $944 million, or $3.77 a share.[7]

As this excerpt suggests, investors and their advisors use earnings per share results to evaluate a corporation's past performance, project its future earnings, and compare its prospects with other investment opportunities.

Because of the importance and widespread use of earnings per share numbers, accountants have developed detailed guidelines for calculating it. One important factor that shapes the presentation of earnings per share is the company's capital structure, which can be either simple or complex.

Companies with Simple Capital Structures

Earnings per share calculations can be simple or complicated, depending on a company's situation. The calculations are not difficult for a company with a **simple capital structure** because it has only common stock and perhaps nonconvertible preferred stock outstanding. That is, a simple capital structure cannot include any options or rights to purchase common stock or any convertible preferred stock or bonds.

Calculating Earnings per Share When the Number of Common Shares Does Not Change

As an easy example of calculating earnings per share, let's assume that a company has issued only common stock and nonconvertible preferred stock. As a further simplification, assume that the number of outstanding common shares does not change during the period. In this situation, the calculation involves determining the amount of the net income that is available to the common stockholders and dividing it by the number of common shares. The amount of income available to the common stockholders is the year's net income less any dividends declared or accumulated on the preferred stock. (If the preferred stock is cumulative, the current year's dividend must be subtracted even if it was not declared.) The following formula applies in this case:

$$\text{Earnings per share} = \frac{\text{Net income} - \text{Preferred dividends}}{\text{Outstanding common shares}}$$

For example, assume that the Blackwell Company earned $40,000 net income in 19X1 and declared dividends of $7,500 on its noncumulative preferred stock. The company had 5,000 common shares outstanding throughout the entire year. Thus:

$$\text{Earnings per share} = \frac{\$40{,}000 - \$7{,}500}{5{,}000 \text{ shares}} = \$6.50$$

[7] "J. C. Penney Expects to Have Record Year for Sales and Profit," *The Wall Street Journal*, May 23, 1994, p. C16.

The calculation becomes more complex if the number of outstanding shares changes during the year. The number may change for a variety of reasons that most often involve sales of additional shares, purchases of treasury stock, and stock dividends or splits.

Finding the Denominator When a Company Sells or Purchases Common Shares

If a company sells additional shares or purchases treasury shares during the year, the denominator of the formula becomes the weighted average of outstanding shares. The idea behind this change is to produce an average amount of earnings accruing to the average number of shares outstanding during the year the income was earned.

For example, suppose that Blackwell Company earned $40,000 in 19X2 and declared preferred dividends of $7,500. As a result, the earnings available to the common stock is again $32,500. Now assume that Blackwell sold 4,000 additional common shares on July 1, 19X2, and purchased 3,000 treasury shares on November 1, 19X2. As a result, 5,000 shares were outstanding for six months, 9,000 shares were outstanding for four months, and 6,000 shares were outstanding for two months. We calculate the weighted-average number of outstanding shares as follows:

Time Period	Outstanding Shares	Fraction of Year	Weighted Average
January–June	5,000	$\frac{6}{12}$	2,500
July–October	9,000	$\frac{4}{12}$	3,000
November–December	6,000	$\frac{2}{12}$	1,000
Weighted-average outstanding shares			6,500

Using the weighted-average number of common shares outstanding for Blackwell, the earnings per share calculation is

$$\text{Earnings per share} = \frac{\$40{,}000 - \$7{,}500}{6{,}500 \text{ shares}} = \$5.00$$

This number appears at the bottom of the company's income statement for 19X2.

Adjusting the Denominator for Stock Splits and Stock Dividends

The number of outstanding shares also can be affected by a stock split or stock dividend during the year. These events do not bring in any additional assets; thus, they do not affect the company's ability to produce earnings for the common stockholders. In effect, the earnings for the year are simply spread out over a larger number of shares. This causes accountants to treat stock splits and stock dividends differently when they calculate the weighted-average number of shares for the year.

When a stock split or stock dividend occurs, the number of shares that were outstanding earlier in the year are retroactively restated to reflect the effects of the stock split or dividend as if it occurred at the beginning of the year. For example, let's reconsider the Blackwell Company example and assume that the stock transactions in 19X2 included a two-for-one stock split on December 1. This split caused the percentage ownership of each share to be cut in half while doubling the number of outstanding shares. The situation is described by this table:

Time Period	Original Shares	Effect of Split	Post-Split Shares
January–June	5,000	2	10,000
July–October	9,000	2	18,000
November	6,000	2	12,000

Then, the numbers in the third column can be inserted into the weighted-average calculation for the new shares:

Time Period	Post-Split Shares	Fraction of Year	Weighted Average
January–June	10,000	6/12	5,000
July–October	18,000	4/12	6,000
November–December	12,000	2/12	2,000
Weighted-average outstanding shares			13,000

This same result can be produced by multiplying the weighted-average of the pre-split shares (6,500) by two.

Blackwell Company's earnings per share for 19X2 under this set of assumptions are

$$\text{Earnings per share} = \frac{\$40{,}000 - \$7{,}500}{13{,}000 \text{ shares}} = \$2.50$$

The same sort of modification is used when stock dividends occur. For example, if the two-for-one stock split had been a 10% stock dividend, the numbers of old outstanding shares would have been multiplied by 1.1 instead of two.

Companies with Complex Capital Structures

Companies with **complex capital structures** have outstanding securities that include options, warrants, bonds, or preferred stock that can be converted into common stock. Determining earnings per share under these circumstances is more complicated because it is not exactly clear how the earnings should be divided among the different securities. In many situations, companies with complex capital structures actually present two sets of earnings per share results. The first one, **primary earnings per share,** represents the most likely case. The second is a worst case result called **fully diluted earnings per share.**

For example, suppose a corporation's convertible preferred stock is outstanding throughout the most recent year. Although the preferred shares were not actually converted to common, they could have been and can be converted at any point. If they had been converted at the beginning of the year, how would the earnings per share have been affected? First, the numerator would be increased because the preferred stock dividends would not have been declared. Instead of being the net income minus the preferred dividends, the numerator would simply be the year's net income. Second, the number of common shares would have been increased by the conversion. Thus, both the numerator and the denominator would be larger, but it is not possible to state whether the net result would have been a larger or smaller earnings per share.

If the outcome of assuming conversion is a smaller earnings per share, the convertible security is said to be a **dilutive** because it reduces (or *dilutes*) the amount of earnings available to each common share. On the other hand, if the outcome of assuming conversion is a larger earnings per share, the convertible security is said to be an **antidilutive security** because it actually increases the amount of earnings available to each common share. Only dilutive securities are used to compute the primary and fully diluted earnings per share.

ILLUSTRATION 14–7 *Reporting Earnings per Share on the Income Statement*

Showing multiple components

Sprint Corporation

	1993	1992	1991
Earnings per common share			
Continuing operations	$1.39	$1.46	$1.41
Discontinued operations	(0.04)		0.15
Extraordinary item	(0.08)	(0.05)	(0.01)
Cumulative effect of changes in accounting principles	(1.12)	0.07	
Total	$0.15	$1.48	$1.55

Showing primary and fully diluted results

Colgate-Palmolive Company

	1993	1992	1991
Earnings per common share, primary			
Income before changes in accounting	$3.38	$2.92	$ .77
Cumulative effect on prior years of accounting changes	(2.30)		
Net income	$1.08	$2.92	$ .77
Earnings per common share, fully diluted			
Income before changes in accounting	$3.15	$2.74	$ .75
Cumulative effect on prior years of accounting changes	(2.10)		
Net income	$1.05	$2.74	$ .75

Courtesy of Sprint Corporation and Colgate-Palmolive Company

Primary Earnings per Share

Based on detailed rules, convertible securities are identified as being equivalent or not equivalent to common stock when they are first issued.[8] If their eventual conversion seems reasonable, the convertible securities are considered to be **common stock equivalents.** The amount of primary earnings per share is calculated as if all dilutive common stock equivalents were converted at the beginning of the period.

Fully Diluted Earnings per Share

In contrast to common stock equivalents that have a high likelihood of being converted, other convertible securities are less likely to be changed into common shares. Nevertheless, if the assumed conversion would have a dilutive effect, the fully diluted calculation is accomplished as if the securities were converted. Actually, the entire process is very complicated and accountants often use special computer software to guide them through the steps.

Presenting Earnings per Share on the Income Statement

Because information about earnings per share is important, corporations must report it on the face of their income statements. Furthermore, they usually report the amount of earnings per share for net income and each of the four main subcategories of income (continuing operations, discontinued segments, extraordinary items, and the effect of accounting principles changes). Illustration 14–4 on page 510 shows Connelly Corporation's earnings per share in section ⑤.

[8] FASB, *Accounting Standards—Current Text* (Norwalk, CT, 1994), sec. E09.122–127. First published as *APB Opinion No. 15*, par. 31, 33, 35–37. Also see *FASB, Statement of Financial Accounting Standards No. 85* (March 1985), par. 2.

Even though some flexibility exists within the accounting guidelines on reporting these components, many companies simply present all the details in one place for the convenience of the financial statement users. Illustration 14–7 provides real examples of earnings per share presentations by Sprint Corporation and Colgate-Palmolive Company. The Sprint example shows the per share effects of the various components of its income for three fiscal years. The Colgate-Palmolive example shows the primary and fully diluted results for the same three years.

Using the Information—The Price-Earnings Ratio

You learned in Chapter 13 that a stock's market value is largely affected by the stream of future dividends expected to be paid out to stockholders. Market value is also affected by expectations for future changes in market value. By comparing the company's earnings per share and its market value per share, investors and other decision makers can obtain information about the stock market's apparent expectations for growth in future earnings, dividends, and market values.

LO 6 Calculate the price-earnings ratio and describe its meaning.

Although it would be possible to make this comparison as a rate of return by dividing the earnings per share by the market value per share, the ratio has traditionally been turned upside-down and calculated as the **price-earnings ratio.** Thus, this ratio is found by dividing the stock's market value by the earnings per share, as shown in this formula:

$$\text{Price-earnings ratio} = \frac{\text{Market value per share}}{\text{Earnings per share}}$$

The ratio may be calculated using the earnings per share reported in the past period. Often, however, analysts calculate the ratio based on the expected earnings per share for the next period. Suppose, for example, that the stock's current market price is $100 per share and that its next year's earnings are expected to be $8 per share. Its price-earning ratio (often abbreviated as the PE ratio) is found as $100/$8, which is 12.5.

As a general rule, stocks with higher PE ratios (generally greater than 12 to 15) are considered more likely to be overpriced while stocks with lower PE ratios (generally less than 5 to 8) are considered more likely to be underpriced. Thus, some investors prefer to sell or avoid buying stocks with high PE ratios while they prefer to buy or hold stocks that have low PE ratios. Investment decisions are not quite that simple, however, because a stock with a high PE ratio may prove to be a good investment if its earnings increase rapidly. On the other hand, a stock with a low PE ratio may prove to be a poor performer. Although the price-earnings ratio is clearly important for investment decisions, it is only one piece of information that investors should consider.

Summary of Chapter in Terms of Learning Objectives

LO 1 In contrast to cash dividends, stock dividends do not transfer corporate assets to stockholders. Stock dividends and stock splits do not affect assets, total stockholders' equity, or the equity attributed to each stockholder. Small stock dividends (≤25%) are recorded by capitalizing retained earnings equal to the market value of the distributed shares. Large stock dividends (>25%) are recorded by capitalizing retained earnings equal to the par or stated value of the issued shares. Stock splits are not recorded through journal entries but should lead to changing the account title for the common stock if it includes the par or stated value.

LO 2 When outstanding treasury shares are repurchased by the corporation that issued them, the cost of the shares is debited to the contra-equity account called Treasury Stock. Its balance is subtracted from total stockholders' equity in the balance sheet. When treasury stock is later reissued, the amount of any proceeds in excess of cost is credited to an account called Contributed Capital, Treasury Stock Transactions. If the proceeds are less than cost, the difference is debited to Contributed Capital, Treasury Stock Transactions to the extent a credit balance exists in that account. Any remaining amount is debited to Retained Earnings. The possibility for ethical abuses in treasury stock transactions has led to extensive guidance for managers and accountants concerning these activities.

LO 3 Most states use statutes to limit dividends and treasury stock purchases to the amount of retained earnings. Companies also enter into contractual situations in which they agree to further limit the amount of dividends, even though they have both the cash and the retained earnings to pay them. Corporations may voluntarily appropriate retained earnings to inform stockholders why dividends are not larger. Often, this information is expressed in a letter to the stockholders.

LO 4 As a method of increasing the usefulness of the information in the income statement, accountants have developed rules to be certain that the statement clearly identifies the results of activities that are expected to continue into the future. This presentation helps decision makers project future income from more appropriate data. Thus, if a company's management has decided to discontinue a segment, the income effects of operating and disposing of the segment are separately reported on the income statement below income from continuing operations. Extraordinary gains or losses are also separated out of the continuing operations and reported lower in the income statement. A similar treatment is required for the cumulative effects of changes in accounting principles. Prior period adjustments for error corrections are not reported on the income statement, but appear on the retained earnings statement or the statement of changes in stockholders' equity. Changes in accounting estimates arise when new information shows the old estimates to be inaccurate. If an accounting estimate is changed, the firm uses the new estimate to calculate income in the current and future periods.

LO 5 Companies with simple capital structures have not issued any securities that are convertible into common stock. These companies calculate earnings per share by dividing net income (less any preferred dividends) by the weighted-average number of outstanding common shares. Companies with complex capital structures have issued securities that are convertible into common stock. These companies often have to report both primary earnings per share and fully diluted earnings per share.

LO 6 The price-earnings ratio of a common stock is closely watched by investors and other decision makers. The ratio is calculated by dividing the current market value per share by the expected earnings per share for the next year. A high ratio often suggests that a stock is overvalued while a low ratio suggests that a stock is undervalued. However, selecting stocks to buy or sell requires a great deal more information.

Demonstration Problem

The Precision Company began 19X1 with the following balances in its stockholders' equity accounts:

Common stock, $10 par, 500,000 shares authorized, 200,000 shares issued and outstanding	$2,000,000
Contributed capital in excess of par	1,000,000
Retained earnings	5,000,000
Total	$8,000,000

All of the outstanding stock was issued for $15 when the company was created.

Part 1. Prepare journal entries to account for the following transactions during 19X1:

Mar. 31	Declared a 20% stock dividend. The market value of the stock was $18 per share.
Apr. 15	Distributed the stock dividend declared on March 31.
June 30	Purchased 30,000 shares of treasury stock at $20 per share.
Aug. 31	Sold 20,000 treasury shares at $26 per share.
Nov. 30	Purchased and retired 50,000 shares at $24 per share.

Part 2. Use the following information to prepare an income statement for 19X1, including earnings per share results for each category of income.

Cumulative effect of a change in depreciation method (net of tax benefit)	$ (136,500)
Expenses related to continuing operations	(2,072,500)
Extraordinary gain on debt retirement (net of tax)	182,000
Gain on disposal of discontinued segment's assets (net of tax)	29,000
Gain on sale of stock investment	400,000
Loss from operating discontinued segment (net of tax benefit)	(120,000)
Income taxes on income from continuing operations	(225,000)
Prior period adjustment for error (net of tax benefit)	(75,000)
Sales	4,140,000
Infrequent loss	(650,000)

Planning the Solution

- Decide whether the stock dividend is a small or large dividend. Then, analyze each event to determine the accounts affected and the appropriate amounts to be recorded.
- Based on the shares of outstanding stock at the beginning of the year and the transactions during the year, calculate the weighted-average number of outstanding shares for the year.
- Assign each of the listed items to an appropriate income statement category.
- Prepare an income statement similar to Illustration 14–4, including appropriate earnings per share results.

Solution to Demonstration Problem

Part 1.

Mar.	31	Stock Dividends Declared	720,000.00	
		Common Stock Dividend Distributable		400,000.00
		Contributed Capital in Excess of Par Value, Common Stock		320,000.00
		Declared a small stock dividend of 20% or 40,000 shares; market value is $18 per share.		
Apr.	15	Common Stock Dividend Distributable	400,000.00	
		Common Stock		400,000.00
		Distributed 40,000 shares of common stock.		
June	30	Treasury Stock, Common	600,000.00	
		Cash		600,000.00
		Purchased 30,000 shares of common stock at $20 per share.		
Aug.	31	Cash	520,000.00	
		Treasury Stock, Common		400,000.00
		Contributed Capital, Treasury Stock Transactions		120,000.00
		Sold 20,000 shares of treasury stock at $26 per share.		

Nov.	30	Common Stock	500,000.00	
		Contributed Capital in Excess of Par Value, Common Stock	250,000.00	
		Retained Earnings	450,000.00	
		Cash		1,200,000.00
		Purchased and retired 50,000 shares at $24 per share.		

Part 2. Calculating the weighted average of outstanding shares:

Time Period	Original Shares	Effect of Dividend	Post-Dividend Shares
January–April 15	200,000	1.2	240,000

Time Period	Post-Dividend Shares	Fraction of Year	Weighted Average
January–June	240,000	6/12	120,000
July–August	210,000	2/12	35,000
September–November	230,000	3/12	57,500
December	180,000	1/12	15,000
Weighted-average outstanding shares			227,500

PRECISION COMPANY
Income Statement
For Year Ended December 31, 19X1

Sales		$4,140,000
Expenses		(2,072,500)
Income taxes		(225,000)
Gain on sale of stock investment		400,000
Infrequent loss		(650,000)
Income from continuing operations		$1,592,500
Discontinued operations:		
Loss from operation of discontinued segment (net of tax benefit)	$(120,000)	
Gain on disposal of discontinued segment's assets (net of tax)	29,000	
Loss from discontinued division		(91,000)
Income before extraordinary items and cumulative effect of a change in accounting principle		$1,501,500
Extraordinary items:		
Extraordinary gain on debt retirement (net of tax)		182,000
Cumulative effect of a change in depreciation method (net of tax benefit)		(136,500)
Net income		$1,547,000
Earnings per share (227,500 average shares outstanding):		
Income from continuing operations		$ 7.00
Loss from discontinued segment		(0.40)
Income before extraordinary gain and cumulative effect of change in accounting principle		$ 6.60
Extraordinary gain		0.80
Cumulative effect of change in accounting principle .		(0.60)
Net income		$ 6.80

Glossary

LO 7 Define or explain the words and phrases listed in the chapter glossary.

Antidilutive securities convertible or exercisable securities that would increase earnings per share when converted or exercised. p. 517

Appropriated retained earnings retained earnings that are voluntarily restricted as a way of informing stockholders that dividends will not be paid. p. 508

Changes in accounting estimates modifications to previous estimates or predictions about future events and outcomes, such as salvage values and the useful lives of operating assets. p. 514

Common stock equivalent a convertible or exercisable security that is reasonably expected to be converted or exercised. p. 518

Complex capital structure a capital structure with options, warrants, bonds, or preferred stock that can be converted into common stock. p. 517

Dilutive securities convertible or exercisable securities that would decrease earnings per share when converted or exercised. p. 517

Earnings per share the amount of income earned by each share of a company's common stock. p. 515

Extraordinary gain or loss a gain or loss that is reported separate from continuing operations because it is both unusual and infrequent. p. 511

Fully diluted earnings per share earnings per share results based on a worst case assumption that all dilutive securities have been converted to common stock. p. 517

Infrequent gain or loss a gain or loss that is not expected to occur again, given the operating environment of the business. p. 511

Large stock dividend a stock dividend that is more than 25% of the corporation's previously outstanding shares. p. 500

Liquidating dividends distributions of corporate assets as a dividend that returns part of the original investment to the stockholders; these distributions are charged to contributed capital accounts. p. 499

Price-earnings ratio the ratio between a company's current market value and its expected earnings per share; used to gain understanding of the market's expectations for the stock. p. 519

Primary earnings per share earnings per share results for a company with a complex structure based on the conversion or exercise of securities that would be reasonably exercised or converted. p. 517

Prior period adjustment an item in the statement of retained earnings as a correction of an error that occurred in a previous year. p. 513

Restricted retained earnings retained earnings that are not available for dividends because of legal or contractual limitations. p. 506

Reverse stock split an action by a corporation to call in its stock and replace it with less than one new share. p. 503

Segment of a business a component of a company's operations that serves a particular line of business or class of customers and that has assets, activities, and financial results of operations that can be distinguished from other parts of the business. p. 509

Simple capital structure a capital structure that consists of no more than common stock and nonconvertible preferred stock; it cannot include any options or rights to purchase common stock or any convertible preferred stock or bonds. p. 515

Small stock dividend a stock dividend that is 25% or less of the corporation's previously outstanding shares. p. 500

Statement of changes in stockholders' equity a financial statement that lists the beginning and ending balances of each equity account and describes all the changes that occurred during the year. p. 514

Stock dividend a corporation's distribution of its own stock to its stockholders without receiving any payment in return. p. 499

Stock split an action by a corporation to call in its stock and replace it with more than one new share. p. 503

Treasury stock stock that was reacquired and is still held by the issuing corporation. p. 504

Unusual gain or loss a gain or loss that is abnormal or otherwise unrelated to the ordinary activities and environment of the business. p. 511

Objective Review

Answers to the following questions are listed at the end of this chapter. Be sure that you decide which is the one best answer to each question *before* you check the answers.

LO 1 Which of the following statements about stock dividends and stock splits is true?

a. A stock split is recorded in the accounts with a debit to Retained Earnings and a credit to the stock account for the par or stated value of the issued shares.

b. A large stock dividend is recorded by capitalizing retained earnings equal to the market value of the distributable shares.

c. Stock dividends and stock splits have equal effects on the total assets and the retained earnings of the issuing corporation.

d. Distributing a stock dividend reduces both cash and stockholders' equity but a stock split does not reduce either cash or equity.

e. Distributing a stock dividend does not transfer corporate assets to the stockholders but does require that retained earnings be capitalized.

LO 2 A corporation's purchase of treasury stock:

a. Does not change the amount of outstanding stock.
b. Increases one asset and decreases another asset.
c. Decreases the amount of issued stock.
d. Reduces both total assets and total stockholders' equity by the same amount.
e. Produces a debit to Retained Earnings.

LO 3 When a corporation appropriates retained earnings:

a. The amount of the appropriation must be equaled by a separate fund of cash.
b. The company is permanently committed to never pay dividends from the appropriated amount.
c. The board of directors voluntarily restricts dividends for a special purpose, and uses the appropriation to indicate why dividends are not going to be declared.
d. The action is recorded by transferring the designated amount from Retained Earnings to a contributed capital account.
e. None of the above.

LO 4 Which of the following gains and losses would be reported as extraordinary?

a. The loss from damages to plant and equipment caused by a meteorite.
b. A gain from exchanging U.K. pounds into U.S. dollars.
c. A settlement paid to a customer injured while using the company's product.
d. A settlement paid to an employee for injuries suffered on the job.
e. None of the above are extraordinary items.

LO 5 During 19X1, Remington Corp. had net income of $250,000 and paid preferred dividends of $70,000. As of January 1, 19X1, the company had 25,000 outstanding common shares and the company purchased 5,000 treasury shares on July 1, 19X1. The earnings per share for 19X1 is:

a. $7.20.
b. $8.00.
c. $9.00.
d. $10.00.
e. $11.11.

LO 6 Which of the following situations produces a price-earnings ratio of 8.0 for the common stock?

a. Earnings per share for the prior year were $1.25, and the price of the stock at the end of the year is $10.00.
b. Earnings per share for the next year are expected to be $2.20, and the price of the stock at the beginning of the year was $17.60.
c. Earnings per share for the next year are expected to be $4.25, and the current price of the stock is $34.00.
d. Earnings per share for the next year are expected to be $3.20, and the market price of the stock at the end of the year is expected to be $25.60.
e. None of the above.

LO 7 A gain or loss that is not unusual but that is not expected to occur again is classified as:

a. Infrequent.
b. Unusual.
c. Extraordinary.
d. Abnormal.
e. Prior period adjustment.

Questions for Class Discussion

1. Why is the term *liquidating dividend* used to describe cash dividends that are debited against contributed capital accounts?
2. What effects does declaring a stock dividend have on the corporation's assets, liabilities, and total stockholders' equity? What effect does the distribution of the stock have?
3. How do accountants distinguish between large and small stock dividends?
4. When accounting for a small stock dividend, what amount of retained earnings should be capitalized?
5. What is the difference between a stock dividend and a stock split?
6. Courts have determined that a stock dividend is not taxable income to stockholders. What concept justifies this decision?
7. Southern Products Corporation bought 15,000 shares of Regional Steel Corporation stock and turned it over to the treasurer of Southern Products for safekeeping. Are these shares appropriately classified as treasury stock?
8. How does the purchase of treasury stock affect the purchaser's assets and total stockholders' equity?
9. Distinguish between issued shares and outstanding shares.
10. Why do state laws place limits on purchases of treasury stock?
11. Identify the four possible major sections of the annual income statement that might appear below income from continuing operations.
12. Where on the income statement would a company report an abnormal gain that is not expected to occur more often than once every two years?
13. During the year just finished, the Daley Company changed its compensation system to pay its sales representatives with a commission and bonuses

instead of salaries. Does this new policy require a prior period adjustment in the financial statements?

14. After taking five years' straight-line depreciation expense for an asset that was expected to have an eight-year useful life, a company decided that the asset would last another six years. Is this decision a change in accounting principle? How would the financial statements describe this change?
15. How are earnings per share results calculated for a corporation with a simple capital structure?
16. How are stock splits and stock dividends treated in the calculation of the weighted-average number of outstanding common shares?
17. What kind of convertible securities are not considered to be common stock equivalents for calculating primary earnings per share?
18. What is the difference between primary earnings per share and fully diluted earnings per share?

19. Refer to the statement of changes in common stockholders' investment for Federal Express Corporation presented in Appendix G at the end of the book. Can you determine the purpose for the company's annual purchases of treasury stock?

20. Refer to the balance sheet for Ben & Jerry's Homemade, Inc., in Appendix G at the end of the book. How many treasury shares of Class A and Class B stock did the company have at the end of its 1992 fiscal year?

Exercises

Exercise 14–1
Stock dividends and per share values
(LO 1)

The stockholders' equity of Porter Construction, Inc., consisted of the following amounts on March 8:

Common stock, $25 par value, 100,000 shares authorized, 40,000 shares issued and outstanding	$1,000,000
Contributed capital in excess of par value, common stock . .	350,000
Total contributed capital	$1,350,000
Retained earnings	450,000
Total stockholders' equity	$1,800,000

On March 8, the stock's market value was $40.00. On that date, the directors declared a 20% stock dividend distributable on March 31 to the March 20 stockholders of record. The stock's market value was $38.00 on April 10.

Required

1. Prepare the journal entries that the company's accountant would use to record the dividend declaration and distribution.
2. One stockholder owned 500 shares on March 8. Calculate the per share and total book values of the investor's shares immediately before and after the declaration on March 8.
3. Calculate the market values of the investor's shares as of March 8 and April 10.

Exercise 14–2
Stock dividends and splits
(LO 1)

On March 31, 19X1, Pacific Management Corporation's common stock was selling for $62 per share and the following information appeared in the stockholders' equity section of its balance sheet as of that date:

Common stock, $20 par value, 60,000 shares authorized, 25,000 shares issued	$ 500,000
Contributed capital in excess of par value, common stock . .	200,000
Total contributed capital	$ 700,000
Retained earnings	660,000
Total stockholders' equity	$1,360,000

Required

1. Assume that the company declares and immediately distributes a 100% stock dividend. The event is recorded by capitalizing the required minimum amount of retained earnings. Answer these questions about the stockholders' equity as it exists after issuing the new shares:

a. What is the retained earnings balance?
b. What is the total amount of stockholders' equity?
c. How many shares are outstanding?

2. Assume that the company implements a two-for-one stock split instead of the stock dividend. Answer these questions about the stockholders' equity as it exists after issuing the new shares:
   a. What is the retained earnings balance?
   b. What is the total amount of stockholders' equity?
   c. How many shares are outstanding?
3. Briefly explain the difference, if any, that an investor would experience if new shares are distributed under a large dividend or a stock split.

Exercise 14–3
Reporting a treasury stock purchase
(LO 2, 3)

On August 15, the stockholders' equity section of the balance sheet for Indelible, Inc., included this information:

Stockholders' Equity

Contributed capital:	
Common stock, $10 par value; 12,000 shares authorized, issued, and outstanding	$120,000
Contributed capital in excess of par value, common stock	36,000
Total contributed capital	$156,000
Retained earnings	144,000
Total stockholders' equity	$300,000

On the next day, the corporation purchased 1,500 shares of treasury stock at $30 per share. Present the stockholders' equity section as it would appear immediately after the purchase.

Exercise 14–4
Journal entries for treasury stock transactions
(LO 2)

Use the information in Exercise 14–3 to develop the accountant's journal entries to record these events for Indelible, Inc.:

1. The purchase of the treasury shares on August 16.
2. The sale of 400 treasury shares on September 1 for cash at $36 per share.
3. The sale of all the remaining treasury shares on September 29 for cash at $25 per share.

Exercise 14–5
Journal entries for stock retirements
(LO 2)

This information appeared in the stockholders' equity section of Winter Sports, Inc.'s balance sheet as of December 31, 19X1:

Common stock, $5 par value, 40,000 shares authorized, 15,000 shares issued and outstanding	$ 75,000
Contributed capital in excess of par value, common stock	165,000
Total contributed capital	$240,000
Retained earnings	190,000
Total stockholders' equity	$430,000

On January 1, 19X2, the company purchased and retired 800 shares of common stock.

1. Determine the average amount of contributed capital per share of outstanding stock.
2. Prepare the journal entries to record the retirement under the following separate situations:
   a. The stock was purchased for $13 per share
   b. The stock was purchased for $16 per share.
   c. The stock was purchased for $30 per share.

Exercise 14–6
Income statement categories
(LO 4)

During 19X1, Simon's Club, Inc., sold its assets in a chain of wholesale outlets. This sale took the company out of the wholesaling business completely. The company still operates its retail outlets.

Following is a lettered list of sections of an income statement:

A. Income from continuing operations
B. Income from operating a discontinued segment
C. Gain or loss from disposing of a discontinued segment
D. Extraordinary gain or loss
E. Cumulative effect of change in accounting principle.

Indicate where each of the nine income-related items for the company would appear on the 19X1 income statement by writing the letter of the appropriate section in the blank beside each item.

	Debit	Credit
___1. Depreciation expense	$175,000	
___2. Gain on sale of segment (net of tax)		$ 450,000
___3. Loss from operating segment sold (net of tax)	370,000	
___4. Salaries expense	360,000	
___5. Sales		1,800,000
___6. Gain on state's condemnation of company property (net of tax)		220,000
___7. Cost of goods sold	920,000	
___8. Effect of change from declining-balance to straight-line depreciation (net of tax)		90,000
___9. Income taxes expense	138,000	

Exercise 14–7
Income statement presentation
(LO 4)

Use the data for the company described in Exercise 14–6 to present its income statement for 19X1.

Exercise 14–8
Accounting for a change in accounting principle
(LO 4)

The Long Company put an asset in service on January 1, 19X1. Its cost was $900,000, its predicted service life was six years, and its expected salvage value was $90,000. The company decided to use double-declining-balance depreciation and recorded these amounts of depreciation expense in the first two years of the asset's life:

19X1	$300,000
19X2	200,000

The scheduled depreciation expense for 19X3 was $133,000. After consulting with the company's auditors, management decided to change to straight-line depreciation in 19X3, without changing either the predicted service life or salvage value. Under this system, the annual depreciation expense for all years in the asset's life would be $135,000. The company faces a 35% income tax rate.

1. Prepare a table like Illustration 14–5 that deals with this situation.
2. How much depreciation expense will be reported on the company's income statement for this asset in 19X3 and in each of the remaining years of the asset's life?
3. What amount will be reported on the company's 19X3 income statement as the after-tax cumulative effect of the change?

Exercise 14–9
Financial statement presentation of income-related items
(LO 4)

Answer the questions about each of the following items related to a company's activities for the year:

a. Although the company has been operating for five years, it had not retired any of its vehicles from active use in past years. However, this year it retired nine vehicles and sold them to a used equipment dealer. According to the company's accounts, the transaction produced a gain of $45,000. Where should this gain appear in the company's income statement, and how should it be labeled?

b. After applying an expected useful life of seven years and no salvage value to depreciate $98,000 of office equipment over the preceding three years, the company decided early this year that the equipment will last only two more years. How much depreciation expense will be reported for the current year and where will it appear in the financial statements? Where will any cumulative adjustment appear?

c. In performing a routine review of the files, a new accountant for the company determined that the company had reported interest expense for the full amount of last year's payment on an installment note payable. The mistake had a material effect on the amount of income in the prior year. Will it be necessary to correct the accounts for this mistake? Where will the correction be reported?

Exercise 14–10
Weighted-average outstanding shares and earnings per share
(LO 5)

A company reported $450,000 of net income for 19X1. It also declared $65,000 of dividends on preferred stock for the same year. At the beginning of 19X1, the company had 90,000 outstanding shares of common stock. These two events changed the number of outstanding shares during the year:

Apr. 30 Sold 60,000 common shares for cash.
Oct. 31 Purchased 36,000 shares of common stock for the treasury.

a. What is the amount of net income available to the common stockholders?
b. What is the weighted-average number of shares of common stock for the year?
c. What is the earnings per share for the year?

Exercise 14–11
Weighted-average shares outstanding and earnings per share
(LO 5)

A company reported $240,000 of net income in 19X1. It also declared $32,500 dividends on preferred stock for the same year. At the beginning of 19X1, the company had 25,000 outstanding shares of common stock. These three events changed the number of outstanding shares during the year:

June 1 Sold 15,000 common shares for cash.
Aug. 31 Purchased 6,500 shares of common stock for the treasury.
Oct. 1 Completed a three-for-one stock split.

a. What is the amount of net income available to the common stockholders?
b. What is the weighted-average number of shares of common stock for the year?
c. What is the earnings per share for the year?

Exercise 14–12
Computing primary and fully diluted earnings per share
(LO 5)

A company's income statement for 19X1 reported that it produced $520,000 of net income during the year. This company has a complex capital structure that includes common stock, common stock equivalents, and other potentially dilutive securities. The weighted-average number of common shares and common stock equivalents for 19X1 was 125,000. The weighted-average number of common shares that would have been outstanding if all dilutive securities had been converted was 160,000. The dilutive securities included convertible preferred stock that received its regular dividend of $50,000 during 19X1.

a. What is the amount of net income available to the common stockholders that would be used to compute primary earnings per share?
b. What is the primary earnings per share for the year?
c. What is the amount of net income available to the common stockholders that would be used to compute fully diluted earnings per share?
d. What is the fully diluted earnings per share for the year?

Exercise 14–13
Computing the price-earnings ratio
(LO 5)

Use the following information to calculate the price-earnings ratio for each case:

	Earnings per Share	Market Value per Share
a.	$ 4.50	$ 43.00
b.	18.00	120.00
c.	3.25	45.00
d.	0.75	18.00
e.	5.00	83.00

Exercise 14–14
Identifying corporate capital structure terms
(LO 7)

Match each of the numbered definitions with the term it best defines. Indicate your answer by writing the letter for the correct term in the blank space next to each description.

A. Common stock equivalent
B. Extraordinary gain or loss
C. Large stock dividend
D. Reverse stock split
E. Small stock dividend
F. Stock split
G. Treasury stock

__1. Gain or loss that is reported separate from continuing operations because it is both unusual and infrequent.

__2. Stock that was reacquired and is still held by the issuing corporation.

__3. Stock dividend that is more than 25% of the corporation's previously outstanding shares.

__4. Action by a corporation to call in its stock and replace it with less than one new share.

__5. Convertible or exercisable security that is reasonably expected to be converted or exercised.

__6. Action by a corporation to call in its stock and replace it with more than one new share.

__7. Stock dividend that is 25% or less of the corporation's previously outstanding shares.

Problems

Problem 14–1
Treasury stock transactions and stock dividends
(LO 1, 2, 3)

The balance sheet for Elizabeth Manufacturing, Inc., reported the following components of stockholders' equity on December 31, 19X1:

Common stock, $10 par value, 100,000 shares authorized, 40,000 shares issued	$400,000
Contributed capital in excess of par value, common stock . .	60,000
Retained earnings	270,000
Total stockholders' equity	$730,000

The company completed these transactions during 19X2:

Jan.	6	Purchased 4,000 shares of treasury stock at $20.00 cash per share.
Mar.	10	The directors declared a $1.50 per share cash dividend payable on April 10 to the April 2 stockholders of record.
Apr.	10	Paid the dividend declared on March 10.
Aug.	1	Sold 1,500 of the treasury shares at $24.00 per share.
Sept.	16	Sold 2,500 of the treasury shares at $17.00 per share.
Dec.	10	The directors declared a $1.60 per share cash dividend payable on January 10, 19X3, to the December 15 stockholders of record. They also declared a 20% stock dividend distributable on January 10, 19X3, to the December 15 stockholders of record. The market value of the stock was $25.00 per share.
	31	Closed the $388,000 credit balance in the Income Summary account to Retained Earnings.
	31	Closed the Cash Dividends Declared and Stock Dividends Declared accounts.

Required

1. Prepare general journal entries to record the transactions and closings for 19X2.
2. Prepare a statement of retained earnings for 19X2.
3. Prepare the stockholders' equity section of the company's balance sheet as of December 31, 19X2.

Problem 14–2
Describing equity changes with journal entries and account balances
(LO 1)

At September 30, the end of the third quarter for Astronomical Adventures, Inc., these balances existed in its stockholders' equity accounts:

Common stock, $12 par value	$360,000
Contributed capital in excess of par value	90,000
Retained earnings	320,000

Over the next three months, the following journal entries were recorded in the company's equity accounts:

Oct.	5	Cash Dividends Declared	60,000.00	
		Common Dividend Payable		60,000.00
	20	Common Dividend Payable	60,000.00	
		Cash		60,000.00
	31	Stock Dividends Declared	75,000.00	
		Common Stock Dividend Distributable		36,000.00
		Contributed Capital in Excess of Par Value, Common Stock		39,000.00
Nov.	15	Common Stock Dividend Distributable	36,000.00	
		Common Stock, $12 Par Value		36,000.00
Dec.	1	Memo—change the title of the common stock account to reflect the new par value of $4 per share.		
	31	Income Summary	210,000.00	
		Retained Earnings		210,000.00
	31	Retained Earnings	135,000.00	
		Cash Dividends Declared		60,000.00
		Stock Dividends Declared		75,000.00

Required

1. Provide explanations for each of the journal entries.
2. Complete the following table showing the balances of the company's equity accounts (including the dividends declared accounts) at each of the indicated dates:

Date	Oct. 5	Oct. 20	Oct. 31	Nov. 15	Dec. 1	Dec. 31
Common stock	$____	$____	$____	$____	$____	$____
Stock dividend distributable	____	____	____	____	____	____
Contributed capital in excess of par	____	____	____	____	____	____
Retained earnings	____	____	____	____	____	____
Less:						
Cash dividends declared	____	____	____	____	____	____
Stock dividends declared	____	____	____	____	____	____
Combined balances of equity accounts	$____	$____	$____	$____	$____	$____

Problem 14–3
Changes in retained earnings
(LO 1, 2, 3)

The equity sections from the 19X1 and 19X2 balance sheets of New Haven Corporation appeared as follows:

Stockholders' Equity
(As of December 31, 19X1)

Common stock, $4 par value, 100,000 shares authorized, 40,000 shares issued	$160,000
Contributed capital in excess of par value, common stock	120,000
Total contributed capital	$280,000
Retained earnings	320,000
Total stockholders' equity	$600,000

Stockholders' Equity
(As of December 31, 19X2)

Common stock, $4 par value, 100,000 shares authorized, 47,400 shares issued, 3,000 in the treasury	$189,600
Contributed capital in excess of par value, common stock	179,200
Total contributed capital	$368,800
Retained earnings ($30,000 restricted)	400,000
Total	$768,800
Less cost of treasury stock	(30,000)
Total stockholders' equity	$738,800

The following events occurred during 19X2:

Jan. 10 A $0.50 per share cash dividend was declared, and the date of record was five days later.

Mar. 17 The treasury stock was purchased.

Apr. 10 A $0.50 per share cash dividend was declared, and the date of record was five days later.

July 10 A $0.50 per share cash dividend was declared, and the date of record was five days later.

Aug. 15 A 20% stock dividend was declared when the market value was $12.00 per share.

Sept. 8 The dividend shares were issued.

Oct. 10 A $0.50 per share cash dividend was declared, and the date of record was five days later.

Required

1. How many shares were outstanding on each of the cash dividend dates?
2. How large were each of the four cash dividends?
3. How large was the capitalization of retained earnings for the stock dividend?
4. What was the price per share paid for the treasury stock?
5. How much income did the company achieve during 19X2?

Problem 14–4
Presenting items in an income statement
(LO 4)

The following table shows the balances from various accounts in the adjusted trial balance for McHenry Corp. as of December 31, 19X1:

		Debit	Credit
a.	Interest earned		$ 8,000
b.	Depreciation expense, equipment	$ 24,000	
c.	Loss on sale of office equipment	16,500	
d.	Accounts payable		28,000
e.	Other operating expenses	65,000	
f.	Accumulated depreciation, equipment		49,000
g.	Gain from settling a lawsuit		28,000
h.	Cumulative effect of change in accounting principle (pre-tax)	42,000	
i.	Accumulated depreciation, buildings		109,000
j.	Loss from operating a discontinued segment (pre-tax)	13,000	
k.	Gain on early settlement of debt (pre-tax)		19,000
l.	Sales		647,000
m.	Depreciation expense, buildings	36,000	
n.	Correction of overstatement of prior year's sales (pre-tax)	10,000	
o.	Gain on sale of discontinued segment's assets (pre-tax)		22,000
p.	Loss from settling a lawsuit	16,000	
q.	Income taxes expense	?	
r.	Cost of goods sold	325,000	

Required

Answer each of these questions by providing detailed schedules:

1. Assuming that the company's income tax rate is 30%, what are the tax effects and after-tax measures of the items labeled as pre-tax?
2. What is the amount of the company's income from continuing operations before income taxes? What is the amount of the company's income taxes expense? What is the amount of the company's income from continuing operations?
3. What is the amount of after-tax income associated with the discontinued segment?
4. What is the amount of income before extraordinary items and the cumulative effect of the change in principle?
5. What is the amount of net income for the year?

Problem 14–5
Changes in accounting principles
(LO 4)

On January 1, 19X1, Fields, Inc., purchased some equipment. Its cost was $400,000 and it was expected to have a salvage value of $20,000 at the end of its five-year useful life. Depreciation was allocated to 19X1 through 19X3 with the declining-balance method at twice the straight-line rate. Early in 19X4, the company concluded that changing to the straight-line method would produce more useful financial statements because it would be consistent with the practices of other firms in the industry.

Required

1. Do generally accepted accounting principles allow Fields, Inc., to change depreciation methods in 19X4?
2. Prepare a schedule that shows the amount of depreciation expense allocated to 19X1 through 19X3 under the declining-balance method.
3. Prepare a schedule that shows the amount of depreciation expense that would have been allocated to 19X1 through 19X3 under the straight-line method.
4. Combine the information from your answers to Parts 2 and 3 in a table like Illustration 14–5 that computes the before- and after-tax cumulative effects of the change. The company's income tax rate is 30%. (For simplicity, round your answers to the nearest dollar.)
5. How should the cumulative effect be reported by the company? Does the cumulative effect increase or decrease net income?
6. How much depreciation expense will be reported on the income statement for 19X4?

Problem 14–6
Earnings per share calculations and presentation
(LO 5)

The original income statements for Safeco, Inc., presented the following information in 19X2, 19X3, and 19X4:

	19X2	19X3	19X4
Sales	$740,000	$850,000	$825,000
Expenses	465,000	520,000	491,000
Income from continuing operations	$275,000	$330,000	$334,000
Loss on discontinued segment	(105,000)		
Income before extraordinary items	$170,000	$330,000	$334,000
Extraordinary gain (loss)		66,000	(140,000)
Net income	$170,000	$396,000	$194,000

The company also experienced some changes in the number of outstanding shares through the following events:

Outstanding shares on December 31, 19X1	10,000
19X2	
Treasury stock purchase on April 1	− 1,000
Issuance of new shares on June 30	+ 3,000
10% stock dividend on October 1	+ 1,200
Outstanding shares on on December 31, 19X2	13,200

19X3	
Issuance of new shares on July 1	+ 4,000
Treasury stock purchase on November 1	− 1,200
Outstanding shares on December 31, 19X3 . .	16,000
19X4	
Issuance of new shares on August 1	+ 5,000
Treasury stock purchase on September 1 . . .	− 1,000
Three-for-one split on October 1	+40,000
Outstanding shares on December 31, 19X4 . .	60,000

Required

1. Calculate the weighted average of the outstanding common shares as of the end of 19X2.
2. Use the results of Part 1 to present the original earnings per share amounts for 19X2 for income from continuing operations, loss on discontinued segment, and net income.
3. Calculate the weighted average of the outstanding common shares as of the end of 19X3.
4. Use the results of Part 3 to present the original earnings per share amounts for 19X3 for income from continuing operations, the extraordinary gain, and net income.
5. Calculate the weighted average of the outstanding common shares as of the end of 19X4.
6. Use the results of Part 5 to present the earnings per share amounts for 19X4 for income from continuing operations, the extraordinary loss, and net income.

Problem 14–7
Analytical essay
(LO 1)

As of December 31, the balance sheet for Helmer Corporation provided this information about the stockholders' equity:

Common stock, $10 par value, 50,000 shares authorized, 30,000 shares issued and outstanding . .	$300,000
Contributed capital in excess of par value, common stock	150,000
Retained earnings	500,000
Total stockholders' equity	$950,000

The company's board of directors wants to decrease the market value of the company's outstanding stock from its current level of $50 per share by increasing the number of outstanding shares from 30,000 to 60,000. They are considering a choice between a two-for-one stock split and a 100% stock dividend.

Required

Write a short essay describing the difference between the two alternatives in terms of:

1. Their effects on the stock.
2. How they would be recorded in the accounts.
3. Their effects on the balance sheet.

Problem 14–8
Analytical essay
(LO 6)

The bookkeeper for Catamaran Corporation, who has almost finished preparing the 19X1 financial statements, has come to you for some advice. This draft of the balance sheet accurately describes the company's stockholders' equity situation:

Preferred stock, $80 par value, 5%, cumulative, 10,000 shares authorized, 6,000 shares issued and outstanding	$480,000
Common stock, $1 par value, 50,000 shares authorized, 36,000 shares issued and outstanding . .	36,000
Contributed capital in excess of par value, common stock	260,000
Retained earnings	125,000
Total stockholders' equity	$901,000

The net income for 19X1 has been correctly measured as $250,000, and the accounts show that no cash dividends were declared on the preferred or common stock. In fact, the only stock transaction that occurred during the year was the sale of 3,000 shares of common stock on May 1, 19X1. The bookkeeper has tentatively calculated earnings per share as follows:

$$\frac{\text{Net income}}{\text{Outstanding common plus preferred as of Dec. 31}} = \frac{\$250{,}000}{36{,}000 + 6{,}000} = \$5.95$$

Required

1. Describe any errors that you find in the calculation of earnings per share and specify the corrections that should be made.
2. Explain how the calculation would be different if the preferred stock is not cumulative and if the additional common shares had been issued through a stock dividend instead of a sale.

Provocative Problems

Provocative Problem 14–1
QualTech, Inc.
(LO 1, 2, 3)

On January 1, 19X1, QualTech, Inc., had the following balances in its stockholders' equity accounts:

Common stock	$ 750,000
Contributed capital in excess of par value, common stock	150,000
Retained earnings	650,000
Total	$1,550,000

The company was authorized to issue 100,000 shares, but had issued only 25,000 shares as of January 1, 19X1. The par value per share was $30. The common stock had the following book values as of December 31:

19X1	$70.00
19X2	30.00
19X3	36.00

At the end of each year, the company paid the following dividends per share:

19X1	$3.50
19X2	1.00
19X3	2.00

On March 1, 19X1, the company declared a 20% stock dividend. The market value of the shares was $40 per share. On August 10, 19X2, the stockholders approved a three-for-one split by increasing the number of authorized shares and reducing the par value per share. On April 5, 19X3, the company purchased 10,000 shares of treasury stock at the price of $50 per share.

Required

Use the preceding facts to find the following information (present your work in appropriate schedules):

1. Determine the par value per share of common stock as of the end of 19X1, 19X2, and 19X3.
2. Determine the number of authorized, issued, and outstanding shares as of the end of 19X1, 19X2, and 19X3.
3. Determine the total par value of the issued shares as of the end of 19X1, 19X2, and 19X3.
4. Determine the balance of contributed capital in excess of par as of the end of 19X1, 19X2, and 19X3.
5. Use the book value per share to determine the total stockholders' equity at the end of 19X1, 19X2, and 19X3.

6. Determine the total amount of retained earnings as of the end of 19X1, 19X2, and 19X3.
7. Use the answer to Part 6 and information about the dividends to determine the amount of net income reported in 19X1, 19X2, and 19X3.

Finally, use the information to complete this table:

	1/1/X1	12/31/X1	12/31/X2	12/31/X3
Common stock:				
Par value per share	______	______	______	______
Authorized shares	______	______	______	______
Issued shares	______	______	______	______
Treasury shares	______	______	______	______
Outstanding shares	______	______	______	______
Account balances:				
Common stock	______	______	______	______
Contributed capital in excess of par	______	______	______	______
Retained earnings	______	______	______	______
Total	______	______	______	______
Less treasury stock	______	______	______	______
Total stockholders' equity	______	______	______	______

Provocative Problem 14–2
Commonwealth Enterprises, Inc.
(LO 4)

Over the last three years, Commonwealth Enterprises, Inc., had experienced the following income results (all numbers are rounded to the nearest thousand dollars):

	19X1	19X2	19X3
Revenues	$11,000	$11,900	$14,600
Expenses	(7,000)	(7,900)	(7,700)
Gains	3,200	2,400	–0–
Losses	(1,200)	(1,900)	(3,900)
Net income	$ 6,000	$ 4,500	$ 3,000

Part 1
Use the information to develop a general prediction of the company's net income for 19X4.

Part 2
A closer analysis of the information shows that the company discontinued a segment of its operations in 19X3. The company's accountant has determined that the discontinued segment produced the following amounts of income:

	19X1	19X2	19X3
Revenues	$7,000	$2,600	$1,600
Expenses	(5,000)	(5,000)	(4,000)
Gains		400	
Losses	(1,200)	(1,500)	(900)
Loss on disposal of segment assets			(1,200)

Use the information to calculate the company's income without the discontinued segment and then develop a general prediction of the company's net income for 19X4.

Part 3
A more in-depth analysis of the company's activity reveals that the company experienced these extraordinary items during the three years when it retired some of its debts before their scheduled maturity dates:

	19X1	19X2	19X3
Extraordinary gain	$2,200	$2,000	
Extraordinary loss			$(1,700)

Use the information to calculate the company's income from continuing operations and develop a general prediction of the company's net income for 19X4.

Provocative Problem 14–3
Apple Computer, Inc.
(LO 1, 2, 3, 4, 5)

Apple Computer, Inc.

The financial statements and footnotes from Apple's 1992 annual report are presented in Appendix F at the end of the book. Use that information to answer the following questions:

1. Does Apple have a simple or complex capital structure?
2. What was Apple's earnings per share in fiscal year 1992? How does this figure compare with the results for 1991?
3. What was the dollar amount of cash dividends declared during 1992?
4. What was the dollar amount of cash dividends paid during 1992? How does this number compare with the dividends declared?
5. What is the par value of the common stock?
6. How many shares of common stock were outstanding at the end of the 1992 fiscal year?
7. Does Apple own shares of treasury stock?
8. Did Apple have any extraordinary gains or losses during 1992?
9. Did Apple have any gains or losses on the disposal of a business segment during 1992?
10. Where did Apple report the debit balance in the account called Notes Receivable from Stockholders? Try to explain why this treatment is reasonable.

Provocative Problem 14–4
As a Matter of Ethics: Essay

ETHICS

Review the "As a Matter of Ethics" case on page 504 and discuss the ethical implications of the directors' tentative decision to avoid announcing Falcon Corporation's new government contract. What actions would you take if you were the financial vice president?

Answers to Objective Review Questions

LO 1 (*e*)	**LO 4** (*a*)	**LO 6** (*c*)
LO 2 (*d*)	**LO 5** (*b*)	**LO 7** (*a*)
LO 3 (*c*)		

CHAPTER

15

Reporting and Using Cash Flows in Decision Making

Cash is the lifeblood of a business enterprise. In a sense, cash is the fuel that keeps a business alive. With cash, employees and suppliers can be paid, loans can be repaid, and owners can receive dividends. But, without cash, none of these things can happen. In simple terms, a business must have an adequate amount of cash to operate. For these reasons, decision makers pay close attention to a company's cash position and the events and transactions causing that position to change. Information about the events and transactions that affect the cash position of a company is reported in a financial statement called the **statement of cash flows.** By studying this chapter, you will learn how to prepare and interpret a statement of cash flows. You also should begin to appreciate the importance of cash flow information in many decision situations.

Learning Objectives

After studying Chapter 15, you should be able to:

1. Describe a statement of cash flows; classify cash flows as operating, investing, or financing activities; and identify some decisions that involve evaluating cash flows.
2. Prepare a statement of cash flows in which cash flows from operating activities are reported according to the direct method and prepare a schedule of noncash investing and financing activities.
3. Calculate cash inflows and outflows by inspecting the noncash account balances of a company and related information about its transactions.
4. Calculate the net cash provided or used by operating activities according to the indirect method and prepare the statement of cash flows.
5. Prepare a working paper for a statement of cash flows so that the net cash flow from operating activities is calculated by the indirect method.
6. Define or explain the words or phrases listed in the chapter glossary.

Why Cash Flow Information Is Important

Information about cash flows can influence decision makers in many ways. For example, if a company's regular operations bring in more cash than they use, investors will value the company higher than if property and equipment must be sold to finance operations. Information about cash flows can help creditors decide whether a company will have enough cash to pay its existing debts as they mature. And, investors, creditors, managers, and other users of financial statements use cash flow information to evaluate a company's ability to meet unexpected obligations. Cash flow information is used by decision makers outside as well as inside the firm to evaluate a company's ability to take advantage of new business opportunities that may arise. Managers within a company use cash flow information to plan day-to-day operating activities and make long-term investment decisions. These are just a few of the many ways that different people use cash flow information.

The importance of cash flow information to decision makers has directly influenced the thinking of accounting authorities. For example, the FASB's objectives of financial reporting clearly reflect the importance of cash flow information. The FASB stated that financial statements should include information about:

- How a business obtains and spends cash.
- Its borrowing and repayment activities.
- The sale and repurchase of its ownership securities.
- Dividend payments and other distributions to its owners.
- Other factors affecting a company's liquidity or solvency.[1]

To accomplish these objectives, a financial statement is needed to summarize, classify, and report the periodic cash inflows and outflows of a business. This information is provided in a statement of cash flows.

Statement of Cash Flows

LO 1 Describe a statement of cash flows; classify cash flows as operating, investing, or financing activities; and identify some decisions that involve evaluating cash flows.

In November 1987, the FASB issued *Statement of Financial Accounting Standards No. 95,* "Statement of Cash Flows." This standard requires businesses to include a statement of cash flows in all financial reports that contain both a balance sheet and an income statement. The purpose of this statement is to present information about a company's cash receipts and disbursements during the reporting period.

Illustration 15–1 is a diagram of the information reported in a statement of cash flows. Note that the illustration shows three categories of cash flows: cash flows from operating activities, cash flows from investing activities, and cash flows from financing activities. Both inflows and outflows are included within each category. Because all cash inflows and outflows are reported, the statement reconciles the beginning-of-period and end-of-period balances of cash plus cash equivalents.

Direct Method of Presenting Cash Flows from Operating Activities

When preparing a statement of cash flows, you can calculate the net cash provided (or used) by operating activities two different ways. One is the **direct method of calculating net cash provided (or used) by operating activities.** The other is the indirect method. When using the direct method, you separately list each major class of operating cash receipts (for example, cash received from customers) and each major class of cash payments (such as payments for merchandise). Then, you subtract the payments from the receipts to determine the net cash provided (or used) by operating activities.

Indirect Method of Presenting Cash Flows from Operating Activities

The **indirect method of calculating net cash provided (or used) by operating activities** is not as informative as the direct method. The indirect method is not as informative because it does not disclose the individual categories of cash inflows and outflows from operating activities. Instead, the indirect method discloses only the net cash provided (or used) by operating activities.

[1] FASB, *Statement of Financial Accounting Concepts No. 1,* "Objectives of Financial Reporting by Business Enterprises" (Norwalk, CT, 1978), par. 49.

ILLUSTRATION 15–1 *Categories of Information in the Statement of Cash Flows*

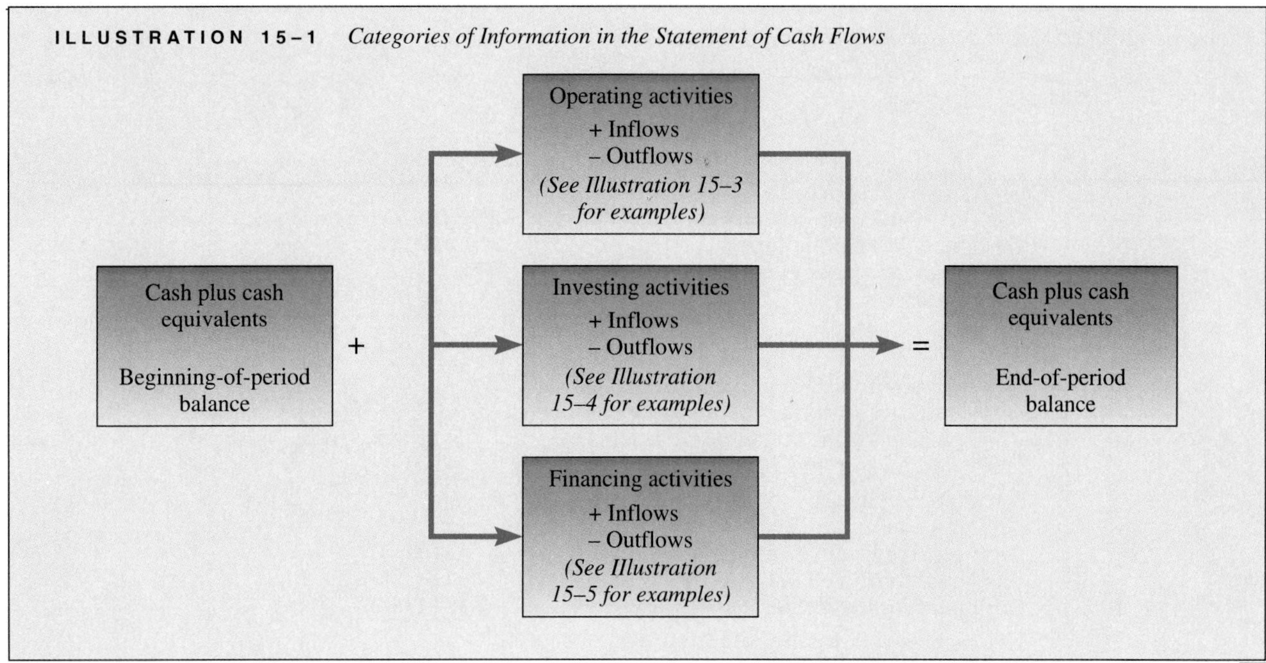

When using the indirect method, list net income first. Next, adjust it for items that are necessary to reconcile net income to the net cash provided (or used) by operating activities. For example, in the calculation of net income, we subtract depreciation expense. However, depreciation expense does not involve a current cash payment. Therefore, add depreciation expense back to net income in the process of reconciling net income to the net cash provided (or used) by operating activities.

The direct method is most informative and is the method that the FASB recommends. However, most companies use the indirect method in spite of the FASB's recommendation. By learning the direct method first, you will find the indirect method easier to understand. Also, managers use the direct method to predict future cash requirements and cash availability. Thus, we explain the direct method next.

The Format of the Statement of Cash Flows (Direct Method)

Illustration 15–2 shows the statement of cash flows for Grover Company. Notice that the major classes of cash inflows and cash outflows are listed separately in the operating activities section of the statement. This is the format of the direct method. The operating cash outflows are subtracted from the operating cash inflows to determine the net cash provided (or used) by operating activities.

Also observe in Illustration 15–2 the other two categories of cash flows reported on the statement of cash flows. In both categories—investing activities and financing activities—we subtract the cash outflows from the cash inflows to determine the net cash provided (or used).

Compare the statement in Illustration 15–2 with the chart in Illustration 15–1. Notice that the beginning and ending balances are called *cash plus cash equivalents* in Illustration 15–1. However, in Illustration 15–2, the beginning and ending balances refer only to *cash*. The balances in Illustration 15–2 are called *cash* because Grover Company does not own any *cash equivalents.*

ILLUSTRATION 15-2 *Statement of Cash Flows (Direct Method)*

GROVER COMPANY
Statement of Cash Flows
For Year Ended December 31, 19X2

Cash flows from operating activities:		
Cash received from customers	$570,000	
Cash paid for merchandise	(319,000)	
Cash paid for wages and other operating expenses	(218,000)	
Cash paid for interest	(8,000)	
Cash paid for taxes	(5,000)	
Net cash provided by operating activities		$ 20,000
Cash flows from investing activities:		
Cash received from sale of plant assets	$ 12,000	
Cash paid for purchase of plant assets	(10,000)	
Net cash provided by investing activities		2,000
Cash flows from financing activities:		
Cash received from issuing stock	$ 15,000	
Cash paid to retire bonds	(18,000)	
Cash paid for dividends	(14,000)	
Net cash used in financing activities		(17,000)
Net increase in cash		$ 5,000
Cash balance at beginning of 19X2		12,000
Cash balance at end of 19X2		$ 17,000

Cash and Cash Equivalents

In *Statement of Financial Accounting Standards No. 95,* the FASB concluded that a statement of cash flows should explain the difference between the beginning and ending balances of cash and cash equivalents. Prior to this new standard, cash equivalents were generally understood to be short-term, temporary investments of cash. As you learned in Chapter 6, however, a cash equivalent must satisfy these two criteria:

1. The investment must be readily convertible to a known amount of cash.
2. The investment must be sufficiently close to its maturity date so that its market value is relatively insensitive to interest rate changes.

In general, only investments purchased within three months of their maturity dates satisfy these criteria.[2]

The idea of classifying short-term, highly liquid investments as cash equivalents is based on the assumption that companies make these investments to earn a return on idle cash balances. Sometimes, however, items that meet the criteria of cash equivalents are not held as temporary investments of idle cash balances. For example, an investment company that specializes in the purchase and sale of securities may buy cash equivalents as part of its investing strategy. Companies that have such investments are allowed to exclude them from the cash equivalents category. However, the companies must develop a clear policy for determining which items to include and which to exclude. These policies must be disclosed in the footnotes to the financial statements and must be followed consistently from period to period.

[2] FASB, *Accounting Standards—Current Text* (Stamford, CT, 1994), sec. C25.106. First published in *Statement of Financial Accounting Standards No. 95,* par. 8.

AS A MATTER OF

Opinion

Ms. Garza earned a BBA degree with a major in accounting at the University of Houston. Upon graduation she joined the audit staff of Ernst & Young where she specialized in bank auditing. She continued her education at The University of Texas at Austin, completing an MBA degree in 1982. Thereafter, Ms. Garza entered banking as a professional and executive lender. Presently, she is senior vice president and metropolitan manager of the Austin area, NationsBank of Texas, N.A.

Ms. Garza has served in a variety of public service positions with organizations such as United Way, the American Heart Association, and Easter Seals.

Mary E. Garza

After I left public accounting and entered the banking industry there was not much emphasis placed on cash flow analysis. As a loan officer, the review of financial statements centered primarily on profitability. However, during the years I have been in banking, there has been a shift in focus to the analysis of cash flows.

We now recognize that a lender must have a complete understanding of a borrower's cash flow in order to better assess both the borrowing needs and repayment sources. This requires historical and projected information about the major types of cash inflows and outflows.

The truth is that cash, and cash alone, is the source of repayment for all loans. Over the years, I have seen many companies, whose financial statements indicated good profitability, experience severe financial problems because the owners or managers lacked a good understanding of the companies' cash flow.

Classifying Cash Transactions

On a statement of cash flows, cash and cash equivalents are treated as a single item. In other words, the statement reports the changes in cash plus cash equivalents. Therefore, cash payments to purchase cash equivalents and cash receipts from selling cash equivalents do not appear on the statement. All other cash receipts and payments are classified and reported on the statement as operating, investing, or financing activities. Within each category, individual cash receipts and payments are summarized in a manner that clearly describes the general nature of the company's cash transactions. Then, the summarized cash receipts and payments within each category are netted against each other. A category provides a net cash flow if the receipts in the category exceed the payments. And, if the payments in a category exceed the receipts, the category is a net use of cash during the period.

Operating Activities

Look at the cash flows classified as **operating activities** in Illustration 15–2. Notice that operating activities generally include transactions that relate to the calculation of net income. However, some income statement items are not related to operating activities. We discuss these items later.

As disclosed in a statement of cash flows, operating activities involve the production or purchase of merchandise and the sale of goods and services to customers. Operating activities also include expenditures that relate to administering the business. In fact, cash flows from operating activities include all cash flows from transactions that are not defined as investing or financing activities. Illustration 15–3 shows typical cash inflows and outflows from operating activities.

ILLUSTRATION 15–3 *Cash Flows from Operating Activities*

Cash Inflows	Cash Outflows
Cash sales to customers.	Payments to employees for salaries and wages.
Cash collections from credit customers.	Payments to suppliers of goods and services.
Receipts of cash dividends from stock investments in other entities.	Payments to government agencies for taxes, fines, and penalties.
Receipts of interest payments.	Interest payments, net of amounts capitalized.
Refunds from suppliers.	Cash refunds to customers.
Cash collected from a lawsuit.	Contributions to charities.

Investing Activities

Transactions that involve making and collecting loans or that involve purchasing and selling plant assets, other productive assets, or investments (other than cash equivalents) are called **investing activities.** Usually, investing activities involve the purchase or sale of assets classified on the balance sheet as plant and equipment, intangible assets, or long-term investments. However, the purchase and sale of short-term investments other than cash equivalents are also investing activities. Illustration 15–4 shows examples of cash flows from investing activities.

The fourth type of receipt listed in Illustration 15–4 involves proceeds from collecting the principal amount of loans. Regarding this item, carefully examine any cash receipts that relate to notes receivable. If the notes resulted from sales to customers, classify the cash receipts as operating activities. Use this classification even if the notes are long-term notes. But, if a company loans money to other parties, classify the cash receipts from collecting the principal of the loans as inflows from investing activities. Nevertheless, the FASB concluded that collections of interest are not investing activities. Instead, they are reported as operating activities.

Financing Activities

The **financing activities** of a business include transactions with its owners and transactions with creditors to borrow money or to repay the principal amounts of loans. Financing activities include borrowing and repaying both short-term loans and long-term debt. However, cash payments to settle credit purchases of merchandise, whether on account or by note, are operating activities. Payments of interest expense are also operating activities. Illustration 15–5 shows examples of cash flows from financing activities.

Noncash Investing and Financing Activities

Some important investing and financing activities do not involve cash receipts or payments during the current period. For example, a company might purchase land and buildings and finance 100% of the purchase by giving a long-term note payable. Although this transaction clearly involves both investing and financing activities, we do not report it in the current period's statement of cash flows because it does not involve a cash inflow or outflow.

Other investing and financing activities may involve some cash receipt or payment but also involve giving or receiving other types of consideration. For example, suppose that you purchase machinery for $12,000 by paying cash of $5,000 and trading in old machinery that has a market value of $7,000. In this case, the statement of cash flows reports only the $5,000 cash outflow for the purchase of machinery. As a result, this $12,000 investing transaction is only partially described in the statement of cash flows.

ILLUSTRATION 15–4 *Cash Flows from Investing Activities*

Cash Inflows	Cash Outflows
Proceeds from selling productive assets (for example, land, buildings, equipment, natural resources, and intangible assets).	Payments to purchase property, plant and equipment, or other productive assets (excluding merchandise inventory).
Proceeds from selling investments in the equity securities of other companies.	Payments to acquire equity securities of other companies.
Proceeds from selling investments in the debt securities of other entities, except cash equivalents.	Payments to acquire debt securities of other entities, except cash equivalents.
Proceeds from collecting the principal amount of loans.	Payments in the form of loans made to other parties.
Proceeds from the sale (discounting) of loans made by the enterprise.	

ILLUSTRATION 15–5 *Cash Flows from Financing Activities*

Cash Inflows	Cash Outflows
Proceeds from issuing equity securities (e.g., common and preferred stock).	Payments of dividends and other distributions to owners.
Proceeds from issuing bonds and notes payable.	Payments to purchase treasury stock.
	Repayments of cash loans.
Proceeds from other short- or long-term borrowing transactions.	Payments of the principal amounts involved in long-term credit arrangements.

The noncash portions of investing and financing activities should *not* be reported in the statement of cash flows. However, they are important events that should be disclosed. To accomplish this disclosure, a company may describe its noncash investing and financing activities in a footnote or a separate schedule. Illustration 15–6 shows an example of how a company might disclose its noncash investing and financing activities.

In Illustration 15–6, notice that the last item describes an exchange of machinery including both the cash and noncash aspects of this transaction. The $5,000 cash payment is reported in Decco Company's statement of cash flows as an investing activity. Nevertheless, the description of noncash investing and financing activities includes both the cash and noncash aspects of the transaction.

Examples of transactions that must be disclosed as noncash investing and financing activities include the following:

- The retirement of debt securities by issuing equity securities.
- The conversion of preferred stock to common stock.
- The leasing of assets in a transaction that qualifies as a capital lease.
- The purchase of long-term assets by issuing a note payable to the seller.
- The exchange of a noncash asset for other noncash assets.
- The purchase of noncash assets by issuing equity or debt securities.

ILLUSTRATION 15-6 *Decco Company—Footnote Describing Noncash Investing and Financing Activities*

The company issued 1,000 shares of common stock for the purchase of land and buildings with fair values of $5,000 and $15,000, respectively.

The company entered into a capital lease obligation of $12,000 for new computer equipment.

The company exchanged old machinery with a fair value of $7,000 and a book value of $8,000 for new machinery valued at $12,000. The balance of $5,000 was paid in cash.

Preparing a Statement of Cash Flows

LO 2 Prepare a statement of cash flows in which cash flows from operating activities are reported according to the direct method and prepare a schedule of noncash investing and financing activities.

The information you need to prepare a statement of cash flows comes from a variety of sources. These include comparative balance sheets at the beginning and the end of the accounting period, an income statement for the period, and a careful analysis of each noncash balance sheet account in the general ledger. However, because cash inflows and cash outflows are to be reported, you might wonder why we do not focus our attention on the Cash account. For the moment, we should at least consider this approach.

Analyzing the Cash Account

All of a company's cash receipts and cash payments are recorded in the Cash account in the general ledger. Therefore, the Cash account would seem to be the logical place to look for information about cash flows from operating, investing, and financing activities. To demonstrate, review this summarized Cash account of Grover Company:

Summarized Cash Account

Balance, 12/31/X1	12,000		
Receipts from customers	570,000	Payments for merchandise	319,000
Proceeds from sale of plant assets	12,000	Payments for wages and other operating expenses	218,000
Proceeds from stock issuance	15,000	Interest payments	8,000
		Tax payments	5,000
		Payments for purchase of plant assets	10,000
		Payments to retire bonds	18,000
		Dividend payments	14,000
Balance, 12/31/X2	17,000		

In this account, the individual cash transactions are already summarized in major types of receipts and payments. For example, the account has only one debit entry for the total receipts from all customers. All that remains is to determine whether each type of cash inflow or outflow is an operating, investing, or financing activity and then place it in its proper category on the statement of cash flows. The completed statement of cash flows appears in Illustration 15–2 on page 540.

While an analysis of the Cash account may appear to be an easy way to prepare a statement of cash flows, it has two serious drawbacks: First, most companies have so many individual cash receipts and disbursements that it is not practical to review them all. Imagine what a problem this analysis would present for IBM, General Motors, Kodak, or Exxon, or even for a relatively small business. Second, the Cash account usually does not contain a description of each cash transaction. Therefore, even though the Cash account shows the amount of each debit and credit, you generally cannot determine the type of transaction by looking at the Cash account. Thus, the Cash account does not

ILLUSTRATION 15-7 *Why an Analysis of the Noncash Accounts Explains the Change in Cash*

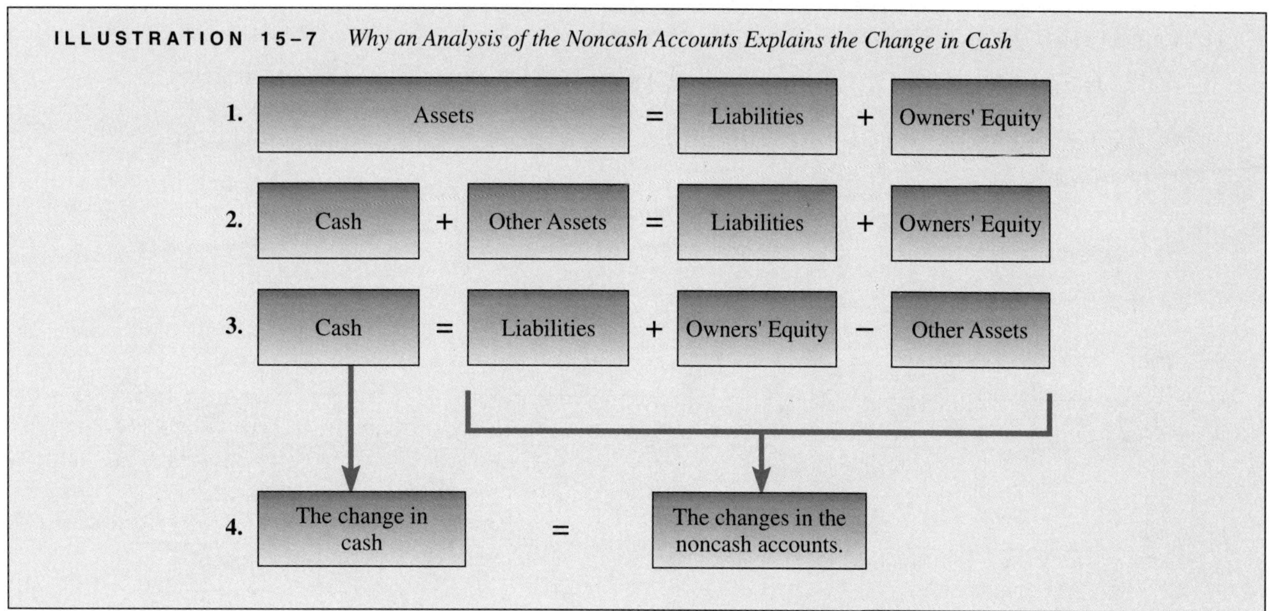

readily provide the information you need to prepare a statement of cash flows. To obtain the necessary information, you must analyze the changes in the noncash accounts.

Analyzing Noncash Accounts to Determine Cash Flows

LO 3 Calculate cash inflows and outflows by inspecting the noncash account balances of a company and related information about its transactions.

When a company records cash inflows and outflows with debits and credits to the Cash account, it also records credits and debits in other accounts. Some of these accounts are balance sheet accounts. Others are revenue and expense accounts that are closed to Retained Earnings, a balance sheet account. As a result, all cash transactions eventually affect noncash balance sheet accounts. Therefore, we can determine the nature of the cash inflows and outflows by examining the changes in the noncash balance sheet accounts. Illustration 15–7 shows this important relationship between the Cash account and the noncash balance sheet accounts.

In Illustration 15–7, notice that the balance sheet equation labeled (1) is expanded in (2) so that cash is separated from the other assets. Then, the equation is rearranged in (3) so that cash is set equal to the sum of the liability and equity accounts less the noncash asset accounts. The illustration then points out in (4) that changes in one side of the equation (cash) must be equal to the changes in the other side (noncash accounts). Part 4 shows that you can fully explain the changes in cash by analyzing the changes in liabilities, owners' equity, and noncash assets.

This overall process has another advantage. The examination of each noncash account also identifies any noncash investing and financing activities that occurred during the period. As you learned earlier, these noncash items must be disclosed, but not on the statement of cash flows.

When beginning to analyze the changes in the noncash balance sheet accounts, recall that Retained Earnings is affected by revenues, expenses, and dividend declarations. Therefore, look at the income statement accounts to help explain the change in Retained Earnings. In fact, the income statement accounts provide important information that relates to the changes in several balance sheet accounts.

Illustration 15–8 summarizes some of these relationships between income statement accounts, balance sheet accounts, and possible cash flows. For example, to determine the cash receipts from customers during a period, adjust

ILLUSTRATION 15-8 *Key Relationships between Income Statement Items and Balance Sheet Accounts*

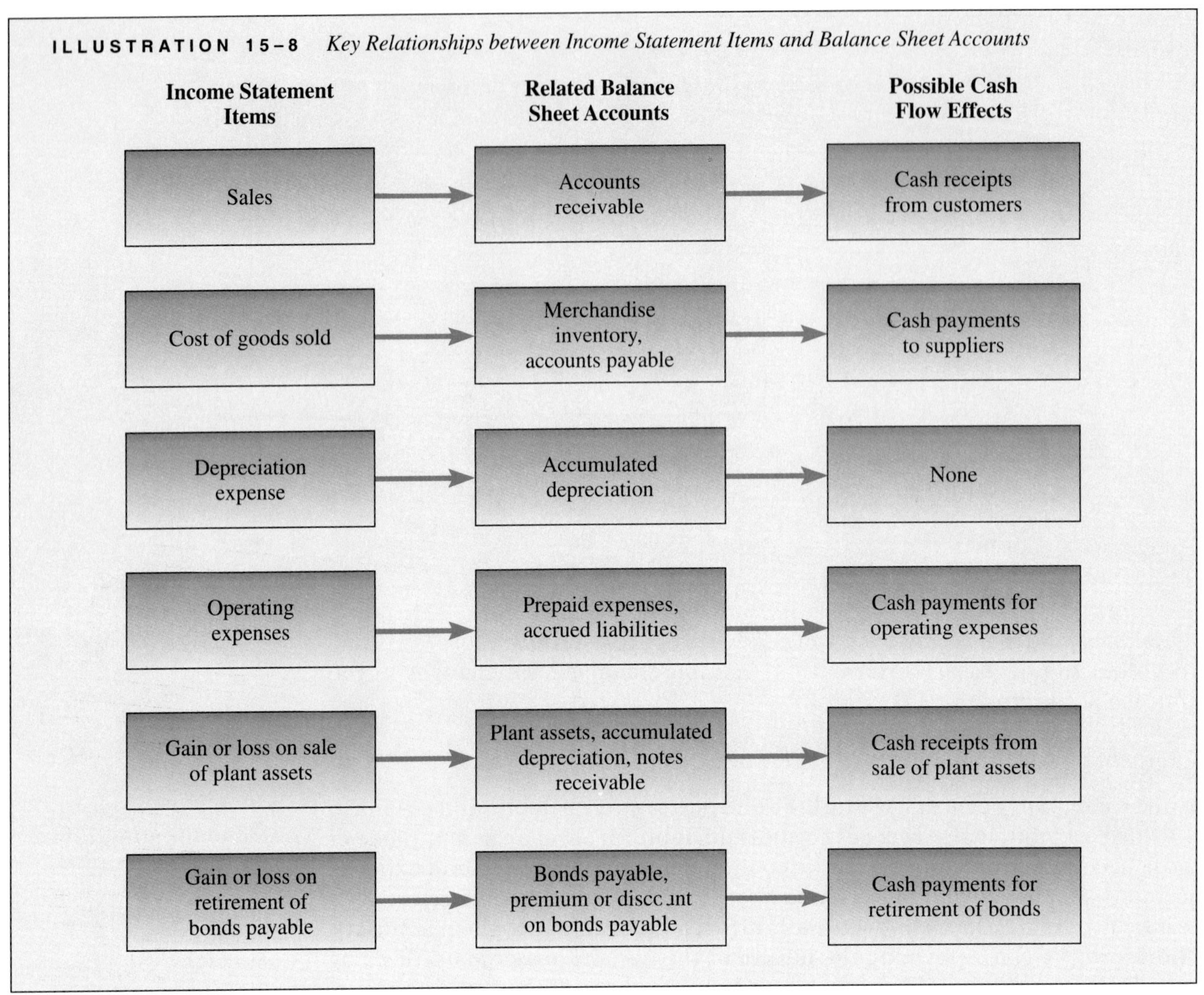

the amount of sales revenue for the increase or decrease in Accounts Receivable.[3] If the Accounts Receivable balance did not change, the cash collected from customers is equal to sales revenue. On the other hand, if the Accounts Receivable balance decreased, cash collections must have been equal to sales revenue plus the reduction in Accounts Receivable. And, if the Accounts Receivable balance increased, the cash collected from customers must have been equal to Sales less the increase in Accounts Receivable.

By analyzing all noncash balance sheet accounts and related income statement accounts in this fashion, you can obtain the necessary information for a statement of cash flows. Next, we illustrate this process by examining the noncash accounts of Grover Company.

[3] This introductory explanation assumes that there is no bad debts expense. However, if bad debts occur and are written off directly to Accounts Receivable, the change in the Accounts Receivable balance will be due in part to the write-off. The remaining change results from credit sales and from cash receipts. This chapter does not discuss the allowance method of accounting for bad debts since it would make the analysis unnecessarily complex at this time.

Grover Company: A Comprehensive Example

Grover Company's December 31, 19X1, and 19X2 balance sheets and its 19X2 income statement are presented in Illustration 15–9. Our objective is to prepare a statement of cash flows that explains the $5,000 increase in cash, based on these financial statements and this additional information about the 19X2 transactions:

a. All accounts payable balances resulted from merchandise purchases.
b. Plant assets that cost $70,000 were purchased by paying $10,000 cash and issuing $60,000 of bonds payable to the seller.
c. Plant assets with an original cost of $30,000 and accumulated depreciation of $12,000 were sold for $12,000 cash. The result was a $6,000 loss.
d. The proceeds from issuing 3,000 shares of common stock were $15,000.
e. The $16,000 gain on the retirement of bonds resulted from paying $18,000 to retire bonds that had a book value of $34,000.
f. Cash dividends of $14,000 were declared and paid.

Operating Activities

We begin the analysis by calculating the cash flows from operating activities. In general, this process involves adjusting the income statement items that relate to operating activities for changes in their related balance sheet accounts.

Cash Received from Customers. The calculation of cash receipts from customers begins with sales revenue. If all sales are for cash, the amount of cash received from customers is equal to sales. However, when sales are on account, you must adjust the amount of sales revenue for the change in Accounts Receivable.

In Illustration 15–9, look at the Accounts Receivable balances on December 31, 19X1, and 19X2. The beginning balance was $40,000, and the ending balance was $60,000. The income statement shows that sales revenue was $590,000. With this information, you can reconstruct the Accounts Receivable account and determine the amount of cash received from customers, as follows:

Accounts Receivable

Balance, 12/31/X1	40,000		
Sales, 19X2	590,000	Collections =	570,000
Balance, 12/31/X2	60,000		

This account shows that the balance of Accounts Receivable increased from $40,000 to $60,000. It also shows that cash receipts from customers are $570,000, which is equal to sales of $590,000 plus the $40,000 beginning balance less the $60,000 ending balance. This calculation can be restated in more general terms like this:

Cash received from customers = Sales − Increase in accounts receivable

And, if the balance of Accounts Receivable decreases, the calculation is:

Cash received from customers = Sales + Decrease in accounts receivable

Now turn back to Illustration 15–2 on page 540. Note that the $570,000 of cash Grover Company received from customers appears on the statement of cash flows as a cash inflow from operating activities.

Cash Payments for Merchandise. The calculation of cash payments for merchandise begins with cost of goods sold and merchandise inventory. For a moment, suppose that all merchandise purchases are for cash and that the ending balance of Merchandise Inventory is unchanged from the beginning balance. In

ILLUSTRATION 15–9 *Financial Statements*

GROVER COMPANY
Balance Sheet
December 31, 19X2 and 19X1

		19X2		19X1
Assets				
Current assets:				
Cash		$ 17,000		$ 12,000
Accounts receivable		60,000		40,000
Merchandise inventory		84,000		70,000
Prepaid expenses		6,000		4,000
Total current assets		$167,000		$126,000
Long-term assets:				
Plant assets	$250,000		$210,000	
Less accumulated depreciation	60,000	190,000	48,000	162,000
Total assets		$357,000		$288,000
Liabilities				
Current liabilities:				
Accounts payable		$ 35,000		$ 40,000
Interest payable		3,000		4,000
Income taxes payable		22,000		12,000
Total current liabilities		$ 60,000		$ 56,000
Long-term liabilities:				
Bonds payable		90,000		64,000
		$150,000		$120,000
Stockholders' Equity				
Contributed capital:				
Common stock, $5 par value	$ 95,000		$ 80,000	
Retained earnings	112,000		88,000	
Total stockholders' equity		207,000		168,000
Total liabilities and stockholders' equity		$357,000		$288,000

GROVER COMPANY
Income Statement
For Year Ended December 31, 19X2

Sales		$ 590,000
Cost of goods sold	$300,000	
Wages and other operating expenses	216,000	
Interest expense	7,000	
Income taxes expense	15,000	
Depreciation expense	24,000	(562,000)
Loss on sale of plant assets		(6,000)
Gain on retirement of debt		16,000
Net income		$ 38,000

this case, the total cash paid for merchandise equals the cost of goods sold. However, this case is not typical. Usually, you expect some change in a company's Merchandise Inventory balance during a period. Also, purchases of merchandise usually are made on account, causing some change in the Accounts Payable balance.

When the balances of Merchandise Inventory and Accounts Payable change, you must adjust cost of goods sold for the changes in these accounts to determine the cash payments for merchandise. This adjustment has two steps. First, combine the change in the balance of Merchandise Inventory with cost of goods sold to determine the cost of purchases during the period.[4] Second, combine the change in the balance of Accounts Payable with the cost of purchases to determine the total cash payments to suppliers of merchandise.

Consider again the Grover Company example. Begin by combining the reported amount of cost of goods sold ($300,000) with the Merchandise Inventory beginning balance ($70,000) and with the ending balance ($84,000) to determine the amount that was purchased during the period. To accomplish this, reconstruct the Merchandise Inventory account as follows:

Merchandise Inventory

Balance, 12/31/X1	70,000		
Purchases =	314,000	Cost of goods sold	300,000
Balance, 12/31/X2	84,000		

This account shows that we add the $14,000 increase in merchandise inventory to cost of goods sold of $300,000 to get purchases of $314,000.

To determine the cash paid for merchandise, adjust purchases for the change in accounts payable. This can be done by reconstructing the Accounts Payable account as follows:

Accounts Payable

		Balance, 12/31/X1	40,000
Payments =	319,000	Purchases	314,000
		Balance, 12/31/X2	35,000

In this account, purchases of $314,000 plus a beginning balance of $40,000 less the ending balance of $35,000 equals cash payments of $319,000. In other words, purchases of $314,000 plus the $5,000 decrease in accounts payable equals cash payments of $319,000.

To summarize the adjustments to cost of goods sold that are necessary to calculate cash payments for merchandise:

$$\text{Purchases} = \text{Cost of goods sold} \begin{bmatrix} + \text{ Increase in merchandise inventory} \\ \textit{or} \\ - \text{ Decrease in merchandise inventory} \end{bmatrix}$$

And,

$$\text{Cash payments for merchandise} = \text{Purchases} \begin{bmatrix} + \text{ Decrease in accounts payable} \\ \textit{or} \\ - \text{ Increase in accounts payable} \end{bmatrix}$$

Now, look at Illustration 15–2 on page 540. Notice that Grover Company's payments of $319,000 for merchandise are reported on the statement of cash flows as a cash outflow for operating activities.

Cash Payments for Wages and Other Operating Expenses. Grover Company's income statement shows wages and other operating expenses of $216,000 (see Illustration 15–9). To determine the amount of cash paid during the period for wages and other operating expenses, we need to combine this amount with the changes in any related balance sheet accounts. In Grover Company's beginning and ending balance sheets in Illustration 15–9, look for prepaid expenses and any accrued liabilities that relate to wages and other operating expenses. In this example, the balance sheets show that Grover Company has prepaid

[4] The amount of purchases is also in the Purchases account in the General Ledger.

expenses but does not have any accrued liabilities. Thus, the adjustment to the expense item is limited to the change in prepaid expenses. The amount of the adjustment can be determined by assuming that all cash payments of wages and other operating expenses were originally debited to Prepaid Expenses. With this assumption, we can reconstruct the Prepaid Expenses account as follows:

Prepaid Expenses

Balance, 12/31/X1	4,000		
Payments =	**218,000**	Wages and other operating expenses	216,000
Balance, 12/31/X2	6,000		

This account shows that prepaid expenses increased by $2,000 during the period. Therefore, the cash payments for wages and other operating expenses were $2,000 greater than the reported expense. Thus, the amount paid for wages and other operating expenses is $216,000 plus $2,000, or $218,000.

In reconstructing the Prepaid Expenses account, we assumed that all cash payments for wages and operating expenses were debited to Prepaid Expenses. However, this assumption does not have to be true for the analysis to work. If cash payments were debited directly to the expense account, the total amount of cash payments would be the same. In other words, the cash paid for operating expenses still equals the $216,000 expense plus the $2,000 increase in prepaid expenses.

On the other hand, if Grover Company's balance sheets had shown accrued liabilities, we would have to adjust the expense for the change in those accrued liabilities. In general terms, the calculation is as follows:

$$\begin{matrix}\text{Cash paid for}\\ \text{wages and other}\\ \text{operating expenses}\end{matrix} = \begin{matrix}\text{Wages and}\\ \text{other}\\ \text{operating}\\ \text{expenses}\end{matrix} \begin{bmatrix}+\text{ Increase in prepaid expenses}\\ \textit{or}\\ -\text{ Decrease in prepaid expenses}\end{bmatrix} \begin{bmatrix}+\text{ Decrease in accrued liabilities}\\ \textit{or}\\ -\text{ Increase in accrued liabilities}\end{bmatrix}$$

Payments for Interest and Taxes. Grover Company's remaining operating cash flows involve cash payments for interest and for taxes. The analysis of these items is similar because both require adjustments for changes in related liability accounts. Grover Company's income statement shows interest expense of $7,000 and income taxes expense of $15,000. To calculate the related cash payments, adjust interest expense for the change in interest payable and adjust income taxes expense for the change in income taxes payable. These calculations are accomplished by reconstructing the liability accounts as follows:

Interest Payable

		Balance, 12/31/X1	4,000
Interest paid =	**8,000**	Interest expense	7,000
		Balance 12/31/X2	3,000

Income Taxes Payable

	Balance, 12/31/X1	12,000
Income taxes paid = 5,000	Income taxes expense	15,000
	Balance, 12/31/X2	22,000

These reconstructed accounts show that interest payments were $8,000 and income tax payments were $5,000. The general form of each calculation is

$$\text{Cash Payment} = \text{Expense} \begin{bmatrix}+\text{ Decrease in related payable}\\ \textit{or}\\ -\text{ Increase in related payable}\end{bmatrix}$$

Both of these cash payments appear as operating items on Grover Company's statement of cash flows in Illustration 15–2 on page 540.

Investing Activities

Investing activities usually involve transactions that affect long-term assets. Recall from the information provided about Grover Company's transactions that the company purchased plant assets and also sold plant assets. Both of these transactions are investing activities.

Purchase of Plant Assets. Grover Company purchased plant assets that cost $70,000 by issuing $60,000 of bonds payable to the seller and paying the $10,000 balance in cash. The $10,000 payment is a cash outflow on the statement of cash flows (see Illustration 15–2). Also, because $60,000 of the purchase was financed by issuing bonds payable, this transaction involves noncash investing and financing activities. It might be described in a footnote as follows:

Noncash investing and financing activities:	
Purchased plant assets	$70,000
Issued bonds payable to finance purchase	60,000
Balance paid in cash	$10,000

Sale of Plant Assets. Grover Company sold plant assets that cost $30,000 when they had accumulated depreciation of $12,000. The result of the sale was a loss of $6,000 and a cash receipt of $12,000. This cash receipt is reported in the statement of cash flows as a cash inflow from investing activities (see Illustration 15–2).

Recall from Grover Company's income statement that depreciation expense was $24,000. Depreciation does not use or provide cash. Note, however, the effects of depreciation expense, the plant asset purchase, and the plant asset sale on the Plant Assets and Accumulated Depreciation accounts. These accounts are reconstructed as follows:

Plant Assets

Debit		Credit	
Balance, 12/31/X1	210,000		
Purchase	70,000	Sale	30,000
Balance 12/31/X2	250,000		

Accumulated Depreciation, Plant Assets

Debit		Credit	
		Balance, 12/31/X1	48,000
Sale	12,000	Depreciation expense	24,000
		Balance, 12/31/X2	60,000

The beginning and ending balances of these accounts were taken from Grover Company's balance sheets (Illustration 15–9). Reconstructing the accounts shows that the beginning and ending balances of both accounts are completely reconciled by the purchase, the sale, and the depreciation expense. Therefore, we did not omit any of the investing activities that relate to plant assets.

Financing Activities

Financing activities usually relate to a company's long-term debt and stockholders' equity accounts. In the information about Grover Company, four transactions involved financing activities. We already discussed one of these, the $60,000 issuance of bonds payable to purchase plant assets, as a noncash investing and financing activity. The remaining three transactions were the retirement of bonds, the issuance of common stock, and the payment of cash dividends.

Payment to Retire Bonds Payable. Grover Company's December 31, 19X1, balance sheet showed total bonds payable of $64,000. Included within this balance for 19X2 were bonds with a carrying value of $34,000 that were retired for an $18,000 cash payment during the year. The income statement reports the $16,000 difference as a gain. The statement of cash flows shows the $18,000 payments as a cash outflow for financing activities (see Illustration 15–2 on page 540).

Notice that the beginning and ending balances of Bonds Payable are reconciled by the $60,000 issuance of new bonds and the retirement of $34,000 of old bonds. The following reconstructed Bonds Payable account shows the results of these activities:

Bonds Payable

		Balance, 12/31/X1	64,000
Retired bonds	34,000	Issued bonds	60,000
		Balance, 12/31/X2	90,000

Receipt from Common Stock Issuance. During 19X2, Grover Company issued 3,000 shares of common stock at par for $5 per share. This $15,000 cash receipt is reported on the statement of cash flows as a financing activity. Look at the December 31, 19X1, and 19X2 balance sheets in Illustration 15–9. Notice that the Common Stock account balance increased from $80,000 at the end of 19X1 to $95,000 at the end of 19X2. Thus, the $15,000 stock issue explains the change in the Common Stock account.

Payment of Cash Dividends. According to the facts provided about Grover Company's transactions, it paid cash dividends of $14,000 during 19X2. This payment is a cash outflow for financing activities. Also, note that the effects of this $14,000 payment and the reported net income of $38,000 fully reconcile the beginning and ending balances of Retained Earnings. The following reconstructed Retained Earnings account shows this:

Retained Earnings

		Balance, 12/31/X1	88,000
Cash dividend	14,000	Net income	38,000
		Balance, 12/31/X2	112,000

We have described all of Grover Company's cash inflows and outflows and one noncash investing and financing transaction. In the process of making these analyses, we reconciled the changes in all of the noncash balance sheet accounts. The change in the Cash account is reconciled by the statement of cash flows, as seen in Illustration 15–2 on page 540.

Reconciling Net Income to Net Cash Provided (or Used) by Operating Activities

As you learned earlier, the FASB recommends that the operating activities section of the statement of cash flows be prepared according to the direct method. Under this method, the statement reports each major class of cash inflows and outflows from operating activities. *However, when the direct method is used, the FASB also requires that companies disclose a reconciliation of net income to the net cash provided (or used) by operating activities.* This reconciliation is precisely what is accomplished by the *indirect* method of calculating the net cash provided (or used) by operating activities. We explain the indirect method next.

The Indirect Method of Calculating Net Cash Provided (or Used) by Operating Activities

When using the indirect method, list net income first. Then, adjust net income to reconcile its amount to the net amount of cash provided (or used) by operating activities. To see the results of the indirect method, look at Illustration 15–10. This illustration shows Grover Company's statement of cash flows with the reconciliation of net income to the net cash provided by operating activities.

ILLUSTRATION 15–10 *Statement of Cash Flows (Indirect Method)*

GROVER COMPANY
Statement of Cash Flows
For Year Ended December 31, 19X2

	Cash flows from operating activities:		
	Net income	$38,000	
	Adjustments to reconcile net income to net cash provided by operating activities:		
(1)	Increase in accounts receivable	(20,000)	
(1)	Increase in merchandise inventory	(14,000)	
(1)	Increase in prepaid expenses	(2,000)	
(1)	Decrease in accounts payable	(5,000)	
(1)	Decrease in interest payable	(1,000)	
(1)	Increase in income taxes payable	10,000	
(2)	Depreciation expense	24,000	
(3)	Loss on sale of plant assets	6,000	
(3)	Gain on retirement of bonds	(16,000)	
	Net cash provided by operating activities		$20,000
	Cash flows from investing activities:		
	Cash received from sale of plant assets	$12,000	
	Cash paid for purchase of plant assets	(10,000)	
	Net cash provided by investing activities		2,000
	Cash flows from financing activities:		
	Cash received from issuing stock	$15,000	
	Cash paid to retire bonds	(18,000)	
	Cash paid for dividends	(14,000)	
	Net cash used in financing activities		(17,000)
	Net increase in cash		$ 5,000
	Cash balance at beginning of 19X2		12,000
	Cash balance at end of 19X2		$17,000

In Illustration 15–10, notice that the net cash provided by operating activities is $20,000. This same amount was reported on the statement of cash flows (direct method) in Illustration 15–2 on page 540. However, these illustrations show entirely different ways of calculating the $20,000 net cash inflow. Under the direct method in Illustration 15–2, we subtracted major classes of operating cash outflows from major classes of cash inflows. By comparison, we include none of the individual cash inflows or cash outflows under the indirect method in Illustration 15–10. Instead, we modify net income to exclude those amounts included in the determination of net income but not involved in operating cash inflows or outflows during the period. Net income is also modified to include operating cash inflows and outflows not recorded as revenues and expenses.

LO 4 Calculate the net cash provided or used by operating activities according to the indirect method and prepare the statement of cash flows.

Illustration 15–10 shows three types of adjustments to net income. The adjustments grouped under the section labeled (1) are for changes in noncash current assets and current liabilities that relate to operating activities. Adjustment (2) is for an income statement item that relates to operating activities but that did not involve a cash inflow or outflow during the period. The adjustments grouped under (3) eliminate gains and losses that resulted from investing and financing activities. These gains and losses do not relate to operating activities.

Adjustments for Changes in Current Assets and Current Liabilities

To help you understand why adjustments for changes in noncash current assets and current liabilities are part of the reconciliation process, we use the transactions of a very simple company as an example. Assume that Simple Company's income statement shows only two items, as follows:

Sales	$20,000
Operating expenses	(12,000)
Net income	$ 8,000

For a moment, assume that all of Simple Company's sales and operating expenses are for cash. The company has no current assets other than cash and has no current liabilities. Given these assumptions, the net cash provided by operating activities during the period is $8,000, which is the cash received from customers less the cash paid for operating expenses.

Adjustments for Changes in Noncash Current Assets

Now assume that Simple Company's sales are on account. Also assume that its Accounts Receivable balance was $2,000 at the beginning of the year and $2,500 at the end of the year. Under these assumptions, cash receipts from customers equal sales of $20,000 minus the $500 increase in Accounts Receivable, or $19,500. Therefore, using the *direct* method, the net cash provided by operating activities is $7,500 ($19,500 − $12,000).

When the *indirect* method is used to calculate the net cash flow, net income of $8,000 is adjusted for the $500 increase in Accounts Receivable to get $7,500 as the net amount of cash provided by operating activities. Both calculations are as follows:

Direct Method	
Receipts from customers ($20,000 − $500)	$19,500
Payments for operating expenses	(12,000)
Cash provided (or used) by operating activities	$ 7,500
Indirect Method	
Net income	$8,000
Less the increase in accounts receivable	(500)
Cash provided (or used) by operating activities	$7,500

Notice that the direct method calculation subtracts the increase in Accounts Receivable from Sales, while the indirect method calculation subtracts the increase in Accounts Receivable from net income.

As another example, assume instead that the Accounts Receivable balance decreased from $2,000 to $1,200. Under this assumption, cash receipts from customers equal sales of $20,000 plus the $800 decrease in Accounts Receivable, or $20,800. By the direct method, the net cash provided by operating activities is $8,800 ($20,800 − $12,000). And when the indirect method is used, the $800 decrease in Accounts Receivable is added to the $8,000 net income to get $8,800 net cash provided by operating activities.

When the indirect method is used, adjustments like those for Accounts Receivable are required for all noncash current assets related to operating activities. When a noncash current asset increases, part of the assets derived from operating activities goes into the increase. This leaves a smaller amount as the net cash inflow. Therefore, when you calculate the net cash inflow using the indirect method, subtract the noncash current asset increase from net income. But when a noncash current asset decreases, additional cash is produced, and you should add this amount to net income. These modifications of income for changes in current assets related to operating activities are as follows:

Net income
Add: Decreases in current assets
Subtract: Increases in current assets
Net cash provided (or used) by operating activities

Adjustments for Changes in Current Liabilities

To illustrate the adjustments for changes in current liabilities, return to the original assumptions about Simple Company. Sales of $20,000 are for cash, and operating expenses are $12,000. However, assume now that Simple Company has Interest Payable as its only current liability. Also assume that the beginning-of-year balance in Interest Payable was $500 and the end-of-year balance was $900. This increase means that the operating expenses of $12,000 were $400 larger than the amount paid in cash during the period. Therefore, the cash payments for operating expenses were only $11,600, or ($12,000 − $400). Under these assumptions, the direct method calculation of net cash provided by operating activities is $8,400, or $20,000 receipts from customers less $11,600 payments for expenses. The indirect method calculation of $8,400 is net income of $8,000 plus the $400 increase in Interest Payable.

Alternatively, if the Interest Payable balance decreased, for example by $300, the cash outflow for operating expenses would have been the $12,000 expense plus the $300 liability decrease, or $12,300. Then, the direct calculation of net cash flow is $20,000 − $12,300 = $7,700. The indirect calculation is $8,000 − $300 = $7,700. In other words, when using the indirect method, subtract a decrease in Interest Payable from net income.

Using the indirect method requires adjustments like those for Interest Payable for all current liabilities related to operating activities. When a current liability decreases, part of the cash derived from operating activities pays for the decrease. Therefore, subtract the decrease from net income to determine the remaining net cash inflow. And when a current liability increases, it finances some operating expenses. In other words, cash was not used to pay for the expense and the liability increase must be added to net income when you calculate cash provided by operating activities. These adjustments for changes in current liabilities related to operating activities are

Net income
Add: Increases in current liabilities
Subtract: Decreases in current liabilities
Net cash provided (or used) by operating activities

One way to remember how to make these modifications to net income is to observe that a *debit* change in a noncash current asset or a current liability is *subtracted* from net income. And, a *credit* change in a noncash current asset or a current liability is *added* to net income.

Adjustments for Operating Items that Do Not Provide or Use Cash

Some operating items that appear on an income statement do not provide or use cash during the current period. One example is depreciation. Other examples are amortization of intangible assets, depletion of natural resources, and bad debts expense.

A company records these expenses with debits to expense accounts and credits to noncash accounts. They reduce net income but do not require cash outflows during the period. Therefore, when a company makes adjustments to net income under the indirect method, it adds these noncash expenses back to net income.

In addition to noncash expenses such as depreciation, net income may include some revenues that do not provide cash inflows during the current period. If net income includes revenues that do not provide cash inflows, subtract the revenues from net income in the process of reconciling net income to the net cash provided by operating activities.

The indirect method adjustments for expenses and revenues that do not provide or use cash during the current period are as follows:

Net income
Add: Expenses that do not use cash
Subtract: Revenues that do not provide cash
Net cash provided (or used) by operating activities

Adjustments for Nonoperating Items

Some income statement items are not related to the operating activities of the company. These gains and losses result from investing and financing activities. Examples are gains or losses on the sale of plant assets and gains or losses on the retirement of bonds payable.

Remember that the indirect method reconciles net income to the net cash provided (or used) by operating activities. Therefore, net income must be modified to exclude gains and losses created by investing and financing activities. In making the modifications under the indirect method, subtract gains from financing and investing activities from net income and add losses back to net income:

Net income
Add: Losses from investing or financing activities
Subtract: Gains from investing or financing activities
Net cash provided (or used) by operating activities

Applying the Indirect Method to Grover Company

LO 5 Prepare a working paper for a statement of cash flows so that the net cash flow from operating activities is calculated by the indirect method.

Determining the net cash flows provided (or used) by operating activities according to the indirect method requires balance sheets at the beginning and end of the period, the current period's income statement, and other information about selected transactions. Illustration 15–9 on page 548 shows the income statement and balance sheet information for Grover Company. Based on this information, Illustration 15–10 presents the indirect method of reconciling net income to net cash provided by operating activities.

Preparing the Indirect Method Working Paper

When a company has a large number of accounts and many operating, investing, and financing transactions, the analysis of noncash accounts can be difficult and confusing. In these situations, a working paper can help organize the information you need to prepare a statement of cash flows. A working paper also makes it easier to check the accuracy of your work.

In addition to Grover Company's comparative balance sheets and income statement presented in Illustration 15–9, the information needed to prepare the working paper follows. The letters identifying each item of information also cross-reference related debits and credits on the working paper.

a. Net income was $38,000.
b. Accounts receivable increased by $20,000.
c. Merchandise inventory increased by $14,000.
d. Prepaid expenses increased by $2,000.
e. Accounts payable decreased by $5,000.
f. Interest payable decreased by $1,000.
g. Income taxes payable increased by $10,000.
h. Depreciation expense was $24,000.
i. Loss on sale of plant assets was $6,000; assets that cost $30,000 with accumulated depreciation of $12,000 were sold for $12,000 cash.
j. Gain on retirement of bonds was $16,000; bonds with a book value of $34,000 were retired with a cash payment of $18,000.
k. Plant assets that cost $70,000 were purchased; the payment consisted of $10,000 cash and issuing $60,000 of bonds payable.
l. Sold 3,000 shares of common stock for $15,000.
m. Paid cash dividends of $14,000.

Illustration 15–11 shows the indirect method working paper for Grover Company. Notice that the beginning and ending balance sheets are recorded on the working paper in the first and fourth monetary columns. Following the balance sheets, we enter information in the Analysis of Changes columns about cash flows from operating, investing, and financing activities and about noncash investing and financing activities. Note that net income is entered as the first item used in computing the amount of cash flows from operating activities.

Entering the Analysis of Changes on the Working Paper

After the balance sheets are entered, we recommend using the following sequence of procedures to complete the working paper:

1. Enter net income as an operating cash inflow (a debit) and as a credit to Retained Earnings.
2. In the statement of cash flows section, adjustments to net income are entered as debits if they increase cash inflows and as credits if they decrease cash inflows. Following this rule, adjust net income for the change in each noncash current asset and current liability related to operating activities. For each adjustment to net income, the offsetting debit or credit should reconcile the beginning and ending balances of a current asset or current liability.
3. Enter the adjustments to net income for income statement items, such as depreciation, that did not provide or use cash during the period. For each adjustment, the offsetting debit or credit should help reconcile a noncash balance sheet account.
4. Adjust net income to eliminate any gains or losses from investing and financing activities. Because the cash associated with a gain must be excluded from operating activities, the gain is entered as a credit in the operating activities section. On the other hand, losses are entered with debits. For each of these adjustments, the related debits and/or credits help reconcile balance sheet accounts and also involve entries to show the cash flow from investing or financing activities.

ILLUSTRATION 15-11

GROVER COMPANY
Working Paper for Statement of Cash Flows (Indirect Method)
For Year Ended December 31, 19X2

	December 31, 19X1	Analysis of Changes Debit	Analysis of Changes Credit	December 31, 19X2
Balance sheet—debits:				
Cash	12,000			17,000
Accounts receivable	40,000	(*b*) 20,000		60,000
Merchandise inventory	70,000	(*c*) 14,000		84,000
Prepaid expenses	4,000	(*d*) 2,000		6,000
Plant assets	210,000	(*k1*) 70,000	(*i*) 30,000	250,000
	336,000			417,000
Balance sheet—credits:				
Accumulated depreciation, plant assets	48,000	(*i*) 12,000	(*h*) 24,000	60,000
Accounts payable	40,000	(*e*) 5,000		35,000
Interest payable	4,000	(*f*) 1,000		3,000
Income taxes payable	12,000		(*g*) 10,000	22,000
Bonds payable	64,000	(*j*) 34,000	(*k2*) 60,000	90,000
Common stock, $5 par value	80,000		(*l*) 15,000	95,000
Retained earnings	88,000	(*m*) 14,000	(*a*) 38,000	112,000
	336,000			417,000
Statement of cash flows:				
Operating activities:				
Net income		(*a*) 38,000		
Increase in accounts receivable			(*b*) 20,000	
Increase in merchandise inventory			(*c*) 14,000	
Increase in prepaid expenses			(*d*) 2,000	
Decrease in accounts payable			(*e*) 5,000	
Decrease in interest payable			(*f*) 1,000	
Increase in income taxes payable		(*g*) 10,000		
Depreciation expense		(*h*) 24,000		
Loss on sale of plant assets		(*i*) 6,000		
Gain on retirement of bonds			(*j*) 16,000	
Investing activities:				
Receipt from sale of plant assets		(*i*) 12,000		
Payment for purchase of plant assets			(*k1*) 10,000	
Financing activities:				
Payment to retire bonds			(*j*) 18,000	
Receipts from issuing stock		(*l*) 15,000		
Payments of dividends			(*m*) 14,000	
Noncash investing and financing activities:				
Purchase of plant assets financed by bonds		(*k2*) 60,000	(*k1*) 60,000	
		337,000	337,000	

5. After reviewing any unreconciled balance sheet accounts and related information, enter the reconciling entries for all remaining investing and financing activities. These include items such as purchases of plant assets, issuances of long-term debt, sales of capital stock, and dividend payments. Some of these may require entries in the noncash investing and financing activities section of the working paper.

6. Confirm the accuracy of your work by totaling the Analysis of Changes columns and by determining that the change in each balance sheet account has been explained.

For Grover Company, these steps were performed in Illustration 15–11:

Step	Entries
1	(*a*)
2	(*b*) through (*g*)
3	(*h*)
4	(*i*) through (*j*)
5	(*k*) through (*m*)

Because adjustments *i*, *j*, and *k* are more complex, we show them in the following debit and credit format. This format is similar to the one used for general journal entries, except that the changes in the Cash account are identified as sources or uses of cash.

		Debit	Credit
i.	Loss from Sale of Plant Assets	6,000.00	
	Accumulated Depreciation	12,000.00	
	Receipt from Sale of Plant Assets	12,000.00	
	Plant Assets		30,000.00
	To describe the sale of plant assets.		
j.	Bonds Payable	34,000.00	
	Payments to Retire Bonds		18,000.00
	Gain on Retirement of Bonds		16,000.00
	To describe the retirement of bonds.		
k1.	Plant Assets	70,000.00	
	Payment to Purchase Plant Assets		10,000.00
	Purchase of Plant Assets Financed by Bonds . . .		60,000.00
	To describe the purchase of plant assets, the cash payment, and the use of noncash financing.		
k2.	Purchase of Plant Assets Financed by Bonds	60,000.00	
	Bonds Payable		60,000.00
	To show the issuance of bonds payable to finance the purchase of plant assets.		

Using the Information—Cash Flows

LO 1 Describe a statement of cash flows; classify cash flows as operating, investing, or financing activities; and identify some decisions that involve evaluating cash flows.

Mary Garza (As a Matter of Opinion, page 541) typifies the attitude of most managers when she emphasizes the importance of understanding and predicting cash flows. Many business decisions are based on cash flow evaluations. For example, creditors evaluate a company's ability to generate cash before deciding whether to loan money to the company. Investors often make similar evaluations before they buy a company's stock. In making these evaluations, cash flows from investing and financing activities are considered. However, special attention is given to the company's ability to generate cash flows from its operations. The cash flows statement facilitates this by separating the investing and financing activity cash flows from the operating cash flows.

To see the importance of identifying cash flows as operating, investing, and financing activities, consider the following three companies. Assume they operate in the same industry and have been in business for several years.

	First Company	Second Company	Third Company
Cash provided (used) by operating activities	$90,000	$40,000	$(24,000)
Cash provided (used) by investing activities:			
Proceeds from sale of operating assets			26,000
Purchase of operating assets	(48,000)	(25,000)	
Cash provided (used) by financing activities:			
Proceeds from issuance of debt			13,000
Repayment of debt	(27,000)		
Net increase (decrease) in cash	$15,000	$15,000	$15,000

Each of the three companies generated a $15,000 net increase in cash. Their means of accomplishing this, however, were very different. First Company's operating activities provided $90,000, which allowed the company to purchase additional operating assets for $48,000 and repay $27,000 of debt. By comparison, Second Company's operating activities provided only $40,000, enabling it to purchase only $25,000 of operating assets. By comparison, Third Company's net cash increase was obtained only by selling operating assets and incurring additional debt; the company's operating activities used $24,000.

The implication of this comparison is that First Company is more capable of generating cash to meet its future obligations than is Second Company; and Third Company is least capable. This evaluation is, of course, tentative and may be contradicted by other information.

Managers analyze cash flows in making a variety of short-term decisions. In deciding whether borrowing will be necessary, managers use the procedures you learned in this chapter to predict cash flows for the next period or periods. These short-term planning situations also may lead to decisions about investing idle cash balances. Another example is deciding whether a customer's offer to buy a product at a reduced price should be accepted or rejected.

Long-term decisions involving new investments usually require detailed cash flow predictions. Companies must estimate cash inflows and outflows over the life of the investment, often extending many years into the future. Other decisions that require cash flow information include deciding whether a product should be manufactured by the company or purchased from an outside supplier and deciding whether a product or a department should be eliminated or retained.

Summary of Chapter in Terms of Learning Objectives

LO 1 The statement of cash flows reports cash receipts and disbursements as operating, investing, or financing activities. Operating activities include transactions related to producing or purchasing merchandise, selling goods and services to customers, and performing administrative functions. Investing activities include purchases and sales of noncurrent assets and short-term investments that are not cash equivalents. Financing activities include transactions with owners and transactions to borrow or repay the principal amounts of long-term and short-term debt.

Many decisions involve evaluating cash flows. Examples are investor and creditor decisions to invest in or loan money to a company. The evaluations include paying attention to the activities that provide or use cash. Managers evaluate cash flows in deciding whether borrowing is necessary, whether cash balances should be invested, and in a variety of other short-term and long-term decisions.

LO 2 In using the direct method to report the net cash provided (or used) by operating activities, major classes of operating cash inflows and outflows are separately disclosed. On the statement, operating cash outflows are subtracted from operating cash inflows to derive the net inflow or outflow from operating activities. This method is encouraged by the FASB but is not required. Also, company managers use the direct method to predict future cash inflows and outflows.

For external reporting, a company must supplement its statement of cash flows with a description of its noncash investing and financing activities. Two examples of these activities are the retirement of debt obligations by issuing equity securities and the exchange of a note payable for plant assets.

LO 3 Cash receipts and payments are recorded in the Cash account and in other noncash balance sheet accounts, or temporary accounts, such as revenues and expenses. The temporary accounts are closed to Retained Earnings. Therefore, to identify the cash receipts and cash payments, analyze the changes in the noncash balance sheet accounts created by income statement transactions and other events. For example, the amount of cash collected from customers is calculated by modifying sales revenues for the change in accounts receivable. Also, cash paid for interest is calculated by adjusting interest expense for the change in interest payable.

LO 4 In using the indirect method to calculate the net cash provided (or used) by operating activities, list the net income and then modify it for these three types of events: (*a*) changes in noncash current assets and current liabilities related to operating activities; (*b*) revenues and expenses that did not provide or use cash; and (*c*) gains and losses from investing and financing activities. If using the direct method, report the reconciliation between net income and net cash provided (or used) by operating activities on a separate schedule.

LO 5 To prepare an indirect method working paper, enter the beginning and ending balances of the balance sheet accounts in columns 1 and 4. Then, establish the three sections of the statement of cash flows (operating, investing, and financing). Enter net income as the first item in the operating activities section. Then, adjust the net income for events (*a*) through (*c*) identified in the preceding paragraph. This process reconciles the changes in the noncash current assets and current liabilities related to operations. Reconcile any remaining balance sheet account changes and report their cash effects in the appropriate sections. Enter noncash investing and financing activities at the bottom of the working paper.

Demonstration Problem

The following summarized journal entries show the total debits and credits to the Pyramid Corporation's Cash account during 19X1. Use the information to prepare a statement of cash flows for 19X1. The cash provided (or used) by operating activities should be presented according to the direct method. In the statement, identify the entry that records each item of cash flow. Assume that the beginning balance of cash was $133,200.

a.	Cash	1,440,000.00	
	Common Stock, $10 par value		360,000.00
	Contributed Capital in Excess of Par Value, Common Stock		1,080,000.00
	Issued common stock for cash.		
b.	Cash	2,400,000.00	
	Notes Payable		2,400,000.00
	Borrowed cash with a note payable.		

c.	Purchases	480,000.00	
	Cash		480,000.00
	Purchased merchandise for cash.		
d.	Accounts Payable	1,200,000.00	
	Cash		1,200,000.00
	Paid for credit purchases of merchandise.		
e.	Wages Expense	600,000.00	
	Cash		600,000.00
	Paid wages to employees.		
f.	Rent Expense	420,000.00	
	Cash		420,000.00
	Paid rent for buildings.		
g.	Cash	3,000,000.00	
	Sales		3,000,000.00
	Made cash sales to customers.		
h.	Cash	1,800,000.00	
	Accounts Receivable		1,800,000.00
	Collected accounts from credit customers.		
i.	Machinery	2,136,000.00	
	Cash		2,136,000.00
	Purchased machinery for cash.		
j.	Investments	2,160,000.00	
	Cash		2,160,000.00
	Purchased investments for cash.		
k.	Interest Expense	216,000.00	
	Notes Payable	384,000.00	
	Cash		600,000.00
	Paid notes and accrued interest.		
l.	Cash	206,400.00	
	Dividends Earned		206,400.00
	Collected dividends from investments.		
m.	Cash	210,000.00	
	Loss on Sale of Investments	30,000.00	
	Investments		240,000.00
	Sold investments for cash.		
n.	Cash	720,000.00	
	Accumulated Depreciation, Machinery	420,000.00	
	Machinery		960,000.00
	Gain on Sale of Machinery		180,000.00
	Sold machinery for cash.		
o.	Common Dividend Payable	510,000.00	
	Cash		510,000.00
	Paid cash dividends to stockholders.		
p.	Income Taxes Payable	480,000.00	
	Cash		480,000.00
	Paid income taxes owed for the year.		
q.	Treasury Stock, Common	228,000.00	
	Cash		228,000.00
	Acquired treasury stock for cash.		

Planning the Solution

- Prepare a blank statement of cash flows with sections for operating, investing, and financing activities.
- Examine each journal entry to determine whether it describes an operating, investing, or financing activity and whether it describes an inflow or outflow of cash.
- Enter the cash effects of the entry in the appropriate section of the statement, being sure to combine similar events, including *c* and *d*, as well as *g* and *h*. For entry *k*, identify the portions of the cash flow that should be assigned to operating and financing activities.
- Total each section of the statement, determine the total change in cash, and add the beginning balance to get the ending balance.

Solution to Demonstration Problem

PYRAMID CORPORATION
Statement of Cash Flows
For Year Ended December 31, 19X1

Cash flows from operating activities:		
g, h. Cash received from customers	$ 4,800,000	
l. Cash received as dividends	206,400	
c, d. Cash paid for merchandise	(1,680,000)	
e. Cash paid for wages	(600,000)	
f. Cash paid for rent	(420,000)	
k. Cash paid for interest	(216,000)	
p. Cash paid for taxes	(480,000)	
Net cash provided by operating activities		$ 1,610,400
Cash flows from investing activities:		
i. Cash paid for purchases of machinery	$(2,136,000)	
j. Cash paid for purchases of investments	(2,160,000)	
m. Cash received from sale of investments	210,000	
n. Cash received from sale of machinery	720,000	
Net cash used in investing activities		(3,366,000)
Cash flows from financing activities:		
a. Cash received from issuing stock	$ 1,440,000	
b. Cash received from borrowing	2,400,000	
k. Cash paid for repayment of note payable	(384,000)	
o. Cash paid for dividends	(510,000)	
q. Cash paid for purchases of treasury stock	(228,000)	
Net cash provided by financing activities		2,718,000
Net increase in cash		$ 962,400
Beginning balance of cash		133,200
Ending balance of cash		$ 1,095,600

Glossary

LO 6 Define or explain the words or phrases listed in the chapter glossary.

Direct method of calculating net cash provided or used by operating activities a calculation of the net cash provided or used by operating activities that lists the major classes of operating cash receipts, such as receipts from customers, and subtracts the major classes of operating cash disbursements, such as cash paid for merchandise. p. 538

Financing activities transactions with the owners of a business or transactions with its creditors to borrow money or to repay the principal amounts of loans. p. 542

Indirect method of calculating net cash provided or used by operating activities a calculation that begins with net income and then adjusts the net income amount by adding and subtracting items that are necessary to reconcile net income to the net cash provided or used by operating activities. p. 538

Investing activities transactions that involve making and collecting loans or that involve purchasing and selling plant assets, other productive assets, or investments other than cash equivalents. p. 542

Operating activities activities that involve the production or purchase of merchandise and the sale of goods and services to customers, including expenditures related to administering the business. p. 541

Statement of cash flows a financial statement that reports the cash inflows and outflows for an accounting period, and that classifies those cash flows as operating activities, investing activities, and financing activities. p. 537

Objective Review

Answers to the following questions are listed at the end of this chapter. Be sure that you decide which is the one best answer to each question *before* you check the answers.

LO 1 A payment in the form of a loan made by a manufacturing company to another company is an example of:

a. A cash flow from operating activities.
b. A cash flow from investing activities.
c. A cash flow from financing activities.
d. A noncash investing and financing activity.
e. A cash payment to purchase a cash equivalent.

LO 2 The following T-account is a summary of the Cash account of Outland Shirt Company.

Summarized Cash Account

Balance, 12/31/X1	5,000		
Receipts from customers	273,000	Payments for merchandise	150,000
Proceeds from dividends from stock investments	4,500	Payments for other operating expenses	105,000
		Interest payments	7,500
		Tax payments	6,000
Proceeds from issuance of bonds payable	75,000	Payments to purchase treasury stock	75,000
Proceeds from sale of stock investment	27,000	Dividend payments	22,500
Balance, 12/31/X2	18,500		

A statement of cash flows prepared according to the direct method would state:

a. Net cash provided (or used) by financing activities, $(22,500).
b. Net cash provided (or used) by investing activities, $31,500.
c. Net cash provided (or used) by operating activities, $4,500.
d. Net cash provided (or used) by investing activities, $(48,000).
e. Net cash provided (or used) by operating activities, $18,500.

LO 3 Snyder Company's Merchandise Inventory account balance decreased during a period from a beginning balance of $32,000 to an ending balance of $28,000. Cost of goods sold for that same period was $168,000. If the Accounts Payable balance increased $2,400 during the period, what was the amount of cash paid for merchandise?

a. $161,600.
b. $166,400.
c. $168,000.
d. $169,600.
e. $174,400.

LO 4 Determine the net cash provided (or used) by operating activities based on the following data:

Net income	$74,900
Decrease in accounts receivable	4,600
Increase in inventory	11,700
Decrease in accounts payable	1,000
Loss on sale of equipment	3,400
Payment of dividends	21,500

a. $48,700.
b. $61,000.
c. $63,400.
d. $70,200.
e. $79,600.

LO 5 In preparing a working paper for a statement of cash flows with the cash flows from operating activities reported according to the indirect method:

a. A decrease in accounts receivable is analyzed with a debit in the statement of cash flows section and a credit in the balance sheet section.
b. A cash dividend paid is analyzed with a debit to retained earnings and a credit in the investing activities section.
c. The analysis of a cash payment to retire bonds payable at a loss would require one debit and two credits.
d. Depreciation expense would not require analysis on the working paper because there is no cash inflow or outflow.
e. None of the above is correct.

LO 6 Transactions with the owners or long-term creditors of the business or that involve borrowing cash on a short-term basis are classified as:

a. Noncash investing and financing activities.
b. Operating activities.
c. Financing activities.
d. Investing activities.
e. None of the above.

Questions for Class Discussion

1. What information is shown on a statement of cash flows?
2. What are the three categories of cash flows shown on a statement of cash flows?
3. What are some examples of items reported on a statement of cash flows as investing activities?
4. What are some examples of items reported on a statement of cash flows as financing activities?

5. When a statement of cash flows is prepared by the direct method, what are some examples of items reported as cash flows from operating activities?
6. A machine that was held as a long-term asset for use in business operations is sold for cash. Where should this cash flow appear on the statement of cash flows?
7. A business purchases merchandise inventory for cash. Where should this cash flow appear on the statement of cash flows?
8. If a corporation pays cash dividends, where on the corporation's statement of cash flows should the payment be reported?
9. A company purchases land for $100,000, paying $20,000 cash and borrowing the remainder on a long-term note payable. How should this transaction be reported on a statement of cash flows?
10. What is the direct method of reporting cash flows from operating activities?
11. What is the indirect method of reporting cash flows from operating activities?
12. Do the direct and indirect methods of calculating cash flows from operating activities lead to the same net amount?
13. Is depreciation a source of cash?
14. On June 3, a company borrowed $50,000 by giving its bank a 60-day, interest-bearing note. On the statement of cash flows, where should this item be reported?
15. When a working paper for the preparation of a statement of cash flows is prepared, all changes in noncash balance sheet accounts are accounted for on the working paper. Why?
16. If a company reports a net income for the year, is it possible for the company to show a net cash outflow from operating activities? Explain your answer.
17. Why are expenses such as depreciation and amortization of goodwill added to net income when cash flow from operations is calculated by the indirect method?
18. A company reports a net income of $15,000 that includes a $3,000 gain on sale of plant assets. Why is this gain subtracted from net income in the process of reconciling net income to the net cash provided or used by operating activities?

19. Refer to the consolidated statement of cash flows for Ben & Jerry's Homemade, Inc., in Appendix G. What type and amount of investing activities took place during the year ended December 26, 1992? What was the largest source of cash to finance these activities?

20. Refer to Federal Express Corporation's consolidated statement of cash flows shown in Appendix G. (*a*) Which method was used to calculate net cash provided by operating activities? (*b*) Why was the increase in receivables subtracted rather than added in the calculation of net cash provided by operating activities during the year ended May 31, 1993?

Exercises

Exercise 15–1
Classifying transactions on statement of cash flows (direct method)
(LO 1)

The following events occurred during the year. Assuming that the company uses the direct method of reporting cash provided by operating activities, indicate the proper accounting treatment for each event listed below by placing an *x* in the appropriate column.

	Statement of Cash Flows			Footnote Describing Noncash Investing and Financing Activities	Not Reported on Statement or in Footnote
	Operating Activities	Investing Activities	Financing Activities		
a. Long-term bonds payable were retired by issuing common stock.	____	____	____	____	____
b. Surplus merchandise inventory was sold for cash.	____	____	____	____	____
c. Borrowed cash from the bank by signing a nine-month note payable.	____	____	____	____	____
d. Paid cash to purchase a patent.	____	____	____	____	____
e. A six-month note receivable was accepted in exchange for a building that had been used in operations.	____	____	____	____	____
f. Recorded depreciation expense on all plant assets.	____	____	____	____	____
g. A cash dividend that was declared in a previous period was paid in the current period.	____	____	____	____	____

Exercise 15–2
Organizing the statement of cash flows and supporting footnote
(LO 1, 2)

Use the following information about the 19X2 cash flows of Forrest Company to prepare a statement of cash flows under the direct method and a footnote describing noncash investing and financing activities.

Cash and cash equivalents balance, December 31, 19X1	$ 50,000
Cash and cash equivalents balance, December 31, 19X2	140,000
Cash received as interest	5,000
Cash paid for salaries	145,000
Bonds payable retired by issuing common stock (there was no gain or loss on the retirement)	375,000
Cash paid to retire long-term notes payable	250,000
Cash received from sale of equipment	122,500
Cash borrowed on six-month note payable	50,000
Land purchased and financed by long-term note payable	212,500
Cash paid for store equipment	47,500
Cash dividends paid	30,000
Cash paid for other expenses	80,000
Cash received from customers	970,000
Cash paid for merchandise	505,000

Exercise 15–3
Calculating cash flows
(LO 3)

In each of the following cases, use the information provided about the 19X1 operations of Benzar Company to calculate the indicated cash flow:

Case A:	Calculate cash received from customers:	
	Sales revenue	$255,000
	Accounts receivable, January 1	12,600
	Accounts receivable, December 31	17,400
Case B:	Calculate cash paid for insurance:	
	Insurance expense	$ 34,200
	Prepaid insurance, January 1	5,700
	Prepaid insurance, December 31	8,550
Case C:	Calculate cash paid for salaries:	
	Salaries expense	$102,000
	Salaries payable, January 1	6,300
	Salaries payable, December 31	7,500

Exercise 15–4
Calculating cash flows
(LO 3)

In each of the following cases, use the information provided about the 19X1 operations of CNA Company to calculate the indicated cash flow:

Case A:	Calculate cash paid for rent:	
	Rent expense	$ 20,400
	Rent payable, January 1	4,400
	Rent payable, December 31	3,600
Case B:	Calculate cash received from interest:	
	Interest revenue	$ 68,000
	Interest receivable, January 1	6,000
	Interest receivable, December 31	7,200
Case C:	Calculate cash paid for merchandise:	
	Cost of goods sold	$352,000
	Merchandise inventory, January 1	106,400
	Accounts payable, January 1	45,200
	Merchandise inventory, December 31	87,600
	Accounts payable, December 31	56,000

Exercise 15–5
Cash flows from operating activities (direct method)
(LO 2, 3)

Use the following income statement and information about changes in noncash current assets and current liabilities to present the cash flows from operating activities using the direct method:

ALAMO DATA COMPANY
Income Statement
For Year Ended December 31, 19X1

Sales		$606,000
Cost of goods sold		297,000
Gross profit from sales		$309,000
Operating expenses:		
Salaries expense	$82,845	
Depreciation expense	14,400	
Rent expense	16,200	
Amortization expense, patents	1,800	
Utilities expense	6,375	121,620
Total		$187,380
Gain on sale of equipment		2,400
Net income		$189,780

Changes in current asset and current liability accounts during the year, all of which related to operating activities, were as follows:

Accounts receivable	$13,500 increase
Merchandise inventory	9,000 increase
Accounts payable	4,500 decrease
Salaries payable	1,500 decrease

Exercise 15–6
Cash flows from operating activities (indirect method)
(LO 3, 4)

Refer to the information about Alamo Data Company presented in Exercise 15–5. Use the indirect method and calculate the cash provided (or used) by operating activities.

Exercise 15–7
Cash flows from operating activities (indirect method)
(LO 4)

Trador Company's 19X1 income statement showed the following: net income, $728,000; depreciation expense, $90,000; amortization expense, $16,400; and gain on sale of plant assets, $14,000. An examination of the company's current assets and current liabilities showed that the following changes occurred because of operating activities: accounts receivable decreased $36,200; merchandise inventory decreased $104,000; prepaid expenses increased $7,400; accounts payable decreased $18,400; other payables increased $2,800. Use the indirect method to calculate the cash flow from operating activities.

Exercise 15–8
Classifying transactions on statement of cash flows (indirect method)
(LO 4)

The following events occurred during the year. Assuming that the company uses the indirect method of reporting cash provided by operating activities, indicate the proper accounting treatment for each event listed below by placing an *x* in the appropriate column(s).

	Statement of Cash Flows			Footnote Describing Noncash Investing and Financing Activities	Not Reported on Statement or in Footnote
	Operating Activities	Investing Activities	Financing Activities		
a. Land for a new plant was purchased by issuing common stock.	______	______	______	______	______
b. Recorded depreciation expense.	______	______	______	______	______
c. Income taxes payable increased by 15% from prior year.	______	______	______	______	______
d. Declared and paid a cash dividend.	______	______	______	______	______
e. Paid cash to purchase merchandise inventory.	______	______	______	______	______
f. Sold plant equipment at a loss.	______	______	______	______	______
g. Accounts receivable decreased during the year.	______	______	______	______	______

Problems

Problem 15–1
Statement of cash flows (direct method)
(LO 1, 2, 3)

Helix Corporation's 19X2 and 19X1 balance sheets carried the following items:

	December 31	
Debits	**19X2**	**19X1**
Cash	$116,000	$ 78,000
Accounts receivable	62,000	54,000
Merchandise inventory	406,000	356,000
Equipment	222,000	198,000
Totals	$806,000	$686,000
Credits		
Accumulated depreciation, equipment	$104,000	$ 68,000
Accounts payable	46,000	64,000
Income taxes payable	18,000	16,000
Common stock, $2 par value	388,000	372,000
Contributed capital in excess of par value, common stock	132,000	108,000
Retained earnings	118,000	58,000
Totals	$806,000	$686,000

An examination of the company's activities during 19X2, including the income statement, shows the following:

a. Sales (all on credit)		$1,328,000
b. Credits to Accounts Receivable during the period were receipts from customers.		
c. Cost of goods sold	$796,000	
d. Purchases of merchandise were on credit.		
e. Debits to Accounts Payable during the period resulted from payments for merchandise.		
f. Depreciation expense	36,000	
g. Other operating expenses (paid with cash)	334,000	
h. Income taxes expense	28,000	1,194,000
i. The only decreases in Income Taxes Payable were payments of taxes.		
j. Net income		$ 134,000

k. Equipment was purchased for $24,000 cash.
l. Eight thousand shares of stock were issued for cash at $5 per share.
m. The company declared and paid $74,000 of cash dividends during the year.

Required

Prepare a statement of cash flows that reports the cash inflows and outflows from operating activities according to the direct method. Show your supporting calculations.

Problem 15–2
Statement of cash flows (indirect method)
(LO 4)

Refer to Helix Corporation's balance sheets presented in Problem 15–1. The additional information about the company's activities during 19X2 is restated as follows:

a. Net income was $134,000.
b. Accounts receivable increased.
c. Merchandise inventory increased.
d. Accounts payable decreased.
e. Income taxes payable increased.
f. Depreciation expense was $36,000.
g. Equipment was purchased for $24,000 cash.
h. Eight thousand shares of stock were issued for cash at $5 per share.
i. The company declared and paid $74,000 of cash dividends during the year.

Required

Prepare a statement of cash flows that reports the cash inflows and outflows from operating activities according to the indirect method.

Problem 15–3
Cash flows working paper (indirect method)
(LO 1, 5)

Refer to the facts about Helix Corporation presented in Problem 15–1 and Problem 15–2. Prepare a statement of cash flows working paper that follows the indirect method of calculating cash flows from operating activities. Identify the debits and credits in the Analysis of Changes columns with letters that correspond to the list in Problem 15–2.

Problem 15–4
Statement of cash flows (direct method)
(LO 1, 2, 3)

Purcell Company's 19X2 and 19X1 balance sheets included the following items:

	December 31	
Debits	**19X2**	**19X1**
Cash	$ 107,750	$153,250
Accounts receivable	130,000	99,250
Merchandise inventory	547,500	505,000
Prepaid expenses	10,750	12,500
Equipment	319,000	220,000
Totals	$1,115,000	$990,000
Credits		
Accumulated depreciation, equipment	$ 69,250	$ 88,000
Accounts payable	176,250	233,250
Short-term notes payable	20,000	12,500
Long-term notes payable	187,500	107,500
Common stock, $5 par value	337,500	312,500
Contributed capital in excess of par value, common stock	65,000	
Retained earnings	259,500	236,250
Totals	$1,115,000	$990,000

Additional information about the 19X2 activities of the company is as follows:

a.	Sales revenue, all on credit		$992,500
b.	Credits to Accounts Receivable during the period were receipts from customers.		
c.	Cost of goods sold	$500,000	
d.	All merchandise purchases were on credit.		
e.	Debits to Accounts Payable during the period resulted from payments to creditors.		
f.	Depreciation expense	37,500	
g.	Other expenses	273,000	
h.	The other expenses were paid in advance and were initially debited to Prepaid Expenses.		
i.	Income taxes expense (paid with cash)	24,250	
j.	Loss on sale of equipment	10,250	845,000
	The equipment cost $93,750, was depreciated by $56,250, and was sold for $27,250.		
k.	Net income		$147,500

l. Equipment that cost $192,750 was purchased by paying cash of $50,000 and by signing a long-term note payable for the balance.
m. Borrowed $7,500 by signing a short-term note payable.
n. Paid $62,750 to reduce a long-term note payable.
o. Issued 5,000 shares of common stock for cash at $18 per share.
p. Declared and paid cash dividends of $124,250.

Required

Prepare a statement of cash flows that reports the cash inflows and outflows from operating activities according to the direct method. Show your supporting calculations. Also prepare a footnote describing noncash investing and financing activities.

Problem 15–5
Statement of cash flows (indirect method)
(LO 4)

Refer to Purcell Company's balance sheets presented in Problem 15–4. The additional information about the company's activities during 19X2 is restated as follows:

a. Net income was $147,500.
b. Accounts receivable increased.
c. Merchandise inventory increased.
d. Prepaid expenses decreased.
e. Accounts payable decreased.
f. Depreciation expense was $37,500.
g. Equipment that cost $93,750 with accumulated depreciation of $56,250 was sold for $27,250 cash, which caused a loss of $10,250.
h. Equipment that cost $192,750 was purchased by paying cash of $50,000 and (*i*) by signing a long-term note payable for the balance.
j. Borrowed $7,500 by signing a short-term note payable.
k. Paid $62,750 to reduce a long-term note payable.
l. Issued 5,000 shares of common stock for cash at $18 per share.
m. Declared and paid cash dividends of $124,250.

Required

Prepare a statement of cash flows that reports the cash inflows and outflows from operating activities according to the indirect method.

Problem 15–6
Cash flows working paper (indirect method)
(LO 1, 5)

Refer to the facts about Purcell Company presented in Problem 15–4 and Problem 15–5. Prepare a statement of cash flows working paper that follows the indirect method of calculating cash flows from operating activities. Identify the debits and credits in the Analysis of Changes columns with letters that correspond to the list for the company presented in Problem 15–5.

Problem 15–7
Analytical essay
(LO 3)

Write a brief essay explaining why, in preparing a statement of cash flows according to the direct method, it is generally better to determine the changes in cash by analyzing the changes in the noncash accounts rather than by examining the Cash account directly. You should include in your essay an explanation of why the changes in cash for the period equal the changes in the noncash balance sheet accounts.

Problem 15–8
Analytical essay
(LO 5)

The following items might be found on a working paper for a statement of cash flows. Write a brief essay describing where each item appears on a working paper for a statement of cash flows according to the indirect method. Also describe the nature of any debits and/or credits that should be entered in the Analysis of Changes columns next to each item, and any balancing entries.

1. Accounts receivable.
2. Depreciation expense.
3. Payment for purchase of plant assets.

Provocative Problems

Provocative Problem 15–1
Griffin Company
(LO 3)

Griffin Company's 19X2 statement of cash flows appeared as follows:

Cash flows from operating activities:		
Cash received from customers	$903,600	
Cash paid for merchandise	(473,550)	
Cash paid for other operating expenses	(244,500)	
Cash paid for income taxes	(26,100)	
Net cash provided by operating activities		$159,450
Cash flows from investing activities:		
Cash received from sale of office equipment	$ 13,950	
Cash paid for store equipment	(21,000)	
Net cash used by investing activities		(7,050)
Cash flows from financing activities:		
Cash paid to retire bonds payable	$ (76,650)	
Cash paid for dividends	(37,500)	
Net cash used in financing activities		(114,150)
Net increase in cash		$ 38,250
Cash balance at beginning of year		47,850
Cash balance at end of year		$ 86,100

Griffin's beginning and ending balance sheets were as follows:

	December 31	
Debits	**19X2**	**19X1**
Cash	$ 86,100	$ 47,850
Accounts receivable	68,250	79,650
Merchandise inventory	312,000	292,950
Prepaid expenses	7,200	3,300
Equipment	271,650	293,400
Totals	$745,200	$717,150
Credits		
Accumulated depreciation, equipment	$123,900	$ 95,100
Accounts payable	57,600	67,500
Income taxes payable	10,200	8,850
Dividends payable	–0–	9,000
Bonds payable	–0–	75,000
Common stock, $10 par value	337,500	337,500
Retained earnings	216,000	124,200
Totals	$745,200	$717,150

An examination of the company's statements and accounts showed:

a. All sales were made on credit.

b. All merchandise purchases were on credit.

c. Accounts Payable balances resulted from merchandise purchases.

d. Prepaid expenses relate to other operating expenses.

e. Equipment that cost $42,750 with accumulated depreciation of $22,200 was sold for cash.

f. Equipment was purchased for cash.

g. The change in the balance of Accumulated Depreciation resulted from depreciation expense and from the sale of equipment.

h. The change in the balance of Retained Earnings resulted from dividend declarations and net income.

Required

Present Griffin's income statement for 19X2. Show your supporting calculations.

Provocative Problem 15–2
Apple Computer, Inc.
(LO 1)

Apple Computer, Inc.

Look in Appendix F at the end of the book to find Apple Computer, Inc.'s statement of cash flows. Based on your examination of that statement, answer the following questions:

1. Was Apple's statement of cash flows prepared according to the direct method or the indirect method?
2. During each of the fiscal years 1992, 1991, and 1990, was the cash provided from operating activities more or less than the cash paid for dividends?
3. In calculating the net cash provided from operating activities, which single item represented the largest addition to net income during 1992? During 1991?
4. In calculating the net cash provided from operating activities, which single item represented the largest subtraction from net income during 1992? During 1991?
5. What was the largest cash inflow from investing activities during 1992?
6. What was the largest cash outflow from investing activities during 1992?
7. Did the company issue any new stock for cash during 1992?
8. Compare the payments to purchase and retire capital stock during 1992 and 1991.

Answers to Objective Review Questions

LO 1 (*b*)	LO 3 (*a*)	LO 5 (*a*)
LO 2 (*a*)	LO 4 (*d*)	LO 6 (*c*)

CHAPTER

16

Analyzing Financial Statements

Chapter 16 demonstrates how to use the information in financial statements to evaluate the activities and financial status of a business. The chapter explains how you can relate the numbers in financial statements to each other and expands your ability to interpret the ratios we described in previous chapters.

Learning Objectives

After studying Chapter 16 you should be able to:

1. Explain the relationship between financial reporting and general purpose financial statements.
2. Describe, prepare, and interpret comparative financial statements and common-size comparative statements.
3. Calculate and explain the interpretation of the ratios, turnovers, and rates of return used to evaluate (*a*) short-term liquidity, (*b*) long-term risk and capital structure, and (*c*) operating efficiency and profitability.
4. State the limitations associated with using financial statement ratios and the sources from which standards for comparison may be obtained.
5. Define or explain the words and phrases listed in the chapter glossary.

Financial Reporting

LO 1 Explain the relationship between financial reporting and general purpose financial statements.

Many people receive and analyze financial information about business firms. These people include managers, employees, directors, customers, suppliers, current and potential owners, current and potential lenders, brokers, regulatory authorities, lawyers, economists, labor unions, financial advisors, and financial analysts. Some of these, such as managers and some regulatory agencies, are able to gain access to specialized financial reports that meet their specific interests. However, the others must rely on the **general purpose financial statements** that companies publish periodically. General purpose financial statements include the (1) income statement, (2) balance sheet, (3) statement of changes in stockholders' equity (or statement of retained earnings), (4) statement of cash flows, and (5) footnotes related to the statements.

Financial reporting is intended to provide useful information to investors, creditors, and others for making investment, credit, and similar decisions. The information should help the users assess the amounts, timing, and uncertainty of prospective cash inflows and outflows.

Financial reporting includes communicating through a variety of means in addition to the financial statements. Some examples are reports filed with the Securities and Exchange Commission, news releases, and management letters or analyses included in annual reports. For an example, look in Appendix F at the section of Apple Computer, Inc.'s annual report called Management Discussion and Analysis of Financial Condition and Results of Operations.

Comparative Statements

LO 2 Describe, prepare, and interpret comparative financial statements and common-size comparative statements.

In analyzing financial information, individual items taken alone usually are not very revealing. However, important relationships exist between items and groups of items. As a result, financial statement analysis involves identifying and describing relationships between items and groups of items and changes in those items.

You can see changes in financial statement items more clearly when amounts for two or more successive accounting periods are placed side by side in columns on a single statement. Statements prepared in this manner are called **comparative statements.** Each financial statement can be presented in this comparative format.

In its simplest form, a comparative balance sheet consists of the amounts from two or more successive balance sheet dates arranged side by side. However, the usefulness of the statement can be improved by also showing each item's dollar amount of change and percentage change. When this is done, large dollar or percentage changes are more readily apparent. Illustration 16–1 shows this type of comparative balance sheet for Microsoft Corporation.

A comparative income statement is prepared in the same way. Amounts for two or more successive periods are placed side by side, with dollar and percentage changes in additional columns. Look at Illustration 16–2 to see Microsoft Corporation's comparative income statement.

Calculating Percentage Increases and Decreases

To calculate the percentage increases and decreases on comparative statements, divide the dollar increase or decrease of an item by the amount shown for the item in the base year. If no amount is shown in the base year, or if the base year amount is negative (such as a net loss), a percentage increase or decrease cannot be calculated.

In this text, percentages and ratios typically are rounded to one or two decimal places. However, there is no uniform practice on this matter. In general, percentages should be carried out far enough to be meaningful. They should not be carried out so far that the important relationships become lost in the length of the numbers.

Analyzing and Interpreting Comparative Statements

In analyzing comparative data, study any items that show significant dollar or percentage changes. Then, try to identify the reasons for each change and, if possible, determine whether they are favorable or unfavorable. For example, in Illustration 16–1, the first item, Cash and short-term investments, shows a $945 million increase (70.3%). To a large extent, this may be explained by the increase in two other items: the $429 million increase in "Common stock and paid-in capital" and the $620 million increase in "Retained earnings."

Note that Microsoft's liabilities increased by $116 million. In light of this, the $945 million increase in "Cash and short-term investments" might appear to be an excessive investment in highly liquid assets that usually earn a low return. However, the company's very strong and liquid financial position indi-

ILLUSTRATION 16–1

MICROSOFT CORPORATION
Comparative Balance Sheet
June 30, 1993, and June 30, 1992
(in millions)

	June 30		Amount of Increase or (Decrease) during 1993	Percent of Increase or (Decrease) during 1993
	1993	1992		
Assets				
Current assets:				
Cash and short-term investments	$2,290	$1,345	$ 945	70.3
Accounts receivable, net of allowances of $76 and $57	338	270	68	25.2
Inventories	127	86	41	47.7
Other	95	69	26	37.7
Total current assets	$2,850	$1,770	$1,080	61.0
Property, plant, and equipment—net	867	767	100	13.0
Other assets	88	103	(15)	(14.6)
Total assets	$3,805	$2,640	$1,165	44.1
Liabilities and Stockholders' Equity				
Current liabilities:				
Accounts payable	$ 239	$ 196	$ 43	21.9
Accrued compensation	86	62	24	38.7
Income taxes payable	127	73	54	74.0
Other	111	116	(5)	(4.3)
Total current liabilities	$ 563	$ 447	$ 116	26.0
Commitments and contingencies	—	—		
Stockholders' equity:				
Common stock and paid-in capital—shares authorized 500; issued and outstanding 282 and 272	1,086	657	429	65.3
Retained earnings	2,156	1,536	620	40.4
Total stockholders' equity	$3,242	$2,193	$1,049	47.8
Total liabilities and stockholders' equity	$3,805	$2,640	$1,165	44.1

cates an outstanding ability to respond to new opportunities such as the acquisition of other companies.

Now look at the comparative income statement for Microsoft in Illustration 16–2. Microsoft's rapid growth is reflected by its 36% increase in net revenues. In fact, we should point out that the growth in 1993 continued a very strong trend established in prior years. (Later, we present data showing that net revenues in 1993 were 467% of net revenues in 1989.) Perhaps the most fundamental reason for this is the company's commitment to research and development. Note that research and development expenses were $470 million in 1993, up $118 million from 1992.

All of the income statement items (except "Other") reflect the company's rapid growth. The increases ranged from 30.7% to 46.4%. Especially note the large $351 million or 41.1% increase in "Sales and marketing." This suggests the company's leadership and strong response to competition in the software industry. Although the dollar increase in "Interest income—net" was only $26 million, this amounted to a 46.4% increase. This is consistent with the

ILLUSTRATION 16-2

MICROSOFT CORPORATION
Comparative Income Statement
For Years Ended June 30, 1993 and 1992
(in millions)

	Years Ended June 30		Amount of Increase or (Decrease) during 1993	Percent of Increase or (Decrease) during 1993
	1993	1992		
Net revenues	$3,753	$2,759	$ 994	36.0
Cost of revenues	633	467	166	35.6
Gross profit	$3,120	$2,292	$ 828	36.1
Operating expenses:				
Research and development	$ 470	$ 352	$ 118	33.5
Sales and marketing	1,205	854	351	41.1
General and administrative	119	90	29	32.2
Total operating expenses	$1,794	$1,296	$ 498	38.4
Operating income	$1,326	$ 996	$ 330	33.1
Interest income—net	82	56	26	46.4
Other*	(7)	(11)	(4)	(36.4)
Income before income taxes	$1,401	$1,041	$ 360	34.6
Provision for income taxes	448	333	115	34.5
Net income	$ 953	$ 708	$ 245	34.6
Earnings per share	$ 3.15	$ 2.41	$0.74	30.7
Weighted average shares outstanding	303	294		

*On this line, the (7) and (11) are shown in parentheses because they represent expenses that are subtracted in the calculation of income. The (4) is in parentheses because the "Other" item decreased from 11 to 7. In the third column, the expense decrease (4) must be added to the $330 and $26 increases in operating income and interest income to reconcile the $360 increase in Income before income taxes.

large increase in Cash and short-term investments reported on the balance sheet.

Trend Percentages

Trend percentages (also known as *index numbers*) can be used to describe changes that have occurred from one period to the next. They also are used to compare data that cover a number of years. To calculate trend percentages:

1. Select a base year and assign each item on the base year statement a weight of 100%.
2. Then, express each item from the statements for the other years as a percentage of its base year amount. To determine these percentages, divide the amounts in the nonbase years by the amount of the item in the base year.

For example, consider the following data for Microsoft Corporation:

	1993	1992	1991	1990	1989
Net revenues	$3,753	$2,759	$1,843	$1,183	$804
Cost of revenues	633	467	362	253	204
Gross profit	$3,120	$2,292	$1,481	$ 930	$600

ILLUSTRATION 16–3 *Trend Lines Showing Percentage Changes in Net Revenues, Cost of Revenues, and Gross Profit*

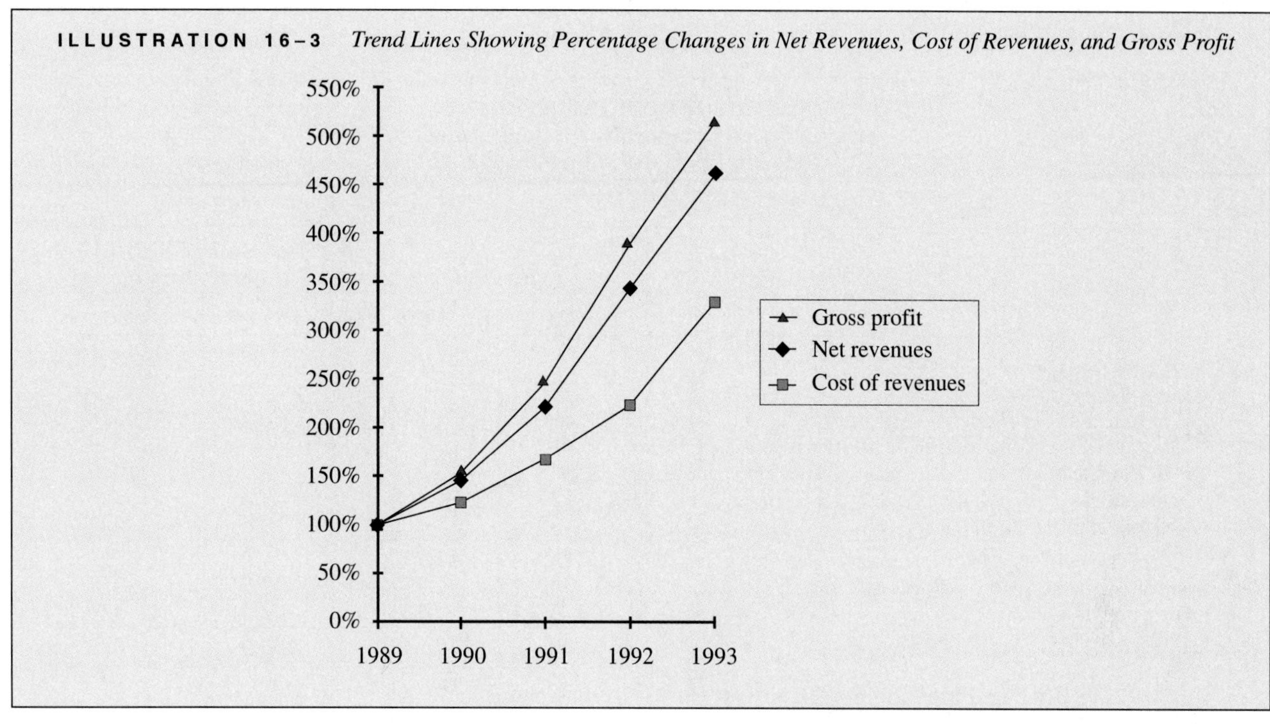

Using 1989 as the base year, we calculate the trend percentages for each year by dividing the dollar amounts in each year by the 1989 dollar amounts. When the percentages are calculated, the trends for these items appear as follows:

	1993	1992	1991	1990	1989
Net revenues	466.8%	343.2%	229.2%	147.1%	100%
Cost of revenues	310.3	228.9	177.5	124.0	100
Gross profit	520.0	382.0	246.8	155.0	100

Illustration 16–3 presents the same data in a graph. A graph can help you identify trends and detect changes in their direction or growth rates. For example, note that the gross profit line and the net revenues line were bending upward from 1989 to 1991 but were essentially straight from 1991 to 1993. In other words, the rates of increase were improving from 1989 to 1991 but were basically unchanged from 1991 to 1993.

A graph also may help you identify and understand the relationships between items. For example, the graph in Illustration 16–3 shows that through 1993, cost of revenues increased at a rate that was somewhat less than the increase in net revenues. Further, the differing trends in these two items had a clear effect on the percentage changes in gross profit. That is, gross profit increased each year at a faster rate than net revenues or cost of revenues.

The analysis of financial statement items also may include the relationships between items on different financial statements. For example, note the following comparison of Microsoft's total assets and net revenues:

	1993	1989	1993 Amount as a Percentage of 1989
Net revenues	$3,753	$804	466.8
Total assets (fiscal year-end)	3,805	721	527.7

ILLUSTRATION 16-4

MICROSOFT CORPORATION
Common-Size Comparative Balance Sheet
June 30, 1993, and June 30, 1992
(in millions)

	June 30		Common-Size Percentages	
	1993	**1992**	**1993**	**1992**
Assets				
Current assets:				
Cash and short-term investments	$2,290	$1,345	60.2	50.9
Accounts receivable, net of allowances of $76 and $57	338	270	8.9	10.2
Inventories	127	86	3.3	3.3
Other	95	69	2.5	2.6
Total current assets	$2,850	$1,770	74.9	67.0
Property, plant, and equipment—net	867	767	22.8	29.1
Other assets	88	103	2.3	3.9
Total assets	$3,805	$2,640	100.0	100.0
Liabilities and Stockholders' Equity				
Current liabilities:				
Accounts payable	$ 239	$ 196	6.3	7.4
Accrued compensation	86	62	2.3	2.3
Income taxes payable	127	73	3.3	2.8
Other	111	116	2.9	4.4
Total current liabilities	$ 563	$ 447	14.8	16.9
Commitments and contingencies	—	—		
Stockholders' equity:				
Common stock and paid-in capital—shares authorized 500; issued and outstanding 282 and 272	1,086	657	28.5	24.9
Retained earnings	2,156	1,536	56.7	58.2
Total stockholders' equity	$3,242	$2,193	85.2	83.1
Total liabilities and stockholders' equity	$3,805	$2,640	100.0	100.0

The rate of increase in total assets was even larger than the increase in net revenues. Was this change favorable? We cannot say for sure. It might suggest that the company is no longer able to use its assets as efficiently as in earlier years. On the other hand, it might mean that the company is poised for even greater growth in future years. Financial statement analysis often leads the analyst to ask questions, without providing one clear answer.

Common-Size Comparative Statements

Although the comparative statements illustrated so far show how each item has changed over time, they do not emphasize the relative importance of each item. Changes in the relative importance of each financial statement item are shown more clearly by **common-size comparative statements.**

In common-size statements, each item is expressed as a percentage of a *base amount.* For a common-size balance sheet, the base amount is usually the amount of total assets. This total is assigned a value of 100%. (Of course, the total amount of liabilities plus owners' equity also equals 100%.) Then, each asset, liability, and owners' equity item is shown as a percentage of total assets

ILLUSTRATION 16–5

MICROSOFT CORPORATION
Common-Size Comparative Income Statement
For Years Ended June 30, 1993 and 1992
(in millions)

	Years Ended June 30		Common-Size Percentages	
	1993	1992	1993	1992
Net revenues	$3,753	$2,759	100.0	100.0
Cost of revenues	633	467	16.9	16.9
Gross profit	$3,120	$2,292	83.1	83.1
Operating expenses:				
Research and development	$ 470	$ 352	12.5	12.8
Sales and marketing	1,205	854	32.1	31.0
General and administrative	119	90	3.2	3.3
Total operating expenses	$1,794	$1,296	47.8	47.0*
Operating income	$1,326	$ 996	35.3	36.1
Interest income—net	82	56	2.2	2.0
Other	(7)	(11)	(0.2)	(0.4)
Income before income taxes	$1,401	$1,041	37.3	37.7
Provision for income taxes	448	333	11.9	12.1
Net income	$ 953	$ 708	25.4	25.7*
Earnings per share	$ 3.15	$ 2.41		
Weighted-average shares outstanding	303	294		

*Does not foot due to rounding.

(or total liabilities plus owners' equity). If you present a company's successive balance sheets in this way, changes in the mixture of the assets or liabilities and equity are more readily apparent.

For example, look at the common-size comparative balance sheet for Microsoft in Illustration 16–4. Note that Cash and short-term investments amounted to 50.9% of total assets at the end of the 1992 fiscal year. By comparison, they were 60.2% of total assets at the end of 1993.

In producing a common-size income statement, the amount of net sales is usually the base amount and is also assigned a value of 100%. Then, each statement item appears as a percentage of net sales. If you think of the 100% sales amount as representing one sales dollar, then the remaining items show how each sales dollar was distributed among costs, expenses, and profit. For example, the comparative income statement in Illustration 16–5 shows that for each dollar of Microsoft's net revenue during 1993, research and development expenses amounted to 12.5 cents. In 1992, research and development consumed 12.8 cents of each sales dollar.

Common-size percentages help the analyst see any potentially important changes in a company's expenses. In the case of Microsoft, the relative size of each expense changed very little from 1992 to 1993.

Many corporate annual reports include graphic presentations such as those in Illustration 16–6 from Microsoft's 1993 report. The pie chart on the left side of the illustration shows the revenues generated by each of the company's product groups. The pie chart on the right shows the revenues by sales channel. In that chart, OEM refers to original equipment manufacturers. In the annual report, the data for these charts did not appear in the financial

ILLUSTRATION 16–6 *Pie-Chart Presentations, Microsoft Corporation*

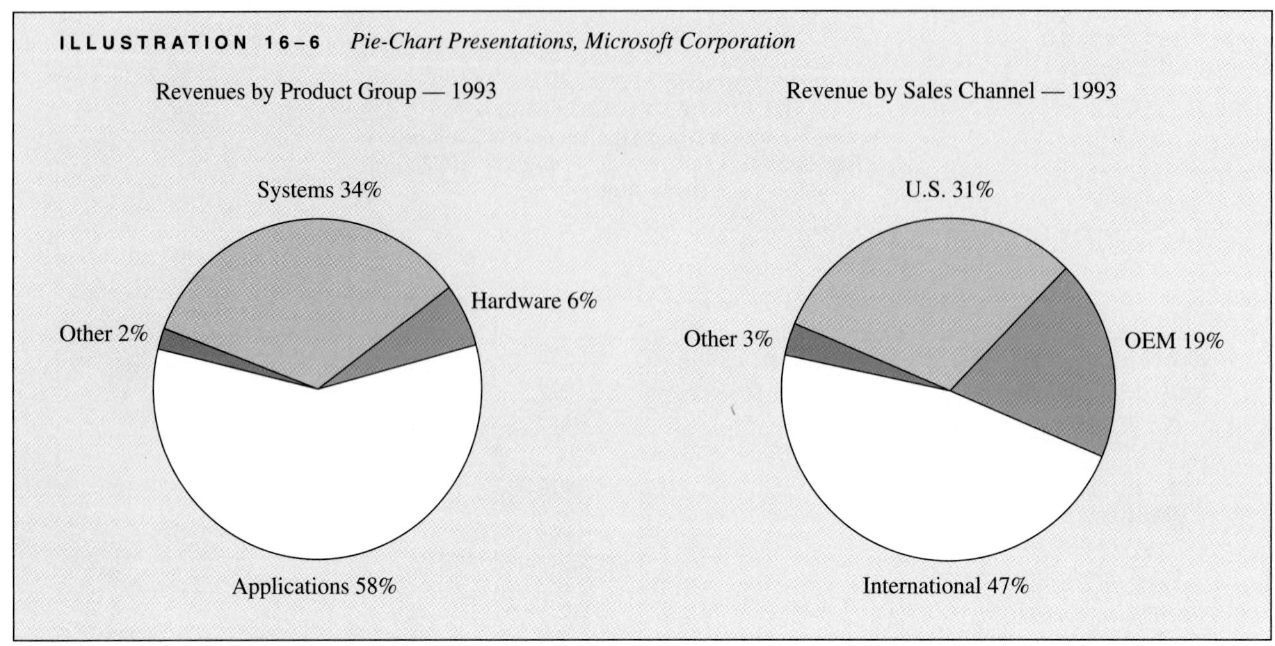

statements. Instead, they were included as part of the discussion and analysis by management.

Analysis of Short-Term Liquidity

LO 3 Calculate and explain the interpretation of the ratios, turnovers, and rates of return used to evaluate (*a*) short-term liquidity, (*b*) long-term risk and capital structure, and (*c*) operating efficiency and profitability.

The amount of current assets less current liabilities is called the **working capital** or *net working capital* of a business. A business must maintain an adequate amount of working capital to meet current debts, carry sufficient inventories, and take advantage of cash discounts. Indeed, a business that runs out of working capital cannot meet its current obligations or continue operations.

Current Ratio

When evaluating the working capital of a business, you must look beyond the dollar amount of current assets less current liabilities. Also consider the relationship between the amounts of current assets and current liabilities. Recall from Chapter 3 that the *current ratio* describes a company's ability to pay its short-term obligations. The current ratio relates current assets to current liabilities, as follows:

$$\text{Current ratio} = \frac{\text{Current assets}}{\text{Current liabilities}}$$

For example, using the information in Illustration 16–1, Microsoft's working capital positions and current ratios at the end of its 1993 and 1992 years were

	June 30, 1993	June 30, 1992
Current assets	$2,850	$1,770
Current liabilities	563	447
Working capital	$2,287	$1,323
Current ratio:		
$2,850/$563	5.1 to 1	
$1,770/$447		4.0 to 1

A high current ratio generally indicates a strong position because a high ratio suggests the company is capable of meeting its current obligations. On the other hand, a company might have a current ratio that is too high. This condition means that the company has invested too much in current assets compared to its needs. Normally, current assets do not generate very much additional revenue. Therefore, if a company invests too much in current assets, the investment is not being used efficiently.

Years ago, bankers and other creditors often used a current ratio of 2 to 1 as a rule of thumb in evaluating the debt-paying ability of a credit-seeking company. A company with a 2 to 1 current ratio was generally thought to be a good credit risk in the short run. However, most lenders realize that the 2 to 1 rule of thumb is not a good test of debt-paying ability. Whether a company's current ratio is good or bad depends on at least three factors:

1. The nature of the company's business.
2. The composition of its current assets.
3. The turnover rate for some of its current assets.

Whether a company's current ratio is adequate depends on the nature of its business. A service company that has no inventories other than supplies and that grants little or no credit may be able to operate on a current ratio of less than 1 to 1 if its sales generate enough cash to pay its current liabilities on time. On the other hand, a company that sells high-fashion clothing or furniture may occasionally misjudge customer demand. If this happens, the company's inventory may not generate as much cash as expected. A company that faces risks like these may need a current ratio of much more than 2 to 1 to protect its liquidity.

Therefore, when you study the adequacy of working capital, consider the type of business under review. Before you decide that a company's current ratio is too low or too high, compare the company's current ratio with ratios of other successful companies in the same industry. Another important source of insight is to observe how the ratio has changed over time.

Keep in mind that the current ratio can be affected by a company's choice of an inventory flow assumption. For example, a company that uses LIFO tends to report a smaller amount of current assets than if it uses FIFO. Therefore, consider the underlying factors before deciding that a given current ratio is acceptable.

Also consider the composition of a company's current assets when you evaluate its working capital position. Cash and short-term investments are more liquid than accounts and notes receivable. And, short-term receivables normally are more liquid than merchandise inventory. Cash can be used to pay current debts at once. But, accounts receivable and merchandise inventory must be converted into cash before payments can be made. Therefore, an excessive amount of receivables and inventory could weaken the company's ability to pay its current liabilities.

One way to take the composition of current assets into account is to evaluate the acid-test ratio. We discuss this next. Then, we examine the turnover rates for receivables and inventories.

Acid-Test Ratio

Recall from Chapter 5 that an easily calculated check on current asset composition is the *acid-test ratio,* also called the *quick ratio.* Quick assets are cash, short-term investments, accounts receivable, and notes receivable. These are the most liquid types of current assets. Calculate the ratio as follows:

$$\text{Acid-test ratio} = \frac{\text{Quick assets}}{\text{Current liabilities}}$$

Using the information in Illustration 16–1, we calculate Microsoft's acid-test ratios as follows:

	June 30, 1993	June 30, 1992
Cash and short-term investments	$2,290	$1,345
Accounts receivable, net of allowances . .	338	270
Total quick assets	$2,628	$1,615
Current liabilities	$ 563	$ 447
Acid-test ratio:		
$2,628/$563	4.7 to 1	
$1,615/$447		3.6 to 1

A traditional rule of thumb for an acceptable acid-test ratio is 1 to 1. However, as is true for all financial ratios, you should be skeptical about rules of thumb. The working capital requirements of a company are also affected by how frequently the company converts its current assets into cash. Thus, a careful analysis of a company's short-term liquidity should include additional analyses of its receivables and inventories.

Accounts Receivable Turnover

One way to measure how frequently a company converts its receivables into cash is to calculate the *accounts receivable turnover.* As you learned in Chapter 7, this is calculated as follows:

$$\text{Accounts receivable turnover} = \frac{\text{Net sales}}{\text{Average accounts receivable}}$$

Although this ratio is widely known as accounts receivable turnover, all short-term receivables from customers normally are included in the denominator. Thus, if a company has short-term notes receivable, those balances should be included with the accounts receivable. In the numerator, the calculation would be more precise if credit sales were used. Usually, however, net sales is used because information about credit sales is not available.

Applying the formula to Microsoft's 1993 fiscal year results, the company's accounts receivable turnover was

$$\frac{\$3,753}{(\$338 + \$270)/2} = 12.3 \text{ times}$$

If accounts receivable are collected quickly, the accounts receivable turnover is high. In general, this is favorable because it means that the company does not have to commit large amounts of capital to accounts receivable. However, an accounts receivable turnover may be too high. This might occur when credit terms are so restrictive they negatively affect sales volume.

Sometimes, the ending accounts receivable balance can substitute for the average balance in calculating accounts receivable turnover. This is acceptable if the effect is not significant. Also, some analysts prefer using gross accounts receivable before subtracting the allowance for doubtful accounts. However, balance sheets may report only the net amount of accounts receivable.

Days' Sales Uncollected

Accounts receivable turnover is only one way to measure how frequently a company collects its accounts. Another method is to calculate the *days' sales uncollected,* which we defined in Chapter 6 as

$$\text{Days' sales uncollected} = \frac{\text{Accounts receivable}}{\text{Net sales}} \times 365$$

Although this formula takes the usual approach of placing accounts receivable in the numerator, short-term notes receivable from customers should be included. To illustrate, we refer to the information about Microsoft in Illustrations 16–1 and 16–2. The days' sales uncollected on June 30, 1993, was

$$\frac{\$338}{\$3{,}753} \times 365 = 32.9 \text{ days}$$

Days' sales uncollected has more meaning if you know the credit terms. A rule of thumb is that days' sales uncollected: (*a*) should not exceed one and one third times the days in the credit period, if discounts are not offered; (*b*) should not exceed one and one third times the days in its discount period, if discounts are offered.

Turnover of Merchandise Inventory

Working capital requirements are also affected by how long a company holds merchandise inventory before selling it. This effect can be measured by calculating *merchandise turnover,* which we defined in Chapter 8 as

$$\text{Merchandise turnover} = \frac{\text{Cost of goods sold}}{\text{Average merchandise inventory}}$$

Using the cost of revenues and inventories information in Illustrations 16–1 and 16–2, we calculate Microsoft's merchandise turnover during 1993 as follows (cost of goods sold is called *cost of revenues* on Microsoft's income statement):

$$\frac{\$633}{(\$127 + \$86)/2} = 5.9 \text{ times}$$

In this calculation, the average inventory was estimated by averaging the beginning and the ending inventories for 1993. In case the beginning and ending inventories do not represent the amount normally on hand, an average of the quarterly inventories may be used, if that is available.

From a working capital point of view, a company with a high turnover requires a smaller investment in inventory than one that produces the same sales with a low turnover. On the other hand, the merchandise turnover may be too high if a company keeps such a small inventory that sales volume is restricted.

Days' Stock on Hand

Recall from Chapter 8 that *days' stock on hand* is another means of evaluating the liquidity of a company's inventory. It relates to inventory in a similar fashion as day's sales uncollected relates to receivables. The calculation is

$$\text{Days' stock on hand} = \frac{\text{Ending inventory}}{\text{Cost of goods sold}} \times 365$$

Applying the formula to Microsoft's 1993 information, we calculate days' stock on hand as

$$\frac{\$127}{\$633} \times 365 = 73.2 \text{ days}$$

Assuming the particular products in inventory are those customers demand, the formula estimates that the inventory will be converted into receivables (or cash) in 73.2 days. If all of Microsoft's sales were credit sales, the conversion of inventory to receivables in 73.2 days plus the conversion of receivables to cash in 32.9 days would suggest that the inventory would be converted into cash in about 106 days (73.2 + 32.9 = 106.1).

Analysis of Long-Term Risk and Capital Structure

LO 3 Calculate and explain the interpretation of the ratios, turnovers, and rates of return used to evaluate (*a*) short-term liquidity, (*b*) long-term risk and capital structure, and (*c*) operating efficiency and profitability.

An analysis of working capital evaluates the short-term liquidity of the company. However, analysts are also interested in a company's ability to meet its obligations and provide security to its creditors over the long run. Indicators of this ability include *debt* and *equity* ratios, the relationship between *pledged assets and secured liabilities,* and the company's capacity to earn *sufficient income to pay its fixed interest charges.*

Debt and Equity Ratios

Financial analysts are always interested in the portion of a company's assets contributed by its owners and the portion contributed by creditors. This relationship is described by the debt ratio you learned about in Chapter 2. That ratio expresses total liabilities as a percentage of total assets. The **equity ratio** provides complementary information by expressing total stockholders' equity as a percentage of total assets.

We calculate the debt and equity ratios of Microsoft Corporation as follows:

	1993	1992
a. Total liabilities (all short-term)	$ 563	$ 447
b. Total stockholders' equity	3,242	2,193
c. Total liabilities and stockholders' equity	$3,805	$2,640
Percentages provided by creditors: (*a*/*c*)	14.8%	16.9%
Percentages provided by stockholders: (*b*/*c*)	85.2%	83.1%

Microsoft's financial statements reflect very little debt compared to most companies. It has no long-term liabilities and, at the end of the 1993 year, its current liabilities provide only 14.8% of the total assets. In general, a company is less risky if it has only a small amount of debt in its capital structure. The larger the portion provided by stockholders, the more losses can be absorbed by stockholders before the remaining assets become inadequate to satisfy the claims of creditors.

From the stockholders' point of view, however, including debt in the capital structure of a company may be desirable, so long as the risk is not too great. If a business can earn a return on borrowed capital that is higher than the cost of borrowing, the difference represents increased income to stockholders. Because debt can have the effect of increasing the return to stockholders, the inclusion of debt is sometimes described as *financial leverage.* Companies are said to be highly leveraged if a large portion of their assets are financed by debt.

Pledged Assets to Secured Liabilities

In Chapter 12, we explained how to use the ratio of pledged assets to secured liabilities to evaluate the risk of nonpayment faced by secured creditors. Recall that the ratio also may provide information of interest to unsecured creditors. The ratio is calculated as follows:

$$\text{Pledged assets to secured liabilities} = \frac{\text{Book value of pledged assets}}{\text{Secured liabilities}}$$

Regardless of how helpful this ratio might be in evaluating the risk faced by creditors, the information needed to calculate the ratio is seldom presented in published financial statements. Thus, it is used primarily by persons who have the ability to obtain the information directly from the company managers.

The usual rule-of-thumb minimum value for this ratio is 2 to 1. However, the ratio needs careful interpretation because it is based on the book value of the pledged assets. As you know, book values are not intended to reflect the amount that would be received for the assets in a liquidation sale. Also, the long-term earning ability of the company with pledged assets may be more important than the value of the pledged assets. Creditors prefer that a debtor be able to pay with cash generated by operating activities rather than with cash obtained by liquidating assets.

Times Fixed Interest Charges Earned

As you learned in Chapter 11, the *times fixed interest charges earned* ratio is often calculated to describe the security of the return offered to creditors. The amount of income before the deduction of interest charges and income taxes is the amount available to pay the interest charges. Calculate the ratio as follows:

$$\text{Times fixed interest charges earned} = \frac{\text{Income before interest and income taxes}}{\text{Interest expense}}$$

The larger this ratio, the greater the security for the lenders. A rule of thumb for this statistic is that creditors are reasonably safe if the company earns its fixed interest charges two or more times each year. Look in Illustration 16–2 and observe that Microsoft did not report interest expense as a separate item. Apparently interest expense is not material; probably it is offset against interest income which is reported as "Interest income—net." Also recall from Illustration 16–1 that Microsoft did not have any long-term debt. Furthermore, few if any of the company's current liabilities would be likely to generate interest expense. As a result, we are not able to calculate a times fixed interest charges earned ratio for Microsoft. Yet, we should again recognize that there appears to be little risk for Microsoft's creditors.

Analysis of Operating Efficiency and Profitability

Financial analysts are especially interested in the ability of a company to use its assets efficiently to produce profits for its owners and thus to provide cash flows to them. Several ratios are available to help you evaluate operating efficiency and profitability.

Profit Margin

The operating efficiency of a company can be expressed in two components. The first is the company's *profit margin.* As you learned in Chapter 4, this ratio describes a company's ability to earn a net income from sales. It is measured by expressing net income as a percentage of revenues. For example, we can use the information in Illustration 16–2 to calculate Microsoft's 1993 profit margin as follows:

$$\text{Profit margin} = \frac{\text{Net income}}{\text{Revenues}} = \frac{\$953}{\$3{,}753} = 25.4\%$$

To evaluate the profit margin of a company, consider the nature of the industry in which the company operates. For example, a publishing company might be expected to have a profit margin between 10 and 15%, while a retail supermarket might have a normal profit margin of 1 or 2%.

Total Asset Turnover

The second component of operating efficiency is *total asset turnover,* which describes the ability of the company to use its assets to generate sales. In Chapter 9, you learned to calculate this ratio as follows:

$$\text{Total asset turnover} = \frac{\text{Net sales}}{\text{Average total assets}}$$

In calculating Microsoft's total asset turnover for 1993, we follow the usual practice of averaging the total assets at the beginning and the end of the year. Taking the information from Illustrations 16–1 and 16–2, the calculation is

$$\frac{\$3{,}753}{(\$3{,}805 + \$2{,}640)/2} = 1.165 \text{ times}^{\star}$$

*Carried to three decimal places to avoid later rounding error.

Both profit margin and total asset turnover describe the two basic components of operating efficiency. However, they also evaluate management performance because the management of a company is fundamentally responsible for its operating efficiency.

Return on Total Assets

Because operating efficiency has two basic components (profit margin and total asset turnover), analysts frequently calculate a summary measure of these components. This summary measure is the *return on total assets* that we discussed in Chapter 10. Recall that the calculation is

$$\text{Return on total assets} = \frac{\text{Net income}}{\text{Average total assets}}$$

Applying this to Microsoft's 1993 year, we calculate return on total assets as

$$\frac{\$953}{(\$3{,}805 + \$2{,}640)/2} = 29.6\%$$

Microsoft's 29.6% return on total assets appears very favorable compared to most businesses. However, you should make comparisons with competing companies and alternative investment opportunities before reaching a final conclusion. Also, you should evaluate the trend in the rates of return earned by the company in recent years.

Earlier, we said that the return on total assets summarizes the two components of operating efficiency—profit margin and total asset turnover. The following calculation shows the relationship between these three measures. Notice that both profit margin and total asset turnover contribute to overall operating efficiency, as measured by return on total assets.

Profit margin	×	Total asset turnover	=	Return on total assets
$\frac{\text{Net income}}{\text{Net sales}}$	×	$\frac{\text{Net sales}}{\text{Average total assets}}$	=	$\frac{\text{Net income}}{\text{Average total assets}}$
For Microsoft Corporation:				
25.4%	×	1.165	=	29.6%

Return on Common Stockholders' Equity

Perhaps the most important reason for operating a business is to earn a net income for its owners. The *return on common stockholders' equity* measures the success of a business in reaching this goal. In Chapter 1, we simplified this calculation by basing it on the beginning balance of owners' equity. However, many companies have frequent transactions that involve issuing and perhaps repurchasing stock during each year. Thus, you should allow for these events by calculating the return based on the average stockholders' equity, as follows:

$$\text{Return on common stockholders' equity} = \frac{\text{Net income} - \text{Preferred dividends}}{\text{Average common stockholders' equity}}$$

Recall from Illustration 16–1 that Microsoft did not have any preferred stock outstanding. As a result, we determine Microsoft's 1993 return as follows:

$$\frac{\$953}{(\$3{,}242 + \$2{,}193)/2} = 35.1\%$$

When preferred stock is outstanding, the denominator in the calculation should be the book value of the common stock. In the numerator, the dividends on cumulative preferred stock must be subtracted whether they were declared or are in arrears. If the preferred is not cumulative, the dividends are subtracted only if declared.

Price Earnings Ratio

Recall from Chapter 14 that the *price earnings ratio* is calculated as follows:

$$\text{Price earnings ratio} = \frac{\text{Market price per share}}{\text{Earnings per share}}$$

Sometimes, the predicted earnings per share for the next period is used in the denominator of the calculation. Other times, the reported earnings per share for the most recent period is used. In either case, the ratio is an indicator of the future growth of and risk related to the company's earnings as perceived by investors who establish the market price of the stock.

During the last three months of Microsoft's 1993 year, the market price of its common stock ranged from a low of \$65.50 to a high of \$98. Using the \$3.15 earnings per share that was reported after the year-end, the price earnings ratios for the low and the high were

$$\text{Low: } \frac{\$65.50}{\$3.15} = 20.8 \qquad \text{High: } \frac{\$98.00}{\$3.15} = 31.1$$

In its 1993 annual report, Microsoft's management reported that it did not expect the 1994 revenue growth rates to be as high as those for 1993. Management also indicated that operating expenses as a percentage of revenues might increase. Nevertheless, the price earnings ratios are much higher than for most companies. No doubt, Microsoft's high ratios reflect the expectation of investors that the company would continue to grow at a much higher rate than most companies.

Dividend Yield

As you learned in Chapter 13, *dividend yield* is a statistic used to compare the dividend-paying performance of different investment alternatives. The formula is

$$\text{Dividend yield} = \frac{\text{Annual dividends per share}}{\text{Market price per share}}$$

Some companies may not declare dividends because they need the cash in the business. For example, Microsoft's 1993 annual report stated that the company had not declared any dividends.

Review of Financial Statement Ratios and Statistics for Analysis

To evaluate short-term liquidity, use these ratios:

$$\text{Current ratio} = \frac{\text{Current assets}}{\text{Current liabilities}}$$

$$\text{Acid-test ratio} = \frac{\text{Cash} + \text{Short-term investments} + \text{Current receivables}}{\text{Current liabilities}}$$

$$\text{Accounts receivable turnover} = \frac{\text{Net sales}}{\text{Average accounts receivable}}$$

$$\text{Days' sales uncollected} = \frac{\text{Accounts receivable}}{\text{Net sales}} \times 365$$

$$\text{Merchandise turnover} = \frac{\text{Cost of goods sold}}{\text{Average merchandise inventory}}$$

$$\text{Days' stock on hand} = \frac{\text{Ending inventory}}{\text{Cost of goods sold}} \times 365$$

To evaluate long-term risk and capital structure, use these ratios:

$$\text{Debt ratio} = \frac{\text{Total liabilities}}{\text{Total assets}}$$

$$\text{Equity ratio} = \frac{\text{Total stockholders' equity}}{\text{Total assets}}$$

$$\text{Pledged assets to secured liabilities} = \frac{\text{Book value of pledged assets}}{\text{Secured liabilities}}$$

$$\text{Times fixed interest charges earned} = \frac{\text{Income before interest and taxes}}{\text{Interest expense}}$$

To evaluate operating efficiency and profitability, use these ratios:

$$\text{Profit margin} = \frac{\text{Net income}}{\text{Net sales revenues}}$$

$$\text{Total asset turnover} = \frac{\text{Net sales}}{\text{Average total assets}}$$

$$\text{Return on total assets} = \frac{\text{Net income}}{\text{Average total assets}}$$

$$\text{Return on common stockholders' equity} = \frac{\text{Net income} - \text{Preferred dividends}}{\text{Average common stockholders' equity}}$$

$$\text{Price earnings ratio} = \frac{\text{Market price per common share}}{\text{Earnings per share}}$$

$$\text{Dividend yield} = \frac{\text{Annual dividends per share}}{\text{Market price per share}}$$

Standards of Comparison

LO 4 State the limitations associated with using financial statement ratios and the sources from which standards for comparison may be obtained.

After computing ratios and turnovers in the process of analyzing financial statements, you then have to decide whether the calculated amounts suggest good, bad, or merely average performance by the company. To make these judgments, you must have some bases for comparison. The following are possibilities:

1. An experienced analyst may compare the ratios and turnovers of the company under review with *subjective* standards acquired from past experiences.

2. For purposes of comparison, an analyst may calculate the ratios and turnovers of a selected group of competing companies in the same *industry*.
3. *Published* ratios and turnovers (such as those provided by Dun & Bradstreet) may be used for comparison.
4. Some local and national trade associations gather data from their members and publish *standard* or *average* ratios for their trade or industry. When available, these data can give the analyst a useful basis for comparison.
5. *Rule-of-thumb* standards can be used as a basis for comparison.

Of these five standards, the ratios and turnovers of a selected group of competing companies normally are the best bases for comparison. Rule-of-thumb standards should be applied with great care and then only if they seem reasonable in light of past experience and the industry's norms.

Summary of the Chapter in Terms of Learning Objectives

LO 1 Financial reporting is intended to provide information that is useful to investors, creditors, and others in making investment, credit, and similar decisions. The information is communicated in a variety of ways, including general purpose financial statements. These statements normally include an income statement, balance sheet, statement of changes in stockholders' equity or statement of retained earnings, statement of cash flows, and the related footnotes.

LO 2 Comparative financial statements show amounts for two or more successive periods, sometimes with the changes in the items disclosed in absolute and percentage terms. In common-size statements, each item is expressed as a percentage of a base amount. The base amount for the balance sheet is usually total assets, and the base amount for the income statement is usually net sales.

LO 3 To evaluate the short-term liquidity of a company, calculate a current ratio, an acid-test ratio, the accounts receivable turnover, the days' sales uncollected, the merchandise turnover, and the days' stock on hand.

In evaluating the long-term risk and capital structure of a company, calculate debt and equity ratios, pledged assets to secured liabilities, and the number of times fixed interest charges were earned.

In evaluating operating efficiency and profitability, calculate profit margin, total asset turnover, return on total assets, and return on common stockholders' equity. Other statistics used to evaluate the profitability of alternative investments include the price earnings ratio and the dividend yield.

LO 4 In deciding whether financial statement ratio values are satisfactory, too high, or too low, you must have some bases for comparison. These bases may come from past experience and personal judgment, from ratios of similar companies, or from ratios published by trade associations or other public sources. Traditional rules-of-thumb should be applied with great care and only if they seem reasonable in light of past experience.

Demonstration Problem

Use the financial statements of Precision Co. to satisfy the following requirements:

1. Prepare a comparative income statement showing the percentage increase or decrease for 19X2 over 19X1.
2. Prepare a common-size comparative balance sheet for 19X2 and 19X1.
3. Compute the following ratios as of December 31, 19X2, or for the year ended December 31, 19X2:

a. Current ratio.
b. Acid-test ratio.
c. Accounts receivable turnover.
d. Days' sales uncollected.
e. Merchandise turnover.
f. Debt ratio.
g. Pledged assets to secured liabilities.
h. Times fixed interest charges earned.
i. Profit margin.
j. Total asset turnover.
k. Return on total assets.
l. Return on common stockholders' equity.

PRECISION COMPANY
Comparative Income Statement
For Years Ended December 31, 19X2 and 19X1

	19X2	19X1
Sales	$2,486,000	$2,075,000
Cost of goods sold	1,523,000	1,222,000
Gross profit from sales	$ 963,000	$ 853,000
Operating expenses:		
Advertising expense	$ 145,000	$ 100,000
Sales salaries expense	240,000	280,000
Office salaries expense	165,000	200,000
Insurance expense	100,000	45,000
Supplies expense	26,000	35,000
Depreciation expenses	85,000	75,000
Miscellaneous expense	17,000	15,000
Total operating expenses	$ 778,000	$ 750,000
Operating income	$ 185,000	$ 103,000
Less interest expense	44,000	46,000
Income before taxes	$ 141,000	$ 57,000
Income taxes	47,000	19,000
Net income	$ 94,000	$ 38,000
Earnings per share	$ 0.99	$ 0.40

PRECISION COMPANY
Comparative Balance Sheet
December 31, 19X2, and December 31, 19X1

	19X2	19X1
Assets		
Current assets:		
Cash	$ 79,000	$ 42,000
Short-term investments	65,000	96,000
Accounts receivable (net)	120,000	100,000
Merchandise inventory	250,000	265,000
Total current assets	$ 514,000	$ 503,000
Plant and equipment:		
Store equipment (net)	$ 400,000	$ 350,000
Office equipment (net)	45,000	50,000
Buildings (net)	625,000	675,000
Land	100,000	100,000
Total plant and equipment	$1,170,000	$1,175,000
Total assets	$1,684,000	$1,678,000
Liabilities		
Current liabilities:		
Accounts payable	$ 164,000	$ 190,000
Short-term notes payable	75,000	90,000
Taxes payable	26,000	12,000
Total current liabilities	$ 265,000	$ 292,000
Long-term liabilities:		
Notes payable (secured by mortgage on building and land)	400,000	420,000
Total liabilities	$ 665,000	$ 712,000

Stockholders' Equity		
Contributed capital:		
Common stock, $5 par value	$ 475,000	$ 475,000
Retained earnings	544,000	491,000
Total stockholders' equity	$1,019,000	$ 966,000
Total liabilities and stockholders' equity	$1,684,000	$1,678,000

Planning the Solution

- Set up a four-column income statement; enter the 19X2 and 19X1 amounts in the first two columns, and then enter the dollar change in the third column and the percentage change from 19X1 in the fourth column.
- Set up a four-column balance sheet; enter the 19X2 and 19X1 amounts in the first two columns, and then compute and enter the amount of each item as a percent of total assets.
- Compute the given ratios using the provided numbers; be sure to use the average of the beginning and ending amounts where appropriate.

Solution to Demonstration Problem

1.

PRECISION COMPANY
Comparative Income Statement
For Years Ended December 31, 19X2 and 19X1

	19X2	19X1	Increase (Decrease) in 19X2 Amount	Percent
Sales	$2,486,000	$2,075,000	$411,000	19.8%
Cost of goods sold	1,523,000	1,222,000	301,000	24.6
Gross profit from sales	$ 963,000	$ 853,000	$110,000	12.9
Operating expenses:				
Advertising expense	$ 145,000	$ 100,000	$ 45,000	45.0
Sales salaries expense	240,000	280,000	(40,000)	(14.3)
Office salaries expense	165,000	200,000	(35,000)	(17.5)
Insurance expense	100,000	45,000	55,000	122.2
Supplies expense	26,000	35,000	(9,000)	(25.7)
Depreciation expense	85,000	75,000	10,000	13.3
Miscellaneous expenses	17,000	15,000	2,000	13.3
Total operating expenses	$ 778,000	$ 750,000	$ 28,000	3.7
Operating income	$ 185,000	$ 103,000	$ 82,000	79.6
Less interest expense	44,000	46,000	(2,000)	(4.3)
Income before taxes	$ 141,000	$ 57,000	$ 84,000	147.4
Income taxes	47,000	19,000	28,000	147.4
Net income	$ 94,000	$ 38,000	$ 56,000	147.4
Earnings per share	$ 0.99	$ 0.40	$ 0.59	147.5

2.

PRECISION COMPANY
Common-Size Comparative Balance Sheet
December 31, 19X2, and December 31, 19X1

	December 31		Common-Size Percentages	
	19X2	19X1	19X2*	19X1*
Assets				
Current assets:				
Cash	$ 79,000	$ 42,000	4.7%	2.5%
Short-term investments	65,000	96,000	3.9	5.7
Accounts receivable (net)	120,000	100,000	7.1	6.0
Merchandise inventory	250,000	265,000	14.8	15.8
Total current assets	$ 514,000	$ 503,000	30.5	30.0
Plant and equipment:				
Store equipment (net)	$ 400,000	$ 350,000	23.8	20.9
Office equipment (net)	45,000	50,000	2.7	3.0
Buildings (net)	625,000	675,000	37.1	40.2
Land	100,000	100,000	5.9	6.0
Total plant and equipment	$1,170,000	$1,175,000	69.5	70.0
Total assets	$1,684,000	$1,678,000	100.0	100.0
Liabilities				
Current liabilities:				
Accounts payable	$ 164,000	$ 190,000	9.7	11.3
Short-term notes payable	75,000	90,000	4.5	5.4
Taxes payable	26,000	12,000	1.5	0.7
Total current liabilities	$ 265,000	$ 292,000	15.7	17.4
Long-term liabilities:				
Notes payable (secured by mortgage on building and land)	400,000	420,000	23.8	25.0
Total liabilities	$ 665,000	$ 712,000	39.4	42.4
Stockholders' Equity				
Contributed capital:				
Common stock, $5 par value	$ 475,000	$ 475,000	28.2	28.3
Retained earnings	544,000	491,000	32.3	29.3
Total stockholders' equity	$1,019,000	$ 966,000	60.5	57.6
Total liabilities and equity	$1,684,000	$1,678,000	100.0	100.0

*Columns may not foot due to rounding.

3. **Ratios for 19X2:**
   a. Current ratio: $514,000/$265,000 = 1.9 to 1
   b. Acid-test ratio: ($79,000 + $65,000 + $120,000)/$265,000 = 1.0 to 1
   c. Average receivables: ($120,000 + $100,000)/2 = $110,000
   Accounts receivable turnover: $2,486,000/$110,000 = 22.6 times
   d. Days' sales uncollected: ($120,000/$2,486,000) × 365 = 17.6 days
   e. Average inventory: ($250,000 + $265,000)/2 = $257,500
   Merchandise turnover: $1,523,000/$257,500 = 5.9 times
   f. Debt ratio: $665,000/$1,684,000 = 39.5%
   g. Pledged assets to secured liabilities:
   ($625,000 + $100,000)/$400,000 = 1.8 to 1
   h. Times fixed interest charges earned: $185,000/$44,000 = 4.2 times
   i. Profit margin: $94,000/$2,486,000 = 3.8%
   j. Average total assets: ($1,684,000 + $1,678,000)/2 = $1,681,000
   Total asset turnover: $2,486,000/$1,681,000 = 1.48 times
   k. Return on total assets: $94,000/$1,681,000 = 5.6%
   or 3.8% × 1.48 = 5.6%
   l. Average total equity: ($1,019,000 + $966,000)/2 = $992,500
   Return on common stockholders' equity: $94,000/$992,500 = 9.5%

Glossary

LO 5 Define or explain the words and phrases listed in the chapter glossary.

Common-size comparative statements comparative financial statements in which each amount is expressed as a percentage of a base amount. In the balance sheet, the amount of total assets is usually selected as the base amount and is expressed as 100%. In the income statement, net sales is usually selected as the base amount. p. 578

Comparative statement a financial statement with data for two or more successive accounting periods placed in columns side by side, sometimes with changes shown in dollar amounts and percentages. p. 574

Equity ratio the portion of total assets provided by stockholders' equity, calculated as stockholders' equity divided by total assets. p. 584

Financial reporting the process of providing information that is useful to investors, creditors, and others in making investment, credit, and similar decisions. p. 573

General purpose financial statements statements published periodically for use by a wide variety of interested parties; include the income statement, balance sheet, statement of changes in stockholders' equity (or statement of retained earnings), statement of cash flows, and related footnotes. p. 573

Working capital current assets minus current liabilities. p. 580

Objective Review

Answers to the following questions are listed at the end of this chapter. Be sure that you decide which is the one best answer to each question *before* you check the answers.

LO 1 Which of the following is not an objective of financial reporting?

a. Financial reporting includes reporting information in general purpose financial statements and in other ways such as news announcements and management discussions in annual reports.

b. Financial reporting should provide information that is useful primarily for meeting the needs of corporation managers.

c. Financial reporting should provide information that is useful to investors and creditors and other users in making investment, credit, and similar decisions.

d. Financial reporting should provide information to help users assess the amounts, timing, and uncertainty of prospective cash inflows and outflows.

e. All of the above are objectives of financial reporting.

LO 2 Given the following information for Moyers Corporation, determine the common-size percentages for gross profit from sales:

	19X2	19X1
Net sales	$134,400	$114,800
Cost of goods sold	72,800	60,200

a. 45.8% in 19X2; 47.6% in 19X1.

b. 113% in 19X2; 100% in 19X1.

c. 12.8% increase during 19X2.

d. 100% in 19X2; 88.8% in 19X1.

e. 54.2% in 19X2; 52.4% in 19X1.

LO 3 Times fixed interest charges earned describes:

a. How fast a company collects its accounts.

b. The security of the return offered to creditors.

c. Short-term liquidity.

d. Operating efficiency and profitability.

e. The protection provided to the secured creditors by the mortgages on the assets.

LO 4 Which of the following may be used as a standard for comparing ratios and turnovers computed in the process of analyzing financial statements?

a. Rule-of-thumb standards.

b. Past experience of the analyst with the company under review as well as other companies.

c. Ratios and turnovers of a selected group of companies competing in the same industry as the one whose statements are under review.

d. Data gathered and published by local and national trade associations as standard or average ratios for their industry.

e. All of the above.

LO 5 Current assets minus current liabilities is (are) called:

a. Quick assets.

b. Working capital.

c. Residual assets.

d. Equity.

e. Net assets.

Questions for Class Discussion

1. Who are the intended users of general purpose financial statements?
2. What statements are usually included in the general purpose financial statements published by corporations?
3. Explain the difference between financial reporting and financial statements.
4. What are common-size comparative financial statements?
5. What items are usually assigned a value of 100% on (*a*) a common-size comparative balance sheet and (*b*) a common-size comparative income statement?
6. Why is working capital given special attention in the process of analyzing balance sheets?
7. What are three factors that would influence your decision as to whether a company's current ratio is good or bad?
8. Suggest several reasons why a 2 to 1 current ratio may not be adequate for a particular company.
9. What does a high accounts receivable turnover indicate about a company's short-term liquidity?
10. What is the significance of the number of days' sales uncollected?
11. Why does merchandise turnover provide information about a company's short-term liquidity?
12. Why is the capital structure of a company, as measured by debt and equity ratios, of importance to financial statement analysts?
13. Why must the ratio of pledged assets to secured liabilities be interpreted with caution?
14. What is the relationship between profit margin, total asset turnover, and return on total assets?
15. Why would a company's return on total assets typically be less than its return on common stockholders' equity?
16. What ratios would you calculate for the purpose of evaluating management performance?

17. Using the financial statements for Federal Express Corporation in Appendix G, calculate Federal Express's return on total assets for the fiscal year ended May 31, 1993.

18. Refer to the financial statements for Ben & Jerry's Homemade, Inc., in Appendix G. Calculate Ben & Jerry's equity ratio as of December 26, 1992.

Exercises

Exercise 16–1
Calculating trend percentages
(LO 2)

Calculate trend percentages for the following items, using 19X0 as the base year. Then, state whether the situation shown by the trends appears to be favorable or unfavorable.

	19X4	19X3	19X2	19X1	19X0
Sales	$377,600	$362,400	$338,240	$314,080	$302,000
Cost of goods sold . . .	172,720	164,560	155,040	142,800	136,000
Accounts receivable . .	25,400	24,400	23,200	21,600	20,000

Exercise 16–2
Reporting percentage changes
(LO 2)

Where possible, calculate percentages of increase and decrease for the following:

	19X2	19X1
Short-term investments	$145,200	$110,000
Accounts receivable	28,080	32,000
Notes payable	38,000	-0-

Exercise 16–3
Calculating common-size percentages
(LO 2)

Express the following income statement information in common-size percentages and assess whether the situation is favorable or unfavorable.

CLEARWATER CORPORATION
Comparative Income Statement
For Years Ended December 31, 19X2 and 19X1

	19X2	19X1
Sales	$960,000	$735,000
Cost of goods sold	576,000	382,200
Gross profit from sales	$384,000	$352,800
Operating expenses	216,000	148,470
Net income	$168,000	$204,330

Exercise 16–4
Evaluating short-term liquidity
(LO 3)

TGA Company's December 31 balance sheets included the following data:

	19X3	19X2	19X1
Cash	$ 61,600	$ 71,250	$ 73,600
Accounts receivable, net	177,000	125,000	98,400
Merchandise inventory	223,000	165,000	106,000
Prepaid expenses	19,400	18,750	8,000
Plant assets, net	555,000	510,000	459,000
Total assets	$1,036,000	$890,000	$745,000
Accounts payable	$ 257,800	$150,500	$ 98,500
Long-term notes payable secured by mortgages on plant assets	195,000	205,000	165,000
Common stock, $10 par value	325,000	325,000	325,000
Retained earnings	258,200	209,500	156,500
Total liabilities and stockholders' equity	$1,036,000	$890,000	$745,000

Required

Compare the short-term liquidity positions of the company at the end of 19X3, 19X2, and 19X1, by calculating: (*a*) the current ratio and (*b*) the acid-test ratio. Comment on any changes that occurred.

Exercise 16–5
Evaluating short-term liquidity
(LO 3)

Refer to the information in Exercise 16–4 about TGA Company. The company's income statements for the years ended December 31, 19X3, and 19X2, included the following data:

	19X3	19X2
Sales	$1,345,000	$1,060,000
Cost of goods sold	$ 820,450	$ 689,000
Other operating expenses	417,100	267,960
Interest expense	22,200	24,600
Income taxes	17,050	15,690
Total costs and expenses	$1,276,800	$ 997,250
Net income	$ 68,200	$ 62,750
Earnings per share	$ 2.10	$ 1.93

Required

For the years ended December 31, 19X3, and 19X2, assume all sales were on credit and calculate the following: (*a*) days' sales uncollected, (*b*) accounts receivable turnover, (*c*) merchandise turnover, and (*d*) days' stock on hand. Comment on any changes that occurred from 19X2 to 19X3.

Exercise 16–6
Evaluating long-term risk and capital structure
(LO 3)

Refer to the information in Exercises 16–4 and 16–5 about TGA Company. Compare the long-term risk and capital structure positions of the company at the end of 19X3 and 19X2 by calculating the following ratios: (*a*) debt and equity ratios, (*b*) pledged assets to secured liabilities, and (*c*) times fixed interest charges earned. Comment on any changes that occurred.

Exercise 16–7
Evaluating operating efficiency and profitability
(LO 3)

Refer to the financial statements of TGA Company presented in Exercises 16–4 and 16–5. Evaluate the operating efficiency and profitability of the company by calculating the following: (*a*) profit margin, (*b*) total asset turnover, and (*c*) return on total assets. Comment on any changes that occurred.

Exercise 16–8
Evaluating profitability
(LO 3)

Refer to the financial statements of TGA Company presented in Exercises 16–4 and 16–5. This additional information about the company is known:

Common stock market price, December 31, 19X3	$30.00
Common stock market price, December 31, 19X2	28.00
Annual cash dividends per share in 19X3	.60
Annual cash dividends per share in 19X2	.30

Required

To evaluate the profitability of the company, calculate the following for 19X3 and 19X2: (*a*) return on common stockholders' equity, (*b*) price earnings ratio on December 31, and (*c*) dividend yield.

Exercise 16–9
Determining income effects from common-size and trend percentages
(LO 2)

Common-size and trend percentages for a company's sales, cost of goods sold, and expenses follow:

	Common-Size Percentages			Trend Percentages		
	19X3	**19X2**	**19X1**	**19X3**	**19X2**	**19X1**
Sales	100.0%	100.0%	100.0%	106.5%	105.3%	100.0%
Cost of goods sold	64.5	63.0	60.2	104.1	102.3	100.0
Expenses	16.4	15.9	16.2	96.0	94.1	100.0

Required

Determine whether the company's net income increased, decreased, or remained unchanged during this three-year period.

Problems

Problem 16–1
Calculating ratios and percentages
(LO 2, 3)

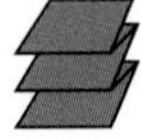

The condensed statements of Stellar Company follow:

STELLAR COMPANY
Comparative Income Statement
For Years Ended December 31, 19X3, 19X2, and 19X1
($000)

	19X3	19X2	19X1
Sales	$148,000	$136,000	$118,000
Cost of goods sold	89,096	85,000	75,520
Gross profit from sales	$ 58,904	$ 51,000	$ 42,480
Selling expenses	$ 20,898	$ 18,768	$ 15,576
Administrative expenses	13,379	11,968	9,735
Total expenses	$ 34,277	$ 30,736	$ 25,311
Income before taxes	$ 24,627	$ 20,264	$ 17,169
State and federal income taxes	4,588	4,148	3,481
Net income	$ 20,039	$ 16,116	$ 13,688

STELLAR COMPANY
Comparative Balance Sheet
December 31, 19X3, 19X2, and 19X1
($000)

	19X3	19X2	19X1
Assets			
Current assets	$24,240	$18,962	$25,324
Long-term investments	–0–	250	1,860
Plant and equipment	45,000	48,000	28,500
Total assets	$69,240	$67,212	$55,684
Liabilities and Stockholders' Equity			
Current liabilities	$10,100	$ 9,980	$ 9,740
Common stock	36,000	36,000	27,000
Other contributed capital	4,500	4,500	3,000
Retained earnings	18,640	16,732	15,944
Total liabilities and stockholders' equity	$69,240	$67,212	$55,684

Required

1. Calculate each year's current ratio.
2. Express the income statement data in common-size percentages.

3. Express the balance sheet data in trend percentages with 19X1 as the base year.
4. Comment on any significant relationship revealed by the ratios and percentages.

Problem 16–2
Calculation and analysis of trend percentages
(LO 2)

The condensed comparative statements of Jasper Company follow:

JASPER COMPANY
Comparative Income Statement
For Years Ended December 31, 19X7–19X1
($000)

	19X7	19X6	19X5	19X4	19X3	19X2	19X1
Sales	$ 797	$ 698	$ 635	$ 582	$ 543	$ 505	$420
Cost of goods sold	573	466	401	351	326	305	250
Gross profit from sales	$ 224	$ 232	$ 234	$ 231	$ 217	$ 200	$170
Operating expenses	170	133	122	90	78	77	65
Net income	$ 54	$ 99	$ 112	$ 141	$ 139	$ 123	$105

JASPER COMPANY
Comparative Balance Sheet
December 31, 19X7–19X1
($000)

	19X7	19X6	19X5	19X4	19X3	19X2	19X1
Assets							
Cash	$ 34	$ 44	$ 46	$ 47	$ 49	$ 48	$ 50
Accounts receivable, net	240	252	228	175	154	146	102
Merchandise inventory	869	632	552	466	418	355	260
Other current assets	23	21	12	22	19	19	10
Long-term investments	-0-	-0-	-0-	68	68	68	68
Plant and equipment, net	1,060	1,057	926	522	539	480	412
Total assets	$2,226	$2,006	$1,764	$1,300	$1,247	$1,116	$902
Liabilities and Equity							
Current liabilities	$ 560	$ 471	$ 309	$ 257	$ 223	$ 211	$136
Long-term liabilities	597	520	506	235	240	260	198
Common stock	500	500	500	420	420	320	320
Other contributed capital	125	125	125	90	90	80	80
Retained earnings	444	390	324	298	274	245	168
Total liabilities and equity	$2,226	$2,006	$1,764	$1,300	$1,247	$1,116	$902

Required

1. Calculate trend percentages for the items of the statements using 19X1 as the base year.
2. Analyze and comment on the situation shown in the statements.

Problem 16–3
Calculation of financial statement ratios
(LO 3)

The 19X2 financial statements of Oltorf Corporation follow:

OLTORF CORPORATION
Income Statement
For Year Ended December 31, 19X2

Sales		$697,200
Cost of goods sold:		
Merchandise inventory, December 31, 19X1	$ 64,800	
Purchases	455,800	
Goods available for sale	$520,600	
Merchandise inventory, December 31, 19X2	62,300	
Cost of goods sold		458,300
Gross profit from sales		$238,900
Operating expenses		122,700
Operating income		$116,200
Interest expense		7,100
Income before taxes		$109,100
Income taxes		17,800
Net income		$ 91,300

OLTORF CORPORATION
Balance Sheet
December 31, 19X2

Assets		Liabilities and Stockholders' Equity	
Cash	$ 18,000	Accounts payable	$ 32,600
Short-term investments	14,700	Accrued wages payable	4,200
Accounts receivable, net	55,800	Income taxes payable	4,800
Notes receivable (trade)	6,200	Long-term note payable, secured by mortgage on plant assets	125,000
Merchandise inventory	62,300		
Prepaid expenses	2,800		
Plant assets, net	306,300	Common stock, $1 par value	180,000
		Retained earnings	119,500
Total assets	$466,100	Total liabilities and stockholders' equity	$466,100

Assume that all sales were on credit. On the December 31, 19X1, balance sheet, the assets totaled $367,500, common stock was $180,000, and retained earnings were $86,700.

Required

Calculate the following: (*a*) current ratio, (*b*) acid-test ratio, (*c*) days' sales uncollected, (*d*) merchandise turnover, (*e*) days' stock on hand, (*f*) ratio of pledged assets to secured liabilities, (*g*) times fixed interest charges earned, (*h*) profit margin, (*i*) total asset turnover, (*j*) return on total assets, and (*k*) return on common stockholders' equity.

Problem 16–4
Comparative analysis of financial statement ratios
(LO 3)

Two companies that operate in the same industry as competitors are being evaluated by a bank that can lend money to only one of them. Summary information from the financial statements of the two companies follows:

	Payless Company	Capital Company
Data from the current year-end balance sheets		
Assets		
Cash	$ 37,400	$ 66,000
Accounts receivable	73,450	112,900
Notes receivable (trade)	16,200	13,100
Merchandise inventory	167,340	263,100
Prepaid expenses	8,000	11,900
Plant and equipment, net	568,900	606,400
Total assets	$871,290	$1,073,400
Liabilities and Stockholders' Equity		
Current liabilities	$120,200	$ 184,600
Long-term notes payable	159,800	210,000
Common stock, $5 par value	350,000	410,000
Retained earnings	241,290	268,800
Total liabilities and stockholders' equity	$871,290	$1,073,400
Data from the current year's income statements		
Sales	$1,325,000	$1,561,200
Cost of goods sold	970,500	1,065,000
Interest expense	14,400	23,000
Income tax expense	24,840	38,700
Net income	135,540	210,400
Beginning-of-year data		
Accounts receivable, net	$ 57,800	$ 106,200
Notes receivable	-0-	-0-
Merchandise inventory	109,600	212,400
Total assets	776,400	745,100
Common stock, $5 par value	350,000	410,000
Retained earnings	189,300	181,200

Required

1. Calculate the current ratio, acid-test ratio, accounts (including notes) receivable turnover, merchandise turnover, days' stock on hand, and days' sale uncollected for the two companies. Then, identify the company that you consider to be the better short-term credit risk and explain why.
2. Calculate the profit margin, total asset turnover, return on total assets, and return on common stockholders' equity for the two companies. Assuming that each company paid cash dividends of $2.00 per share and each company's stock can be purchased at $25 per share, calculate their price earnings ratios and dividend yields. Also, identify which company's stock you would recommend as the better investment and explain why.

Problem 16–5
Analysis of working capital
(LO 3)

Metro Corporation began the month of March with $750,000 of current assets, a current ratio of 2.5 to 1, and an acid-test ratio of 1.1 to 1. During the month, it completed the following transactions:

Mar.	4	Bought $85,000 of merchandise on account. (The company uses a perpetual inventory system.)
	10	Sold merchandise that cost $68,000 for $113,000.
	12	Collected a $29,000 account receivable.
	17	Paid a $31,000 account payable.
	19	Wrote off a $13,000 bad debt against the Allowance for Doubtful Accounts account.
	24	Declared a $1.25 per share cash dividend on the 40,000 shares of outstanding common stock.
	28	Paid the dividend declared on March 24.
	29	Borrowed $85,000 by giving the bank a 30-day, 10% note.
	30	Borrowed $100,000 by signing a long-term secured note.
	31	Used the $185,000 proceeds of the notes to buy additional machinery.

Required

Prepare a schedule showing Metro's current ratio, acid-test ratio, and working capital after each of the transactions. Round calculations to two decimal places.

Problem 16–6
Analytical essay
(LO 3)

Kerbey Company and Telcom Company are similar firms that operate within the same industry. The following information is available:

	Kerbey			Telcom		
	19X3	19X2	19X1	19X3	19X2	19X1
Current ratio	1.8	1.9	2.2	3.3	2.8	2.0
Acid-test ratio	1.1	1.2	1.3	2.9	2.6	1.7
Accounts receivable turnover	30.5	25.2	29.2	16.4	15.2	16.0
Merchandise turnover	24.2	21.9	17.1	14.5	13.0	12.6
Working capital	$65,000	$53,000	$47,000	$126,000	$98,000	$73,000

Required

Write a brief essay comparing Kerbey and Telcom based on the preceding information. Your discussion should include their relative ability to meet current obligations and to use current assets efficiently.

Problem 16–7
Analytical essay
(LO 3)

Snowden Company and Comet Company are similar firms that operate within the same industry. Comet began operations in 19X7 and Snowden in 19X1. In 19X9, both companies paid 7% interest to creditors. The following information is available:

	Snowden			Comet		
	19X9	19X8	19X7	19X9	19X8	19X7
Total asset turnover	3.3	3.0	3.2	1.9	1.7	1.4
Return on total assets	9.2	9.8	9.0	6.1	5.8	5.5
Profit margin	2.6	2.7	2.5	3.0	3.2	3.1
Sales	$800,000	$740,000	$772,000	$400,000	$320,000	$200,000

Required

Write a brief essay comparing Snowden and Comet based on the preceding information. Your discussion should include their relative ability to use assets efficiently to produce profits. Also comment on their relative success in employing financial leverage in 19X9.

Provocative Problems

Provocative Problem 16–1
Skinner Company
(LO 2, 3)

In your position as controller of Skinner Company, you are responsible for keeping the board of directors informed about the financial activities and status of the company. In preparing for the next board meeting, you have calculated the following ratios, turnovers, and percentages to enable you to answer questions:

	19X6	19X5	19X4
Sales trend	137.00	125.00	100.00
Selling expenses to net sales	9.8%	13.7%	15.3%
Sales to plant assets	3.5 to 1	3.3 to 1	3.0 to 1
Current ratio	2.6 to 1	2.4 to 1	2.1 to 1
Acid-test ratio	0.8 to 1	1.1 to 1	1.2 to 1
Merchandise turnover	7.5 times	8.7 times	9.9 times
Accounts receivable turnover	6.7 times	7.4 times	8.2 times
Total asset turnover	2.6 times	2.6 times	3.0 times
Return on total assets	8.8%	9.4%	10.1%
Return on stockholders' equity	9.75%	11.50%	12.25%
Profit margin	3.3%	3.5%	3.7%

Required

Using the preceding data, answer each of the following questions and explain your answers.

1. Is it becoming easier for the company to meet its current debts on time and to take advantage of cash discounts?
2. Is the company collecting its accounts receivable more rapidly?
3. Is the company's investment in accounts receivable decreasing?
4. Are dollars invested in inventory increasing?
5. Is the company's investment in plant assets increasing?
6. Is the stockholders' investment becoming more profitable?
7. Is the company using its assets efficiently?
8. Did the dollar amount of selling expenses decrease during the three-year period?

Provocative Problem 16–2
Apple Computer, Inc.
(LO 2, 3)

Apple Computer, Inc.

Refer to the 11-year financial history and the consolidated balance sheet contained in the financial statements of Apple Computer, Inc., in Appendix F, to answer the following questions:

1. Using 1990 as the base year, calculate trend percentages for 1990–1992 for the total net sales, total costs and expenses, operating income, and net income.
2. Calculate common-size percentages for 1992 and 1991 for the following categories of assets: total current assets; net property, plant, and equipment; and other assets.
3. Calculate the high and low price earnings ratio for 1992.
4. Calculate the dividend yield for 1992 using the high stock price for the year.
5. Calculate the debt and equity ratios for 1992.

Answers to Objective Review Questions

LO 1 (*b*)
LO 2 (*a*)
LO 3 (*b*)
LO 4 (*e*)
LO 5 (*b*)

APPENDIX

C

Accounting Principles, the FASB's Conceptual Framework, and Alternative Valuation Methods

Accounting principles or concepts are not laws of nature. They are broad ideas developed as a way of *describing* current accounting practices and *prescribing* new and improved practices. In Appendix C, you will learn about some new accounting concepts that the FASB developed in an effort to guide future changes and improvements in accounting. You also will learn about some major alternatives to the historical cost measurements reported in conventional financial statements. Studying these alternatives will help you understand the nature of the information that is contained in conventional statements. In addition, it will help you grasp the meaning of new reporting practices that may occur in future years.

Learning Objectives

After studying Appendix C, you should be able to:

1. Explain the difference between descriptive concepts and prescriptive concepts, and the difference between bottom-up and top-down approaches to the development of accounting concepts.
2. Describe the major components in the FASB's conceptual framework.
3. Explain why conventional financial statements fail to adequately account for price changes.
4. Use a price index to restate historical cost/nominal dollar costs into constant purchasing power amounts and to calculate purchasing power gains and losses.
5. Explain the current cost approach to valuation, including its effects on the income statement and balance sheet.
6. Explain the current selling price approach to valuation.
7. Define or explain the words and phrases listed in the appendix glossary.

ACCOUNTING PRINCIPLES AND THE FASB'S CONCEPTUAL FRAMEWORK

Descriptive and Prescriptive Accounting Concepts

To fully understand the importance of financial accounting concepts or principles, you must realize that they serve two purposes: First, they provide general descriptions of existing accounting practices. In doing this, concepts and principles serve as guidelines that help you learn about accounting. Thus, after learning how the concepts or principles are applied in a few situations,

LO 1 Explain the difference between descriptive concepts and prescriptive concepts, and the difference between bottom-up and top-down approaches to the development of accounting concepts.

you develop the ability to apply them in different situations. This is easier and more effective than memorizing a very long list of specific practices.

Second, these concepts or principles help accountants analyze unfamiliar situations and develop procedures to account for those situations. This purpose is especially important for the Financial Accounting Standards Board (FASB), which is charged with developing uniform practices for financial reporting in the United States and with improving the quality of such reporting.

In prior chapters, we defined and illustrated several important accounting principles. These principles, which follow, describe in general terms the practices currently used by accountants.

Generally Accepted Principles		
Business entity principle	Full-disclosure principle	Objectivity principle
Conservatism principle	Going concern principle	Revenue recognition principle
Consistency principle	Matching principle	
Cost principle	Materiality principle	Time-period principle

To help you learn accounting, we first listed these principles in Chapter 1 (p. 23) and have referred to them frequently in later chapters. Although these ideas are labeled *principles,* in this discussion we use the term *concepts* to include these principles as well as other general rules developed by the FASB. The FASB also uses the word *concepts* in this general manner.

The preceding concepts are useful for teaching and learning about accounting practice and are helpful for dealing with some unfamiliar transactions. As business practices have evolved in recent years, however, these concepts have become less useful as guides for accountants to follow in dealing with new and different types of transactions. This problem has occurred because the concepts are intended to provide general descriptions of current accounting practices. In other words, they describe what accountants currently do; they do not necessarily describe what accountants should do. Also, since these concepts do not identify weaknesses in accounting practices, they do not lead to major changes or improvements in accounting practices.

Because the FASB is charged with improving financial reporting, its first members decided that a new set of concepts should be developed. They also decided that the new set of concepts should not merely *describe* what was being done under current practice. Instead, the new concepts should *prescribe* what ought to be done to make things better. The project to develop a new set of prescriptive concepts was initiated in 1973, and quickly became known as the FASB's *conceptual framework project.*

However, before we examine the concepts developed by the FASB, we need to look more closely at the differences between descriptive and prescriptive uses of accounting concepts.

The Processes of Developing Descriptive and Prescriptive Accounting Concepts

Sets of concepts differ in how they are developed and used. In general, when concepts are intended to describe current practice, they are developed by looking at accepted specific practices, and then making some general rules to encompass them. This bottom-up approach is diagrammed in Illustration C–1, which shows the arrows going from the practices to the concepts. The outcome of the process is a set of general rules that summarize practice and that can be used for education and for solving some new problems. For example, this approach leads to the concept that assets are recorded at cost. However, these kinds of concepts often fail to show how new problems should be solved. For example, the concept that assets are recorded at cost does not provide much direct guidance for situations in which assets have no cost because they are donated to a company by a local government. Further, because these concepts

ILLUSTRATION C-1 *A "Bottom-Up" Process of Developing Descriptive Accounting Concepts*

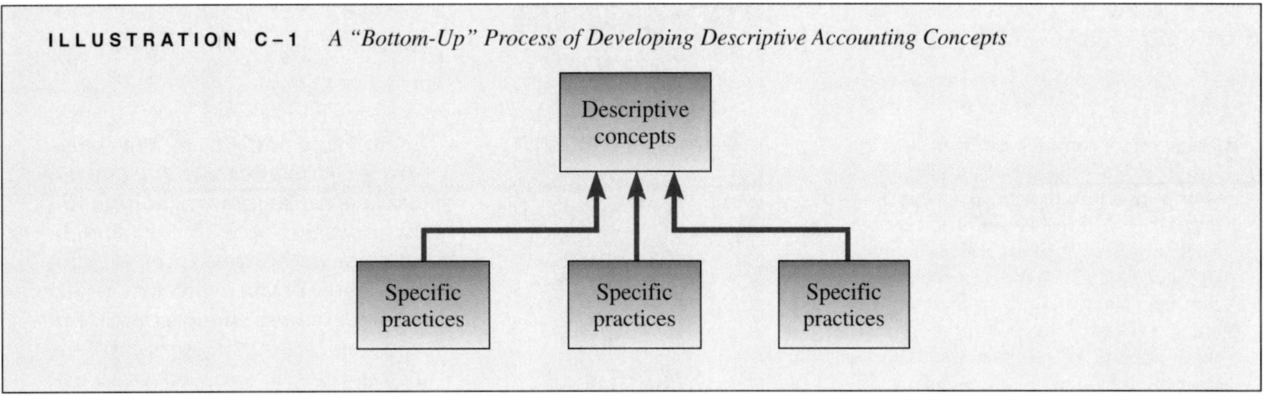

ILLUSTRATION C-2 *A "Top-Down" Process of Developing Prescriptive Accounting Concepts*

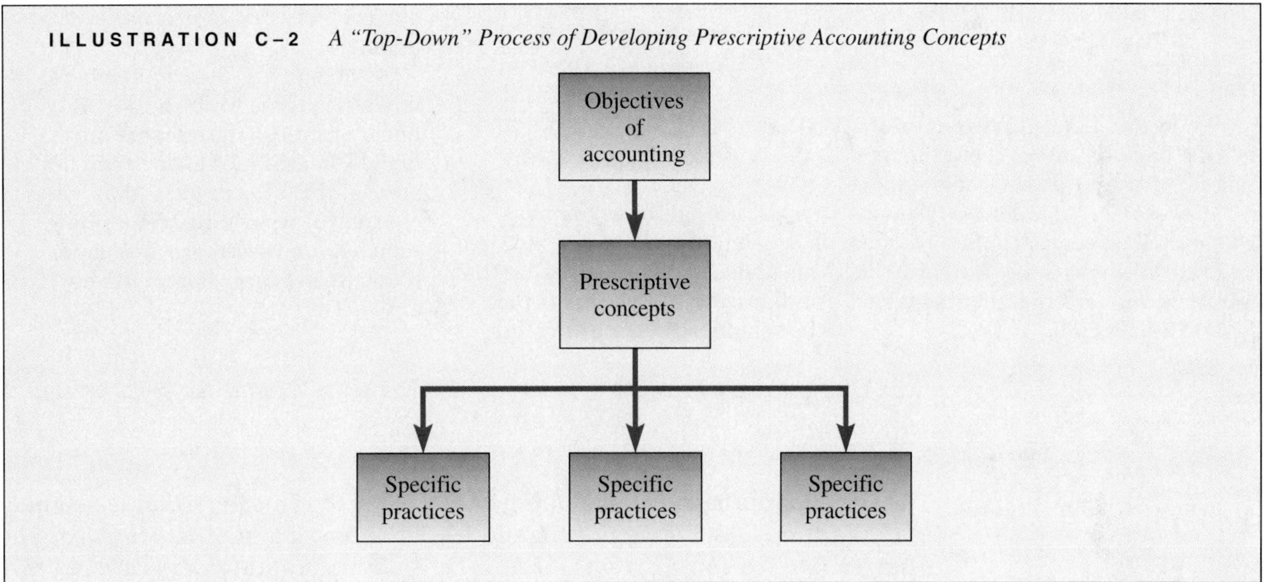

are based on the presumption that current practices are adequate, they do not lead to the development of new and improved accounting methods. To continue the example, the concept that assets are initially recorded at cost does not encourage asking the question of whether they should always be carried at that amount.

In contrast, if concepts are intended to *prescribe* improvements in accounting practices, they are likely to be designed by a top-down approach (Illustration C-2). Note that the top-down approach starts with broad accounting objectives. The process then generates broad concepts about the types of information that should be reported. Finally, these concepts should lead to specific practices that ought to be used. The advantage of this approach is that the concepts are good for solving new problems and evaluating old answers; its disadvantage is that the concepts may not be very descriptive of current practice. In fact, the suggested practices may not be in current use.

Since the FASB uses accounting concepts to prescribe accounting practices, the Board uses a top-down approach to develop its conceptual framework. The Board's concepts are not necessarily more correct than the previously developed concepts. However, the new concepts are intended to provide better guidelines for developing new and improved accounting practices. The Board has stated that it will use them as a basis for its future actions and already has used them to justify important changes in financial reporting.

AS A MATTER OF

Opinion

Dennis R. Beresford, CPA

Mr. Beresford graduated from the University of Southern California in 1961 with a B.A. degree in accounting. After working 10 years in the Los Angeles office of Ernst & Ernst (now Ernst & Young), he was assigned to that firm's national office and made a partner. In 1987, he was appointed to the Financial Accounting Standards Board and named as its chairman. In 1991, he was reappointed for a second term, which will expire in 1997. Among his honors is the designation as the Beta Alpha Psi "Accountant of the Year" for 1986.

When the conceptual framework was being created, some thought that it would provide immediate answers for standard-setting issues. However, it could never do that all by itself. Rather, the framework is a tool that helps the FASB do its job.

Because getting to right answers depends on asking the right questions, I've come to realize that perhaps the most critical part of the standard-setting process is identifying and stating the issues properly. That's exactly what the conceptual framework helps us do by providing us with common objectives and terms. In effect, the conceptual framework brings discipline to those who participate in the standard-setting process. This discipline helps the Board to ask the right questions. It also helps other participants comment on our projects in a more consistent manner.

Although all Board members might not agree which answer to a question is best, the odds are much higher that the best answer will be among the alternatives that we consider if we ask the right questions. As a result, we are more likely to ultimately adopt the best answer.

The FASB's Conceptual Framework

LO 2 Describe the major components in the FASB's conceptual framework.

The FASB's approach to developing its conceptual framework is diagrammed in Illustration C–3. Between 1978 and 1985, the Board issued six *Statements of Financial Accounting Concepts (SFAC)*. These concepts statements are not the same as the FASB's *Statements of Financial Accounting Standards (SFAS)*. The *SFAS*s are authoritative statements of generally accepted accounting principles that must be followed. The *SFAC*s are guidelines the Board uses in developing new standards. Accountants are not required to follow the *SFAC*s in practice.

The Objectives of Financial Reporting

The FASB's first *Statement of Financial Accounting Concepts (SFAC 1)* identified the broad objectives of financial reporting (Illustration C–3). The first and most general objective stated in *SFAC 1* is to "provide information that is useful to present and potential investors and creditors and other users in making rational investment, credit, and similar decisions."[1] From this beginning point in *SFAC 1,* the Board expressed other more specific objectives. These objectives recognize (1) that financial reporting should help users predict future cash flows, and (2) that information about a company's resources and obligations is useful in making such predictions. All the concepts in the conceptual framework are intended to be consistent with these general objectives. Of course, present accounting practice already provides information about a company's resources and obligations. Thus, although the conceptual

[1] FASB, *Statement of Financial Accounting Concepts No. 1,* "Objectives of Financial Reporting by Business Enterprises" (Norwalk, CT, 1978), par. 34.

ILLUSTRATION C-3 *The FASB's Conceptual Framework*

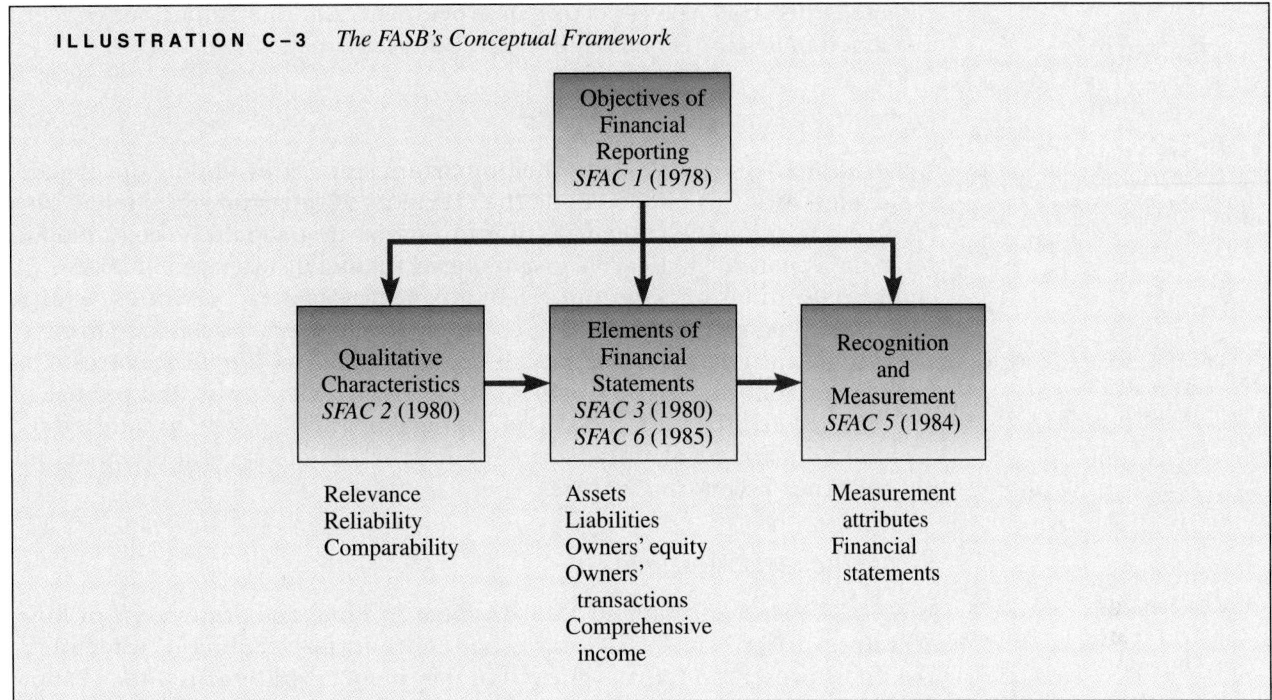

framework is intended to be prescriptive of new and improved practices, the concepts in the framework are also descriptive of many current practices.

The Qualities of Useful Information

Illustration C–3 shows that the next step in the conceptual framework project was to identify the qualities (or qualitative characteristics) that financial information should have if it is to be useful in decision making. The Board discussed the fact that information can be useful only if it is understandable to users. However, the users are assumed to have the training, experience, and motivation to analyze financial reports. With this decision, the Board indicated that financial reporting should not try to meet the needs of unsophisticated or other casual report users.

In *SFAC 2,* the FASB said that information is useful if it is (1) relevant, (2) reliable, and (3) comparable. Information is *relevant* if it can make a difference in a decision. Information has this quality when it helps users predict the future or evaluate the past and is received in time to affect their decisions.

Information is *reliable* if users can depend on it to be free from bias and error. Reliable information is verifiable and faithfully represents what is supposed to be described. In addition, users can depend on information only if it is neutral. This means that the rules used to produce information should not be designed to lead users to accept or reject any specific decision alternative.

Information is *comparable* if users can use it to identify differences and similarities between companies. Comparability is possible only if companies follow uniform practices. However, even if all companies uniformly follow the same practices, comparable reports do not result if the practices are not appropriate. For example, comparable information would not be provided if all companies were to ignore the useful lives of their assets and depreciate all assets over two years.

Comparability also requires consistency (see Chapter 8, page 300), which means that a company should not change its accounting practices unless the change is justified as a reporting improvement. Another important concept discussed in *SFAC 2* is materiality (see Chapter 7, page 274).

Elements of Financial Statements

Illustration C–3 shows that another important step in developing the conceptual framework was to determine the elements of financial statements. This involved defining the categories of information that should be contained in financial reports. The Board's discussion of financial statement elements includes definitions of important elements such as assets, liabilities, equity, revenues, expenses, gains, and losses. In earlier chapters, we referred to many of these definitions when we explained various accounting procedures. The Board's pronouncement on financial statement elements was first published in 1980 as *SFAC 3.* In 1985, *SFAC 3* was replaced by *SFAC 6,* which modified the discussion of financial statement elements to include several elements for not-for-profit accounting entities.[2]

Recognition and Measurement

In *SFAC 5,* "Recognition and Measurement in Financial Statements of Business Enterprises," the FASB established concepts for deciding (1) when items should be presented (or recognized) in the financial statements, and (2) how to assign numbers to (or measure) those items. In general, the Board concluded that items should be recognized in the financial statements if they meet the following criteria: (1) *definitions*—the item meets the definition of an element of financial statements; (2) *measurability*—it has a relevant attribute measurable with sufficient reliability; (3) *relevance*—the information about it is capable of making a difference in user decisions, and (4) *reliability*—the information is representationally faithful, verifiable, and neutral.

The question of how items should be measured raises the fundamental question of whether financial statements should be based on cost or on value. Since this question is quite controversial, the Board's discussion of this issue is more descriptive of current practice than it is prescriptive of new measurement methods.

In *SFAC 5,* the Board stated that a full set of financial statements should show:

1. Financial position at the end of the period.
2. Earnings for the period. (This concept is very similar to the concept of net income used in current practice.)
3. Comprehensive income for the period. (This new concept is broader than earnings and includes all changes in owners' equity other than those that resulted from transactions with the owners. Some changes in asset values are included in this concept but are excluded from earnings.)
4. Cash flows during the period.
5. Investments by and distributions to owners during the period.

We should note that *SFAC 5* was the first official pronouncement to call for the presentation of a statement of cash flows. The statement of cash flows is now required under *SFAS 95,* which was issued two years after *SFAC 5.*

---

[2] Among the six *Statements of Financial Accounting Concepts* issued by the FASB, one *(SFAC 4)* is directed toward accounting by not-for-profit organizations. Although *SFAC 4* is important, it is beyond the scope of this course.

ALTERNATIVE ACCOUNTING VALUATION SYSTEMS

Conventional Financial Statements Fail to Account for Price Changes

LO 3 Explain why conventional financial statements fail to adequately account for price changes.

All accountants agree that conventional financial statements provide useful information for making economic decisions. However, many accountants also believe that conventional financial statements fail to adequately account for the impact of changing prices. Sometimes, this makes the statements misleading. That is, the statements may imply certain facts that are inconsistent with the real state of affairs. As a result, the information in the statements may lead decision makers to make decisions inconsistent with their objectives.

Failure to Account for Price Changes on the Balance Sheet

In what ways do conventional financial statements fail to account for changing prices? The general problem is that transactions are recorded in the historical number of dollars paid. Usually, these amounts are not adjusted even though subsequent price changes may dramatically change the value of the purchased items.[3] For example, Old Company purchased 10 acres of land for $25,000. Then, at the end of each accounting period, Old Company presented a balance sheet showing "Land . . . $25,000." Six years later, after price increases of 97%, New Company purchased 10 acres of land that was next to and nearly identical to Old Company's land. New Company paid $49,250 for the land. Comparing the conventional balance sheets of the two companies reveals the following balances:

	Old Company	New Company
Land	$25,000	$49,250

Without knowing the details that led to these balances, a statement reader is likely to conclude that either New Company has more land than Old Company or that New Company's land is more valuable. In reality, both companies own 10 acres that are of equal value. The entire difference between the prices paid by the two companies is explained by the 97% price increase between the two purchase dates. That is, $\$25,000 \times 1.97 = \$49,250$.

Failure to Account for Price Changes on the Income Statement

The failure of conventional financial statements to adequately account for changing prices also shows up in the income statement. For example, assume that in the previous example, the companies purchased machines instead of land. Also, assume that the machines of Old Company and New Company are identical except for age; both are being depreciated on a straight-line basis over a 10-year period with no salvage value. As a result, the annual income statements of the two companies show the following:

	Old Company	New Company
Depreciation expense, machinery	$2,500	$4,925

[3] An exception to this general rule is the reporting of certain investments in debt and equity securities at their fair (market) values. This exception is explained in Chapters 7 and 10.

Although assets of equal value are being depreciated, the income statements show depreciation expense for New Company that is 97% higher than Old Company's. This is inconsistent with the fact that both companies own identical machines affected by the same depreciation factors. Furthermore, although Old Company appears more profitable, it must pay more income taxes due to the apparent extra profits. Also, if Old Company's selling prices are linked to its costs, it may not recover the full replacement cost of its machinery through the sale of its products.

Valuation Alternatives to Conventional Measurements of Cost

There are three basic alternatives to the historical cost measurements presented in conventional financial statements without adjustment for changing prices. These alternatives are:

1. Historical costs adjusted for changes in the general price level.
2. Current replacement cost valuations.
3. Current selling price valuations.

We discuss each of these in the remaining sections of Appendix C.

Adjusting Historical Costs for General Price Level Changes

LO 4 Use a price index to restate historical cost/nominal dollar costs into constant purchasing power amounts and to calculate purchasing power gains and losses.

One alternative to conventional financial statements is to restate dollar amounts of cost incurred in earlier years for changes in the general price level. In other words, a specific dollar amount of cost in a previous year can be restated as the number of dollars that would have been expended if the cost had been paid with dollars that have the current amount of purchasing power.

For example, assume the general price index shown at right for December of 19X1 through 19X7. Then, assume that a firm purchased assets for $1,000 in December 19X1 and purchased assets for $1,500 in December 19X2. The 19X1 cost of $1,000 correctly states the number of monetary units (dollars) expended in 19X1. Also, the 19X2 cost of $1,500 correctly states the number of monetary units expended in 19X2. However, in a very important way, the 19X1 monetary units do not mean the same thing as the 19X2 monetary units. A dollar (one monetary unit) in 19X1 represented a different amount of purchasing power than a dollar in 19X2. Both of these dollars represent different amounts of purchasing power than a dollar in 19X7.

Year	Price Index
19X1	92.5
19X2	100.0
19X3	109.5
19X4	123.7
19X5	135.0
19X6	150.0
19X7	168.0

To communicate the total amount of purchasing power given up for the assets, the historical number of monetary units must be restated in dollars with the same amount of purchasing power. For example, the total amount of cost incurred during 19X1 and 19X2 may be stated in the purchasing power of 19X2 dollars or the purchasing power of 19X7 dollars. These calculations are presented in Illustration C–4.

Conventional financial statements disclose revenues, expenses, assets, liabilities, and owners' equity in the historical monetary units exchanged when the transactions occurred. As such, they are sometimes called **historical cost/nominal dollar financial statements.** This emphasizes the difference between conventional statements and historical cost/constant purchasing power statements. **Historical cost/constant purchasing power accounting** uses a general price index to restate the dollar amounts on conventional financial statements into amounts that represent current general purchasing power.

The same principles for determining depreciation expense, cost of goods sold, accruals of revenue, and so forth, apply to both historical cost/nominal

ILLUSTRATION C-4 *Expressing Costs in Constant Purchasing Power*

Year Cost Was Incurred	Monetary Units Expended (*a*)	Price Index Factor for Adjustment to 19X2 Dollars (*b*)	Historical Cost Stated in 19X2 Dollars (*a* × *b* = *c*)	Price Index Factor for Adjustment to 19X7 Dollars (*d*)	Historical Cost Stated in 19X7 Dollars (*c* × *d*)
19X1	$1,000	100/92.5 = 1.08108	$1,081	168/100 = 1.68000	$1,816*
19X2	1,500		1,500	168/100 = 1.68000	2,520
Total cost	$2,500		$2,581		$4,336

* An alternative calculation is $1,000 × (168.0/92.5) = $1,816.

dollar statements and historical cost/constant purchasing power statements. The same generally accepted accounting principles apply to both. The only difference between the two is that constant purchasing power statements reflect adjustments for general price level changes and nominal dollar statements do not.

The Impact of General Price Changes on Monetary Items

Some assets and liabilities are defined as monetary items. **Monetary assets** represent money or claims to receive a fixed amount of money. **Monetary liabilities** are obligations that are fixed in terms of the amount owed. The number of dollars to be received or paid does not change even though the purchasing power of the dollar may change. Examples of monetary items include cash, accounts receivable, accounts payable, and notes payable.

Because the amount of money that will be received or paid is fixed, a monetary item is not adjusted for general price level changes on a historical cost/constant purchasing power balance sheet. For example, assume that $800 in cash was owned at the end of 19X2. Regardless of how the price level has changed since the cash was acquired, the amount to be reported on the December 31, 19X2, historical cost/constant purchasing power balance sheet is $800.

Although monetary items are not adjusted on the balance sheet, they do involve special risks. When the general price level changes, monetary items create **purchasing power gains and losses.** Owning monetary assets during a period of inflation results in a loss of purchasing power. Owing monetary liabilities during a period of inflation results in a gain of purchasing power. During a period of deflation, the effects are just the opposite. Monetary assets result in purchasing power gains and monetary liabilities result in purchasing power losses.

For example, assume that a company has a cash balance of $800 on December 31, 19X2, which resulted from the following:

Cash balance, December 31, 19X1	$ 200
Cash receipts, assumed to have been received uniformly throughout the year	1,500
Cash disbursements, assumed to have been made uniformly throughout the year	(900)
Cash balance, December 31, 19X2	$ 800

Also assume that the general price index was 150.0 at the end of 19X1; that it averaged 160.0 throughout 19X2; and was 168.0 at the end of that year. As the price level increased throughout 19X2, the purchasing power of the cash declined. To calculate the loss during the year, the beginning cash balance and each receipt or disbursement must be adjusted for price changes to the end of the year. Then, the adjusted balance is compared with the actual balance to determine the loss. The calculation is as follows:

	Nominal Dollar Amounts	Price Index Factor for Restatement to December 31, 19X2	Restated to December 31, 19X2	Gain or (Loss)
Beginning balance	$ 200	168.0/150.0 = 1.12000	$ 224	
Receipts	1,500	168.0/160.0 = 1.05000	1,575	
Disbursements	(900)	168.0/160.0 = 1.05000	(945)	
Ending bal. adjusted . . .			$ 854	
Ending balance, actual . .	$ 800		(800)	
Purchasing power loss . .				$(54)

Stated in terms of general purchasing power at year-end, the beginning cash balance plus receipts less disbursements was $854. Since the company has only $800 on hand, the $54 difference is a loss of general purchasing power.

In the preceding calculation, note that we adjusted the receipts and disbursements from the *average* price level during the year (160.0) to the ending price level (168.0). Because we assumed the receipts and disbursements occurred uniformly throughout the year, we used the average price level to approximate the price level at the time each receipt and disbursement took place. If receipts and disbursements do not occur uniformly, then we must separately adjust each receipt and each disbursement from the price level at the time of the receipt or disbursement to the price level at year-end.

The calculation of purchasing power gains and losses that result from owing monetary liabilities is the same as it is for monetary assets. Assume, for example, that a note payable for $300 was outstanding on December 31, 19X1, when the price index was 150.0. On April 5, 19X2, when the price index was 157.0, a $700 increase in the note resulted in a $1,000 balance that remained outstanding throughout the rest of 19X2. On December 31, 19X2, the price index was 168.0. On the historical cost/constant purchasing power balance sheet for December 31, 19X2, the note payable is reported at $1,000. The purchasing power gain or loss during 19X2 is calculated as follows:

	Nominal Dollar Amounts	Price Index Factor for Restatement to December 31, 19X2	Restated to December 31, 19X2	Gain or (Loss)
Beginning balance	$ 300	168.0/150.0 = 1.120	$ 336	
April 5 increase	700	168.0/157.0 = 1.070	749	
Ending bal. adjusted . . .			$ 1,085	
Ending balance, actual . .	$1,000		(1,000)	
Purchasing power gain . .				$85

Stated in terms of general purchasing power at year-end, the amount borrowed was $1,085. Since the company can pay the note with $1,000, the $85 difference is a gain in general purchasing power earned by the firm.

To determine a company's total purchasing power gain or loss during a year, the accountant must analyze each monetary asset and each monetary liability. The final gain or loss is then described as the *purchasing power gain (or loss) on net monetary items owned or owed.*

ILLUSTRATION C–5 *Reporting the Effects of Price Changes on Monetary and Nonmonetary Items*

	When the General Price Level Rises (Inflation)		When the General Price Level Falls (Deflation)	
Financial Statement Item	**Balance Sheet Adjustment Required**	**Income Statement Gain or Loss**	**Balance Sheet Adjustment Required**	**Income Statement Gain or Loss**
Monetary assets	No	Loss	No	Gain
Nonmonetary assets	Yes	None	Yes	None
Monetary liabilities	No	Gain	No	Loss
Nonmonetary equities and liabilities . .	Yes	None	Yes	None

The Impact of General Price Changes on Nonmonetary Items

Nonmonetary items include stockholders' equity and all assets and liabilities that are not fixed in terms of the number of monetary units to be received or paid. Land, equipment, intangible assets, and many product warranty liabilities are examples of nonmonetary items. The prices of **nonmonetary assets** tend to increase or decrease over time as the general price level increases or decreases. Similarly, the amounts needed to satisfy **nonmonetary liabilities** tend to change with changes in the general price level.

To reflect these changes on historical cost/constant purchasing power balance sheets, nonmonetary items are adjusted for price level changes that occur after the items were acquired. For example, assume that $500 was invested in land (a nonmonetary asset) at the end of 19X1, and the investment was still held at the end of 19X7. During this time, the general price index increased from 92.5 to 168.0. The historical cost/constant purchasing power balance sheets would disclose the following amounts:

Asset	December 31, 19X1, Historical Cost/Constant Purchasing Power Balance Sheet (*a*)	Price Index Factor for Adjustment to December 31, 19X7 (*b*)	December 31, 19X7, Historical Cost/Constant Purchasing Power Balance Sheet (*a* × *b*)
Land	$500	168.0/92.5 = 1.81622	$908

The $908 shown as the investment in land at the end of 19X7 has the same amount of general purchasing power as $500 at the end of 19X1. Thus, no change in general purchasing power is recognized from holding the land.

Illustration C–5 summarizes the impact of general price level changes on monetary and nonmonetary items. The illustration shows which items require adjustments to prepare a historical cost/constant purchasing power balance sheet. It also shows which items generate purchasing power gains and losses recognized on a constant purchasing power income statement.

Current Cost Valuations

As we said before, all prices do not change at the same rate. In fact, when the general price level is rising, some specific prices may be falling. If this were not so, if all prices changed at the same rate, then historical cost/constant purchasing power accounting would report current values on the financial statements.

For example, suppose that a company purchased land for $50,000 on January 1, 19X1, when the general price index was 135.0. Then, the price level increased until December 19X2, when the price index was 168.0. A historical

LO 5 Explain the current cost approach to valuation, including its effects on the income statement and balance sheet.

cost/constant purchasing power balance sheet for this company on December 31, 19X2, would report the land at $50,000 × 168.0/135.0 = $62,222. If all prices increased at the same rate during that period, the market value of the land would have increased from $50,000 to $62,222, and the company's historical cost/constant purchasing power balance sheet would coincidentally disclose the land at its current value.

Because all prices do not change at the same rate, however, the current value of the land may differ substantially from the historical cost/constant dollar amount of $62,222. For example, assume that the company had the land appraised and determined that its current value on December 31, 19X2, was $80,000. The difference between the original purchase price of $50,000 and the current value of $80,000 is explained as follows:

Unrealized holding gain	$80,000 − $62,222 = $17,778
Adjustment for general price level increase	$62,222 − $50,000 = 12,222
Total change	$80,000 − $50,000 = $30,000

In this case, the historical cost/constant purchasing power balance sheet would report land at $62,222, which is $17,778 ($80,000 − $62,222) less than its current value. This illustrates an important fact about historical cost/constant purchasing power accounting: it does not attempt to report current value. Rather, historical cost/constant purchasing power accounting restates original transaction prices into equivalent amounts of current, *general* purchasing power. The balance sheets display current values only if current, *specific* purchasing power is the basis of valuation.

Current Costs on the Income Statement

When the current cost approach to accounting is used, the reported amount of each expense, or **current cost,** is the number of dollars that would have been needed at the time the expense was incurred to acquire the consumed resources. For example, assume that the annual sales of a company included an item sold in May for $1,500. The item had been acquired on January 1 for $500. Also, suppose that in May, at the time of the sale, the cost to replace this item was $700. Then, the annual current cost income statement would show sales of $1,500 less cost of goods sold of $700. In other words, when an asset is acquired and then held for a time before it expires, the historical cost of the asset usually is different from its current cost at the time it expires. Current cost accounting measures the amount of expense as the cost to replace the asset at the time the asset expires or is sold.

The result of measuring expenses in current costs is that revenue is matched with the current (at the time of the sale) cost of the resources used to earn the revenue. Thus, operating profit is not greater than zero unless revenues are large enough to replace all of the resources consumed in the process of producing those revenues. Those who argue for current costs believe that operating profit measured in this fashion provides an improved basis for evaluating the effectiveness of operating activities.

Current Costs on the Balance Sheet

On the balance sheet, current cost accounting reports assets at the amounts that would have to be paid to purchase them as of the balance sheet date. Liabilities are reported at the amounts that would have to be paid to satisfy the liabilities as of the balance sheet date. Note that this valuation basis is similar to historical cost/constant purchasing power accounting in that a distinction exists between monetary and nonmonetary assets and liabilities.

Monetary assets and liabilities are fixed in amount regardless of price changes. Therefore, monetary items are not adjusted for price changes. All of the nonmonetary items, however, must be evaluated at each balance sheet date to determine the best estimate of current cost.

For a moment, think about the large variety of assets reported on balance sheets. Given that there are so many different assets, you should not be surprised that accountants have difficulty obtaining reliable estimates of current costs. In some cases, they use price indexes that relate to specific categories of assets. Such specific price indexes may provide the most reliable source of current cost information. In other cases, when an asset is not new and has been partially depreciated, its current cost can be estimated by determining the cost to acquire a similar but new asset. Depreciation on the old asset is then based on the current cost of the new asset. Clearly, the accountant's professional judgment is an important factor in developing current cost data.

Current Selling Price Valuations

LO 6 Explain the current selling price approach to valuation.

In the previous discussion, you learned that conventional financial statements generally report historical costs in nominal dollars. That is, adjustments usually are not made for price changes. We also explained how accountants use a general price level index to adjust the nominal dollar amounts to measure the historical costs in terms of a constant purchasing power. Next, we discussed the alternative of reporting current (replacement) costs in the financial statements.

The final alternative to be considered is the reporting of assets (and liabilities) at current selling prices. On the balance sheet, this means assets would be reported at the amounts that would be received if the assets were sold. Similarly, liabilities would be reported at the amounts that would have to be paid to settle or eliminate the liabilities. The financial press describes this selling price approach to valuation as *mark to market accounting.*

The argument for reporting the current selling prices of assets is based on the idea that the alternative to owning an asset is to sell it. Thus, the sacrifice a business makes to hold an asset is the amount it would receive if the asset were sold. Further, the benefit derived from owing a liability is the amount the business avoids paying by not eliminating the liability. If these current selling prices are reported on the balance sheet, the stockholders' equity represents the net amount of cash that would be realized by liquidating the business. This net liquidation value is the amount that could be invested in other projects if the business were liquidated. Therefore, one can argue that net liquidation value is the most relevant basis for evaluating whether the income the company earns is enough to justify remaining in business.

Some proponents of the current selling price approach believe that it should be applied to assets but not to liabilities. Others argue that it applies equally well to both. Still others believe that it should be applied only to assets held for sale. They would not apply it to assets held for use in the business.

A related issue is whether to report the adjustments to selling price as gains and losses in the income statement. Some businesses, especially banks, argue that reporting such gains or losses causes excessive fluctuations in their reported net incomes. As an alternative to reporting the gains or losses on the income statement, they may be shown in stockholders' equity on the balance sheet as "unrealized gains and losses."

As Chapters 7 and 10 explain, a very recent pronouncement by the FASB (*SFAS 115*) requires companies to use the selling price approach to valuation for some assets. Investments in trading securities are reported at their fair (market) values, with the related changes in fair values reported on the income statement. Investments in securities available for sale are also reported at their fair values, but the related changes in fair values are not reported on the income statement. Instead, they are reported as part of stockholders' equity.

Summary of the Appendix in Terms of Learning Objectives

LO 1 Some accounting concepts provide general descriptions of current accounting practices. Other concepts prescribe the practices accountants should follow. These prescriptive concepts are most useful in developing accounting procedures for new types of transactions and making improvements in accounting practice. A bottom-up approach to developing concepts examines current practices and then develops concepts to provide general descriptions of those practices. In contrast, a top-down approach begins by stating accounting objectives, and from there, develops concepts that prescribe the types of accounting practices accountants should follow.

LO 2 The FASB's conceptual framework begins with *SFAC 1* by stating the broad objectives of financial reporting. Next, *SFAC 2* identifies the qualitative characteristics accounting information should possess. The elements contained in financial reports are defined in *SFAC 6* and the recognition and measurement criteria to be used are identified in *SFAC 5*.

LO 3 Conventional financial statements report transactions in the historical number of dollars received or paid. Therefore, the statements are not adjusted to reflect general price level changes or changes in the specific prices of the items reported.

LO 4 To restate a historical cost/nominal dollar cost in terms of constant purchasing power, multiply the nominal dollar cost by a factor that represents the change in the general price level since the cost was incurred. On the balance sheet, monetary assets and liabilities should not be adjusted for changes in prices. However, purchasing power gains or losses result from holding monetary assets and owing monetary liabilities during a period of general price changes.

LO 5 Current costs on the balance sheet are the dollar amounts that would be spent to purchase the assets at the balance sheet date. On the income statement, current costs are the dollar amounts that would be necessary to acquire the consumed assets on the date they were consumed.

LO 6 Reporting current selling prices of assets and liabilities is supported by those who believe the balance sheet should show the net cost of not selling the assets and settling the liabilities. Some argue for applying selling price valuations to all assets and liabilities, or to marketable investments and marketable liabilities only, or to assets only. The related gains and losses may be reported on the income statement, but some would show them as unrealized stockholders' equity items on the balance sheet.

Glossary

LO 7 Define or explain the words and phrases listed in the appendix glossary.

Current cost In general, the cost that would be required to acquire (or replace) an asset or service at the present time. On the income statement, the number of dollars that would be required, at the time the expense is incurred, to acquire the resources consumed. On the balance sheet, the amounts that would have to be paid to replace the assets or satisfy the liabilities as of the balance sheet date. p. 612

Historical cost/constant purchasing power accounting an accounting system that adjusts historical cost/nominal dollar financial statements for changes in the general purchasing power of the dollar. p. 608

Historical cost/nominal dollar financial statements conventional financial statements that disclose revenues, expenses, assets, liabilities, and owners' equity in terms of the historical monetary units exchanged at the time the transactions occurred. p. 608

Monetary assets money or claims to receive a fixed amount of money; the number of dollars to be received does not change regardless of changes in the purchasing power of the dollar. p. 609

Monetary liabilities fixed amounts that are owed; the number of dollars to be paid does not change regardless of changes in the general price level. p. 609

Nonmonetary assets assets that are not claims to a fixed number of monetary units, the prices of which therefore tend to fluctuate with changes in the general price level. p. 611

Nonmonetary liabilities obligations that are not fixed in terms of the number of monetary units needed to satisfy them, and that therefore tend to fluctuate in amount with changes in the general price level. p. 611

Purchasing power gains or losses the gains or losses that result from holding monetary assets and/or owing monetary liabilities during a period in which the general price level changes. p. 609

Objective Review

Answers to the following questions are listed at the end of this appendix. Be sure that you decide which is the one right answer to each question *before* you check the answers.

LO 1 The FASB's conceptual framework is intended to:

a. Provide a historical analysis of accounting practice.
b. Describe current accounting practice.
c. Provide concepts that attempt to prescribe what should be done in accounting practice.
d. Describe every situation that may be encountered in accounting practice and prescribe an accounting principle for each one.
e. None of the above is correct.

LO 2 That a business should be consistent from year to year in its accounting practices most directly relates to the FASB's concept that information reported in financial statements should be:

a. Relevant.
b. Material.
c. Reliable.
d. Measurable.
e. Comparable.

LO 3 The following selected information is from the conventional balance sheets of Company A and Company B:

	Company A	Company B
Cash	$ 24,000	$ 40,000
Equipment, net	96,000	102,200
Land	130,000	157,800
Total assets	$250,000	$300,000

Based on this information, which of the following statements is true?

a. Company B's assets are worth $50,000 more than Company A's assets.
b. Company A's assets are worth at least $16,000 less than Company B's assets.
c. If Company A and Company B own identical equipment and depreciate the equipment on the same basis, Company A must have purchased its machinery at an earlier date than Company B.
d. If Company A and Company B own identical tracts of land, Company B must have purchased its land at a later date than Company A.
e. The relative values of Company A's and Company B's assets cannot be determined from this conventional balance sheet information.

LO 4 Foster Company purchased 150 acres of land for $100,000 in 19X1 when the general price index was 145.0 and the specific price index for land was 142.0. In December 19X4, the general price index was 150.0 and the specific price index for land was 140.0. The purchasing power gain or (loss) pertaining to land that would be reported on the 19X4 historical cost/constant purchasing power income statement would be (rounded to the nearest dollar):

a. $ –0– .
b. $ 3,448.
c. $(3,448).
d. $ 1,408.
e. $(1,408).

LO 5 In the current cost approach to accounting:

a. All balance sheet items are restated to reflect general price level changes.
b. On the balance sheet, nonmonetary items are restated to reflect general price level changes.
c. On the balance sheet, monetary items are restated to reflect general price level changes.
d. Nonmonetary assets are reported at the amounts that would have to be paid to purchase them as of the balance sheet date.
e. None of the above is correct.

LO 6 If current selling price valuations were used to account for the assets and liabilities of a business:

a. Gains and losses from changing market values would not be recorded.
b. Losses from changing market values would be recorded but not gains.
c. All accountants agree that gains and losses from changes in market values would be reported on the income statement.
d. Some accountants believe that gains and losses from changes in market values should be accumulated and reported on the balance sheet as unrealized gains and losses.
e. None of the above is correct.

LO 7 Obligations that are not fixed in terms of the number of monetary units needed to satisfy them, and that therefore tend to fluctuate in amount with changes in the general price level, are called:

a. Monetary assets.
b. Monetary liabilities.
c. Nonmonetary assets.
d. Nonmonetary liabilities.
e. Current liabilities.

Questions for Class Discussion

1. Can a concept be used descriptively and prescriptively?
2. What is the starting point in a top-down approach to developing accounting concepts?
3. What is the starting point in a bottom-up approach to developing accounting concepts?
4. Explain the difference between the FASB's *Statements of Financial Accounting Concepts* and the *Statements of Financial Accounting Standards.*
5. Which three qualitative characteristics of accounting information did the FASB identify as being necessary if the information is to be useful?
6. What is implied by saying that financial information should have the qualitative characteristic of relevance?
7. What are the characteristics of accounting information that make it reliable?
8. What is the meaning of the phrase *elements of financial statements?*
9. What are the four criteria an item should satisfy to be recognized in the financial statements?
10. Some people argue that conventional financial statements fail to adequately account for inflation. What general problem with conventional financial statements generates this argument?
11. What is the fundamental difference in the adjustments made under current cost accounting and under historical cost/constant purchasing power accounting?
12. What are historical cost/nominal dollar financial statements?
13. What is the difference between monetary and nonmonetary assets?
14. Describe the meaning of *operating profit* under a current cost accounting system.
15. What is meant by the current selling price valuation of a liability?

Exercises

Exercise C–1
Adjusting costs for historical cost/constant purchasing power statements
(LO 5)

A company's plant and equipment consisted of land purchased in late 19X1 for $460,000, machinery purchased in late 19X3 for $154,000, and a building purchased in late 19X5 for $210,000. Values of the general price index for December of 19X1 through 19X8 are as follows:

19X1	100.0
19X2	106.5
19X3	111.0
19X4	121.3
19X5	128.0
19X6	139.0
19X7	144.0
19X8	153.0

Required

1. Assuming the preceding price index adequately represents end-of-year price levels, calculate the amount of each asset's cost that would be shown on a historical cost/constant purchasing power balance sheet for (*a*) December 31, 19X7, and (*b*) December 31, 19X8. Ignore any accumulated depreciation. Round calculations to three decimals.
2. Would the historical cost/constant purchasing power income statement for 19X8 disclose any purchasing power gain or loss as a consequence of holding these assets? If so, how much?

Exercise C–2
Classifying monetary and nonmonetary items
(LO 5 and 6)

Determine whether the following are monetary or nonmonetary items:

1. Notes payable.
2. Merchandise inventory.
3. Copyrights.
4. Savings accounts.
5. Common stock.
6. Product warranties liability.
7. Wages payable.
8. Contributed capital in excess of par value, common stock.

9. Accounts receivable.
10. Goodwill.
11. Prepaid insurance.
12. Computer equipment.
13. Retained earnings.
14. Prepaid rent.

Exercise C–3
Calculating amounts for current cost statements
(LO 6)

A company purchased land in 19X1 at a cost of $730,000 and in 19X2 at a cost of $357,000. What is the current cost of these land purchases in (*a*) 19X3 and (*b*) 19X4, given the following specific price index for land costs?

19X1	104.0
19X2	100.0
19X3	109.2
19X4	117.0

Exercise C–4
Calculating general purchasing power gain or loss
(LO 5)

Calculate the general purchasing power gain or loss in 19X2 given the following information (round calculations to three decimals):

Time period	Price Index
December 19X1	95.6
Average during 19X2	100.2
December 19X2	105.0

a. The cash balance on December 31, 19X1, was $74,000. During 19X2, cash sales occurred uniformly throughout the year and amounted to $452,000. Payments of expenses also occurred evenly throughout the year and amounted to $315,000. Accounts payable of $22,500 were paid in December.

b. Accounts payable amounted to $52,000 on December 31, 19X1. Additional accounts payable amounting to $97,000 were recorded evenly throughout 19X2. The only payment of accounts during the year was $22,500 in late December.

Problems

Problem C–1
Adjusting costs to historical cost/constant purchasing power amounts
(LO 5)

Garson Company purchased machinery for $330,000 on December 31, 19X1. It expected the equipment to last five years and to have no salvage value; straight-line depreciation was to be used. It sold the equipment on December 31, 19X5, for $82,000. End-of-year general price index numbers were as follows:

19X1	106.0
19X2	110.1
19X3	117.0
19X4	122.3
19X5	128.9

Required

(Round answers to the nearest whole dollar.)

1. What should be presented for the machinery and accumulated depreciation on a historical cost/constant purchasing power balance sheet dated December 31, 19X4? Hint: Depreciation is the total amount of cost that has been allocated to expense. Therefore, the price index number that is used to adjust the nominal dollar cost of the asset should also be used to adjust the nominal dollar amount of depreciation.
2. How much depreciation expense should be shown on the historical cost/constant purchasing power income statement for 19X4?
3. How much depreciation expense should be shown on the historical cost/constant purchasing power income statement for 19X5?
4. How much gain on the sale of the machinery should be reported on the historical cost/nominal dollar income statement for 19X5?

5. After adjusting the machinery's cost and accumulated depreciation to the end-of-19X5 price level, how much gain in (loss of) purchasing power was realized on the sale of the machinery?

Problem C–2
Calculating purchasing power gain or loss
(LO 5)

Parker Company had three monetary items during 19X2: cash, accounts receivable, and accounts payable. The changes in these accounts during the year were as follows:

Cash:	
Beginning balance	$ 90,500
Cash proceeds from sale of building (in May 19X2)	51,200
Cash receipts from customers (spread evenly throughout the year)	359,400
Payments of accounts payable (spread evenly throughout the year)	(274,700)
Dividends declared and paid in July 19X2	(44,000)
Payments of other cash expenses during August 19X2	(77,800)
Ending balance	$104,600
Accounts receivable:	
Beginning balance	$ 92,800
Sales to customers (spread evenly throughout the year)	375,600
Cash receipts from customers (spread evenly throughout the year)	(359,400)
Ending balance	$109,000
Accounts payable:	
Beginning balance	$115,000
Merchandise purchases (spread evenly throughout the year)	231,600
Special purchase December 31, 19X2	47,500
Payments of accounts payable (spread evenly throughout the year)	(274,700)
Ending balance	$119,400

General price index numbers at the end of 19X1 and during 19X2 are as follows:

December 19X1	196.4
January 19X2	202.1
May 19X2	211.0
July 19X2	214.1
August 19X2	215.6
December 19X2	217.0
Average for 19X2	214.8

Required

Calculate the general purchasing power gain or loss experienced by Parker Company in 19X2. Round all amounts to the nearest whole dollar.

Problem C–3
Historical cost/nominal dollars, historical cost/constant purchasing power, and current costs
(LO 4, 5, and 6)

Longhorn Corporation purchased a tract of land for $574,000 in 19X1, when the general price index was 127.4. At the same time, a price index for land values in the area of Longhorn's tract was 133.1. In 19X2, when the general price index was 134.6 and the specific price index for land was 142.5, Longhorn bought another tract of land for $296,000. In late 19X7, the general price index is 157.2 and the price index for land values is 174.0.

Required

1. In preparing a balance sheet at the end of 19X7, show the amount that should be reported for land based on:
   a. Historical cost/nominal dollars.
   b. Historical cost/constant purchasing power.
   c. Current costs.
   (Round all amounts to the nearest whole dollar.)

2. In Longhorn's December 19X7 meeting of the board of directors, one director insists that Longhorn has earned a gain in purchasing power as a result of owning the land. A second director argues that there could not have been a purchasing power gain or loss since land is a nonmonetary asset. Which director do you think is correct? Explain your answer.

Problem C–4
Analytical essay
(LO 1, 2, 3)

Write a brief essay that explains the difference between descriptive and prescriptive concepts and that explains why the FASB's conceptual framework is designed to be prescriptive. Also discuss the question of whether specific concepts can be both descriptive and prescriptive.

Answers to Objective Review Questions

LO 1 (*c*)
LO 2 (*e*)
LO 3 (*e*)
LO 4 (*e*)
LO 5 (*a*)
LO 6 (*d*)
LO 7 (*d*)

APPENDIX

D

Special Journals

Even in small businesses, the quantity of data that is processed through the accounting system is large. As a result, the accounting system should be designed so that the data can be processed efficiently. This appendix explains some general procedures and techniques that you can use with a manual accounting system to efficiently process data. Computerized systems often involve the same components but, of course, the specific procedures used by the bookkeeper are different.

Learning Objectives

After studying Appendix D, you should be able to:

1. Explain how special journals save posting labor and state the type of transaction that is recorded in each journal when special journals are used.
2. Journalize and post transactions when special journals are used.
3. Define or explain the words and phrases listed in the appendix glossary.

Reducing Writing and Posting Labor

LO 1 Explain how special journals save posting labor and state the type of transaction that is recorded in each journal when special journals are used.

The General Journal is a flexible journal in which you can record any transaction. However, each debit and credit entered in a General Journal must be individually posted. As a result, a firm that uses a General Journal to record all the transactions of its business requires much time and labor to post the individual debits and credits.

One way to reduce the writing and the posting labor is to divide the transactions of a business into groups of similar transactions and to provide a separate **special journal** for recording the transactions in each group. For example, most of the transactions of a merchandising business fall into four groups: sales on credit, purchases on credit, cash receipts, and cash disbursements. When a special journal is provided for each group, the journals are

1. A Sales Journal for recording credit sales.
2. A Purchases Journal for recording credit purchases.
3. A Cash Receipts Journal for recording cash receipts.
4. A Cash Disbursements Journal for recording cash payments.
5. A General Journal for all the miscellaneous transactions not recorded in the special journals and also for adjusting, closing, and correcting entries.

The following illustrations show how special journals save time in journalizing and posting transactions. They do this by providing special columns for accumulating the debits and credits of similar transactions. These journals allow you to post the amounts entered in the special columns as column totals rather than as individual amounts. For example, you can save posting labor if you record credit sales for a month in a Sales Journal like the one at the top of Illustration D–1. As the illustration shows, you do not post the credit sales to the general ledger accounts until the end of the month. Then, you calculate the total sales for the month and post the total as one debit to Accounts Receivable and as one credit to Sales. Only seven sales are recorded in the illustrated journal. However, if you assume the 7 sales represent 700 sales, you can better appreciate the posting labor saved by making only one debit to Accounts Receivable and one credit to Sales.

The special journal in Illustration D–1 is also called a **columnar journal** because it has columns for recording the date, the customer's name, the invoice number, and the amount of each credit sale. Only credit sales are recorded in it, and they are recorded daily, with the information about each sale placed on a separate line. Normally, the information is taken from a copy of the sales ticket or invoice prepared at the time of the sale.

Posting the Sales Journal

LO 2 Journalize and post transactions when special journals are used.

When customer accounts are maintained in a subsidiary ledger, a Sales Journal is posted as shown in Illustration D–1. The individual sales recorded in the Sales Journal are posted each day to the proper customer accounts in the Accounts Receivable Ledger. These daily postings keep the customer accounts up-to-date. This is important in granting credit because the person responsible for granting credit should know the amount the credit-seeking customer currently owes. The source of this information is the customer's account, and if the account is not up-to-date, an incorrect decision may be made.

Note the check marks in the Sales Journal's Posting Reference column. They indicate that the sales recorded in the journal were individually posted to the customer accounts in the Accounts Receivable Ledger. Check marks rather than account numbers are used because customer accounts may not be numbered. When the accounts are not numbered, they are arranged alphabetically in the Accounts Receivable Ledger so they can be located easily.

In addition to the daily postings to customer accounts, the Sales Journal's Amount column is totaled at the end of the month. Then, the total is debited to Accounts Receivable and credited to Sales. The credit records the month's revenue from charge sales. The debit records the resulting increase in accounts receivable.

Identifying Posted Amounts

When posting several journals to ledger accounts, you should indicate in the Posting Reference column before each posted amount the journal and the page number of the journal from which the amount was posted. Indicate the journal by using its initial. Thus, items posted from the Cash Disbursements Journal carry the initial *D* before their journal page numbers in the Posting Reference columns. Likewise, items from the Cash Receipts Journal carry the letter *R*. Those from the Sales Journal carry the initial *S*. Items from the Purchases Journal carry the initial *P*, and from the General Journal, the letter *G*.

Cash Receipts Journal

A Cash Receipts Journal that is designed to save labor through posting column totals must be a multicolumn journal. A multicolumn journal is necessary because different accounts are credited when cash is received from different sources. For example, the cash receipts of a store normally fall into three groups: (1) cash from credit customers in payment of their accounts,

ILLUSTRATION D-1

Sales Journal Page 3

Date		Account Debited	Invoice Number	PR	Amount
Feb.	2	James Henry	307	√	450.00
	7	Albert Smith	308	√	500.00
	13	Sam Moore	309	√	350.00
	15	Paul Roth	310	√	200.00
	22	James Henry	311	√	225.00
	25	Frank Booth	312	√	175.00
	28	Albert Smith	313	√	250.00
	28	Total—Accounts Receivable, Dr.; Sales, Cr.			2,150.00
					(106/413)

Individual amounts are posted daily to the subsidiary ledger.

Total is posted at the end of the month to the general ledger accounts.

Accounts Receivable Ledger

Frank Booth

Date		PR	Debit	Credit	Balance
Feb.	25	S3	175.00		175.00

James Henry

Date		PR	Debit	Credit	Balance
Feb.	2	S3	450.00		450.00
	22	S3	225.00		675.00

Sam Moore

Date		PR	Debit	Credit	Balance
Feb.	13	S3	350.00		350.00

Paul Roth

Date		PR	Debit	Credit	Balance
Feb.	15	S3	200.00		200.00

Albert Smith

Date		PR	Debit	Credit	Balance
Feb.	7	S3	500.00		500.00
	28	S3	250.00		750.00

General Ledger

Accounts Receivable No. 106

Date		PR	Debit	Credit	Balance
Feb.	28	S3	2,150.00		2,150.00

Sales No. 413

Date		PR	Debit	Credit	Balance
Feb.	28	S3		2,150.00	2,150.00

Note that the customer accounts are in a subsidiary ledger and the financial statement accounts are in the **General Ledger.** If you have not yet studied Chapter 7, read pages 264–266 for an explanation of subsidiary ledgers and controlling accounts.

Explanation columns are omitted from the accounts due to a lack of space.

(2) cash from cash sales, and (3) cash from miscellaneous sources. Note in Illustration D–2 that a special column is provided for the credits that result when cash is received from each of these sources.

Cash from Credit Customers

When a Cash Receipts Journal similar to Illustration D–2 is used to record cash received in payment of a customer's account, the customer's name is entered in the Journal's Account Credited column. The amount credited to the customer's account is entered in the Accounts Receivable Credit column, and the debits to Sales Discounts and Cash are entered in the journal's last two columns.

Look at the Accounts Receivable Credit column. First, observe that this column contains only credits to customer accounts. Second, the individual credits are posted daily to the customer accounts in the subsidiary Accounts Receivable Ledger. Third, the column total is posted at the end of the month as a credit to the Accounts Receivable controlling account. This is the normal recording and posting procedure when using special journals and controlling accounts with subsidiary ledgers. Transactions are normally entered in a special journal column and the individual amounts are then posted to the subsidiary ledger accounts and the column totals are posted to the general ledger accounts.

Cash Sales

After cash sales are entered on one or more cash registers and totaled at the end of each day, the daily total is recorded with a debit to Cash and a credit to Sales. When using a Cash Receipts Journal like Illustration D–2, enter the debits to Cash in the Cash Debit column, and the credits in a special column headed Sales Credit. By using a separate Sales Credit column, you can post the total cash sales for a month as a single amount, the column total. (Although cash sales are normally journalized daily based on the cash register reading, cash sales are journalized only once each week in Illustration D–2 to shorten the illustration.)

At the time they record daily cash sales in the Cash Receipts Journal, some bookkeepers, as in Illustration D–2, place a check mark in the Posting Reference (PR) column to indicate that no amount is individually posted from that line of the journal. Other bookkeepers use a double check (√√) to distinguish amounts that are not posted to customer accounts from amounts that are posted.

Miscellaneous Receipts of Cash

Most cash receipts are from collections of accounts receivable and from cash sales. However, other sources of cash include borrowing money from a bank or selling unneeded assets. The Other Accounts Credit column is for receipts that do not occur often enough to warrant a separate column. In most companies, the items entered in this column are few and are posted to a variety of general ledger accounts. As a result, postings are less apt to be omitted if these items are posted daily.

The Cash Receipts Journal's Posting Reference column is used only for daily postings from the Other Accounts and Accounts Receivable columns. The account numbers in the Posting Reference column indicate items that were posted to general ledger accounts. The check marks indicate either that an item (like a day's cash sales) was not posted or that an item was posted to the subsidiary Accounts Receivable Ledger.

ILLUSTRATION D-2 *Cash Receipts Journal*

Cash Receipts Journal — Page 2

Date		Account Credited	Explanation	PR	Other Accounts Credit	Accts. Rec. Credit	Sales Credit	Sales Discounts Debit	Cash Debit
Feb.	7	Sales	Cash sales	√			4,450.00		4,450.00
	12	James Henry	Invoice, 2/2	√		450.00		9.00	441.00
	14	Sales	Cash sales	√			3,925.00		3,925.00
	17	Albert Smith	Invoice, 2/7	√		500.00		10.00	490.00
	20	Notes Payable	Note to bank	245	1,000.00				1,000.00
	21	Sales	Cash sales	√			4,700.00		4,700.00
	23	Sam Moore	Invoice, 2/13	√		350.00		7.00	343.00
	25	Paul Roth	Invoice, 2/15	√		200.00		4.00	196.00
	28	Sales	Cash sales	√			4,225.00		4,225.00
	28	Totals			1,000.00	1,500.00	17,300.00	30.00	19,770.00
					(√)	(106)	(413)	(415)	(101)

Individual amounts in the Other Accounts Credit and Accounts Receivable Credit columns are posted daily.

Total is not posted.

Totals posted at the end of the month.

Accounts Receivable Ledger

Frank Booth

Date		PR	Debit	Credit	Balance
Feb.	25	S3	175.00		175.00

James Henry

Date		PR	Debit	Credit	Balance
Feb.	2	S3	450.00		450.00
	12	R2		450.00	-0-
	22	S3	225.00		225.00

Sam Moore

Date		PR	Debit	Credit	Balance
Feb.	13	S3	350.00		350.00
	23	R2		350.00	-0-

Paul Roth

Date		PR	Debit	Credit	Balance
Feb.	15	S3	200.00		200.00
	25	R2		200.00	-0-

Albert Smith

Date		PR	Debit	Credit	Balance
Feb.	7	S3	500.00		500.00
	17	R2		500.00	-0-
	28	S3	250.00		250.00

General Ledger

Cash — No. 101

Date		PR	Debit	Credit	Balance
Feb.	28	R2	19,770.00		19,770.00

Accounts Receivable — No. 106

Date		PR	Debit	Credit	Balance
Feb.	28	S3	2,150.00		2,150.00
	28	R2		1,500.00	650.00

Notes Payable — No. 245

Date		PR	Debit	Credit	Balance
Feb.	20	R2		1,000.00	1,000.00

Sales — No. 413

Date		PR	Debit	Credit	Balance
Feb.	28	S3		2,150.00	2,150.00
	28	R2		17,300.00	19,450.00

Sales Discounts — No. 415

Date		PR	Debit	Credit	Balance
Feb.	28	R2	30.00		30.00

Month-End Postings

At the end of the month, the amounts in the Accounts Receivable, Sales, Sales Discounts, and Cash columns of the Cash Receipts Journal are posted as column totals. However, the transactions recorded in any journal must result in equal debits and credits to general ledger accounts. Therefore, to be sure that the total debits and credits in a columnar journal are equal, you must *crossfoot* the column totals before posting them. To *foot* a column of numbers is to add it. To crossfoot, add the debit column totals and add the credit column totals; then compare the two sums for equality. For Illustration D–2, the two sums appear as follows:

Debit Columns		**Credit Columns**	
Sales discounts debit	$ 30	Other accounts credit	$ 1,000
Cash debit	19,770	Accounts receivable credit . .	1,500
		Sales credit	17,300
Total	$19,800	Total	$19,800

Because the sums are equal, you may assume that the debits in the journal equal the credits.

After crossfooting the journal to confirm that debits equal credits, post the totals of the last four columns as indicated in each column heading. As for the Other Accounts column, do not post the column total because the individual items in this column are posted daily. Note in Illustration D–2 the check mark below the Other Accounts column. The check mark indicates that the column total was not posted. The account numbers of the accounts to which the remaining column totals were posted are in parentheses below each column.

Posting items daily from the Other Accounts column with a delayed posting of the offsetting items in the Cash column (total) causes the General Ledger to be out of balance during the month. However, this does not matter because posting the Cash column total causes the offsetting amounts to reach the General Ledger before the trial balance is prepared.

Purchases Journal

You can use a Purchases Journal with one money column to record purchases of merchandise on credit. However, a Purchases Journal usually is more useful if it is a multicolumn journal in which all credit purchases on account are recorded. Such a journal may have columns similar to those in Illustration D–3. In the illustrated journal, the invoice date and terms together indicate the date on which payment for each purchase is due. The Accounts Payable Credit column is used to record the amounts credited to each creditor's account. These amounts are posted daily to the individual creditor accounts in a subsidiary Accounts Payable Ledger.

In Illustration D–3, note that each line of the Account column shows the subsidiary ledger account that should be posted for the amount in the Accounts Payable Credit column. The Account column also shows the general ledger account to be debited when a purchase involves an amount recorded in the Other Accounts Debit column.

In this illustration, note the separate column for purchases of office supplies on credit. A separate column such as this is useful whenever several transactions involve debits to a particular account. The Other Accounts Debit column in Illustration D–3 allows the Purchases Journal to be used for all purchase transactions involving credits to Accounts Payable. The individual amounts in the Other Accounts Debit column typically are posted daily to the indicated general ledger accounts.

ILLUSTRATION D-3 *Purchases Journal*

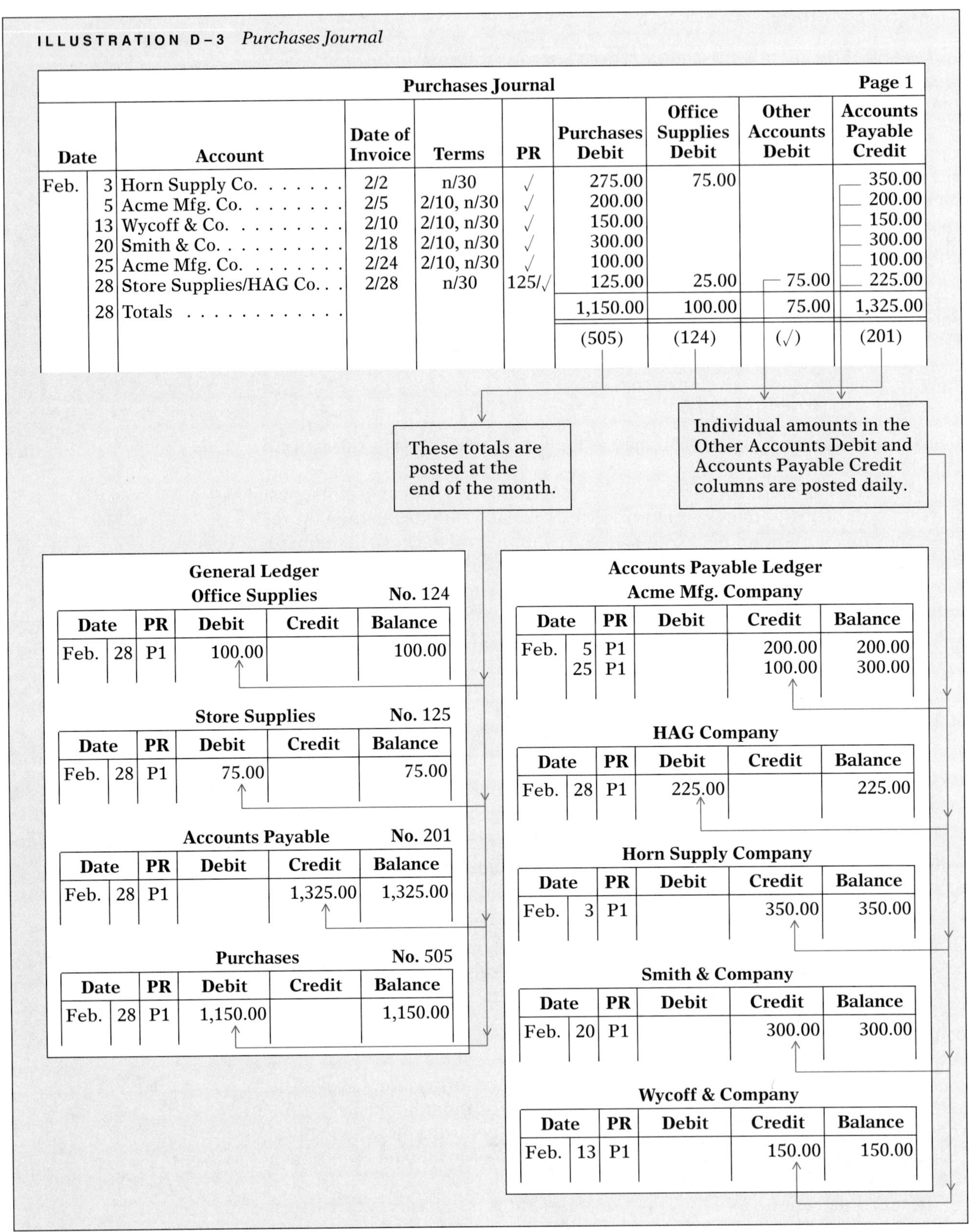

Purchases Journal — Page 1

Date		Account	Date of Invoice	Terms	PR	Purchases Debit	Office Supplies Debit	Other Accounts Debit	Accounts Payable Credit
Feb.	3	Horn Supply Co.	2/2	n/30	√	275.00	75.00		350.00
	5	Acme Mfg. Co.	2/5	2/10, n/30	√	200.00			200.00
	13	Wycoff & Co.	2/10	2/10, n/30	√	150.00			150.00
	20	Smith & Co.	2/18	2/10, n/30	√	300.00			300.00
	25	Acme Mfg. Co.	2/24	2/10, n/30	√	100.00			100.00
	28	Store Supplies/HAG Co. . .	2/28	n/30	125/√	125.00	25.00	75.00	225.00
	28	Totals				1,150.00	100.00	75.00	1,325.00
						(505)	(124)	(√)	(201)

General Ledger

Office Supplies — No. 124

Date		PR	Debit	Credit	Balance
Feb.	28	P1	100.00		100.00

Store Supplies — No. 125

Date		PR	Debit	Credit	Balance
Feb.	28	P1	75.00		75.00

Accounts Payable — No. 201

Date		PR	Debit	Credit	Balance
Feb.	28	P1		1,325.00	1,325.00

Purchases — No. 505

Date		PR	Debit	Credit	Balance
Feb.	28	P1	1,150.00		1,150.00

Accounts Payable Ledger

Acme Mfg. Company

Date		PR	Debit	Credit	Balance
Feb.	5	P1		200.00	200.00
	25	P1		100.00	300.00

HAG Company

Date		PR	Debit	Credit	Balance
Feb.	28	P1	225.00		225.00

Horn Supply Company

Date		PR	Debit	Credit	Balance
Feb.	3	P1		350.00	350.00

Smith & Company

Date		PR	Debit	Credit	Balance
Feb.	20	P1		300.00	300.00

Wycoff & Company

Date		PR	Debit	Credit	Balance
Feb.	13	P1		150.00	150.00

At the end of the month, all of the column totals except the Other Accounts Debit column are posted to the appropriate general ledger accounts. After this is done, the balance in the Accounts Payable controlling account should equal the sum of the account balances in the subsidiary Accounts Payable Ledger.

ILLUSTRATION D-4 *Cash Disbursements Journal*

Cash Disbursements Journal — Page 2

Date		Ch. No.	Payee	Account Debited	PR	Other Accounts Debit	Accounts Payable Debit	Purchases Discounts Credit	Cash Credit
Feb.	3	105	L. & N. Railroad . . .	Transportation-In . .	508	15.00			15.00
	12	106	East Sales Co.	Purchases	505	25.00			25.00
	15	107	Acme Mfg. Co.	Acme Mfg. Co.	√		200.00	4.00	196.00
	15	108	Jerry Hale	Salaries Expense . .	622	250.00			250.00
	20	109	Wycoff & Co.	Wycoff & Co.	√		150.00	3.00	147.00
	28	110	Smith & Co.	Smith & Co.	√		300.00	6.00	294.00
	28		Totals			290.00	650.00	13.00	927.00
						(√)	(201)	(507)	(101)

Individual amounts in the Other Accounts Debit column and Accounts Payable Debit column are posted daily.

Totals posted at the end of the month.

Accounts Payable Ledger

Acme Mfg. Company

Date		PR	Debit	Credit	Balance
Feb.	5	P1		200.00	200.00
	15	D2	200.00		-0-
	25	P1		100.00	100.00

HAG Company

Date		PR	Debit	Credit	Balance
Feb.	28	P1		225.00	225.00

Horn Supply Company

Date		PR	Debit	Credit	Balance
Feb.	3	P1		350.00	350.00

Smith & Company

Date		PR	Debit	Credit	Balance
Feb.	20	P1		300.00	300.00
	28	D2	300.00		-0-

Wycoff & Company

Date		PR	Debit	Credit	Balance
Feb.	13	P1		150.00	150.00
	20	D2	150.00		-0-

General Ledger

Cash — No. 101

Date		PR	Debit	Credit	Balance
Feb.	28	R2	19,770.00		19,770.00
	28	D2		927.00	18,843.00

Accounts Payable — No. 201

Date		PR	Debit	Credit	Balance
Feb.	28	P1		1,325.00	1,325.00
	28	D2	650.00		675.00

Purchases — No. 505

Date		PR	Debit	Credit	Balance
Feb.	12	D2	25.00		25.00
	28	P1	1,150.00		1,175.00

Purchases Discounts — No. 507

Date		PR	Debit	Credit	Balance
Feb.	28	D2		13.00	13.00

Transportation-In — No. 508

Date		PR	Debit	Credit	Balance
Feb.	3	D2	15.00		15.00

Salaries Expense — No. 622

Date		PR	Debit	Credit	Balance
Feb.	15	D2	250.00		250.00

ILLUSTRATION D–5 *A Sales Journal with a Column for Sales Taxes Payable*

Sales Journal

Date		Account Debited	Invoice Number	PR	Accounts Receivable Debit	Sales Taxes Payable Credit	Sales Credit
Dec.	1	D. R. Horn	7–1698		103.00	3.00	100.00

The Cash Disbursements Journal or Check Register

The Cash Disbursements Journal, like the Cash Receipts Journal, has columns so that you can post repetitive debits and credits in column totals. The repetitive cash payments involve debits to the Accounts Payable controlling account and credits to both Purchases Discounts and Cash. Most companies usually purchase merchandise on credit. Therefore, a Purchases column is not needed. Instead, the occasional cash purchase is recorded as shown on line 2 of Illustration D–4.

Observe that the illustrated journal has a column headed Check Number (Ck. No.). To gain control over cash disbursements, all payments except for very small amounts should be made by check.[1] The checks should be prenumbered by the printer and should be entered in the journal in numerical order with each check's number in the column headed Ck. No. This makes it possible to scan the numbers in the column for omitted checks. When a Cash Disbursements Journal has a column for check numbers, it is often called a **Check Register.**

To post a Cash Disbursements Journal or Check Register similar to Illustration D–4, do the following. Each day, post the individual amounts in the Other Accounts Debit column to the appropriate general ledger accounts. Also on a daily basis, post the individual amounts in the Accounts Payable Debit column to the named creditors' accounts in the subsidiary Accounts Payable Ledger. At the end of the month, after you crossfoot the column totals, post the Accounts Payable Debit column total to the Accounts Payable controlling account. Then, post the Purchases Discounts Credit column total to the Purchases Discounts account and post the Cash Credit column total to the Cash account. Because the items in the Other Accounts column are posted individually, do not post the column total.

Sales Taxes

Many cities and states require retailers to collect sales taxes from their customers and to periodically remit these taxes to the city or state treasurer. When using a columnar Sales Journal, you can have a record of the taxes collected by adding special columns in the journal as shown in Illustration D–5.

As we described earlier in the chapter, the column totals of a Sales Journal are typically posted at the end of each month. This, of course, includes crediting the Sales Taxes Payable account for the total of the Sales Taxes Payable column. The individual amounts in the Accounts Receivable column are posted daily to the customer accounts in the Accounts Receivable Ledger. The individual amounts in the Sales Taxes Payable and Sales columns are not posted.

A business that collects sales taxes on its cash sales may use a special Sales Taxes Payable column in its Cash Receipts Journal.

[1] In Chapter 6, we discuss a system that controls small payments made with currency and coins.

ILLUSTRATION D–6

Sales Returns and Allowances Journal

Date		Account Credited	Explanation	Credit Memo No.	PR	Amount
Oct.	7	Robert Moore	Defective merchandise	203	✓	10.00
	14	James Warren	Defective merchandise	204	✓	12.00
	18	T. M. Jones	Not ordered	205	✓	6.00
	23	Sam Smith	Defective merchandise	206	✓	18.00
	31	Sales Returns and Allowances, Dr.;	Accts. Receivable, Cr.			46.00
						(414/106)

Sales Invoices as a Sales Journal

To save labor, some retailers avoid using Sales Journals for credit sales. Instead, they post each sales invoice total directly to the customer's account in the subsidiary Accounts Receivable Ledger. Then, they place copies of the invoices in numerical order in a binder. At the end of the month, they total all the invoices of that month, and make a general journal entry to debit Accounts Receivable and credit Sales for the total. In effect, the bound invoice copies act as a Sales Journal. Such a procedure is known as direct posting of sales invoices.

Sales Returns

A business that has only a few sales returns may record them in a General Journal with an entry like the following:

Oct.	17	Sales Returns and Allowances	414	17.50	
		Accounts Receivable—George Ball . . .	106/✓		17.50
		Customer returned merchandise.			

The debit of the entry is posted to the Sales Returns and Allowances account. The credit is posted to both the Accounts Receivable controlling account and the customer's account. Note the account number and the check mark, 106/✓, in the PR column on the credit line. This indicates that both the Accounts Receivable controlling account in the General Ledger and the George Ball account in the Accounts Receivable Ledger were credited for $17.50. Both were credited because the balance of the controlling account in the General Ledger will not equal the sum of the customer account balances in the subsidiary ledger unless both are credited.

A company with a large number of sales returns can save posting labor by recording them in a special Sales Returns and Allowances Journal similar to Illustration D–6. Note that this is in keeping with the idea that a company can design and use a special journal for any group of similar transactions if there are enough transactions to warrant the journal. When using a Sales Returns and Allowances Journal to record returns, the amounts in the journal are posted daily to the customers' accounts. Then, at the end of the month, the journal total is posted as a debit to Sales Returns and Allowances and as a credit to Accounts Receivable.

General Journal Entries

When special journals are used, a General Journal is always necessary for adjusting, closing, and correcting entries and for a few transactions that cannot be recorded in the special journals. If a Sales Returns and Allowances Journal is not provided, some of these transactions are sales returns, purchases returns, and purchases of plant assets.

Summary of the Appendix in Terms of Learning Objectives

LO 1 Columnar journals are designed so that repetitive debits to a specific account are entered in a separate column. The same is done for repetitive credits. As a result, the column totals can be posted as single amounts, thereby eliminating the need to post individually each debit and credit.

Those using special journals enter all credit sales in a Sales Journal. Purchases on credit are entered in a Purchases Journal. They enter all cash receipts in the Cash Receipts Journal, and all cash payments by check are entered in the Cash Disbursements Journal (or Check Register). Any transactions that cannot be entered in the special journals are entered in the General Journal.

LO 2 To enter a transaction when using special journals, first decide which journal must be used. Second, record the transaction in accordance with the columns provided in the journal and the nature of the transaction.

When posting transactions from special journals to the accounts, post individual debits and credits to subsidiary Accounts Receivable and Accounts Payable Ledgers daily. Other amounts that must be posted individually also may be posted daily. Normally, the columns of each special journal are totaled and crossfooted at the end of each month. Then, the column totals are posted to the appropriate General Ledger accounts.

Glossary

LO 3 Define or explain the words and phrases listed in the appendix glossary.

Check Register a book of original entry for recording cash payments by check. p. 628

Columnar journal a book of original entry having columns, each of which is designated as the place for entering specific data about each transaction of a group of similar transactions. p. 622

General Ledger the ledger that contains the financial statement accounts of a business. p. 621

Special journal a book of original entry that is designed and used for recording only a specified type of transaction. p. 620

Objective Review

Answers to the following questions are listed at the end of this appendix. Be sure that you decide which is the one best answer to each question *before* you check the answers.

LO 1 When special journals are used:

a. A General Journal is not used.

b. All cash payments by check are recorded in the Cash Disbursements Journal.

c. All purchase transactions are recorded in the Purchases Journal.

d. All sales transactions are recorded in the Sales Journal.

e. All cash receipts except from cash sales of merchandise are recorded in the Cash Receipts Journal.

LO 2 Travor Company uses special journals to record accounting data. Travor does not offer any sales discounts for credit sales. The following transactions occurred in the month of May:

May 1 Credit sale to Fairview Company, $1,200.
10 Cash sale to Frisco, Inc., $500.
20 Payment in full received from Fairview Company for May 1 sale.
31 Credit sale to Haley Corporation, $750.

In posting the transactions from the special journals to the accounts, Travor Company:

a. Would not post anything in the subsidiary Accounts Receivable Ledger for Fairview Company because payment in full was received within the same month of the sale.

b. Would post $500 in the subsidiary Accounts Receivable Ledger for Frisco, Inc.

c. Would post a $1,950 credit to the Sales account from the Sales Journal.

d. Would post a $1,200 credit to the Sales account from the Cash Receipts Journal.

e. Would post a $2,450 debit to the Accounts Receivable account from the Sales Journal.

Questions for Class Discussion

1. How does a columnar journal save posting labor?
2. When special journals are used, separate special journals normally are used to record each of four different types of transactions. What are these four types of transactions?
3. Why should sales to and receipts of cash from credit customers be recorded and posted daily?
4. Both credits to customer accounts and credits to miscellaneous accounts are individually posted from a Cash Receipts Journal similar to the one in Illustration D–2. Why not put both kinds of credits in the same column and thus save journal space?
5. What procedures allow copies of a company's sales invoices to be used as a Sales Journal?
6. When a general journal entry is used to record a returned credit sale, the credit of the entry must be posted twice. Does this cause the trial balance to be out of balance? Why or why not?
7. How does one tell from which journal a particular amount in a ledger account was posted?

Exercises

Exercise D–1
Special journals
(LO 1)

Sampson Iron Works uses a Sales Journal, a Purchases Journal, a Cash Receipts Journal, a Cash Disbursements Journal, and a General Journal like the ones described in the appendix. Sampson recently completed the following transactions. List the transaction letters and next to each letter give the name of the journal in which the transaction would be recorded.

a. Paid a creditor.
b. Sold merchandise for cash.
c. Purchased merchandise on credit.
d. Sold merchandise on credit.
e. Gave credit to a customer for merchandise purchased on credit and returned.
f. Borrowed money from the bank.
g. Purchased shop supplies on credit.
h. Signed a promissory note for the purchase of office equipment.
i. Paid an employee's salary.
j. Recorded adjusting and closing entries.

Exercise D–2
The Sales Journal
(LO 1, 2)

Fletcher's Frozen Foods uses a Sales Journal, a Purchases Journal, a Cash Receipts Journal, a Cash Disbursements Journal, and a General Journal. The following transactions occurred during the month of February:

Feb. 2 Sold merchandise to M. Stohl for $356 cash, Invoice No. 5703.
5 Purchased merchandise on credit from Campbell Company, $2,035.
7 Sold merchandise to E. Jason for $950; terms 2/10, n/30; Invoice No. 5704.
8 Borrowed $5,000 by giving a note to the bank.
12 Sold merchandise to L. Patrick for $223, terms n/30, Invoice No. 5705.
16 Received $931 from E. Jason to pay for the purchase of February 7.
19 Sold used store equipment to Green Acres for $500.
25 Sold merchandise to P. Sumo for $428, terms n/30, Invoice No. 5706.

Required

On a sheet of notebook paper, draw a Sales Journal like the one in Illustration D–1. Journalize the February transactions that should be recorded in the Sales Journal.

Exercise D–3
The Cash Receipts Journal
(LO 1, 2)

Landmark Map Company uses a Sales Journal, a Purchases Journal, a Cash Receipts Journal, a Cash Disbursements Journal, and a General Journal. The following transactions occurred during the month of September:

Sept. 3 Purchased merchandise on credit for $2,900 from Pace Supply Co.
7 Sold merchandise on credit to N. Jamal for $800, subject to a $16 sales discount if paid by the end of the month.

Sept. 9 Borrowed $1,750 by giving a note to the bank.
13 Received a capital contribution of $3,500 from R. Galindo, the owner of the company.
18 Sold merchandise to T. Byrd for $199 cash.
22 Paid Pace Supply $2,900 for the merchandise purchased on September 3.
27 Received $784 from N. Jamal in payment of the September 7 purchase.
30 Paid salaries of $1,500.

Required

On a sheet of notebook paper, draw a multicolumn Cash Receipts Journal like the one that appears in Illustration D–2. Journalize the September transactions that should be recorded in the Cash Receipts Journal.

Exercise D–4
The Purchases Journal
(LO 1, 2)

Gem Industries uses a Sales Journal, a Purchases Journal, a Cash Receipts Journal, a Cash Disbursements Journal, and a General Journal. The following transactions occurred during the month of July:

July 1 Purchased merchandise on credit for $7,190 from Angel, Inc., terms n/30.
8 Sold merchandise on credit to H. Baruk for $1,300, subject to a $26 sales discount if paid by the end of the month.
10 J. Powers, the owner of the business, contributed $2,500 cash to the business.
14 Purchased store supplies from Steck & Vaughn on credit for $145, terms n/30.
17 Purchased office supplies on credit from King Mart for $310, terms n/30.
24 Sold merchandise to V. Valdi for $467 cash.
28 Purchased store supplies from Hadlock's for $79 cash.
29 Paid Angel, Inc., $7,190 for the merchandise purchased on July 1.

Required

On a sheet of notebook paper, draw a multicolumn Purchases Journal like that in Illustration D–3. Journalize the July transactions that should be recorded in the Purchases Journal.

Exercise D–5
The Cash Disbursements Journal
(LO 1, 2)

Neon Art Supply uses a Sales Journal, a Purchases Journal, a Cash Receipts Journal, a Cash Disbursements Journal, and a General Journal. The following transactions occurred during the month of March:

Mar. 3 Purchased merchandise for $1,850 on credit from Paige, Inc.; terms 2/10, n/30.
9 Issued Check No. 210 to Mott & Son to buy store supplies for $369.
12 Sold merchandise on credit to C. Klempt for $625, terms n/30.
17 Issued Check No. 211 for $1,000 to repay a note payable to City Bank.
20 Purchased merchandise for $4,700 on credit from LeBeck's; terms 2/10, n/30.
29 Issued Check No. 212 to LeBeck's to pay the amount due for the purchase of March 20, less the discount.
31 Paid salary of $1,500 to B. Eldon by issuing Check No. 213.
31 Issued Check No. 214 to Paige, Inc., to pay the amount due for the purchase of March 3.

Required

On a sheet of notebook paper, draw a multicolumn Cash Disbursements Journal like the one that appears in Illustration D–4. Journalize the March transactions that should be recorded in the Cash Disbursements Journal.

Exercise D–6
General Journal transactions
(LO 1, 2)

The Nostalgic Book Shop uses a Sales Journal, a Purchases Journal, a Cash Receipts Journal, a Cash Disbursements Journal, and a General Journal. The following transactions occurred during the month of November:

Nov. 2 Purchased merchandise on credit for $1,900 from The Randolph Co.; terms 2/10, n/30.

Nov. 6 Borrowed $2,500 by signing a note with the bank.
12 The owner, I.M. Nowalski, contributed an automobile worth $13,500 to the business.
15 Issued Check No. 1006 to Scott Supply House to buy shop supplies for $530.
16 Sold merchandise on credit to W. Ryder for $1,100, terms n/30.
19 W. Ryder returned $90 of merchandise originally purchased on November 16.
21 Issued Check No. 1007 to Scofield's to pay the $715 due from an October 23 purchase.
28 Returned $170 of defective merchandise to The Randolph Co. from the November 2 purchase.
30 Accrued salaries payable were $1,240.

Required

Journalize the November transactions that should be recorded in the General Journal.

Exercise D–7
Special journal transactions
(LO 1)

Simonetti Pharmacy uses the following journals: Sales Journal, Purchases Journal, Cash Receipts Journal, Cash Disbursements Journal, and General Journal. On June 5, Simonetti purchased merchandise priced at $15,000, subject to credit terms of 2/10, n/30. On June 14, the pharmacy paid the net amount due. However, in journalizing the payment, the bookkeeper debited Accounts Payable for $15,000 and failed to record the cash discount. Cash was credited for the actual amount paid. In what journals would the June 5 and the June 14 transactions have been recorded? What procedure is likely to discover the error in journalizing the June 14 transaction?

Exercise D–8
Posting to subsidiary ledger accounts
(LO 2)

At the end of May, the Sales Journal of Cowtown Leather Goods appeared as follows:

Sales Journal

Date		Account Debited	Invoice Number	PR	Amount
May	6	Bud Smith	190		1,780.00
	10	Don Holly	191		2,040.00
	17	Sandy Ford	192		960.00
	25	Don Holly	193		335.00
	31	Total			5,115.00

Cowtown had also recorded the return of merchandise with the following entry:

May	20	Sales Returns and Allowances	165.00	
		Accounts Receivable—Sandy Ford		165.00
		Customer returned merchandise.		

Required

1. On a sheet of notebook paper, open a subsidiary Accounts Receivable Ledger that has a T-account for each customer listed in the Sales Journal. Post to the customer accounts the entries in the Sales Journal, and any portion of the general journal entry that affects a customer's account.
2. Open a General Ledger that has T-accounts for Accounts Receivable, Sales, and Sales Returns and Allowances. Post the Sales Journal and any portion of the general journal entry that affects these accounts.
3. Prepare a list or schedule of the accounts in the subsidiary Accounts Receivable Ledger and add their balances to show that the total equals the balance in the Accounts Receivable controlling account.

Exercise D–9
Posting from special journals to T-accounts
(LO 2)

Following are the condensed journals of Tip-Top Trophy Shop. The journal column headings are incomplete in that they do not indicate whether the columns are debit or credit columns.

Sales Journal

Account	Amount
Jack Heinz	2,700
Trudy Stone	7,400
Wayne Day	3,000
Total	13,100

Purchases Journal

Account	Amount
Frasier Corp.	3,400
Sultan, Inc.	6,500
McGraw Company . .	1,700
Total	11,600

General Journal

. . .	. .	Sales Returns and Allowances	400.00	
		Accounts Receivable—Jack Heinz		400.00
	. .	Accounts Payable—Frasier Corp.	850.00	
		Purchases Returns and Allowances		850.00

Cash Receipts Journal

Account	Other Accounts	Accounts Receivable	Sales	Sales Discounts	Cash
Jack Heinz		2,300		46	2,254
Sales			1,950		1,950
Notes Payable	3,500				3,500
Sales			525		525
Trudy Stone		7,400		148	7,252
Store Equipment . . .	200				200
Totals	3,700	9,700	2,475	194	15,681

Cash Disbursements Journal

Account	Other Accounts	Account Payable	Purchases Discounts	Cash
Prepaid Insurance . .	960			960
Sultan, Inc.		6,500	195	6,305
Frasier Corp.		2,550	51	2,499
Store Equipment . . .	1,570			1,570
Totals	2,530	9,050	246	11,334

Required

1. Prepare T-accounts on notebook paper for the following general ledger and subsidiary ledger accounts. Separate the accounts of each ledger group as follows:

General Ledger Accounts

Cash
Accounts Receivable
Prepaid Insurance
Store Equipment
Accounts Payable
Notes Payable
Sales
Sales Returns and Allowances
Sales Discounts
Purchases
Purchases Returns and Allowances
Purchases Discounts

Accounts Receivable Ledger Accounts

Wayne Day
Jack Heinz
Trudy Stone

Accounts Payable Ledger Accounts

Frasier Corp.
McGraw Company
Sultan, Inc.

2. Without referring to any of the illustrations in the chapter that show complete column headings for the journals, post the journals to the proper T-accounts.

Comprehensive Problem

Regis Company
(LO 1, 2)

(If the Working Papers that accompany this text are not available, omit this comprehensive problem.)

Assume it is Monday, August 1, the first business day of the month, and you have just been hired as the accountant for Regis Company, which operates with monthly accounting periods. All of the company's accounting work has been completed through the end of July and its ledgers show July 31 balances. During your first month on the job, you record the following transactions:

Aug. 1 Issused Check No. 1236 to Republic Management Co. in payment of the August rent, $2,650. (Use two lines to record the transaction. Charge 80% of the rent to Rent Expense, Selling Space and the balance to Rent Expense, Office Space.)

2 Sold merchandise on credit to L&M Company, Invoice No. 5725, $4,300. (The terms of all credit sales are 2/10, n/30.)

2 Issued a $125 credit memorandum to Prime, Inc., for defective merchandise sold on July 28 and returned for credit. The total selling price (gross) was $3,375.

3 Received a $570 credit memorandum from Signature Products for merchandise received on July 29 and returned for credit.

4 Purchased on credit from Discount Supplies: merchandise, $26,480; store supplies, $410; and office supplies, $59. Invoice dated August 4, terms n/10 EOM.

5 Received payment from Prime, Inc., for the remaining balance from the sale of July 28 less the August 2 return and the discount.

8 Issued Check No. 1237 to Signature Products to pay for the $5,070 of merchandise received on July 29 less the August 3 return and a 2% discount.

9 Sold store supplies to the merchant next door at cost for cash, $250.

10 Purchased office equipment on credit from Discount Supplies, invoice dated August 10, terms n/10 EOM, $2,910.

11 Received payment from L&M Company for the August 2 sale less the discount.

11 Received merchandise and an invoice dated August 10; terms 2/10, n/30; from Mayfair Corp., $6,300.

12 Received a $610 credit memorandum from Discount Supplies for defective office equipment received on August 10 and returned for credit.

15 Issued Check No. 1238, payable to Payroll, in payment of sales salaries, $3,800, and office salaries, $2,250. Cashed the check and paid the employees.

15 Cash sales for the first half of the month, $42,300. (Such sales are normally recorded daily. They are recorded only twice in this problem to reduce the repetitive entries.)

15 *Post to the customer and creditor accounts. Also, post individual items that are not included in column totals at the end of the month to the general ledger accounts. (Such items are normally posted daily, but you are asked to post them only twice each month because they are few in number.)*

16 Sold merchandise on credit to L&M Company, Invoice No. 5726, $2,850.

17 Received merchandise and an invoice dated August 14; terms 2/10, n/60; from Tranh Industries, $9,750.

19 Issued Check No. 1239 to Mayfair Corp. in payment of its August 10 invoice less the discount.

22 Sold merchandise on credit to Anchor Services, Invoice No. 5727, $4,900.

23 Issued Check No. 1240 to Tranh Industries in payment of its August 14 invoice less the discount.

Aug. 24 Purchased on credit from Discount Supplies: merchandise, $5,800; store supplies, $450; and office supplies, $200. Invoice dated August 24, terms n/10 EOM.

25 Received merchandise and an invoice dated August 23; terms 2/10, n/30; from Signature Products, $2,200.

26 Sold merchandise on credit to Franzetti Corp., Invoice No. 5728, $10,150.

26 Issued Check No. 1241 to HP&L in payment of the July electric bill, $918.

29 The owner of Regis Company, Walt Regis, used Check No. 1242 to withdraw $5,000 from the business for personal use.

30 Received payment from Anchor Services for the August 22 sale less the discount.

30 Issued Check No. 1243, payable to Payroll, in payment of sales salaries, $3,800, and office salaries, $2,250. Cashed the check and paid the employees.

31 Cash sales for the last half of the month were $47,180.

31 *Post to the customer and creditor accounts. Also, post individual items that are not included in column totals at the end of the month to the general ledger accounts.*

31 Foot and crossfoot the journals and make the month-end postings.

Required

1. Enter the transactions in the appropriate journals and post when instructed to do so.
2. Prepare a trial balance in the Trial Balance columns of the provided work sheet form and complete the work sheet using the following information:
   a. Expired insurance, $395.
   b. Ending store supplies inventory, $1,880.
   c. Ending office supplies inventory, $360.
   d. Estimated depreciation of store equipment, $405
   e. Estimated depreciation of office equipment, $235.
   f. Ending merchandise inventory, $126,000.
3. Prepare a multiple-step classified August income statement, an August statement of changes in owner's equity, and an August 31 classified balance sheet.
4. Prepare and post adjusting and closing entries.
5. Prepare a post-closing trial balance. Also prepare a list of the Accounts Receivable Ledger accounts and a list of the Accounts Payable Ledger accounts. Total the balances of each to confirm that the totals equal the balances in the controlling accounts.

Answers to Objective Review Questions

LO 1 (*b*)

LO 2 (*c*)

APPENDIX

Present and Future Values: An Expansion

The concept of present value is introduced and applied to accounting problems in Chapters 11 and 12. This appendix is designed to supplement those presentations with additional discussion, more complete tables, and additional homework exercises. In studying this appendix, you will also learn about the concept of future value.

Learning Objectives

After studying Appendix E, you should be able to:

1. Explain what is meant by the present value of a single amount and the present value of an annuity, and be able to use tables to solve present value problems.
2. Explain what is meant by the future value of a single amount and the future value of an annuity, and be able to use tables to solve future value problems.

Present Value of a Single Amount

LO 1 Explain what is meant by the present value of a single amount and the present value of an annuity, and be able to use tables to solve present value problems.

The present value of a single amount to be received or paid at some future date may be expressed as:

$$p = \frac{f}{(1 + i)^n}$$

where

p = Present value
f = Future value
i = Rate of interest per period
n = Number of periods

For example, assume that \$2.20 is to be received one period from now. It would be useful to know how much must be invested now, for one period, at an interest rate of 10% to provide \$2.20. We can calculate that amount with this formula:

$$p = \frac{f}{(1 + i)^n} = \frac{\$2.20}{(1 + .10)^1} = \$2.00$$

Alternatively, we can use the formula to find how much must be invested for two periods at 10% to provide \$2.42:

$$p = \frac{f}{(1 + i)^n} = \frac{\$2.42}{(1 + .10)^2} = \$2.00$$

Note that the number of periods (n) does not have to be expressed in years. Any period of time such as a day, a month, a quarter, or a year may be used. However, whatever period is used, the interest rate (i) must be compounded for the same period. Thus, if a problem expresses n in months, and i equals 12% per year, then 1% of the amount invested at the beginning of each month is earned that month and added to the investment. Thus, the interest is compounded monthly.

A present value table shows present values for a variety of interest rates (i) and a variety of numbers of periods (n). Each present value is based on the assumption that the future value (f) is 1. The following formula is used to construct a table of present values of a single future amount:

$$p = \frac{1}{(1 + i)^n}$$

Table E–1 on page 642 is a table of present values of a single future amount and is often called a *present value of 1* table.

Future Value of a Single Amount

LO 2 Explain what is meant by the future value of a single amount and the future value of an annuity, and be able to use tables to solve future value problems.

The following formula for the present value of a single amount can be modified to become the formula for the future value of a single amount with a simple step:

$$p = \frac{f}{(1 + i)^n}$$

By multiplying both sides of the equation by $(1 + i)^n$, the result is

$$f = p \times (1 + i)^n$$

For example, we can use this formula to determine that \$2.00 invested for one period at 10% will increase to a future value of \$2.20:

$$\begin{aligned} f &= p \times (1 + i)^n \\ &= \$2.00 \times (1 + .10)^1 \\ &= \$2.20 \end{aligned}$$

Alternatively, assume that \$2.00 will remain invested for three periods at 10%. The \$2.662 amount that will be received after three periods is calculated with the formula as follows:

$$\begin{aligned} f &= p \times (1 + i)^n \\ &= \$2.00 \times (1 + .10)^3 \\ &= \$2.662 \end{aligned}$$

A future value table shows future values for a variety of interest rates (i) and a variety of numbers of periods (n). Each future value is based on the assumption that the present value (p) is 1. Thus, the formula used to construct a table of future values of a single amount is

$$f = (1 + i)^n$$

Table E–2 on page 643 is a table of future values of a single amount and is often called a *future value of 1* table.

In Table E–2, look at the row where $n = 0$ and observe that the future value is 1 for all interest rates because no interest is earned.

Observe that a table showing the present values of 1 and a table showing the future values of 1 contain exactly the same information because both tables are based on the same equation. As you have seen, this equation

$$p = \frac{f}{(1 + i)^n}$$

is nothing more than a reformulation of

$$f = p \times (1 + i)^n$$

Both tables reflect the same four variables *p, f, i,* and *n*. Therefore, any problem that can be solved with one of the two tables can also be solved with the other.

For example, suppose that a person invests $100 for five years and expects to earn 12% per year. How much should the person receive after five years? To solve the problem using Table E–2, find the future value of 1, five periods from now, compounded at 12%. In the table, $f = 1.7623$. Thus, the amount to be accumulated over five years is $176.23 ($100 × 1.7623).

Table E–1 shows that the present value of 1, discounted five periods at 12% is 0.5674. Recall that the relationship between present value and future value may be expressed as:

$$p = \frac{f}{(1 + i)^n}$$

This formula can be restated as:

$$p = f \times \frac{1}{(1 + i)^n}$$

In turn, it can be restated as:

$$f = \frac{p}{\dfrac{1}{(1 + i)^n}}$$

Because we know from Table E–1 that $1/(1 + i)^n$ equals 0.5674, the future value of $100 invested for five periods at 12% is

$$f = \frac{\$100}{0.5674} = \$176.24$$

In summary, the future value can be found two ways. First, we can multiply the amount invested by the future value found in Table E–2. Second, we can divide the amount invested by the present value found in Table E–1. As you can see in this problem, immaterial differences can occur between these two methods through rounding.

Present Value of an Annuity

LO 1 Explain what is meant by the present value of a single amount and the present value of an annuity, and be able to use tables to solve present value problems.

An annuity is a series of equal payments occurring at equal intervals, such as three annual payments of $100 each. The present value of an annuity is defined as the present value of the payments one period prior to the first payment. Graphically, this annuity and its present value (*p*) may be represented as follows:

```
     $100  $100  $100
o-----o-----o-----o
p
```

One way to calculate the present value of this annuity finds the present value of each payment with the formula and adds them together. For this example, assuming an interest rate of 15%, the calculation is

$$p = \frac{\$100}{(1 + .15)^1} + \frac{\$100}{(1 + .15)^2} + \frac{\$100}{(1 + .15)^3} = \$228.32$$

Another way calculates the present value of the annuity by using Table E–1 to compute the present value of each payment and then taking their sum:

First payment:	$p = \$100 \times 0.8696 =$	\$ 86.96
Second payment:	$p = \$100 \times 0.7561 =$	75.61
Third payment:	$p = \$100 \times 0.6575 =$	65.75
Total:	$p =$	\$228.32

We can also use Table E–1 to solve the problem by first adding the table values for the three payments and then multiplying this sum by the \$100 amount of each payment:

From Table E–1:	$i = 15\%, n = 1, p =$	0.8696
	$i = 15\%, n = 2, p =$	0.7561
	$i = 15\%, n = 3, p =$	0.6575
	Sum =	2.2832
	Present value = 2.2832 × \$100 =	\$228.32

An easier way to solve the problem uses a different table that shows the present values of annuities, like Table E–3 on page 643, which is often called a *present value of an annuity of 1* table. Look at Table E–3 on the row where $n = 3$ and $i = 15\%$ and observe that the present value is 2.2832. Thus, the present value of an annuity of 1 for three periods, discounted at 15%, is 2.2832.

Although a formula is used to construct a table showing the present values of an annuity, you can construct one by adding the amounts in a present value of 1 table.[1] Examine Table E–1 and Table E–3 to confirm that the following numbers were drawn from those tables:

From Table E–1		**From Table E–3**	
$i = 8\%, n = 1$	0.9259		
$i = 8\%, n = 2$	0.8573		
$i = 8\%, n = 3$	0.7938		
$i = 8\%, n = 4$	0.7350		
Total	3.3120	$i = 8\%, n = 4$	3.3121

The minor difference in the results occurs because the numbers in the tables have been rounded.

In addition to the preceding methods, you can use preprogrammed business calculators and spreadsheet computer programs to find the present value of annuities.

Future Value of an Annuity

LO 2 Explain what is meant by the future value of a single amount and the future value of an annuity, and be able to use tables to solve future value problems.

Just as an annuity has a present value, it also has a future value. The future value of an annuity is the accumulated value of the annuity payments and interest as of the date of the final payment. Consider the earlier annuity of three annual payments of \$100. The points in time at which the present value (p) and the future value (f) occur are:

```
         $100   $100   $100
o--------o------o------o
p                      f
```

[1] The formula for the present value of an annuity of 1 is:

$$p = \frac{1 - \dfrac{1}{(1+i)^n}}{i}$$

Note that the first payment is made two periods prior to the point at which the future value is determined. Therefore, for the first payment, $n = 2$. For the second payment, $n = 1$. Since the third payment occurs on the future value date, $n = 0$.

One way to calculate the future value of this annuity uses the formula to find the future value of each payment and adds them together. Assuming an interest rate of 15%, the calculation is

$$f = \$100 \times (1 + .15)^2 + \$100 \times (1 + .15)^1 + \$100 \times (1 + .15)^0 = \$347.25$$

Another way calculates the future value of the annuity by using Table E–2 to find the sum of the future values of each payment:

First payment:	$f = \$100 \times 1.3225 =$	\$132.25
Second payment:	$f = \$100 \times 1.1500 =$	115.00
Third payment:	$f = \$100 \times 1.0000 =$	100.00
Total:	$f =$	\$347.25

A third approach adds the future values of three payments of 1 and multiplies the sum by \$100:

From Table E–2:	$i = 15\%, n = 2, f =$	1.3225
	$i = 15\%, n = 1, f =$	1.1500
	$i = 15\%, n = 0, f =$	1.0000
	Sum $=$	3.4725
	Future value $= 3.4725 \times \$100 =$	\$347.25

A fourth and easier way to solve the problem uses a table that shows the future values of annuities, often called a *future value of an annuity of 1* table. Table E–4 on page 644 is such a table. Note in Table E–4 that when $n = 1$, the future values are equal to 1 ($f = 1$) for all rates of interest because the annuity consists of only one payment and the future value is determined on the date of the payment. Thus, the future value equals the payment.

Although a formula is used to construct a table showing the future values of an annuity of 1, you can construct one by adding the amounts in a future value of 1 table like Table E–2.[2] Examine Table E–2 and Table E–4 to confirm that the following numbers were drawn from those tables:

From Table E–2		From Table E–4	
$i = 8\%, n = 0$	1.0000		
$i = 8\%, n = 1$	1.0800		
$i = 8\%, n = 2$	1.1664		
$i = 8\%, n = 3$	1.2597		
Total	4.5061	$i = 8\%, n = 4$	4.5061

Minor differences may occur because the numbers in the tables have been rounded.

You can also use business calculators and spreadsheet computer programs to find the future values of annuities.

Observe that the future value in Table E–2 is 1.0000 when $n = 0$ but the future value in Table E–4 is 1.0000 when $n = 1$. Why does this apparent contradiction arise? When $n = 0$ in Table E–2, the future value is determined on the

[2] The formula for the future value of an annuity of 1 is

$$f = \frac{(1 + i)^n - 1}{i}$$

date that the single payment occurs. Thus, no interest is earned and the future value equals the payment. However, Table E–4 describes annuities with equal payments occurring each period. When $n = 1$, the annuity has only one payment, and its future value also equals 1 on the date of its final and only payment.

Summary of the Appendix in Terms of Learning Objectives

LO 1 The present value of a single amount to be received at a future date is the amount that could be invested now at the specified interest rate to yield that future value. The present value of an annuity is the amount that could be invested now at the specified interest rate to yield that series of equal periodic payments. Present value tables and business calculators simplify calculating present values.

LO 2 The future value of a single amount invested at a specified rate of interest is the amount that would accumulate at a future date. The future value of an annuity to be invested at the specified rate of interest is the amount that would accumulate at the date of the final equal periodic payment. Future value tables and business calculators simplify calculating future values.

TABLE E–1 *Present Value of 1 Due in n Periods*

	Rate											
Periods	**1%**	**2%**	**3%**	**4%**	**5%**	**6%**	**7%**	**8%**	**9%**	**10%**	**12%**	**15%**
1	0.9901	0.9804	0.9709	0.9615	0.9524	0.9434	0.9346	0.9259	0.9174	0.9091	0.8929	0.8696
2	0.9803	0.9612	0.9426	0.9246	0.9070	0.8900	0.8734	0.8573	0.8417	0.8264	0.7972	0.7561
3	0.9706	0.9423	0.9151	0.8890	0.8638	0.8396	0.8163	0.7938	0.7722	0.7513	0.7118	0.6575
4	0.9610	0.9238	0.8885	0.8548	0.8227	0.7921	0.7629	0.7350	0.7084	0.6830	0.6355	0.5718
5	0.9515	0.9057	0.8626	0.8219	0.7835	0.7473	0.7130	0.6806	0.6499	0.6209	0.5674	0.4972
6	0.9420	0.8880	0.8375	0.7903	0.7462	0.7050	0.6663	0.6302	0.5963	0.5645	0.5066	0.4323
7	0.9327	0.8706	0.8131	0.7599	0.7107	0.6651	0.6227	0.5835	0.5470	0.5132	0.4523	0.3759
8	0.9235	0.8535	0.7894	0.7307	0.6768	0.6274	0.5820	0.5403	0.5019	0.4665	0.4039	0.3269
9	0.9143	0.8368	0.7664	0.7026	0.6446	0.5919	0.5439	0.5002	0.4604	0.4241	0.3606	0.2843
10	0.9053	0.8203	0.7441	0.6756	0.6139	0.5584	0.5083	0.4632	0.4224	0.3855	0.3220	0.2472
11	0.8963	0.8043	0.7224	0.6496	0.5847	0.5268	0.4751	0.4289	0.3875	0.3505	0.2875	0.2149
12	0.8874	0.7885	0.7014	0.6246	0.5568	0.4970	0.4440	0.3971	0.3555	0.3186	0.2567	0.1869
13	0.8787	0.7730	0.6810	0.6006	0.5303	0.4688	0.4150	0.3677	0.3262	0.2897	0.2292	0.1625
14	0.8700	0.7579	0.6611	0.5775	0.5051	0.4423	0.3878	0.3405	0.2992	0.2633	0.2046	0.1413
15	0.8613	0.7430	0.6419	0.5553	0.4810	0.4173	0.3624	0.3152	0.2745	0.2394	0.1827	0.1229
16	0.8528	0.7284	0.6232	0.5339	0.4581	0.3936	0.3387	0.2919	0.2519	0.2176	0.1631	0.1069
17	0.8444	0.7142	0.6050	0.5134	0.4363	0.3714	0.3166	0.2703	0.2311	0.1978	0.1456	0.0929
18	0.8360	0.7002	0.5874	0.4936	0.4155	0.3503	0.2959	0.2502	0.2120	0.1799	0.1300	0.0808
19	0.8277	0.6864	0.5703	0.4746	0.3957	0.3305	0.2765	0.2317	0.1945	0.1635	0.1161	0.0703
20	0.8195	0.6730	0.5537	0.4564	0.3769	0.3118	0.2584	0.2145	0.1784	0.1486	0.1037	0.0611
25	0.7798	0.6095	0.4776	0.3751	0.2953	0.2330	0.1842	0.1460	0.1160	0.0923	0.0588	0.0304
30	0.7419	0.5521	0.4120	0.3083	0.2314	0.1741	0.1314	0.0994	0.0754	0.0573	0.0334	0.0151
35	0.7059	0.5000	0.3554	0.2534	0.1813	0.1301	0.0937	0.0676	0.0490	0.0356	0.0189	0.0075
40	0.6717	0.4529	0.3066	0.2083	0.1420	0.0972	0.0668	0.0460	0.0318	0.0221	0.0107	0.0037

TABLE E-2 *Future Value of 1 Due in* n *Periods*

Periods	Rate 1%	2%	3%	4%	5%	6%	7%	8%	9%	10%	12%	15%
0	1.0000	1.0000	1.0000	1.0000	1.0000	1.0000	1.0000	1.0000	1.0000	1.0000	1.0000	1.0000
1	1.0100	1.0200	1.0300	1.0400	1.0500	1.0600	1.0700	1.0800	1.0900	1.1000	1.1200	1.1500
2	1.0201	1.0404	1.0609	1.0816	1.1025	1.1236	1.1449	1.1664	1.1881	1.2100	1.2544	1.3225
3	1.0303	1.0612	1.0927	1.1249	1.1576	1.1910	1.2250	1.2597	1.2950	1.3310	1.4049	1.5209
4	1.0406	1.0824	1.1255	1.1699	1.2155	1.2625	1.3108	1.3605	1.4116	1.4641	1.5735	1.7490
5	1.0510	1.1041	1.1593	1.2167	1.2763	1.3382	1.4026	1.4693	1.5386	1.6105	1.7623	2.0114
6	1.0615	1.1262	1.1941	1.2653	1.3401	1.4185	1.5007	1.5869	1.6771	1.7716	1.9738	2.3131
7	1.0721	1.1487	1.2299	1.3159	1.4071	1.5036	1.6058	1.7138	1.8280	1.9487	2.2107	2.6600
8	1.0829	1.1717	1.2668	1.3686	1.4775	1.5938	1.7182	1.8509	1.9926	2.1436	2.4760	3.0590
9	1.0937	1.1951	1.3048	1.4233	1.5513	1.6895	1.8385	1.9990	2.1719	2.3579	2.7731	3.5179
10	1.1046	1.2190	1.3439	1.4802	1.6289	1.7908	1.9672	2.1589	2.3674	2.5937	3.1058	4.0456
11	1.1157	1.2434	1.3842	1.5395	1.7103	1.8983	2.1049	2.3316	2.5804	2.8531	3.4785	4.6524
12	1.1268	1.2682	1.4258	1.6010	1.7959	2.0122	2.2522	2.5182	2.8127	3.1384	3.8960	5.3503
13	1.1381	1.2936	1.4685	1.6651	1.8856	2.1329	2.4098	2.7196	3.0658	3.4523	4.3635	6.1528
14	1.1495	1.3195	1.5126	1.7317	1.9799	2.2609	2.5785	2.9372	3.3417	3.7975	4.8871	7.0757
15	1.1610	1.3459	1.5580	1.8009	2.0789	2.3966	2.7590	3.1722	3.6425	4.1772	5.4736	8.1371
16	1.1726	1.3728	1.6047	1.8730	2.1829	2.5404	2.9522	3.4259	3.9703	4.5950	6.1304	9.3576
17	1.1843	1.4002	1.6528	1.9479	2.2920	2.6928	3.1588	3.7000	4.3276	5.0545	6.8660	10.7613
18	1.1961	1.4282	1.7024	2.0258	2.4066	2.8543	3.3799	3.9960	4.7171	5.5599	7.6900	12.3755
19	1.2081	1.4568	1.7535	2.1068	2.5270	3.0256	3.6165	4.3157	5.1417	6.1159	8.6128	14.2318
20	1.2202	1.4859	1.8061	2.1911	2.6533	3.2071	3.8697	4.6610	5.6044	6.7275	9.6463	16.3665
25	1.2824	1.6406	2.0938	2.6658	3.3864	4.2919	5.4274	6.8485	8.6231	10.8347	17.0001	32.9190
30	1.3478	1.8114	2.4273	3.2434	4.3219	5.7435	7.6123	10.0627	13.2677	17.4494	29.9599	66.2118
35	1.4166	1.9999	2.8139	3.9461	5.5160	7.6861	10.6766	14.7853	20.4140	28.1024	52.7996	133.176
40	1.4889	2.2080	3.2620	4.8010	7.0400	10.2857	14.9745	21.7245	31.4094	45.2593	93.0510	267.864

TABLE E-3 *Present Value of an Annuity of 1 per Period*

Periods	Rate 1%	2%	3%	4%	5%	6%	7%	8%	9%	10%	12%	15%
1	0.9901	0.9804	0.9709	0.9615	0.9524	0.9434	0.9346	0.9259	0.9174	0.9091	0.8929	0.8696
2	1.9704	1.9416	1.9135	1.8861	1.8594	1.8334	1.8080	1.7833	1.7591	1.7355	1.6901	1.6257
3	2.9410	2.8839	2.8286	2.7751	2.7232	2.6730	2.6243	2.5771	2.5313	2.4869	2.4018	2.2832
4	3.9020	3.8077	3.7171	3.6299	3.5460	3.4651	3.3872	3.3121	3.2397	3.1699	3.0373	2.8550
5	4.8534	4.7135	4.5797	4.4518	4.3295	4.2124	4.1002	3.9927	3.8897	3.7908	3.6048	3.3522
6	5.7955	5.6014	5.4172	5.2421	5.0757	4.9173	4.7665	4.6229	4.4859	4.3553	4.1114	3.7845
7	6.7282	6.4720	6.2303	6.0021	5.7864	5.5824	5.3893	5.2064	5.0330	4.8684	4.5638	4.1604
8	7.6517	7.3255	7.0197	6.7327	6.4632	6.2098	5.9713	5.7466	5.5348	5.3349	4.9676	4.4873
9	8.5660	8.1622	7.7861	7.4353	7.1078	6.8017	6.5152	6.2469	5.9952	5.7590	5.3282	4.7716
10	9.4713	8.9826	8.5302	8.1109	7.7217	7.3601	7.0236	6.7101	6.4177	6.1446	5.6502	5.0188
11	10.3676	9.7868	9.2526	8.7605	8.3064	7.8869	7.4987	7.1390	6.8052	6.4951	5.9377	5.2337
12	11.2551	10.5753	9.9540	9.3851	8.8633	8.3838	7.9427	7.5361	7.1607	6.8137	6.1944	5.4206
13	12.1337	11.3484	10.6350	9.9856	9.3936	8.8527	8.3577	7.9038	7.4869	7.1034	6.4235	5.5831
14	13.0037	12.1062	11.2961	10.5631	9.8986	9.2950	8.7455	8.2442	7.7862	7.3667	6.6282	5.7245
15	13.8651	12.8493	11.9379	11.1184	10.3797	9.7122	9.1079	8.5595	8.0607	7.6061	6.8109	5.8474
16	14.7179	13.5777	12.5611	11.6523	10.8378	10.1059	9.4466	8.8514	8.3126	7.8237	6.9740	5.9542
17	15.5623	14.2919	13.1661	12.1657	11.2741	10.4773	9.7632	9.1216	8.5436	8.0216	7.1196	6.0472
18	16.3983	14.9920	13.7535	12.6593	11.6896	10.8276	10.0591	9.3719	8.7556	8.2014	7.2497	6.1280
19	17.2260	15.6785	14.3238	13.1339	12.0853	11.1581	10.3356	9.6036	8.9501	8.3649	7.3658	6.1982
20	18.0456	16.3514	14.8775	13.5903	12.4622	11.4699	10.5940	9.8181	9.1285	8.5136	7.4694	6.2593
25	22.0232	19.5235	17.4131	15.6221	14.0939	12.7834	11.6536	10.6748	9.8226	9.0770	7.8431	6.4641
30	25.8077	22.3965	19.6004	17.2920	15.3725	13.7648	12.4090	11.2578	10.2737	9.4269	8.0552	6.5660
35	29.4086	24.9986	21.4872	18.6646	16.3742	14.4982	12.9477	11.6546	10.5668	9.6442	8.1755	6.6166
40	32.8347	27.3555	23.1148	19.7928	17.1591	15.0463	13.3317	11.9246	10.7574	9.7791	8.2438	6.6418

TABLE E-4 *Future Value of an Annuity of 1 per Period*

	Rate											
Periods	1%	2%	3%	4%	5%	6%	7%	8%	9%	10%	12%	15%
1	1.0000	1.0000	1.0000	1.0000	1.0000	1.0000	1.0000	1.0000	1.0000	1.0000	1.0000	1.0000
2	2.0100	2.0200	2.0300	2.0400	2.0500	2.0600	2.0700	2.0800	2.0900	2.1000	2.1200	2.1500
3	3.0301	3.0604	3.0909	3.1216	3.1525	3.1836	3.2149	3.2464	3.2781	3.3100	3.3744	3.4725
4	4.0604	4.1216	4.1836	4.2465	4.3101	4.3746	4.4399	4.5061	4.5731	4.6410	4.7793	4.9934
5	5.1010	5.2040	5.3091	5.4163	5.5256	5.6371	5.7507	5.8666	5.9847	6.1051	6.3528	6.7424
6	6.1520	6.3081	6.4684	6.6330	6.8019	6.9753	7.1533	7.3359	7.5233	7.7156	8.1152	8.7537
7	7.2135	7.4343	7.6625	7.8983	8.1420	8.3938	8.6540	8.9228	9.2004	9.4872	10.0890	11.0668
8	8.2857	8.5830	8.8923	9.2142	9.5491	9.8975	10.2598	10.6366	11.0285	11.4359	12.2997	13.7268
9	9.3685	9.7546	10.1591	10.5828	11.0266	11.4913	11.9780	12.4876	13.0210	13.5795	14.7757	16.7858
10	10.4622	10.9497	11.4639	12.0061	12.5779	13.1808	13.8164	14.4866	15.1929	15.9374	17.5487	20.3037
11	11.5668	12.1687	12.8078	13.4864	14.2068	14.9716	15.7836	16.6455	17.5603	18.5312	20.6546	24.3493
12	12.6825	13.4121	14.1920	15.0258	15.9171	16.8699	17.8885	18.9771	20.1407	21.3843	24.1331	29.0017
13	13.8093	14.6803	15.6178	16.6268	17.7130	18.8821	20.1406	21.4953	22.9534	24.5227	28.0291	34.3519
14	14.9474	15.9739	17.0863	18.2919	19.5986	21.0151	22.5505	24.2149	26.0192	27.9750	32.3926	40.5047
15	16.0969	17.2934	18.5989	20.0236	21.5786	23.2760	25.1290	27.1521	29.3609	31.7725	37.2797	47.5804
16	17.2579	18.6393	20.1569	21.8245	23.6575	25.6725	27.8881	30.3243	33.0034	35.9497	42.7533	55.7175
17	18.4304	20.0121	21.7616	23.6975	25.8404	28.2129	30.8402	33.7502	36.9737	40.5447	48.8837	65.0751
18	19.6147	21.4123	23.4144	25.6454	28.1324	30.9057	33.9990	37.4502	41.3013	45.5992	55.7497	75.8364
19	20.8109	22.8406	25.1169	27.6712	30.5390	33.7600	37.3790	41.4463	46.0185	51.1591	63.4397	88.2118
20	22.0190	24.2974	26.8704	29.7781	33.0660	36.7856	40.9955	45.7620	51.1601	57.2750	72.0524	102.444
25	28.2432	32.0303	36.4593	41.6459	47.7271	54.8645	63.2490	73.1059	84.7009	98.3471	133.334	212.793
30	34.7849	40.5681	47.5754	56.0849	66.4388	79.0582	94.4608	113.283	136.308	164.494	241.333	434.745
35	41.6603	49.9945	60.4621	73.6522	90.3203	111.435	138.237	172.317	215.711	271.024	431.663	881.170
40	48.8864	60.4020	75.4013	95.0255	120.800	154.762	199.635	259.057	337.882	442.593	767.091	1779.09

Objective Review

Answers to the following questions are listed at the end of this appendix. Be sure that you decide which is the one best answer to each question *before* you check the answers.

LO 1 Smith & Company is considering making an investment that would pay $10,000 every six months for three years. The first payment would be received in six months. If Smith & Company requires an annual return of 8%, which of the following statements is true?

a. In determining the future value of the annuity, $n = 6$ and $i = 8\%$.

b. In determining the present value of the annuity, $n = 3$ and $i = 8\%$.

c. Smith & Company should be willing to invest no more than $25,771.

d. Smith & Company should be willing to invest no more than $46,229.

e. Smith & Company should be willing to invest no more than $52,421.

LO 2 On May 9, Frank and Cindy Huber received news that they had inherited $150,000 from one of Cindy's distant relatives. They decided to deposit the money in a savings account that yields an 8% annual rate of interest. They plan on quitting their jobs to travel around the country when the inheritance equals $299,850. How many years will it be before Frank and Cindy are able to quit working?

a. 2.

b. 8.

c. 9.

d. 10.

e. 11.

Exercises

Exercise E-1
Present value of an amount
(LO 1)

Jasper Company is considering an investment which, if paid for immediately, is expected to return $172,500 five years hence. If Jasper demands a 9% return, how much will it be willing to pay for this investment?

LCV Company invested $529,000 in a project expected to earn a 12% annual rate of return. The earnings will be reinvested in the project each year until the entire investment is liquidated 10 years hence. What will the cash proceeds be when the project is liquidated?

Exercise E–2
Future value of an amount
(LO 2)

Cornblue Distributing is considering a contract that will return $200,400 annually at the end of each year for six years. If Cornblue demands an annual return of 7% and pays for the investment immediately, how much should it be willing to pay?

Exercise E–3
Present value of an annuity
(LO 1)

Sarah Oliver is planning to begin an individual retirement program in which she will invest $1,200 annually at the end of each year. Oliver plans to retire after making 30 annual investments in a program that earns a return of 10%. What will be the value of the program on the date of the last investment?

Exercise E–4
Future value of an annuity
(LO 2)

Kevin Smith has been offered the possibility of investing $0.3152 for 15 years, after which he will be paid $1. What annual rate of interest will Smith earn? (Use Table E–1 to find the answer.)

Exercise E–5
Interest rate on an investment
(LO 1)

Laura Veralli has been offered the possibility of investing $0.5268. The investment will earn 6% per year and will return Veralli $1 at the end of the investment. How many years must Veralli wait to receive the $1? (Use Table E–1 to find the answer.)

Exercise E–6
Number of periods of an investment
(LO 1)

Tom Albertson expects to invest $1 at 15% and, at the end of the investment, receive $66.2118. How many years will elapse before Albertson receives the payment? (Use Table E–2 to find the answer.)

Exercise E–7
Number of periods of an investment
(LO 2)

Ed Teller expects to invest $1 for 35 years, after which he will receive $20.4140. What rate of interest will Teller earn? (Use Table E–2 to find the answer.)

Exercise E–8
Interest rate on an investment
(LO 2)

Helen Fanshawe expects an immediate investment of $9.3936 to return $1 annually for 13 years, with the first payment to be received in one year. What rate of interest will Fanshawe earn? (Use Table E–3 to find the answer.)

Exercise E–9
Interest rate on an investment
(LO 1)

Ken Priggin expects an investment of $7.6061 to return $1 annually for several years. If Priggin is to earn a return of 10%, how many annual payments must he receive? (Use Table E–3 to find the answer.)

Exercise E–10
Number of periods of an investment
(LO 1)

Steve Church expects to invest $1 annually for 40 years and have an accumulated value of $95.0255 on the date of the last investment. If this occurs, what rate of interest will Church earn? (Use Table E–4 to find the answer.)

Exercise E–11
Interest rate on an investment
(LO 2)

Bitsy Brennon expects to invest $1 annually in a fund that will earn 8%. How many annual investments must Brennon make to accumulate $45.7620 on the date of the last investment? (Use Table E–4 to find the answer.)

Exercise E–12
Number of periods of an investment
(LO 2)

Bill Lenehan financed a new automobile by paying $3,100 cash and agreeing to make 20 monthly payments of $450 each, the first payment to be made one month after the purchase. The loan was said to bear interest at an annual rate of 12%. What was the cost of the automobile?

Exercise E–13
Present value of an annuity
(LO 1)

Exercise E–14
Future value of an amount
(LO 2)

Stephanie Powell deposited $4,900 in a savings account that earns interest at an annual rate of 8%, compounded quarterly. The $4,900 plus earned interest must remain in the account 10 years before it can be withdrawn. How much money will be in the account at the end of the 10 years?

Exercise E–15
Future value of an annuity
(LO 2)

Sally Sayer plans to have $90 withheld from her monthly paycheck and deposited in a savings account that earns 12% annually, compounded monthly. If Sayer continues with her plan for 2½ years, how much will be accumulated in the account on the date of the last deposit?

Exercise E–16
Present value of bonds
(LO 1)

Stellar Company plans to issue 12%, 15-year, $500,000 par value bonds payable that pay interest semiannually on June 30 and December 31. The bonds are dated December 31, 19X1, and are to be issued on that date. If the market rate of interest for the bonds is 10% on the date of issue, what will be the cash proceeds from the bond issue?

Exercise E–17
Future value of an amount plus an annuity
(LO 2)

Travis Company has decided to establish a fund that will be used 10 years hence to replace an aging productive facility. The company makes an initial contribution of $150,000 to the fund and plans to make quarterly contributions of $60,000 beginning in three months. The fund is expected to earn 12%, compounded quarterly. What will be the value of the fund 10 years hence?

Exercise E–18
Present value of an amount
(LO 1)

McCoy Company expects to earn 10% per year on an investment that will pay $756,400 six years hence. Use Table E–2 to calculate the present value of the investment.

Exercise E–19
Future value of an amount
(LO 2)

Comet Company invests $216,000 at 7% per year for nine years. Use Table E–1 to calculate the future value of the investment nine years hence.

Answers to Objective Review Questions

LO 1 (*e*)   **LO 2** (*c*)

APPENDIX

F

Financial Statements and Related Disclosures from Apple Computer Inc.'s 1992 Annual Report

CONSOLIDATED STATEMENTS OF INCOME

(In thousands, except per share amounts)

THREE FISCAL YEARS ENDED SEPTEMBER 25, 1992	1992	1991	1990
Net sales	$7,086,542	$6,308,849	$5,558,435
Costs and expenses:			
Cost of sales	3,991,337	3,314,118	2,606,223
Research and development	602,135	583,046	478,019
Selling, general and administrative	1,687,262	1,740,293	1,728,508
Restructuring costs and other	—	224,043	33,673
	6,280,734	5,861,500	4,846,423
Operating income	805,808	447,349	712,012
Interest and other income, net	49,634	52,395	66,505
Income before income taxes	855,442	499,744	778,517
Provision for income taxes	325,069	189,903	303,622
Net income	$ 530,373	$ 309,841	$ 474,895
Earnings per common and common equivalent share	$ 4.33	$ 2.58	$ 3.77
Common and common equivalent shares used in the calculations of earnings per share	122,490	120,283	125,813

See accompanying notes.

CONSOLIDATED BALANCE SHEETS

SEPTEMBER 25, 1992, AND SEPTEMBER 27, 1991	1992	1991
		(Dollars in thousands)
ASSETS:		
Current assets:		
Cash and cash equivalents	$ 498,557	$ 604,147
Short-term investments	936,943	288,572
Accounts receivable, net of allowance for doubtful accounts of $83,048 ($53,993 in 1991)	1,087,185	907,159
Inventories	580,097	671,655
Prepaid income taxes	199,139	222,980
Other current assets	256,473	169,097
Total current assets	3,558,394	2,863,610
Property, plant, and equipment:		
Land and buildings	255,808	198,107
Machinery and equipment	516,335	485,872
Office furniture and equipment	155,317	146,433
Leasehold improvements	208,180	205,602
	1,135,640	1,036,014
Accumulated depreciation and amortization	(673,419)	(588,036)
Net property, plant, and equipment	462,221	447,978
Other assets	203,078	182,009
	$ 4,223,693	$ 3,493,597
LIABILITIES AND SHAREHOLDERS' EQUITY:		
Current liabilities:		
Notes payable	$ 184,461	$ 148,566
Accounts payable	426,936	357,084
Accrued compensation and employee benefits	142,382	119,468
Income taxes payable	78,382	14,857
Accrued marketing and distribution	187,767	136,712
Accrued restructuring costs	105,038	162,365
Other current liabilities	300,554	277,999
Total current liabilities	1,425,520	1,217,051
Deferred income taxes	610,803	509,870
Commitments and contingencies	—	—
Shareholders' equity:		
Common stock, no par value; 320,000,000 shares authorized; 118,478,825 shares issued and outstanding in 1992 (118,385,899 shares in 1991)	282,310	278,865
Retained earnings	1,904,519	1,492,024
Accumulated translation adjustment	541	(2,377)
	2,187,370	1,768,512
Notes receivable from shareholders	—	(1,836)
Total shareholders' equity	2,187,370	1,766,676
	$ 4,223,693	$ 3,493,597

See accompanying notes.

CONSOLIDATED STATEMENTS OF SHAREHOLDERS' EQUITY

(In thousands)

	Common Stock Shares	Common Stock Amount	Retained Earnings	Accumulated Translation Adjustment	Notes Receivable from Shareholders	Total Shareholders' Equity
Balance at September 29, 1989	126,270	$ 315,279	$ 1,175,899	$ (1,868)	$ (3,564)	$ 1,485,746
Common stock issued under stock option and purchase plans, including related tax benefits	3,804	105,977	—	—	(5,798)	100,179
Repurchase of common stock	(14,715)	(284,701)	(284,855)	—	—	(569,556)
Repayment of notes receivable from shareholders	—	—	—	—	3,329	3,329
Cash dividends	—	—	(53,783)	—	—	(53,783)
Accumulated translation adjustment	—	—	—	6,010	—	6,010
Net income	—	—	474,895	—	—	474,895
Balance at September 28, 1990	115,359	136,555	1,312,156	4,142	(6,033)	1,446,820
Common stock issued under stock option and purchase plans, including related tax benefits	7,377	253,523	—	—	(744)	252,779
Repurchase of common stock	(4,350)	(111,213)	(73,464)	—	—	(184,677)
Repayment of notes receivable from shareholders	—	—	—	—	4,941	4,941
Cash dividends	—	—	(56,509)	—	—	(56,509)
Accumulated translation adjustment	—	—	—	(6,519)	—	(6,519)
Net income	—	—	309,841	—	—	309,841
Balance at September 27, 1991	118,386	278,865	1,492,024	(2,377)	(1,836)	1,766,676
Common stock issued under stock option and purchase plans, including related tax benefits	4,093	155,388	—	—	—	155,388
Repurchase of common stock	(4,000)	(151,943)	(60,682)	—	—	(212,625)
Repayment of notes receivable from shareholders	—	—	—	—	1,836	1,836
Cash dividends	—	—	(57,196)	—	—	(57,196)
Accumulated translation adjustment	—	—	—	2,918	—	2,918
Net income	—	—	530,373	—	—	530,373
Balance at September 25, 1992	118,479	$ 282,310	$ 1,904,519	$ 541	$ —	$ 2,187,370

See accompanying notes.

CONSOLIDATED STATEMENTS OF CASH FLOWS

(In thousands)

THREE FISCAL YEARS ENDED SEPTEMBER 25, 1992	1992	1991	1990
Cash and cash equivalents, beginning of the period	$ 604,147	$ 374,682	$ 438,300
Operations:			
Net income	530,373	309,841	474,895
Adjustments to reconcile net income to cash generated by operations:			
Depreciation and amortization	217,182	204,433	202,686
Net book value of property, plant, and equipment retirements	14,687	6,955	2,186
Changes in assets and liabilities:			
Accounts receivable	(180,026)	(145,291)	30,956
Inventories	91,558	(316,182)	119,904
Prepaid income taxes	23,841	(97,445)	(8,356)
Other current assets	(87,376)	(5,738)	(63,261)
Accounts payable	69,852	16,509	6,418
Income taxes payable	63,525	(18,384)	(52,549)
Accrued restructuring costs	(57,327)	162,365	—
Other liabilities	96,524	3,570	112,064
Deferred income taxes	100,933	8,038	138,922
Cash generated by operations	883,746	128,671	963,865
Investments:			
Purchase of short-term investments	(2,121,341)	(610,696)	(1,424,427)
Proceeds from short-term investments	1,472,970	944,533	1,172,668
Purchase of property, plant, and equipment	(194,853)	(218,348)	(224,305)
Other	(69,410)	(57,165)	(97,467)
Cash generated by (used for) investment activities	(912,634)	58,324	(573,531)
Financing:			
Increase in short-term borrowings	35,895	25,936	65,879
Increases in common stock and related tax benefits, net of changes in notes receivable from shareholders	157,224	257,720	103,508
Repurchase of common stock	(212,625)	(184,677)	(569,556)
Cash dividends	(57,196)	(56,509)	(53,783)
Cash generated by (used for) financing activities	(76,702)	42,470	(453,952)
Total cash generated (used)	(105,590)	229,465	(63,618)
Cash and cash equivalents, end of the period	$ 498,557	$ 604,147	$ 374,682
Supplemental cash flow disclosures:			
Cash paid during the year for:			
Interest	$ 8,778	$ 9,755	$ 6,361
Income taxes	$ 98,330	$ 265,755	$ 211,642

See accompanying notes.

Notes to Consolidated Financial Statements

Summary of Significant Accounting Policies

Basis of Presentation

The consolidated financial statements include the accounts of Apple Computer, Inc. and its wholly owned subsidiaries (the Company). Intercompany accounts and transactions have been eliminated. The Company's fiscal year-end is the last Friday in September.

Revenue Recognition

The Company recognizes revenue at the time products are shipped. Provision is made currently for estimated product returns and price protection that may occur under Company programs.

Foreign Currency Translation

Gains and losses resulting from foreign currency translation are accumulated as a separate component of shareholders' equity until the foreign entity is sold or liquidated. Gains and losses resulting from foreign currency transactions are immaterial and are included in the statement of income.

Financial Instruments

The Company hedges certain portions of its exposure to foreign currency and interest rate fluctuations through a variety of strategies and instruments, including forward foreign exchange contracts; foreign currency options; and interest rate swaps, options, caps, and floors. Gains and losses associated with these financial instruments are recorded currently in income, unless the instrument hedges a firm commitment or existing underlying position. In this case, any gains and losses are deferred and included as a component of the related transaction. Generally, the interest element of the foreign currency instruments is recognized over the life of the contract.

Cash, Cash Equivalents, and Short-Term Investments

All highly liquid investments with a maturity of three months or less at the date of purchase are considered to be cash equivalents; investments with maturities between three and twelve months are considered to be short-term investments. Short-term investments are carried at cost plus accrued interest, which approximates market. A substantial portion of the Company's cash, cash equivalents, and short-term investments is held by foreign subsidiaries and is generally in U.S. dollar–denominated holdings. Amounts held by foreign subsidiaries would be subject to U.S. income taxation upon repatriation to the United States to meet domestic cash needs; the Company's financial statements fully provide for any related tax liability on amounts that may be remitted.

Income Taxes

U.S. income taxes have not been provided on a cumulative total of $133 million of undistributed earnings of certain of the Company's foreign subsidiaries. It is intended that these earnings will be indefinitely invested in operations outside the United States. Except for such indefinitely invested earnings, the Company provides federal and state income taxes currently on undistributed earnings of foreign subsidiaries. The Company has not elected early adoption of Financial Accounting Standard No. 109, Accounting for Income Taxes (FAS 109). FAS 109 becomes effective no later than the beginning of the Company's 1994 fiscal year. The Company believes that FAS 109, when adopted, will not have a material effect on its financial position or results of operations.

Earnings per Share

Earnings per share are computed using the weighted average number of common and dilutive common equivalent shares attributable to stock options outstanding during the period.

Inventories

Inventories are stated at the lower of cost (first-in, first-out) or market.

Property, Plant, and Equipment

Property, plant, and equipment is stated at cost. Depreciation and amortization is computed by use of declining balance and straight-line methods over the estimated useful lives of the assets.

Reclassifications

Certain prior year amounts on the Consolidated Statements of Cash Flows, as well as on the Income Taxes and Industry Segment and Geographic Information footnotes, have been reclassified to conform to the current year presentation.

Inventories

Inventories consist of the following:

(In thousands)

	1992	1991
Purchased parts	$ 150,147	$ 154,812
Work in process	94,790	72,301
Finished goods	335,160	444,542
	$ 580,097	$ 671,655

Notes Payable

As of September 25, 1992, notes payable represent unsecured commercial paper borrowings of approximately $184 million at varying interest rates. The weighted average interest rate was approximately 3.5%, and the average days to maturity was 30 days. As of September 27, 1991, notes payable represent unsecured commercial paper borrowings of approximately $149 million at varying interest rates. The weighted average interest rate was approximately 5.5%, and the average days to maturity was 29 days. Interest expense in each of the three years ended September 25, 1992, was immaterial.

Restructuring of Operations

In the third quarter of 1991, the Company initiated a plan to restructure its operations worldwide. In connection with this plan, the Company recorded a $197.5 million charge to operating expenses ($122 million, or $1.02 per share, after taxes) during the third quarter. The restructuring charge for 1991 included $114.5 million of estimated facilities, equipment, and other expenses and $83 million of estimated employee-related expenses associated with the consolidation, relocation, and termination of certain operations and employees. The Company continues to phase in the 1991 restructuring plan. Spending associated with certain actions of the plan may extend well beyond the implementation of the actions. For example, lease payments under noncancelable leases generally extend for some period of time beyond the closing of the facilities.

Commitments and Contingencies

Lease Commitments

The Company leases various facilities and equipment under noncancelable lease arrangements. The major facilities leases are for terms of 5 to 10 years and generally provide renewal options for terms of up to 5 additional years. Rent expense under all operating leases was approximately $160 million, $163 million, and $139 million in 1992, 1991, and 1990, respectively. Future minimum lease payments under these noncancelable operating leases as of September 25, 1992, are as follows:

	(In thousands)
1993	$ 121,585
1994	100,312
1995	66,855
1996	43,348
1997	30,248
Later years	59,670
Total minimum lease payments	$ 422,018

In July 1991, a subsidiary of the Company formed a partnership, Cupertino Gateway Partners, with a local real estate developer for the purpose of constructing a campus-type office facility to be leased to the Company by the partnership. The Company executed six noncancelable leases with the partnership to lease the buildings for terms of approximately 17 years. As of September 25, 1992, the Company accounted for its 50% investment in the partnership under the equity method.

On November 11, 1992, subsequent to the date of the independent auditor's report, the Company modified the terms of the partnership agreement, which included an agreement by the Company to extend permanent financing for the project, not to exceed $158 million on an as-needed basis. The permanent financing will replace the construction loan and return substantially all of the partner's initial capital contributions. Because of the modifications to the terms of the partnership agreement, the Company will consolidate the partnership into its operations and record a minority interest beginning in fiscal 1993. As a result of the Company's future consolidation of the partnership, total future minimum lease payments to the partnership of approximately $427 million have been excluded from the preceding table.

A portion of the future minimum lease payments presented in the preceding table is attributable to leases for facilities that were subject to the Company's restructuring actions initiated in the third quarter of 1991. Future lease payments associated with these facilities were provided for in the Company's 1991 third quarter restructuring reserve, and therefore do not represent future operating expenses. Minimum lease payments may decline in the future, as the leases for facilities subject to restructuring actions are terminated or otherwise completed.

Off-Balance-Sheet Risk and Concentrations of Credit

At September 25, 1992, the Company had approximately $538 million in forward foreign exchange contracts in various currencies. The Company also enters into foreign currency options, both purchased and sold, generally to protect against currency exchange risks associated with certain probable, but not firmly committed, transactions. Risk of loss on purchased foreign currency put options is limited to premiums paid for the options. The face value of the Company's sold foreign currency call options at September 25, 1992, totaled approximately $577 million.

In addition, the Company has entered into interest rate risk management agreements with certain financial institutions. At September 25, 1992, the Company had outstanding interest rate risk management agreements with a total notional amount of approximately $610 million. The agreements have maturities ranging from six months to three years and generally require the Company to pay a floating interest rate based on London InterBank Offered Rates and to receive interest at a fixed rate. Though the notional amounts of the Company's interest rate risk management agreements are an indication of the volume of these transactions, the amounts potentially subject to credit risk are generally limited to the amounts, if any, by which the counterparties' obligations exceed the obligations of the Company.

The counterparties to the agreements relating to the Company's investments and foreign currency and interest rate risk management financial instruments consist of a number of major international financial institutions. The Company does not believe there is significant risk of nonperformance by these counterparties, because the Company continuously monitors its positions and the credit ratings of such counterparties, and limits the amount of agreements and contracts it enters into with any one party.

The Company distributes its products principally through third-party computer resellers and various educational channels. Concentrations of credit risk with respect to trade receivables are limited because of flooring arrangements for selected customers with third-party financing companies and because the Company's customer base consists of large numbers of geographically diverse customers dispersed across many industries.

Income Taxes

The provision for income taxes consists of the following:

(In thousands)

	1992	1991	1990
Federal:			
Current	$ 108,512	$ 106,162	$ 93,047
Deferred	100,355	22,131	138,632
	208,867	128,293	231,679
State:			
Current	26,935	26,866	28,593
Deferred	13,891	(9,591)	5,050
	40,826	17,275	33,643
Foreign:			
Current	65,144	40,614	51,416
Deferred	10,232	3,721	(13,116)
	75,376	44,335	38,300
Provision for income taxes	$ 325,069	$ 189,903	$ 303,622

The foreign provision for income taxes is based on foreign pretax earnings of approximately $611 million, $464 million, and $521 million in 1992, 1991, and 1990, respectively.

Deferred (prepaid) income taxes result from timing differences between years in the recognition of certain revenue and expense items for financial and tax reporting purposes. The sources of timing differences and the related tax effects are as follows:

(In thousands)

	1992	1991	1990
Income of foreign subsidiaries not taxable in current year	$ 71,429	$ 103,912	$ 145,900
Warranty, bad debt, and other expenses	21,381	(84,924)	(11,719)
Depreciation	(3,398)	(11,989)	(20,919)
Inventory valuation	(1,940)	(16,691)	(2,315)
State income taxes	(10,959)	4,585	2,972
Other individually immaterial items	47,965	21,368	16,647
Total deferred taxes	$ 124,478	$ 16,261	$ 130,566

A reconciliation of the provision for income taxes, with the amount computed by applying the statutory federal income tax rate (34% in each of 1992, 1991, and 1990) to income before taxes, is as follows:

(In thousands)

	1992	1991	1990
Computed expected tax	$ 290,850	$ 169,913	$ 264,696
State taxes, net of federal benefit	26,945	11,401	22,204
Research and development tax credit	(7,000)	(13,000)	(8,000)
Indefinitely invested earnings of foreign subsidiaries	(31,280)	(13,940)	—
Other individually immaterial items	45,554	35,529	24,722
Provision for income taxes	$ 325,069	$ 189,903	$ 303,622
Effective tax rate	38%	38%	39%

The Company's federal income tax returns for 1981 through 1986 have been examined by the Internal Revenue Service (IRS). All contested issues for the years 1981 through 1983 have been resolved. During 1990, the IRS proposed tax deficiencies for the years 1984 through 1986, and the Company made prepayments thereon in 1991. The Company is contesting these alleged deficiencies and is pursuing administrative and judicial remedies. Management believes that adequate provision has been made for any adjustments that may result from these examinations.

Preferred Stock

Five million shares of preferred stock have been authorized for issuance in one or more series. The Board of Directors is authorized to fix the number and designation of any such series and to determine the rights, preferences, privileges, and restrictions granted to or imposed on any such series.

Common Stock

Shareholder Rights Plan

The Company has adopted a shareholder rights plan and distributed a dividend of one right to purchase one share of common stock (a "Right") for each outstanding share of common stock of the Company. The Rights become exercisable in certain limited circumstances involving a potential business combination transaction of the Company and are initially exercisable at a price of $200 per share. Following certain other events after the Rights have become exercisable, each Right entitles its holder to purchase for $200 an amount of common stock of the Company, or, in certain circumstances, securities of the acquiror, having a then-current market value of two times the exercise price of the Right. The Rights are redeemable and may be amended at the Company's option before they become exercisable. Until a Right is exercised, the holder of a Right, as such, has no rights as a shareholder of the Company. The Rights expire on April 19, 1999.

Stock Option Plans

The Company has in effect a 1990 Stock Option Plan (the 1990 Plan) and a 1987 Executive Long Term Stock Option Plan (the 1987 Plan). The 1981 Stock Option Plan terminated in October 1990. Options granted before that date remain outstanding in accordance with their terms. Options may be granted under the 1990 Plan to employees, including officers and directors who are employees, at not less than the fair market value on the date of grant. These options generally become exercisable over varying periods, based on continued employment, and generally expire ten years after the grant date. The 1990 Plan permits the granting of incentive stock options, nonstatutory stock options, and stock appreciation rights.

The 1987 Plan permits the granting of nonstatutory options to certain officers of the Company to purchase Apple common stock at prices not less than 75% of the fair market value on the date of grant. Options under the 1987 Plan are not exercisable for 18 months after the date of grant, and then become exercisable at varying rates over the subsequent seven years, based on continued service to the Company.

Summarized information regarding the Company's stock option plans as of September 25, 1992, is as follows:

(In thousands, except per share amounts)

	Number of Shares	Price per Share
Outstanding at September 27, 1991	14,856	\$7.50–\$68.00
Granted	3,436	
Exercised	(3,214)	\$7.50–\$68.00
Expired or canceled	(616)	
Outstanding at September 25, 1992	14,462	\$7.50–\$68.00
Exercisable	6,435	
Reserved for issuance	19,639	
Available for future grant	5,177	

Employee Stock Purchase Plan

The Company has an employee stock purchase plan (the Purchase Plan) under which substantially all employees may purchase common stock through payroll deductions at a price equal to 85% of the lower of the fair market values as of the beginning or end of the offering period. Stock purchases under the Purchase Plan are limited to 10% of an employee's compensation. As of September 25, 1992, approximately 1,078,000 shares were reserved for future issuance under the Purchase Plan. In September 1992, the Board of Directors adopted an amendment to the Purchase Plan to increase the number of shares reserved for issuance by 2 million shares, subject to shareholder approval in January 1993.

Stock Repurchase Programs

In September 1990, the Board of Directors authorized the purchase of up to 10 million shares of the Company's common stock in the open market. No shares were repurchased under this authorization in fiscal 1990. During 1992 and 1991, the Company repurchased approximately 4.0 million and 4.4 million shares respectively, in the open market under this repurchase program.

Savings Plan

The Company has an employee savings plan (the Savings Plan) that qualifies as a deferred salary arrangement under Section 401(k) of the Internal Revenue Code. Under the Savings Plan, participating U.S. employees may defer a portion of their pretax earnings, up to the Internal Revenue Service annual contribution limit (\$8,728 for calendar year 1992). The Company matches 30% to 50% of each employee's contributions, depending on length of service, up to a maximum of 6% of the employee's earnings. The Company's matching contributions to the Savings Plan were \$11.1 million, \$10.6 million, and \$8.6 million in 1992, 1991, and 1990, respectively.

Litigation

In March 1988, the Company filed suit in the U.S. District Court for the Northern District of California (the Court) against Microsoft Corporation (Microsoft) and Hewlett-Packard Company (HP), alleging that their Microsoft Windows 2.03 and HP NewWave computer programs infringe the Company's registered audiovisual copyrights protecting the Macintosh user interface. Microsoft and HP each filed separate answers setting forth affirmative defenses and counterclaims against the Company, seeking declaratory relief and unspecified monetary damages (including punitive damages).

In 1989, the Court ruled that a 1985 license agreement relating to Windows Version 1.0 did not constitute a complete defense to the Company's claim because the visual displays of Windows 2.03 are fundamentally different from those of Windows Version 1.0; the visual display elements of Windows Version 1.0 that are used in Windows 2.03 are licensed; and the visual displays in Windows 2.03 that are not licensed are those relating to the use of overlapping main application windows and the appearance and manipulation of icons. The Court also confirmed that the license does not extend to visual displays added by HP in its NewWave software, which operates in conjunction with Windows 2.03.

On April 16, 1990, the Company filed a motion for partial summary judgment, asking the Court to hold that the Company's copyrights for the Lisa® and Macintosh computers are valid and to strike the defendants' defenses challenging the validity and scope of protection of those copyrights. Microsoft and HP each filed a motion for partial summary judgment, challenging the validity of the Company's copyrights and seeking to narrow the scope of protection. Each also continued to argue that additional visual displays relating to overlapping main application windows and the use and manipulation of icons should be deemed licensed.

On March 6, 1991, the Court issued a ruling acknowledging the originality of the Company's copyrighted works. By an order dated June 15, 1991, the Court granted the Company's request to supplement its complaint to add Windows 3.0 and NewWave 3.0 to the lawsuit, but denied its request to add a claim against Microsoft for breach of the 1985 license agreement, rescission, and unfair competition.

By stipulation the parties agreed to the voluntary dismissal of the following claims: Microsoft's counterclaims for tortious interference with contract, intentional interference with prospective business advantage, disparagement of property, slander of title, and unfair business practices; HP's counterclaims for intentional interference with prospective and existing business relations and unfair business practices; and the Company's claim for unfair competition.

By an order dated July 25, 1991, the Court (i) dismissed Microsoft's claim that the Company breached the 1985 license agreement, (ii) dismissed an HP counterclaim to the extent that it raised the issue of the originality of the Company's copyrights, (iii) stayed all litigation on HP's antitrust counterclaim, (iv) held that the originality of the Company's copyrights had already been established and that the Company was not obligated to prove the originality of each element or feature of its works, and (v) ordered all discovery of fact witnesses to be completed by January 31, 1992, and all discovery of expert witnesses to be completed by February 28, 1992. Subsequent to that hearing, both Microsoft and HP moved for reconsideration of the Court's order that upheld the originality of the Company's copyrighted works.

By an order dated August 14, 1991, the Court granted defendants' motion for reconsideration on the issue of originality, holding that defendants may attempt to establish that individual elements in the Company's copyrighted works are not original. According to the Court's order, to meet their burden, defendants must prove that the Company's expression of component features was directly copied from prior work. Further, the Court rejected defendants' arguments that elements that cannot be protected should be excluded from the infringement analysis, holding that the entire works will be examined for substantial similarity.

On April 14, 1992, the Court issued a ruling on motions filed by the parties, which substantially narrowed the scope of the issues in the case and was not favorable to the Company. The Court held that most of the Windows and NewWave interface elements were either licensed by the Company to Microsoft, or made up of elements common to the Company that cannot be protected.

On August 7, 1992, the Court entered an order disposing of various motions that had been filed by the parties, including the Company's motion for reconsideration of the Court's April 14, 1992, order. In that order, the Court (i) held that many of the similarities alleged by the Company were not entitled to copyright protection, (ii) ruled that, with respect to Windows, four of the similarities may be entitled to protection, but only against virtual copying and, with respect to NewWave, a few additional similarities alleged by the Company were protectible, and (iii) declined to extend protection to the overall arrangement and organization of the Macintosh work.

During a telephone conference on August 10, 1992, the Court requested additional briefs by the parties identifying those issues that remain to be decided. The defendants have each filed briefs requesting the Court to enter final judgment in their favor, dismissing the Company's claim. No dates have been set for the completion of motions or for rulings from the Court on the remaining issues in the case.

The Company believes the resolution of this matter will not have a material adverse effect on its financial condition and results of operations as reported in the accompanying financial statements.

In February 1989, Apple Corps Ltd. and Apple Corps S.A., each unaffiliated with the Company, filed suit in the High Court of Justice, Chancery Division, London, England, against the Company and two of its European subsidiaries. The complaint alleged that the defendants were in breach of a trademark coexistence agreement entered into among the parties in 1981, pursuant to which the parties agreed to certain restrictions on the use and registration of their respective "Apple" trademarks. On October 9, 1991, the parties entered into a settlement agreement, pursuant to which the Company paid to Apple Corps Ltd. $26.5 million.

In 1984, class action complaints were filed in Federal District Court and California State Court against the Company and 14 of its officers and directors, alleging violations of federal and state securities laws, based on the Company's alleged failure to make certain disclosures regarding the Lisa computer and the "Twiggy" disk drive during the period from November 12, 1982, to September 23, 1983. A fund of $16 million was created to settle the case under an agreement approved by the court in March 1992.

In May 1991, class action complaints were filed in Federal District Court against the Company and certain of its officers and directors, alleging violations of federal securities laws, based on the Company's alleged misleading statements during the period from January 17, 1991, to April 30, 1991, regarding the Company's business prospects and outlook for growth in earnings. A fund of $3.8 million was created to settle the case under an agreement approved by the Court in May 1992.

A substantial portion of the amount paid for settlement in the two securities class action cases was provided by the Company's insurance coverage.

Industry Segment and Geographic Information

The Company operates in one principal industry segment: the design, manufacture, and sale of personal computing products. The Company's products are sold primarily to the business, education, home, and government markets. Products are distributed principally through third-party computer resellers.

Geographic financial information is as follows:

(In thousands)

	1992	1991	1990
Net sales to unaffiliated customers:			
United States	$ 3,885,042	$ 3,484,534	$ 3,241,061
Europe	1,950,039	1,824,641	1,545,091
Pacific and Canada	1,251,461	999,675	772,283
Total net sales	$ 7,086,542	$ 6,308,850	$ 5,558,435
Transfers between geographic areas (eliminated in consolidation):			
United States	$ 934,673	$ 774,059	$ 559,069
Europe	246,745	147,713	33,531
Pacific and Canada	979,566	1,099,448	373,118
Total transfers	$ 2,160,984	$ 2,021,220	$ 965,718
Operating income:			
United States	$ 245,810	$ 9,036	$ 229,016
Europe	301,865	222,893	367,499
Pacific and Canada	246,181	227,690	103,770
Eliminations	11,952	(12,235)	11,727
Interest and other income, net	49,634	52,362	66,505
Income before income taxes	$ 855,442	$ 499,746	$ 778,517
Identifiable assets:			
United States	$ 1,536,705	$ 1,440,332	$ 1,054,169
Europe	767,765	734,836	591,534
Pacific and Canada	456,472	461,555	350,966
Eliminations	(43,716)	(56,693)	(27,455)
Corporate assets	1,506,467	913,567	1,006,493
Total assets	$ 4,223,693	$ 3,493,597	$ 2,975,707

Net sales to unaffiliated customers is based on the location of the customers. Transfers between geographic areas are recorded at amounts generally above cost and in accordance with the rules and regulations of the respective governing tax authorities. Operating income consists of total net sales less operating expenses, and does not include either interest and other income, net, or income taxes. U.S. operating income is net of corporate expenses. Identifiable assets of geographic areas are those assets used in the Company's operations in each area. Corporate assets include cash and cash equivalents, joint-venture investments, and short-term investments.

REPORT OF ERNST & YOUNG, INDEPENDENT AUDITORS

TO THE SHAREHOLDERS AND BOARD OF DIRECTORS OF APPLE COMPUTER, INC.

We have audited the accompanying consolidated balance sheets of Apple Computer, Inc. as of September 25, 1992, and September 27, 1991, and the related consolidated statements of income, shareholders' equity, and cash flows for each of the three fiscal years in the period ended September 25, 1992. These financial statements are the responsibility of the Company's management. Our responsibility is to express an opinion on these financial statements based on our audits.

We conducted our audits in accordance with generally accepted auditing standards. Those standards require that we plan and perform the audit to obtain reasonable assurance about whether the financial statements are free of material misstatement. An audit includes examining, on a test basis, evidence supporting the amounts and disclosures in the financial statements. An audit also includes assessing the accounting principles used and significant estimates made by management, as well as evaluating the overall financial statement presentation. We believe that our audits provide a reasonable basis for our opinion.

In our opinion, the financial statements referred to above present fairly, in all material respects, the consolidated financial position of Apple Computer, Inc. at September 25, 1992, and September 27, 1991, and the consolidated results of its operations and its cash flows for each of the three fiscal years in the period ended September 25, 1992, in conformity with generally accepted accounting principles.

Ernst & Young

San Jose, California
October 14, 1992

APPENDIX

G

Financial Statements (excluding footnotes) from the Annual Reports of Federal Express Corporation and Ben and Jerry's Homemade, Inc.

Consolidated Statements of Operations

FEDERAL EXPRESS CORPORATION AND SUBSIDIARIES

Years ended May 31 In thousands, except per share amounts	1993	1992	1991
REVENUES	**$ 7,808,043**	$ 7,550,060	$ 7,688,296
OPERATING EXPENSES:			
Salaries and employee benefits (Notes 8 and 9)	**3,807,493**	3,637,080	3,438,391
Rentals and landing fees (Note 4)	**658,138**	672,341	650,001
Depreciation and amortization	**579,896**	577,157	562,207
Fuel	**495,384**	508,386	663,327
Maintenance and repairs	**404,639**	404,311	449,394
Restructuring charges (Note 13)	**(12,500)**	254,000	121,000
Other	**1,497,820**	1,473,818	1,551,850
	7,430,870	7,527,093	7,436,170
OPERATING INCOME	**377,173**	22,967	252,126
OTHER INCOME (EXPENSE):			
Interest, net (Note 1)	**(160,923)**	(164,315)	(181,880)
Gain on disposition of aircraft and related equipment	**4,633**	2,832	11,375
Other, net	**(17,307)**	(8,312)	(8,679)
Payroll tax loss (Note 13)	**–**	–	(32,000)
	(173,597)	(169,795)	(211,184)
INCOME (LOSS) BEFORE INCOME TAXES AND CUMULATIVE EFFECT OF CHANGE IN ACCOUNTING PRINCIPLE	**203,576**	(146,828)	40,942
PROVISION (CREDIT) FOR INCOME TAXES (Note 7)	**93,767**	(33,046)	35,044
INCOME (LOSS) BEFORE CUMULATIVE EFFECT OF CHANGE IN ACCOUNTING PRINCIPLE	**109,809**	(113,782)	5,898
CUMULATIVE EFFECT OF CHANGE IN ACCOUNTING FOR POSTRETIREMENT BENEFITS, NET OF TAX BENEFIT OF $34,287 (Note 9)	**(55,943)**	–	–
NET INCOME (LOSS)	**$ 53,866**	$ (113,782)	$ 5,898
EARNINGS (LOSS) PER SHARE (Note 6):			
Before cumulative effect of change in accounting principle	**$ 2.01**	$ (2.11)	$ .11
Cumulative effect of change in accounting for postretirement benefits (Note 9)	**(1.03)**	–	–
	$ .98	$ (2.11)	$ .11
AVERAGE SHARES OUTSTANDING (Note 6)	**54,719**	53,961	53,350

The accompanying Notes to Consolidated Financial Statements are an integral part of these statements.

Consolidated Balance Sheets

FEDERAL EXPRESS CORPORATION AND SUBSIDIARIES

May 31 In thousands	1993	1992
ASSETS		
CURRENT ASSETS:		
Cash and cash equivalents	**$ 155,456**	$ 78,177
Receivables, less allowance for doubtful accounts of $31,308 and $32,074	**922,727**	899,773
Spare parts, supplies and fuel	**164,087**	158,062
Prepaid expenses and other	**63,573**	69,994
Deferred income taxes (Note 7)	**133,875**	–
Total current assets	**1,439,718**	1,206,006
PROPERTY AND EQUIPMENT, AT COST (Notes 3, 4 and 11):		
Flight equipment	**2,843,253**	2,540,350
Package handling and ground support equipment	**1,413,793**	1,352,659
Computer and electronic equipment	**947,913**	851,686
Other	**1,501,250**	1,433,212
	6,706,209	6,177,907
Less accumulated depreciation and amortization	**3,229,941**	2,766,610
Net property and equipment	**3,476,268**	3,411,297
OTHER ASSETS:		
Goodwill (Note 1)	**432,215**	487,780
Equipment deposits and other assets (Note 11)	**444,863**	358,103
Total other assets	**877,078**	845,883
	$ 5,793,064	$ 5,463,186

The accompanying Notes to Consolidated Financial Statements are an integral part of these balance sheets.

	1993	1992
LIABILITIES AND STOCKHOLDERS' INVESTMENT		
CURRENT LIABILITIES:		
Current portion of long-term debt (Note 3)	**$ 133,797**	$ 155,257
Accounts payable	**554,111**	430,130
Accrued expenses (Note 2)	**761,357**	799,468
Total current liabilities	**1,449,265**	1,384,855
LONG-TERM DEBT, LESS CURRENT PORTION (Note 3)	**1,882,279**	1,797,844
DEFERRED INCOME TAXES (Note 7)	**72,479**	123,715
OTHER LIABILITIES (Note 1)	**717,660**	577,050
COMMITMENTS AND CONTINGENCIES (Notes 11 and 12)		
COMMON STOCKHOLDERS' INVESTMENT (Note 6):		
Common stock, $.10 par value; 100,000 shares authorized, 54,743 and 54,100 shares issued	**5,474**	5,410
Additional paid-in capital	**699,385**	672,727
Retained earnings	**969,515**	906,555
	1,674,374	1,584,692
Less treasury stock and deferred compensation related to stock plans	**(2,993)**	(4,970)
Total common stockholders' investment	**1,671,381**	1,579,722
	$ 5,793,064	$ 5,463,186

Consolidated Statements of Cash Flows

FEDERAL EXPRESS CORPORATION AND SUBSIDIARIES

Years ended May 31 In thousands	1993	1992	1991
OPERATING ACTIVITIES			
Net income (loss)	**$ 53,866**	$ (113,782)	$ 5,898
Adjustments to reconcile income (loss) to net cash provided by operating activities:			
Depreciation and amortization	**579,896**	577,157	562,207
Provision for uncollectible accounts	**33,552**	31,670	59,721
Provision (credit) for deferred income taxes and other	**19,910**	(75,219)	36,935
(Gain) loss from disposals of property and equipment	**(5,648)**	1,810	(1,621)
Cumulative effect of accounting change	**55,943**	–	–
Changes in assets and liabilities, net of effects from purchases and dispositions of businesses:			
(Increase) decrease in receivables	**(41,535)**	(727)	20,431
(Increase) decrease in other current assets	**(5,813)**	61,749	(21,904)
Increase in accounts payable, accrued expenses and other liabilities	**13,651**	33,620	131,500
Other, net	**21,259**	4,543	(5,768)
Net cash provided by operating activities	**725,081**	520,821	787,399
INVESTING ACTIVITIES			
Purchases of property and equipment, including deposits on aircraft of $177,564 $212,291 and $92,587	**(1,023,723)**	(915,878)	(1,027,736)
Proceeds from disposition of property and equipment:			
Sale-leaseback transactions	**216,444**	400,433	275,347
Other	**5,984**	12,851	5,699
Purchase of businesses, net of cash acquired	**–**	–	(24,322)
Other, net	**1,992**	621	–
Net cash used in investing activities	**(799,303)**	(501,973)	(771,012)
FINANCING ACTIVITIES			
Proceeds from debt issuances	**878,499**	437,709	910,703
Principal payments on debt	**(737,334)**	(507,283)	(916,430)
Proceeds from stock issuances (includes treasury)	**24,512**	19,272	31,241
Purchases of treasury stock	**(472)**	(3,099)	(23,565)
Other, net	**(13,704)**	(4,962)	857
Net cash provided by (used in) financing activities	**151,501**	(58,363)	2,806
Net increase (decrease) in cash and cash equivalents	**77,279**	(39,515)	19,193
Cash and cash equivalents at beginning of period	**78,177**	117,692	98,499
Cash and cash equivalents at end of period	**$ 155,456**	$ 78,177	$ 117,692
SUPPLEMENTAL DISCLOSURE OF CASH FLOW INFORMATION			
Cash paid for:			
Interest (net of capitalized interest)	**$ 162,648**	$ 178,943	$ 190,054
Income taxes	**188,943**	89,729	36,500

Non-cash investing and financing activities:

In November 1992, approximately $73,000 of secured debt related to a portion of the purchase price of one MD-11 aircraft acquired by the Company was assumed by a third party in a sale-leaseback of the aircraft.

The accompanying Notes to Consolidated Financial Statements are an integral part of these statements.

Consolidated Statements of Changes in Common Stockholders' Investment

FEDERAL EXPRESS CORPORATION AND SUBSIDIARIES

In thousands, except common shares	Common Stock	Additional Paid-in Capital	Retained Earnings	Treasury Stock	Deferred Compen-sation
BALANCE AT MAY 31, 1990	$ 5,315	$ 639,676	$ 1,010,090	$ (21)	$ (5,873)
Purchase of treasury stock	–	–	–	(23,565)	–
Issuance of common and treasury stock under employee incentive plans (1,141,283 shares)	48	12,369	(4,483)	23,572	642
Amortization of deferred compensation	–	–	–	–	1,252
Foreign currency translation adjustment	–	–	3,700	–	–
Net income	–	–	5,898	–	–
BALANCE AT MAY 31, 1991	5,363	652,045	1,015,205	(14)	(3,979)
Purchase of treasury stock	–	–	–	(3,099)	–
Issuance of common and treasury stock under employee incentive plans (554,269 shares)	47	20,682	(287)	3,081	(2,792)
Amortization of deferred compensation	–	–	–	–	1,833
Foreign currency translation adjustment	–	–	5,419	–	–
Net loss	–	–	(113,782)	–	–
BALANCE AT MAY 31, 1992	5,410	672,727	906,555	(32)	(4,938)
Purchase of treasury stock	–	–	–	(472)	–
Issuance of common and treasury stock under employee incentive plans (655,938 shares)	64	26,658	(85)	468	(393)
Amortization of deferred compensation	–	–	–	–	2,374
Foreign currency translation adjustment	–	–	9,179	–	–
Net income	–	–	53,866	–	–
BALANCE AT MAY 31, 1993	**$ 5,474**	**$ 699,385**	**$ 969,515**	**$ (36)**	**$ (2,957)**

The accompanying Notes to Consolidated Financial Statements are an integral part of these statements.

CONSOLIDATED BALANCE SHEET ASSETS

26

	December 26, 1992	December 28, 1991
Current assets:		
Cash and cash equivalents	$ 7,356,133	$ 6,704,006
Accounts receivable, less allowance for doubtful accounts: $350,000 in 1992 and 1991	8,849,326	6,939,975
Income taxes receivable	306,193	
Inventories	17,089,857	8,999,666
Deferred income taxes	1,730,000	984,000
Prepaid expenses	208,996	107,325
Total current assets	35,540,505	23,734,972
Property, plant and equipment	39,312,513	28,496,080
Less accumulated depreciation	12,575,088	9,196,551
	26,737,425	19,299,529
Investments	25,200,000	
Other assets	728,885	21,598
	$ 88,206,815	$ 43,056,099

ASSETS — THINGS THE COMPANY OWNS.
- CASH
- ACCOUNTS RECEIVABLE · MONEY OWED TO THE COMPANY
- INVENTORY · MANUFACTURED PRODUCTS WAITING TO BE SOLD, ALSO INGREDIENTS, PACKAGING & SUPPLIES
- PROPERTY, PLANT & EQUIPMENT · BUILDINGS, MACHINERY, TRUCKS ETC. DEPRECIATION IS THE PART OF THE VALUE OF THESE ASSETS THAT HAS BEEN USED UP, BASED ON HOW LONG IT IS EXPECTED TO LAST.
- PREPAID EXPENSES, DEFERRED INCOME TAXES, OTHER ASSETS · THESE ARE MISCELLANEOUS OTHER PURCHASED ASSETS THE COMPANY HAS THAT HAVE VALUE.

...2 MILLION 67, 2 MILLION 68, 2 MILLION 69, ...

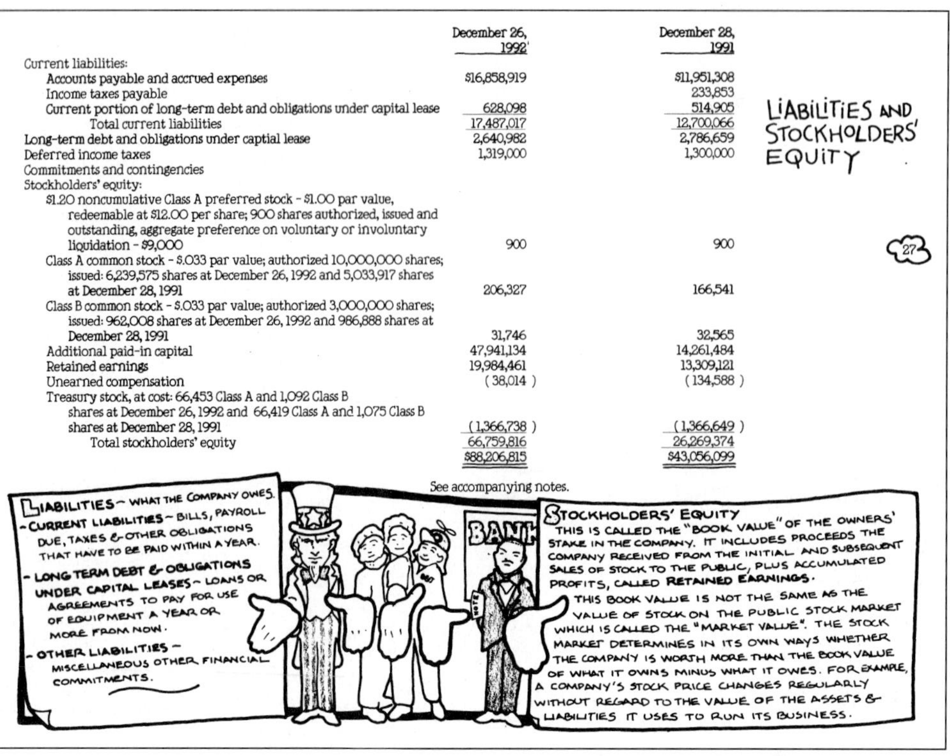

	December 26, 1992	December 28, 1991
Current liabilities:		
Accounts payable and accrued expenses	$16,858,919	$11,951,308
Income taxes payable		233,853
Current portion of long-term debt and obligations under capital lease	628,098	514,905
Total current liabilities	17,487,017	12,700,066
Long-term debt and obligations under captial lease	2,640,982	2,786,659
Deferred income taxes	1,319,000	1,300,000
Commitments and contingencies		
Stockholders' equity:		
$1.20 noncumulative Class A preferred stock - $1.00 par value, redeemable at $12.00 per share; 900 shares authorized, issued and outstanding, aggregate preference on voluntary or involuntary liquidation - $9,000	900	900
Class A common stock - $.033 par value; authorized 10,000,000 shares; issued: 6,239,575 shares at December 26, 1992 and 5,033,917 shares at December 28, 1991	206,327	166,541
Class B common stock - $.033 par value; authorized 3,000,000 shares; issued: 962,008 shares at December 26, 1992 and 986,888 shares at December 28, 1991	31,746	32,565
Additional paid-in capital	47,941,134	14,261,484
Retained earnings	19,984,461	13,309,121
Unearned compensation	(38,014)	(134,588)
Treasury stock, at cost: 66,453 Class A and 1,092 Class B shares at December 26, 1992 and 66,419 Class A and 1,075 Class B shares at December 28, 1991	(1,366,738)	(1,366,649)
Total stockholders' equity	66,759,816	26,269,374
	$88,206,815	$43,056,099

See accompanying notes.

CONSOLIDATED STATEMENT OF INCOME

	Years Ended December 26, 1992	December 28, 1991	December 29, 1990
Net sales	$ 131,968,814	$ 96,997,339	$ 77,024,037
Cost of sales	94,389,391	68,500,402	54,202,387
Gross profit	37,579,423	28,496,937	22,821,650
Selling, general and administrative expenses	26,242,761	21,264,214	17,639,357
Operating income	11,336,662	7,232,723	5,182,293
28 Other income (expenses):			
Interest income	394,817	147,058	296,329
Interest expense	(181,577)	(736,248)	(868,736)
Other	(235,765)	(139,627)	(136,578)
	(22,525)	(728,817)	(708,985)
Income before income taxes	11,314,137	6,503,906	4,473,308
Income taxes	4,638,797	2,764,523	1,864,063
Net income	$ 6,675,340	$ 3,739,383	$ 2,609,245
Net income per common share	$ 1.07	$ 0.67	$ 0.50
Weighted average number of common shares outstanding	6,253,825	5,572,368	5,224,667

See accompanying notes.

STATEMENT OF INCOME

- NET SALES – THIS IS THE TOTAL SALES OF THE COMPANY MINUS THE VALUE OF PRODUCT DISCOUNTED OR RETURNED.
- COST OF SALES – WHAT IT COST TO MAKE & STORE THE PRODUCTS UNTIL THEY ARE SOLD. INCLUDES INGREDIENTS, PACKAGING, LABOR COSTS, & THE COST TO RUN PRODUCTION & STORAGE MACHINERY.
- GROSS PROFIT – NET SALES MINUS COST OF SALES.
- SELLING & ADMINISTRATIVE EXPENSES – THESE ARE THE COSTS OF MARKETING & SELLING THE PRODUCT AFTER IT HAS BEEN MADE, PLUS ALL OF THE ADMINISTRATIVE COSTS TO RUN THE COMPANY.
- OPERATING INCOME – GROSS PROFIT MINUS SELLING, GENERAL & ADMINISTRATIVE EXPENSES. THIS MEASURES HOW MUCH A COMPANY EARNS (BEFORE TAXES) FROM THE CORE BUSINESS IT IS IN.
- INCOME BEFORE TAXES, INCOME TAXES & NET INCOME – INCOME TAXES ARE THE AMOUNT OF FEDERAL & STATE TAXES PAID OR DUE BASED ON THE COMPANY'S BOOK INCOME. SUBTRACTING THOSE TAXES FROM INCOME BEFORE TAXES RESULTS IN NET INCOME OR THE "BOTTOM LINE". (REMEMBER, BEN & JERRY'S HAS TWO "BOTTOM LINES."

CONTINUED →

CONSOLIDATED STATEMENT OF CASH FLOWS

Years Ended	12/26/92	12/28/91	12/29/90
Cash flows from operating activities:			
Net income	$ 6,675,340	$ 3,739,383	$ 2,609,245
Adjustments to reconcile net income to net cash provided by operating activities:			
Depreciation and amortization	3,455,720	2,980,826	2,320,666
Provision for doubtful accounts receivable		100,000	88,000
Deferred income taxes	(727,000)	(294,000)	91,000
Amortization of unearned compensation	96,574	77,162	
(Gain) Loss on disposition of assets	(14,232)	13,250	3,666
Stock awards	57,000	302,601	
Changes in assets and liabilities:			
Accounts receivable	(1,909,351)	(1,995,530)	(1,462,567)
Income tax receivable/payable	(540,046)	(98,441)	390,413
Inventories	(8,090,191)	1,083,476	(6,086,592)
Prepaid expenses	(101,671)	10,601	72,363
Other assets	93,656		
Accounts payable and accrued expenses	4,907,611	4,399,156	3,198,786
Net cash provided by operating activities	3,903,410	10,318,484	1,224,980
Cash flows from investing activities:			
Additions to property, plant and equipment	(10,447,007)	(4,034,124)	(2,597,635)
Proceeds from sale of property, plant and equipment	105,084	70,000	42,500
Increase in investments	(25,200,000)		
Changes in other assets	(836,657)		
Net cash used for investing activities	(36,378,580)	(3,964,124)	(2,555,135)
Cash flows from financing activities:			
Borrowings on short-term debt		8,900,000	
Repayments of short-term debt		(8,900,000)	
Repayments of long-term debt and capital leases	(534,231)	(439,002)	(348,731)
Net proceeds from issuance of common stock	33,661,528	95,325	81,763
Payment of bond redemption costs		(102,867)	
Net cash provided by (used for) financing activities	33,127,297	(446,544)	(266,968)
Increase (decrease) in cash and cash equivalents	652,127	5,907,816	(1,597,123)
Cash and cash equivalents at beginning of year	6,704,006	796,190	2,393,313
Cash and cash equivalents at end of year	$ 7,356,133	$6,704,006	$ 796,190

See accompanying notes.

29

CONSOLIDATED STATEMENT OF STOCKHOLDERS' EQUITY

30

	Preferred Stock	Common Stock Class A	Common Stock Class B
	Par Value	Par Value	Par Value
Balance at December 30, 1989	$ 900	$131,909	$38,383
Net income			
Common Stock forfeited under restricted stock plan (306 Class A shares and 150 Class B shares)			
Common Stock issued under stock purchase plan (12,462 shares)		411	
Conversion of Class B shares to Class A shares (78,048 shares)		2,576	(2,576)
Conversion of subordinated debentures to Class A shares (644 shares)		21	
Balance at December 29, 1990	900	134,917	35,807
Net income			
Common stock issued under restricted stock plan (53,450 Class A shares)			
Amortization of unearned compensation			
Conversion of Class B shares to Class A shares (98,230 shares)		3,242	(3,242)
Conversion of subordinated debentures to Class A shares (847,804 shares)		27,976	
Common stock forfeited under restricted stock plan (40 Class Ashares and 20 Class B shares)			
Common stock issued under stock purchase plan (12,292 Class A shares)		406	
Common stock contributed (89,624 Class A shares)			
Balance at December 28, 1991	900	166,541	32,565
Net income			
Common stock issued through public offering (1,170,000 Class A shares)		38,610	
Common stock issued under stock purchase plan (8,778 Class A shares)		291	
Common stock issued under restricted stock plan (2,000 Class A shares)		66	
Common stock forfeited under restricted stock plan (34 Class A shares and 17 Class B shares)			
Conversion of Class B to Class A shares (24,880 shares)		819	(819)
Amortization of unearned compensation			
Balance at December 26, 1992	$ 900	$ 206,327	$ 31,746

(STATEMENT OF INCOME CONTINUED)

- NET INCOME PER COMMON SHARE - USING THE WEIGHTED AVERAGE NUMBER OF SHARES "OUTSTANDING," THIS IS A CALCULATION OF HOW MUCH OF THE COMPANY'S NET INCOME CAN BE ASSIGNED TO INDIVIDUAL'S SHARES. SOMETIMES CALLED "EARNINGS PER SHARE," THIS IS AN IMPORTANT YARDSTICK FOR COMPARING A COMPANY'S PERFORMANCE IN THE CURRENT PERIOD (A YEAR OR A QUARTER) TO PERFORMANCE IN A PREVIOUS PERIOD.

BEN&JERRY'S HOMEMADE INC.

CHER HOULDER

CERTIFICATE OF STOCK

Additional Paid-in Capital	Retained Earnings	Unearned Compensation	Treasury Stock Class A Cost	Treasury Stock Class B Cost	
$6,302,851	$6,960,493	$ 0	($24,729)	($4,413)	
	2,609,245				
			(534)	(264)	
82,149					
4,978					
6,389,978	9,569,738	0	(25,263)	(4,677)	
	3,739,383				
(53,450)		(211,750)	567,907		31
		77,162			
5,925,527					
			(71)	(35)	
94,919					
1,904,510			(1,904,510)		
14,261,484	13,309,121	(134,588)	(1,361,937)	(4,712)	
	6,675,340				
33,467,490					
155,226					
56,934					
			(59)	(30)	
		96,574			
$47,941,134	$19,984,461	$ (38,014)	$ (1,361,996)	$ (4,742)	

See accompanying notes.

WOW AGAIN. I'M BEGINNING TO THINK I CAN FIGURE THIS OUT!
HERE'S THE TEST. FLIP THROUGH THE FINANCIAL STATEMENTS IN THIS ANNUAL REPORT & TAKE A HARD LOOK AT THEM. READ THE MANAGEMENT'S DISCUSSION & ANALYSIS & THE FOOTNOTES. GO AHEAD - YOU CAN DO IT. THEN THINK OF THE QUESTIONS YOU WANT TO ASK. CALL OR WRITE TO OUR INVESTOR RELATIONS STAFF. SEE IF YOU CAN STUMP 'EM. I DARE YOU.
OOH! WHAT A CHALLENGE. SEE YOU AT THE ANNUAL MEETING!
TO BE CONTINUED-NEXT YEAR.

Index

Check Figures

Problem	Check Figure
1–1	Net income, $9,250
1–2	Ending capital balance, $30,220
1–3	Modified return on equity, 8.1%
1–4	Ending capital balance, $28,080
1–5	Co. C, 12/31/X2 assets, $86,000
1–6	No check figure
1–7	No check figure
1–8	No check figure
2–1	Total debits in trial balance, $152,600
2–2	Total debits in trial balance, $84,500
2–3	Cash account balance, $18,225
2–4	Total credits in trial balance, $34,827
2–5	Ending capital balance, $47,000
2–6	No check figure
2–7	No check figure
Serial Problem	Cash account balance, $22,030
3–1	Insurance expense, $4,104
3–2	Ending capital balance, $31,050
3–3	Current ratio, 1.8
3–4	Net income, $81,300
3–5	No check figure
3–6	No check figure
3–7	Total assets, $276,000
3–8	No check figure
3–9	No check figure
3–10	No check figure
Serial Problem	Net income for three months, $4,070
4–1	Ending capital balance, $37,190
4–2	Total assets, $74,450
4–3	Total assets, $189,100
4–4	Total debits in adjusted trial balance, $266,300
4–5	Ending capital balance, $51,240
4–6	No check figure
4–7	No check figure
Serial Problem	Total credits in post-closing trial balance, $49,440
5–1	Total cost of goods purchased, $5,128
5–2	Part 5, total expenses, $163,400
5–3	Second closing entry: debit to Income Summary, $213,750
5–4	Second closing entry: debit to Income Summary, $188,750

Problem	Check Figure
5–5	Part 3, total expenses, $81,750
5–6	No check figure
5–7	No check figure
6–1	July 31, Cash, $234.65 Cr.
6–2	Cash credits, $275.00; $362.65; $142.80
6–3	Reconciled balance, $39,164
6–4	Reconciled balance, $28,195
6–5	No check figure
6–6	No check figure
7–1	Part 3, Unrealized Holding Gain (Loss), $15,122 Cr.
7–2	No check figure
7–3	Part 1c, Bad Debts Expense, $23,085 Dr.
7–4	Part 2, Bad Debts Expense, $17,520 Dr.
7–5	19X2, Bad Debts Expense, $22,339.50 Dr.
7–6	No check figure
7–7	12/31/X3, Short-Term Investments, Fair Value Adjustment, $46,376 Dr.
7–8	No check figure
7–9	No check figure
8–1	Cost of units sold, $517,000; $614,500; $564,958
8–2	Net income, $80,920; $78,400; $79,998
8–3	No check figure
8–4	Lower of cost or market, $369,778; $352,966; $347,078
8–5	Inventory shortage at cost, $15,616
8–6	Estimated March 31 inventory, $942,410
8–7	No check figure
9–1	Part 3, Depreciation Expense, Land Improvements (Two), $2,962.50
9–2	Part 3, 19X1, depreciation expense, $16,406.25
9–3	Part 1, year 4, units-of-production depreciation expense, $22,320
9–4	Dec. 31, 19X2, Accum. Depr., Heavy Equipment, $24,337
9–5	July 5, 19X3, Loss on Exchange of Delivery Trucks, $3,054
9–6	Nov. 2, 19X5, Gain on Sale of Machinery, $4,353.75
9–7	No check figure
10–1	Part 2, Depletion of Mineral Deposit, $558,000
10–2	Goodwill, $95,000 or $68,400
10–3	Part 1, carrying value per share, $13.95
10–4	Part 2, Unrealized Holding Gain (Loss), $19,555 Cr.
10–5	Part 2, 19X1 total foreign exchange gain, $1,214.64

Problem	Check Figure
10–6	No check figure
11–1	12/31/X1, estimated liability balance, $2,015 credit
11–2	Total interest for Eastern Bank note, $1,050
11–3	Total income tax expense, $7,480
11–4	Plan C present value, $103,431
11–5	Net liability as of December 31, 19X3, $50,850
11–6	Total take-home pay, $5,677.30
11–7	Part 3, net income for Adams Co., $17,000
11–8	No check figure
11–9	No check figure
12–1	Part 2, interest for period ending 11/30/X4, $3,339
12–2	Part 1, premium, $5,952
12–3	Total interest expense, $91,986
12–4	Total interest expense, $8,708
12–5	Interest for period ending 6/30/X2, $4,073
12–6	Ending balance as of 4/30/X4, $98,378
12–7	Ending balance as of 6/30/X3, $80,894
12–8	No check figure
12–9	No check figure
13–1	Total equity, $179,000
13–2	Total equity, $695,000
13–3	Part 1b, total to common, $26,500
13–4	Part 4, book value per share of common, $56.25
13–5	Part 1c, income to Evers, $21,640
13–6	No check figure
13–7	No check figure

Problem	Check Figure
14–1	Retained earnings, Dec. 31, 19X2, $338,500
14–2	Total equity, Dec. 31, $920,000
14–3	Net income, $248,000
14–4	Net income, $130,550
14–5	After-tax cumulative effect, $59,920
14–6	19X4 earnings per share, $3.64
14–7	No check figure
14–8	Part 1, earnings per share, $6.46
15–1	Net cash provided by operating activities, $96,000
15–2	Net cash provided by operating activities, $96,000
15–3	Analysis of Changes column totals, $386,000
15–4	Net cash provided by operating activities, $66,750
15–5	Net cash provided by operating activities, $66,750
15–6	Analysis of Changes column totals, $1,030,750
15–7	No check figure
15–8	No check figure
16–1	Part 3, 19X3 total assets, 124.34
16–2	Part 1, 19X7 total assets, 246.8
16–3	No check figure
16–4	No check figure
16–5	Mar. 31 working capital, $360,000
16–6	No check figure
16–7	No check figure
C–1	Part 4, gain on sale of machinery, $16,000
C–2	Net purchasing power loss, $8,994
C–3	Part 1c, $1,111,815
C–4	No check figure

COMPREHENSIVE LIST OF ACCOUNTS USED IN EXERCISES AND PROBLEMS

Current Assets

101 Cash
102 Petty cash
103 Cash equivalents
104 Short-term investments
105 Short-term investments, fair value adjustment
106 Accounts receivable
107 Allowance for doubtful accounts
108 Legal fees receivable
109 Interest receivable
110 Rent receivable
111 Notes receivable
115 Subscriptions receivable, common stock
116 Subscriptions receivable, preferred stock
119 Merchandise inventory
120 _____ inventory
121 _____ inventory
124 Office supplies
125 Store supplies
126 _____ supplies
128 Prepaid insurance
129 Prepaid interest
130 Prepaid property taxes
131 Prepaid rent

Long-Term Investments

141 Investment in _____ stock
142 Investment in _____ bonds
143 Long-term investments, fair value adjustment
144 Investment in _____
145 Bond sinking fund

Plant Assets

151 Automobiles
152 Accumulated depreciation, automobiles
153 Tricks
154 Accumulated depreciation, trucks
155 Boats
156 Accumulated depreciation, boats
157 Professional library
158 Accumulated depreciation, professional library
159 Law library
160 Accumulated depreciation, law library
161 Furniture
162 Accumulated depreciation, furniture
163 Office equipment
164 Accumulated depreciation, office equipment
165 Store equipment
166 Accumulated depreciation, store equipment
167 _____ equipment
168 Accumulated depreciation, _____ equipment
169 Machinery
170 Accumulated depreciation, machinery
173 Building _____
174 Accumulated depreciation, building _____
175 Building _____
176 Accumulated depreciation, building _____
179 Land improvements _____
180 Accumulated depreciation, land improvements _____
181 Land improvements _____
182 Accumulated depreciation, land improvements _____
183 Land

Natural Resources

185 Mineral deposit
186 Accumulated depletion, mineral deposit

Intangible Assets

191 Patents
192 Leasehold
193 Franchise
194 Copyrights
195 Leasehold improvements
196 Organization costs

Current Liabilities

201 Accounts payable
202 Insurance payable
203 Interest payable
204 Legal fees payable
207 Office salaries payable
208 Rent payable
209 Salaries payable
210 Wages payable
211 Accrued payroll payable
214 Estimated warranty liability
215 Income taxes payable
216 Common dividend payable
217 Preferred dividend payable
218 State unemployment taxes payable
219 Employees' federal income taxes payable
220 Employees' income taxes payable
221 Employees' medical insurance payable
222 Employees' retirement program payable
223 Employees' union dues payable
224 Federal unemployment taxes payable
225 FICA taxes payable
226 Estimated vacation pay liability

Unearned Revenues

230 Unearned consulting fees
231 Unearned legal fees
232 Unearned property management fees
233 Unearned _____ fees
234 Unearned _____
235 Unearned janitorial revenue
236 Unearned _____ revenue
238 Unearned rent
240 Short-term notes payable
241 Discount on short-term notes payable

COMPREHENSIVE LIST OF ACCOUNTS USED IN EXERCISES AND PROBLEMS
(Continued)

Unclassified Liabilities

245 Notes payable

Long-Term Liabilities

251 Long-term notes payable
252 Discount on notes payable
255 Bonds payable
256 Discount on bonds payable
257 Premium on bonds payable
258 Deferred income tax liability

Owner's Equity

Proprietorships and Partnerships

301 _____, capital
302 _____, withdrawals
303 _____, capital
304 _____, withdrawals
305 _____, capital
306 _____, withdrawals

Corporate Contributed Capital

307 Common stock, $ _____ par value
308 Common stock, no par
309 Common stock, subscribed
310 Common stock dividend distributable
311 Contributed capital in excess of par value, common stock
312 Contributed capital in excess of stated value, no-par common stock
313 Contributed capital from the retirement of common stock
314 Contributed capital, treasury stock transactions
315 Preferred stock
316 Contributed capital in excess of par value, preferred stock
317 Preferred stock subscribed

Retained Earnings

318 Retained earnings
319 Cash dividends declared
320 Stock dividends declared

Other Owner's Equity

321 Treasury stock, common
322 Unrealized holding gain (loss)

Revenues

401 _____ fees earned
402 _____ fees earned
403 _____ services revenue
404 _____ services revenue
405 Commissions earned
406 Rent earned
407 Dividends earned
408 Earnings from investment in _____
409 Interest earned
410 Sinking fund earnings
413 Sales
414 Sales returns and allowances
415 Sales discounts

Cost of Goods Sold Items

502 Cost of goods sold
505 Purchases
506 Purchases returns and allowances
507 Purchases discounts
508 Transportation-in

Expenses

Depletion, Amortization, and Depreciation Expenses

601 Amortization expense, _____
602 Amortization expense, _____
603 Depletion expense, _____
604 Depreciation expense, boats
605 Depreciation expense, automobiles
606 Depreciation expense, building _____
607 Depreciation expense, building _____
608 Depreciation expense, land improvements _____
609 Depreciation expense, land improvements _____
610 Depreciation expense, law library
611 Depreciation expense, trucks
612 Depreciation expense, _____ equipment
613 Depreciation expense, _____ equipment
614 Depreciation expense, _____
615 Depreciation expense, _____

Employee Related Expenses

620 Office salaries expense
621 Sales salaries expense
622 Salaries expense
623 _____ wages expense
624 Employees' benefits expense
625 Payroll taxes expense

Financial Expenses

630 Cash over and short
631 Discounts lost
632 Factoring fee expense
633 Interest expense

Insurance Expenses

635 Insurance expense, delivery equipment
636 Insurance expense, office equipment
637 Insurance expense, _____

Rental Expenses

640 Rent expense
641 Rent expense, office space
642 Rent expense, selling space
643 Press rental expense
644 Truck rental expense
645 _____ rental expense

Supplies Expense

650 Office supplies expense
651 Store supplies expense
652 _____ supplies expense
653 _____ supplies expense